THE ROUTLEDGE COMPANION
TO FAMILY BUSINESS

The Routledge Companion to Family Business offers a definitive survey of a field that has seen rapid growth in research in recent years. Edited by leading scholars with contributions from the top minds in family business from around the world, this volume provides researchers and scholars with a comprehensive understanding of the state of the discipline.

Over 25 chapters address a wide variety of subjects, providing readers with a thorough review of the key research themes in the modern family firm, such as corporate social responsibility and bank debt rationing. International examples cover a wide range of economies including China, Europe, and Latin America.

The book will appeal to undergraduates, postgraduates, and business instructors seeking a definitive view of the issues and solutions that affect and support family business.

Franz W. Kellermanns is the Addison H. & Gertrude C. Reese Endowed Chair in International Business and Professor of Management at the University of North Carolina – Charlotte, USA. He holds a joint appointment with the Center for Family Business at the WHU–Otto Beisheim School of Management, Germany.

Frank Hoy is the Paul R. Beswick Professor of Innovation and Entrepreneurship at Worcester Polytechnic Institute, USA.

THE ROUTLEDGE COMPANION TO FAMILY BUSINESS

Edited by Franz W. Kellermanns and Frank Hoy

Routledge
Taylor & Francis Group

LONDON AND NEW YORK

First published 2017
by Routledge
4 Park Square, Milton Park, Abingdon, Oxon OX14 4RN

and by Routledge
605 Third Avenue, New York, NY 10017

First issued in paperback 2022

Routledge is an imprint of the Taylor & Francis Group, an informa business

Publisher's Note
The publisher has gone to great lengths to ensure the quality of this reprint
but points out that some imperfections in the original copies may be
apparent.

Library of Congress Cataloging in Publication Data
Names: Kellermanns, Franz W., editor. | Hoy, Frank, editor.
Title: The Routledge companion to family business /
[edited by] Franz Kellermanns & Frank Hoy.
Description: New York, NY : Routledge, 2016.
Identifiers: LCCN 2016009888 | ISBN 9781138919112 (hbk) |
ISBN 9781315688053 (ebk) Subjects: LCSH: Family-owned business
enterprises. | Family corporations. Classification: LCC HD62.25 .R68 2016 |
DDC 658—dc23 LC record available at https://lccn.loc.gov/2016009888

ISBN 13: 978-1-03-247718-3 (pbk)
ISBN 13: 978-1-138-91911-2 (hbk)
ISBN 13: 978-1-315-68805-3 (ebk)

DOI: 10.4324/9781315688053

Typeset in Bembo
by codeMantra

CONTENTS

List of Figures   *xi*

List of Tables   *xiii*

Notes on Contributors   *xv*

1 Introduction to the Family Business Companion   1
   Franz W. Kellermanns and Frank Hoy

PART I
Strategic Management   **13**

2 What Do We Know About Succession in Family Businesses?
   Mapping Current Knowledge and Unexplored Territory   15
   Carolin Decker, Katharina Heinrichs, Peter Jaskiewicz, and Sabine B. Rau

3 Agency Theory in Family Firm Research: Accomplishments
   and Opportunities   45
   Kristen Madison, Zonghui Li, and Daniel T. Holt

4 Long-Term Orientation: Reviewing the Past and Identifying Future
   Opportunities for Family Business Research   70
   Jeffrey A. Chandler, Miles A. Zachary, Keith H. Brigham, and G. Tyge Payne

5 Upper Echelons in Family Firms: What We Know and
   Still Can Learn About Family-TMT-Involvement   90
   Torben Tretbar, Marko Reimer, and Utz Schäffer

6 Familiness, Socioemotional Wealth, and Internationalization of
Family Firms: A Review of Capabilities and Motivations in
Different Modes of Internationalization 118
Anne Sluhan

7 Socioemotional Wealth Preservation in Family Firms: A Source of Value
Destruction or Value Creation? 143
Ionela Neacsu, Geoffrey Martin, and Luis Gómez-Mejía

8 Family Firms, Stakeholder Relationships, and Competitive Advantage:
A Review and Directions for Future Research 159
J. Kirk Ring, Jessica Brown, and Curtis F. Matherne

9 Credit Rationing in Family Firms: Short-Term vs. Long-Term
Bank Debt Rationing 175
Tensie Steijvers and Wim Voordeckers

10 Multi-Family Offices across the Globe: Recent Developments
and Future Research 195
Carolin Decker

PART II
Entrepreneurship **209**

11 Innovation and Family Business Research: A Review
and Future Directions 211
Nils D. Kraiczy and Andreas Hack

12 Open Innovation: A Literature Review and Recommendations
for Family Business Research 241
Jasper Brinkerink, Anita Van Gils, Yannick Bammens, and Martin Carree

13 Market Orientation and Innovativeness in Family Firms: The Moderating
Influence of Organizational Social Consciousness 267
Clay Dibrell, Cristina Bettinelli, and Kathleen Randerson

14 Corporate Entrepreneurship in Family Business: The When and How 281
*Tommaso Minola, Giovanna Campopiano, Mara Brumana, Lucio Cassia,
and Robert Paul Garrett*

15 Portfolio Entrepreneurship in Family Firms: Taking Stock
and Moving Forward 311
Naveed Akhter

PART III

Organizational Behavior   **329**

16 Family Involvement and Corporate Social Responsibility in
    Small- and Medium-Sized Family Firms   331
    Giovanna Campopiano and Alfredo De Massis

17 Bad Blood in the Boardroom: Antecedents and Outcomes of
    Conflict in Family Firms   349
    Andrew C. Loignon, Franz W. Kellermanns, Kimberly A. Eddleston,
    and Roland E. Kidwell

18 Conflict in Family Business in the Light of Systems Theory   367
    Arist von Schlippe and Hermann Frank

19 More Than a Feeling: The Promise of Experimental Approaches
    for Building Affective and Cognitive Microfoundations of Family
    Firm Behavior   385
    David S. Jiang and Timothy P. Munyon

20 Finding Benevolence in Family Firms: The Case of Stewardship Theory   401
    Matthias Waldkirch and Mattias Nordqvist

PART IV

Family Science   **415**

21 The Heart of the Matter: Family Processes Affect Family Businesses   417
    Sharon M. Danes and Kathryn Stafford

22 Uncovering the 'Missing Variable': The Family in Family
    Business Research   432
    Thomas Rieg and Sabine Rau

23 The Janus Effect: Psychopathy in Family Business   459
    Reginald L. Tucker, Kristen K. Shanine, and James G. Combs

PART V

Special Topics: Country   **481**

24 Family Business Research in China: A Field in the Light
    of Traditional Culture and Transforming Society   483
    Jing Xi, Shanshan Zhang, Linlin Jin, and Garrett Holloway

25 Founders and Successors in China's Family Firms: What Should
We Expect from the Rising Generation? 506
Milton Ming Wang and Michael Carney

26 A Review of the Academic Literature on Family Business in Spanish 522
María Concepción López-Fernández, Ana María Serrano-Bedia,
Marta Pérez-Pérez, Remedios Hernández-Linares, and Manuel Palma-Ruiz

27 Contextual Factors That Affect Selection and Use of Governance Structures
in Latin American Family Enterprises 549
Isabel C. Botero and Gonzalo Gómez Betancourt

28 Family Business in Latin America: The Case of Mexico 567
Edgar Rogelio Ramírez Solís, Verónica Ilián Baños Monroy, and Lucía Alejandra
Rodríguez Acevez

29 Family Business Centers 580
Donna Boone Parsons and Cindy Clarke

Index *591*

FIGURES

4.1	Long-Term Orientation Literature Overview	81
6.1	Overlap of Family, Ownership, and Management	120
12.1	Factors Affecting Open Innovation in (Family) SMEs	256
13.1	Market Orientation and Firm Innovativeness Moderated by Organizational Social Consciousness in Family Firms	276
14.1	Overarching Framework of Family Business Developmental Dimensions and Corporate Entrepreneurship	302
16.1	Proposed Theoretical Model	337
17.1	Path Model Summarizing Relationships	352
22.1	Analytical Framework for the Literature Review	436
22.2	Methodologies Employed	437
23.1	Conceptual Model	469
24.1	Increase in Terms of Enterprise Number During 2013–2014	485
24.2	Registered Capital of Enterprises During 2013–2014	485
24.3	Tax Amount of Enterprises During 2013–2014	486
24.4	Industry Distribution of CFB in 2015	486
24.5	Established Time of CFB by 2015	487
24.6	Annual Revenue of CFB in 2015	487
24.7	Succession Stage of CFB in 2015	487
24.8	Temporal Analysis of Article Publication	489
24.9	Productivity of Journals	491
25.1	Differences Between Founders and Successors	517
26.1	Total Percentages of Family Business Articles Retrieved from Dialnet's Categories	524
26.2	Total Percentages of Family Business Articles Retrieved from Dialnet's Sub-Categories	524
26.3	Productivity of Family Business Articles per Country	525

26.4 Number of Publications on Family Business per Year   529
26.5 Strategic Matrix Results   533
27.1 Influence of Societal Culture on Selection and Use of Corporate
      Governance Structures and Policies   554
27.2 Characteristics of Latin American Enterprises That Affect
      the Selection and Use of Governance Structures   559

TABLES

2.1	Studies on Succession According to Process Stages and Levels of Analysis	18
2.2	Factors Affecting Post-Succession Performance	32
3.1	Family Firm Agency Theory Research	49
4.1	Sample Definitions of Long-Term Orientation and Related Terms in Family Business Research	76
4.2	Measures of Long-Term Orientation in Family Business Research	79
6.1	Review: Family Firm Motivations and Capabilities for Internationalization Based on Entry Mode	129
7.1	The Negative and Positive Effects of SEW Preservation	153
9.1	Pairwise Correlations	181
9.2	Descriptive Statistics	182
9.3	Estimation of the 'Demand-Supply Disequilibrium' Models for Long- and Short-Term Bank Debt	185
9.4	Proportion Credit Rationed Family and Nonfamily Firms (1994–2001)	187
9.5	Frequency of Credit Rationing of Family Firms	187
9.6	Comparison of Profile of Long-Term Credit Rationed Versus Long-Term Non-Credit Rationed Family Firms	188
10.1	The Activity System Design Framework Applied to Multi-Family Offices	198
11.1	Type of Studies	213
11.2	Theoretical Perspectives	213
11.3	Empirical Studies Analyzed in the Review	217
12.1	Overview of Literature on Open Innovation in Family and Nonfamily SMEs	245
13.1	Descriptives and Correlations of Family Firms	274
13.2	Firm Innovativeness in Family Firms with 2-Way Interaction	275
14.1	Family Business Developmental Dynamics	286
14.2	Findings from the Literature Review: CE Along Family Business Developmental Dynamics	294
15.1	Selected Studies on Portfolio Entrepreneurship	314
15.2	Studies on Portfolio Entrepreneurship in the Family Firm Context	316
16.1	Means, Standard Deviations, and Correlations	340
16.2	Hierarchic Logit Regression for CSR Engagement in Family Firms	341

17.1	Strategies for Reducing Family Conflict and Limiting the Fredo Effect	359
18.1	Differences Between the Logics	373
19.1	Experimental Design Steps and Recommendations	388
22.1	Journals and Articles Reviewed for the Literature Review	435
22.2	Classification and Summary of Reviewed Articles	450
23.1	Psychopathy and Family Studies	463
24.1	CFB's Economic Contribution	485
24.2	Journal Distribution of CFB Articles	490
24.3	Authors with More Than Five Articles	492
24.4	Researchers and Their Articles in English	493
24.5	Result of High Frequency Keyword Clustering Analysis	495
24.6	Comparison of English and Chinese FB Research	503
26.1	Search Criteria Used in Dialnet	523
26.2	Number of Articles on Family Business in Spanish per Country	525
26.3	Journals in Dialnet That Have Published at Least Three Articles on Family Business	526
26.4	Search Criteria Used in Web of Science and Scopus Databases	527
26.5	Productivity per Country	529
26.6	Most Productive Journals on Family Business Literature in Spanish	530
26.7	Most Productive Authors on Family Business Studies in Spanish	531
26.8	Most Productive Institutions on Family Business Studies in Spanish	531
26.9	Main Groups of Co-words Identified Using Hierarchical Clustering Analysis	533
26.10	Comparative Methodological Parameters	538
26.11	Primary Topics Covered (Benavides-Velasco, Quintana-Garcia, and Guzman-Parra 2013 Versus Web of Science and Scopus)	539
27.1	Effects of Culture on Corporate Governance Based on Each Environment	553

Appendix

Appendix 5.A	List of Relevant Articles	102
Appendix 5.B	Mapping of Dependent Variables and Upper-Echelons Themes	109
Appendix 9.A	Definitions of Variables of Demand-Supply Disequilibrium Models	190
Appendix 11.A	Highly Ranked Journals Publishing Family Business Articles	236

CONTRIBUTORS

Editors

Frank Hoy is the Paul R. Beswick Professor of Innovation and Entrepreneurship and the Director of the Collaborative for Entrepreneurship and Innovation at Worcester Polytechnic Institute. Dr. Hoy earned his Ph.D. at Texas A&M University where he developed a small business outreach program for the Texas Agricultural Extension Service. Subsequently, he became the Director of the Small Business Development Center for the State of Georgia. He moved from the University of Georgia to Georgia State University in 1988 as the Carl R. Zwerner Professor of Family-Owned Businesses. From 1991 to 2001 Dr. Hoy was the Dean of the College of Business Administration and from 2001 to 2009 the Director of the Entrepreneurship Centers at the University of Texas at El Paso. His most recent books are *Entrepreneurial Family Firms* (with Pramodita Sharma, 2010) and *Small Business Management* (17th ed. with William Petty and Leslie Palich, 2014).

Franz W. Kellermanns is the Addison H. & Gertrude C. Reese Endowed Chair in International Business and Professor of Management in the Belk College of Business at the University of North Carolina – Charlotte. His research interests include international business, strategy process, and entrepreneurship with a focus on family business research. He is an Editor of *Entrepreneurship Theory and Practice* and former Associate Editor of *Family Business Review*. He has published in journals such as *Organization Science, Journal of Management, Journal of Management Studies, Journal of Organizational Behavior, Journal of Business Venturing, Entrepreneurship Theory and Practice, Family Business Review, Academy of Management Learning and Education*, etc. He serves on the Editorial Boards of *Journal of Business Venturing, Journal of Management, Journal of Management Studies, Group and Organization Management, Family Business Review, Journal of Family Business Strategy*, and *Strategic Entrepreneurship Journal*.

Chapter Authors

Naveed Akhter is a doctoral candidate and lecturer in Entrepreneurship and Strategy at Jönköping International Business School, Jönköping University, Sweden. He teaches and conducts research in the areas of entrepreneurship, strategy, and family firms. The primary focus of his doctoral dissertation is enduring entrepreneurship and exit strategies in family business portfolios. He is a member of Entrepreneurship and Organization & Management Theory divisions of the Academy of Management.

Yannick Bammens is an Assistant Professor of Management at the Maastricht University School of Business and Economics, Department of Organization and Strategy, the Netherlands. His research centers on innovation management and corporate governance, with a special interest in the setting of founder- and family-led enterprises. His work in this field received several best paper awards at international conferences and appeared in various academic journals such as *Family Business Review*, *Journal of Management*, and *Journal of Product Innovation Management*. Yannick also serves on the editorial review board of *Family Business Review*.

Verónica Ilián Baños Monroy is a Professor of Entrepreneurship at Tecnológico de Monterrey, Mexico. She received her M.Sc. A. from Tecnológico de Monterrey (ITESM), a Ph.D. in Administrative Science from the Universidad Nacional Autónoma de México (UNAM) and a second Ph.D. in International Business from the Universidad Autónoma de Madrid (UAM) in Spain. She studies the succession process and innovation in family firms. She has served as a Visiting Professor at the University of San Diego. She has also published articles in different international academic journals. She currently serves as a full-time Professor and as a Family Business Consultant in the Entrepreneurship Division at Tecnológico de Monterrey, Campus Guadalajara; she teaches courses in Family Business and Service Management at the undergraduate and masters levels.

Gonzalo Gómez Betancourt is the Director of the Family Business and Business Policy areas at INALDE Business School, Universidad de La Sabana, Colombia. He obtained his Ph.D. in Management at IESE – University of Navarra in Spain. His research interest includes: typologies of family business (FB), corporate governance in FB, factors that influence strategy and performance in FB, emotional intelligence in FB, ownership responsibilities in FB. He serves on IFERA board of directors and is the Liaison Officer to IFERA fellows.

Cristina Bettinelli is an Assistant Professor of Management at the University of Bergamo, Italy. She earned her Ph.D. from the University of Bergamo where she majored in Strategic Management and did part of her graduate studies at Harvard University. Areas of research interest include corporate governance, entrepreneurship, family firms, and small–medium firms. Her research has been published in academic journals including *Family Business Review*, *Journal of Family Business Strategy*, *Small Business Economics*, *Futures*, and *Management Decision*. She is on the editorial review boards of *Family Business Review* as well as a special issue guest editor for *International Journal of Entrepreneurship and Small Business* and *Journal of Small Business Management*. She has taught management, entrepreneurship, and international business courses at the undergraduate and graduate level (master). She has received the best 2011 paper award from *Family Business Review*; the excellent reviewer award from *Family Business Review* for 2011 and 2012; the distinguished reviewer award in 2014 from the *Academy of Management Conference (Entrepreneurship Division)*; the *Small Business Management Journal* editor's choice award in 2015; and the best unpublished research award from the *Family Firm Institute* in 2015.

Isabel C. Botero is an Assistant Professor of Entrepreneurship and Family Enterprise in the Department of Management at Stetson University, Florida, and Research Principal at Fediuk Botero LLC. She obtained her Ph.D. from Michigan State University. Her research interests include communication in and about family firms, governance issues in family firms, and influence processes in organizations. She serves as the Co-Leader of the Successful Transgenerational Entrepreneurship Practices (STEP) at Stetson University.

Keith H. Brigham, Ph.D., is the Kent R. Hance Professor in Entrepreneurship at the Rawls College of Business at Texas Tech University where he is the Director of Entrepreneurship Programs. His primary research interests are in entrepreneurial cognition, temporal orientation, and family business. His research has been published in a number of journals such as *Business Ethics Quarterly*, *Entrepreneurship Theory and Practice*, *Family Business Review*, *The Leadership Quarterly*, *Journal of Business Venturing*, and *Organizational Research Methods*. Dr. Brigham has won several best paper awards and university-wide teaching awards. He currently serves on the editorial review boards of *Entrepreneurship Theory and Practice*, *Family Business Review*, *Group & Organization Management*, and *Strategic Entrepreneurship Journal*.

Jasper Brinkerink is a Ph.D. candidate at the Maastricht University School of Business and Economics, Department of Organization and Strategy, the Netherlands. For his dissertation, he studies innovation management in the context of small and medium-sized (family) enterprises. Research interests beyond his thesis include the effects of large capital investments on a firm's productivity and the energy efficiency of firms. His work received the best conference research paper award at the IFERA 2015 annual conference in Hamburg.

Jessica Brown is originally from the Central Coast of New South Wales, Australia and graduated with a Bachelor's degree in Business Administration from Newman University in Wichita, Kansas. She is currently pursuing her Master's degree in Business Administration, with a concentration in Finance, at Wichita State University in Wichita, Kansas, where she also works for the Director of the Kansas Family Business Forum. Jessica recently concluded a research project on all family business forums within the United States.

Mara Brumana is Research Fellow at the University of Bergamo, Italy. She is also a member of the Research Center for Young and Family Enterprise (CYFE). Her research interests lie at the intersection of entrepreneurship, organization theory, and international business, with a particular focus on family firms' entrepreneurial initiatives, strategic change, and power relationships within multinational corporations.

Giovanna Campopiano is an Assistant Professor at the Chair of Business Administration and Family Entrepreneurship at the Witten Institute for Family Business (WIFU), University of Witten/Herdecke, Germany. She has published, among others, in *Family Business Review*, *Journal of Family Business Strategy*, *Journal of Small Business Management*, and *Journal of Business Ethics*. Her research interests mainly focus on management issues in Family Business in relation to corporate social responsibility, sustainability, growth, governance, and entrepreneurial activities.

Michael Carney is the Concordia University Research Chair in Strategy and Entrepreneurship at the John Molson School of Business, Montréal and Visiting Professor at Renmin University of China. He has published extensively on the corporate and organizational strategies of Asia's family-owned business groups and on the development of the global institutional environment of international aviation. His research focuses on entrepreneurship and the comparative analysis of business, financial and governance systems and their influence upon the development of firm capabilities and strategic assets, and national competitiveness. He is currently editor-in-chief of the *Asia Pacific Journal of Management*. His research is published in *Academy of Management Journal*, *Asia Pacific Journal of Management*, *Corporate Governance: An International Review Entrepreneurship Theory and Practice*, *Journal of Management*, *Journal of Management Studies*, *Management and Organization Review*, *Organizations Studies*, and *Strategic Management Journal*.

Martin Carree is a Full Professor of Industrial Organization (since 2003) and Head of the Department of Organization and Strategy at the School of Business and Economics of Maastricht University, the Netherlands. He received his Ph.D. in 1997 from Erasmus University Rotterdam. He has published in a range of international refereed journals in the fields of entrepreneurship, applied econometrics, regional economics, competition policy, industrial dynamics, and innovation studies.

Lucio Cassia is a Full Professor in Strategic Management and Entrepreneurship. He teaches strategic management, corporate strategy, competition and growth, and entrepreneurial strategy in graduate, post-graduate, and Ph.D. programs. He is currently leading research, education, and consulting on entrepreneurship, business strategy, and family business. His main interests are in technology-based start-ups, high-tech companies, innovation tools, and patterns of growth of small and medium enterprises. With particular focus on the topics of youth entrepreneurship, growth of family businesses, managerial succession, and generational change, Lucio promoted and founded the Research Center for Young and Family Enterprise (CYFE). He has published 10 books and over 150 papers in academic and professional journals.

Jeffrey A. Chandler is a Ph.D. student at the Rawls College of Business at Texas Tech University. He received his Bachelor of Business Administration at the University of Texas at Tyler and his Master of Business Administration at the University of North Texas. His research interests include temporal orientation, organizational identity, signaling theory, corporate entrepreneurship, and family business.

Cindy Clarke was raised in a family-owned business (Jack and Jill Nursery School) in Weaverville, North Carolina. Cindy has been the Executive Director of the UNC Asheville Family Business Forum since 2006. The Forum is a continuing education program for family-owned and privately-held businesses. Under her guidance the Forum has increased its membership and number of strategic partners; created the position as a key component of business relations at the University; is well-known for its quality programs from leading national experts, and hosted national family brands such as Bush Brother Beans, White Castle Burgers, Crane and Company, the Brown-Foreman Corporation, The McIlhenny Company, and LL Bean. She has been a guest on and producer of numerous radio talk shows focusing on family business challenges, led workshops for business owners at area community colleges, civic, and business organizations. The UNC Asheville Family Business Forum will host the Family Enterprise Research Conference in 2017.

James (Jim) Combs completed his Ph.D. at Louisiana State University and is currently the Dr. Phillips Chair of American Private Enterprise at the University of Central Florida. His research interests are primarily in the areas of franchising, family business, research synthesis, and executive compensation, and appears in journals such as the *Academy of Management Journal*, *Strategic Management Journal*, *Journal of Management*, *Journal of Business Venturing*, *Entrepreneurship Theory and Practice*, and *Organizational Research Methods*. Jim has served as an Associate Editor at the *Academy of Management Journal*, and is currently an Editor at *Entrepreneurship Theory and Practice*. He has served on the Executive Committee of the Business Policy and Strategy Division of the Academy of Management, and as the President of the Southern Management Association (SMA) where he is also a Fellow. Jim teaches entrepreneurship and strategic management at the doctoral and masters levels.

Sharon M. Danes is a Professor in the Family Social Science Department at the University of Minnesota and one of the authors of the Sustainable Family Business Theory. She has authored over 150 refereed research articles, book chapters, and outreach publications emphasizing the intersection of economic and social decision making. She has received over $1,050,000 of research and educational grants in recent years; the most recent grant was from National Science Foundation. She has been a Juran Faculty Scholar, Juran Center for Leadership in Quality, Carlson School of Management, University of Minnesota. She is a Past-Chair of the Family Business Section of the U.S. Association for Small Business and Entrepreneurship. She serves on several editorial boards of research journals.

Carolin Decker is a Professor of Management and Organization at the University of Bremen, Germany. Her research interests include family businesses and family offices, the governance of interorganizational relationships (for example, strategic alliances and buyer–supplier relationships), and organizational decline and recovery (for example, divestiture and turnaround strategies). Carolin mainly conducts quantitative research. She has published her research in journals including *Academy of Management Perspectives*, *British Journal of Management*, *Journal of Retailing*, *Industry and Innovation*, *European Management Journal*, and *Organizational Dynamics*.

Alfredo De Massis is Professor of Entrepreneurship & Family Business at the Free University of Bozen-Bolzano, Italy and Lancaster University Management School, England, where he is Director of the School's Centre for Family Business. In September 2015, *Family Capital* ranked him among the world's top 25 star professors for family business. He serves as Chair of the Family Business Research SIG at the European Academy of Management (EURAM) and as member of the Academic Advisory Board of the Institute for Family Business (IFB) Research Foundation. Alfredo's research interests focus on family business. On these topics, he has published widely in leading academic and professional journals. In the past few years, Alfredo has co-edited nine special issues in journals like *Entrepreneurship Theory and Practice*, *California Management Review*, *Journal of Product Innovation Management*, *Global Strategy Journal*, *Small Business Economics*, and *International Journal of Management Reviews*. He serves on the Editorial Boards of *Entrepreneurship Theory and Practice*, *Family Business Review*, *Strategic Entrepreneurship Journal*, and *Journal of Family Business Strategy*. His research has been featured in various media outlets including the *Financial Times*, *Reuters*, and *Harvard Business Review*.

Clay Dibrell is an Associate Professor of Management, holder of the William Gresham, Jr., Entrepreneurial Professorship at the University of Mississippi, and a U.S. Fulbright Scholar. He earned his Ph.D. from the University of Memphis where he majored in Strategic Management and minored in International Business. Areas of research interest include family enterprises, innovation, and environmental sustainability. His research is forthcoming or has been published in leading academic journals, including: *Entrepreneurship Theory and Practice*, *Family Business Review*, *Journal of Family Business Strategy*, *Journal of Business Ethics*, *Journal of Small Business Management*, *Small Business Economics*, *Journal of Business Research*, *IEEE Transactions on Engineering Management*, *Industrial Marketing Management*, *Management International Review*, and *Journal of World Business*. He is an associate editor of the *Journal of Family Business Strategy*, and on the editorial review boards of *Family Business Review* and *Journal of World Business*, as well as a special issue guest editor for multiple journals. He has taught entrepreneurship, strategic management, and international business courses at the undergraduate, MBA, doctorate, and/or EMBA levels in the U.S., Europe, and Australia. His interest in entrepreneurship and small business is, in part, derived from his family, where both of his grandfathers either started or ran small businesses, his father-in-law and mother-in-law ran a successful small business before retiring, and his father founded and managed a successful radio station for over 30 years.

Kimberly A. Eddleston is the Schulze Distinguished Professor of Entrepreneurship and Professor of Entrepreneurship & Innovation at the D'Amore-McKim School of Business, Northeastern University, Massachusetts. She also holds the Daniel and Dorothy Grady Research Fellowship and is a research fellow at the University of St. Gallen, Switzerland. Her research focuses on family businesses and the careers of entrepreneurs. Professor Eddleston is an associate editor of the *Journal of Business Venturing* and serves on the editorial board of multiple journals including *Entrepreneurship Theory & Practice, Family Business Review, Journal of Family Business Strategy, Group & Organization Management*, and *Strategic Entrepreneurship Journal*. Her research has appeared in prestigious journals such as the *Academy of Management Journal, Strategic Management Journal, Journal of Applied Psychology, Journal of International Business Studies, Academy of Management Perspectives, Journal of Business Venturing, Entrepreneurship Theory and Practice*, and *Journal of Management Studies*.

Hermann Frank is a Professor at WU Vienna, Austria, visiting Professor at University Witten/Herdecke, Germany, and the Director of the Research Institute for Family Business at WU Vienna. He is associate editor of the Journal of Small Business Management and editorial board member of several entrepreneurship and small business journals. He has published his research in Entrepreneurship Theory and Practice, Entrepreneurship and Regional Development, Journal of Family Business Strategy, and International Small Business Journal among many others. His research interests focus on family business, especially familiness, family governance, conflicts in family business, and corporate entrepreneurship.

Robert Garrett is an Assistant Professor of Entrepreneurship at the University of Louisville and earned his Ph.D. from Indiana University in 2008. He has published in *Organization Science, Entrepreneurship Theory and Practice, Journal of Product Innovation Management, Journal of Business Venturing*, and other entrepreneurship journals. His primary area of research emphasis is on internal corporate venturing. He serves on the editorial board of *Entrepreneurship Theory and Practice*.

Luis R. Gómez-Mejía is a Professor of Management at the WP Carey School of Business, Arizona State University. He was the Ray and Milan Siegfried Professor of Management at the Mendoza College of Business in Notre Dame, the Benton Cocanougher Chair in Business at Texas A & M University, and faculty member at Arizona State University, where he was a Council of 100 Distinguished Scholar, a Regents Professor, and Arizona Heritage Chair holder. Gómez-Mejía has received numerous awards in his professional career, including the Outstanding Alumni Award from the University of Minnesota (given to approximately two out of every 50,000 graduates from the University of Minnesota), Doctor Honoris Causa at Carlos III University, Spain, and Regents Professor (awarded to less than 1 percent of Arizona State University faculty). He was inducted into the Hall of Fame of the Academy of Management (given to 33 Academy of Management members out of approximately 20,000 members). He has also received numerous awards for his research, including best paper in the *Academy of Management Journal*, best paper in *Administrative Science Quarterly*, and highest impact paper from the Entrepreneurship Division of

Academy of Management. Gómez-Mejía, who has been named in several studies as one of the top management scholars in the world, has published more than 200 articles and 15 books in various management areas. His research interests cover international management, family business, strategic management, and executive compensation. His research has appeared in the best management journals: *Academy of Management Journal, Academy of Management Review, Strategic Management Journal,* and *Administrative Science Quarterly.* His research has been cited more than 12,000 times. Luis Gómez-Mejía was an elected member of the Board of Governors of the Academy of Management and served as president of the Personnel/Human Resources Division of the Academy of Management (with approximately 2,500 members). He was elected for three terms as president of the Iberoamerican Academy of Management (an affiliate of the Academy of Management), which covers Spain/Portugal, all of Latin America, as well as the Hispanic faculty in U.S. universities.

Andreas Hack is the Director of the Institute of Organization and Human Resource Management and Professor of Human Resource Management at the University of Bern in Switzerland. He is also affiliated with the Witten Institute for Family Business of the Witten/Herdecke University in Germany. His research interests include leadership and decision-making behavior in the context of family firms and small and medium-sized firms. He has published in leading innovation, entrepreneurship, and family business journals such as *Journal of Product Innovation Management, Entrepreneurship Theory and Practice, Small Business Economics, Journal of Small Business Management, British Journal of Management,* and *Family Business Review,* among others.

Katharina Heinrichs is a Ph.D. graduate from WHU-Otto Beisheim School of Management in Vallendar, Germany. Her Ph.D. thesis focuses on succession in family businesses, with parts of it published in *Entrepreneurship Theory and Practice.* She held a scholarship from the EQUA Foundation during her Ph.D. studies and is now working for a German family business.

Remedios Hernández-Linares is a Lecturer in the Department of Financial Economy and Accounting of the University of Extremadura, Spain. Her primary research interests include family businesses, business strategy, entrepreneurship, and higher education learning. *remedioshl@unex.es*

Garrett Holloway is an Organizational Science doctoral student at the University of North Carolina at Charlotte. He earned a Master's Degree in Industrial-Organizational Psychology from Radford University, Virginia, and a Bachelor's Degree in Psychology from Louisiana State University. He may be contacted at ghollow3@uncc.edu.

Daniel T. Holt is an Associate Professor of Management in the College of Business at Mississippi State University. He received his Ph.D. in Management from Auburn University, Alabama. Prior to joining the faculty at Mississippi State University, he served in the U.S. Air Force, serving as an engineer in Central America, Asia, and the Middle East and as a professor at the Air Force Institute of Technology at Wright-Patterson Air Force Base. Daniel's research interests include family business, entrepreneurship, measurement methods, and organizational change. His research has appeared in *Family Business Review, Entrepreneurship Theory and Practice, Journal of Applied Psychology,* and *Journal of Management Studies.*

Peter Jaskiewicz is a CIBC Distinguished Professor and an Associate Professor at Concordia University in Montreal, Canada. He conducts quantitative and qualitative research on family business and entrepreneurship. His current research interests involve transgenerational entrepreneurship, executive team compensation, nepotism, corporate reputation, and succession planning. His research has been widely published in journals such as *Journal of Management Studies*, *Journal of Business Venturing*, *Journal of Management*, *Family Business Review*, *Entrepreneurship Theory and Practice*, and *Academy of Management Learning & Education*.

David S. Jiang is a Ph.D. candidate in Organizations and Strategy at the University of Tennessee and an incoming Assistant Professor of Entrepreneurship at Georgia Southern University. His research interests integrate psychological approaches to emotion, motivation, and social behavior with entrepreneurship and family business research.

Linlin Jin is an Associate Professor at the Guangdong University of Technology, School of Management, Department of Management Science and Engineering China. He earned his Master's Degree and Ph.D. in Management Science and Engineering from Beijing Institute of Technology, China. After that, he worked for two years as a postdoctoral in organizational behavior in Sun Yat-sen University, China. His research interest is in TMT and scientific research teams. His research papers have been published in academic journals including *International Journal of Human Resource Management*, and *Social Behavior and Personality*. He has been granted Chinese National Fund of Natural Science for his research on scientific research teams' innovation. He once worked in Tennessee University at Knoxville for one year as a visiting scholar. Courses he teaches include Operation Management, Statistics, Managerial System Engineering, and Strategic Management. He may be contacted at jinlinlin@gdut.edu.cn.

Roland Kidwell is a Professor of Management and Chair of the Department of Management Programs in the College of Business at Florida Atlantic University in Boca Raton. His research currently focuses on family firms and franchisor-franchisee relationships. His research has been published in *Academy of Management Review*, *Journal of Management*, *Journal of Business Venturing*, *Entrepreneurship Theory and Practice*, *Journal of Business Ethics*, *Journal of Family Business Strategy*, *Journal of Management History*, and *Human Resource Management*. He is past Chair of the Management History Division of the Academy of Management, and previously served as its division's Chair, Scholarly Program Chair, and Professional Development Workshop Chair.

Nils D. Kraiczy is a Senior Research Assistant at the Institute of Organization and Human Resource Management of the University of Bern in Switzerland. He received his Ph.D. from the WHU – Otto Beisheim School of Management in Germany. His research interests include innovation management of small and medium-sized firms with a focus on family firms. He has published his research in the *Journal of Product Innovation Management*, *Journal of Business Research*, *International Journal of Innovation Management*, *Journal of Business Economics*, *Entrepreneurship Theory and Practice*, and *Small Business Economics*, among others.

Zonghui Li is a Ph.D. candidate in management in the College of Business at Mississippi State University. Previously, she earned her Ph.D. from Nanjing University, China with research interests in international business. Prior to joining the Ph.D. program at Mississippi State University, she visited North Dakota State University as a visiting scholar. Her current research interests include corporate governance, organizational change, and family business. Her research has been published in *Journal of Management Studies*.

Andrew C. Loignon is an Assistant Professor of Management at NEOMA Business School. Andrew's current research interests focus on work groups and teams, quantitative methodologies, and social class in the workplace.

María Concepción López-Fernández is an Associate Professor of Management in the Department of Business Administration of the University of Cantabria (UC), Spain. She holds the Banco Santander Chair of Family Business at the UC, and is the president of the Entrepreneurship and Business Creation Section of the Scientific Association of Economics and Business (ACEDE) in Spain. She has served as Dean of the Business School and as Vice-President of the UC. Her published research appears in journals such as *Organization and Environment*, *Tourism Management*, *Cornell Hospitality Quarterly*, *R&D Management*, *Total Quality Management*, *Journal of Small Business Management*, and *International Journal of Production Research*. Her primary research interests include family firms, business strategy and structure, innovation management, entrepreneurship, organizational flexibility, and tourism.

Kristen ("Kincy") Madison is an Assistant Professor of Management in the College of Business at Mississippi State University. She received her Ph.D. in Organizations and Strategy from the University of Tennessee. She has a B.S. in Management and a M.S. in Human Resources, both from Auburn University, Alabama. Kincy's research interest is family business, with a focus on topics that intersect strategic management and human resources, such as governance, leadership, and competitive advantage. Her research has appeared in *Family Business Review*, *Journal of Family Business Strategy*, and *Academy of Management Perspectives*.

Geoff Martin is an Associate Professor of Strategy at Melbourne Business School. He has worked as a chartered accountant, in finance roles with investment banks, and as a strategy consultant. He completed his Ph.D. in Management at IE Business School in Madrid, Spain, before joining Melbourne Business School in 2012. His research interests cover strategic decision making, executive compensation, risk-taking, and corporate governance. Geoff has published in the leading practitioner and academic journals, including *Harvard Business Review*, the *Academy of Management Journal*, *Strategic Management Journal*, *Entrepreneurship Theory and Practice*, *Journal of Business Ethics*, and *Human Resource Management*.

Curtis Matherne is an Associate Professor of Management in the B.I. Moody III College of Business Administration at the University of Louisiana at Lafayette. He received his doctorate in organizational behavior from Mississippi State University. His research interests include ethical behaviors and identity dynamics in organizational settings, focusing primarily on family owned businesses. His work has appeared in *Entrepreneurship Theory and Practice*, *Family Business Review*, *Journal of Behavioral and Applied Management*, *Strategic Organization*, and *Journal of Leadership, Accountability and Ethics* and he currently serves on the editorial review board of *Family Business Review*. Prior to entering academia, Dr. Matherne earned his MBA with an emphasis in finance from the University of Southern Mississippi and worked as a corporate financial analyst for Isle of Capri Casinos, Inc. headquarters. Dr. Matherne is a native of Biloxi, MS and currently resides in Youngsville, LA.

Tommaso Minola is co-founder and the Director of the Research Center for Young and Family Enterprise (CYFE) of the University of Bergamo, Italy, where he is Lecturer in the fields of Technology Management, Entrepreneurship and Strategy. He is TOFT Visiting Professor at Jönköping International Business School, Sweden. His research and teaching is focused on entrepreneurship, family business, technological innovation, and technology transfer. His work has been published in several academic journals such as: *Strategic Entrepreneurship Journal*, *Small Business Economics*, *Journal of Small Business Management*, *R&D Management*, and *The Journal of Technology Transfer*. He is member of several academic and professional associations on entrepreneurship and family business, and reviewer for major international journals in the field. He has also been Technology Manager and the Director of Technology Incubator at Politecnico di Milano.

Timothy P. Munyon earned his Ph.D. at Florida State University and is an Assistant Professor of Management and the Ray & Joan Myatt Faculty Research Fellow at the Haslam College of Business, the University of Tennessee. His research interests include social influence, affect and emotion, and human resource management practices.

Ionela Neacsu is an Assistant Professor in the Strategy and Innovation Department at the ESC Rennes School of Business, France. She has worked as a Postdoctoral Researcher in the Strategic Management Department at the IESE Business School, Spain, before joining ESC Rennes School of Business in 2016. Ionela holds a Ph.D. in Business Administration and Quantitative Methods from Universidad Carlos III de Madrid (since 2015). Her research interests cover corporate governance, family business, strategic decision making, and executive compensation. Ionela has presented her work over the past years in international conferences, including the annual meetings of the Academy of Management and Strategic Management Society.

Mattias Nordqvist is a Professor in Business Administration and the Hamrin International Professor of Family Business, and the Director of the Center for Family Enterprise and Ownership (CeFEO) at Jönköping International Business School, Sweden. He is also a Visiting Professor at Swedish University of Agricultural Sciences Nordqvist is a former co-Director of the Global STEP Project and Visiting Scholar at Babson College, Massachusetts, University of Alberta, Canada, and Bocconi University, Italy. He has served on the board of the International Family Enterprise Research Academy (IFERA). Nordqvist is a recipient of the Young Entrepreneurship Researcher Award from the Swedish Entrepreneurship Forum and the Swedish Agency for Economic and Regional Growth. He is a founding associate editor of the *Journal of Family Business Strategy* and serves on the editorial board of several journals.

Manuel Palma-Ruiz is a Professor in the Department of Administration, Business and Finance at the School of Business and Humanities at Tecnológico de Monterrey, Campus Chihuahua, Mexico. He has been a visiting scholar at the University of Cantabria, Spain, serving as a coordinator of the Banco Santander Chair of Family Business, and guest professor of Family Business in the Department of Business Administration. Palma-Ruiz is a member of alumni associations such as the Walton International Scholarship Program in U.S.A., Fundación Carolina in Spain, and the National Council for Science and Technology (CONACYT) in Mexico. His current research interests include strategic management and entrepreneurship with a focus on family firms.

Donna Parsons took her first job in the family business at age 8. She has worked for over twenty years as a principal in her family's consulting firm serving family-owned businesses across North America. Her work as a consultant led her to an adjunct teaching position where she discovered a passion for working with students in the classroom. As a consultant, Donna provided developmental support in the creation of and, then, served for eight years as the faculty liaison to the UNC Asheville Family Business Forum. Currently, she is an Assistant Professor of Business at Mars Hill University in Mars Hill, North Carolina. She holds an MBA from the University of Tennessee and is a Ph.D. Candidate in Business Administration from the Sobey School of Business at Saint Mary's University in Halifax, Nova Scotia. She has published in international journals in the area of gender in organizations. Donna's current research interests include gender and women in family firms.

G. Tyge Payne, Ph.D., is the Georgie G. Snyder Professor of Strategic Management at the Rawls College of Business, Texas Tech University. His research interests include configurations, family business, firm-level entrepreneurship, organizational ethics, multi-level methods, social capital, and temporality. Published research appears in journals such as *Business Ethics Quarterly*, *Entrepreneurship Theory and Practice (ET&P)*, *Family Business Review (FBR)*, *Journal of Business Ethics*, *Journal of Management (JOM)*, *Journal of Management Studies*, *Journal of Small Business Management (JSBM)*, *Organizational Research Methods*, *Organization Science*, and *Strategic Entrepreneurship Journal (SEJ)*, among others. Dr. Payne is currently an Associate Editor for *FBR*. He is also on the editorial review boards of *ET&P*, *Group and Organization Management*, *JSBM*, *JOM*, and *SEJ*.

Marta Pérez-Pérez is an Assistant Professor of Operations Management in the Department of Business Administration, University of Cantabria, Spain. Her primary interests are the effects of organizational flexibility on firm performance, entrepreneurship, family firm, and bibliometric analysis. Published research appears in journals such as *Journal of Small Business Management* or *International Journal of Production Research*.

Kathleen Randerson is an Associate Professor of Entrepreneurship at EDC Paris Business School. She earned her Ph.D. from the Université de Grenoble Alpes. She is also a visiting professor at the University of Bergamo, Italy, where she teaches entrepreneurship and international business. Her research interests include Corporate Entrepreneurship, Entrepreneurial Orientation, Internationalisation, and Family Entrepreneurship. Her works are forthcoming or have been published in both French language and international refereed journals such as *La Revue Française de Gestion*, *Management & Avenir*, *la Revue de l'Entrepreneuriat*, *M@n@gement*, the *International Journal of Entrepreneurship and Small Business*, *Futures*, and the *Journal of Family Business Strategy*, as well as a special issue guest editor for several journals. She is currently the Coordinator of the ECSB special interest group dedicated to Corporate Entrepreneurship and Chair of the Communications Committee of the Entrepreneurship Division of the Academy of Management.

Sabine Rau is a Professor of Entrepreneurship and Family Business at King's College London. Before going back to academia again, Professor Rau founded her own business before joining her family's business. She re-started her academic career as a Research Fellow at INSEAD in 2001. In 2003 Professor Rau took over the presidency of the international family business researchers, ifera (www.ifera.org), which she led until 2007. She serves on several boards as an independent Director such as the Aufsichtsrat of Steuler (www.steuler.de), a hidden champion from Germany. Professor Rau has published in various journals such as *Strategic Management Journal*, *Journal of Business Venturing*, *Family Business Review*, *Journal of Business Research*, *Entrepreneurship Theory and Practice*, *Small Business Economics*, *Entrepreneurship and Regional Development*, and others. Her research focus is on the influence of family onto the business and vice versa. Topics such as succession, governance, and family specific resources and its influence on performance are central to her research.

Marko Reimer is an Assistant Professor at the Institute of Management Accounting and Control of WHU Otto Beisheim School of Management in Germany. He obtained his doctoral degree from the TU Berlin in 2011. His research focusses on upper echelons and top management teams. In current projects, he explores how top management teams and middle managers interact in strategy formulation and implementation. Marko's work has been presented at several international conferences and published in top-tier management journals such as *Organization Studies* and *Human Resource Management.*

Thomas Rieg is currently working at TRUMPF, a family-owned business in the machine tool industry. Previously, he completed his Ph.D. and worked as a research assistant at the Institute for Family Business Research at WHU – Otto Beisheim School of Management in Germany. He has studied business administration and economics on an undergraduate and postgraduate level at the University of Mannheim in Germany. Furthermore, he holds a Master's degree from Queen's University in Canada. His research focuses on the interplay of family dynamics, governance, and innovation in family firms and has been published in the *Academy of Management Proceedings* (2015) as well as several practitioner-oriented outlets.

J. Kirk Ring is an Assistant Professor of Management in the College of Business at Louisiana Tech University. He received his doctorate in business strategy and entrepreneurship from Mississippi State University. His research interests include family firms (stakeholder relationships, decision making, socioemotional wealth, agency relationships, identity), entrepreneurship (opportunity recognition, business models, innovation), strategic decision making, and corporate governance. His work has appeared in *The Family Business Review, Entrepreneurship Theory and Practice, Journal of Behavioral and Applied Management, Journal of Management Education, Journal of Entrepreneurship and Public Policy, Venture Capital,* and *American Journal of Entrepreneurship,* and he currently serves on the editorial review board for *Family Business Review.* Dr. Ring was previously an Associate Professor of Management at Wichita State University where he held the position of Director of the Kansas Family Business Forum.

Lucía Rodríguez-Aceves is a Professor of Entrepreneurship at Tecnológico de Monterrey, Mexico. She received her Ph.D. in Business Administration from EGADE Business School. Her research interests include knowledge management and strategy in family firms, with a special focus on using social network analysis. She participates in the Global Knowledge Research Network and the Iberoamerican Knowledge Systems Community. Currently, she serves as a full-time professor in the Entrepreneurship Division at Tecnológico de Monterrey, Campus Guadalajara; she teaches courses in entrepreneurship and innovation at the undergraduate level.

Edgar Rogelio Ramírez Solís is a Professor of Management at Tecnológico de Monterrey, Mexico. He received his Master in Planning and Communication from ITESO University, a Ph.D. in Administrative Science from the Universidad Nacional Autónoma de México (UNAM), and a second Ph.D. in International Business from the Universidad Autónoma de Madrid (UAM) in Spain. His research interests include family firms with a special interest in strategy and corporate governance practices. He has served as a Visiting Professor at the University of San Diego, California. He has also published articles in different international academic journals. Currently serves as a Full Professor and as a Family Business Consultant in the Marketing and Business Department at Tecnológico de Monterrey, Campus Guadalajara; he teaches courses in Family Business and Strategic Management at the undergraduate and masters levels.

Utz Schäffer is the Director of the Institute of Management Accounting and Control (IMC) of WHU – Otto Beisheim School of Management in Vallendar, Germany. His primary research area is the counterpart role of the Finance Function (i.e., the role of controllers, financial directors, and CFOs) as part of organized learning and critique. Utz's research has been published in journals such as *Contemporary Accounting Research, European Accounting Review, Journal of Management & Governance* and *Management Accounting Research.* He also serves as co-editor of *Journal of Management Control,* the leading journal for management control in the German-language area, and *Controlling and Management Review,* a major German-language practitioner journal on management accounting and control. In addition, Utz is co-author of the leading German-language textbook *Einführung in das Controlling* (15th edition), which has been translated into Chinese, English, Russian, and Polish. In addition to his academic career, Utz Schäffer gained practical experience as a consultant for McKinsey & Company and serves on the Board of Trustees of the Internationaler Controller Verein (International Controller Association).

Arist v. Schlippe is a Professor at the University of Witten/Herdecke, Germany, and the Director of the WIFU (Witten Research Institute for Family Business). Graduation and Ph.D. in psychology, postdoctoral lecture qualification in clinical psychology and psychotherapy, licensed psychological psychotherapist, licensed teacher for systemic therapy and supervision. He is editor of *Familiendynamik* the most prominent journal for family psychology/therapy in Germany. His research fields cover all psychological issues in FB such as family strategy and management, specific conflicts, and succession.

Ana María Serrano-Bedia is an Associate Professor of Operations Management in the Department of Business Administration of the University of Cantabria, Spain. She is the Vice Director of the Banco Santander Chair of Family Business at the University of Cantabria. Her primary interests are the effects of quality and environmental management systems on organizational strategies, R&D and innovation management, organizational flexibility, entrepreneurship, and family firm. She has published in journals such as *Organization and Environment, Tourism Management, Cornell Hospitality Quarterly, R&D Management, Total Quality Management, Journal of Small Business Management,* and *International Journal of Production Research.*

Kristen Shanine completed her Ph.D. at the University of Alabama and is an Assistant Professor of Management at Middle Tennessee State University. Her research applies concepts from organizational behavior to better understand Entrepreneurship and Family Business. Her primary research applies theory from Psychology and Sociology to Family Business in an effort to better understand the family factors that influence succession failure. She has published in journals such as the *Journal of Occupational Health Psychology* and *Journal of Occupational and Organizational Psychology.*

Anne Sluhan is a Ph.D. Fellow and lecturer in the Department of International Economics and Management at Copenhagen Business School. She earned a Bachelor of Arts at Wittenberg University, a Master of Arts at the University of Toronto, and a Master of Business Administration at Copenhagen Business School. She recently spent time at the University of North Carolina, Charlotte as a visiting scholar. Her research interests span the areas of international business, corporate governance, corporate social responsibility, and organizational commitment with a focus on family business research.

Kathryn Stafford is an Associate Professor at the Ohio State University in the Department of Consumer Sciences. She teaches graduate and undergraduate courses in management theory, family business management, and quantitative methods. She has studied economic analyses of employed wives' use of resources, managerial decisions of home-based workers, and managerial practices of family business owners. For over a decade she has collaborated with members of the Family Business Research Group to collect the first panel data from a national sample of family business owners and their families. From the results, they have proposed the first holistic model of family firms, obtained reliable estimates of the economic impact of family firms, and have begun to distinguish between beneficial practices for family firms in the short and long run. She has published in professional journals, and her research has been featured in *The Wall Street Journal*, *Time*, and *Newsweek*.

Tensie Steijvers is Associate Professor of Accounting at the Research Center for Entrepreneurship and Family Firms (RCEF) at Hasselt University, Belgium. She obtained her Ph.D. at Hasselt University. Her research interests include corporate governance, professionalization, and financing in a family business context. She has published in various peer-reviewed journals including *Family Business Review*, *Journal of Family Business Strategy*, *Accounting and Business Research*, *Journal of Small Business Management*, *Small Business Economics*. *Journal of Banking & Finance*, *Accounting & Finance*, and *Journal of Economic Surveys*. She is currently a member of the review board of *Family Business Review*.

Torben Tretbar obtained his doctoral degree at WHU – Otto Beisheim School of Management in Germany in 2015 and currently works in the Investment Management department of The Linde Group. His research focusses on the influence of family firm owners' involvement in the top management team on organizational outcomes. In particular, his empirical studies investigate how family involvement alters the family's emphasis on socioemotional wealth preservation and the pursuit of ambidexterity in family firms. Results of his dissertation have been presented at several international conferences such as the 4. EIASM Workshop on Top Management Teams and Business Strategy Research in 2013.

Reginald Tucker is a doctoral student whose research interest centers on entrepreneurial psychology. His primary research interest is in how dark triad traits (machiavellianism, narcissism, and psychopathy) influence entrepreneurial cognition, behaviors, and firm outcomes. His research investigates the conventional wisdom that dark triad traits ultimately lead to individual self-destruction and organizational failure. He has presented at the Academy of Management and Western Academy of Management and has published in the *Journal of Business Ethics*.

Anita Van Gils is an Associate Professor in the Department of Organization and Strategy at Maastricht University, the Netherlands. Her research and teaching deal with entrepreneurship and small business management, strategy, and innovation. In particular, she focuses on strategic alliances and corporate governance issues in an SME and family business context. Her research has resulted in international publications in journals and books, amongst which *Small Business Economics*, *Journal of Small Business Management*, *International Small Business Journal*, *Entrepreneurship and Regional Development*, *Corporate Governance: An International Review*, and *European Management Journal*. She is also an associate editor of the *Journal of Family Business Strategy*.

Wim Voordeckers is a Professor of Entrepreneurial Finance and Governance at the Research Center for Entrepreneurship and Family Firms (RCEF) at Hasselt University, Belgium, of which he is the Academic Director. He obtained his Ph.D. at Hasselt University. His research interests include corporate governance and board behaviour in family firms and financing issues in family SMEs. He has published in various peer-reviewed journals including: *Journal of Banking & Finance*, *Small Business Economics*, *Family Business Review*, *Corporate Governance: an International*

Review, Journal of Small Business Management, International Journal of Management Reviews, Entrepreneurship and Regional Development, Journal of Business Ethics, Journal of Management & Organization, Journal of Family Business Strategy, and *Journal of Economic Surveys.* He is currently associate editor of the *Family Business Review.* He is also the author of several family business management and governance textbooks.

Matthias Waldkirch is a Ph.D. candidate at Jönköping International Business School, Sweden, and is affiliated with the Centre of Family Enterprise and Ownership. His main research interest is in strategy and strategic leadership in family firms, with a special focus on non-family management and the role of non-family chief executive officers. He is co-editor of the book *Theoretical Perspectives on Family Businesses,* published by Edward Elgar in 2015.

Milton Ming Wang is a doctoral candidate at Renmin University of China. His major interests are corporate governance and business policy in emerging markets. Currently, he is a member of the Academy of Management. He has published in top Chinese management journals such as *Management World* and *China Industrial Economy,* as well as an international journal, *Frontiers of Business Research in China.*

Jing Xi has a Ph.D. and a Master's Degree in business administration from Jinan University, China. Currently, Dr. Xi is an associate professor at the Guangdong University of Technology, School of Management, Department of Business Administration, China. Her research interests are in the areas of family business research, human resource management, and behavioral decision making, with a specific focus on intergenerational succession and relationship governance in family business. She has hosted two research projects regarding family business sponsored by Chinese national fund, one is on non-family-member employees' organizational identification, and the other is on next-generation offspring's identity as a successor to take over the family business. She won best research awards (second class) from International Symposium on Entrepreneurship and Family Business (China) in 2014 and 2015. She teaches Organizational Behavior, Human Resource Management, and Knowledge Management at undergraduate and graduate level (master). She once worked in Tennessee University at Knoxville for one year as a visiting scholar.

Miles A. Zachary is an Assistant Professor of Management in the College of Business & Economics at West Virginia University. His research broadly considers the sociocognitive elements of organizations that influence organizational outcomes and stakeholder relationships over time, including organization identity/image, impression management, and social evaluations. His research has been featured in professional journals including *Journal of Management, Strategic Entrepreneurship Journal, Family Business Review, Journal of the Academy of Marketing Science, Business Horizons, Journal of the Academy of Business and Economics,* and *Journal of International Business and Cultural Studies.*

Shanshan Zhang is a Management Science graduate student at the Guangdong University of Technology, China. She got her Bachelor's degree from the Hunan University of Humanities, China.

1

INTRODUCTION TO THE FAMILY BUSINESS COMPANION

Franz W. Kellermanns and Frank Hoy

Family firm research has seen an exponential growth in output, quality and topics studies (e.g., Debicki, Matherne, Kellermanns, & Chrisman, 2009). Despite the youth of the field, growing academic interest has been documented through the publication of annotated bibliographies (e.g, De Massis, Sharma, Chua, & Chrisman, 2012; Hoy & Laffranchini, 2014), reflection pieces (Sharma, Chrisman, & E. Gersick, 2012), literature reviews (e.g., Gedajlovic, Carney, Chrisman, & Kellermanns, 2012), meta-analyses (e.g., Carney, Essen, Gedajlovic, & Heugens, 2014; O'Boyle, Pollack, & Rutherford, 2012) and edited volumes (e.g., Melin, Nordqvist, & Sharma, 2013).

The Routledge Companion to Family Business is an edited volume that builds on the growing body of knowledge and the wealth of recent research with the intent to add substantial value to the field. To achieve this objective, we utilized a tri-pronged approach. First, we organized the volume based on general areas. The chapters are grouped based on their wider affiliation to the strategic management, entrepreneurship, organizational behavior, and family science. In addition, we added a special topics area, which reviews country or regional aspects of the family firm literature. Second, while choosing the aforementioned topics, we have strongly emphasized areas that were under-researched, or that are not easily accessible to research. For example, while the interest in family science related work is growing (e.g., Morris & Kellermanns, 2013), this type of research has yet to fully inform mainstream family firm literature. Similarly, research in organizational behavior in family firms, maybe with the exception of family firm conflict (e.g., Kellermanns & Eddleston, 2004), is under-researched as the family firm literature developed from a strategic management perspective (Sharma, Chrisman, & Chua, 1997). In addition, some chapters summarize the literature published in "non-English publications." These chapters can provide both new research ideas, as well as highlight differences in cultural and research traditions. Lastly, we chose to provide a mix of papers that provides reviews of current research as well as new and innovative trajectories for future research, trying to make *The Routledge Companion to Family Business* a true companion for both researchers and practitioners. Below we discuss the individual sections in more detail and summarize the individual chapters.

Part I: Strategic Management

The strategic management literature served as the birth place of the wider entrepreneurship literature and also more specifically the field of family business. Considering this early origin, it is not surprising that much of the family firm literature is dominated by strategy oriented research even today.

Yet, such a focus is not surprising, as strategy permeates wide areas of interest in family firm research. From succession to financial and non-financial goals and the various family firm-specific characteristics have led themselves to compare process between family and non-family firms as well as resulted in a more differentiated understanding of the potential heterogeneity of family firms themselves.

This first section provides a mix of papers focusing on classical strategic management theories and topics (e.g., upper echelons, agency theory). In addition to review oriented pieces, new foci in the field of family business are also discussed (e.g, socio-emotional wealth, finance). As such these papers provide not only good overviews of key research areas in the realm strategic family firm research, but also offer insightful agendas for future research.

Below we summarize the nine chapters in this section.

Chapter 2: Decker, Heinrichs, Jaskiewicz, Rau

This chapter focuses on a key topic of family firm research, namely family firm succession. It provides a rigorous analysis of the literature and provides significant value by classifying the studies based on succession process stages (i.e., preparation, successor choice, exploration and implementation, incumbent's withdrawal and post succession success) as well as highlighting the level of analysis (i.e., individual, organizational, environmental). This comprehensive approach then allows the authors to identify research gaps in each of the identified succession stages as well as to do general future research, advocating a holistic framework for studying family firm succession.

Chapter 3: Madison, Li, Holt

Madison, Li and Holt provide a review of 67 empirically grounded agency theory studies in the realm of family firms. This chapter provides a detailed summary table of the analyzed studies. The paper discusses both agency problems, which are abundant in family firms, due to the involvement of the family in the firm. Further, governance related issues are discussed, detailing remedies for agency problems and their potential for enhancing family firm performance. The resulting analysis concludes in discussion of future research opportunities.

Chapter 4: Chandler, Zachary, Brigham, Payne

Long-term orientation is of high interest for family firm researchers, as it may explain why family firms behave differently than non-family firms. It further offers complementary insights to some of the chapters in this book (e.g., agency, succession). This chapter provides a comprehensive review of the construct. Their review of the construct covers both the roots of the construct in the non-business literature and highlights its development in the business and economic field, before turning to long-term orientation in the family firm literature. The review provides an overview of definitions and operationalizations as well as detailed suggestions for future research.

Chapter 5: Tretbar, Reimer, Schäffer

Tretbar, Reimer and Schäffer contribute to the ongoing debate on the effect of family involvement on performance. Their chapter provides a detailed literature review on family involvement in the top management team (TMT) and its implications for family firm performance drawing on the upper echelon literature. It does not only provide an excellent template for literature reviews but provides a comprehensive discussion of strategic processes affected by family involvement in the TMT. The tables in this chapter provide a key resource for authors interested in this topic, and the future research section highlights a multitude of research ideas on TMT processes, and family values and the family as "supra TMT."

Chapter 6: Sluhan

The chapter by Sluhan provides a review on family firm internationalization. It extends prior research, particularly recent reviews, and meta-analyses, which have concluded that family ownership is not related to the degree of internationalization. This chapter instead focuses on how the internationalization process is different for family firms. The paper first reviews the motivations and capabilities necessary for internationalization before elaborating on specific equity and non-equity modes of internationalization. In addition to comprehensive literature review tables, the chapter also advances areas for future research.

Chapter 7: Neacsu, Martin, Gómez-Mejía

The chapter by Neacsu Martin and Gómez-Mejía discusses socio-emotional wealth (SEW), a topic of strong interest in the recent family firm literature that has experienced exponential growth in recent years. Their focus, however, is not solely the positive aspects that were widely associated with the discussion of SEW. Instead, the paper provides a balanced assessment of value creation and destroying processes of the effects of SEW loss aversion. The resulting Table 7.1, provides a comprehensive summary of both positive and negative aspects of SEW. Yet, the authors conclude that family ownership has at worst neutral effect and at best a positive performance relationship.

Chapter 8: Ring, Brown, Matherne

Family firm research often exclusively focuses on family members and their goals and resulting utilities. Not surprisingly, the chapter by Ring, Brown and Matherne, which discusses stakeholders in relation to family firms, devotes a significant part of the paper to the analysis of family members' interests. It goes further by also discussing additional internal stakeholder groups in family firms as well as the external stakeholder. The paper further provides an exhibit of the 20 most cited articles on stakeholder definitional and salience issues, as well as a list of the most influential articles on descriptive, instrumental and normative approach. Thus, providing a useful guide for readers interested in the topic area. The article concludes with implications for practice as well as extensive suggestions for future research.

Chapter 9: Steijvers and Voordeckers

While the finance literature has discovered the family firm context as a useful context, particularly related to agency literature, the topics of finance (and accounting) have also entered mainstream family firm research. Steijvers and Voordeckers, which are part of the latter growing research stream, discuss the phenomenon of credit rationing. Their sample of 1000 Belgian SMEs shows that 35.3 percent of family firms vs. 23 percent of non-family firms experience more long-term than short-term credit rationing. This study highlights the juxtaposition of the desire of long-term debt that family firms prefer, as it does not dilute equity and the potential lack of supply of such debt.

Chapter 10: Decker

Families who have created wealth through business ownership face decisions regarding conserving and growing the wealth for future generations, and applying the wealth in ways that adhere to family values. One strategy has been the formation of family offices. These are organizational entities designed for multiple purposes, e.g., to nurture coordination, continuity, and even harmony among family members; to provide advice on wealth management, taxation and investment; and, more and more, to create value for individuals and families in different national environments. Decker examines the business model formation of multi-family offices and the evolution of their global standardization, leading to propositions for future research.

Part II: Entrepreneurship

Much of the early literature on family businesses encouraged the 'professionalization' of the firm. The implication was that family-owned enterprises suffer from nepotism in the negative sense of placing incompetent relatives into positions of responsibility. Recommended solutions were typically the education and development of family members to qualify them to be senior executives and the employment of non-family managers with relevant credentials for their positions. The expectation was that the company would transition from the entrepreneurial founder to a team of effective administrators.

In recent years, it has become understood that entrepreneurial behavior is more than launching an enterprise. It can be reflected in a variety of ways, typically in the infusion of innovation, such as new products, new markets, new business models, even spin-offs from the original firm. This represents the concept that entrepreneurship continues as the company grows, matures, and transitions from one generation to the next.

This section of the *Companion* interrelates entrepreneurship with family business. We find the words innovation and opportunity injected throughout the chapters. The authors investigate a wide variety of approaches to entrepreneurial traits and behaviors. They summarize relevant preceding literature and propose paths for future investigations. The five chapters constituting this section are summarized below.

Chapter 11: Kraiczy and Hack

Kraiczy and Hack extend the earlier work of De Massis, Frattini, and Lichtenthaler (2013) by applying the latter's Input-Mediation-Output (IMO) framework to the increased and more recent contributions to the family business innovation literature. Kraiczy and Hack then proceed to assess the studies from an ability-willingness perspective. They note that they have taken a broad view of innovation rather than limiting their analyses, as De Massis and colleagues did, to technological innovation. They found evidence, albeit inconsistent, that there are family influences on innovation, and they feel their ability-willingness examination may help resolve some of those inconsistencies. The increased attention to innovation in scholarly studies reflects multiple definitions of innovation, suggesting further analysis of family firms and innovation with more focused definitions of the variables.

Chapter 12: Brinkerink, Van Gils, Bammens, Carree

Trying to ascertain consistencies in studies of family firms is complicated by the heterogeneity of the entities under investigation, as noted by Brinkerink and his colleagues. They thoroughly examine the literature related to open innovation in family firms and acknowledge how industry, size, level of education, participation by non-family executives all influence the desirability and ability of firms to engage in open innovation. The point to the fact that open innovation can entail both inbound and outbound activity. These observations lead them to urge more longitudinal research, especially with attempts to capture life cycle changes. While they avoid reaching subjective judgments in their conclusions, they demonstrate the enormous role of communication in open systems environments that could put firms with closed systems in jeopardy.

Chapter 13: Dibrell, Bettinelli, Randerson

Although entrepreneurial behavior is often associated with venture creation, it can also be reflected through many types of actions in existing businesses. Dibrell, Bettinelli and Randerson address innovativeness as exemplary of entrepreneurial behavior. They specifically focus on the impact the interaction of market orientation and social consciousness may have on family firm innovation. Firm innovativeness in this study is reflected as developing new products, upgrading existing products, introducing specialty products, and innovative market techniques. As the authors point out in their literature review, the integration of family values into strategic behavior by firm leadership has been reflected in samples of family businesses demonstrating greater social responsibility than non-family businesses. This chapter extends our understanding of how family values may translate into behaviors that foster innovativeness by firms. It adds a new dimension to the role that socioemotional wealth may play in promoting entrepreneurial behavior in business performance. The implication that social consciousness may have positive consequences for innovation by businesses should stimulate further research.

Chapter 14: Minola, Campopiano, Brumana, Cassia, Garrett

In the academic discipline of management, family business research is often seen as a sub-field of entrepreneurship. Family business scholars, on the other hand, recognize that the fields overlap, but have distinctly separate characteristics as well. A review of the family business literature suggests that attention to entrepreneurship is relatively recent, with prior research dominated by governance, succession, and finance. A number of studies have drawn from corporate entrepreneurship, but most have focused on how to develop entrepreneurial traits and behaviors in family members as they enter and progress in the firms. Minola and his colleagues provide an in-depth review of how corporate entrepreneurship has been treated in family business studies and find some differences from its application in non-family enterprises. They label their findings as 'fragmented,' then offer a model for grasping the role of corporate entrepreneurship in family business with proposals for future research. In particular, they conclude that life cycle models may offer promise for enabling family and business leaders to implement strategies.

Chapter 15: Akhter

Akhter provides a much-needed status report on portfolio entrepreneurship in family firms. This under-researched subject may prove to be one of the most critical components of global economic growth, given the massive roles family business groups play in many countries. This chapter contains a comprehensive review of the current body of knowledge regarding portfolio entrepreneurship and a classification scheme to help guide future research. Akhter identifies multiple research gaps stemming from their classifications. A critical outcome of research into this concept could be a new appreciation for family business through the recognition that they have greater impacts through multiple businesses, and that they may survive longer than generally recognized resulting through continuation through numerous entities rather than a single enterprise.

Part III: Organizational Behavior

Similar to the field of entrepreneurship, where more topics related to organizational behavior have been investigated, the field of family firm research is on the cusp of experiencing similar patterns. While conflict in the family firm is a "traditional" family firm research topic, and as such also represented in this book by two chapters.

While the family firm literature has often seen the family firm as positive (for exceptions see Schulze, Lubatkin, & Dino, 2003; Schulze, Lubatkin, Dino, & Buchholtz, 2001), and this positive focus is also represented in this set of papers, we find that some of the authors caution about being overly optimistic about the family firm and highlight critical aspects of the management of the family firm.

Thus, Part III of the book not only makes a push for including more topics in the realm of organizational behavior, but also asks us to develop a balanced view of the positive and negative aspects that family firm are exposed to due to the involvement of the family. Indeed, the next section of the book focuses on the omitted variable in family firm research, the "family." This section is comprised of five chapters, which are summarized below.

Chapter 16: Campopiano and De Masssis

Corporate social responsibility (CSR) has become a growing topic of interest. Campopiano and De Massis show that for 131 Italian small and mid-size businesses family firms increasing degree of family involvement leads to a significant impact of the engagement in CSR. Specifically, they show that higher family ownership, higher ownership dispersion amongst family members as well as later stage generational control decreases CSR. The study thus both adds to the understanding of the effect of family involvement as well as the wider CSR literature.

Chapter 17: Loignon, Kellermanns, Eddleston, Kidwell

This chapter is one of two chapters on conflict in this book, stressing the importance of conflict as a research topic for family firms. Specifically, Loignon, Kellermanns, Eddleston and Kidwell review the empirical findings on the effects of three types of conflict (cognitive-, process- and relationship-conflict) on outcomes variables (performance) and identify the moderators of the relationships. In addition, the chapter highlights the "Fredo effect" and its role in generating conflict in family firms. Various conflict management techniques are also briefly discussed. The review results in the development of a model that summarizes the current proposed and tested relationships in this literature.

Chapter 18: von Schlippe and Frank

The second conflict chapter, by von Schlippe and Frank, takes a system theoretical approach to conflict. They argue that the systems of family, business, and ownership operate on different systems logic, which they summarize in Table 18.1. They argue that these systems cannot be reconciled. Inevitably leading to system inherent conflicts, which can, through the escalation, lead to a parasitic conflict system. They stress that family businesses are emotional arenas, in which conflict can easily arise. The authors propose consciousness raising as an intervention to mitigate the inherent paradoxes of the three systems logics colliding.

Chapter 19: Jiang and Munyon

Understanding how goals and emotions affect behavior is a worthy area of research. Yet, data to investigate these potentially contentious factors that nobody, particularly not family firms, are very forthcoming in disclosing, provides a problem for advancing our knowledge in this area. Jiang and Munyon argue that experiments should be considered to further investigate cognitive micro-foundations that drive family firm behavior. As such, they provide useful suggestions on the design and execution of such experiments and are prone to generate an experimental research branch in family firm research.

Chapter 20: Waldkirch and Nordqvist

The final chapter in this section discusses "stewardship theory." While this particular theory has often been utilized to explain positive performance effects in family firms and thus could be easily classified as a strategic management topic, yet as stewardship theory stresses positive behavior, the chapter found a home in the organizational behavior section. Waldkirch and Nordqvist after reviewing the model of man and the general tenants of stewardship behavior, review its application in the family business literature. The authors then take a critical stance toward stewardship theory, as they argue that focusing on utility maximization without an ethical dimension is highly problematic.

Part IV: Family Science

More and more, we are seeing the family business literature criticized for placing emphasis on the business at the expense of the family. There is a rich body of knowledge in family science that is increasingly being drawn from. The authors of the chapters in this section of the *Companion* seek to accelerate that process. They introduce numerous citations from family science and propose strategies for studying how businesses and families interact with and influence one another.

The authors point out that we do not always agree on what a family actually is, and those disagreements may have national and cultural origins. Several concerns emerge: Are scholars effectively communicating with one another regarding their samples and observations? Are meaningful comparisons across international and cultural boundaries being made? How applicable are our normative, descriptive and even empirical models if we are using different definitions of family?

If we comprehend what one another is describing regarding the family, then we are positioned to better document and interpret processes by which the family influences the business, both positively and negatively, and vice versa. In this part of the book, we also explore psychological approaches to understanding the family and business relationship. Controlling psychological predispositions may be a less viable approach than recognizing the effects of the psychological characteristics and devising strategies for coping with them.

Part IV of the book may be seen as a call to action to integrate disciplines in our research. We have moved forward on the integration of family business and entrepreneurship. There would appear to be value in reaching further beyond business disciplines and into family science. The three chapters that are summarized below make up section IV.

Chapter 21: Danes and Stafford

In the SAGE Handbook of Family Business (Melin, Nordqvist and Sharma, 2014), Danes (2014) proposed family processes as a promising direction for future research in the family business discipline. We are pleased that she pressed forward in that direction with her co-author Stafford with this chapter. Processes involve making and acting on decisions by family members individually or jointly, but which are largely unseen patterns. The unseen aspect raises issues associated with observing and reporting on phenomena. Thus, Danes and Stafford make a valuable contribution by offering detailed explanations of how to conduct investigations of family processes. The authors make a strong case for family processes impacting firm performance.

Chapter 22: Rieg and Rau

How can we perform family business research if we do not know what a "family" is? Rieg and Rau raise this critical question as they attempt to determine how to operationalize *family* as a variable. They report a wide variety of definitions of families in their literature review and list multiple characteristics, ultimately grouping their observations into two categories: dyads and whole families. Looking beyond this chapter, we find in Botero and Gómez Betancourt's chapter on Latin America that the perception of family can be influenced by culture, religion and political and legal environment. A fundamental conclusion to be drawn from Rieg and Rau is the need to include a family science perspective into family business research and to articulate how the family is defined and measured.

Chapter 23: Tucker, Shanine, Combs

Tucker, Shanine and Combs remind us that personality characteristics of individuals can have positive and negative effects on others, regardless of the stereotypes associated with those characteristics. In this chapter, they introduce positive impacts of psychopathy. Psychopaths lack remorse when they harm others, yet they may also lead teams, engage in strategic thinking, and instill vision for those with whom they interact. The authors provide evidence that psychopaths may be more dysfunctional as family members than in businesses that they operate. They contend that, in turn, family members may place constraints on the psychopath's ability to manage the family firm. This chapter could foster many directions for future research, in particular, investigations indicating how psychopathy can be recognized and channeled toward positive outcomes.

Part V: Special Topics: Country

In this section of the *Companion*, we review family business-related subject matter in China, Latin America, and North America. It will come as no surprise that there are some consistencies in research findings and some variations across international borders. A critical contribution of the chapters on China and Latin America is the insight they provide through their analyses of scholarly publications in languages other than English. Much of the work cited is being introduced to larger audiences for the first time.

It is also not surprising that national and cultural differences are reported by authors as they compare the research findings with those from other regions. These comparisons also document that there are both similarities and differences in the concentration of scholars on topics.

Enterprise governance is found to be a major subject of interest globally. The role of and relationship to governmental agencies, on the other hand, is treated differently in different regions.

Another observation made by authors in this section of the book is that there is variation in research methodologies. Publications coming out of the regions and countries vary based on sample size and characteristics, data collection procedures, variable selection and definitions, emphasis on qualitative versus quantitative approaches, and analytical techniques. These findings are essential for researchers across the globe to be able to assess conclusions and applications and to be able to replicate investigations for comparative purposes. The six chapters comprising this section are summarized below:

Chapter 24: Xi, Zhang, Jin, Holloway

The family business literature is presently dominated by studies from Europe and North America published in English-language journals and books. Authors who are bi- or multi-lingual are able to site foreign language contributions, but far too little becomes internationally circulated. Xi, Zhang, Jin and Holloway present and review the rich body of knowledge that is being compiled in China. They offer comparisons with English-language publications. The authors discovered two subject areas receiving far more attention in China than other locations: traditional culture and social transformation. These findings may serve as a springboard for comparative research.

Chapter 25: Wang and Carney

The chapter by Wang and Carney examines the remarkable transformations occurring in China due to those who founded ventures when free enterprise began emerging in the country begin passing their businesses along to the next generation. China provides a laboratory setting where scholars can observe whether practices that are viewed as normal and acceptable in other countries apply in an environment where the transfer of ownership and management is new and occurring under unique political and cultural conditions. Wang and Carney introduce a set of propositions that suggest some significant distinctions between founders and prospective successors – distinctions that have implications for sustainability and growth, but also for conflict. There is the potential for much to be learned from what Chinese family businesses are experiencing.

Chapter 26: López-Fernández, Serrano-Bedia, Pérez-Pérez, Hernández-Linares, Palma-Ruiz

Similar to Xi et al. in their chapter, López-Fernández, Serrano-Bedia, Pérez-Pérez, Hernández-Linares, and Palma-Ruiz make an important contribution by introducing English-language scholars to a compilation of Spanish-language publications, giving particular attention to Spain. Thanks to these sets of authors, along with the other chapter from China and the one from Columbia, we are exposed to research findings published in the two most widely used languages in the world. López-Fernández and her colleagues organized their literature review into clusters. Spanish-language family business researchers have been studying the continuity of firms over time, corporate governance, both external and internal cultures and their influence, performance, and size. López-Fernández et al. report comparisons and contrasts with English-language published research for both subject matter and methodologies. Interestingly, they also include comparisons and contrasts between studies in Spain and studies in Latin America. These comparisons suggest numerous paths for future research.

Chapter 27: Botero and Gómez Betancourt

Botero and Gómez Betancourt introduce us to cultural issues in Latin America. Looking at the country of Columbia as an example, they examine how culture influences govern practices in family firms. Columbia is the third largest country by population in Latin America. It typifies the region in the shift it has experienced toward urban population centers, a civil law system, and the influence of the Roman Catholic Church. Botero and Gómez Betancourt report a number of governance characteristics that beg for further research. They found boards of public companies to be dominated by family members, and the key decision makers to be male and members of senior generations, regardless of their daily direct involvement in the firm. These observations run counter to normative recommendations for family business governance. This calls for compiling evidence to determine the impact of differences in governance and the fit within larger cultures.

Chapter 28: Ramírez Solís, Baños Monroy, Rodríguez Aceves

As with the Botero and Gómez Betancourt study of Latin America and Columbia, Ramírez Solís, Baños Monroy and Rodríguez Aceves describe a national economic environment in which family enterprises play a large role. The overview of Latin America's economic conditions affecting family businesses in the two chapters is consistent and complementary. Ramírez Solís and his colleagues argue that Mexico possesses a history and set of characteristics that make it the most representative of Latin American countries. Their review of the literature shows that culture, succession, and corporate governance have been dominant themes of family business research. Once again, a key observation is the importance of local and regional context on understanding the dynamics of family firms.

Chapter 29: Parsons and Clarke

Parsons and Clarke present a review of family business centers in North America, predominantly in the United States. Why an interest in family business centers? They have been extensively introduced in a variety of forms in the United States, fulfilling a need suffered by practitioners. For scholars, they offer entry. Not only can they serve as databases, but they also build trust relationships with universities, resulting in greater access to information. In their chapter, Parsons and Clarke briefly explain the historic development of centers and describe various models which have gained acceptance in local markets. They address assessment issues, particularly those associated with the accreditation of associated business schools. They demonstrate that, in addition to serving as sources of data, centers in and of themselves may prove to be subjects of family business research.

Contributions

Drawing from the diversity of topics, approaches, observations, and conclusions of the chapters in this *Companion*, we find that the authors have summarized and advanced the field in numerous ways. Several of the authors provide retrospectives that capture how far the body of knowledge in family business has advanced in such a short period of time. From their reviews, we find that:

- topics under study have expanded from narrow research streams, predominantly interpersonal relationships, governance, and succession, to a broad range of issues addressing both family and firm, the behaviors of individuals and the interaction with the global economy, the preparation of prospective successors and the exit of senior generations, and much more;

- methodologies have advanced, moving away from participant observation, anecdotal evidence, and mixed samples, to the implementation of macroeconomic databases, rigorous data collection, and analysis, and more carefully designed and selected samples;
- atheoretical descriptions have been replaced by the application of theories and practices from diverse but related fields and through the development of theories and models within the family business discipline.

Additionally, the authors give us pathways to future research contributions. Each chapter suggests extensions of what we have learned to date and gaps in the literature that need to be filled. Several authors pose challenging new questions that may lead to answers that will have practical implications for family business owners and leaders. We offer an example below from each Part of *The Companion*:

- In Part I, Strategy, the review of the socioemotional wealth (SEW) theory of family business identifies the need to determine whether the desire of family members for SEW improves or decreases performance.
- In Part II, Entrepreneurship, the question is raised about how findings from the corporate entrepreneurship literature may enable family firms to implement strategies more effectively.
- In Part III, Organizational Behavior, there are two chapters that critique generally accepted theories of conflict in family firms, proposing new models for scholars to test with expectations that family members can resolve negative conflicts and acquire benefits from positive conflicts.
- In Part IV, Family Science, a novel recommendation is made to study how improved knowledge of the behaviors of psychopathic family members may have positive effects for both the family and the business.
- In Part V, Special Topics: Countries, authors provide extensive support for comparative studies of the influences of legal, cultural, social and other environments on firms that are doing business both within countries and across international boundaries. Attempts to generalize observations globally may be dysfunctional to both families and firms.

A critical purpose of compiling and presenting the information in the chapters of this book is to stimulate further research into what is finally being recognized as the predominant form of business worldwide.

Conclusion

Our chapters cover strategic management, entrepreneurship, organizational behavior, family science and special topics with a country/regional focus. We provide review pieces, critical pieces as well as empirical papers with a mix of topics and implications tailored to academics and practitioners alike. We hope that you will find these chapters interesting and helpful in your own pursuit of understanding family firms better.

References

Carney, M., Essen, M. V., Gedajlovic, E. R., & Heugens, P. P. M. A. R. (2014). What Do We Know About Private Family Firms? A Meta-Analytical Review. *Entrepreneurship Theory & Practice*.

De Massis, A., Sharma, P., Chua, J. H., & Chrisman, J. J. (2012). *Family Business Studies: An Annotated Bibliography*. Northhampton, MA: Edward Elgar.

Debicki, B. J., Matherne, C. F., Kellermanns, F. W., & Chrisman, J. J. (2009). Family business research in the new millennium: An overview of the who, the where, the what, and the why. *Family Business Review, 22*(2), 151–166.

Gedajlovic, E., Carney, M., Chrisman, J. J., & Kellermanns, F. W. (2012). The adolescence of family firm research: Taking stock and planning for the future. *Journal of Management, 38*(4), 1010–1037.

Hoy, F., and Laffranchini, G. (2014). 'Managing family business,' in Griffin, R. (ed.) Oxford Bibliographies in Management, New York: Oxford University Press.

Kellermanns, F. W., & Eddleston, K. (2004). Feuding families: When conflict does a family firm good. *Entrepreneurship: Theory & Practice, 28*(3), 209–228.

Melin, L., Nordqvist, M., & Sharma, P. (eds.). (2013). *Handbook of Family Business.* London: Sage Publications.

Morris, L., & Kellermanns, F. W. (2013). Family relations and family businesses: A note from the guest editors. *Family Relations, 62*, 379–383.

O'Boyle, E. H., Pollack, J. M., & Rutherford, M. W. (2012). Exploring the relation between family involvement and firms' financial performance: A meta-analysis of main and moderator effects. *Journal of Business Venturing, 27*, 1–18.

Schulze, W. S., Lubatkin, M. H., & Dino, R. N. (2003). Toward a theory of agency and altruism in family firms. *Journal of Business Venturing, 18*(4), 473–490.

Schulze, W. S., Lubatkin, M. H., Dino, R. N., & Buchholtz, A. K. (2001). Agency relationships in family firms: Theory and evidence. *Organization Science, 12*(2), 99–116.

Sharma, P., Chrisman, J. J., & Chua, J. H. (1997). Strategic management of the family business: Past research and future challenges. *Family Business Review, 10*(1), 1–36.

Sharma, P., Chrisman, J. J., & E. Gersick, K. (2012). 25 years of family business review: Reflections on the past and perspectives for the future. *Family Business Review, 25*(1), 5–15.

PART I

Strategic Management

2

WHAT DO WE KNOW ABOUT SUCCESSION IN FAMILY BUSINESSES?

Mapping Current Knowledge and Unexplored Territory

Carolin Decker, Katharina Heinrichs,
Peter Jaskiewicz, and Sabine B. Rau

Introduction

Succession, which includes the set of "actions, events, and organizational mechanisms by which leadership at the top of the firm, and often ownership, are transferred" (Le Breton-Miller, Miller, and Steier 2004, 305), is one of the most important issues in the field of family business (Chua, Chrisman, and Sharma 2003). A first literature review was conducted by Handler (1994), who identified five streams of research. Since then, scholars have generated a vast body of literature on succession in family businesses. Considering the sheer number of publications, it would seem that succession is over-published. A closer look at the results, however, indicates that the literature on succession remains non-cumulative and disjointed (Chittoor and Das 2007; Long and Chrisman 2007, 2013). To lay the groundwork for theory development, we provide a systematic analysis of peer-reviewed studies that have been published since Handler's (1994) seminal literature review.

With our chapter we contribute to family business research in three ways. First, we focus on succession research that adheres to the methodological standards set by Tranfield, Denyer, and Smart (2003). Following a thorough keyword search and a systematic assessment of research papers fit for this review, 95 studies were selected with respect to their bibliographical information, theoretical foundation, research design, and main findings.

Second, unlike previous reviews, we analyze the succession process across three levels of analysis and considering various aspects and stages: Prior literature reviews have traditionally focused on selected aspects of succession, such as antecedents (De Massis, Chua, and Chrisman 2008; Le Breton-Miller et al. 2008, 2004), psychological factors (Filser, Kraus, and Märk 2013), research methods (Brockhaus 2004), or theoretical perspectives (Nordqvist, Wennberg, and Hellerstedt 2013). They have also put a stronger emphasis on management (Brockhaus 2004; De Massis et al. 2008; Long and Chrisman 2004, 2008, 2013) than on ownership (Nordqvist et al. 2013). In contrast, we describe succession as a process involving changes in both management and ownership and comprising three levels of analysis. We review the literature according to the "five stages" specified by Le Breton-Miller et al. (2004): *preparation, choice of a successor, exploration and implementation, incumbent owner-manager withdrawal,* and *post-succession.* As such, we extend Handler's work and consolidate extant research since 1994, mapping current academic knowledge on the entire succession process at all levels of analysis.

Third, we elaborate on paths for future research. In addition to recommendations related to each stage of the succession process, we suggest that researchers should embrace a holistic approach that studies succession across levels of analysis and over time. In so doing, future research can generate insights that extend those from studies on isolated and single succession factors.

The remainder of this article is structured as follows: First, we elaborate on the approach chosen for study selection and analysis. Second, we outline the findings of our review based on the pre-specified stages and levels. Finally, we discuss implications for future research on succession.

A Systematic Selection and Assessment of Studies on Succession

Following the principles for a systematic review suggested by Tranfield et al. (2003), we identified a list of keywords based on the succession literature, and then conferred with two experienced researchers in the field, ultimately deciding upon a list of 28 keywords: *family business, family firm, handover/hand over, heir, heritage, incumbent, inheritance, junior generation, last will, MBO/MBI, next generation, offspring, older generation, passing the baton, predecessor, privately held business, privately owned business, retirement, retiring, senior generation, succeeding, succession process, succession, successor, takeover, take over, testament, transfer, transition.* Search strings were constructed by combining the keywords *family business, family firm, privately owned business,* and *privately held business* with the remaining 24, resulting in a total of 96 (24 × 4) search strings. To ensure that all studies included in this review originated from the family business field, these four keywords were included in all possible search strings. Examples include [succession AND family business], [succession AND privately owned business], and [predecessor AND family firm].

We started writing this literature review with a focus on studies in peer-reviewed journals. These studies were considered to meet high-quality standards because of the systematic peer-review processes that scientific journals usually apply (Light and Pillemer 1984). Whenever we were not familiar with a particular journal, we availed ourselves of help from field experts.

We proceeded as follows. First, we selected the top 20 management journals, ranked by their Citation Impact Factor (CIF) for the year 2009 in the management subset of the Thomson Reuters Web of Science (formerly ISI Web of Knowledge). Second, we added *Journal of Family Business Strategy,* a relatively new peer-reviewed field journal that was not part of the top 20 list but was expected to include many studies on succession, since family business research is relatively young compared with other disciplines (Siebels and Knyphausen-Aufseß 2012). The first issue of this journal was published in March 2010. Third, family business research is multi-disciplinary and frequently focuses on how the family affects firm performance and governance (Colli 2013; Mazzi 2011; Siebels and Knyphausen-Aufseß 2012). As a result, in order to broaden our knowledge base, we also added top field journals in finance and economics that might include research on family businesses.

This selection process yielded 36 journals, namely *Academy of Management Journal, Academy of Management Review, Administrative Science Quarterly, American Economic Review, Decision Sciences, Econometrica, Entrepreneurship Theory and Practice, Family Business Review, International Journal of Management Reviews, International Small Business Journal, Journal of Banking and Finance, Journal of Business Venturing, Journal of Corporate Finance, Journal of Family Business Strategy, Journal of Finance, Journal of Financial Economics, Journal of International Business Studies, Journal of Management, Journal of Management Studies, Journal of Operations Management, Journal of Political Economy, Journal of Small Business Management, MIS Quarterly, OMEGA International Journal of Management*

Science, Organization Science, Organizational Behavior and Human Decision Processes, Organizational Research Methods, Personnel Psychology, Quarterly Journal of Economics, Research in Organizational Behavior, Review of Financial Studies, Small Business Economics, Strategic Management Journal, Strategic Organization, Supply Chain Management, and Technovation.

The literature search was conducted using EBSCO (Business Source Premier) and Science-Direct, as well as a manual search. The search strings were used for analyses of titles, abstracts, and author-provided keywords. A total of 493 studies relevant to any aspect of succession in family firms were retrieved. We then excluded studies that focused on anecdotal evidence and/or non-family businesses, which reduced our total to 95 studies (24 conceptual papers, 29 qualitative studies, and 42 quantitative approaches).

We classified this prior literature into five stages and three levels of analysis because we viewed succession as a process on multiple levels of analysis (e.g., Cadieux, Lorrain, and Hugron 2002; Ellul, Pagana, and Panunzi 2010; Filser et al. 2013; Ibrahim, Soufani, and Lam 2001; Lam 2011; Long and Chrisman 2013; Rubenson and Gupta 1996; Santiago 2000; Wasserman 2003). With respect to these multiple levels, we focused on *individual*, *organizational*, and *environmental* levels of analysis. On the organizational level, we further distinguished the dimensions of *family*, *business*, *management*, and *ownership* (Pieper and Klein 2007). The results are depicted in Table 2.1, which summarizes the level(s) of analysis applied to each study and how each study contributes to the organizational dimensions of family, business, management, and ownership for each stage of the succession process.

In the following sections, we synthesize the existing research based on the pre-specified stages and dimensions.

Succession Preparation (Stage 1)

Our review shows that the first stage of the succession process, succession preparation, has been studied mainly with a focus on either *the next generation's intention and decision to join the family business* or *succession planning*. In addition, research on the *socialization of the next generation* has been a blind spot in the literature.

The Next Generation's Intention and Decision to Join the Family Business

Studies on the next generation examine the question of *what drives the next generation's decision to join and take over the family business*. These studies focus predominantly on individual characteristics.

The more the family scions aim at realizing personal goals, exploring their own career paths, and/or breaking free from the family's tradition, the weaker is their intention to join the family business, unless employment opportunities in the labor market are less attractive (Stavrou 1999; Stavrou and Swiercz 1998). The decision to join the family business is driven by the family heirs' commitment, which is based on desire, obligation, opportunity cost, and need (Sharma and Irving 2005). It can be fostered by their past involvement in the business (Stavrou; 1999) and the predecessor's encouragement (Dumas, Dupuis, Richer, and St.-Cyr 1995). Interestingly, daughters are more likely to receive control of the family business from their fathers than their mothers. Mothers tend to resign from their positions rather reluctantly (Vera and Dean 2005).

Gender plays a major role in this stage of the succession process. It interacts with other factors, such as nationality, birth order, and industry context. For instance, Stavrou (1999) reveals that male descendants in the Far East and female heirs in Europe are generally more likely to join the family business than are any other offspring from the United States, Europe, or the Far

Table 2.1 Studies on Succession According to Process Stages and Levels of Analysis

			Levels of Analysis					
					Organizational			
Succession Process Stages	Central Questions	Studies [Methods]	Individual	Family	Business	Management	Ownership	Environmental
Intention and Decision to Join	What drives the next generation's decision to join and take over the family business?	Dumas et al. (1995) [ql]	x	x		x		
		Stavrou and Swiercz (1998) [qn]	x	x	x			
		Stavrou (1999) [qn]	x		x			
		Sharma and Irving (2005) [con]	x					
		Vera and Dean (2005) [ql]	x	x	x			
		Schröder et al. (2011) [qn]	x					
		Overbeke et al. (2013) [ql]	x			x		
Preparation	Succession Planning How do internal and external factors affect the importance and extensiveness of succession planning?	Fiegener et al. (1994) [qn]		x		x		
		Harvey and Evans (1994) [con]		x	x	x		
		Lansberg and Astrachan (1994) [qn]		x		x		
		Mandelbaum (1994) [qn]				x		
		Fiegener et al. (1996) [qn]			x			
	How are these factors managed?	Harveston et al. (1997) [qn]	x	x	x	x	x	
		Davis and Harveston (1998) [qn]	x	x	x	x	x	
		Berman-Brown and Coverly (1999) [qn]	x	x		x	x	
		Janjuha-Jivraj and Woods (2002) [ql]	x	x		x		x
		Sharma et al. (2003b) [qn]	x	x		x		
		Westhead (2003) [qn]	x		x			
		Marshall et al. (2006) [qn]	x		x	x	x	
		Motwani et al. (2006) [qn]		x		x		
		DeNoble et al. (2007) [ql]	x			x		
		Tatoglu et al. (2008) [qn]				x		
		Gagné et al. (2011) [qn]	x			x		x
		Sardeshmukh and Corbett (2011) [qn]	x			x		x

Socialization	How are potential successors socialized in the family business?	García-Álvarez et al. (2002) [ql]	x		x		x	
Successor Choice	To what extent is the decision to select a successor influenced by a candidate's attributes and by organizational characteristics and needs?	Kirby and Lee (1996) [qn]				x		x
		Keating and Little (1997) [ql]	x		x	x		x
		Chrisman et al. (1998) [qn]			x			
		Sharma and Rao (2000) [qn]			x			
		Lee et al. (2003) [con]	x		x		x	x
		Royer et al. (2008) [qn]	x				x	
		Aguilera and Crespi-Cladera (2012) [con]		x	x		x	
Transfer of Knowledge and Social Capital	How can the transfer of knowledge and social capital be managed?	Cabrera-Suárez et al. (2001) [con]	x		x	x		x
		Steier (2001) [ql]	x				x	
		Giovannoni et al. (2011) [ql]	x				x	
Transfer of Leadership / Exploration and Implementation	When and how should leadership be transferred to the next generation? What barriers exist? What are the determinants of a successful transfer of leadership? How can the transfer of leadership be managed?	Goldberg (1996) [qn/ql]	x		x	x		x
		Kimhi (1997) [con]	x				x	
		Matthews et al. (1999) [con]			x			
		Shepherd and Zacharakis (2000) [qn]				x		
		Bachkaniwala et al. (2001) [ql]			x	x		x
		Howorth and Ali (2001) [ql]			x	x		x
		Perricone et al. (2001) [ql]	x		x		x	
		Dyck et al. (2002) [ql]					x	
		Murray (2003) [ql]					x	
		Lambrecht (2005) [ql]	x		x		x	
		Yan and Sorenson (2006) [con]			x			
		Haberman and Danes (2007) [ql]	x		x	x		x
		Cater and Justis (2009) [ql]	x		x	x		x
		Janjuha-Jivraj and Spence (2009) [con]	x		x		x	
		Ellul et al. (2010) [qn]			x			
		Salvato and Corbetta (2013) [ql]	x		x		x	

(Continued)

Succession Process Stages	Central Questions	Studies [Methods]	Levels of Analysis						
			Individual	Family	Business	Management	Organizational	Ownership	Environmental
Transfer of Ownership	What are the nature, characteristics, and effects of family relationship dynamics on the transfer of ownership? How do internal and external challenges affect ownership transition?	Dunn (1999) [ql]	x	x					
		Bjuggren and Sund (2001) [con]							x
		Bjuggren and Sund (2002) [con]							x
		Burkart et al. (2003) [con]					x		x
		Thomas (2002) [ql]					x		
		Bjuggren and Sund (2005) [con]							x
		Brun de Pontet et al. (2007) [qn]	x				x		
		Wiklund et al. (2013) [qn]	x	x	x		x		
Incumbent's Withdrawal	What problems need to be addressed after management and ownership have been passed to the next generation? How does a predecessor's role change?	Cadieux (2007) [ql]	x						
		Kim and DeVaney (2003) [qn]	x	x	x		x		
		Harvey and Evans (1995) [con]	x	x			x		
Satisfaction	What drives satisfaction with succession in family businesses?	Sharma et al. (2001) [con]	x				x		
		Sharma et al. (2003a) [qn]	x				x		
		Howorth et al. (2004) [ql]					x	x	
		Morris et al. (1997) [qn]	x	x			x		
		King (2003) [qn]	x						
		Stavrou et al. (2005) [qn]	x	x			x		
		Venter et al. (2005) [qn]	x	x			x		
		Fahed-Sreih and Djoundourian (2006) [qn]	x				x		
		Pérez-González (2006) [qn]	x	x			x		

Post-Succession								
Post-Succession Perfor-mance	What are the determinants of a successful business transition? How does succession affect family business performance?	Bennedsen et al. (2007) [qn]			x	x	x	
		Chittoor and Das (2007) [ql]				x	x	
		Cucculelli and Micucci (2008) [qn]			x	x	x	x
		Diwisch et al. (2009) [qn]	x					
		Mitchell et al. (2009) [con]			x	x		
		Molly et al. (2010) [qn]			x	x		
		Amore et al. (2011) [qn]			x	x	x	x
		Blumentritt et al. (2013) [con]	x		x	x		
		Chung and Luo (2013) [qn]	x	x	x	x	x	x
		Eddleston et al. (2013) [qn]	x		x	x		
Failed Succession	What factors impede intra-family succession??	Miller et al. (2003) [ql]	x	x	x	x		
		De Massis et al. (2008) [con]	x	x	x	x	x	x
General Process	What factors affect and are affected by the succession process in general?	Rubenson and Gupta (1996) [con]	x					
		Santiago (2000) [ql]	x	x	x	x		
		Ibrahim et al. (2001) [ql]	x	x		x		
		Cadieux et al. (2002) [ql]	x	x	x	x		
		Wasserman (2003) [ql/qn]			x		x	
		Lam (2011) [ql]	x					
Reviews on Succession		Handler (1994) [con]	x	x	x	x	x	
		Brockhaus (2004) [con]	x	x	x	x	x	x
		Le Breton-Miller et al. (2004) [con]	x	x	x	x	x	x
		Bagby (2004) [con]			x		x	
		Nordqvist et al. (2013) [con]	x	x	x	x	x	

East. In Europe, the later the potential heirs are born (i.e., the older the predecessors are upon the birth of their offspring), the lower the likelihood that they will become successors while the relationship between birth order and succession is the reverse among descendants in the Far East. Evidence from Canada illustrates the persistence of primogeniture, in which the eldest son takes over the business (Dumas et al. 1995). Whether descendants decide to join can also be affected by the industry. Although female descendants may be interested in the family business, they tend to opt against succession if the firm operates in a male-dominated industry (Schröder, Schmitt-Rodermund, and Arnaud 2011).

Daughters' intentions and self-assessments are strongly influenced by cues about gender roles that they receive from family members, teachers, friends, and other associates when they are young. Because of the limitations that are presupposed by gender roles, daughters are often blind to their own possibilities for succession in the family business. In many cases, nothing less than, critical events are required to initiate daughters' consideration of this succession possibility (Overbeke, Bilimoria, and Perelli 2013).

In summary, the next generation's decision to join the family business is a necessary condition for effective intra-family succession. Extending the existing findings—for example, with research on potential successors' self-efficacy, family communication patterns, and social network members' educational backgrounds, as well as on cross-country comparisons (Hollingsworth and Boyer 1997; Whitley 1999)—may further enhance the existing knowledge about the next generation's likelihood to opt for the family business.

Succession Planning

Studies on succession planning primarily examine *how internal and external factors affect succession planning*. Most family business scholars agree that succession should be planned in order to be effective (Harvey and Evans 1994; Kimhi 1997; Santiago 2000; Sharma and Rao 2000). However, succession is rarely planned well in advance (Berman-Brown and Coverly 1999; Kirby and Lee 1996; Mandelbaum 1994); in addition, succession planning might be important, but it is not necessarily essential to the long-term survival of family businesses (Astrachan and Kolenko 1994; Santiago 2000).

Incumbents' characteristics—such as age, education, and goal adjustment capacities—affect the extensiveness of succession planning, as does their intended retirement date/age (Gagné, Wrosch, and Brun de Pontet 2011). Harveston, Davis, and Lyden (1997) further revealed a gender effect: Individual characteristics have a stronger impact on succession planning in male-led than in female-led family businesses. In addition, higher owner age is positively associated with formal succession plans (Marshall et al. 2006). Paradoxically, higher owner age negatively affects cooperative conflict management, an aspect that is positively related to formal succession planning. Thus, higher owner age is directly associated with formal succession plans but indirectly influences behavioral practices that interfere with succession planning. These findings may explain why an incumbent's desire to keep the business in the family is not necessarily a driver of succession planning (Motwani, Levenburg, Schwarz, and Blankson 2006; Sharma, Chrisman, and Chua 2003b). A predecessor's goal adjustment capacities, such as disengagement and reengagement, and his or her trust in the successor are strong drivers of the agreement on a retirement date. Family business owners with high goal-reengagement capacities who trust in their successors' abilities set an earlier retirement date than others. More precisely, not only are these owners able to reduce the psychological commitment to their former activities and responsibilities, but they are also likely to replace their former goals with alternative goals (Gagné et al. 2011).

Family adaptability and cohesion are affected by the family's commitment to the business and the quality of the relationship between the owner-manager and the successor (Lansberg and Astrachan 1994). Although the influence of individual characteristics on succession planning declines over generations, the impact of the family on the succession process remains constant across generations (Davis and Harveston 1998); in addition, depending on the cultural context and individual roles of family members, those who are not involved in the business also affect succession planning. For instance, in Asian family firms in the United Kingdom, the heir's mother is a crucial buffer between generations (Janjuha-Jivraj and Woods 2002).

Results on the relationship between company size and the extent of succession planning are mixed. Fiegener, Brown, Prince, and File (1994) revealed that company size has no effect on successor development and succession planning. Motwani et al. (2006), however, showed that in larger family businesses, succession planning is more important. Organizational characteristics, such as size and formality, influence succession planning differently in male-led than in female-led organizations (Harveston et al. 1997). In addition, poor firm performance can compel owners to initiate succession planning (Westhead 2003).

An important factor at the management level in terms of succession planning is the availability of a trusted successor. If a successor is not available, owner-managers will be less likely to engage in succession planning. Therefore, successor development systems are needed (Motwani et al. 2006). Fiegener et al. (1994) specified differences between family and non-family business successor development systems. Family business owner-managers favor more personal, relationship-centered approaches while non-family business managers favor formalized, task-oriented approaches. The predecessor usually has the final say in determining the method of successor selection (Tatoglu, Kula, and Glaister 2008). Effective successors must be able to acquire company and industry-specific knowledge rapidly and must have the cognitive ability to exploit that knowledge (Cater and Justis 2009; Sardeshmukh and Corbett 2011). They are supposed to manage relations with key external stakeholders and gain experience in strategic planning (Fiegener, Brown, Prince, and File 1996). Predecessors should view themselves as manager-builders during the preparation stage of successors and support successors while they acquire the required task experience (Cater and Justis 2009).

If tacit knowledge or social capital is needed to run the business successfully, often a family offspring is chosen and developed as a potential successor (DeNoble, Ehrlich, and Singh 2007). The transfer of tacit knowledge to a non-family candidate is more difficult; this fact influences the selection and succession planning process (Cabrera-Suárez, De Saá-Pérez, and García-Almeida 2001; Steier 2001). Regarding the time and mode of entry, Harvey and Evans (1994) suggest that there are distinct, predictable, and multiple stages in siblings' career development that are suited to an offspring's entry into the family business. Because the needs of family businesses and successors vary from family to family, there is no general recommendation for the best entry time. However, proactively managing the children's entry into a family business is essential and should begin early in the children's lives to prevent succession paralysis (Lambrecht 2005).

Comparatively little is known about how succession planning is affected by economic performance of the business prior to succession and by different ownership structures. Although Harveston et al. (1997) include the ownership dimension, they do not provide evidence that access to capital and family funding play a greater role in succession planning in male-led than in female-led family businesses. Similarly, although it is posited that ethnicity influences succession (Janjuha-Jivraj and Woods 2002), our knowledge about succession planning in different cultural contexts, including that of immigrant family firms, is limited. Furthermore, analysis of family business heterogeneity (Chua, Chrisman, Steier, and Rau 2012) has not yet been considered in the context of succession, although different types of family businesses might use different approaches to succession planning.

Literature Gap: Socialization of the Next Generation

The socialization of the next generation remains largely a blind spot in research on family business succession. This is surprising, considering that the few existing studies that consider this factor suggest that this is an important topic. Lambrecht (2005), for instance, found that proactive involvement of family scions in the business facilitates succession. Moreover, when García-Álvarez, López-Sintas, and Gonzalvo (2002) studied 13 male Spanish founders to explore *how potential successors are socialized in family businesses*, they identified four founder types: the founder of the family tradition, the founder-achiever, the founder-strategist, and the founder-inventor. Based on these types, differences exist in the nature of the values that are passed on to the successors. "Strategist-type founders emphasize self-fulfillment and business as an end, whereas the other three groups of founders—although they agree on business as a means as a value for transmission—opt for different blends of psychosocial values" (García-Álvarez et al. 2002, 196). Whether, for example, an early stimulating environment with entrepreneurial role models or whether authoritative parenting affects the development of successors as positively as it influences entrepreneurs (Steinberg 2001) may be a building block for a future theory of succession.

Having completed our analysis of the succession preparation stage (Stage 1), we now move to the second stage of the succession process: the choice of a successor.

The Choice of a Successor (Stage 2)

Research on the choice of a successor focuses on the extent to which the decision to select a successor is influenced by the *attributes of the potential heir* and by *organizational characteristics and needs*. However, little is known about the role of different *decision-making processes and country-specific institutionalized frameworks*.

Attributes of the Potential Heir

Family firms can choose successors from among family members and individuals outside the family. Intra-family "successions are not necessarily better when staffed by professionals from outside the family as opposed to individuals from within the family. This succession selection is contingent on the abilities and training of the successor heirs" (Aguilera and Crespi-Cladera 2012, 68). Evidence from Chrisman, Chua, and Sharma (1998), Sharma and Rao (2000), and Keating and Little (1997) implies that across different national backgrounds, integrity and commitment to the business are the most important successor attributes, while birth order and gender are least important. Considering the persistence of primogeniture, these findings are surprising and might indicate that successor attributes interact with other contextual variables.

Organizational Characteristics and Needs

Drawing on the South Asian example, Lee, Lim, and Lim suggest that "if a family business is highly idiosyncratic, the family will prefer to appoint its offspring to head its business, even though the offspring may be less competent than nonfamily managers. The exception to this is when the offspring is so poorly qualified that the survival of the business will be jeopardized with such an appointment" (2003, 663). Based on data from 35 family firms, Kirby and Lee

(1996) proposed that firm size has no impact on successor selection. More recent evidence, based on 5,334 Danish limited liability companies, by Bennedsen, Nielsen, Pérez-González, and Wolfenzon (2007), focused on the performance implications of CEO succession and shows that smaller firms and families with male eldest children are more likely to appoint family CEOs than are larger firms or families with eldest children that are female. In addition, if family business-specific knowledge is highly relevant and the need for industry-specific general or technical knowledge is weak, family members are regularly selected. External successors are preferred when education, work experience, and success in other firms in the same industry are considered relevant (Royer, Simons, Boyd, and Rafferty 2008).

Research Gap: Decision-Making Processes and Country-Specific Frameworks

Despite important findings on desirable characteristics of successors, our knowledge on how successors are selected is still rudimentary at best. For instance, the question of how decision-making styles (namely, *crown heir, horse race, coup d'état, comprehensive search*; Friedman and Olk 1995) and country-specific institutionalized frameworks (e.g., *primogeniture, adoption*) affect the outcomes of succession processes has not yet been addressed.

Referring to country-specific frameworks, the consideration of the national business systems approach may provide new thought-provoking impulses for theory-building (Whitley 1999). National contexts differ in terms of legal, regulatory and sociopolitical institutions that affect the likelihood and extent to which particular succession practices will be adopted—with any such adoptions determining not only the type of successor but also the post-succession performance of family businesses (Carney, Gedajlovic, and Strike 2014).

After a successor has been chosen in this second stage of the succession process, the third stage—exploration and implementation—begins.

Exploration and Implementation (Stage 3)

The third stage of the succession process, exploration and implementation, involves the preparation for and implementation of the transfers of ownership and leadership. We review these transfers separately before pointing out that little is known about *the role of shocks* at this critical stage of the succession process.

Transfer of Ownership

Studies on the transfer of ownership usually focus on family and environmental levels of analysis. The former considers *relational and emotional aspects* while the latter focus on *economic and legal issues*.

Relational and Emotional Aspects

The early exit of shareholders, especially of those not involved in day-to-day operations, represents one of the most salient challenges in succession. Transfer of ownership is largely accompanied by anxiety, which tempers the emotional equilibrium of the individuals involved. The predecessor and the successor are trapped by the need to maintain an emotional equilibrium while, for instance, the predecessor plans for retirement and both decide on the timing of the transfer of wealth and power. The process of transferring ownership differs between families, based on a family's values, regime, and life cycle (Dunn 1999). This process is also influenced by the traditions, laws, and tax regimes of the country and culture in which the family firm operates (Carney et al. 2014). For an incumbent who is usually the head of both the family and the business, it may be difficult to hand over control to a successor and abandon ownership, as this dual role typically brings high personal and emotional value (Brun de Pontet, Wrosch, and Gagné 2007). Under conditions of high ownership dispersion, the intention to maintain emotional equilibrium leads to competing motivations that can be addressed in one of two ways. The first is to maintain ongoing communication with all shareholders, and the second is to implement practices that facilitate timely action to meet the needs of all parties (Thomas 2002).

Other important conditions pertain to family structure and embeddedness. For instance, Wiklund, Nordqvist, Hellerstedt, and Bird (2013) showed that the relationship between ownership dispersion and the likelihood of intra-family ownership transfer follows an inverted-u-shaped pattern. Moreover, the higher the number of potential adult heirs, the higher will be the likelihood of an intra-family ownership transition. Conversely, the availability of many young potential heirs does not drive the likelihood of an intra-family ownership transition. Wiklund et al. (2013) also show that when multiple generations are involved in managing the business, an intra-family ownership transition is more likely to take place than an external one. Firms with a CEO from the owner-family are also more likely to be passed on to other family members than are firms with a non-family CEO.

Economic and Legal Issues

National legal systems significantly affect ownership transition. For example, in Sweden, many successions failed because the country lacked a legal system that facilitated intra-family ownership transitions. Families could therefore hardly preserve their idiosyncratic knowledge through unburdened intra-family succession (Bjuggren and Sund 2001, 2002). As a result, Sweden abolished gift and inheritance taxes as of January 1st, 2005 (Bjuggren and Sund 2005).

There are strong indicators that estate tax rates influence the efficiency of ownership transfers (Davis et al. 1996) and the outcome of these transfers for entire economies (Wahl 2003). During and after the transfer of ownership to the next generation, there is a decrease in financial investment that is more severe if the firm is in a country with a strict inheritance regime that requires hefty inheritance tax payments (Ellul et al. 2010).

Moreover, the legal protection of shareholders across countries affects how ownership succession is implemented. In countries with strong legal protection of minority shareholders, founders tend to hire professional managers and sell off the firm after going public. If a country offers intermediate protection of minority shareholders, a founder may still hire a professional manager, but the founding family nevertheless usually remains a large shareholder in order to monitor this new manager (i.e., ensure there is no abuse of managerial discretion) and ultimately protect the interests of all shareholders. Finally, in a country that offers weak protection of minority shareholders, the founding family must continue to run the firm or cede control to a professional manager who is closely tied to the family (Burkart, Panunzi, and Shleifer 2003).

Transfer of Leadership

Studies on the transfer of leadership refer to the issues of *when and how leadership should be transferred.* Moreover, they address the question of *how tacit knowledge and social capital should be transferred.* These studies focus on individual, organizational, and environmental levels of analysis.

When and How Leadership Should be Transferred

Two aspects affect the timing of the transfer of leadership control. First, the parent can delay the transfer of power to a child due to the results of a self-categorization process (Matthews, Moore, and Fialko 1999). Second, the presence of binding borrowing constraints promotes a premature transfer of leadership control (Kimhi 1997). On the individual and family levels of analysis, the ability of successive generations to acquire skills that enable them to identify new market niches (Perricone, Earle, and Taplin 2001), to rely on harmonious rather than contentious relationships (Howorth and Ali 2001), to utilize social capital and trust (Perricone et al. 2001), and to establish mentoring relationships (Goldberg 1996) fosters a successful transfer. A precondition is the outgoing generation's benevolence by passing the leadership to the next generation. This benevolence is rewarded by confirming the outgoing generation's legacy within the family and possibly the wider community (Janjuha-Jivraj and Spence 2009).

Development of successors' leadership skills can be promoted by external advisors. Advisors facilitate the process through which a successor's leadership is gradually accepted by all actors involved by taking on a transitional leadership role alongside incumbent leaders and the selected successor. This serves as a bridge between the former and the new leadership configuration in family firms (Salvato and Corbetta 2013).

On the business level, effective succession depends on individuals' abilities to continue to sustain the viability of the business (Goldberg 1996). Interactions between members involved in leadership transfer processes can either foster or impede the transition of power—depending on how family members cope with power structures and depending on their relationships, both individually and as a group—so in order to assess and balance all such interactions, transfer processes should reflect multiple perspectives within the family and the business (Haberman and Danes 2007). In addition, if a successor must buy into the family business, he or she will be more likely to appreciate the rules that allowed him or her to lead the business, and thus more likely to value the business more highly and less likely to sell it due to high financial or behavioral sunk costs (Shepherd and Zacharakis 2000).

Culture also affects the nature of the leadership transfer. South Asian family businesses are a case in point: The next generation's interest in taking over the business is largely affected by education, external employment opportunities, growth expectations for the business, strong dependence on co-ethnic customers, and the availability of other succession options such as buyouts and trade sales (Bachkaniwala, Wright, and Ram 2001). In Chinese family business transitions, Confucian values are a factor. These values, which include, for example, respectful family relationships, are related to stronger acceptance of succession decisions (Yan and Sorenson 2006). Cultural differences also lead to differences in successors' prerequisites. For example, in contrast to Anglo-American cultures, in Portugal, less-educated, less-experienced, and less-qualified sons are preferred over better educated daughters (Howorth and Ali 2001).

Three methods of transferring leadership are conceivable: balance, imbalance and disintegration from inadequate exploration, and imbalance and disintegration due to the continuance of the business. Balance fosters the continuance of the family business while imbalance is more likely to lead to its disintegration (Murray 2003). Lambrecht (2005) revealed five ways to transfer a business to the next generation. One, the successor takes the lead. Two, succession is initiated at the explicit request of the incumbent. Three, the successor has a sense of moral duty to engage in succession. Four, succession occurs by an institutionalized or at least previously decided way (e.g., primogeniture). Five, the incumbent give the successor a gentle push in the direction he or she perceives to be the best. Another option to transfer the business to the next generation may be added to Lambrecht's (2005) five pre-specified ways: succession may occur unexpectedly through the sudden death of the incumbent.

From a process perspective, the tasks related to the transfer of leadership to the next generation can be compared to a 4x100 relay race, with shared tasks that include sequence, timing, passing the baton, and communication. Interestingly, the conditions and events fostering a successful transfer of leadership do not necessarily enhance firm performance. Vice versa, the transfer of leadership may be impeded by events and circumstances dedicated to increasing performance (Dyck, Mauws, Starke, and Mischke 2002).

How Tacit Knowledge and Social Capital Should be Transferred

Research alluding to the question of *how the transfer of knowledge and social capital is managed* mainly focuses on the management level (Cabrera-Suárez et al. 2001; Giovannoni, Maraghini, and Riccaboni 2011; Steier 2001). However, the competitive advantage of family businesses often involves tacit knowledge that is experienced solely by family members (Lee et al. 2003). A challenge to succession is, therefore, the transfer of this knowledge to the designated successor (Jaskiewicz, Uhlenbruck, Balkin, and Reay 2013). Cabrera-Suárez et al. (2001), using the resource-based view, developed an integrative model that asserts that knowledge transfer is affected by the business and the family context, the quality of the predecessor-successor relationship, and the training of the successor. Jaskiewicz et al. (2013) proposed that tacit knowledge management can be more effective in the context of family than non-family business. The authors elaborated on this point, in that high-quality social exchange relationships are most common among family members. Such relationships are critical in order to understand, share, and protect tacit knowledge. When considering that tacit knowledge can be a critical resource for competitive advantage and organizational success (e.g., Coff, Coff, and Eastvold 2006), we understand why its transfer in the context of succession remains an important research topic in family business research.

Steier (2001) examines how social capital is managed and transferred. Social capital, defined as "the actual and potential resources individuals obtain from knowing others, being part of a social network with them, or merely from being known to them and having a good reputation" (Steier 2001, 260), can be created, transferred, and managed in four ways: one, in an unplanned, sudden succession; two, in a rushed succession; three, in a natural immersion; and four, in a planned succession and deliberate transfer. Further, there are seven means of managing social capital, including deciphering existing network structures, attaining legitimacy, using management accounting practices to provide a shared language, and clarifying optimal roles. In the case of a planned and deliberate transfer (Steier 2001), the use of management accounting practices that provide a shared language represents a key tool in the transfer of knowledge, especially if a successor from outside the family is appointed (Giovannoni et al. 2011).

In summary, effectively sharing tacit knowledge and social capital with the designated successor can be critical for his or her future success in the family firm.

Research Gap: The Role of Shocks

Existing research has provided many important insights on how ownership, management, tacit knowledge, and social capital should ideally be passed on to a successor. However, in reality, a large percentage of these transfers fail because of unforeseen shocks and resulting complications. Therefore more research is needed on how shocks such as illness, depression, addiction, and death of the predecessor or successor can adversely affect the exploration and implementation of each of these transfers. Similarly, whether and how familial issues (e.g., divorce, marriage, parenthood) and environmental issues (e.g., a change in inheritance tax laws, an introduction of governance codes that restrict family involvement in firms) can derail these crucial transfers requires more attention in research.

Now, after having discussed the third stage of the succession process, we move on to the fourth of five stages: the incumbent's withdrawal.

The Incumbent's Withdrawal (Stage 4)

Research on the incumbent's withdrawal focuses on resulting *threats and opportunities for the business* and *the predecessor's new role in the business.* Most studies focus on dimensions that pertain to the individual and organizational (namely, family and business) levels of analysis.

Threats and Opportunities for the Business

After the transition of the business to the successor is complete, conflicts between a predecessor and successor often emerge because of a lack of trust in the successor, insufficient communication, changes in leadership style and business strategy, the predecessor's reluctance to cede his or her informal power, and/or the predecessor's continued involvement in important decisions (Harvey and Evans 1995). Questions of how the predecessor retires and how his or her future roles are defined are also essential. The predecessor's age affects the time of withdrawal (Kim and DeVaney 2003; Marshall et al. 2006). When owner-managers have a better education, more income, and more tax-deferred retirement accounts, and when they work more hours per week, they tend to retire earlier (Kim and DeVaney 2003).

The Predecessor's New Role in the Business

The withdrawal stage represents an important time for predecessors. During a shared leadership phase, the predecessor acts as a supervisor, teacher, and/or introducer. These roles change during the withdrawal stage: The predecessor should now act as an administrator, symbol, and safeguard, thus as a type of consultant (Cadieux 2007). However, many predecessors seek a transfer of leadership to another person while retaining ownership, hence, "Controlling ownership may be symbolic of the owner's ultimate resistance to letting go" (Brun de Pontet et al. 2007, 349). More studies exploring this topic would be desirable.

Research Gap: Cross-Cultural Differences Regarding the Predecessor's Withdrawal

While research has focused on how withdrawal by the predecessor affects both his or her relationship with the successor and the family business, little is known about what triggers this withdrawal. Thus, an analysis of how the predecessor's withdrawal could be triggered, managed, and completed across family firms and cultures would not only fill this gap but also offer important insights into the least disruptive and most beneficial processes for family firms.

While most research assumes the succession process ends at this fourth stage, more recent studies point to the need to add a fifth stage: post-succession (Le Breton-Miller et al. 2004).

Post-Succession (Stage 5)

Studies on post-succession performance focus on *what predicts an effective succession, how succession affects firm performance*, and *what ensures satisfaction from succession*. Factors for individual, family, business, and management levels are often considered. Conversely, ownership and environmental aspects remain largely overlooked. These latter two factors, however, can play major roles in failed succession processes.

What Predicts an Effective Succession?

Successful business transitions require a combination of individual-, family-, and management-level factors. The preparation level of heirs, leader personality, family and business culture, the quality of the relationship between predecessor and successor, and family business managers' planning and control activities predict whether a transition will be successful (Fahed-Sreih and Djoundourian 2006; Morris, Williams, Allen, and Avila 1997). When heirs are well-prepared, family relationships are trust-based and affable, and families engage in financial planning, successions tend to be smoother. Accordingly, characteristics of intra-family relationships are important drivers of effective successions (Morris et al. 1997).

How Succession Affects Firm Performance

Both the definition and measurement of succession-time and post-succession firm performance differ across studies. Frequently used variables include financial structure, sales, asset growth (King 2003; Mitchell, Hart, Valcea, and Townsend 2009; Molly, Laveren, and Deloof 2010; Morris et al. 1997), employment growth (Diwisch, Voithofer, and Weiss 2009; Morris et al. 1997), perceptions of succession effectiveness or firm growth (Eddleston, Kellermanns, Floyd, Crittenden, and Crittenden 2013; Venter, Boshoff, and Maas 2005), and longevity/continuity (Fahed-Sreih and Djoundourian 2006).

The study of succession-time and post-succession performance has led to mixed results. Based on objective financial data, some authors argue that there is no relationship between the nature of the transition process and post-succession performance (Molly et al. 2010; Morris et al. 1997). However, studies based on individual perceptions of profitability report other results. For instance, Venter et al. (2005) showed that profitability is influenced by a successor's willingness to take over the firm, his or her level of preparation, and the quality of the relationship between the successor and the predecessor.

Additional succession-time and post-succession firm performance measures include the level of firm debt and growth (Amore, Minichilli, and Corbetta 2011; Chittoor and Das 2007; Molly et al. 2010) and the change of the number of employees (Diwisch et al. 2009). Chittoor and Das (2007) asserted that the professionalization of management, defined as the transfer of management control to a non-family manager, leads to superior succession-time firm performance. This finding lends support to the assertion that separation of ownership and management results in improved firm performance (Burkart et al. 2003) while intra-family successions tend to be negatively related to firm performance. Family-CEO underperformance is particularly high in fast-growing industries, in industries with a highly skilled labor force, in relatively large firms, and in firms with foreign ownership (Bennedsen et al. 2007; Chung and Luo 2013). In contrast, on average, firms managed by non-family CEOs fail to show improvements in firm performance for some time only when they need to restructure poorly performing companies after succession (Cucculelli and Micucci 2008; Pérez-González 2006).

The transfer from the first to the second generation negatively influences a firm's debt. This effect is reversed in transitions to later generations. Firm growth decreases after the handover from the first to the second generation. However, in successions to later generations, no effect on growth can be identified (Molly et al. 2010). The appointment of a non-family CEO causes a significant increase in debt financing around succession. The increase in debt is greater when the firm is younger and fast-growing when the family exerts influence on managerial decision-making through the board of directors, and when the new CEO has limited access to alternative funding sources (Amore et al. 2011). Finally, Diwisch et al. (2009) revealed significant and positive employment growth effects post-succession.

The successor's capability is related to an increase in sales in the third year after succession (King 2003). Successor discretion, defined as the extent to which a successor is able and willing to formulate, modify, and enact plans for the renewal of the company, affects the degree to which successors are able to take the risks necessary to maintain the family firm's entrepreneurial edge and maximize family wealth. Put differently, there are individual-level differences in successor discretion that are influenced by firm-level factors such as wealth preservation-based inertia, post-succession predecessor involvement, and "familiness" (Mitchell et al. 2009).

Inconsistent findings may be due to the fact that the relationship between antecedents and post-succession performance is contingent on yet unknown factors. For example, economic context (e.g., developed versus emerging economies) might influence the relationship between successor choice and firm performance. The research of Chung and Luo (2013) yielded a result seemingly in keeping with this economic-context notion: Although outsiders outperform family successors in firms with high family ownership and in group-affiliated firms, the researchers found that outsider performance premium was significantly reduced in Taiwan, a developed country. Another possible contingency factor is the generation managing the firm. For example, strategic and succession planning may fuel firm growth, but they are most conducive to growth in firms transitioning to the second generation; they do not strongly nurture growth in firms transitioning to the third generation. In fact, while *succession* planning can somewhat promote growth in third-or-later-generation family firms, *strategic* planning appears in these situations to be negatively related to growth (Eddleston et al. 2013).

Altogether, these results, depicted in Table 2.2, illustrate Blumentritt, Mathews, and Marchisio's (2013) assertion that post-succession performance is driven by a great variety of more or less interdependent individual decisions and contextual factors. These findings also echo Mazzi's findings on the family firm-performance linkage, that "the relationship is complex and very likely to be moderated or mediated by factors not included in the analysis" (2011, 176). The results thus bear potential for future studies considering multiple levels of analysis. A contingency approach may, therefore, be interesting if we assume that there is no single best way to achieve satisfactory post-succession performance for family firms in general.

What Ensures Satisfaction From Succession?

Studies examining this question focus on the individual and management levels of analysis. Five antecedents lead to a satisfactory intra-family succession, namely, the predecessor's propensity to step aside, the successor's propensity to take over the business, succession planning, an agreement to continue the business, and the acceptance of individual roles (Sharma, Chrisman, and Chua 2003a; Sharma, Chrisman, Pablo, and Chua 2001; Venter et al. 2005).

If a suitable family successor is not available, a management buyout (MBO) or a management buy-in (MBI) may be viable options. In these cases, drivers of satisfactory succession outcomes are low information asymmetries, high levels of trust, good relationships, and coordinative

Table 2.2 Factors Affecting Post-Succession Performance

Studies	Sample	Independent Variables	Dependent Variables	Findings
Morris et al. (1997)	209 heads of family firms; U.S.A.	preparation of heirs, family and business relationships, planning and control, characteristics of the transition	post-transition performance (financial structure, sales, asset growth)	Family business transitions occur more smoothly when heirs are better prepared, relationships among family members are trust-based and affable, and family businesses engage in more planning for taxation and wealth transfer purposes. Post-transition performance is positively affected by the education level of the heirs.
King (2003)	29 predecessors and successors; U.S.A.	successor capability	adjusted gross sales	To the extent that business size and complexity change over the three years following succession, there is a significant tendency for businesses with successors of higher potential capabilities to show a growth in adjusted sales. Businesses with successors of lower capabilities show either lower growth or an actual reduction in adjusted sales growth.
Stavrou et al. (2005)	30 leaders of family firms; Cyprus	leader personality, cultural configuration (firm, family, board), success factors	success of the transition	Successful intergenerational transitions in family firms involve collaborative family and participative business cultures. This cultural configuration is related mostly to Extraverted-Sensing–Thinking-Judging leaders. A shift in the board culture between the generations may suggest a necessary change for the firm's growth and long-term success.
Venter et al. (2005)	332 owner-managers and successors in SMEs; South Africa	willingness to take over, rewards, trust, needs alignment, relation between owner-manager and successor, family harmony, preparation level	perceived success of the succession process (satisfaction, continued business profitability)	Successor-related factors affecting satisfaction are the willingness of the successor to take over and the relationship between the owner-manager and the successor. Profitability is affected by the willingness of the successor to take over the business, the preparation level of the successor, and the relationship between the successor and the owner-manager. The relationship between the owner-manager and the successor is influenced by the extent to which interpersonal relationships in the family are harmonious.
Fahed-Sreih and Djoundourian (2006)	114 family firms; Lebanon	planning and control, family relations, attitudes	firm age: young versus mature	Older firms are more inclined to use a participatory decision-making process, as evidenced by more reliance on advisory boards. A larger proportion of older firms relative to younger ones hold family meetings and have formal redemption and liquidity plans.

Study	Sample	Independent variables	Dependent variable	Findings
Pérez-González (2006)	335 management transitions; U.S.A.	CEO succession, inherited control	firm performance (operating ROA, net income to assets, market-to-book ratio)	Promoting family CEOs in publicly traded corporations significantly hurts performance. Declines in performance are pertinent in firms that appoint family CEOs who did not attend a selective undergraduate institution. Comparable firms that promote non-family CEOs do not experience negative changes in performance.
Bennedsen et al. (2007)	5,334 CEO successions; Denmark	CEO succession, number of spouses, number of children, gender ratio, gender of first child	firm performance (ROA, ROCE, likelihood of bankruptcy and liquidation)	The gender of the first child is unlikely to affect firm outcomes. Family successions have a negative effect on firm performance. Family-CEO underperformance is high in fast-growing industries, industries with a highly skilled labor force, large firms, and firms with foreign ownership. Professional, non-family CEOs provide valuable services to the organizations they head.
Chittoor and Das (2007)	3 family business groups; India	professionalization of management	post-succession performance	Succession to a non-family manager has a positive effect on performance. Four mechanisms enhance performance: (1) planned exit mechanisms for family members; (2) a successor with moderate experience within the business; (3) key professional managers on the board of directors; and (4) moderate ownership of key managers in the business.
Cucculelli and Micucci (2008)	229 family firms; Italy	CEO succession, inherited management, sectoral level of competition	firm performance (ROA, ROS)	Inherited management negatively affects performance. This decrease is concentrated among founder-run firms that outperform sectoral average profitability before succession. The decrease in post-succession performance is larger for heir-managed firms than for companies managed by unrelated CEOs.
Diwisch et al. (2009)	1,101 family firms; Austria	completed successions, planned successions	employment growth	Succession has a significant and positive effect on employment growth, which becomes stronger over time. However, there is no significant difference in employment growth between firms that plan to transfer the firm in the next 10 years and those that do not, thus authors reject the "shadow of succession" hypothesis.
Mitchell et al. (2009)	n/a	successor discretion	productive change	Successor discretion can affect productive change following succession in a family business.
Molly et al. (2010)	152 SMEs; Belgium	family business transfer in first and later generations	debt rate, firm growth (operating ROA)	A transfer from the first to the second generation negatively influences the firm's debt rate. Successions between later generations positively affect debt. In first-generation firms, growth decreases after the transition, whereas in next-generation firms, there is no effect on growth. A family firm's profitability is not significantly affected by succession.

(Continued)

Studies	Sample	Independent Variables	Dependent Variables	Findings
Amore et al. (2011)	2,484 family firms; Italy	CEO succession, financial and governance variations, debt and financial flexibility	financial policies	Appointing non-family CEOs causes an increase in debt financing. The increase in debt is greater when the firm is younger and fast-growing, the family has influence on managerial decision making, and the incoming CEO has limited access to alternative funding sources. The increase in debt induced by professional successions occurs primarily when the incoming manager can exploit spare borrowing capacity.
Blumentritt et al. (2013)	n/a	individual choices	total family/firm welfare	Game theory provides a solid foundation from which to observe, explain, and make predictions about succession in family businesses. Game theory offers a means of observing actors through an integrated model that can account for interdependencies among actors and the ramifications of one actor's decisions on the decisions of others. The construction of utility functions forces a complete assessment of what is important to each actor.
Chung and Luo (2013)	4,316 firm-year cases (573 firms); Taiwan	successor origin, family involvement, business group, industry, foreign institutional investment	performance premium	Given the weak market for institutions, successors' access to social networks and the legitimacy conferred by important stakeholders are crucial to successors' abilities to garner resources and support, which in turn benefits firm profitability.
Eddleston et al. (2013)	107 family firms; U.S.A.	strategic planning, succession planning, generation	firm growth	The degree to which strategic planning and succession planning are associated with family firm growth depends on the generation managing the firm. Both forms of planning are most conducive to the growth of first-generation firms, but neither form of planning confers much growth for second-generation firms. For third-and-beyond generation firms, the benefits of succession planning tend to reemerge, whereas strategic planning is negatively associated with their level of growth.

Notes: Based on their dependent variables, 16 studies are classified as pertaining to post-succession performance. These studies are listed in chronological order.

forms of negotiation behavior. Compared to intra-family succession, process- rather than individual-level factors drive satisfaction; that is, the way the MBO/MBI process is conducted is decisive (Howorth, Westhead, and Wright 2004).

Research Gap: Failed (Family) Succession

While most studies focus on effective successions and their drivers, for far too long, researchers have ignored the fertile research ground stemming from family businesses that failed at succession. Focusing on *factors impeding intra-family succession* and an analysis of teaching-oriented case studies, De Massis et al. (2008) specified five categories of factors that impede succession: individual-level factors that are either successor- or predecessor-related (e.g., a potential successor's lack of ability or motivation); relational factors (e.g., conflicts in parent-child or other family relationships, or a lack of trust in and commitment to potential successors); financial factors (e.g., inability to sustain the tax burden or to find financial resources for payouts to possible heirs); contextual factors (e.g., a change in business performance or the loss of key customers or suppliers); and process factors (e.g., inadequate communication or a misleading evaluation of the gaps between business needs and the potential successor's abilities).

Miller, Steier, and Le Breton-Miller (2003) identified three patterns of failed successions. The first pattern is a conservative succession characterized by a newly appointed CEO who is still depending on his or her predecessor. The shadow of the parents guides strategies and organizations that are locked in the past. The second pattern is a wavering succession in which the newly appointed CEO wants to put his or her stamp on the business but is uncertain about how to proceed. This uncertainty leads to indecision and a reversal of the new CEO's initiatives. The third instance is the rebellious succession, in which the newly appointed CEO rejects the predecessor's legacy and past practices.

Taken together, these past studies show that individual, familial, and organizational factors can impede the effectiveness of successions. However, the existing research also illustrates that little is yet known about how the dispersion of family ownership before and after succession affects whether succession fails or succeeds. For instance, will the equal division of firm ownership among next generation members undermine the successor's positive results with the family firm? Similarly, little is known about how environmental aspects shape succession outcomes. Inheritance tax laws, prevalent cultural norms, and common family traditions incentivize families to decide on a particular succession route. But just because a chosen route appears familiar or obvious, it is not necessarily the one that will most likely lead to an effective succession. More research is needed on these topics.

Discussion

A plethora of studies have focused on succession in family firms. Similarly, various reviews of the body of succession research have summarized what we know and what still needs to be studied. In this review, we have built upon prior work; yet at the same time, our work differs from past reviews in important ways.

First, we believe that succession research has been over-published but under-studied. While research standards have increased over the last decades, many older studies on succession use basic methodological standards at best. In contrast to past reviews, our study is the first to provide a comprehensive review of succession research that adhered to reasonable methodological standards, as set by Tranfield et al. (2003). Our review thereby lays a potentially stronger, though smaller, foundation for what we know about succession.

Second, prior reviews have focused on particular aspects of succession, such as antecedents (De Massis et al. 2008; Le Breton-Miller et al. 2004), psychological factors (Filser et al. 2013), and factors pertaining to management succession (Brockhaus 2004; De Massis et al. 2008; Long and Chrisman 2013). In contrast, we describe succession as a process involving management and ownership succession and synthesize insights from studies independent of their levels of analysis.

Moreover, Le Breton-Miller et al. (2004) explained that succession encompasses five stages, namely, *preparation, choice of a successor, exploration and implementation, incumbent owner-manager withdrawal*, and *post-succession*. Most reviews, however, focus on the first four stages at best. The most recent review of family succession research that we considered (De Massis et al. 2008), for instance, focuses on factors that prevent succession, and thereby necessarily excludes the final stage, post-succession. Our review thus goes beyond prior reviews on the topic by looking at the entire succession process and across levels of analysis.

Third, we not only draw a more complete (and solid) map of succession knowledge but also provide an updated overview of research gaps that still require attention. Our holistic view of succession aims to overcome the isolated analyses of single factors at particular stages of the succession process in order to employ a more integrated approach that sheds light on the interactions and interdependencies of factors across stages of the succession process and across levels of analysis. We elaborate on this point in the following section.

Implications

A Holistic Framework for Studying Family Firm Succession

Our literature review shows that in addition to economic factors (e.g., Bachkaniwala et al. 2001; Giovannoni et al. 2011; Pérez-González 2006), psychological factors (e.g., García-Álvarez et al. 2002; Haberman and Danes 2007; Sharma and Rao 2000), and sociological factors (e.g., Howorth and Ali 2001; Perricone et al. 2001) on the individual and organizational levels of analysis, factors on the environmental level (i.e., the strength of market institutions, prevalent corporate governance rules, non-preventive tax laws; Bjuggren and Sund 2001; Burkart et al. 2003; Chung and Luo 2013; Ellul at al. 2010) need to be considered in succession research. Only when holistic models capture all of these factors across levels of analysis can a more in-depth understanding of succession processes, their antecedents, and their outcomes be gained.

We suggest that intra-family succession is "effective" if the family preserves its influence on the business, if the business is thriving, and if the family is flourishing. As a result, first, the family must identify practices that allow it to preserve influence on the business in the long run (e.g., Janjuha-Jivraj and Woods 2002; Mandelbaum 1994; Sardeshmukh and Corbett 2011; Tatoglu et al. 2008). Ideally, the family and its business are rooted in an environment that supports the development of such practices (e.g., Bennedsen et al. 2007; Bjuggren and Sund 2002; Carney et al. 2014).

Second, based on the establishment of such practices, a potential family heir must consider the current situation and potential future of the firm in her or his decision about whether or not to join the family business (e.g., Bachkaniwala et al. 2001; Bennedsen et al. 2007; Goldberg 1996; Kirby and Lee 1996). The more qualified the potential heir is, the more relevant the pre-succession growth and performance of the family business will be to his or her decision to join.

Third, the family needs to be flourishing. Specifically, it should be perceived as supportive, harmonious, and cohesive by potential family heirs (e.g., Jaskiewicz, Combs, and Rau 2015; Lansberg and Astrachan 1994; Perricone et al. 2001) to maximize the chances of winning over a potential heir. For instance, prescribed gender roles regularly dissuade competent female potential heirs from joining the business, reducing the potential size of the pool of family successors by roughly half (Overbeke et al. 2013).

Related to the third point, we believe that a variety of norms, values, and goals contribute to succession. For instance, a major stream of family business research focuses on socioemotional wealth (SEW)—the effective value that family members derive from firm control (Gómez-Mejía, Haynes, Núñez-Nickel, Jacobson, and Moyano-Fuentes 2007). The prevailing paradigm within this stream of research is that a family's pursuit of SEW hurts performance and thereby undermines the long-term sustainability of the firm. We encourage researchers to study the role of SEW in the context of succession, but also ask them to do so in more holistic ways: First, recent studies show that only some families are able to pursue simultaneously socioemotional and economic goals during the succession process (Jaskiewicz, Heinrichs, Rau, and Reay 2015). Future research will, therefore, need to analyze how organizational succession processes can encompass the pursuit of socioemotional and financial goals. Second, researchers commonly think of SEW as an antecedent of firm performance or an outcome of family influence. In the context of succession, researchers might consider the successful pursuit of SEW as an important antecedent of effective family succession and an important indicator of cohesive families. Maybe it is through the pursuit of SEW that families can maintain their strong identification with the firm, motivate the next generation to consider a career in the family business, and nurture the affective commitment of family members working in the firm (Deephouse and Jaskiewicz 2013). In summary, holistic succession research needs to import novel paradigms from other research contexts in order to broaden and refine existing theory. A holistic approach, however, will not ignore the complex web of intricate linkages that might exist between the pursuit of SEW, for example, and pertinent factors across the five stages of succession and various levels of analysis.

Based on this general framework, we encourage future researchers to consider the many interactions between factors across levels of analysis and stages of the succession process. For instance, potential conflicts may spill over from the business to the family because of the chosen succession process. One such scenario considers institutionalized succession rules, such as primogeniture, which have an impact on the family and its members. In the case of primogeniture, the firstborn knows that he or she will become the leader of the family business while all other offspring can independently choose their future paths. By contrast, when children compete for succession, such competition can lead to siblings following similar educational paths, as well as to ongoing competitive aggressiveness that, in turn, might result in a high propensity to take risks in order to become the designated successor. Put differently, what appears right for the business is not necessarily right for the family and vice versa. Recent studies on succession in family firms indicate that only about one-third of families are able to institutionalize succession processes that strengthen both the business and the family; the rest damage the family, the business, or both (Jaskiewicz, Heinrichs, et al. 2015). By considering such interactions, future research will hopefully succeed at identifying safe paths through the maze that succession processes represent to most family firms. We use the context of family in the following section to draw attention to an exciting and largely neglected dimension that needs to be considered in more detail in future research on succession.

Research on the Role of Families in Succession

Our literature review illustrates the multidisciplinary character of succession research. Other disciplines, such as family science (James, Jennings, and Breitkreuz 2013), psychology (Filser et al. 2013), and business history (Colli 2013), can provide additional insights. For instance, following James et al. (2013), we plead for a stronger focus on the effects of family structure and involvement on the succession process in order to increase our knowledge about the circumstances under which the family's impact on succession is likely to be positive and when this impact is likely to be negative. "Transformation in the general context in which economic activity takes place (market dynamism, technology, institutional and legal settings) can either emphasize the positive role of family ties and trust creation, or the negative effects of excessive 'familism'" (Colli 2013, 581). In a similar vein, Bennedsen et al. (2007) showed that overall gender composition of potential family heirs affects the choice between a family and a non-family CEO. Mehrotra, Morck, Shim, and Wiwattanakantang (2013) provided insights into the instruments that Japanese families use to keep their businesses in the family across generations. Adult adoption and arranged marriages are legitimate tools when family heirs are not available or when potential family successors lack the necessary talent and/ or education to run the business successfully. Although the cultural embeddedness of these findings arouses suspicion about their generalization across countries, Mehrotra, Morck, Shim, and Wiwattanakantang (2011) indicated that these mechanisms might also work in countries other than Japan.

These findings advance the idea of viewing families as organizations in themselves (Klein 2008). Although the family is the defining element that differentiates a "family firm" from a "non-family firm," until now, its perceived impact on succession has primarily been based on the characteristics of the relationship between the predecessor and the successor (e.g., Cabrera-Suárez et al. 2001; Cater and Justis 2009; Fahed-Sreih and Djoundourian 2006; Goldberg 1996; Ibrahim et al. 2001). Intercultural comparisons need to go beyond this status quo. For instance, future research should shed light on the effects of parallel and sequential marriages on successor preparation and selection.

Overall, many valuable insights on particular aspects of succession have been gained, but we lack a holistic theory that considers interactions between factors at all levels of analysis across all stages of the succession process. The future, therefore, holds many promising avenues that will allow us to not only expand our understanding of succession processes in family firms but also to help family firms succeed in these transitions.

References

Aguilera, Ruth. V., and Rafael Crespi-Cladera. 2012. "Firm family firms: Current debates of corporate governance in family firms." *Journal of Family Business Strategy* 3: 66–69.

Amore, Mario D., Alessandro Minichilli, and Guido Corbetta. 2011. "How do managerial successions shape corporate financial policies in family firms?" *Journal of Corporate Finance* 17: 1016–1027.

Astrachan, Joseph H., and Thomas A. Kolenko. 1994. "A neglected factor explaining family business success: Human resource practices." *Family Business Review* 7 (3): 251–262. doi:10.1111/j.1741-6248.1994.00251.x.

Bachkaniwala, Darshan, Mike Wright, and Monder Ram. 2001. "Succession in South Asian family businesses in the U.K." *International Small Business Journal* 19 (4): 15–27. doi:10.1177/0266242601194001.

Bagby, D. Ray. 2004. "Enhancing succession research in the family firm: A commentary on "Toward an integrative model of effective fob succession." *Entrepreneurship Theory and Practice* 28 (4): 329–333. doi: 10.1111/j.1540-6520.2004.00048.x.

Bennedsen, Morton, Kasper M. Nielsen, Francisco Pérez-González, and Daniel Wolfenzon. 2007. "Inside the family firm: The role of families in succession decisions and performance." *Quarterly Journal of Economics* 122 (2): 647–691. doi:10.1162/qjec.122.2.647.

Berman-Brown, Reva, and Roger Coverly. 1999. "Succession planning in family businesses: A study from East Anglia, U.K." *Journal of Small Business Management* 37 (1): 93–97.

Bjuggren, Per-Olof, and Lars-Göran Sund. 2001. "Strategic decision making in intergenerational successions of small- and medium-size family-owned businesses." *Family Business Review* 14 (1): 11–24. doi:10.1111/j.1741-6248.2001.00011.x.

Bjuggren, Per-Olof, and Lars-Göran Sund. 2002. "A transaction cost rationale for transition of the firm within the family." *Small Business Economics* 19 (2): 123–133. doi:10.1023/A:1016289106477.

Bjuggren, Per-Olof, and Lars-Göran Sund. 2005. "Organization of transfers of small and medium-sized enterprises within the family: Tax law considerations." *Family Business Review* 18 (4): 1305–319. doi:10.1111/j.1741-6248.2005.00050.x.

Blumentritt, Tim, Timothy Mathews, and Gaia Marchisio. 2013. "Game theory and family business succession: An introduction." *Family Business Review* 26: 51–67. doi:10.1177/0894486512447811.

Brockhaus, Robert H. 2004. "Family business succession: Suggestions for future research." *Family Business Review* 17 (2): 165–177. doi:10.1111/j.1741-6248.2004.00011.x.

Brun de Pontet, Stéphanie, Carsten Wrosch, and Marylene Gagné. 2007. "An exploration of the generational differences in levels of control held among family businesses approaching succession." *Family Business Review* 20 (4): 337–354. doi:10.1111/j.1741-6248.2007.00103.x.

Burkart, Mike, Fausto Panunzi, and Andrei Shleifer. 2003. "Family firms." *Journal of Finance* 58 (5): 2167–2201. doi:10.1111/1540-6261.00601.

Cabrera-Suárez, Katiuska, Petra De Saá-Pérez, and Desiderio García-Almeida. 2001. "The succession process from a resource- and knowledge-based view of the family firm." *Family Business Review* 14 (1): 37–48. doi:10.1111/j.1741-6248.2001.00037.x.

Cadieux, Louise. 2007. "Succession in small and medium-sized family businesses: Toward a typology of predecessor roles during and after instatement of the successor." *Family Business Review* 20 (2): 95–109. doi:10.1111/j.1741-6248.2007.00089.x.

Cadieux, Louise, Jean Lorrain, and Pierre Hugron. 2002. "Succession in women-owned family businesses: A case study." *Family Business Review* 15 (1): 17–30. doi:10.1111/j.1741-6248.2002.00017.x.

Carney, Michael, Eric Gedajlovic, and Vanessa M. Strike. 2014. "Dead money: Inheritance law and the longevity of family firms." *Entrepreneurship Theory and Practice* 38: 1261–1283. doi:10.1111/etap.12123.

Cater, John J., III, and Robert T. Justis. 2009. "The development of successors from followers to leaders in small family firms." *Family Business Review* 22 (2): 109–124. doi:10.1177/0894486508327822.

Chittoor, Raveendra, and Ranjan Das. 2007. "Professionalization of management and succession performance: A vital linkage." *Family Business Review* 20 (1): 65–79. doi:10.1111/j.1741-6248.2007.00084.x.

Chrisman, James J., Jess H. Chua, and Pramodita Sharma. 1998. "Important attributes of successors in family businesses: An exploratory study." *Family Business Review* 11 (1): 19–34. doi:10.1111/j.1741-6248.1998.00019.x.

Chua, Jess H., James J. Chrisman, and Pramodita Sharma. 2003. "Succession and nonsuccession concerns of family firms and agency relationship with nonfamily managers." *Family Business Review* 16 (2): 89–108. doi:10.1111/j.1741-6248.2003.00089.x.

Chua, Jess H., James J. Chrisman, Lloyd P. Steier, and Sabine B. Rau. 2012. "Sources of heterogeneity in family firms: An introduction." *Entrepreneurship Theory and Practice* 36 (6): 1103–1113. doi:10.1111/j.1540-6520.2012.00540.x.

Chung, Chi-Nien, and Xiaowei R. Luo. 2013. "Leadership succession and firm performance in an emerging economy: Successor origin, relational embeddedness, and legitimacy." *Strategic Management Journal* 34 (3): 338–357. doi:10.1002/smj.2011.

Coff, Russell W., David C. Coff, and Roger Eastvold. 2006. "The knowledge-leveraging paradox: How to achieve scale without making knowledge imitable." *Academy of Management Review* 31: 452–465. doi:10.5465/AMR.2006.20208690.

Colli, Andrea. 2013. "Family firms between risks and opportunities: A literature review." *Socio-Economic Review* 11 (3): 577–599. doi:10.1093/ser/mwt010.

Cucculelli, Marco, and Giacinto Micucci. 2008. "Family succession and firm performance: Evidence from Italian family firms." *Journal of Corporate Finance* 14 (1): 17–31.

Davis, John A., Jeffrey Swartz, Elizabeth B. Blakely, Christopher Chang, José M. Eyzaguirre, Robert Mattson, and John D. Pettker. 1996. "A comparison of four countries' estate laws and their influence on family companies." *Family Business Review* 9 (3): 285–294. doi:10.1111/j.1741-6248.1996.00285.x.

Davis, Peter S., and Paula D. Harveston. 1998. "The influence of family on the family business succession process: A multi-generational perspective." *Entrepreneurship Theory and Practice* 22 (3): 31–53.

De Massis, Alfredo, Jess H. Chua, and James J. Chrisman. 2008. "Factors preventing intra-family succession." *Family Business Review* 21 (2): 183–199. doi:10.1111/j.1741-6248.2008.00118.x.

DeNoble, Alex, Sanford Ehrlich, and Gangaram Singh. 2007. "Toward the development of a family business self-efficacy scale: A resource-based perspective." *Family Business Review* 20 (2): 127–140. doi:10.1111/j.1741-6248.2007.00091.x.

Deephouse, David L., and Peter Jaskiewicz. 2013. "Do family firms have better reputations than non-family firms? An integration of socioemotional wealth and social identity theories." *Journal of Management Studies* 50 (3): 337–360. doi:10.1111/joms.12015.

Diwisch, Denise S., Peter Voithofer, and Christoph R. Weiss. 2009. "Succession and firm growth: Results from a non-parametric matching approach." *Small Business Economics* 32 (1): 45–56. http://www.jstor.org/stable/40344531.

Dumas, Colette, Jean P. Dupuis, Francine Richer, and Lousie St.-Cyr. 1995. "Factors that influence the next generation's decision to take over the family farm." *Family Business Review* 8 (2): 99–120. doi:10.1111/j.1741-6248.1995.00099.x.

Dunn, Barbara. 1999. "The family factor: The impact of family relationship dynamics on business-owning families during transitions." *Family Business Review* 12 (1): 41–60. doi:10.1111/j.1741-6248.1999.00041.x.

Dyck, Bruno, Michael Mauws, Frederick A. Starke, and Gary A. Mischke. 2002. "Passing the baton: The importance of sequence, timing, technique and communication in executive succession." *Journal of Business Venturing* 17 (2): 143–162. doi:10.1016/S0883-9026(00)00056-2.

Eddleston, Kimberly A., Franz W. Kellermanns, Steven W. Floyd, Victoria L. Crittenden, and William F. Crittenden. 2013. "Planning for growth: Life stage differences in family firms." *Entrepreneurship Theory and Practice* 37 (6): 1177–1202. doi:10.1111/etap.12002.

Ellul, Andrew, Marco Pagana, and Fausto Panunzi. 2010. "Inheritance law and investment in family firms." *American Economic Review* 100 (5): 2414–2450. doi:10.1257/aer.100.5.2414.

Fahed-Sreih, Josiane, and Salpie Djoundourian. 2006. "Determinants of longevity and success in Lebanese family businesses: An exploratory study." *Family Business Review* 19 (3): 225–234.

Fiegener, Mark K., Bonnie M. Brown, Russ A. Prince, and Karen M. File. 1994. "A comparison of successor development in family and nonfamily businesses." *Family Business Review* 7 (4): 313–329. doi:10.1111/j.1741-6248.1994.00313.x.

Fiegener, Mark K., Bonnie M. Brown, Russ A. Prince, and Karen M. File. 1996. "Passing on strategic vision: Favored modes of successor preparation by CEOs of family and nonfamily firms." *Journal of Small Business Management* 34 (3): 15–26.

Filser, Matthias, Sascha Kraus, and Stefan Märk. 2013. "Psychological aspects of succession in family business management." *Management Research Review* 36 (3): 256–277. doi:10.1108/01409171311306409.

Friedman, Stewart D., and Paul Olk. 1995. "Four ways to choose a CEO: Crown heir, horse race, coup d'état, and comprehensive search." *Human Resource Management* 34 (1): 141–164. doi:10.1002/hrm.3930340109.

Gagné, Marylène, Carsten Wrosch, Stéphanie Brun de Pontet. 2011. "Retiring from the family business: The role of goal adjustment capacities." *Family Business Review* 24 (4): 292–304. doi:10.1177/0894486511410688.

García-Álvarez, Ercilia, Jordi López-Sintas, and Pilar S. Gonzalvo. 2002. "Socialization patterns of successors in first- to second-generation family businesses." *Family Business Review* 15 (3): 189–203. doi:10.1111/j.1741-6248.2002.00189.x.

Giovannoni, Elena, Maria P. Maraghini, and Angelo Riccaboni. 2011. "Transmitting knowledge across generations: The role of management accounting practices." *Family Business Review* 24 (2): 126–150. doi:10.1177/0894486511406722.

Goldberg, Steven D. 1996. "Research Note: Effective successors in family-owned businesses: Significant elements." *Family Business Review* 9 (2): 185–197. doi:10.1111/j.1741-6248.1996.00185.x.

Gómez-Mejía, Luis R., Katalin T. Haynes, Manuel Núñez-Nickel, Kathryn J. L. Jacobson, and José Moyano-Fuentes. 2007. "Socioemotional wealth and business risks in family-controlled firms: evidence from Spanish olive oil mills." *Administrative Science Quarterly* 52 (1): 106–137. doi:10.2189/asqu.52.1.106.

Haberman, Heather, and Sharon M. Danes. 2007. "Father-daughter and father-son family business management transfer comparison: Family FIRO model application." *Family Business Review* 20 (2): 163–184. doi:10.1111/j.1741-6248.2007.00088.x.

Handler, Wendy C. 1994. "Succession in family business: A review of the research." *Family Business Review* 7 (2): 133–157. doi:10.1111/j.1741-6248.1994.00133.x.

Harveston, Paula D., Peter S. Davis, and Julie A. Lyden. 1997. "Succession planning in family business: The impact of owner gender." *Family Business Review* 10 (4): 373–396. doi:10.1111/j.1741-6248.1997.00373.x.

Harvey, Michael, and Rodney E. Evans. 1994. "The impact of timing and mode of entry on successor development and successful succession." *Family Business Review* 7 (3): 221–236. doi:10.1111/j.1741-6248.1994.00221.x.

Harvey, Michael, and Rodney E. Evans. 1995. "Life after succession in the family business: Is it really the end of problems?" *Family Business Review* 8 (1): 3–16. doi:10.1111/j.1741-6248.1995.00003.x.

Hollingsworth, J. Rogers, and Robert Boyer. 1997. *Contemporary capitalism. The embeddedness of institutions.* Cambridge: Cambridge University Press.

Howorth, Carole, and Zahra A. Ali. 2001. "Family business succession in Portugal: An examination of case studies in the furniture industry." *Family Business Review* 14 (3): 231–244. doi:10.1111/j.1741-6248.2001.00231.x.

Howorth, Carole, Paul Westhead, and Mike Wright. 2004. "Buyouts, information asymmetry and the family management dyad." *Journal of Business Venturing* 19 (4): 509–534. doi:10.1016/j.jbusvent.2003.04.002.

Ibrahim, A. Bakr, Khaled Soufani, and Jose Lam. 2001. "A study of succession in a family firm." *Family Business Review* 14 (3): 245–258. doi:10.1111/j.1741-6248.2001.00245.x.

James, Albert E., Jennifer E. Jennings, and Rhonda S. Breitkreuz. 2013. "Worlds apart? Rebridging the distance between family science and family business research." *Family Business Review* 25: 87–108. doi:10.1177/0894486511414271.

Janjuha-Jivraj, Shaheena, and Laura J. Spence. 2009. "The nature of reciprocity in family firm succession." *International Small Business Journal* 27 (6): 702–719. doi:10.1177/0266242609344252.

Janjuha-Jivraj, Shaheena, and Adrian Woods. 2002. "Successional issues within Asian family firms: Learning from the Kenyan experience." *International Small Business Journal* 20 (1): 77–94. doi:10.1177/0266242602201006.

Jaskiewicz, Peter, James G. Combs, and Sabine B. Rau. 2015. "Entrepreneurial legacy: Toward a theory of how some family firms nurture transgenerational entrepreneurship." *Journal of Business Venturing* 30 (1): 29–49. doi:10.1016/j.jbusvent.2014.07.001.

Jaskiewicz, Peter, Katharina Heinrichs, Sabine B. Rau, and Trish Reay. 2015. "To be or not to be: How family firms manage family and commercial logics in succession." *Entrepreneurship Theory and Practice*, in press. doi:10.1111/etap.12146.

Jaskiewicz, Peter, Klaus Uhlenbruck, David B. Balkin, and Trish Reay. 2013. "Can nepotism be a source of competitive advantage? A social exchange perspective on types of nepotism." *Family Business Review* 26 (2): 121–139. doi:10.1177/0894486512470841.

Keating, Norah C., and Heather M. Little. 1997. "Choosing the successor in New Zealand family farms." *Family Business Review* 10 (2): 157–171. doi:10.1111/j.1741-6248.1997.00157.x.

Kim, Haejeong, and Sharon A. DeVaney. 2003. "The expectation of partial retirement among family business owners." *Family Business Review* 16 (3): 199–210. doi:10.1111/j.1741-6248.2003.tb00014.x.

Kimhi, Ayal. 1997. "Intergenerational succession in small family businesses: Borrowing constraints and optimal timing of succession." *Small Business Economics* 9 (4): 309–318. doi:10.1023/A:1007987731337.

King, Sandra. 2003. "Organizational performance and conceptual capability: The relationship between organizational performance and successors' capability in a family-owned firm." *Family Business Review* 16 (3): 173–182. doi:10.1111/j.1741-6248.2003.tb00012.x.

Kirby, David A., and Thomas J. Lee. 1996. "Research Note: Succession management in family firms in the North East of England." *Family Business Review* 9 (1): 75–81. doi:10.1111/j.1741-6248.1996.00075.x.

Klein, Sabine B. 2008. "Commentary and extension: Moderating the outcome of identity confirmation in family firms." *Entrepreneurship Theory and Practice* 32 (6): 1083–1088. doi:10.1111/j.1540-6520.2008.00274.x.

Lam, Wing. 2011. "Dancing to two tunes: Multi-entity roles in the family business succession process." *International Small Business Journal* 29 (5): 508–533. doi:10.1177/0266242610376357.

Lambrecht, Johan. 2005. "Multigenerational transition in family businesses: A new explanatory model." *Family Business Review* 18 (4): 267–282. doi:10.1111/j.1741-6248.2005.00048.x.

Lansberg, Ivan, and Joseph H. Astrachan. 1994. "Influence of family relationships on succession planning and training: The importance of mediating factors." *Family Business Review* 7 (1): 39–59. doi:10.1111/j.1741-6248.1994.00039.x.

Le Breton-Miller, Isabelle, Danny Miller, and Llyod P. Steier. 2004. "Toward an integrative model of effective FOB succession." *Entrepreneurship Theory and Practice* 28 (4): 305–328. doi:10.1111/j.1540-6520.2004.00047.x.

Lee, Khai. S., Guan H. Lim, and Wei S. Lim. 2003. "Family business succession: Appropriation risk and choice of successor." *Academy of Management Review* 28 (4): 657–666. http://www.jstor.org/stable/30040754.

Light, Richard J., and David B. Pillemer. 1984. *Summing up: The science of reviewing research.* Cambridge: Harvard University Press.

Long, Rebecca G., and James J. Chrisman. 2013. "Management succession in family businesses." In *The Sage Handbook of Family Business*, edited by Leif Melin, Mattias Nordqvist and Pramodita Sharma, 249–268. London, UK: Sage Publications.

Mandelbaum, Leonard. 1994. "Small business succession: The educational problem." *Family Business Review* 7 (4): 369–375. doi:10.1111/j.1741-6248.1994.00369.x.

Marshall, James P., Ritch Sorenson, Keith Brigham, Elizabeth Wieling, Alan Reifman, and Richard S. Wampler. 2006. "The paradox for the family firm CEO: Owner age relationship to succession-related processes and plans." *Journal of Business Venturing* 21 (3): 348–368. doi:10.1016/j.jbusvent.2005.06.004.

Matthews, Charles H., Terrence W. Moore, and Anne S. Fialko. 1999. "Succession in family firms: A cognitive categorization perspective." *Family Business Review* 12 (2): 159–169. doi:10.1111/j.1741-6248.1999.00159.x.

Mazzi, Chiara. 2011. "Family business and financial performance: Current state of knowledge and future research challenges." *Journal of Family Business Strategy* 2 (3): 166–181. doi:10.1016/j.jfbs.2011.07.001.

Mehrotra, Vikas, Randall Morck, Jungwook Shim, and Yupana Wiwattanakantang. 2011. "Must love kill the family firm? Some exploratory evidence." *Entrepreneurship Theory and Practice* 35 (6): 1121–1148. doi:10.1111/j.1540-6520.2011.00494.x.

Mehrotra, Vikas, Randall Morck, Jungwook Shim, and Yupana Wiwattanakantang. 2013. "Adoptive expectations: Rising sons in Japanese family firms." *Journal of Financial Economics* 108 (3): 840–854. doi:10.1016/j.jfineco.2013.01.011.

Miller, Danny, Lloyd P. Steier, and Isabelle Le Breton-Miller. 2003. "Lost in time: Intergenerational succession, change, and failure in family business." *Journal of Business Venturing* 18 (4): 513–531. doi:10.1016/S0883-9026(03)00058-2.

Mitchell, J. Robert, Timothy A. Hart, Sorin Valcea, and David M. Townsend. 2009. "Becoming the boss: Discretion and postsuccession success in family firms." *Entrepreneurship Theory and Practice* 33 (6): 1201–1218. doi:10.1111/j.1540-6520.2009.00341.x.

Molly, Vincent, Eddy Laveren, and Marc Deloof. 2010. "Family business succession and its impact on financial structure and performance." *Family Business Review* 23 (2): 131–147. doi:10.1177/0894486510365062.

Morris, Michael H., Roy O. Williams, Jeffrey A. Allen, and Ramon A. Avila. 1997. "Correlates of success in family business transitions." *Journal of Business Venturing* 12 (5): 385–401. doi:10.1016/S0883-9026(97)00010-4.

Motwani, Jaideep, Nancy M. Levenburg, Thomas V. Schwarz, and Charles Blankson. 2006. "Succession planning in SMEs: An empirical analysis." *International Small Business Journal* 24 (5): 471–495. doi:10.1177/0266242606067270.

Murray, Barbara. 2003. "The succession transition process: A longitudinal perspective." *Family Business Review* 16 (1): 17–33. doi:10.1111/j.1741-6248.2003.00017.x.

Nordqvist, Mattias, Karl Wennberg, Massimo Bau, and Karin Hellerstedt. 2013. "An entrepreneurial process perspective on succession in family firms." *Small Business Economics* 40: 1087–1122. doi:10.1007/s11187-012-9466-4.

Overbeke, Kathyann K., Diana Bilimoria, and Sheri Perelli. 2013. "The dearth of daughter successors in family businesses: Gendered norms, blindness to possibility, and invisibility." *Journal of Family Business Strategy* 4 (3): 201–212. doi:10.1016/j.jfbs.2013.07.002.

Pérez-González, Francisco. 2006. "Inherited control and firm performance." *American Economic Review* 96 (5): 1559–1588. doi:10.2139/ssrn.320888.

Perricone, Philip J., John R. Earle, and Ian M. Taplin. 2001. "Patterns of succession and continuity in family-owned businesses: Study of an ethnic community." *Family Business Review* 14 (2): 105–122. doi:10.1111/j.1741-6248.2001.00105.x.

Pieper, Torsten M., and Sabine B. Klein. 2007. "The bullseye: A systems approach to modeling family firms." *Family Business Review* 20 (4): 301–319. doi:10.1111/j.1741-6248.2007.00101.x.

Royer, Susanne, Roland Simons, Britta Boyd, and Alannah Rafferty. 2008. "Promoting family: A contingency model of family business succession." *Family Business Review* 21 (1): 15–30. doi:10.1111/j.1741-6248.2007.00108.x.

Rubenson, George C., and Gupta, Anil K. 1996. "The initial succession: A contingency model of founder tenure." *Entrepreneurship Theory and Practice* 21 (2): 21–35.

Salvato, Carlo, and Guido Corbetta. 2013. "Transitional leadership of advisors as a facilitator of successors' leadership construction." *Family Business Review* 26 (3): 235–255. doi:10.1177/0894486513490796.

Santiago, Andrea L. 2000. "Succession experience in Philippine family businesses." *Family Business Review* 13 (1): 15–40. doi:10.1111/j.1741-6248.2000.00015.x.

Sardeshmukh, Shruti R., and Andrew C. Corbett. 2011. "The duality of internal and external development of successors: Opportunity recognition in family firms." *Family Business Review* 24 (2): 111–125. doi:10.1177/0894486510391783.

Schröder, Elke, Eva Schmitt-Rodermund, and Nicolas Arnaud. 2011. "Career choice intentions of adolescents with a family business background." *Family Business Review* 24 (4): 305–321. doi:10.1177/0894486511416977.

Sharma, Pramodita, James J. Chrisman, and Jess H. Chua. 2003a. "Predictors of satisfaction with the succession process in family firms." *Journal of Business Venturing* 18 (5): 667–687. doi:10.1016/S0883-9026(03)00015-6.

Sharma, Pramodita, James J. Chrisman, and Jess H. Chua. 2003b. "Succession planning as planned behavior: Some empirical results." *Family Business Review* 16 (1): 1–15. doi:10.1111/j.1741-6248.2003.00001.x.

Sharma, Pramodita, James J. Chrisman, Amy L. Pablo, and Jess H. Chua. 2001. "Determinants of initial satisfaction with the succession process in family firms: A conceptual model." *Entrepreneurship Theory and Practice* 25 (3): 17–35.

Sharma, Pramodita, and P. Gregory Irving. 2005. "Four bases of family business successor commitment: Antecedents and consequences." *Entrepreneurship Theory and Practice* 29 (1): 13–33. doi:10.1111/j.1540-6520.2005.00067.x.

Sharma, Pramodita, and A. Srinivas Rao. 2000. "Successor attributes in Indian and Canadian family firms: A comparative study." *Family Business Review* 13 (4): 313–330. doi:10.1111/j.1741-6248.2000.00313.x.

Shepherd, Dean A., and Andrew Zacharakis. 2000. "Structuring family business succession: An analysis of the future leader's decision making." *Entrepreneurship Theory and Practice* 24 (4): 25–39.

Siebels, Jan-Folke, and Dodo zu Knyphausen-Aufseß. 2012. "A review of theory in family business research: The implications for corporate governance." *International Journal of Management Reviews* 14: 280–304. doi:10.1111/j.1468-2370.2011.00317.x.

Stavrou, Eleni T. 1999. "Succession in family businesses: Exploring the effects of demographic factors on offspring intentions to join and take over the business." *Journal of Small Business Management* 37 (3): 43–61.

Stavrou, Eleni T., and Paul M. Swiercz. 1998. "Securing the future of the family enterprise: A model of offspring intentions to join the business." *Entrepreneurship Theory and Practice* 23 (2): 19–39.

Stavrou, Eleni T., Tonia Kleanthous, and Tassos Anastasiou. 2005. "Leadership personality and firm culture during hereditary transitions in family firms: Model development and empirical investigation." *Journal of Small Business Management* 43 (2): 187–206.

Steier, Lloyd P. 2001. "Next-generation entrepreneurs and succession: An exploratory study of modes and means of managing social capital." *Family Business Review* 14 (3): 259–276. doi:10.1111/j.1741-6248.2001.00259.x.

Steinberg, Laurence. 2001. "We know some things: Parent-adolescent relationships in retrospect and prospect." *Journal of Research on Adolescence* 11 (1): 1–19. doi:10.1111/1532-7795.00001.

Tatoglu, Ekrem, Veysel Kula, and Keith W. Glaister. 2008. "Succession planning in family-owned businesses: Evidence from Turkey." *International Small Business Journal* 26 (2): 155–180. doi:10.1177/0266242607086572.

Thomas, Jill. 2002. "Freeing the shackles of family business ownership." *Family Business Review* 15 (4): 321–336. doi:10.1111/j.1741-6248.2002.00321.x.

Tranfield, David, David Denyer, and Palminder Smart. 2003. "Towards a methodology for developing evidence-informed management knowledge by means of systematic review." *British Journal of Management* 14 (3): 207–222. doi:10.1111/1467-8551.00375.

Venter, Eduard, Christo Boshoff, and Ger Maas. 2005. "The influence of successor-related factors on the succession process in small and medium-sized family businesses." *Family Business Review* 18 (4): 283–303. doi:10.1111/j.1741-6248.2005.00049.x.

Vera, Carolina F., and Michelle A. Dean. 2005. "An examination of the challenges daughters face in family business succession." *Family Business Review* 18 (4): 321–345. doi:10.1111/j.1741-6248.2005.00051.x.

Wahl, Jenny B. 2003. "From riches to riches: Intergenerational transfer and the evidence from estate tax returns." *Social Science Quarterly* 84 (2): 278–296. doi:10.1111/1540-6237.8402004.

Wasserman, Noam. 2003. "Founder-CEO succession and the paradox of entrepreneurial success." *Organization Science* 14 (2): 149–172.

Westhead, Paul. 2003. "Succession decision-making outcomes reported by private family companies." *International Small Business Journal* 21 (4): 369–401.

Whitley, Richard. 1999. *Divergent capitalisms: The social structuring and change of business systems.* Oxford: Oxford University Press.

Wiklund, Johan, Mattias Nordqvist, Karin Hellerstedt, and Miriam Bird. 2013. "Internal versus external ownership transition in family firms: An embeddedness perspective." *Entrepreneurship Theory and Practice* 37 (6): 1319–1340. doi:10.1111/etap.12068.

Yan, Jun, and Ritch Sorenson. 2006. "The effect of Confucian values on succession in family business." *Family Business Review* 19 (3): 235–250. doi:10.1111/j.1741-6248.2006.00072.x.

3

AGENCY THEORY IN FAMILY FIRM RESEARCH

Accomplishments and Opportunities

Kristen Madison, Zonghui Li, and Daniel T. Holt

"Agency theory offers a rich and fruitful frame of reference by which the peculiar problems of family businesses might be studied."

—Chrisman, Chua, and Litz, 2004: 351

Introduction

Agency theory has received considerable research attention since its migration into the family firm literature (Le Breton-Miller and Miller 2009; Madison et al. 2016; Shukla et al. 2014). Knowledge can be gained by this migration, such as new insights regarding agency theory, or importantly, the uniqueness, behavior, performance, and competitive advantage of family firms. Accordingly, the first objective of this chapter is to provide an overview of agency theory and its general tenets. We then transition to reviewing and synthesizing agency theory's use in the family firm literature, with a focus on both the content and methods of the articles. While we acknowledge that agency theory has been extensively reviewed in the extant family firm literature (e.g., Chrisman et al. 2005; Madison et al. 2016), our review differs by its focus on empirical articles. Accordingly, not only are we able to document the empirical support that demonstrates how agency theory has been extended by the family firm context, but we are able to examine the methodology employed in these studies. We conclude the chapter with suggestions for future research opportunities that can further extend theory, reduce methodological limitations, and provide additional insights into the family firm.

Theory and Context

Every theory should contain three necessary elements; namely, the *what, how,* and *why* (Whetten 1989). The *what* seeks to describe the phenomenon and the associated factors in a comprehensive but parsimonious way, the *how* describes the relationship between the factors, and the *why* explains the rationale underlying the selected factors and their proposed relationships (Reay and Whetten 2011; Whetten 1989). Theories should also be generalizable, but instead often suffer from boundary conditions and limitations when context, like the *where* is taken into consideration (Lee and O'Neill 2003; Smith and Hitt 2005; Whetten 1989). Context refers to "situational opportunities and constraints that affect the occurrence and meaning of organizational behavior as well as functional relationships between variables" (Johns 2006: 386).

We consider both theory and context in this chapter. We first provide an overview of agency theory organized by the theoretical elements of *what*, *how*, and *why*. We then transition to the element of *where* by reviewing agency theory specifically within family firm research to assess its strength and generalizability with contextual considerations. We refer to the family firm context as the unique opportunities, challenges, and resulting behavior and performance implications arising from residing at the intersection of the family system and the business system. Family control frees family firms from the formalized, short-term-oriented demands often imposed by capital markets. At the same time, however, family influence often leads to the pursuit of non-economic goals that the family values, sometimes at the expense of economic returns, leading to emotional and inflexible attachment to existing assets and strategies.

What

Agency theory is one of the most widely used theories in management (Daily et al. 2003; Wasserman 2006), and family firms in particular (Madison et al., 2016). Broadly, agency theory is about the relationship between two parties, the principal (owner) and the agent (manager; Eisenhardt 1989; Jensen and Meckling 1976; Ross 1973). More specifically, it examines this relationship from a behavioral and a structural perspective. Theory suggests that given the chance, agents will behave in a self-interested manner, behavior that may conflict with the principal's interest (Chrisman et al. 2004; Eisenhardt 1989; Jensen and Meckling 1976; Wiseman et al. 2012). As such, principals will enact structural mechanisms that monitor the agent in order to curb the opportunistic behavior and better align the parties' interests (Cruz et al. 2010; Eisenhardt 1989; Fama and Jensen 1983).

How

Firm performance by way of cost minimization and greater efficiencies is the desired outcome of the agency theory perspective (Corbetta and Salvato 2004; Fama 1980). Theory suggests that agency costs are incurred to alleviate the agency problems associated with the separation of the firm's ownership and management (Eisenhardt 1989; Jensen and Meckling 1976; Karra et al. 2006; Lee and O'Neill 2003; Wasserman 2006). Separation of ownership and management is a key component of agency theory; the principal delegates work to the agent, and the agent is expected to act in the best interest of the principal (Ross 1973; Wiseman et al. 2012). However, when the interest of the principal is not aligned with the interest of the agent, and when the principal lacks the information to assess the agent's behavior, an agency problem is created (Eisenhardt 1989; Karra et al. 2006; Lee and O'Neill 2003; Ross 1973). Agency problems are categorized as moral hazard or adverse selection (Chrisman et al. 2004; Eisenhardt 1989; Karra et al. 2006). A moral hazard agency problem is when the agent lacks effort in the scope of the employment relationship (Chrisman et al. 2004; Ross 1973). It is considered a form of opportunistic behavior that includes free-riding, shirking, and perk-consumption (Chrisman et al. 2004; Chua et al. 2009; Karra et al. 2006). An adverse selection agency problem is when the agent lacks the ability or skills to competently behave in the scope of the employment relationship (Eisenhardt 1989; Fama 1980; Schulze et al. 2001).

Agency problems can be reduced in two ways (Eisenhardt 1989). The first is to create a governance structure that enables the principal to monitor and assess the actual behavior of the agent (Anderson and Reeb 2004; Chrisman et al. 2007). This structure includes, for example, reporting procedures, additional management, or a board of directors (Donaldson and Davis 1991). The second is to create a governance structure where the employment contract is based on actual outcomes (Eisenhardt 1989). For example, compensation incentive plans, where the agent receives incentives for high firm performance, fall into this category (Chrisman et al. 2007). This shifts the risk to the agent, thereby creating alignment between the principal and agent's interests (Davis et al. 1997; Eisenhardt 1989). In sum, the principal can choose to establish a governance structure based on the agent's actual behavior or the outcomes of that behavior (Eisenhardt 1989). Either choice creates agency costs for the principal (Jensen and Meckling 1976).

Why

The underlying assumption of agency theory is based on the economic model of man (Davis et al. 1997; Eisenhardt 1989; Jensen and Meckling 1976). This model assumes that individuals seek to optimize their own utility. In the principal-agent relationship, an agent is hired to maximize the principal's utility (Ross 1973). However, agency theory assumes agents will instead behave opportunistically because they too are self-serving. Therefore, the principal enacts mechanisms to minimize losses to their own utility (Davis et al. 1997; Eisenhardt 1989; Jensen and Meckling 1976; Ross 1973).

Where

As described, agency theory contains the essential elements of theory. It has predictive and explanatory power as shown in the descriptions of the *what, how,* and *why*. However, the question remains as to whether agency theory is adequate and relevant when context is taken into consideration. In other words, are expansions necessary or boundary conditions or limitations apparent if the *where* is considered? To assess its strength and generalizability, the next section of this chapter examines agency theory within family firms, an important organizational context. Family firms represent a unique context for several reasons. Family-controlled firms differ from their nonfamily controlled counterparts along several important dimensions. On the one hand, families have little need to monitor management as their equity stakes overlap considerably with their own. On the other, large equity stakes give families considerable discretion to implement strategies that serve the family, providing them with incentives to monitor management more closely and the voting power to discipline them should they engage in unproductive, opportunistic activities.

Literature Review

Although family firms are deemed the most prevalent and oldest organizational type, scholarly investigations of these businesses pale in comparison (Goel et al. 2012). Scholars stress that family firm research "should describe why family businesses are distinct, how the uniqueness builds, and how and under what conditions this may lead to a competitive advantage" (Klein et al. 2005a: 333). Accordingly, family firm governance and its related performance implications have been a topic of interest due to the unique structures and dynamics brought about by residing at the intersection of the family system and the business system (Goel et al. 2012). Since agency theory addresses governance and firm performance, it is not surprising that it has become a prominent lens in family firm research (Chrisman et al. 2005; Goel et al. 2012; Le Breton-Miller and Miller 2009), and as such, is the focus of our review.

Family firm agency theory articles were found through an electronic and manual search of the literature using combinations of keywords such as *family firm, family business, family enterprise* plus *agency theory* or *agency costs*. Family firm articles citing the seminal theoretical works (e.g., Jensen and Meckling 1976; Eisenhardt 1989) were also reviewed to determine appropriateness for inclusion. To be considered for inclusion, the theoretical underpinning for the empirical model had to be agency theory.

Characteristics of the Literature

This search process yielded 89 articles grounded in agency theory within the context of family firms. These articles appeared in 22 journals across several disciplines and were published between 2000 and 2014. The articles comprised 18 conceptual articles and 71 empirical articles. Four of the empirical articles were qualitative in nature, and 67 were quantitative. We focus specifically on the quantitative articles for this review because we are interested in the methodological approaches associated with these articles. Table 3.1 provides an alphabetical list and the characteristics of these 67 articles. The focus of our literature review is twofold; we first synthesize the content of agency theory articles, and second we analyze the methodology. We then present future research suggestions that can further extend theory while simultaneously addressing the methodical limitations in extant investigations.

Content of the Literature

Agency Problems. At the heart of agency theory is the separation of ownership and management and the problems that arise from this separation (Eisenhardt 1989). This owner-manager conflict is referred to as a Type I agency problem (Villalonga and Amit 2006). However, it was assumed that family firms are not susceptible to Type I agency problems due to a lack of separation among owners and managers (Chrisman et al. 2004; Goel et al. 2012; Jensen and Meckling 1976); and therefore, agency perspectives remained absent in this organizational context. However, the work of Schulze and his colleagues challenged this logic (Schulze et al. 2001; Schulze et al. 2003a, 2003b), and began an important stream of literature. This stream seeks to conceptually and empirically demonstrate that family firms are indeed susceptible to agency problems. Unique to the family firm, research supports nontraditional agency problems such as those created by asymmetric altruism (Moores 2009; Schulze et al. 2001; Schulze et al. 2003a, 2003b) and entrenched family ownership (Block 2012; Moores 2009; Nicholson 2008).

Altruism is often regarded as a selfless other-serving behavior but is presented in a different light by agency theorists (Eddleston et al. 2008). Agency theory perspectives refer to altruism as asymmetric, which describes behavior that is exploitable and not reciprocated (Chua et al. 2009; Wright and Kellermanns 2011). It can cause harm to the family firm by creating both moral hazard and adverse selection agency problems (Schulze et al. 2001; Schulze et al. 2003a). Moral hazard problems are created by asymmetric altruism when parents are overly generous to their children and their children take advantage of this act by shirking or free-riding in the employment relationship (Dawson 2011; Eddleston et al. 2008; Schulze et al. 2001, 2003a). This agency problem then becomes worse because family firm leaders don't often monitor the behavior of other family members in the firm (Chua et al. 2011; Eddleston et al. 2010). Adverse selection agency problems are created when family firms hire family members who may be less qualified and skilled than nonfamily members for the position (Karra et al. 2006; Schulze et al. 2001, 2003a), and may even pay them more generously (Chua et al. 2009). These agency problems created by asymmetric altruism are shown to decrease the performance of the family firm

Table 3.1 Family Firm Agency Theory Research

Source	Key Theoretical Findings	Sample	Location	Data Analysis	Response Rate	Random Sampling	Alternative Measures or Explanation	Correlation Matrix	Temporal Ordering
Ali, Chen, and Radhakrishnan (2007)	Family firms have lower principal-manager agency costs but higher principal-principal agency costs than nonfamily firms. Disclosure practices are different between family and nonfamily firms due to these agency problems.	177 family firms & 323 nonfamily firms	US	Regression	NA	No	Yes	No	Longitudinal
Anderson, Duru, and Reeb (2009)	Transparency helps mitigate the principal-principal agency problem	2000 firms	US	Regression	NA	No	Yes	Yes	Longitudinal
Anderson, Mansi, and Reeb (2003)	Family firms outperform nonfamily firms; family ownership structures reduce the shareholder-bondholder agency problem and are associated with lower cost of debt financing	252 firms	US	Regression	NA	No	Yes	No	Longitudinal
Anderson and Reeb (2003a)	Family firms outperform nonfamily firms; family ownership structures reduce agent behavior (opportunism)	141 family & 262 nonfamily firms	US	Regression	NA	No	Yes	Yes	Longitudinal
Anderson and Reeb (2003b)	Family ownership reduces principal-principal agency problems; minority shareholders benefit from higher levels of family ownership.	319 firms	US	Regression	NA	No	Yes	Yes	Longitudinal
Anderson and Reeb (2004)	Agency structures apply in family firms; family directors monitor business; independent directors monitor family	141 family & 262 nonfamily firms	US	Regression	NA	No	Yes	Yes	Longitudinal
Andres (2008)	Family firms outperform nonfamily firms; families can successfully balance both Agency I and Agency II problems	103 family firms & 172 nonfamily firms	Germany	Regression	NA	No	Yes	Yes	Longitudinal

(Continued)

Source	Key Theoretical Findings	Sample	Location	Data Analysis	Response Rate	Random Sampling	Alternative Measures or Explanation	Correlation Matrix	Temporal Ordering
Asaba (2013)	Family firms invest more than nonfamily firms because of their reduced agency costs; self-interested managers underinvest.	184 firms (approximately 1/3 family firms)	Japan	Regression	NA	No	Yes	Yes	Time-lagged longitudinal
Barth, Gulbrandsen, and Schone (2005)	Family firms are less productive than nonfamily firms, unless managed by nonfamily. Findings support moral hazard agency problem	220 family firms & 218 nonfamily firms	Norway	Regression	NA	No	Yes	No	Cross-sectional
Bartholomeusz and Tanewski (2006)	Family and nonfamily firms have different governance structures that impact firm performance. To improve firm performance, family firms should adopt transparent structures and implement independent monitoring.	50 family firms & 50 nonfamily firms	Australia	Regression	NA	No	Yes	No	Cross-sectional
Ben-Amar and André (2006)	Principal-principal agency problems are reduced with increased family ownership and in countries with legal institutions that protect minority shareholders	327 acquisitions by 232 firms	Canada	Regression	NA	No	No	No	Cross-sectional
Block (2010)	Examines the agency relationship between family owners (agents) and society (principal). Family firms downsize less than nonfamily firms because of their reputational concerns	414 firms	US	Regression	NA	No	Yes	Yes	Time-lagged longitudinal
Block (2012)	Family ownership fosters agent behavior (moral hazard and information asymmetry)	154 family firms	US	Regression	NA	No	Yes	Yes	Longitudinal

Citation	Findings	Sample	Country	Method					Design
Braun and Sharma (2007)	CEO duality does not affect family firm performance; agency structures protect minority shareholders	84 family firms	US	Regression	NA	No	No	Yes	Cross-sectional
Cai, Luo, and Wan (2012)	Family CEOs reduce principal-agent costs that outweigh the principal-principal costs and enhance firm performance in China	351 firms	China	Regression	NA	No	No	Yes	Longitudinal
Chen, Chen, Cheng, and Shevlin (2010)	Family firms are less tax aggressive the principal-principal agency conflict impacts the level of the family firm's tax aggressiveness.	476 family firms & 527 nonfamily firms	US	Regression	NA	No	Yes	Yes	Longitudinal
Chen, Gray, and Nowland (2013)	Nonfamily managers are used by controlling families to extend their influence within their firms, increasing agency costs to minority shareholders (i.e., nonfamily can be an agency concern to minority shareholders)	536 family firms	Taiwan	Regression	NA	No	Yes	Yes	Cross-sectional
Chen, Hsu, and Chang (2014)	Family ownership reduces agency costs; family ownership increases internationalization (i.e., make long-term investments in the business despite the risks)	217 firms	Taiwan	Regression	NA	No	Yes	Yes	Time-lagged longitudinal
Chirico and Bau (2014)	Inverted U-shaped relationship between % family on TMT and firm performance. Prevalence of stewardship and agency behaviors depends on the extent of family influence and market dynamism.	199 family firms	Switzerland	Regression	33.61%	No	No	Yes	Cross-sectional
Choi, Park, and Hong (2012)	In emerging economies, agency theory may not adequately explain the relationship between ownership and innovation performance.	301 firms	Korea	Regression	NA	No	No	Yes	Cross-sectional

(Continued)

Source	Key Theoretical Findings	Sample	Location	Data Analysis	Response Rate	Random Sampling	Alternative Measures or Explanation	Correlation Matrix	Temporal Ordering
Chrisman, Chua, Kellermanns, and Chang (2007)	Family managers are agents; agency structures increase firm performance	208 family firms	US	Regression	18%	No	No	Yes	Cross-sectional
Chrisman, Chua, and Litz (2004)	Agency structures with family involvement decrease agency problems	901 family firms & 240 nonfamily firms	US	Regression	21.30%	No	No	Yes	Cross-sectional
Chua, Chrisman, and Sharma (2003)	Traditional agency problems operate in family businesses when they increase in size and employ nonfamily managers	272 family firms	Canada	Regression	28%	No	No	Yes	Cross-sectional
Cruz, Gómez-Mejía, and Becerra (2010)	CEO perceptions and trust impact agency contracts and implementation of agency structures	122 family firms	US	Regression	11%	No	Yes	Yes	Cross-sectional
Cucculelli, Mannarino, Pupo, and Ricotta (2014)	Family firms are less efficient than nonfamily firms due to unique agency costs (altruism and family entrenchment)	1835 family firms & 1085 nonfamily firms	Italy	Regression	NA	No	Yes	No	Cross-sectional
Dawson (2011)	Investors associate family and business negatively; prefer to invest in professional family firms	35 private equity firms	Italy	Regression	81.40%	No	No	No	Cross-sectional
De Maere, Jorissen, and Uhlaner (2014)	Agency and resource dependence theory are used to show that separation of ownership and management helps avoid bankruptcy (due to board monitoring) and increases a firm's resources (due to board capital)	116 bankrupt firms matched with 116 non-bankrupt firms	Belgium	Regression	NA	No	Yes	Yes	Cross-sectional

Study	Key findings	Sample	Country	Method					Design
De Massis, Kotlar, Campopiano, and Cassia (2013)	Nonlinear relationship: family ownership and management (alignment/lower information asymmetries) reduces agency costs to the point where the lack of external monitoring allows for opportunistic behavior to prevail	787 firms	Italy	Regression	NA	No	Yes	Yes	Cross-sectional
George, Wiklund, and Zahra (2005)	CEO and TMT ownership levels are negatively associated with the scale and scope of internationalization. This indicates agent behavior (opportunistic risk aversion)	889 firms	Sweden	Regression	36%	No	No	Yes	Cross-sectional
Gnan, Montemerlo, and Huse (2013)	Results indicate that family councils (relational stewardship perspective) partially substitute for corporate governance mechanisms (contractual agency perspective); agency and stewardship theory can complement one another.	243 family firms	Italy	MANOVA	3.20%	No	Yes	No	Cross-sectional
Gómez-Mejía, Larraza-Kintana, and Makri (2003)	Differing agency relationships affect pay structures. Family CEOs receive less pay than professional managers; family ties protect a CEO from bearing excessive personal risk but increase business risk.	253 family firms	US	Regression	NA	No	Yes	Yes	Longitudinal
Gómez-Mejía, Núñez-Nickel, and Gutierrez (2001)	Executive entrenchment causes agency problems in family firms	276 firms	Spain	Regression	NA	No	Yes	Yes	Cross-sectional
González, Guzmán, Pombo, and Trujillo (2015)	Family involvement on the board reduces CEO turnover; serve as mediators in family conflicts (reducing agency problems within families) and effectively monitor performance of CEOs.	523 firms	Columbia	Regression	NA	No	Yes	No	Time-lagged longitudinal

(Continued)

Source	Key Theoretical Findings	Sample	Location	Data Analysis	Response Rate	Random Sampling	Alternative Measures or Explanation	Correlation Matrix	Temporal Ordering
Graves and Shan (2013)	Family firms outperform nonfamily firms; they have higher profit margins which can be attributed to having lower agency costs. Results can also be explained in that family leaders are altruistic stewards of the family wealth.	4217 firms	Australia	Regression	NA	No	Yes	Yes	Longitudinal
Herrero (2011)	Family firms outperform nonfamily firms; have reduced agency problems	58 family & 33 nonfamily firms	Spain	Regression	NA	No	Yes	No	Cross-sectional
Jaskiewicz and Klein (2007)	Both theories explain board composition: Agency = low goal alignment (need larger boards, more outside members); Stewardship = high goal alignment	351 family firms	Germany	Regression	6.09%	No	Yes	Yes	Cross-sectional
Kappes and Schmid (2013)	Family firms have longer time horizons than nonfamily firms; agency perspective explains differences (family firms are long-term oriented; nonfamily want short-term gains)	701 firms	Germany	Regression	NA	No	Yes	No	Longitudinal
Klein, Shapiro, and Young (2005b)	Agency: aligning principal-manager goals and reducing information asymmetry is important to investors. Stewardship: board of directors should be an advisor, not a monitor	263 family and nonfamily firms	Canada	Regression	NA	No	Yes	Yes	Cross-sectional
Kuo and Hung (2012)	Agency problem of free cash flow may lead to overinvestment, information asymmetry between firms and external capital markets may cause underinvestment; independent boards mitigate these effects of family control	1115 firms	Taiwan	Regression	NA	No	Yes	Yes	Longitudinal

Reference	Description	Sample	Country	Method					
Liang, Li, Yang, Lin, and Zheng (2013)	Family involvement in boards strengthens the positive relationship between R&D investment and innovation; family involvement in management weakens it. Not all types of family involvement reduce agency problems.	102 family firms	China	Regression	NA	No	No	Yes	Longitudinal
Luo and Chung (2013)	Examines agency relationships in the institutional context. Family control creates varying levels of agency costs and performance depending on the pattern of family control and the strength of market institutions.	631 firms	Taiwan	Regression	NA	No	Yes	Yes	Longitudinal
Maseda, Iturralde, and Arosa (2014)	Proportion of outside members has a differing relationship with family firm performance across generations. No relationship by the third generation; results indicate boards serve as advisors rather than as monitors.	341 family firms	Spain	Regression	24.71%	No	Yes	Yes	Cross-sectional
Maury (2006)	Family controlled firms have reduced Agency I problems but suffer from Agency II problems. Increased transparency and policy is necessary to protect minority shareholders.	1672 firms	Western Europe	Regression	NA	No	Yes	No	Cross-sectional
McConaughy (2000)	Family CEOs receive less pay than nonfamily CEOs and their pay is less sensitive to performance. Nonfamily CEOs need pay incentives to align their interests.	82 family firms (45 family CEOs; 37 nonfamily CEOs)	US	Regression	NA	No	No	No	Cross-sectional
McConaughy, Matthews, and Fialko (2001)*	Firms controlled by the founding family have greater value, operate more efficiently, and carry less debt. This is because they have reduced agency costs.	219 family firms	US	Univariate analysis	NA	No	No	No	Cross-sectional

(Continued)

Source	Key Theoretical Findings	Sample	Location	Data Analysis	Response Rate	Random Sampling	Alternative Measures or Explanation	Correlation Matrix	Temporal Ordering
Michiels, Voordeckers, Lybaert, and Steijvers (2012)	Family firms face agency costs; assumed because they use performance-based compensation. Agency costs appear to be lower in later generational stages.	529 family firms	US	Regression	NA	No	No	Yes	Cross-sectional
Miller, Le Breton–Miller, and Lester (2010)	Powerful owners prevent opportunistic acquisitions by managers: Family ownership is negatively related with acquisition volume and positively related with acquisition diversification.	898 family and nonfamily firms	US	Regression	NA	No	Yes	Yes	Longitudinal
Miller, Le Breton–Miller, Minichilli, Corbetta, and Pittino (2014)	Blends agency and behavioral agency theory governance structures. Nonfamily CEOs do best for a firm's performance when working alone and monitored by multiple major owners (agency); Family CEOs impact on performance doesn't vary much with regard to ownership and leadership structures (SEW).	893 family firms	Italy	Regression	NA	No	Yes	Yes	Longitudinal
Miller, Minichilli, and Corbetta (2013)	Supports both agency and stewardship theories; depends on the context of ownership and management; there must be an appropriate fit.	2522 family firms	Italy	Regression	NA	No	Yes	Yes	Longitudinal
Mustakallio, Autio, and Zahra (2002)	Blends social capital theory with agency theory to demonstrate that relational and contractual governance structures are important.	192 family firms	Finland	SEM	46%	No	No	Yes	Cross-sectional

Study	Findings	Sample	Country	Method	%				Design
Naldi, Nordqvist, Sjöberg, and Wiklund (2007)	Family firms take less risk, and risk is negatively related to performance. Results indicate the need for formal agency structures to monitor the family and their business decisions.	265 family firms & 431 nonfamily firms	Sweden	Regression	28%	No	No	No	Cross-sectional
Peake and Watson (2014)	Family firms are less likely to use contracts among owners (a measure of formal control); family firms with economic goals, rather than family goals, are more likely to use contracts.	423 family and nonfamily firms	US	Regression	NA	No	Yes	Yes	Cross-sectional
Pieper, Klein, and Jaskiewicz (2008)	Both theories explain board presence: Agency = low goal alignment, have board; Stewardship = high goal alignment, no board	714 family firms	Germany	Discriminant analysis; regression	12.90%	No	Yes	No	Cross-sectional
Pindado, Requejo, and Torre (2012)	Family firms adopt higher dividend payments; used as a governance mechanism to overcome the agency conflict between the controlling family and minority investors.	482 family firms & 163 nonfamily firms	Eurozone	Regression	NA	No	Yes	Yes	Time-lagged longitudinal
Prencipe, Markarian, and Pozza (2008)	Both theories explain why family firms are less sensitive to short-term performance and stock fluctuations; agency and stewardship structures facilitate long-term orientations.	23 family & 21 nonfamily firms	Italy	Regression	NA	No	No	Yes	Longitudinal
Randoy and Goel (2003)	Agency structures (monitoring) are more relevant in nonfounder firms but are redundant in founding family-led firms.	68 firms	Norway	Regression	NA	No	Yes	Yes	Longitudinal
Schulze, Lubatkin, and Dino (2003a)	Proportion of family ownership influences board conduct.	1464 family firms	US	Regression	10.30%	No	Yes	Yes	Cross-sectional

(Continued)

Source	Key Theoretical Findings	Sample	Location	Data Analysis	Response Rate	Random Sampling	Alternative Measures or Explanation	Correlation Matrix	Temporal Ordering
Schulze, Lubatkin, and Dino (2003b)	Family firms have unique agency problems; created by altruism	883 family firms	US	Regression	10.30%	No	No	Yes	Cross-sectional
Schulze, Lubatkin, Dino, and Buchholtz (2001)	Altruism creates agency problems; family firms must incur agency costs.	1376 family firms	US	Regression; Cluster analysis	10.30%	No	No	Yes	Cross-sectional
Sciascia and Mazzola (2008)	Family management decreases performance: infers family agent behavior (lack professional competencies and oriented toward nonfinancial goals). Stewardship effects do not outweigh agency costs.	620 firms	Italy	Regression	4.10%	Yes	No	Yes	Cross-sectional
Sciascia, Mazzola, Astrachan, and Pieper (2012)	Stewardship is advantageous for internationalization; agency structures should govern the business and the family.	1035 family firms	US	Regression	41%	No	No	Yes	Cross-sectional
Sieger, Zellweger, and Aquino (2013)	Psychological ownership can align interests of agents and principals, thus reducing agency costs of monitoring.	714 firms	Switzerland & Germany	Regression	9.50%	No	No	Yes	Cross-sectional
Songini and Gnan (2015)	Family involvement in governance had a negative relationship with agency cost control mechanisms; Family management had a positive relationship with agency cost control mechanisms; no relationship between cost controls and firm performance	146 family firms	Italy	SEM	15%	No	No	No	Cross-sectional

Tsai, Hung, Kuo, and Kuo (2006)	Family firms need to refine governance systems; agency theory is not suitable for family firms.	63 family & 241 nonfamily firms	Taiwan	Regression	NA	No	Yes	Yes	Cross-sectional
Villalonga and Amit (2006)	Demonstrate that agency conflicts between shareholders are relevant in the US and affect firm performance. Firms can have Agency I and II problems.	508 firms	US	Regression	NA	No	Yes	No	Longitudinal
Westhead and Howorth (2006)	Management rather than ownership structure drives financial performance and pursuit of nonfinancial goals.	240 family firms	UK	Regression	48%	No	No	Yes	Cross-sectional
Zahra (2005)	Family ownership and management promote entrepreneurship, but long tenures of CEO founders do not. Agency theory research leads to contradictory conclusions.	209 family firms	US	Canonical analysis	24.85%	No	No	No	Cross-sectional

Note: * Does not use control variables in the model.

(Eddleston et al. 2010; Wright and Kellermanns 2011) and to create the need family firms are burdened with to incur agency costs by implementing governance mechanisms to monitor and assess behavior (Chua et al. 2009; Lubatkin et al. 2007).

Entrenched family ownership can also create unique family firm agency problems. Entrenchment is defined as "the relational contract between owners and managers that enable both to occupy key positions in the firm for a significant duration" (Moores 2009: 172). Family ownership is often described as effective because it reduces Type I agency problems associated with the separation of owners and managers (Anderson and Reeb 2003b; Chirico et al. 2011; Jensen and Meckling 1976; Tsai et al. 2006). However, some research suggests that family ownership is not effective because family dynamics and conflicts are difficult to monitor. With ineffective monitoring, moral hazard agency problems may increase, inhibiting productivity (Block 2012). Furthermore, the emotional attachment the owning family has on the firm may inhibit sound business decisions, decreasing firm performance further (Nicholson 2008).

Additionally, family ownership can create agency problems specific to family firms, referred to as Type II agency problems (Ali et al. 2007; Goel et al. 2012; Villalonga and Amit 2006). Instead of the Type I owner-manager conflict, the Type II represents the conflict between majority and minority shareholders (i.e., family and nonfamily shareholders; Villalonga and Amit 2006). An example of a Type II agency problem manifests itself in the misalignment of shareholder goals; family firms often pursue noneconomic goals at the expense of financial gain (Gómez-Mejía et al. 2007). Diverting resources to pursue the family's noneconomic agendas may negatively impact firm performance (Chrisman et al. 2004), thus creating conflicts between family and nonfamily shareholders.

In conclusion, the literature provides support that agency problems are indeed prevalent in the family firm context and is important for two reasons. First, this literature challenged the original agency theory research that argued agency problems did not exist in organizations typified by the convergence of ownership and management (i.e., Eisenhardt 1989; Fama and Jensen 1983; Jensen and Meckling 1976). In doing so, a host of nontraditional agency problems specific to family firms (i.e., asymmetric altruism, family entrenchment, Type II agency problems) was brought to light, thus expanding agency theory into the realm of the family firm. Second, this realization allows for continued agency research within a family firm context, but with a different focus. It allows scholars to research whether other tenets of agency theory are applicable to family firms. Accordingly, the next section shifts the focus away from agency problems and instead focuses on the governance mechanisms agency theorists call for to mitigate agency problems.

Agency Governance. Research supports agency theory's applicability within family firms by examining the firm-level governance mechanisms and their relationship with firm performance. For example, research investigates boards of directors (Anderson and Reeb 2004; Braun and Sharma 2007; Gersick and Feliu 2014; Goel et al. 2014), incentive compensation (Chrisman et al. 2007), and monitoring activities (Chrisman et al. 2007) as agency mechanisms used to mitigate agency problems and subsequently increase performance. Anderson and Reeb (2004) examine board independence and family influence to support their contention that an agency lens is applicable to family firms. They conclude that monitoring mechanisms such as a board of directors are necessary; outside board members monitor the family, and family board members monitor the business (Anderson and Reeb 2004). Likewise, Chrisman and his colleagues (2007) explore the motivations and control of family firm managers to determine if they are agents or stewards. They conclude that family managers are agents because family firms using governance mechanisms prescribed by agency theory (i.e., monitoring, incentive compensation) have higher levels of performance (Chrisman et al. 2007). Braun and Sharma (2007) explore CEO duality and demonstrate that the separation of positions is a beneficial governance structure for family firm performance.

Instead of a focus on performance, others have focused on perceptions. Cruz and her colleagues (2010) examine how agency contracts are affected by the CEO's perceptions of the top management team. In line with agency theory, they suggest that monitoring and incentive mechanisms are implemented based on the CEO's trust perceptions of top managers. In the family firm context, they suggest that the presence of top managers who are related to the CEO and the level of family ownership in the firm affect these perceptions. Dawson (2011) examines the perceptions of private equity firms as they assess the attractiveness of family firms. She finds that investors prefer professionalized family firms, described as businesses that have agency prescriptions in place such as formal human resource management practices and the presence of nonfamily managers (Dawson, 2011).

In conclusion, this group of family firm articles focuses on the remedies prescribed by agency theory that are theorized to positively impact firm performance. Importantly, this research provides support that agency governance mechanisms, such as the presence of a board of directors, incentive compensation plans, and monitoring activities serve their theorized purpose within family firms. Similar to agency problem research, this research expands the boundary conditions of agency theory by supporting its governance mechanisms and related outcomes within a new organizational context.

Methods of the Literature

As suggested, the cornerstone of much of the agency theory research is that family involvement in the firm creates or causes unique agency conditions that influence the subsequent performance of the firm. Given the importance of research methods in establishing and validating these causal inferences, we examine the extent to which agency theory research includes research designs that effectively guard against key threats to causality and confounded results. Causal relationships can be inferred when three conditions are met. First, the cause and effect variables covary (Van de Ven 2007). Second, the cause precedes the effect in time (Van de Ven 2007). Third, alternative explanations for the covariance between cause and effect variables are eliminated (Cook and Campbell 1979). While exhaustively meeting these criteria is impossible, researchers can more confidently infer causal relationships as these conditions are addressed more thoroughly with a line of solid evidence being preferred over several lines of evidence of questionable quality.

The first criterion, covariation between cause and effect variables, suggests that a change in one variable is accompanied by a change in another (Van de Ven 2007). Presenting a correlation matrix that includes all the study variables provides a rather straightforward means to demonstrate covariance. Given the importance of covariation to causality (Van de Ven 2007), these matrices would be expected to be ubiquitous; however, reviews of the entrepreneurship literature have indicated that not all studies report these matrices (e.g., Crook et al. 2010). Indeed, we find this to be the case in our review of the family firm agency theory literature, finding that only 48 studies (71.6 percent) reported a covariation matrix.

Second, it is critical to establish that the cause precedes the effect, suggesting that the change in the cause variable occurs before the change in the effect variable (i.e., the agency conditions cause changes in outcomes; Van de Ven 2007). The ability to test whether an effect is actually caused by the hypothesized variable is limited when researchers rely on cross-sectional data where the cause and effect variables are collected at the same point in time. Hence, from a temporal perspective, causal influences can be inferred more confidently with longitudinal data or, at the very least, cross-sectional data using time-lagged variables. In our review, most of the investigations are cross-sectional in nature (59.7 percent), whereas some are time-lagged (7.5 percent) or longitudinal (32.8 percent articles).

The final criterion, the elimination of alternative explanations, suggests that if the influences of external forces are not eliminated it is impossible to assess the extent to which the external forces may be causing the effect (Van de Ven 2007). The ability to eliminate alternative explanations can be influenced by sampling design (Cook and Campbell 1979). Specifically, because of sampling bias, relationships reflected in the data may not accurately reflect the relationships in the population when small, nonrandom samples are used. Examining the sampling methods of the studies in our review, the majority (56.7 percent) examine differences between family and nonfamily firms. As such, the samples included both types of firms (391 family firms and 381 nonfamily firms, on average). The remainder of articles assesses family firm heterogeneity by examining agency theory within a sample of family firms only (498 family firms on average). Investigations use secondary data (64.2 percent) or primary data (35.8 percent). Of those using primary data, the average response rate is 23.80 percent. Samples of firms in North America (US and Canada) and Europe are equally represented (28 and 27 of the articles, respectively); firm samples from Asia (9 articles), Australia (2 articles), and South America (1 article) are also represented. Unfortunately, only one article used a random sample; in this study, the authors drew a random sample of 15,517 firms from the Italian population of nearly 5 million firms (Sciascia and Mazzola 2008).

Ruling out alternative explanations can also be accomplished by incorporating statistical control variables into the research design (Atinc et al. 2012; Becker 2005). By including theoretically meaningful control variables, variance in the dependent variable that is attributable to the alternative explanation is accounted for *a priori*, enabling researchers to assess the extent to which the remaining variance in the effect is explained by the hypothesized cause (Atinc et al. 2012). Given that regression is the data analysis approach in the overwhelming majority of investigations (60 of 67 articles; other approaches included structural equation modeling, cluster analysis, and canonical analysis), we expected a large percentage of articles in our data set to use control variables. Indeed, among the agency theory articles examined, all but one made use of control variables. In addition, authors often provided the proper rationale, theoretical reasoning, or citations to explain why a particular control variable was included. Schulze et al. (2003a, 2003b), for instance, argued that covariates were to reduce variance that was extraneous to the research question and could potentially confound the interpretation of the findings. In each article, the authors controlled for firm age, justifying this variable as it might be linked to the performance outcome studied due to a selection bias where older firms were in the sample just because they had survived and were successful.

Finally, by not accounting for endogeneity, scholars are not able to eliminate several alternative explanations, leading to incorrect generalizations. The problem of endogeneity arises when the cause that is hypothesized to have a particular effect is influenced directly by that effect. While a number of statistical techniques exist to test for such problems, these methods are just beginning to appear in the family business research (e.g., Patel and Cooper 2014). In fact, these methods were used in only 21 (31.3 percent) of the articles examined. This is particularly important in family firms where the involvement of the family clearly may influence the performance of the firm but the performance of the firm may also influence the family's involvement, especially the family's involvement in the day-to-day operations.

In summary, our review of the methodology employed in family firm agency theory studies reveals that our ability to effectively infer causality may be inhibited. Although roughly two-thirds of the studies include correlation matrices, only one-third are time-lagged or longitudinal, and only one-third rule out alternative explanations by accounting for endogeneity concerns.

Furthermore, the samples are not random and often are relatively small with low response rates, which gives rise to generalizability concerns. Given the importance of research methods in establishing and validating causal inferences, we incorporate methodological remedies as we present our future research opportunities.

Future Research Opportunities

In this section, we present three future research opportunities that can further extend theory while simultaneously addressing the methodical limitations revealed from extant investigations. The first opportunity for future agency theory research specifically relates to causality, within the theory and the methods. The theorized outcome of agency theory is firm performance, which is often supported in the family firm literature (e.g., Anderson and Reeb 2004; Chrisman et al. 2007; Braun and Sharma 2007; Gersick and Feliu 2014; Goel et al. 2014). However, studies tend to ignore the reasons why there is a link between agency governance and firm performance. Agency theory prescribes governance mechanisms to curb opportunistic behavior thus resulting in increased performance (Eisenhardt 1989; Jensen and Meckling 1976). However, just because governance mechanisms are in place and performance levels are high, does not necessarily mean opportunistic behavior was thwarted; there could be other factors contributing to high levels of performance even in the presence of opportunistic behavior. To account for this possibility, governance, behavior, and performance must be considered. Extant studies neglect to consider behavior as the linking pin between structure and performance; therefore, it should be examined in future studies. For example, research could examine productive work behavior as the missing link; it is an appropriate proxy for capturing a lack of opportunistic behavior (i.e., shirking, free-riding), and has been conceptually and empirically linked to increased firm performance (Gerhart and Milkovich 1992; Huselid 1995).

Additionally, effective research designs and statistical techniques can further support causality. For example, a longitudinal approach that captures variables at several intervals to determine the change in behavior and performance over time as a result of governance mechanisms implemented is warranted. Longitudinal studies can also capture the potential dynamic nature of governance and how that may change over time or generations (Madison et al., 2016). More effective statistical techniques, such as including a correlation matrix or control variables such as past performance, would assist in ruling out alternative explanations and increase our ability to infer causality. The more thoroughly these conditions are addressed, the more confidence researchers have that a causal relationship exists.

The second opportunity for future research is at the intersection of agency theory problems (i.e., opportunistic behavior) and sampling techniques. Current agency theory research assumes that managers are a homogeneous group. Agency theorists subscribe to the idea that self-serving behavior is curbed by the use of governance mechanisms (Eisenhardt 1989; Jensen and Meckling 1976). However, in a family firm context, it is likely that managers are both family and nonfamily members. As such, different behaviors may result between the two groups (Chua et al. 2009; Davis et al. 2010). For example, agency problems are created by asymmetric altruism, but this line of research focuses solely on family members (i.e., parent-child) (e.g., Schulze et al. 2001; Schulze et al. 2003a). There is a need for research to address the relationship between family and nonfamily members. Agency mechanisms may curb the assumed opportunistic behavior of family members, but do they have the same effect on nonfamily members? If not, what are the resulting performance implications for the family firm? Accordingly, future research is needed that addresses agency problems and outcomes with considerations of kinship status.

From a methodological perspective, this infers that more research is needed that addresses the heterogeneity among family firms. As evidenced in our review, most research, particularly early family firm research, addresses the differences between family and nonfamily firms (Chrisman et al. 2005). More research is necessary to examine differences within and between family firms to provide additional insights. It has been suggested that there is more variation within family firms than in comparison with nonfamily firms (Chrisman and Patel 2012), and these variations can help explain performance differentials. Furthermore, when family firm research can look inside the firms, examinations between family and nonfamily employees can be made. Some studies have shown that family and nonfamily employees behave differently, thus impacting performance (e.g., Madison and Kellermanns 2013). This also implies that respondents are a key concern in family firm research. Results may be misleading if studies continue to mix survey responses from family and nonfamily employees or only have family members represented in the sample.

The third opportunity resides at the intersection of agency governance mechanisms and sampling techniques. Governance mechanisms can be categorized as formal (i.e., monitoring activities, human resource policies) or social (i.e., informal meetings, get-togethers; Mustakallio et al. 2002). Family firm literature is heavily focused on formal governance mechanisms like boards of directors (e.g., Anderson and Reeb 2004; Braun and Sharma 2007), incentive compensation plans (e.g., Chrisman et al. 2007; Schulze et al. 2001), strategic planning (e.g., Chrisman et al. 2004), or human resources practices (Dawson 2011). Importantly, agency research is "concerned with describing the governance mechanisms that solve the agency problem" (Eisenhardt 1989: 59); however, research neglects to consider the impact of social governance mechanisms, and thus should be a consideration for future research.

From a methodological perspective, scholars could explore this opportunity cross-culturally. As shown in our review, the majority of family firm agency theory research is from North America and Europe. As such, results may not be generalizable to other geographic contexts and cultures, such as those in South America. Collective-oriented cultures, such as South America, tend to focus on family harmony and relationships (Strike 2012). It may be plausible that in these cultures, social governance mechanisms are of more importance to family firms and their performance than formal governance. As such, cross-culture samples would provide valuable insight into the heterogeneity of family firms and strengthen the generalizability of findings.

Conclusion

Like others (e.g., Le Breton-Miller and Miller 2009; Madison et al. 2016; Shukla et al. 2014), our review suggests that agency theory is indeed applicable in a family firm context. The literature supports that agency problems are prevalent and uniquely created in family firms. Accordingly, agency costs must be incurred to mitigate these problems. Meaning, agency governance mechanisms, such as boards of directors, compensation incentive plans, and monitoring activities, are deemed necessary in family firms to curb opportunistic self-interested agent behavior and thus reap firm level performance benefits. Other governance structures, however, could be considered in future research to determine their applicability in altering the unique agent behavior problems found in family firms. Gersick and Feliu (2014), for instance, offered an atheoretical, description of unique governance practices in family firms to include formal (e.g., blockholding, dual class stock systems, and shareholder agreements) and informal, family specific (e.g., family offices and family assemblies) practices. Our review suggests that agency theory offers the theoretical lens to hypothesize and explore how each may influence specific agency problems (i.e., principal-principal problems) and the subsequent performance of the family firm.

Assessing actual agent behavior is also warranted; in doing so, the behavior of family and non-family employees could be assessed to determine if the prescriptions of agency theory hold equivocally across employee types. Furthermore, supporting and validating causal inferences through the methodological approaches in future research is of utmost importance. Our review, unlike others who have reviewed agency theory and governance in family firms (cf. Gersick and Feliu 2014; Goel et al. 2014; Shukla et al. 2014), examined the strength of our causal inferences regarding agency relationships in family firms. While several findings were encouraging (i.e., the prevalent use of control variables), endogeneity testing has been limited. These tests are critical as family involvement may have a causal influence several on variables such as performance as well as an outcome which is dependent on the same variable. In conclusion, agency theory is an applicable theoretical perspective for family firm governance and performance research; however, more research is necessary to fully comprehend the impact of agency governance on the behaviors within and among family firms.

References

★References marked with an asterisk indicate studies included in the table.

★Ali, A., Chen, T.-Y., and Radhakrishnan, S. 'Corporate disclosures by family firms.' *Journal of Accounting and Economics* 44, no. 1 (2007): 238–286.

★Anderson, R.C., Duru, A., and Reeb, D.M. 'Founders, heirs, and corporate opacity in the United States.' *Journal of Financial economics* 92, no. 2 (2009): 205–222.

★Anderson, R.C., Mansi, S.A., and Reeb, D.M. 'Founding family ownership and the agency cost of debt.' *Journal of Financial economics* 68, no. 2 (2003): 263–285.

★Anderson, R.C., and Reeb, D.M. 'Founding family ownership and firm performance: Evidence from the S&P 500.' *The Journal of Finance* 58, no. 3 (2003a): 1301–1327.

★Anderson, R.C., and Reeb, D.M. 'Founding-family ownership, corporate diversification, and firm leverage.' *Journal of Law and Economics* 46, no. 2 (2003b): 653–684.

★Anderson, R.C., and Reeb, D.M. 'Board composition: Balancing family influence in S&P 500 firms.' *Administrative Science Quarterly* 49, no. 2 (2004): 209–237.

★Andres, C. 'Large shareholders and firm performance – An empirical examination of founding-family ownership.' *Journal of Corporate Finance* 14, no. 4 (2008): 431–445.

★Asaba, S. 'Patient investment of family firms in the Japanese electric machinery industry.' *Asia Pacific Journal of Management* 30, no. 3 (2013): 697–715.

Atinc, G., Simmering, M.J., and Kroll, M.J. 'Control variable use and reporting in macro and micro management research.' *Organizational Research Methods* 15 (2012): 57–74.

★Barth, E., Gulbrandsen, T., and Schønea, P. 'Family ownership and productivity: The role of owner-management.' *Journal of Corporate Finance* 11, no. 1–2 (2005): 107–127.

★Bartholomeusz, S., and Tanewski, G.A. 'The relationship between family firms and corporate governance.' *Journal of Small Business Management* 44, no. 2 (2006): 245–267.

Becker, T.E. 'Potential problems in the statistical control of variables in organizational research: A qualitative analysis with recommendations.' *Organizational Research Methods* 8, no. 3 (2005): 274–289.

★Ben-Amar, W., and André, P. 'Separation of ownership from control and acquiring firm performance: The case of family ownership in Canada.' *Journal of Business Finance & Accounting* 33, no. 3–4 (2006): 517–543.

★Block, J. 'Family management, family ownership, and downsizing: Evidence from S&P 500 firms.' *Family Business Review* 23, no. 2 (2010): 109–130.

★Block, J.H. 'R&D investments in family and founder firms: An agency perspective.' *Journal of Business Venturing* 27, no. 2 (2012): 248–265.

★Braun, M., and Sharma, A. 'Should the CEO also be chair of the board? An empirical examination of family-controlled public firms.' *Family Business Review* 20, no. 2 (2007): 111–126.

★Cai, D, Luo, J., and Wan, D. 'Family CEOs: Do they benefit firm performance in China?.' *Asia Pacific Journal of Management* 29, no. 4 (2012): 923–947.

★Chen, E.T., Gray, S., and Nowland, J. 'Family representatives in family firms.' *Corporate Governance: An International Review* 21, no. 3 (2013): 242–263.

★Chen, H.-L., Hsu, W.-T., and Chang, C.-Y. 'Family ownership, institutional ownership, and internationalization of SMEs.' *Journal of Small Business Management* 52, no. 4 (2014): 771–789.

*Chen, S., Chen, X., Cheng, Q., and Shevlin, T. 'Are family firms more tax aggressive than non-family firms?.' *Journal of Financial Economics* 95, no. 1 (2010): 41–61.

*Chirico, F., and Bau, M. 'Is the family an "Asset" or "Liability" for firm performance? The moderating role of environmental dynamism.' *Journal of Small Business Management* 52, no. 2 (2014): 210–225.

Chirico, F., Ireland, R.D., and Sirmon, D.G. 'Franchising and the family firm: Creating unique sources of advantage through "Familiness."' *Entrepreneurship Theory and Practice* 35, no. 3 (2011): 483–501.

*Choi, S.B., Park, B.I., and Hong, P. 'Does ownership structure matter for firm technological innovation performance? The case of Korean firms.' *Corporate Governance: An International Review* 20, no. 3 (2012): 267–288.

*Chrisman, J.J., Chua, J.H., Kellermanns, F.W., and Chang, E.P. 'Are family managers agents or stewards? An exploratory study in privately held family firms.' *Journal of Business Research* 60, no. 10 (2007): 1030–1038.

*Chrisman, J.J., Chua, J.H., and Litz, R.A. 'Comparing the agency costs of family and non-family firms: Conceptual issues and exploratory evidence.' *Entrepreneurship Theory and Practice* 28, no. 4 (2004): 335–354.

Chrisman, J.J., Chua, J.H., and Sharma, P. 'Trends and directions in the development of a strategic management theory of the family firm.' *Entrepreneurship Theory and Practice* 29, no. 5 (2005): 555–576.

Chrisman, J.J., and Patel, P.C. 'Variations in R&D investments of family and nonfamily firms: Behavioral agency and myopic loss aversion perspectives.' *Academy of Management Journal* 55, no. 4 (2012): 976–997.

Chua, J.H., Chrisman, J.J., and Bergiel, E.B. 'An agency theoretic analysis of the professionalized family firm.' *Entrepreneurship Theory and Practice* 33, no. 2 (2009): 355–372.

Chua, J.H., Chrisman, J.J., Kellermanns, F., and Wu, Z. 'Family involvement and new venture debt financing.' *Journal of Business Venturing* 26, no. 4 (2011): 472–488.

*Chua, J.H., Chrisman, J.J., and Sharma, P. 'Succession and nonsuccession concerns of family firms and agency relationship with nonfamily managers.' *Family Business Review* 16, no. 2 (2003): 89–107.

Cook, T.D., and Campbell, D.T. *Quasi-experimentation: Design & analysis issues for field settings*. Boston: Houghton Mifflin, 1979.

Corbetta, G., and Salvato, C. 'Self-serving or self-actualizing? Models of man and agency costs in different types of family firms: A commentary on "comparing the agency costs of family and non-family firms: Conceptual issues and exploratory evidence."' *Entrepreneurship Theory and Practice* 28, no. 4 (2004): 355–362.

Crook, T.R., Shook, C.L., Morris, M.L., and Madden, T.M. 'Are we there yet? An assessment of research design and construct measurement practices in entrepreneurship research.' *Organizational Research Methods* 13, no. 1 (2010): 192–206.

*Cruz, C.C., Gómez-Mejía, L.R., and Becerra, M. 'Perceptions of benevolence and the design of agency contracts: CEO-TMT relationships in family firms.' *Academy of Management Journal* 53, no. 1 (2010): 69–89.

*Cucculelli, M., Mannarino, L., Pupo, V., and Ricotta, F. 'Owner-Management, Firm Age, and Productivity in Italian Family Firms.' *Journal of Small Business Management* 52, no. 2 (2014): 325–343.

Daily, C.M., Dalton, D.R., and Rajagopalan, N. 'Governance through ownership: Centuries of practice, decades of research.' *Academy of Management Journal* 46, no. 2 (2003): 151–158.

Davis, J.H., Allen, M.R., and Hayes, H.D. 'Is blood thicker than water? A study of stewardship perceptions in family business.' *Entrepreneurship: Theory & Practice* 34, no. 6 (2010): 1093–1116.

Davis, J.H., Schoorman, F.D., and Donaldson, L. 'Toward a stewardship theory of management.' *Academy of Management review* 22, no. 1 (1997): 20–47.

*Dawson, A. 'Private equity investment decisions in family firms: The role of human resources and agency costs.' *Journal of Business Venturing* 26, no. 2 (2011): 189–199.

*De Maere, J., Jorissen, A., and Uhlaner, L.M. 'Board Capital and the Downward Spiral: Antecedents of Bankruptcy in a Sample of Unlisted Firms.' *Corporate Governance: An International Review* 22, no. 5 (2014): 387–407.

*De Massis, A., Kotlar, J., Campopiano, G., and Cassia, L. 'The impact of family involvement on SMEs' performance: Theory and evidence.' *Journal of Small Business Management* (2014). doi: 10.1111/jsbm.12093.

Donaldson, L., and Davis, J.H. 'Stewardship theory or agency theory: CEO governance and shareholder returns.' *Australian Journal of Management* 16, no. 1 (1991): 49–64.

Eddleston, K.A., Chrisman, J.J., Steier, L.P., and Chua, J.H. 'Governance and trust in family firms: An introduction.' *Entrepreneurship Theory and Practice* 34, no. 6 (2010): 1043–1056.

Eddleston, K.A., Kellermanns, F.W., and Sarathy, R. 'Resource configuration in family firms: Linking resources, strategic planning and technological opportunities to performance.' *Journal of Management Studies* 45, no. 1 (2008): 26–50.

Eisenhardt, K.M. 'Agency theory: An assessment and review.' *Academy of Management Review* 14, no. 1 (1989): 57–74.

Fama, E.F. 'Agency Problems and the Theory of the Firm.' *The Journal of Political Economy* 88, no. 2 (1980): 288–307.

Fama, E.F., and Jensen, M.C. 'Separation of ownership and control.' *Journal of Law and Economics* 26, no. 2 (1983): 301–325.

★George, G., Wiklund, J., and Zahra, S.A. 'Ownership and the internationalization of small firms.' *Journal of Management* 31, no. 2 (2005): 210–233.

Gerhart, B.A., and Milkovich, G.T. 'Employee compensation: Research and practice.' In *Handbook of Industrial and Organizational Psychology*, edited by Marvin D. Dunnette and Leaetta M. Hough, vol. 3, 481–569. Palo Alto, CA: Consulting Psychologists Press, 1992.

Gersick Kelin, and Neus Feliu. "Governing the family enterprise: Practices, Performance, and Research." In Leif Melin, Mattias Nordqvist, and Pramodita Sharma (Editors), *Sage Handbook of Family Business.* Thousand Oaks, CA: Sage Publishing (2014).

★Gnan, L., Montemerlo, D., and Huse, M. 'Governance systems in family SMEs: The substitution effects between family councils and corporate governance mechanisms.' *Journal of Small Business Management* 53, no. 2 (2015): 355–381.

Goel, S., Jussila, I., and Ikaheimonen, T. 'Governance in family firms: A review and research agenda.' In Leif Melin, Mattias Nordqvist, and Pramodita Sharma (Editors), *Sage Handbook of Family Business.* Thousand Oaks, CA: Sage Publishing (2014).

Goel, S., Mazzola, P., Phan, P.H., Pieper, T.M., and Zachary, R.K. 'Strategy, ownership, governance, and socio-psychological perspectives on family businesses from around the world.' *Journal of Family Business Strategy* 3, no. 2 (2012): 54–65.

Gómez-Mejía, L.R., Haynes, K.T., Núñez-Nickel, M., Jacobson, K.JL., and Moyano-Fuentes, J. 'Socio-emotional wealth and business risks in family-controlled firms: Evidence from Spanish olive oil mills.' *Administrative Science Quarterly* 52, no. 1 (2007): 106–137.

★Gómez-Mejía, L.R., Larraza-Kintana, M., and Makri, M. 'The determinants of executive compensation in family-controlled public corporations.' *Academy of Management Journal* 46, no. 2 (2003): 226–237.

★Gómez-Mejía, L.R., Núñez-Nickel, M., and Gutierrez, I. 'The role of family ties in agency contracts.' *Academy of Management Journal* 44, no. 1 (2001): 81–95.

★González, M., Guzmán, A., Pombo, C., and Trujillo, M.-A. 'The role of family involvement on CEO Turnover: Evidence from Colombian Family Firms.' *Corporate Governance: An International Review* 23, no. 3 (2015): 266–284.

★Graves, C., and Shan, Y.G. 'An empirical analysis of the effect of internationalization on the performance of unlisted family and nonfamily firms in Australia.' *Family Business Review* 27, no. 2 (2013):142–160.

★Herrero, I. 'Agency costs, family ties, and firm efficiency.' *Journal of Management* 37, no. 3 (2011): 887–904.

Huselid, M.A. 'The impact of human resource management practices on turnover, productivity, and corporate financial performance.' *Academy of Management Journal* 38, no. 3 (1995): 635–672.

★Jaskiewicz, P., and Klein, S. 'The impact of goal alignment on board composition and board size in family businesses.' *Journal of Business Research* 60, no. 10 (2007): 1080–1089.

Jensen, M.C., and Meckling, W.H. 'Theory of the firm: Managerial behavior, agency costs and ownership structure.' *Journal of Financial Economics* 3, no. 4 (1976): 305–360.

Johns, G. 'The essential impact of context on organizational behavior.' *Academy of Management Review* 31, no. 2 (2006): 386–408.

Karra, N., Tracey, P., and Phillips, N. 'Altruism and agency in the family firm: Exploring the role of family, kinship, and ethnicity.' *Entrepreneurship Theory and Practice* 30, no. 6 (2006): 861–877.

★Kappes, I, and Schmid, T. 'The effect of family governance on corporate time horizons.' *Corporate Governance: An International Review* 21, no. 6 (2013): 547–566.

★Klein, P., Shapiro, D., and Young, J. 'Corporate governance, family ownership and firm value: The Canadian evidence.' *Corporate Governance: An International Review* 13, no. 6 (2005b): 769–784.

Klein, S.B., Astrachan, J.H., and Smyrnios, K.X. 'The F-PEC scale of family influence: Construction, validation, and further implication for theory.' *Entrepreneurship Theory and Practice* 29, no. 3 (2005a): 321–339.

★Kuo, Y.-P., and Hung, J.H. 'Family Control and Investment-Cash Flow Sensitivity: Moderating Effects of Excess Control Rights and Board Independence.' *Corporate Governance: An International Review* 20, no. 3 (2012): 253–266.

Le Breton-Miller, I., and Miller, D. 'Agency vs. stewardship in public family firms: A social embeddedness reconciliation.' *Entrepreneurship Theory and Practice* 33, no. 6 (2009): 1169–1191.

Lee, P.M., and O'Neill, H.M. 'Ownership structures and R&D investments of U.S. and Japanese firms: Agency and stewardship perspectives.' *Academy of Management Journal* 46, no. 2 (2003): 212–225.

*Liang, Q., Li, X., Yang, X., Lin, D., and Zheng, D. 'How does family involvement affect innovation in China?.' *Asia Pacific Journal of Management* 30, no. 3 (2013): 677–695.

Lubatkin, M.H., Durand, R., and Ling, Y. 'The missing lens in family firm governance theory: A self-other typology of parental altruism.' *Journal of Business Research* 60, no. 10 (2007): 1022–1029.

*Luo, X.R., and Chung, C.-N. 'Filling or abusing the institutional void? Ownership and management control of public family businesses in an emerging market.' *Organization Science* 24, no. 2 (2013): 591–613.

Madison, K., Holt, D.T., Kellermanns, F.W., and Ranft, A.L. 'Viewing family firm behavior and governance through the lens of agency and stewardship theories.' *Family Business Review* (2016): doi: 10.1177/0894486515594292.

Madison, K., and Kellermanns, F.W. 'Is the spiritual bond bound by blood? An exploratory study of spiritual leadership in family firms.' *Journal of Management, Spirituality & Religion* 10, no. 2 (2013): 159–182.

*Maseda, A, Iturralde, X., and Arosa, B. 'Impact of outsiders on firm performance over different generations of family-owned SMEs.' *Journal of Small Business Management* (2014): doi: 10.1111/jsbm.12119.

*Maury, B. 'Family ownership and firm performance: Empirical evidence from Western European corporations.' *Journal of Corporate Finance* 12, no. 2 (2006): 321–341.

*McConaughy, D.L. 'Family CEOs vs. nonfamily CEOs in the family-controlled firm: An examination of the level and sensitivity of pay to performance.' *Family Business Review* 13, no. 2 (2000): 121–131.

*McConaughy, D.L., Matthews, C.H., and Fialko, A.S. 'Founding family controlled firms: Performance, risk, and value.' *Journal of Small Business Management* 39, no. 1 (2001): 31–49.

*Michiels, A., Voordeckers, W., Lybaert, N., and Steijvers, T. 'CEO compensation in private family firms pay-for-performance and the moderating role of ownership and management.' *Family Business Review* 26, no. 2 (2013): 140–160.

*Miller, D., Breton-Miller, L., and Lester, R.H. 'Family ownership and acquisition behavior in publicly-traded companies.' *Strategic Management Journal* 31, no. 2 (2010): 201–223.

*Miller, D., Breton-Miller, L., Minichilli, A., Corbetta, G., and Pittino, D. 'When do non-family CEOs outperform in family firms? Agency and behavioral agency perspectives.' *Journal of Management Studies* 51, no. 4 (2014): 547–572.

*Miller, D., Minichilli, A., and Corbetta, G. 'Is family leadership always beneficial?.' *Strategic Management Journal* 34, no. 5 (2013): 553–571.

Moores, K. 'Paradigms and theory building in the domain of business families.' *Family Business Review* 22, no. 2 (2009): 167–180.

*Mustakallio, M., Autio, E., and Zahra, S.A. 'Relational and contractual governance in family firms: Effects on strategic decision making.' *Family Business Review* 15, no. 3 (2002): 205–222.

*Naldi, L., Nordqvist, M., Sjöberg, K., and Wiklund, J. 'Entrepreneurial orientation, risk-taking, and performance in family firms.' *Family Business Review* 20, no. 1 (2007): 33–47.

Nicholson, N. 'Evolutionary psychology, organizational culture, and the family firm.' *The Academy of Management Perspectives* 22, no. 2 (2008): 73–84.

Patel, P.C., and Cooper, D. 'Structural power equality between family and non-family TMT members and the performance of family firms.' *Academy of Management Journal* 57, no. 6 (2014): 1624–1649.

*Peake, W.O., and Watson, W. 'Ties that bind? A mediation analysis exploring contract use in family versus nonfamily firms.' *Journal of Small Business Management* (2014): doi: 10.1111/jsbm.12105.

*Pieper, T.M., Klein, S.B., and Jaskiewicz, P. 'The impact of goal alignment on board existence and top management team composition: Evidence from family-influenced businesses.' *Journal of Small Business Management* 46, no. 3 (2008): 372–394.

*Pindado, J., Requejo, I., and Torre, C. 'Do family firms use dividend policy as a governance mechanism? Evidence from the Eurozone.' *Corporate Governance: An International Review* 20, no. 5 (2012): 413–431.

*Prencipe, A., Markarian, G., and Pozza, L. 'Earnings management in family firms: Evidence from R&D cost capitalization in Italy.' *Family Business Review* 21, no. 1 (2008): 71–88.

*Randøy, T., and Goel, S. 'Ownership structure, founder leadership, and performance in Norwegian SMEs: Implications for financing entrepreneurial opportunities.' *Journal of Business Venturing* 18, no. 5 (2003): 619–637.

Reay, T., and Whetten, D.A. 'What constitutes a theoretical contribution in family business?.' *Family Business Review* 24, no. 2 (2011): 105–110.

Ross, S.A. 'The economic theory of agency: The principal's problem.' *The American Economic Review* 63, no. 2 (1973): 134–139.

*Schulze, W.S., Lubatkin, M.H., and Dino, R.N. 'Exploring the agency consequences of ownership dispersion among the directors of private family firms.' *Academy of Management Journal* 46, no. 2 (2003a): 179–194.

*Schulze, W.S., Lubatkin, M.H., and Dino, R.N. 'Toward a theory of agency and altruism in family firms.' *Journal of Business Venturing* 18, no. 4 (2003b): 473–490.

*Schulze, W.S., Lubatkin, M.H., Dino, R.N., and Buchholtz, A.K. 'Agency relationships in family firms: theory and evidence.' *Organization Science* 12, no. 2 (2001): 99–116.

*Sciascia, S., and Mazzola, P. 'Family involvement in ownership and management: Exploring nonlinear effects on performance.' *Family Business Review* 21, no. 4 (2008): 331–345.

*Sciascia, S., Mazzola, P., Astrachan, J.H., and Pieper, T.M. 'The role of family ownership in international entrepreneurship: Exploring nonlinear effects.' *Small Business Economics* 38, no. 1 (2012): 15–31.

Shukla, P., Carney, M. and Gedajlovic, E. 'Economic theories of family firms.' In Leif Melin, Mattias Nordqvist, and Pramodita Sharma (Editors), *Sage Handbook of Family Business*. Thousand Oaks, CA: Sage Publishing (2014).

*Sieger, P., Zellweger, T., and Aquino, K. 'Turning agents into psychological principals: aligning interests of non-owners through psychological ownership.' *Journal of Management Studies* 50, no. 3 (2013): 361–388.

Smith, K.G., and Hitt, M.A. *Great Minds in Management: The Process of Theory Development*. New York, NY: Oxford University Press, 2005.

*Songini, L., and Gnan, L. 'Family involvement and agency cost control mechanisms in family small and medium-sized enterprises.' *Journal of Small Business Management* 53, no. 3 (2015): 581–841.

Strike, V.M. 'Advising the family firm: Reviewing the past to build the future.' *Family Business Review* 25, no. 2 (2012): 156–177.

*Tsai, W.-H., Hung, J.-H., Kuo, Y.-C., and Kuo, L. 'CEO tenure in Taiwanese family and nonfamily firms: An agency theory perspective.' *Family Business Review* 19, no. 1 (2006): 11–28.

Van de V., Andrew H. *Engaged Scholarship: A Guide for Organizational and Social Research*. Oxford, UK: Oxford University Press, 2007.

*Villalonga, B., and Amit, R. 'How do family ownership, control and management affect firm value?.' *Journal of Financial Economics* 80, no. 2 (2006): 385–417.

Wasserman, N. 'Stewards, agents, and the founder discount: Executive compensation in new ventures.' *Academy of Management Journal* 49, no. 5 (2006): 960–976.

*Westhead, P., and Howorth, C. 'Ownership and management issues associated with family firm performance and company objectives.' *Family Business Review* 19, no. 4 (2006): 301–316.

Whetten, D.A. 'What constitutes a theoretical contribution?.' *Academy of Management Review* 14, no. 4 (1989): 490–495.

Wiseman, R.M., Cuevas-Rodríguez, G., and Gómez-Mejía, L.R. 'Towards a social theory of agency.' *Journal of Management Studies* 49, no. 1 (2012): 202–222.

Wright, M., and Kellermanns, F.W. 'Family firms: A research agenda and publication guide.' *Journal of Family Business Strategy* 2, no. 4 (2011): 187–198.

*Zahra, S.A. 'Entrepreneurial risk taking in family firms.' *Family Business Review* 18, no. 1 (2005): 23–40.

4

LONG-TERM ORIENTATION

Reviewing the Past and Identifying Future Opportunities for Family Business Research

Jeffrey A. Chandler, Miles A. Zachary,
Keith H. Brigham, and G. Tyge Payne

Time is inherent in the decisions and actions of organizations and, therefore, crucial to an organization's success and longevity (Bluedorn & Denhardt, 1988). Conceptions of time are often manifested as a cultural artifact (Gurvitch, 1964), a resource (Doob, 1971, McGrath & Rotchford, 1983), or an event horizon (Das, 1986), which collectively influence how managers frame decisions (e.g., Agor, 1986; Burke & Miller, 1999; Dane & Pratt, 2007; De Dreu, 2003) and subsequent outcomes (e.g., Balkundi, & Harrison, 2006; Harrison, Price, Gavin, & Florey, 2002). For instance, employees' perceptions regarding the length of a deadline have been demonstrated to affect the pace of work (e.g., Kelly & McGrath, 1985), productivity (e.g., Andrews & Farris, 1972), and job performance (e.g., Peters, O'Connor, Pooyon, & Quick, 1984). Also, product or market entry decisions and outcomes are influenced by timing (Zachary, Gianiodis, Payne, & Markman, 2015) and based both on organizational and environmental time pressures (Mitchell, 1989; Perez-Nordtvedt, Payne, Short, and Kedia, 2008).

For family businesses, the influence of time may be even more pronounced as family business leaders seek to draw on their own history and traditions in order to manage current business concerns, all while simultaneously looking to the future (Brockhaus, 2004). Relative to non-family businesses, family businesses must deal with a number of unique issues that are temporally driven, such as succession planning (Davis & Harveston, 1998; Handler, 1994), maintaining family business continuity and harmony (Lambrecht & Lievens, 2008; Malone, 1989), and preserving a strong reputation (Miller & Le Breton-Miller, 2005). Indeed, research suggests that family businesses that are able to reconcile the various and often paradoxical temporal factors are more successful than other family businesses (Le Breton-Miller & Miller, 2006). Hence, family business managers, in particular, would benefit from a greater understanding of the interdependencies and balance that is needed between honoring the past, exploiting the present, and exploring and preparing for the future (Le Breton-Miller & Miller, 2011).

Although family business scholars have historically acknowledged the intrinsic nature of time, more recent research has centered on long-term orientation as a defining temporal construct (Brigham, Lumpkin, Payne, & Zachary, 2014). Long-term orientation (LTO) refers to "the tendency to prioritize the long-range implications and impact of decisions and actions that come to fruition after an extended time period" (Lumpkin & Brigham, 2011: p. 1152). LTO is comprised of three component dimensions – continuity, futurity, and perseverance – and serves as a dominant logic that influences the cognitions and strategic decision-making criteria of the dominant coalition, which is typically the family in family businesses (Lumpkin & Brigham, 2011). Accordingly, an LTO is a shared schema that helps managers to process information, consider alternatives, and develop solutions to problems in keeping with its long-run objectives (cf. Prahalad & Bettis, 1986).

While the proliferation of research on LTO within and beyond the family business discipline is encouraging, its conceptual roots, empirical developments, and meaningful gaps are not well understood. As a result, research on LTO risks becoming confounded and fragmented. With a central objective of helping clarify and advance the LTO construct, this chapter first reviews the extant literature, both across a variety of scholarly disciplines and specifically within the family business domain, then identifies some opportunities for future development. More specifically, this manuscript traces the origins and early work on LTO to reveal its various conceptualizations, associated theories, antecedents, consequences, and measures. Then, using this synthesized information, we assess the nomological structure of LTO – a critical step toward further establishing construct validity (Cronbach & Meehl, 1955) – to identify gaps and highlight future research opportunities. Overall, our intention is to apply the LTO logic to the LTO construct itself – to trace the past, assess the present state, and begin to chart the future of LTO.

The Development of the Long-Term Orientation Construct

LTO – often referred to more generally as long-termism or temporal orientation – has been examined across a wide variety of disciplines and at different levels of analysis (i.e., individual, group, organizational, and societal). Non-business disciplines, such as anthropology, linguistics, and sociology, have had a major impact on the development of LTO by providing a strong foundation for understanding how people view and apply time to various aspects of life, including work. Scholars in economics, marketing, finance, accounting, and management have then utilized these perspectives to extend our general understanding of LTO, particularly as it applies to business and economic settings, including the family business context.

Foundations from Non-Business Literature

As anthropology is the study of past and present humans, temporal orientation has been viewed by anthropologists as a cultural artifact, capturing if and how conceptions of time differ between distinct groups of people, such as nations. Most cultures recognize that time is unidirectional and unrepeatable, and is defined by the appearance and disappearance of objects or events (Casasanto & Boroditsky, 2008). Moreover, most people recognize that time is finite, bookended by birth and death. Yet, how time is treated within different cultures can differ significantly. For example, Hofstede and colleagues (Hofstede, 1984; Hofstede & Bond, 1988) described certain cultures as long-term or short-term oriented depending on the relative emphasis on the future or present. Originally termed 'Confucian dynamism,' Hofstede (1984) referred to LTO as "the fostering of virtues oriented towards future rewards, in particular, perseverance and thrift" (p. 359). Specifically, cultures that are more long-term oriented tend to place more emphasis on pragmatic rewards systems and the desire to save or store provisions that can be later utilized for adaptation and survival (Hofstede, 1984). Conversely, short-term oriented cultures deemphasize adaptation in favor of tradition, preservation, and ensure compliance with rigid social obligations. More recently, business scholars have extended Hofstede's work by conceptualizing LTO as a cultural dimension in order to examine its effect on multiple constructs such as international buyer-seller relationships (e.g., Cannon, Doney, Mullen & Peterson, 2010; Lee & Dawes, 2005), trust (e.g., Wang, Siu & Barnes, 2008), and ethics (e.g., Arli & Tjiptono, 2014; Moon & Franke 2000; Nevins, Bearden & Money, 2007; Tsui & Windsor, 2001).

Language within communications and linguistics has also been examined and observed to influence how people approach the concept of time. While one-dimensional directional terms assigned to describing time such as "ahead" or "behind" tend to be consistent across languages (Clark, 1973; Traugott, 1978), other spatial frames tend to differ between languages and, hence, cultures and societies. In a series of experiments, Casasanto and Boroditsky (2008) found that individuals speaking English referenced time almost exclusively as 'horizontal,' whereas individuals speaking Mandarin considered time in more 'vertical' terms. Referencing time as exclusively 'horizontal,' the English-speaking individuals emphasized continuity by framing time as a dimension of the past, present, and future. In contrast, the Mandarin speakers, referencing time as a 'vertical' dimension, framed time as a static snapshot of the present, which does not have a before or after. This study also demonstrated that Mandarin speakers vary in their vertical conception of time depending on what age they learned the language, suggesting that language is a powerful framing mechanism that influences perceptions, decisions, and actions.

Similar to research in anthropology, sociologists largely recognize that the way societies conceptualize and experience time is fundamental to their decision to plan and prepare for the future. Extensive research has focused on how society treats time, generally suggesting that time is dynamic and tends to change across different historical periods and societies (Ferrarotti, 1985; Kumar, 2009). In traditional societies (i.e., pre-industrial), time was often considered cyclically, where people structured their behaviors based on seasons. With modernization and globalization, clock-time has become more standardized, shifting from more cyclical views of time to more linear (Adam, 1990, 1995; Ferrarotti, 1985; Gronmo, 1989); it has also become more influential. Indeed, Daly (1996) argued that more advanced technology has led to a more constant barrage of high levels of information and activities, which compresses time into shorter and more chaotic segments. As such, individuals see the present as fragmented and increasingly difficult (if not impossible) to manage (Daly, 1996). Likewise, Nowotny (1994) suggested that an extended present – the situation in which the speed of change is so fast that the future seems ever-present or out of sight – reduces the salience of the future, resulting in an inability of individuals to conceptualize and plan for the future. Hence, individuals are likely to feel out of control, deconstructing the previously linear relationship between the past, present, and future, and may ultimately lead to a failure to plan for the future.

Scholars have also suggested that the meaning of the future changes based on time *and* space. Under conditions of uncertainty, Bauman (1998) argued that individuals who feel less constrained by time and more constrained by space (i.e., resources) are likely to view the future apprehensively or as a threat (Sennett, 1998). Conversely, individuals less limited by space but constrained by time may view the future as risky, but manageable (Bauman, 1998). Such research demonstrates how LTO can be coupled with uncertainty to explain individuals' attitudes and behaviors towards all aspects of life, but particularly work.

Development in the Business and Economics Literature

Areas of research within business and economics have also explored how temporal orientation affects individuals and organizations, mainly through its impact on decision-making. Fundamentally, a temporal orientation underlies the common and important economic assumption that individuals choose to substitute work or leisure in the present for future work or leisure.

This assumption is ubiquitous in economics (as well as accounting and finance), and, as such, is common in a number of economic theories. For example, Milton Friedman's permanent income hypothesis makes predictions of how individuals distribute their consumption decisions over their lifetime. Friedman (1957) argued that individual spending decisions are a function of both their current and future income. Accordingly, changes in consumer spending habits reflect changes in permanent income – defined as an expected average income – rather than changes in temporary income, such as a tax rebate or bonus. Thus, Friedman (1957) incorporates the notion of time and temporality into how consumers frame their income and consumption decisions.

Behavioral economic principles, acknowledging the tradeoffs and uncertainty inherent in intertemporal choices of costs and benefits (Lowenstein & Thaler, 1989), have also contributed to the development of the LTO construct. A topic of increasing importance in behavioral economics is temporal discounting, which refers to "the fact that the present, subjective value of a reward decreases as the delay until its receipt increases" (Myerson et al., 2003: p. 620). For example, Myerson and Green (1995) argued that the rate of discounting is adversely affected by the amount of the delayed reward such that the subjective value of the reward decreases (in both linear and non-linear forms) as the delay increases (holding the value of the reward constant). In a set of experiments, Myerson and colleagues (2003) found that the rate at which the subjective value of a reward decreased was significantly higher for lower rewards than greater rewards; this finding suggests that the subjective value of smaller rewards are much lower than greater rewards. As such, individuals may be more likely to engage in short-term actions when rewards are smaller.

Business scholars have also argued that managers develop a short-term orientation due to pressure for expected market returns (Drucker, 1986; Laverty, 1996) and higher costs of capital (Jacobs, 1991). As a result, organizational managers may focus too narrowly on short-run profits and neglect the long-term outcomes of their organization. Scholars have found that this corporate myopia reflects managers' underlying emphasis on bottom-line results (Latham & Braun, 2010), distributions of costs and benefits (Souder & Bromiley, 2012), securing fluid and impatient capital (Jacobs, 1991), and stock prices (Samuel, 2000); of course, short-term decisions come at the expense of future investments. Utilizing the concept of intertemporal choice, scholars have advanced the development of time in research by examining its impact on issues such as policy reform processes (Freytag & Renaud, 2007), long-run growth (Edmans, 2009), shareholder myopia (Samuel, 2000), and managerial myopia (Laverty, 2004; Miller, 2002; Wahal & McConnell, 2000).

In the marketing literature, scholars have utilized LTO to emphasize the importance of relationships and interactions between people and organizations (e.g., Anderson & Narus, 1990; Anderson & Weitz, 1989; Ganesan, 1994). Gummesson (1987), for instance, argued that existing marketing concepts are unrealistic and should be replaced with newer ideas that emphasize building long-term, interactive relationships between suppliers and customers. Subsequently, scholars in the marketing discipline have primarily studied the determinants of LTO in buyer-seller and interfirm relationships (e.g., Lee & Dawes, 2005; Narver & Slater, 1990; Ryu, Park, & Min, 2007). Notably, Ganesan (1994) suggested that LTO in a buyer-seller relationship is a function of two main factors: mutual dependence and trust. To the degree that mutual dependence and trust exist between two parties, the buyer-seller relationship will inspire a longer-term approach to business decisions. Indeed, the underlying theme of LTO in the marketing literature reflects a commitment to building and maintaining relationships that persist over time (Anderson & Weitz, 1989; Ganesan, 1994).

In finance and accounting research, LTO has primarily been utilized to examine intertemporal decision making with regard to financial investments (Bebchuk & Stole, 1993; Fama, 1998) and budgetary or accounting-based controls (Van der Stede, 2000). For example, a number of studies suggest that accounting-based controls may influence managers to neglect long-term effectiveness to protect themselves from the downside risk of missing budget targets (Hill; 1988; Lukka, 1988; Merchant, 1990; Merchant & Bruns, 1986; Onsi, 1973, Schiff & Lewin, 1970). However, Van der Stede (2000) suggested that if the appropriate competitive strategy is pursued, business unit managers will be able to create more slack, which allows them to make more long-term decisions.

LTO has also played an important role in the management literature, which also serves as the basis for much of the research in family business. Management scholars have studied the relationship between temporal orientation and managerial investment decisions (Souder & Bromily, 2012), organizational strategic orientations (Venkatraman, 1989), survival strategies (Hall, 1980), and individual characteristics of managers, such as planning preferences (Das, 1987). Other scholars have examined how individuals conceptualize the temporal distance of the past and the future (Zacher & Frese, 2009). For example, Bluedorn and Standifer (2006) examined how temporal depth, defined as an individual's conceptual distance between the present and the past or future, influences employees and managers in organizations. Scholars have also examined whether organizational decision makers adopt a more long-term or short-term approach to decision making when faced with different environmental conditions (Covin & Selvin, 1989). Generally, management research suggests that an organization's temporal orientation is influential with regards to its influence on decision making.

Long-Term Orientation in the Family Business Literature

Building on the extensive literature that pervades many social science disciplines, LTO has emerged as a prominent topic in family business research (e.g., Brigham, et al., 2014; Le-Breton Miller & Miller, 2006; Lumpkin & Brigham, 2011; Lumpkin, Brigham & Moss, 2010). There are several reasons for this adoption in family business studies. First, family business owners and managers generally act as stewards, rather than agents, and are often compelled to remain within the family business significantly longer than non-family businesses (Miller & Le Breton-Miller, 2005). In fact, the average CEO tenure for publicly-traded family businesses is greater than 15 years, as compared to non-family businesses where CEOs typically last less than 5 years (Miller & Le Breton-Miller, 2005). Second, the family business owners/managers tend to have a significant financial stake in the business, which may represent the cumulative investment of the business. Accordingly, family business managers may be more willing to sacrifice dividend payouts and short-term financial goals in favor of on-going investments and longer-term outcomes (Hoopes & Miller, 2006). Third, managing the family business is likely to be a more personal affair, intertwining the reputation of the individuals (i.e., managers and employees) with the business (Davis, Schoorman, & Donaldson, 1997; Gómez-Mejía et al., 2007). Hence, managers of family businesses are often highly concerned about the reputation, as well as other non-financial performance outcomes of the business (Le Breton-Miller & Miller, 2006; Miller & Le Breton-Miller, 2005). Overall, there is ample reason to examine the LTO construct in family businesses because it helps explain, relative to each other and non-family businesses, differences in how family businesses operate and differences in outcomes.

Methods for Review of Family Business Literature

To more fully assess the current state of LTO research within the family business field of study, we systematically reviewed the relevant literature to assess the definitions, theories, antecedents, consequences, and empirical approaches scholars have utilized to study the LTO construct. Our intention was not an exhaustive review of any and all articles on the subject, but rather to sample the highest quality research. Hence, we focused on the family business articles published in the most recognized journals in management, entrepreneurship, and family business: *Academy of Management Journal (AMJ), Academy of Management Review (AMR), Administrative Science Quarterly (ASQ), Entrepreneurship Theory & Practice (ETP), Family Business Review (FBR), Journal of Business Ethics (JBE), Journal of Business Venturing (JBV), Organization Science (OS), Strategic Entrepreneurship Journal (SEJ),* and *Strategic Management Journal (SMJ).*

In terms of process, we first searched the above-listed journals within the EBSCOhost and ABI/INFORM databases using the terms *long-term orientation, long-term investment, long-term value, long-term activities, managing for the long run,* and *organization longevity.* This initial search resulted in a total of 357 articles. We then examined these articles more closely to arrive at a final sample of 65 articles to utilize in this review. Articles were selected for inclusion if they extensively utilized, either theoretically or empirically, LTO in the family business context. Restated, we excluded articles that only mentioned LTO and did not explicitly utilize or discuss the construct, or a closely related one, in detail. For the 65 sampled articles, we then assessed their use of LTO across four areas: 1) definitions, 2) antecedents of LTO (with associated theories), 3) consequences or outcomes of LTO (with associated theories), and 4) empirical approaches to measurement and testing of LTO. The following section discusses each of these areas of interest in more detail.

Definitions

Family business scholars have suggested a number of definitions associated with LTO; these are summarized in Table 4.1. One of the most popular ways of defining the construct is through the financial investments of family businesses. For instance, Hoopes and Miller (2006) build on theories of economic choices to frame LTO in terms of the managerial preference for receiving payment immediately or in the future. The authors argue that decisions on ownership concentration in family businesses reflect either short-term or long-term investment choices, which include not monitoring (i.e., to sell or maintain their stock ownership), non-pecuniary consumption (i.e., hiring less competent family members over more qualified employees), or financial profit (i.e., consuming the profit or reinvesting the profit back into the business). In a similar fashion, Miller and Le-Breton Miller (2005) argue that family businesses use long-term investments such as innovation, R&D funding, quality enhancement, and branding to build up the reputation of the business and accommodate future family generations in succession planning. Many other scholars similarly define LTO as reflective of financial investments, couched in terms such as longer investment horizons (Stein, 1988; 1989), extended time horizon (Zellweger, 2007), long-term value (Salvato & Melin, 2008), and long-term investments (Allouche, Amann, Jaussaud, & Kurashina, 2008; Anderson, Duru, & Reeb, 2012). Despite slight differences, scholars generally argue that managers of family businesses generally prioritize long-range investment decisions to avoid managerial myopia (Stein, 1988) and reduce the marginal risk of investment decisions (Zellweger, 2007).

Family business scholars have also approached the LTO construct from a planning or activity-based perspective, utilizing terms such as long-term oriented activities (Duo, Zhang, & Su, 2014), long-term goal orientation (Cater & Schwab, 2008), long-term plans (Jorissen, Laveren, Martens, & Reheul, 2005), organizational survival and longevity (Colli 2012; Fahed-Sreih & Djoundourian, 2006; Sharma & Salvato, 2013; Vallejo, 2009; Zellweger, Nason, & Nordqvist, 2012), and managing for the long-run (Le Breton-Miller & Miller, 2006). Essentially, these scholars emphasize long-range activities such as those associated with charities (Duo et al., 2014) or production and operations processes (Jorissen et al., 2005).

Table 4.1 Sample Definitions of Long-Term Orientation and Related Terms in Family Business Research

Term	Sample Definition	Journal References
Long-term investment	The managerial preference of receiving payment immediately or in the future.	Allouche, Amann, Jaussaud, & Kurashina, 2008; Anderson, Duru & Reeb, 2012; Hoopes & Miller, 2006; Miller & Le Breton-Miller, 2005
Extended-time horizon	The reflection of future-oriented business activities and investment choices.[1]	Zellweger, 2007
Long-term value	The ability to create value over generations in terms of financial outcomes and strategic sustainability.	Salvato & Melin, 2008
Long-term oriented activities	Future-oriented actions that represent family values and preferences such as charitable donations.[1]	Duo, Zhang & Su, 2014
Long-term goal orientation	The long-term time horizon of the family business goals.	Cater & Schwab, 2008
Organizational survival and longevity	Companies that are able to persist in the long run.	Colli 2012; Fahed-Sreigh & Djoundourian, 2006; Sharma & Salvato, 2013
Managing for the long-run	To manage not for short-term profits but for very long-term market success and for the benefit of all organizational stakeholders.	Le Breton-Miller & Miller, 2006
Long-term perspective	A perspective that prioritizes the future and long-term success of the company.[1]	Sciascia & Mazzola, 2008
Long-term focus	A businesses emphasis on long-term value creation.	McVey & Draho, 2005
Long-term plans	A long-term outlook to the formal planning approaches of the family business.[1]	Jorissen, Laveren, Martens & Reheul, 2005
Long-term orientation (LTO)	The tendency to prioritize the long-range implications and impact of decisions and actions that come to fruition after an extended time period.	Allison, McKenny & Short, 2013; Brigham, Lumpkin, Payne & Zachary, 2014; Chrisman, Sharma, Steier, & Chua, 2013; Eddleston, Kellermanns, & Zellweger, 2012; Le Breton-Miller & Miller, 2006; Lumpkin & Brigham, 2011; Lumpkin, Brigham & Moss, 2010; Zahra, Hayton, & Salvato, 2004

[1] Terms were not explicitly defined. Meaning of the term is inferred in order to construct a sample definition.

Scholars have also framed the temporal orientation of family businesses as how the future is perceived. In such cases, key terms include long-term perspective (Sciascia & Mazzola, 2008), long-term values (Salmi & Sharafutdinova, 2008) and long-term focus (McVey & Draho, 2005). However, the most prominent term used to define a family business' futuristic perspective is long-term orientation (Allison, McKenny, & Short, 2013; Anderson & Reeb, 2003; Brigham et al., 2014; Chrisman, Sharma, Steier, & Chua, 2013; Eddleston, Kellermanns, & Zellweger, 2012;

Le Breton-Miller & Miller, 2006; Lumpkin & Brigham, 2011; Lumpkin et al., 2010; Zahra, Hayton, & Salvato, 2004). LTO is defined by Lumpkin and Brigham (2011) as "the tendency to prioritize the long-range implications and impact of decisions and actions that come to fruition after an extended time period" (p.1152).

Overall, our assessment of the various definitions suggests that, although the exact terms may vary, the broad notion of temporal orientation is a prevalent component in family business research (e.g., Brigham et al., 2014) and there has been some convergence around the label of LTO by family business scholars. Also, while the notion of LTO is based on the temporal orientation and decision-making biases associated with individuals, the LTO construct has been almost exclusively applied at the organizational level of analysis (i.e., the family business).

Antecedents

In terms of the antecedents to LTO, the literature has primarily focused on the characteristics of family businesses that incent or enable them to prioritize the future. Scholars have argued that the unique structure of family businesses allows managers to inherently be more long-term oriented than managers in non-family businesses (e.g., Anderson & Reeb, 2003; James, 1999; Le Breton-Miller & Miller, 2006). Generally, scholars have approached LTO using either agency theory (e.g., Chrisman & Patel, 2012; Patel & Fiet, 2011) or stewardship theory (e.g., Eddleston et al., 2012; Goel, Jussila, & Ikaheimonen, 2014). Using an agency theory perspective, family businesses are viewed as owner-managed (or at least have family owners in upper management), which inherently aligns incentives of principal and agent (Hoopes & Miller, 2006; Le Breton-Miller & Miller, 2006; Lumpkin & Brigham, 2011). Also, a concentrated ownership structure of family businesses is argued to reduce monitoring costs, which allows the family business to develop a resource surplus and unique competitive opportunities (Hoopes & Miller, 2006).

Stewardship theory, on the other hand, suggests that family business managers and employees are less inclined to act opportunistically due to the implicit family relationships that exist (Donaldson & Davis, 1991; Eddleston et al., 2012). Indeed, James (1999) suggested that a defining feature of families in business is their willingness to make sacrifices now to benefit the business and family members in the future. As such, scholars have argued for the importance of a family culture of stewardship, which can positively influence LTO-related activities and outcomes such as employee commitment (Zahra et al., 2008) and R&D spending (Miller & Le Breton-Miller, 2006). Collectively, such research seems to indicate that stewardship attitudes and behaviors instigated by family members in the business can help bring about a positive organizational culture that affects non-family employees and managers as well.

Recent studies have also considered socio-emotional wealth (SEW) as a central explanation for higher levels of LTO in family businesses. Gómez-Mejía and colleagues (2007) argued that family businesses are willing to incur significant risk and financial loss in an effort to preserve SEW, which is the "non-financial aspects of the firm that meet the family's affective needs, such as identity, the ability to exercise family influence, and the perpetuation of the family dynasty" (p. 106). This willingness to maintain SEW influences how family business managers approach the decision-making time horizon (Chrisman, Chua, & Steier, 2011). Specifically, it suggests that family business managers may be willing to forgo short-term financial opportunities or activities that mitigate their risk in favor of the long-run preservation of family values, community standing, and family organization identity (Gómez-Mejía et al., 2007). Additionally, scholars have suggested other similar antecedents of LTO, such as concerns for preserving family wealth

(Lumpkin & Brigham, 2011), long CEO tenures (Ensley, 2006), high levels of social interaction (Mustakallio, Autio, & Zahra, 2002), and concerns for developing a sustainable business to pass on to future generations (Le Breton-Miller & Miller, 2006; Long & Chrisman, 2014). In particular, Kappes and Schmid (2013) tie LTO to considerations for the well-being of future generations (i.e., trans-generational concerns) and the use of patient capital.

Consequences

Family business research has largely used LTO to help draw important distinctions between family and non-family businesses. A number of studies have considered the relationship between LTO and performance (e.g., Anderson & Reeb, 2003; Villalonga & Amit, 2006). Indeed, LTO has been proposed as a unique source of competitive advantage for family businesses (e.g., Gómez-Mejía et al., 2007; James, 1999), which may help to explain why family businesses often outperform non-family businesses (Anderson & Reeb, 2003; Villalonga and Amit, 2006). For example, Pearson and colleagues (2008) use social capital theory to argue that "familiness" can be competitively advantageous because it supports long-term oriented attitudes and behaviors. Overall, LTO and family business performance are argued to be positively related, although empirical research has yet to sufficiently examine this relationship.

Scholars have also examined the relationship between LTO and risk taking (e.g., Lumpkin & Brigham, 2011; Sharma, Chrisman, & Chua 1997; Zahra et al., 2004). Some studies have suggested that family businesses with high levels of LTO will reflect a "conservative" preference for less risky decisions in order to sustain and preserve wealth over time (e.g. Lumpkin & Brigham, 2011; Schulze, Lubatkin, & Dino, 2002). In contrast, other scholars have suggested that long-term oriented family businesses tend to engage in more risk-taking behavior (e.g. Zahra et al., 2004). Zellweger (2007) somewhat reconciled these conflicting perspectives by arguing that long-term oriented family businesses invest in projects that are both low-risk and high-risk by undertaking strategies that allow the business to persevere and out pace competitors. Furthermore, the duality of the LTO to risk relationship is also demonstrated in studies of SEW (e.g., Gómez-Mejía et al., 2007).

Understandably, LTO has been examined in relation to sustainability efforts. Researchers suggest that LTO leads to businesses that emphasize longer-term projects (Anderson & Reeb, 2003), continual short-term projects (Zahra et al., 2004), and socially-responsible projects (Delmas & Gergaud, 2014). For example, Dou and colleagues (2014) suggested that the anticipation of the needs of future generations encourages sustainable business decisions, and thus family businesses with higher levels of LTO will be more likely to adapt sustainable activities such as eco-certifications. Indeed, it is the emphasis on the long-term survival and growth of the family and the business that encourages family businesses to seek sustainability.

Scholars have also examined how LTO affects the resilience of family businesses under adverse conditions (e.g., Chrisman et al., 2011; Essen, Strike, Carney, & Sapp, 2015; McVey & Draho, 2005). Specifically, McVey and Draho (2005) argued that family businesses with a long-term focus are less likely to respond to external pressures for higher current earnings and more likely to strengthen the companies' relationships with customers, suppliers, and capital providers (p. 135). In addition, Essen and colleagues (2015) found evidence that family businesses possessing an LTO are more resilient during a financial crisis and out perform non-family businesses. That being said, family businesses that misunderstand or confuse the relationships between the past, present, and future are likely to be less resilient in the face of crisis (Lumpkin & Brigham, 2011). Thus, the relationship between LTO and resilience may be more complex than research to date suggests.

Lastly, prior research shows that entrepreneurship in family businesses may be influenced by LTO (Lumpkin & Brigham, 2011). For example, Patel and Fiet (2011) linked LTO to business windows of opportunity. Also, Eddleston and colleagues (2012) utilized stewardship theory to investigate the key factors that drive corporate entrepreneurship in family businesses; these authors found evidence that LTO is one of the key determinants of corporate entrepreneurship. Finally, scholars have linked LTO to the entrepreneurial orientation (EO) construct (Lumpkin et al., 2010; Zahra et al., 2004). Most notably, Lumpkin and colleagues (2010) conceptually linked the LTO construct to all five dimensions of EO arguing that LTO is positively associated with innovativeness, pro-activeness, and autonomy, but negatively associated with the risk-taking and competitive aggressiveness.

Measures

Despite the prevalence of the LTO concept in family business research, one of the most challenging obstacles for researchers is its operationalization (e.g., Brigham et al., 2014; Lumpkin & Brigham, 2011). Scholars have attempted to measure the LTO construct by using a number of different approaches, but a reliable and valid measure has yet to be agreed upon. Table 4.2 summarizes the different measures of LTO in the family business literature.

Typically, researchers have utilized archival data to establish proxies for LTO. Specifically, family business scholars have operationalized LTO through measures such as asset durability (e.g., Souder & Bromiley, 2012), R&D expenditures (e.g., Chrisman & Patel, 2012; Souder & Shaver, 2010), and the sum of R&D and capital expenditures (e.g., Anderson et al., 2012). Of these, R&D expenditures is the most popular proxy for LTO, which essentially suggests that the R&D investment activities reflect the overarching long-term perspective of the company. However, there is evidence suggesting that R&D expenditures is not an appropriate proxy for LTO (e.g., Chrisman & Patel, 2012).

Scholars have also measured LTO through survey instruments (e.g., Bearden, Money & Nevins, 2006; Eddleston et al., 2012; Laforet, 2013; Vallejo, 2009; Zahra et al., 2004). Laforet (2013), for instance, developed an item measurement for future orientation through mailed questionnaires of 500 random family business owners across the UK. Similarly, Eddleston and

Table 4.2 Measures of Long-Term Orientation in Family Business Research

Measurement	*Representative Examples*
R&D expenditures	Chrisman & Patel, 2012; Souder & Shaver, 2010
Sum of R&D expenditures and capital expenditures	Anderson, Duru & Reeb, 2012
Performance measures	Colli, 2012
Asset durability	Souder & Bromiley, 2012
Time horizon in financial investment decisions	James, 1999
Survey Instrument	Bearden, Money & Nevins, 2006; Eddleston, Kellermanns & Zellweger, 2012; Laforet, 2013; Vallejo, 2009; Zahra, Hayton & Salvato, 2004
Interviews	Cassia, De Massis & Pizzurno, 2012
Semi-structured interviews	Cater & Schwab, 2008; Cater & Justis, 2010; Gómez-Mejía, Haynes, Nunez-Nickel, Jacobson & Moyano-Fuentes, 2007
Content-analysis	Brigham, Lumpkin, Payne & Zachary, 2014

colleagues (2012) developed a four-item measure of LTO based on work by Zellweger (2007), which considered the implications of an expanded time horizon on investment activities. One of the difficulties of survey-based measures of LTO is whether perceptions of "long-term" differ between respondents. However, research has yet to examine this issue.

Family business scholars have also examined the LTO construct through case-based field work (e.g., Cater & Schwab, 2008; Cater & Justis, 2010), grounded theory (e.g., Cassia, De Massis & Pizzurno, 2012), and content analysis (e.g., Brigham et al., 2014). For instance, Cassia and colleagues (2012), using a grounded theory approach, collected data through in-depth interviews with the family business' top management team, informal conversations, and personal observation. They also utilized archival data obtained from company documents, company catalogs, and family information to extend and support their arguments. In a similar qualitative fashion, Garcia-Alvarez and colleagues (2002) gathered data in fieldwork over a six-month period using a semi-structured interview protocol. Through this qualitative approach, the authors obtained 28 values, one of which being LTO. In addition, Brigham et al. (2014) developed a content analysis dictionary of the three LTO dimensions: continuity, futurity, and perseverance. Brigham and colleagues (2014) validated the content analysis dictionary on two different samples of firm shareholder letters. Content analysis has been used commonly in the family business literature (e.g., McKenny, Short, Zachary, & Payne, 2011; Short, Payne, Brigham, Lumpkin, & Broberg, 2009; Zachary, McKenny, Short, & Payne, 2011), and, unlike other measures of LTO, the technique provides a more direct means to operationalize the LTO construct at the organizational level that may help avoid biases (Short & Palmer, 2007).

Recommendations for Future Research

Our review of LTO in the family business literature suggests that while the notion of an LTO is prevalent and there does seem to be some basic agreement among researchers regarding its definition and role in the organization, there is still much work and refinement that needs to be done with respect to the construct. In this section, we will discuss some of the future research opportunities with respect to the development and application of the LTO construct in family business research. We summarize our findings as well as opportunities for future research in Figure 4.1.

Most of the family business studies considering LTO have emphasized its forward-looking elements. However, recent conceptualizations have argued that LTO should be viewed as a multidimensional construct and that futurity is just one dimension, along with perseverance and continuity (Brigham et al., 2014; Lumpkin et al., 2010). This is a more dynamic and holistic view of temporal orientation that includes not only the future but the past and present as well. The ability to incorporate past and current temporal considerations along with the future can help us better understand family business, which while often characterized as focusing on future outcomes, often involves a rich history, founder legacies, and the involvement of multiple generations. This powerful influence of the past, along with present concerns that are often associated more with the "business" aspect of a family business, are important future areas of study that could be better understood through the holistic conceptualization of LTO.

While temporal orientation has been conceptualized and measured from the individual to the societal level, our review of the family business literature reveals that most researchers discussed and operationalized LTO from a management perspective and at the organizational level of analysis. Thus, for application to family business research, the development of organizational-level measures of LTO would seem most relevant. However, we find that a number of different proxy measures are used to assess LTO at the organizational level and that

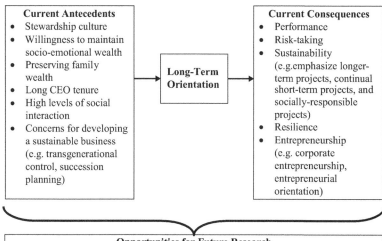

Figure 4.1 Long-Term Orientation Literature Overview

most of these only try to assess the future-based dimension of a multidimensional construct. There has been some progress with the introduction and validation of new measures (e.g., Brigham et al., 2014), but there is a strong need for more measurement development. We would caution, however, that organizational-level constructs and measures should be elevated up from individual-level constructs and measures with great care (McKenny, Short, & Payne, 2013).

With respect to LTO construct development and measurement, we believe that it may be helpful to look at the historical development of a popular and well-researched firm-level orientation – specifically entrepreneurial orientation (EO). Recently, Covin and Lumpkin (2011) reflected on the development of EO and noted that, after several decades of research, there was still debate with respect to EO as a dispositional or behavioral phenomenon, a unidimensional or multidimensional construct, and whether it should be assessed by formative or reflective measurement models. While our review of the LTO construct in the family business literature does not show any clear consensus on these issues, it is likely that these questions will need to be addressed in the future development of the LTO construct. Thus, we encourage family business researchers to keep these issues in mind as they work to further develop the LTO construct.

In our review, we highlight that temporal assumptions are central to many of the theories and frameworks applied to understanding family business. Agency theory proposes that there can be a misalignment between agents (managers) who, motivated by self-interest, may be more focused on short-run actions and outcomes than principals. Conversely, stewardship theory implies that some managers may naturally adopt more of a long-term mindset (cf. Davis et al., 1997). It is interesting that both of these prevalent theories are built on different assumptions with respect to managerial goals and time. We suggest it is critical that the notions of short-term and long-term be better defined and developed, and that an important step in this direction is the refinement of the LTO construct. Consensus as to what we mean by long-term versus short-term and validated measures would allow for more specificity and further our understanding regarding the temporal mechanics at play when applying these theories to questions of interest in family business research. Furthermore, temporal assumptions are also either explicit or implicit in many other theoretical perspectives and frameworks utilized in family business research. For example, SEW (Gómez-Mejía et al., 2007) and transgenerational control (Chrisman & Patel, 2012; Le-Breton Miller & Miller, 2006) are emerging frameworks that rely on temporal assumptions. These perspectives would be strengthened and would gain increased utility with the further development of the LTO construct.

As demonstrated in our review, LTO has long been identified as a potential key distinguishing characteristic of family businesses (e.g., Miller & Le Breton-Miller, 2005) and recent research has provided empirical support that family businesses do generally have a greater LTO than non-family businesses (Brigham et al., 2014). While identifying between-group differences of family and non-family businesses is important, we argue that the application of LTO will be most valuable in understanding within-group differences of family businesses. Family businesses are heterogeneous and while they may generally possess higher levels of LTO than non-family businesses, we would also expect that there is a large degree of variance among family businesses. Understanding the antecedents and factors that lead to more LTO in some family businesses and not others is a promising future research avenue. Additionally, given that LTO may vary among family businesses, it may be an important variable in explaining differences in firm behaviors, strategies, and ultimately, both financial and non-economic outcomes.

There have been recent calls for more multilevel and cross-level research in the study of family business (McKenny, Payne, Zachary, & Short, 2014). At the individual level, differences in LTO within family businesses may help to explain strategic inconsistencies or turmoil. Along the lines of research on principal-principal conflict (e.g., Young, Peng, Ahlstrom, Bruton, & Jiang, 2008), competition and contestation over decision making may likely arise between individuals with divergent conceptions of time (i.e., LTO), especially those that are mutually-exclusive. Scholars interested in the micro-foundations of LTO should investigate whether heterogeneity among family business owners and managers leads to conflict and whether that conflict spills over into operations and outcomes. Indeed, such research should help to clarify the mechanisms by which individual conceptions of time translate to a shared schema or dominant logic (cf. Brigham et al., 2014).

Another rich area for future research might be to look at temporal congruence across levels. For example, following a Person-Organization (PO) Fit (Kristof, 1996) approach – which suggests a host of individual and organizational benefits when there is a match between relevant individual and organizational needs and values (Cable & Edwards, 2004) – LTO could be assessed at the organizational level and matched with an individual's temporal frame. In other words, it may be that the positive outcomes of LTO are contingent upon the LTO-related value congruence between an organization (i.e., a family business) and its employees (Edwards & Cable, 2009). Conversely, when misfit exists, it may be that LTO engenders negative attitudes and behaviors (Brigham, De Castro, & Shepherd, 2007). Such research might suggest that the influences of LTO on organizational processes and performance may be limited by the temporal tolerance of its employees, and thus may stress recruitment and selection mechanisms as critical for maintaining temporal fit.

As discussed earlier in our review, family business scholars have begun to explore both the antecedents and consequences of LTO. However, many of the proposed relationships as to what factors might lead to a higher LTO in family businesses and what outcomes might be affected by a higher level of LTO have not been empirically tested. Furthermore, simple cross-sectional designs limit the ability to infer causality among LTO and potential antecedents and consequences.

Indeed, we suggest that the relationship among LTO and many other factors may often be recursive. For example, Miller and Le Breton-Miller (2005) argued that family businesses that "manage for the long run" will outperform those that do not. The assumption is that increased performance is a result of a greater LTO. However, it is also possible that increased performance results in slack resources that allow a business to pursue more long-term goals and thus serves to reinforce or strengthen a LTO over time. Performance, therefore, could be considered both a consequence and an antecedent of LTO. Future scholars, for example, could examine the recursive nature of LTO and performance by analyzing repeated measures longitudinal data with seemingly unrelated regression, which allows for the simultaneous linear analysis of systems of related data. Combined with more nuanced temporal theory such as spiral theory (Masuch, 1985), it could be argued that the LTO-performance relationship is characterized by amplifying-deviating loops or patterns of interaction that serve to reinforce the relationship over time until disrupted by an exogenous event. Overall, more longitudinal research is needed to better understand the complex causal and potentially looped relationships between LTO and its related constructs.

Conclusion

The Danish existentialist philosopher Søren Kierkegaard (1843) wrote that "life can only be understood backwards; but it must be lived forwards." His message suggests that while we must look to our past to explain our history, we can only move forward to live it. Family businesses, by their very nature, tend to draw on their own histories more extensively when considering decisions that impact their future. As such, the LTO construct seemingly plays in important role in the family business, particularly when it is defined by dimensions of the past, present, and future. Overall, our review has revealed a rich heritage upon which our current understanding of LTO and its related components is framed. Looking to the future, our hope is that this review will help aid family business scholars in the development and application of the LTO construct.

References

Adam, Barbara. 1990. *Time and Social Theory.* Cambridge.

Adam, Barbara. 1995. *Timewatch: The Social Analysis of Time.* Cambridge.

Agor, Weston H. 1986. "How Top Executives Use Their Intuition to Make Important Decisions." *Business Horizons* 29, no. 1: 49–53.

Allison, Thomas H., Aaron Francis McKenny, and Jeremy C. Short. 2013. "Integrating Time Into Family Business Research: Using Random Coefficient Modeling to Examine Temporal Influences on Family Firm Ambidexterity." *Family Business Review* 27, no. 1: 20–34.

Allouche, José, Bruno Amann, Jacques Jaussaud, and Toshiki Kurashina. 2008. "The Impact of Family Control on the Performance and Financial Characteristics of Family Versus Nonfamily Businesses in Japan: A Matched-Pair Investigation." *Family Business Review* 21, no. 4: 315–329.

Anderson, Erin, and Barton Weitz. 1989. "Determinants of Continuity in Conventional Industrial Channel Dyads." *Marketing Science* 8, no. 4: 310–323.

Anderson, James C., and James A. Narus. 1990. "A Model of Distributor Firm and Manufacturer Firm Working Partnerships." *Journal of Marketing* 54, no. 1: 42–58.

Anderson, Ronald C., Augustine Duru, and David M. Reeb. 2012. "Investment Policy in Family Controlled Firms." *Journal of Banking & Finance* 36, no. 6: 1744–1758.

Anderson, Ronald C., and David M. Reeb. 2003. "Founding-Family Ownership and Firm Performance: Evidence from the S&P 500." *Journal of Finance* 58, no. 3: 1301–1328.

Andrews, Frank M., and George F. Farris. 1972. "Time Pressure and Performance of Scientists and Engineers: A Five-Year Panel Study." *Organizational Behavior and Human Performance* 8, no. 2: 185–200.

Arli, Denni, and Fandy Tjiptono. 2014. "The end of religion? Examining the Role of Religiousness, Materialism, and Long-Term Orientation on Consumer Ethics in Indonesia." *Journal of Business Ethics* 123, no. 3: 385–400.

Balkundi, Prasad, and David A. Harrison. 2006. "Ties, Leaders, and Time in Teams: Strong Inference about Network Structure's Effects on Team Viability and Performance." *Academy of Management Journal* 49, no. 1: 49–68.

Bauman, Zygmunt. 1998. *Globalization: The Human Consequences*. Columbia University Press.

Bearden, William O., R. Bruce Money, and Jennifer L. Nevins. 2006. "A Measure of Long-Term Orientation: Development and Validation." *Journal of the Academy of Marketing Science* 34, no. 3: 456–467.

Bebchuk, Lucian Arye, and Lars A. Stole. 1993. "Do Short-Term Objectives Lead to Under- or Overinvestment in Long-Term Projects?." *Journal of Finance* 48, no. 2: 719–730.

Bluedorn, Allen C., and Rhetta L. Standifer. 2006. "Time and the Temporal Imagination." *Academy of Management Learning & Education* 5, no. 2: 196–206.

Bluedorn, Allen C., and Robert B. Denhardt. 1988. "Time and Organizations." *Journal of Management* 14, no. 2: 299–320.

Brigham, Keith H., G. T. Lumpkin, G. Tyge Payne, and Miles A. Zachary. 2014. "Researching Long-Term Orientation: A Validation Study and Recommendations for Future Research." *Family Business Review* 27, no. 1: 72–88.

Brigham, Keith H., Julio O. De Castro, and Dean A. Shepherd. 2007. "A Person-Organization Fit Model of Owner-Managers' Cognitive Style and Organizational Demands." *Entrepreneurship Theory and Practice* 31, no. 1: 29–51.

Brockhaus, Robert H. 2004. "Family Business Succession: Suggestions for Future Research." *Family Business Review* 17, no. 2: 165–177.

Burke, Lisa A., and Monica K. Miller. 1999. "Taking the Mystery Out of Intuitive Decision Making." *Academy of Management Executive* 13, no. 4: 91–99.

Cable, Daniel M., and Jeffrey R. Edwards. 2004. "Complementary and Supplementary Fit: A Theoretical and Empirical Integration." *Journal of Applied Psychology* 89, no. 5: 822–834.

Cannon, Joseph P., Patricia M. Doney, Michael R. Mullen, and Kenneth J. Petersen. 2010. "Building Long-Term Orientation in Buyer–Supplier Relationships: The Moderating Role of Culture." *Journal of Operations Management* 28, no. 6: 506–521.

Casasanto, Daniel, and Lera Boroditsky. 2008. "Time in the Mind: Using Space to Think About Time." *Cognition* 106, no. 2: 579–593.

Cassia, Lucio, Alfredo De Massis, and Emanuele Pizzurno. 2012. "Strategic Innovation and New Product Development in Family Firms: An Empirically Grounded Theoretical Framework." *International Journal of Entrepreneurial Behavior & Research* 18, no. 2: 198–232.

Cater III, John James, and Robert T. Justis. 2010. "The Development and Implementation of Shared Leadership in Multi-Generational Family Firms." *Management Research Review* 33, no. 6: 563–585.

Cater, John, and Andreas Schwab. 2008. "Turnaround Strategies in Established Small Family Firms." *Family Business Review* 21, no. 1: 31–50.

Chrisman, James J., Jess H. Chua, and Lloyd P. Steier. 2011. "Resilience of Family Firms: An Introduction." *Entrepreneurship Theory and Practice* 35, no. 6: 1107–1119.

Chrisman, James J., Jess H. Chua, and Reginald Litz. 2003. "A Unified Systems Perspective of Family Firm Performance: An Extension and Integration." *Journal of Business Venturing* 18, no. 4: 467–472.

Chrisman, James J., and Pankaj C. Patel. 2012. "Variations in R&D Investments of Family and Nonfamily Firms: Behavioral Agency and Myopic Loss Aversion Perspectives." *Academy of Management Journal* 55, no. 4: 976–997.

Chrisman, James J., Pramodita Sharma, Lloyd P. Steier, and Jess H. Chua. 2013. "The Influence of Family Goals, Governance, and Resources on Firm Outcomes." *Entrepreneurship: Theory & Practice* 37, no. 6: 1249–1261.

Clark, Herbert H. 1973. "The Language-As-Fixed-Effect Fallacy: A Critique of Language Statistics in Psychological Research." *Journal of Verbal Learning and Verbal Behavior* 12, no. 4: 335–359.

Colli, A. 2012. "Contextualizing Performances of Family Firms: The Perspective of Business History." *Family Business Review* 25, no. 3: 243–257.

Covin, Jeffrey G., and Dennis P. Slevin. 1989. "Strategic Management of Small Firms in Hostile and Benign Environments." *Strategic Management Journal* 10, no. 1: 75–87.

Covin, Jeffrey G., and G. T. Lumpkin. 2011. "Entrepreneurial Orientation Theory and Research: Reflections on a Needed Construct." *Entrepreneurship Theory and Practice* 35, no. 5: 855–872.

Cronbach, Lee J., and Paul E. Meehl. 1955. "Construct Validity in Psychological Tests." *Psychological Bulletin* 52, no. 4: 281–301.

Daly, Kerry. 1996. *Families & Time: Keeping Pace in a Hurried Culture*. Vol. 7. Sage Publications.

Dane, Erik, and Michael G. Pratt. 2007. "Exploring Intuition and Its Role in Managerial Decision Making." *Academy of Management Review* 32, no. 1: 33–54.

Das, Tushar Kanti. 1986. *The Subjective Side of Strategy Making: Future Orientations and Perceptions of Executives.* Praeger Publishers.

Das, Tushar K. 1987. "Strategic Planning and Individual Temporal Orientation." *Strategic Management Journal* 8, no. 2: 203–209.

Davis, James H., F. David Schoorman, and Lex Donaldson. 1997. "Toward a Stewardship Theory of Management." *Academy of Management Review* 22, no. 1: 20–47.

Davis, Peter S., and Paula D. Harveston. 1998. "The Influence of Family on the Family Business Succession Process: A Multi-Generational Perspective." *Entrepreneurship Theory and Practice* 22, no. 3: 31–54.

De Dreu, Carsten KW. 2003. "Time Pressure and Closing of the Mind in Negotiation." *Organizational Behavior and Human Decision Processes* 91, no. 2: 280–295.

Delmas, Magali A., and Olivier Gergaud. 2014. "Sustainable Certification for Future Generations: The Case of Family Business." *Family Business Review* 27, no. 3: 228–243.

Donaldson, Lex, and James H. Davis. 1991. "Stewardship Theory or Agency Theory: CEO Governance and Shareholder Returns." *Australian Journal of Management* 16, no. 1: 49–64.

Doob, Leonard W. 1971. "Patterning of time." Yale: Yale University Press.

Dou, Junsheng, Zhongyuan Zhang, and Emma Su. 2014. "Does Family Involvement Make Firms Donate More? Empirical Evidence from Chinese Private Firms." *Family Business Review* 27, no. 3: 259–274.

Drucker, Peter Ferdinand. 1986. *The Changed World Economy.* Council on Foreign Relations.

Eddleston, Kimberly A., Franz W. Kellermanns, and Thomas M. Zellweger. 2012. "Exploring the Entrepreneurial Behavior of Family Firms: Does the Stewardship Perspective Explain Differences?" *Entrepreneurship Theory and Practice* 36, no. 2: 347–367.

Edmans, A. 2009. "Blockholder Trading, Market Efficiency, and Managerial Myopia." *Journal of Finance* 64, no. 6: 2481–2513.

Edwards, Jeffrey R., and Daniel M. Cable. 2009. "The Value of Value Congruence." *Journal of Applied Psychology* 94, no. 3: 654–677.

Ensley, Michael. 2006. "Family Businesses Can Out-Compete: As Long as They are Willing to Question the Chosen Path." *Entrepreneurship Theory and Practice* 30, no. 6: 747–754.

Essen, Marc, Vanessa M. Strike, Michael Carney, and Stephen Sapp. 2015. "The Resilient Family Firm: Stakeholder Outcomes and Institutional Effects." *Corporate Governance: An International Review* 23, no. 3: 167–183.

Fahed-Sreih, Josiane, and Salpie Djoundourian. 2006. "Determinants of Longevity and Success in Lebanese Family Businesses: An Exploratory Study." *Family Business Review* 19, no. 3: 225–234.

Fama, Eugene F. 1998. "Market Efficiency, Long-Term Returns, and Behavioral Finance." *Journal of Financial Economics* 49, no. 3: 283–306.

Ferrarotti, Franco. 1985. "Historical Roots of Social Science." *Society* 22, no. 5: 15–17.

Freytag, Andreas, and Simon Renaud. 2007. "From Short-Term to Long-Term Orientation—Political Economy of the Policy Reform Process." *Journal of Evolutionary Economics* 17, no. 4: 433–449.

Friedman, Milton. 1957. "Theory of the Consumption Function." Princeton, NJ: Princeton University Press.

Ganesan, Shankar. 1994. "Determinants of Long-Term Orientation in Buyer-Seller Relationships." *Journal of Marketing* 58, no. 2: 1–19.

García-Álvarez, Ercilia, Jordi López-Sintas, and Pilar Saldaña Gonzalvo. 2002. "Socialization Patterns of Successors in First- to Second-Generation Family Businesses." *Family Business Review* 15, no. 3: 189–203.

Goel, Sanjay, Iiro Jussila, and Tuuli Ikäheimonen. 2014. "Governance in Family Firms: A Review and Research Agenda." *The Sage Handbook of Family Business*, edited by Leif Melin, Mattias Nordqvist, and Pramodita Sharma. 226–248. Sage Publications.

Gómez-Mejía, Luis R., Katalin Takács Haynes, Manuel Núñez-Nickel, Kathyrn JL Jacobson, and José Moyano-Fuentes. 2007. "Socioemotional Wealth and Business Risks in Family-Controlled Firms: Evidence from Spanish Olive Oil Mills." *Administrative Science Quarterly* 52, no. 1: 106–137.

Gronmo, Sigmund. 1989. "Concepts of Time: Some Implications for Consumer Research." *Advances in Consumer Research* 16, no. 1: 39–435.

Gummesson, Evert. 1987. "The New Marketing—Developing Long-Term Interactive Relationships." *Long Range Planning* 20, no. 4: 10–20.

Gurvitch, Georges. 1964. *The Spectrum of Social Time.* Vol. 8. Springer Science & Business Media.

Hall, William K. 1980. "Survival Strategies in a Hostile Environment." *Harvard Business Review* 58, no. 5: 75–85.

Handler, Wendy C. 1994. "Succession in Family Business: A Review of the Research." *Family Business Review* 7, no. 2: 133–157.

Harrison, David A., Kenneth H. Price, Joanne H. Gavin, and Anna T. Florey. 2002. "Time, Teams, and Task Performance: Changing Effects of Surface- and Deep-Level Diversity on Group Functioning." *Academy of Management Journal* 45, no. 5: 1029–1045.

Hill, Charles WL. 1988. "Internal Capital Market Controls and Financial Performance in Multidivisional Firms." *The Journal of Industrial Economics* 37, no. 1: 67–83.

Hofstede, Geert. 1984. *Culture's Consequences: International Differences in Work-Related Values.* Vol. 5. Sage Publications.

Hofstede, Geert, and Michael Harris Bond. 1988. "The Confucius Connection: From Cultural Roots to Economic Growth." *Organizational Dynamics* 16, no. 4: 5–21.

Hoopes, David G., and Danny Miller. 2006. "Ownership Preferences, Competitive Heterogeneity, and Family-Controlled Businesses." *Family Business Review* 19, no. 2: 89–101.

Jacobs, Michael T. 1991. *Short-Term America: The Causes and Cures of our Business Myopia.* Harvard Business School Press.

James, Harvey S. 1999. "Owner as Manager, Extended Horizons, and the Family Firm." *International Journal of the Economics of Business* 6, no. 1: 41–55.

Jorissen, Ann, Eddy Laveren, Rudy Martens, and Anne-Mie Reheul. 2005. "Real Versus Sample-Based Differences in Comparative Family Business Research." *Family Business Review* 18, no. 3: 229–246.

Kappes, Imke, and Thomas Schmid. 2013. "The Effect of Family Governance on Corporate Time Horizons." *Corporate Governance: An International Review* 21, no. 6: 547–566.

Kelly, Janice R., and Joseph E. McGrath. 1985. "Effects of Time Limits and Task Types on Task Performance and Interaction of Four-Person Groups." *Journal Of Personality & Social Psychology* 49, no. 2: 395–407.

Kierkegaard, Søren. 1843. *Fear and Trembling.*

Kristof, Amy L. 1996. "Person-Organization Fit: An Integrative Review of Its Conceptualizations, Measurement, and Implications." *Personnel Psychology* 49, no. 1: 1–49.

Kumar, Krishan. 2009. *From Post-Industrial to Post-Modern Society: New Theories of the Contemporary World.* John Wiley & Sons.

Laforet, Sylvie. 2013. "Innovation Characteristics of Young and Old Family-Owned Businesses." *Journal of Small Business and Enterprise Development* 20, no. 1: 204–224.

Lambrecht, Johan, and Jozef Lievens. 2008. "Pruning the Family Tree: An Unexplored Path to Family Business Continuity and Family Harmony." *Family Business Review* 21, no. 4: 295–313.

Latham, Scott, and Michael Braun. 2010. "Does Short-Termism Influence Firm Innovation? An Examination of S&P 500 Firms, 1990–2003." *Journal of Managerial Issue* 22, no. 3: 368–382.

Laverty, Kevin J. 1996. "Economic 'Short-Termism': The Debate, the Unresolved Issues, and the Implications for Management Practice and Research." *Academy of Management Review* 21, no. 3: 825–860.

Laverty, Kevin J. 2004. "Managerial Myopia or Systemic Short-Termism? The Importance of Managerial Systems in Valuing the Long-Term." *Management Decision* 42, no. 8: 949–962.

Le Breton-Miller, Isabelle and Danny Miller. 2006. "Why Do Some Family Businesses Out-Compete? Governance, Long-Term Orientations, and Sustainable Capability." *Entrepreneurship Theory and Practice* 30, no. 6: 731–746.

Le Breton-Miller, Isabelle and Danny Miller. 2011. "Commentary: Family Firms and the Advantage of Multitemporality." *Entrepreneurship Theory and Practice* 35, 6: 1171–1177.

Lee, Don Y., and Philip L. Dawes. 2005. "Guanxi, Trust, and Long-Term Orientation in Chinese Business Markets." *Journal of International Marketing* 13, no. 2: 28–56.

Loewenstein, George, and Richard H. Thaler. 1989. "Anomalies: Intertemporal Choice." *The Journal of Economic Perspectives* 3, no. 4: 181–193.

Long, Rebecca G., and James J. Chrisman. 2014. "Management Succession in Family Business" In *The Sage Handbook of Family Business*, edited by Leif Melin, Mattias Nordqvist, and Pramodita Sharma, 249–268. Sage Publications.

Lukka, Kari. 1988. "Budgetary Biasing in Organizations: Theoretical Framework and Empirical Evidence." *Accounting, Organizations and Society* 13, no. 3: 281–301.

Lumpkin, G. T., and Keith H. Brigham. 2011. "Long-Term Orientation and Intertemporal Choice in Family Firms." *Entrepreneurship Theory and Practice* 35, no. 6: 1149–1169.

Lumpkin, G. T., Keith H. Brigham, and Todd W. Moss. 2010. "Long-term orientation: Implications for the Entrepreneurial Orientation and Performance of Family Businesses." *Entrepreneurship and Regional Development* 22, no. 3–4: 241–264.

Malone, Stewart C. 1989. "Selected Correlates of Business Continuity Planning in the Family Business." *Family Business Review* 2, no. 4: 341–353.

Masuch, Michael. 1985. "Vicious Circles in Organizations." *Administrative Science Quarterly* 30, no. 1: 14–33.

McGrath, Joseph E., and Nancy L. Rotchford. 1983. "Time and Behavior in Organizations." *Research in Organizational Behavior* 5, no. 1: 57–101.

McKenny, Aaron. F., G. Tyge Payne, Miles. A. Zachary, and Jeremy. C. Short. 2013. "Multilevel Analysis in Family Business Studies." In *The Sage Handbook of Family Business*, edited by Leif Melin, Mattias Nordqvist, and Pramodita Sharma, 594–608. Sage Publications.

McKenny, Aaron F., Jeremy C. Short, and G. Tyge Payne. 2013. "Using Computer-Aided Text Analysis to Elevate Constructs an Illustration Using Psychological Capital." *Organizational Research Methods* 16, no. 1: 152–184.

McKenny, Aaron F., Jeremy C. Short, Miles A. Zachary, and G. Tyge Payne. 2011. "Assessing Espoused Goals in Private Family Firms Using Content Analysis." *Family Business Review* 25, no. 3: 298–317.

McVey, Henry, and Jason Draho. 2005. "US Family-Run Companies–They May Be Better Than You Think." *Journal of Applied Corporate Finance* 17, no. 4: 134–143.

Merchant, Kenneth A. 1990. "The Effects of Financial Controls on Data Manipulation and Management Myopia." *Accounting, Organizations and Society* 15, no. 4: 297–313.

Merchant, Kenneth A., and William J. Bruns. 1986. "Measurements to Cure Management Myopia." *Business Horizons* 29, no. 3: 56–64.

Miller, Danny, and Isabelle Le Breton-Miller. 2005. *Managing For the Long Run: Lessons in Competitive Advantage from Great Family Business.* Harvard Business Press.

Miller, Kent D. 2002. "Knowledge Inventories and Managerial Myopia." *Strategic Management Journal* 23, no. 8: 689–706.

Mitchell, Will. 1989. "Whether and When? Probability and Timing of Incumbents' Entry Into Emerging Industrial Subfields." *Administrative Science Quarterly* 34, no. 2: 208–230.

Moon, Young Sook, and George R. Franke. 2000. "Cultural Influences on Agency Practitioners' Ethical Perceptions: A Comparison of Korea and the US." *Journal of Advertising* 29, no. 1: 51–65.

Mustakallio, Mikko, Erkko Autio, and Shaker A. Zahra. 2002. "Relational and Contractual Governance in Family Firms: Effects on Strategic Decision Making." *Family Business Review* 15, no. 3: 205–222.

Myerson, Joel, and Leonard Green. 1995. "Discounting of Delayed Rewards: Models of Individual Choice." *Journal of the Experimental Analysis of Behavior* 64, no. 3: 263–276.

Myerson, Joel, Leonard Green, J. Scott Hanson, Daniel D. Holt, and Sara J. Estle. 2003. "Discounting Delayed and Probabilistic Rewards: Processes and Traits." *Journal of Economic Psychology* 24, no. 5: 619–635.

Narver, John C., and Stanley F. Slater. 1990. "The Effect of a Market Orientation on Business Profitability." *Journal of Marketing* 54, no. 4: 20–35.

Nevins, Jennifer L., William O. Bearden, and Bruce Money. 2007. "Ethical Values and Long-Term Orientation." *Journal of Business Ethics* 71, no. 3: 261–274.

Nowotny, Helga. 1994. *Time: The Modern and Postmodern Experience.* Cambridge, MA: Blackwell Publisher.

Onsi, Mohamed. 1973. "Factor Analysis of Behavioral Variables Affecting Budgetary Slack." *Accounting Review* 48, no. 3: 535–548.

Patel, Pankaj C., and James O. Fiet. 2011. "Knowledge Combination and the Potential Advantages of Family Firms in Searching for Opportunities." *Entrepreneurship Theory and Practice* 35, no. 6: 1179–1197.

Pearson, Allison W., Jon C. Carr, and John C. Shaw. 2008. "Toward a Theory of Familiness: A Social Capital Perspective." *Entrepreneurship Theory and Practice* 32, no. 6: 949–969.

Pérez-Nordtvedt, Liliana, G. Tyge Payne, Jeremy C. Short, and Ben L. Kedia. 2008. "An Entrainment-Based Model of Temporal Organizational Fit, Misfit, and Performance." *Organization Science* 19, no. 5: 785–801.

Peters, Lawrence H., Edward J. O'Connor, Abdullah Pooyan, and James C. Quick. 1984. "Research Note: The Relationship between Time Pressure and Performance: A Field Test of Parkinson's Law." *Journal of Organizational Behavior* 5, no. 4: 293–299.

Prahalad, Coimbatore Krishnarao, and Richard A. Bettis. 1986. "The Dominant Logic: A New Linkage between Diversity and Performance." *Strategic Management Journal* 7, no. 6: 485–501.

Ryu, Sungmin, Jeong Eun Park, and Soonhong Min. 2007. "Factors of Determining Long-Term Orientation in Interfirm Relationships." *Journal of Business Research* 60, no. 12: 1225–1233.

Salmi, Asta, and Elmira Sharafutdinova. 2008. "Culture and Design in Emerging Markets: The Case of Mobile Phones in Russia." *Journal of Business & Industrial Marketing* 23, no. 6: 384–394.

Salvato, Carlo, and Leif Melin. 2008. "Creating Value Across Generations in Family-Controlled Businesses: The Role of Family Social Capital." *Family Business Review* 21, no. 3: 259–276.

Samuel, Cherian. 2000. "Does Shareholder Myopia Lead to Managerial Myopia? A First Look." *Applied Financial Economics* 10, no. 5: 493–505.

Schiff, Michael, and Arie Y. Lewin. 1970. "The Impact of People on Budgets." *Accounting Review* 45, no. 2: 259–268.

Schulze, William S., Michael H. Lubatkin, and Richard N. Dino. 2002. "Altruism, Agency, and the Competitiveness of Family Firms." *Managerial and Decision Economics* 23, no. 4–5: 247–259.

Sciascia, Salvatore, and Pietro Mazzola. 2008. "Family Involvement in Ownership and Management: Exploring Nonlinear Effects on Performance." *Family Business Review* 21, no. 4: 331–345.

Sennett, Richard. 1998. *The Corrosion of Character: The Personal Consequences of Work in the New Capitalism.* WW Norton & Company.

Sharma, P., and C. Salvato. 2013. "Family Firm Longevity: A Balancing Act between Continuity and Change." In *A Global Revolution: The Endurance of Large Family Businesses Around the World*, edited by Paloma F. Perez and Andrea Colli, 34–56. Cambridge University Press.

Sharma, Pramodita, James J. Chrisman, and Jess H. Chua. 1997. "Strategic Management of the Family Business: Past Research and Future Challenges." *Family Business Review* 10, no. 1: 1–35.

Short, Jeremy C., and Timothy B. Palmer. 2007. "The Application of DICTION to Content Analysis Research in Strategic Management." *Organizational Research Methods* 11, no. 4: 727–752.

Short, Jeremy C., G. Tyge Payne, Keith H. Brigham, G. T. Lumpkin, and J. Christian Broberg. 2009. "Family Firms and Entrepreneurial Orientation in Publicly Traded Firms: A Comparative Analysis of the S&P 500." *Family Business Review* 22, no. 1: 9–24.

Souder, David, and J. Myles Shaver. 2010. "Constraints and Incentives for Making Long Horizon Corporate Investments." *Strategic Management Journal* 31, no. 12: 1316–1336.

Souder, David, and Philip Bromiley. 2012. "Explaining Temporal Orientation: Evidence from the Durability of Firms' Capital Investments." *Strategic Management Journal* 33, no. 5: 550–569.

Stein, Jeremy C. 1988. "Takeover Threats and Managerial Myopia." *Journal of Political Economy* 96, no. 1: 61–80.

Stein, Jeremy C. 1989. "Efficient Capital Markets, Inefficient Firms: A Model of Myopic Corporate Behavior." *Quarterly Journal of Economics* 104, no. 4: 655–669.

Traugott, Elizabeth Closs. 1978. "On the Expression of Spatio-Temporal Relations in Language" *Universals of Human Language* 3, no. 1: 369–400.

Tsui, Judy, and Carolyn Windsor. 2001. "Some Cross-Cultural Evidence on Ethical Reasoning." *Journal of Business Ethics* 31, no. 2: 143–150.

Vallejo, Manuel Carlos. 2009. " Analytical Model of Leadership in Family Firms under Transformational Theoretical Approach: An Exploratory Study." *Family Business Review* 22, no. 2: 136–150.

Van der Stede, Wim A. 2000. "The Relationship between Two Consequences of Budgetary Controls: Budgetary Slack Creation and Managerial Short-Term Orientation." *Accounting, Organizations and Society* 25, no. 6: 609–622.

Venkatraman, Natarajan. 1989. "Strategic Orientation of Business Enterprises: The Construct, Dimensionality, and Measurement." *Management Science* 35, no. 8: 942–962.

Villalonga, Belen, and Raphael Amit. 2006. "How Do Family Ownership, Control, and Management Affect Firm Value?" *Journal of Financial Economics* 80, no. 2: 385–417.

Wahal, Sunil, and John J. McConnell. 2000. "Do Institutional Investors Exacerbate Managerial Myopia?" *Journal of Corporate Finance* 6, no. 3: 307–329.

Wang, Cheng Lu, Noel YM Siu, and Bradley R. Barnes. 2008. "The Significance of Trust and Renqing in the Long-Term Orientation of Chinese Business-to-Business Relationships." *Industrial Marketing Management* 37, no. 7: 819–824.

Young, M. N., Peng, M. W., Ahlstrom, D., Bruton, G. D., & Jiang, Y. 2008. "Corporate Governance in Emerging Economies: A Review of the Principal-Principal Perspective." *Journal of Management Studies* 45, no. 1: 196–220.

Zachary, Miles A., Aaron McKenny, Jeremy C. Short, and G. Tyge Payne. 2011. "Family Business and Market Orientation Construct Validation and Comparative Analysis." *Family Business Review* 24, no. 3: 233–251.

Zachary, Miles A., Peter T. Gianiodis, G. Tyge Payne, and Gideon D. Markman. 2015. "Entry Timing Enduring Lessons and Future Directions." *Journal of Management* 41, no. 5: 1388–1415.

Zacher, Hannes, and Michael Frese. 2009. "Remaining Time and Opportunities at Work: Relationships between Age, Work Characteristics, and Occupational Future Time Perspective." *Psychology and Aging* 24, no. 2: 487–493.

Zahra, Shaker A., James C. Hayton, and Carlo Salvato. 2004. "Entrepreneurship in Family vs. Non-Family firms: A Resource-Based Analysis of the Effect of Organizational Culture." *Entrepreneurship Theory and Practice* 28, no. 4: 363–381.

Zahra, Shaker A., James C. Hayton, Donald O. Neubaum, Clay Dibrell, and Justin Craig. 2008. "Culture of Family Commitment and Strategic Flexibility: The Moderating Effect of Stewardship." *Entrepreneurship Theory and Practice* 32, no. 6: 1035–1054.

Zellweger, Thomas. 2007. "Time Horizon, Costs of Equity Capital, and Generic Investment Strategies of Firms." *Family Business Review* 20, no. 1: 1–15.

Zellweger, Thomas Markus, Robert S. Nason, and Mattias Nordqvist. 2012. "From Longevity of Firms to Transgenerational Entrepreneurship of Families Introducing Family Entrepreneurial Orientation." *Family Business Review* 25, no. 2: 136–155.

5

UPPER ECHELONS IN FAMILY FIRMS

What We Know and Still Can Learn About Family-TMT-Involvement

Torben Tretbar, Marko Reimer, and Utz Schäffer

Introduction

Building on Hambrick and Mason's (1984) seminal work, mountains of research have investigated the impact of top managers on their organization in terms of strategy and performance (Finkelstein, Hambrick & Cannella 2009). More recently, family firm researchers have adopted the upper echelons perspective to provide new insights into how family involvement in the top management team (TMT) affects the firm (Minichilli, Corbetta & MacMillan 2010). The overarching contribution of this stream of research has been a deeper understanding of family-TMT-involvement as a source of heterogeneity in family firms (Chua, Chrisman, Steier & Rau 2012).

Despite this contribution, the research stream has produced conflicting theoretical arguments and empirical results. As our literature review reveals, the most prominent variable studied is firm performance, but it is unclear whether family managers influence it positively or negatively. Whereas some authors conceptualize family managers as stewards who are highly capable of managing their firm, others view them as untalented agents who primarily serve the family's interests and who are unable to manage a firm (Chrisman, Chua, Kellermanns & Chang 2007; Miller, Minichilli & Corbetta 2013). Conflicting results have also been obtained for several other firm-level variables, ranging from entrepreneurial activities to accounting choices (Huybrechts, Voordeckers & Lybaert 2013; Pazzaglia, Mengoli & Sapienza 2013; Sirmon, Arregle, Hitt & Webb 2008; Stockmans, Lybaert & Voordeckers 2010). Thus, it appears that family-TMT-involvement is indeed a source of heterogeneity in family firms (Chua et al. 2012). However, its implications for the firm seem to be more complex than presented in many studies.

The research objective of our study is to support a structured approach for exploring the effects of family-TMT-involvement. To do so, we analyze 50 articles and provide a structured literature review that describes the proposed implications of family-TMT-involvement (Short 2009) and we derive a future research agenda to further enhance our understanding of family-TMT-involvement. We draw on upper echelons research, which has been explicitly dedicated to the effects of top managers on firm-level outcomes (Hambrick & Mason 1984). Many of the constructs proposed in upper echelons research also apply to the TMTs of family firms (Minichilli et al. 2010). Furthermore, the field has generated knowledge for more than 30 years and has faced several challenges that are also evident in studies on family–TMT-involvement. In particular, upper echelons research has struggled with using demographic proxies and identified measures to capture the processes in the TMT more precisely (Finkelstein et al. 2009). These approaches are potentially valuable to scholars in the field of family–TMT-involvement. As the future research section shows, several potential links exist between work on upper echelons and family–TMT-involvement that may explain the conflicting evidence.

Our contribution is two-fold. First, family firm scholars can benefit from our overview. The review identifies previous studies that relate family–TMT-involvement to their dependent variables, the selection of a research field, and the inclusion of control variables for confounding mechanisms. Hence, scholars can draw on the literature review when developing their theoretical arguments and designing their research. Such knowledge is potentially also of value for stakeholders of family firms (e.g., non-family shareholders, banks, and non-family managers). It enables them to understand how family influences the firm in which they are interested.

Second, the future research agenda is a starting point from which to improve our understanding of the implications of family–TMT-involvement. Family firm research has largely overlooked the findings from the upper echelons literature, despite the fact that upper echelon effects are equally present in the TMTs of both family and non-family firms (Minichilli et al. 2010; Patel & Cooper 2014). Neglecting these effects in research on family–TMT-involvement may explain why family firm researchers report inconclusive results. Likewise, upper echelons research can benefit from being combined with the knowledge gained regarding family–TMT-involvement, which has also produced a variety of conflicting results. Potentially, this is because upper echelons research has not accounted sufficiently for the influence of entrepreneurial families (Anderson & Reeb 2003; Carpenter, Geletkanycz & Sanders 2004; Minichilli et al. 2010).

Procedure of Literature Review

Identification of Articles

The selection of relevant papers followed prior literature reviews on family firms (De Massis, Frattini & Lichtenthaler 2013; Salvato & Moores 2010). In particular, we searched the 33 journals that De Massis, Sharma, Chua and Chrisman (2011) identified as having published impactful research on family firms. Because of their relevance for family firms and general management research, respectively, the *Journal of Family Business Strategy* and *Strategic Management Journal* were added to the list (Short 2009). To exclude early-stage family firm research, which tend to lack clear theory development and rigorous empirical methods, we restricted the search of articles to those published from 1996 onwards (Bammens, Voordeckers & van Gils 2011; De Massis et al. 2011). Our results include all articles available from these journals at the end of February 2014.

All journals were searched for the following terms (in the title, abstract, or keywords): "family business" or "family firm" or "family owned" or "family enterprise" (following De Massis et al. 2011) and "chairman" or "CEO" or "CEOs" or "executive" or "management" or "manager" or "managers" or "officer" or "TMT" or "TMTs" (adopted from Nielsen 2010). As a result, we obtained 373 articles.

After reading the abstracts, we excluded all papers that did not study family–TMT-involvement on organizational outcomes with a quantitative research approach. We identified 50 studies as relevant to our research endeavor. The high number of irrelevant articles is consistent with other literature reviews on family firms (Pukall & Calabro 2014).

Coding Scheme

We relied on the rich upper echelons literature to build a guiding framework for coding the articles. Our framework included four categories, split into individual and team-level research (Hambrick 2007). On the individual level, the category "*Upper echelon-related characteristics*" captures arguments traditionally found in the upper echelons literature, focusing on the experiences and characteristics of managers (e.g. their functional background, tenure, or social capital). In addition, the family-specific category "*explicit strategic preferences*" addresses the strategic choices made by family managers because of their specific family background (e.g., choosing to pursue family goals such as socio-emotional wealth or acting as long-term oriented stewards of the firm). On the team level, the first category is "*TMT composition, interaction, and decision-making processes.*" In traditional upper echelons research, this sub-stream has investigated the entire TMT. Hence, it is designed to capture articles that address research on family-TMT-involvement and that explicitly focus on the team level, thereby acknowledging that individual differences between family and non-family managers may have implications for the entire team. Lastly, "*family as supra-TMT*" has been adapted from the upper echelons research on boards (e.g. how board composition and other facets of supra-TMTs affect organizational outcomes). The purpose of this category is to capture research linking family-TMT-involvement to the entire family, thereby extending the range of decision makers to the firm's owners, similar to the board and supra-TMT-approach.

Each of the articles was carefully investigated with regard to the coding categories. To do this, we read the introduction, theoretical background, hypotheses development, and discussion sections of the papers and extracted the main theoretical arguments proposed for how and why family-TMT-involvement matters. Afterwards, we assigned these arguments to the coding scheme to provide a structured overview of the theoretical constructs assigned to family-TMT-involvement by previous researchers.

Overview of Results

The progress of research on family-TMT-involvement over time indicates a trend for more research in later years. Between 1996 and 2006, only seven papers were published, whereas in 2013 (our last full observation year) alone twelve papers were published. In Appendix A, we list all relevant articles and their key findings (note that each article may have applied several upper echelon themes and could therefore be classified into more than one coding category). The first category of the coding scheme, upper echelon-related characteristics is picked up by twenty-two family firm articles. The related category of explicit strategic preferences, which also captures differences on the individual level, is the most prominent theme in the family firm literature, appearing in thirty-five articles. On the team level, ten studies address TMT-focused aspects, and 10 other studies examine the family as a supra-TMT.

Regarding the dependent variables, the majority of articles (26) focus on financial or market performance. Interestingly, only five articles consider growth as a performance outcome, even though these data are potentially easier to obtain. With regard to the antecedents of performance outcomes, entrepreneurial activities of the family firm are investigated in light of family-TMT-involvement in ten articles, followed by capital structure and accounting choices. Less common issues include HR policies, financial management techniques, internationalization, TMT processes, and management practices.

Forms of Family-TMT-Involvement

Family-TMT-involvement has been studied in various forms. In the review, the presence of a family CEO was most prominent, mentioned in thirty-three articles. Additionally, nine articles looked at the ratio or number of family members in the TMT. Aside from these frequently used proxies for family-TMT-involvement, a range of articles used composite measures of family-TMT-involvement to capture how dominant the family is in the TMT. For example, Casillas and Moreno (2010) summed up three dummy variables to measure the following: whether the managing director is a family member, whether more than half of the TMT consists of family members, and whether the firm's strategy is essentially designed by family members. Similarly, Dekker, Lybaert, Steijvers and Depaire (2013) used a composite measure that aggregates the presence of each of the following: a family CEO, family members in the TMT, and family directors. Furthermore, several articles used dichotomous measures, taking the value of 1 if the TMT included family or non-family managers (Claver, Rienda & Quer, 2009; Stockmans et al. 2010) or if the daily operations of the firm were in family hands (Wu, Chua & Chrisman 2007). Beyond solely counting the family managers present in the TMT, Le Breton-Miller, Miller and Lester (2011) measured the percentage of shares held by family members active in the firm (even though this potentially includes shares held by family employees not part of the TMT).

Additionally, several studies considered the specific family roles of TMT members. In particular, six studies investigated whether multiple generations of the family were involved in the TMT. Similarly, Ensley and Pearson (2005) distinguished between non-family TMTs, familial TMTs (TMTs with family members but without a clear leader, such as siblings or cousins), and parental TMTs (TMTs with a parent-child constellation). Lastly, Di Giuli, Caselli and Gatti (2011) and Filbeck and Lee (2000) focused on specific business roles other than the CEO, namely whether the CFO position was held by a family member.

How Family-TMT-Involvement Influences Organizational Outcomes

This section focuses on upper echelons themes reflected in the coding scheme and presents in more detail how the family firm literature has adapted those themes. We emphasize upper echelon themes and not the proxies or organizational outcomes because the patterns that distinguish family from non-family managers are repetitive. Put differently, the same arguments have been applied to various proxies and dependent variables. Appendix B additionally links the current knowledge on family-firm-specific upper echelon effects to dependent variables and highlights the diffuse implications that family-TMT-involvement may have for the firm. For almost all the dependent variables studied more than once, contradictory findings have been obtained.

Upper Echelon-Related Characteristics

Twenty-two studies have considered differences related to the characteristics studied in upper echelons research. They agree that non-family managers usually are more talented than family managers because the latter are promoted for kinship rather than competence and are chosen from a relatively small group of family members (Block, Jaskiewicz & Miller 2011; Lin & Hu 2007). In contrast, because non-family managers are chosen from a larger talent pool and not for their kinship, they bring in a larger repertoire of management skills (Miller, Le Breton-Miller, Minichilli, Corbetta & Pittino 2014). Consequently, firms in which the family manager has been chosen based on primogeniture are particularly subject to poor management (Bloom & van Reenen 2007).

In addition to superior managerial talent, non-family managers benefit from their experience outside the family firm. Hence, they have a greater network outside the organization (Mazzola, Sciascia & Kellermanns 2013; Sciascia & Mazzola 2008) and bring in additional knowledge and perspectives (Di Giuli et al. 2011; Kraiczy, Hack & Kellermanns 2014; Mazzola et al. 2013). They make decisions more objectively (Filbeck & Lee 2000) and are more likely to reorganize the firm in case of poor performance (Cucculelli & Marchionne 2012). Furthermore, they perceive more growth opportunities than family managers (Amore, Minichilli & Corbetta 2011).

Yet, some researchers have argued that family managers also bring in positive ability effects into family firms. Because the family internally shares knowledge about the firm, family managers have a deep understanding of the business and a strong internal network within the firm (Herrero 2011). Furthermore, family managers provide social capital outside the organization (Kowalewski, Talavera & Stetsyuk 2010), because their emphasis on socio-emotional wealth preservation keeps them engaged in long-term relationships with customers and suppliers (Kim & Gao 2013).

Explicit Strategic Preferences

The vast majority of the articles argue that family managers affect their firms through their strategic preferences. Because of their family status, their preferences differ from non-family managers, and these preferences are imposed on the firm. Some articles suggest that family managers act as agents of the owning family and serve family interests in their decision making. With regard to non-family managers, some of the studies explicitly argue that they either serve their own interests (Huybrechts et al. 2013; McConaughy 2000; Michiels, Voordeckers, Lybaert & Steijvers 2013; Minichilli et al. 2010; Yang 2010) or make decisions based on economic rationales (Casillas, Moreno & Barbero 2011; Dekker et al. 2013; Sirmon et al. 2008; Stockmans et al. 2010).

Contrary to the perspective of family managers imposing family goals on the firm, several authors instead argue that family managers act as stewards when making strategic choices. Family managers share a long common history with the firm as a social entity (Block 2010). Thus, they have a deep relationship with the firm (Andres 2008). Their most important interest is the firm's success, and they choose to maximize firm performance over pursuing family goals (Sciascia & Mazzola 2008; Zahra, Neubaum & Larraneta 2007).

These two perspectives, family managers as either agents or stewards, may appear contradictory. However, some authors note that it is sometimes difficult to disentangle them, particularly because stewardship behavior involves investments in farsighted activities such as research and development and asset purchases that can preserve the family's long-term economic and socio-emotional wealth (Landry, Fortin & Callimaci 2013; Le Breton-Miller et al. 2011). Similarly, Block (2010) argues that family managers care about the firm's reputation for reasons of stewardship, whereas Berrone, Cruz and Gómez-Mejía (2012) identify corporate reputation as a dimension of socio-emotional wealth. Lin and Hu (2007) further show that family CEOs improve firm performance, but only if the family has high cash flow rights. Thus, they act as stewards only if it is in the family's interest, again highlighting the difficulty in distinguishing between the interest of the family and the firm.

TMT Composition, Interaction, and Decision-Making Processes

In addition to the two research strands focusing on individual differences between family and non-family managers, several authors have investigated how such individual differences affect the entire TMT and its decision-making processes, thereby acknowledging the potential cross-level effects of individual differences on the entire TMT. Casillas and Moreno (2010) argue that family managers' ownership shares, close relationship to the family, and willingness to maintain control over the firm encourage them to make centralized decisions. In turn, decisions are made faster, which can affect the eventual outcome and implementation of those decisions.

Looking at the relationship between family and non-family managers, Minichilli et al. (2010) highlight the potential for fault lines. In particular, family and non-family managers can separate into two factional groups that do not cooperate well with each other. Thus, the firm benefits most in terms of profitability if it is either entirely managed by family members or entirely managed by non-family members. In contrast, a mix of family and non-family members is detrimental to performance, as it inhibits effective decision-making in the TMT.

From an information processing perspective, researchers have focused on the family-TMT-ratio (Kraiczy et al. 2014) and generational diversity (Kellermanns, Eddleston, Barnett & Pearson 2008; Kraiczy et al. 2014; Sciascia, Mazzola & Chirico 2013). Regarding the family-TMT-ratio, the smaller the proportion of external managers in the TMT, the less diverse the TMT is in terms of external perspectives (Kraiczy et al. 2014). As upper echelons theory suggests, the TMT then lacks the cognitive capacity to process complex information and is subject to groupthink (Carpenter et al. 2004; Hambrick & Mason 1984). Consequently, it cannot transform cognitive input, such as TMT innovation orientation, into output, such as new products (Kraiczy et al. 2014). With regard to generational diversity in the TMT, the opposite effect is proposed. The knowledge and perspectives of different generations tend to be diverse (Kraiczy et al. 2014; Ling & Kellermanns 2010; Sciascia et al. 2013). Hence, when multiple generations are involved in the TMT, decision-making benefits from additional insights (Kellermanns et al. 2008). Eventually, this promotes constructive debate within the TMT (Sciascia et al. 2013).

Family as a Supra-TMT

Ten studies consider family-TMT-involvement in light of the cross-level effects with the family. These studies investigate how individual differences between family and non-family managers may be interrelated with the entire family. Two papers link the family's objectives to the inclination of family managers to pursue family goals. They interpret the family's choice to appoint a family manager as a signal of the family's emphasis on socio-emotional wealth (Gulbrandsen 2005; Naldi, Cennamo, Guido & Gómez-Mejía 2013). Including family managers in the TMT increases the family's ability to influence the firm, which is the key dimension of socioemotional wealth (Berrone et al. 2012). As Gulbrandsen (2005) notes, family owners who have delegated operational responsibility to external managers "*have demonstrated that they have a more relaxed view of control*" (p. 62). In contrast, family owners who emphasize their socioemotional wealth are less likely to appoint external managers (Vandekerkhof, Steijvers, Hendriks & Voordeckers 2014). Hence, the presence of family managers may be understood as an indication of the family's control orientation. By interpreting family-TMT-involvement this way, researchers can extract more information from the presence of family managers than from simply assuming that the family goals are more salient. Instead, it conveys a message regarding the firm as a source of non-economic utility for the family (Mazzola et al. 2013).

Similarly, generational diversity in the TMT indicates a focus on long-term intentions for continuity and survival (Casillas et al. 2011). Hence, the number of generations involved in the firm's management reflects the family's emphasis on the renewal of family bonds through dynastic succession, another dimension of socio-emotional wealth (Berrone et al. 2012). Overall, the family may be aware of individual differences between family and non-family managers and may use this knowledge when selecting either type of manager, showing the interrelations between the team and individual levels of analysis regarding family-TMT-involvement.

Several studies have additionally focused on how processes and interaction patterns within the family depend on family-TMT-involvement. In discussing the potential implications of family conflicts on the firm, these studies disagree on whether family-TMT-involvement increases or decreases conflict. On the one hand, Kraiczy et al. (2014) claim that family-TMT-involvement raises emotional issues, which family managers transfer to the TMT. Hence, family-TMT-involvement is associated with an increase in family-induced relationship conflict and is detrimental to the effectiveness of decision-making processes. On the other hand, it is argued that family members trust family managers to a greater extent than they trust non-family managers (Livingston 2007). Such trust facilitates active communication within the TMT and between the TMT and the owning family (De Massis, Kotlar, Campopiano & Cassia 2013). Therefore, the presence of family managers also reduces intra-family conflicts between owners and the TMT (De Massis et al. 2013), hence supporting more effective decision making within the firm.

Researchers on generational involvement in the firm have supported conflicting views as well. According to Zahra et al. (2007), involving multiple generations in the business facilitates the transfer of the family's identity to the younger generation, thereby creating stronger cohesion within the family. This stronger cohesion enables the family to better resolve relational issues and likewise encourages family members to share ideas and thoughts (Ensley & Pearson 2005). Yet, the involvement of multiple generations in the firm can also complicate family relationships (Sciascia et al. 2013).

Interrelations Between the Categories

The individual-level effects of family-TMT-involvement have largely been studied in isolation, and some empirical evidence suggests that some linkages exist between them. For example, Miller et al. (2014) find that co-CEO arrangements involving family and non-family CEOs hamper the non-family CEO's performance. They reason that non-family CEOs, in this case, are distracted from business issues. Hence, a team process within the TMT limits the possibility for non-family CEOs to exploit their superior abilities. Similarly, additional family managers can improve firm performance only if the CEO is also from the family because a non-family CEO would distract them from doing what is best for the firm (Minichilli et al. 2010).

Non-linear effects of family-TMT-involvement additionally point out that the variety of individual differences add up and that the effects of family managers depend on the composition of the TMT, particularly regarding how many other family managers are in the TMT (Mazzola et al. 2013; Sciascia & Mazzola 2008). Low levels of family-TMT-involvement may benefit firm performance because family managers induce stewardship and monitor the behavior of external managers. Likewise, external managers contribute by using their superior managerial abilities and ensuring that the family managers do not only serve family goals. However, at high levels of family involvement, the TMT is faced with greater family conflict. In addition, family managers have the power to pursue non-economic family-driven goals, and few or no external managers bring in superior managerial skills. Hence, family-TMT-involvement eventually becomes harmful for firm performance. Sciascia et al. (2013) propose a similar relationship for generational diversity and entrepreneurial orientation: when generational diversity is low, generational conflict is low and additional generations may provide additional insights. However, when generational diversity reaches high levels, the conflict outweighs the benefits of additional cognitive diversity.

In addition to the composite effects of individual differences, the individual strategic preferences of family managers may depend on their and the family's characteristics. First, tenure has been found to decrease differences between family and non-family CEOs, because non-family

CEOs develop psychological ownership over time and therefore act in a similar manner to family CEOs (Huybrechts et al. 2013). Second, from a family perspective, longevity goals indicate the family's desire for transgenerational control and should therefore be reflected in stewardship-like behavior of family managers (Kim and Gao 2013). Third, in acquired firms, the family puts less emphasis on its goal of socio-emotional wealth preservation and instead pursues economic goals, as it is not as attached as it is to non-acquired firms (Pazzaglia et al. 2013). Fourth, Vandemaele and Vancauteren (2015) found that socio-emotional wealth-driven goals are less important in later-stage firms, and thus family CEOs are more inclined to pay out dividends in these firms.

Future Research Avenues

This empirical evidence varies widely in its implications, perhaps because most articles focus on individual differences, either in strategic preferences or characteristics similar to those proposed in the upper echelons literature. However, as Hambrick (2007) points out, the explanatory power of research on top executives is better when the focus is on teams rather than individuals. Thus, family firm research can benefit from studying individual differences between family and non-family managers in light of their interrelations with the entire team of decision makers, which includes the TMT and family (Carpenter et al. 2004; Finkelstein et al. 2009; March & Simon 1993).

We next point out some areas for research that are based on upper echelons research and that address the study of such cross-level effects between family-TMT-involvement and the broader team of decision makers. First, upper echelons research has adopted many team processes to TMTs and extensively studied the interaction between the CEO and the TMT (Carpenter et al. 2004; Stoker, Grutterink & Kolk 2012). Applying such team processes and interfaces specifically to family firms can advance our understanding of how individual differences between family and non-family managers influence the TMTs of family firms, as we describe in the first research area. Second, upper echelons research has acknowledged the influence of the firm's board members and owners in supra-TMTs (Finkelstein et al. 2009). Extending the range of actors to the board and owners is particularly applicable to family firms, where owners often actively engage in the firm. The second research area, therefore, focuses on the supra-TMT as a potential area for further family firm research. Last, upper echelons research is essentially grounded in individual values (Hambrick & Mason 1984). Such individual values are often shaped within the family (Hambrick & Brandon 1988). Thus, family managers may transfer familial values into the firm as discussed in the third research area.

Research Area One: TMT Processes

TMT Decision Making

As the literature review revealed, some family firm studies have already acknowledged the importance of teams in decision making and have focused on processes in the family and the TMT rather than the strategic choices and the managerial ability of isolated actors. These studies have argued that family members are a potential source of diversity in family firm TMTs but have yielded contradictory results (Kraiczy et al. 2014; Ling & Kellermanns 2010). The upper echelons literature helps to clarify because it has already generated knowledge on TMT composition. As Harrison and Klein (2007) point out, diversity occurs as separation, variety, and disparity. Diversity as separation refers to differences in general attitudes and values; diversity as variety refers to differences in information, knowledge, and experiences; and diversity in disparity refers to differences in social assets and resources such as pay or status. The examples of family-induced diversity studied so far mainly focus on diversity as separation and variety, arguing that family managers have a family-oriented attitude and bring a certain set of information. Yet, the disparity dimension can add particularly valuable knowledge regarding family-TMT-involvement. Family managers often are more powerful than non-family managers because of their ownership stake and the legitimacy provided by their family status (Greve & Mitsuhashi 2007; Michiels et al. 2013; Mitchell, Agle, Chrisman & Spence 2011).

Minichilli et al. (2010) have conducted research in this area and found a u-shaped relationship between the ratio of family members in the TMT and firm performance. They argue that fault lines between family and non-family managers hinder information exchange in the TMT when both groups are present. Thus, the TMT's information exchange is best when the firm is managed solely by either family or non-family managers. Their results suggest that family firms benefit more from better cooperation among one group of managers than they suffer from the loss of diversity among both groups (Carpenter et al. 2004). Potentially, this is because the differences in status inhibit the TMT from utilizing the benefits of differences in separation or variety. Patel and Cooper (2014) provide further insights on this topic: their findings indicate that firm performance benefits from structural power equality between family and non-family TMT members. Firms with balanced power between both groups may experience improved interaction processes whereas imbalanced power can hinder effective decision processes.

Future research can take the work of upper echelon scholars as a starting point for studying team processes as mediators between family-TMT-involvement and firm outcomes. The upper echelons literature provides a rich base for family firm research. Nielsen (2010) provides a list of team processes as mediators between diversity and outcome, adding significant explanatory power to empirical studies on TMT heterogeneity. These processes include debate, collaborative effort, consensus, interpersonal conflict, agreement seeking, information sharing, and team dynamics. Furthermore, behavioral integration in the TMT might differ depending on the level of family managers (Simsek, Veiga, Lubatkin & Dino 2005). Given Ensley and Pearson's (2005) exploratory finding that such processes differ between TMTs with and without family members, pursuing this avenue is likely to return significant results and interesting findings.

Future research might study whether certain conditions lead to factional groups and fault lines caused by the disparity between family and non-family managers. For example, the existence of groups formed according to the managers' family status may be less likely when the family's ownership has been dispersed among several branches and family ties have weakened (Gersick, Davis, Hampton & Lansberg 1997). Future research might also consider whether the presence of certain family actors (e.g. the founder, the head of household, or the family's younger generation) increase the fault lines between family and non-family members.

CEO-TMT Interface

Another stream of research in the TMT literature has focused on the interface between the CEO and the TMT (e.g., Arendt, Priem & Ndofor 2005; Buyl et al. 2011; Cao, Simsek & Zhang 2010; Heyden, Reimer & Van Doorn in press; Ling et al. 2008). The central tenet of this research is that the CEO is the most powerful actor with regard to organizational decision making, but that organizational outcomes also are influenced by the TMT. Thus, one way by which the CEO's characteristics eventually influence organizational outcomes is the processes that those characteristics trigger within the TMT (Carmeli, Tishler & Edmondson 2012; Hambrick 2007; Reina, Zhang & Peterson 2014).

It also would be interesting to study the CEO-TMT interface with an explicit focus on the specifics of family firms. One avenue to study is whether family CEOs induce higher levels of trust in the TMT, which fosters open discussion of and learning from mistakes (Carmeli et al. 2012). Such trust may, for example, stem from the fact that family CEOs engage in fewer lay-offs and thus other TMT members are less afraid of losing their jobs because of mistakes (Le Breton-Miller & Miller 2006; Sirmon & Hitt 2003; Sraer & Thesmar 2007). Furthermore, the family CEOs potential desire for socio-emotional wealth preservation can result in long-term compensation and centralization of authority, both influencing the TMTs emphasis on entrepreneurial activities (Ling, Simsek, Lubatkin & Veiga 2008). Last, family firm research might consider transformational leadership. Colbert, Kristof-Brown, Bradley and Barrick (2008) argue that transformational leaders create congruence in the TMT regarding organizational goals. In particular, they understand and communicate the goals that are important to the organization. Furthermore, they use rhetorical strategies to ensure that followers attend to, understand, and remember the strategic direction. Finally, transformational CEOs behave consistently with their goals. Thus, if the CEO leads in a transformational way, then the other TMT members might perceive the CEO's family oriented goals as important and act in congruence with these goals (Reina et al. 2014).

Some research has focused on the interface between the CEO and specific actors (Menz 2012). Miller et al. (2014) already provided first evidence by studying co-CEO arrangements and found that family co-CEOs hamper the performance of non-family co-CEOs because family co-CEOs distract non-family ones from focusing on business activities. Future research might, for example, emphasize co-CEO arrangements and investigate whether co-CEO arrangements are beneficial to the family firm in some situations, e.g. in the case of low TMT diversity (Marcel 2010). Furthermore, such a study might investigate the specific division of labor. Bergfeld and Weber (2011) found that the family makes strategic decisions, whereas non-family managers are responsible for the day-to-day implementation of such decisions. It may be worthwhile to study the intention of co-CEO arrangements, as the family co-CEO's role can range from actively setting the strategy to only monitoring the non-family CEO.

Despite these rich research avenues, little research has investigated TMT processes in family firms. Future research on family-TMT-involvement can benefit from team-related research to understand the processes within the team. Such research can also benefit from studying how family and non-family CEOs interact with their teams to make strategic decisions.

Research Area Two: Family as Supra-TMT

Future research might continue to expand TMT research to the broader family by focusing on the interface between the family and the TMT. Empirical evidence supports the influence of family owners on the TMT. Even when they are not part of the TMT, family owners influence the firm's innovation strategy by advising instead of simply monitoring the TMT (Matzler, Veider, Hautz & Stadler 2015). To do this, family owners employ a variety of formal and informal governance mechanisms (van den Berghe & Carchon 2002), such as family councils and controlling boards (Michiels et al. 2013). In a qualitative study, Bergfeld and Weber (2011) found that owners use these bodies to align the firm's innovation strategy with family goals. In such an arrangement, family owners define the long-term growth paths but leave the execution to the firm's TMT. Entrepreneurial families potentially may be involved in setting the firm's strategy because their own economic and socio-emotional wealth is often exclusively tied to the firm (Carney 2005; Gersick et al. 1997). Hence, they have a strong motivation to ensure that the firm's strategy is aligned with family goals (Baysinger, Kosnik & Turk 1991; Lee & O'Neill 2003).

Studying the family as a supra-TMT may thus help to capture the entire range of influential actors at the apex of family firms. As shown in the literature review, the presence of family managers is potentially an indication of the family's goals. It would thus be worthwhile to more explicitly study how family owners' preferences differ, depending on whether they are actively involved in the firm's management. Furthermore, it might be worthwhile to investigate the family's structure. For example, one research stream studies family ownership dispersion and argues that ownership passes from a controlling owner stage to a sibling partnership to a cousin consortium (Gersick et al. 1997; Schulze, Lubatkin & Dino 2003). In the final stage, the firm is owned by many family owners who are, to a large extent, not employed in the firm (De Massis et al. 2013; Sciascia, Nordqvist, Mazzola & De Massis 2014). Along with the dispersion of ownership, the cognitive base and family network is extended, and families in dispersed ownership structures are more heterogeneous than families with concentrated ownership in one branch (Campopiano, De Massis, & Chirico 2014; Miller et al. 2014). Although this development is associated with more comprehensive information processing, it also increases goal and relational conflict within the family, particularly when not all branches are actively involved in the firm (Le Breton-Miller et al. 2011; Lubatkin, Schulze, Ling & Dino 2005; Miller et al. 2013; Spriggs, Yu, Deeds & Sorenson 2013).

Based on these findings, dispersion of family ownership appears to have effects similar to TMT heterogeneity; it increases the variety of perspectives but potentially leads to less effective decision-making processes (Carpenter et al. 2004; Certo, Lester, Dalton & Dalton 2006). As a consequence, conflicting empirical results regarding the relationship between family ownership dispersion and firm performance have been published (De Massis et al. 2013, De Massis, Kotlar, Campopiano & Cassia 2014; Miller et al. 2013; Miller et al. 2014). To provide more detail in this area, future research might consider how the interaction of family ownership dispersion and family-TMT-involvement affects team decision making processes (e.g., those described in research area one) and link family ownership dispersion to antecedents of firm performance (e.g., innovation strategy).

Research Area Three: Family Values

A topic deeply rooted in the original upper echelons framework of Hambrick and Mason (1984) are the values of top managers. These values may be of particular interest in family firms because the family is among the institutions that influence the values of individuals, especially during adolescence (Hambrick & Brandon 1988). Thereby, the family's values are one way by which family practices can influence the family's firm or at least the way future generations act within the firm.

Hambrick and Brandon (1988) developed a framework of six values specifically dedicated to studying individual values of top executives: collectivism, duty, rationality, novelty, materialism, and power. Collectivism refers to individuals who value the wholeness of humankind and of social systems and who regard and respect all people. Such individuals are likely to put group interests over their personal goals and to gather information from multiple sources (Ling, Zhao & Baron 2007; Simsek et al. 2005). Because they value their individual interests less, collectivistic family managers may consider how their decisions affect the entire group, which includes non-family stakeholders of the firm. Thus, collectivistic family managers are likely to act more as stewards of the firm than individualistic family managers (Corbetta & Salvato 2004). Further, by gathering input from various sources, collectivistic family managers may involve non-family managers in decision-making processes, reducing faultiness and reaping the benefits of exchanging knowledge from a variety of internal (family) and external perspectives (Ling & Kellermanns 2010). Yet, by consulting a variety of people, collectivistic family managers may need to reduce their decision-making speed, thus giving up one advantage of their powerful position (Casillas & Moreno 2010; Ling et al. 2007).

The other values proposed by Hambrick and Brandon (1988) can also influence the implications of family-TMT-involvement. Family cultures that value duty emphasize the integrity of reciprocal relationships, obligation, and loyalty. If such reciprocal relationships include non-family stakeholders, then these relationships may relate to decision-making processes in a similar manner as collectivism. However, if the family values reciprocal relationships mainly within the family, then family managers are likely to make decisions based on their family's interests. Such a family-oriented duty increases the salience of family goals over stewardship (Mitchell et al. 2011). If focused on one specific family branch, the duty may also increase the intra-family conflict arising from family-TMT-involvement (De Massis et al. 2013). For family members who are characterized by rationality, however, it is unlikely that they emphasize family needs when making decisions, as they take actions based on facts rather than emotions. Power-oriented family managers may deepen fault lines between non-family and family managers (especially themselves), thus potentially reducing the decision quality of the entire TMT (Minichilli et al. 2010). Materialistic family managers may make decisions based on economic rather than non-economic goals, which may reduce the importance of socio-emotional wealth as a reference point (Gómez-Mejía, Haynes, Nuñez-Nickel, Jacobson & Moyano-Fuentes 2007). Lastly, family managers who are open to novelty may also be more open to innovative activities, thereby overcoming the risk aversion often attributed to them (Huybrechts et al. 2013).

Family values may affect family-TMT-involvement. Therefore, these values should help explain how family managers influence their firm. The study of collectivism, in particular, can enhance family firm research as it can influence several mechanisms simultaneously, thereby providing a solid foundation upon which to argue for the implications of family managers on firm-level outcomes. Hence, future research might investigate family-TMT-involvement in light of family values.

Conclusion

Our literature review provides family firm scholars with an overview of the current knowledge on how family-TMT-involvement affects firm-level outcomes. The results show that researchers have investigated individual top manager differences mostly from the perspective of explicit strategic preferences, which was not part of the original upper echelons model (Finkelstein et al. 2009; Hambrick & Mason 1984). To further extend the field, family firm research can move beyond these individual differences and focus on the TMT and the broader family. First, studying team processes can help to improve our understanding of how family-specific mechanisms affect decision processes. Second, by considering not only the TMT but also family owners, family firm research may adopt the idea of a supra-TMT and capture the effects of a broader range of influential decision makers. Last, including family values may help to explain the conditions under which family-related mechanisms are more apparent and how the family influences the firm via family-TMT-involvement.

Appendix 5.A List of Relevant Articles

Author (Year)	Dependent Variable(s)	Coding Categories	Key Finding
Amore, Minichilli and Corbetta (2011)	Capital structure	Upper echelon–related characteristics	Family firms raise debt when appointing non-family CEOs, because they are more capable of bringing in growth opportunities than family CEOs. Given the family's reluctance toward external equity, they issue debt to finance growth opportunities.
Anderson and Reeb (2003)	Financial performance Market performance	Upper echelon–related characteristics Explicit strategic preferences	Family CEOs pursue family goals and are less capable of management than non-family CEOs, thereby producing inferior performance.
Andres (2008)	Financial performance Market performance	Explicit strategic preferences	Family firms outperform when the family is active in the firm's management, because that increases its relationship with the firm and thereby fosters stewardship behavior.
Barth, Gulbrandsen and Schonea (2005)	Productivity	Upper echelon–related characteristics	Non-family managers are positively related to productivity because they are selected from a larger talent pool and are therefore more capable.
Bennedsen, Nielsen, Pérez-González and Wolfenzon (2007)	Financial performance	Upper echelon–related characteristics	Family CEOs underperform because they lack of managerial ability.
Block (2010)	HR practices	Explicit strategic preferences	Because of their long history with the firm and their secure employment, family managers may behave as stewards and face less need to engage in downsizing in response to low profitability. Non-family managers, however, are evaluated on short-term profitability and therefore more often engage in downsizing.
Bloom and van Reenen (2007)	Management practices	Upper echelon–related characteristics	Family CEOs selected based on primogeniture employ poor management practices. However, when selected from a larger talent pool within the family, family CEOs manage their firm no worse than external CEOs.
Casillas and Moreno (2010)	Growth	Explicit strategic preferences TMT composition, interaction, and decision making processes	Family involvement facilitates the transformation of innovations into growth because of long-term orientation and centralized and speedy decision making. However, it dampens the transformation of risk-taking into growth because of the family's risk aversion.

Casillas, Moreno and Barbero (2011)	Entrepreneurial activities	TMT composition, interaction, and decision making processes Family as supra-TMT	Next-generational involvement increases cognitive diversity in the TMT and the family's focus on long-term orientation. It positively relates to entrepreneurial orientation in dynamic environments, and negatively in stable environments.
Chen, Chen and Cheng (2008)	Accounting choices	Explicit strategic preferences	Family CEOs issue less earnings forecasts but more early warnings, because they share the family's long-term investment horizon and transfer the family's reputation concerns to the firm.
Chrisman et al. (2007)	Financial performance	Explicit strategic preferences	Monitoring and incentives improve the performance of family-managed firms, indicating that family managers are agents of their own branch and need to be monitored.
Claver, Rienda and Quer (2009)	Internationalization	Upper echelon-related characteristics	Non-family managers introduce the knowledge and skills family firms need to pursue internationalization activities.
Cucculelli and Micucci (2008)	Financial performance	Upper echelon-related characteristics	An intra-family succession of the CEO position is often associated with decreased performance, because family successors are less capable of managing the firm. That decrease is particularly strong in competitive environments with high managerial complexity.
De Massis et al. (2013)	Financial performance	Family as supra-TMT	High levels of family involvement in management mitigate some disadvantages of dispersed family ownership, particularly the disadvantage that some family owners pursue opportunistic behaviors at the expense of others. High involvement also reduces the intra-family relationship conflicts arising from the fear of such behavior. Thus, family-TMT-involvement moderates the relationship of family ownership dispersion and firm performance.
Dekker, Lybaert, Steijvers and Depaire (2013a)	Financial performance	Upper echelon-related characteristics Explicit strategic preferences	Non-family managers positively influence firm performance when financial control systems are weak and when authority is decentralized. The reason is that non-family managers are more professional and do not need to be monitored, because they are interested in improving performance and need sufficient amounts of decision-making authority to work effectively.
Di Giuli, Caselli and Gatti (2011)	Financial management techniques	Upper echelon-related characteristics	The presence of an external CFO enhances the firm's willingness to make use of sophisticated financial products.

(Continued)

Author (Year)	Dependent Variable(s)	Coding Categories	Key Finding
Ensley and Pearson (2005)	TMT processes	TMT composition, interaction, and decision-making processes; Family as supra-TMT	The social system within the family is interlinked with TMT processes. Parental family TMTs, where leadership is clearly defined, exhibit higher potency, cohesion, shared cognition, and lower relationship conflict than non-family TMTs. However, family TMTs without such clear leadership show lower potency, cohesion, shared cognition, and higher relationship conflict than non-family TMTs. Their idea conflict is comparable to non-family TMTs and is greater than in parental TMTs.
Filbeck and Lee (2000)	Financial management techniques	Upper echelon-related characteristics	Firms with non-family CFOs engage more in calculating payback periods and average rates of return, whereas firms with family CFOs make more use of sensitivity analysis and cash management. Thus, it is unclear whether external CFOs provide more or less sophisticated financial management techniques to the family firm.
González, Guzmán, Pombo and Trujillo (2013)	Capital structure	Explicit strategic preferences	Family CEOs take less debt, because they transfer the family's risk aversion to the firm.
Gulbrandsen (2005)	HR practices	Family as supra-TMT	If the firm is family managed, then the family is inclined to maintain control over the firm and therefore less open to autonomous workgroups, job autonomy, subcontractors, and workers hired from external agencies.
Herrero (2011)	Productivity	Upper echelon-related characteristics; Explicit strategic preferences	In small firms with low complexity, family CEOs benefit from their deep firm knowledge and likewise monitor whether other employees act in accordance with family goals. This allows family CEOs to achieve superior efficiency compared to non-family CEOs.
Huybrechts et al. (2013)	Entrepreneurial activities	Explicit strategic preferences	Family CEOs take less risk than non-family CEOs, because they aim to reduce the family's risk. Yet, the effect holds only at low tenure, because over time, the non-family CEO adopts family goals as well.
Isakov and Weisskopf (2014)	Financial performance; Market performance	Upper echelon-related characteristics; Explicit strategic preferences	Family members have superior skills and stewardship incentives, which lead to higher performance.

Study	Dependent variable	Theoretical focus	Main findings
Kellermanns, Eddleston, Barnett and Pearson (2008)	Growth Entrepreneurial activities	TMT composition, interaction, and decision-making processes	Generational diversity fosters entrepreneurial behavior, because new generations bring new perspectives and perceive innovative activities as more important for the firm's long-term success. Entrepreneurial behavior thus mediates the relationship between generational diversity and growth.
Kim and Gao (2013)	Composite performance measure	Upper echelon-related characteristics Explicit strategic preferences	Family managers have superior social capital and behave as stewards if the family has longevity goals, producing superior performance. Otherwise, they rather nurture their family.
Kowalewski, Talavera and Stetsyuk (2010)	Financial performance	Upper echelon-related characteristics	In an unstable political and legal environment, firm performance benefits from a family CEO's social capital.
Kraiczy et al. (2014a)	Entrepreneurial activities	Upper echelon-related characteristics Explicit strategic preferences TMT composition, interaction, and decision-making processes Family as supra-TMT	High levels of family–TMT-involvement hinder the firm from transforming TMT innovation orientation into new product portfolio performance, because family managers lack skills and transfer the family's conflict and risk aversion to the firm. Yet, generational diversity has the opposite effect, as younger generations are more open to innovation and bring additional perspectives to the TMT.
Landry, Fortin and Callimaci (2013)	Capital structure	Explicit strategic preferences	Family CEOs conduct less asset leasing than non-family CEOs, because purchasing assets fosters their socioemotional wealth as a means to accumulate wealth for subsequent generations.
Le Breton-Miller et al. (2011)	Entrepreneurial activities	Explicit strategic preferences	Family managers extract resources to serve their family. This also applies to the involvement of multiple generations, because the later generations are less attached to the firm and more interested in extracting resources for private benefits.
Lin and Hu (2007)	Financial performance Market performance	Upper echelon-related characteristics Explicit strategic preferences	Family CEOs improve firm performance when the family has high cash flow rights; non-family CEOs improve firm performance under high managerial complexity.
Mehrotra, Morck, Shim and Wiwattanakantang (2013)	Financial performance Market performance Growth	Upper echelon-related characteristics Family as supra-TMT	Adopted heirs are beneficial for firm performance in Japan, because they usually are adopted for their talent. Furthermore, they foster competition within the family, thereby increasing the performance of blood heirs.
Miller and Le Breton-Miller (2011)	Entrepreneurial activities	Explicit strategic preferences	Family managers nurture the family and therefore avoid risks and extract resources, which hinder entrepreneurial activities.

(Continued)

Author (Year)	Dependent Variable(s)	Coding Categories	Key Finding
Miller, Le Breton-Miller and Lester (2011)	Market performance Entrepreneurial activities	Explicit strategic preferences	Family CEOs take the role of family nurturers and therefore pursue non-growth strategies.
Miller et al. (2014)	Financial performance	Upper echelon-related characteristics Explicit strategic preferences TMT composition, interaction, and decision-making processes	The performance difference between family and non-family CEOs depends on a complex configuration. In particular, non-family CEOs outperform under dispersed family ownership, where the family can monitor the non-family CEO and benefits from his or her superior managerial capability. However, when the ownership is concentrated, the non-family CEO underperforms, because he or she is then not well-monitored and pursues self-serving goals. Further, he or she underperforms when a co-CEO arrangement with a family member distracts him from business activities.
Miller et al. (2013)	Financial performance	Upper echelon-related characteristics Explicit strategic preferences	Family CEOs outperform non-family CEOs in small firms with concentrated ownership, because their managerial ability is sufficient and the concentrated ownership structure limits intra-family conflict. However, non-family CEOs outperform in large firms with dispersed ownership, because the family CEO suffers from inferior ability, whereas intra-family conflict causes him or her to extract resources for family reasons. In small firms with dispersed ownership and large firms with concentrated ownership, the superior/inferior managerial ability of family CEOs are offset by their desire to act in the firm's best interest or to nurture the family, respectively.
Minichilli et al. (2010)	Financial performance	Explicit strategic preferences TMT composition, interaction, and decision-making processes	Family CEOs outperform non-family CEOs because of their stewardship behavior. This is particularly strong when the firm is not listed, because the family CEO then does not face market pressure. Further, a U-shape relationship exists between the family–TMT-ratio and performance, because of faultlines in the case of a mix with both family and non-family managers. Last, the family–TMT-ratio is most positively related to performance if the CEO is also from the family and the firm is not listed, which is the best scenario for stewardship behavior. In contrast, if the firm is listed and the CEO is not from the family, then the family–TMT-ratio negatively relates to performance, because family managers then may not behave as stewards.

Study	Outcome	Dimension	Findings
Naldi et al. (2013)	Financial performance	Explicit strategic preferences; Family as supra-TMT	The presence of a family CEO is a choice the family makes in order to preserve its SEW. The family CEO's activities to preserve SEW are in turn beneficial for performance in industrial sectors characterized by informal rules and long-term relationships, and are detrimental to performance in listed firms.
Oswald, Muse and Rutherford (2009)	Growth	Explicit strategic preferences	Family managers decrease the performance of their firm, because they pursue family-oriented non-economic goals.
Pazzaglia et al. (2013)	Accounting choices	Explicit strategic preferences	Family CEOs in acquired firms conduct earnings management but refrain from earnings management in non-acquired firms. Thus, family CEOs nurture the family in acquired firms and preserve their SEW in non-acquired firms.
Randøy and Goel (2003)	Financial performance; Market performance	Explicit strategic preferences	Family firms' performance suffers from family CEOs in contexts characterized by strong monitoring, because family managers monitor non-family employees and ensure that they pursue family goals. Thus, the governance mechanism is redundant here. In contrast, family firms benefit from family CEOs in contexts of weak monitoring.
Sciascia & Mazzola (2008)	Composite performance measure	Upper-echelon–related characteristics; Explicit strategic preferences; TMT composition, interaction, and decision-making processes; Family as supra-TMT	Stewardship behavior by family managers is salient at low levels of family–TMT-involvement, while inferior ability, family conflict, and non-economic family goals are salient at high levels of family–TMT-involvement, producing an inverse U-shaped effect. Yet, the findings show that the effect of family–TMT-involvement on performance is always negative, arguing against the stewardship predictions for low levels of family–TMT-involvement.
Sciascia, Mazzola and Chirico (2013)	Entrepreneurial activities	TMT composition, interaction, and decision-making processes; Family as supra-TMT	At low levels, generational diversity is positively associated with entrepreneurial orientation, because it induces multiple perspectives. Yet, the relationship turns around at high levels of generational diversity, because family relationships become more complicated.
Sirmon et al. (2008)	Financial performance; Internationalization; Entrepreneurial activities	Explicit strategic preferences; Family as supra-TMT	Family CEOs bring diverse family voices to the table when making decisions and make decisions based on the family's long-term horizon. Therefore, their presence reduces concerns about imitability when deciding on R&D investments or internationalization, thereby improving firm performance.

(Continued)

Author (Year)	Dependent Variable(s)	Coding Categories	Key Finding
Srae and Thesmar (2007)	Financial performance Market performance Growth HR practices Capital structure	Upper-echelon-related characteristics Explicit strategic preferences	Non-family CEOs reduce cost of capital, because they bring in business expertise. Yet, family CEOs need to pay lower wages, because they seek transfer the family's long-term orientation to the firm and therefore engage less in hiring and firing activities. Overall, family CEOs outperform non-family CEOs.
Stockmans et al. (2010)	Accounting choices	Explicit strategic preferences	Descendant family CEOs engage in less earnings management than founder CEOs, because family goals do not require earnings management in the descendant stage. Non-family CEOs also engage in less earnings management, because they have no interest in doing so.
Vandemaele and Vancauteren (2015)	Capital structure	Explicit strategic preferences	Family CEOs pay out less dividends than non-family CEOs, because retaining resources in the firm helps them to preserve the family's SEW. This tendency is stronger when the board is also dominated by the family and the family CEO's power increases. It is even stronger in early generational firms, where the family puts more emphasis on its SEW and the family CEO therefore pursues this family goal.
Westhead and Howorth (2006)	Composite performance measure	Upper-echelon-related characteristics Explicit strategic preferences	Family CEOs pursue family goals and are less capable of management than non-family CEOs, thereby producing inferior financial performance.
Wu, Chua and Chrisman (2007)	Capital structure	Explicit strategic preferences	Family managers prefer debt over public equity, because public equity implies a strong loss of control and therefore conflicts with family goals.
Yang (2010)	Accounting choices	Explicit strategic preferences	Family CEOs engage less in earnings management than non-family CEOs, because they do not need to signal short-term results and instead act in alignment with the family's long-term goals.
Zahra et al. (2007)	Entrepreneurial activities	Explicit strategic preferences TMT composition, interaction, and decision-making processes Family as supra-TMT	Higher levels of family involvement increase the number of managers with a strong sense of obligation to the firm. Generational diversity further signals the appreciation of multiple perspectives in the firm, the younger generation's commitment to the firm, and that the family has overcome some of its intra-generational conflict. Both types of management leverage the benefits of knowledge sharing and strengthen its effect on technological capabilities.

Appendix 5.B Mapping of Dependent Variables and Upper-Echelons Themes

Dependent Variable	Individual Level		Team Level
	Upper-Echelon-Related Characteristics	*Explicit Strategic Preferences*	*TMT Composition, Interaction, and Decision-Making Processes*	*Family as Supra-TMT*
Accounting choices		*Earnings management* • Family managers conduct earnings management to nurture their family financially • Family managers conduct earnings management to preserve their SEW • Family managers refrain from earnings management because it harms their family's SEW • Family managers conduct less earnings management because they do not need to signal short-term results *Disclosure* • Family managers transfer the family's reputation concerns to the firm and therefore issue more early warnings		
Capital structure	• Non-family managers bring in more ideas for growth, causing the family to increase debt • Non-family managers improve the capital structure, because they have more financial expertise	• Family managers incur less debt, because debt is potentially risky for the family • Family managers prefer debt over equity, because the family loses control with equity • Family managers would rather purchase than lease assets, because that enhances their SEW • Family managers pay out less dividends, because internal funding helps to preserve the family's SEW		

(Continued)

Dependent Variable	Individual Level		Team Level	
	Upper-Echelon-Related Characteristics	*Explicit Strategic Preferences*	*TMT Composition, Interaction, and Decision-Making Processes*	*Family as Supra-TMT*
Entrepreneurial activities	• Family managers lack the skill to transform innovation orientation into new products	• Family managers transfer the family's long-term orientation to the firm • Family managers are strongly committed to the firm, which benefits the firm's technological capabilities • Family managers extract resources for the family, reducing the resources available for innovation • Family managers transfer the family's risk aversion to the firm, hindering innovation	• Family managers make decisions more centralized, fostering the transformation of innovation into growth • Younger generations bring in multiple perspectives, fostering innovation	• Family managers bring more family voices to the table, which improves relationships of the TMT and the family and increases the family's willingness to innovate • Younger generations in the business signal that the family has overcome some of its intra-family conflict. Their presence is therefore beneficial for innovation. • Young generations involved in the firm might complicate family relationships and be detrimental to innovation • Family managers transfer family conflict to the TMT, hindering innovation
Growth		• Family managers transfer the family's risk aversion to the firm • Family managers transfer the family's long-term orientation to the firm	• Younger generations bring in new ideas for innovation, which eventually leads to growth	

HR policies		• Family managers face no pressure of losing their jobs and therefore do not engage in downsizing to increase performance measures • Family managers engage in less hiring and firing activities because of their long-term orientation • Family managers support the family's control orientation and therefore are less open to autonomous workgroups, subcontractors, and temporary workers from external agencies	
Internationalization	Non-family managers bring in the knowledge and skills the firm needs to pursue international activities	• Family managers benefit from the family's long-term orientation, potentially reducing concerns about the risks of internationalization	• Family managers bring more family voices to the table, which improves relationships in the family and increases its willingness to pursue international activities
Management practices	• Family managers selected from a small talent pool employ poor management practices		
Performance (financial/ market/ productivity/ composite)	• Family managers provide social capital in informal environments • Family CEOs have superior knowledge of the firm	• Family managers are interested in maximizing performance • Family managers transfer the family's long-term orientation to the firm, improving long-term performance	• Family managers bring more family voices to the table, which improves relationships in the family and increases firm performance

(*Continued*)

Dependent Variable	Individual Level		Team Level	
	Upper-Echelon-Related Characteristics	Explicit Strategic Preferences	TMT Composition, Interaction, and Decision-Making Processes	Family as Supra-TMT
	• Family managers lack the ability to maximize performance, because they are selected from a small talent pool	• Family managers transfer the family's SEW to the firm, which is beneficial in informal environments and detrimental in formal ones • Family managers pursue non-economic goals, hampering firm performance		• Family branches might mistrust other branches less if those branches are represented in the TMT • Family managers might be in conflict with other family branches if they are involved in the TMT and nurture their own branch
TMT processes (explicitly measured)			• TMTs with family influence exhibit higher levels of potency, cohesion, and shared cognition	• TMTs with family influence might suffer from relational conflict if there is no clear family member with decision authority

References

Amore, M. D., Minichilli, A., & Corbetta, G. (2011) 'How do managerial successions shape corporate financial policies in family firms?,' *Journal of Corporate Finance*, 17(4), 1016–1027.

Anderson, R. C., & Reeb, D. M. (2003) 'Founding-family ownership and firm performance: Evidence from the S&P 500,' *Journal of Finance*, 58(3), 1301–1328.

Andres, C. (2008) 'Large shareholders and firm performance - An empirical examination of founding-family ownership,' *Journal of Corporate Finance*, 14(4), 431–445.

Arendt, L. A., Priem, R. L., & Ndofor, H. A. (2005) 'A CEO-adviser model of strategic decision making,' *Journal of Management*, 31(5), 680–699.

Bammens, Y., Voordeckers, W., & van Gils, A. (2011) 'Boards of directors in family businesses: A literature review and research agenda,' *International Journal of Management Reviews*, 13(2), 134–152.

Baysinger, B. D., Kosnik, R. D., & Turk, T. A. (1991) 'Effects of board and ownership structure on corporate R&D strategy,' *Academy of Management Journal*, 34(1), 205–214.

Bergfeld, M.-M. H., & Weber, F.-M. (2011) 'Dynasties of innovation: Highly performing German family firms and the owners' role for innovation,' *International Journal of Entrepreneurship and Innovation Management*, 13(1), 80–94.

Berrone, P., Cruz, C. C., & Gómez-Mejía, L. R. (2012) 'Socioemotional wealth in family firms: theoretical dimensions, assessment approaches, and agenda for future research,' *Family Business Review*, 25(3), 258–279.

Block, J. (2010) 'Family management, family ownership, and downsizing: Evidence from S&P 500 firms,' *Family Business Review*, 23(2), 109–130.

Block, J., Jaskiewicz, P., & Miller, D. (2011) 'Ownership versus management effects on performance in family and founder companies: A Bayesian reconciliation,' *Journal of Family Business Strategy*, 2(4), 232–245.

Bloom, N., & van Reenen, J. (2007) 'Measuring and explaining management practices across firms and countries,' *Administrative Science Quarterly*, 122(4), 1351–1408.

Buyl, T., Boone, C., Hendriks, W., & Matthyssens, P. (2011) 'Top management team functional diversity and firm performance: The moderating role of CEO characteristics,' *Journal of Management Studies*, 48(1), 151–177.

Campopiano, G., De Massis, A., & Chirico, F. (2014) 'Firm philanthropy in small- and medium-sized family firms: The effects of family involvement in ownership and management,' *Family Business Review*, 27(3), 244–258.

Cao, Q., Simsek, Z., & Zhang, H. (2010) 'Modelling the joint impact of the CEO and the TMT on organizational ambidexterity,' *Journal of Management Studies*, 47(7), 1272–1296.

Carmeli, A., Tishler, A., & Edmondson, A. C. (2012) 'CEO relational leadership and strategic decision quality in top management teams: The role of team trust and learning from failure,' *Strategic Organization*, 10(1), 31–54.

Carney, M. (2005) 'Corporate governance and competitive advantage in family-controlled firms,' *Entrepreneurship: Theory & Practice*, 29(3), 249–265.

Carpenter, M. A., Geletkanycz, M. A., & Sanders, G. W. (2004) 'Upper echelons research revisited: Antecedents, elements, and consequences of top management team composition,' *Journal of Management*, 30(6), 749–778.

Casillas, J. C., & Moreno, A. M. (2010) 'The relationship between entrepreneurial orientation and growth: The moderating role of family involvement,' *Entrepreneurship & Regional Development*, 22(3–4), 265–291.

Casillas, J. C., Moreno, A. M., & Barbero, J. L. (2011) 'Entrepreneurial orientation of family firms: Family and environmental dimensions,' *Journal of Family Business Strategy*, 2(2), 90–100.

Certo, S. T., Lester, R. H., Dalton, C. M., & Dalton, D. R. (2006) 'Top management teams, strategy and financial performance: A meta-analytic examination,' *Journal of Management Studies*, 43(4), 813–839.

Chrisman, J. J., Chua, J. H., Kellermanns, F. W., & Chang, E. P. (2007) 'Are family managers agents or stewards? An exploratory study in privately held firms,' *Journal of Business Research*, 60(10), 1030–1038.

Chrisman, J. J., Chua, J. H., & Sharma, P. (2005) 'Trends and directions in the development of a strategic management theory of the family firm,' *Entrepreneurship: Theory & Practice*, 29(5), 555–575.

Chua, J. H., Chrisman, J. J., Steier, L. P., & Rau, S. B. (2012) 'Sources of heterogeneity in family firms: An introduction,' *Entrepreneurship: Theory & Practice*, 36(6), 1103–1113.

Claver, E., Rienda, L., & Quer, D. (2009) 'Family firms' international commitment: The influence of family-related factors,' *Family Business Review*, *22*(2), 125–135.

Colbert, A. E., Kristof-Brown, A. L., Bradley, B. H., & Barrick, M. R. (2008) 'CEO transformational leadership: The role of goal importance congruence in top management teams,' *Academy of Management Journal*, *51*(1), 81–96.

Corbetta, G., & Salvato, C. (2004) 'Self-serving or self-actualizing? Models of man and agency costs in different types of family firms: A commentary on "Comparing the agency costs of family and non-family firms: Conceptual issues and exploratory evidence,"' *Entrepreneurship: Theory & Practice*, *28*(4), 355–362.

Cucculelli, M., & Marchionne, F. (2012) 'Market opportunities and owner identity: Are family firms different,' *Journal of Corporate Finance*, *18*(3), 476–495.

De Massis, A., Frattini, F., & Lichtenthaler, U. (2013) 'Research on technological innovation in family firms: Present debates and future directions,' *Family Business Review*, *26*(1), 10–31.

De Massis, A., Kotlar, J., Campopiano, G., & Cassia, L. (2013) 'Dispersion of family ownership and the performance of small-to-medium size private family firms,' *Journal of Family Business Strategy*, *4*(3), 166–175.

De Massis, A., Kotlar, J., Campopiano, G., & Cassia, L. (2014) 'The impact of family involvement on SMEs' performance: Theory and evidence,' *Journal of Small Business Management*, doi:10.1111/jsbm.12093.

De Massis, A., Sharma, P., Chua, J. H., & Chrisman, J. J. (2011) '*Family business studies: An annotated bibliography*,' Northhampton, MA: Edward Elgar.

Dekker, J., Lybaert, N., Steijvers, T., & Depaire, B. (2013) 'The effect of family business professionalization as a multidimensional construct on firm performance,' *Journal of Small Business Management*, doi:10.1111/jsbm.12082.

Di Giuli, A., Caselli, S., & Gatti, S. (2011) 'Are small family firms financially sophisticated?,' *Journal of Banking & Finance*, *35*(11), 2931–2944.

Ensley, M. D., & Pearson, A. W. (2005) 'An exploratory comparison of the behavioral dynamics of top management teams in family and nonfamily new ventures: Cohesion, conflict, potency, and consensus,' *Entrepreneurship: Theory & Practice*, *29*(3), 267–284.

Filbeck, G., & Lee, S. (2000) 'Financial management techniques in family businesses,' *Family Business Review*, *13*(3), 201–216.

Finkelstein, S., Hambrick, D. C., & Cannella, A. A. (2009) *Strategic leadership: Theory and research on executives, top management teams, and boards. Strategic management series*, New York: Oxford University Press.

Gersick, K. E., Davis, J. A., Hampton, M. M., & Lansberg, I. (1997) *Generation to generation: Life cycles of the family business*, Boston, MA: Harvard Business School Press.

Gómez-Mejía, L. R., Haynes, K. T., Nuñez-Nickel, M., Jacobson, K. J. L., & Moyano-Fuentes, J. (2007) 'Socioemotional wealth and business risks in family-controlled firms: Evidence from Spanish olive oil mills,' *Administrative Science Quarterly*, *52*(1), 106–137.

Greve, H. R., & Mitsuhashi, H. (2007) 'Power and glory: Concentrated power in top management teams,' *Organization Studies*, *28*(8), 1197–1221.

Gulbrandsen, T. (2005) 'Flexibility in Norwegian family-owned enterprises,' *Family Business Review*, *18*(1), 57–76.

Hambrick, D. C. (2007) 'Upper Echelons theory: An update,' *Academy of Management Review*, *32*(2), 334–343.

Hambrick, D. C., & Brandon, G. L. (1988) Executive values. In D. C. Hambrick (Ed.), *Strategic management policy and planning: Vol. 2. The executive effect: Concepts and methods for studying top managers* (pp. 3–34), Greenwich, CT: Jai Press.

Hambrick, D. C., & Mason, P. A. (1984) 'Upper echelons: The organization as a reflection of its top managers,' *Academy of Management Review*, *9*(2), 193–206.

Harrison, D. A., & Klein, K. J. (2007) 'What's the difference? Diversity constructs as separation, variety, or disparity in organizations,' *Academy of Management Review*, *32*(4), 1199–1228.

Herrero, I. (2011) 'Agency costs, family ties, and firm efficiency,' *Journal of Management*, *37*(3), 887–904.

Heyden, M. L. M., Reimer, M., & Van Doorn, S. (in press) 'Innovating beyond the horizon: CEO career horizon, top management composition, and R&D intensity,' *Human Resource Management*.

Huybrechts, J., Voordeckers, W., & Lybaert, N. (2013) 'Entrepreneurial risk taking of private family firms: The influence of a nonfamily CEO and the moderating effect of CEO tenure,' *Family Business Review*, *26*(2), 161–179.

Kellermanns, F. W., Eddleston, K. A., Barnett, T., & Pearson, A. W. (2008) 'An exploratory study of family member characteristics and involvement: Effects on entrepreneurial behavior in the family firm,' *Family Business Review*, 21(1), 1–14.

Kim, Y., & Gao, F. Y. (2013) 'Does family involvement increase business performance? Family-longevity goals' moderating role in Chinese family firms,' *Journal of Business Research*, 66(2), 265–274.

Kowalewski, O., Talavera, O., & Stetsyuk, I. (2010) 'Influence of family involvement in management and ownership on firm performance: Evidence from Poland,' *Family Business Review*, 23(1), 45–59.

Kraiczy, N. D., Hack, A., & Kellermanns, F. W. (2014) 'New product portfolio performance in family firms,' *Journal of Business Research*, 67(6), 1065–1073.

Landry, S., Fortin, A., & Callimaci, A. (2013) 'Family firms and the lease decision,' *Journal of Family Business Strategy*, 4(3), 176–187.

Le Breton-Miller, I., & Miller, D. (2006) 'Why do some family businesses out-compete? Governance, long-term orientations, and sustainable capability,' *Entrepreneurship: Theory & Practice*, 30(6), 731–746.

Le Breton-Miller, I., Miller, D., & Lester, R. H. (2011) 'Stewardship or agency? A social embeddedness reconciliation of conduct and performance in public family businesses,' *Organization Science*, 22(3), 704–721.

Lee, P. M., & O'Neill, H. (2003) 'Ownership structures and R&D investments of U.S. and Japanese firms: Agency and stewardship perspectives,' *Academy of Management Journal*, 46(2), 212–225.

Lin, S.-h., & Hu, S.-y. (2007) 'A family member or professional management? The choice of a CEO and its impact on performance,' *Corporate Governance: An International Review*, 15(6), 1348–1362.

Ling, Y., & Kellermanns, F. W. (2010) 'The effects of family firm specific sources of TMT diversity: The moderating role of information exchange frequency,' *Journal of Management Studies*, 47(2), 322–344.

Ling, Y., Simsek, Z., Lubatkin, M. H., & Veiga, J. F. (2008) 'Transformational leadership's role in promotiong corporate entrepreneurship: Examining the CEO-TMT interface,' *Academy of Management Journal*, 51(3), 557–576.

Ling, Y., Zhao, H., & Baron, R. A. (2007) 'Influence of founder-CEOs' personal values on firm performance: Moderating effects of firm age and size?,' *Journal of Management*, 33(5), 673–696.

Livingston, L. (2007) 'Control sales in family firms,' *Family Business Review*, 20(1), 49–64.

Lubatkin, M. H., Schulze, W. S., Ling, Y., & Dino, R. N. (2005) 'The effects of parental altruism on the governance of family-managed firms,' *Journal of Organizational Behavior*, 26(3), 313–330.

Lubatkin, M. H., Simsek, Z., Ling, Y., & Veiga, J. F. (2006) 'Ambidexterity and performance in small- to medium-sized firms: The pivotal role of top management team behavioral integration,' *Journal of Management*, 32(5), 646–672.

Marcel, J. J. (2010) 'Why top management team characteristics matter when employing a Chief Operating Officer: A strategic contingency perspective,' *Strategic Management Journal*, 30(6), 647–658.

March, J. G., & Simon, H. A. (1993) *Organizations* (2nd ed), Cambridge, Mass., USA: Blackwell.

Matzler, K., Veider, V., Hautz, J., & Stadler, C. (2015) 'The impact of family ownership, management, and governance on innovation,' *Journal of Product Innovation Management*, 32(3), 319–333.

Mazzola, P., Sciascia, S., & Kellermanns, F. W. (2013) 'Non-linear effects of family sources of power on performance,' *Journal of Business Research*, 66(4), 568–574.

McConaughy, D. L. (2000) 'Family CEOs vs. nonfamily CEOs in the family-controlled firm: An examination of the level and sensitivity of pay to performance,' *Family Business Review*, 13(2), 121–131.

Menz, M. (2012) 'Functional top management teams: A review, synthesis, and research agenda,' *Journal of Management*, 38(1), 45–80.

Michiels, A., Voordeckers, W., Lybaert, N., & Steijvers, T. (2013) 'CEO compensation in private family firms: Pay-for-performance and the moderating role of ownership and management,' *Family Business Review*, 26(2), 140–160.

Miller, D., Le Breton-Miller, I., Minichilli, A., Corbetta, G., & Pittino, D. (2014) 'When do non-family CEOs outperform in family firms? Agency and behavioral agency perspectives,' *Journal of Management Studies*, 51(4), 547–572.

Miller, D., Minichilli, A., & Corbetta, G. (2013) 'Is family leadership always beneficial?,' *Strategic Management Journal*, 34(5), 553–571.

Minichilli, A., Corbetta, G., & MacMillan, I. C. (2010) 'Top management teams in family-controlled companies: "Familiness," "faultlines," and their impact on financial performance,' *Journal of Management Studies*, 47(2), 205–222.

Mitchell, R. K., Agle, B. R., Chrisman, J. J., & Spence, L. J. (2011) 'Toward a theory of stakeholder salience in family firms,' *Business Ethics Quarterly*, *21*(2), 235–255.

Naldi, L., Cennamo, C., Guido, C., & Gómez-Mejía, L. R. (2013) 'Preserving socioemotional wealth in family firms: Asset or liability? The moderating role of business context,' *Entrepreneurship: Theory & Practice*, *37*(6), 1341–1360.

Nielsen, S. (2010) 'Top management team diversity: A review of theories and methodologies,' *International Journal of Management Reviews*, *12*(3), 301–316.

Patel, P. C., & Cooper, D. (2014) 'Structural power equality between family and non-family TMT members and the performance of family firms,' *Academy of Management Journal*, *57*(6), 1624–1649.

Pazzaglia, F., Mengoli, S., & Sapienza, E. (2013) 'Earnings quality in acquired and nonacquired family firms: A socioemotional wealth perspective,' *Family Business Review*, *26*(4), 374–386.

Pukall, T. J., & Calabro, A. (2014) 'The internationalization of family firms: A critical review and integrative model,' *Family Business Review*, *27*(2), 103–125.

Reimer, M., Schäffer, U., & Tretbar, T. (2015) Upper Echelons in family firms: What we know and still have to learn about family-TMT-involvement, *unpublished working paper*.

Reina, C. S., Zhang, Z., & Peterson, S. J. (2014) 'CEO grandiose narcissism and firm performance: The role of organizational identification,' *The Leadership Quarterly*, *25*(5), 958–971.

Salvato, C., & Moores, K. (2010) 'Research on accounting in family firms: Past accomplishments and future challenges,' *Family Business Review*, *23*(3), 193–215.

Schulze, W. S., Lubatkin, M. H., & Dino, R. N. (2003) 'Exploring the agency consequences of ownership dispersion among the directors of private family firms,' *Academy of Management Journal*, *46*(2), 179–194.

Sciascia, S., & Mazzola, P. (2008) 'Family involvement in ownership and management: Exploring nonlinear effects on performance,' *Family Business Review*, *21*(4), 331–345.

Sciascia, S., Mazzola, P., & Chirico, F. (2013) 'Generational involvement in the top management team of family firms: Exploring nonlinear effects on entrepreneurial orientation,' *Entrepreneurship: Theory & Practice*, *37*(1), 69–85.

Sciascia, S., Nordqvist, M., Mazzola, P., & De Massis, A. (2014) 'Family ownership and R&D intensity in small- and medium-sized firms,' *Journal of Product Innovation Management*, doi: 10.1111/jpim.12204.

Short, J. C. (2009) 'The art of writing a review article,' *Journal of Management*, *35*(6), 1312–1317.

Simsek, Z., Veiga, J. F., Lubatkin, M. H., & Dino, R. N. (2005) 'Modeling the multilevel determinants of top management team behavioral integration,' *Academy of Management Journal*, *48*(1), 69–84.

Sirmon, D. G., Arregle, J. L., Hitt, M. A., & Webb, J. W. (2008) 'The role of family influence in firms' strategic responses to threat of imitation,' *Entrepreneurship: Theory & Practice*, *32*(6), 979–998.

Sirmon, D. G., & Hitt, M. A. (2003) 'Managing resources: Linking unique resources, management, and wealth creation in family firms,' *Entrepreneurship: Theory & Practice*, *27*(4), 339–358.

Smith, B. F., & Amoako-Adu, B. (1999) 'Management succession and financial performance of family controlled firms,' *Journal of Corporate Finance*, *5*(4), 341–368.

Spriggs, M., Yu, A., Deeds, D., & Sorenson, R. L. (2013) 'Too many cooks in the kitchen: Innovative capacity, collaborative network orientation, and performance in small family businesses,' *Family Business Review*, *26*(1), 32–50.

Sraer, D., & Thesmar, D. (2007) 'Performance and behavior of family firms: Evidence from the french stock market,' *Journal of the European Economic Association*, *5*(4), 709–751.

Stockmans, A., Lybaert, N., & Voordeckers, W. (2010) 'Socioemotional wealth and earnings management in private family firms,' *Family Business Review*, *23*(3), 280–294.

Stoker, J. I., Grutterink, H., & Kolk, N. J. (2012) 'Do transformational CEOs always make the difference? The role of TMT feedback seeking behavior,' *The Leadership Quarterly*, *23*(3), 582–592.

van den Berghe, L. A. A., & Carchon, S. (2002) 'Corporate governance practices in Flemish family business,' *Corporate Governance: An International Review*, *10*(3), 225–245.

Vandekerkhof, P., Steijvers, T., Hendriks, W., & Voordeckers, W. (2014) 'The effect of organizational characteristics on the appointment of nonfamily managers in private family firms: the moderating role of socioemotional wealth,' *Family Business Review*, doi:10.1177/0894486513514274.

Vandemaele, S., & Vancauteren, M. (2015) 'Nonfinancial goals, governance, and dividend payout in private family firms,' *Journal of Small Business Management*, *53*(1), 166–182.

Wu, Z., Chua, J. H., & Chrisman, J. J. (2007) 'Effects of family ownership and management on small business equity financing,' *Journal of Business Venturing*, *22*(6), 875–895.

Yang, M. L. (2010) 'The impact of controlling families and family CEOs on earnings management,' *Family Business Review*, *23*(3), 266–279.

Yu, A., Lumpkin, G. T., Sorenson, R. L., & Brigham, K. H. (2012) 'The landscape of family business outcomes: A summary and numerical taxonomy of dependent variables,' *Family Business Review*, *25*(1), 33–57.

Zahra, S. A., Neubaum, D. O., & Larraneta, B. (2007) 'Knowledge sharing and technological capabilities: The moderating role of family involvement,' *Journal of Business Research*, *60*(10), 1070–1079.

6

FAMILINESS, SOCIOEMOTIONAL WEALTH, AND INTERNATIONALIZATION OF FAMILY FIRMS

A Review of Capabilities and Motivations in Different Modes of Internationalization

Anne Sluhan

Introduction

Family-owned firms have unique advantages for internationalization including reduced agency costs for speedy and flexible decision-making, patient and survivability capital for long-term investment, social capital for easier and lower cost access to external finance, and resources including, but not limited to, formal and informal networks. Despite these advantages, scholars suggest that the afore-mentioned advantages are undermined by family owners' conservative attitudes toward investment diversification, a lack of professional experience on international markets, less willingness to hire out-side professional managers, less willingness to utilize professional training, and a reluctance to secure external financial resources for fear of losing family control of the firm (Banalieva & Eddleston, 2011).

Due to the prevalence of family-controlled companies around the world, it is relevant to focus on the ways in which they internationalize. Indeed, the global phenomenon of family firm internation-alization offers researchers a rich field of inquiry not only due to the dominance of family firms on a global scale but also since they have been deemed to behave differently than non-family businesses.

Thus far, empirical studies have found that family ownership is generally unrelated to the degree of internationalization (see meta-analysis by Arregle, Duran, Hitt, & van Essen, 2014; and reviews by Kontinen & Ojala, 2010; and Pukall & Calabrò, 2013). While these studies provide valuable insights on the relationship between family ownership and the degree of international-ization, the varied capabilities and motivations for family firms to engage in internationalization are not specifically mentioned. Since the decision to internationalize is a critical, complex, and risk-creating strategic decision for any firm, it is a relevant topic for the literature to better understand the ways in which family firms internationalize compared with other types of firms, not least because of the prevalence of the family firm's dominant ownership and governance structure around the world (Arregle, Naldi, Nordqvist, & Hitt, 2012). Yet in current discussions in the international business literature related to the impact of family ownership attributes and their influence on internationalization, results seem to be inconsistent.

Internationalization requires a firm to engage in a risk-heavy and uncertainty-rich strategic decision-making process, and since scholarly work up to this point suggests that family firm internationalization is undermined by a tendency of this type of firm to act conservatively, this chapter intends to reconcile these seemingly contrary notions of family firm internationalization by reviewing the extant literature. This chapter: 1) presents the relevance of family firms in organizational studies, 2) describes how the literature considers family firms to be differentiated from non-family firms, 3) investigates how this differentiation affects family firm behavior – in particular with regard to family firm motivations and capabilities in the process of internationalization, 4) reviews the extant literature on family firm motivations and capabilities vis à vis internationalization, and 5) structures a literature review within a frame of varying entry modes. This chapter contributes to the family firm literature in that it presents the extant empirical work on family firm internationalization by focusing on the various motivations and capabilities of family firms when choosing entry mode. Finally, as its main contribution to the literature, this chapter highlights some unresolved issues in the field of family firm internationalization. Before specifying motivations and capabilities for internationalization, the next section presents the relevance of family firms to the field of organizational studies.

Family Firms as a Dominant Organizational Form

Family firms are defined as an organizational form in which a family (or group of families) exerts power over the firm and its strategic direction by leveraging control via ownership, management, or board involvement (Pieper, Klein, & Jaskiewicz, 2008). Family-owned and family-controlled firms account for approximately 90 percent of all companies worldwide (Aldrich & Cliff, 2003) and are the most common organizational form in both advanced and developing economies. Families are involved in establishing, organizing, and operating approximately 70–85 percent of firms in the United States (Chirico, Sirmon, Sciascia, & Mazzola, 2011; Neubauer & Lank, 1998 and South European countries Gómez-Mejía, 2012), respectively, and as many as 95 percent of all firms around the world (Gómez-Mejía, Haynes, Núñez-Nickel, Jacobson, & Moyano-Fuentes, 2007; La Porta, Lopez-de-silanes, Shleifer, & Vishny, 2002; Lumpkin, Steier, & Wright, 2011). In the United States alone, family businesses account for more than half of GDP—including at least one-third of the Fortune 500 firms (e.g. Cargill, Motorola, Ford, Microsoft) and employ over 80 percent of the total US workforce (Chirico et al., 2011). Founding families are present in one-third of the S&P 500 (Anderson & Reeb, 2003) and the Fortune 500 companies (Shleifer & Vishny, 1986). In Asia, over two-thirds of the firms are controlled by founding families or individuals (Claessens, Djankov, Fan, & Lang, 2002). In Western Europe, approximately 44 percent of publicly-listed firms are family controlled (Faccio & Lang, 2002).

Despite the continuing significant global economic impact of family firms, the field of family business research remains relatively young. Since family firms are a prevalent form of business around the world (Anderson & Reeb, 2003; Chrisman, Chua, & Litz, 2004), it is not surprising that interest in family business as an academic research field has grown in recent years (Dyer & Sanchez, 1998; Zahra & Sharma, 2004). Growing interest has resulted in a significant increase in family business studies conducted as well as the accumulation of new knowledge about family business as a phenomenon (Sharma, 2004). Challenges to studying family entrepreneurship abound, however, since family businesses exist within complex relationships with their business families. This means the field of family business studies endeavors to minimize complexity and to reach consensus about a definition for the family business. Varying definitions include elements such as ownership (Barnes & Hershon, 1976; Bernard, 1975; Gallo & Sveen, 1991; Lansberg, 1988), management participation (Handler, 1989), employment, governance structure

(Dreux, 1990), intention and vision (Chua, Chrisman, & Sharma, 1999), and family involvement based on power, experience, and culture (Klein, Astrachan, & Smyrnios, 2005). It is widely acknowledged that family businesses involve complex relationships and dependencies between the business, the family, and the environment (Donckels & Fröhlich, 1991). These complex interrelationships create a challenge for research, as highlighted in Bird, Welsch, Astrachan, and Pistrui's (2002) review noting the challenges faced by family business researchers to establish clear definitive boundaries for family firms due to the complexity of interrelationships between the domains of the family and the business (Moores, 2009). These domains have been combined and studied to better understand what it means to be a family business thanks to recent contributions of researchers from the fields of corporate governance, finance, management, strategy, entrepreneurship, psychology, and sociology. Thus the theory and study of family business have evolved significantly over the last 20 years. But while the field has undergone significant transformations, and while scholars generally agree that family businesses do differ from non-family businesses, they have yet to reach consensus about what exactly distinguishes family firms from non-family firms.

Thus, at this stage of study we can review and assess what work our scholarly colleagues have produced to move the field towards a better understanding of the distinguishing characteristics that affect family firm behavior. If we better understand whether and how family firms differentiate themselves from other types of organizations, we may be better able to understand their decisions regarding internationalization.

Family Firms as a Differentiated Organizational Form

An enduring discussion within the family business literature concerns how family firms can be distinguished from non-family firms (Chrisman, Chua, & Sharma, 2005; Chrisman, Steier, & Chua, 2008). Unlike non-family firms, family businesses are a synthesis of four significant organizational characteristics: family ownership/control, strategic influence of a family in day-to-day management of the firm, the intention/possibility for trans-generational continuity, and a concern for family relationships, all of which determine outcomes specific to family firms. These organizational characteristics are embedded in overlapping systems of a family business entity: management, ownership, and family (Lansberg, 1988; Tagiuri & Davis, 1996).

In particular, the differentiating factor of family has now been shown to be a variable that affects behavior at different levels of analysis (individual, group, and firm) and which impacts how the firm is managed (Dyer, 2003). Reasons for a distinction between family and non-family

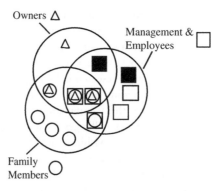

Figure 6.1 Overlap of Family, Ownership, and Management

firms can be found in two family characteristics that illustrate relationships and drive behavior in family firms: family goals and values (Dyer, 1986; Fukuyama, 1995; Tagiuri & Davis, 1992).

Family goals are by and large to develop, support, and care for family members. Unlike family goals, business goals are generally based on profits, efficiency, and financial measures. Ultimately, research shows that the qualities and intrinsic nature of family firms determine their distinctive character and behavior (Dawson & Mussolino, 2014), much of which is a combination of the aforementioned family goals mixed with business goals. Such distinctive behavior has been labeled particularism (Carney, 2005), meaning that owners of family firms view the firms as theirs and they, therefore, intervene in business decisions using non-financial qualifiers that may be with/without rational-calculative criteria (Dawson & Mussolino, 2014). This type of behavior is driven by nonfinancial motivations.

Consequently, scholars have sought ways to understand these behavioral complexities by defining family firms based on nonfinancial characteristics such as family involvement (Astrachan, Klein, & Smyrnios, 2002); familiness (Habbershon & Williams, 1999; Hitt & Sirmon, 2003); the so-called 'essence' of the family firm, which highlights the vision and the trans-generational intention of the controlling family (Chrisman et al., 2005); and socioemotional wealth, which refers to the stock of affect-related value that family principals have invested in the firm (Berrone, Cruz, Gómez-Mejía, & Larraza-Kintana, 2010).

The literature has supported the notion that family involvement differentiates a family firm from a non-family firm due to its inimitable idiosyncratic bundle of resources and capabilities – referred to as "familiness" – that result from the interacting and overlapping systems of the family, the business entity, the ownership structure, as well as the individual family members (Habbershon, Williams, & MacMillan, 2003). This bundle of resources and capabilities motivates strategic behavior that differs from non-family firm behavior (Arregle, Hitt, Sirmon, & Very, 2007; Carney, 2005; Verbeke & Kano, 2012).

To better understand the potential range of behavioral complexities in family businesses, one must study the three systems governing the firm. Each of the three systems – management, ownership, and family – sustains a spectrum of goals that impacts firm behavior. This spectrum of goals incorporates a range of perceived wealth in the family firm: from financial wealth on the one side to non-financial wealth on the other. Whereas financial wealth relies on a traditional measurement of return on investment, non-financial wealth captures a more emotion-based value that a family derives from its controlling position in a firm (Gómez-Mejía & Cruz, 2011). Within its range of both financial and non-financial variables, family-specific resources are bundled and help to determine firm identity and ultimately vision and strategic goals.

Derived from both the resource-based view of the firm and from systems theory, the above-mentioned notion of familiness refers to this unique bundle of resources resulting from the interaction of the family and business systems (Habbershon & Williams, 1999; Habbershon et al., 2003). According to Zellweger, Eddleston, and Kellermanns (2010), familiness is a multidimensional construct that describes a "rare and inimitable family-based resource" that is central to family firm identity. Firm identity can then be intentionally projected to external stakeholders via the firm's image (Zellweger, Kellermanns, Eddleston, & Memili, 2012). Dimensions of familiness include human resources (reputation and experience), organizational resources (decision making and learning), and process resources (relationships and networks) (Irava & Moores, 2010). Familiness is also comprised of structural dimensions (social interactions and networks), cognitive dimensions (shared vision and purpose, as well as unique language, stories, and culture), and relational dimensions (trust, norms, obligations, and identity) (Pearson, Carr, & Shaw, 2008). Finally, familiness includes the dimension of family involvement, essence, and organizational identity (Zellweger et al., 2010). Outcomes of familiness include nonfinancial performance results, such as the preservation of family ties or transgenerational value creation (Chrisman, Steier, & Chua, 2003); a strong sense of commitment to the business (Carmon, Miller, Raile, & Roers, 2010); organizational identity (Carmon et al., 2010); social capital (Ensley & Pearson, 2005); strategic flexibility (Zahra, Hayton, Neubaum, Dibrell, & Craig, 2008), market orientation (Cabrera-Suárez, de la Cruz Déniz-Déniz, & Martín-Santana, 2011); shared understanding and shared values in top management teams which lead to increased leadership team cohesion (Ensley & Pearson, 2005); revenue, capital structure, growth, and perceived performance (Rutherford & Holt, 2008); and superior levels of financial performance and competitive advantage over time (Zahra et al., 2008; Zellweger & Nason, 2008). The characteristics of familiness also produce unique motivations and capabilities of family firms when they consider building international strategies, which will be reviewed in the next section of this paper.

Like the notion of familiness, but derived from the behavioral agency model (Wiseman & Gómez-Mejía, 1998), another theoretical framework that helps to explain affect-related behavioral complexities within family firms is socioemotional wealth (SEW). SEW, an overarching construct that captures family firm idiosyncrasy and heterogeneity, brings intangible and non-financial factors into the analysis of family firms. The behavioral agency model (Wiseman & Gómez-Mejía, 1998), upon which SEW is based, assumes that firms make decisions depending upon the perspective of the firm's dominant principal. In the case of a family firm, dominant principals are family owners, directors, managers, and employees (Berrone et al., 2010), and thus SEW argues that one major concern for these family principals involves the potential loss of their asset(s). Family principals tend to frame strategic issues in terms of how a threat might affect not only their financial investment but also their non-financial investment (SEW). Within SEW, five non-financial elements affect in firm behavior. According to the model, if one or more of these individual non-financial elements are threatened, family principals will first consider these elements and how they might expose their overall socioemotional endowment at risk before making a decision for the business.

SEW reconciles previous approaches to understanding distinct family firm behaviors, in that it allows for differential risk preferences, it accounts for non-financial aspects of involvement (ownership, employment), and it considers both positive and negative consequences of non-economic aspects of doing business. SEW is characterized by emotional needs for identity and family influence and the preservation of the family dynasty (Gómez-Mejía et al., 2007). The non-financial elements within SEW include *F*amily control and influence, *I*dentification of family members with the firm, *B*inding social ties, *E*motional attachment of family members, and *R*enewal of family bonds to the firm through dynastic succession (FIBER) (Berrone, Cruz, & Gómez-Mejía, 2012). According to the FIBER model, when one or more of these non-financial elements are threatened, family principals will first consider the socioemotional endowment when making decisions for the business. The main point of SEW is that when family involvement is high, firms are more likely to be driven by a belief that risks are counterbalanced by nonfinancial benefits rather than exclusively by potential financial gains (Berrone et al., 2012). Preserving the family's SEW represents a key goal for a controlling family (Gómez-Mejía et al., 2007) and it is this attribute that helps to explain why family firms behave in distinctly different strategic ways from non-family firms (Berrone et al., 2012).

Thus, Berrone, Cruz, and Gómez-Mejía (2012) maintain that perceived threats to SEW may drive the family to make decisions that are not driven by an economic logic, and they may even be willing to put the firm at risk to preserve their non-financial endowment. Indeed, Pukall and Calabrò (2013) suggest that family principals tend not to be risk averse or risk prone, but rather they tend to be generally loss averse. Fernández and Nieto (2014) highlight that family firms are loss averse when the SEW is threatened due to the potential risk for reduction of family control, and that they exhibit a preference for lower levels of internationalization that will, thus, ensure family control over the firm. Ultimately, depending upon the situation, principals would be willing to take risks with the main reference point of SEW. This implies that in an extreme situation—for example, a possibility to internationalize or under a threat of bankruptcy—family owners could be more willing to take a risk than their nonfamily business peers due to their commitment to the firm (Chrisman & Patel, 2012; Fernández & Nieto, 2014). This approach to managing and leveraging the business seems to offer insight into one more way in which family firms differ from their non-family counterparts. Ultimately, SEW helps to explain how stakeholders' goals of protecting their non-financial investments in the firm influence business decisions and processes.

An ever-growing body of literature has begun to address how this set of preservation goals can potentially conflict with financial objectives of the firm. Since the literature outlines how family firms behave distinctively differently from non-family firms thanks to, amongst other reasons, the involvement of non-financial characteristics of ownership, employment, governance, and strategy building, it would follow that when considering risk and return, family firms could approach the process of internationalization differently than non-family firms. Considerable scholarly attention has been given to the process of internationalization, which can be a primary way for firms to achieve financial growth. A number of studies have, however, demonstrated that family principals often view internationalization/diversification as a potential threat to SEW (Gómez-Mejía et al., 2007). The following section outlines how preservation goals affect firm behavior: in particular with regard to family firm motivations and capabilities vis à vis internationalization.

Family Firm Motivations and Capabilities for Internationalization

The decision to internationalize is a critical, complex, and risk-creating strategic decision for any firm. Since family firms dominate the global business environment in terms of ownership and governance models, it would follow that the study of family firm internationalization offers international business scholars a rich topic for exploration. Family influence creates patterns of goals and strategies that are often articulated, structured, and implemented in ways that can be radically different from non-family firms (Salvato & Corbetta, 2014). Among other things, the inimitable bundle of resources embedded in family firms create an opportunity to investigate the various ways in which family businesses make the decision to go abroad when compared with other types of firms.

The current debate amongst international business and management scholars about the impact of family ownership attributes on internationalization has created inconsistent results. Prior empirical studies have presented both positive (Carr & Bateman, 2009; Zahra, 2003) and negative effects (Fernández & Nieto, 2006; Graves & Thomas, 2006; Hautz, Mayer, & Stadler, 2013) of family ownership on firm internationalization. Other studies find no statistically significant impact (Cerrato & Piva, 2010; Pinho, 2007). In their recent meta-analysis, Arregle, Duran, Hitt, & van Essen (2014) generally find that family firms are not statistically significantly different from non-family firms in their international activities. For other helpful recent reviews, also see Kontinen & Ojala (2010) and Pukall & Calabro (2014).

This review of empirical studies on family firm internationalization uncovers great variance and inconclusive results about the motivations and capabilities of family firms in the internationalization process. Previous studies considered family controlled SMEs and their internationalization strategies, yet these studies primarily focused on export behavior (Fernández & Nieto, 2006). More recent empirical literature has begun to investigate other modes of internationalization, in particular outward foreign direct investment (FDI), but these studies are few and far between. While FDI is considered to be a riskier mode of entry than export, FDI is a significant internationalization strategy that can meet company demands that would not be met via export. For example, gaining access to lower-cost production in target countries and overcoming trade barriers. It might be that empirical results in the extant literature create a less-than-precise picture of family firm motivations and capabilities vis à vis internationalization due to their primary focus on export modes.

Therefore, in an attempt to more clearly outline family firm motivations and capabilities for internationalization, this chapter pays particular attention to classifying internationalization into two broad categories of entry modes: non-equity based and equity-based. Within the non-equity based modes of internationalization, two forms of internationalization are referred to in the literature: export and international sales. Equity-based modes of internationalization – also referred to as outward foreign direct investment – in this review include Greenfield ventures, mergers, acquisitions, and joint ventures.

In terms of structure, first, this chapter outlines family-related factors that have been found in the reviewed empirical analyses regardless of internationalization mode. Thereafter, family firm motivations and capabilities are divided into non-equity and equity modes of internationalization as represented in extant literature, since empirical studies tend to specify these classifications.

Family Firm Motivations and Capabilities in (Non-Specific Modes of) Internationalization

On the motivation side of family firm behavior, a key differentiator in family firms is SEW. As previously outlined, the dimensions of FIBER are *F*amily control and influence, *I*dentification of family members with the firm, *B*inding social ties, *E*motional attachment of family members, and *R*enewal of family bonds to the firm through dynastic—or trans-generational—succession (Berrone et al., 2012).

Specifically, the *F* dimension results in a fear of loss of control and influence in the process of internationalization. Internationalization implies a change to strategy and organizational structure. In order to maximize the family's own utilities—as suggested by agency theory—fewer international entrepreneurship activities are expected, as this means taking risks with their own assets as well as losing control. Family owners show suspicion of this organizational redesign because they fear changes in ownership and management that might negatively influence their decision-making power. Consequently, the fear of losing control makes family firms rather forgo international activities in order to maintain their decision-making power (Bhaumik, Driffield, & Pal, 2010; Gallo & Sveen, 1991) and thus discourages sizable global expansions (Chen, Hsu, & Chang, 2014; Sanchez-Bueno & Usero, 2014).

The *I* dimension implies that family owners tend to impose family-derived common values, goals, and organizational culture, which may cause conflicts with foreign values and practices (Muñoz-Bullón & Sánchez-Bueno, 2012). The *B* dimension implies that family firms value kinship and reciprocal social connections in foreign operations (Sciascia, Mazzola, Astrachan, & Pieper, 2012), which may restrict their location choices abroad. The *E* dimension suggests that family owners attach emotional benefits to the firm, which may result in weak management of investment funds (Graves & Thomas, 2006). Lastly, the *R* dimension outlines an intention to ensure continuity and firm survival over the long run. This suggests that family owners value long-term projects for trans-generational succession (Jess H Chua, Chrisman, Kellermanns, & Wu, 2011), which leads to both fear of the higher inherent risk associated with foreign assets and ventures (Dyer, 2006; Gómez-Mejía, Makri, & Kintana, 2010).

According to Claver, Rienda, & Quer (2009), the family-related factor of long-term vision (Daily & Dollinger, 1992; Gersick, Davis, Hampton, & Lansberg, 1997; Harris, Martinez, & Ward, 1994; Tagiuri & Davis, 1992) is a necessary motivation/capability of a family firm when considering international expansion. If family owner-managers consider internationalization to be essential for long-term business development, the family would want to pursue the strategy despite risks and damage to short-term returns (Zahra, 2003). A long-term perspective, combined with the presence of outside management and directors, may lead these companies to choose entry modes that involve greater resource commitment over the long-term (Claver, Rienda, & Quer, 2009b).

Ultimately, the desire to preserve SEW reduces the incentive towards internationalization particularly if investing abroad may potentially reduce SEW. Thus, the dimensions of SEW generally imply that family firms are relatively less motivated to invest abroad.

Regarding capabilities, in some studies family firms have been shown to have less access to capital, a lack of knowledge and access to qualified personnel (Fernández & Nieto, 2006), and have been shown to have less developed information and control systems (Tsang, 2002a). In their study about the effect of family involvement in new venture debt financing, Chua, Chrisman, Kellermanns, and Wu (2011) show family firms have the capability to mobilize their social capital through family involvement in the firm so as to improve the firm's access to debt financing of new ventures. Family firms, thanks to fewer agency problems, are also capable of making speedy and flexible decisions (Gallo & Pont, 1996) which allow the firm to swiftly decide to internationalize once they are ready to commit. The long-term orientation of family firms encourages internationalization, since it leads to a capability to commit more strongly to fulfill strategies – including internationalization – and therefore allows family firms to dedicate higher levels of resources to overcome potential drawbacks.

Family Firm Motivations and Capabilities in Non-equity Modes of Internationalization

In terms of non-equity modes of internationalization – e.g., export, international sales, contractual agreements, and franchising – the empirical literature shows exports and international sales might imply different motivations and capabilities than in equity-based modes of market entry.

In their study of 10,579 family-owned Spanish manufacturing firms from 1991–96 concerning influential factors for SME internationalization strategies, Fernández and Nieto (2005) confirm a negative relationship between family ownership and export orientation and show that family firms are less likely to internationalize than non-family firms due to their motivation to maintain control of the firm. Arrival of new generations in the family firm, however, positively influence export orientation, as does corporate ownership. In terms of export orientation, Fernández and Nieto find therefore that as time progresses and generations changeover, SMEs gain resources necessary to further internationalize as the family firms maintain stable relationships with other firms through shareholding or agreements aimed to promote international expansion.

Okoroafo and Perryy (2010) support this result. They show in a study of 196 manufacturing firms in Ohio, USA that the likelihood of a firm to participate in export activities increases as subsequent generations to the founder/owner arrive on the scene. On the capabilities side, Fernández and Nieto (2006) show that family SMEs face difficulties in building a portfolio of strategic capabilities and resources thus making international success through the mode of export more challenging. In the same study, they also show corporate ownership to be a positive indicator for the scale of family SME internationalization.

According to Calabrò & Mussolino (2013) it is a critical factor within family SMEs that they face two opposing forces within the firms: the possibility to exploit opportunities across borders drives them to grow and seek expansion beyond their traditional markets, while the wish to maintain family control encourages stability and more risk-averse behavior by developing lower-risk projects by engaging in low-equity investments as they internationalize. This study shows that both formal and informal governance mechanisms – in particular at the board level – can coexist in a complementary way that positively influences SME export intensity.

Gallo and Pont (1996) find both facilitating factors as well as restricting factors to internationalization in their study of 450 Spanish manufacturing firms that conduct export activities. The facilitating factors they find in this study are issues of family control: for example, the possibility to create work opportunities for other family members in various countries thus ensuring they maintain family control of the business. As well, the motivation to ensure patient returns confirms a long-term orientation in their sample. On the capabilities side, Gallo and Pont find that agent alignment in their sample of firms facilitates speedy decision-making and a possibility of alliances with other family firms abroad. Restricting factors to internationalization – or anti-capabilities if you will – found in their sample firms include product orientation to the domestic consumer, a lack of preparedness of family members to internationalize, resistance of management towards internationalization, an unwillingness to form alliances with other firms, as well as intra-firm power struggles.

Zahra (2003) outlines in her study of 2379 US manufacturing firms based in southern states[1] that the percentage share of family ownership in the business is positively related to its level of internationalization when referring to international sales. She argues that the positive effect of family ownership is reinforced when family members also participate in management of the firm and concludes that if family members actively participate in management, their motivation will be more cautious toward internationalization, since to make an overseas investment usually involves a long return on investment and therefore implies a reduction in family wealth in the short run. On the capabilities side of non-equity modes of internationalization, Zahra notes that in the family firms engaged in international sales that were studied, they had a strong capability characterized by intense communication among their members. This capability can lower the risks associated with strategic moves that require a longer return on investment and altruism, which means owners are expected to devote resources necessary to protect their investments.

In their study of 902 Chinese privately held SMEs, Liang, Wang, and Cui (2014) distinguish between two forms of family control: family ownership and family management. They predict that family involvement in management will have a negative relationship with export propensity because owners fear potential financial and SEW losses. Yet contrary to their prediction, their study finds that when family members are more actively involved in management, export propensity increases. The positive relationship between export propensity and family management involvement in this study suggests that exports – especially if carried out through distributors/ agents – might require fewer managerial capabilities than the skill set required to do direct exports. This study also assesses family control vis à vis outward FDI, as outlined in a later section.

According to Graves and Thomas' study of 890 Australian exporters (2006), the managerial capabilities of family SMEs lag behind those of their non-family counterparts. In terms of capability lag, family firms were significantly less likely to employ an outside manager or to utilize professional training at the domestic level and at moderate levels of internationalization when compared to their nonfamily counterparts. Family firms were significantly less likely to develop strategic plans or utilize quality assurance at the domestic level of internationalization when compared to their non-family counterparts. Graves and Thomas contribute to the RBV theory of internationalization by providing empirical support for the positive association between a firm's managerial capabilities and the extent of internationalization.

In the vein of managerial and operational capabilities for internationalization, Merino, Monreal-Pérez, and Sánchez-Marín (2014) study 500 Spanish manufacturing firms that export, and consider whether family SMEs are able to overcome their lack of resources necessary for internationalization (e.g. financial, human, marketing) through focused family-specific resources (e.g. trust, altruism, social capital, and network ties). This study provides evidence that the expertise and capabilities of different generations of family owners and employees, combined with the family business culture, positively affect the export activities of family SMEs. Conversely, factors related to family ownership and management does not show significant influence on internationalization, experience, and culture.

Family Firm Motivations and Capabilities in Equity Modes of Internationalization

The literature on family firm internationalization via equity modes of entry contain similar themes regarding motives and skills as those found in non-equity modes of entry. As previously mentioned, the empirical studies available on family firm motivations and capabilities in equity modes—specifically mergers, acquisitions, joint ventures, and greenfield investments—are few and results are inconsistent. For example, Bhaumik, Driffield, and Pal (2010) find that while family control and concentrated ownership in the Indian pharmaceutical and automotive industries could be optimal in their home institutional environments, family ownership and management has a detrimental impact on outward investments. In striking contrast, Kuo, Kau, Chang, & Chiu (2012) find that family firms are likely to choose joint ventures more often than non-family firms due to their need for local partners and to help with management of the firm. Furthermore, in cases of higher levels of international experience, Kuo et al's study shows that family firms more aggressively pursue investment in a wholly-owned subsidiary than non-family firms. These disparate results are just two that can be found in the small pool of available empirical work on equity modes of family firm internationalization done thus far. These similar themes reiterate the elements of SEW. For example, family control and the motivation for independence remains a main issue.

In their study of listed Japanese firms in Japan, Abdellatif, Amman, and Jaussaud (2010) find that family firms establish fewer joint ventures than non-family firms. The authors confirm that this result implies that family firms prefer to remain independent when compared to non-family firms.

As discussed earlier vis à vis non-equity modes of internationalization, Liang et.al (2014) find in their study of privately-held Chinese SMEs that family involvement in management has an inverted-U-shaped relationship with the likelihood of outward foreign direct investment. Thus, on the motivation side, this empirical study seems to indicate that family-managed firms are more reticent to invest heavily internationally and they prefer to minimize risk by committing fewer firm resources via a non-equity mode (i.e., export). Less risk implies a lower likelihood of loss of SEW. Thus, this study indicates how family firm strategies are designed and executed to fulfill the management/ownership motivation to preserve and enhance SEW. Since SEW serves as a primary driver in owner prioritization as shown in this study, the importance of SEW in forming firm strategies varies with the degree of family involvement in management and the degree of family ownership.

On the capabilities side, for example, family involvement in management mostly affects the managerial capabilities and resources related to international expansion. In contrast, family ownership influences the motivation side towards internationalization strategy via owner risk preference and long-term orientation. Ultimately, a higher family ownership stake decreases the likelihood of exporting because owners fear potential financial and SEW losses, but as outlined in this study, that negative relationship reaches a threshold, after which owners are more likely to take more significant risks due to their desire to preserve long-term SEW in the form of transgenerational succession. This study shows evidence of how family control can affect FDI decisions in SMEs, which extends extant evidence of SME internationalization through export behavior.

Family owners have been shown to exhibit a few distinctive characteristics that create advantages in relation to outward FDI.

First, family control may promote flexibility and speedy decision-making vis à vis internationalization (Chen et al., 2014; Fernández & Nieto, 2006). This capability enables firms to respond to rapid changes in the international marketplace, which consequently increases the potential for success in internationalization (Chen et al., 2014).

Second, family-controlled firms are characterized as long-term oriented. Thus, their patient capital can be considered to be a capability enabling long-term commitment to investments in internationalization (Abdellatif et al., 2010; Carr & Bateman, 2009; Claver et al., 2009b; Gallo & Pont, 1996). For instance, internationalization was found to be positively associated with speed (Gallo & Pont, 1996), flexibility, and intuition (Tsang, 2002b) in family firm decision making.

Third, owners possess family-specific capabilities such as trust, family social capital, dynastic stability, and network ties (Casillas, Moreno, & Acedo, 2010; Jess H. Chua, Chrisman, Kellermanns, & Wu, 2011; Segaro, 2012). For example, in their study of international joint ventures, Swinth and Vinton (1993) show that JVs between family firms are more likely to succeed than those between family firms and non-family firms. They find that this can be explained by the fact that family firms – even across different cultural contexts – share similar values by which they conduct business. Specifically, trust, loyalty, and commitment to the transgenerational continuation of the firm within the family are mentioned as the values that contribute to the family firm capability pool.

Family firms also exhibit lower borrower-lender agency costs which result in a lower probability of managerial opportunism (Jess H. Chua et al., 2011). These advantages provide the firm a capability to leverage external financial capital with preferential borrowing terms (Anderson, Mansi, & Reeb, 2003), which is helpful for large-scale investments abroad.

In their sample of 146 family firms that had at least undergone one succession process, and had a minimum of EUR 40 million turnover in diverse industries, Puig and Perez (2009) show that these firms had accumulated internal intangible assets over a long period of time. These accumulated intangible assets create key family firm capabilities in the areas of marketing, branding, and negotiation skills that facilitate execution of international projects which become of primary importance for firms following Spain's accession to the EU.

The empirical literature also outlines disadvantages when it comes to family firm motivations and capabilities affecting equity-based outward FDI. In Sanchez-Sellero, Rosell-Martinez, & García-Vazquez's study of 1288 Spanish manufacturing firms (2014) they find that excessive family control can impede changes in management styles, staffing policies, and other operational decisions, which ultimately impede firm productivity and absorptive capacity from FDI (Gulbrandsen, 2005). Additionally, they find that family management has a significant negative influence on absorptive capacity through FDI, thus asserting that firms who are run by people who are not members of the same family—those who are sourced from a broader pool of professional managers—are more skilled at absorbing spillover effects from FDI.

Table 6.1 Review: Family Firm Motivations and Capabilities for Internationalization Based on Entry Mode

	Non-Specified Entry Mode			Non-Equity Entry Modes: e.g., Export, International Sales, Contractual Agreements, & Franchising				Equity Entry Modes: e.g., Greenfield, Mergers, Acquisitions, Joint Ventures			
	Concept (Fiber)	*Effect*	*Reference*	*Concept (Fiber)*	*Effect*	*Reference*	*Entry mode*	*Concept (Fiber)*	*Effect*	*Reference*	*Entry Mode*
	(F)AMILY CONTROL	Fear of losing control makes family firms rather forgo international activities in order to maintain their decision-making power	Gallo & Sveen 1991; Bhaumik et al. 2010; Chen, Hsu, & Chang, 2014; Sanchez-Bueno & Usero, 2014	**(F)AMILY CONTROL**	FFs less likely to internationalize than NFFs due to motivation to maintain control of the firm. Arrival of new generations in the family firm, however, positively influence export orientation, as does corporate ownership.	Fernández and Nieto (2005)	Export	**(F)AMILY CONTROL**	While family control & concentrated ownership in the Indian pharmaceutical & automotive industries could be optimal in their home institutional environments, family ownership & management has a detrimental impact on outward investments	Bhaumik, Driffield, and Pal (2010)	Outward FDI
		Due to family involvement in the firm, family firms have the capability to mobilize their social capital to improve the firm's access to debt financing of new ventures.	Chua, Chrisman, Kellermanns, & Wu, 2011		The likelihood of a firm to participate in export activities increases as subsequent generations to the founder/owner arrive on the scene.	Okorofo & Perryy, 2010	Export		Finds that FFs establish fewer JVs than NFFs. The result implies that FFs prefer to remain independent when compared to NFFs.	Abdellatif, Amman, and Jaussaud (2010)	Joint ventures

(Continued)

Non-Specified Entry Mode			Non-Equity Entry Modes: e.g., Export, International Sales, Contractual Agreements, & Franchising				Equity Entry Modes: e.g., Greenfield, Mergers, Aquisitions, Joint Ventures			
Concept (Fiber)	Effect	Reference	Concept (Fiber)	Effect	Reference	Entry mode	Concept (Fiber)	Effect	Reference	Entry Mode
	Thanks to fewer agency problems due to family control, firms are capable of making speedy and flexible decisions, which allows the firm to swiftly decide to internationalize once they are ready to commit.	Gallo & Garcia Pont, 1996		The possibility to exploit international opportunities drives growth & search for expansion. Wish to maintain family control encourages stability and more risk-averse behavior: develop lower-risk projects through low-equity investments.	Calabrò & Mussolino, 2013	Export		This study shows evidence of how family control can affect FDI decisions in SMEs, which extends extant evidence of SME internationalization through export behavior.	Liang et.al (2014)	Outward FDI
				Facilitating factors for internationalization are issues of family control (e.g, possibility to create work opportunities for other family members in various countries thus ensuring they maintain family control of the business) Also, agent alignment facilitates speedy decision-making & possibility of alliances w/other family firms abroad.	Gallo & Pont, 1996	Alliances		Family control may promote flexibility & speedy decision making vis à vis internationalization, which in turn enables firms to respond to rapid changes in the international marketplace, thus increasing potential for international success.	Chen, Hsu, & Chang, 2014; Fernandez & Nieto, 2006	Outward FDI

Two types of control: family ownership & family management. They predict that family involvement in management will have a negative relationship with export propensity because owners fear potential financial and SEW losses. Yet contrary to their prediction, their study finds that when family members are more actively involved in management, export propensity increases. The positive relationship between export propensity and family management involvement in this study suggests that exports – especially if carried out through distributors/agents— might require fewer managerial capabilities than the skill set required to do direct exports.

Liang, Wang, & Cui, 2014

Export

Lower borrower–lender agency costs which results in lower probability of managerial opportunism

Chua, Chrisman, Kellermanns, & Wu, 2011

Outward FDI

(Continued)

Non-Specified Entry Mode			Non-Equity Entry Modes: e.g., Export, International Sales, Contractual Agreements, & Franchising				Equity Entry Modes: e.g., Greenfield, Mergers, Acquisitions, Joint Ventures			
Concept (Fiber)	Effect	Reference	Concept (Fiber)	Effect	Reference	Entry mode	Concept (Fiber)	Effect	Reference	Entry Mode
(I)DENTIFICATION	Family owners tend to impose family-derived common values, goals, and organizational culture, which may cause conflicts with foreign values and practices	Munoz-Bullón & Sanchez-Bueno, 2012	(I)DENTIFICATION	According to Graves' study of 890 Australian exporters (2006), managerial capabilities of family SMEs lag behind NFF counterparts, FFs less likely to hire outside management/utilize professional training, and FFs less likely to develop strategic plans or utilize QA when compared to NFF counterparts.	Graves 2006	Export	(I)DENTIFICATION	Excessive family control can impede changes in management styles, staffing policies, & other operational decisions, which ultimately impede firm productivity & absorptive capacity from FDI.	Sanchez-Sellero, Rosell-Martinez, & García-Vazquez, 2014	Outward FDI

(B)INDING SOCIAL TIES			
(B)INDING SOCIAL TIES	Sciascia, Mazzola, Astrachan, & Pieper, 2012		B dimension implies that family firms value kinship and reciprocal social connections in foreign operations which may restrict their location choices abroad.
(B)INDING SOCIAL TIES	Zahra, 2003	Int'l sales	In the family firms engaged in international sales studied, their capability is characterized by intense communication among their member owners.
	Merino, Monreal-Pérez, & Sánchez-Marín, 2014	Export	Re: managerial & operational capabilities for internationalization, this study of 500 Spanish manufacturing firms that export considers whether family SMEs are able to overcome lack in resources nec. for internationalization (e.g. financial, human, marketing) through focused family-specific resources (e.g. trust/ altruism/social capital/ network ties). Provides evidence that the expertise and capabilities of different generations of family owners/ employees, combined w/FF culture, positively affect export activities of FFs.
(B)INDING SOCIAL TIES	Kuo, Kau, Chang, & Chu (2012)		Finds that FFs are likely to choose JVs more often than NFFs due to their need for local partners & to help with management of the firm.
(B)INDING SOCIAL TIES	Swinth and Vinton (1993)	JVs	JVs between FFs are more likely to succeed than those between FFs and NFFs. This can be explained by the fact that family firms – even across different cultural contexts—share similar values by which they conduct business: specifically, trust, loyalty, and commitment to transgenerational continuation of the firm.

(Continued)

	Non-Specified Entry Mode		Non-Equity Entry Modes: e.g., Export, International Sales, Contractual Agreements, & Franchising				Equity Entry Modes: e.g., Greenfield, Mergers, Acquisitions, Joint Ventures			
Concept (Fiber)	Effect	Reference	Concept (Fiber)	Effect	Reference	Entry mode	Concept (Fiber)	Effect	Reference	Entry Mode
(E)MOTIONAL ATTACHMENT TO THE FIRM	Family owners attach emotional benefits to the firm, which may result in weak management of investment funds	Graves & Thomas, 2004	(E)MOTIONAL ATTACHMENT TO THE FIRM	Family managers emotionally attached to firm, which negatively influences levels of commitment to internationalization when compared with NF management. This study opens up for future research into the relative importance of both types of managers as far as international commitment is concerned.	Claver, E.; Rienda, L.; Quer, D., 2009	Export, contractual agreements	(E)MOTIONAL ATTACHMENT TO THE FIRM			
(R) ENEWAL OF FAMILY BONDS TO THE FIRM	Intention to ensure continuity & firm survival over the long run. This suggests family owners value long-term projects to ensure transgenerational succession, which leads to both fear of the higher inherent risk associated with foreign assets and ventures.	Chua, Chrisman, Kellermanns, Wu, 2011; Gibb Dyer, 2006; Gómez-Mejía et al., 2010, Claver, Rienda, & Quer, 2009	(R) ENEWAL OF FAMILY BONDS TO THE FIRM	Motivation to ensure patient returns confirms a long-term orientation in their sample.	Gallo & Pont, 1996	Strategic alliances	(R)ENEWAL OF FAMILY BONDS TO THE FIRM	Higher family ownership stake decreases the likelihood of exporting b/c owners fear potential financial and SEW losses, but this study shows that negative relationship reaches a threshold, after which owners are more likely to take more significant risks due to their desire to preserve long-term SEW in the form of transgenerational succession.	Liang et.al (2014)	Outward FDI

The family-related factor of long-term vision is a necessary motivation/capability of a family firm when considering international expansion. If family owner-managers consider internationalization to be essential for long-term business development, the family would want to pursue the strategy despite risks and damage to short-term returns. A long-term perspective, combined with the presence of outside management and directors, may lead these companies to choose entry modes that involve greater resource commitment over the long-term.	Daily & Dollinger, 1993; Gersick, Davis, Hampton McCollom, & Lansberg, 1997; Harris, Martinez, & Ward, 1994; Tagiuri & Davis, 1992; Zahra, 2003; Claver et al., 2009.	
The capability of intense communication can lower the risks associated with strategic moves that require a longer return on investment and altruism, which means owners are expected to devote resources necessary to protect their investments.	Zahra, 2003	Int'l sales
FFs are characterized as long-term oriented. Their patient capital is a capability enabling long-term commitment to investments in internationalization	Abdellatif, Amann, & Jaussaud, 2010; Carr & Bateman, 2009; Claver et al, 2009; Gallo & Pont, 1996	Outward FDI

(Continued)

Non-Specified Entry Mode			Non-Equity Entry Modes: e.g., Export, International Sales, Contractual Agreements, & Franchising				Equity Entry Modes: e.g., Greenfield, Mergers, Acquisitions, Joint Ventures			
Concept (Fiber)	Effect	Reference	Concept (Fiber)	Effect	Reference	Entry mode	Concept (Fiber)	Effect	Reference	Entry Mode
				Long-term vision is a key element of the international expansion of family firms & presence of external managers in the family firm may lead these companies to choose entry modes involving greater ressource commitment.	Claver, E.; Rienda, L.; Quer, D., 2009	Export, contractual agreements		Shows firms had accumulated internal intangible assets over a long period of time. These accumulated intangible assets create key family firm capabilities that facilitate execution of international projects which become of primary importance for firms following Spain's accession to the EU.	Puig and Perez (2009)	FDI

Implications for Future Research

This review has shown a great degree of variance and inconclusive results about the motivations and capabilities of family firms to internationalize. In particular, the scarcity of studies on how and why family firms choose a specific mode of entry leaves much potential for further scholarly work at a time when FDI is becoming an increasingly important internationalization strategy for SMEs (Liang et al., 2014). Since FDI has been shown empirically to be a risk-heavy and uncertainty rich strategic decision-making process that might meet company demands not possible via export activity, and while the complexities the bundled resources within familiness and socioemotional wealth have yet to be explored specifically within this context of outward FDI, we recommend further work in this direction.

For example, the notions of familiness and socioemotional wealth have enhanced our understanding of what it means to be a family business. These notions encourage us to migrate away from a dichotomy of the family firm. This migration inherently accepts a new and complex view of firm behavior, which subsequently further complicates investigation. The complex bundles of resources comprising familiness/SEW within the family firm would be fruitful to investigate. Since the dimensions of familiness and socioemotional wealth are not, as yet, easily measurable, further investigation might help to take these abstract concepts that otherwise help to form motivations and capabilities of family firm systems. As Rau suggests, investigation of where family-specific bundles of resources qualify as valuable, rare, inimitable, and non-substitutable offer opportunities to empirically connect elements of familiness to a competitive (dis)advantage of the family firms while also showing moderating and/or mediating effects of these elements on firm behavior (Rau, 2014). Examples could include further work on Segaro's (2012) theoretical and conceptual contribution about the relationship between familiness and internationalization: specifically governance systems, social capital, and human capital (including managerial capabilities and international experience dimensions in top management teams and boards of directors in family-controlled SMEs). Another avenue of investigation could include a systematic analysis of the way in which family firms approach FDI. Familiness and SEW affect the decision-making process, and one could extend Tsang's comparative study of the process by which Chinese and Taiwanese family firms and non-family firms collect and analyze data in anticipation of FDI and place such a study into a different institutional setting. Such an extension could address another significant theme not addressed in this chapter: the role of institutional differences in family firm internationalization. Finally, at the intersection of the international business literature and the family business literature, scholars could further investigate family firm internationalization and firm performance. Specifically, future research could consider not only financial measurements of performance (e.g. revenues, innovation, and efficiency) but could also extend measurement to include non-financial performance objectives of family firms (e.g., preservation of SEW) (Fernández & Nieto, 2014).

Conclusion

Despite assertions that unique family firm advantages for internationalization—e.g. reduced agency costs for swift and flexible decision-making, patient capital for long-term investment, and social capital for lower cost access to venture financing—, are undermined by conservative attitudes towards diversification, lack of international professional experience, and a closed attitude towards hiring outside professional managers, the literature reviewed herein shows that family firms are, in fact, internationalizing in many different ways and affected by a number of family firm specific motivations and capabilities.

Although the literature reviewed herein fails to provide conclusive results about the way in which family firms are motivated to choose specific modes of internationalization, this chapter hopefully achieves its intended goal of outlining the relevance of family firms within the organizational sciences, describing how the notions of familiness and socioemotional wealth differentiates family firms from non family firms, frames how the literature has begun to assess the ways in which familiness and SEW affect family firm behavior with particular focus on the process of internationalization, and provides a structured overview of the literature classified into various modes of entry (unspecified, non-equity based, and equity-based modes). Finally, this chapter touches upon some unresolved issues within the field of family firm internationalization and recommends further avenues of scholarly study.

Note

1 Georgia, Tennessee, South Carolina, North Carolina, and Virginia

References

Abdellatif, M., Amann, B., & Jaussaud, J. 2010. Family Versus Nonfamily Business: A Comparison of International Strategies. *Journal of Family Business Strategy*, 1(2): 108–116.

Aldrich, H. E., & Cliff, J. E. 2003. The Pervasive Effects of Family on Entrepreneurship: Toward a Family Embeddedness Perspective. *Journal of Business Venturing*, 18(5): 573–596.

Anderson, R. C., Mansi, S. a., & Reeb, D. M. 2003. Founding Family Ownership and The Agency Cost of Debt. *Journal of Financial Economics*, 68(2): 263–285.

Anderson, R. C., & Reeb, D. M. 2003. Founding-Family Ownership and Firm Performance: Evidence from the S & P 500. *Journal of Finance*, LVIII(3): 1301–1328.

Arregle, J., Hitt, M. A., Sirmon, D. G., & Very, P. 2007. The Development of Organizational Social Capital: Attributes of Family Firms. *Journal of Management Studies*, 44(January).

Arregle, J.-L., Duran, P., Hitt, M. A., & van Essen, M. 2014. Is Family Firms' Internationalization Special? A Meta-Analysis. *Journal of International Business Studies*, 1–46.

Arregle, J.-L., Naldi, L., Nordqvist, M., & Hitt, M. A. 2012. Internationalization of Family-Controlled Firms: A Study of the Effects of External Involvement in Governance. *Entrepreneurship Theory and Practice*, 36(6): 1115–1143.

Astrachan, J. H., Klein, S. B., & Smyrnios, K. X. 2002. The F-PEC Scale of Family Influence: A Proposal for Solving the Family Business Definition Problem. *Family Business Review*, 15(1): 45–58.

Banalieva, E. R., & Eddleston, K. A. 2011. Home-region focus and performance of family firms: The role of family vs non-family leaders. *Journal of International Business Studies*, 42(8): 1060–1072.

Barnes, L. B., & Hershon, S. A. 1976. Transferring Power in The Family Business. *Harvard Business Review*, 54(4): 105–114.

Bernard, B. 1975. The Development of Organisation Structure in the Family Firm. *Journal of General Management*, 3(1): 42–60.

Berrone, P., Cruz, C. C., & Gómez-Mejía, L. R. 2012. Socioemotional Wealth in Family Firms: Theoretical Dimensions, Assessment Approaches, and Agenda for Future Research. *Family Business Review*, 25(3): 258–279.

Berrone, P., Cruz, C. C., Gómez-Mejía, L. R., & Larraza-Kintana, M. 2010. Socioemotional Wealth and Corporate Responses to Institutional Pressures: Firms Pollute Less? *Administrative Science Quarterly*, 55(1): 82–113.

Bhaumik, S., Driffield, N., & Pal, S. 2010. Does Ownership Structure of Emerging Market Firms Affect their Outward FDI? The Case of Indian Automotive and Pharmaceutical Sectors. *Journal of International Business Studies*, 41(3): 437–450.

Bird, B., Welsch, H., Astrachan, J. H., & Pistrui, D. 2002. Family Business Research: The Evolution of an Academic Field. *Family Business Review*, 15(4): 337–350.

Cabrera-Suárez, M. K., de la Cruz Déniz-Déniz, M., & Martín-Santana, J. D. 2011. Familiness and Market Orientation: A Stakeholder Approach. *Journal of Family Business Strategy*, 2(1): 34–42.

Calabrò, A., & Mussolino, D. 2013. How Do Boards of Directors Contribute to Family SME Export Intensity? The Role of Formal and Informal Governance Mechanisms. *Journal of Management and Governance*, 17: 363–403.

Carmon, A. F., Miller, A. N., Raile, A. N. W., & Roers, M. M. 2010. Fusing family and firm: Employee perceptions of perceived homophily, organizational justice, organizational identification, and organizational commitment in family businesses. *Journal of Family Business Strategy*, 1(4): 210–223.

Carney, M. 2005. Corporate Governance and Competitive Advantage in Family-Controlled Firms. *Entrepreneurship Theory and Practice*. http://onlinelibrary.wiley.com/doi/10.1111/j.1540–6520.2005.00081.x/full.

Carr, C., & Bateman, S. 2009. International Strategy Configurations of the World's Top Family Firms. *Management International Review*, 49(6): 733–758.

Casillas, J. C., Moreno, A. M., & Acedo, F. J. 2010. Internationalization of Family Businesses: A Theoretical Model Based on International Entrepreneurship Perspective. *Global Management Journal*, 3(2).

Cerrato, D., & Piva, M. 2010. The Internationalization of Small and Medium-Sized Enterprises: The Effect of Family Management, Human Capital and Foreign Ownership. *Journal of Management & Governance*, 16(4): 617–644.

Chen, H.-L., Hsu, W.-T., & Chang, C.-Y. 2014. Family Ownership, Institutional Ownership, and Internationalization of SMEs. *Journal of Small Business Management*, 52(2): 771–789.

Chirico, F., Sirmon, D. G., Sciascia, S., & Mazzola, P. 2011. Resource orchestration in family firms: Investigating how entrepreneurial orientation, generational involvement, and participative strategy affect performance. *Strategic Entrepreneurship Journal*, 5: 307–326.

Chrisman, J. J., Chua, J. H., & Litz, R. A. 2004. Comparing the Agency Costs of Family and Non-Family Firms: Conceptual Issues and Exploratory Evidence. *Entrepreneurship Theory and Practice*, 28(4): 335–354.

Chrisman, J. J., Chua, J. H., & Sharma, P. 2005. Trends and directions in the development of a strategic management theory of the family firm. *Entrepreneurship Theory and Practice*, 555–576.

Chrisman, J. J., & Patel, P. C. 2012. Variations in R & D Investments of Family and Nonfamily Firms : Behavioral Agency and Myopic Loss Aversion Perspectives. *Academy of Management Journal*, 55(4): 976–997.

Chrisman, J. J., Steier, L. P., & Chua, J. H. 2003. Creating Wealth in Family Firms through Managing Resources: Comments and Extensions. *Entrepreneurship, Theory, and Practice …*, 27(4): 359–366.

Chrisman, J. J., Steier, L. P., & Chua, J. H. 2008. Toward a Theoretical Basis for Understanding the Dynamics of Strategic Performance in Family Firms. *Entrepreneurship, Theory, and Practice …*, 32(662): 935–947.

Chua, J. H., Chrisman, J. J., Kellermanns, F. W., & Wu, Z. 2011. Family involvement and new venture debt financing. *Journal of Business Venturing*, 26: 472–488.

Chua, J. H., Chrisman, J. J., & Sharma, P. 1999. Defining the family business by behavior. *Entrepreneurship, Theory, and Practice …*, 19–40.

Claessens, S., Djankov, S., Fan, J. P. H., & Lang, L. H. P. 2002. Disentangling the Incentive and Entrenchment Effects of Large Shareholdings. *The Journal of Finance*, 57(6): 2741–2771.

Claver, E., Rienda, L., & Quer, D. 2009a. The Influence of Family-Related Factors. *Family Business Review*, 22(2): 125–135.

Claver, E., Rienda, L., & Quer, D. 2009b. Family Firms' International Commitment The Influence of Family-Related Factors. *Family Business Review*, (March).

Daily, C. M., & Dollinger, M. J. 1992. An Empirical Examination of Ownership Structure in Family and Professionally Managed Firms. *Family Business Review*, 5(2): 117–136.

Dawson, A., & Mussolino, D. 2014. Exploring what makes family firms different: Discrete or overlapping constructs in the literature? *Journal of Family Business Strategy*, 5(2): 169–183.

Donckels, R., & Fröhlich, E. 1991. Are Family Businesses Really Different? European Experiences from STRATOS. *Family Business Review*, 4(2): 149–160.

Dreux, D. R. 1990. Financing Family Business: Alternatives to Selling Out or Going Public. *Family Business Review*, 3(3): 225–243.

Dyer, W. G. 1986. *Cultural Change in Family Firms: Anticipating and Managing Business and Family Transitions.* San Francisco: Jossey-Bass.

Dyer, W. G. 2003. The Family: The missing variable in organizational research. *Entrepreneurship, Theory, and Practice …*, 401–416.

Dyer, W. G. 2006. Examining the "Family Effect" on Firm Performance. *Family Business Review*, 19(4): 253–273.

Dyer, W. G., & Sanchez, M. 1998. Current State of Family Business Theory and Practice as Reflected in Family Business Review 1988–1997. *Family Business Review*, 11(4): 287–295.

Ensley, M. D., & Pearson, A. W. 2005. An Exploratory Comparison of The Behavioral Dynamics of Top Management Teams in Family and Nonfamily New Ventures: Cohesion, Conflict, Potency, and Consensus. *Entrepreneurship Theory and Practice*, 29(3): 267–284.

Faccio, M., & Lang, L. H. P. 2002. The Ultimate Ownership of Western European Corporations. *Journal of Financial Economics*, 65(3): 365–395.

Fernández, Z., & Nieto, M. 2005. Internationalization Strategy of Small and Medium Sized Family Businesses: Some Influential Factors. *Family Business Review*, 18(1): 77–89.

Fernández, Z., & Nieto, M. J. 2006. Impact of Ownership on the International Involvement of SMEs. *Journal of International Business Studies*, 37(3): 340–351.

Fernández, Z., & Nieto, M. J. 2014. Internationalization of Family Firms. In L. Melin, M. Nordqvist, & P. Sharma (Eds.), *The SAGE Handbook of Family Business*: 403–423.

Fukuyama, F. 1995. *Trust: The Social Virtues and the Creation of Prosperity*. New York: Free Press.

Gallo, M. A., & Pont, C. G. 1996. *Important Factors in Family Business Internationalization*, 9(1): 45–59.

Gallo, M. A., & Sveen, J. 1991. Internationalizing the Family Business: Facilitating and Restraining Factors. *Family Business Review*, 4: 181–190.

Gersick, K. E., Davis, J. A., Hampton, M. M., & Lansberg, I. S. 1997. *Generation to Generation: Life Cycles of the Family Business*. Harvard Business School Press, http://books.google.com/books?hl=en&lr=&id=-CcGUxSCJqcC&oi=fnd&pg=PR7&dq=Generation+to+Generation:+Life+Cycles+of+the+Family+Business&ots=RgcTznwL1o&sig=OPbW9chPvUQxDdrpHhlsM7jhWxw.

Gómez-Mejía, L. R. 2012. Socioemotional wealth in the family business. *FERC*. Montreal.

Gómez-Mejía, L. R., & Cruz, C. C. 2011. The bind that ties: Socioemotional wealth preservation in family firms. *The Academy of Management Annals*, 5(June 2011): 653–707.

Gómez-Mejía, L. R., Haynes, K. T., Núñez-Nickel, M., Jacobson, K. J. L., & Moyano-Fuentes, J. 2007. Socioemotional Wealth and Business Risks in Family-controlled Firms: Evidence from Spanish Olive Oil Mills. *Administrative Science Quarterly*, 52: 106–137.

Gómez-Mejía, L. R., Makri, M., & Kintana, M. L. 2010. Diversification Decisions in Family-Controlled Firms. *Journal of Management Studies*, 47(2): 223–252.

Graves, C., & Thomas, J. 2006. Internationalization of Australian Family Businesses: A Managerial Capabilities Perspective. *Family Business Review*, XIX(3).

Gulbrandsen, T. 2005. Flexibility in Norwegian family-owned enterprises. *Family Business Review*, 18(1): 57–76.

Habbershon, T. G., & Williams, M. L. 1999. A Resource-Based Framework for Assessing the Strategic Advantages of Family Firms. *Family Business Review*, 12(1): 1–25.

Habbershon, T. G., Williams, M., & MacMillan, I. C. 2003. A Unified Systems Perspective of Family Firm Performance. *Journal of Business Venturing*, 18(4): 451–465.

Handler, W. C. 1989. Methodological Issues and Considerations in Studying Family Businesses. *Family Business Review*, 2(3): 257–276.

Harris, D., Martinez, J. I., & Ward, J. L. 1994. Is Strategy Different for the Family-Owned Business? *Family Business Review*, 7(2): 159–174.

Hautz, J., Mayer, M. C. J., & Stadler, C. 2013. Ownership Identity and Concentration: A Study of their Joint Impact on Corporate Diversification. *British Journal of Management*, 24: 102–126.

Hitt, M. A., & Sirmon, D. G. 2003. Managing Resources: Linking Unique Resources, Management, and Wealth Creation in Family Firms. *Entrepreneurship Theory and Practice*, 27(4): 339–358.

Irava, W. J., & Moores, K. 2010. Clarifying the Strategic Advantage of Familiness: Unbundling Its Dimensions and Highlighting Its Paradoxes. *Journal of Family Business Strategy*, 1(3): 131–144.

Klein, S. B., Astrachan, J. H., & Smyrnios, K. X. 2005. The F-PEC Scale of Family Influence: Construction, Validation, and Further Implication for Theory. *Entrepreneurship, Theory, and Practice …*, 29(3): 321–339.

Kontinen, T., & Ojala, A. 2010. The Internationalization of Family Businesses: A Review of Extant Research. *Journal of Family Business Strategy*, 1(2): 97–107.

Kuo, A., Kao, M. S., Chang, Y. C., & Chiu, C. F. 2012. The Influence of International Experience on Entry Mode Choice: Difference Between Family and Non-Family Firms. *European Management Journal*, 30(3): 248–263.

La Porta, R., Lopez-de-silanes, F., Shleifer, A., & Vishny, R. 2002. *Investor Protection and Corporate Valuation*, LVII(3).

Lansberg, I. S. 1988. The Succession Conspiracy. *Family Business Review*, 1(2): 119–143.

Liang, X., Wang, L., & Cui, Z. 2014. Chinese Private Firms and Internationalization: Effects of Family Involvement in Management and Family Ownership. *Family Business Review*, 27: 126–141.

Lumpkin, G. T., Steier, L., & Wright, M. 2011. *Strategic Entrepreneurship in Family Business*, 306: 285–306.

Merino, F., Monreal-Pérez, J., & Sánchez-Marín, G. 2014. Family SMEs' Internationalization: Disentangling the Influence of Familiness on Spanish Firms' Export Activity. *Journal of Small Business Management*, 1–21.

Moores, K. 2009. Paradigms and Theory Building in the Domain of Business Families. *Family Business Review*, 22(2): 167–180.

Muñoz-Bullón, F., & Sánchez-Bueno, M. J. 2012. Do Family Ties Shape the Performance Consequences of Diversification? Evidence From the European Union. *Journal of World Business*, 47: 469–477.

Neubauer, F., & Lank, A. G. 1998. *The Family Business*. London: MacMillan Business.

Okoroafo, S., & Perryy, M. 2010. Generational Perspectives of the Export Behavior of Family Businesses. *International Journal of Economics and Finance*, 19(3): 15–24.

Pearson, A. W., Carr, J. C., & Shaw, J. C. 2008. Toward a Theory of Familiness: A Social Capital Perspective. *Entrepreneurship Theory and Practice*, 32(6): 949–969.

Pieper, T. M., Klein, S., & Jaskiewicz, P. 2008. The Impact of Goal Alignment on Board Composition and Board Size in Family Businesses. *Journal of Small Business Management*, 46(3): 372–394.

Pinho, J. C. 2007. The Impact of Ownership: Location-Specific Advantages and Managerial Characteristics on SME Foreign Entry Mode Choices. *International Marketing Review*, 24(6): 715–734.

Puig, N., & Pérez, P. F. 2009. A Silent Revolution: The Internationalisation of Large Spanish Family Firms. *Business History*, 51(3): 462–483.

Pukall, T. J., & Calabrò, A. 2013. The Internationalization of Family Firms: A Critical Review and Integrative Model. *Family Business Review*, (June 2013). http://fbr.sagepub.com/cgi/doi/10.1177/0894486513491423.

Pukall, T. J., & Calabrò, A. 2014. The Internationalization of Family Firms: A Critical Review and Integrative Model. *Family Business Review*, 27(2): 103–125.

Rau, S. B. 2014. Resource-based view of family firms. In L. Melin, M. Nordqvist, & P. Sharma (Eds.), *The SAGE Handbook of Family Business*: 321–340.

Rutherford, M. W., & Holt, D. T. 2008. Examining the Link and Performance: Can the F-PEC Untangle the Family Business Theory Jungle ? *Entrepreneurship Theory and Practice*, (804): 1089–1110.

Salvato, C. C., & Corbetta, G. 2014. Strategic Content and Process in Family Business. In L. Melin, M. Nordqvist, & P. Sharma (Eds.), *The SAGE Handbook of Family Business*: 295–321.

Sanchez-Bueno, M. J., & Usero, B. 2014. How May the Nature of Family Firms Explain the Decisions Concerning International Diversification? *Journal of Business Research*, 67: 1311–1320.

Sánchez-Sellero, P., Rosell-Martínez, J., & García-Vázquez, J. M. 2014. Absorptive Capacity from Foreign Direct Investment in Spanish Manufacturing Firms. *International Business Review*, 23: 429–439.

Sciascia, S., Mazzola, P., Astrachan, J. H., & Pieper, T. M. 2012. The Role of Family Ownership in International Entrepreneurship: Exploring Nonlinear Effects. *Small Business Economics*, 38: 15–31.

Segaro, E. 2012. Internationalization of Family SMEs: The Impact of Ownership, Governance, and Top Management Team. *Journal of Management and Governance*, 16: 147–169.

Sharma, P. 2004. An Overview of the Field of Family Business Studies: Current Status and Directions for the Future. *Family Business Review*, 17(1): 1–36.

Shleifer, A., & Vishny, R. W. 1986. Large Shareholders and Corporate Control. *Journal of Political Economy*, 94(3): 461–488.

Swinth, R. L., & Vinton, K. L. 1993. Do Family-Owned Businesses Have a Strategic Advantage in International Joint Ventures? *Family Business Review*, 6(1): 19–30.

Tagiuri, R., & Davis, J. A. 1992. On The Goals of Successful Family Companies. *Family Business Review*, 5(1): 43–62.

Tagiuri, R., & Davis, J. 1996. Bivalent Attributes of the Family Firm. *Family Business Review*, 9(2): 199–208.

Tsang, E. W. K. 2002a. Learning From Overseas Venturing Experience: The Case of Chinese Family Businesses. *Journal of Business Venturing*, 17: 21–40.

Tsang, E. W. K. 2002b. Internationalizing the Family Firm: A Case Study of a Chinese Family Business. *Journal of Small Business Management*, 200139(1): 88–94.

Verbeke, A., & Kano, L. 2012. The Transaction Cost Economics Theory of the Family Firm: Family-Based Human Asset Specificity and the Bifurcation Bias. *Entrepreneurship: Theory and Practice*, 36(6): 1183–1205.

Wiseman, R. M., & Gómez-Mejía, L. R. 1998. A Behavioral Agency Model of Management Risk Taking. *Academy of Management Review*, 23(1): 133–153.

Zahra, S. A. 2003. International Expansion of U.S. Manufacturing Family Businesses: The Effect of Ownership and Involvement. *Journal of Business Venturing*, 18(4): 495–512.

Zahra, S. A., & Sharma, P. 2004. Family Business Research: A Strategic Reflection. *Family Business Review*, 17(4): 331–346.

Zahra, S., Hayton, J. C., Neubaum, D. O., Dibrell, C., & Craig, J. 2008. Culture of Family Commitment and Strategic Flexibility: The Moderating Effect of Stewardship. *Entrepreneurship: Theory & Practice*, 32(6): 1035–1054.

Zellweger, T. M., Eddleston, K. A., & Kellermanns, F. W. 2010. Exploring the Concept of Familiness: Introducing Family Firm Identity. *Journal of Family Business Strategy*, 1: 54–63.

Zellweger, T. M., Kellermanns, F. W., Eddleston, K. a., & Memili, E. 2012. Building a Family Firm Image: How Family Firms Capitalize on Their Family Ties. *Journal of Family Business Strategy*, 3(4): 239–250.

Zellweger, T. M., & Nason, R. S. 2008. A Stakeholder Perspective on Family Firm Performance. *Family Business Review*, 21(3): 203–216.

7

SOCIOEMOTIONAL WEALTH PRESERVATION IN FAMILY FIRMS

A Source of Value Destruction or Value Creation?

Ionela Neacsu[1], Geoffrey Martin, and Luis Gómez-Mejía

The role played by large family owners and minority shareholders in influencing firm strategic decisions has been widely analyzed in the management literature (e.g., Block 2010, 2012; Chrisman and Patel 2012; Deephouse and Jaskiewicz 2013; Feldman et al. 2014; Gómez-Mejía et al. 2010, 2014; Grossman and Hart 1986; Miller et al. 2010; Muñoz-Bullon and Sanchez-Bueno 2011; Patel and Chrisman 2014; Shleifer and Vishny 1986). According to the growing body of research exploring the interplay between family and non-family shareholders, family owners are prone to make strategic decisions that follow their own subjective rules—triggered by their own risk preference—rather than make choices based on objective financial criteria which presumably would be more beneficial to non-family shareholders (Anderson et al. 2012; Chua et al. 2015). Given this conflict of interests between family and non-family shareholders, powerful family owners may develop an "us-against-them" mentality (Kellermanns et al. 2012) that leads them to use their control and influence over the business to alter firm strategic decision-making in ways that advance their family interests. That is, family owners purportedly obtain private benefits from the firm at the expense of other firm stakeholders (Berkman et al. 2009; Fan and Wong 2002; Grossman and Hart 1986). In fact, family owners' prioritization of family goals is likely to influence the future of the firm since it affects the allocation of internal resources, the relationship with non-family stakeholders, as well as the work environment (Hitt et al. 2009). For instance, senior executives of family firms may allocate considerable levels of resources and capabilities to achieve family goals, which may have negative consequences for firm performance (Shleifer and Vishny 1986).

Given family owners' intentions to exercise control and influence over the family firm—often at the expense of non-family stakeholders—the research question we revisit in this book chapter is: 'How does family ownership influence firm performance?' Although a large body of literature has addressed this question by examining the differences in performance results between family and non-family firms, the findings remain contradictory and the conclusions are mixed (e.g., Dyer 2006; Miller et al. 2007; Schulze et al. 2001, 2003). Further confounding this stream of literature, family firms are generally found to outperform non-family firms, despite their purported pursuit of non-financial objectives (see extensive review by Amit and Villalonga 2014). One possible explanation for these equivocal findings is that the definition used for classifying a firm as family-owned differs considerably between studies, given 'family-owned' is a relatively arbitrary measurement (Amit and Villalonga 2014). That is, the proxy used can depend on both the subjective perception of researchers and more objective criteria, such as the percentage of family ownership and the number of family members in management positions or on the board of directors (Dyer 2006).

The relationship between family firm's aspiration to achieve family-centered non-economic goals (flow) and the accumulation of effective resources that have non-economic utility (stock) is likely to represent a source of heterogeneity among family firms (Chua et al. 2015). As Chua and colleagues argue, family firms driven by non-economic flow are more likely to take aggressive strategic decisions (making them more risk-willing) relative to family firms driven by non-economic stock. Given that riskier strategic actions are associated with high economic returns (Fama and French 1992), the distinction between stocks and flows of non-economic wealth may help explain differences in performance among family firms. Lastly, a diverse set of contingencies such as firm size, the nature of the sample, generational stage or the type of firm may all be behind these mixed results (Villalonga and Amit 2006; Morck et al. 2004). For instance, Naldi and colleagues (2013) compared firms led by family CEOs and firms led by non-family CEOs across two types of business environments, namely industrial districts and publicly listed firms in Italy. Their findings show that family firms with a family member as CEO outperform family firms with a non-family CEO when analyzed based on industrial districts, and underperform them when the firms are publicly traded. That is, having a family CEO at the helm improves firm performance in industrial districts where the social norms and tacit rules are of greater importance, and becomes a burden in publically traded companies, where broader stakeholder management has more importance. Similarly, Villalonga and Amit (2006) and Miller et al. (2007) report that family firms outperform non-family firms, yet only when the founder remains involved. We conclude that, although the family influence on firm's decisions is indubitable, the impact of family ownership on firm performance remains an open research question. Our intention is to revisit this issue from the perspective of the socioemotional wealth (SEW) preservation theory (Gómez-Mejía et al. 2007), which "has gained great traction in family business research in recent years" (Schulze and Kellermanns 2015).

Socioemotional Wealth Theory

Because the SEW construct has been used in family firm research for less than 10 years, most prior research on family business performance has not relied on SEW as a theoretical lens. The purpose of this chapter is to reexamine prior literature, focusing on the question of whether SEW preservation in family businesses helps create or destroy firm value. Specifically, we reinterpret prior results using the logic of loss aversion in the context of SEW, derived from the behavioral agency model (BAM; Wiseman and Gómez-Mejía 1998). Consistent with prospect theory (Kahneman and Tversky 1979; Tversky and Kahneman 1992) BAM's predictions draw on the concept of loss aversion, which suggests that individuals prefer to preserve the accumulated value of their wealth rather than pursue strategic decisions with uncertain prospective gains. BAM's main objective is to analyze managerial agents' risk preferences in response to the wealth-at-risk (or risk bearing) associated with compensation. Family firm literature applies this logic to decision making of the firm's principals – often comparing family principals' decision making to non-family firm principals. Hence, instead of analyzing decisions of managerial agents, family firm scholars have examined loss aversion of family principals with respect to their stock of SEW.

SEW is an umbrella term coined by Gómez-Mejía and colleagues (2007) to capture the whole set of non-pecuniary endowments that the family has embedded in the firm. This would include, for instance, enjoyment of family control over the business, granting family members job security and financial benefits, assuring the transgenerational control of the family business, as well as securing the family's reputation and status in the community (see Berrone et al. 2012, for a discussion of various SEW dimensions). As a consequence of these family-specific utilities, family owners are considered loss averse to SEW. That is, when making risky strategic decisions, family firms will trade off economic and non-economic goals. For instance, family firms engage in lower R&D investments (Block 2012; Chrisman and Patel 2012; Gómez-Mejía et al. 2014; Muñoz-Bullon and Sanchez-Bueno 2011; Patel and Chrisman 2014), less international diversification (Gómez-Mejía et al., 2010; Miller et al., 2010), fewer unrelated acquisitions (Gómez-Mejía, Patel and Zellweger in press), lower asset divestiture (Feldman et al. 2014), lower cooperative participation (Gómez-Mejía et al. 2007) and invest more in environmental programs (Berrone et al. 2010), among others, to protect SEW and prolong the family control over the firm, even if these actions are detrimental to the "bottom line." This trade-off between socioemotional and financial benefits is likely to provide one explanation as to why the evidence regarding family firms' performance relative to non-family firms is mixed or conflicting.

Contrary to non-family firms that are primarily interested in maximizing firm financial results, family firms think of performance in a broader sense, comprising both pecuniary and socioemotional forms of wealth (Gómez-Mejía et al. 2011). Thus, to family owners, the firm's value includes both socioemotional and financial endowments (Zellweller et al. 2012). Expanding on this idea, McKenny and colleagues (2012) suggest integrating family firms' non-financial (or socioemotional) benefits into a multidimensional performance measure. However, measuring family firm performance from a multidimensional perspective represents a challenge for researchers trying to understand how family ownership and control influence firm results. For instance, under financial distress, family firms may increase R&D investments despite that this could lead to a reduction in SEW (Gómez-Mejía et al. 2014). As R&D investments imply that part of family control and influence needs to be delegated to external experts, the family firm becomes dependent on external parties from outside the family area of influence. In a similar fashion, when exposed to greater potential for bankruptcy, family firms may engage in greater diversification (Gómez-Mejía et al. 2010), join a cooperative (Gómez-Mejía et al. 2007), or even replace a long-tenured family CEO with an external executive (Gómez-Mejía et al. 2001).

Applying a behavioral agency logic (Wiseman and Gómez-Mejía 1998), family owners consider both economic and socioemotional reference points when framing the possible outcomes of their strategic decisions in terms of gains and losses. Given that SEW preservation depends on the firm's survival, SEW loss avoidance represents a priority as long as the firm is not suffering from financial distress (Chrisman and Patel 2012). However, as performance hazard decreases, family firms will be more prone to make strategic decisions motivated by both financial and socioemotional considerations, with the latter moving to the forefront if the firm is financially secure (Chrisman and Patel 2012). That is, in order to ensure firm survival and the preservation of the family-specific endowment, family owners need to guarantee their firm's economic sustenance. This might explain why SEW preservation may not lead to lower economic performance, except perhaps if we consider opportunity costs of SEW loss avoidance when the firm is performing relatively well (for instance, family owners may make "suboptimal" economic investments, such as lower R&D, to protect SEW when the firm is not in financial danger; Gómez-Mejía et al. 2014; Chrisman and Patel 2012). Thus, overall family firms, despite the SEW loss aversion motive, may slightly outperform non-family firms. This conclusion is consistent with firm performance differences between family and non-family based on dozens of prior empirical studies recently reviewed by Amit and Villalonga (2014).

Value Destruction as the Offspring of SEW Loss Aversion

Despite the non-pecuniary benefits family owners obtain from preserving SEW, the family firm literature is still exploring how this family-specific socioemotional endowment affects strategic decision-making processes and firm performance. According to the SEW logic, family controlled firms are concerned with the preservation of SEW as their main goal, often at the expense of financial performance. That is, since family owners have most of their wealth (financial and non-financial) invested in the firm, they face severe consequences in case of failed strategic actions (Gedajlovic et al. 2004). As such, family firm's loss aversion to SEW results in family owners' tendency to avoid strategic decisions that may threaten SEW even when they have the potential to increase the firm's financial returns (Berrone et al. 2010; Deephouse and Jaskiewicz 2013; Gómez-Mejía et al. 2007, 2010, in press; Leitterstorf and Rau 2014; Zellweller et al. 2012).

Moreover, family owners deal with the negative consequences of their desire to protect SEW at the expense of other financial benefits, such as strong conflicts of interest between family members (Zellweger and Astrachan 2008) or between family owners and external stakeholders (Fan and Wong 2002). These conflicts may have severe negative implications for the survival of the family business as they could tear the firm apart, ultimately leading to a forced sale, liquidation or a merger. That is, the duality of family members' role inside the firm— family member and employee—is likely to make it difficult to achieve both socioemotional and financial goals (Berrone et al. 2012). Other family-specific characteristics such as sibling rivalry or identity conflicts (Schulze et al. 2001) are likely to accentuate the conflict between the different roles family members assume, making family members less likely to nurture the family firm's stakeholders (Kellermanns et al. 2012). According to Kellermanns and colleagues (2012), family-centric behavior is negatively associated with proactive stakeholder engagement. That is, such conflicts are strongly associated with a lower engagement of firm employees and reduced job satisfaction. Even when family employees are not able to leave the firm because of family ties with the rest of family members, the negative impact of such constrains is likely to be reflected in a hostile relationship with other employees, both family, and non-family, resulting in lower productivity.

Schulze and colleagues (2001) argue that family ownership and control may also represent a liability, due to a decrease in the firm's entrepreneurial behavior that may negatively influence firm growth and performance. Given the family's intention to protect and prolong its socioemotional endowment over the long run, family shareholders may become more conservative (risk averse) in their strategic actions. Presumably, this translates into weaker performance because family businesses are considered to be conservative, unwilling to change, and introverted, which is the opposite of the entrepreneurial spirit that might lead to higher returns (Naldi et al. 2007). This creates a problem for family firms given that: (1) obtaining superior results has been associated with risk taking, the so called "high risk/high return" paradigm (Miller and Bromiley 1990; Sanders and Hambrick 2007); and (2) family firms are argued to be more risk averse than non-family firms (Basu et al. 2009; McConaughy et al. 2001; Mishra and McConaughy1999). Since family owners are less diversified than non-family shareholders, they are also more likely to bear the brunt of downturns in their chosen industry without the benefit of diversified investments stemming from having wealth spread across businesses with negatively correlated returns. That is, the family firm's wealth (financial and socioemotional) could be significantly affected by the negative results of failed risky choices due to a lack of diversification. As a result, since high returns are generally associated with taking high risks, family firm's vulnerability to losses will cause them to avoid high risk; high return strategies that may come at the expense of family's socioemotional wealth.

Gómez-Mejía and colleagues (2007) offer strong theoretical and empirical support for the hypothesis that family firms may choose to preserve SEW at the expense of financial benefits. Based on a population of Spanish olive oil mills, the authors show that family firms are less likely to join a cooperative that would bring them financial benefits in order to preserve their SEW. That is, family firms prefer to remain independent even if this decision would imply assuming greater business risks due to a higher probability of failure and lower performance. In a similar fashion, researchers have shown that family firms are less likely than non-family firms to engage in corporate diversification (Anderson and Reeb 2003b; Gómez-Mejía et al. 2010). According to Gómez-Mejía and colleagues (2011), firm diversification represents a threat to family owners' SEW for several reasons. First, firm diversification may require extra funding from external parties who would gain power over the strategic decision-making process of the family firm and consequently weaken family owners' ability to control and influence the family business. Second, diversification projects may also require hiring external expertise, leading to an increase in the information asymmetry between family owners and managers and ultimately reduce family owners' authority and monitoring ability. Lastly, by introducing new products and technologies or entering new markets, family's authorities and traditions would be threatened, leading to a decrease in SEW. Gómez-Mejía and colleagues (2010) also found that family firms are less eager to engage in international diversification that would decrease the family firm's dependence on local revenues, reduce the risk profile of the firm and therefore the cost of capital. Family owners' concern for SEW preservation may also slow rates of growth, reduce the investments in product development, as well as diminish the firm's ability to accumulate capital (Gómez-Mejía et al. 2014; Schulze and Kellermanns 2015). Likewise, family firms are less likely to use debt financing, suffering the consequences associated with their undiversified wealth and higher risk (Schulze et al. 2003).

The preservation of family SEW is also prone to restrain the family firm's innovative behavior for various reasons, as presented by Block and colleagues (2013). First, family owners' desire to exercise control and influence over the firm's strategic decisions may, in fact, diminish the firm's access to financial capital with potential to dilute family control, such that innovation projects with significant resonance are unlikely to be funded. Second, family shareholders' desire to appoint family members to key positions within the firm may restrain the managerial expertise needed to undertake sound innovation projects. Third, family owners' desire to pass the family legacy to next generations (transgenerational) control (Berrone et al. 2010), or the motivation for dynastic succession (Berrone et al. 2012), may in fact expose family members' inability to manage their firm and thus reflect their failure to engage in the innovation that is crucial for their firm's competitiveness. Lastly, most innovation projects are characterized by high levels of uncertainty. As such, family firms are inclined to invest in innovation projects with lower economic and technological relevance than non-family firms, even when controlling for the level of R&D spending (Block et al. 2013). That is, family firms will not only invest less in R&D than their non-family counterparts but will choose those innovation projects with inferior economic and technological impact. It follows that, by investing less in R&D projects, family firms' growth and survival are at risk (especially in high technology markets), whereas a constant investment level may allow firms to remain competitive in the market (Gómez-Mejía et al. 2011).

Similar to the case of R&D investments, Feldman and colleagues (2014) show that family owners may choose to retain rather than divest firm assets, motivated by their intentions to provide management positions for future family generations and prolong established relationships with firm stakeholders such as employees, buyers, and suppliers. The authors also mention that family firms may protect themselves from short-term market pressures by introducing control measures such as dual-class stock, high board representations, pyramids and voting arrangements.

Faccio and colleagues (2001) demonstrated that in an East Asian empirical context, due to conflict of interests that emerge between family members, family firms are worse performers than non-family firms. According to Anderson and Reeb (2003), among Fortune-500 firms, dual share classes, hierarchies and voting arrangements are likely to weaken the founder's positive effect on firm value that we have referred to previously (cf.Villalonga and Amit 2006). According to Anderson and Reeb (2003a), conflict of interest between owners and managers are more costly in non-family firms relative to founder firms, and less costly in next-generations family firms relative to non-family firms. In addition, the effect of descendant CEOs on firm value is negatively associated with family firms owned by second-generation family members but positively associated with third-generation family firms.

Managerial entrenchment is also related to SEW preservation as the family is reluctant to replace one of its own, despite poor performance outcomes (Gómez-Mejía et al. 2001). Given that family managers tend to be relatively free from performance accountability, they tend to achieve longer tenures than their contributions would justify. According to McConaughy (2000), the tenure of family members holding executive positions tends to be three times longer than the tenure of non-family executives. Likewise, Gómez-Mejía and colleagues (2001) found that family CEOs' tenure is about seven years longer than the tenure of non-family CEOs when the probability of firm failure is high. Cruz et al. (2010) report that for similar performance levels the tenure of family CEOs is four times greater on average than the tenure of non-family CEOs. Some researchers argue that the main cause of managerial entrenchment is family altruism, resulting from a high concentration of family ownership (Stulz 1988) or from family owner's incapability to discipline another family member (Schulze et al. 2003). Thus, family managers' entrenchment may negatively affect firm performance. In support of these findings, Gómez-Mejía and colleagues (2003) show that, as industry-wide risk increases, family owners will increase family CEO's compensation to account for the possibility of firm failure or takeover, which would represent a threat to CEO's position within the firm.

Family members' altruism among each other has been found by Gómez-Mejía and colleagues (2001) and Schulze and colleagues (2001) to lead to poor performance. According to Schulze and colleagues (2001), family firms that have developed governance mechanisms able to curb altruism are better performers relative to firms which didn't adopt such measures. In a similar fashion, Gómez-Mejía and colleagues (2001) argue in their study based on the population of Spanish family newspapers that these organizations were less likely to dismiss family member CEOs than non-family firms owing to family altruism. However, when the family CEO was fired and replaced, performance improved significantly relative to the performance of non-family firms that also named new CEOs. In consequence, when family firms delay the decision to replace inefficient CEOs due to altruism, they are likely to negatively affect firm performance on a longer period.

Cucculelli and Micucci (2008) also found that family management has a negative impact on firm performance and this effect is stronger in competitive markets. According to the authors, family characteristics with a potentially positive impact on performance (stewardship, lower agency costs, long-term orientation and firm-specific investments) are significantly reduced when the firm is controlled by family members. For instance, family owners' desire to maintain control over the firm may lead them to assign family members to the board, which will negatively affect non-family stakeholders (Kellermanns et al. 2012). In addition, hiring outsiders for key positions within the firm is likely to be discouraged in family firms (Gómez-Mejía et al. 2010; Kets de Vries 1993). Although this tendency can be explained from a socioemotional point of view, there are also other factors impacting it, such as limited resources and capabilities, as well as the size of the firm (Gómez-Mejía et al. 2011). In fact, even when hiring outsiders, family owners will try to instill new employees with family values and rules to preserve their socioemotional endowment. It follows that family owners' desire to control the family business and appoint family members to key positions within the firm may lead to dysfunctional conservatism, unqualified management, and strategic involution (Miller and Le Breton-Miller 2014). Although these consequences may align with family's socioemotional objectives, they ultimately decrease firm performance, reduce the chances of firm survival, and lead to discontent non-family stakeholders (Schulze and Kellermanns 2015).

Nevertheless, family owners' loss aversion to SEW does not mean that they ignore the financial consequences of their strategic choices. It is more likely that, under family ownership, firms are willing to indulge the costs and uncertainty associated with certain strategic decisions led by the belief that the prospective financial gains are counterbalanced by family-specific noneconomic benefits. Next, we are offering evidence for the purported positive effect of SEW on family firm performance.

Value Creation as the Offspring of SEW Loss Aversion

As discussed above, family firms have idiosyncratic firm-specific non-utilitarian endowment in the form of socioemotional wealth (Gómez-Mejía et al. 2007). As a result of this non-pecuniary investment, family principals' financial and socioemotional risk bearing (wealth-at-risk) leads them to subjectively value their firm higher than owners of non-family firms (Zellweger et al. 2012). Empirical evidence shows that, because of a strong association between the firm and the family name, public attacks to firm's reputation could have devastating consequences on the future of the family business (Westhead et al. 2001). As a consequence, family firms are prone to achieve higher levels of corporate social responsibility and community service in order to protect or enhance family firm's image and reputation in society (Berrone et al. 2010; Dyer and Whetten 2006). It follows that family firms are more likely than owners of non-family firms to closely monitor managers' strategic decision-making process to ensure that they will not expose the family firm to financial losses that would ultimately lead to dramatic reputational (and thus SEW) losses.

Amit and colleagues (2015) argue in their research study based on publicly listed Chinese firms that family firms may, in fact, outperform non-family firms when institutional efficiency is high. This is consistent with the seminal agency literature (cf. Berle and Means 1932; Jensen and Meckling 1976) arguing that the concentration of ownership has a positive effect on firm value given a reduction in the conflict of interest appearing between owners and managers. Since the family name has great visibility, family owners will be more strongly linked with the business relative to their non-family counterparts, making them more committed and loyal to their business (Ward and Dolan 1998). Family members are willing to work intensively, in many cases even without extra compensation, and are flexible regarding their responsibilities in order to assure firms' survival and success. In addition, family members are usually involved in the family firm starting at early ages in order to understand how the business works, the attributes of firm customers, suppliers, and competitors, and have received intensive training from experienced family leaders (Dyer 1992). Such an apprenticeship can lead to a considerable competitive advantage relative to non-family firms without access to such a profound learning process. Other scholars propose that family firms are also better at attracting loyal customers and offering higher quality service due to the goodwill and truthfulness inspired by the family name and reputation and the commitment to their customers (Dyer 2006; Dollinger 1995). In sum, from the resource-based point of view, "firms with assets that are valuable, rare, inimitable, and nonsubstitutable may be able to create a sustainable competitive advantage" (Dyer 2006: 262), implying that such resources may improve family firm performance.

It follows that elements of SEW such as dynastic succession, strong social ties between the family firm members, the importance of family identity within the firm and family transgenerational control can make the family firm more competitive and thus survive over the long-term. Given their longer-term orientation (Miller and Le Breton-Miller 2005), family firms are also more likely than non-family firms to invest in patient strategies that result in building lasting relationships with firm's stakeholders such as suppliers and customers to acquire social capital and goodwill (Carney 2005). Consequently, in times of financial distress, this type of non-financial capital represents a social protection for firm's capital (Godfrey 2005). In short, the challenge for family owners is to guarantee firm survival by using SEW as a resource that enhances the firm's long-term competitive advantage.

We have mentioned that family firms tend to under-invest in R&D despite the potential negative effect on long-term competitiveness. However, there is also potentially a bright side to family firm's unique R&D approach. Given that family firms are more prone than non-family firms to have a better understanding of the family business and processes, there is likely to be lower information asymmetry between owners and managers (Miller and Le Breton-Miller, 2005; Ward, 2004). As a result, although family firms may invest less in R&D projects relative to non-family firms (Chen and Hsu 2009; Chrisman and Patel 2012; Patel and Chrisman 2013; Gómez-Mejía et al. 2014), once the decision to make the investment was taken, they may obtain lower agency costs and more successful R&D investments (Block 2012).

Family firms are also able to attract unique physical and financial capital to be used by the firm. According to Sirmon and Hitt (2003), family firms possess survivability capital, which represents the joint financial resources of the family, able to provide the firm with greater slack relative to those firms (non-family) that don't have access to it. Family owners may use financial resources from the family members uninvolved in the business as well, which protects the firm against major financial problems and contributes to the growth of the family firm. Some authors argue that family firms represent fertile grounds for entrepreneurial behaviors, necessary for firm foundation and evolution (Aldrich and Cliff 2003). According to Zahra (2005), goal convergence between family members and the firm, as well as goal continuity across family generations working within the firm may foster entrepreneurial behaviors. Together with a long-term orientation and lasting social relationships this may all contribute to greater perseverance in the pursuit of opportunities (Kellermanns et al. 2008), ultimately leading to an improvement in firm performance.

Founder involvement has often been argued to improve the performance of family firms (Amit and Villalonga 2006; Anderson and Reeb 2003a). This is explained by the fact that family members' identification with the firm, control and influence weakens as the firm changes its status from founding-family business to later generations family ownership (Gómez-Mejía et al. 2007). In other words, as family owners' desire to preserve SEW weakens from one generation to another, the use of SEW as a main reference point for strategic decision-making is also likely to decrease, inducing managers to make decisions aimed at improving firm's financial results (Anderson and Reeb 2003a). Similarly, founders have been argued to be more growth focused because they are less impeded by family non-economic priorities (Le Breton-Miller and Miller 2008).

Family firms' strategic decision-making process is also strongly influenced by family owners' desire to pass the business to future family generations, what is known as dynastic succession (Berrone et al. 2012; Chrisman and Patel 2012; Gómez-Mejía et al. 2011). According to Anderson and Reeb (2003a), because of blood ties between family members, family owners view their business as an asset to be passed to future family generations and not wealth to be spent during their reign. Thus, in order to ensure the transgenerational transfer of family ownership and control (or dynastic succession; Berrone et al. 2012), family firms need to make strategic decisions that strengthen firm longevity. Such long-term objectives are achieved when family firms' strategic decisions are characterized by three elements: futurity, continuity, and perseverance (Lumpkin and Brigham 2011). Futurity refers to a prospective orientation of firm's strategic decisions; continuity requires the appreciation of firm's legacy, values, and traditions while perseverance implies the firm's ability to accept short-term sacrifices in order to attain long-term objectives.

Several family business scholars have argued that family firms may be indeed longer-term oriented than non-family firms given their intention to assure the transgenerational continuity of family control and influence (Anderson and Reeb 2003a; Arregle et al. 2007; Gómez-Mejía et al. 2011; James 1999; Kets de Vries 1993; Le Breton-Miller and Miller 2006; Miller et al. 2010; Sirmon and Hitt 2003; Zellweger and Astrachan 2008; Zellweger et al. 2012). That is, family firms may take strategic decisions intended to help the future family generations continue to enjoy the emotional and economic benefits of ownership, which may not necessarily produce economic gains in the shorter term (Block 2010; Casson 1999; James 1999). Since family owners are interested in achieving non-utilitarian benefits such as preserving the family's legacy, traditions, control and influence across generations (Gómez-Mejía et al. 2007), developing strong relationships with firm stakeholders (Berrone et al. 2012; Block 2010) or building a strong social position and image (Arregle et al. 2007), they are less pressured by external shareholders to obtain short-term results. According to Sirmon and Hitt (2003), family firms are more likely than non-family firms to invest in "patient capital," which is a type of financial capital without threat of liquidation on the short-term. Lastly, family owners may have greater self-efficacy and thus be more prudent in their risk taking behaviors, so that overall risk-taking is more successful (Martin et al. 2015)

Given that long-term horizons of firm strategic decisions may lead to superior performance in the long run (Drucker 1986; Jensen and Murphy 1990; Laverty 1996; Marginson and McAulay 2008; Mueller and Reardon 1993; Walsh and Seward 1990), family firms' desire to protect and prolong SEW across family generations may, in fact, lead to an alignment between the economic and family goals when analyzed over the long-term. Theoretical work examining family firm's temporal orientation relative to non-family firms supports the idea that the former type of ownership has longer-term horizons than the latter. For instance, family firms are more likely than their non-family counterparts to develop market loyalty, highly skilled employees and stable relationships with external stakeholders to ensure firm longevity (Arregle et al. 2007; Carney 2005; Chrisman et al. 2009; Miller et al. 2010). Family firms are also more likely to have concentrated ownership, lengthy executive tenure, and superior business expertise, all being associated with a long-term orientation (Le Breton-Miller and Miller 2006) and thus, with superior performance. A greater accumulation of slack resources, taking a less strategic risk and having a lower bankruptcy risk (Gentry et al. 2014) may also be precedents of superior performance results for family businesses. These findings may partly explain why, despite the negative consequences of SEW preservation (for instance, nepotism, managerial entrenchment, conflicts between family members, excessive control and influence over the firm as such; Gómez-Mejía et al. 2011, Schulze and colleagues 2001, 2003), family firms may in fact outperform non-family firms (Amit and Villalonga 2014; Amit et al. 2015).

Powerful stakeholders are also likely to influence the strategic decision making of family firms and thus their performance outcomes (Bromiley 1991; Wright et al. 1996). For instance, powerful external shareholders (blockholders) are likely to resist family firms' intentions to pursue non-economic (socioemotional) goals (Anderson and Reeb 2004; Thomsen and Pedersen 2000). According to Harrison and colleagues (2010), firms need to satisfy the demands of their shareholders. That is, even though family owners' preferences for specific strategic decisions may be driven by their desire to protect and prolong SEW, they will still need to get the approval of external shareholders in order to initiate their investment plans (Cennamo et al. 2012). That is, family firms are likely to develop a strong shareholder orientation in order to protect and preserve their socioemotional wealth and reputation (Cennamo et al. 2009). As a consequence, blockholders' power to gain control over the firms' strategic decisions (Thomsen and Pedersen 2000) is likely to weaken family owners' ability to pursue socioemotional objectives and favor more economic-driven decisions with a positive effect on firm's short-term performance. In a similar fashion, firm creditors (debt holders) represent another key class of stakeholders with significant influence over the family firms' strategic decision-making process (Schulze et al. 2003). This happens because creditors are highly interested in debt repayment and thus are less inclined to encourage family owners' intentions to make strategic decisions led by socioemotional rather than financial objectives. Therefore, through the presence of debt holders on the board of directors or their power to influence managers' strategic decisions through debt agreements, family owners' discretion to preserve SEW in a manner prejudicial to firm performance is likely to be mitigated.

Summary and Conclusions

This chapter has analyzed the impact of SEW preservation logic on family firm performance. The cumulative evidence from theoretical and empirical studies reviewed here suggests that family owners' desire to protect and prolong SEW can have both positive and negative implications for firm. That is, strategic decisions that encourage SEW preservation may also expose the family firm to performance hazard and increased employment risk when the non-utilitarian benefits are not also balanced by financial considerations. Our review of the literature suggests that, rather than being entirely concerned with the preservation of SEW, family firms face a trade-off between socioemotional and economic objectives. For instance, Chrisman and Patel (2012) argue that SEW preservation takes priority in family firms as long as their performance doesn't decline relative to aspirations. The authors argue that when performance doesn't meet aspirations, the SEW goals will become less important for family owners, making them more myopic in their strategic decision-making. That is, when firm failure due to poor performance results becomes a threat—leading to a complete loss of SEW—family firms are more likely to take shorter-term strategic decisions to improve their economic situation. In a similar fashion, Gómez-Mejía and colleagues (2014) show that family and non-family firms are more similar in their strategic decision making in a low-performance context, driven by the fear of losing all their SEW as a consequence of firm failure. It follows that, when firm performance is above aspirations, socio-emotional goals are more likely to influence the strategic decisions of family firms, leading to a divergence from non-family firms' strategic decision-making.

Given the complexity of most strategic decisions, prior empirical findings on the relationship between family ownership, strategic choices and performance outcomes may be open to alternative interpretations. For instance, R&D investments can be both short-term (tactical) and long-term (strategic) (Smit and Ankum 1993). Likewise, asset divestiture can be considered to be both a resistance to short-term market pressure (Feldman et al. 2014) or value destroying on the long-term since it doesn't make use of opportunities specific to low-performing firms with valuable assets (Berry 2010). Similarly, local and international diversification may decrease firm risk in the short-term, but over the long-term reduces firm returns and thus threatens the firm's

Table 7.1 The Negative and Positive Effects of SEW Preservation

Negative Aspects of SEW	Positive Aspects of SEW
1. Less diversified shareholders	1. Control measures such as dual-class stock, high board representations, pyramids and voting arrangements protect family firms from short-term market shocks
2. Family owners purportedly obtain private benefits from the firm at the expense of other firm stakeholders	2. Lower agency costs
3. Allocation of considerable levels of resources and capabilities to guide the company in a particular direction, with negative consequences for firm performance	3. Long-term orientation
4. Dysfunctional conservatism	4. Invest in patient strategies that result in building lasting relationships with firm's stakeholders
5. Strategic involution	5. Higher levels of corporate social responsibility and community service
6. Slow rates of growth	6. Encourage firm-specific investments
7. Low investments in product development	7. Attract loyal customers, offering higher quality service
8. Diminished ability to accumulate capital	8. Superior business expertise
9. Less access to debt financing	9. Greater accumulation of slack resources
10. Lower R&D investments	10. Less strategic risk taking
11. Less local and international diversification	11. Lower bankruptcy risk
12. Lower asset divestiture	12. More successful R&D investments
13. Lower cooperative participation	13. Attract survivability capital
14. Unqualified management	14. Invest in "patient capital"
15. Nepotism and family altruism	15. Enhances futurity, continuity, and perseverance
16. Managerial entrenchment	16. Strong social ties between the family firm members
17. Conflicts between family members	17. Intentions for family transgenerational control
18. Excessive control and influence over the firm	18. Family stewardship: committed and loyal family members, that work intensively and are flexible regarding their responsibilities
19. Strong conflicts of interest between family members or between family owners and external stakeholders	19. Intensive training from experienced family leaders
20. Sibling rivalry and identity conflicts	20. Good knowledge of the family business
21. Lower entrepreneurial behavior (more conservative, unwilling to change, risk averse, introverted)	21. Considerable competitive advantage relative to non-family firms without access to a profound learning process

competitive position (Morck et al. 2004). The literature suggests that family firm's failure to make such strategic decisions may be explained by family owners' desire to exercise transgenerational control and influence over the firm—as socioemotional objectives—rather than based on performance considerations. However, we could also conclude from the aforementioned literature that the accumulated family-specific resources and capabilities allow family firms to obtain a long-term competitive advantage (Rau 2014) that is likely to contribute to outperformance relative to non-family firms (Amit and Villalonga 2014; Amit et al. 2015).

Consequently, a sensible conclusion from this review is that SEW loss aversion, which has been well established in the family business literature, may lead to suboptimal performance choices by family owners when the firm is doing relatively well (representing an opportunity cost); yet the same loss aversion will not put the firm in financial danger because this will also imply a potential loss in SEW (and in the extreme, the total loss of both SEW and the family's financial endowment if the case of firm failure). Another way of looking at this is that SEW loss aversion may induce family owners to "satisfice" rather than maximize when it comes to the pursuit of financial returns, and that paradoxically this may help in ensuring firm survival and in general offer some slight performance advantages over non-family firms (by promoting a long-term orientation, by avoiding imprudent risk taking, by having access to "patient capital," by enjoying greater reputation in the community, by having more continuity at the top and a more stable workforce).

In short, the effect of SEW preservation on firm performance may be both negative and positive (which we have summarized in Table 7.1); yet the fact that family firms, in general, tend to outperform non-family firms (Amit and Villalonga 2014) suggests that at worst, the performance consequence of SEW loss aversion is neutral (because the positives and the negatives cancel each other out). At best the net performance effect is positive, as a result of those SEW aspects that may enhance firm performance.

In terms of a future research agenda, the net impact of SEW preservation on firm performance needs further theoretical and empirical development before it can be considered a main characteristic of the family firm. Although the SEW logic provides a comprehensive theoretical framework to help us understand family firm behavior relative to non-family firm (that may ultimately provide a platform for a theory of the family firm), a more fine-grained theoretical and empirical research is still necessary. For instance, given the complexity of the SEW concept, future research could analyze which specific aspects of SEW are more likely to have a strong impact on firm behaviors and performance (cf. Miller and Le-Breton Miller 2014). Perhaps there are mediating behaviors that will further elucidate why family firm performance differs from non-family? Another interesting research question that deserves further examination is related to the causal effect between family owner's desire to protect and prolong SEW and firm performance. That is, do family firms achieve superior performance (relative to non-family firms) as a consequence of their desire to preserve and enhance SEW, or is it that family firms have dual socioemotional and economic objectives that may, in fact, be compatible over the long-term? Or do family owners outperform despite their commitment to emotional objectives that conflict with financial objectives? The generational stage also appears to be instrumental in differences between family and non-family firms (cf. Amit and Villalonga 2006), however, research examining the behavioral differences between different generations of family firms and how they impact performance is sparse. Further studies may need to address these research questions through the lens of a more comprehensive theoretical model that can explain both family owners' preference for dual—socioemotional and economic—objectives and contingencies (moderators) that make family firms behave similarly to non-family firms (and thus achieve similar performance levels).

Note

1 Corresponding author.

References

Aldrich, H. E., & Cliff, J. E. (2003) 'The pervasive effects of family on entrepreneurship: Toward a family embeddedness perspective,' *Journal of Business Venturing* 18(5): 573–596.

Amihud, Y. & B. Lev (1981) 'Risk reduction as a managerial motive for conglomerate mergers,' *Bell Journal of Economics* 12: 605–617.

Amit, R., Ding, Y., Villalonga, B., & Zhang, H. (2015) 'The role of institutional development in the prevalence and performance of entrepreneur and family-controlled firms,' *Journal of Corporate Finance* 31: 284–305.

Amit, R. & Villalonga, B. (2014) 'Financial performance of family firms,' In L. Melin, M. Nordqvist, and P. Sharma (eds.), *The SAGE Handbook of family business,* London: Sage, 157–178.

Anderson, R.C., Duru, A., & Reeb, D.M. (2012) 'Investment policy in family controlled firms,' *Journal of Banking & Finance* 36: 1744–1758.

Anderson, R. C., & Reeb, D. M. (2003a) 'Founding-family ownership and firm performance: Evidence from the S&P 500,' *Journal of Finance* 1301–1328.

Anderson, R. C., & Reeb, D. M. (2003b) 'Founding–family ownership, corporate diversification, and firm leverage,' *Journal of Law and Economics* 46(2): 653–684.

Anderson, R. C., & Reeb, D. M. (2004) 'Board composition: Balancing family influence in S&P 500 firms,' *Administrative Science Quarterly* 49(2): 209–237.

Arregle, J. L., Hitt, M. A., Sirmon, D. G., & Very, P. (2007) 'The development of organizational social capital: Attributes of family firms,' *Journal of Management Studies* 44(1): 73–95.

Basu, N., Dimitrova, L., & Paeglis, I. (2009) 'Family control and dilution in mergers,' *Journal of Banking & Finance* 33(5): 829–841.

Berkman, H., Cole, R. A., & Fu, L. J. (2009) 'Expropriation through loan guarantees to related parties: Evidence from China,' *Journal of Banking & Finance* 33(1): 141–156.

Berle, A., & Means, G. (1932) 'The modern corporate and private property,' New York, NY: McMillian.

Berrone, P., Cruz, C., & Gómez-Mejía, L. R. (2012) 'Socioemotional wealth in family firms theoretical dimensions, assessment approaches, and agenda for future research,' *Family Business Review* 25(3): 258–279.

Berrone, P., Cruz, C., Gómez-Mejía, L. R., & Larraza-Kintana, M. (2010) 'Socioemotional wealth and corporate responses to institutional pressures: Do family-controlled firms pollute less?,' *Administrative Science Quarterly* 55(1): 82–113.

Berry, H. (2010) 'Why do firms divest?,' *Organization Science* 21(2): 380–396.

Bertrand, M., & Schoar, A. (2006) 'The role of family in family firms,' *The Journal of Economic Perspectives* 73–96.

Block, J., Miller, D., Jaskiewicz, P., & Spiegel, F. (2013) 'Economic and technological importance of innovations in large family and founder firms an analysis of patent data,' *Family Business Review* 26(2): 180–199.

Block, J.H. (2012) 'R&D investments in family and founder firms: An agency perspective,' *Journal of Business Venturing* 27(2): 248–265.

Block, J.H. (2010) 'Family management, family ownership and downsizing: evidence from S&P 500 firms,' *Family Business Review* 23(2): 1–22.

Bromiley, P. (1991) 'Testing a causal model of corporate risk taking and performance,' *Academy of Management Journal* 34(1): 37–59.

Carney, M. (2005) 'Corporate governance and competitive advantage in family–controlled firms,' *Entrepreneurship Theory and Practice* 29(3): 249–265.

Casson, M. (1999) 'The economics of the family firm,' *Scandinavian Economic History Review* 47(1): 10–23.

Cennamo, C., Berrone, P., Cruz, C., & Gómez–Mejía, L. R. (2012) 'Socioemotional wealth and proactive stakeholder engagement: Why family–controlled firms care more about their stakeholders,' *Entrepreneurship Theory and Practice* 36(6): 1153–1173.

Cennamo, C., Berrone, P., & Gómez–Mejía, L. R. (2009) 'Does stakeholder management have a dark side?,' *Journal of Business Ethics* 89(4): 491–507.

Chen, H. L., & Hsu, W. T. (2009) 'Family ownership, board independence, and R&D investment,' *Family Business Review* 22(4): 347–362.

Chrisman, J. J., Chua, J. H., Sharma, P., & Yoder, T. R. (2009) 'Guiding family businesses through the succession process,' *The CPA Journal* 79(6): 48.

Chrisman, J. J., & Patel, P. C. (2012) 'Variations in R&D investments of family and nonfamily firms: Behavioral agency and myopic loss aversion perspectives,' *Academy of Management Journal* 55(4): 976–997.

Chua, J. H., Chrisman, J. J., & De Massis, A. (2015) 'A closer look at socioemotional wealth: Its flows, stocks, and prospects for moving forward,' *Entrepreneurship Theory & Practice* 39(2): 173–182.

Cruz, C. C., Gómez-Mejía, L. R., & Becerra, M. (2010) 'Perceptions of benevolence and the design of agency contracts: CEO-TMT relationships in family firms,' *Academy of Management Journal* 53(1): 69–89.

Cucculelli, M., & Micucci, G. (2008) 'Family succession and firm performance: Evidence from Italian family firms,' *Journal of Corporate Finance* 14(1): 17–31.

Deephouse, D. L., & Jaskiewicz, P. (2013) 'Do family firms have better reputations than non–family firms? An integration of socioemotional wealth and social identity theories,' *Journal of Management Studies* 50(3): 337–360.

Dollinger M. J. (1995) *Entrepreneurship: Strategies and Resources*. Boston, MA: Irwin.

Drucker, P. (1986) 'A crisis of capitalism.,' *Wall Street Journal* 30: 31.

Dyer, W. G. (2006) 'Examining the "family effect" on firm performance,' *Family Business Review* 19(4): 253–273.

Dyer, W. G., & Whetten, D. A. (2006) 'Family firms and social responsibility: Preliminary evidence from the S&P 500,' *Entrepreneurship Theory and Practice* 30(6): 785–802.

Dyer Jr, W. G. (1992) *The entrepreneurial experience: Confronting career dilemmas of the start-up executive*. The Jossey-Bass Management Series. San Francisco, CA: Jossey-Bass, Inc.

Faccio, M., Lang, L. H., & Young, L. (2001) 'Dividends and expropriation,' *American Economic Review* 54–78.

Fama, E. F., & French, K. R. (1992) 'The cross-section of expected stock returns,' *Journal of Finance* 47: 427–486.

Fama, E. F., & Jensen, M. C. (1985) 'Organizational forms and investment decisions,' *Journal of Financial Economics* 14(1): 101–119.

Fan, J. P., & Wong, T. J. (2002) 'Corporate ownership structure and the informativeness of accounting earnings in East Asia,' *Journal of Accounting and Economics* 33(3): 401–425.

Feldman, E. R., Amit, R. R., & Villalonga, B. (2014) 'Corporate divestitures and family control,' *Strategic Management Journal* DOI: 10.1002/smj.2329.

Gedajlovic, E., Lubatkin, M. H., & Schulze, W. S. (2004) 'Crossing the threshold from founder management to professional management: A governance perspective,' *Journal of Management Studies* 41(5): 899–912.

Gentry, R., Dibrell, C., & Kim, J. (2014). 'Long-term orientation in publicly traded family businesses: Evidence of a dominant logic,' *Entrepreneurship Theory and Practice* DOI: 10.1111/etap.12140.

Godfrey, P. C. (2005) 'The relationship between corporate philanthropy and shareholder wealth: A risk management perspective,' *Academy of Management Review* 30(4): 777–798.

Gómez-Mejía, L. R., Campbell, J. T., Martin, G., Hoskisson, R. E., Makri, M., & Sirmon, D. G. (2014) 'Socioemotional wealth as a mixed gamble: Revisiting family firm R&D investments with the behavioral agency model,' *Entrepreneurship Theory and Practice* 38(6): 1351–1374.

Gómez-Mejía, L. R., Cruz, C., Berrone, P., & De Castro, J. (2011) 'The bind that ties: Socioemotional wealth preservation in family firms,' *The Academy of Management Annals* 5(1): 653–707.

Gómez-Mejía, L. R., Haynes, K. T., Núñez-Nickel, M., Jacobson, K. J., & Moyano-Fuentes, J. (2007) 'Socioemotional wealth and business risks in family-controlled firms: Evidence from Spanish olive oil mills,' *Administrative Science Quarterly* 52(1): 106–137.

Gómez-Mejía, L. R., Larraza-Kintana, M., & Makri, M. (2003) 'The determinants of executive compensation in family-controlled public corporations,' *Academy of Management Journal* 46(2): 226–237.

Gómez-Mejía, L. R., Makri, M., & Kintana, M. L. (2010) 'Diversification decisions in family–controlled firms,' *Journal of Management Studies* 47(2): 223–252.

Gómez-Mejía, L. R., Nunez-Nickel, M., & Gutierrez, I. (2001) 'The role of family ties in agency contracts,' *Academy of Management Journal* 44(1): 81–95.

Gómez-Mejía, L.R., Patel, C., & Zellweger, T. (in press) 'In the horns of the dilemma: socioemotional wealth, financial wealth and acquisitions in family firms,' *Journal of Management* 1–50.

Grossman, S. J., & Hart, O. D. (1986) 'The costs and benefits of ownership: A theory of vertical and lateral integration,' *The Journal of Political Economy* 691–719.

Harrison, J. S., Bosse, D. A., & Phillips, R. A. (2010) 'Managing for stakeholders, stakeholder utility functions, and competitive advantage,' *Strategic Management Journal* 31(1): 58–74.

Hitt, M.A., Ireland, R.D., & Hoskisson, R.E. (2009) *Strategic management: Competitiveness and globalization, concepts and cases,* (8th ed.) Mason, OH: South-Western.

James, H. S. (1999) 'Owner as manager, extended horizons and the family firm,' *International Journal of the Economics of Business* 6(1): 41–55.

Jensen, M. C., & Meckling, W. H. (1976) 'Theory of the firm: Managerial behavior, agency costs and ownership structure,' *Journal of Financial Economics* 3(4): 305–360.

Jensen, M. C., & Murphy, K. J. (1990) 'Performance pay and top-management incentives,' *Journal of Political Economy* 225–264.

Kahneman, D., & Tversky, A. (1979) 'Prospect theory: An analysis of decision under risk,' *Econometrica: Journal of the Econometric Society* 263–291.

Kellermanns, F. W., Eddleston, K. A., Barnett, T., & Pearson, A. (2008) 'An exploratory study of family member characteristics and involvement: Effects on entrepreneurial behavior in the family firm,' *Family Business Review* 21(1): 1–14.

Kellermanns, F.W., Eddleston, K., & Zellweger, T. (2012) 'Extending the socioemotional wealth perspective: A look at the dark side,' *Entrepreneurship: Theory & Practice* 36(6): 1175–1182.

Kets de Vries, M. F. (1993) 'The dynamics of family controlled firms: The good and the bad news,' *Organizational Dynamics* 21(3): 59–71.

Laverty, K. J. (1996) 'Economic "short-termism": The debate, the unresolved issues, and the implications for management practice and research,' *Academy of Management Review* 21(3): 825–860.

Le Breton-Miller, I., & Miller, D. (2006) 'Why do some family businesses out–compete? Governance, long–term orientations, and sustainable capability,' *Entrepreneurship Theory and Practice* 30(6): 731–746.

Le Breton-Miller, I., & Miller, D. (2008) 'To grow or to harvest? Governance, strategy and performance in family and lone founder firms,' *Journal of Strategy and Management* 1(1): 41–56.

Leitterstorf, M. P., & Rau, S. B. (2014) 'Socioemotional wealth and IPO underpricing of family firms,' *Strategic Management Journal* 35(5): 751–760.

Lumpkin, G.T., & Brigham, K. H. (2011) 'Long–term orientation and intertemporal choice in family firms,' *Entrepreneurship Theory and Practice* 35(6): 1149–1169.

Marginson, D., & McAulay, L. (2008) 'Exploring the debate on short–termism: A theoretical and empirical analysis,' *Strategic Management Journal* 29(3): 273–292.

Martin, G., Washburn, N., Makri, M., & Gómez–Mejía, L. R. (2015) 'Not all Risk Taking is Born Equal: The Behavioral Agency Model and CEO's Perception of Firm Efficacy,' *Human Resource Management* 54(3): 483–498.

McConaughy, D. L. (2000) 'Family CEOs vs. nonfamily CEOs in the family–controlled firm: An examination of the level and sensitivity of pay to performance,' *Family Business Review* 13(2): 121–131.

McConaughy, D. L., Matthews, C. H., & Fialko, A. S. (2001) 'Founding family controlled firms: Performance, risk, and value,' *Journal of Small Business Management* 39(1): 31–49.

McConaughy, D. L., Walker, M. C., Henderson, G.V., & Mishra, C. S. (1998) 'Founding family controlled firms: Efficiency and value,' *Review of Financial Economics* 7(1): 1–19.

McKenny, A. F., Short, J. C., Zachary, M. A., & Payne, G.T. (2012) 'Assessing espoused goals in private family firms using content analysis,' *Family Business Review* 25(3): 298–317.

Miller, D., & Le Breton-Miller, I. (2005) *Managing for the long run: Lessons in competitive advantage from great family businesses.* Harvard Business Press.

Miller, D. & Le Breton-Miller, L. (2014) 'Deconstructing socioemotional wealth,' *Entrepreneurship Theory and Practice* 38(4): 713–720.

Miller, D., Le Breton–Miller, I., & Lester, R. H. (2010) 'Family ownership and acquisition behavior in publicly–traded companies,' *Strategic Management Journal* 31(2): 201–223.

Miller, D., Le Breton-Miller, I., Lester, R. H., & Cannella, A. A. (2007) 'Are family firms really superior performers?,' *Journal of Corporate Finance* 13(5): 829–858.

Miller, K. D., & Bromiley, P. (1990) 'Strategic risk and corporate performance: An analysis of alternative risk measures,' *Academy of Management Journal* 33(4): 756–779.

Mishra, C. S., & McConaughy, D. L. (1999) 'Founding family control and capital structure: The risk of loss of control and the aversion to debt,' *Entrepreneurship Theory and Practice* 23: 53–64.

Morck, R., Wolfenzon, D., & Yeun, B. (2004) *Corporate governance, economic entrenchment and growth.* NBER Working Paper, n. 10692.

Mueller, D. C., & Reardon, E. A. (1993) 'Rates of return on corporate investment,' *Southern Economic Journal* 430–453.

Muñoz-Bullón, F., & Sanchez-Bueno, M. J. (2011) 'The impact of family involvement on the R&D intensity of publicly traded firms,' *Family Business Review* 24(1): 62–70.

Naldi, L., Cennamo, C., Corbetta, G., & Gómez–Mejía, L. (2013) 'Preserving socioemotional wealth in family firms: Asset or liability? The moderating role of business context,' *Entrepreneurship Theory and Practice* 37(6): 1341–1360.

Naldi, L., Nordqvist, M., Sjöberg, K., & Wiklund, J. (2007) 'Entrepreneurial orientation, risk taking, and performance in family firms,' *Family Business Review* 20(1): 33–47.

Patel, P. C., & Chrisman, J. J. (2014) 'Risk abatement as a strategy for R&D investments in family firms,' *Strategic Management Journal* 35(4): 617–627.

Rau, S. B. (2014) 'Resource-based view of family firms,' In L. Melin, M. Nordqvist, and P. Sharma (eds.), *The SAGE Handbook of family business*. London: Sage, 157–178.

Sanders, W. G., & Hambrick, D. C. (2007) 'Swinging for the fences: The effects of CEO stock options on company risk taking and performance,' *Academy of Management Journal* 50(5): 1055–1078.

Schulze, W. S., & Kellermanns, F. W. (2015) 'Reifying socioemotional wealth,' *Entrepreneurship Theory and Practice* 39(3): 447–459.

Schulze, W. S., Lubatkin, M. H., Dino, R. N., & Buchholtz, A. K. (2001) 'Agency relationships in family firms: Theory and evidence,' *Organization Science* 12(2): 99–116.

Schulze, W. S., Lubatkin, M. H., & Dino, R. N. (2003) 'Toward a theory of agency and altruism in family firms,' *Journal of Business Venturing* 18(4): 473–490.

Shleifer, A., & Vishny, R. W. (1986) 'Large shareholders and corporate control,' *The Journal of Political Economy* 461–488.

Sirmon, D. G., & Hitt, M. A. (2003) 'Managing resources: Linking unique resources, management, and wealth creation in family firms,' *Entrepreneurship Theory and Practice* 27(4): 339–358.

Smit, H. T., & Ankum, L. A. (1993) 'A real options and game-theoretic approach to corporate investment strategy under competition,' *Financial Management* 241–250.

Stulz, R. (1988) 'On takeover resistance, managerial discretion, and shareholder wealth,' *Journal of Financial Economics* 20(1/2): 25–54.

Thomsen, S., & Pedersen, T. (2000) 'Ownership structure and economic performance in the largest European companies,' *Strategic Management Journal* 21(6): 689–705.

Tversky, A., & Kahneman, D. (1992) 'Advances in prospect theory: Cumulative representation of uncertainty,' *Journal of Risk and Uncertainty,* 5(4), 297–323.

Villalonga, B., & Amit, R. (2006) 'How do family ownership, control and management affect firm value?,' *Journal of Financial Economics* 80(2): 385–417.

Zahra, S. A. (2005) 'Entrepreneurial risk taking in family firms,' *Family Business Review* 18(1): 23–40.

Zellweger, T. M., & Astrachan, J. H. (2008) 'On the emotional value of owning a firm,' *Family Business Review* 21(4): 347–363.

Zellweger, T. M., Kellermanns, F. W., Chrisman, J. J., & Chua, J. H. (2012) 'Family control and family firm valuation by family CEOs: The importance of intentions for transgenerational control,' *Organization Science* 23(3): 851–868.

Walsh, J. P., & Seward, J. K. (1990) 'On the efficiency of internal and external corporate control mechanisms,' *Academy of Management Review* 15(3): 421–458.

Ward, J., & Dolan, C. (1998) 'Defining and describing family business ownership configurations,' *Family Business Review* 11(4): 305–310.

Ward, J. L. (2004) *Perpetuating the family business: 50 lessons learned from long lasting, successful families in business.* Palgrave Macmillan.

Westhead, P., Cowling, M., & Howorth, C. (2001) 'The development of family companies: Management and ownership imperatives,' *Family Business Review* 14(4): 369–385.

Wiseman, R. M., & Gómez-Mejía, L. R. (1998) 'A behavioral agency model of managerial risk taking,' *Academy of Management Review* 23(1): 133–153.

Wright, P., Ferris, S. P., Sarin, A., & Awasthi, V. (1996) 'Impact of corporate insider, blockholder, and institutional equity ownership on firm risk taking,' *Academy of Management Journal* 39(2): 441–458.

8

FAMILY FIRMS, STAKEHOLDER RELATIONSHIPS, AND COMPETITIVE ADVANTAGE

A Review and Directions for Future Research

J. Kirk Ring, Jessica Brown, and Curtis F. Matherne

Introduction

Stakeholder theory is concerned with the relationships between the firm and stakeholders, as well as how these relationships affect processes and outcomes for all parties involved (Jones and Wicks 1999). Rather than only adhering to the demands of shareholders, stakeholder theory is founded upon the idea that all stakeholders have inherent worth that should be considered during managerial decision making (Donaldson and Preston 1995) and this multifaceted focus will potentially result in different decisions made than if only shareholders were important. A significant amount of research has been conducted on stakeholder theory and the variety of academic work by scholars from multiple disciplines has resulted in some authors continuing to disagree upon how to use the theory to explain performance, be it economic, social, environmental, etc. (Mitchell et al. 1997). Where authors do agree is companies have an assortment of relationships with groups of individuals who are affected by and can affect decisions made by the firm (Freeman 1984). These groups of individuals are called stakeholders.

It is widely accepted in management literature that Freeman is the source of stakeholder theory. Many authors also look towards multiple-constituency theory which preceded stakeholder theory. Similarities between the two theories are evident, although the concepts delivered in stakeholder theory are more closely aligned to factors affecting modern day business.

Overall, this theory concentrates on how the wants and needs of various groups affect decision-making processes (Hillman and Keim 2001), as well as how managers interact jointly with stakeholders to create value for the firm. If managers disregard certain groups' needs, these stakeholders may withhold participation, cooperation or commitment, leading to inefficiencies and the potential for reduced value creation and profitability. Therefore, skillfully managing stakeholder relationships to create as much value as possible, offers the potential for competitive advantage in the marketplace if competitors are not as adept. Additionally, executives must be able to reconsider ways to address problems when stakeholder interests conflict because they could, in turn, create additional value for distribution to multiple stakeholder groups (Harrison, Bosse, and Phillips 2010).

Family business research has received attention regarding stakeholder relationships and how the relationships affect the performances of these firms (e.g., Sharma 2001; Zellweger and

Nason 2008). Family businesses are defined as businesses governed or managed by a family or group of families that have the intention to shape and pursue the vision of the business while also intending to pass on the business to future generations of the family (Chua, Chrisman, and Sharma 1999). Regardless of the family business definition utilized, one consistent issue arises. Family businesses are owned and/or operated by a group of individuals who are family. This distinct group of individuals who are family members provides an important area for focus when considering stakeholder theory. First, the family has both the opportunity and power to make decisions based on their own stakeholder group's needs. This level of power over decision-making is not as readily available to top management in non-family firms and non-family firm management does not have the common familial bond that family firms possess. Second, the family stakeholder group in family firms has been described as one that has more than economic performance of the business as an important goal (e.g., Gómez-Mejía et al. 2007; Zellweger and Nason 2008). Adhering to goals based on noneconomic issues that are often related to the family stakeholder group's needs or core values may significantly alter the strategic decisions of the business as compared to non-family businesses.

The remainder of this chapter will discuss family business strategy in regards to the tenets of stakeholder theory, which include the identification, competition, priority, and treatment of stakeholder groups. We will review what has been accomplished to date and areas that may be fruitful avenues for future research. Finally, suggestions for members of family businesses will be provided.

The Origins of Stakeholder

Stakeholder theory can be traced to Freeman (1984) where he argued management within organizations should be concerned about the interests of individuals and groups other than shareholders when making strategic decisions. Up until this time, the corporate governance literature relied heavily on the idea of maximizing shareholder returns and often this literature was identified as lacking a systematic way of taking into account more than profitability for shareholders. The two key assumptions (Tantalo and Priem 2015) that have guided stakeholder theory's development are: (1) the claims or goals of one stakeholder group are in competition with the remaining stakeholder groups and managers must balance these claims in through trade-offs (Bridoux and Stoelhorst, 2014; Freeman 2010; Freeman, Harrison, and Wicks 2007); and (2) shareholders hold a place of superiority over all other stakeholders. Freeman et al. (2007) explain that the classic process for managing stakeholders involves four fundamental actions when addressing a strategic issue: identify the stakeholder groups that can be affected or can affect the decision making process, assess the stakes of each group and their relevance, determine the management team's current effectiveness in meeting these stakeholder group's needs or expectations, and lastly, adjust managerial and company actions to adhere to the claims of the incongruent stakeholder claims (Tantalo and Priem 2015).

Governmental entities and the public at large have shown positive interest in the concept of making decisions that include the concerns of many types of stakeholders (e.g., Donaldson and Preston 1995). Although, within businesses and academic literature, one of the more significant debates results from disagreement upon whether or not the definition utilized for stakeholders is too broad or restrictive. In other words, what groups can be considered stakeholders and how do we demarcate between groups? What groups are most important and what groups can we ignore? Owing to this issue, Freeman's (1984) definition has been altered many times over in an effort to reduce the breadth of potential stakeholders but his definition remains as the foundation for the field in identifying stakeholders.

Mitchell and colleagues (1997) reviewed the literature concerning the identification of stakeholder groups and proposed an interesting way to understand the process managers undergo. Their stakeholder identification process suggests that managerial perceptions of three stakeholder attributes—power, legitimacy, and urgency—may affect the salience of stakeholders, where salience is "the degree to which managers give priority to competing stakeholder claims" (Agle et al. 1999, 507). Indeed, the combination of the stakeholder's power to influence the firm, the legitimacy of the stakeholder's relationship with the firm, and the urgency of the stakeholder's claims on the firm will affect the decisions made by managers depending on how salient the managers perceive these attributes to be. This was a change in direction for stakeholder theory because it supplements efforts by others to simplify the stakeholder concept through classification schemes. By clarifying how stakeholder groups become salient in the eyes of managers it, in turn, is clearer how stakeholders can affect firm decision making (Bundy, Shropshire, and Buckhholtz 2013). Mitchell et al.'s (1997) argument presuppose that it is critical to stakeholder theory to understand that only when the manager perceives an identified stakeholder group to be salient will their needs be met. Please see Exhibit 8.1 for a list of the 20 most cited articles on stakeholder definitional and salience issues.

Mitchell et al.'s (1997) salience theory is helpful because of the disagreement concerning "who are the stakeholders of the firm?" This most basic question can be difficult to answer considering the broad nature of the definition of stakeholders first proposed by Freeman (1984). By looking at stakeholders as any person, group, or entity who can affect or is affected by the actions of the organization, research has been limited in the ability to rule out virtually any group or individual as a stakeholder.

Common themes amongst the relatively many views of what constitutes a stakeholder include identifying stakeholders based on their significance to the firm's core capabilities, their economic and moral interests, and survival (e.g., Berman et al. 1999). Stakeholders are often categorized as internal or external, primary or secondary, social or non-social, etc. There are even further nuanced categorizations such as how Clarkson (1995) describes stakeholders in terms of risk, be it involuntary (the firm can affect stakeholders regardless of affiliation with the firm), or voluntary (stakeholders who purposefully put themselves in harm's way through such activities as employment, investment, etc.). Describing stakeholders in this way effectively reduces those who can be stakeholders of a firm to only individuals or entities that can lose or gain something (a stake) (Mitchell et al. 1997). No matter how the categorization is developed, the literature has consistently taken said categories and then explained how stakeholders try to influence the organization's decision-making process so that it meets their needs. The strategic management literature also emphasizes the active management of stakeholder interests (Mainardes, Alves, and Raposo 2011). The actions directed toward improving stakeholder relationships with the firm and further integrating stakeholder claims into strategic planning and decision-making is a key objective (Cennamo et al. 2012).

As stakeholder theory developed in the last four decades, the research can be divided into three different approaches (Donaldson and Preston 1995; Friedman and Miles 2006): descriptive, instrumental, and normative. The instrumental and normative approaches received the most significant attention from academic research. The instrumental approach is goal-based, where stakeholders are seen as part of the strategy of the firm. This line of research is not surprising considering a central goal of all strategy research is to further understand what management practices can be related to company performance (Rumelt, Schendel, and Teece 1995). However, the normative approach is morality-based, where firms act in a more ethical sense (Chua et al. 2012). It provides an underlying basis for stakeholder theory in that its main assumption is the intrinsic value of any one stakeholder should not take priority over other stakeholders.

Exhibit 8.1 – Top 20 Cited Stakeholder Definition and Salience Articles

Agle, B. R., Mitchell, R. K., and Sonnenfeld, J. A. (1999). Who matters to Ceos? An investigation of stakeholder attributes and salience, corporate performance, and Ceo values. *Academy of Management Journal, 42*(5), 507–525.

Buchholz, R. A., and Rosenthal, S. B. (2005). Toward a contemporary conceptual framework for stakeholder theory. *Journal of Business Ethics, 58*(1–3), 137–148.

Buysse, K., and Verbeke, A. (2003). Proactive environmental strategies: A stakeholder management perspective. *Strategic Management Journal, 24*(5), 453–470.

Cragg, W., and Greenbaum, A. (2002). Reasoning about responsibilities: Mining company managers on what stakeholders are owed. *Journal of Business Ethics, 39*(3), 319–335.

Driscoll, C., and Starik, M. (2004). The primordial stakeholder: Advancing the conceptual consideration of stakeholder status for the natural environment. *Journal of Business Ethics, 49*(1), 55–73.

Dunham, L., Freeman, R. E., and Liedtka, J. (2006). Enhancing stakeholder practice: A particularized exploration of community. *Business Ethics Quarterly, 16*(01), 23–42.

Eesley, C. E., and Lenox, M. J. (2006, August). Secondary stakeholder actions and the selection of firm targets. In *Academy of Management Proceedings* (Vol. 2006, No. 1, pp. B1–B6). Academy of Management.

Henriques, I., and Sadorsky, P. (1999). The relationship between environmental commitment and managerial perceptions of stakeholder importance. *Academy of Management Journal, 42*(1), 87–99.

Jawahar, I. M., and McLaughlin, G. L. (2001). Toward a descriptive stakeholder theory: An organizational life cycle approach. *Academy of Management Review, 26*(3), 397–414.

Jones, T. M., Felps, W., and Bigley, G. A. (2007). Ethical theory and stakeholder–related decisions: The role of stakeholder culture. *Academy of Management Review, 32*(1), 137–155.

Knox, S., and Gruar, C. (2007). The application of stakeholder theory to relationship marketing strategy development in a non–profit organization. *Journal of Business Ethics, 75*(2), 115–135.

Mitchell, R. K., Agle, B. R., and Wood, D. J. (1997). Toward a theory of stakeholder identification and salience: Defining the principle of who and what really counts. *Academy of Management Review, 22*(4), 853–886.

Pajunen, K. (2006). Stakeholder influences in organizational survival. *Journal of Management Studies, 43*(6), 1261–1288.

Parent, M. M., and Deephouse, D. L. (2007). A case study of stakeholder identification and prioritization by managers. *Journal of Business Ethics, 75*(1), 1–23.

Phillips, R., Freeman, R. E., and Wicks, A. C. (2003). What stakeholder theory is not. *Business Ethics Quarterly, 13*(04), 479–502.

Post, J. E., Preston, L. E., and Sachs, S. (2002). *Redefining the corporation: Stakeholder management and organizational wealth.* Stanford University Press.

Ryan, L. V., and Schneider, M. (2003). Institutional investor power and heterogeneity. *Business & Society, 42*(4)398–429.

Winn, M. I. (2001). Building stakeholder theory with a decision modeling methodology. *Business & Society, 40*(2), 133–166.

Wolfe, R. A., and Putler, D. S. (2002). How tight are the ties that bind stakeholder groups? *Organization Science, 13*(1), 64–80.

All stakeholders should receive equitable treatment when decisions are to be made. Emotional attachments and social ties are more likely to form and become quite important for the firm.

Although the descriptive approach has not been explored as vigorously as the instrumental and normative approaches, stakeholder theory has most frequently been approached from a descriptive viewpoint. This approach, "attempts to explain certain firm characteristics and behaviors based on how organizations view and interact with their constituencies" (Bingham et al. 2011). By being descriptive, authors provide a common language for the community of scholars to convey their understanding of the relationships between the firm and its stakeholders. While simply basing stakeholder theory in descriptive terms is inadequate (Waddok and Graves 1997), a description does offer necessary information to later be used when making instrumental predictions regarding causality and performance. Please see Exhibit 8.2 for the most influential scholarly articles published on the descriptive, instrumental, and normative approaches.

In summary, stakeholder theory seeks to understand how managers of companies identify stakeholders who can affect or be affected by firm activities. Firms enter into relationships with stakeholders who could be internal or external to the firm and may include groups such as employees, suppliers, buyers, government entities, charities, the environment, etc. Stakeholder theory is interested in how management decides which needs from which stakeholder group to adhere to and why they make these decisions. The benefits of stakeholder management include increased trust from stakeholders, stakeholder commitment to the firm, increased capabilities to create competitive advantage, greater firm legitimacy, and increased company financial and social performance (Choi and Wang 2009; Freeman 2010; Freeman et al. 2007; Freeman et al. 2010; Graves and Waddock 1994; Hillman and Keim 2001). Lastly, the theory is interested in success on multiple levels including both economic success and noneconomic success through better relationships, increased social performance, and ability to meet environmental goals (e.g., Kroeger and Weber 2014).

Family Firms as Nested Stakeholder Relationships

Stakeholder theory is especially relevant to family firm studies since the family unit that owns and/or controls the business comprises a major stakeholder group. In family firm research, there is general agreement that the definition of a family firm must take into account the role that family members play in the decision-making process, along with the family's ability to create capabilities and resources that are unique to the firm (Chrisman, Chua, and Steier 2003b; Habbershon, Williams, and MacMillan 2003; Pearson, Carr, and Shaw 2008). In addition to the family group, the family firm is regularly described as a heterogeneous entity consisting of two additional systems (Gersick, Davis, and Hampton 1997). These systems consist of the ownership group and the management group. Not only are these three systems a "useful tool for understanding different goals and expectations, sources of interpersonal conflicts, role dilemmas, priorities and boundaries in family firms" (Sharma 2001, 5), but they also identify the major internal stakeholders of family businesses: owners, managers, and family. Stakeholder management (Laplume, Sonpar, and Litz 2008) in family firm research has commonly focused upon how the needs, goals, or wants of the family have the potential to be as influential as the economic needs of the ownership or management group (Gómez-Mejía et al. 2007) because the leaders of the business may hold the position of being a family member, owner, and manager simultaneously. By having leaders in control of the decision-making process who are potentially members of several different and powerful stakeholder groups, the competing claims of stakeholders may increase the amount of conflict between stakeholders (Mitchell et al. 2011). In other words, stakeholder theory's assumption that claims of various stakeholders will be in competition for attention and resources from the top management team may be magnified in a family firm owing to this issue of power and control.

Exhibit 8.2 – Contributions to Stakeholder Theory Approaches

Descriptive

Frooman, J. (1999). Stakeholder influence strategies. *Academy of Management Review, 24*(2), 191–205.

Jawahar, I. M., and McLaughlin, G. L. (2001). Toward a descriptive stakeholder theory: An organizational life cycle approach. *Academy of Management Review, 26*(3), 397–414.

Mitchell, R. K., Agle, B. R., and Wood, D. J. (1997). Toward a theory of stakeholder identification and salience: Defining the principle of who and what really counts. *Academy of Management Review, 22*(4), 853–886.

Normative

Donaldson, T., and Dunfee, T. W. (1999). *Ties that bind: A social contracts approach to business ethics.* Boston, MA: Harvard Business Press.

Gibson, K. (2000). The moral basis of stakeholder theory. *Journal of Business Ethics, 26*(3), 245–257.

Hendry, J. (2001). Missing the target: Normative stakeholder theory and the corporate governance debate. *Business Ethics Quarterly, 11*(01), 159–176.

McWilliams, A., and Siegel, D. (2001). Corporate social responsibility: A theory of the firm perspective. *Academy of Management Review, 26*(1), 117–127.

Phillips, R. A. (1997). Stakeholder theory and a principle of fairness. *Business Ethics Quarterly, 7*(01), 51–66.

Instrumental

Agle, B. R., Mitchell, R. K., and Sonnenfeld, J. A. (1999). Who matters to CEOs? An investigation of stakeholder attributes and salience, corporate performance, and CEO values. *Academy of Management Journal, 42*(5), 507–525.

Berman, S. L., Wicks, A. C., Kotha, S., and Jones, T. M. (1999). Does stakeholder orientation matter? The relationship between stakeholder management models and firm financial performance. *Academy of Management Journal, 42*(5), 488–506.

Jones, T. M. (1995). Instrumental stakeholder theory: A synthesis of ethics and economics. *Academy of Management Review, 20*(2), 404–437.

Normative/Instrumental

Jones, T. M., and Wicks, A. C. (1999). Convergent stakeholder theory. *Academy of Management Review, 24*(2), 206–221.

McWilliams, A., and Siegel, D. (2001). Corporate social responsibility: A theory of the firm perspective. *Academy of Management Review, 26*(1), 117–127.

Ruf, B. M., Muralidhar, K., Brown, R. M., Janney, J. J., and Paul, K. (2001). An empirical investigation of the relationship between change in corporate social performance and financial performance: A stakeholder theory perspective. *Journal of Business Ethics, 32*(2), 143–156.

The Family Stakeholder Group

As noted, within the tenets of stakeholder theory, the family unit wields much power and influence in the direction and operation of the family firm. If the family stakeholder group has the potential to make decisions in their own best interest and sometimes not in the best interest of the business, it is important to understand what goals the family may try to achieve. A focus on profit maximization by the majority of mainstream strategy literature appears to not fit with the family firm subset. Family firms do not have the sole objective of profit maximization because they display preference toward goals with noneconomic outcomes (Chrisman, Chua, and Litz 2004). Empirical differences began to emerge between family and non-family firms in areas such as executive pay (Combs et al. 2010; Gómez-Mejía, Larraza-Kintana, and Makri 2003), international diversification (Berrone, Cruz, Gómez-Mejía, and Larraza-Kintana 2010), human resource management practices (Cruz, Fiffira, and Gómez-Mejía 2011), and firm risk-taking (Gómez-Mejía et al. 2007). Each of these studies contributed to the concept of socioemotional wealth (SEW) (e.g., Gómez-Mejía et al. 2007), where SEW represents those firm characteristics that meet the controlling family's affective needs such as the ability to exercise power, identity, and family dynasty continuation. SEW is an extension of the behavioral agency model. The behavioral agency model states that choices made within a firm rest primarily with the reference point of key decision makers. These key decision makers will attempt to preserve their accumulated endowment in the firm (Wiseman and Gómez-Mejía 1998).

In family firms, it is argued that the key reference point for decision makers is from the family's point of view and their accumulated endowment is considered to be socioemotional. Preserving socioemotional wealth may be vital and therefore, it can serve as a primary focus when making decisions (Cennamo et al. 2012). Gómez-Mejía and colleagues (2007) posit that when there is an opportunity to increase the endowment of SEW or the danger of a loss in SEW, the family will potentially decide upon a course of action that is not economically driven. In other words, the family will knowingly put the business at risk in an effort so as to preserve SEW. For example, unqualified family members are often hired into family firms and are difficult to forcefully remove from the business when their performance does not meet company standards. The desire for harmony amongst the family stakeholder group is in direct conflict with the desire to have employees who increase the profitability of the firm through their actions.

The family stakeholder group may be inclined to protect specific stakes such as: providing financial benefits and security to the family members of the firm; providing the opportunity for growth; social/reputation advancement; autonomy to family members; and providing job security to family members. Chrisman and colleagues (2003) suggested that not only do family firms focus on providing employment for family members but they also want those employment opportunities to provide avenues for growth and development of family members' knowledge and skills. A prime example of assisting in the development of their family members is the use of university led executive training programs as well as university-led family business associations or forums. Currently, in the United States, there are nearly 50 family business membership programs that provide university outreach programming in areas such as leadership, succession planning, human resource management training, family estate planning, development of family meetings, etc. One such association can be found at Wichita State University where the Center for Entrepreneurship houses the Kansas Family Business Forum. This particular program has served more than 150 family owned businesses over a 20-year period. Other examples of family business forums can be found at Fresno State University, University of Arkansas, University of Massachusetts, Loyola University, Northeastern University, etc. Many family business associations are also tied to executive training programs for key managerial skills including improving supervisory skills, transformational leadership, managing non-family members, emotional intelligence, communication skills, and conflict resolution skills. Outside of the United States some of the well-known forums are: the Canadian Association of Family Enterprises, which is a nationwide association with chapters in various regions; the Witten Institute for Family Business in Germany; and Loedstar, which is an international forum that holds events in Europe primarily and has specific forums for London and Dubai.

Each of these programs requires a financial commitment from the business to support the growth and development of a subset of individuals within the business who receive this benefit owing to their familial status. Rather than simply putting money into the development of the most promising employees, regardless of their last name, family business leaders are in many instances protecting their SEW. Subsequently, the family's continued control of the business will be intact through the development of the next generation of family leaders in their business. Additional monetary commitment may come in the form of contracting with the growing family business consulting market. In one such instance, the Family Business Consulting Group located in Atlanta, GA in the United States boasts the assistance of over 2,300 clients in 70 countries around the world (http://www.thefbcg.com/benefits/where-we-work/). Indeed, family business leaders are willingly diverting resources away from pure, economically driven objectives and are instead placing time and money into the protection, or even enhancement, of their SEW.

Family firms may also differ in their level of stakeholder influence when looking at the life cycle of the family firm, which has been traditionally based upon the generational stages of the firm (Gersick et al. 1997). As a family firm moves from the first to subsequent generations "ownership tends to get dispersed in a somewhat episodic and 'stepwise' fashion over a relatively long period of time, with shares usually passed from parent to child around the time of the principal owner's retirement and/or death" (Schulze, Lubatkin, and Dino 2003, 182). In general, family firms are described as moving between three significantly different stages of ownership dispersion and this subsequently has the potential to affect management control as well. These stages are designated as the controlling owner, sibling partnership, and cousin consortium phases (Gersick et al. 1997).

The controlling owner phase normally occurs as the business is founded and suggests that the founding family possesses the majority of the equity in the firm as well as manages the firm with near total control. In this instance, there is significant overlap in the family, ownership, and management groups and the salience of each internal stakeholder group has the potential to create significant conflict. When the business is passed down to the next generation of the business through a succession event, multiple children may become owners/managers and in turn, the business moves into the sibling partnership phase. Sibling partnerships result in the likelihood of the family stakeholder group's claims to become increasingly salient. Additionally, the stakeholder claims of the family group will often increase in breadth at this time. There may be an increased desire to hire additional family members such as in-laws, a growing desire to consume some of the free cash flow of the business for perquisites owing to a diminishing bootstrapping mindset, etc. Lastly, when the firm encounters yet another succession event, it will move into the cousin consortium phase where ownership dispersion is again broadened to more family members (Gersick et al. 1997). The cousin consortium phase also sees continued broadening of the needs of the family. Ownership is now dispersed amongst a larger group of family members and therefore the profitability of the firm likely provides less to each individual family member than in previous governance structures. Therefore, it is necessary to grow the business or decrease costs in an effort to increase profit margins. Owing to these issues, management of the business could move to professional non-family managers with better skills in accomplishing these business goals. The result of increased non-family management upon meeting the needs of the family stakeholder group could be quite dramatic.

Although Gersick's model is applicable in many societies across the globe, it may not be universally appropriate. Many externalities influence family business practices, including national context, ethnicity, and religion (Hoy and Pu 2012). Specifically, the Chinese community may deem Gersisk's model invalid as the one-child policy upheld in China almost diminishes the sibling partnership phase. Salience within the family stakeholder group will decrease, and the desire to hire family members also decreases. The cousin consortium phase, preceded by the sibling partnership phase, also suffers. Therefore, the Chinese community will rely heavily on other internal stakeholders, such as those discussed below, rather than family internal stakeholders.

Other Internal Stakeholders

Beyond the family unit, non-family managers and employees are likely the most studied stakeholder group in family business research. Non-family managers have been included in research topics such as justice perceptions (Barnett and Kellermanns 2006), agency cost analysis (Chrisman et al. 2007), firm growth (Ward, 1997), organizational social capital (Arregle et al. 2007), stakeholder perceptions of culture and management practices (Poza, Alfred, and Maheshwari 1997), and board composition (Anderson and Reeb 2004). Overall, the studies of non-family managers and employees has taken on the task of trying to understand how the relationship of the non-family stakeholder group with the family is developed over time, how well their needs as a group are met, what autonomy they possess to meet their own needs and the needs of the business, as well as their commitment to the goals of the business and family, be it economic or non-economic goals. For example, in Poza et al. (1997), the authors find that family CEOs perceive their actions more favorably than non-family managers in regards to decision making, culture, and succession. They suggest that increased communication with the non-family managers may alleviate the incongruence of perceptions but likely will not remove it altogether. From a stakeholder perspective, the authors argue that meeting the needs of the family for hiring, promotion, and compensation is perceived by the family CEO as equitable since the family members are part of the family stakeholder group and eventual owners of the business. This would encourage the full commitment of family members to the business. From the perspective of the non-family managers though, these actions may be taken as nepotism and favoritism, as well as unwarranted business expenses that reduces the growth potential for non-family managers in their own careers and financial rewards.

External Stakeholders

The external stakeholders of a family firm are not inherently different than non-family firms. These stakeholders include such groups as suppliers, customers, the community, charities, non-profits, competitors, and the environment. As suggested previously, the influence of the family unit on the decisions of the business, as well as the relationships between the family stakeholder group and all other stakeholders, is where research has focused.

Family business research has argued that family firms perform well from the standpoint of corporate social performance, where corporate social performance is "comprehensive assessment of the firm's voluntary actions to improve conditions with associate stakeholder groups" (Bingham et al. 2011, 566). Empirically, the results have been positive. Some research suggests that family firms contribute significantly to charitable organizations (Ylvisaker, 1990). Many family businesses have also begun to create their own family foundations as a way to create a legacy of their own in the world external to the business (Sharma, Chrisman, and Chua 1997). One example of a family foundation that provides benefit to the family unit but also increases the legitimacy of the family's principle business is the Cabela Family Foundation in the United States. The Cabela family founded Cabela's Outdoor World in 1961 and it has since turned into one of the largest outdoor products retailers in the world with net sales revenues in excess of $3.65B in 2014. The *company* operates the Cabela's Outdoor Fund which promotes conservation and hunting, camping, and boating, while the *family* operates the Cabela Family Foundation which provides grants to causes designated by the family, including outdoor and conservation initiatives. In each foundation, the business is being influenced by the personal actions of the family to consider the family's legacy as environmental conservationists when utilizing excess cash flow. Margolis and Walsh (2003) and Morck and Yeung (2004) would argue through agency theory that these actions are instead done only to protect the interests of the family and that they are not truly benevolent in their actions. Bingham and colleagues (2011) address these inconsistent descriptions by assessing the corporate social performance of family firms through a stakeholder identity approach. They argue that family firms typically take on a relational identity orientation toward their stakeholders whereas non-family firms take on an individualistic identity orientation. The result of these differences is that they find family firms with high levels of family involvement demonstrate greater levels of corporate social performance toward a wide range of stakeholder groups.

Family firms have been found to be more responsive to the environment as a stakeholder group. For example, Sharma and Sharma (2011) draw upon the theory of planned behavior and state that family firms develop a proactive environmental strategy. The authors argue that family businesses are shaped by the involvement of the family and because of the family's attitudes, subjective norms, and perceived behavioral control they are able to pursue strategies to meet the needs of the environment. Further, the capability to accomplish these type goals increases when the family has higher levels of involvement and when the family believes that the subjective norms of meeting environmental needs benefit their firm. Family firms are expected to want to meet the needs of the environment because the family stakeholder group typically possesses a long-term strategic focus (Gentry, Dibrell, and Kim 2014), family members maintain leadership positions for extended periods of time, the family highly identifies with the business (Matherne, Ring, and McKee 2011), and environmental success may gain SEW endowments for later generations of the family (Sharma and Sharma 2011). The authors go on to suggest that family firms that maintain relatively low levels of relationship conflict within the family stakeholder group may be more successful in meeting environmental goals by diverting resources toward strategies that help the environment.

Berrone and colleagues (2010) also studied why family firms have been able to better meet environmental needs and they were able to show empirically in a sample of US firms that they polluted less through better emissions reporting. These authors argued that firms controlled by a family stakeholder group would respond more readily to institutional pressures involving the environment. The pursuit of environmentally friendly strategies can be quite costly and the results are most likely to be ambiguous at best. Therefore, many firms have difficulty in deciding the amount of resources to dedicate toward common initiatives such as carbon credits, planting trees, recycling, green materials and packaging, etc. Berrone et al. (2010) state that the family stakeholder group may believe environmentally friendly practices provide additional social legitimacy as well as the potential for increased SEW.

Implications for Future Research and Practice

Although much has been accomplished in the fields of stakeholder theory and family business research, additional work remains. We believe that the following suggestions for future research may offer scholars with the opportunity to successfully contribute to both fields simultaneously.

First, family business advising is a growing part of the consulting market and has received recent attention from family business research. In 2013, the Family Business Review published a special issue on family business advising (Reay, Pearson, and Dyer 2013). In this issue, Salvato and Corbetta (2013) highlight the role that advisors play as facilitators of leadership construction in family business successors. The authors investigate how the succession process may be improved by providing a significant mentoring relationship to next generation family members. In essence, they seek to understand how mentoring may turn into a form of shared leadership of the business between the advisor and the successor. Although the authors looked at this activity as one that may prove to be effective in developing leaders, from a stakeholder standpoint we ask "How might the advisor/successor relationship alter the salience of various stakeholder claims?" We expect that a significant difference may exist when choosing advisors with different areas of expertise, as well as whether or not they have extensive experience working solely with family owned companies. For example, an advisor brought in for leadership development and executive coaching that lacks understanding of the issues regarding SEW and the stakeholder claims of the family group may be less apt to understand the important issues regarding conflict resolution amongst family members within the business. Further evidence of this issue is seen in Barbara and Hasso (2013) where they found that use of an accountant as the family business advisor had a significant effect on sales growth and business survival. We believe one should also question how the use of an accountant affects the family stakeholder group's desire to increase or protect SEW. Stakeholder theorists have already begun to address the issues of executive succession processes (Friedman and Olk 1995) and leader power sharing (Heller 1997). There appears to be potential for using this work as a background for better understanding how advisors assist successors in their transition to top management, as well as how these successors can successfully manage the competing claims of stakeholders during this turbulent time of transition (Taylor 1995). Lastly, Naldi, Chirico, Kellermanns, and Campopiano (2015) explored the dynamic between family firm performance and family members serving in an advising capacity. In a study of Swedish family firms, the authors observed a direct relationship between performance and number of family advisors in the form of an inverted U-shape and a moderating effect between firm generation and performance. First generation firms had a positive relationship with performance and later generation firms had an inverted U-shape relationship.

Second, de Luque, Washburn, Waldman, and House (2008) explain how a stakeholder orientation by CEOs can result in the perception that the CEO is a visionary leader and when this perception held by stakeholders it increases their commitment. The result is better overall firm performance (Parma et al. 2010). The authors' data collection provided insight to the differences between leaders who primarily emphasize economic values, rather than stakeholder values. Those emphasizing economic values were perceived as autocratic leaders and employees were less apt to increase their efforts when this perception prevailed. We believe that these findings may address the seemingly negative connotation that family firms' focus too heavily on non-economic goals (Cennamo et al. 2012; Chua et al. 1999; Gómez-Mejía et al. 2007) and this focus could instead create a positive perception by stakeholder groups. When coupling this predominant decision-making value with the long-term orientation of family firms (Chrisman et al. 2003b), it is conceivable to argue that the stakeholders associated with a family firm will see the leader of the business as a visionary leader and in turn increase their efforts. This may be yet another way to explain why family firms are believed to outperform non-family firms (Miller et al. 2007).

Next, it would be interesting to investigate how stakeholder relationships in family firms change over time. How might stakeholder engagement strategies change when a family firm moves from a sibling partnership to a cousin consortium governance structure (Gersick et al. 1997)? Will family managers become increasingly influenced by the stakes of the family stakeholder group as this group grows and its needs escalate? Are some stakeholder relationships in the family firm disrupted more or less than others during a time of succession? And, is it possible for actions to be taken leading up to the succession process to enshrine the legacy of certain stakeholder relationships?

Lastly, Tantalo and Priem (2015) addressed directly *how* firms may be able to create value for multiple stakeholder groups simultaneously by discussing a new concept they call "stakeholder synergy." Stakeholder synergy is the ability of the top management team to "identify novel combinations of different utilities, each valued by different stakeholder groups" (Tantalo and Priem 2015), and then to deploy strategies to meet the needs of each group at the same time. Mechanisms to achieve the deployment of these strategies include:

1. increasing the utility of a single stakeholder group without decreasing the utility of another group;
2. finding complementary needs across multiple stakeholder groups and meeting them simultaneously;
3. "follow-on" results of a singular action or a complementary action, such as increased stakeholder commitment and trust, will lead to additional synergies between and amongst various stakeholder groups.

Following Tantalo and Priem (2015), we believe it would be interesting for family firm research to investigate whether or not there are consistent types of stakeholder needs that could be complementary and, hence, provide opportunities for complementary actions. For example, the need to develop leaders of the next generation of family members may encourage the family stakeholder group to place resources into leadership training programs for family members. As policies for this type program are created, it would behoove the top management team to consider equitable ways to also include non-family members in leadership training. The results may be a protection of the family's socioemotional endowment and an overall increase in leadership abilities throughout the company. What other human resource areas could address complementary needs of different internal stakeholder groups in the family firm? What needs of external stakeholders may consistently be complementary with the needs of the family stakeholder group? The stakeholder synergy concept may also help identify strategies to deal with the significant salience of the family stakeholder group (Mitchell et al. 2011). Stakeholder synergy could offer new options for dealing with nonessential stakeholder groups, as well as essential stakeholders (Tantalo and Priem 2015) such as the family stakeholder group.

From a practical standpoint, consistency in organizational practices may be especially important in family businesses. Similar to the example provided previously for the development of a leadership training program in a family firm, the equitable treatment of family and non-family members may result in increased effort by the entirety of the employee complement. Barnett and Kellermanns (2006) argue that low levels of family influence had little impact on justice perceptions of human resource practices by non-family members in family firms. They also theorize that moderate levels of family influence in the firm will result in positive perceptions of human resource practices, but high levels of family influence will have negative effects on perceptions of justice in human resource practices. Practitioners in family firms should be actively seeking opportunities to find stakeholder synergy and to then create policies that reflect equity through distributive and procedural justice. By listening closely to stakeholders when interacting with them, finding synergistic ways to meet the needs of multiple groups simultaneously, and then providing explanations to each stakeholder group about the subsequent decisions made (Harrison et al. 2010), it is possible to manage stakeholders' perceptions of the family who is in charge of the business.

Additionally, current family firm leaders should consider how the relationships of certain primary stakeholder groups could be damaged during the transition to the next generation of family members into leadership roles in the business. For example, understanding the needs of stakeholders requires intimate interaction with these groups. In the case of suppliers or key customers to the firm, the stakeholder relationship could become strained if a family successor is not properly provided with the opportunity to build a relationship with these firms or customers. Family firm consultants and family business researchers have both expanded significantly upon the idea that one major succession problem is the management of key relationships in the firm. We reiterate their suggestion here and encourage family firm leaders to help their successors focus very specifically on the needs of key stakeholder groups. This will require intimate interaction with each group and may lead to the continued perception of the family being visionary leaders of the firm.

Conclusion

Stakeholder theory began (Freeman 1984) as a way to explain how companies can increase the breadth of information utilized when making decisions for their firms. Stakeholders may be affected or can affect the firm in a myriad of ways and this should be recognized as important, rather than only focusing on the effect of shareholder needs upon decision-making processes. Although much work remains to be accomplished, the combination of stakeholder theory and family firm research offers unique contributions to our understanding of these literature streams. The family stakeholder group desires to meet its own socioemotional wealth goals (Gómez-Mejía et al. 2007) and meeting these needs may not be 100 percent contradictory to the economic goals of the business. Opportunities are abundant to specify how stakeholders of the family firm affect profitability, justice perceptions, leadership, and organizational culture. The opportunities for practitioners to learn how to increase their effectiveness and competitive advantage in the marketplace appear to be significant as well.

References

Agle, B. R., Mitchell, R. K., and Sonnenfeld, J. A. (1999) 'Who matters to CEOs? An investigation of stakeholder attributes and salience, corporate performance, and CEO values,' *Academy of Management Journal,* 42(5): 507–525.

Anderson, R. C., and Reeb, D. M. (2004) 'Board composition: Balancing family influence in S&P 500 firms,' *Administrative Science Quarterly,* 49(2): 209–237.

Arregle, J., Hitt, M. A., Sirmon, D. G., and Very, P. (2007) 'The development of organizational social capital: Attributes of family firms,' *Journal of Management Studies,* 44(1): 73–95.

Barbera, F., and Hasso, T. (2013) 'Do we need to use an accountant? The sales growth and survival benefits to family SMEs,' *Family Business Review,* 26(3): 271–292.

Barnett, T., and Kellermanns, F.W. (2006) 'Are we family and are we treated as family? Nonfamily employees' perceptions of justice in the family firm,' *Entrepreneurship Theory & Practice,* 30(6): 837–854.

Berman, S. L., Wicks, A. C., Kotha, S., and Jones, T. M. (1999) 'Does stakeholder orientation matter? The relationship between stakeholder management models and firm financial performance,' *Academy of Management Journal,* 42(5): 488–506.

Berrone, P., Cruz, C., Gómez-Mejía, L.R., and Larraza-Kintana, M. (2010) 'Socioemotional wealth and corporate responses to institutional pressures: Do family-controlled firms pollute less?,' *Administrative Science Quarterly,* 55: 82–113.

Bingham, J. B., Dyer, W. G. Jr., Smith, I., and Adams, G. L. (2011) 'A stakeholder identity orientation approach to corporate social performance in family firms,' *Journal of Business Ethics,* 99(4): 565–585.

Bridoux, F., and Stoelhorst, J. W. (2014) 'Microfoundations for stakeholder theory: Managing stakeholders with heterogeneous motives,' *Strategic Management Journal,* 35(1): 107–125.

Bundy, J., Shropshire, C., and Buchholtz, A. K. (2013) 'Strategic cognition and issue salience: Toward an explanation of firm responsiveness to stakeholder concerns,' *Academy of Management Review,* 38(3): 352–376.

Cennamo, C., Berrone, P., Cruz, C., and Gómez-Mejía, L. R. (2012) 'Socioemotional wealth and proactive stakeholder engagement: Why family-controlled firms care more about their stakeholders,' *Entrepreneurship Theory & Practice,* 36(6): 1153–1173.

Choi, J., and Wang, H. (2009) 'Stakeholder relations and the persistence of corporate financial performance,' *Strategic Management Journal,* 30: 895–907.

Chrisman, J. J., Chua, J. H., Kellermanns, F. W., and Chang, E. P. C. (2007) 'Are family managers agents or stewards? An exploratory study in privately held family firms,' *Journal of Business Research,* 60: 1030–1038.

Chrisman, J. J., Chua, J. H., and Litz, R. (2004) 'Comparing the agency costs of family and nonfamily firms: Conceptual issues and exploratory evidence,' *Entrepreneurship Theory & Practice,* 28(4): 335–354.

Chrisman, J. J., Chua, J. H., and Steier, L. (2003) 'An introduction to theories of family business,' *Journal of Business Venturing,* 18(4): 441–448.

Chua, J. H., Chrisman, J. J., and Sharma, P. (1999) 'Defining the family business by behavior,' *Entrepreneurship: Theory & Practice,* 23(4): 19–39.

Chua, J. H., Chrisman, J. J., Steier, L. P., and Rau, S. B. (2012) 'Sources of Heterogeneity in Family Firms: An Introduction,' *Entrepreneurship: Theory and Practice,* 36(6): 1103–1113.

Clarkson, M. E. (1995) 'A Stakeholder Framework for Analyzing and Evaluating Corporate Social Performance,' *Academy of Management Review,* 20(1): 92–117.

Cruz, C., Firfiray, S., and Gómez-Mejía, L.R. (2011) 'Socioemotional wealth and human resource management in family firms,' in A. Joshi, H. Liao, & J. Martocchio (eds.), *Personnel and Human Resource Management* (Vol. 30, pp. 159–219), Bingley, UK: Emerald Publishing Company.

De Luque, S., Washburn, M. F., Waldman, D. A., and House, R. J. (2008) 'Unrequited profit: How stakeholder and economic values relate to subordinates' perceptions of leadership and firm performance,' *Administrative Science Quarterly,* 53(4): 626–654.

Donaldson, T., and Preston, L. E. (1995) 'The stakeholder theory of the corporation: Concepts, evidence, and implications,' *Academy of Management Review,* 20(1): 65–91.

Freeman, R. E. (1984) *Strategic Management: A Stakeholder Approach,* Englewood Cliffs, NJ: Prentice Hall.

Freeman R. E. (2010) 'Managing for stakeholders: trade-offs or value creation,' *Journal of Business Ethics,* 96: 7–9.

Freeman, R. E., Harrison, J. S., and Wicks, A. C. (2007) *Managing for Stakeholders: Survival, Reputation and Success,* New Haven, CT: Yale University Press.

Freeman, R. E., Harrison, J. S., Wicks, A. C., Parmar, B., and de Colle, S. (2010) *Stakeholder Theory: The State of the Art,* Cambridge, UK: Cambridge University Press.

Friedman, A., and Miles, S. (2006) *Stakeholders: Theory and Practice,* Oxford: Oxford University Press.

Friedman, S. D., and Olk, P. (1995) 'Four ways to choose a CEO: Crown heir, horse race, coup d'etat & comprehensive search,' *Human Resource Management,* 34(1): 141–164.

Gentry, R., Dibrell, C., and Kim, J. (2014), in press. 'Long-term orientation in publicly traded family businesses: Evidence of a dominant logic,' *Entrepreneurship Theory & Practice.*

Gersick, K. E., Davis, J. A., Hampton, M. M., and Lansberg, I. (1997) *Generation to Generation: Life Cycles of the Family Business,* Boston, MA: Harvard Business School Press.

Gómez-Mejía, L. R., Haynes, K. T., Nuñez-Nickel, M., Jacobson, K. J. L., and Moyana-Fuentes, J. (2007) 'Socioemotional wealth and business risks in family-controlled firms: Evidence from Spanish olive oil mills,' *Administrative Science Quarterly,* 52(1): 106–137.

Gómez-Mejía, L.R., Larraza-Kintana, M., and Makri, M. (2003) 'The determinants of executive compensation in family-controlled public corporations,' *Academy of Management Journal,* 46(2): 226–237.

Graves, S. B., and Waddock, S. A. (1994) 'Institutional owners and corporate social performance,' *Academy of Management Journal*, 37(4): 1034–1046.

Habbershon, T. G., Williams, M., and MacMillan, I. C. (2003) 'A unified systems perspective of family firm performance,' *Journal of Business Venturing*, 18(4): 451.

Harrison, J. S., Bosse, D. A., and Phillips, R. A. (2010) 'Managing for stakeholders, stakeholder utility functions, & competitive advantage,' *Strategic Management Journal*, 31(1): 58–74.

Heller, F. (1997) 'Leadership and power in a stakeholder setting,' *European Journal of Work & Organizational Psychology*, 6: 567–579.

Hillman, A. J., and Keim, G. D. (2001a) 'Shareholder value, stakeholder management, and social issues: What's the bottom line?,' *Strategic Management Journal*, 22(2): 125–139.

Hillman, A. J., and Keim, G. D. (2001b) 'Shareholder value, stakeholder management, and social issues: What's the bottom line?,' *Strategic Management Journal*, 26: 159–180.

Hoy, F., and Pu, H. (2012) 'Reconsidering Models for Investigating Family Firms: Variants from China,' *Entrepreneurship Research Journal*, 2(4): 1–18.

Hutton, J. (1999) *The Stakeholders Society*, London: Blackwell.

Jones, T. M., and Wicks, A. C. (1999) 'Convergent stakeholder theory,' *Academy of Management Review*, 24(2): 206.

Kroeger, A., and Weber, C. (2014) 'Developing a conceptual framework for measuring social value creation,' *Academy of Management Review*, 39(4): 513–540.

Laplume, A. O, Sonpar, K., and Litz, R. A. (2008) 'Stakeholder theory: Reviewing a theory that moves us,' *Journal of Management*, 34(6): 1152–1189.

Mainardes, E. W., Alves, H., and Raposo, M. (2011) 'Stakeholder theory: Issues to resolve,' *Management Decision*, 49(2): 226–252.

Margolis, J. D., and Walsh, J. P. (2003) 'Misery loves companies: Rethinking social initiatives by business,' *Administrative Science Quarterly*, 48: 268–305.

Matherne, C. F., Ring, J. K., and McKee, D. (2011) 'Multiple Social Identifications and the Family Firm,' *Journal of Behavioral and Applied Management*, 13(1): 24–43.

Miller, D., Le Breton-Miller, I., Lester, R. H., and Cannella, A. A. Jr. (2007) 'Are family firms really superior performers?,' *Journal of Corporate Finance*, 13(5): 829–858.

Mitchell, R. K., Agle, B. R., Chrisman, J. J., and Spence, L. J. (2011) 'Toward a theory of stakeholder salience in family firms,' *Business Ethics Quarterly*, 21(2): 235–255.

Mitchell, R. K., Agle, B. R., and Wood, D. J. (1997) 'Toward a theory of stakeholder identification and salience: Defining the principle of who and what really counts,' *Academy of Management Review*, 22(4): 853–886.

Morck, R., and Yeung, B. (2004) 'Family control and the rent-seeking society.' *Organizational Dynamics*, 12: 39–46.

Naldi, L., Chirico, F., Kellermanns, F. W., and Campopiano, G. (2015) 'All in the family? An exploratory study of family member advisors and firm performance,' *Family Business Review*, 28(3): 227–242.

Pearson, A. P., Carr, J. C., and Shaw, J. C. (2008) 'Toward a theory of familiness: A social capital perspective,' *Entrepreneurship Theory & Practice*, 32(6): 949–969.

Poza, E. J., Algred, T., and Maheshwari, A. (1997) 'Stakeholder perceptions of culture and management practices in family and family firms – A preliminary report,' *Family Business Review*, 10(2): 135–155.

Reay, T., Pearson, W. P., and Dyer, W. G. (2013) 'Advising family enterprise: Examining the role of family firm advisors,' *Family Business Review*, 26(3): 209–214.

Rumelt, R. P., Schendel, D. E., and Teece, D. J. (1995) *Fundamental Issues in Strategy: A Research Agenda for the 1990s* (Paperback), Boston, MA: Harvard Business School Press Books.

Salvato, C., and Corbetta, G. (2013) 'Transitional leadership of advisors as a facilitator of successors' leadership construction,' *Family Business Review*, 26(3): 235–254.

Schulze, W. S., Lubatkin, M. H., and Dino, R. N. (2003) 'Exploring the agency consequences of ownership dispersion among the directors of private family firms,' *Academy of Management Journal*, 46(2): 179–194.

Sharma, P. (2001) 'Stakeholder management concepts in family firms,' in *Proceedings of 12th Annual Conference of International Association of Business and Society* 254–259.

Sharma, P., Chrisman, J. J., and Chua, J. H. (1997) 'Strategic management of the family business: Past research and future challenges,' *Family Business Review*, 10(1): 1–35.

Sharma, P. and Sharma, S. (2011) 'Drivers of proactive environmental strategy in family firms,' *Business Ethics Quarterly*, 21(2): 309–334.

Tantalo, C. and Priem, R. L. (2015), in press. 'Value creation through stakeholder synergy,' *Strategic Management Journal.*

Taylor, B. (1995) 'The new strategic leadership – Driving change, getting results,' *Long Range Planning,* 28(5): 71–81.

Waddok, S. A., and Graves, S. B. (1997) 'The corporate social performance-financial performance link,' *Strategic Management Journal,* 14(4): 3030–3319.

Ward, J. L. (1997) 'Growing the family business: Special challenges and best practices,' *Family Business Review,* 10(4): 323–337.

Where we work. (2015). Retrieved May 25, 2015, from http://www.thefbcg.com/benefits/where-we-work/.

Wiseman, R. and Gómez-Mejía, L.R. (1998) 'A behavioural agency model of managerial risk taking,' *Academy of Management Review,* 25: 133–152.

Ylvisaker, P. N. (1990) 'Family foundations: High risk, high reward,' *Family Business Review,* 3(4): 331–335.

Zellweger, T. M., and Nason, R. S. (2008) 'A stakeholder perspective on family firm performance,' *Family Business Review,* 21(3), 203–216.

9

CREDIT RATIONING IN FAMILY FIRMS

Short-Term vs. Long-Term Bank Debt Rationing

Tensie Steijvers and Wim Voordeckers[1]

Introduction

Extent research found that financing decisions in family firms and the resulting capital structure differ substantially from those of their nonfamily counterparts (e.g. Croci et al. 2011; Romano et al. 2000; Schmid 2013; Koropp et al. 2014). Surprisingly, there is less agreement about the direction of the effect. While several studies reported that (some types of) family firms use more debt (e.g. Romano et al. 2000; Croci et al. 2011; Gottardo and Moisello 2014), others found the opposite effect (e.g. McConaughy et al. 2001; Schmid 2013; Ampenberger et al. 2013) or no systematic effect (e.g. Anderson and Reeb 2003). Several theoretical explanations for differences in debt ratios have been proposed of which the specific control motivations of family owners rank ahead.

However, an overlooked aspect of this debate is the fact that the debt ratio of a firm is the result of demand as well as supply side considerations. The proportion of debt used by a family firm will not only depend on the financial attitudes and beliefs towards debt of the founding family (Matthews et al. 1994; Koropp et al. 2013) but also on the potential credit rationing behavior of financial institutions towards private family firms (Robb and Robinson 2014; Crespi and Martin-Oliver 2015). Indeed, dark side effects of family ownership like nepotism, special dividend payouts, and excessive executive remuneration may refrain a bank from approving a loan request from a family firm (Anderson and Reeb 2003; Steijvers and Voordeckers 2009a), leading to higher credit rationing among family firms. Therefore, the aim of this paper is to explain the debt ratio of private family versus nonfamily SMEs using a demand-supply framework. In addition, we investigate whether family SMEs are more credit rationed than nonfamily firms in the Belgian context which is exemplary for the Continental European bank-based system (Degryse and Van Cayseele 2000). Credit rationing occurs if the demand for loans exceeds the supply at the ruling price (interest rate). The rational expectation is that an excess demand for debt would cause the opportunistic suppliers to increase the price, until quantity demanded equals quantity supplied. However, this typical market mechanism does not function in the bank loan market which may lead to the existence of credit rationing for SMEs (Stiglitz and Weiss 1981). We focus on SMEs because, when external financing sources are needed in order to ensure continuity and to realize growth, SMEs and especially those in bank-based financial systems have to rely partly on bank loans since collecting money on the public capital market is often a difficult and costly task (Bhattacharya and Thakor 1993; Berger and Udell 1998; Robb and Robinson 2014).

This article contributes to the literature in several ways. First, we investigate potential differences in capital structure between family and nonfamily SMEs by using a demand and supply framework which allows us to estimate simultaneous the impact of credit demand factors and credit rationing on the capital structure. Therefore, we measure credit rationing by estimating a demand-supply disequilibrium model for bank debt by which firms are endogenously classified in rationed versus non-rationed firms (Atanasova and Wilson 2004; Vijverberg 2004; Ogawa and Suzuki 2000). This simultaneous estimation approach allows firms to switch throughout time between the categories of rationed and non-rationed firms thereby going further than prior studies investigating differences in leverage of private firms from a supply side perspective (e.g. Cole 2013; Robb and Robinson 2014; Crespi and Martin-Oliver 2015). The model is estimated using a large panel data set of annual accounts of small and medium-sized Belgian firms for the period 1994–2001 which can be considered as an economic expansion period in Europe (Bengoechea et al. 2006). We chose this long economic expansion period as prior studies showed that differences in leverage between family and nonfamily firms are different in expansion and crisis periods (Crespi and Martin-Oliver 2015). Secondly, we investigate the distinction between long-term and short-term bank debt rationing. Although this distinction was never made in existing credit rationing studies, there are several theoretical reasons, grounded in the debt maturity and agency theory literature, to argue that SMEs would incur a higher probability of being long-term bank debt rationed rather than short-term bank debt rationed.

The remaining part of the paper is organised as follows. The upcoming section on Credit Rationing provides an overview of the theoretical credit rationing literature which is the foundation of our empirical research. Furthermore, we discuss the theoretical arguments for making a distinction in our study between credit rationing for long- versus short-term bank debt and develop our hypotheses. In the next section, we describe the empirical methodology, formulating the disequilibrium model of corporate bank lending to be estimated, as well as the data. The estimation results are presented in the subsequent section. Concluding remarks and suggestions for further research are provided.

Credit Rationing

Background

Economic theory states that there exists an equilibrium in the market when demand equals supply or the Walrasian market clearing level is reached. However, in the market for bank debt, an equilibrium different from that point may exist. Instead, equilibrium is reached at the bank-optimal interest rate (Stiglitz and Weiss 1981). At this interest rate, the demand for bank debt may exceed the supply and credit rationing occurs. Numerous researchers have tried to find a theoretical explanation for the existence of credit rationing. Jaffee and Russell (1976) and Stiglitz and Weiss (1981) were the first to introduce information asymmetry in the analysis of the credit decision. Stiglitz and Weiss (1981) conclude that banks will rather ration credit than increase the interest rate due to adverse selection and moral hazard problems. Credit rationed firms will be prepared to pay a higher interest rate. However, if a bank accepts this higher (than bank-optimal) interest rate, it will attract higher risk borrowers while lower risk borrowers drop out (adverse selection effect). Consequently, the expected return for the bank will increase at a slower rate than the interest rate and will even decrease after a certain interest rate is exceeded. In order to avoid this negative effect, banks will not charge a (market clearing) interest rate above the bank-optimal interest rate. Moreover, the interest rate will also influence the borrower in his selection of projects. If the bank increases the interest rate, the borrower will prefer higher risk projects above low-risk projects, decreasing again the expected return for the bank (moral hazard effect). Stiglitz and Weiss conclude that there are no competitive forces leading to an equilibrium between demand and supply. Moreover, the behavior of borrowers cannot be monitored costlessly. Consequently, a bank may prefer to ration credit rather than increasing the interest rate until equilibrium is reached.

The model of Stiglitz and Weiss gave rise to many theoretical models trying to explain credit rationing, taking into account the existence of information asymmetry (e.g. Blinder and Stiglitz 1983; Besanko and Thakor 1987a, 1987b; Williamson 1986; Milde and Riley 1988). Most models conclude that information asymmetry leads to credit rationing when the information problem remains unresolved. Information asymmetry is the foundation for credit rationing: the expected return increases non-monotonously when the interest rate increases.

Credit Rationing for Long-Term vs. Short-Term Bank Debt

In the SME finance and debt maturity literature, several theoretical arguments have been developed which point to the existence of a demand-supply market for short-term bank debt and one for long-term bank debt for SMEs, which are interrelated markets. From this literature, we argue that debt rationing may occur in one market but not in the other, i.e. SMEs may be long-term bank debt rationed but not short-term bank debt rationed. As far as we know, this distinction was never made in existing empirical studies concerning credit rationing. The evidence we found in previous research is rather anecdotal (Cull et al., 2006) or indirect in nature and deducted from the debt maturity literature (e.g. Scherr and Hulburt 2001; Berger et al. 2005).

A distinctive feature of the debt market for small business finance is the existence of information and agency problems arising from the fact that small firms are informational opaque (Barnea et al. 1980, 1985; Pettit and Singer 1985; Berger and Udell 1998). This informational opaqueness causes difficulties to assess the long-term credibility of the debtor, causing an adverse selection problem (Akerlof 1970; Jaffee and Russel 1976; Leland and Pyle 1977; Stiglitz and Weiss 1981; Cosci 1993). The probability of the occurrence of an adverse event or of suffering financial distress is larger as the maturity of the loan increases. SMEs are also very flexible, facilitating the ability to move into risk shifting behavior, giving rise to moral hazard problems such as asset substitution (Arrow 1963, 1968; Jensen and Meckling 1976; Stiglitz and Weiss 1981). The asset substitution problem is especially prevalent when obtaining long-term bank debt: especially debt with a longer maturity offers more opportunities to alter the projects in subtle ways or even switch from low-risk to high-risk projects (Berger and Udell 1998).

In order to cope with the informational opacity in a small firm context and the resulting agency problem, the use of a shorter loan maturity in debt contracts can offer a solution (e.g. Myers 1977; Barnea et al. 1980; Smith and Warner 1979; Berlin and Mester 1992). The short debt maturity forces the SMEs to frequently renegotiate with the financial institution and clear the informational opaqueness that causes difficulties to assess the long-term credibility of the debtor (Ortiz-Molina and Penas 2006; Berger and Udell 2005).

Not only banks but also SMEs make the distinction between the demand for long-term and short-term bank debt. Due to their initial informational opaqueness, SMEs are inclined to signal their creditworthiness by demanding short-term bank debt (Flannery 1986). Throughout time, they get the opportunity to show their qualities and to build up a reputation. Short-term finance offers the possibility to incorporate this positive information, increasing the credit availability and decreasing the interest rate (Diamond 1991, 1993). As the information asymmetry is reduced and the positive traits of the firm are known by the bank, SMEs would rather demand long-term bank debt instead of subsequent short-term bank debt.

Given these arguments, we argue that studying the demand and supply for long- and short-term bank debt separately, adds new insights to the credit rationing debate. The results of the empirical studies by Berger et al. (2005) and Ortiz-Molina and Penas (2006) support the proposition that shorter loan maturities serve to mitigate the problems associated with asymmetric information. Results by Berger et al. (2005), suggest that maturities increase when the informational asymmetries are reduced. Also, Barclay and Smith (1995) and Stohs and Mauer (1996) empirically confirm the positive correlation between firm size and debt maturity. Moreover, related empirical capital structure research by Van der Wijst and Thurik (1993), Chittenden et al. (1996) and Hall et al. (2004) points out that, for certain determinants of the total leverage degree, the sign of the regression coefficient masks two opposite effects for long and short-term debt. In addition, Guiso (1998) concludes in his study that, a large share of short-term financial liabilities at high-tech firms, considerably increases the probability of a firm being credit rationed. This result indirectly suggests that these firms coping with credit rationing for long-term bank debt, substitute long-term bank debt by short-term debt including short-term *bank* debt. These findings provide justification for a more thoroughly empirical investigation of the existence as well as the differences in profiles of long-term and short-term bank debt rationed firms.

Control Considerations and the Demand for Bank Debt in Private Family Firms

The choice for a financing source (i.e. debt-equity choice) is often the consequence of control considerations (Schmid 2013) which seem to play a more prominent role in private family firms than in their nonfamily counterparts. Indeed, private family firms differ from other organizational forms in that managerial choices are motivated by economic as well as noneconomic objectives (Gómez-Mejía et al. 2011). Family owners obtain important utilities from these noneconomic objectives which are labeled as the family's socioemotional wealth (Gómez-Mejía et al. 2007). A key dimension of the family's socioemotional wealth is the desire to keep family control and influence over the firm (Berrone et al. 2012). Family owners are reluctant to use financing sources which dilute their perceived control over the family firm like external equity (Koropp et al. 2014). Consequently, family firms are expected to have a stronger preference for non-control-diluting securities such as bank debt than nonfamily firms (Croci et al. 2011). This control argument is especially valid for the choice between equity and long-term debt as additional financing source for the financing of new long-term investment projects. Hence, the argument mainly applies for the demand of long-term loans and less for the demand of short-term loans as firms generally strive to match the maturities of their assets and liabilities (Heyman et al. 2008). Therefore, we propose that especially the preference for long-term loans is higher in family firms compared to nonfamily firms:

Hypothesis 1

Family firms will have a higher preference for long-term bank loans than nonfamily firms.

Agency Problems and the Supply of Bank Debt in Private Family Firms

As explained above, asymmetric information and agency problems play an important role in the existence of credit rationing. The existence and the scope of agency problems in private family firms have been the topic of academic debate for several decades. Traditional agency theory predicts that family ownership and management mitigate potential principal-agent conflicts. Indeed, agency problems may occur when ownership and control are separated, a situation less common in private family firms (Fama and Jensen 1983). Moreover, family bonds and parental altruism will withhold family agents from demonstrating self-serving behavior (Schulze et al.

2003). In addition, the concentration of ownership in the hands of family members places the family in a strong position to monitor the management team and alleviates agency problems such as asset substitution behavior (Steijvers and Voordeckers 2009a). Family owners usually have a longer investment horizon and a focus on the long-term survival of the firm with the objective to continue the firm as family firm across generations (Sirmon and Hitt 2003) and will strive to establish and maintain a strong reputation (Huybrechts et al. 2011). These characteristics reduce agency costs of debt and consequently the risk for debtholders (Steijvers et al. 2010). Following these arguments, financial institutions will more easily approve loan requests of family firms. Accordingly, family firms are expected to be less credit rationed than nonfamily firms.

However, other studies argue that the unchallenged discretion of family owners may lead to self-control problems (Lubatkin et al. 2005) such as risk shifting behavior, special dividend payouts (Michiels et al. 2015), excessive compensation (Anderson and Reeb 2003), nepotism (Perez-Gonzalez 2006) and managerial entrenchment (Gómez-Mejía et al. 2001) which may harm the interests of debtholders. These potential agency problems may make financial institutions more cautious and vigilant when dealing with family firms and may result in fewer approvals of credit requests with a longer term. In this case, banks may ration long-term credit or may decide to approve a credit with a shorter maturity. Consequently, we hypothesize that:

Hypothesis 2

Financial institutions will supply less long-term loans and more short-term loans to private family firms in comparison with nonfamily firms.

Taking Hypothesis 1 and Hypothesis 2 together, we can infer conclusions from credit rationing behavior of banks towards family firms in comparison with nonfamily firms. As family firms are expected to have a higher demand for long-term loans while simultaneously financial institutions will supply less long-term loans to family firms, we infer that a higher proportion of private family firms will experience long-term credit rationing. Additionally, long-term credit rationing is expected to be higher than short-term credit rationing.

Hypothesis 3a

A higher proportion of private family firms will experience long-term credit rationing compared to private nonfamily firms.

Hypothesis 3b

A higher proportion of private family firms will experience long-term credit rationing compared to short-term credit rationing.

Data and Methodology

Data

Detailed financial information of 320,000 Belgian companies is collected each year by the National Bank of Belgium. This information is available on the Bel-First DVD-ROM of Bureau Van Dijk. From this database, we select the private small and medium-sized firms according to Belgian law[2], not active in the agriculture, forestry or financial sector and having more than 10 employees. All firms in the population are limited companies ('NV') or limited liability companies ('(E)BVBA'). The published accounts meet all the requirements set by the National Bank of Belgium. This criterion provides us with a population of 16,095 firms.

From this population, we select a random sample of 1,000 firms.[3] For the small and medium-sized firms in this sample, we gather detailed financial data for the period 1994–2001. This selected time frame allows us to estimate the regression models for a long economic expansion period which provides findings for demand-supply mechanisms in the credit market under stable economic conditions (Bengoechea et al. 2006). Indeed, the study of Crespi and Martin-Oliver (2015) found that differences in leverage between family and nonfamily firms are different in expansion and crisis periods which may complicate the estimation of the models when mixing time periods with different economic conditions. In addition, the 1994–2001 time frame is characterized by stable financial regulatory conditions under the Basel I Accord. After the removal of outliers, we obtain an unbalanced data set consisting of 6,068 published accounts, with 1998 used as reference year: all firms in our data set existed in 1998. Our dataset consists of 3,730 published accounts of family firms, representing 61.5 percent of the sample.

A possible exit of failed firms and entry of newly established firms in our sample, reduces a potential survivorship and selection bias. Moreover, as Maddala (1986) suggests, making use of these microdata avoids the aggregation bias problem. The aggregation bias problem is common in empirical studies on credit rationing that use macro-level data (e.g. Pazarbasioglu 1997; Barajas and Steiner 2002; Hurlin and Kierzenkowski 2002; Ikhide 2003).

Table 9.1 reports the correlation matrix. Table 9.2 presents descriptive statistics of the sample. The average firm in our sample is 19 years in operation and has 8,625,000 euros (median: 1,806,000 euros) in total assets. It reports a solvency of 30.1 percent and a return on equity of 16.8 percent. The average SME finances 25.6 percent of its assets with trade credit, 8.7 percent with internally generated funds, 17.3 percent with bank finance, consisting of 10.6 percent long-term bank finance and 6.73 percent short-term bank finance.

A Demand-Supply Disequilibrium Model

The amount of bank debt received depends on the interaction of the desired demand and the supply of bank debt if the equilibrium or market-clearing interest rate is lower than the bank-optimal interest rate r^* from the model of Stiglitz and Weiss (1981). If the equilibrium interest rate exceeds the bank-optimal interest rate, the transaction is determined by the supply of bank debt.

In this study, credit rationing can occur in a market in equilibrium as defined by Stiglitz and Weiss (1981). In other words, in *equilibrium*, meaning that the bank demands the bank-optimal interest rate, the credit market can, from the traditional Walrasian point of view, be in *disequilibrium*. We assume that the interest rates are 'sticky' and do not equilibrate the market in every period considered. We are thus considering equilibrium rationing in our study: the price persistently stays at a level implying an excess demand which is consistent with rational lender behavior based on asymmetric information problems encountered.

In order to take into account the existence of a (permanent) disequilibrium in the market (credit rationing), the simultaneous equation model stated below, being a disequilibrium model, will be estimated (Maddala and Nelson 1974; Atanasova and Wilson 2004):

$$L_t^d = \beta_1 x'_{1t} + u_{1t}$$
$$L_t^s = \beta_2 x'_{2t} + u_{2t} \qquad (1)$$
$$L_t = \min(L_t^d, L_t^s)$$

The model consists of a demand equation L_t^d, a supply equation L_t^s and a transaction equation L_t. The transaction equation L_t, being the dependent variable in this study, is the amount of long-term (or short-term) bank debt actually received in year t. Only this amount can be perceived. L_t^d and L_t^s represent the amount of bank debt demanded and supplied, but are not observed by

Table 9.1 Pairwise Correlations

	1	2	3	4	5	6	7	8	9	10	11	12	13
1 Long-term bank debt	1												
2 Short-term bank debt	-0.04***	1											
3 Family firm	0.04***	-0.05***	1										
4 Assets	-0.03*	0.03***	-0.13***	1									
5 Asset rotation	-0.17***	0.04***	-0.12***	0.07***	1								
6 LT growth	0.02*	0.02	-0.03*	0.01	0.01	1							
7 Cash flow	0.15***	-0.18***	0.03***	-0.06***	-0.12***	-0.01	1						
8 Net trade credit	0.10***	-0.10***	0.10***	0.01	-0.08***	0.01	-0.07***	1					
9 Group dummy	-0.08***	0.10***	-0.26***	0.11***	0.06***	0.02*	-0.04***	-0.06***	1				
10 Firm age	0.01	-0.08***	0.09***	0.01	0.03*	-0.03**	-0.10***	-0.01	-0.01	1			
11 Solvency	-0.21***	-0.21***	0.14***	0.09***	-0.04***	-0.03**	0.09***	-0.16***	-0.03**	0.10***	1		
12 Interest cover	-0.08***	-0.02*	-0.08***	0.01	0.11***	-0.01	0.03*	-0.02	0.08***	-0.08***	0.04***	1	
13 Trade credit	-0.02*	0.04***	-0.01	-0.09***	0.10***	0.04***	-0.04***	0.37***	0.01	-0.01	-0.22***	0.01	1

*, **, *** Correlation is significant at the 0.1 level, 0.05 level, 0.01 level (2-tailed).

Table 9.2 Descriptive Statistics

Variable	Mean	Median	Std. dev.	Min.	Max.
Firmage (in years)	19	16	13.46	3	91
Total assets (000)	8,625	1,806	46,624	50	902,587
Value added/assets	0.6330	0.5313	0.4843	-0.68	6.85
Cash flow/assets	0.0987	0.0867	0.1061	-0.83	1.15
Trade credit/assets	0.2561	0.2297	0.1727	0	1.00
Long-term growth	0.6630	0.1725	9.7891	-0.96	723.66
Solvency	0.3010	0.2685	0.2275	-0.99	0.97
Return On Equity	0.1680	0.1238	0.3784	-4.64	7.82
Interestcover	4.7422	-0.74	47.1624	-98	979
Fixed assets/assets	0.2668	0.2210	0.2102	0	0.98
Short-term bank debt/assets	0.0673	0.0075	0.1151	0	1.21
Long-term bank debt/assets	0.1060	0.0483	0.1380	0	0.94
N of obs. = 6,068					

any external party. Ex-ante, we do not know if the transaction amount[4] of debt is the amount demanded by the firm or the result of a constraint set by the bank which was not prepared to offer the demanded amount of bank debt ('unknown sample separation,' Maddala, 1987). The vectors x'_{1t} and x'_{2t} reflect the exogenous independent variables, β_1 and β_2 their coefficients, and u_{1t} and u_{2t} the disturbances. The selection of the exogenous independent variables is discussed in the following sections. A detailed explanation of these variables can be found in appendix A. The disequilibrium model, as described in (1), will be estimated twice: once for measuring credit rationing concerning long-term bank debt and once for short-term bank debt. Short-term bank debt is defined as bank debt with a duration of less than or equal to 1 year; long-term bank debt is defined as bank debt with a duration of more than 1 year.

Demand Equation

The vector x'_{1t} in the demand equation consists of those variables measuring the desired demand for bank loans. Our main variable of interest is a dummy variable indicating whether the firm is a family firm or not. Most definitions of family firms in academic literature, using characteristics related to involvement in management, governance, and ownership, cannot be used to identify family firms in our database due to the lack of data. Therefore, we made use of the following criteria, in order to identify family firms in an indirect way: (a) the name of one of the directors (member of the board)[5] is part of the firm name; (b) the firm consists of more than one director and minimum two of them have the same last name; (c) one of the directors home address is the same as the firm address; (d) minimum two directors of the firm do not have the same last name but do live at the same private address. If one or more of these criteria are applicable to the firm, it is classified as a 'family firm.' A study by Voordeckers and Van Gils (2003) showed that these indirect criteria well approximate the usual family firm definitions based on family involvement in ownership and management (Chua et al. 1999).

We also added several control variables. Based on the pecking order theory (Myers 1984), we expect that firms possessing more internal financial resources, measured by the generated cash flow, desire less bank debt (Sealey 1979; Perez 1998; Ogawa and Suzuki 2000; Shen 2002; Atanasova and Wilson 2004). The pecking order predicts that firms will only move on to bank finance when the internal resources are inadequate. Firms characterized by a higher level of activity, measured by assets and asset rotation, are expected to demand more (bank) finance (Perez 1998; Ogawa and Suzuki 2000; Atanasova and Wilson 2004).

The agency theory predicts that firms with more growth opportunities, in this study measured by an intangibles dummy, prefer equity above bank debt. Growth opportunities increase the agency costs related to the conflict between lender and shareholder (Myers 1977; Jensen 1986). However, the actual growth of the firm, measured by asset growth, is expected to be positively related to the demand for bank debt. Growing firms need more financial resources in order to finance growth: internal resources are insufficient and firms have to descend in the pecking order (Cressy and Olofsson 1997; Berger and Udell 1998). Trade credit can be used as a substitute (Petersen and Rajan 1994; Biais et al. 1995; Atanasova and Wilson 2004) or a complement (Elliehausen and Wolken 1993; Biais and Gollier 1997; Petersen and Rajan 1997) for bank finance. We expect that firms using more trade credit would actually desire more bank debt since trade credit is an expensive source of finance. In this study, we use net trade credit taking into account the use of accounts receivable, the extension of payment to its customers. The net effect of both matters if we want to consider trade credit as a financing source. Intra-group finance, measured by means of a group-dummy, can be an important substitute for bank debt. We expect that firms belonging to a group structure desire less bank debt. Financial resources can be transferred within the group by means of participations, loans or trade credit and should be easier to obtain (Deloof and Jegers 1999). Finally, in the demand function, we also control for the year of analysis and the industry in which the firm operates.

Supply Equation

The vector x'_{2t} in the supply equation consists of the firm risk indicators measured by the family firm dummy, firmage, solvency, interest cover and industry (Perez 1998; Shen 2002; Atanasova and Wilson 2004). We expect that younger firms, as well as firms having a lower solvency or interest cover, represent a higher risk for the bank and reduce the supply of bank debt. Comparable to the demand function, we also include four dummy variables in the supply function representing the industries. Based on the signaling value of collateral, we expect that firms being able to offer more assets as collateral to the bank are supplied with more bank debt (Ogawa and Suzuki 2000; Shen 2002; Atanasova and Wilson 2004). Collateral minimizes the asymmetry of information between bank and firm (Chan and Kanatas 1985). The positive signaling value of trade credit, suggested by Biais and Gollier (1997), implies that suppliers giving trade credit to a firm, signal the creditworthiness of the firm receiving trade credit. This could increase the supply of bank debt. We use two measures: the use of trade credit and a trade credit dummy with value '1' if the firm is offered more trade credit than the industry average. Moreover, a bank will be more eager to offer bank debt if a firm belongs to a group structure (Ogawa and Suzuki 2000). The group affiliation is measured by a shareholder dummy and a participation dummy. Finally, we also take into account the interest rate uncertainty measured by the standard deviation of the interest rate (Calcagnini and Iacobucci 1997). We hypothesize that a higher volatility of interest rates makes banks less eager to offer debt.

Estimation of a Disequilibrium Model

The simultaneous equation model described in (1), being a disequilibrium model with unknown sample separation, can be described as a 'switching regression model with endogenous switching.' The amount of debt obtained (perceived) is equal either to the amount of debt demanded or the amount of debt supplied. The endogenous switching feature implies that firms that appear to be credit rationed in year t, can switch to the group of non-credit rationed firms in another year of analysis (Ogawa and Suzuki 2000).

This model can be estimated by means of a full information maximum likelihood model (FIML). Contrary to other system estimations (e.g. 3SLS), FIML takes into account the existence of a possible disequilibrium in the market for which the model is estimated (Maddala 1986). The FIML estimators are consistent and asymptotically normally distributed (Hartley and Mallela 1977; Eliason 1993).

After estimating the demand and supply model for corporate (short-term and long-term) bank lending, we derive the probability that any observation, being firm i in period t, is credit rationed (Gersovitz 1980; Maddala 1986). Following Gersovitz (1980), Maddala (1986) and Atanasova and Wilson (2004), we take into consideration the probability, conditional on the observed transaction:

$$P \left(L_t^d < L_t^s \mid L_t \right), \tag{2}$$

We classify an observation, firm i in period t, as belonging to the supply function and thus being credit rationed, if this probability is smaller than 0.5.

Thus:

$$P\left(L_t^d < L_t^s \mid L_t\right) = \int_{L_t}^{\infty} g\left(L_t, L_t^s\right) d L_t^s / h\left(L_t\right) \tag{3}$$

where, according to Maddala (1986), $h(L_t)$, the unconditional density of L_t, is defined as

$$h\left(L_t\right) = \lambda_t h\left(L_t \mid L_t = L_t^d\right) + \left(1 - \lambda_t\right) h\left(L_t \mid L_t = L_t^s\right)$$

$$= \int_{L_t}^{\infty} g\left(L_t, L_t^s\right) d L_t^s + \int_{L_t}^{\infty} g\left(L_t, L_t^d\right) d L_t^d \tag{4}$$

Lee (1983) shows that this classification rule, also used in our empirical study, is optimal in the sense that the total probability of misclassifications is minimized.

Results

Hypotheses Testing

Starting values for the switching regression models are estimated, based on Ordinary Least Squares, which were considered superior to a vector of null values (Eliason 1993). The Newton-Raphson algorithm was used to converge to the maximum. The results of the estimation of the switching regression models with endogenous switching for long- and short-term bank debt are reported in table 9.3.

With respect to Hypothesis 1, results in table 9.3 suggest that family firms have a higher preference for long-term bank debt ($\beta = 0.0189$, $p<0.05$). This finding supports hypothesis 1. This suggests that family firms seem to avoid the loss of control due to external capital investment. When external finance is needed to finance investments, family firms would rather rely on long-term bank finance (e.g. Romano et. al. 2000). No significant effect was found in the analysis of short-term bank debt.

Table 9.3 Estimation of the 'Demand-Supply Disequilibrium' Models for Long- and Short-Term Bank Debt

Variable	(a) Long-Term Bank Debt		(b) Short-Term Bank Debt	
DEMAND EQUATION	Coeff.	Std. dev.	Coeff.	Std. dev.
Family firm	0.0189***	0.007	0.0061	0.0039
Assets	0.1792***	0.012	0.0873***	0.0072
Assets rotation	-0.0004***	0.00003	-0.00003	0.00003
Intangibles dummy	-0.0113	0.008	0.0275***	0.0052
LT growth	0.0001	0.0002	0.00134**	0.0005
Cash flow	0.2911***	0.024	-0.1596***	0.0137
Net trade credit	0.1126***	0.012	-0.0732***	0.0070
Group dummy	-0.0345***	0.007	0.0174***	0.0039
Year dummy[d]				
1995	-0.0098	0.0106	0.0079	0.0067
1996	-0.0131	0.0104	0.0011	0.0065
1997	-0.0126	0.0105	-0.0043	0.0066
1998	0.0077	0.0107	-0.0013	0.0067
1999	-0.0045	0.0105	-0.0020	0.0067
2000	0.0007	0.0107	-0.0131**	0.0066
2001	0.0109	0.0106	0.0018	0.0067
Industry [b]				
Building	-0.0372***	0.009	-0.0080	0.0055
Retail	-0.0153*	0.008	0.0224***	0.0051
Services	0.030***	0.009	-0.0173***	0.0049
Constant	-6.3829***	2.2690	-6.2384***	1.4277
SUPPLY EQUATION				
Family firm	0.0110	0.010	-0.0070	0.0160
Firmage	-0.0290 ***	0.006	-0.0197**	0.0098
Industry [b]				
Building	0.0123	0.012	0.0348*	0.0182
Retail	-0.0418***	0.010	-0.0246	0.0167
Services	-0.0019	0.013	0.0981***	0.0330
Solvency	-0.8385***	0.026	-0.9918***	0.0355
Interestcover	-0.0001	0.0001	-0.00003	0.00006
Assets	0.7645***	0.029	0.8699***	0.0475
Trade credit	-0.1940***	0.015	-0.1330***	0.0226
Trade credit dummy	-0.2092***	0.011	-0.2259***	0.0163
Shareholder dummy	-0.0014	0.009	-0.0268*	0.0146
Participation dummy	0.0057	0.009	0.0413***	0.0151
Std dev. interest rate[c]	0.0290	0.018	0.0180	0.0196
Constant	11.150**	5.258	2.9413	6.5233
Covariance matrix				
Std. dev. Supply	0.1270***		0.1111***	
Std. dev. Demand	0.1651***		0.1197***	
Start Log likelihood	917.29		2,476.4	
Final Log likelihood	3,221.31		4,210.82	

Notes: Std. dev. calculated based on the second deviation (Newton). An asterisk *, **, *** denotes significance at 10 percent, 5 percent or 1 percent level. [b] manufacturing industry as comparison category. [c] 'Std. dev. interest rate' is the standard deviation of the short-term interest rate for the analysis of short-term bank debt and the standard deviation for the long-term interest rate for the analysis of long-term bank debt (see Appendix A). [d] Year dummies with 1994 as comparison category.

Concerning Hypothesis 2, results in table 9.3 suggest that neither the supply of long-term nor short-term loans are different between family and nonfamily firms. Therefore, we do not find support for Hypothesis 2.

After estimating the simultaneous equation models consisting of the demand and supply functions for short and long-term bank debt, the conditional probabilities $P(L_t^d < L_t^s | L_t)$ can be obtained for each firm i in each year t. Table 9.4 presents the results on the proportion of credit rationed family firms and nonfamily firms for each year t during the period 1994–2001.

Based on table 9.4, we can confirm hypothesis 3a. For each year during the period 1994–2001, a significantly higher proportion of family firms experienced long-term bank debt rationing compared to nonfamily firms (p-value <0.01). Over the entire period 1994–2001, we observe long-term bank debt rationing in 35.3 percent of the private family firms, while only 23.0 percent of the nonfamily firms experience this type of rationing. With respect to short-term credit rationing, there is less difference between family firms and nonfamily firms: 9 percent of the private family firms cope with this type of rationing compared to 5.9 percent of the nonfamily firms. For 1998, 1999 and 2001, there is even no significant difference in the proportion of short-term credit rationing between family firms and nonfamily firms. Table 9.4 also indicates that a significantly higher proportion of family firms copes with long-term credit rationing (35.3 percent) compared to short-term credit rationing (9.0 percent). Therefore, we can confirm hypothesis 3b. Given the large difference between the proportion of long- and short-term debt rationing, we further investigate the practical relevance of both types of credit rationing. Therefore, Table 9.5 provides us with additional information on how often each Belgian family firm copes with credit rationing during the period 1994–2001.

Despite the fact that, over the entire period, 35.3 percent of the family firm observations are characterized by long-term bank debt rationing, 37.3 percent of the family firms never coped with long-term bank debt rationing during the period 1994–2001. On the other hand, 48.6 percent of the family firms were during two or more years confronted with credit rationing for long-term bank debt, which is significantly higher compared to the percentage of 39.3 percent for our total sample of family and nonfamily SMEs.

For short-term bank debt, credit rationing seems to be a minor problem: 78.5 percent of the private family firms never experienced short-term credit rationing during the period 1994–2001 while 6.9 percent of the family firms only suffered one out of eight years with this type of credit rationing. The minor importance of credit rationing for short-term bank debt is in line with the debt maturity literature, set out in the section entitled Credit Rationing for Long-Term vs. Short-Term Bank Debt. A longer term of the loan provides family SMEs the opportunity to switch from low to high-risk projects ('moral hazard'). As loan duration falls, the reputation effect seems to become much more important and the risk of moral hazard behaviour is reduced (Berger and Udell 1998). Moreover, long-term loans require a long-term judgment of the creditor on the creditworthiness of the debtor. The chance of occurrence of an adverse event becomes larger, as the time period of the loan is enlarged (Mann 1997). By means of a succession of bank debt contracts of short-term, the bank can force the family SME to negotiate on a regular basis in order to receive a new short-term loan and thus minimize the 'adverse selection' problem (Pettit and Singer 1985; Hutchinson 1995).

Robustness Checks

In order to check the robustness of our estimated switching regression models (and the resulting proportion of credit rationed firms), several alternative disequilibrium models were tested. First, the model presented in Table 9.3 was re-estimated, taking into account possible spillover effects between the market for long-term and short-term bank debt. We include the amount of

Table 9.4 Proportion Credit Rationed Family and Nonfamily firms (1994–2001)

Year	Credit Rationing for Long-Term Bank Debt in:		Credit Rationing for Short-Term Bank Debt in:	
	Family firms	*Nonfamily firms*	*Family firms*	*Nonfamily firms*
2001	36.1%	22.1%	8.4%	7.5%
2000	35.0%	24.0%	8.7%	5.9%
1999	32.5%	24.2%	7.7%	6.4%
1998	36.8%	23.8%	9.4%	7.0%
1997	36.8%	21.1%	10.1%	4.4%
1996	34.1%	24.6%	9.5%	6.0%
1995	34.5%	19.3%	9.6%	3.7%
1994	37.2%	24.6%	8.9%	5.4%
1994–2001	35.3%	23.0%	9.0%	5.9%

Table 9.5 Frequency of Credit Rationing of Family Firms

Number of Years Coping with Credit Rationing	Credit Rationing for Long-Term Bank Debt	Credit Rationing for Short-Term Bank Debt
0 year	37.2%	78.5%
1 year	14.0%	6.9%
2 years	8.9%	5.1%
3 years	9.6%	3.5%
4 years	8.1%	2.5%
5 years	4.9%	0.5%
6 years	4.7%	0.7%
7 years	5.6%	1.1%
8 years	6.7%	1.1%

short-term bank debt received as an independent variable in the disequilibrium model for long-term bank debt while including the amount of long-term bank debt received as an independent variable in the disequilibrium model for short-term bank debt (results not reported).

We also re-estimated the model from Table 9.3, using other proxies for several variables: in the supply function the interest cover was replaced by 'cash flow/assets,' the shareholder dummy and participation dummy were replaced by one 'group dummy.' In addition, since Table 9.2 reveals that many SMEs do not resort to short-term bank debt, we re-estimated the switching regression model for short-term bank debt without the observations with value '0' for the dependent variable. In either model, no significant changes with respect to significance, signs of the parameters or percentage of credit rationed firms were found (results not reported).

Comparison of Profiles of Long-term Credit Rationed and Non Credit Rationed Firms

In this section, we focus on the most prevalent type of credit rationing being long-term bank debt rationing. We compare the profiles of the median family firm coping with credit rationing for long-term bank debt with the median family firm not coping with this type of credit rationing. Table 9.6 shows the descriptive statistics for these two groups of family firms.

Table 9.6 Comparison of Profile of Long-Term Credit Rationed Versus Long-Term Non-Credit
Rationed Family Firms

	Credit Rationed	Non-Credit Rationed
	Median	Median
Trade credit/ total assets	29.1%	21.0%
Cash flow/ total assets	9.97%	8.3%
Tangible fixed assets/total assets	21.4%	26.3%
Value added/ total assets	0.54	0.54
Total assets	1,596,000 euro	1,516,000 euro
Firmage	19 year	16 year
Growth of assets (on 1 year)	7.6%	2.84%
Long-term growth (on 3 years)	18.8%	15.3%
Solvency	46%	22.8%
Return on Equity	11.2%	12.04%
Interestcover	-2.00	-0.92

Table 9.6 reveals that the median credit rationed family firm turns to alternative financing sources: trade credit and internal cash flow. There is a significant difference in median between the group of credit rationed and non-credit rationed family firms in our sample (respectively 29.2 percent versus 21.0 percent for trade credit and 9.97 percent versus 8.3 percent for cash flow). However, there is no significant difference in size between both groups of firms: the median asset size for both groups is situated around 1,550,000 euros.

Furthermore, the median credit rationed family firm with respect to long-term bank debt can be characterized as a firm with a remarkable (fast) growth. Non rationed family firms seem to grow less and especially less fast. Small fast-growing Belgian family firms consider the access to financial resources as one of the most important obstacles for continuing growth (Grant Thornton Survey 2002). Moreover, this finding is consistent with Carpenter and Petersen (2002) stating that fast-growing firms are the firms most subject to financing constraints. Myers (1977) indicates that firms have to take risks in order to grow and to take advantage of its growth opportunities. The probability of moral hazard behavior is more prevalent at firms experiencing strong growth. If a bank grants long-term bank loans to a firm, the advantages and proceeds of risk taking and growth of the firm will go to the owners of the firm. The bank will only receive the principal and interest amount. If the experienced growth cannot be realized and the loan cannot be repaid, the bank suffers the complete loss of non-repayment of the loan.

Conclusion and Suggestions for Further Research

This study advances our understanding of differences in financing choices and constraints in private family versus nonfamily firms in the Belgian context which is representative of the Continental European bank-based system. Using a large unbalanced panel data set for the period 1994–2001 consisting of 1,000 Belgian SMEs and 6,068 published accounts, we examine the bank debt ratio of family versus nonfamily firms by estimating disequilibrium models of demand and supply for long- and short-term corporate bank loans. Contrary to most previous studies that use an exogenous classification between rationed and non-rationed firms (e.g. Moyen 2004;

Cunningham 2004; Alti 2003; Fazzari et al. 2000), we endogenously classify firms as credit rationed or not (Atanasova and Wilson 2004). In our study, we avoid the use of an ex-ante splitting criterion (e.g. firm size, use of trade credit, firm age, relationship strength) which can only be a crude *proxy* for distinguishing between credit rationed and non-credit rationed firms. Moreover, by making no ex-ante separation in two groups, we allow firms to switch between the group of credit rationed and non-credit rationed firms from one year to another.

The results support our hypothesis that private family firms will have a higher preference for non-control-diluting securities such as bank debt. When making the distinction between short-term and long-term debt, we find that family firms have a higher preference for long-term debt than nonfamily firms which is also in line with the first hypothesis. With respect to the supply of bank debt, we do not find any significant difference between family firms and nonfamily firms which is not in line with the second hypothesis. We speculate that an explanation for this puzzling finding could be found in the collateral requirements of the loan contract. Steijvers and Voordeckers (2009a) found that family firms are more likely to pledge personal collateral as this type of collateral is better suited to cope with the idiosyncratic agency problems in private family firms. Putting personal assets at stake will make a family entrepreneur less inclined to engage in a self-interested behavior. As a result, banks will not make a distinction between family versus nonfamily firms in their supply of long-term debt. However, to compensate for the potentially higher agency problems, banks will demand more stringent collateral requirements.

Concerning credit rationing, our results are in line with our hypotheses. The results suggest that the percentage of credit rationed firms is related to debt maturity. Credit rationing for long-term bank debt seems to be posing more of a problem to Belgian family firms: during the period 1994–2001, 35.3 percent of the family firms experience credit rationing for long-term bank debt while only 9 percent of the family firms cope with credit rationing for short-term bank debt. Moreover, results indicate that family firms (35.3 percent) experience significantly more long-term credit rationing compared to nonfamily firms (23 percent).

This study has several limitations which provide important opportunities for future research. First, due to data limitations, we could not include any qualitative elements in our analysis. The length of the relationship with the bank, the number of banks an SME works with, the frequency of contact between SME and bank, the number of bank products a firm buys and corporate governance issues might also have an influence on the supply of bank debt, being part of the disequilibrium model estimated. Including these elements in the analysis may further extend our results. Second, this study uses the 1994–2001 time frame which represents a period of economic expansion and uniform financial regulatory conditions under Basel I. Whereas the Basel I Capital Accord treated all corporate lending alike, the Basel II (2004) and Basel III (2009) Capital Accords requires greater amounts of capital for higher risk lending (Steijvers and Voordeckers 2009b). The effect of these capital requirements on the credit supply for SMEs is unclear and seems to depend on the classification of SME loans in the asset portfolio (retail or corporate) (Altman and Sabato 2005; Saurina and Trucharte 2004). Therefore, it would be interesting to investigate in future research whether and to which extent our results hold given the recently changed capital requirements for the banking industry (Basel III).

Notes

1 Corresponding author: Tensie Steijvers, Hasselt University, RCEF Research Center, Martelarenlaan 42, B-3500 Hasselt, Belgium, Tel. +32 11 268627, Fax: +32 11 268700, e-mail address: tensie.steijvers@ uhasselt.be Wim Voordeckers, Hasselt University, RCEF Research Center, Martelarenlaan 42, B-3500 Hasselt, Belgium, e-mail address: wim.voordeckers@uhasselt.be.

2 The definition used for 'Small and medium-sized firms' is set forward by Belgian law (Royal decree dd 17th February 2000): firms which do not exceed more than one of the following criteria: maximum of

50 employees; maximum annual sales of 6,250,000 euro;maximum total of assets per year of 3,125,000 euro; and do not have more than 100 employees.

3 A confidence interval of respectively 95 percent and 98 percent would require panel data of a sample of 375 firms and 2,792 firms. In order to balance reliability on the one hand and feasibility on the other hand, we decided to opt for the middle course and select panel data of a sample of 1,000 firms, representing a confidence interval of more than 96 percent.

4 Note that in this model, no absolute values are used. These absolute values are expressed as ratios: they are divided by the total number of assets of the previous year t-1. Using ratios avoids the possible problem of heteroskedasticity in the sample.

5 Belgium has a one-tier board system. Limited liability companies ("Naamloze Vennootschap") have the legal obligation to have at least three directors (with the exception of some special cases).

Appendix 9.A Definitions of Variables of Demand-Supply Disequilibrium Models

Variable	Definition
Short-term bank debt	Short-term bank debt received/total assets in year t-1
Long-term bank debt	Long-term bank debt received/total assets in year t-1
Level of activity	
Assets	Total assets in year t/total assets in year t-1
Asset rotation	Value of production (added value) / (tangible fixed assets + intangible assets + preliminary flotation)
Growth	
Intangibles dummy	= 1 if investment in intangible assets in year t > 0
LT growth	(total assets in year t − total assets in year t-3) / total assets in year t-3
Internal financial resources	
Cash flow	Cash flow / total assets in year t −1
Substitute finance	
Net trade credit	Trade credit (short-term) − accounts receivable (short-term)/ total assets in year t-1
Group dummy	=1 if the SME has one or more shareholders or/and participations
Organisation	
Family firm	Based on ex ante criteria; Family firm= 1 if : • the name of one or more of the directors of the firm is incorporated in the firm name; • or the firm has more than one director and at least two of them have the same last name; • or one of the directors resides at the firm address; • or at least two of the directors of the firm do not have the same last name but reside at the same private address
Risk degree	
Firmage	Ln (1+ age of the firm in years)
Solvency	Equity/total assets in year t
Interestcover	Operating income before taxes/ financial debt cost in year t
Collateral	
Assets	Total assets in year t/total assets in year t-1
Trade credit	
Trade credit	Trade credit (short-term)/total assets in year t-1

Trade credit dummy	=1 if the SME has a higher ratio 'trade credit/total assets' than the industry average ratio for SMEs
Intragroup finance	
Shareholder dummy	=1 if the SME has one or more shareholders
Participation dummy	=1 if the SME has one or more participations
Interest rate uncertainty	
Std. dev. interest rate	= for long-term bank debt: standard deviation of the interest rate on a long-term Belgian government bond (10 years) in year t
	= for short-term bank debt: standard deviation of the short-term interest rate LIBOR in year t
Control variables	
Year dummies	= 1 if the observation belongs to year t with t= 1994… 2001
Industry dummies	
Production industry	=1 if the SME is an industrial firm (NACE code 15–41)
Building & construction	=1 if the SME is a building/construction firm (NACE code 45)
Retail	=1 if the SME is a retail firm (NACE code 50–52)
Services	=1 if the SME is a service firm (NACE code 55–93)

References

Akerlof, George A. 1970. "The market for lemons: quality uncertainty and the market mechanisms." *Quarterly Journal of Economics* 84(3): 488–500.

Alti, A. 2003. "How sensitive is investment to cash flow when financing is frictionless?" *Journal of Finance* 58(2): 707–722.

Altman, E. and G. Sabato. 2005. "Effects of the new Basel Capital Accord on bank capital requirements for SMEs." *Journal of Financial Services Research* 28 (1/2/3): 15–42.

Ampenberger, M., Schmid, T., Achleitner, A.-K., and C. Kaserer. 2013. "Capital structure decisions in family firms: empirical evidence from a bank-based economy." *Review of Managerial Science* 7: 247–275.

Anderson, R. and D. Reeb. 2003. 'Founding-family ownership and firm performance: evidence from the S&P 500.' *Journal of Finance* 58(3): 1301–28.

Arrow, K. J. 1963. "Uncertainty and the welfare economics of medical care." *American Economic Review* 53(5): 941–973.

Arrow, K. J. 1968. "The economics of moral hazard: further comment." *American Economic Review* 58(3): 537–539.

Atanasova, C.V., and N.Wilson. 2004. "Disequilibrium in the UK corporate loan market." *Journal of Banking and Finance* 28: 595–614.

Barajas, A., and R. Steiner. 2002. "Credit stagnation in Latin America." IMF Working Paper 02/53.

Barclay, M. J., and C. Smith. 1995. "The maturity structure of corporate debt." *Journal of Finance* 50(2): 609–631.

Barnea, Amir, Robert A. Haugen, and Lemma W. Senbet. 1980. "A rationale for debt maturity structure and call provisions in the agency theoretic framework." *Journal of Finance* 35: 1223–1234.

Bengoechea, P., Camacho, M. and G. Perez-Quiros. 2006. "A useful tool for forecasting the Euro-area business cycle phases." *International Journal of Forecasting* 22: 735–749.

Berger, Allen N., and Gregory F. Udell. 1992. "Some evidence on the empirical significance of credit rationing." *Journal of Political Economy* 100(5): 1047–1077.

Berger, Allen N., and Gregory F. Udell. 1998. "The economics of small business finance: the roles of private equity and debt markets in the financial growth cycle." *Journal of Banking and Finance* 22: 613–673.

Berger, Allen N., and Gregory F. Udell. 2005. "Small business and debt finance." In Handbook of entrepreneurship research: an interdisciplinary survey and introduction, edited by Zoltan J. Acs and David B. Audretsch, pp. 299–329. Springer, Kluwer Academic Publishers.

Berger, Allen N., Marco A. Espinosa-Vega, W. Scott Frame, and Nathan H. Miller. 2005. "Debt maturity, risk and asymmetric information." *Journal of Finance* 60(6): 2895–2923.

Berlin, Mitchell, and Loretta J. Mester. 1992. "Debt covenants and renegotiation." *Journal of Financial Intermediation* 2(2): 95–133.

Berrone, P., Cruz, C., and L.R. Gómez-Mejía. 2012. "Socioemotional wealth in family firms: Theoretical dimensions, assessment approaches, and agenda for future research." *Family Business Review* 25(3): 258–279.

Besanko, David, and Anjan Thakor. 1987a. "Collateral and rationing: sorting equilibria in monopolistic and competitive credit markets." *International Economic Review* 28(3): 671–689.

Besanko, David, and Anjan Thakor. 1987b. "Competitive equilibrium in the credit market under asymmetric information." *Journal of Economic Theory* 42: 167–182.

Bhattacharya, Sudipto, and Anjan Thakor. 1993. "Contemporary banking theory." *Journal of Financial Intermediation* 3: 2–50.

Biais, Bruno, and Christian Gollier. 1997. "Trade credit and credit rationing." *Review of Financial Studies* 10(4): 903–937.

Biais, Bruno, Pierre Hillion, and Jean Francois Malécot. 1995. "La structure financière des entreprises: une investigation empirique sur données françaises." *Economie et Prévision* 120: 15–28.

Blinder, Alan S., and Joseph E. Stiglitz. 1983. "Money, credit constraints, and economic activity." *American Economic Review* 73: 297–302.

Calcagnini, Giorgio, and Donato Iacobucci. 1997. "Small firm investment and financing decisions: An option value approach." *Small Business Economics* 9(6): 491–502.

Carpenter, Robert E., and Bruce C. Petersen. 2002. "Is the growth of small firms constrained by internal finance?" *Review of Economics and Statistics* 84(2): 298–310.

Chan, Yuk Shee, and George Kanatas. 1985. "Asymmetric valuation and the role of collateral in loan agreements." *Journal of Money, Credit and Banking* 17: 85–95.

Chittenden, Francis, Graham Hall, and Patrick Hutchinson. 1996. "Small firm growth, access to capital markets and financial structure: review of issues and an empirical investigation." *Small Business Economics* 8(1): 59–67.

Chua, J. H., Chrisman, J. J., and P. Sharma. 1999. "Defining the family business by behaviour." *Entrepreneurship Theory and Practice* 27(4): 19–39.

Cole, Rebel A. 2013. "What do we know about the capital structure of privately held US firms? Evidence from the surveys of small business finance." *Financial Management* 42(4): 777–813.

Cosci, Stefania. 1993. "Credit rationing and asymmetric information." Aldershot: Dartmouth.

Crespi, Rafel and Alfredo Martin-Oliver. 2015. "Do family firms have better access to external finance during crises?" *Corporate Governance: An International Review* 23(3): 249–265.

Cressy, Robert, and Christer Olofsson. 1997. "The financial conditions for Swedish SMEs: survey and research agenda." *Small Business Economics* 9(2): 179–194.

Croci, E., Doukas, J., and H. Gonenc. 2011. Family Control and Financing Decisions, *European Financial Management* 17(5): 860–897.

Cull, Robert, Lance E. Davis, Naomi R. Lamoreaux, and Jean-Laurent Rosenthal. 2006. "Historical financing of small- and medium-size enterprises." *Journal of Banking and Finance* 30: 3017–3042.

Cunningham, Rose. 2004. "Finance constraints and inventory investment: empirical tests with panel data." Working Paper 2004–38, Bank of Canada.

Degryse, H., and P. Van Cayseele. 2000. "Relationship lending within a bank-based system: Evidence from European small business data." *Journal of Financial Intermediation* 9(1): 90–109.

Deloof, Marc, and Marc Jegers. 1999. "Trade credit, corporate groups and the financing of Belgian firms." *Journal of Business, Finance and Accounting* 26(7–8): 945–966.

Diamond, Douglas W. 1991. "Debt maturity structure and liquidity risk." *Quarterly Journal of Economics* 106(3): 709–737.

Diamond, Douglas W. 1993. "Seniority and maturity of debt contracts." *Journal of Financial Economics* 33(3): 341–368.

Eliason, Scott R. 1993. "Maximum likelihood estimation: Logic and practice." Quantitative Applications in the Social Sciences 96, Sage University Paper 07–096.

Elliehausen, Gregory E., and John D. Wolken. 1993. "The demand for trade credit: An investigation of motives for trade credit use by small businesses." Board of Governors of the Federal Reserve System, Washington, Federal Reserve Bulletin October 1993.

Fama, E., and M. Jensen. 1983. "Separation of ownership and control." *Journal of Law and Economics* 26: 301–25.

Fazzari, Steven, Glenn R. Hubbard, and Bruce Petersen. 2000. "Investment-cash flow sensitivities are useful: a comment on Kaplan and Zingales." *Quarterly Journal of Economics* 115(2): 695–705.

Flannery, Mark J. 1986. "Asymmetric information and risky debt maturity choices." *Journal of Finance* 41(1): 19–37.

Gersovitz, Mark. 1980. "Classification probabilities for the disequilibrium model." *Journal of Econometrics* 14(2): 239–246.

Gómez-Mejía, L. R., Cruz, C., Berrone, P., and J. De Castro 2011. "The bind that ties: Socioemotional wealth preservation in family firms." *Academy of Management Annals* 5(1): 653–707.

Gómez-Mejía, L. R., Haynes, K., Nunez-Nickel, M., Jacobson, K. J. L., and J. Moyano-Fuentes. 2007. "Socioemotional wealth and business risks in family-controlled firms: Evidence from Spanish olive oil mills." *Administrative Science Quarterly* 52(1): 106–137.

Gómez-Mejía, L., Nuñez-Nickel, M., and I. Gutierrez. 2001. "The role of family ties in agency contracts." *Academy of Management Journal* 44(1): 81–95.

Gottardo, P., and A.-M. Moisello. 2014. "The capital structure choices of family firms. Evidence from Italian medium-large unlisted firms." *Managerial Finance* 40(3): 254–275.

Grant Thornton Survey 2002. "SME Survey." London.

Guiso, Luigi. 1998. "High-tech firms and credit rationing." *Journal of Economic Behavior and Organization* 35(1): 39–59.

Hall, Graham C., Patrick J. Hutchinson, and Nicos Michaelas. 2004. "Determinants of the capital structures of European SMEs." *Journal of Business Finance and Accounting* 31(5–6): 711–728.

Hartley, Michael J., and Parthasaradhi Mallela. 1977. "The asymptotic properties of a maximum likelihood estimator for a model of markets in disequilibrium." *Econometrica* 45(5): 1205–1220.

Heyman, D., Deloof, M., and H. Ooghe. 2008. "The financial structure of private held Belgian firms." *Small Business Economics* 30: 301–313.

Hurlin, Christoph, and Rafal Kierzenkowki. 2002. "A theoretical and empirical assessment of the bank lending channel and loan market disequilibrium in Poland." National Bank of Poland, Working Paper nr.22.

Hutchinson, Robert W. 1995. "The capital structure and investment decisions of the small owner-managed firm: Some exploratory issues." *Small Business Economics* 7: 231–239.

Huybrechts, J., W. Voordeckers, N. Lybaert, and S. Vandemaele 2011, "The distinctiveness of family firm intangibles: A review and suggestions for future research." *Journal of Management & Organization* 17(2): 268–287.

Ikhide, Sylvanus. 2003. "Was there a credit crunch in Namibia between 1996–2000?" *Journal of Applied Economics* 6(2): 269–290.

Jaffee, Dwight M., and Thomas Russell. 1976. "Imperfect information, uncertainty, and credit rationing." *Quarterly Journal of Economics* 90(4): 651–666.

Jensen, Michael C. 1986. "The agency costs of free cash flow, corporate finance, and takeovers." *American Economic Review* 76(2): 323–329.

Jensen, Michael C., and William H. Meckling. 1976. "Theory of the firm: managerial behavior, agency costs and ownership structure." *Journal of Financial Economics* 3(4): 305–360.

Koropp, C., Grichnik, D., and F. Kellermanns. 2013. "Financial Attitudes in Family Firms: The Moderating Role of Family Commitment." *Journal of Small Business Management* 51(1): 114–137.

Koropp, C., Kellermanns, F.W., Grichnik, D., and L. Stanley. 2014. "Financial decision making in family firms: An adaptation of the theory of planned behavior." *Family Business Review* 27(4): 307–327.

Lee, Lung-Fei. 1983. "Regime classification in the disequilibrium market models." Discussion Paper #93, Center for Econometrics and Decision Sciences, University of Florida.

Leland, Hayne E., and David H. Pyle. 1977. "Information asymmetries, financial structure, and financial intermediaries." *Journal of Finance* 32(2): 371–387.

Lubatkin, M., Schulze, W., Ling, Y., and R. Dino. 2005. "The effects of parental altruism on the governance of family-managed firms." *Journal of Organizational Behavior* 26: 313–30.

Maddala, G.S. 1986. "Disequilibrium, self-selection, and switching models." In Handbook of econometrics Vol. III., edited by Zvi Griliches and Michael D. Intriligator, pp. 1634–1682. Elsevier Science Publishers BV.

Maddala, G.S., and Forrest D. Nelson. 1974. "Maximum likelihood methods for models of markets in disequilibrium." *Econometrica* 42(6): 1013–1030.

Mann, Ronald J. 1997. "Explaining the pattern of secured debt." *Harvard Law Review* 110: 625–683.

Matthews, C., Vasudevan, D., Barton, S., and R. Apana. 1994. "Capital structure decision making in privately held firms: Beyond the finance paradigm." *Family Business Review* 7(4): 349–367.

McConaughy, D.L., Matthews, H.C., and A.S. Fialko. 2001. "Founding Family Controlled Firms: Performance, Risk, and Value." *Journal of Small Business Management* 39(1): 31–49.

Michiels, A., W. Voordeckers, N. Lybaert, and T. Steijvers. 2015. "Dividends and family governance practices in private family firms." *Small Business Economics* 44: 299–314.

Milde, Hellmut, and John G. Riley. 1988. "Signaling in credit markets." *Quarterly Journal of Economics* 103(1): 101–129.

Moyen, N. 2004. "Investment-cash flow sensitivities: constrained versus unconstrained firms." *Journal of Finance* 59(5): 2061–2093.

Myers, Steward C. 1977. "Determinants of corporate borrowing." *Journal of Financial Economics* 5(2): 147–175.

Myers, Steward C. 1984. "The capital structure puzzle." *Journal of Finance* 39(3): 575–592.

Ogawa, Kazuo, and Kazuyuki Suzuki. 2000. "Demand for bank loans and investment under borrowing constraints: a panel study of Japanese firm data." *Journal of the Japanese and International Economics* 14: 1–21.

Ortiz-Molina, Hernan, and Maria Penas. 2006. "Lending to small businesses: The role of loan maturity in addressing information problems." Center Discussion paper nr. 2004–99, May 2006.

Pazarbasioglu, Ceyla. 1997. "A credit crunch? Finland in the aftermath of the banking crisis." *IMF Staff Papers* 44(3): 315–327.

Perez, Stepen J. 1998. "Testing for credit rationing: an application of disequilibrium econometrics." *Journal of Macroeconomics* 20(4): 721–739.

Pérez-González, F. 2006. "Inherited control and firm performance." *American Economic Review* 96(5): 1559–1588.

Petersen, Mitchell A., and Raghuram G. Rajan. 1994. "Benefits of lending relationships: Evidence from small business data." *Journal of Finance* 49(1): 3–37.

Petersen, Mitchell A., and Raghuram G. Rajan. 1997. "Trade credit: Theories and evidence." *Review of Financial Studies* 10(3): 661–691.

Pettit, R. Richardson, and Ronald Singer. 1985. "Small business finance: A research agenda." *Financial Management* 14(3): 47–60.

Robb, Alicia M., Robinson and David T. Robinson. 2014. "The capital structure decisions of new firms." *Review of Financial Studies* 27(1): 153–179.

Romano, Claudio, George Tanewski, and Kosmas X. Smyrnios. 2000. "Capital structure decision making: A model for family business." *Journal of Business Venturing* 16(3): 285–310.

Saurina, J., and C. Trucharte. 2004. "The impact of Basel II on lending to small-and medium-sized firms: a regulatory policy assessment based on Spanish credit register data." *Journal of Financial Services Research* 26(2): 121–144.

Scherr, Frederick C., and Heather M. Hulburt. 2001. "The debt maturity structure of small firms." *Financial Management* 30(1): 85–111.

Schmid, T. 2013. "Control considerations, creditor monitoring, and the capital structure of family firms." *Journal of Banking & Finance* 37: 257–272.

Schulze, W., Lubatkin, M. and R. Dino. 2003. "Exploring the agency consequences of ownership dispersion among the directors of private family firms." *Academy of Management Journal* 46(2): 179–94.

Sealey, Charles W. 1979. "Credit rationing in the commercial loan market: Estimates of a structural model under conditions of disequilibrium." *Journal of Finance* 34(3): 689–702.

Shen, Chung-Hua. 2002. "Credit rationing for bad companies in bad years: Evidence from bank loan transaction data." *International Journal of Finance and Economics* 7: 261–278.

Sirmon, D., and M. Hitt. 2003. "Managing resources: linking unique resources, management, and wealth creation in family firms." *Entrepreneurship: Theory & Practice* 27(4): 339–358.

Smith, Clifford W., and Jerold B. Warner. 1979. "On financial contracting: An analysis of bond covenants." *Journal of Financial Economics* 7(2): 117–162.

Steijvers T. and W. Voordeckers. 2009a. "Private family ownership and the agency costs of debt." *Family Business Review* 22(4): 333–346.

Steijvers T. and W. Voordeckers. 2009b, 'Collateral and credit rationing: A review of recent studies as a guide for future research.' *Journal of Economic Surveys* 23(5), 924–946.

Steijvers T., W. Voordeckers and K. Vanhoof. 2010, "Collateral, relationship lending and family firms." *Small Business Economics* 34: 243–259.

Stiglitz, Joseph, and Andrew Weiss. 1981. "Credit rationing in markets with imperfect information." *American Economic Review* 71(3): 393–410.

Stohs, Mark Hoven, and David C. Mauer. 1996. "The determinants of corporate debt maturity structure." *Journal of Business* 69(3): 279–312.

Van der Wijst, Nico, and Roy Thurik. 1993. "Determinants of small firm debt ratios: An analysis of retail panel data." *Small Business Economics* 5(1): 55–65.

Vijverberg, Chu-Ping C. 2004. "An empirical financial accelerator model: Small firms' investment and credit rationing." *Journal of Macroeconomics* 26(1): 101–129.7.

Voordeckers, W. and A. Van Gils. 2003. "Governance in het Vlaamse Familiebedrijf." Research paper Instituut voor het Familiebedrijf.

Williamson, Stephen D. 1986. "Costly monitoring, financial intermediation and equilibrium credit rationing." *Journal of Monetary Economics* 18(2): 159–179.

10

MULTI-FAMILY OFFICES ACROSS THE GLOBE

Recent Developments and Future Research

Carolin Decker

Introduction

Over the last decades, there has been an increase in the number of affluent individuals in the Americas, Europe, and Asia (Beaverstock, Hubbard, and Short 2004; Rosplock 2014). Many of their fortunes originate from the complete or partial sale of a family business (a "liquidity event"), inheritance, ongoing entrepreneurial and investment activities, or "new" sources of private wealth based on work in the financial services industry that has led to a client segment including, for example, investment bankers, hedge fund managers and corporate lawyers with high salaries and bonuses (Beaverstock, Hall, and Wainwright 2013; Wessel et al. 2014). Be they "old" multi-generational business families or new financial elites, they are often served by family offices. These specialist institutions aim at nurturing the continuity, harmony, and coordination of the families and their businesses (Daniell and Hamilton 2010; Gilding, Gregory, and Cosson 2015) and exist in different forms: while a single-family office provides services typically to a blood-related family, a multi-family office may serve multiple, unrelated families (Decker and Lange 2013).

Multi-family offices have strongly increased in popularity and interest in the financial domain all over the world for several reasons. First, single-family offices increasingly outsource services to larger multi-family offices. In addition, many single-family offices alter themselves into more cost-efficient multi-family offices over time as a result of the growing number of family members and their increasingly complex demands (Decker and Lange 2013), although some might face outcomes below their expectations. Second, many companies from different segments in the financial services industry, such as accounting, taxation, or financial planning, and global banking institutions diversify into the potentially lucrative business with the "super-rich" and denote themselves as multi-family offices (Hauser 2001; Rosplock and Hauser 2014). Third, there is an increasing internationalization of affluent families, their entrepreneurial activities, and the geographic dispersion of their members (Lowenhaupt 2008; Welsh et al. 2013). Families, especially in Europe and Asia, become more and more multi-jurisdictional. They need advice in, for instance, wealth management, taxation, investment, or inheritance law from each jurisdiction where their members live. Family offices are expected to manage investments in foreign countries, conduct cross-border transactions, and hire internationally experienced advisors (Lowenhaupt 2008; Rosplock and Hauser 2014). Compared to the much smaller single-family offices, multi-family offices tend to have a better resource endowment to meet these expectations (Decker and Lange 2013).

Because of the increasing popularity of multi-family offices, I concentrate on this form in this chapter. Different national contexts may foster the interpretation of activities and practices, to the extent that they are adopted, in different ways (Tempel and Walgenbach 2007). Indeed, "many practices observed in other institutional contexts may be at odds with strongly and widely held beliefs and norms in a local institutional environment" (Sanders and Tuschke 2007: 52). Interestingly, our knowledge on how multi-family offices do business in different national contexts is limited. We do not know whether their business models are characterized by global standardization or local adaptation. Proponents of different streams of institutional theory have discussed the tension between global standardization and local adaptation (Tempel and Walgenbach 2007). Drawing on this debate, I ask *how multi-family offices create value for affluent individuals and their families in different national contexts.*

This chapter is structured as follows: first, in the next section, I elaborate on the business model-concept and apply it to multi-family offices. Second, I then use two institutionalist traditions in organization theory to discuss the tension between the global standardization and the local adaptation of activities performed for affluent individuals and their families. Finally, in the concluding section, I elaborate on implications for future research and management practice.

Servicing Affluent Families: Business Models of Multi-Family Offices

The Business Model: Creating Value for Stakeholders

The theoretical and practical value and the definition of the business model-concept are still subject to vivid debates (Casadesus-Masanell and Ricart 2010; George and Bock 2011; Lambert and Davidson 2013). Nonetheless, since the mid-1990s it has been widely used across disciplines (Lecocq, Demil, and Ventura 2010), such as strategy (Zott and Amit 2008), entrepreneurship (Morris, Schindehutte, and Allen 2005), innovation (Chesbrough and Rosenbloom 2002), e-commerce (Amit and Zott 2001; Mahadevan 2000), and marketing (Sorescu et al. 2011).

Business models explain the value created by an organization by specifying activity systems and factors driving their perceived value. Value creation refers to the product/service mix, the organization's role in creating and delivering products and services, and how a product or a service is provided to customers (Morris, Schindehutte, and Allen 2005). Put differently, it focuses on how an organization satisfies its customers' needs and creates a customer surplus while making money in doing so (Zott and Amit 2010; Zott, Amit, and Massa 2011).

An activity system is "a set of interdependent organizational activities centered on a focal firm, including those conducted by the focal firm, its partners, vendors or customers, etc." (Zott and Amit 2010: 217). It comprises three *design elements*:

First, *activity content* describes *what* activities are performed (Zott and Amit 2010). Because most clients are business families (Welsh et al. 2013), services span both the family and the business domains, such as wealth management, family business assistance, asset management or real estate (Beaverstock, Hall, and Wainwright 2013; Decker and Lange 2013; Wessel et al. 2014).

Second, *activity structure* describes *how* these activities are linked (Zott and Amit 2010). Many client families, especially those with globally dispersed members and various entrepreneurial activities, prefer a structure that captures a family's needs in their entirety. Other clients use their family offices for selected services only, requiring a well-defined area of expertise (Hauser 2001; Lowenhaupt 2008).

Third, *activity governance* specifies *who* is involved in creating and performing the services within and across organizational and geographic boundaries (Zott and Amit 2010).

These elements are connected by four *design themes* which drive the perceived value created by a business model, namely *novelty* (introducing new products or services or presenting them in a unique way), *lock-in* (implementing mechanisms for retaining clients), *complementarities* (generating synergies by bundling activities), and *efficiency* (minimizing transaction costs) (Amit and Zott 2001; Zott and Amit 2010).

In the next section, I apply the business model-concept to multi-family offices. Table 10.1 summarizes the definitions of the design elements and the design themes in general and provides specific examples of value-creating activities from the multi-family office context.

Placing the Family in the Foreground

Design elements and design themes translate the logic behind how multi-family offices serve affluent individuals and their families in distinct activities and value propositions. They can generally be addressed to different stakeholder groups (Casadesus-Masanell and Ricart 2010; Doganova and Eyquem-Renault 2009). Clients constitute particularly important stakeholders (Demil, Lecocq, and Ricart 2015), because "the business model revolves around customer-focused value creation" (Zott, Amit, and Massa 2011: 1031). This point is essential for multi-family offices because their success largely depends on their responsiveness to their client families' needs and the alignment of their expectations with the selected structures and activities to govern the families and their fortunes (Hauser 2001; Zellweger and Kammerlander 2015).

First, multi-family offices provide services that are designed to apply to the families' circumstances and may enhance their continuity and legacy (Daniell and Hamilton, 2010; Gilding, Gregory, and Cosson 2015; Rosplock 2014). These services must fit with the increasing complexity of family structures and needs. Generally, the more branches and generations are involved, the more useful it can be to centralize the family's wealth management. An example is the Fleming family, the founding family of Fleming Family & Partners, a multi-family office. It has its roots in an investment business dating back to 1873. The family's banking business was sold in 2000. The family was then in its fifth generation and comprised about 130 members. It decided to keep its family trust company and use this as a basis to establish a firm serving the members of the Fleming family and other affluent families (Decker and Lange 2013). Many families are likely to be *involved* in the compilation of the services that are intended for their use (Hauser 2001; Welsh et al. 2013). In many multi-family offices, this active involvement, that is typical for single-family offices, is not part of the usual business model (Rosplock 2014). Involvement is likely, if the families that are served, simultaneously act as owners of their multi-family offices. For instance, the Phipps family fully owns U.S.-based Bessemer Trust. The Fleming family, jointly with company directors and staff, holds a 60 percent stake in Fleming Family & Partners, that is based in London. The Stanhope family office gave 10 percent of its equity to five prominent UK and European families that, in return, allowed this organization to manage their assets (Decker and Lange 2013).

Second, the previous point may indicate that exclusiveness is key, but caution is necessary when considering what exclusiveness means in this context. Clients of multi-family offices are well-informed due to their backgrounds as entrepreneurs, investors, and family business owners. A case in point is Andreas Jacobs, a member of Germany's Jacobs coffee roaster dynasty. As an offspring of a prominent business family and based on his own experience, he knows what wealthy families need. Because of a certain dissatisfaction with the services provided by financial services institutions, he and a non-family partner founded Focam, a German multi-family

Table 10.1 The Activity System Design Framework Applied to Multi-Family Offices

Design Elements	General Definition[a]	Application to Multi-Family Offices[b]
Activity Content	What kind of activities are adopted and performed?	Four strands of activities: • asset protection (e.g., stock holding, conflict management, tax and succession planning, family education) • asset management (e.g., estate management, risk management, design of investment strategies, asset allocation) • asset control (e.g., reporting and financial accounting) • "concierge services" (e.g., coordinating philanthropic activities, walking the dog or selecting schools for the children)
Activity Structure	How are the activities linked and sequenced?	Possible approaches: • full range of services (holistic) or • selected type or certain group of services (specialized)
Activity Governance	Who performs the activities?	Networked partners ("value is created in concert by a firm and a plethora of partners, for multiple users"; Amit, Zott, and Massa 2011, 1029): e.g, family office managers and advisors, business partners (e.g., law firms, investment advisors, specialists in taxation, art experts), outsourcing vendors, extent of family involvement, etc.
Novelty	Introducing new products or services or presenting them in a unique way	Exclusiveness: Organization of activities and range of services provided (investment and non-investment services), unique investment opportunities, independent advice, long-term orientation
Lock-In	Implementing mechanisms for retaining clients	
Complementarities Efficiency	Generating synergies by bundling activities minimizing transaction costs	• generating economies of scale and scope (e.g., joint investment opportunities or "club deals," sharing knowledge and experience with other affluent families) • increasing transparency and cost efficiency by centralizing investment activities and wealth management and by separating family wealth from business activities

[a] Terms and definitions adopted from Amit and Zott (2010, 222).
[b] Examples adopted from Decker and Lange (2013, 2014) and Decker and Günther (2015).

office. Jacobs and other experts in the family office industry agree that affluent individuals and their families do not only demand unique investment opportunities but first and foremost *independent* advice. Investment advisors should not over-emphasize the products of their own institutions or any particular provider. They are expected to select products from a range of external providers. On the one hand, this commitment to "open architecture" has fostered the rise of the multi-family office in the last decade (Decker and Lange 2013). On the other hand, multi-family offices will rarely reap sustainable benefits from the exclusiveness of financial products, if they just sell the goods generated by other financial companies and banking institutions. These are also directly available from these providers. Hence, the exclusiveness of a business model of a multi-family office is less likely to focus on *what* products and services this specialist institution sells but more likely on *how* it *organizes* its activities for the families (Demil, Lecocq, and Ricart 2015; Sorescu et al. 2011). Moreover, the *range* of services provided is important: "Rather than the focus purely on investments, families are returning to the priority of having help with their non-investment services" (Rosplock and Hauser 2014: 14). For example, some multi-family offices provide services pertaining to the preparation of the next generation (that is, family education) and the implementation and management of family foundations (Decker and Lange 2013).

Third and related to the organization of activities, affluent individuals, and their families are demanding clients. Most families require strong commitment. A case in point is Pictet & Cie that considers itself as a problem-solver for its client families. These do not want to deal with many different advisors over time but expect a single person or team – that is, one entry point – to be familiar with their financial and personal affairs in the long run and engage in direct and frequent interactions with them (Decker and Lange 2013; Hauser 2001).

Although it is well understood that old, multi-generational business families comprise increasingly numerous members, that these members are more and more geographically dispersed and internationally oriented, and that their entrepreneurial and investment activities are increasingly global in scope (Lowenhaupt 2008; Rosplock 2014), it is an open question how homogeneous or heterogeneous the business models of multi-family offices are across countries. The following section focuses on this question based on two streams of institutional theory.

Institutional Perspectives on Multi-Family Offices

Two institutionalist traditions in organization theory provide thought-provoking impulses regarding the business models of multi-family offices operating in different national contexts. They both suggest that organizations adjust their activities to the environments in which they are operating but provide different solutions regarding the homogenization of activities (Tempel and Walgenbach 2007). In the following subsections, I elaborate on these traditions in organization theory and the insights that they provide in more detail. I summarize these insights in three propositions.

New Institutionalism: Global Standardization of Business Models

Standardization of business models will be likely, if the members of an organizational field are subject to strong homogenizing forces (DiMaggio and Powell 1983). An organizational field is a group of actors whose behaviors are guided by cultural-cognitive, normative and regulative institutions (Scott 2001). These institutions foster conformity of activities of the actors in an organizational field even across national boundaries (Beckert 2010; DiMaggio and Powell 1983;

Meyer and Rowan 1977). They interact and affect each other, because they come together around, for example, joint projects, common enterprises, central issues or shared agendas (for example, Hoffman 1999; Schüßler, Rüling, and Wittneben 2014).

Based on the criteria established by DiMaggio and Powell (1983: 148), exploratory findings by Decker and Lange (2014) indicate that multi-family offices constitute a global organizational field in which these homogenizing forces exert influence.

First, there is a high *extent of interaction* among multi-offices, particularly through specialized associations and regular meetings, such as the *Financial Times* Family Office Forum. The extent of communication has substantially increased among family offices from North America, Europe and Asia in the last decade.

Second, *interorganizational patterns of coalition* among multi-family offices can be specified, for example, with regard to regulation. Although multi-family offices are competitors in the marketplace, they use collective action for influencing policy-makers in their favor (Decker and Lange 2014).

Third, multi-family offices face an *increase in the information load* with which they must cope, for example, more regulation and multiple jurisdictions, increasingly complex financial products and services in a broad range of areas, and the emergence of new asset classes (Carney, Gedajlovic, and Strike 2014; Lowenhaupt 2008).

Fourth, the *mutual awareness* among multi-family offices is growing. This fact is illustrated by, for example, the yearly *Bloomberg* Top 50 ranking. The institutions included in this ranking attract worldwide attention and high media coverage, promoting their status as "role models" for other family offices in different parts of the world.

It is likely that these developments have a homogenizing influence on how multi-family offices all over the world do business and that they foster a global standardization of their business models.

National Business-Systems: Local Adaptation of Business Models

Proponents of the national business systems-approach claim that activities must be adapted to the local context in which they are used (Whitley 1999). These contexts are shaped by national institutions that affect the adoption of business models that have originally been developed in other contexts. Local adaptation will be likely if a business model contradicts to the usually valid norms and beliefs in a local environment (Sanders and Tuschke 2007). "Against the background of the business-systems approach, it can be assumed that such elements and practices, if they are adopted, are used or interpreted in different ways in different societal contexts and are decoupled to different extents from the activities of organizations because institutions limit and direct the development of organizational forms and practices" (Tempel and Walgenbach 2007: 13). Cross-country comparisons support this issue. For instance, although both the German and French car industries implemented the ISO 9000 quality norms for production in the 1990s, their comparison reveals that, in doing so, these national industries followed completely different trajectories (Casper and Hancké 1999).

Referring to multi-family offices, the context-dependent interpretation of organizational forms and activities is clearly discernible. National regulators, such as the SEC (*Securities and Exchange Commission*) in the U.S., the BaFin (*Bundesanstalt für Finanzdienstleistungsaufsicht*) in Germany, the *Agency for the Development of the Financial Centre* in Luxembourg, or the FIDC (*Dubai International Financial Centre*), have all developed their own definitions of (types of) family offices (Krause and Klebeck 2012). These definitions do not only influence the emergence of patterns of a coalition (Decker and Lange 2014) but also reflect the impact of national institutions on the forms, activities, and persistence of organizations in different institutional settings (Carney, Gedajlovic, and Strike 2014).

Prior studies indicate that the rationales behind business models differ depending on the contexts in which they are applied (Lambert and Davidson 2013; Patzelt, Knyphausen-Aufseß, and Nikol 2008; Sorescu et al. 2011). Therefore, heterogeneity among the business models of multi-family offices operating in different national settings is likely. Legislation is an important factor. Referring to national inheritance laws, Carney, Gedajlovic, and Strike (2014) illustrate how different legislative frameworks affect the longevity of family-controlled businesses.

There are also cultural differences between families from different regions. For example, the multi-family office-concept is less successful in Asia than in Europe or the Americas. Despite the rising number of "super-rich" in Asia, the prevailing economic culture is not necessarily conducive to the establishment of multi-family offices. "There is a deep-rooted mistrust among tycoons, who fear that the managers of multi-family offices could divulge confidential information" (Decker and Lange 2013: 300). Thus, heterogeneity in how multi-family offices all over the world do business for affluent individuals and their families is likely.

In the following section, the two streams of institutional reasoning outlined above are applied to multi-family offices in order to show how pressures for both homogeneity and heterogeneity exert influence on their business models.

Business Models of Multi-Family Offices: Homogeneity *and* Heterogeneity!

The neo-institutionalist literature acknowledges that actors constituting organizational fields are not necessarily fully homogeneous but also contain elements of heterogeneity. For example, empirical evidence by Quirke (2013), focusing on private schools in Toronto, illustrates that this field is "patchy." That is, there is a relatively high organizational diversity in terms of, for example, structures, applied logics, and responses to technical demands. Obviously, fields comprise dimensions in which pressures to homogeneity may be stronger or weaker. Quirke's (2013) finding fosters the idea that organizations in a field are not completely similar but comprise distinct actors that orient their activities toward each other in selected areas (Wooten and Hoffman 2008). More precisely, they can simultaneously have homogeneous and heterogeneous dimensions. Selected activities of particular importance for the organizations may converge.

Quirke's (2013) finding has implications for the business model-concept and the activities performed by multi-family offices operating within and across national contexts. Drawing on activity systems and value propositions, I elaborate on these implications below.

Heterogeneous Activity Systems

As outlined above, business models consist of design elements and design themes (Zott and Amit 2010). Turning to the design elements, the decisions of multi-family offices on activity content (for example, tasks related to asset management, asset protection, asset control, and "concierge services"), activity structure (for example, the choice between holistic or specialized service offerings), and activity governance (the extent to which activities involve business partners inside and outside the organization as well as members of the client families) are purely structural choices. The upper half of Table 10.1 includes examples of these design elements in the multi-family office context.

All types of organizations can put more or less emphasis on each of these design elements and combine them in a variety of ways without changing their clients' perceptions of their potential to create value. These decisions on design elements always lead to different and viable configurations of activities (Zott and Amit 2007, 2010). To put it in a nutshell, there is no single best way to configure activity systems.

Moreover, the national origins of these specialist institutions may lead to divergence in the activities performed for their client families across the globe. As, for example, national legislations affect the activities and the persistence of family businesses (Carney, Gedajlovic, and Strike 2014), it is fairly straightforward to conclude that national institutions also impact the content, structure and governance of the activities performed by multi-family offices.

Thus, due to the possibility to make various structural choices leading to many different viable combinations and the potential of national institutions to affect these activity systems, the heterogeneity referring to the design elements of the business models of multi-family offices all over the world is likely.

Hypothesis 1

Choices of activity content, activity structure and activity governance are likely to promote the heterogeneity of the business models of multi-family offices across national contexts.

Homogeneous Value Propositions on the Corporate Level

The possible configurations of design elements do not drive differences in the perceived value creation potential of organizations. As shown above, Amit and Zott (2001) suggest four design themes that act as value drivers within the possible configurations of design elements. Based on this literature, we should expect that the differences between the business models, which are perceived by actual and prospective client families, are driven by these design themes because they constitute the actual drivers of the value which is to be created for the clients (Zott, Amit, and Massa 2011). Examples for design themes in the multi-family office context are depicted in the lower half of Table 10.1.

In the selected field, however, one should take into account that, on average, affluent families frequently express very similar needs across countries, be the multi-family office concept new or well-established in a national context (Decker and Lange 2013; Rosplock and Hauser 2014). As the application of the criteria outlined by DiMaggio and Powell (1983) on multi-family offices has revealed, there are strong homogenizing forces (Decker and Lange 2014). These are likely to affect the design themes inherent in the business models of the multi-family offices in several ways.

First, *novelty* is a value driver of a business model of a multi-family office, because the affluent and well-informed clients generally appreciate unique investment opportunities in various fields and independent advice (Decker and Günther 2015). In addition, as families become increasingly multi-jurisdictional, innovative ways to get access to, for example, tax and investment advice or global information on entrepreneurial opportunities or philanthropy to preserve a family's legacy are appreciated (Rosplock 2014; Rosplock and Hauser 2014).

Second, many if not most client families aim at preserving and increasing their wealth for subsequent generations (Beaverstock, Hall, and Wainwright 2013; Daniell and Hamilton 2010; Wessel et al. 2014). Multi-family offices provide advice to families over several generations. The design theme of *lock-in* refers to the clients' expectations of a multi-family office's long-term orientation of the relationship with its clients and of many years of experience in serving wealthy families (Decker and Lange 2014).

Third, the business models of multi-family offices bear chances to create *complementarities*. For instance, multi-family offices can collect and assess information on industries in which their clients have or have had a family business, such that families can make thorough investment decisions. As multi-family offices serve multiple families, they can also provide the opportunity to meet other families and arrange "club deals." These equity investments comprise several investing families and individuals who pool their assets together to jointly acquire a majority interest in a project while each investor alone has a minority interest. With each party acquiring a small stake of a project, each investor's individual entrepreneurial risk is reduced (Decker and Günther 2015).

Fourth, the rise of the multi-family office all over the world shows that *efficiency* is a major concern for these specialist institutions and the families behind them. The popularity of this family office-form is often driven by the families' need to, for instance, buy specialized services instead of establishing a full-service single-family office because of the desire to delegate and centralize the wealth management needs of the family members and the high amount of resources needed to maintain such an institution in the long run (Rosplock 2014).

Thus, overall, the design themes included in the business models of multi-family offices all over the world hardly differ, leading to homogeneity on the corporate level in the value propositions perceived by affluent individuals and their families.

Hypothesis 2

Novelty, lock-in, complementarities, and efficiency are likely to promote the homogeneity of the business models of multi-family offices across national contexts.

Heterogeneity in the Emphasis Put on Design Themes on the Local Level

Up to now, only a few multi-family offices operate in various countries. However, because families are increasingly international, and their members are more and more geographically dispersed, there are promising opportunities for multi-family offices to internationalize (for example, by establishing subsidiaries abroad). This internationalization implies the chance to increase the heterogeneity internally in the design themes of the business models, i.e., on the local level. For instance, client families whose members are spread across countries may benefit from the global presence of a multi-family office in terms of subsidiaries and branches in different regions. This bears the potential of a broader knowledge base, for example, referring to taxation or inheritance law in and across different jurisdictions (Lowenhaupt 2008). In that vein, Rosplock and Hauser (2014, 18) recommend establishing "one global stop" multi-family offices for families with an increasingly global footprint as a promising future trend.

This global presence can be a chance for a multi-family office to differentiate itself from its competitors by designing custom-tailored, country-specific activities that reflect, for example, either more efficiency- or more novelty-oriented business models in the subsidiaries established in different countries. While an efficiency-oriented business model focuses on the organization of activities that increase the transaction efficiency for the involved actors, a novelty-oriented business model refers to innovative ways to organize activities (Zott and Amit 2008).

By transferring and implementing activities in other contexts, the international client families' local needs can be considered. Put differently, a globally operating multi-family office must delineate the ways in which it transacts with its client families in different ways, depending on the location of the individual family members. For example, families in the Gulf region often have access to a wide array of concierge services that are usually provided by the family managers in their businesses. They are less likely to demand novel concierge services but rather, for instance, "best practices" for the tax-efficient transition of the family business from the founder to the next generation. Clients in Latin America are more concerned with security issues. They may appreciate novel service offerings for their family members, for example, in the field of personal security, which help discourage kidnappers attracted by the family wealth (Rosplock and Hauser 2014).

To put it briefly, on the corporate level, the business models of multi-family offices may be perceived as relatively homogenous across countries, but on the local level, the emphasis put by the subsidiaries of the globally operating multi-family offices on different design themes may vary.

Hypothesis 3

If multi-family offices implement subsidiaries across the globe, internal variation in the emphasis put on the design themes of their business models will be likely, leading to an increase in internal heterogeneity of the business models across subsidiaries.

The analysis so far has shown that different configurations of the content, structure and governance of the activities performed by multi-family offices are possible, promoting hetero-geneity. Because of the similar expectations of the client families across the globe, the value propositions are relatively homogeneous on the corporate level. Multi-family offices having subsidiaries in different countries, such as many of the institutions included in *Bloomberg*'s yearly ranking of the Top 50 family offices (Decker and Lange 2014), have the chance to increase their internal heterogeneity (that is, on the subsidiary level) by adapting the design themes of their business models to the local needs of the members of their international client families.

The concluding section sheds light on the implications that these insights provide for research and practice.

Discussion and Implications

The application of the business model-concept and its combination with two institutionalist traditions in organization theory raise some issues, which may warrant future empirical research.

First, industry-specific studies on business models are relatively numerous, because it is widely accepted that design elements and design themes differ based on the industries in which business models are applied (for example, Amit and Zott 2001; Patzelt, Knyphausen-Aufseß, and Nikol 2008; Sorescu et al. 2011). However, although the need for studies on the creation and use of business models in different national contexts has been openly specified (Demil, Lecocq, and Ricart 2015: 8), our knowledge on whether or to what extent the business models of organizations in a selected industry differ across countries is limited. Exploratory evidence based on corporate-level data of *Bloomberg*'s Top 50 family offices illustrates that there is a high degree of homogeneity in the business models. Marginal differences in how these world-renowned multi-family offices do business mainly result from various possible configurations of the design elements. Contrary to the assumptions outlined by the propo-nents of the national business-systems approach (for example, Whitley 1999), the observed marginal heterogeneity of the business models is neither driven by the design themes nor by the regional embeddedness of the analyzed multi-family offices (Decker and Lange 2014). As these findings draw on secondary data from corporate websites of a limited number of multi-family offices, they do not provide insights into the internal variation in the emphasis put on the design themes of the business models. Survey-based measurement approaches (for example, Morris, Schindehutte, and Allen 2005; Zott and Amit 2007) targeting both corporate and local (subsidiary) levels of multi-family offices operating in different countries would be more informative in this regard. Those studies would benefit from the cooperation of researchers working in different countries and using the same measurement instrument for capturing the business models of multi-family offices across these countries.

Second, this essay purely focuses on the drivers of homogeneity or heterogeneity in the business models of multi-family offices. It hardly reflects on the value created for the involved actors. Future studies can specify the relevant performance outcomes of the business models of multi-family offices, thereby considering that any performance measurement should include "the family relationship appeal that is their strongest attribute" (Hauser 2001, 15). The emphasis put on the family includes the requirement to conceive of two-sided measurement approaches. These capture the performance outcomes of the multi-family offices, on the one hand, and the value created for the client families (that is, the extent to which the needs of the affluent individuals and their families are satisfied, and a customer surplus is created), on the other hand (Zott and Amit 2010). Value can thereby refer to different forms (Amit, Zott, and Massa 2011). Economic value focuses on the financial benefit that the multi-family offices and their clients reap. Social value can be created, for instance, by helping a family to adopt a sustainable investment strategy and use its fortune for social projects (Decker and Günther 2015).

Third, the measurement of the business models of multi-family offices across countries and the assessment of their potential to create value for increasingly international families reflects the fact that the business model-concept is appealing for management practice (George and Bock 2011; Lecocq, Demil, and Ventura 2010). Similarly, the interest in both single- and multi-family offices seems to be stronger in the practical sphere than in academia. The abundance of working papers and media coverage produced by managers, consultants, and journalists compared to the relatively limited number of scientific studies in strategy and entrepreneurship illustrates this issue. Combining institutionalist perspectives with the business model-concept bears the opportunity to reconcile practice and theory. Affluent individuals and their families need valid instruments to assess the usefulness of the business models that family offices implement. Frequently, they neither know the available options to professionalize the management of their wealth nor how beneficial these options are to ensure the continuity and coordination of their families and their fortunes within and across jurisdictions (Rosplock 2014). This chapter can at least be a starting-point for the development of an instrument capturing configurations of activities and how multi-family offices aim at creating value for their clients in and across national contexts as well as on and across levels of analysis.

Overall, I hope that the infusion of two institutionalist traditions in reflections on the business models of multi-family offices across countries will provide many opportunities for further studies and inspire the development of innovative research designs.

References

Amit, R., and Zott, C. (2001) 'Value creation in e-business.' *Strategic Management Journal* 22: 493–520. DOI: 10.1002/smj.187.

Beaverstock, J.V., Hall, S., and Wainwright, T. (2013) 'Servicing the super-rich: New financial elites and the rise of the private wealth management retail ecology.' *Regional Studies* 47(6): 834–849. DOI: 10.1080/00343404.2011.587795.

Beaverstock, J.V., Hubbard, P., and Short, J.R. (2004) 'Getting away with it? Exposing the geographies of the super-rich.' *Geoforum* 35: 401–407. DOI: 10.1016/j.geoforum.2004.03.001.

Beckert, J. (2010) 'How do fields change? The interrelations of institutions, networks, and cognition in the dynamics of markets.' *Organization Studies* 31(5): 605–627. DOI: 10.1177/0170840610372184.

Carney, M., Gedajlovic, E., and Strike, V.M. (2014) 'Dead money: Inheritance law and the longevity of family firms.' *Entrepreneurship Theory and Practice* 38: 1261–1283. DOI: 10.1111/etap.12123.

Casadesus-Masanell, R., and Ricart, J.E. (2010) 'From strategy to business models and onto tactics.' *Long Range Planning* 43: 195–215. DOI: 10.1016/j.lrp.2010.01.004.

Casper, S., and Hancké R. (1999) 'Global quality norms within national production regimes: ISO 9000 standards in the French and German car industries.' *Organization Studies* 20(6): 961–985.

Chesbrough, H., and Rosenbloom, R.S. (2002) 'The role of the business model in capturing value from innovation: Evidence from Xerox Corporation's technology spin-off companies.' *Industrial and Corporate Change* 11(3): 529–555. DOI: 10.1093/icc/11.3.529.

Daniell, Mark H., and Sara S. Hamilton. (2010) *Family Legacy and Leadership*. Singapore: John Wiley & Sons (Asia).

Decker, C., and Günther, C. (2016) 'Coordinating family entrepreneurship: When money seeks opportunity.' *International Journal of Entrepreneurial Venturing* 8(1): 46–61.

Decker, C., and Lange, K.S.G. (2013) 'Exploring a secretive organization: What can we learn about family offices from the public sphere?' *Organizational Dynamics* 42: 298–306. DOI: 10.1016/j.orgdyn.2013.07.008.

Decker, C., and Lange, K.S.G. (2014) *The Global Field of Multi-Family Offices: Business Models as Communication Devices.* Paper presented at the Academy of Management Annual Meeting 2014, Philadelphia, USA.

Demil, B., Lecocq, X., and Ricart, J.E. (2015) 'Introduction to the *SEJ* special issue on business models: Business models within the domain of strategic entrepreneurship.' *Strategic Entrepreneurship Journal* 9: 1–11. DOI: 10.1002/sej.1194.

DiMaggio, P.J., and Powell, W.W. (1983) 'The iron cage revisited: Institutional isomorphism and collective rationality in organizational fields.' *American Sociological Review* 48: 147–160.

Doganova, L., and Eyquem-Renault, M. (2009) 'What do business models do? Innovation devices in technology entrepreneurship.' *Research Policy* 38: 1559–1570. DOI: 10.1016/j.respol.2009.08.002.

George, G.G., and Bock, A.J. (2011) 'The business model in practice and its implications for entrepreneurship research.' *Entrepreneurship Theory and Practice* 35: 83–111. DOI: 10.1111/j.1540-6520.2010.00424.x.

Gilding, M., Gregory, S., and Cosson, B.B. (2015) 'Motives and outcomes in family business succession planning.' *Entrepreneurship Theory and Practice* 39: 299–312. DOI: 10.1111/etap.12040.

Hauser, B. (2001) 'The Family Office: Insight into their development in the U.S., a proposed prototype, and advice for adaptation in other countries.' *Journal of Wealth Management* 4: 9–17.

Hoffman, A.J. (1999) 'Institutional evolution and change: Environmentalism and the U.S. chemical industry.' *Academy of Management Journal* 42: 351–371.

Krause, M., and Klebeck, U. (2012) 'Family Office und AIFM-Richtlinie [Family office and AIFM norms].' *Betriebs-Berater* 34: 2063–2068.

Lambert, S.C., and Davidson, R.A. (2013) 'Applications of the business model in studies of enterprise success, innovation and classification: An analysis of empirical research from 1996 to 2010.' *European Management Journal* 31: 668–681. DOI: 10.1016/j.emj.2012.07.007.

Lecocq, X., Demil, B., and Ventura, J. (2010) 'Business model as a research program in strategic management: An appraisal based on Lakatos.' *M@n@gement* 13(4): 214–225.

Lowenhaupt, C.A. (2008) 'Freedom from wealth and the contemporary global family: A new vision for family wealth management.' *Journal of Wealth Management* 11: 21–29.

Mahadevan, B. (2000) 'Business models for internet-based e-commerce: An anatomy.' *California Management Review* 42(4): 55–69.

Meyer, J.W., and Rowan, B. (1977) 'Institutionalized organizations: Formal structure as myth and ceremony.' *American Journal of Sociology* 83(2): 340–363.

Morris, M., Schindehutte, M., and Allen, J. (2005) 'The entrepreneur's business model: Toward a unified perspective.' *Journal of Business Research* 58: 726–735. DOI: 10.1016/j.jbusres.2003.11.001.

Patzelt, H., zu Knyphausen-Aufseß, D., and Nikol, P. (2008) 'Top management teams, business models, and performance of biotechnology ventures: An upper echelons perspective.' *British Journal of Management* 19: 205–221. DOI: 10.1111/j.1467-8551.2007.00552.x.

Quirke, L. (2013) 'Rogue resistance: Sidestepping isomorphic pressures in a patchy institutional field.' *Organization Studies*, 34(11): 1675–1699. DOI: 10.1177/0170840613483815.

Rosplock, K. (2014) *The Complete Family Office Handbook. A Guide for Affluent Families and the Advisors Who Serve Them.* Hoboken, NJ: John Wiley & Sons.

Rosplock, K., and Hauser, B.R. (2014) 'The family office landscape: Today's trends and five predictions for the family office of tomorrow.' *Journal of Wealth Management* 17(3): 9–19.

Sanders, W., Gerard, and Tuschke, A. (2007) 'The adoption of institutionally contested organizational practices: The emergence of stock option pay in Germany.' *Academy of Management Journal* 50: 33–56. DOI: 10.5465/AMJ.2007.24160889.

Schüßler, E., Rüling, C., and Wittneben, B.B.F. (2014) 'On melting summits: The limitations of field-configuring events as catalysts of change in transnational climate policy.' *Academy of Management Journal* 57: 140–171. DOI: 10.5465/amj.2011.0812.

Scott, W. R. (2001) *Institutions and Organizations.* 2nd ed., Thousand Oaks, CA: Sage.

Sorescu, A., Frambach, R. T., Singh, J., Rangaswamy, A., and Bridges, C. (2011) 'Innovations in retail business models.' *Journal of Retailing* 87S(1): S3-S16. DOI: 10.1016/j.jretai.2011.04.005.

Tempel, A., and Walgenbach, P. (2007) 'Global standardization of organizational forms and management practices? What new institutionalism and the business-systems approach can learn from each other.' *Journal of Management Studies* 44: 1–24. DOI: 10.1111/j.1467-6486.2006.00644.x.

Welsh, D.H.B., Memili, E., Rosplock, K., Roure, J., and Segurado, J.L. (2013) 'Perceptions of entrepreneurship across generations in family offices: A stewardship theory perspective.' *Journal of Family Business Strategy* 4: 213–226. DOI: 10.1016/j.jfbs.2013.07.003.

Wessel, S., Decker, C., Lange, K.S.G., and Hack, A. (2014) 'One size does *not* fit all: Entrepreneurial families' reliance on family offices.' *European Management Journal* 32(1): 37–45. DOI: 10.1016/j.emj.2013.08.003.

Whitley, R. (1999) *Divergent Capitalisms: The Social Structuring and Change of Business Systems.* Oxford: Oxford University Press.

Wooten, M., and Hoffman, A.J. (2008) 'Organizational fields: Past, present and future.' In *The Sage Handbook of Organizational Institutionalism,* edited by Royston Greenwood, Christine Oliver, Roy Suddaby, and Kerstin Sahlin, 130–147. London: Sage Publications.

Zellweger, T., and Kammerlander, N. (2015) 'Family, wealth, and governance: An agency account.' *Entrepreneurship Theory and Practice*, forthcoming.

Zott, C., and Amit, R. (2007) 'Business model design and the performance of entrepreneurial firms.' *Organization Science* 18(2): 181–199. DOI: 10.1287/orsc.1060.0232.

Zott, C., and Amit, R. (2008) 'The fit between product market strategy and business model: Implications for firm performance.' *Strategic Management Journal* 29: 1–26. DOI: 10.1002/smj.642.

Zott, C., and Amit, R. (2010) 'Business model design: An activity system perspective.' *Long Range Planning* 43(2–3): 216–226. DOI: 10.1016/j.lrp.2009.07.004.

Zott, C., Amit, R., and Massa, L. (2011) 'The business model: Recent developments and future research.' *Journal of Management* 37(4): 1010–1042. DOI: 10.1177/0149206311406265.

PART II

Entrepreneurship

11

INNOVATION AND FAMILY BUSINESS RESEARCH

A Review and Future Directions

Nils D. Kraiczy and Andreas Hack

Introduction

Research on innovation in family firms is continuously increasing and has recently reached a peak of attention. The leading academic journal on innovation research, the *Journal of Product Innovation Management*, has published a special issue on this topic, which shows that research on innovation in family firms has started to attract attention not only of the family business research community but also of the innovation research community. Additionally, one of the leading general management journals, the *Academy of Management Journal*, has recently published a meta-analysis on innovation input and output in family firms (Duran et al. 2015), which further shows the great interest in this topic. However, this meta-analysis only includes studies published through 2012, which omits the recent results of an increasing number of studies.

This is not a surprising development because the ability to be innovative in niche markets has been identified as a characteristic of the strong, or even dominant, competitive positions of "Hidden Champions" in their industries. "Hidden Champions" are successful small and medium-sized enterprises, 70 percent of which are family firms (Simon 2009). The driver of this innovation success may well be the family, which distinguishes family firms from nonfamily firms. However, how can a family influence innovation in a family firm, and does the firm always benefit from family influence?

In their attempts to answer this question, family business researchers have analyzed family influence spanning the innovation process. A review of technological innovations in family firms by De Massis, Frattini, and Lichtenthaler (2013) applied an input-mediation-output (IMO) framework to structure relevant literature concerning family influence on innovation inputs, innovation activities, and innovation outputs. The authors analyzed 23 studies that were published through 2012. Since 2012, the number of studies focusing on innovation in family businesses has increased dramatically. Hence, a review may help structure the literature and derive gaps and future research.

First, we briefly describe the method used to identify the existing literature on innovation in family businesses. In the literature review, we examine the theoretical frameworks that have been applied in the context of innovation in family business. Second, we adopt the IMO approach used by De Massis, Frattini, and Lichtenthaler (2013) to structure the literature concerning family influence on innovation spanning the innovation process. Third, we move one step forward by analyzing the studies from an ability-willingness perspective that may help explain family firm innovative behavior (Chrisman et al. 2015; De Massis et al. 2014). Last, we discuss limitations of the current state of research and present avenues for future research.

Method

To review the research on innovation in family business, we focused on studies in which innovation is central to the article. We searched for articles in the Web of Science, a database by Thomson Reuter. To consider only high-quality research, we restricted our search to journals ranked grade 3 or higher in the subject areas entrepreneurship and small business management, general management, ethics and social responsibility, innovation, organization studies, and strategy in the recently published ABS Academic Journal Guide (42 journals in total). Additionally, we included journals from the Financial Times 45-journal ranking that were not included in the chosen subject areas of the ABS Academic Journal Guide and journals that focus specifically on family firms (i.e., *Journal of Family Business Strategy,* and *Journal of Family Business Management*). All journals appear in the Appendix.

To be considered, the articles had to meet three criteria: (1) one or more keywords related to family business research, including the article title, topic, and abstract (i.e., "family business," "family firm," "family enterprise," "familiness," "family-owned," "family-managed," "non-family," or "nonfamily"); (2) one or more keywords related to innovation including the article title and abstract (i.e., "innovation," "innovativeness," "innovative," "R&D," "new product," "technology," "ambidexterity," "absorptive capacity," or "patent"); and (3) publication on or before May 2015. In addition to the electronic database search, we conducted a manual title search for each journal considered to ensure inclusion of all relevant articles.

Our initial search resulted in a total of 95 articles. After reading the abstract of each article, 56 articles were excluded because the research was not focused on innovation in family firms. For example, we excluded studies that largely focused on the entrepreneurial orientation (EO) construct, which includes innovativeness but only as a subdimension of EO. We also excluded qualitative studies with only a single case study. Hence, our search resulted in 39 articles in 15 different journals: *Academy of Management Journal* (2), *Academy of Management Review* (1), *Entrepreneurship Theory and Practice* (4), *Family Business Review* (7), *Journal of Business Ethics* (2), *Journal of Business Research* (1), *Journal of Business Venturing* (1), *Journal of Family Business Management* (2), *Journal of Family Business Strategy* (4), *Journal of Product Innovation Management* (8), *Journal of Small Business Management* (3), *Research Policy* (1), *Small Business Economics* (2), and *Strategic Management Journal* (1).

Table 11.1 presents the different types of studies that were found. Most studies (20) are empirical and quantitative and compare family firms with nonfamily firms.

Theoretical Perspectives

Family business research focusing on innovation has used a number of well-established theories to explain the differences between family firms and nonfamily firms as well as differences within the group of family firms concerning their innovation behavior. We provide a brief description of each theory and its application in the context of innovation in family firms in the following. Table 11.2 presents the theories and the frequency of their application to family business innovation research.

Agency Theory

Agency theory is theoretically based on divergent interests, opportunistic behavior, and asymmetric information; it addresses the conflict of interest between a principal and an agent.

Table 11.1 Type of Studies

Type of Study		#	Comparative Studies (Family and Nonfamily Firms)	Non-comparative Studies (Only Family Firms)
Non-empirical	Conceptual	5	–	5
	Commentary	1	–	1
	Review	1	1	–
	Sum	7	1	6
Empirical	Qualitative	3	1	2
	Quantitative	28	20	8
	Meta analysis	1	1	–
	Sum	32	22	10
	Total	39	23	16

Table 11.2 Theoretical Perspectives

Theoretical Perspective	Frequency
Agency theory	7
Resource-based view	5
Behavioral agency model	5
Socioemotional wealth	4
Upper echelon theory	3

An agency problem may occur, for example, if the agent has better information than the principal (i.e., the problem of asymmetric information) or if the informed agent may fear the costs associated with a decision and therefore favor less risky decisions over risky decisions (i.e., problem of moral hazard).

In family firm research, agency cost considerations are ambiguous. Some authors suggest that agency problems are mitigated in family firms because ownership and management are often not separated or that family firm owners have a strong incentive to monitor their agents because most of their wealth is invested in the family firm and they intend to transfer the firm to the next generation (Chrisman, Chua, and Litz 2004). However, other authors argue that agency problems increase due to altruism and less self-control (Schulze, Lubatkin, and Dino 2003b, a, 2002).

In the context of innovation and family firms, agency theory is often used when analyzing R&D investments as input to the innovation process. For example, Block (2012) applies agency theory in his study and argues that due to the uncertainty concerning the outcome of R&D investments, investments in R&D may lead to an agency problem between the owners and the managers of a family firm.

Resource-Based View

Another theoretical perspective that has often been used in family business innovation research is the resource-based view (RBV). The RBV suggests that resources that are valuable, rare, inimitable, and non-substitutable can result in a competitive advantage for the firm. Family firms possess a unique bundle of resources, the so-called "familiness," which is distinctive to a firm because of family involvement. Sirmon and Hitt (2003) identify five family firm-specific resources that have the potential to provide competitive advantages for family firms. These resources are human capital, social capital, survivability capital, patient financial capital, and governance structure.

In the context of innovations, family firms offer unique resources that can improve innovative projects. In particular, the human capital of the family and the ownership structures of family firms are unique resources that bring knowledge to create new ideas and financial capital to develop these ideas into innovations.

For example, Matzler et al. (2015) use the RBV to explain how capabilities shape innovation because families may have particular capabilities that enable them to be more effective in their innovation efforts than a nonfamily firm would be. Furthermore, they argue that the deployment of idiosyncratic resources unique to family firms requires a strong involvement of families in management and governance. Hence, having more family members involved in management and governance increases the likelihood that a firm can deploy these family-specific resources.

Behavioral Agency Model

Building on agency and prospect theory, the behavioral agency model (BAM) suggests that executive risk-taking varies across and within different forms of monitoring and that agents may exhibit risk-seeking and risk-averse behaviors (Wiseman and Gómez-Mejía 1998). Furthermore, the BAM suggests that the behavioral preferences of individuals are shaped by problem framing and loss aversion (Kahneman 1991; Wiseman and Gómez-Mejía 1998). Although loss aversion implies that individuals are more concerned with avoiding losses than with obtaining gains, problem framing implies that choices are viewed from a perspective of gains or losses, usually in reference to current asset endowments (Kahneman and Tversky 1979) or, in family firms, in reference to socioemotional wealth (Gómez-Mejía et al. 2007). The BAM helps overcome the limitations of agency theory and explain the risk-taking behavior of family firms because this theory does not imply that family firms are inevitably risk averse or that their risk preferences are constant (Chrisman and Patel 2012).

In the context of innovation, the BAM suggests that to preserve socioemotional wealth (SEW), loss-averse family firms usually invest less in R&D than nonfamily firms. For example, Chrisman and Patel (2012) apply the BAM and extend this theoretical perspective with the myopic loss-aversion framework. They show that family firms usually invest less in R&D than nonfamily firms but that the variability of their investments is greater due to differences in the compatibility of long- and short-term family goals with the economic goals of a family firm. Additionally, their study indicates that when the performance of a family firm is below aspiration levels, family goals and economic goals tend to converge. In this situation, the R&D investments of family firms increase and the variability of those investments decreases compared with nonfamily firms.

Socioemotional Wealth

In family firms, the primary reference of potential gains or losses is SEW (Gómez-Mejía et al. 2011). SEW describes nonfinancial aspects of a firm that meet the family's affective needs such as identity, the ability to exercise family influence, and the perpetuation of the family dynasty. Hence, it describes the utility family owners derive from the noneconomic aspect of a firm. Gómez-Mejía et al. (2007) introduced SEW based on the BAM and assumed that the risk-taking behavior of family owners is affected by how their decisions might affect their SEW. Accordingly, SEW and the BAM are closely related theoretical concepts and cannot be clearly separated from one another. However, whereas most studies that apply BAM as a theoretical framework also use SEW, not all of the studies that apply SEW as a theoretical framework also use the BAM explicitly. Because innovation is always related to risk, SEW has recently been applied to predict family firm innovative behavior.

For example, Kraiczy, Hack, and Kellermanns (2015) explore how the organizational context (i.e., ownership by top management team family members and the generation in charge of the family firm) of family firms interacts with CEO risk-taking propensity to affect new product portfolio innovativeness. Their results show that the organizational context of family firms affects the positive relationship between CEO risk-taking propensity and new product portfolio innovativeness. Specifically, the relationship between CEO risk-taking propensity and new product portfolio innovativeness is weaker if levels of ownership by top management team (TMT) family members are high, which would indicate high levels of SEW; thus, SEW is a strong and important reference point. Additionally, the effect of CEO risk-taking propensity on new product portfolio innovativeness is stronger in family firms at earlier generational stages, which is also related to high levels of SEW, making SEW a strong and important reference point.

Upper Echelon Theory

Recently, upper echelon theory (UET) has been applied in the context of innovation in family firms. UET is an information processing theory that explains how executives act under conditions of bounded rationality (Hambrick and Mason 1984). Based on their interpretation of situations, executives make decisions that are influenced by their experience, personality, and values. According to UET, executives' personalized interpretations of situations directly affect their strategic choices and behaviors.

Because of the discretion of the executives, these choices and behaviors are reflected in innovation-related decisions such as R&D investments and go/kill decisions on innovation projects.

For example, Kraiczy, Hack, and Kellermanns (2014) investigate interaction effects between TMT innovation orientation and two family firm-specific sources of TMT diversity: the number of involved generations and the ratio of family members in the TMT. Their results show that although TMT innovation orientation has a more positive influence on new product portfolio performance when multiple generations participate in the TMT, a more negative influence on new product portfolio performance exists when the ratio of family members in the TMT is high. The results indicate that family firm-specific TMT diversity needs careful analysis because each source of TMT diversity may affect family firm performance differently.

Conclusion

Based on this plurality of theoretical perspectives, research on innovation in family firms has pursued different topics spanning the innovation process. Most of these theories can be applied to predict both positive and negative effects of family influence on innovation. For example, the RBV suggests that family firms can benefit from a unique resource bundle but, conversely, that family firms have also been characterized by resource scarcity. Similarly, agency theory predicts that agency conflicts may arise between the family firm owner and the manager, which may mitigate innovation but, conversely, when the family firm is managed by a family member these agency conflicts should disappear, which may have a positive effect on innovation. Taken together, from a theoretical perspective, it is difficult to predict the effect of family influence on innovation. Specifically, according to SEW and the BAM, effects can be contradictory. In the next step, we examine the empirical evidence that is based on the different theoretical perspectives presented above.

Research Review

Input-Mediation-Output Framework

De Massis, Frattini, and Lichtenthaler (2013) reviewed and systemized 23 peer-reviewed journal articles on technological innovation in family firms with the use of an innovation inputs-innovation activities-innovation output-framework. The results of this literature review show that family influence has direct effects on innovation inputs (e.g., R&D investments), innovation activities (e.g., a new product development process), and innovation outputs (e.g., number of new products), and moderating effects on the relationships between these steps of technological innovation.

Because we focused our review only on articles published in high-ranked journals and did not restrict it to technological innovation, not all papers reviewed by De Massis, Frattini, and Lichtenthaler (2013) are included in this study, and vice versa. In a first step, we assign the studies according to the IMO framework used by De Massis, Frattini, and Lichtenthaler (2013). We distinguish between studies that compare family with nonfamily firms and studies that focus only on family firms. In a second step, we apply the ability-willingness perspective to extend previous findings and explain why results have been inconsistent.

Except for the meta analysis by Duran et al. (2015), Table 11.3 presents all of the empirical studies included in the review (N = 31) and provides detailed information for each study.

Studies Focusing on Differences between Family and Nonfamily Firms Concerning Innovation

Most of the articles reviewed in this study applied comparative research designs (67.74 percent 20 quantitative studies and 1 qualitative study) to identify differences between family and nonfamily firms in their analyses.

Innovation Inputs

Our review shows that most studies focus on family influence on R&D-related measures such as R&D investment (Chrisman and Patel 2012; Gómez-Mejía et al. 2014; Patel and Chrisman 2014; Sirmon et al. 2008), change in R&D investment (Kotlar, De Massis, et al. 2014; Kotlar, Fang, et al. 2014), and R&D intensity (Block 2012; Muñoz-Bullón and Sanchez-Bueno 2011; Schmid et al. 2014; Sciascia et al. 2015) as innovation input. All of these studies use objective measures and analyze solely family influence on this input factor, not examining how these investments transform in innovation activities or innovation outcomes. Considering only direct effects, family influence, which is primarily measured by family ownership and management, on R&D-related measures is negative (e.g., Muñoz-Bullón and Sanchez-Bueno 2011; Sciascia et al. 2015). Adding context variables changes this effect. For example, when the gap between aspirations and performance (i.e., gap between current performance and both historical performance and competitors' performance) is negative, family firms increase R&D investments more than nonfamily firms do (Chrisman and Patel 2012). Furthermore, research shows that when institutional ownership and diversification increase, family firms are more likely to invest in R&D (Gómez-Mejía et al. 2014). Analyzing threats of imitation, Sirmon et al. (2008) show that family-influenced firms are less rigid in their responses to threats of imitation and reduce their R&D investments and internationalization significantly less than firms without family influence.

Table 11.3 Empirical Studies Analyzed in the Review

#	Author (Year)	Sample	Theoretical Framework	Research Design	Innovation Measure	Input, Activity, Output	Willingness to Innovate	Ability to Innovate	Key Findings
1	Allison, McKenny, and Short (2014)	149 S&P 500 firms, USA, various industries, only family firms	–	Quantitative, panel data, hierarchical linear modeling	Organizational ambidexterity (exploration orientation), R&D intensity	Activity	High willingness due to economic goals	High ability due to management, low levels of turnover and the presence of strong familial bonds	Family firm ambidexterity is stable over time, but is punctuated by dramatic changes. Level of innovation required to compete in an industry is a predictor of changes in exploration versus exploitation over time among family firms.
2	Beck et al. (2011)	111 family firms, SME, Belgium and Netherlands, various industries, only family firms	–	Quantitative, multiple regression analysis	Innovation	Construct including output	Low willingness of later generations due to greater conservativeness focus on preserving family wealth	High ability of later generations due to an innovation-oriented culture, equal and participative involvement in decision making and professionalism	Market orientation mediates the relationship between generational stage and innovation. Later generations have a negative effect on market orientation, which reduces innovation.
3	Block (2012)	154 S&P 500 firms, USA, R&D-intensive industries, family and nonfamily firms	Agency theory	Quantitative, panel data regression	R&D intensity	Input	–	High ability due to ownership and management	Family ownership is negatively associated with the level of R&D
4	Block and Spiegel (2013)	326 German regions with the locations of 526 medium- to large-scale family firms in innovative industries, only family firms	–	Quantitative, multiple regression analysis	Regional innovation activity measured by the number of granted patents	Output	High willingness due to long-term orientation and strong local roots	High ability due to ownership	Regions with a higher family firm density also show higher levels of innovation output, as measured by the number of successful patent applications

(Continued)

#	Author (Year)	Sample	Theoretical Framework	Research Design	Innovation Measure	Input, Activity, Output	Willingness to Innovate	Ability to Innovate	Key Findings
5	Block et al. (2013)	248 S&P 500 firms, USA, various industries, family and nonfamily firms	Socioemotional wealth	Quantitative, count data regression	Patent citations	Output	Low willingness due to pursuit of SEW	High ability due to ownership and management	Family-managed firms receive fewer patent citations compared with other firms
6	Chrisman and Patel (2012)	965 S&P 1500 firms, USA, manufacturing industry, family and nonfamily firms	Behavioral agency model, myopic loss aversion framework	Quantitative, panel data regression	R&D investment	Input	Low willingness due to loss aversion with respect to their socioemotional wealth and focus on short-term family goals	High ability due to ownership, management, and governance	Family firms generally invest less in R&D. Family firms increase R&D investments more than nonfamily firms when the gap between aspirations and performance is negative. The variability of investments in R&D is greater among family firms than among nonfamily firms. Performance below aspirations reduces the variability of investments in R&D more in family firms than in nonfamily firms.
7	Classen et al. (2012)	167 firms, SME, Belgium and Netherlands, manufacturing industry, family firms and nonfamily firms	Behavioral theory of the firm	Quantitative, multiple regression analysis	Search breadth	Activity	Low willingness due to maintenance of SEW	High ability due to ownership and management. Low ability due to their limited cognitive diversity and absorptive capacity	Family firms have a lower search breadth than nonfamily firms.

#									
8	Classen et al. (2014)	2087 firms, SME, Germany, various industries, family and nonfamily firms	Exploratory	Quantitative, CDM model	Probability of investing in innovation, innovation intensity, product innovation output, process innovation output	Input and output	–	High ability due to ownership	Family firms have a higher propensity to invest in innovation at all. Conditional on investing in innovation, these firms do so less intensively than nonfamily firms do. Family firms tend to outperform nonfamily firms in terms of process innovation outcomes when controlling for innovation investment. Given the level of product and process innovation, family firms underperform concerning labor productivity in comparison to nonfamily firms.
9	Craig and Dibrell (2006)	391 firms, SME, USA, various industries, family and nonfamily firms	Stewardship theory	Quantitative, multiple regression analysis	Firm innovation	Construct including input, activity, and output	–	High ability due to ownership and management; High ability due to more flexible structures and decision-making processes and less formal monitoring and control mechanisms	Family firms are able to facilitate environmentally friendly firm policies associated with improved firm innovation and greater financial performance more effectively than nonfamily firms can.
10	Craig, Dibrell, and Garrett (2014)	359 firms, USA, food processing industry, family and nonfamily firms	Resource-based view, upper echelon theory	Quantitative, structural equation modeling	Firm innovativeness	Construct including input, activity, and output	–	High ability due to family mission, family control, and family culture; High ability due to flexible planning systems	Family influence positively influences family culture; that family culture improves the ability of families to be strategically flexible. This flexibility positively affects firm innovativeness, subsequently benefiting firm performance.

(Continued)

#	Author (Year)	Sample	Theoretical Framework	Research Design	Innovation Measure	Input, Activity, Output	Willingness to Innovate	Ability to Innovate	Key Findings
11	De Massis et al. (2015)	10 firms, Italy, various industries, family and nonfamily firms	Resource-based view, agency theory, stewardship theory, behavioral theory	Qualitative, exploratory	Product innovation process (strategy, organization, climate)	Activity	–	High ability due to ownership and management	Family firms differ from nonfamily firms concerning product innovation strategies and organization of the innovation process.
12	Gómez-Mejía et al. (2014)	610 firms, USA, high-technology industries, family and nonfamily firms	Behavioral agency model, mixed gamble	Quantitative, panel data regression	R&D investment	Input	Low willingness due to loss aversion with respect to their socioemotional wealth	High ability due to ownership and management	Family firms are less prone to invest in R&D compared with nonfamily firms. As institutional ownership increases, family firms are more likely to invest in R&D. As related diversification increases, family firms are more likely to invest in R&D.
13	Grundström, Öberg, and Öhrwall Rönnbäck (2012)	10 firms, SME, Sweden, manufacturing industry, only family firms	–	Qualitative, multiple case study	Innovativeness, innovation intensity	Output	Low willingness due to retention of family tradition	High ability due to family member as successor (ownership, management)	Values related to a firm's context, influenced by the divesting party and by the choice of successor, create inertia to the extent that only minor changes in innovation orientation are possible. External owners may focus largely on growth and new ways of innovating, whereas family-controlled firms diversify to avoid abandoning previous businesses. Intermediating factors, such as customer involvement, type of SME, and the acquirers' motives, influence the innovative organizational culture and create explanatory links to innovation intensity and methodologies of innovation.

	Author	Sample/Context	Theory	Method	Topic	Output/Activity	Willingness	Ability	Main findings
14	Hauck and Prügl (2015)	81 firms, Austria, tourism industry, only family firms	Socioemotional wealth	Quantitative, multiple regression analysis	Perceived suitability of the succession phase for innovation activities	Output	High willingness due to family adaptability	High ability due to family member as successor (ownership, management)	Socioemotional factors have both dark and bright sides in the context of innovation. Family adaptability and a family member's closeness to the firm are positively associated with perceiving the succession phase as an opportunity for innovation.
15	Kammerlander and Ganter (2015)	7 firms, Germany, consumer goods industry, only family firms	Attention-based view, sense-making theory	Qualitative, multiple case studies	Family firms' adaptation to discontinuous technological change	Activity	Willingness depends on the noneconomic goals of the family CEO. High willingness due to the goal of family power and control	High ability due to ownership and management	Family CEO's specific noneconomic goals determine whether the CEO assesses a discontinuous technology as sufficiently relevant to warrant a reaction from the firm and constrain the set of considered responses. The outcome of this sense-making process determines the organization's response. Over time, family CEOs might re-evaluate the emerging trend based on their goals and adapt organizational moves according.
16	Kashmiri and Mahajan (2014)	107 firms, USA, various industries, only family firms	Social-identity theory	Quantitative, event study, panel data regression	Shareholder value impact of firms' new product introductions	Output	High willingness due to motivation to protect firm reputation	High capability to translate strong motivation into their firm's more trustworthy product-related behavior	Presence of the founding family's name as part of a family firm's name acts as a valuable firm resource, increasing the abnormal stock returns surrounding the firm's new product introductions.

(Continued)

#	Author (Year)	Sample	Theoretical Framework	Research Design	Innovation Measure	Input, Activity, Output	Willingness to Innovate	Ability to Innovate	Key Findings
									Superior returns to family-named firms' new product introductions are partially mediated by these firms' history of ethical product-related behavior: family-named firms, particularly those with corporate branding, and those wherein a founding family member holds the CEO or chairman position, are more likely to exhibit a history of avoiding such product-related controversies as product safety issues and deceptive advertising.
17	Kotlar et al. (2013)	1540 firms, Spain, manufacturing industry, family and nonfamily firms	Behavioral agency model	Quantitative, panel data regression	External technology acquisition (R&D contracting)	Input	Low willingness due to perseveration of authority and identity foundations of socioemotional wealth	High ability due to ownership and management	Family firms are generally more reluctant to acquire external technology; and the effect of negative aspiration performance gaps becomes less relevant as family management is higher. Family firms become more favorable to considering the adoption of an open approach to technology development when some protection mechanisms increase the managers' perceptions of control over the technology trajectory.
18	Kotlar, De Massis, et al. (2014)	437 firms, Spain, manufacturing industry, family and nonfamily firms	Strategic reference point theory	Quantitative, panel data regression	Change in R&D investment	Input	Low willingness due to pursuance of family-centered goals	High ability due to ownership and management	Family firms are less likely to change their level of R&D investments across periods. This general tendency is moderated by the influence of reference points distributed along internal and external reference dimensions.

#	Author	Sample	Theory	Method	DV	Type	Willingness	Ability	Findings
									Unabsorbed slack resources exert a negative influence on change in R&D investments and internal performance hazard positively affects change in R&D investments, whereas family management positively moderates both of these relationships.
									External performance hazard positively influences change in R&D investments, whereas competitors' market power, buyers' and suppliers' bargaining power negatively influence change in R&D investments.
									However, family management negatively moderates the effect of external performance hazard and positively moderates the effect of competitors' market power, buyers' and suppliers' bargaining power.
19	Kotlar, Fang, et al (2014)	431 firms, Spain, manufacturing industry, family and nonfamily firms	Behavioral theory of the firm, resource dependency theory	Quantitative, panel data regression	Change in R&D investment	Input	Low willingness due to noneconomic goals	High ability due to ownership and management	Family firms react more strongly to increasing supplier bargaining power when their profitability reference points have been reached.
									For family firms, a negative profitability–aspiration gap negatively moderates the positive effect of a change in supplier bargaining power on R&D investment variation, such that the effect is weaker.

(*Continued*)

#	Author (Year)	Sample	Theoretical Framework	Research Design	Innovation Measure	Input, Activity, Output	Willingness to Innovate	Ability to Innovate	Key Findings
20	Kraiczy, Hack, and Kellermanns (2014)	77 firms, SME, Germany, manufacturing industry, only family firms	Upper echelon theory	Quantitative, multiple regression analysis	New product portfolio performance	Construct including output	High willingness due to multiple generations in the TMT Low willingness due to high ratio of family members in the TMT	High ability due to CEO's discretion	Results indicate that family-induced diversity in the TMT has opposing moderating effects. A positive relationship exists between TMT innovation orientation and new product portfolio performance when multiple generations are involved in the TMT TMT innovation orientation and new product portfolio performance experience a negative relationship when the ratio of family members in the TMT is high.
21	Kraiczy, Hack, and Kellermanns (2015)	114 firms, SME, Germany, manufacturing industry, only family firms	Socioemotional wealth, upper echelon theory	Quantitative, multiple regression analysis	New product portfolio innovativeness	Construct including output	Low willingness due to high levels of ownership by family members on the TMT High willingness due to closeness to founding generation	High ability due to CEO's discretion	CEO risk-taking propensity has a positive effect on new product portfolio innovativeness. The relationship between CEO risk-taking propensity and new product portfolio innovativeness is weaker if levels of ownership by family members on the TMT are high (high SEW). The effect of CEO risk-taking propensity on new product portfolio innovativeness is stronger in family firms at earlier generational stages (high SEW).
22	Llach et al. (2012)	88 firms, Spain, manufacturing industry, family and nonfamily firms	–	Quantitative, matched-pair design	Reduction of R&D other innovation dimensions in a recession	Input and output	Low willingness due to risk aversion	High ability due to ownership	Family firms have a significantly higher reduction of R&D in a recession environment than nonfamily firms do.

23	Matzler et al. (2015)	134 firms, Germany, various industries, family and nonfamily firms	Resource-based view, agency theory	Quantitative, panel data regression	Innovation input (R&D intensity), innovation output (patents intensity, citation intensity)	Input and output	Low willingness due to risk aversion (innovation input)	High ability due to ownership, management, and governance High ability due to unique social capital building (innovation output)	Family participation in management and governance has a negative effect on innovation input and a positive influence on innovation output.
24	Muñoz-Bullón and Sanchez-Bueno (2011)	736 firms, Canada, various industries, family and nonfamily firms	Agency theory	Quantitative, panel data regression	R&D intensity	Input	Low willingness due to risk aversion	High ability due to ownership and control Low ability due to limited access to human and financial resources, CEO tenure and age, the agency costs of possible altruism, the relationship between family members and minority shareholders	Family firms in record lower R&D intensity compared with nonfamily firms
25	Nieto, Santamaria, and Fernandez (2015)	15,173 observations, Spain, various industries, family and nonfamily firms	Agency theory	Quantitative, panel data regression	Innovation behavior (innovation effort, R&D), sources of innovation (internal, external), innovation result (incremental, radical)	Input, activity, and output	Low willingness due to risk aversion	High ability due to ownership and management Low ability due to agency costs and resource constraints	Family firms make fewer innovation efforts and are less inclined to turn to external sources of innovation such as technological collaboration than nonfamily firms. Family firms are more likely to achieve incremental than radical innovations.

(*Continued*)

#	Author (Year)	Sample	Theoretical Framework	Research Design	Innovation Measure	Input, Activity, Output	Willingness to Innovate	Ability to Innovate	Key Findings
26	Patel and Chrisman (2014)	874 S&P 1500 firms, USA, various industries, family and nonfamily firms	Behavioral agency theory, risk abatement	Quantitative, panel data regression	R&D investment	Input	Willingness depends on the aspiration level	High ability due to ownership and management	When performance is above aspiration levels, the investments in R&D of family firms will decrease the variability of sales more than will the investments in R&D of nonfamily firms. When performance is below aspiration levels, the investments in R&D of family firms will increase the variability of sales more than will the investments in R&D of nonfamily firms.
27	Schmid et al. (2014)	641 firms, Germany, various industries, family and nonfamily firms	Agency theory	Quantitative, panel data regression	R&D intensity	Input	High willingness due to long-term orientation	High ability due to control, management, and supervision	R&D intensity is higher in firms that are actively managed by the family. This positive effect disappears if we follow previous research and use R&D information from financial statements. Family-managed firms report too conservative R&D expenditures, particularly if they face financial constraints. This leads to an under-estimation of R&D intensity in these firms if accounting figures are used.

| 28 | Sciascia et al. (2015) | 240 firms, SME, Italy, various industries, family and nonfamily firms | Behavioral agency model, socioemotional wealth | Quantitative, multiple regression analysis | R&D intensity | Input | Willingness depends on the overlap between family wealth and firm equity | High ability due to ownership | In SMEs in which there is a high overlap between family wealth and firm equity, the relationship between family ownership and R&D intensity is negative due to family owners' greater desire to protect SEW. If the overlap between family's total wealth and single firm equity is low, the relationship between family ownership and R&D intensity is positive because the low overlap reduces the family's loss aversion propensity, fostering R&D intensity. |
| 29 | Sirmon et al. (2008) | 2531 firms, SME, France, manufacturing industry, family and nonfamily firms | Resource-based view, threat rigidity | Quantitative, multiple regression analysis | R&D investment | Input | High willingness to innovate in threat situations due to long-term orientation and higher incentives to monitor. Both reduce persistence and overemphasis on efficiency | High ability to innovate in threat situations due to higher particularism, extensive interactions between family owners, favor for open communication and preference of organic organizational structures | Family-influenced firms are less rigid in their responses to threats of imitations, reducing their R&D investments and internationalization significantly less than firms without family influence. |

(*Continued*)

#	Author (Year)	Sample	Theoretical Framework	Research Design	Innovation Measure	Input, Activity, Output	Willingness to Innovate	Ability to Innovate	Key Findings
30	Spriggs et al. (2013)	199 firms, USA, various industries, only family firms	Resource-based view, agency theory	Quantitative, multiple regression analysis	Innovative capacity	Activity	–	High ability to benefit from innovative capacity if ownership dispersion is high due to higher information exchange Low ability due to more difficult goal alignment, higher probability of ownership conflicts, and diminished flexibility and speed in decision making – and vice versa if ownership dispersion is low	Innovative capacity has a positive effect on small family firm performance. This effect is stronger if concentrated ownership is combined with high collaborative network orientation or dispersed ownership is combined with low collaborative network orientation.
31	Wagner (2010)	252 S&P 500 firms, USA, various industries, family and nonfamily firms	–	Quantitative, panel data regression	Innovation with high social benefits (environmental innovation, CSR innovation, part of firm's mission is the provision of products or services for the economically disadvantaged)	Output	High willingness to innovate with high social benefits due to (1) long-term orientation, (2) concern about ones positive reputation, and (3) supportiveness of protecting the environment and other social issues	High ability to innovate with high social benefits due to higher organizational flexibility	Being a family firm positively moderates the relationship between corporate social performance and innovation with high social benefits.

Three studies focus not only on innovation inputs but also on outputs (Llach et al. 2012; Classen et al. 2014; Matzler et al. 2015). In an exploratory study, Classen et al. (2014) find that family firms have a higher propensity to invest in innovation at all; however, conditional on investing in innovation, these companies do so less intensively than their nonfamily counterparts do. Furthermore, family firms tend to outperform nonfamily firms in terms of process innovation outcomes when controlling for innovation investment. Given the level of product and process innovation, family firms underperform concerning labor productivity in comparison to nonfamily firms. Llach et al. (2012) show that family firms only differ from nonfamily firms in R&D efforts because family firms decrease R&D-related measures, whereas nonfamily firms increase them. For other indicators of innovation, such as product innovation, cooperation, organizational innovation and product-related services, no differences were found. The study by Matzler et al. (2015) analyzes R&D intensity (innovation input), patents intensity and citation intensity (innovation outputs) and finds that family participation in management and governance has a negative effect on innovation input and a positive influence on innovation output.

Innovation Activities

Focusing specifically on innovation activities, studies have analyzed search breadth (Classen et al. 2012) and product innovation process (De Massis et al. 2015). Classen et al. (2012) investigate the differences in the diversity of cooperation partners used for innovation-related activities (i.e., search breadth). Their results show that family firms have a lower search breadth than their nonfamily counterparts. In a qualitative study, De Massis et al. (2015) analyze differences in the product innovation process between family and nonfamily firms. Their analysis shows that family firms differ from nonfamily firms in product innovation strategies, innovation climate, and organization of the innovation process. Specifically, family firms focus on incremental new products by applying an open approach, relying on collaborations with external sources of knowledge and technologies, whereas nonfamily firms invest both in incremental and radical innovations, with only sporadic collaborations with external partners. In family firms, the predominant organizational climate is largely informal, unstructured, and risk averse, whereas nonfamily firms are highly structured and more risk taking.

Innovation Outputs

Two studies focus solely on innovation outputs by using innovation with high social benefits (i.e., environmental innovation, corporate social responsibility innovation, and provision of products or services for the economically disadvantaged) (Wagner 2010) and patent citations (Block et al. 2013) as measures.

The study by Wagner (2010) analyzes an indirect effect of family influence on the link between corporate social performance and innovation. The results show that being a family firm positively moderates this relationship. Block et al. (2013) use the number of patent citations that a patent portfolio receives not only as a measure of economic and technological importance but also as a measure of the radicalness of innovations. Their results show that family-managed firms are less likely to produce innovations of a radical and exploratory nature, whereas, for founder-managed firms, the opposite seems to be true. Even when controlling for R&D spending, family-managed firms produce innovations with low economic and technological importance.

Comprehensive Studies

Nieto, Santamaria, and Fernandez (2015) include in their study measures of innovation input (i.e., R&D intensity), innovation activity (i.e., R&D contracting and technological collaboration), and innovation output (i.e., incremental product innovations and radical product innovations). They find that family firms invest less in R&D and are less inclined to turn to external sources of innovation such as technological collaboration than are nonfamily firms. Furthermore, their results show that family firms are more likely to achieve incremental innovations than radical innovations. Analyzing firm innovation and firm innovativeness, Craig and Dibrell (2006) and Craig, Dibrell, and Garrett (2014) use constructs in their studies, which include items of innovation inputs, activities, and outputs. Craig and Dibrell (2006) find that family firms are better able to facilitate environmentally friendly firm policies associated with improved firm innovation and greater financial performance more effectively than their nonfamily counterparts are. Craig, Dibrell, and Garrett (2014) show that family influence positively influences family culture, which, in turn, improves the ability of families to be strategically flexible and that this flexibility positively affects firm innovativeness.

Studies Focusing on Differences within the Group of Family Firms Concerning Innovation

Innovation Inputs

Studies analyzing heterogeneity among family firms with a focus on innovation inputs have not been found. To the best of our knowledge, no research exists on this topic. We discuss this finding as an avenue for future research.

Innovation Activities

Organizational ambidexterity is defined as the ability of an organization to simultaneously pursue both explorative (discontinuous) and exploitative (incremental) innovation (O'Reilly and Tushman 2004). Exploration and exploitation can be described as innovation activities. Although exploration is related to search, experimentation, and variance increase, exploitation increases productivity and efficiency through improved execution and variance reduction (March 1991). Allison, McKenny, and Short (2014) analyze how family firm ambidexterity changes over time due to temporal-, firm-, and industry-level factors. They find that family firm ambidexterity is stable over time, though it is punctuated by dramatic changes. They also find that the level of innovation required to compete in an industry is a predictor of changes over time in exploration versus exploitation in family firms.

Absorptive capacity (AC) is defined as the ability of a firm to recognize the value of new, external information, assimilate it, and apply it to commercial ends (Cohen and Levinthal 1990), which is critical to its innovative capabilities. In a conceptual study, Andersén (2015) focuses on the effect of familiness on this innovation activity and argues that due to higher levels of social capital, familiness is positively related to the ability to transform and use external knowledge (i.e., realized AC). Furthermore, he indicates that firms with high levels of familiness are likely to be inferior in acquiring and assimilating external knowledge (i.e., potential AC).

Using multiple case studies, Kammerlander and Ganter (2015) applied a quantitative approach to analyzing how family CEOs' managerial attention response patterns affect family firms' adaptation to discontinuous technological change. Specifically, the study shows that noneconomic goals of the family CEO determine whether he/she assesses a discontinuous technology as sufficiently relevant to warrant a reaction from the firm and constrain the set of considered responses.

Innovation Outputs

Most of the studies analyzing the heterogeneity of family firms with regard to innovation focus on innovation outputs. Block and Spiegel (2013) analyze the regional innovation activity of family firms measured by the number of granted patents. They find that regions with a higher family firm density show higher levels of innovation output. Another objective measure is applied by Kashmiri and Mahajan (2014), who analyze the shareholder value effect of firms' new product introductions. Their results show that the presence of the founding family's name as part of a family firm's name acts as a valuable firm resource, increasing the abnormal stock returns surrounding the firm's new product introductions. Superior returns to family-named firms' new product introductions are partially mediated by these firms' history of ethical product-related behavior; family-named firms, particularly those with corporate branding and those wherein a founding family member holds the CEO or chairman position, are more likely to exhibit a history of avoiding such product-related controversies as product safety issues and deceptive advertising.

Grundström, Öberg, and Öhrwall Rönnbäck (2012) applied a qualitative approach using multiple case studies to analyze family influence on innovation outputs. They analyze succession and the ability to innovate in family firms. Their results show that family firms taken over by family members tend to focus on incremental innovation and showed low innovation intensity. These family firms depended on partners for developing ideas and were, therefore, adopters rather than innovators. Compared with family firms kept within the family, those taken over by external parties that attempted to implement change in the firms tended to be more growth oriented. However, following the succession in a family firm, attitudes toward innovativeness largely remain focused on incremental innovations in established frames, regardless of whether the family firm passes to a family member or an external party. Focusing also on succession, Hauck and Prügl (2015) find that family adaptability and a family member's closeness to the firm are positively related to perceiving the succession phase as an opportunity for innovation.

Three studies use constructs to measure innovation outputs of family firms. While Kraiczy, Hack, and Kellermanns (2014) focus on the performance of the new product portfolio, Kraiczy, Hack, and Kellermanns (2015) focus on the innovativeness of the new product portfolio; both employed self-reported and subjective assessment measures from the executives of the family firm. Kraiczy, Hack, and Kellermanns (2014) analyze the effect of family-induced diversity in the top management team (TMT) on the relationship between TMT innovation orientation and new product portfolio performance. Their results indicate that family-induced diversity in the TMT has opposing moderating effects. Although a positive relationship exists between TMT innovation orientation and new product portfolio performance when multiple generations are involved in the TMT, TMT innovation orientation and new product portfolio performance experience a negative relationship when the ratio of family members in the TMT is high. Kraiczy, Hack, and Kellermanns (2015) focus on

CEOs and the effect of their risk-taking propensity on new product portfolio performance. They find that CEO risk-taking propensity has a positive effect on new product portfolio innovativeness in family firms. More interestingly, their results also show opposing effects of different family influence variables. Specifically, the relationship between CEO risk-taking propensity and new product portfolio innovativeness is weaker if levels of ownership by family members on the TMT are high, which describes a situation in which SEW is a strong reference point. Furthermore, the effect of CEO risk-taking propensity on new product portfolio innovativeness is stronger in family firms at earlier generational stages, which also describes a situation in which SEW is a strong reference point. Beck et al. (2011) analyze the relationship between the generational stage of the family firm and innovation. The results show that later generations are less innovative.

Ability-Willingness Perspective

Although or because various theories have been applied in family business innovation research, results have not always been consistent. Recent research has introduced the ability-willingness framework to explain family firm innovation (Chrisman et al. 2015), which may help to overcome these inconsistencies. Whereas ability describes the discretion of the family to act, willingness describes the disposition of the family to act. Ability includes the latitude in selecting the goals of the firm and in choosing among a wider range of options (Hambrick and Finkelstein 1987, Morck, Shleifer, and Vishny 1988). In contrast, willingness describes "the disposition of the family owners to engage in idiosyncratic behavior based on the goals, intentions, and motivations that drive the owner to influence the firm's behavior in directions diverging from those of nonfamily firms or the institutional norms among family firms" (Chrisman et al. 2015: 311). In family firms, "ability and willingness are necessary but individually insufficient conditions; sufficiency requires both, not just one or the other" (De Massis et al. 2014: 345).

Ability

Families who are the owners of family firms, have the discretion to direct, allocate, add to, or dispose of available family firm resources to innovate (De Massis et al. 2014). This discretion varies with the degree of family influence and may be affected by context factors.

Two important conditions affect family firms' ability to influence innovation. First, family ownership, which can be defined as the foundation of family influence, is compulsory to generate discretion. A higher level of family ownership is associated with a higher of level family discretion to affect decisions such as innovation. Second, family management, which describes the active involvement of family members in the top management team, can further increase the discretion to act. If a family is the sole owner of the firm and family members are actively involved in the management, the ability of the family to innovate is highest. Indeed, most studies focus on the ability to act by focusing on family ownership and family management (e.g., Gómez-Mejía et al. 2014; Kotlar, Fang, et al. 2014).

Additionally, research has described family firms as having further abilities that increase the basic ability to innovate. For example, Sirmon et al. (2008) argue that family firms have a higher ability to innovate in threat situations due to higher particularism, extensive interactions between family owners, a preference for open communication, and a preference for organic organizational structures. Another study by Wagner (2010) assigns a higher ability to innovate with high social benefits to family firms due to their higher organizational flexibility. Similarly,

Craig, Dibrell, and Garrett (2014) find family firms to be more innovative because of their strategic flexibility, which results from the family culture. Spriggs et al. (2013) state that family firms have a higher ability to benefit from innovative capacity if ownership dispersion is high due to higher information exchange. However, such firms also show a lower ability due to more difficult goal alignment, higher probability of ownership conflicts, and diminished flexibility and speed in decision making – and vice versa, if ownership dispersion is low.

Conversely, research also found ability decreasing factors. For example, Andersén (2015) argue that family firms have a low ability to increase potential absorptive capacity due to low external orientation and stability. Classen et al. (2012) find that family firms have a low ability to show high search breadth because of their limited cognitive diversity and absorptive capacity. Muñoz-Bullón and Sanchez-Bueno (2011) state that family firms have a low ability to invest in R&D due to limited access to human and financial resources, CEO tenure and age, the agency costs of possible altruism, and the relationship between family members and minority shareholders. Similarly, Nieto, Santamaria, and Fernandez (2015) describe family firms as having a low ability to be innovative due to agency costs and resource constraints. Furthermore, Allison, McKenny, and Short (2014) argue that low levels of turnover and the presence of strong familial bonds decrease the ability to innovate (i.e., change in family firm ambidexterity over time is gradual and continuous with a linear trend) because these low levels of turnover indicate organizational inertia and strong family bonds may result in less-risky change trajectories.

Willingness

Whereas the ability to innovate is always considered in the studies because it determines family influence, the willingness of the family to innovate has received less attention in the literature. However, family firms' possession of the ability to innovate does not necessarily indicate that they are also willing to do so. Hence, analyzing willingness is important to understand and predict family firm innovative behavior. The literature has identified factors associated with why family firms are more or less willing to innovate. Specifically, context factors affect the level of family firms' willingness to be innovative. Thus, research has identified factors that describe family firms as having both lower and higher willingness.

Because the literature describes family firms often as risk averse, the preservation of SEW (e.g., Gómez-Mejía et al. 2014; Kraiczy, Hack, and Kellermanns 2015) and risk aversion (e.g., Nieto, Santamaria, and Fernandez 2015; Llach et al. 2012) have been the most often used factors related to a lower willingness of family firms to innovate. For example, Block et al. (2013) analyze patent citations of family and nonfamily firms, which have been shown in the literature to reflect the economic and technological importance of innovations. The authors argue that family firms have a lower willingness to be innovative because they try to preserve SEW by pursuing incremental innovation projects that often are not protected by patent. The uncertainty associated with challenging innovation projects may threaten family control and therefore SEW. Their findings show that with increasing ownership of a family (i.e., increasing ability to innovate), a low willingness of the family to innovate becomes reflected in fewer patent citations. However, this low willingness is only theoretically assumed and not measured in the study. Furthermore, SEW-related factors such as preservation of authority and identity, focus on non-economic goals (Kotlar, Fang, et al. 2014), pursuance of family-centered goals (Kotlar, De Massis, et al. 2014), and retention of family tradition (Grundström, Öberg, and Öhrwall Rönnbäck 2012) have been used to assign a lower willingness to innovate to family firms.

Focusing on risk aversion, Muñoz-Bullón and Sanchez-Bueno (2011) argue that family firms' willingness to invest in R&D is low because these investments are uncertain and risky. Although family firms have the ability to invest in R&D due to ownership and control, the authors assign a low ability to family firms due to limited access to human and financial resources, CEO tenure and age, the agency costs of possible altruism, and the relationship between family members and minority shareholders. Their results indicate that the low willingness and low ability to invest in R&D result in lower R&D intensity compared with nonfamily firms. However, except ownership, ability, and willingness measures were only theoretically applied and not measured in the study.

Conversely, research has also assigned factors to family firms that result in higher willingness to innovate. Most often, the long-term orientation of family firms has been described as a motivator for family firms to innovate (e.g., Wagner 2010; Block and Spiegel 2013). For example, Schmid et al. (2014) argue that family firms are willing to invest more in R&D than nonfamily firms because family firms are long-term oriented. However, this positive effect disappears if R&D information is used from financial statements. It appears that family firms report too conservative R&D expenditures. Furthermore, Sirmon et al. (2008) assume that family firms are more willing to innovate in threat situations due to their long-term orientation and higher incentives to monitor. Their findings show that family firms are less rigid in their responses to threats of imitation and reduce their R&D investments and their internationalization significantly less than nonfamily firms.

Kashmiri and Mahajan (2014) found that the presence of the founding family's name as part of a family firm's name acts as a valuable firm resource, increasing the abnormal stock returns surrounding the firm's new product introductions. They identified the willingness of the family to protect firm reputation as the reason for this result.

Studies by Chrisman and Patel (2012), Kammerlander and Ganter (2015), Patel and Chrisman (2014), and Sciascia et al. (2015) argue that willingness to innovate is dependent on other factors. For example, Chrisman and Patel (2012) assume in their study that family firms have a lower willingness to invest in R&D due to loss aversion with respect to their socioemotional wealth and a focus on short-term family goals. However, this low willingness changes when the performance is below aspiration levels and family goals and economic goals tend to converge. In this situation, family firms are more willing to invest in R&D relative to nonfamily firms. Additionally, focusing on performance aspiration, Patel and Chrisman (2014) find that when performance exceeds aspirations, family firms manage socioemotional and economic objectives by making exploitative R&D investments that lead to more reliable and less risky sales levels. However, performance below aspirations leads to exploratory R&D investments that result in potentially higher but less reliable sales levels. Hence, the willingness of the family to invest in R&D depends on whether the performance is above or below the aspiration level.

Kammerlander and Ganter (2015) assume that willingness to innovate depends on the noneconomic goals of the family CEO. Their study shows that the family CEO's specific noneconomic goals (i.e., power and control, transgenerational value, maintenance of family reputation, the continuance of personal ties, or personal affect associated with the family business) determine whether the CEO assesses an emerging technology as sufficiently relevant to warrant a reaction from the firm. Specifically, willingness to innovate is high when the goal of the CEO is "family power and control." Sciascia et al. (2015) argue that willingness to invest in R&D depends on the overlap of family wealth and firm equity. In small and medium-sized enterprises with a high overlap between family wealth and firm equity, family ownership has a negative effect on R&D intensity due to family owners' willingness to protect SEW. If the overlap between a family's total wealth and single firm equity is low, the effect of family ownership on R&D intensity is positive because the low overlap reduces the family's loss aversion propensity, fostering R&D intensity.

These studies reveal the variability in the willingness of family firms to innovate by considering performance aspirations as a context factor. Hence, family firms' willingness to innovate is not likely to be static but rather will be dynamic and depends on context factors.

Discussion, Limitations, and Directions for Future Research

Our review presents the current state of innovation and family business research. As more and more researchers get interested in innovation in family businesses, we provide a comprehensive and up-to-date overview that future research can build on. Compared with the review by De Massis, Frattini, and Lichtenthaler (2013) and the meta-analysis by Duran et al. (2015), which both included studies published in 2012 or earlier, our review considers the recent increase in the number of published studies focusing on innovation topics in family firms by analyzing studies published through May 2015. Furthermore, our review provides an overview of the most applied theories in this area, which has not been done previously. Going one step further, our review extends the IMO approach by De Massis, Frattini, and Lichtenthaler (2013) with an ability-willingness perspective, which analyzes the literature concerning the questions, "Can family businesses innovate?" (ability) and "Are family businesses willing to innovate?" (willingness). This perspective is a recent approach that has been applied to family business research (Chrisman et al. 2015; De Massis et al. 2014) to help increase the understanding of family business behavior.

The current state of research reveals weaknesses that offer promising avenues for future research.

First, most of the studies focus on the effect of family influence on innovation inputs. Innovation inputs are critical for the innovation process because they determine the realization of innovation projects. Hence, the bulk of the research has focused on family influence on R&D-related measures. What we have learned from this research is that family firms invest occasionally more and occasionally less in R&D depending on context factors such as performance aspiration levels. However, what we do not know is how these innovation inputs transform in innovation activities and innovation outputs. A recent meta-analysis by Duran et al. (2015) showed that although family firms invest less in innovation than nonfamily firms, their innovation output of the former is higher. A holistic approach may help increase our understanding of the innovation process in family firms. Therefore, longitudinal research designs appear to be the most promising approaches because these can accompany, for example, a new product project from its funding to its market introduction.

Second, research has often focused on direct effects without considering context variables. As recent research has shown, context variables are likely to change the direction of direct effects. Hence, considering other context variables such as environmental dynamism or competitive pressure may further increase our understanding of family firm innovative behavior.

Third, future research is encouraged to include not only variables that measure the ability of family firms to innovate but also the willingness of family firms to innovate. Most studies use willingness theoretically to predict family firm innovative behavior. Kraiczy, Hack, and Kellermanns (2014) measure in their study top management team innovation orientation, a construct, which may be adapted to the families to determine their attitudes toward innovation. Furthermore, preservation of SEW, which has been often used to describe family firms that have a lower willingness to innovate, may be directly measured with the FIBER scale developed by Berrone, Cruz, and Gómez-Mejía (2012). Because the importance of SEW may differ among family firms, this heterogeneity must be considered. Kraiczy, Hack, and Kellermanns (2015) used ownership by family members on the TMT and generational stage as proxies for a high relevance of SEW as a reference point for family firms. Future research is encouraged to extend this indirect approach to measuring SEW importance by using direct measurement.

Fourth, research analyzing heterogeneity among family firms has mostly focused on innovation inputs. We encourage future research to investigate differences among family firms concerning innovation activities and outputs. Why are some family firms more innovative or more successful with innovation than other family firms? Where in the innovation process is family influence beneficial and where is it detrimental?

Fifth, current topics in innovation research such as open innovation (West and Bogers 2014), radical product innovation capability (Slater, Mohr, and Sengupta 2014), and social innovation (Schweitzer et al. 2015) must be considered in family business research to follow recent developments in innovation research.

Conclusion

Research on innovation in family firms has revealed differences between family and nonfamily firms and among family firms. Although we know that family firms are able to innovate, we know little about the willingness of family firms to innovate. Recent research has started to analyze context factors that may help increase our understanding. Additionally, a meta-analysis revealed that family firms are more effective in their innovation endeavors (Duran et al. 2015). Although family firms invest less, they obtain higher innovation outputs. Future research is encouraged to investigate context factors that determine family innovative behavior, to measure family firms' willingness to innovate directly, and to analyze more deeply the transformation of innovation inputs in innovation outputs in family firms.

Appendix 11.A Highly Ranked Journals Publishing Family Business Articles

Grade 3, 4, and 4★ Journals of the ABS Journal Ranking 2015		# of Relevant Studies
Entrepreneurship and Small Business Management		
Entrepreneurship Theory and Practice	Grade 4	4
Journal of Business Venturing	Grade 4	1
Strategic Entrepreneurship Journal	Grade 4	–
Entrepreneurship and Regional Development	Grade 3	–
Family Business Review	Grade 3	7
International Small Business Journal	Grade 3	–
Journal of Small Business Management	Grade 3	3
Small Business Economics	Grade 3	2
Journal of Family Business Strategy	*Not ranked*	4
Journal of Family Business Management	*Not ranked*	2
General Management, Ethics and Social Responsibility		
Academy of Management Journal	Grade 4★	2
Academy of Management Review	Grade 4★	1
Administrative Science Quarterly	Grade 4★	–

Grade 3, 4, and 4★ Journals of the ABS Journal Ranking 2015		*# of Relevant Studies*
Journal of Management	Grade 4★	–
British Journal of Management	Grade 4	–
Business Ethics Quarterly	Grade 4	–
Journal of Management Studies	Grade 4	–
Academy of Management Perspectives	Grade 3	–
Business and Society	Grade 3	–
California Management Review	Grade 3	–
European Management Review	Grade 3	–
Harvard Business Review	Grade 3	–
International Journal of Management Reviews	Grade 3	–
Journal of Business Ethics	Grade 3	2
Journal of Business Research	Grade 3	1
Journal of Management Inquiry	Grade 3	–
MIT Sloan Management Review	Grade 3	–
Innovation		
Journal of Product Innovation Management	Grade 4	8
Research Policy	Grade 4	1
R and D Management	Grade 3	–
Technovation	Grade 3	–
Organisation Studies		
Organization Science	Grade 4★	–
Human Relations	Grade 4	–
Leadership Quarterly	Grade 4	–
Organization Studies	Grade 4	–
Organizational Research Methods	Grade 4	–
Group and Organization Management	Grade 3	–
Organization	Grade 3	–
Research in Organizational Behavior	Grade 3	–
Research in the Sociology of Organizations	Grade 3	–
Strategy		
Strategic Management Journal	Grade 4★	1
Global Strategy Journal	Grade 3	–
Long Range Planning	Grade 3	–
Strategic Organization	Grade 3	–
Additional Financial Times Top 45 Journals		
Accounting, Organisations and Society	Grade 4★	–
Accounting Review	Grade 4★	–
American Economic Review	Grade 4★	–
Contemporary Accounting Research	Grade 4★	–
Econometrica	Grade 4★	–
Human Resource Management	Grade 4	–
Information Systems Research	Grade 4★	–
Journal of Accounting and Economics	Grade 4★	–
Journal of Accounting Research	Grade 4★	–

(Continued)

Grade 3, 4, and 4★ Journals of the ABS Journal Ranking 2015		# of Relevant Studies
Journal of Applied Psychology	Grade 4	–
Journal of Consumer Psychology	Grade 4★	–
Journal of Consumer Research	Grade 4★	–
Journal of Finance	Grade 4★	–
Journal of Financial and Quantitative Analysis	Grade 4	–
Journal of Financial Economics	Grade 4★	–
Journal of International Business Studies	Grade 4★	–
Journal of Marketing	Grade 4★	–
Journal of Marketing Research	Grade 4★	–
Journal of Operations Management	Grade 4★	–
Journal of Political Economy	Grade 4★	–
Journal of the American Statistical Association	Grade 4	–
Management Science	Grade 4★	–
Marketing Science	Grade 4★	–
MIS Quarterly	Grade 4★	–
Operations Research	Grade 4★	–
Organizational Behaviour and Human Decision Processes	Grade 4	–
Production and Operations Management	Grade 4	–
Quarterly Journal of Economics	Grade 4★	–
Rand Journal of Economics	Grade 4	–
Review of Accounting Studies	Grade 4	–
Review of Financial Studies	Grade 4★	–

★ The guide rates a journal 4★ if it is rated in the highest category by at least three out of five non-university based listings (Financial Times 45, Dallas List, VHB, Australian Deans' List, CNRS).

References

Allison, T.H., McKenny, A.F., and Short J.C. (2014) 'Integrating time into family business research: Using random coefficient modeling to examine temporal influences on family firm ambidexterity.' *Family Business Review* 27 (1):20–34.

Andersén, J. (2015) 'The absorptive capacity of family firms.' *Journal of Family Business Management* 5 (1):73–89.

Beck, L., Janssens, W., Debruyne, M., and Lommelen, T. 2011. 'A study of the relationships between generation, market orientation, and innovation in family firms.' *Family Business Review* 24 (3):252–272.

Berrone, P., Cruz, C., and Gómez-Mejía, L.R. (2012) 'Socioemotional wealth in family firms: Theoretical dimensions, assessment approaches, and agenda for future research.' *Family Business Review* 25 (3):258–279.

Block, J.H. (2012) 'R&D investments in family and founder firms: An agency perspective.' *Journal of Business Venturing* 27 (2):248–265.

Block, J.H., and Spiegel, F. (2013) 'Family firm density and regional innovation output: An exploratory analysis.' *Journal of Family Business Strategy* 4 (4):270–280.

Block, J., Miller, D., Jaskiewicz, P., and Spiegel F. (2013) 'Economic and technological importance of innovations in large family and founder firms: An analysis of patent data.' *Family Business Review* 26 (2):180–199.

Chrisman, J.J., Chua, J.H., De Massis, A., Frattini, F. and Wright, M. (2015) 'The ability and willingness paradox in family firm innovation.' *Journal of Product Innovation Management* 32 (3):310–318.

Chrisman, J.J., Chua, J.H., and Litz, R.A. (2004) 'Comparing the agency costs of family and non-family firms: Conceptual issues and exploratory evidence.' *Entrepreneurship Theory and Practice* 28 (4):335–354.

Chrisman, J.J., and Patel, P.C. (2012) 'Variations in R&D investments of family and nonfamily firms: Behavioral agency and myopic loss aversion perspectives.' *Academy of Management Journal* 55 (4):976–997.

Classen, N., Carree, M., Gils, A., and Peters, B. (2014) 'Innovation in family and non-family SMEs: An exploratory analysis.' *Small Business Economics* 42 (3):595–609.

Classen, N., Gils, A.V., Bammens, Y., and Carree, M. (2012) 'Accessing resources from innovation partners: The search breadth of family SMEs.' *Journal of Small Business Management* 50 (2):191–215.

Cohen, W.M., and Levinthal, D.A. (1990) 'Absorptive Capacity: A New Perspective on Learning and Innovation.' *Administrative Science Quarterly* 35 (1):128–152.

Craig, J.B., and Dibrell, C. (2006) 'The natural environment, innovation, and firm performance: A comparative study.' *Family Business Review* 19 (4):275–288.

Craig, J.B., Dibrell, C., and Garrett, R. (2014) 'Examining relationships among family influence, family culture, flexible planning systems, innovativeness and firm performance.' *Journal of Family Business Strategy* 5 (3):229–238.

De Massis, A., Frattini, F., and Lichtenthaler, U. (2013) 'Research on technological innovation in family firms: Present debates and future directions.' *Family Business Review* 26 (1):10–31.

De Massis, A., Frattini, F., Pizzurno, E., and Cassia, L. (2015) 'Product innovation in family versus nonfamily firms: An exploratory analysis.' *Journal of Small Business Management* 53 (1):1–36.

De Massis, A., Kotlar, J., Chua, J.H., and Chrisman, J.J. (2014) 'Ability and willingness as sufficiency conditions for family-oriented particularistic behavior: Implications for theory and empirical studies.' *Journal of Small Business Management* 52 (2):344–364.

Duran, P., Kammerlander, N., van Essen, M., and Zellweger, T. (2015) 'Doing more with less: Innovation input and output in family firms.' *Academy of Management Journal*, doi: 10.5465/amj.2014.0424.

Gómez-Mejía, L.R., Campbell, J.T., Martin, G., Hoskisson, R.E., Makri, M., and Sirmon, D.G. (2014) 'Socioemotional wealth as a mixed gamble: Revisiting family firm R&D investments with the behavioral agency model.' *Entrepreneurship Theory and Practice* 38 (6):1351–1374.

Gómez-Mejía, L.R., Cruz, C., Berrone, P., and De Castro, J., (2011) 'The bind that ties: Socioemotional wealth preservation in family firms.' *Academy of Management Annals* 5 (1):653–707.

Gómez-Mejía, L.R., Haynes, K.T., Núñez-Nickel, M., Jacobson, K.J.L., and Moyano-Fuentes, J. (2007) 'Socioemotional wealth and business risks in family-controlled firms: Evidence from Spanish olive oil mills.' *Administrative Science Quarterly* 52 (1):106–137.

Grundström, C., Öberg, C., and Rönnbäck, A.Ö. (2012) 'Family-owned manufacturing SMEs and innovativeness: A comparison between within-family successions and external takeovers.' *Journal of Family Business Strategy* 3 (3):162–173.

Hambrick, D.C., and Finkelstein, S. (1987) 'Managerial discretion: A bridge between polar views of organizational outcomes.' *Research in Organizational Behavior* 9 (2):369–406.

Hambrick, D.C., and Mason, P.A. (1984) 'Upper echelons: The organization as a reflection of its top managers.' *Academy of Management Review* 9 (2):193–206.

Hauck, J., and Prügl, R. (2015) 'Innovation activities during intra-family leadership succession in family firms: An empirical study from a socioemotional wealth perspective.' *Journal of Family Business Strategy*, doi: 10.1016/j.jfbs.2014.11.002.

Kahneman, D. (1991) 'Anomalies: The Endowment Effect, Loss Aversion, and Status Quo Bias.' *The Journal of Economic Perspectives* 5 (1):193–206.

Kahneman, D., and Tversky, A. (1979) 'Prospect theory: An analysis of decision under risk.' *Econometrica* 47 (2):263–291.

Kammerlander, N., and Ganter, M. (2015) 'An attention-based view of family firm adaptation to discontinuous technological change: Exploring the role of family CEOs' noneconomic goals.' *Journal of Product Innovation Management* 32 (3):361–383.

Kashmiri, S., and Mahajan, V. (2014) 'A rose by any other name: Are family firms named after their founding families rewarded more for their new product introductions?' *Journal of Business Ethics* 124 (1):81–99.

Kotlar, J., De Massis, A., Fang, H., and Frattini, F. (2014) 'Strategic reference points in family firms.' *Small Business Economics* 43 (3):597–619.

Kotlar, J., De Massis, A., Frattini, F., Bianchi, M., and Fang, H. (2013) 'Technology acquisition in family and nonfamily firms: A longitudinal analysis of Spanish manufacturing firms.' *Journal of Product Innovation Management* 30 (6):1073–1088.

Kotlar, J., Fang, H., De Massis, A., and Frattini, F. (2014) 'Profitability goals, control goals, and the R&D investment decisions of family and nonfamily firms.' *Journal of Product Innovation Management* 31 (6):1128–1145.

Kraiczy, N.D., Hack, A., and Kellermanns, F.W. (2014) 'New product portfolio performance in family firms.' *Journal of Business Research* 67 (6):1065–1073.

Kraiczy, N.D., Hack, A., and Kellermanns, F.W. (2015) 'What makes a family firm innovative? CEO risk-taking propensity and the organizational context of family firms.' *Journal of Product Innovation Management* 32 (3):334–348.

Llach, J., Marquès, P., Bikfalvi, A., Simon, A., and Kraus, S. (2012) 'The innovativeness of family firms through the economic cycle.' *Journal of Family Business Management* 2 (2):96–109.

March, J.G. (1991) 'Exploration and exploitation in organizational learning.' *Organization Science* 2 (1):71–78.

Matzler, K., Veider, V., Hautz, J., and Stadler, C. (2015) 'The impact of family ownership, management, and governance on innovation.' *Journal of Product Innovation Management* 32 (3):319–333.

Morck, R., Shleifer, A., and Vishny, R.W. (1988) 'Management ownership and market valuation: An empirical analysis.' *Journal of Financial Economics* 20 (1/2):293–315.

Muñoz-Bullón, F., and Sanchez-Bueno, M.J. (2011) 'The impact of family involvement on the R&D intensity of publicly traded firms.' *Family Business Review* 24 (1):62–70.

Nieto, M.J., Santamaria, L., and Fernandez, Z. (2015) 'Understanding the innovation behavior of family firms.' *Journal of Small Business Management* 53 (2):382–399.

O'Reilly, C.A., and Tushman, M.L. (2004) 'The ambidextrous organization.' *Harvard Business* 82 (4):74–81.

Patel, P.C., and Chrisman, J.J. (2014) 'Risk abatement as a strategy for R&D investments in family firms.' *Strategic Management Journal* 35 (4):617–627.

Schmid, T., Achleitner, A-K., Ampenberger, M., and Kaserer, C. (2014) 'Family firms and R&D behavior – New evidence from a large-scale survey.' *Research Policy* 43 (1):233–244.

Schulze, W.S., Lubatkin, M.H., and Dino, R.N. (2002) 'Altruism, agency, and the competitiveness of family firms.' *Managerial and Decision Economics* 23 (4/5):247–259.

Schulze, W.S., Lubatkin, M.H., and Dino, R.N. (2003a) 'Exploring the agency consequences of ownership dispersion among the directors of private family firms.' *Academy of Management Journal* 46 (2):179–194.

Schulze, W.S., Lubatkin, M.H., and Dino, R.N. (2003b) 'Toward a theory of agency and altruism in family firms.' *Journal of Business Venturing* 18 (4):473–490.

Schweitzer, F., Rau, C., Gassmann, O., and van den Hende, E. (2015) 'Technologically reflective individuals as enablers of social innovation.' *Journal of Product Innovation Management*, doi: 10.1111/jpim.12269.

Sciascia, S., Nordqvist, M., Mazzola, P., and De Massis, A. (2015) 'Family ownership and R&D intensity in small- and medium-sized firms.' *Journal of Product Innovation Management* 32 (3):349–360.

Simon, H. (2009) Hidden champions of the twenty-first century, doi. New York: Springer.

Sirmon, D.G., Arregle, J-L., Hitt, M.A., and Webb, J.W. (2008) 'The role of family influence in firms' strategic responses to threat of imitation.' *Entrepreneurship Theory and Practice* 32 (6):979–998.

Sirmon, D.G., and Hitt, M.A. (2003) 'Managing resources: Linking unique resources, management, and wealth creation in family firms.' *Entrepreneurship Theory and Practice* 27 (4):339–358.

Slater, S.F., Mohr, J.J., and Sengupta, S. (2014) 'Radical product innovation capability: Literature review, synthesis, and illustrative research propositions.' *Journal of Product Innovation Management* 31 (3):552–566.

Spriggs, M., Yu, A., Deeds, D., and Sorenson, R.L. (2013) 'Too many cooks in the kitchen: Innovative capacity, collaborative network orientation, and performance in small family businesses.' *Family Business Review* 26 (1):32–50.

Wagner, M. (2010) 'Corporate social performance and innovation with high social benefits: A quantitative analysis.' *Journal of Business Ethics* 94 (4):581–594.

West, J., and Bogers, M. (2014) 'Leveraging external sources of innovation: A review of research on open innovation.' *Journal of Product Innovation Management* 31 (4):814–831.

Wiseman, R.M., and Gómez-Mejía, L.R. (1998) 'A behavioral agency model of managerial risk taking.' *Academy of Management Review* 23 (1):133–153.

12

OPEN INNOVATION

A Literature Review and Recommendations for Family Business Research

*Jasper Brinkerink, Anita Van Gils, Yannick Bammens,
and Martin Carree*

Keywords: Open innovation, Small- and Medium-sized Enterprises, Family Firms

Introduction

By exchanging core organizational resources with their environment and renewing social interactions within and outside the family, family firms are able to build and sustain competitive advantage over many generations (Arrègle et al. 2007; Salvato and Melin 2008). Nevertheless, how the relational resources and capabilities of family firms can facilitate their innovation performance has not received much attention in our field (De Massis, Frattini, and Lichtenthaler 2013). In line with Duran et al. (2015) we believe that the opportunities residing within the networks of family firms may help explain why family businesses achieve similar or even higher innovation output compared to nonfamily firms, despite their structurally lower investments in innovation (Carney et al. 2015). We propose that valuable new insights can be obtained by applying concepts from the open innovation literature (e.g., Chesbrough 2003; Dahlander and Gann 2010) to the empirical context of family firms. As family ownership is more prevalent and more likely to affect goal setting and firm behavior among smaller, mostly private businesses than in large public corporations (Carney et al. 2015), a thorough review of open innovation in the context of small- and medium-sized enterprises (hereafter SMEs) is executed. Supplemented with the knowledge so far developed by the few family firm specific open innovation studies, this review should provide a solid base for future research on open innovation in family firms.

This chapter is structured as follows: To introduce the reader to the concept of open innovation, in *Section 2* we will commence with a brief discussion of its definition, theoretical origins, and its main dimensions. Subsequently, in *Section 3* we review the general SME literature on the opportunities and challenges that open models of innovation bring about, after which in *Section 4* we discuss the effect family involvement may have on open innovation and delineate questions for further research within the family business field.

Open Innovation

From a 'Closed' to an 'Open' view: A New Innovation Paradigm Emerges

Consistent with a Schumpeter Mark II view on the origin of innovations (Schumpeter 1942), the strategic management and innovation literature has traditionally approached the

241

development of new products and processes as an inherently closed process. Each predominantly large organization conducts its own research and development (hereafter R&D) and uses the produced knowledge to develop and commercialize its own products, services or processes. However, more in line with the earlier ideas of Schumpeter (1934), many business scholars recognize that valuable ideas and technologies may originate outside the boundaries of large corporations and actually reside within smaller companies (Acs and Audretsch 1988), public research institutions (Lee 1996), business clients or end users (Von Hippel 1986). Aggregating these findings, Chesbrough (2003) observes that more often than not, large technology companies closely monitor and source their external environment for emerging ideas or technologies. Also, these businesses are actively looking for external opportunities for valorizing their own knowledge. As such, they use *"purposive inflows and outflows of knowledge to accelerate internal innovation, and expand the markets for external use of innovation"* (Chesbrough, Vanhaverbeke, and West 2006, 1). This broad scope of interaction with external parties in the innovation process is coined 'open innovation,' and is, hence, offset against the traditional 'closed' view elaborated before (Chesbrough 2003; Chesbrough, Vanhaverbeke, and West 2006; Gassmann 2006).

In his initial work, Chesbrough (2003) integrates ideas from various well-established streams of business research, such as the literature on strategic alliances (e.g., Hagedoorn and Duysters 2002; Hamel 1991; Mowery, Oxley, and Silverman 1996; Narula and Hagedoorn 1999), research on user innovation (Von Hippel 1986), the absorptive capacity literature (Cohen and Levinthal 1990; Zahra and George 2002), literature on knowledge spillovers (Jaffe, Trajtenberg, and Henderson 1992), collaboration networks (Ahuja 2000), the notion of dynamic capabilities (Teece, Pisano, and Shuen 1997) as well as the seminal work of David Teece on why some firms profit from innovation and others do not (1986). Furthermore, in line with the resource-based view of the firm (Barney 1991; Wernerfelt 1984), Chesbrough (2003) acknowledges each firm to possess a unique combination of resources. However, he deviates from the mostly inward focused perspective of the resource based view, which poses the isolated ownership of valuable, rare and inimitable resources to be the source of superior firm profitability. Rather, the focus shifts to the lack of certain essential resources needed in the innovation process of the focal firm. Consequently, acquiring these resources externally to enhance one's own innovation process serves as a key strategy for securing the competitiveness of the firm (Chesbrough and Appleyard 2007).

Inbound and Outbound Open Innovation

Open innovation can be classified along two broad dimensions. Inbound open innovation refers to the acquisition of external knowledge to enhance the internal innovation process and complement internal R&D (Chesbrough and Crowther 2006; Huizingh 2011). Examples of activities involving inbound open innovation are formal arrangements such as acquisitions, joint ventures, inward licensing of intellectual property or contracting knowledge workers of other organizations (Gassmann, Enkel, and Chesbrough 2010), or less formal actions such as involving suppliers, business clients or lead-users in the front-end of the innovation process (Gassmann, Sandmeier, and Wecht 2006). Outbound open innovation refers to the transfer and subsequent commercialization of knowledge, technology or other resources developed in-house through external channels (Chesbrough and Crowther 2006). Examples of outbound open innovation activities are the patenting and subsequent outward licensing of intellectual property, strategic divestments and the creation of spin-off firms (Chesbrough 2003; Enkel, Gassmann, and Chesbrough 2009; Huizingh 2011).

Opening Up the Innovation Process Across Business Contexts

The open innovation paradigm initially centered on the behavior of big firms in high-tech industries. For instance, all examples used by Chesbrough in his initial work (2003) to illustrate the open innovation model are of high-technology firms in industries such as the pharmaceutical industry (Millenium/Takeda), computer hard- and software (IBM) and the semi-conductor industry (Intel). Though the vast majority of open innovation research still is conducted in the empirical context of large, high-tech firms (cf. West and Bogers 2014), the application of the open innovation paradigm is slowly extending towards different business contexts and industries. To add external validity to the open innovation model, scholars have studied the application of open innovation practices in (mostly large) firms in more mature and traditional industries (e.g., Chesbrough and Crowther 2006; Chiaroni, Chiesa, and Frattini 2011; Spithoven, Clarysse, and Knockaert 2011). A general observation is that, following the high-tech sectors, also firms in traditional industries are adopting a more open model of innovation (Chesbrough and Crowther 2006; Chiaroni, Chiesa, and Frattini 2011). Interestingly, whereas high-tech firms mostly search for complementary technologies, firms from mature industries seem to open their innovation process predominantly to access external market knowledge (Grimpe and Sofka 2009).

Also small and medium-sized enterprises have increasingly adopted open innovation models, as shown by an exploratory study by Van de Vrande et al. (2009). Although in absolute terms SMEs engage in fewer open innovation activities, these firms are more 'open' than larger corporations if one considers relative figures (Spithoven, Vanhaverbeke, and Roijakkers 2013). SMEs actively involve customers, suppliers and other members of their external network in the innovation process. Mostly, SMEs engage in open innovation for market related motives, for example to reach niche customers or to increase their market share (Lee et al. 2010; Van de Vrande et al. 2009). However, technology sourcing may also be attractive to SMEs. As resource and cognitive limitations may inhibit conducting the complete innovation process in-house, SMEs may not have any other choice than to incorporate external knowledge and technology in the development of new products. These pressures are especially salient when SMEs are active in markets characterized by high technological complexity and radical product changes (Dahlander and Gann 2010; Pullen et al. 2012). Other authors studying open innovation in an SME context corroborate these findings and establish open innovation as a highly interesting model to pursue for SMEs, as it will enable these companies to overcome the 'smallness' liabilities that present barriers to innovate for them (e.g., Colombo, Piva, and Rossi-Lamastra 2014; Parida, Westerberg, and Frishammar 2012; Wynarczyk, Piperopoulos, and McAdam 2013). However, some scholars maintain a critical stance and argue that in certain contexts open innovation may not be a valid strategic choice for SMEs (e.g., Oakey 2013). Next we will review the literature on open innovation in SMEs, to shed further light on why, when and how (family and nonfamily) SMEs may profit from opening up their innovation process.

Open Innovation in SMEs: Opportunities and Challenges

The reviewed literature on open innovation in (family) SMEs was obtained by executing the following steps early 2015: First of all we retrieved the majority of sources by searching for a combination of the terms 'open innovation,' 'openness' or 'opening' on the one hand and 'small medium enterprises,' 'SME,' 'small,' 'medium' or 'family' on the other, in Google Scholar and ISI Web of Knowledge. Second, a screening of an extensive range of peer-reviewed journals was performed. These journals were included as leading family business, strategic management, entrepreneurship and innovation journals in Anne-Will Harzing's Journal Quality List (2014) and/or identified as prominent 'open innovation outlets' by Dahlander and Gann (2010, 701). The selected journals can be found in the notes accompanying Table 12.1. Third and final, we employed a 'snowballing approach,' in which we browsed the reference lists reported in the studies obtained through the first two steps for further useful sources. The main characteristics and contributions of the final set of 32 reviewed studies are summarized in Table 12.1.

The key findings in the literature will be integrated and discussed with respect to the merits of collaborating with other organizations in the innovation process and specific opportunities for inbound and outbound open innovation activities. Additionally, we will discuss the main hampering factors experienced by SMEs in implementing a more open innovation model. The reader will notice that most SME studies in our review do not explicitly distinguish family from nonfamily firms in their respective samples (see the second column of Table 12.1). However, based on our extensive knowledge of the presence of family firms among SMEs in most economies (e.g., Astrachan and Shanker 2003; Flören 1998; Klein 2000), one can safely assume that the samples used in most of the studies include many family SMEs. Especially big representative survey data sets, such as the Community Innovation Survey data (e.g., Barge-Gil 2010; Laursen and Salter 2006; Spithoven, Vanhaverbeke, and Roijakkers 2013) or data obtained from seemingly representative samples of broad manufacturing industries (e.g., Huang and Rice 2009; Moreno-Menéndez and Casillas 2014; Nieto and Santamaría 2010; Tomlinson and Fai 2013) have been amply proven in family business studies to contain large shares of family firms (e.g., Chrisman et al. 2007; Classen et al. 2014). Therefore, one should keep in mind that in the remainder of this review, when we discuss 'SMEs' we are implicitly talking about family SMEs as well, even if the original authors do not take family involvement into account. The limited number of studies that does explicitly study family firms will be discussed in Section 4 to highlight those aspects of open innovation that are particularly salient for family SMEs. Together, the SME and family SME open innovation literatures provide a solid knowledge base upon which future family business research can build.

Opportunities

The relatively small resource bases inherent to SMEs poses constraints on the internal capacity for developing new products or processes (Hewitt-Dundas 2006). This 'liability of smallness' (e.g., Dahlander and Gann 2010; Parida, Westerberg, and Frishammar 2012; Spithoven, Vanhaverbeke, and Roijakkers 2013) manifests itself in limited access to financial resources (Beck and Demirgüç-Kunt 2006; Carpenter and Petersen 2002), human capital (Madrid-Guijarro, García, and Van Auken 2009) and in general in a lack of organizational structures supporting innovation (Pullen et al. 2009).

Because of increasingly rapid technological change and shortening product life cycles facing many SMEs, their limited research budgets and relatively small pools of research personnel strongly inhibit the capability of these firms to respond fast enough to their changing environment. These limitations may partially be overcome if SMEs broaden their search area for innovative technologies beyond the boundaries of their firm. Actively searching the environment for complementary external knowledge significantly improves innovative performance (Fu 2012; Laursen and Salter 2006; Lee et al. 2010; Nieto and Santamaría 2010; Parida, Westerberg, and Frishammar 2012). In fact, externally sourced knowledge complements internal R&D (Laursen and Salter 2006; Wynarczyk 2013) and as such may enable SMEs to bridge the innovation gap with large firms (Nieto and Santamaría 2010).

Where then should SMEs search for complementary technological knowledge and resources? Recent research indicates that publicly funded research centers, such as universities

Table 12.1 Overview of Literature on Open Innovation in Family and Nonfamily SMEs

Authors (Year)	Explicit Focus on Family Firms?	Goal of Study	Deployed Theories and Theoretical Concepts	Data Used in Study	Key Conclusions of Study
Barge-Gil (2010)	No	To assess the relationship between degree of openness and firm characteristics.	Absorptive capacity	Spanish CIS panel data with 10,875 observations.	Medium-sized firms both have the need and the absorptive capacity to engage in open innovation. Small firms have the need for openness, but lack the absorptive capacity.
Bianchi, Campodall'Orto, Frattini & Vercesi (2010)	No	Providing a practical tool for assessing viable opportunities for out-licensing a firm's technologies.	–	Application of tool to one particular packaging company.	Licensing their technology to other firms presents an interesting alternative to reach the market for SMEs with bounded resources. The authors develop a tool which SMEs can use to see if their technology could be interesting for other firms. Cognitive boundaries make it difficult for small firms to identify alternative applications for their technology. Furthermore, disclosing their intellectual property without losing their technology is difficult for SMEs. Small businesses often have a hard time negotiating a favorable position in collaboration agreements.
Brunswicker & Vanhaverbeke (2015)	No	Exploring how SMEs engage in external knowledge sourcing.	–	Sample of 1,411 European SMEs from 7 industry groups.	SMEs that have open innovation relationships with various types of partners show the best innovation performance. Especially deep interaction with direct and indirect customers fosters innovation success. SMEs need to have innovation strategy and development processes in place to facilitate successful open innovation. Also, formal innovation project control mechanisms facilitate the success of open innovation activities.

(Continued)

Authors (Year)	Explicit focus on family firms?	Goal of study	Deployed theories and theoretical concepts	Data used in study	Key conclusions of study
Burcharth & Fosfuri (2015)	No	Test the relationship between institutionalized socialization practices and the negative attitudes towards external knowledge, the so-called not-invented-here (NIH) syndrome.	Social identity theory; Organizational socialization	Survey data on 169 Danish SMEs from medium- to high-tech manufacturing sectors.	Institutionalized socialization processes lead to a more negative stance towards external knowledge. Technologically specialized firms are more positive or open towards external knowledge. Interestingly, in these highly technologically specialized firms, institutionalized socialization processes have a positive effect on the attitude towards external knowledge.
Burcharth, Knudsen & Sondergaard (2014)	No	Assess how the not-invented-here (NIH) and the not-shared-here syndrome (NSH) impact the engagement of SMEs in open innovation practices.	–	Survey data on 331 Danish manufacturing SMEs.	Inbound (through NIH) and outbound (through NSH) open innovation practices are negatively influenced by the attitudes of employees towards the acquisition and sharing of knowledge. The impact of these attitudes can be effectively diminished by using specific types of training programs.
Classen, Van Gils, Bammens & Carree (2012)	Yes	Investigating differences in use of external cooperation partners between family and nonfamily SMEs.	Behavioral theory; Socioemotional wealth; Absorptive capacity	Sample of 167 Dutch and Belgian manufacturing SMEs.	Among SMEs, those with significant family ownership apply less broad search for external resources along various types of partners.

Author (Year)		Purpose	Theory	Sample	Findings
De Massis, Frattini, Pizzurno & Cassia (2015)	Yes	Studying how family firms manage product innovation.	Resource based view; Agency theory; Stewardship theory; Behavioral theory	Multiple case studies, based on data from 10 SMEs: 5 family–owned, 5 nonfamily firms.	Family firms might prefer to set up collaborations with partners (e.g., universities, research centers) that do not involve potential control losses. With suppliers only if strong IP regimes prevent involuntary knowledge spillovers. Horizontal collaboration (i.e., with potential competitors) is not very popular among family SMEs, probably because of potential threats to the family's socioemotional wealth.
Drechsler & Natter (2012)	No	Investigating the drivers of openness.	Absorptive capacity	German CIS data on 2,422 firms.	Factors that prevent firms from opening up are lack of technological and market knowledge, ineffective IP protection and imitation threats. Factors that increase firm openness are the need for financial funding in innovation and effectiveness of a firm's IP protection mechanisms.
Fu (2012)	No	Investigating the moderating effect of open innovation on the relationship between incentive schemes and innovation.	Agency theory	406 British manufacturing and business service firms.	Open innovation can give small firms easier and greater access to (inter)national markets. Actively searching for complementary external knowledge significantly improves innovative output. Several challenges: Risk of losing valuable knowledge. Also, larger budget constraints for SMEs makes that investment in open innovation should go at the expense of internal R&D. Opening up the innovation process brings about high coordination costs. Furthermore, information shortage makes choosing the right partner difficult. Shortage of time and money make open innovation difficult to pursue for SMEs. Openness and incentives act as substitutes in their effect on innovativeness.
Huang & Rice (2009)	No	Testing interaction effects between open innovation strategies and absorptive capacity.	Absorptive capacity	Panel set of 292 Australian manufacturing SMEs.	Technology acquisition alone has negative effects on innovation. Only when accompanied by sufficient absorptive capacity will it benefit SME innovation performance. Networking has strong positive implications for innovation, but only if the SME has sufficient absorptive capacity.

(Continued)

Authors (Year)	Explicit focus on family firms?	Goal of study	Deployed theories and theoretical concepts	Data used in study	Key conclusions of study
Kotlar, De Massis, Frattini, Bianchi & Fang (2013)	Yes	Capturing the impact of behavioral considerations on the technology acquisition decisions of family and nonfamily firms.	Behavioral theory	Panel data set on 1,540 companies in 20 Spanish manufacturing industries.	There is a negative relationship between technology acquisition and family management. External acquisition of technology forces family managers to give up part of their discretionary control over innovation trajectories, which they do not want. Among family firms, the effect of negative performance aspiration gaps on external technology acquisition is smaller than among nonfamily firms. The acquisition of external technologies is more attractive for family firms when their technology can be protected by means of intellectual property rights.
Lasagni (2012)	No	Investigating the role of external relationships in small business innovativeness.	Absorptive capacity	490 SMEs from six European countries.	Active relationships with suppliers and users enhance innovation. Also, relationships with research institutes are proven to be effective.
Laursen & Salter (2006)	No	Linking search strategy, in terms of search depth and breadth, to innovative performance.	Absorptive capacity	CIS survey data on 2,707 UK manufacturing firms.	External information can complement knowledge created through internal R&D. Collaborating with multiple partners is beneficial for innovation outcomes. Also, the strength of the collaborations determines innovative performance. There are both an optimal depth and breadth of collaborative ties. Too many ties and too deep relationships cause over-complexity and over-embeddedness.
Lecocq & Demil (2006)	No	Investigating an open innovation system in a low-tech setting.	–	Data on 193 companies playing a role in the tabletop role-playing game industry.	The core of a business model may be already developed by incumbents. Through that, entry barriers in an industry can be significantly lower if a company decides to join an open innovation system. New/small firms therefore do not have to build the core technology themselves if they join open innovation system.

Author (Year)	Family firm	Aim	Theory	Data	Findings
Lee, Park, Yoon & Park (2010)	No	Developing understanding of open innovation in the SME context and to suggest the input of a network intermediary in facilitating innovation.	–	Survey data from 2,743 Korean SMEs and larger firms.	Networks of collaborating SMEs generate shorter time-to-market of innovative ideas, because firms can focus on activities that lie closest to their core. Furthermore, market uncertainty can be reduced by effective networking. Also, collaboration may enhance the creation of other innovative ideas. Networking gives access to much needed external financial and human capital. Allying with network intermediaries enhances innovation opportunities. High transaction costs are named as the biggest network-challenge for SMEs. Imitation of valuable technological assets is a risk when engaging in open innovation.
Moreno-Menéndez & Casillas (2014)	No	Studying the relationship between open innovation and internationalization.	Network theory; Resource based view	Sample of 424 Spanish manufacturing SMEs.	Open innovation is instrumental to internationalization, because it requires firms to develop internal capabilities for managing international relationships. International innovation networks give access to foreign contacts, and international opportunities.
Nieto & Santamaria (2010)	No	Analyzing how collaboration serves as an important innovation input factor for SMEs.	–	Panel data set containing data on 1,300 Spanish manufacturing firms.	Technological collaboration allows SMEs to bridge the innovation gap with large firms. Specifically regarding product innovation, collaboration is a key input. Working with vertical partners is especially crucial for performance.
Nieto, Santamaria & Fernández (2015)	Yes	Examining the innovation behavior of family firms.	Resource based view; Agency theory	Unbalanced panel data set of Spanish manufacturing firms containing 15,173 observations.	Family firms are less prone to engage in technological collaboration to access external resources, suggesting that certain aspects of family influence may hinder opening up innovation.

(Continued)

Authors (Year)	Explicit focus on family firms?	Goal of study	Deployed theories and theoretical concepts	Data used in study	Key conclusions of study
Oakey (2013)	No	Relating the open innovation concept to the context of high-tech SMEs.	–	Conceptual study.	Open innovation may not fit with the confidentiality required in the development of high-technology small firms. As such, not engaging in open innovation may also be a valid strategic choice.
Padilla-Meléndez, Del Aguila-Obra & Lockett (2013)	No	Exploring the role of social capital in enabling knowledge transfer and exchange between higher education institutions and spin-off SMEs.	Social capital	18 in depth semi-structured interviews and a semi-structured questionnaire.	Knowledge transfer and exchange is an attractive option for SMEs to gain access to new technologies. SMEs are often not aware of developments in universities and other research organizations, resulting in missed opportunities. Ensuring formal agreement on expectations concerning partners'' behavior and commitment is vital.
Parida, Westerberg & Frishammar (2012)	No	Investigating the effect of four open innovation activities on innovation performance of SMEs.	Absorptive capacity	Survey data from 252 Swedish high-tech SMEs.	Scouting technology externally helps SMEs in pursuit of radical innovation. Depending on the type of innovation pursued, horizontal and/ or vertical collaboration enhance innovative performance. SMEs suffer from their smallness in the sense that it imposes constraints on resources and capabilities.
Pullen, Weerd-Nederhof, Groen & Fisscher (2012)	No	Building on configuration theory, this paper examines multiple network relationships simultaneously in relation to innovation performance.	Configuration theory	Survey data on 60 SMEs in the Dutch medical devices sector, triangulated with 50 interviews.	The most successful innovators serve as suppliers to distributors rather than selling directly to end consumers. Complementarity within an NPD network is the most important prerequisite for successful innovation. A key challenge is to retain a business-like approach to networking. The best performing innovators have a relatively closed NPD networking approach.

Author (year)		Purpose	Perspective	Data	Key findings
Roper & Hewitt-Dundas (2013)	No	Exploring the open innovation catalyzing function of publicly funded R&D centers.	Absorptive capacity	Monitored data on the external connections of 18 R&D centers.	Publicly funded research centers offer relatively open access to new knowledge and as such may enhance innovation opportunities for SMEs. A high need exists to ensure the fit between the research focus of publicly funded R&D centers and the needs of smaller firms.
Spithoven, Vanhaverbeke & Roijakkers (2013)	No	Exploring how SMEs and larger firms differ in their use of open innovation practices, and the extent to which these firms benefit from open innovation practices.	–	CIS data from 967 Belgian innovative firms.	SMEs benefit more from the use of protection mechanisms than larger firms; perhaps they patent more efficiently, or only the innovations with the greatest market potential. Open innovation activities contribute to relative revenues from new products only for smaller companies, corroborating the view that SMEs depend more on networking. SMEs do not have enough financial and human resources to systematically search their environment for relevant external knowledge and benefit less from external search. SMEs generate fewer marketable products from their open innovation initiatives than larger firms.
Theyel (2013)	No	Assessing the adoption of open innovation practices during different value chain activities.	Resource based view; Dynamic capabilities; Value chain perspective	Survey data on 293 US manufacturing SMEs.	Opportunities for collaboration exist across all value chain activities. Not all forms of collaboration positively relate to innovation performance. Rather, it depends on partner choice (i.e., supplier or customer). Also, it may depend on the mode of collaboration (in terms of value chain activity).
Tomlinson & Fai (2013)	No	Conducting a broader measurement of SME co-operation to capture the multi-scalar and multi-dimensional nature of cooperation	Absorptive capacity	Survey data on 371 UK manufacturing SMEs.	Cooperation with suppliers enhances product and process innovation. Cooperation with buyers enhances product innovation. Horizontal collaboration does not affect innovative performance. In spite of the potential gains from cooperative innovation efforts, SMEs may shy away from them because the inherent difficulties of nurturing such relationships

(Continued)

Authors (Year)	Explicit focus on family firms?	Goal of study	Deployed theories and theoretical concepts	Data used in study	Key conclusions of study
Vahter, Love & Roper (2014)	No	Exploring whether and how the benefits of openness in innovation are different for small firms compared to medium and large ones.	Absorptive capacity	Panel data set on Irish manufacturing firms, containing 3842 observations.	Although SMEs have fewer linkages than large firms, innovative linkages contribute more to innovative sales for SMEs than for larger firms. SMEs thus seem to have more to gain from collaboration than larger firms. There is an optimal amount of linkages, too few will offer limited opportunities, too many will result in too high coordination costs. This limit is reached earlier by SMEs than by large firms.
Van der Meer (2007)	No	Descriptive analysis of adoption of open innovation in Dutch industry.	-	Survey data from 814 Dutch firms.	The biggest challenge lies in the flexible and open way of handling business models. Many SME entrepreneurs recognize their 'normal' way of thinking in open innovation principles.
Van de Vrande, De Jong, Vanhaverbeke & De Rochemont (2009)	No	Investigating if open innovation practices are also applied by SMEs, and identifying motivations and hampering factors concerning the engagement in open innovation activities.	-	Survey data on 605 innovative Dutch manufacturing SMEs.	SMEs are increasingly adopting open innovation approaches. Market-related motivations (such as better serving existing customers and opening up new markets) are the biggest motivation for SMEs to open up their innovation process. Customers form a fertile ground for innovative ideas. Informal open innovation practices such as customer involvement and networking are less capital intensive and as such particularly interesting for resource-constrained SMEs. Especially in the pursuit for external technology, SMEs find it difficult to connect with reliable and qualitatively sound partners. Dealing with increased external contacts presents SMEs with a number of organizational and cultural issues. Uncommitted employees and resistance to change are also often mentioned as hampering factors.

Vanhaverbeke, Vermeersch & De Zutter (2012)	No	Research report on how SMEs and start-ups can benefit from open innovation strategies.	–	Multiple case-studies on 10 SMEs from Belgium, Denmark, and the Netherlands.	Collaboration seems particularly likely to happen with the SME's value chain partners. Cooperation with technology partners is less common among SMEs. In changing their business model, SMEs need to rely on innovation partners. IP management in partnerships is important to avoid tensions in the network. In order to capture maximum value from collaborative innovation, SMEs need to organize themselves internally to learn from their partners.
Wincent, Anokhin & Boter (2009)	No	Studying how boards of open innovation networks should be organized in order to enhance the innovative status of network participants.	–	Longitudinal data on 53 Swedish strategic small-firm networks.	Networks of collaborating SMEs may appoint network boards. These boards are most effective at either low or high rates of member renewal.
Wynarczyk (2013)	No	Assessing the impact of open innovation practices on the innovation capability and export performance of SMEs.	Absorptive capacity	Survey data on 64 UK science and technology based SMEs.	Open innovation significantly predicts SME export performance. Open innovation complements R&D in achieving international competitiveness. SMEs lack knowledge and awareness of external opportunities.

Note: Several studies that specifically focus on (open source) software SMEs (e.g., Colombo, Piva, and Rossi-Lamastra 2014; Gruber and Henkel 2006) are neither included in the summary table, nor in the review of challenges and opportunities. Though certain common principles apply, the empirical context is too different from the more traditionally operating SMEs that are typically family owned. The following journals were included in the literature search: *Academy of Management Annals, Academy of Management Journal, Academy of Management Review, Administrative Science Quarterly, California Management Review, Creativity and Innovation Management, Economics of Innovation and New Technology, Entrepreneurship and Regional Development, Entrepreneurship Theory and Practice, Family Business Review, Industrial and Corporate Change, Industry and Innovation, International Small Business Journal, International Journal of Entrepreneurial Behavior and Research, International Journal of Technology Management, Journal of Business Venturing, Journal of Engineering and Technology Management, Journal of Business Research, Journal of Family Business Strategy, Journal of Management Studies, Journal of Management, Journal of Product Innovation Management, Journal of Small Business Management, Management Science, MIT Sloan Management Review, Organization Science, R&D Management, Research Policy, Research-Technology Management, Small Business Economics, Strategic Management Journal, Strategic Organization, Technovation.*

and polytechnics, offer relatively open and low-cost access to new knowledge and as such may enhance the innovation opportunities for some SMEs (Lasagni 2012; Padilla-Meléndez, Del Aguila-Obra, and Lockett 2013; Roper and Hewitt-Dundas 2013). Other inbound open innovation opportunities for SMEs can be found across the firm's value chain partners (Theyel 2013). First, looking upstream, suppliers offer a fertile ground for innovative ideas, for example concerning product design or streamlining of production processes (Lasagni 2012; Tomlinson and Fai 2013). Second, downstream relationships may offer cheap yet very effective advice for SMEs on how to improve their products. Indeed, actively involving customers in the development of new products positively affects the innovation performance of SMEs (Brunswicker and Vanhaverbeke 2015) and increases the revenues generated from new and improved products (Tomlinson and Fai 2013). In sum, vertical partners are a great source of performance-enhancing external knowledge (Nieto and Santamaría 2010; Parida, Westerberg, and Frishammar 2012) and are more likely to be used as such by SMEs than (horizontal) competitors (Vanhaverbeke, Vermeersch, and De Zutter 2012). However, even collaboration with competitors may succeed. Networks of collaborating SMEs function best when intermediaries act as brokers between potential innovation partners (Lee et al. 2010) and a group level governance structure mitigates misappropriation concerns (Wincent, Anokhin, and Boter 2009).

Smallness liabilities faced by SMEs do not only create difficulties regarding the development of technologies. In general having limited market power and few marketing resources (Knight 2000) and relatively narrow cognitive boundaries (Bianchi et al. 2010), SMEs also have a hard time finding commercial applications for their internally developed technologies, which significantly deters their innovation potential (Hewitt-Dundas 2006). Moreover, even if opportunities are identified, due to time and resource constraints exploiting proprietary technologies through the in-house development of new products based on these technologies is often hard for SMEs (Bianchi et al. 2010).

Through strategically pursuing outbound open innovation activities, SMEs may find applications for their technologies by using more effective external pathways to the market, which require fewer resources to be invested (Bianchi et al. 2014). Moreover, by allowing commercialization of the firm's knowledge outside its boundaries, redundant or otherwise unused technologies can be taken off the shelves and generate additional profits. Following this reasoning, utilizing external market opportunities is a dominant motivation for SMEs to open up their innovation process (Van de Vrande et al. 2009). Rightly so, as the time-to-market for innovative ideas can be significantly reduced by effective networking (Lee et al. 2010), and (international) markets can be accessed easier and to a larger extent by connecting with the right innovation partners (Fu 2012; Moreno-Menéndez and Casillas 2014; Wynarczyk 2013).

In a similar vein, the typically specialized knowledge of SMEs may be leveraged by connecting their niche technologies to business models of which the core has already been developed by industry incumbents, thereby allowing for synergies and significantly lowering the entry barriers in new industries (Lecocq and Demil 2006). By acknowledging that the full internal development of products may be unfeasible and subsequently joining such systems of open innovation, SMEs can focus on the activities that lie closest to their core and the overall innovation process is more resource efficient (Lee et al. 2010). As a viable mode of external commercialization, Bianchi et al. (2010) propagate the strategic out-licensing of proprietary technology and develop a practical tool which SMEs can use to assess the external uses of these technologies. Although Bianchi et al. (2010) stress the difficulties SMEs seem to encounter in finding external applications for their technologies, encouraging findings by Spithoven, Vanhaverbeke, and Roijakkers (2013) show that SMEs profit to a larger extent from their patented technologies.

Challenges

If both the external sourcing of complementary technologies and the external commercialization of proprietary technology offer ample potential benefits, why are some SMEs still hesitant to open up their firm's boundaries? Throughout the literature studied for this review, a number of common themes resonate, together capturing the main challenges and hampering factors experienced by SMEs in the implementation of a more open model of innovation. First, cognitive boundaries imposed by limited financial, managerial and network resources make that SMEs often lack the knowledge and awareness of external opportunities (Drechsler and Natter 2012; Spithoven, Vanhaverbeke, and Roijakkers 2013; Wynarczyk 2013), both residing within the business environment (Bianchi et al. 2010; Van de Vrande et al. 2009) and at universities and other knowledge institutes (Padilla-Meléndez, Del Aguila-Obra, and Lockett 2013; Roper and Hewitt-Dundas 2013). Second, and related to this lack of awareness and information, comes the difficulty SMEs experience in choosing partners of appropriate quality (Fu 2012). Third, reliability of partners is sometimes hard to assess prior to establishing the partnership (Van de Vrande et al. 2009). The risk of involuntarily losing their valuable intellectual property (Bianchi et al. 2010; Drechsler and Natter 2012; Fu 2012) and consequently the risk of imitation of their technology by competitors (Lee et al. 2010) may be a justifiable reason for SMEs not to engage in collaborative innovation initiatives (Oakey 2013). Fourth, SMEs need to have certain formal innovation- and development structures and processes in place (Brunswicker and Vanhaverbeke 2015; Van de Vrande et al. 2009) to secure sufficient absorptive capacity for assimilating the additional knowledge inflow (Barge-Gil 2010; Huang and Rice 2009). These required organizational structures may pose too much of a burden on resource-constrained SMEs. Fifth, the transaction and coordination costs involved in maintaining and controlling open innovation ties are often perceived as very high (Fu 2012; Lee et al. 2010; Padilla-Meléndez, Del Aguila-Obra, and Lockett 2013), and sometimes judged to outweigh the benefits of increasing the SME's openness (Tomlinson and Fai 2013). Indeed, research shows that there are both an optimal number of open innovation partners and an optimal 'depth' of the relationships with these partners; too many ties will create over-complexity, whereas too 'deep' ties may result in over-embeddedness (Laursen and Salter 2006). These findings are confirmed by Vahter, Love, and Roper (2014), who also show that this 'optimal number' of ties is lower for SMEs than for larger firms, as SMEs have too little managerial capacity to handle bigger portfolios of open innovation partners. Sixth and last, both towards the inflow of external knowledge (labeled the not-invented-here syndrome) and the outflow of internally developed knowledge (the not-sold-here virus) organizational members of SMEs often take on a negative attitude (Burcharth and Fosfuri 2015; Burcharth, Knudsen, and Søndergaard 2014). This negative attitude forces SMEs to shy away from open innovation activities (Burcharth, Knudsen, and Søndergaard 2014), which supports the observation by Van de Vrande et al. (2009) that uncommitted employees and a general resistance to change are among the top factors hampering the successful implementation of a more open model of innovation.

To conclude, our discussion of opportunities and challenges elicits several factors that shape the degree to which SMEs apply and profit from open innovation activities. These factors either affect the desirability of using open or closed innovation strategies or relate more to the ability to do so, as we visualize in the matrix in Figure 12.1.

The desirability of adopting an open innovation model is increased by prospects of easier market access and a shorter time-to-market, as well as shortening product life cycles or the possession of technology which is not used internally and may thus be commercialized externally. On the other hand, internal resistance to both the adoption of external knowledge and the sharing of own ideas, and the risk of involuntary knowledge spillovers decrease the desirability

	Factors affecting ability	Factors affecting desirability
Factors favoring open innovation	Limited internal research budgets Limited internal research personnel Specialized knowledge and technologies (Family) social capital*	Decreasing product life cycles Easier market access Shorter time to market No internal use for technologies Desirability of connectedness*
Factors favoring closed innovation	Limited awareness of open innovation opportunities Lack of supporting organizational structures for open innovation Limited diversity in management*	Not-invented-here and not-sold-here attitudes Risk of involuntary knowledge spillovers Protection of control and broder socioemotional wealth*

* = Additional factors argued to be more important for family firms

Figure 12.1   Factors Affecting Open Innovation in (Family) SMEs

of open innovation models. The desire to pursue either a closed or an open innovation model is however not a sufficient condition for successful implementation of the chosen approach. Certain capabilities are essential to the feasibility and effectiveness of either innovation model (Lichtenthaler and Lichtenthaler 2009). The possession of certain resources or capabilities (e.g., niche technologies and highly specialized knowledge), or the lack of those (e.g., limited internal research budgets and personnel bases) are factors that push SMEs towards more open models of innovation. Conversely, the ability to engage in open innovation activities is negatively affected by other factors (e.g., the lack of awareness of open innovation opportunities and supporting structures), thus advocating a relatively closed innovation strategy.

Barge-Gil (2010) illustrates the tensions that may arise between issues of ability and desirability. His findings suggest that although both small and medium-sized companies have a need for a fairly open innovation model, the smallest firms may lack certain abilities to incorporate external knowledge in their innovation process and therefore find it difficult to increase their openness relative to medium-sized firms. However, the aggregate findings of Barge-Gil (2010) do not explain why for so many smaller firms open innovation seems to come as a second nature (Van Der Meer 2007; Vanhaverbeke, Vermeersch, and De Zutter 2012). SMEs are heterogeneous in the innovation trajectories they wish to follow (e.g., Mangematin et al. 2003) and the nature of the innovations they pursue (i.e., radical or incremental innovation; process or product innovation, see for example Massa and Testa 2008). Hence, abilities and desires may play out differently among different SMEs. Future studies may therefore aim to disentangle the highly heterogeneous population of SMEs and investigate which characteristics of these firms facilitate proper alignment of desirability and ability regarding the implementation of open innovation models.

A commonly identified source of SME heterogeneity is the presence or absence of a dominant business family, which may bring about various strategic implications (Habbershon and Williams 1999). We believe that family involvement in the business, which may manifest itself through family ownership, family management or less formal channels of influence on strategic behavior (Astrachan, Klein, and Smyrnios 2002), affects various aspects of open innovation. In the final section, we will therefore assess the current state of our knowledge on the impact of family involvement on the openness of SMEs and integrate this knowledge in the broader context of technological innovation in family SMEs, thereby identifying several broad opportunities for future research.

Family Influence on Open Innovation: Terra Incognita

Current Knowledge

The knowledge base regarding the effect of family involvement on a firm's open innovation activities is rather limited (cf. De Massis, Frattini, and Lichtenthaler 2013). This is remarkable, since family firms are renowned for their highly idiosyncratic relationship building- and maintenance skills (Arrègle et al. 2007; Cennamo et al. 2012), suggesting that these businesses may have access to a very specific array of open innovation opportunities. Sirmon and Hitt (2003) propose that the rich social capital of business families, together with their patient capital and transgenerational outlook allows family firms to derive more value from their cooperative behavior. The stewardship characteristics of family businesses further increase the desirability of building connections with external stakeholders (Miller, Le Breton-Miller, and Scholnick 2008). Moreover, ample research has established that family businesses, both publicly traded organizations and private SMEs, systematically invest fewer financial resources in R&D compared to firms without family ownership (Block 2012; Carney et al. 2015; Chrisman and Patel 2012; Classen et al. 2014). Family firms may thus be at a disadvantage when it comes to autonomously generating sufficient innovative output to secure the long-term, transgenerational family involvement which so often is at the heart of their strategic interests (Le Breton-Miller and Miller 2006; Lumpkin and Brigham 2011; Lumpkin, Brigham, and Moss 2010; Zellweger et al. 2012). To secure their long-term existence, family businesses may therefore have to rely more on collaborative innovation modes than their nonfamily counterparts.

The studies conducted till thus far unanimously focus on the search and acquisition of external (technological) resources to enhance the internal innovation process, in line with the inbound dimension of open innovation. Contrary to the motivations outlined before, common findings are that family firms search and acquire external technological resources to a lower extent than firms without significant family involvement (Classen et al. 2012; Kotlar et al. 2013; Nieto, Santamaria, and Fernández 2015). More specific, Classen et al. (2012) establish that Dutch and Belgian family manufacturing SMEs search their environment less broadly than nonfamily SMEs, making use of a less diverse set of partners in the innovation process. Similarly, Nieto, Santamaria, and Fernández (2015) find in their analysis of a large sample of Spanish firms that family businesses are less inclined to turn to external sources for innovation. Furthermore, they find that technological collaboration is avoided by family firms. Additional robustness is provided by Kotlar et al. (2013), who show that family firms acquire significantly less external R&D than other companies. Moreover, negative performance aspiration gaps provide less of an incentive to acquire external technologies for family firms than for nonfamily businesses.

These findings raise the question whether the lower use of external technologies by family SMEs is grounded in issues of ability or desirability. Based on the argumentation and findings in these respective studies, the answer seems to be a bit of both (cf. Figure 12.1). On the one hand, the lower engagement in inbound open innovation is attributed to limited cognitive diversity, partially due to the restricted access to qualified human capital family firms encounter (Classen et al. 2012). This lack of qualified managerial talent, combined with relatively low absorptive capacity derived from their aforementioned limited internal research base constrain family firms in the search for-, and assimilation of external knowledge (Classen et al. 2012; Nieto, Santamaria, and Fernández 2015). On the other hand, though, to gain access to external technologies, a certain level of disclosure of sensitive information related to the core technology of the family firm may be necessary. In addition, partners may require a certain voice in the decision making process (Nieto, Santamaria, and Fernández 2015). Including too many external parties in the innovation process might, therefore, come at the expense of the control the family has over the strategic direction of the firm and, hence, the independence family owners typically prioritize (Kotlar et al. 2013; Nieto, Santamaria, and Fernández 2015). As this control facilitates the preservation of the family's socioemotional wealth (e.g., Gómez-Mejía et al. 2011), refraining from external technology acquisition may be a deliberate and rational choice (Classen et al. 2012). Qualitative evidence gathered by De Massis et al. (2015) highlights that through a fear of involuntary knowledge spillovers and diminished control, potential socioemotional wealth losses indeed form a key motivation for family firms to abstain from technological collaborations with other businesses.

Both the ability and desirability issues outlined in the previous paragraph can be somewhat counterbalanced. Regarding the former, Classen et al. (2012) show that family SMEs gain in terms of search breadth and opportunity recognition if they are led by a CEO who underwent university education. Furthermore, including nonfamily managers in the top management team is beneficial for the family SME's external outlook, especially when the inclusion of outsiders increases the educational background diversity of the top management team (Classen et al. 2012). With regard to the 'desirability' problem, family firms seem less reluctant to engage in collaborative innovation initiatives when misappropriation risks are mitigated. Therefore, sourcing technological resources from parties that require less control over the application of these resources, such as universities or other public research centers, may offer relatively 'safe' opportunities for family firms (De Massis et al. 2015). Additionally, in contexts characterized by strong intellectual property regimes, family businesses are less afraid of involuntary knowledge spillovers, which mitigates the negative attitude towards technological collaboration (De Massis et al. 2015; Kotlar et al. 2013).

Clearly, though the discussed studies offer the first insight, a lot remains to be uncovered regarding the relevance of open innovation models for family firms. To facilitate a broader investigation, in the final section we will delineate several research directions that may guide and encourage family business scholars in the process of bringing forward our knowledge regarding this matter.

Future Research

Antecedents to openness: Desirability and ability

The desirability and ability factors discussed before deserve more attention in future studies. Regarding the desirability of open innovation, prior work (Classen et al. 2012; De Massis et al. 2015; Kotlar et al. 2013) already highlights the importance family firm owners attach to maintaining control over their firm's activities to protect their socioemotional wealth. Hence, control concerns negatively influence the desirability of open innovation activities. However, recent discourse stresses the multidimensionality of socioemotional wealth and encourages scholars to consider nonfinancial aspects of family firm ownership beyond firm control (e.g., Berrone, Cruz, and Gómez-Mejía 2012; Miller and Le Breton-Miller 2014). Other, perhaps more positive aspects of socioemotional wealth, such as reputation building (Deephouse and Jaskiewicz 2013) or the family's concern for transgenerational continuity (Lumpkin and Brigham 2011) may increase the attractiveness of setting up and nurturing collaborative relationships.

Similarly, deeper understanding is needed concerning the ability of family firms to benefit from open innovation opportunities. Recent studies highlight family firms' limitations regarding human capital and abortive capacity (Classen et al. 2012). What we do not know, however, is how the quality of family firms' rich social capital (Sirmon and Hitt 2003), rather than the number of collaborative ties, enables family firms to extract valuable knowledge from their environment. Family firms have benefits when it comes to maintaining long-term quality relationships with close stakeholders such as customers and suppliers (Bingham et al. 2011; Schmieder 2014). Their reputation of trustworthiness is likely to enhance family firms' attractiveness as innovation partners, and may consequently lead to more opportunities for collaboration (Huybrechts et al. 2011). Some caution should be used though if trustworthiness is signaled by family firms to attract innovation partners. When trust in an open innovation relationship becomes a unidirectional construct and the innovation partner behaves as a free rider, or the family firm gets over-embedded in the sharing of knowledge and resources, the future of the family business can be seriously harmed (Steier and Muethel 2014). Future research should model and test factors affecting the ability of family firms to open up, and as such create a better understanding of explanatory mechanisms linking family involvement and open innovation.

Open innovation activities and outcomes

Given the focus on inbound open innovation activities in the research conducted to date (Classen et al. 2012; Kotlar et al. 2013; Nieto, Santamaria, and Fernández 2015), research on outbound open innovation seems warranted. Additionally, scholars may want to assess the relative emphasis on inbound versus outbound open innovation displayed by family businesses. On the one hand, given their in-house focus on developing incremental innovations (Carnes and Ireland 2013; Patel and Chrisman 2014), family firms may choose to periodically insource more radically novel technologies. Subsequently, little opportunity is left for licensing out the family firm's own incremental improvements. On the other hand, the deep and specialized knowledge of family firms, often established over multiple generations of family involvement, may add to the attractiveness of their technologies for other firms and therefore give family firms the opportunity to sell or out-license their technology at a premium (cf. Bendixen, Bukasa, and Abratt 2004). Following Hoy (2014), we recommend the use of life cycle stage models to assess the research challenges above, as these models have illustrated their explanatory and predictive power for strategic management behavior.

Further insights can be gained by assessing how the desires and abilities of family firms affect the screening and selection of innovation partners and the governance of their innovation partnerships and collaborations. For example, the emphasis on socioemotional wealth maintenance may cause a preference for partnering with other family firms sharing similar sensitivities, or with knowledge institutes (universities, public research centers) to mitigate misappropriation and control loss risks (De Massis et al. 2015). Along similar lines, it would be interesting to investigate whether family firms prefer formal agreements to limit misappropriation risks or undue external interferences, or (after meticulous upfront screening and selection) trust-based informal agreements in which contractual stipulations put fewer limits on the family's discretion in pursuing their idiosyncratic socioemotional wealth agenda (cf. Chrisman et al. 2015).

Recent work suggests that (private) family firms, although having smaller research budgets, are more efficient in the conversion of these research inputs in innovation output (Duran et al. 2015). These authors partially attribute the superior conversion rate of innovation inputs to the better network access of family firms. In line with Sirmon and Hitt (2003), Duran et al. argue that family firms are better at extracting value from their cooperative innovation efforts and therefore require fewer internal R&D investments. Future research should aim to explain how family firms benefit from open innovation and whether their 'innovation efficiency' relative to nonfamily firms can indeed be attributed to their superior use of open innovation opportunities.

Family firm heterogeneity

Given the rather embryonic state of research on this topic, the outlined research areas deserve deep investigation both regarding the differences between firms with and without family involvement, as well as differences among the heterogeneous population of family-owned firms (Sharma 2004). Heterogeneity among family firms may arise from differences in goals, governance structures, and resources (Chrisman et al. 2013; Chua et al. 2012).

Differentiating on goals, the various dimensions of socioemotional wealth (e.g., Berrone, Cruz, and Gómez-Mejía 2012) may be valued differently in each family firm and preservation of these socioemotional benefits may thus lead to diverse noneconomic goals (Chrisman et al. 2012; Zellweger et al. 2012). Furthermore, the competitive situation a family firm finds itself in may change the relative importance of noneconomic and economic goals of family firms (Chua et al. 2012). Accordingly, how differences in these goals affect family firms' engagement in open innovation activities deserves more scholarly attention.

Heterogeneity may also stem from differences in governance structures. For example, the inclusion of nonfamily members in the top management may increase the ability of family firms to engage in open innovation activities (Classen et al. 2012). Also, differentiating family firms based on which generation(s) has (have) control over the business may lead to interesting findings. For example, Kellermanns et al. (2008) find that involvement of multiple generations in the family business increases the entrepreneurial behavior of family firms. Does this then also hold for the engagement in open innovation? Furthermore, many family businesses are part of larger family business groups. Control motivations play a big role within these groups (Masulis, Pham, and Zein 2011). Morck and Yeung (2003) illustrate the danger of business families blocking innovation in their more peripheral businesses, to protect themselves from what they coin 'creative self-destruction' of their core business. Taking a more positive perspective though, if a business family owns a diverse group of businesses, cross-fertilization of technologies may actually enhance innovation within the group (Belenzon and Berkovitz 2010) and subsequently decrease the need for opening up the firm (group)'s boundaries. Taking into account whether partnerships are set up within family business groups or with external firms would not only expand our knowledge but may be imperative as failure to do so might lead to flawed analyses of empirical data through unjust omission of important information. Scholars should thus use caution when investigating inter-firm collaborations of family firms.

Family firms have access to heterogeneous pools of resources and the accumulation of resources in family firms is path dependent (Chua et al. 2012). The depth and richness of social and human capital available to the family firm differ and are highly idiosyncratic to the involved family (Arrègle et al. 2007; Sorensen and Bierman 2009). Additionally, differences can be observed as to how family firms finance their business (Danes et al. 2009). How these variations in resource availability relate to family firm engagement in open innovation may serve as an interesting avenue for future research.

The interactions of family firm heterogeneity aspects may pose further research opportunities. For example, the goal setting of family firms is argued to be dependent on the generational stage of the family firm (Berrone, Cruz, and Gómez-Mejía 2012; Gómez-Mejía et al. 2011). Researchers may study how family firm goals affect their engagement in open innovation activities during different generational stages. Related to the generational stage of the family firm is the succession of key family members in the firm, often a difficult process (Cabrera-Suárez, De Saá-Pérez, and García-Almeida 2001; Daspit et al. 2015). The transfer of social capital resources from family incumbents to family successors may be vital to the long-term success of open innovation practices. How family firms' handling of the succession process affects the benefits family businesses derive from open innovation practices remains to be uncovered.

Research methods

The limited literature on open innovation in family firms mainly builds on cross-sectional data and is mostly restricted to one level of analysis (i.e., the firm). Longitudinal data or historical analyses will facilitate researchers to better capture the influence of business life cycle changes, generational transitions or environmental dynamics on the desirability and ability dimensions of family businesses to engage in open innovation, as well as its outcomes. Furthermore, given that multiple partners are involved in open innovation relationships, next to organization or individual-level variables, group, and inter-organizational variables will have to be added to the empirical data of scholars in order to fully grasp the complex dynamics of open innovation in and among family firms. Multilevel analysis techniques are recommended to analyze the nested data.

In conclusion, we are confident that a deeper and finer-grained understanding of the innovation process of family SMEs can be created by investigating how these firms derive value from their external relationships and leverage the knowledge available in their networks to enhance their firm's innovation performance. This literature review on open innovation will hopefully inspire family business scholars to direct their attention towards this promising topic.

References

Acs, Zoltan J., and David B. Audretsch. 1988. "Innovation in large and small firms: An empirical analysis." *The American Economic Review* 78 (4):678–690.

Ahuja, Gautam. 2000. "Collaboration networks, structural holes, and innovation: A longitudinal study." *Administrative Science Quarterly* 45 (3):425–455.

Arrègle, Jean-Luc, Michael A. Hitt, David G. Sirmon, and Philippe Very. 2007. "The development of organizational social capital: Attributes of family firms." *Journal of Management Studies* 44 (1):73–95.

Astrachan, Joseph H., and Melissa C. Shanker. 2003. "Family businesses' contribution to the US economy: A closer look." *Family Business Review* 16 (3):211–219.

Astrachan, Joseph H., Sabine B. Klein, and Kosmas X. Smyrnios. 2002. "The F-PEC scale of family influence: A proposal for solving the family business definition problem." *Family Business Review* 15 (1):45–58.

Barge-Gil, Andrés. 2010. "Open, semi-open and closed innovators: towards an explanation of degree of openness." *Industry and Innovation* 17 (6):577–607.

Barney, Jay. 1991. "Firm resources and sustained competitive advantage." *Journal of Management* 17 (1):99–120.

Beck, Thorsten, and Asli Demirgüç-Kunt. 2006. "Small and medium-size enterprises: Access to finance as a growth constraint." *Journal of Banking and Finance* 30 (11):2931–2943.

Belenzon, Sharon, and Tomer Berkovitz. 2010. "Innovation in business groups." *Management Science* 56 (3):519–535.

Bendixen, Mike, Kalala A. Bukasa, and Russell Abratt. 2004. "Brand equity in the business-to-business market." *Industrial Marketing Management* 33 (5):371–380.

Berrone, Pascual, Cristina Cruz, and Luis R. Gómez-Mejía. 2012. "Socioemotional wealth in family firms: Theoretical dimensions, assessment approaches, and agenda for future research." *Family Business Review* 25 (3):258–279.

Bianchi, Mattia, Federico Frattini, José Lejarraga, and Alberto Di Minin. 2014. "Technology exploitation paths: Combining technological and complementary resources in new product development and licensing." *Journal of Product Innovation Management* 31 (S1):146–169.

Bianchi, Mattia, Sergio Campodall'Orto, Federico Frattini, and Paolo Vercesi. 2010. "Enabling open innovation in small- and medium-sized enterprises: How to find alternative applications for your technologies." *R&D Management* 40 (4):414–431.

Bingham, John B., W. Gibb Dyer Jr, Isaac Smith, and Gregory L. Adams. 2011. "A stakeholder identity orientation approach to corporate social performance in family firms." *Journal of Business Ethics* 99 (4):565–585.

Block, Joern H. 2012. "R&D investments in family and founder firms: An agency perspective." *Journal of Business Venturing* 27 (2):248–265.

Brunswicker, Sabine, and Wim Vanhaverbeke. 2015. "Open innovation in small and medium-sized enterprises (SMEs): External knowledge sourcing strategies and internal organizational facilitators." *Journal of Small Business Management* 53 (4):1241–1263.

Burcharth, Ana Luiza Araújo, and Andrea Fosfuri. 2015. "Not invented here: How institutionalized socialization practices affect the formation of negative attitudes toward external knowledge." *Industrial and Corporate Change* 24 (2):281–305.

Burcharth, Ana Luiza Araújo, Mette Praest Knudsen, and Helle Alsted Søndergaard. 2014. "Neither invented nor shared here: The impact and management of attitudes for the adoption of open innovation practices." *Technovation* 34 (3):149–161.

Cabrera-Suárez, Katiuska, Petra De Saá-Pérez, and Desiderio García-Almeida. 2001. "The succession process from a resource-and knowledge-based view of the family firm." *Family Business Review* 14 (1):37–46.

Carnes, Christina Matz, and R. Duane Ireland. 2013. "Familiness and innovation: Resource bundling as the missing link." *Entrepreneurship Theory and Practice* 37 (6):1399–1419.

Carney, Michael, Marc Van Essen, Eric R. Gedajlovic, and Pursey P. M. A. R. Heugens. 2015. "What do we know about private family firms? A meta-analytical review." *Entrepreneurship Theory and Practice* 39 (3):513–544.

Carpenter, Robert E., and Bruce C. Petersen. 2002. "Is the growth of small firms constrained by internal finance?" *Review of Economics and Statistics* 84 (2):298–309.

Cennamo, Carmelo, Pascual Berrone, Cristina Cruz, and Luis R. Gómez-Mejía. 2012. "Socioemotional wealth and proactive stakeholder engagement: Why family-controlled firms care more about their stakeholders." *Entrepreneurship Theory and Practice* 36 (6):1153–1173.

Chesbrough, Henry W. 2003. *Open innovation: The new imperative for creating and profiting from technology.* Cambridge, MA: Harvard Business Press.

Chesbrough, Henry W., and Adrienne K. Crowther. 2006. "Beyond high tech: Early adopters of open innovation in other industries." *R&D Management* 36 (3):229–236.

Chesbrough, Henry W., and Melissa M. Appleyard. 2007. "Open innovation and strategy." *California Management Review* 50 (1):57–76.

Chesbrough, Henry W., Wim Vanhaverbeke, and Joel West. 2006. *Open innovation: Researching a new paradigm.* Oxford, UK: Oxford University Press.

Chiaroni, Davide, Vittorio Chiesa, and Federico Frattini. 2011. "The open innovation journey: How firms dynamically implement the emerging innovation management paradigm." *Technovation* 31 (1):34–43.

Chrisman, James J., Jess H. Chua, Alfredo De Massis, Federico Frattini, and Mike Wright. 2015. "The ability and willingness paradox in family firm innovation." *Journal of Product Innovation Management* 32 (3):310–318.

Chrisman, James J., Jess H. Chua, Allison W. Pearson, and Tim Barnett. 2012. "Family involvement, family influence, and family-centered non-economic goals in small firms." *Entrepreneurship Theory and Practice* 36 (2):267–293.

Chrisman, James J., Jess H. Chua, Franz W. Kellermanns, and Erick P.C. Chang. 2007. "Are family managers agents or stewards? An exploratory study in privately held family firms." *Journal of Business Research* 60 (10):1030–1038.

Chrisman, James J., and Pankaj C. Patel. 2012. "Variations in R&D investments of family and nonfamily firms: Behavioral agency and myopic loss aversion perspectives." *Academy of Management Journal* 55 (4):976–997.

Chrisman, James J., Pramodita Sharma, Lloyd P. Steier, and Jess H. Chua. 2013. "The influence of family goals, governance, and resources on firm outcomes." *Entrepreneurship Theory and Practice* 37 (6):1249–1261.

Christensen, Jens F., Michael H. Olesen, and Jonas S. Kjaer. 2005. "The industrial dynamics of open innovation - Evidence from the transformation of consumer electronics." *Research Policy* 34 (10):1533–1549.

Chua, Jess H., James J. Chrisman, Lloyd P. Steier, and Sabine B. Rau. 2012. "Sources of heterogeneity in family firms: An introduction." *Entrepreneurship Theory and Practice* 36 (6):1103–1113.

Classen, Nicolas, Anita Van Gils, Yannick Bammens, and Martin Carree. 2012. "Accessing resources from innovation partners: The search breadth of family SMEs." *Journal of Small Business Management* 50 (2):191–215.

Classen, Nicolas, Martin Carree, Anita Van Gils, and Bettina Peters. 2014. "Innovation in family and non-family SMEs: an exploratory analysis." *Small Business Economics* 42 (3):595–609.

Cohen, Wesley M., and Daniel A. Levinthal. 1990. "Absorptive capacity: a new perspective on learning and innovation." *Administrative Science Quarterly* 35 (1):128–152.

Colombo, Massimo G., Evila Piva, and Cristina Rossi-Lamastra. 2014. "Open innovation and within-industry diversification in small and medium enterprises: The case of open source software firms." *Research Policy* 43 (5):891–902.

Dahlander, Linus, and David M. Gann. 2010. "How open is innovation?" *Research Policy* 39 (6):699–709.

Danes, Sharon M., Kathryn Stafford, George Haynes, and Sayali S. Amarapurkar. 2009. "Family capital of family firms: Bridging human, social, and financial capital." *Family Business Review* 22 (3):199–215.

Daspit, Joshua J., Daniel T. Holt, James J. Chrisman, and Rebecca G. Long. 2015. "Examining family firm succession from a social exchange perspective: A multiphase, multistakeholder review." *Family Business Review*. doi: 10.1177/0894486515599688.

De Massis, Alfredo, Federico Frattini, and Ulrich Lichtenthaler. 2013. "Research on technological innovation in family firms: Present debates and future directions." *Family Business Review* 26 (1):10–31.

De Massis, Alfredo, Federico Frattini, Emanuele Pizzurno, and Lucio Cassia. 2015. "Product innovation in family versus nonfamily firms: an exploratory analysis." *Journal of Small Business Management* 53 (1):1–36.

Deephouse, David L., and Peter Jaskiewicz. 2013. "Do family firms have better reputations than non-family firms? An integration of socioemotional wealth and social identity theories." *Journal of Management Studies* 50 (3):337–360.

Drechsler, Wenzel, and Martin Natter. 2012. "Understanding a firm's openness decisions in innovation." *Journal of Business Research* 65 (3):438–445.

Duran, Patricio, Nadine Kammerlander, Marc Van Essen, and Thomas M. Zellweger. 2015. "Doing more with less: Innovation input and output in family firms." *Academy of Management Journal*. doi: 10.5465/amj.2014.0424.

Enkel, Ellen, Oliver Gassmann, and Henry W. Chesbrough. 2009. "Open R&D and open innovation: exploring the phenomenon." *R&D Management* 39 (4):311–316.

Flören, Roberto H. 1998. "The significance of family business in the Netherlands." *Family Business Review* 11 (2):121–134.

Fu, Xiaolan. 2012. "How does openness affect the importance of incentives for innovation?" *Research Policy* 41 (3):512–523.

Gardet, Elodie, and Shady Fraiha. 2012. "Coordination modes established by the hub firm of an innovation network: the case of an SME bearer." *Journal of Small Business Management* 50 (2):216–238.

Gassmann, Oliver. 2006. "Opening up the innovation process: Towards an agenda." *R&D Management* 36 (3):223–228.

Gassmann, Oliver, Ellen Enkel, and Henry W. Chesbrough. 2010. "The future of open innovation." *R&D Management* 40 (3):213–221.

Gassmann, Oliver, Patricia Sandmeier, and Christoph H. Wecht. 2006. "Extreme customer innovation in the front-end: Learning from a new software paradigm." *International Journal of Technology Management* 33 (1):46–66.

Gómez-Mejía, Luis R., Cristina Cruz, Pascual Berrone, and Julio De Castro. 2011. "The bind that ties: socioemotional wealth preservation in family firms." *Academy of Management Annals* 5 (1):653–707.

Grimpe, Christoph, and Wolfgang Sofka. 2009. "Search patterns and absorptive capacity: Low-and high-technology sectors in European countries." *Research Policy* 38 (3):495–506.

Gruber, Marc, and Joachim Henkel. 2006. "New ventures based on open innovation - an empirical analysis of start-up firms in embedded Linux." *International Journal of Technology Management* 33 (4):356–372.

Habbershon, Timothy G., and Mary L. Williams. 1999. "A resource-based framework for assessing the strategic advantages of family firms." *Family Business Review* 12 (1):1–25.

Hagedoorn, John, and Geert Duysters. 2002. "External sources of innovative capabilities: the preferences for strategic alliances or mergers and acquisitions." *Journal of Management Studies* 39 (2):167–188.

Hamel, Gary. 1991. "Competition for competence and interpartner learning within international strategic alliances." *Strategic Management Journal* 12 (S1):83–103.

Harzing, Anne-Will. 2014. *Journal Quality List*. (52nd ed., online report). www.harzing.com.

Hewitt-Dundas, Nola. 2006. "Resource and capability constraints to innovation in small and large plants." *Small Business Economics* 26 (3):257–277.

Hoy, Frank. 2014. "Entrepreneurial venturing for family business research." In *The SAGE handbook of family business*, edited by Leif Melin, Mattias Nordqvist and Pramodita Sharma. London, UK: SAGE.

Huang, Fang, and John Rice. 2009. "The role of absorptive capacity in facilitating "open innovation" outcomes: A study of Australian SMEs in the manufacturing sector." *International Journal of Innovation Management* 13 (02):201–220.

Huizingh, Eelko K.R.E. 2011. "Open innovation: State of the art and future perspectives." *Technovation* 31 (1):2–9.

Huybrechts, Jolien, Wim Voordeckers, Nadine Lybaert, and Sigrid Vandemaele. 2011. "The distinctiveness of family-firm intangibles: A review and suggestions for future research." *Journal of Management & Organization* 17 (2):268–287.

Jaffe, Adam B., Manuel Trajtenberg, and Rebecca Henderson. 1992. "Geographic localization of knowledge spillovers as evidenced by patent citations." *The Quarterly Journal of Economics* 108 (3):577–598.

Kellermanns, Franz W., Kimberly A. Eddleston, Tim Barnett, and Allison Pearson. 2008. "An exploratory study of family member characteristics and involvement: Effects on entrepreneurial behavior in the family firm." *Family Business Review* 21 (1):1–14.

Klein, Sabine B. 2000. "Family businesses in Germany: Significance and structure." *Family Business Review* 13 (3):157–181.

Knight, Gary. 2000. "Entrepreneurship and marketing strategy: The SME under globalization." *Journal of International Marketing* 8 (2):12–32.

Kotlar, Josip, Alfredo De Massis, Federico Frattini, Mattia Bianchi, and Hanqing Fang. 2013. "Technology acquisition in family and nonfamily firms: A longitudinal analysis of spanish manufacturing firms." *Journal of Product Innovation Management* 30 (6):1073–1088.

Lasagni, Andrea. 2012. "How can external relationships enhance innovation in SMEs? New evidence for Europe." *Journal of Small Business Management* 50 (2):310–339.

Laursen, Keld, and Ammon Salter. 2006. "Open for innovation: the role of openness in explaining innovation performance among UK manufacturing firms." *Strategic Management Journal* 27 (2):131–150.

Le Breton-Miller, Isabelle, and Danny Miller. 2006. "Why do some family businesses out-compete? Governance, long-term orientations, and sustainable capability." *Entrepreneurship Theory and Practice* 30 (6):731–746.

Lecocq, Xavier, and Benoît Demil. 2006. "Strategizing industry structure: The case of open systems in a low-tech industry." *Strategic Management Journal* 27 (9):891–898.

Lee, Sungjoo, Gwangman Park, Byungun Yoon, and Jinwoo Park. 2010. "Open innovation in SMEs–An intermediated network model." *Research Policy* 39 (2):290–300.

Lee, Yong S. 1996. "'Technology transfer'and the research university: A search for the boundaries of university-industry collaboration." *Research Policy* 25 (6):843–863.

Lichtenthaler, Ulrich, and Eckhard Lichtenthaler. 2009. "A capability-based framework for open innovation: Complementing absorptive capacity." *Journal of Management Studies* 46 (8):1315–1338.

Lumpkin, G. Thomas, and Keith H. Brigham. 2011. "Long-term orientation and intertemporal choice in family firms." *Entrepreneurship Theory and Practice* 35 (6):1149–1169.

Lumpkin, G. Thomas, Keith H. Brigham, and Todd W. Moss. 2010. "Long-term orientation: Implications for the entrepreneurial orientation and performance of family businesses." *Entrepreneurship and Regional Development* 22 (3–4):241–264.

Madrid-Guijarro, Antonia, Domingo García, and Howard Van Auken. 2009. "Barriers to innovation among Spanish manufacturing SMEs." *Journal of Small Business Management* 47 (4):465–488.

Mangematin, Vincent, Stéphane Lemarié, Jean-Pierre Boissin, David Catherine, Frédéric Corolleur, Roger Coronini, and Michel Trommetter. 2003. "Development of SMEs and heterogeneity of trajectories: The case of biotechnology in France." *Research Policy* 32 (4):621–638.

Massa, Silvia, and Stefania Testa. 2008. "Innovation and SMEs: Misaligned perspectives and goals among entrepreneurs, academics, and policy makers." *Technovation* 28 (7):393–407.

Masulis, Ronald W., Peter Kien Pham, and Jason Zein. 2011. "Family business groups around the world: Financing advantages, control motivations, and organizational choices." *Review of Financial Studies* 24 (11):3556–3600.

Miller, Danny, and Isabelle Le Breton-Miller. 2014. "Deconstructing socioemotional wealth." *Entrepreneurship Theory and Practice* 38 (4):713–720.

Miller, Danny, Isabelle Le Breton-Miller, and Barry Scholnick. 2008. "Stewardship vs. stagnation: An empirical comparison of small family and non-family businesses." *Journal of Management Studies* 45 (1):51–78.

Morck, Randall, and Bernard Yeung. 2003. "Agency problems in large family business groups." *Entrepreneurship Theory and Practice* 27 (4):367–382.

Moreno-Menéndez, Ana M., and Jose C. Casillas. 2014. "Open innovation and internationalization behavior: The case of Spanish firms." In *Open innovation through strategic alliances: Approaches for product, technology, and business model creation*, edited by Refik Culpan. New York, NY: Palgrave Macmillan.

Mowery, David C., Joanne E. Oxley, and Brian S. Silverman. 1996. "Strategic alliances and interfirm knowledge transfer." *Strategic Management Journal* 17 (S2):77–91.

Narula, Rajneesh, and John Hagedoorn. 1999. "Innovating through strategic alliances: moving towards international partnerships and contractual agreements." *Technovation* 19 (5):283–294.

Nieto, María Jesús, and Lluís Santamaría. 2010. "Technological collaboration: bridging the innovation gap between small and large firms." *Journal of Small Business Management* 48 (1):44–69.

Nieto, María Jesús, Lluís Santamaria, and Zulima Fernández. 2015. "Understanding the innovation behavior of family firms." *Journal of Small Business Management* 53 (2):382–399.

Oakey, Raymond P. 2013. "Open innovation and its relevance to industrial research and development: The case of high-technology small firms." *International Small Business Journal* 31 (3):319–334.

Padilla-Meléndez, Antonio, Ana R. Del Aguila-Obra, and Nigel Lockett. 2013. "Shifting sands: Regional perspectives on the role of social capital in supporting open innovation through knowledge transfer and exchange with small and medium-sized enterprises." *International Small Business Journal* 31 (3):296–313.

Parida, Vinit, Mats Westerberg, and Johan Frishammar. 2012. "Inbound open innovation activities in high-tech SMEs: The impact on innovation Performance." *Journal of Small Business Management* 50 (2):283–309.

Patel, Pankaj C., and James J. Chrisman. 2014. "Risk abatement as a strategy for R&D investments in family firms." *Strategic Management Journal* 35 (4):617–627.

Pullen, Annemien J.J., Petra C. Weerd-Nederhof, Aard J. Groen, and Olaf A.M. Fisscher. 2012. "Open innovation in practice: Goal omplementarity and closed NPD networks to explain differences in innovation performance for SMEs in the medical devices sector." *Journal of Product Innovation Management* 29 (6):917–934.

Pullen, Annemien J.J., Petra C. Weerd-Nederhof, Aard J. Groen, Michael Song, and Olaf A.M. Fisscher. 2009. "Successful patterns of internal SME characteristics leading to high overall innovation performance." *Creativity and Innovation Management* 18 (3):209–223.

Roper, Stephen, and Nola Hewitt-Dundas. 2013. "Catalysing open innovation through publicly-funded R&D: A comparison of university and company-based research centres." *International Small Business Journal* 31 (3):275–295.

Salvato, Carlo, and Leif Melin. 2008. "Creating value across generations in family-controlled businesses: The role of family social capital." *Family Business Review* 21 (3):259–276.

Schmieder, Joe. 2014. *Innovation in the family business: Succeeding through generations*. New York, NY: Palgrave Macmillan.

Schumpeter, Joseph A. 1934. *The theory of economic development: An inquiry into profits, capital, credit, interest, and the business cycle*. Cambridge, MA: Harvard University Press.

Schumpeter, Joseph A. 1942. *Capitalism, socialism and democracy*. New York, NY: Harper and Brothers.

Sharma, Pramodita. 2004. "An overview of the field of family business studies: Current status and directions for the future." *Family Business Review* 17 (1):1–36.

Sirmon, David G., and Michael A. Hitt. 2003. "Managing resources: Linking unique resources, management, and wealth creation in family firms." *Entrepreneurship Theory and Practice* 27 (4):339–358.

Sorensen, Ritch L., and Leonard Bierman. 2009. "Family capital, family business, and free enterprise." *Family Business Review* 22 (3):193–195.

Spithoven, André, Bart Clarysse, and Mirjam Knockaert. 2011. "Building absorptive capacity to organise inbound open innovation in traditional industries." *Technovation* 31 (1):10–21.

Spithoven, André, Wim Vanhaverbeke, and Nadine Roijakkers. 2013. "Open innovation practices in SMEs and large enterprises." *Small Business Economics* 41 (3):537–562.

Steier, Lloyd, and Miriam Muethel. 2014. "Trust and family business." In *The SAGE handbook of family business*, edited by Leif Melin, Mattias Nordqvist and Pramodita Sharma. London, UK: SAGE.

Teece, David J. 1986. "Profiting from technological innovation: Implications for integration, collaboration, licensing and public policy." *Research Policy* 15 (6):285–305.

Teece, David J., Gary Pisano, and Amy Shuen. 1997. "Dynamic capabilities and strategic management." *Strategic Management Journal* 18 (7):509–533.

Theyel, Nelli. 2013. "Extending open innovation throughout the value chain by small and medium-sized manufacturers." *International Small Business Journal* 31 (3):256–274.

Tomlinson, Philip R., and Felicia M. Fai. 2013. "The nature of SME co-operation and innovation: A multi-scalar and multi-dimensional analysis." *International Journal of Production Economics* 141 (1):316–326.

Vahter, Priit, James H. Love, and Stephen Roper. 2014. "Openness and innovation performance: Are small firms different?" *Industry and Innovation* 21 (7–8):553–573.

Van de Vrande, Vareska, Jeroen P.J. De Jong, Wim Vanhaverbeke, and Maurice De Rochemont. 2009. "Open innovation in SMEs: Trends, motives and management challenges." *Technovation* 29 (6):423–437.

Van Der Meer, Han. 2007. "Open innovation–the Dutch treat: challenges in thinking in business models." *Creativity and Innovation Management* 16 (2):192–202.

Vanhaverbeke, Wim, Ine Vermeersch, and Stijn De Zutter. 2012. Open innovation in SMEs: How can small companies and start-ups benefit from open innovation strategies? Research report, available at: www.flandersdc.be.

Von Hippel, Eric. 1986. "Lead users: a source of novel product concepts." *Management Science* 32 (7):791–805.

Wernerfelt, Birger. 1984. "A resource-based view of the firm." *Strategic Management Journal* 5 (2):171–180.

West, Joel, and Marcel Bogers. 2014. "Leveraging external sources of innovation: A review of research on open innovation." *Journal of Product Innovation Management* 31 (4):814–831.

Wincent, Joakim, Sergey Anokhin, and Håkan Boter. 2009. "Network board continuity and effectiveness of open innovation in Swedish strategic small-firm networks." *R&D Management* 39 (1):55–67.

Wynarczyk, Pooran. 2013. "Open innovation in SMEs: A dynamic approach to modern entrepreneurship in the twenty-first century." *Journal of Small Business and Enterprise Development* 20 (2):258–278.

Wynarczyk, Pooran, Panagiotis Piperopoulos, and Maura McAdam. 2013. "Open innovation in small and medium-sized enterprises: An overview." *International Small Business Journal* 31 (3):240–255.

Zahra, Shaker A., and Gerard George. 2002. "Absorptive capacity: A review, reconceptualization, and extension." *Academy of Management Review* 27 (2):185–203.

Zellweger, Thomas M., Franz W. Kellermanns, James J. Chrisman, and Jess H. Chua. 2012. "Family control and family firm valuation by family CEOs: The importance of intentions for transgenerational control." *Organization Science* 23 (3):851–868.

13

MARKET ORIENTATION AND INNOVATIVENESS IN FAMILY FIRMS

The Moderating Influence of Organizational Social Consciousness

Clay Dibrell, Cristina Bettinelli, and Kathleen Randerson

All family firms begin with the founder of the firm engaging in an entrepreneurial action to either start the venture or through some form of acquisition. The founder takes the risk and responsibility, and by extension, the shadow of this risk bears upon the founder's family. Following the call of Bettinelli, Fayolle, and Randerson (2014) and Uhlaner, Kellermanns, Eddleston, and Hoy (2012) to further explore how entrepreneurship permeates and invigorates family firms, we have chosen to study the entrepreneurial behaviors exhibited between the family and the firm in this book chapter. Further, as family firms are often an active member of the community in which they are embedded (e.g., Dyer & Whetten, 2006), we consider the extent to which family firms perceive their external environment (e.g., market orientation, social environment) and engage in entrepreneurial behaviors, such as innovativeness.

Although there have been many studies on market orientation (e.g., Narver & Slater, 1990) and its linkages with innovation (e.g., Beck, Janssens, Debruyne, & Lommelen, 2011; Dibrell, Craig, & Hansen, 2011), Zachary, McKenny, Short, and Payne (2011) suggest additional consideration of how market orientation affects entrepreneurial behaviors (e.g., innovativeness) in family firms is needed. Likewise, other family business scholars (e.g., Campopiano, De Massis & Chirico, 2014; Kellermanns, Dibrell, & Cruz, 2014; Van Gils, Dibrell, Neubaum, & Craig, 2014) call for a better understanding of how family emotions and images are linked with stakeholders. In response to these different appeals, we argue the impact of an organization's social consciousness (i.e., a firm which attempts to solve social problems through alignment of the firm's interests and its stakeholders, Dibrell, Craig, Kim, & Johnson, 2015) may contribute to our knowledge, and such an approach within an entrepreneurial family firm context is presently missing.

More recently, family business scholars have considered how family firms employ market orientation (i.e., a firm's orientation to its competitors, customers, and interfunctional coordination, Narver & Slater, 1990) to gain a competitive advantage (Tokarczyk, Hansen, Green, & Down, 2007; Zachary et al., 2011) through such efforts as firm innovation (Beck et al., 2011). Antithetically, family firms have been construed as being strategically conservative (Chrisman & Patel, 2012), often not willing to engage in R&D activities (Patel & Chrisman, 2014) unless threatened. On the other hand, family firms show a greater proclivity to engage in corporate social responsibility than nonfamily firms (e.g., Craig & Dibrell, 2006; Neubaum, Dibrell, & Craig, 2012; Uhlaner, van Goor-Balk, & Masurel, 2004). They are often more willing to engage in corporate social responsibility activities at the cost of profit maximization to embed themselves in their local communities (Berrone, Cruz, Gómez-Mejía, & Larraza-Kintana, 2010) and improve the reputation to increase socioemotional wealth (Cennamo, Berrone, Cruz, & Gómez-Mejía, 2012). Overall, there has been limited understanding of how market orientation, corporate social responsibility, and entrepreneurial behaviors are exhibited in family firms and the extent to which these behaviors exist in family firms.

In this current research, we propose that the interaction between market orientation, organizational social consciousness, and the family will augment the effect of market orientation on firm innovativeness. We argue that family firms who strategically emphasize their market orientation and organizational social consciousness will have increased levels of entrepreneurial behaviors than family firms who place less weight on these strategic orientations. To summate, we ask: is the relationship between market orientation and firm innovativeness moderated by organizational social consciousness in family firms? If so, how does the interaction of market orientation and organizational social consciousness affect innovativeness in family firms?

Our study contributes to the family entrepreneurship literature in multiple ways. First, we consider the alignment of stakeholders (i.e., market orientation) and broader social interests (i.e., organizational social consciousness) in relation to entrepreneurial behaviors (i.e., firm innovativeness) and socioemotional wealth creation (non-economic benefits for the family firm). Second, the construct of organizational social consciousness, or social orientation, is introduced to better elucidate why family firms are able to attain a competitive advantage. Third, we discover that in concert market orientation and organizational social consciousness lead to increasing innovativeness. Fourth, we further inform the strategic conservatism-entrepreneurial behavior conversation in regards to family firm behaviors.

We organize this chapter by beginning with a relevant literature review of market orientation, family entrepreneurship, and organizational social consciousness, as well as hypothesis development. Then, we present our methodology and provide the results of our hypothesis testing. Finally, we discuss our findings and implications for both researchers and practitioners.

Literature Review and Hypotheses

Narver and Slater (1990) established a culture-based approach to market orientation, characterized by employees that strive to provide superior value to customers resulting in a competitive advantage through a greater understanding of what customers want, how competitors respond, and the capability of employees to disseminate and to coordinate this information across and within departments. The outcome of a market-oriented approach is the increased likelihood of the provision of superior value to customers, widely considered key for maximizing long-term profitability.

Further, research has consistently exhibited a strong positive relationship between market orientation and innovativeness (Beck et al., 2011; Dibrell et al., 2011). Market orientation is comprised of three sub-components: competitor, customer, and interfunctional coordination (Narver & Slater, 1990). For competitor orientation, firms monitor the strategic actions of their competitors, and then attempt to reduce the impact of these initiatives or to proactively start new competitive initiatives to find and to keep customers. Customer orientation, similarly to competitive orientation, is to focus on and to predict the needs of the customer and then satisfy these needs. In both instances, the culture of the firm is oriented towards these two external constituencies. Interfunctional coordination is the dissemination of this external information among the internal areas of the firm. Interfunctional coordination is needed in order to deliver the needed strategic outcomes provided through the competitor and customer orientations (Slater & Narver, 1999; Hansen, Dibrell, & Down, 2006).

Innovativeness is an entrepreneurial behavior, which is often considered to be critical for the survival of the firm (Cohen & Winn, 2007; Lumpkin & Dess, 1996). Likewise, innovativeness has been positively identified as a key competitive competence in family firms (e.g., Craig, Dibrell, & Garrett, 2014). These authors state innovativeness is the "propensity of a firm to engage in innovative actions that materialize over time…[and] is an idiosyncratic family-influenced resource attribute" (2014: 232). Innovativeness may be manifested through new services, products, and/or processes (Slevin & Covin, 1995).

While it has been generally found that market-oriented firms are more prone to innovate to meet their customers' demand for products and services (Dibrell et al., 2011), extant literature has also stressed that family firms' orientation towards the market may have different antecedents and consequences (e.g., Beck et al., 2011). Indeed, market orientation is not a mere result of a rational strategic choice, rather the result of, and bound to a firm's specific culture. Thus, the way market orientation is implemented and related to a firm's innovativeness may depend on the organization's culture.

In the case of family firms, for example, market orientation seems to be promoted by some inherent and distinct qualities and resources that have been summarized under the term "familiness" (Tokarczyk et al., 2007). The extent to which a family firm's market orientation is translated into innovativeness depends very much on how these familiness qualities contribute to the creation of an appropriate environment that could facilitate, or hinder such development.

Some scholars have argued that one of the typical family business attributes is related to conservatism (e.g., Carney, Van Essen, Gedajlovic, & Heugens, 2015). Family firms seem to be particularly susceptible to remaining conservative and avoiding taking risks such as investing in R&D (Chrisman & Patel, 2012; Zahra, 2005). This tendency to become conservative, unwilling or unable to translate the information gained from the market into innovations, may be due to the fact that family members need to preserve a lasting legacy and mitigate the risk of destroying family economic or socioemotional wealth (Sharma, Chrisman, & Chua, 1997; Kellermanns et al., 2014). Thus, family firm leaders may be more likely to seek wealth preservation rather than wealth creation, and this may make them more hesitant to pursue innovations or engagement with their customers (Kellermanns, Eddleston, & Zellweger, 2012).

Conversely, we argue that there are at least three familiness qualities that may support a positive relationship between market orientation and innovativeness. First, close relations among family members, fast communication, and frequent interactions offer the cultural context that may facilitate the translation of identified market needs into appropriate innovations (Frank, Lueger, Nosé, & Suchy, 2010). Second, family members accumulate and transmit from generation to generation their lifelong exposure to business experience, this unique business acumen can be a determinant when it relation to interpreting in new ways customer needs to innovate (Pearson, Carr, & Shaw, 2008). Third, most family firms typically distinguish themselves for being relatively more flexible than nonfamily firms and for preferring dialogues without barriers and based on mutual respect (Sciascia, Clinton, Nason, James, & Rivera-Algarin, 2013). This communication approach may allow for identification and engagement of new opportunities to attain a rapid response to customers' needs through innovative solutions (Hoy, 2008). Following this logic, we present our first hypothesis:

Hypothesis 1

In family firms, market orientation is positively related to innovativeness.

Changing societal expectations regarding corporate social responsibility have continued to evolve from one of neglect or apathy to a greater concern for how the firm responds to its external stakeholders (Chan, 2005, Bergamaschi & Randerson, forthcoming). Firms are increasingly responding by being more proactive, such as a greater regard for natural environmental issues (Craig & Dibrell, 2006). Organizational social consciousness is indicative of the extent that "socially conscious organizations will engage in opportunities to predict and to solve social problems through alignment of the organization's interest with those of the social participants" (Dibrell et al., 2015: 592). As such, organizational consciousness may be defined, "as the transparent dimension that ties the organization together and forms a sense of meaning that jointly holds the organization as one" (Dibrell et al., 2015: 592).

Although much of the extant research on corporate social responsibiity activities focuses on large corporations, extending the investigation to family firms is pertinent since family values are transmitted to the business, such as long-term orientation, respect for, and protection of the employees, strong ties with the social and business community, integrity and continuity in the business policies, and concern for reputation (Miller & Le Breton-Miller, 2005; Neubauer, 1998; Ward, 2011) for example. In addition, much of this literature adopts an economic view of corporate social responsibility activities, meaning that firms will undertake such initiatives solely in the perspective of gaining a short-term competitive advantage (Bergamaschi & Randerson, forthcoming). Understanding how the inherent features of family businesses can support a more evolved perspective of corporate social responsibility is of great importance. In particular, it seems interesting to better understand how family firms behave in the social context and how the relationship between market orientation and innovativeness is for family firms that face corporate social responsibility challenges.

For instance, we know that Maignan et al. (1999) hypothesized that firms' market orientation would be positively related to corporate citizenship proactivity. This supposition was largely based on the views of Narver and Slater's (1990) idea that market oriented firms were particularly sensitive to any stakeholder which affects long-term performance. While research has investigated the corporate social responsibility of family firms (e.g., Uhlaner et al., 2004), studies have neglected concurrently investigating market orientation, organizational social consciousness, and innovativeness in family *and* nonfamily firms.

In the Sharma and Vredenburg (1998) study, family firms which were characterized to be proactive firms and actively engaged in corporate social responsibilities (e.g., natural environmental policy) were discovered to support opportunity seeking and experimentation. In other words, a strong natural environmental policy may result in enhanced innovativeness as firms are more open to, and aware of, societal/consumer trends and may be more proactive. Following this logic within the context of organizational social consciousness, it can be argued that a firm which has a high social consciousness will enlarge the field of information considered relevant by a firm, thereby increasing the number of ideas that can lead to innovations.

Family businesses have unique cultures which derive from the overlap of family, management, and ownership (Tagiuri & Davis, 1996), which has been empirically demonstrated to positively influence competitive advantages of these firms (e.g., Tokarczyk, et al., 2007; Zahra, Hayton, Neubaum, Dibrell, & Craig, 2008). Due to family firms' unique culture, extant literature has shown that family and nonfamily firms are different in terms of social consciousness. For example, Adams, Taschian, and Shore (1996) compared the ethical practices of family and nonfamily businesses and found that, while family businesses did not often have a formal code of ethics, they were more likely to exhibit ethical behaviors through their actions. Gallo (2004) found that family businesses were more attentive than nonfamily business to the common good of the community. Dyer and Whetten (2006) studied businesses in the S&P 500 and found that

that family firms were more likely than nonfamily firms to be more fully engaged in socially responsible concerns.

More recently, Berrone et al. (2010), in their study of firms who were required to report their emission levels to regulatory agencies, found that family businesses presented significantly better environmental performance than their nonfamily counterparts. These differences can be attributed to the different cultural approach that family firms have and also to the fact that family firms seem to be more motivated to protect family assets and are concerned about the family firm's reputation (Dyer and Whetten, 2006).

Likewise, an organization's culture can induce an orientation toward the market (Narver & Slater, 1990) and toward corporate social responsibility (Uhlaner et al., 2004). Indeed, Aguinis and Glavas (2012) have indicated that at a firm level of analysis, instrumental and normative social responsibility motivations usually interact with other relevant firm attributes such as employee engagement and market orientation (Aguinis and Glavas, 2012) to influence firm behavior. Additionally, the values of the family are exhibited in the culture of the firm (e.g., Tokarczyk, et al., 2007; Zachary et al., 2011) and will positively enhance the effects of a firm's market orientation and social consciousness in relation to firm innovativeness to a greater extent than in nonfamily firms. For example, Delmas and Gergaud (2014) find that the intention to pass ownership and control to the next generation (considered as a unique family firm characteristic), is determinant in fostering a long-term orientation and engagement in both market-based and prosocial actions. In other words, in family firms, the alignment of stakeholders (i.e., market orientation) and social interests of the firm (i.e., organizational social consciousness) may contribute to increasing the extent of entrepreneurial behaviors in the form of firm innovativeness. Therefore, we posit our second hypothesis:

Hypothesis 2

In family firms, organizational social consciousness positively moderates the relationship between market orientation and family firm innovativeness, such that as organizational social consciousness increases, the relationship between market orientation and firm innovativeness increases.

Methodology

To test our hypotheses, we employed a survey research design. Sampling from the food processing industry, a questionnaire was mailed to the CEO of 2,297 firms located in Arizona, Idaho, Nevada, Oregon, Utah, and Washington. After removing 750 potential respondents from the sample pool due to issues such as against firm policy and incorrect addresses, 193 mostly completed questionnaires were returned, resulting in a final response rate of 12.5 percent.

The food processing industry was selected for multiple reasons. First, these firms produce products for human consumption. These products must be consistently safe and of good quality, which will influence the reputation of the firm. Second, food processing firms, working in the food chain, must be aware of what their customers' demand, due to the often limited shelf life of their produced inventory, which provides the firms with more immediate market feedback. Third, by limiting the sample to one industry, effects associated with the industry in which the firm operates are controlled for through the research design.

We further tested for the effects of common method bias through a one factor test, resulting in nine factors with Eigen values greater than 1. The first factor accounted for 23.26 percent of the 63.35 percent total variance indicating that common bias is not a primary concern. Likewise, we tested for non-response bias and found no significant differences between the first and last wave of respondent answers, suggesting the sample is representative of the population of food processors. For firm size, a broad range of firms had one to five employees (n = 54) to larger organizations consisting of 500 to 9,000 employees (n = 15). However, approximately 81 percent of the firms were under 100 full-time employees. For firm age, a preponderance of firms were 20 years or older (n = 133), followed by firms aged 10 to 20 years (n = 56). As we are interested in potential differences between family and nonfamily firms and following the guidance provided by Zahra et al. (2008), we asked respondents if they considered their firms to be a family firm. If respondent perceived their firm to be a family firm, then the firm was classified as a family firm, resulting in our final sample of family (n = 142) and nonfamily firms (n = 51). Considering that family firms are the most prevalent organizational form (Faccio & Lang, 2002; Holderness, 2009), this distribution of family and nonfamily firms may be expected.

Firm Innovativenes

Firm innovativeness encompasses all processes within the organization which are related to creating new products or services. We drew upon the work of Dibrell, Davis, and Craig (2008) who consider "the strategic emphasis placed on innovation" (2008: 203). The anchors for this scale ranged from 1 = not at all to 7 = very great extent, with the scale consisting of the following 4-items which asked respondents to indicate the extent to which their company emphasizes the following: (1) Developing new products; (2) Upgrading; (3) Specialty products; and, (4) Innovative market techniques. The mean score of items was used for this scale, as well as for the other constructs in this study.

Market Orientation

Following the approach employed by Narver and Slater (1990), we utilized a single market orientation score for hypotheses testing, which contained the customer, competitor, and interfunctional coordination sub-dimensions. Anchors for the scale ranged from 1 = Not at All to 5 = To an Extreme Extent, with the following items: (1) We constantly monitor our level of commitment and orientation to serving customers' needs; (2) We rapidly respond to competitive actions that threaten us; (3) All of our business functions (e.g., marketing/sales, manufacturing, etc.) are integrated in serving the needs of our target markets; (4) All of our business functions (e.g., marketing/sales, manufacturing, etc.) are integrated in serving the needs of our target markets; (5) Our salespeople regularly share information within our organization concerning competitors' strategies; (6) All the departments in our business are responsive to each other's needs and requests; (7) Our strategy for competitive advantage is based on our understanding of customer needs; (8) Top management regularly discusses competitors' strengths and strategies; (9) Our top managers from across the business regularly visit our current and prospective customers; (10) Our business strategies are driven by our beliefs about how we can create greater value for customers; (11) We target customers where we have an opportunity for competitive advantage; (12) We freely communicate information about our successful and unsuccessful customer experiences across our business; (13) We measure customer satisfaction systematically and frequently; (14) Our managers understand how everyone in our business can contribute to creating customer value; and (15) We give close attention to after-sales service.

Organizational Social Consciousnes

Drawn from the social entrepreneurship literature, we employed the Dibrell et al. (2015) three-item scale, which focused on how the firm uses its resources to innovatively solve social problems of its stakeholders. The questionnaire stem for this scale asked respondents to "please indicate the extent your business emphasizes each of these activities," using a 7-point Likert-type scale with the following anchors: (1) = Not At All; (4) = To a Moderate Extent; and, (7) To an Extreme Extent. The three items were: (1) Pursuit of opportunities for social problems; (2) Use of socially innovative business models; and, (3) Creation of innovations to solve social problems.

Control Variables

We used six control variables as part of our study. To control for the potential confounding effects of firm age and firm size (i.e., the number of full-time employees), we collected continuous demographic data on these two measures, with a natural log transformation for each measure. Similarly, we controlled for a firm's costs relative to its competitors to ascertain the ability of the firm to control its cost, the perceived extent of industry dynamism and the flexibility of the firm to respond to changes in its external environment, which both may affect a firm's emphasis on innovativeness. Lastly, we considered the extent to which the firm engages in recycling, as it has been demonstrated to effect a firm's level of innovativeness (Craig & Dibrell, 2006).

Analysis

Construct validity was tested through the use of confirmatory factor analyses using LISREL 8.52. To calculate the descriptive statistics, coefficient alphas, the correlation matrix, and conduct the regression analysis, we utilized SPSS 21.0. For hypothesis testing, we employed OLS regression, as we are examining interaction terms using cross-sectional data, using hierarchical moderated regression analysis (Jaccard & Turrisi, 2003). We tested four regression models, the first model including only control variables, then adding market orientation in the second step, followed by the organizational social consciousness construct, before adding the interaction term. With the inclusion of the interaction term, the variables of interest were mean-centered to reduce the effects of collinearity in the construction of interaction term.

Results

As provided in Table 13.1, the correlation results suggest that the different constructs are within an acceptable range ($r = -.11$ to $r = .45$), and there are relationships which merit further investigation with few signs of collinearity. Likewise, all variance inflation factor scores are under 1.6, well below the 10.0 threshold. Through a two-phase CFA approach to test for measurement invariance among the different constructs, we employed confirmatory factory analysis with maximum likelihood estimation. First, we tested the five-factor unconstrained factor model ($\chi^2 = 770.24$, d.f. = 367; CFI = .94; Delta2 = .94; RMSEA = .076; SRMR = .077), with all items loading above a .40 cutoff on their respective factors, supporting convergent validity, with the exception of one item in market orientation, which was dropped from further analysis. Second, we compared the unconstrained factor model to a constrained factor model. For the constrained five-factor model, all paths in the Φ matrix were set to one to create a baseline comparison model to gauge how well our studied model (i.e., unconstrained model) fit the data. In the constrained factor model ($\chi^2 = 1957.44$, d.f. = 377; CFI = .79; Delta2 = .79; RMSEA = .15; SRMR = .12), the factors were not allowed to correlate, while in the unconstrained factor model the factors were allowed to correlate. The unconstrained factor model fit the data significantly better than the constrained factor model ($\Delta\chi^2 = 1187.20$; d.f. = 10; $p < .05$), suggesting discriminant validity. In addition, the average variance extracted and composite reliabilities for the studied constructs are reported in Table 13.1.

Table 13.1 Descriptives and Correlations of Family Firms[1]

	Mean (SD)	Coefficient Alpha	Composite Reliability	Average Variance Extracted	1	2	3	4	5	6	7	8
1. Firm Innovativeness	4.21 (1.46)	.79	.80	49.73								
2. Firm Age	27.75 (26.78)	—			-.01							
3. Number of Employees	116.43 (427.10)	—			.14	.38**						
4. Firm Costs	2.12 (1.54)	—			.07	.05	.01					
5. Industry Dynamism	2.55 (1.85)	—			.29**	.05	-.01	.05				
6. Strategic Flexibility	3.56 (.77)	.85	.85	49.08	.32**	-.11	-.03	.12	.17*			
7. Environmental Recycling	3.12 (1.33)	.66	.67	70.50	.36**	.08	.23**	-.06	.09	.11		
8. Market Orientation	3.74 (.68)	.87	.88	35.54	.45**	.02	.09	.02	.19*	.44**	.18*	
9. Org. Social Consciousness	3.10 (1.50)	.87	.88	70.61	.35**	-.06	.01	-.06	.19*	.12	.40**	.25**

* Correlation is significant at the 0.05 level (two-tailed).
** Correlation is significant at the 0.01 level (two-tailed).
[1] In order to maintain statistical power for regression analysis, the linear trend at point technique was utilized to replace a few missing variables (Olinsky, Chen, & Harlow, 2003).

Our first hypothesis stated market orientation is positively related to firm innovativeness, while the second hypothesis suggested a two-way moderation between market orientation and social consciousness. As evidenced in Table 13.2, we found strong support ($b = .26$; $p < .01$; two-tailed) for Hypothesis 1, which falls in line with previous research (e.g., Dibrell et al., 2011).

To test for Hypothesis 2, a weakly significant relationship ($b = -.13$; $p < .10$; two-tailed) was discovered for family firms between market orientation and social consciousness indicating preliminary support for this hypothesis. The interaction term was graphed for further interpretation. As seen in Figure 13.1, the slope for high-market orientation and high-organizational social consciousness for family firms is positive providing support for Hypothesis 2. Overall, the adjusted R^2 for the full model with only the family firm sample was .336.

Discussion and Conclusion

This research focuses on shedding light upon family entrepreneurial behaviors, more specifically how family values and culture influence entrepreneurial behaviors of the firm. Indeed, although family firms have been considered as strategically conservative, even when the needed innovations are market driven (Chrisman & Patel, 2012; Miller and Le Breton-Miller, 2005; Uhlaner et al., 2012), we show here that family firms do behave entrepreneurially by engaging in innovative behaviors. These firms even have a double advantage: they are able to rely on their specificities to translate their market orientation into innovations, and this relationship becomes stronger when

Table 13.2 Firm Innovativeness in Family Firms with 2-Way Interaction[1]

Variable/Step	Model 1	Model 2	Model 3	Model 4
Firm Age	−.15†	−.15†	−.13†	−.13†
Number of Employees	.15†	.11	.12	.11
Firm Costs	.06	.07	.08	.08
Industry Dynamism	.22**	.20**	.18**	.20**
Strategic Flexibility	.22**	.07	.07	.08
Environmental Recycling	.28***	.25***	.20**	.23**
Market Orientation		.32***	.30***	.26**
Org. Social Consciousness			.13†	.13†
Market Orientation x Org. Social Consciousness				−.13†
R^2	.274	.350	.364	.378
R^2 (adjusted)	.242	.316	.326	.336
F-value	8.51***	10.32***	9.51***	8.91***
ΔR^2		.076	.014	.014
Partial F (for ΔR^2)		15.67***	2.84†	2.98†

†$p < .10$ (two-tailed)
*$p < .05$ (two-tailed)
**$p < .01$ (two-tailed)
***$p < .001$ (two-tailed)
[1]Reported results are standardized regression coefficients.

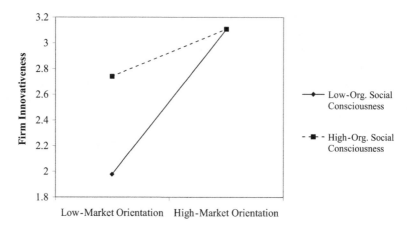

Figure 13.1   Market Orientation and Firm Innovativeness Moderated by Organizational Social Consciousness in Family Firms

an organizational social consciousness is concurrently emphasized. Market orientation and organizational social consciousness interact leading to higher levels of innovativeness.

Our findings show that the antecedents of entrepreneurial behaviors in family firms. Market orientation directly influences innovativeness, and the relationship between market orientation and innovativeness is enhanced by the firm's social orientation, leading to higher levels of innovativeness. We find that in family firms, the alignment of stakeholders (i.e., market orientation) and the firm's social interests (i.e., organizational social consciousness) contributes to entrepreneurial behaviors (i.e., firm innovativeness).

Family firms mobilize three of their idiosyncratic features (Craig, et al., 2014) to offer new products, services, and/or processes. First, they leverage on the family cultural context to induce the transformation of identified market needs into appropriate innovations (Frank, et al., 2010). Second, they use the stock of business acumen accumulated over generations to decipher customer needs to innovate (Pearson, et al., 2008; Hoy & Sharma, 2010). Third, they adopt management styles based on participation and mutual respect, resulting in greater flexibility (Sciascia, Clinton, Nason, James, & Rivera-Algarin, 2013).

The propensity of family firms to engage in corporate social responsibility activities derives directly from the integration of family values in the firm. Values such as long-term orientation, respect for, and protection of the employees, strong ties with the social and business community, integrity and continuity in the business policies, and concern for reputation (Miller & Le Breton-Miller, 2005; Neubauer, 1998; Ward, 2011) may weigh on the decision to undertake and maintain such activities. Whereas generally speaking nonfamily firms may undertake these activities with the aim of gaining a short-term competitive advantage and economic profit, family firms do so simply because it expresses the values they hold, through socioemotional wealth (Berrone et al., 2010; Kellermanns et al., 2012). We find evidence that on the contrary, social orientation contributes not only to the potential for socioemotional wealth but may also add to firm performance by supporting innovation.

This work also demonstrates the pertinence of organizational social consciousness as a construct to more effectively understand why family firms are able to attain long-term competitive advantage, as these firms are more engaged in their communities (Sharma & Sharma, 2010). Likewise, organizational social consciousness may be positively associated with the extent of socioemotional wealth in families (Berrone et al., 2010). Developing research based on organizational social consciousness would enlighten the socioemotional wealth literature and the futures of corporate social responsibility activities, helping family firms move toward more evolved models of corporate social responsibility (Bergamasci & Randerson, forthcoming).

For managers of family firms, our findings provide increasing evidence of the importance of aligning the social values of the family and the firm together. The social values of the family are embedded in the family business (Hoy & Sharma, 2010; Ward, 2011), and the resulting alignment of social values between the organization and its stakeholders is critical in increasing the effectiveness of market orientation strategies in strengthening firm innovativeness. Managers should strive to nurture an organizational culture which considers the social values of both the family and its stakeholders. In addition, we see the strength of market orientation to firm innovativeness. Seemingly, the benefits of market orientation are strong, and managers should continue to strategically emphasize this orientation in a family business. Family firms can draw upon their social values to be more innovative, which creates a unique competitive advantage.

Our analysis does suffer from limitations. Our use of cross-sectional data limits our findings, as well as increases the potential for common method bias, although the marginally significant interaction term diminishes these concerns. The findings of our study are limited only to other firms residing in industries which share similar attributes as the food processing industry. Our use of a single respondent may pose additional limitations of our findings as it provides only one perspective of the different attributes studied and does not consider other perspectives such as family and nonfamily employees.

Our study does not account for the heterogeneity of family firms. Miller, Le Breton-Miller, Lester, and Cannella (2007) discover lone-founding firms behave differently than family firms where the founder is not present, with the lone founder firms often acting more entrepreneurially. In our study, we were unable to test for this potential effect within the family firm context due to limitations of the data. However, firm age which may be considered a coarse proxy of the founder effects (i.e., a younger firm may be more likely to have the founder still heavily engaged in the strategic orientation of the firm), and our results in Table 13.2 indicate that firm age was not significant. This finding suggests lone founder effects may be diminished in our findings.

In future research, scholars may wish to consider how family firm heterogeneity, as well as the extent of family involvement in the family business, may influence the market orientation-organizational social consciousness-innovativeness relationship. For example, do lone-founder firms place a greater strategic emphasis on the market orientation to innovativeness relationship with less attention given to organizational social consciousness, compared to family firms with high family involvement and the founder no longer involved providing extensive emphasis on the organizational social consciousness at the possible expense of market orientation?

Scholars may also wish to consider organizational social consciousness as a possible proxy for socioemotional wealth, as have other corporate social responsibility behaviors been suggested to be a proxy (e.g., Berrone et al., 2010). If so, can the benefits associated with socioemotional wealth which accrues to the family be realized by employees, such as nonfamily employees? Is the strength of the relationship in the social values between the family firm and the employees the same for employees who are family members and employees who are not family members? How does this alignment or misalignment for nonfamily employees influence socioemotional wealth? Lastly, organizational social consciousness may be considered a measure of the social orientation of the firm, and further refinement of this scale to include additional family values which may directly influence the family firm's level of innovativeness is warranted.

Although family firms may be considered to be strategically conservative, we find that family firms who are able to integrate market orientation and organizational social consciousness behave more entrepreneurially than those family firms which do not engage in these activities.

There seems to be a strong link between the ability to understand the firm's customer and competitors (i.e., market orientation) and comprehending the social needs of the firm's stakeholders. Overall, an organization's strategic awareness of these different stakeholders provides a more open, communicative, innovative, and ultimately entrepreneurial work environment in family firms.

References

Adams, Janet S., Armen Taschian, and Ted H. Shore. "Ethics in family and non-family owned firms: An exploratory study." *Family Business Review* 9, no. 2 (1996): 157–170.

Aguinis, Herman, and Ante Glavas. "What we know and don't know about corporate social responsibility a review and research agenda." *Journal of Management* 38, no. 4 (2012): 932–968.

Beck, Lien, Wim Janssens, Marion Debruyne, and Tinne Lommelen. "A study of the relationships between generation, market orientation, and innovation in family firms." *Family Business Review*, 24, no. 3 (2011): 252–272.

Bergamaschi, M., & K. Randerson, K. "The futures of family businesses and the development of corporate social responsibility." *Futures: The Journal of Policy, Planning and Futures Studies*. (Forthcoming).

Berrone, Pascual, Cristina Cruz, Luis R. Gómez-Mejía, and Martin Larraza-Kintana. "Socioemotional wealth and corporate responses to institutional pressures: Do family-controlled firms pollute less?" *Administrative Science Quarterly* 55, no. 1 (2010): 82–113.

Bettinelli, Cristina, Alain Fayolle, and Kathleen Randerson. "Family entrepreneurship: A developing field." *Foundations and Trends (R) in Entrepreneurship* 10, no. 3 (2014): 161–236.

Campopiano, Giovanna, Alfredo De Massis, and Francesco Chirico. "Firm philanthropy in small-and medium-sized family firms the effects of family involvement in ownership and management." *Family Business Review* 27, no. 3 (2014): 244–258.

Carney, Michael, Marc Van Essen, Eric R. Gedajlovic, and Pursey PMAR Heugens. "What do we know about private family firms? A meta-analytical review." *Entrepreneurship Theory and Practice*, 39, no. 3 (2015): 513–544.

Cennamo, Carmelo, Pascual Berrone, Cristina Cruz, and Luis R. Gómez-Mejía. "Socioemotional wealth and proactive stakeholder engagement: Why family-controlled firms care more about their stakeholders." *Entrepreneurship Theory and Practice* 36, no. 6 (2012): 1153–1173.

Chan, Ricky YK. "Does the natural-resource-based view of the firm apply in an emerging economy? A survey of foreign invested enterprises in China." *Journal of Management Studies* 42, no. 3 (2005): 625–672.

Chrisman, James J., and Pankaj C. Patel. "Variations in R&D investments of family and nonfamily firms: Behavioral agency and myopic loss aversion perspectives." *Academy of Management Journal* 55, no. 4 (2012): 976–997.

Cohen, Boyd, and Monika I. Winn. "Market imperfections, opportunity and sustainable entrepreneurship." *Journal of Business Venturing* 22, no. 1 (2007): 29–49.

Craig, Justin, and Clay Dibrell. "The natural environment, innovation, and firm performance: A comparative study." *Family Business Review* 19, no. 4 (2006): 275–288.

Craig, Justin B., Clay Dibrell, and Robert Garrett. "Examining relationships among family influence, family culture, flexible planning systems, innovativeness and firm performance." *Journal of Family Business Strategy* 5, no. 3 (2014): 229–238.

Dibrell, Clay, Justin B. Craig, and Eric N. Hansen. "How managerial attitudes toward the natural environment affect market orientation and innovation." *Journal of Business Research* 64, no. 4 (2011): 401–407.

Dibrell, Clay, Justin B. Craig, Jaemin Kim, and Aaron J. Johnson. "Establishing how natural environmental competency, organizational social consciousness, and innovativeness relate." *Journal of Business Ethics* 127, no. 3 (2015): 591–605.

Dibrell, Clay, Peter S. Davis, and Justin Craig. "Fueling innovation through information technology in SMEs*." *Journal of Small Business Management* 46, no. 2 (2008): 203–218.

Delmas, Magali A., and Olivier Gergaud. "Sustainable certification for future generations: The case of family business." *Family Business Review* 27, no. 3 (2014): 228–243.

Donnelley, Robert G. "The family business." *Family Business Review* 1, no. 4 (1988): 427–445.

Dyer, W. Gibb, and David A. Whetten. "Family firms and social responsibility: Preliminary evidence from the S&P 500." *Entrepreneurship Theory and Practice* 30, no. 6 (2006): 785–802.

Faccio, Mara, and Larry HP Lang. "The ultimate ownership of Western European corporations." *Journal of Financial Economics* 65, no. 3 (2002): 365–395.

Frank, Hermann, Manfred Lueger, Lavinia Nosé, and Daniela Suchy. "The concept of 'Familiness': Literature review and systems theory-based reflections." *Journal of Family Business Strategy* 1, no. 3 (2010): 119–130.

Gallo, Miguel Ángel. "The family business and its social responsibilities." *Family Business Review* 17, no. 2 (2004): 135–149.

Hansen, Eric, Clay Dibrell, and Jon Down. "Market orientation, strategy, and performance in the primary forest industry." *Forest Science* 52, no. 3 (2006): 209–220.

Holderness, Clifford G. "The myth of diffuse ownership in the United States." *Review of Financial Studies* 22, no. 4 (2009): 1377–1408.

Hoy, Frank. "Organizational learning at the marketing/entrepreneurship interface." *Journal of Small Business Management* 46, no. 1 (2008): 152–158.

Hoy, Frank, & Pramodita Sharma. *Entrepreneurial family firms.* Englewood Cliffs, NJ: Prentice Hall, 2010.

Jaccard, James, and Robert Turrisi. *Interaction effects in multiple regression.* Vol. 72. Sage, 2003.

Kellermanns, Franz W., Clay Dibrell, and Cristina Cruz. "The role and impact of emotions in family business strategy: New approaches and paradigms." *Journal of Family Business Strategy* 5, no. 3 (2014): 277–279.

Kellermanns, Franz W., Kimberly A. Eddleston, and Thomas M. Zellweger. "Extending the socioemotional wealth perspective: A look at the dark side." *Entrepreneurship Theory and Practice* 36, no. 6 (2012): 1175–1182.

Lumpkin, G. Tom, and Gregory G. Dess. "Clarifying the entrepreneurial orientation construct and linking it to performance." *Academy of Management Review* 21, no. 1 (1996): 135–172.

Maignan, Isabelle, Odies Collins Ferrell, and G. Tomas M. Hult. "Corporate citizenship: cultural antecedents and business benefits." *Journal of the Academy of Marketing Science* 27, no. 4 (1999): 455–469.

Miller, Danny, and Isabelle Le Breton-Miller. *Managing for the long run: Lessons in competitive advantage from great family businesses.* Harvard Business Press, 2005.

Miller, Danny, Isabelle Le Breton-Miller, Richard H. Lester, and Albert A. Cannella. "Are family firms really superior performers?" *Journal of Corporate Finance* 13, no. 5 (2007): 829–858.

Narver, John C., and Stanley F. Slater. "The effect of a market orientation on business profitability." *The Journal of Marketing* (1990): 20–35.

Neubauer, Fred, and Alden G. Lank. *The family business: Its governance for sustainability.* Macmillan, 1998.

Neubaum, Donald O., Clay Dibrell, and Justin B. Craig. "Balancing natural environmental concerns of internal and external stakeholders in family and non-family businesses." *Journal of Family Business Strategy* 3, no. 1 (2012): 28–37.

Olinsky, Alan, Shaw Chen, and Lisa Harlow. "The comparative efficacy of imputation methods for missing data in structural equation modeling." *European Journal of Operational Research* 151, no. 1 (2003): 53–79.

Patel, Pankaj C., and James J. Chrisman. "Risk abatement as a strategy for R&D investments in family firms." *Strategic Management Journal* 35, no. 4 (2014): 617–627.

Pearson, Allison W., Jon C. Carr, and John C. Shaw. "Toward a theory of familiness: A social capital perspective." *Entrepreneurship Theory and Practice* 32, no. 6 (2008): 949–969.

Sciascia, Salvatore, Eric Clinton, Robert S. Nason, Albert E. James, and Juan O. Rivera-Algarin. "Family communication and innovativeness in family firms." *Family Relations* 62, no. 3 (2013): 429–442.

Sharma, Pramodita, James J. Chrisman, and Jess H. Chua. "Strategic management of the family business: Past research and future challenges." *Family Business Review* 10, no. 1 (1997): 1–35.

Sharma, Pramodita, and Sanjay Sharma. "Drivers of proactive environmental strategy in family firms." *Business Ethics Quarterly* 21, no. 02 (2011): 309–334.

Sharma, Sanjay, and Harrie Vredenburg. "Proactive corporate environmental strategy and the development of competitively valuable organizational capabilities." *Strategic Management Journal* 19, no. 8 (1998): 729–753.

Slater, Stanley F., and John C. Narver. "Market-oriented is more than being customer-led." *Strategic Management Journal* 20, no. 12 (1999): 1165–1168.

Slevin, Dennis P., and Jeffrey G. Covin. "Entrepreneurship as firm behavior: A research model." *Advances in Entrepreneurship, Firm Emergence, and Growth* 2 (1995): 175–224.

Tagiuri, Renato, and John Davis. "Bivalent attributes of the family firm." *Family Business Review* 9, no. 2 (1996): 199–208.

Tokarczyk, John, Eric Hansen, Mark Green, and Jon Down. "A Resource-Based View and Market Orientation Theory Examination of the Role of 'Familiness' in Family Business Success." *Family Business Review* 20, no. 1 (2007): 17–31.

Uhlaner, Lorraine M., Franz W. Kellermanns, Kimberly A. Eddleston, and Frank Hoy. "The entrepreneuring family: A new paradigm for family business research." *Small Business Economics* 38, no. 1 (2012): 1–11.

Uhlaner, Lorraine M., H. J. M. van Goor-Balk, and Enno Masurel. "Family business and corporate social responsibility in a sample of Dutch firms." *Journal of Small Business and Enterprise Development* 11, no. 2 (2004): 186–194.

Van Gils, Anita, Clay Dibrell, Donald O. Neubaum, and Justin B. Craig. "Social Issues in the Family Enterprise." *Family Business Review* 27, no. 3 (2014): 193–205.

Ward, John L. *Keeping the family business healthy: How to plan for continuing growth, profitability, and family leadership.* Palgrave Macmillan, 2011.

Zachary, Miles A., Aaron McKenny, Jeremy Collin Short, and G. Tyge Payne. "Family business and market orientation construct validation and comparative analysis." *Family Business Review* 24, no. 3 (2011): 233–251.

Zahra, Shaker A. "Entrepreneurial risk taking in family firms." *Family Business Review* 18, no. 1 (2005): 23–40.

Zahra, Shaker A., James C. Hayton, Donald O. Neubaum, Clay Dibrell, and Justin Craig. "Culture of family commitment and strategic flexibility: The moderating effect of stewardship." *Entrepreneurship Theory and Practice* 32, no. 6 (2008): 1035–1054.

14

CORPORATE ENTREPRENEURSHIP IN FAMILY BUSINESS

The When and How

Tommaso Minola, Giovanna Campopiano, Mara Brumana,
Lucio Cassia, and Robert Paul Garrett

Introduction

Entrepreneurial endeavors are not limited to individual efforts in matching environmental opportunities and resources to create wealth. Since "entrepreneurial attitudes and behaviors are necessary for firms of all sizes to prosper and flourish" (Barringer and Bluedorn, 1999: 256), modern corporations are systematically challenged to find new ways of serving markets, innovating new products, and dynamically organizing resources and capabilities in order to foster entrepreneurship as an enduring organizational behavior (Busenitz and Barney, 1997). In the domain of entrepreneurship, scholars are increasingly interested in investigating the phenomenon of corporate entrepreneurship (CE) as the set of entrepreneurial activities and strategies that firms can leverage to prosper and grow, developing from start-up to the maturity phase when the firm has to rejuvenate itself to survive (Kuratko, Hornsby, and Montagno, 1990; Markides, 1998; Hitt et al., 1999; Stringer, 2000). The overarching framework of CE, as suggested by Sharma and Chrisman (1999), comprehensively integrates innovation, corporate venturing, and strategic renewal. These entrepreneurial activities also have positive effects on firm performance (Kuratko, Hornsby, and Montagno, 1990; McGrath, Venkataraman, and MacMillan, 1992; Knight, 1997; Zahra, Nielsen, and Bogner, 1998). Most important, CE represents a source of constant renewal and allows repeated acts of entrepreneurship through a firm's development pattern.

CE scholars have recently found great interest in the case of family firms. Family firms are defined as businesses "governed and/or managed with the intention to shape and pursue the vision of the business held by a dominant coalition controlled by members of the same family or a small number of families in a manner that is potentially sustainable across generations of the family or families" (Chua, Chrisman, and Sharma, 1999: 25); and they represent a particularly rich context for the study of CE (Hall, Melin, and Nordqvist, 2001). Besides, family firms account for the vast majority of firms in most economies (IFERA, 2003). Given their unique concern for sustained regeneration and transgenerational succession, the development of CE is specifically critical to family firms (Nordqvist and Melin, 2010). Transgenerational entrepreneurship—i.e., the process through which a family uses and develops entrepreneurial

281

mindsets, family-influenced resources, and capabilities—in particular, allows family firms to consistently adopt innovative, risky and proactive strategic postures. Based on this, they can create value across generations and uniquely support the longevity of the business activity (Zellweger, Nason, and Nordqvist, 2012).

Research has shown that family firms are potentially different in their engagement in entrepreneurial activities with respect to other businesses. Family-centered economic and non-economic goals, together with particularistic power structures, incentives and norms that often characterize these firms (Carney, 2005; Harris et al., 1994), severely affect strategic and entrepreneurial processes (Kellermanns et al., 2008). "For these reasons, the intersection of research in family business and corporate entrepreneurship presents fertile ground for future research efforts" (McKelvie et al., 2014: 341).

The uniqueness and ubiquity of family firms have fostered their recognition by management and entrepreneurship scholars (De Massis et al., 2012). At the same time, their rich behavioral and organizational diversity has prompted family business research to contribute and inform mainstream management and entrepreneurship theories (Sharma, Chrisman, and Gersick, 2012). Whereas most of the aforementioned strategic dimensions of CE in family firms have received attention from recent empirical contributions (Kellermanns and Eddleston, 2006) and research systematizations (McKelvie et al., 2014; Sciascia and Bettinelli, 2013), there seems to be one major gap that still undermines the establishment of the field—thus calling for urgent investigation—that is, the temporal dimension. Indeed, there is room to further understand how antecedents, boundaries, and processes of CE vary along the dynamic development of family firms over time. The inter- or multi-generation nature of enterprising families (Cruz and Nordqvist, 2012) and the role of different family system configurations (Kellermanns and Eddleston, 2006) have received some attention in the scholarly investigation about CE; however, we miss an understanding of the extent to which the recently developed body of research on CE in family firms has explicitly integrated these elements and has conceptualized the temporal evolution of family businesses. In particular, based on the extant body of knowledge, we formulate two research questions: (a) How can the complexity of family firms' dynamic evolution contribute to explain family firm engagement in CE in different moments in time? (b) To what extent has research on CE acknowledged this, and which major areas of contribution remain untapped?

To address this, this study first investigates the dynamic nature of CE in family firms. To assess whether Hoy's (2006) claim, that family firms' entrepreneurial initiatives should be investigated considering the "complicating factor of life cycles," has been sufficiently explored by literature, we focus on the role of temporal dynamics in a sample of 75 papers on CE in family firms from scholarly journals; in particular, we explore the individual and joint impact of different developmental dimensions of family firms on CE activities and strategies. Because of their distinctive characteristics in terms of ownership and governance, management, and long-term orientation, family firms have to simultaneously cope with multiple life cycles (individual, familial, ownership, corporate, etc.) in order to innovate and prosper (Gersick et al., 1997). Drawing on the Family Business System Model (Tagiuri and Davis, 1996) we concentrate on the role of ownership, business, and family developmental stages and cycles (Gersick et al., 1997). In that view, these developmental dimensions can be seen as interacting variables that impact the family firms' entrepreneurial behavior (Hoy, 2006). Family firms offer a unique perspective to clarify the complex process of CE and its triggers. Therefore, family firms represent a particularly insightful domain to explore the "when" question of CE (Hoy, 2006; McKelvie et al., 2014). Second, this research provides an explorative conceptual development based on the most prominent theoretical conceptualization of family firms' developmental dimension (Gersick et al., 1997) and CE (Kuratko et al., 2010), to define theoretical and empirical gaps and suggest future research directions.

The chapter is structured as follows. The next section develops the theoretical foundation of our work by clarifying the domain of CE and the developmental nature of family firms. The third section provides a literature review of CE in family firms by specifically assessing the extent to which such developmental nature is accounted for by the scholarly debate. The fourth section builds an agenda for future research. The fifth session discusses and concludes the chapter.

Theoretical Framework

CE and Family Business

CE refers to the set of entrepreneurial activities that can help a firm to grow from its early stage, through maturity, and rejuvenate to survive a corporate or market decline (Kuratko et al., 1990). CE is an umbrella concept that includes phenomena ranging from new firm creation to corporate venturing, from innovation to internationalization (Sharma and Chrisman, 1999). A number of definitions have been provided in extant literature (McKelvie et al., 2014). One of the cornerstones in the field is considered the definition by Guth and Ginsberg (1990) that encompasses two main components of CE: the creation of new ventures within existing organizations (*corporate venturing*) and the transformation of organizations via *strategic renewal*.

Covin and Miles (1999) define CE through a broader approach, considering concepts such as *sustained regeneration, organizational rejuvenation*, and *domain redefinition*. In parallel, Sharma and Chrisman (1999) identified three domains within which CE should be investigated; these are *corporate venturing, innovation*, and *strategic renewal*. Their study summarized and framed the diverse past contributions, discussing also the broad variety of terms used for the entrepreneurial efforts within an existing organization, such as *corporate entrepreneurship* (Burgelman, 1983; Zahra, 1991); *corporate venturing* (Biggadike, 1979); *intrapreneuring* (Pinchot, 1985); *internal corporate entrepreneurship* (Jones and Butler, 1992); *internal entrepreneurship* (Vesper, 1984); *strategic renewal* (Guth and Ginsberg, 1990); and *venturing* (Hornsby et al., 1993).

Entrepreneurial Orientation (EO) is a construct central to the scholarly conversation on corporate entrepreneurship (Hoskisson et al., 2011). EO focuses on the extent to which firms are characterized by a decision-making style that is proactive, risk-taking, and innovative as they pursue opportunities (Miller, 1983; Covin and Slevin, 1990). Most studies find that EO enhances firm performance, but they also highlight the importance of boundary conditions. For example, previous research has assessed the contingent role of firm resources (Wiklund and Shepherd, 2003), firm culture (Burgelman, 1984), firm structure (Green, Covin, and Slevin, 2008), social capital (Stam and Elfring, 2008), as well as environmental attributes (Covin and Slevin, 1989; Lumpkin and Dess, 2001; Wiklund and Shepherd, 2005; Zahra and Covin, 1995). Firms exhibiting EO are characterized as "geared towards innovation in the product market field by carrying out risky initiatives, and which are the first to develop innovations in a proactive way in an attempt to defeat their competitors" (Miller, 1983, p. 771). With respect to CE, it has to be acknowledged that EO may play a different role according to the different extension of the concept adopted by scholars in their investigations (George and Marino, 2011). Indeed, while EO has been considered a direct measure of CE in some cases (e.g., Kemelgor, 2002), in other studies it has been considered a strategic posture that represents an antecedent (e.g., Lumpkin and Dess, 1996; Zahra, 1991) or a conditioning factor (Dess and Lumpkin, 2005) of CE. However, even if Miller's (1983) foundational definition of EO as a strategic posture is distinct from CE from a procedural point of view, following numerous recent works (Covin and Lumpkin, 2011; Memili, Lumpkin, and Dess, 2010), we frame EO as "orientation towards corporate entrepreneurship actions," as Zahra points out (1991, p. 272). Based on this, and in line with recent reviews (e.g., McKelvie et al., 2014), we will include EO in our review of CE.

In the field of CE, scholars have addressed several issues, which have been studied according to different levels of analysis and during multiple stages of the life cycle of a venture. A number of researchers, in particular, have developed a stream of this research field asking whether the family has a role in fostering CE, and in building the context to develop a venture entrepreneurially. Moreover, the ubiquity of family businesses in the world (Anderson and Reeb, 2003) and their important contribution to economies across the world (Villalonga and Amit, 2009) prompted scholars to investigate entrepreneurial activities in family businesses. Family businesses represent a particular type of enterprise as the presence of the family unquestionably affects the business. Investment horizons, risk aversion, diversification plans, and return aspirations (Thomsen and Pedersen, 2000) have different value for different owners. Ownership structure, therefore, affects the firm's entrepreneurial activities and innovation outcomes (Hoskisson et al., 2002). Moreover, family involvement in ownership and governance generates resource bundles unique to the family firm (Habbershon and Williams, 1999), such as social capital (Sirmon and Hitt, 2003), human capital (Sardeshmukh and Corbett, 2011) and *patient* financial capital (Muñoz-Bullón and Sanchez-Bueno, 2011). These resources and processes distinctly affect family firms' tendency to rely on CE. Furthermore, the distinctive incentives, power structures, and legitimacy norms that characterize family firms (Gedajlovic and Carney, 2010; Gedajlovic, Lubatkin, and Schulze, 2004; Jensen and Meckling, 1976) have been shown to create particular advantages and barriers that may significantly affect their entrepreneurial behaviors.

However, Chrisman, Chua, and Sharma (2005) argued that our knowledge about CE activities of family businesses is comparatively underdeveloped in comparison to what we know about CE in general. To contribute in this stream, Hoy (2006) suggests disentangling the different dynamic mechanisms of family influence on CE; in this vein, we introduce the developmental model of family firms drawing on Gersick et al. (1997).

Family Business Developmental Dimensions

Family businesses can be described as three independent but overlapping subsystems – business, ownership and family (Tagiuri and Davis, 1996). The three-circle model, by separating these three domains, is a very useful tool for clarifying the motivations, perspectives and hence behaviors of individuals differently positioned in the system, as well as for understanding conflicts, priorities, and boundaries in family firms. For example, the decision to distribute or reinvest dividends may be better understood considering each participant position in the three-circle model: a family member, who is an owner but not involved in the business, may prefer dividends to be distributed; conversely, a family member working in the family firm without owning its shares may prefer dividends to be reinvested in order to expand the business and create career opportunities.

In order to make the three-circle model more suitable to the reality of family and business organization, Gersick et al. (1997) advance an additional dimension to be considered: time. As a matter of fact, the model provided by Tagiuri and Davis (1996) is static and does not consider that ownership, as well as business and family systems, change over time, developing across generations, as the family and the firm grow.

Among the different approaches to handling time, Gersick et al. (1997) initially suggest the adoption of the life cycle as a paradigm to model how ownership, business and family systems change (Hoy, 2006). Life cycles have been borrowed from biological evolution theories, and to some extent they can provide relevant insights according to the cyclic metaphor of birth, growth, maturity, decline, and renewal of organizations, as well as families, products or industries (e.g., Hoy, 1995; Scott, 1971). However, this model may appear too simplistic. The development of each dimension can follow a different approach, and therefore, different perspectives may be adopted to represent the evolution of each dimension over time. Indeed, there are firms that intentionally remain small in terms of size and organizational complexity for a long time, especially in family-run companies (e.g., Carland et al., 1984). Or, it is possible to find family businesses where ownership is concentrated along the generations as a pruning strategy is adopted in the succession process (Lambrech and Lievens, 2008).

The main drawback in adopting a standard life cycle approach relates to the fact that it is mostly suitable for entities whose development is ascribable to biological timetables. When considering organizations, and in particular family firms, it is also necessary to think about the social and economic conditions that continuously change (Hareven, 1978). Moreover, the difficulty to identify exact stages in life cycles, due to the continuity of family business system development, led Gersick et al. (1997) to think of more sophisticated perspectives. Indeed, it might be simplistic to consider that each system's structure changes according to a fixed path, as it is the case of ownership or business systems that may remain static over time and across generations, as well as suddenly change several times in a very short period of time. For example, equity may be transferred back and forth within and between generations, or consolidate and grow for a long period (Gersick et al., 1997); and there may be firms entering a growth phase after the maturity stage, or have several growth peaks and declines while still in the startup stage (Greiner, 1997). Indeed, it is the "biological metaphor of life cycle" that does not allow for nonlinearity, unpredictability and emergence (Wales, Monsen, and McKelvie, 2011); instead, it may be worth following an approach to growth and evolution that considers the dynamic nature of firms' development, adopting a framework that allows to consider developmental dimensions beyond the simplistic view of subsequent stage-based life cycles (Levie and Lichtenstein, 2010).

The Three-Dimensional Developmental Model proposed by Gersick and colleagues (1997) goes beyond the biological metaphor of life cycle and thus provide a useful framework to investigate the development of FBs over time. The dynamics of family firms, indeed, are analyzed through a combination of stages across ownership, family and businesses. The progression from one form to another along the three dimensions is portrayed as developmental since it is possible to find, at least partially, a predictable sequence of these forms while the business family ages and the business changes in terms of growth and complexity over time (Gersick et al., 1997). "Thinking developmentally" about these three dimensions means, on the one hand, taking into account the temporal evolution of the family firm's ownership structure, development of family issues—such as the entry of a new generation, the authority transfer from parents to children, the relationships between siblings and cousins—as well as organizational change. On the other hand, it allows a certain degree of flexibility in the description of family firms' developmental patterns.

In Table 14.1 we briefly describe the characteristics, the idiosyncratic challenges and managerial issues in each stage of the three developmental dimensions.

Ownership Developmental Dimension

The Ownership Developmental Dimension (ODD) describes the development of ownership as the factor that intrinsically characterizes the family business as such. Beyond the firm name or the employment of family members, it is the family ownership that defines the family business (Nordqvist, 2005). Changes in ownership, an event of small entity, can represent a dramatic change in firm identity and strategy, and in turn, affect its behaviors and business processes (Miller, Le Breton-Miller, and Lester, 2011). The developmental thinking, as opposed to rigid life cycle reasoning, is of particular value in analyzing ownership; even when single owners change, ownership structure can remain static for generations. Conversely, in most cases, ownership dilution is a slow, on-going process, that is subject to a continuous and long transitional process, rather than static

Table 14.1 Family Business Developmental Dynamics

Ownership Developmental Dimension (ODD)

Stage (characteristics)	Key Challenges	Keywords
Controlling Owner Stage (ownership control consolidated in one individual or couple; other owners, if any, have only token holdings and do not excercise signbificant ownership authority)	Capitalization	Family firm financing (psychological strings attachment) and effect on risk perception
		Exit (split or sell) and decision about venture capital involvement
	Balancing unitary control with input from key stakeholders	Autonomy of control
		Clarity and efficiency
		Leadership concentration/authority
		Competition among offspring for the owner-manager's attention, approval and favor (contingent to FDD)
	Choosing an ownership structure for the next generation	Ownership dispersion choice and effect on institutional investors involvement/governance mechanisms + effect on progression along the ODD
Sibling Partnership Stage (two or more siblings with ownership control; effective control in the hands of one sibling generation)	Developing a process for shared control among owners	Unquestioned autonomy
		Close relationship parents-offspring (legacy)
		Legitimacy of the quasi-parental leader
		Procedural justice (how the first among equals leader was chosen)
		Lack of individual leadership (in the case of truly egalitarian arrangement)
	Defining the role of non-employed owners	Principal-principal agency conflict (employed vs non-employed owners)
		Obligations to non-employed siblings
		Governance structure (role of the board of directors)
		Communication issues and decentralization of responsibilities (see Ling et al. 2008 AMJ)
	Retaining capital	Easier access to debt for growth
		Balance of priority between dividends (driven by personal leasure or personal investments - external venturing) or reinvestment (innovation and internal corporate venturing)
		Mutual influence of these two characteristics (if banks see an unbalance they are less willing to extend their funds)
	Controlling the factional orientation of family branches	Conflict in the sibling group and role of in-laws
		Mistrust
		Family branches

Stage (characteristics)	Key Challenges	Keywords
Cousin Consortium Stage (many cousin shareholders; mixture of employed and non-employed owners)	Managing the complexity of the family and the shareholder group	Distance from the founder (legacy) Political issues Family identity Non-employed owners tend to focus on dividends and question their continued investment in the company Role of board of directors
	Creating a family business capital market	Unplanned demands by cousins to be cashed out Objectivity, fairness, patience, and role of outside professionals (interaction ODD – BDD) help internal market for shares that smoth the overall processes of the family business
Business Developmental Dimension (BDD)		
Start-up Business (informal organizational structure, with owner–manager at the center; one product)	Survival Rational analysis vs the dream	Market entry Business planning Understanding technology Financial intertwining Ability to analyze objectively Feed their passion Lateral thinking/strategic flexibility (considering other related business ventures which could be more successful) – (this could be enhanced in later stages of the ODD) Family pressures may keep away from/encourage entrepreneurial dreams (interaction ODD – BDD) children feeling of deprivation of attention and affection
Expansion/ Formalization Business (increasingly functional structure; multiple products or business lines)	Evolving the owner–manager role and professionalizing the business Strategic planning Organizational systems and policies Cash management	More formal hierarchy Professional hiring Authority delegation (ambivalence: facilitations but also conflicts – e.g. start-stop pattern) Product quality and availability Insufficient funds and open to external investors Complex relationship between strategy and structure Information gathering and analysis as a way to see new opportunities Management and control systems (e.g. ERP) Orientation towards external investors
Mature Business (organizational structure supporting stability; stable or declining customer base, with modest growth; divisional structure run by senior management team; wel-established organizational routines)	Strategic refocus	Systematic analysis to generate new options for new business Discussion Role of the board of directors

(Continued)

Stage (characteristics)	Key Challenges	Keywords
	Management and ownership commitment	Career advancement opportunities for both family and non-family managers
		Role of non-family managers (experience, expertise, buffer against inappropriate family influence, supervision and mentoring of the next generation of family managers) interaction with ODD/FDD
		Incentive tactics
		Recruitment tactics
	Reinvestment	Balance economics vs non-economics and family-centered vs non-family centered goals (e.g. temptation among the owners to treat the company as a static and automatic source of income)
Family Developmental Dimension (FDD)		
Young Business Family Stage (adult generation under forty; children, if any, under 18)	Creating a workable marriage enterprise	Dream ("Marriage enterprise" is the system that the couple builds to accomplish its dream of partnership and family
		Style: enmeshed/disengaged
		Distribution of power (for example, husband/father in control, shared authority, spouse co-preneurship, matriarchies, …)
	Making initial decisions about the relationship between work and family	Special pressures in business families (demands of the business, dynamics with the extended family; work-parenting dilemmas)
		Need of a strong sense of identity (as a separate young family)
	Working out relationships with the extended family	Balance between sides of the extended family
		Family involvement in the business
		Marriage approval by the business-owning extended family
	Raising children	Pushing back the horizon of the future
		Psychological legacy of the firm
Entering the Business Stage (senior generation between 35 and 55; junior generation in teens and 20s)	Managing the midlife transition	Leadership
		Self-Assessment (From exploration, achievement focus, commitment-making to maximum authority, senior status and control)
	Separation and individuation of the younger generation	Brothers and sisters make important decisions (childhood relationships shaped by parents, evolve into adult sibling relationships)
		Birth order
		Differentiation (the centrifugal force of sibling groups acting to pull individuals apart)
		Identification (the centripetal force that holds siblings together)
	Facilitating a good process for initial career decisions	Continuity for the business
		Ownership vs managerial involvement
		Ownership dispersion
		Parent control
		Dynamic of offspring involvement
		Parents' aspirations for their children

Stage (characteristics)	Key Challenges	Keywords
Working Together Stage (senior generation between 50 and 65; junior generation between 20 and 45)	Fostering cross-generational cooperation and communication	Communication (Emotional tone of interactions; quality in terms of honesty, openness, consistency) and other linking mechanisms In-laws (into the emotional dynamics of the business family, but often without access to information of the siblings-spouses)
	Encouraging productive conflict management	Authority Collaboration Conflict as an inevitable aspect of family life
	Managing the three-generation working together family	Positive bonds enhancing vitality Clarity of the middle generation's authority compromised
Passing the Baton Stage (senior generation age 60 and above)	Senior generation disengagement from the business	Succession/Transition Continuity/Preservation Fear (siblings' fear of differentiation; offspring's fear of being perceived as greedy; spouse's fear of loss of identity and activities; family's fear of the leader's death)
	Generational transfer of family leadership	Emotional issues Transfer of power and leadership

(Summary based on Gersick et al., 1997)

and discrete-event evolution. Nonetheless, hybrid situations between different ownership stages are not infrequent, and sometimes they even last for several years. Therefore, even if the progressive approach through sequences partially describes much of family business ownership evolution, a loose interpretation should be given to this developmental phenomenon.

The first stage (*controlling owner*) is characterized by the centrality of the founder, in terms of entrepreneurial leadership, managerial processes, and governance. The board, if included at all, has mostly a nominal value and plays no real advisory role (Miller et al., 2011). Governance processes are quite simple and based on the nature of the relationship between the owner and both family and non-family stakeholders. At this stage, firms are normally small, undercapitalized and quite extensively dependent on the owner's and his family's wealth. The embeddedness of family financial provision is quite common at this stage, and implies a number of socioemotional obligations, norms, and interdependence among family members—the phenomenon is known as 'money with psychological strings attached'—that consistently condition firms strategy, risk-taking and growth propensity (Au and Kwan, 2009). In this case, the role of the family as an investor is extremely important (Habbershon and Pistrui, 2002) and limits individual discretion in growing the business. At this stage, the principal also faces a trade-off, exacerbated by resource dependence toward stakeholders internal and external to the firm, in balancing unitary control and leadership with key stakeholders' involvement. While central authority grants clarity, efficiency and quick decisional processes (Ward, 1997), stakeholder involvement may support strategic diversity, resource access and legitimacy of the business as a shelter to the liability of newness (Stinchcombe, 1965). Finally, during the controlling owner stage, the familial nature of firm ownership unavoidably introduces a number of issues related to the persistence of the firm as a family enterprise. Owners have, in fact, to consider offspring harmony and competition (Ward, 1997), prospective ownership dilution and/or split among different ventures (Rosa et al., 2013) as well as ownership structure and governance of the family enterprise that allow a smooth control relinquishment in line with family and business needs. Needless to say, many families (e.g., culture, generational involvement) and business developmental considerations (e.g., financial prosperity, growth) moderate this process. Indeed, it is also worth considering that especially cultural aspects may affect the way family owners plan the main decisions regarding their business. While Gersick et al. (1997) basically refer to the American conjugal family, different models may instead prevail in other contexts, like the Japanese stem family with two or three generations sharing the same household and providing mutual insurance under the same roof, or the Chinese patrilinear family, with male descendants living together with wives and children until a dissolution happens when the parents pass away (Morioka 1967).

The next stage suggested by Gersick et al. (1997) refers to family businesses that have longer survived and are normally larger; the authors refer to the *sibling partnership stage*, which is characterized, among others, by the crucial challenge of defining a shared but also effective control. Whether this happens through quasi-parental leadership, 'first among equal' form or truly egalitarian arrangement (Grote, 2003), the outcome of this process is crucial to the survival of the firm; it is in fact the result of a complex fit between the overall family style and sibling history, on the one hand, and ownership structure itself, on the other. Family concerns, in particular, are dynamically dependent on the entrepreneurial legacy embedded in the (very diverse) set of relationship that next generation members have with parents (Chirico et al., 2011) and the perceived procedural justice regarding how the leadership was chosen. At this stage non-employee family owners start becoming relevant, in terms of claims and conditioning effects on the business; a sort of agency problem raises, that engenders conflicts among two types of principals (employed vs. not-employed) and affects priorities in the allocation of resources, strategic choices between harvesting and investing (such as deciding whether or not to invest in a new venture), and in turn affects the family business as a whole.

At the final stage (*cousin consortium*), the ownership structure, together with the family and the organization, has grown in complexity. Managing complexity is truly a key challenge that can threaten business survival to a large extent. As a result of this, complex coalitions, political motivation, and identity conflict are quite recurrent at this stage (Shepherd and Haynie, 2009). They affect information and knowledge sharing within the family business, thus enhancing agency and transaction costs. Risk taking and innovation, as well as new administrative routines, are seriously hampered by this complexity. Objectivity, fairness, and patience are common remedies to the inefficiency inherent to this stage. For this reason, the professionalization of both family and non-family members is often a crucial process for the survival of the organization. At this stage, the firm has to prepare for exit plans of family owners and internal financial markets for shares that help ownership transition smoothness and effectiveness (Ward, 1997). This exit/entry process can profoundly change business identity and strategies, but it can also serve as a powerful trigger to entrepreneurial and new venturing processes. Clearly this depends much on other aspects of the developmental model suggested by Gersick et al. (1997), such as the business developmental stage, discussed in the remainder of the chapter.

Business Developmental Dimension

The Business Developmental Dimension (BDD) describes the development of the family business over time. Within the Three-Dimensional Developmental Model theorized by Gersick, the BDD covers three stages—start-up, expansion and formalization, and maturity—and focuses on two key indicators of organizational change: growth, in terms of sales, volume, and number of employees, and complexity of the organizational structure. Particularly, the ability to objectively analyze the 'dreamed' project and to lateral think about it are key in the *start-up business stage, which* corresponds to the founding of the company and the following years when survival is in question. During this phase, a premature commitment to a personal or family dream could retain the entrepreneur from considering more successful business ventures and this tendency is likely to be enhanced in later stages of the ODD because of a lock-in in family legacy. More formal hierarchy, professional hiring, and delegation to non-family members, are among the managerial issues to face, as the business expands and organizational complexity increases (*expansion/formalization*). Authority delegation, in particular, is ambivalent because can facilitate the decision-making process, but also generate conflict (Hatak and Roessl, 2015). The expansion and formalization stage may last few years or be a long phase of gradual evolution, also depending on external conditions, competition, technology change, and product life cycle. The final stage of the BDD corresponds to a phase of stasis—*maturity*—with an organizational structure supporting stability and very modest expectations about growth. The mature business stage appears to be the most insightful in terms of interaction among the different developmental dimensions. For instance, it is in this phase that non-family managers become increasingly influential: they act as experience and expertise providers, a buffer against inappropriate family influence in management, and they can also play a role in the supervision and mentoring of the next generation of family members. This acts as a possible trigger on their propensity towards firm's professionalization and transgenerational entrepreneurship (Hall and Nordqvist, 2008). Moreover, during the expansion/formalization phase FBs leverage on growth and organizational complexity to meet ODD and FDD needs, namely an evolving ownership group and a developing family.

Overall, the literature has focused on corporate governance dynamics as they insightfully and uniquely evolve along the whole business developmental dimension. Recent contributions (e.g., Filatotchev et al., 2006) postulate a process view of corporate governance. Changes in the scope and function of governance mechanism are necessary as the company evolves from early stages towards maturity and, eventually, decline and these are associated with increasing agency costs. These dynamics also concern family firms where agency costs are confined in the early stages of the business because of altruism, but then increase as the venture becomes larger and more established (Karra et al., 2006). It is therefore particularly interesting to observe business development dynamics in family firms, as they might affect family firms' entrepreneurial attitude and behavior (Kellermanns and Eddleston, 2006; Kellermanns et al., 2008).

Family Developmental Dimension

With respect to the three circle model, the third dimension that has to be considered as relevant for a family business relates to the family and in particular to the evolving relationships among family members (Tagiuri and Davis, 1996). Labeled as business families, these groups of people involved in a business, and simultaneously linked by blood ties, have to face several issues that change over time: the family evolves and its development is not free from a number of challenges. Along the family developmental dimension, it is possible to identify four steps (or stages) that stress the most important phases of the life of the family considered as a unit (Gersick et al, 1997). Therefore, in the beginning, the *young business family* has to deal with the creation of a 'marriage enterprise' characterized by its style with respect to the role of each partner, whether they enmesh business and private life or instead try to separate the two systems as much as possible, thus caring about the balance between work and family, and responding to the pressures coming from their extended families, discussing to what extent to involve members from both parties. Later on (*entering the business*), the family has to recognize the role of the leaders who self-assess as incumbents, while teen and young adult offspring grow in the family business atmosphere. Afterward, there is a phase (*entering the business*) when all family members work together and thus communication, collaboration and, in general, linking mechanisms become extremely relevant in order to avoid disruptive conflicts. Finally—*passing the baton*—succession issues emerge; these, while in-depth investigated in management literature, are mainly neglected if the focus is specifically on family sociological issues. The amount of challenges that business families face reveals the importance of this developmental dimension, and this aspect has been investigated from multidisciplinary perspectives. For example, historians have nurtured an interest in analyzing, according to a developmental perspective, the roles and behaviors of families involved in business, in order to examine how the family changes as each individual enters into and exits from different roles over time, as well as to explain how individual and group timings synchronize (Hareven, 1978).

Thus, family dynamics may affect to some extent the behaviors of individuals working into the family business. Moreover, the managerial issues that the business family faces in each stage (see Table 14.1) may affect the decisions regarding CE of this type of firms.

Corporate Entrepreneurship and Family Business Developmental Dimensions: Evidence From the Existing Literature

Considering the paramount growth of research in the last decades about CE in family firms, this chapter aims to assess both conceptual elaboration and empirical validations of the life cycle and developmental arguments.

In this section, we systematize the debate on CE in FB and explore the role of different and coexisting life cycles on family firms' entrepreneurial behavior. The ultimate objectives are: (a) to assess the extent to which scholarly contributions in the field have accounted for the developmental dimensions of the family business system; (b) to define theoretical and empirical gaps; (c) to suggest future research directions.

In performing the review of the literature, on which the findings of this study are based, we searched for published articles in journals with a peer-reviewed evaluation process and proceedings of conferences, available on Scopus database in the time period 1990-November 2013. To ensure substantive relevance of the potential articles, we based our search algorithm on the conceptualization of corporate entrepreneurship provided in literature, and thus looked for the combination of the following research keywords in the title, the abstract, or the paper keywords: Famil★ AND Ventur★; Famil★ AND "Entrepreneurial orientation"; Famil★ AND Renewal★; Famil★ AND "Corporate entrepreneur★"; Famil★ AND "Strategic entrepreneur★"; Famil★ AND (startup★ OR start-up★ OR spin★); Famil★ AND Intrapreneur★; Famil★ AND Rejuvenation (Sharma and Chrisman, 1999). This process led us to select 936 papers. To guarantee the relevance of the articles we read all the abstracts checking for a discussion related to family business. Indeed, most papers discuss the role of family background or clearly revolve around phenomena of new firm creation, and were thus withdrawn from the sample. The authors independently selected the articles dealing with family business and corporate entrepreneurship. For any misalignment in abstracts decisions, the authors considered the whole manuscript for each case and discussed together its selection in the final sample. This procedure led us to finally focus on 75 articles on CE in FB.

The descriptive statistics of the final sample highlight an increase in the number of papers published on this topic. The first article looking at CE in FB appeared in 1998 in the Cambridge Journal of Economics (Antonelli and Marchionatti, 1998). From there up to 2009 a maximum of three papers per year have been published, but, starting from 2010, the yearly publications on this topic have increased exponentially reaching a maximum of 18 in 2010 (15 and 13 contributions have been published in 2011 and 2012 respectively, 8 in 2013[1]). The increasing trend suggests that this is a growing field of research deserving attention from scholars in the last years. Moreover, we found a broad number of journals hosting these publications. The journals that include the highest number of papers each are: *Family Business Review* (8 contributions), *Entrepreneurship: Theory and Practice* (8), *International Journal of Entrepreneurship and Innovation Management* (6), *Journal of Family Business Strategy* (5), *Entrepreneurship and Regional Development* (5), *Journal of Business Venturing* (4). Concerning the type of papers, 20 percent of the selected articles are conceptual; they contribute to theories development and thus provide propositions to advance theory and knowledge on family business. Among the empirical papers, 40 percent are qualitative studies, i.e. single case study or multiple case studies, while the remaining are quantitative studies.

With specific reference to the topics addressed by the 75 contributions, they focus on different aspects and typologies of CE – such as, new venture creation (see for example, Kodithuwakku and Rosa, 2002; Marchisio et al., 2010), strategic renewal (see for example, Salvato et al., 2010; Cassia et al., 2012), and EO (see for example, Naldi et al., 2007; Casillas and Moreno, 2010; Casillas, Moreno, and Barbero, 2010; Lumpkin et al., 2010). Some topics emerge as recurrent; such as the effect of succession on CE dynamics (see for example, Casillas and Moreno, 2010; Pistrui et al., 2010; Welsh et al., 2013), internationalization as a specific type of CE domain (see for example, Abdellatif et al., 2010; Yang, 2012; Piva et al., 2013), and the specific CE patterns in high-technology industries (see for example, Block, 2012; Block et al., 2013; Piva et al., 2013). Finally, the most recurrent theoretical approaches used to investigate CE in FB are agency and stewardship theories (see for example, Zahra, 2005; Habbershon, 2006; Wong, Chang, and Chen, 2010; Eddleston et al., 2012; Welsh et al., 2013), resource-based view (see for example, Kickul et al., 2010; Chirico et al., 2012) and socio-emotional wealth perspective (see for example, Gómez-Mejía et al., 2011; Block et al., 2013).

Looking specifically at the dynamic nature of CE in FB, the 75 contributions reveal that, despite the claim that temporal dynamics represent an important topic to be addressed (Hoy, 2006; Lumpkin et al., 2011), life cycles or the broader concept of developmental dimensions (Gersick et al., 1997), are very seldom referred to (Table 14.2 lists the contributions among the initial sample of 75 papers which, at least to some extent, take into account temporal dynamics).

With particular reference to the ownership and family developmental dimensions, some empirical and conceptual indeterminacies arise concerning the evolution of the FB entrepreneurial behavior. A number of contributions suggest a growing pattern of CE along the ownership and family developmental dimensions. This is interpreted with arguments such as: growth of the family resulting in the need to grow the number of entrepreneurial activities (Marchisio et al., 2010; Webb et al., 2010; Gómez-Mejía et al., 2011), increasing long-term orientation (Lumpkin et al., 2010), higher availability of resources, such as organizational social capital, managerial capabilities, internal autonomy and successors' discretion (Mitchell et al., 2009; Wang and Poutziouris, 2010; Zahra, 2010; Jones et al., 2013), and greater heterogeneity of the decision-making group (Webb et al., 2010). In one of the case studies analyzed by Marchisio and colleagues (2010), for instance, the growth of the family boosts corporate venturing activities as a way to avoid conflicts: "while having several family members working together in the core business could have engendered conflict, external venturing offered opportunities to separate conflicting individuals and to involve more family members who otherwise would not willingly work together" (p. 367). Similarly, Webb and colleagues (2010) propose that family's growth may enhance the need for exploration activities, even in stable markets: "if a firm is divided among the founder's multiple children and the children desire stable or increasing cash flows from the business, the family firm's performance must necessarily multiplicatively grow. Exploitation within a stable market may be insufficient to meet the growing family's heightened goals" (p. 74). Moreover, according to the authors, CE initiatives increase along the ODD because the group of decision makers within a family-controlled firm becomes heterogeneous over time and this heterogeneity replaces affective conflicts with cognitive ones. The latter, in turn, are likely to keep the group from settling on suboptimal decisions.

Table 14.2 Findings from the Literature Review: CE Along Family Business Developmental Dynamics

Year	Journal	Authors	Title	Type of CE	Empirical/ Conceptual	Quantitative/ Qualitative	Findings (FDD/ODD/ BDD)	CE Along the DD
2002	Journal of Business Venturing	Kodithuwakku, S.S., Rosa, P.	The entrepreneurial process and economic success in a constrained environment	Venturing activities	Empirical	Qualitative	Family firms in the controlling owner and start-up business phases generating other venture activities (core business related). RBV justification **(ODD*BDD)**	
2005	Family Business Review	Zahra, S.A.	Entrepreneurial risk taking in family firms	EO (risk-taking)	Empirical	Quantitative	***Multigenerational involvement*** has a positive influence on risk-taking	
2006	Entrepreneurship: Theory and Practice	Hoy, F.	The complicating factor of life cycles in corporate venturing	Venturing activities	Conceptual		Life cycles are moderating variables, complicating the ability of firm leaders to be entrepreneurial **(ODD*BDD*FDD)**	
2006	Entrepreneurship: Theory and Practice	Kellermanns, F.W., Eddleston, K.A.	Corporate entrepreneurship in family firms: A family perspective	EO	Empirical	Quantitative	***Multigenerational involvement*** has a positive influence on EO	
2008	Family Business Review	Kellermanns, F.W., Eddleston, K.A., Barnett, T., Pearson, A.	An exploratory study of family member characteristics and involvement: Effects on entrepreneurial behavior in the family firm	Venturing activities	Empirical	Quantitative	***Multigenerational involvement*** has a positive influence on venturing activities	

Year	Journal	Authors	Title	Focus	Type	Method	Findings	Direction
2009	Entrepreneurship: Theory and Practice	Mitchell, J.R., Hart, T.A., Valcea, S., Townsend, D.M.	Becoming the boss: Discretion and postsuccession success in family firms	Strategic renewal	Conceptual		CE increases along the **ODD** because of successors' discretion	Increase
2010	Entrepreneurship and Regional Development	Salvato, C., Chirico, F., Sharma, P.	A farewell to the business: Championing exit and continuity in entrepreneurial family firms	Exit	Empirical	Qualitative	In a declining and sibling partnership stages exit could be discarded by the family firm because of a lock-in in family legacy **(ODD*BDD)**	
2010	Entrepreneurship and Regional Development	Marchisio, G., Mazzola, P., Sciascia, S., Miles, M., Astrachan, J.	Corporate venturing in family business: The effects on the family and its members	Venturing activities	Empirical	Qualitative	CV as a way to avoid conflicts between family members in later-generations **(ODD)**. CV increases because of family growth	Increase
2010	Journal of Family Business Strategy	Webb, J.W., Ketchen, DJ., Ireland, R.D.	Strategic entrepreneurship within family-controlled firms: Opportunities and challenges	Strategic entrepreneurship (Innovation through exploration)	Conceptual		Family's growth **(ODD)** enhance the need for exploration activities. Strategic entrepreneurship increases along the **ODD** because of group heterogeneity leading to cognitive conflicts	Increase
2010	Entrepreneurship and Regional Development	Lumpkin, G.T., Brigham, K.H., Moss, T.W.	Long-term orientation: Implications for the entrepreneurial orientation and performance of family businesses	EO	Conceptual		EO increases along the **ODD** because of long-term orientation	Increase

(*Continued*)

Year	Journal	Authors	Title	Type of CE	Empirical/ Conceptual	Quantitative/ Qualitative	Findings (FDD/ODD/ BDD)	CE Along the DD
2010	International Journal of Entrepreneurial Behaviour and Research	Wang, Y., Poutziouris, P.	Entrepreneurial risk taking: Empirical evidence from UK family firms	EO (risk taking)	Empirical	Quantitative	Risk taking increases along the **ODD** because of resources availability	Increase
2010	Journal of Management Studies	Zahra, S.A.	Harvesting family firms' organizational social capital: A relational perspective	Venturing activities	Empirical	Quantitative	Equity investment in new ventures increases along the **ODD** and the **BDD** because of organizational social capital availability	Increase
2010	International Small Business Journal	Chirico, F., Nordqvist, M.	Dynamic capabilities and trans-generational value creation in family firms: The role of organizational culture	EO, Innovation, Strategic Renewal	Empirical	Qualitative	CE decreases along the **ODD** because of conflicts among family members	Decrease
2010	International Journal of Entrepreneurship and Innovation Management	Pistrui, D., Murphy, P.J., Deprez-Sims, A.-S.	The transgenerational family effect on new venture growth strategy	Venturing activities	Empirical	Quantitative	EO decreases along the **ODD** as it is replaced by family orientation	Decrease

Year	Journal	Authors	Title	Construct	Type	Method	Findings	Effect
2010	Corporate Governance	Wong, Y.-J., Chang, S.-C., Chen, L.-Y.	Does a family-controlled firm perform better in corporate venturing?	Venturing activities (joint ventures)	Empirical	Quantitative	Better CE initiatives (IVs) along the **BDD** because of outsiders and their managerial skills	Increase
2011	Academy of Management Annals	Gómez-Mejía, L.R., Cruz, C., Berrone, P., de Castro, J.	The Bind that ties: Socioemotional wealth preservation in family firms	CE	Conceptual		Maturity and decline stages (**BDD**) drive R&D investments and technological diversification	Increase
2011	Strategic Entrepreneurship Journal	Lumpkin, G.T., Steier, L., Wright, M.	Strategic entrepreneurship in family business	Strategic CE initiatives	Conceptual		CE decreases along the **ODD** because of conflicts among family members	Decrease
2011	International Journal of Entrepreneurship and Innovation Management	Moog, P., Mirabella, D., Schlepphorst, S.	Owner orientations and strategies and their impact on family business	EO	Empirical	Qualitative	EO decreases along the **ODD** as it is replaced by family orientation	Decrease
2011	Family Business Review	Sardeshmukh, S.R., Corbett, A.C.	The duality of internal and external development of successors: Opportunity recognition in family firms	Venturing activities	Empirical	Quantitative	Growth stage (**BDD**) entails greater opportunities and hence an increase in CE initiatives	Increase
2012	Business History	Yacob, S.	Trans-generational renewal as managerial succession: The Behn Meyer story (1840–2000)	Strategic renewal	Empirical	Qualitative	Exit as a way to avoid decline by a family firm in the cousin consortium stage (**ODD★BDD**)	Decrease

(Continued)

Year	Journal	Authors	Title	Type of CE	Empirical/ Conceptual	Quantitative/ Qualitative	Findings (FDD/ODD/ BDD)	CE Along the DD
2012	Journal of Business Venturing	Parker, S.C., Van Praag, C.M.	The entrepreneur's mode of entry: Business takeover or new venture start?	Business take over or new venture start	Empirical	Quantitative	When there are many siblings it is less likely that an acquisition takes place, because there is great competition among offspring to be the successor (**ODD**)	Decrease
2012	Journal of Business Venturing	Block, J.H.	R&D investments in family and founder firms: An agency perspective	EO (R&D intensity)	Empirical	Quantitative	Over time, family firms may become hostile to change because of family altruism (**ODD**)	Decrease
2012	International Journal of Entrepreneurial Behaviour and Research	Cassia, L.A., De Massis, A., Pizzurno, E.	Strategic innovation and new product development in family firms: An empirically grounded theoretical framework	Innovation and new product development	Empirical	Qualitative	Innovation decreases along the **ODD** because of risk aversion	Decrease
2012	Small Business Economics	Cruz, C., Nordqvist, M.	Entrepreneurial orientation in family firms: A generational perspective	EO	Empirical	Quantitative	EO increases along the **BDD** because of the role of non-family managers	Increase

				EO	Empirical	Qualitative	Increase / Decrease
2012	Small Business Economics	Zellweger, T., Sieger, P.	Entrepreneurial orientation in long-lived family firms	EO	Empirical	Qualitative	Each of the five components of EO has a different path along the **ODD**
2013	Business History	Jones, O., Ghobadian, A., O'Regan, N., Antcliff V.	Dynamic capabilities in a sixth-generation family firm: Entrepreneurship and the Bibby Line	Strategic renewal	Empirical	Qualitative	Increase — CE initiatives increase along the **ODD** because of managerial capabilities and skills. Decline stage (**BDD**) drives CE initiatives
2013	Journal of Family Business Strategy	Welsh, D.H.B., Memili, E., Rosplock, K., Roure, J., Segurado, J.L.	Perceptions of entrepreneurship across generations in family offices: A stewardship theory perspective	CE perceptions and actions	Empirical	Qualitative	Decrease — CE perceptions and actions decrease along the **ODD** because of legacy
2013	Asia Pacific Journal of Management	Au, K., Chiang, F.F.T., Birtch, T.A., Ding, Z.	Incubating the next generation to venture: The case of a family business in Hong Kong	Joint ventures and spin-offs creation	Empirical	Qualitative	Increase — *Multigenerational involvement* has a positive influence on entrepreneurial initiatives. CE initiatives increase along the **BDD** because of professionalization.

Other authors advocate a decreasing pattern of CE along the ownership and family developmental dimensions; this is explained by increasing family concerns and conflicts among the family members (Chirico and Nordqvist, 2010; Lumpkin et al., 2011; Parker and Van Praag, 2012), family altruism (Block, 2012), family orientation (Pistrui et al., 2010; Moog et al., 2011), legacy (Welsh et al., 2013) and risk aversion (Cassia et al., 2012). For example, Parker and Van Praag (2012) argue that, when there are many siblings, it is less likely that an acquisition takes place, because there is great competition among offspring to be the successor. Looking at entrepreneurial perceptions and actions along the ODD, Welsh and colleagues (2013) find that later generations perceive themselves to be less entrepreneurial than the first one. This is due to a lock-in in family legacy, namely the pressure not to lose the family capital created by previous generations, and may impact the ultimate sustainability of the family business if a wealth preservation, rather than growth, mindset confines or even prohibits entrepreneurship.

Some papers refer to the effect of multigenerational involvement, which can occur at different stages of the ownership developmental dimension's stage. The joint involvement of two or more generations increases proclivity for CE and EO (Zahra, 2005; Kellermanns and Eddleston, 2006; Kellermanns et al., 2008; Au et al., 2013). According to these authors, first generation family businesses are often started upon on innovative ideas and mindsets, but, after a few years, they often lose their entrepreneurial spirit and tend to maintain the status quo. When multiple generations are involved, instead, the organization benefits from a variety of inputs and individual perspectives, valuable assets for developing entrepreneurial ideas.

In our sample of papers, there is a consensus regarding a growing engagement in CE along the family firm's BDD. This is enabled by factors such as an increasing access of firms to a stock of idle resources (Kellermanns et al., 2008) and organizational social capital (Zahra, 2010). These resources, indeed, are leveraged to grow and renew the business thanks to values, norms and attitudes which characterize membership in the business family and which support entrepreneurial behavior (Nordqvist and Melin, 2010). Moreover, CE initiatives are fostered by managerial capabilities, professionalization and outsiders' involvement in family firms' board of directors (Wong et al., 2010; Au et al., 2013), as growing family firms become aware that it is necessary to involve non-family members. With respect to specific life cycle stages, evidence suggests that the growth stage entails greater opportunities and hence an increase of CE initiatives (Sardeshmukh and Corbett, 2011). As the firm matures and grows, it will invest in related businesses, with the family members filling key positions (Gómez-Mejía et al., 2011). The decline stage also offers some triggers towards CE initiatives as sources of renewal (Jones et al., 2013), in particular, R&D investments and technological diversification (Gómez-Mejía et al., 2011).

In addition to recognizing the current stage along one specific developmental dimension at a time, the simultaneous evolution of different developmental dimensions (ownership, family, business, but also industry, product, technology and market) illustrates the complex synchronization of life cycles that – distinctively for family firms – could help explain firm's engagement in CE (Hoy, 2006). However, as it clearly emerges from Table 14.2, the joint effect of the developmental dimensions is highly overlooked. The joint effect of the ownership and business developmental dimensions has been captured by three in-depth case studies. In the first, Kodithuwakku and Rosa (2002) report the case of family firms in the controlling owner (ODD) and start-up business (BDD) phases generating other venture activities related to the core business of the mother company. The paper builds upon the resource-based view and, according to the authors, the opportunities to pursue CE initiatives increase with the amount of resources available. Both the other two papers that consider the joint effect of the ownership and business developmental dimensions deal with family firms' exit strategies. Particularly, Salvato, Chirico and Sharma (2010) observe a family firm in the sibling partnership (ODD) and declining (BDD) stages, and show how exit strategies, although viable and attractive, have been discarded by the firm because of a lock-in in family legacy. Exit, as a specific type of entrepreneurial initiative, instead, is pursued to avoid decline (BDD) by a family firm in the cousin consortium stage (ODD) in the case analyzed by Yacob (2012). Taken together, the last two papers seem to suggest that family legacy is higher in the second phase of the ODD than in the third one, BDD being equal.

With specific reference to EO, Cruz and Nordqvist (2012) adopt a generational perspective to explore its determinants in family firms. According to the authors, the antecedents of EO, both internal (non-family managers and non-family investors) and external (environmental dynamism and technological opportunities), are influenced by the ODD. Particularly, environmental factors are more important to predict EO in second-generation family firms compared to first- and third-and-beyond-generation family firms. Access to non-family resources, instead, drives EO to a greater extent in third-and-beyond-generation family firms. These findings can also be interpreted looking at the BDD. In more mature and larger family firms, non-family managers may have more discretion to drive entrepreneurship, and bring new perspectives, ideas, and managerial capabilities to revitalize the organization. EO thus increases along the BDD. A dynamic view of EO in long-lived family firms is provided by Zellweger and Sieger (2012) who highlight the need to disentangle the five components of the construct – autonomy, innovativeness, risk-taking, proactiveness, and competitive aggressiveness. According to the three case studies analyzed, the authors propose the following link between EO components and the ODD: internal autonomy increases as later family generations join the firm; generational changes positively impact both internal and external innovativeness; long-lived family firms display higher levels of ownership risk and lower levels of both performance hazard and control risk; proactiveness fluctuates over time, with periods of low levels of proactiveness combined with proactive moves (for example after the transition from the second to the third generation); finally, competitive aggressiveness decreases over time due to reputation concerns of the controlling family.

In summary, the fragmentary results emerged by the literature presented above indicate the need to develop a deeper understanding of the dynamic nature of CE in FB. Particularly, the evidence suggests the need for a more fine-grained reasoning about the time dimension of CE in FB, as well as larger and more rigorous effort to extend and test the developmental dimensions' approach. In the following section, we introduce some future research directions based on a developmental perspective.

Discussion and Future Research Directions

Our review and conceptual model of CE in family businesses suggest that the developmental perspective may be useful in explaining several important questions in entrepreneurial family firms. The following figure shows an overarching framework of what is discussed in this section.

First, researchers may use the developmental approach to investigate the relationship between *why* and *when* family businesses engage in CE. As family businesses grow and mature, they undergo a variety of transitions that may affect their willingness to engage in CE over time. For example, as management becomes increasingly professionalized (BDD), do family businesses exhibit a greater tendency or aptitude towards behaving entrepreneurially as a way to retain talented managers? Additionally, does the growth in family size that accompanies second and third generational involvement in the business (FDD) and the likely related phenomenon of ownership dispersion (ODD) create incentives to subsidize the increasingly larger-sized family and ownership groups? Are new business projects or new products driven by these goals? We believe that recognizing these distinctive motivations, related to specific developmental dimensions and

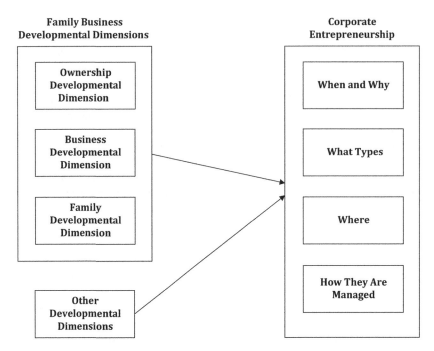

Figure 14.1 Overarching Framework of Family Business Developmental Dimensions and Corporate Entrepreneurship

firm goals, may further the understanding of family firms' entrepreneurial behavior and help reconcile apparently contradicting findings. This may also apply to non-family firms facing ownership transitions, considering for example the pattern from private to public ownership, or the ownership structure before and after an M&A. Moreover, progressing along the ODD, given that the role of non-employed family owners becomes increasingly relevant, is this likely to influence the entrepreneurial behavior of the family, for example the choice between harvesting and investing in a new venture? This kind of questions could particularly benefit from a perspective that takes into account the *joint* effect of different and coexisting developmental dimensions. For instance, with reference to the previous mentioned examples, when a family firm evolves along the BDD—namely, increasingly involves non-family managers, becomes more professionalized and hence interested to undertake entrepreneurial initiatives—but still is in the first stages of ODD and FDD, it will not perceive the growth pressure coming from an evolving ownership group and a developing family: will this affect proclivity to engage in CE? Which developmental dimension will prevail, and why? All these questions may further the debate on the long-term orientation of family firms; these are often referred to as culturally disposed toward "long-term value creating activities that have a low probability of success, but are important for new business creation and revenue generation" (Zahra, Hayton and Salvato, 2004: 367). Considering that in a family business many dimensions are extremely relevant and their development can strongly affect the corporate entrepreneurial behavior, it cannot be overlooked whether these dimensions develop in a synchronic way or not and according to which pattern. Indeed, further research may investigate the role of time on entrepreneurial behavior, in terms for example of rhythms, order and duration of activities aimed at new venture creation (Sharma, Salvato, and Reay, 2014: 14), but also looking at the individual development that interacts with the familial one into a family business. As literature has shown that aging leaders show a decreasing level of engagement in the firm's activities unless there is a high degree of legacy (Zacher, Rosing, and Frese, 2011), an intriguing research question may revolve around the role of entrepreneurial legacy in family firms (Jaskiewicz, Combs, and Rau, 2015), in fostering corporate entrepreneurship over time.

Second, the developmental perspective may also provide a useful paradigm for researchers interested in *how* CE is manifested by family firms as they move through the ownership, business and family developmental dimensions. This line of investigation may consider two different aspects of CE: the form of the entrepreneurial initiative, and the link between the new business domain and the existing businesses of the parenting firm. The first aspect involves the examination of *what types* of initiatives are pursued by family businesses. For example, at different stages of the business developmental dimension, do family firms have a predisposition for external venturing, internal venturing, strategic rejuvenation, business domain redefinition, etc. (Sharma and Chrisman, 1999)? It may be that early-stage family firms engage in CE by spawning their own new businesses from within the existing structure because they lack the resources, i.e., financial capital, to fund or acquire external new business opportunities. But, as they mature, these same family businesses may have both the management and the financial capital to initiate a portfolio of investments in external ventures, i.e., a corporate venture capital approach to CE. The second aspect of this approach to future research is to explore *where* the family business does venture, in terms of which new business domains are explored. Initially, a family firm may be more likely to explore new business domains that are at least in some way related to its current business(es). In this way, a family firm early in its business developmental dimension can leverage the knowledge that it possesses in business related to its core, rather than occupying much of its time acquiring new knowledge. Later, when the firm is more mature and professionalized, perhaps it more likely ventures into business domains that are truly novel and unrelated to its current business(es). This trend clearly depends much on other aspects of the developmental model, such as legacy. As highlighted discussing the papers by Salvato et al. (2010) and Yacob (2012), the pressure not to lose the family capital created by previous generations is probably higher in the second phase of the ODD than in the third one, BDD being equal; hence, cousin consortium stage family firms will more likely direct their entrepreneurial effort towards unrelated businesses. Accordingly, the joint effect of the three developmental dimensions on the *how* of CE in family firms has to be taken into account. Useful paradigms that might be used to explore these research questions include knowledge stock and flows (Dierickx and Cool, 1989) and exploration/exploitation (Schildt et al., 2005).

Third, scholars looking at CE in family businesses may use the developmental perspective to understand *how CE initiatives are managed* through different stages. For example, the literature on corporate venturing has long explored how ventures are structured and the degree of autonomy allowed for those ventures (e.g., Simon, Houghton, and Gurney, 1999; Burgelman and Valikangas, 2005; Garrett and Covin, 2014). It may be that early life cycle stage family firms do structure and manage their entrepreneurial initiatives in such a way that those initiatives are "in the spotlight" and/or are carefully controlled by the parenting firm. However, as family firms become more professional and mature (BDD), as well as distant from the founder stage (ODD), initiatives may be structured more independently and managed with greater autonomy. Implications may exist for prescribing which management techniques and structures may be optimal for different types of ventures at different stages of the three developmental dimensions and at the intersection among them.

Future research also should consider testing similar conceptual models to the one we have presented via empirical analysis. Considering the sensitivity of this kind of data—especially the ones related to the family and ownership developmental dimensions—case study and other empirical strategies (e.g., ethnography) are considered as a particularly appropriate research methodology. While difficult to access, such data may provide a wealth of information on the corporate venturing process, especially as it is presented within family firms. Understanding the dynamic nature of entrepreneurial behavior in family firms is a timely topic that merits further consideration.

These intuitions open new avenues for future research that can benefit from a further discussion about the theoretical perspectives useful to discuss the temporal evolution of CE in family firms. The three-circle model (Tagiuri and Davis, 1996) has driven family business literature to focus on management theories that could explain the behavior of this form of business in light of the intersection of family, ownership and business systems. Indeed, agency and behavioral agency, stewardship, a resource-based view of the firm and dynamic capabilities, as well as organizational identity have been adopted both in family business research (e.g., Chrisman et al., 2010), and to investigate CE-related issues (e.g., McKelvie et al., 2014). Thus, also when time enters into the debate, family firms' behavior may be described in light of these different theoretical assumptions. Further research can focus on the contraposition of agency theory and stewardship theory (e.g., Le Breton-Miller, Miller, and Lester, 2011), looking at how managerial autonomy evolves as the family firm changes along the three developmental dimensions. Indeed, if on the one hand managerial autonomy is necessary to empower especially the middle management in order to identify and exploit new business opportunities, on the other hand too much managerial autonomy can result in opportunistic behavior (Shimizu, 2012). Analyzing this trade-off along, and at the intersection of family, ownership, and business developmental dimensions, would be informative about family firms' behavior.

As regards resources, it would be valuable to investigate how and when family firms rely on different forms of capital, as for example social instead of human or financial capital to develop their entrepreneurial initiatives, or leverage on their dynamic capabilities. Furthermore, when these family firms leverage on the available resources to create alliances and networks, and how this in turn, affects CE, deserves further attention. Looking at behavioral agency model and the overarching concept of socioemotional wealth, it could be interesting to explore when and how family firms change their mix of economic and non-economic goals along the three developmental dimensions.

Moreover, as we look at the effect of temporal dynamics, contingency theory and institutional theory offer alternative perspectives to investigate the phenomenon. Thus, new research avenues can arise when looking at CE at the interaction of the three developmental dimensions with other elements, external to the family business development, which evolve over time as well. Considering the type of industry and its life-cycle, or whether the firm is working in a high-tech sector, may have an impact on the entrepreneurial opportunities and choices made. Product life cycle and market life cycle may also affect the firm's behavior and entrepreneurial activities since their development may destroy and create opportunities for firms (Hoy, 2006). For example, industry characteristics and dynamics represent one of the most compelling elements that firms have to consider in their competitive environment. Industry characteristics, such as the relative importance of innovation and technological change as well as the extent to which capital intensity and sunk costs matter, have been studied in relation to firm's survival, and change over time, especially in the short run (Audretsch et al., 1997; Strotman, 2007).

In addition, other contextual factors at the country level, like taking into account whether the firm operates in an emerging or developed economy, can affect the entrepreneurial firm behavior along and at the intersection of the three developmental dimensions. In addition, the institutional context, norms and pressures have an impact on family firms and their entrepreneurial activities over time and this phenomenon can be of interest to examine.

Conclusion

This chapter contributes to the literature in several ways. We add to entrepreneurship research by showing the conditions under which previously entrepreneurial people or organizations change and stop being entrepreneurial (Miller and Friesen, 1984) as well as non-entrepreneurial organizations become entrepreneurial and then sustain such effort (Kuratko, 2010). In addition, given the ubiquity of family firms and their dominance of entrepreneurial firms, we contribute by indicating family business systems as a potential internal trigger of CE processes, a dimension that has been mostly overlooked by extant research (Kuratko et al., 2010; Phan et al., 2009). We also add to family business literature, by shedding light on how development and change over time can foster or inhibit longevity and sustainability of the firm through CE activities and strategies. Finally, we speak to strategic management scholars, by looking at individual and organizational antecedents of enduring entrepreneurship phenomena, as opposed to infrequent or non-recurring entrepreneurial strategies and organizational practices.

Our work also informs practitioners, as it sheds light on phenomena drawn from real-world business situations. Managerial challenges related to growing the speed of innovation and entrepreneurship processes interact, and often conflict, with multiple life cycle logics and timing (especially in technology-intensive sectors). Against the common wisdom that family firms are conservative, risk averse, and reluctant to innovate (at least beyond the founder's generation), we reinforce the importance of non-conventional views of family firms who indeed can innovate and rejuvenate, even in later stages, thus often representing "the oxygen that feeds the fire of entrepreneurship" (Rogoff and Heck, 2003). Finally, our work gathers new perspectives on the complexity (and evolutionary change) of families as social institutions, representing a great opportunity for entrepreneurship and opportunity exploitation (Aldrich and Cliff, 2003).

Based on our reading of the literature, we believe that there are still opportunities to introduce new perspectives and research efforts and hence advance the field much further than we have heretofore seen. The directions suggested above represent a starting point, offering a retrospective view and pointing the way to new avenues of research.

Note

1 The data obtained for 2013 are partial, since we conducted the search on November 2013.

References

Abdellatif, M., Amann, B., and Jaussaud, J. (2010). Family versus nonfamily business: A comparison of international strategies. *Journal of Family Business Strategy, 1*(2), 108–116.

Aldrich, H. E., and Cliff, J. E. (2003). The pervasive effects of family on entrepreneurship: Toward a family embeddedness perspective. *Journal of Business Venturing, 18*(5), 573–596.

Anderson, R. C., and Reeb, D. M. (2003). Founding-family ownership and firm performance: Evidence from the S&P 500. *Journal of Finance*, 1301–1328.

Antonelli, C., and Marchionatti, R. (1998). Technological and organisational change in a process of industrial rejuvenation: The case of the Italian cotton textile industry. *Cambridge Journal of Economics, 22*(1), 1–18.

Au, K., Chiang, F. F., Birtch, T. A., and Ding, Z. (2013). Incubating the next generation to venture: The case of a family business in Hong Kong. *Asia Pacific Journal of Management, 30*(3), 749–767.

Au, K., and Kwan, H. K. (2009). Start-up capital and Chinese entrepreneurs: The role of family. *Entrepreneurship Theory and Practice, 33*(4), 889–908.

Audretsch, D. B., Houweling, P., and Thurik, A. R. (1997). *New firm survival: Industry versus firm effects* (No. 97–063/3). Tinbergen Institute Discussion Paper.

Barringer, B. R., and Bluedorn, A. C. (1999). The relationship between corporate entrepreneurship and strategic management. *Strategic Management Journal, 20*(5), 421–444.

Biggadike, R. (1979). The risky business of diversification. *Harvard Business Review, 57*(3), 103–111.

Block, J., Miller, D., Jaskiewicz, P., and Spiegel, F. (2013). Economic and technological importance of innovations in large family and founder firms an analysis of patent data. *Family Business Review, 26*(2), 180–199.

Block, J. H. (2012). R&D investments in family and founder firms: An agency perspective. *Journal of Business Venturing, 27*(2), 248–265.

Burgelman, R. A. (1983). A process model of internal corporate venturing in the diversified major firm. *Administrative Science Quarterly, 28*(2), 223–244.

Burgelman, R. A. (1984). Designs for corporate entrepreneurship in established firms. *California Management Review, 26*(3), 154–166.

Burgelman, R., and Valikangas, L. (2005). Venturing cycles. *MIT Sloan Management Review, 46*(4), 26–34.

Busenitz, L. W., and Barney, J. B. (1997). Differences between entrepreneurs and managers in large organizations: Biases and heuristics in strategic decision-making. *Journal of Business Venturing, 12*(1), 9–30.

Carland, J. W., Hoy, F., Boulton, W. R., and Carland, J. A. C. (1984). Differentiating entrepreneurs from small business owners: A conceptualization. *Academy of Management Review, 9*(2), 354–359.

Carney, M. (2005). Corporate governance and competitive advantage in family-controlled firms. *Entrepreneurship Theory and Practice, 29*(3), 249–265.

Casillas, J. C., and Moreno, A. M. (2010). The relationship between entrepreneurial orientation and growth: The moderating role of family involvement. *Entrepreneurship and Regional Development, 22*(3–4), 265–291.

Casillas, J. C., Moreno, A. M., and Barbero, J. L. (2010). A configurational approach of the relationship between entrepreneurial orientation and growth of family firms. *Family Business Review, 23*(1), 27–44.

Cassia, L., De Massis, A., and Pizzurno, E. (2012). Strategic innovation and new product development in family firms: An empirically grounded theoretical framework. International *Journal of Entrepreneurial Behavior & Research, 18*(2), 198–232.

Chirico, F., and Nordqvist, M. (2010). Dynamic capabilities and trans-generational value creation in family firms: The role of organizational culture. *International Small Business Journal, 28*(5), 487–504.

Chirico, F., Nordqvist, M., Colombo, G., and Mollona, E. (2012). Simulating Dynamic Capabilities and Value Creation in Family Firms: Is Paternalism an "Asset" or a "Liability"? *Family Business Review, 25*(3), 318–338.

Chirico, F., Sirmon, D. G., Sciascia, S., and Mazzola, P. (2011). Resource orchestration in family firms: investigating how entrepreneurial orientation, generational involvement, and participative strategy affect performance. *Strategic Entrepreneurship Journal, 5*(4), 307–326.

Chrisman, J. J., Chua, J. H., and Sharma, P. (2005). Trends and directions in the development of a strategic management theory of the family firm. *Entrepreneurship Theory and Practice, 29*(5), 555–576.

Chrisman, J. J., Kellermanns, F. W., Chan, K. C., and Liano, K. (2010). Intellectual foundations of current research in family business: An identification and review of 25 influential articles. *Family Business Review, 23*(1), 9–26.

Chua, J. H., Chrisman, J. J., and Sharma, P. (1999). Defining the family business by behavior. *Entrepreneurship Theory and Practice, 23*(4), 19–39.

Covin, J. G., and Lumpkin, G. T. (2011). Entrepreneurial orientation theory and research: Reflections on a needed construct. *Entrepreneurship Theory and Practice, 35*(5), 855–872.

Covin, J. G., and Miles, M. P. (1999). Corporate entrepreneurship and the pursuit of competitive advantage. *Entrepreneurship Theory and Practice, 23*(3), 47–63.

Covin, J. G., and Slevin, D. P. (1990). New venture strategic posture, structure, and performance: An industry life cycle analysis. *Journal of Business Venturing, 5*(2), 123–135.

Cruz, C., and Nordqvist, M. (2012). Entrepreneurial orientation in family firms: A generational perspective. *Small Business Economics, 38*(1), 33–49.

De Massis, A., Sharma, P., Chua, J. H., and Chrisman, J. J. (2012). *Family business studies: An annotated bibliography*. Edward Elgar Publishing.

Dess, G. G., and Lumpkin, G. T. (2005). The role of entrepreneurial orientation in stimulating effective corporate entrepreneurship. *Academy of Management Executive, 19*(1), 147–156.

Dierickx, I., and Cool, K. (1989). Asset stock accumulation and sustainability of competitive advantage. *Management Science, 35*(12), 1504–1511.

Eckhardt, J. T., and Shane, S. A. (2003). Opportunities and entrepreneurship. *Journal of Management, 29*(3), 333–349.

Eddleston, K. A., Kellermanns, F. W., and Zellweger, T. M. (2012). Exploring the entrepreneurial behavior of family firms: does the stewardship perspective explain differences? *Entrepreneurship Theory and Practice, 36*(2), 347–367.

Filatotchev, I., Toms, S., and Wright, M. (2006). The firm's strategic dynamics and corporate governance life-cycle. *International Journal of Managerial Finance*, 2(4), 256–279.

Gedajlovic, E., and Carney, M. (2010). Markets, hierarchies, and families: Toward a transaction cost theory of the family firm. *Entrepreneurship Theory and Practice*, 34(6), 1145–1172.

Gedajlovic, E., Lubatkin, M. H., and Schulze, W. S. (2004). Crossing the threshold from founder management to professional management: A governance perspective. *Journal of Management Studies*, 41(5), 899–912.

George, B. A., and Marino, L. (2011). The epistemology of entrepreneurial orientation: Conceptual formation, modeling, and operationalization. *Entrepreneurship Theory and Practice*, 35(5), 989–1024.

Gersick, K. E., Davis, J. A., Hampton, M. M., and Lansberg, I. (1997). *Generation to generation: Life cycles of the family business*. Boston: Harvard Business School Press.

Gómez-Mejía, L. R., Cruz, C., Berrone, P., and De Castro, J. (2011). The bind that ties: Socioemotional wealth preservation in family firms. *Academy of Management Annals*, 5(1), 653–707.

Green, K. M., Covin, J. G., and Slevin, D. P. (2008). Exploring the relationship between strategic reactiveness and entrepreneurial orientation: The role of structure–style fit. *Journal of Business Venturing*, 23(3), 356–383.

Greiner, L. E. (1997). Evolution and revolution as organizations grow: A company's past has clues for management that are critical to future success. *Family Business Review*, 10(4), 397–409.

Grote, J. (2003). Conflicting generations: A new theory of family business rivalry. *Family Business Review*, 16(2), 113–124.

Guth, W. D., and Ginsberg, A. (1990). Guest editors' introduction: Corporate entrepreneurship. *Strategic Management Journal*, 11(4), 5–15.

Habbershon, T. G. (2006). Commentary: A framework for managing the familiness and agency advantages in family firms. *Entrepreneurship Theory and Practice*, 30(6), 879–886.

Habbershon, T. G., and Pistrui, J. (2002). Enterprising families domain: Family-influenced ownership groups in pursuit of transgenerational wealth. *Family Business Review*, 15(3), 223–237.

Habbershon, T. G., and Williams, M. L. (1999). A resource-based framework for assessing the strategic advantages of family firms. *Family Business Review*, 12(1), 1–25.

Hall, A., Melin, L., and Nordqvist, M. (2001). Entrepreneurship as radical change in the family business: Exploring the role of cultural patterns. *Family Business Review*, 14(3), 193–208.

Hall, A., and Nordqvist, M. (2008). Professional management in extended family business: Toward an extended understanding. *Family Business Review*, 21(1), 51–69.

Hareven, T. K. (1978). Cycles, courses and cohorts: Reflections on theoretical and methodological approaches to the historical study of family development. *Journal of Social History*, 12(1), 97–109.

Harris, D., Martinez, J. I., and Ward, J. L. (1994). Is strategy different for the family-owned business? *Family Business Review*, 7(2), 159–174.

Hatak, I. R., and Roessl, D. (2015). Relational competence-based knowledge transfer within intrafamily succession: An experimental study. *Family Business Review*, 28(1), 10–25.

Hitt, M. A., Ireland, R. D., Camp, S. M., and Sexton, D. L. (2001). Strategic entrepreneurship: Entrepreneurial strategies for wealth creation. *Strategic Management Journal*, 22(6–7), 479–491.

Hitt, M. A., Nixon, R. D., Hoskisson, R. E., and Kochhar, R. (1999). Corporate entrepreneurship and cross-functional fertilization: Activation, process and disintegration of a new product design team. *Entrepreneurship Theory and Practice*, 23(3), 145–167.

Hornsby, J. S., Naffziger, D. W., Kuratko, D. F., and Montagno, R. V. (1993). An interactive model of the corporate entrepreneurship process. *Entrepreneurship Theory and Practice*, 17(2), 29–37.

Hoskisson, R. E., Covin, J., Volberda, H. W., and Johnson, R. A. (2011). Revitalizing entrepreneurship: The search for new research opportunities. *Journal of Management Studies*, 48(6), 1141–1168.

Hoskisson, R. E., Hitt, M. A., Johnson, R. A., and Grossman, W. (2002). Conflicting voices: The effects of institutional ownership heterogeneity and internal governance on corporate innovation strategies. *Academy of Management Journal*, 45(4), 697–716.

Hoy, F. (1995). Researching the entrepreneurial venture. In Katz, J. A., and Brockhaus, R. H. Sr. (eds.), *Advances in entrepreneurship, firm emergence, and growth* (Vol. 2, pp. 145–174). Greenwich, CT: JAI Press.

Hoy, F. (2006). The complicating factor of life cycles in corporate venturing. *Entrepreneurship Theory and Practice*, 30(6), 831–836.

IFERA. (2003). Family businesses dominate. *Family Business Review*, 16(4), 235–240.

Ireland, R. D., Hitt, M. A., Camp, S. M., and Sexton, D. L. (2001). Integrating entrepreneurship and strategic management actions to create firm wealth. *Academy of Management Executive*, 15(1), 49–63.

Jaskiewicz, P., Combs, J. G., and Rau, S. B. (2015). Entrepreneurial legacy: Toward a theory of how some family firms nurture transgenerational entrepreneurship. *Journal of Business Venturing*, 30(1), 29–49.

Jensen, M. C., and Meckling, W. H. (1976). Theory of the firm: Managerial behavior, agency costs and ownership structure. *Journal of Financial Economics, 3*(4), 305–360.

Jones, G. R., and Butler, J. E. (1992). Managing internal corporate entrepreneurship: An agency theory perspective. *Journal of Management, 18*(4), 733–749.

Jones, O., Ghobadian, A., O'Regan, N., and Antcliff, V. (2013). Dynamic capabilities in a sixth-generation family firm: Entrepreneurship and the Bibby Line. *Business History, 55*(6), 910–941.

Karra, N., Tracey, P., and Phillips, N. (2006). Altruism and agency in the family firm: Exploring the role of family, kinship, and ethnicity. *Entrepreneurship Theory and Practice, 30*(6), 861–877.

Kellermanns, F. W., and Eddleston, K. A. (2006). Corporate entrepreneurship in family firms: A family perspective. *Entrepreneurship Theory and Practice, 30*(6), 809–830.

Kellermanns, F. W., Eddleston, K. A., Barnett, T., and Pearson, A. (2008). An exploratory study of family member characteristics and involvement: Effects on entrepreneurial behavior in the family firm. *Family Business Review, 21*(1), 1–14.

Kemelgor, B. H. (2002). A comparative analysis of corporate entrepreneurial orientation between selected firms in the Netherlands and the USA. *Entrepreneurship and Regional Development, 14*(1), 67–87.

Kickul, J., Liao, J., Gundry, L., and Iakovleva, T. (2010). Firm resources, opportunity recognition, entrepreneurial orientation and performance: the case of Russian women-led family businesses. *International Journal of Entrepreneurship and Innovation Management, 12*(1), 52–69.

Knight, G. A. (1997). Cross-cultural reliability and validity of a scale to measure firm entrepreneurial orientation. *Journal of Business Venturing, 12*(3), 213–225.

Kodithuwakku, S. S., and Rosa, P. (2002). The entrepreneurial process and economic success in a constrained environment. *Journal of Business Venturing, 17*(5), 431–465.

Kuratko, D., Montagno, R., and Hornsby, J. (1990). Developing an intrapreneurial assessment instrument for an effective corporate entrepreneurial environment. *Strategic management journal, 11*, 49–58.

Kuratko, D. F. (2010). Corporate entrepreneurship: An introduction and research review. In Acs, Z. J., and Audretsch, D., *Handbook of entrepreneurship research* (pp. 129–163). New York: Springer.

Lambrecht, J., and Lievens, J. (2008). Pruning the family tree: An unexplored path to family business continuity and family harmony. *Family Business Review, 21*(4), 295–313.

Le Breton-Miller, I., Miller, D., and Lester, R. H. (2011). Stewardship or agency? A social embeddedness reconciliation of conduct and performance in public family businesses. *Organization Science, 22*(3), 704–721.

Levie, J., and Lichtenstein, B. B. (2010). A terminal assessment of stages theory: Introducing a dynamic states approach to entrepreneurship. *Entrepreneurship Theory and Practice, 34*(2), 317–350.

Lumpkin, G. T., Brigham, K. H., and Moss, T. W. (2010). Long-term orientation: Implications for the entrepreneurial orientation and performance of family businesses. *Entrepreneurship and Regional Development, 22*(3–4), 241–264.

Lumpkin, G. T. and Dess, G. G. (1996). Clarifying the entrepreneurial orientation construct and linking it to performance. *Academy of Management Review, 21*(1), 135–172.

Lumpkin, G. T., and Dess, G. G. (2001). Linking two dimensions of entrepreneurial orientation to firm performance: The moderating role of environment and industry life cycle. *Journal of Business Venturing, 16*(5), 429–451.

Lumpkin, G. T., Steier, L., and Wright, M. (2011). Strategic entrepreneurship in family business. *Strategic Entrepreneurship Journal, 5*(4), 285–306.

Marchisio, G., Mazzola, P., Sciascia, S., Miles, M., and Astrachan, J. (2010). Corporate venturing in family business: The effects on the family and its members. *Entrepreneurship and Regional Development, 22*(3–4), 349–377.

Markides, C. (1998). Strategic innovation in established companies. *MIT Sloan Management Review, 39*(3), 31.

McGrath, R. G., Venkataraman, S., and MacMillan, I. C. (1992, August). Measuring outcomes of corporate venturing: An alternative perspective. In *Academy of Management Proceedings, 1*, 85–89.

McKelvie, A., McKenney, A. F., Lumpkin, G. T., and Short, J. C. (2014). Corporate entrepreneurship in family businesses: Past contributions and future opportunities. In Melin, L., Nordqvist, M., and Sharma, P., *SAGE Handbook of family business* (Vol. 17, pp. 340–363), Sage.

Memili, E., Lumpkin, G. T., and Dess, G. G. (2010). Entrepreneurial orientation: The driving force for corporate entrepreneurship. In Mazzola, P., and Kellermanns, F. W. (eds.), *Handbook of research on strategy process* (Vol. 15, pp. 326–349). Edward Elgar Publishing.

Miller, D. (1983). The correlates of entrepreneurship in three types of firms. *Management Science, 29*(7), 770–791.

Miller, D., and Friesen, P. H. (1984). A longitudinal study of the corporate life cycle. *Management Science*, *30*(10), 1161–1183.

Miller, D., Le Breton-Miller, I., and Lester, R. H. (2011). Family and lone founder ownership and strategic behaviour: Social context, identity, and institutional logics. Journal of *Management Studies*, *48*(1), 1–25.

Mitchell, J. R., Hart, T. A., Valcea, S., and Townsend, D. M. (2009). Becoming the boss: Discretion and post-succession success in family firms. *Entrepreneurship Theory and Practice*, *33*(6), 1201–1218.

Moog, P., Mirabella, D., and Schlepphorst, S. (2011). Owner orientations and strategies and their impact on family business. *International Journal of Entrepreneurship and Innovation Management*, *13*(1), 95–112.

Morioka, K. (1967). Life cycle patterns in Japan, China, and the United States. *Journal of Marriage and the Family*, *29*(3), 595–606.

Muñoz-Bullón, F., and Sanchez-Bueno, M. J. (2011). The impact of family involvement on the R&D intensity of publicly traded firms. *Family Business Review*, *24*(1), 62–70.

Naldi, L., Nordqvist, M., Sjöberg, K., and Wiklund, J. (2007). Entrepreneurial orientation, risk taking, and performance in family firms. *Family Business Review*, *20*(1), 33–47.

Nordqvist, M. (2005). Understanding the role of ownership in strategizing: A study of family firms.

Nordqvist, M., and Melin, L. (2010). Entrepreneurial families and family firms. *Entrepreneurship and Regional Development*, *22*(3–4), 211–239.

Parker, S. C., and van Praag, C. M. (2012). The entrepreneur's mode of entry: Business takeover or new venture start? *Journal of Business Venturing*, *27*(1), 31–46.

Phan, P. H., Wright, M., Ucbasaran, D., and Tan, W. L. (2009). Corporate entrepreneurship: Current research and future directions. *Journal of Business Venturing*, *24*(3), 197–205.

Pinchot III, G. (1985). *Intrapreneuring: Why you don't have to leave the corporation to become an entrepreneur*. University of Illinois at Urbana-Champaign's Academy for Entrepreneurial Leadership Historical Research Reference in Entrepreneurship.

Pistrui, D., Murphy, P. J., and Deprez-Sims, A. S. (2010). The transgenerational family effect on new venture growth strategy. *International Journal of Entrepreneurship and Innovation Management*, *12*(1), 3–16.

Piva, E., Rossi-Lamastra, C., and De Massis, A. (2013). Family firms and internationalization: An exploratory study on high-tech entrepreneurial ventures. *Journal of International Entrepreneurship*, *11*(2), 108–129.

Porter, L. W., and Lawler, E. E. (1968). *Managerial attitudes and performance*. Homewood, IL: Richard D. Irwin, Inc.

Rogoff, E. G., and Heck, R. K. Z. (2003). Evolving research in entrepreneurship and family business: Recognizing family as the oxygen that feeds the fire of entrepreneurship. *Journal of Business Venturing*, *18*(5), 559–566.

Rosa, P., Howorth, C., and Cruz, A. D. (2013). Habitual and portfolio entrepreneurship and the family in business. In Melin, L., Nordqvist, M., and Sharma, P., *SAGE handbook of family business* (Vol. 18, pp. 364–382), Sage.

Salvato, C., Chirico, F., and Sharma, P. (2010), A farewell to the business: Championing exit and continuity in entrepreneurial family firms. *Entrepreneurship and Regional Development: An International Journal*, *22*(3–4), 321–348.

Sardeshmukh, S. R., and Corbett, A. C. (2011). The duality of internal and external development of successors: opportunity recognition in family firms. *Family Business Review*, *24*(2), 111–125.

Schildt, H. A., Maula, M. V., and Keil, T. (2005). Explorative and exploitative learning from external corporate ventures. *Entrepreneurship Theory and Practice*, *29*(4), 493–515.

Sciascia, S., and Bettinelli, C. (2013). Part III: Corporate Entrepreneurship in Context: 1. Corporate Entrepreneurship in Family Businesses: past, present and future research. *M@n@gement*, *16*(4), 422–432.

Scott, B. R. (1971). *Stages of corporate development—Part I*. Boston: Intercollegiate Case Clearing House, Harvard University.

Sharma, P., and Chrisman, J. (1999). Toward a reconciliation of the definitional issues in the field of corporate entrepreneurship. *Entrepreneurship Theory and Practice*, *23*(3), 11–27.

Sharma, P., Chrisman, J. J., and Gersick, K. E. (2012). 25 years of family business review: reflections on the past and perspectives for the future. *Family Business Review*, *25*(1), 5–15.

Sharma, P., Salvato, C., and Reay, T. (2014). Temporal dimensions of family enterprise research. *Family Business Review*, *27*(1), 10–19.

Shepherd, D., and Haynie, J. M. (2009). Family business, identity conflict, and an expedited entrepreneurial process: A process of resolving identity conflict. *Entrepreneurship Theory and Practice*, *33*(6), 1245–1264.

Shimizu, K. (2012). Risks of corporate entrepreneurship: Autonomy and agency issues. *Organization Science*, *23*(1), 194–206.

Simon, M., Houghton, S. M., and Gurney, J. (1999). Succeeding at internal corporate venturing: Roles needed to balance autonomy and control. *Journal of Applied Management Studies*, *8*(2), 145–159.

Sirmon, D. G., and Hitt, M. A. (2003). Managing resources: Linking unique resources, management, and wealth creation in family firms. *Entrepreneurship Theory and Practice*, *27*(4), 339–358.

Stam, W., and Elfring, T. (2008). Entrepreneurial orientation and new venture performance: The moderating role of intra-and extraindustry social capital. *Academy of Management Journal*, *51*(1), 97–111.

Stinchcombe, A. L. (2000). Social structure and organizations. In Joel, A. C., and Baum, F. D. (Eds), *Economics Meets Sociology in Strategic Management*, *17*, 229–259. Emerald Group Publishing Limited.

Strotmann, H. (2007). Entrepreneurial survival. *Small Business Economics*, *28*(1), 87–104.

Tagiuri, R., and Davis, J. (1996). Bivalent attributes of the family firm. *Family Business Review*, *9*(2), 199–208.

Thomsen, S., and Pedersen, T. (2000). Ownership structure and economic performance in the largest European companies. *Strategic Management Journal*, *21*(6), 689–705.

Vesper, K. H. (1984). *Three faces of corporate entrepreneurship: A pilot study*. University of Washington. Graduate School of Business.

Villalonga, B., and Amit, R. (2009). How are US family firms controlled? *Review of Financial Studies*, *22*(8), 3047–3091.

Wales, W., Monsen, E., and McKelvie, A. (2011). The organizational pervasiveness of entrepreneurial orientation. *Entrepreneurship Theory and Practice*, *35*(5), 895–923.

Wang, Y., and Poutziouris, P. (2010). Entrepreneurial risk taking: Empirical evidence from UK family firms. *International Journal of Entrepreneurial Behaviour and Research*, *16*(5), 370–388.

Ward, J. L. (1997). Growing the family business: Special challenges and best practices. *Family Business Review*, *10*(4), 323–337.

Webb, J. W., Ketchen Jr, D. J., and Ireland, R. D. (2010). Strategic entrepreneurship within family-controlled firms: Opportunities and challenges. *Journal of Family Business Strategy*, *1*(2), 67–77.

Welsh, D. H., Memili, E., Rosplock, K., Roure, J., and Segurado, J. L. (2013). Perceptions of entrepreneurship across generations in family offices: A stewardship theory perspective. *Journal of Family Business Strategy*, *4*(3), 213–226.

Wiklund, J., and Shepherd, D. (2003). Research notes and commentaries: Knowledge-based resources, entrepreneurial orientation, and the performance of small and medium-sized businesses. *Strategic Management Journal*, *24*(13), 1307–1314.

Wiklund, J., and Shepherd, D. (2005). Entrepreneurial orientation and small business performance: a configurational approach. *Journal of Business Venturing*, *20*(1), 71–91.

Wong, Y. J., Chang, S. C., and Chen, L. Y. (2010). Does a Family-controlled Firm Perform Better in Corporate Venturing? *Corporate Governance: An International Review*, *18*(3), 175–192.

Yacob, S. (2012). Trans-generational renewal as managerial succession: The Behn Meyer story (1840–2000). *Business History*, *54*(7), 1166–1185.

Yang, N. (2012). Small businesses and international entrepreneurship in the economic hard time: A global strategic perspective. *International Journal of Entrepreneurship*, *16*, 113–131.

Zacher, H., Rosing, K., and Frese, M. (2011). Age and leadership: The moderating role of legacy beliefs. *The Leadership Quarterly*, *22*(1), 43–50.

Zahra, S. A. (1991). Predictors and financial outcomes of corporate entrepreneurship: An exploratory study. *Journal of Business Venturing*, *6*(4), 259–285.

Zahra, S. A. (2005). Entrepreneurial risk taking in family firms. *Family Business Review*, *18*(1), 23–40.

Zahra, S. A. (2010). Harvesting family firms' organizational social capital: A relational perspective. *Journal of Management Studies*, *47*(2), 345–366.

Zahra, S. A., and Covin, J. G. (1995). Contextual influences on the corporate entrepreneurship-performance relationship: A longitudinal analysis. *Journal of Business Venturing*, *10*(1), 43–58.

Zahra, S. A., Hayton, J. C., and Salvato, C. (2004). Entrepreneurship in family vs. Non-Family firms: A Resource-Based analysis of the effect of organizational culture. *Entrepreneurship Theory and Practice*, *28*(4), 363–381.

Zahra, S. A., Nielsen, A. P., and Bogner, W. C. (1998). Corporate entrepreneurship, knowledge, and competence development. AUBret.

Zellweger, T., Nason, R., and Nordqvist, M. (2012). From longevity of firms to transgenerational entrepreneurship of families: Introducing family entrepreneurial orientation. *Family Business Review*, *25*(2), 136–155.

Zellweger, T., and Sieger, P. (2012). Entrepreneurial orientation in long-lived family firms. *Small Business Economics*, *38*(1), 67–84.

15

PORTFOLIO ENTREPRENEURSHIP IN FAMILY FIRMS

Taking Stock and Moving Forward

Naveed Akhter

Introduction

Entrepreneurship plays an important role in society by creating wealth, enhancing economic prosperity and fostering growth (Shane and Venkataraman 2000, Venkataraman 1997). However, the notion that entrepreneurs start single ventures has been challenged by scholars who have identified a special breed of entrepreneurs who rely on endeavors with multiple income streams (Carter, Tagg, and Dimitratos 2004, MacMillan 1986, Rosa and Scott 1999, Ucbasaran, Westhead, and Wright 2001). Indeed, not all entrepreneurs create just one business, and growth-seeking entrepreneurs, in particular, tend to engage in multiple business activities simultaneously—in addition to their primary business—by means of portfolio entrepreneurship (Alsos, Carter, and Ljunggren 2014, Carter 1999, Carter and Ram 2003, Carter et al. 2004). Portfolio entrepreneurship is defined as the "simultaneous ownership of several businesses" (Carter and Ram 2003, 371); it contributes to the overall society and the economy and is regarded as a fundamental element to understanding entrepreneurship and growth (see also Alsos and Kolvereid 1998, Carter and Ram 2003, Jaffe and Lane 2004, MacMillan 1986, Wright, Westhead, and Sohl 1998). As previously reported, portfolio entrepreneurship frequently results in significantly greater sales, employment growth, innovation and firm survival (e.g., McGaughey 2007, Ucbasaran et al. 2008, Wiklund and Shepherd 2008).

Despite the importance of portfolio entrepreneurship to the field of entrepreneurship research, the consensus on its contribution to society and the economy (Westhead and Wright 2015, 1998, Wiklund and Shepherd 2008), and the wide prevalence of multiple business ownership (Alsos and Carter 2006, McGaughey 2007, Westhead and Wright 1998), there remains a dearth of research on portfolio entrepreneurship in general and in the context of family firms in particular (Carter and Ram 2003, Cruz, Howorth, and Hamilton 2013, DeTienne and Chirico 2013, Rosa 1999, Rosa and Scott 1999, Sieger et al. 2011, Wright et al. 1998). A closer look at the previous literature on portfolio entrepreneurship offers a number of insights that hint that the family firm context might be important. First, the owners of family firms engage in portfolio activities for the sustainability of their businesses across generations and in view of the longtime horizon, which allows them to rely on multiple businesses to diversify risk and activity types

(Carter and Ram 2003, Cruz, Hamilton, and Jack 2012, Miller and Le Breton-Miller 2005, Sirmon, Hitt, and Ireland 2007, Zellweger 2007). Second, the context of family firms extends itself further because family firms frequently control more than one company (i.e., a portfolio of firms) for the sake of avoiding succession issues and creating a variety of employment opportunities for the next generation (Jaffe and Lane 2004, Rosa, Balunywa, and Iacobucci 2005, Sieger et al. 2011, Zellweger, Nason, and Nordqvist 2012). Finally, family owners search for substitute income opportunities when the core/legacy business faces hostile situations (cf. Carter and Ram 2003, DeTienne and Chirico 2013, Jaffe and Lane 2004, Manikutty 2000).

Given that family circumstances may encourage family firms to engage in entrepreneurial activities (Alsos et al. 2014, Arregle et al. 2007, Carter and Ram 2003, Chrisman et al. 2012, Cruz et al. 2013, Plate, Schiede, and von Schlippe 2010), different socio-emotional and resource-related reasons may affect each addition of a satellite business to the portfolio (cf. Robson et al. 2012a, Sieger et al. 2011, Zellweger 2007, Zellweger et al. 2012). For instance, the resources acquired through the family play a significant role in the development of a business portfolio (Alsos et al. 2014, Sieger et al. 2011); in other words, the family often provides an important resource base for business activities (Alsos et al. 2014, Brigham and Payne 2015, Cruz, Hamilton, et al. 2012, Robson et al. 2012b, Sirmon and Hitt 2003). Moreover, recent studies have found that family owners seek trusted team members because they are more willing to show collective commitment toward entrepreneurial ventures, particularly with respect to overcoming succession issues through portfolio entrepreneurship (Cruz et al. 2013, Cruz, Hamilton, et al. 2012, Iacobucci and Rosa 2010). Thus, keeping the business within the family by creating opportunities through a portfolio approach is likely to positively affect portfolio activities and outcomes (Carter and Ram 2003, DeTienne and Chirico 2013, Sieger et al. 2011, Zellweger et al. 2012).

In light of the growing interest of owners to engage in portfolio entrepreneurship in the context of family firms—in addition to the possible processes regarding sustainable and transgenerational family firms to which it can lead—this field is likely to remain highly relevant and warrant further exploration. Thus, the primary objective of this research is to highlight the importance and relevance of portfolio entrepreneurship in the context of family firms by reviewing and synthesizing the previous literature and, then, to develop a future research agenda and path to move forward in this important and interesting field. Although work on portfolio family firms remains in its nascent stage of development, we highlight those important gaps that are likely to inform future theoretical implications.

The remainder of this paper is structured as follows. First, we briefly describe the method used to identify the relevant previous research. Then, we review the contributions to date regarding portfolio entrepreneurship and family firms, which is followed by a section on a future research agenda and the identification of research gaps. The final section presents the final conclusions.

Research Methods

Prior research on portfolio entrepreneurship in general and on portfolio entrepreneurship in family firms, in particular, is fragmented because the field remains in its infancy (Parker 2014, Ucbasaran et al. 2008, Ucbasaran, Wright, and Westhead 2003). In selecting our studies for this review, we have taken the definition of portfolio entrepreneurship as the simultaneous ownership of multiple businesses as our starting point (Carter and Ram 2003). The keywords we used in our search criteria included *habitual entrepreneurs, portfolio entrepreneurs, multiple ownership* and *business groups* (cf. Carter 1998a, Iacobucci and Rosa 2010, Iacobucci and Rosa 2005, Wiklund and Shepherd 2008). The broad research identified that there are limited scholarships available focused primarily on portfolio entrepreneurship, particularly with respect to family firm portfolios. We learned that generally the published articles on habitual entrepreneurs compare three different types of entrepreneurs: novice, serial and portfolio (e.g., Westhead and Wright 1998). However, there is a significant gap and need for a deeper understanding of portfolio entrepreneurship in the context of family firms.

Our final selection of 27 articles (see Table 15.1) is based on criteria in which portfolio entrepreneurship is either the sole focus of the article or equally weighted in comparison with novice and serial entrepreneurs and includes articles that are relevant to family business studies. Our starting point was Carter and Ram (2003)'s theoretical review work on portfolio entrepreneurship – where the authors mentioned the context of family business (along with the *unit of analysis* and *process of development of a portfolio*) as an important avenue for future research on portfolio entrepreneurship. Therefore, our review and identified future research agenda is a revisit to Carter and Ram (2003), mapping how the field has evolved in relation to the family firm context after their review piece. Next, we found that out of 27 articles, only 9 focused specifically on portfolio entrepreneurship in family firms (See Table 15.2). The journals considered (*with* relevant articles in the area of portfolio entrepreneurship and family firms) are the most relevant entrepreneurship journals, such as *Entrepreneurship and Regional Development, Entrepreneurship Theory and Practice, Journal of Business Venturing, Regional Studies, Strategic Entrepreneurship Journal, International Small Business Journal, Small Business Economics* and *Family Business Review.* After selecting the 27 relevant articles, we carefully read and analyzed the material, which helped us identify potential research areas for future study.

After grouping the articles in terms of the methods used, we noted that 9 of the 27 articles were identified as qualitative studies (e.g., Alsos et al. 2014, Cruz et al. 2013, Cruz, Hamilton, et al. 2012, Huovinen and Tihula 2008, Iacobucci and Rosa 2010, McGaughey 2007, Michael-Tsabari, Labaki, and Zachary 2014, Sieger et al. 2011, Ucbasaran, Wright, and Westhead 2003), 13 were identified as quantitative studies (e.g., Alsos and Carter 2006, Carter et al. 2004, Iacobucci and Rosa 2005, Robson et al. 2012a, b, Thorgren and Wincent 2015, Ucbasaran, Westhead, and Wright 2009, Ucbasaran, Westhead, et al. 2003, Ucbasaran et al. 2010, Westhead, Ucbasaran, and Wright 2003, Westhead et al. 2005, Wiklund and Shepherd 2008, Zellweger et al. 2012), 4 were identified as theoretical studies (e.g., DeTienne and Chirico 2013, Jaffe and Lane 2004, Parker 2014, Rerup 2005), and 1 was a literature review (e.g., Carter and Ram 2003). Focusing on family business studies in the portfolio entrepreneurship setting, we identified 6 qualitative studies (e.g., Alsos et al. 2014, Cruz et al. 2013, Cruz, Hamilton, et al. 2012, Iacobucci and Rosa 2010, Michael-Tsabari et al. 2014, Sieger et al. 2011), 1 quantitative study (e.g., Zellweger et al. 2012), and 2 theoretical studies (e.g., DeTienne and Chirico 2013, Jaffe and Lane 2004). Due to the limited studies on both quantitative and qualitative methods, we did not expand our arguments regarding which method requires further attention because we believe at this early stage that it is necessary to explore this field using a variety of methodological approaches. Finally, our review identified an important future research direction based on the themes highlighted in our review process. We broadly grouped articles based on their suggestions for future research. These themes were categorized as *Triggers, Setting,* and *Performance.* First, articles that suggested that the different motives of portfolio entrepreneurs should be examined were grouped under 'triggers.' For example, Zellweger et al. (2012), Cruz et al. (2013) and Iacobucci and Rosa (2010) suggested examining how family owners have different sets of motivations than individual entrepreneurs in establishing a portfolio of firms. Articles that suggested looking at rural (agricultural) vs. urban portfolios as well as different industries and country contexts were grouped under *Settings.* For instance, Iacobucci and Rosa (2010), Cruz et al. (2013) and Alsos et al. (2014) suggested investigating the activities of portfolio entrepreneurship in a variety of contexts. We also noted that 15 of 22 empirical articles in our review relied on data sets from Europe (see Table 15.1), which further reinforces the need to explore portfolio

Table 15.1 Selected Studies on Portfolio Entrepreneurship

Study	Type - Method	Sample - Setting	Family Firms	Purpose and Objective	Future Research Suggestion
Carter and Ram (2003)	Review	-	-	Review the previous research and identify areas for future research	Multiple units of analysis Context Process
Ucbasaran, Westhead, et al. (2003)	Quantitative	Europe	-	How novice and habitual entrepreneurs differ in terms of opportunity recognition	Heterogeneity: Prior experience Ownership
Ucbasaran, Wright, and Westhead (2003)	Qualitative	Europe	-	A human capital perspective on habitual entrepreneurs	Process
Westhead et al. (2003)	Quantitative	Europe	-	Difference between novice, serial and portfolio entrepreneurs	From identification to exit Full scope of activities Performance
Carter et al. (2004)	Quantitative	Europe	-	Investigating multiple income sources of business owners	In-depth investigation of Performance
Jaffe and Lane (2004)	Theoretical	-	Family	How to sustain a family dynasty	In-depth empirical studies
Westhead et al. (2005)	Quantitative	Europe	-	Difference between the characteristics of novice, serial and portfolio entrepreneurs	Quantitative and qualitative studies
Remp (2005)	Theoretical	-	-	Learning from past experience	Empirical studies
Iacobucci and Rosa (2005)	Quantitative	Europe	-	Growth and diversification of business groups	Performance issues Exit and divestitures
Alsos and Carter (2006)	Quantitative	Europe	-	How the transfer of resources impacts the performance of the new venture	Case studies Process of emergence Settings
McGaughey (2007)	Qualitative	Australia	-	Portfolios and their contributions to international new ventures	Quantitative and qualitative longitudinal studies Processes
Huovinen and Tihula (2008)	Qualitative	Europe	-	How do entrepreneurs learn and how can learning be seen in their entrepreneurial activities	Quantitative and qualitative studies Role of family in failure
Wiklund and Shepherd (2008)	Quantitative	Europe	-	Investigate the organizational mode chosen for portfolio entrepreneurship	Role of resources Assessment and characteristics of new entry
Ucbasaran et al. (2009)	Quantitative	Europe	-	Entrepreneurs' prior business ownership experience and their opportunity identification behavior	Separate studies on novice and repeat entrepreneurs

Reference	Method	Region	Family	Focus	Future research areas
Iacobucci and Rosa (2010)	Qualitative	Europe	Family	To examine the role of entrepreneurial teams in the formation and dynamics of business groups	More theoretical exploration under different contexts; Unit of analysis from individual to group
Urbasaran et al. (2010)	Quantitative	Europe	-	Prior business ownership failure experience more or less likely to report comparative optimism than novice entrepreneurs	Exits; Failures; Harvest; Entrepreneurial process
Sieger et al. (2011)	Qualitative	South America/ Europe	Family	The process of portfolio entrepreneurship and the role of human and social capital	Quantitative studies; Explore other pool of resources
Zellweger et al. (2012)	Quantitative	North America	Family	To offer an alternative to the intra-firm succession approach to studying the longevity of family firms	The role of family in transgenerational family firms
Robson et al. (2012a)	Quantitative	Africa	-	Prior business ownership experience, is associated with the opportunity exploitation outcome relating to the intensity of exporting	Performance of all firms in the portfolio; Contexts
Robson et al. (2012b)	Quantitative	Africa	-	Prior business ownership experience, is associated with seven types of product and work practices innovation	Performance; Contexts; Different Industry Settings
Cruz, Hamilton, et al. (2012)	Qualitative	North America	Family	How an entrepreneurial culture can be continued so that more businesses might be created by members of a family	Geographical Contexts
Cruz et al. (2013)	Qualitative	North America	Family	The role of teams in portfolio entrepreneurship	Family as unit of analysis; Contexts; Team exit
DeTienne and Chirico (2013)	Theoretical		Family	Exit strategies in family firms and family firm portfolios	Empirical studies
Parker (2014)	Theoretical	-	-	Occupational choices between novice, serial and portfolio entrepreneurs	Case studies; Different country contexts; Risk- and performance-related issues
Alsos et al. (2014)	Qualitative	Europe	Family	The role of family ties in multiple ownership of businesses in the farm sector	Explore and compare the findings in urban households
Michael-Tsabari et al. (2014)	Qualitative	-	Family	Entrepreneurial behavior of a multinational family firm over generations	Methodological considerations
Thorgren and Wincent (2015)	Quantitative	Europe	-	Role of passion in habitual entrepreneurship	Individual and team explanations of passion

Table 15.2 Studies on Portfolio Entrepreneurship in the Family Firm Context

Study	Study Type	Future Research Suggestion	Themes
Jaffe and Lane (2004)	Theoretical	In-depth empirical studies	Setting Performance
Iacobucci and Rosa (2010)	Empirical	Unit of analysis from individual to group More theoretical exploration under different contexts	Trigger Setting
Sieger et al. (2011)	Empirical	Quantitative exploration Family vs. non-family firms Reputation as a resource	Methods Setting Performance
Zellweger et al. (2012)	Empirical	The role of family in transgenerational family firms	Trigger Performance
Cruz, Hamilton, et al. (2012)	Empirical	Different geographical contexts	Setting
Cruz et al. (2013)	Empirical	Family as the unit of analysis Context Team exit	Trigger Setting Performance
DeTienne and Chirico (2013)	Theoretical	Empirical studies	Methods Performance
Alsos et al. (2014)	Empirical	Explore and compare the findings in urban households	Setting Performance
Michael-Tsabari et al. (2014)	Empirical	Methodological considerations	Setting Methods

firms in different contexts and particularly in emerging markets in which portfolio firms are more common; as indicated by Carter and Ram (2003, 374), "[s]cholars have remarked upon the prevalence of multiple business ownership, particularly in developing economies." Finally, articles that suggested exploring how a portfolio performs over time were grouped under 'performance.' For instance, Jaffe and Lane (2004), Cruz et al. (2013) and DeTienne and Chirico (2013) proposed examining how performance and outcome issues impact portfolio entrepreneurship. The remainder of this section reviews and discusses the past research and directions for future research involving portfolio entrepreneurship in family firms.

An Overview of Prior Research

Portfolio Entrepreneurship

Entrepreneurs with past experience in founding, owning or managing a business are considered habitual entrepreneurs (Ucbasaran et al. 2008). Further categorization divides them into serial and portfolio entrepreneurs; that is, serial entrepreneurs exploit multiple business opportunities in 'sequence,' i.e., one at a time, whereas portfolio entrepreneurs act as 'parallel founders' (Alsos and Kolvereid 1998, MacMillan 1986, Parker 2014, Westhead and Wright 1998). Our focus is on the latter.

Portfolio entrepreneurship can refer to the simultaneous ownership of multiple firms (Carter and Ram 2003) or the establishment of multiple ventures that operate in parallel to one another (Alsos and Kolvereid 1998). This type of ownership of several businesses is established to foster firm growth and risk diversification (Alsos and Kolvereid 1998, Carter 1998a, Rosa 1998). An increasing number of entrepreneurs are indeed focusing on owning multiple businesses to generate multiple sources of returns (Alsos and Carter 2006, Carter et al. 2004, Ucbasaran et al. 2001). Generating multiple income sources may lead to the creation of a specific type of firm with specific dynamics (Carter 1998a, b). For instance, satellites that are established in different industry settings may have different characteristics and require a different set of resources than satellites established in the same industry settings (cf. Carter 1998a, Sieger et al. 2011).

Portfolio entrepreneurs are found to be innovative and risk taking, which makes them willing and able to start multiple businesses simultaneously (Robson et al. 2012b, Rosa and Scott 1999, Sieger et al. 2011, Wiklund and Shepherd 2008). As such, portfolio entrepreneurs are generally considered individuals showing striving and ambitious behavior motivation, innovation (cf. Mulholland 1997, Ram 1994, Rosa 1998, Rosa and Scott 1999, Westhead et al. 2005, Wiklund and Shepherd 2008) and 'entrepreneurial diversification' (Rosa and Scott 1999, Sieger et al. 2011, Wiklund and Shepherd 2008). Portfolio entrepreneurs are interested in creating a pool of income-generating opportunities that enhance their overall economic progress rather than focusing exclusively on growing a single venture (Carter and Ram 2003, Carter et al. 2004, Wheelock and Baines 1998, Wiklund and Shepherd 2008). Portfolio entrepreneurs may also be motivated to own multiple businesses for motives that have little to do with growth, innovation and diversification (cf. Thorgren and Wincent 2015). For instance, they may find that the passion they have for starting a new business leads them to become portfolio entrepreneurs (MacMillan 1986, Murnieks, Mosakowski, and Cardon 2014, Rosa and Scott 1999, Westhead et al. 2005). Furthermore, Thorgren and Wincent (2015, 219) stated, "Multiple venturing efforts also increase autonomy and the chances of doing things entirely by free will, which particularly facilitate harmonious passion."

Entrepreneurs' past experiences are vital in ultimately driving them to establish and efficiently manage their firms (MacMillan and Katz 1992, Rerup 2005, Robson et al. 2012a). Alsos and Kolvereid (1998, 103), stated that, portfolio entrepreneurs "[l]earn from their earlier founding attempts, have the opportunity to analyze what went wrong and what went right, and eventually adopt the "technology" of entrepreneurship." The previous argument reflects that the similarities between prior business experience and present circumstances are crucial to an entrepreneur's ability to discover and exploit new opportunities (Rerup 2005, 455, Westhead and Wright 1999). Thus, studies advocate that the impact of entrepreneurs' past experiences is extremely noteworthy (e.g., Rerup 2005, Ucbasaran et al. 2009, Ucbasaran, Westhead, et al. 2003, Ucbasaran, Wright, Westhead, et al. 2003). Moreover, Westhead et al. (2003), Westhead et al. (2005), and Alsos and Carter (2006) found that portfolio entrepreneurship leads to the growth of firms due to the expert knowledge of portfolio entrepreneurs, established ties, and resource sharing among firms in a portfolio. These factors collectively show that the several forms of human, social and cultural capital are all significant factors of portfolio entrepreneurship (cf. Sieger et al. 2011, Wiklund and Shepherd 2008).

Together, these aspects require further research to yield conclusive results, particularly when the level of analysis shifts from firms and individuals to groups and families. Next, we further discuss the link between portfolio entrepreneurship and family firms.

Portfolio Entrepreneurship in Family Firms

It is somehow an "implicit assumption in most studies of family firms is that a family firm consists of only a single business entity" (Zellweger et al. 2012, 5). This perspective, however, fails to consider the many "business families [that] are often engaged in several businesses," or in a portfolio of activities (Zellweger et al. 2012, 15). Extant literature argues that family characteristics and resources available at the family's disposal are important in portfolio processes (Alsos et al. 2014, Rosa 1998, Sieger et al. 2011). However, the dearth of studies on portfolio family firms (see Tables 15.1 and 15.2) contrasts with the importance and wide prevalence of portfolio entrepreneurship in the family firm context and thus warrants further exploration (e.g., Cruz et al. 2013, DeTienne and Chirico 2013, Michael-Tsabari et al. 2014, Sieger et al. 2011). The literature suggests that portfolio entrepreneurship plays an even more significant role due to the nature of the phenomenon and its implications for family firms (Ram and Holliday 1993, Sieger et al. 2011). For example, owners of family firms are frequently involved in portfolio activities for purposes of risk management, while simultaneously keeping the legacy/core business intact (Carter and Ram 2003). The context of family firms also makes the succession, establishment and management of multiple businesses relatively easy due to the emotional bonds between family members (Cruz et al. 2013, Sieger et al. 2011, Zellweger et al. 2012). Nevertheless, the complex nature of family relationships may also affect portfolio entrepreneurship in family firms (Berrone, Cruz, and Gómez-Mejía 2012, DeTienne and Chirico 2013, Sieger et al. 2011). For instance, the decisions related to portfolio entry and divestment are often based on the socioemotional considerations of family owners (cf. DeTienne and Chirico 2013, Gómez-Mejía et al. 2007).

The family has also been observed to play an important role in deciding whether a family firm will engage in portfolio entrepreneurship, particularly with respect to generational succession (Breton-Miller and Miller 2006, Jaffe and Lane 2004, Sieger et al. 2011, Zellweger 2007). Family firms may undertake portfolio entrepreneurship to ensure the family's continued existence, even under negative market conditions (Carter and Ram 2003, Mulholland 1997). Portfolio entrepreneurship also offers more opportunities for family members to become part of the business by creating multiple sources of income (Carter and Ram 2003, Cruz et al. 2013, Ram and Holliday 1993). The additional income may be utilized to develop the core business further and to promote its growth, or it may simply be utilized by the family (Carter and Ram 2003, Ram 1994, Sieger et al. 2011).

Family firms may even be able to manage the portfolio entrepreneurship process more efficiently than non-family firms due to the greater control they exercise over resources and decisions (Cruz et al. 2013, Iacobucci and Rosa 2010). For instance, Carter and Ram (2003, 376) explained that when "family members join the business, the enterprise partially fragments to accommodate their individual needs and expectations for business autonomy and control." Family firms may also benefit from their close social ties when developing a portfolio (Alsos et al. 2014, Chirico, Ireland, and Sirmon 2011, Cruz et al. 2013). For example, the social capital entailed in the development of portfolio entrepreneurship in family firms may be promoted by household and kin connections (cf. Alsos et al. 2014, Cruz, Justo, and De Castro 2012, Sieger et al. 2011, Sirmon and Hitt 2003, Steier 2007).

In general, we find agreement in the literature regarding the importance of the role of portfolio entrepreneurship in exploiting opportunities for the progress and growth of firms, particularly in the context of family firms. Going one step further, we explore portfolio entrepreneurship in the context of family firms by identifying potential future research areas.

Future Research Agenda

The review of the portfolio entrepreneurship literature up to this point reveals an inspiring and gradually expanding body of work. Indeed, looking back more than a decade after the publication of the Carter and Ram (2003) review in which the authors touched upon the context of family business as relevant to further explore portfolio entrepreneurship, we have only recently witnessed the growing interest of family business scholars in this field. In particular, our review of the previous research shows that since 2010, scholars have increasingly explored the phenomenon of multiple business ownership in the dynamic field of family business, intending to advance this line of research. Carter and Ram (2003) noted that "[t]he context for portfolio approaches in the small business sector often hinges on understanding the family-business nexus. Thus, there is a need to focus on both the family circumstances that may affect business decisions and also the economic conditions facing a business" (Carter and Ram 2003, 377).

Thus, the lack of studies on portfolio entrepreneurship in the context of family firms persists, and our review notes this major research gap in the family firm area. This research gap reveals the following important and interesting future research directions: 1) to explore opportunities to study family firms' triggers to indulge in portfolio activities, 2) to explore how the different settings and sizes of portfolio family firms affect our understanding of their activities, and 3) to examine the performance and outcomes of portfolio family firms.

Triggers for Portfolio Family Firms

Commonly found triggers to indulge in multiple business ownership include profit maximization and risk diversification (Sieger et al. 2011, Wiklund and Shepherd 2008). Several studies highlight the triggers specific to family firms, such as providing jobs for the next generation and/or protecting the legacy business by establishing new satellite firms to facilitate the succession process (Sieger et al. 2011). Indeed, with some exceptions (Alsos et al. 2014, Cruz et al. 2013, Michael-Tsabari et al. 2014), the three main triggers to start satellite businesses identified above require further in-depth exploration (cf. Parker 2014).

The literature suggests that for a family firm to attain sustainability across generations, much depends on the intentions and willingness of the next generation to work for the family business. As suggested by Goel et al. (2012, 56), analyzing the family system in the context of the business system requires an understanding as to "why some family members enter the family business and others do not." Indeed, the commitment and intention of the next-generation family members to work for their family business has been suggested to be an important factor of firm sustainability, especially during economic crises (Dawson et al. 2015, Sharma and Irving 2005). This is a crucial enquiry, as the portfolio setting offers the possibility of exploring the next generation's motivations and intentions to work in the business (Alsos et al. 2014, Rosa et al. 2005). A family firm may endow the next generation not only with a set of resources but also with a platform to start a business of their own choice (Sieger et al. 2011, Zellweger, Sieger, and Halter 2011). This platform can motivate the next generation of business owners to remain in the business and can thus affect the family firm's sustainability (cf. Jaskiewicz, Combs, and Rau 2015, Nordqvist and Zellweger 2010, Zellweger et al. 2012), which is important because most of the literature reveals that the next generation commonly loses interest in running the family business. Portfolio entrepreneurship in the setting of family firms may reveal the reasons why some family owners stay in the business. For instance, Ram and Holliday (1993) noted that entrepreneurs tend to establish new businesses in addition to their core business not because of the demand in the market but rather because of the desire to accommodate family members' needs.

Similarly, succession is a core activity in family businesses, and a majority of family firms face succession-related issues. The central problem stems from family relationships that complicate business activity and a CEO talent pool restricted to a few family members (Le Breton-Miller, Miller, and Steier 2004, Zellweger et al. 2012). The setting of portfolio entrepreneurship is a good fit to help solve succession crises in family businesses. As suggested in the literature, although portfolio entrepreneurship facilitates the succession process (Sieger et al. 2011, Zellweger et al.

2012), it has been widely neglected in the literature. For example, Zellweger et al. (2012, 2) argued that "existing family firm survival studies tend to neglect the portfolio of entrepreneurial activities of business families beyond a core company and most traditional longevity studies fail to acknowledge other (appropriate) forms of succession beyond passing on the baton within the family, such as the sale of the firm as way to harvest value and create new opportunities for the family." The addition of new satellite businesses is a way to overcome the problem of family conflicts regarding succession (cf. Ram and Holliday 1993, Zellweger et al. 2012). In other words, multiple successions can occur in a portfolio firm and can accommodate multiple family members in the available pool.

Family firms are also considered more protective of their legacy/core business due to socio-emotional considerations (DeTienne and Chirico 2013). In a portfolio entrepreneurship setting, it is more likely that the owners of a family business will show more emotional attachment to the legacy/core business than to the satellites founded later (Feldman 2013, Rouse 2015). Family owners may become involved in portfolio activities to allow them to diversify risk and feel more confident about their legacy/core business activity in terms of its survival and sustainability (Nordqvist and Zellweger 2010, Rosa et al. 2005). Taken together, the research gaps identified are as follows:

Research Gap 1

What are the triggers and motives for family owners to indulge in portfolio entrepreneurship compared with non-family firms?

Research Gap 2

When and why do next-generation family members consider satellite businesses as their career choice intention, and how does this consideration affect the overall sustainability of the family business portfolio?

Research Gap 3

How and why can portfolio entrepreneurship act as the possible solution for a succession crisis in a family business portfolio?

Research Gap 4

How and why do family owners strive to support the legacy/core business versus other satellites in the setting of portfolio entrepreneurship?

Setting and Size of Portfolio Family Firms

The previous literature shows that the portfolio entrepreneurship approach takes different forms in different contexts (Cruz, Hamilton, et al. 2012, Westhead et al. 2003) (i.e., portfolio entrepreneurship in farm-based family firms compared with urban settings and different industrial, structural and country contexts). Interestingly, portfolio entrepreneurship activities and the contexts where these activities are embedded may influence each other (Lang, Fink, and Kibler 2014, Ucbasaran et al. 2001, Welter 2011, Westhead et al. 2003). Carter (1999) explored the additional income sources in the form of satellite businesses that portfolio entrepreneurs might enter—apart from their legacy/core businesses—in a farm setting. Alsos et al. (2014) recently explored family household and kinship issues in portfolio entrepreneurship in the context of family farms. Jaffe and Lane (2004) discussed how large business groups emerge, which are referred to as dynasties, in multiple contexts. These business groups are characterized by different developmental paths, structures and sizes; small, medium and large enterprises (see Brigham and Payne 2015, Carter 1998b, Jaffe and Lane 2004).

Our review also highlights that most empirical studies have been conducted in a European setting (Cruz et al. 2013, Westhead and Wright 1998). However, portfolio entrepreneurship in family firms is a common practice in Asian, North American, South American and African settings (e.g., Cruz et al. 2013, Guillen 2000, Manikutty 2000, Robson et al. 2012a, Sieger et al. 2011, Zellweger et al. 2012), and there are many family firms in those settings—from small and medium-sized firms to substantial business dynasties—that can provide a greater understanding of this phenomenon (cf. Khanna 2000, Khanna and Yafeh 2005). For instance, portfolio entrepreneurship family firms may suggest a different perspective when applied to businesses conducted in emerging economies that feature unique social, political and economic conditions (Khanna 2000, Khanna and Palepu 2000, Khanna and Rivkin 2001, Khanna and Yafeh 2005, Manikutty 2000).

The notable aspects of portfolio entrepreneurship can also be viewed in informal and illegal entrepreneurship. For instance, Webb et al. (2009, 492) stated, "between what is legal in a society and what some large groups consider to be legitimate in that society (besides illegal activities), allows an informal economy to emerge." Informal entrepreneurship refers to these " activities through which entrepreneurs operate and transact specifically outside of formal institutional boundaries yet remain within the boundaries of informal institutions" (Webb, Ireland, and Ketchen 2014, 2; see also Webb et al., 2009). Illegal entrepreneurship refers to activities and businesses dealing with illegal products or services (e.g. drug dealers) (Aidis and Van Praag 2007, Light 1977). A large number of businesses with multiple firms prevail in the setting of informal or illegal economies (Khanna and Palepu 2000, Webb et al. 2014), which fall under informal/illegal institutions (Webb et al. 2013, Webb et al. 2009). In such conditions, where informal and illegal institutes prevail, there is a high likelihood of suspicious activities, especially within the umbrella of a portfolio of firms. For instance, actual owners of the ventures may be hidden when illegitimate or illegal peripheral activities are carried out in the core/legacy business. This activity may be especially prevalent in family firm contexts. As argued by Adams, Taschian, and Shore (1996) and Litz and Turner (2013), surprisingly family firms may have relatively low levels of codes of conduct and are less formal than non-family firms. Classic examples include the mafia olive oil import business, through which money was laundered in the USA, and present-day criminal organizations in Italy, commonly organized by family affiliations, or drug cartels with intertwined informal and illegal activities in Mexico. In this way, portfolio entrepreneurship can be used by a (criminal) family to disguise activities. Another example is currently present in China. Families have one primary firm, which becomes a controlling investor in a second company, which is a controlling investor in a third. For companies three or four places along the chain, the original firm appears to own a small share, but the firm actually exercises control through the intermediaries.

Thus, it is notable that different settings, farm-based family firms compared with urban portfolio entrepreneurship family firms, firms of different sizes of portfolio groups, country or regional settings and informal or illegal economies may have a substantial impact on portfolio family firms and their dynamics. Taken together, the research gaps identified are as follows:

Research Gap 5

To what extent does the setting – i.e., farm-based portfolio entrepreneurship family firms vs. urban portfolio entrepreneurship family firms – impact on family involvement and decision making in the business? How a family firm contributes and it is challenged by different farm and urban settings?

Research Gap 6

How does the size of the portfolio affect the overall sustainability and collaboration among the family members of portfolio entrepreneurship family firms?

Research Gap 7

To what extent do different cultural settings – and particularly the family characteristics specific to a culture – influence the emergence of portfolio entrepreneurship family firms?

Research Gap 8

Is portfolio entrepreneurship used to mask informal or illegal activities? If yes, how?

Research Gap 9

To what extent do informal rules and conduct of a family firm foster the founding of core/satellite firms for informal or illegal activities?

The Performance and Outcome of Portfolio Family Firms

Scholars argue that firms owned by portfolio entrepreneurs may perform better than single-venture firms. However, there remains no consistency in these results with respect to being identified in the family business context, in particular. Studies argue that there is a positive relationship between performance and portfolio entrepreneurship, which results in transgenerational entrepreneurship (Zellweger et al. 2012), increased survival rates (Cruz et al. 2013) and (possibly) conflict mitigation (Carter and Ram 2003). Our review suggests that portfolio entrepreneurship can be used as a tool for transgenerational entrepreneurship and can represent a solution to many conflicts among family members (Zellweger et al. 2012). Habbershon, Nordqvist, and Zellweger (2010, 1) define transgenerational entrepreneurship as "the processes through which a family uses and develops entrepreneurial mindsets and family influenced resources and capabilities to create new streams of entrepreneurial, financial and social value across generations." This is an important outcome and performance indicator for portfolio family firms. Moreover, by mitigating conflicts, it may also suggest the increased survival of family firms across generations (Cruz et al. 2013). As noted by Carter and Ram (2003, 375), "[t]he circumstances in which family businesses may decide to engage in portfolio approaches include; the division of the business [and entry into new businesses] to accommodate the succession of multiple siblings." This succession process leads to reduced relational conflicts among siblings (Chirico and Salvato 2008). Hence, portfolio entrepreneurship in family firms may be understood as a multiple ownership strategy for family survival (Mulholland 1997).

Carter and Ram (2003, 378) argued that "[t]he wider literature suggests that economic conditions that may influence the decision to engage in portfolio approaches." The literature also proposes that economic conditions may influence the decision not only to engage in portfolio activities but also to divest/exit the businesses at times. For instance, Sharma and Manikutty (2005, 295) argued that "[c]hanges in the environment require strategic responses on the part of a firm (such as readjustment of the business portfolio and divestment of unproductive resources), so as to enable regeneration and renewal." This notion is particularly salient in the case of family firms in which family owners are socioemotionally more attached to—and more reluctant to divest from—the legacy/core business (DeTienne and Chirico 2013, Feldman 2015, Feldman, Amit, and Villalonga 2014, Jaskiewicz et al. 2015).

Exit and divestiture is another important outcome and performance indicator for portfolio entrepreneurship firms. However, with the exception to DeTienne and Chirico (2013), who explored the process and exit strategies in portfolio firms, no other prior studies are found in this domain. This lack of research on the performance and outcomes—such as the exit behaviors of family owners—of portfolio firms is surprising (DeTienne and Chirico 2013) because it is important to examine the entirety of portfolio entrepreneurship, from initial motivations to the outcome and performance of the portfolio as a whole, as well as the performance of satellite businesses and their influence on the portfolio. Indeed, it is of utmost importance because portfolio entrepreneurs exit from their ventures multiple times in their careers due to both family- and business-related issues (DeTienne and Chirico 2013, Ucbasaran et al. 2010). We may then see different reasons for divesting satellite businesses and not divesting the legacy business. For instance, DeTienne and Chirico (2013, 10) suggested that "[w]hen it comes to selling or liquidating subsequent businesses in the portfolio (whether new venture creations or acquisitions) family owners may behave very much like a traditional investor (e.g., a venture capitalist) wherein profit and value maximization, not emotions – determine behavior." As the emergence and the development of portfolio businesses is about not only entry and growth issues but also exit, divestment and declining circumstances, it becomes relevant to study portfolio entrepreneurship development as a non-linear process (cf. Michael-Tsabari et al. 2014, Rosa et al. 2005). Thus, we have identified the following overall research gaps:

Research Gap 10

How and why are family owners perceived to be more entrepreneurial in portfolio entrepreneurial firms than in single ventures? Are they really more entrepreneurial, and do they really achieve higher-level (financial, non-financial) performance?

Research Gap 11

How does the portfolio entrepreneurship approach and entries into new businesses mitigate conflicts regarding transgenerational ownership?

Research Gap 12

How and why do family firms exit the setting of portfolio entrepreneurship family firms? Why do family owners choose to exit a satellite or a core business? Why do family owners choose to exit some satellites and not others? How does exit influence the overall sustainability and endurance of portfolio entrepreneurship family firms?

Research Gap 13

What is the effect of declining performance of the legacy business on the overall portfolio, and how does it influence exit decisions in dynamic (hostile) versus non-dynamic environments?

Conclusion

Looking back over previous reviews and research on portfolio entrepreneurship, the purpose of this article was to take stock of prior research on portfolio entrepreneurship in the particular context of family firms and to propose a future research agenda by identifying the relevant gaps in current scholarship. Although the present review identifies many valuable scholarly contributions to portfolio entrepreneurship, there are notable opportunities to be discussed. In this article, we note what needs to be further researched in terms of the limited body of work on portfolio entrepreneurship and family businesses. Additionally, except for some research (e.g., Carter and Ram 2003, Cruz et al. 2013, DeTienne and Chirico 2013, Michael-Tsabari et al. 2014, Sieger et al. 2011) that links portfolio entrepreneurship and family businesses, little research examines the motivations specific to family owners that might trigger such owners to engage in creating a portfolio of businesses. Surprisingly, there is also little research that links portfolio entrepreneurship to family firms in different settings, cultures, environments, and (informal or illegal) economies or that distinguishes small and medium-sized portfolio family firms from large family business groups. There are also significant gaps in the extant research regarding the study of the performance of the overall portfolio and its impact on the overall endurance, sustainability and/or exit strategies of portfolio entrepreneurship family firms. However, it is also promising to observe that in the last few years, research on portfolio entrepreneurship and family businesses has begun to converge. We believe that we will understand more about portfolio entrepreneurship in the context of family firms and what it enables within organizations if we focus on the owning family—albeit in different ways and with different actors—in a variety of contexts. Thus, our research stands to reveal more of the advantages, tensions, and challenges of portfolio family firms.

References

Adams, Janet S., Armen Taschian, and Ted H Shore. 1996. "Ethics in family and non-family owned firms: An exploratory study." *Family Business Review* 9 (2):157–170.

Aidis, Ruta, and Mirjam Van Praag. 2007. "Illegal entrepreneurship experience: Does it make a difference for business performance and motivation?" *Journal of Business Venturing* 22 (2):283–310.

Alsos, Gry Agnete, and Sara Carter. 2006. "Multiple business ownership in the Norwegian farm sector: Resource transfer and performance consequences." *Journal of Rural Studies* 22 (3):313–322.

Alsos, Gry Agnete, Sara Carter, and Elisabet Ljunggren. 2014. "Kinship and business: How entrepreneurial households facilitate business growth." *Entrepreneurship & Regional Development* 26 (1–2):97–122.

Alsos, Gry Agnete, and Lars Kolvereid. 1998. "The business gestation process of novice, serial, and parallel business founders." *Entrepre.neurship Theory and Practice* 22 (4):101–114.

Arregle, Jean-Luc, Michael A. Hitt, David G. Sirmon, and Philippe Very. 2007. "The Development of Organizational Social Capital: Attributes of Family Firms." *Journal of Management Studies* 44 (1):73–95.

Berrone, Pascual, Cristina Cruz, and Luis R. Gómez-Mejía. 2012. "Socioemotional wealth in family firms theoretical dimensions, assessment approaches, and agenda for future research." *Family Business Review* 25 (3):258–279.

Brigham, Keith H, and G Tyge Payne. 2015. "The transitional nature of the multifamily business." *Entrepreneurship Theory and Practice* 39 (6): 1339–1347.

Carter, Sara. 1998a. "The economic potential of portfolio entrepreneurship: enterprise and employment contributions of multiple business ownership." *Journal of Small Business and Enterprise Development* 5 (4):297–306.

Carter, Sara. 1998b. "Portfolio entrepreneurship in the farm sector: Indigenous growth in rural areas?" *Entrepreneurship & Regional Development* 10 (1):17–32.

Carter, Sara. 1999. "Multiple business ownership in the farm sector: Assessing the enterprise and employment contributions of farmers in Cambridgeshire." *Journal of Rural Studies* 15 (4):417–429.

Carter, Sara, and Monder Ram. 2003. "Reassessing portfolio entrepreneurship." *Small Business Economics* 21 (4):371–380.

Carter, Sara, Stephen Tagg, and Pavlos Dimitratos. 2004. "Beyond portfolio entrepreneurship: multiple income sources in small firms." *Entrepreneurship & Regional Development* 16 (6):481–499.

Chirico, Francesco, and Carlo Salvato. 2008. "Knowledge integration and dynamic organizational adaptation in family firms." *Family Business Review* 21 (2):169–181.

Chirico, Francesco, R. Duane Ireland, and David G. Sirmon. 2011. "Franchising and the family firm: Creating unique sources of advantage through 'Familiness.'" *Entrepreneurship Theory and Practice* 35 (3):483–501.

Chrisman, James J., Jess H. Chua, Allison W. Pearson, and Tim Barnett. 2012. "Family involvement, family influence, and family-centered non-economic goals in small firms." *Entrepreneurship Theory and Practice* 36 (2):267–293.

Cruz, Allan Discua, Eleanor Hamilton, and Sarah L. Jack. 2012. "Understanding entrepreneurial cultures in family businesses: A study of family entrepreneurial teams in Honduras." *Journal of Family Business Strategy* 3 (3):147–161.

Cruz, Allan, Carole Howorth, and Eleanor Hamilton. 2013. "Intrafamily entrepreneurship: The formation and membership of family entrepreneurial teams." *Entrepreneurship Theory and Practice* 37 (1):17–46.

Cruz, Cristina, Rachida Justo, and Julio O. De Castro. 2012. "Does family employment enhance MSEs performance?: Integrating socioemotional wealth and family embeddedness perspectives." *Journal of Business Venturing* 27 (1):62–76.

Dawson, Alexandra, Pramodita Sharma, P., Gregory Irving, and Joel Marcus. 2015. "Predictors of Later-Generation Family Members' Commitment to Family Enterprises." *Entrepreneurship Theory and Practice* 39 (3):545–569.

DeTienne, and Dawn R. 2013. "Exit strategies in family firms: How socioemotional wealth drives the threshold of performance." *Entrepreneurship Theory and Practice* 37 (6):1297–1318.

Feldman, Emilie R. 2013. "Legacy divestitures: Motives and implications." *Organization Science* 25 (3):815–832.

Feldman, Emilie R. 2015. "Corporate Spinoffs and Analysts' Coverage Decisions: The Implications for Diversified Firms." *Strategic Management Journal* 37 (7): 1196–1219.

Feldman, Emilie R., Raphael Raffi Amit, and Belén Villalonga. 2014. "Corporate divestitures and family control." *Strategic Management Journal* 37 (3): 429–446.

Goel, Sanjay, Pietro Mazzola, Phillip H. Phan, Torsten M. Pieper, and Ramona K. Zachary. 2012. "Strategy, ownership, governance, and socio-psychological perspectives on family businesses from around the world." *Journal of Family Business Strategy* 3 (2):54–65.

Gómez-Mejía, Luis R., Katalin Takács Haynes, Manuel Núñez-Nickel, Kathryn J.L. Jacobson, and José Moyano-Fuentes. 2007. "Socioemotional wealth and business risks in family-controlled firms: Evidence from Spanish olive oil mills." *Administrative Science Quarterly* 52 (1):106–137.

Guillen, Mauro F. 2000. "Business groups in emerging economies: A resource-based view." *Academy of Management Journal* 43 (3):362–380.

Habbershon, Timothy G., Mattias Nordqvist, and Thomas Zellweger. 2010. "Transgenerational entrepreneurship." *Transgenerational Entrepreneurship: Exploring Growth and Performance in Family Firms Across Generations*:1–38.

Huovinen, Jari, and Sanna Tihula. 2008. "Entrepreneurial learning in the context of portfolio entrepreneurship." *International Journal of Entrepreneurial Behavior & Research* 14 (3):152–171.

Iacobucci, Donato, and Peter Rosa. 2005. "Growth, diversification, and business group formation in entrepreneurial firms." *Small Business Economics* 25 (1):65–82.

Iacobucci, Donato, and Peter Rosa. 2010. "The growth of business groups by habitual entrepreneurs: The role of entrepreneurial teams." *Entrepreneurship Theory and Practice* 34 (2):351–377.

Jaffe, Dennis T., and Sam H. Lane. 2004. "Sustaining a family dynasty: key issues facing complex multigenerational business-and investment-owning families." *Family Business Review* 17 (1):81–98.

Jaskiewicz, Peter, James G. Combs, and Sabine B Rau. 2015. "Entrepreneurial legacy: Toward a theory of how some family firms nurture transgenerational entrepreneurship." *Journal of Business Venturing* 30 (1):29–49.

Khanna, Tarun. 2000. "Business groups and social welfare in emerging markets: Existing evidence and unanswered questions." *European Economic Review* 44 (4):748–761.

Khanna, Tarun, and Jan W. Rivkin. 2001. "Estimating the performance effects of business groups in emerging markets." *Strategic Management Journal* 22 (1):45–74.

Khanna, Tarun, and Krishna Palepu. 2000. "The future of business groups in emerging markets: Long-run evidence from Chile." *Academy of Management Journal* 43 (3):268–285.

Khanna, Tarun, and Yishay Yafeh. 2005. "Business Groups and Risk Sharing around the World." *The Journal of Business* 78 (1):301–340.

Lang, Richard, Matthias Fink, and Ewald Kibler. 2014. "Understanding place-based entrepreneurship in rural Central Europe: A comparative institutional analysis." *International Small Business Journal* 32 (2):204–227.

Le Breton-Miller, and Danny Miller. 2006. "Why Do Some Family Businesses Out-Compete? Governance, Long-Term Orientations, and Sustainable Capability." *Entrepreneurship Theory and Practice* 30 (6):731–746.

Le Breton-Miller, Danny Miller, and Lloyd P. Steier. 2004. "Toward an integrative model of effective FOB succession." *Entrepreneurship Theory and Practice* 28 (4):305–328.

Light, Ivan. 1977. "The ethnic vice industry, 1880–1944." *American Sociological Review:* 464–479.

Litz, Reginald A., and Nick Turner. 2013. "Sins of the father's firm: Exploring responses to inherited ethical dilemmas in family business." *Journal of Business Ethics* 113 (2):297–315.

MacMillan, I. 1986. "To really learn about entrepreneurship, let's study habitual entrepreneurs." *Journal of Business Venturing* 1 (3):241–243.

MacMillan, Ian C., and Jerome A. Katz. 1992. "Idiosyncratic milieus of entrepreneurial research: The need for comprehensive theories." *Journal of Business Venturing* 7 (1):1–8.

Manikutty, Sankaran. 2000. "Family business groups in India: A resource-based view of the emerging trends." *Family Business Review* 13 (4):279–292.

McGaughey, Sara L. 2007. "Hidden ties in international new venturing: The case of portfolio entrepreneurship." *Journal of World Business* 42 (3):307–321.

Michael-Tsabari, Nava, Rania Labaki, and Ramona Kay Zachary. 2014. "Toward the cluster model: The family firm's entrepreneurial behavior over generations." *Family Business Review* 27 (2):161–185.

Miller, Danny, and Isabelle Le Breton-Miller. 2005. *Managing for the Long Run: Lessons in Competitive Advantage from Great Family Businesses:* Harvard Business Press.

Mulholland, Kate. 1997. "The family enterprise and business strategies." *Work, Employment & Society* 11 (4):685–711.

Murnieks, Charles Y., Elaine Mosakowski, and Melissa S. Cardon. 2014. "Pathways of passion: Identity centrality, passion, and behavior among entrepreneurs." *Journal of Management* 40 (6):1583–1606.

Nordqvist, M., and T. Zellweger eds. 2010. *Transgenerational Entrepreneurship: Exploring Growth and Performance in Family Firms across Generations.* Cheltenham, UK and Brookfield, US: Edward Elgar.

Parker, Simon C. 2014. "Who become serial and portfolio entrepreneurs?" *Small Business Economics* 43 (4):887–898.

Plate, Markus, Christian Schiede, and Arist von Schlippe. 2010. "Portfolio entrepreneurship in the context of family owned businesses." *Transgenerational entrepreneurship: Exploring growth and performance of family firms across generations:* 96–123.

Ram, Monder. 1994. *Managing to Survive: Working Lives in Small Firms:* Blackwell Business.

Ram, Monder, and Ruth Holliday. 1993. "Relative merits: family culture and kinship in small firms." *Sociology* 27 (4):629–648.

Rerup, Claus. 2005. "Learning from past experience: Footnotes on mindfulness and habitual entrepreneurship." *Scandinavian Journal of Management* 21 (4):451–472.

Robson, Paul J.A., Charles K. Akuetteh, Paul Westhead, and Mike Wright. 2012a. "Exporting intensity, human capital and business ownership experience." *International Small Business Journal* 30 (4):367–387.

Robson, Paul J.A., Charles K. Akuetteh, Paul Westhead, and Mike Wright. 2012b. "Innovative opportunity pursuit, human capital and business ownership experience in an emerging region: Evidence from Ghana." *Small Business Economics* 39 (3):603–625.

Rosa, P., W. Balunywa, and D. Iacobucci. 2005. "Habitual entrepreneurship and the family business: A transgenerational perspective." *Frontiers of Entrepreneurship Research.*

Rosa, Peter. 1998. "Entrepreneurial processes of business cluster formation and growth by 'habitual' entrepreneurs." *Entrepreneurship Theory and Practice* 22 (4):43–62.

Rosa, Peter. 1999. "The prevalence of multiple owners and directors in the SME sector: Implications for our understanding of start-up and growth." *Entrepreneurship & Regional Development* 11 (1):21–37.

Rosa, Peter, and M. Scott. 1999. "Entrepreneurial diversification, business-cluster formation, and growth." *Environment and Planning C: Government and Policy* 17 (5):527–547.

Rouse, Elizabeth D. 2015. "Beginning's end: How founders psychologically disengage from their organizations." *Academy of Management Journal*:amj. 2013.1219.

Shane, Scott, and Sankaran Venkataraman. 2000. "The promise of entrepreneurship as a field of research." *Academy of Management Review* 25 (1):217–226.

Sharma, Pramodita, and P. Gregory Irving. 2005. "Four bases of family business successor commitment: Antecedents and consequences." *Entrepreneurship Theory and Practice* 29 (1):13–33.

Sharma, Pramodita, and S. Manikutty. 2005. "Strategic divestments in family firms: Role of family structure and community culture." *Entrepreneurship Theory and Practice* 29 (3):293–311.

Sieger, Philipp, Thomas Zellweger, Robert S. Nason, and Eric Clinton. 2011. "Portfolio entrepreneurship in family firms: a resource-based perspective." *Strategic Entrepreneurship Journal* 5 (4):327–351.

Sirmon, David G., and Michael A. Hitt. 2003. "Managing resources: Linking unique resources, management, and wealth creation in family firms." *Entrepreneurship Theory and Practice* 27 (4):339–358.

Sirmon, David G., Michael A. Hitt, and R. Duane Ireland. 2007. "Managing firm resources in dynamic environments to create value: Looking inside the black box." *Academy of Management Review* 32 (1):273–292.

Steier, Lloyd. 2007. "New venture creation and organization: A familial sub-narrative." *Journal of Business Research* 60 (10):1099–1107.

Thorgren, Sara, and Joakim Wincent. 2015. "Passion and habitual entrepreneurship." *International Small Business Journal* 33 (2):216–227.

Ucbasaran, Deniz, Gry Agnete Alsos, Paul Westhead, and Mike Wright. 2008. "Habitual entrepreneurs." *Foundations and Trends in Entrepreneurship* 4 (4):309–450.

Ucbasaran, Deniz, Paul Westhead, and Mike Wright. 2001. "The focus of entrepreneurial research: Contextual and process issues." *Entrepreneurship Theory and Practice* 25 (4):57–80.

Ucbasaran, Deniz, Paul Westhead, and Mike Wright. 2009. "The extent and nature of opportunity identification by experienced entrepreneurs." *Journal of Business Venturing* 24 (2):99–115.

Ucbasaran, Deniz, Paul Westhead, Mike Wright, and Martin Binks. 2003. "Does entrepreneurial experience influence opportunity identification?" *The Journal of Private Equity* 7 (1):7–14.

Ucbasaran, Deniz, Paul Westhead, Mike Wright, and Manuel Flores. 2010. "The nature of entrepreneurial experience, business failure and comparative optimism." *Journal of Business Venturing* 25 (6):541–555.

Ucbasaran, Deniz, Mike Wright, and Paul Westhead. 2003. "A longitudinal study of habitual entrepreneurs: Starters and acquirers." *Entrepreneurship & Regional Development* 15 (3):207–228.

Ucbasaran, Deniz, Mike Wright, Paul Westhead, and Lowell W Busenitz. 2003. "The impact of entrepreneurial experience on opportunity identification and exploitation: Habitual and novice entrepreneurs." *Advances in Entrepreneurship, Firm Emergence and Growth* 6:231–263.

Venkataraman, Sankaran. 1997. "The distinctive domain of entrepreneurship research." *Advances in entrepreneurship, Firm Emergence and Growth* 3 (1):119–138.

Webb, Justin W., Garry D. Bruton, Laszlo Tihanyi, and R. Duane Ireland. 2013. "Research on entrepreneurship in the informal economy: Framing a research agenda." *Journal of Business Venturing* 28 (5):598–614.

Webb, Justin W., R. Duane Ireland, and David J. Ketchen. 2014. "Toward a greater understanding of entrepreneurship and strategy in the informal economy." *Strategic Entrepreneurship Journal* 8 (1):1–15.

Webb, Justin W., Laszlo Tihanyi, R. Duane Ireland, and David G. Sirmon. 2009. "You say illegal, I say legitimate: Entrepreneurship in the informal economy." *Academy of Management Review* 34 (3):492–510.

Welter, F. 2011. "Contextualizing Entrepreneurship-Conceptual Challenges and Ways Forward." *Entrepreneurship Theory and Practice* 35 (1):165–184. doi: 10.1111/j.1540–6520.2010.00427.x.

Westhead, Paul, Deniz Ucbasaran, and Mike Wright. 2003. "Differences between private firms owned by novice, serial and portfolio entrepreneurs: Implications for policy makers and practitioners." *Regional Studies* 37 (2):187–200.

Westhead, Paul, Deniz Ucbasaran, Mike Wright, and Martin Binks. 2005. "Novice, serial and portfolio entrepreneur behaviour and contributions." *Small Business Economics* 25 (2):109–132.

Westhead, Paul, and Mike Wright. 1998. "Novice, portfolio, and serial founders: Are they different?" *Journal of Business Venturing* 13 (3):173–204.

Westhead, Paul, and Mike Wright. 1999. "Contributions of novice, portfolio and serial founders located in rural and urban areas." *Regional Studies* 33 (2):157.

Westhead, Paul, and Mike Wright. 2015. "The habitual entrepreneur phenomenon." *International Small Business Journal (Virtual Special Issue).*:1–16.

Wheelock, Jane, and Susan Baines. 1998. "Dependency or self-reliance? The contradictory case of work in UK small business families." *Journal of Family and Economic Issues* 19 (1):53–73.

Wiklund, Johan, and Dean A. Shepherd. 2008. "Portfolio entrepreneurship: Habitual and novice founders, new entry, and mode of organizing." *Entrepreneurship Theory and Practice* 32 (4):701–725.

Wright, M, P Westhead, and J Sohl. 1998. "Editors." *Introduction: Habitual Entrepreneurs and Angel Investors,' Entrepreneurship Theory and Practice* 22 (4):5–21.

Zellweger, Thomas. 2007. "Time horizon, costs of equity capital, and generic investment strategies of firms." *Family Business Review* 20 (1):1–15.

Zellweger, Thomas, Philipp Sieger, and Frank Halter. 2011. "Should I stay or should I go? Career choice intentions of students with family business background." *Journal of Business Venturing* 26 (5):521–536.

Zellweger, Thomas, Robert S Nason, and Mattias Nordqvist. 2012. "From longevity of firms to transgenerational entrepreneurship of families introducing family entrepreneurial orientation." *Family Business Review* 25 (2):136–155.

PART III

Organizational Behavior

16

FAMILY INVOLVEMENT AND CORPORATE SOCIAL RESPONSIBILITY IN SMALL- AND MEDIUM-SIZED FAMILY FIRMS

Giovanna Campopiano and Alfredo De Massis

Introduction

The corporate world pays increasing attention to face social issues, as firms care and spend resources and efforts towards environmental protection, safety, and health of employees, welfare and well-being of their communities, and in general to behave as responsible corporate citizens (Matten and Crane, 2005). Research has addressed this topic for decades, and several concepts emerged in different fields, from social entrepreneurship to corporate social responsibility, from social innovation to stakeholder management. The boundaries among these concepts are blurred, and strongly dependent on the theoretical lenses adopted as well as the streams of literature considered. Management, entrepreneurship, business ethics are instances of different fields, which definitely makes the topic multidisciplinary. While a focus on Social Entrepreneurship, and the difficulties in defining it and its main discussion areas, mainly refers to the mainstream entrepreneurship field (Mair and Marti, 2006; Peredo and McLean, 2006; see recent research avenues as reviewed by Pierre, von Friedrichs, and Wincent, 2014), the concept of Corporate Social Responsibility (CSR) belongs to other fields of research. The main difference relies on whether a social or a commercial aim is pursued by the organization. While social entrepreneurship deals with entrepreneurial activities with an embedded social purpose and driven to create social value, CSR pertains to the realm of ventures whose ultimate scope is to generate and increase personal and shareholder wealth (Austin, Stevenson, and Wei-Skillern, 2006). Thus, social entrepreneurship is broadly defined as the "process of creating value by combining resources in new ways that are intended primarily to exploit opportunities for creating social value" (Pierre et al., 2014: 44), and only currently the debate has centered around the extent to which social enterprises should pursue also commercial aims (e.g., Lundström and Zhou, 2014). Corporate social responsibility, instead, is meant as an evolving corporate strategy, which has an increasing importance among the (for-profit) firm activities (Carroll and Shabana, 2010). CSR, which is the focus of this chapter, has been debated for a long time in literature and the concept has evolved from claiming that the only responsibility of a business is to make profits (Friedman, 1979) to emphasizing the volunteering character of corporate initiatives aimed at benefiting its stakeholders and society, beyond any legal requirements (e.g., Crane and Matten, 2007; McWilliams and Siegel, 2001). In this study, we adopt a definition of CSR consistent with this latest idea of accomplishing initiatives beyond what is required by law: "A firm is socially responsible if it commits to integrate social and environmental concerns in its business operations and in its interaction with the stakeholders on a voluntary basis" (European Commission, 2011). This definition embeds both the volunteering aspect of responsible actions undertaken by firms and the strategic stakeholder management of private businesses.

In management studies, the focus is especially on the analysis of the factors determining the extent to which firms engage in socially responsible practices. One of the most discussed factors is size: there are studies focusing on the differences between large corporations and small- and medium-sized enterprises (SMEs), for instance, with respect to the level of knowledge of the topic, the extent to which CSR is integrated into the actual firm activities and disseminated among the corporate stakeholders (Blombäck and Wigren, 2009). Recently a debate has arisen on the relevance that SMEs place on these issues, since they are often acknowledged to be unaware of CSR in terms of formal definition and concept, although they are actually involved in some socially responsible activities (Russo and Perrini, 2010), and it thus seems that they do not perceive it as part of their strategy, or at least as an important activity for the sustainability of the firm. This debate can be further enriched considering the family business context, where the presence of a family involved in the business activities may directly influence the importance of socially responsible activities for the family business itself (e.g., Campopiano and De Massis, 2015). Whether a family firm is more or less engaged in CSR activities is indeed especially related to the idiosyncratic characteristics of this form of business organization, defined as a firm owned and managed by a family or a small group of families in order to pursue the vision of the business and to be sustainable across generations (Chua, Chrisman, and Sharma 1999). The overlap of ownership, family and business systems (Tagiuri and Davis, 1996) may affect the definition of the above mentioned vision (De Massis, Kotlar, Chua, and Chrisman, 2014b) and thus also whether engaging in socially responsible activities may be relevant or not.

Overall, research on corporate social responsibility has suggested that, beyond size, a number of factors may affect the commitment of firms, and in particular SMEs, to corporate social responsibility, such as the motivations to engage in socially responsible activities (e.g., Campopiano, Da Massis, and Cassia, 2012), the industry in which the firm operates, whether the firm specifically serves business or consumer markets, the country of origin, and whether the firm works in a developing or industrialized world, which can be considered as meaningful drivers of CSR strategies (Blombäck and Wigren, 2009). Considering the relationship between factors related to the ownership and governance of the firm and CSR engagement may further improve our understanding of family firms' behavior. Indeed, few studies consider family involvement in a firm as an antecedent of CSR behavior (Adams et al., 1996; Berrone et al., 2010; Deniz and Suarez, 2005; Dyer and Whetten, 2006; Niehm et al., 2008; Uhlaner et al., 2004), CSR reporting (Campopiano and De Massis, 2015), philanthropic engagement (Atkinson and Galaskiewicz, 1988; Campopiano, De Massis, and Chirico, 2014; Litz and Stewart, 2000), and the role of values in CSR engagement (e.g., Marques, Presas, and Simon, 2014). These studies mainly rely on arguments based on different theoretical premises to assess family firms' behavior towards CSR, discuss if they are more or less ethical or socially concerned than non-family firms, and uncover whether and why family firms are a heterogeneous sample with respect to CSR. Results are contrasting and we argue that the involvement of the family in the business is an important explanatory variable to predict CSR engagement of small- and medium-sized family businesses.

In an attempt to fill an existing gap in the literature, this study aims to investigate how family involvement affects the engagement of private small- and medium-sized family firms in corporate social responsibility. In the next section, we provide the theoretical arguments used to build the hypotheses; the third section presents the methodology adopted to collect data and perform the analyses; the fourth section shows the results while the fifth one provides a discussion. The last section outlines the conclusions, acknowledges the limitations of the study and draws future research directions.

Theoretical Background and Hypotheses Development

Literature on corporate social responsibility in family business has been rooted in different and contrasting theories. Family firms' conduct, with respect to the whole set of stakeholders, is dependent on a number of factors and cannot neglect the presence of the family as one of the stakeholders involved. The simultaneous presence of ownership, family and business systems may affect family firms' behavior towards CSR, and the main element affecting the extent to which a business is considered highly intertwined with the family is family involvement, which widely varies in terms of degree of family ownership, intra-family ownership dispersion, and generation controlling the business, thus making family firms heterogeneous (De Massis et al., 2013; De Massis et al., 2015; Sciascia and Mazzola, 2008).

In our attempt to take into account ongoing debates on family business social conduct and overcome the limitations of this literature, we rely on two different theoretical lenses. More specifically, we propose that two concepts, i.e. reputation and self-interest, already adopted as theoretical lenses in the family business field (e.g., Chen et al., 2008; Danes et al., 2008; Dyer and Whetten, 2006; Miller et al., 2008; Niehm et al., 2008) are useful to address the issue under investigation and offer a contribution to literature. These two elements have their roots in legitimacy and agency theories respectively, and can thus help to explain the phenomenon from two different, but complementary, perspectives. Moreover, reputation on the one side and self-interest on the other have been widely used in extant literature as relevant elements that can be borrowed to investigate the issues at a corporate level, since we refer to corporate reputation and self-interest in terms of benefits that the family business can earn from CSR engagement.

Reputation

One of the main arguments supporting that family firms have an incentive to engage in corporate social responsibility refers to their propensity to build and maintaining their reputation so as to be legitimated in the communities in which the firm operates. Corporate reputation is built on the idea that a firm is assigned a positive reputation because of a number of desirable characteristics (Davies et al., 2003; Fombrun, 1996). Stakeholders, therefore, assess the firm's actions and update their view of the firm and its character in the light of these actions. As legitimacy theory suggests, firms that want to build a good reputation certainly face a critical strategic issue, and thus, need to find ways to improve their existing reputation and avoid unintentionally damaging it (Love and Kraatz, 2009). Literature depicts three different perspectives on reputation: (i) positive reputation is assigned to firms that have traits that are highly valued since they may be considered as predictors of the firms' future behavior (Fombrun and Van Riel, 2004); (ii) good reputation is given to firms with an organization's symbolic conformity with institutional, context-specific standards and categories; and (iii) high reputation is closely tied to organizational outputs, such as high quality products and services, and great financial results (Shapiro, 1983).

Private small- and medium-sized firms, especially, put great emphasis on the reputation that the community and the firm's stakeholders have of the firm (e.g., Carter and Dukerich, 1998; Dowling, 1986; Fombrun, 1996). Moreover, a firm's reputation is acknowledged to be affected by quality of management, company's financial soundness and its demonstration of social concerns, so that reputation is useful to enhance the long-term sustainability of a business (Barney, 1991; Eddleston, Kellermanns, and Sarathy, 2008; James, 2006; Morris et al., 1997); furthermore, it also supports market share during industry downturns and increases the stability of the business (Fombrun, 1996).

This is even more relevant for family firms that have incentives to be socially responsible in order to maintain a positive image, since a good reputation among the key stakeholders may be considered as a form of social insurance, protecting not only the firm's but also the family's assets in times of crisis (Dunn, 1996; Godfrey, 2005; Whetten and Mackey, 2005). More attention to foster a good reputation of the business is one of the ways a family business may nurture its continuity in the long run (Miller et al., 2008). In addition, the importance of reputation is even exacerbated for family firms, since family wealth is usually intertwined with their business success, the family name is usually associated with the business (Deephouse and Jaskiewicz, 2013), and the investment of the family into the business is often quite difficult to be liquidated with respect, for example, to an investment into a public company (Wiklund, 2006).

However, previous studies have found that not all family firms are equally concerned with CSR, and they are heterogeneous with respect to their attitudes towards social issues. For instance, Deniz and Suarez (2005) in their study classified family firms according to the different degrees of engagement in CSR activities. Reputation among the main stakeholders of the firm can, therefore, be a main aim that the family business wants to pursue through its engagement in CSR. It is not trivial, however, that all family businesses consider CSR as the best investment in order to build and maintain a reputation, and even the relevance of reputation itself may depend on the degree of involvement of the family in the business.

Self-Interest

A second element that plays an important role in explaining family firms' social conduct is self-interest, highly related to family altruism. Rooted in the agency theory, from a utilitarian point of view, altruism plays the role of a connector between the welfare of one individual and that of others (Schulze et al., 2003b). It is a concept that well suits family firms, where for example parents exhibit high levels of benevolence with respect to their children not only because they are closely linked, but also because their own interests, and those of the business, would be damaged if they act less benevolently (Karra et al., 2006). Therefore, they are basically self-interested, since they want to protect their own interests (Morck and Yeung, 2004), and their conduct may result in behaviors that could disadvantage company employees and other stakeholders, or in competing in the marketplace in ways that could be clearly harmful (Schulze et al., 2001). Accordingly, family altruism is defined as the powerful force within family life and, by extension, within the family business, that on the one hand makes the parents care for their offspring, makes family members consider each other, and fosters loyalty and commitment to the family and firm; and on the other hand gives both parents and children incentives to take actions that can threaten the welfare of the family and firm (Schulze et al., 2003b: 474). Family altruism may thus be harmful to the firm if the family's and friends' interests prevail over the business ones when, for example, the family hires and holds unqualified managers and employees just because of blood ties (Schultze et al., 2003b).

On the one hand, according to the family altruism perspective, self-interested family firms may disregard engagement in CSR as a core objective of their firm and do not consider it at all among its strategic and operative activities; on the other hand, a positive view of family altruism allows to take into high consideration the sustainability of the family business, that will be transferred to future generations. This behavior of family firms is referred to in the literature as stewardship towards the family business, since the owners of the firm care about the future of young generations and their business (Miller et al., 2008), so that CSR may be considered as a viable way to achieve this goal. We argue that the presence of a family in a business is an important factor to understand whether and why family firms engage in CSR.

In sum, in the literature there are contrasting arguments that attempt to predict family business behavior. We aim to find out whether and to what extent different dimensions of family involvement in the business affect private small- and medium-sized family firms engagement in corporate social responsibility.

Hypotheses

The arguments examined above suggest that family firms behave differently from non-family firms depending on the importance they attach to reputation and self-interest since these two elements emerge from prior literature as critically important in explaining family firms' corporate behavior and provide arguments to predict CSR engagement in family firms. The role played by the degree of involvement of the family in the business deserves specific attention in order to discuss the socially responsible behavior of the family firm.

The degree of family involvement in ownership may indeed affect engagement in CSR and thus the relationships with firm stakeholders. Even if it has been stated that the presence of the family within the shareholders' pool increases the importance of family reputation in the community, whether the family controls a small or large fraction of the business makes a difference. When family ownership is low, the family itself is not the only actor to shape the firm strategy, and there may be different interests resulting in possible owner–owner agency problems, if the owners of the family business exploit their information and pursue their own interests to the detriment of other shareholders (Bertrand and Schoar, 2006; Morck et al., 2005; Wasserman, 2006). Non-family shareholders may, therefore, prioritize business interests over family control goals, as the group of shareholders is overall less susceptible to family relationships, and thus more likely to create robust connections with other business stakeholders (Le Breton-Miller et al., 2011). In this context, family members can make decisions that increase their personal wealth, for example requiring high dividends at the end of the year (Schulze et al., 2003a), thus reducing the possibility to invest in social issues and making family altruism overwhelm the potential benefits of reputational gains. Conversely, CSR may become a means to build and hold the relationships with firm stakeholders, so that family owners care about the business and thus avoid potential conflicts with the other shareholders prioritizing in the meantime the family business reputation.

Where family control of votes is significant, instead, the owners no longer feel any pressure to meet external stakeholders' claims (Miller, Le Breton-Miller, and Lester, 2013), and they can put in practice the strategies that better suit their own parochial interests (Morck et al., 2005). In fact, with high family ownership, family ties among firm owners have priority over ties with organizational stakeholders such as employees, customers, suppliers and competitors (Granovetter, 1985; Uzzi, 1996), since family identity, values, and goals will definitively affect business conduct, because of the strong structural ties among family members (Stryker, 1987). CSR, in this case, may lose its importance and it may thus be more likely that family firms, where substantial equity is in the hands of the family, disregard and neglect corporate social responsibility in their firm, preferring a self-interested family agenda. Overall, these arguments suggest that while reputational considerations lead family firms with a low degree of family ownership to engage in CSR, self-interest is the prioritized driver of avoiding CSR in case of high degree of family ownership, that can be summarized in the first hypothesis as follows:

Hypothesis 1

In family firms, the degree of family ownership negatively affects engagement in CSR.

Another important aspect of family involvement is intra-family ownership dispersion, i.e. the dispersion of family ownership among family members (e.g., De Massis et al., 2013). Taking into account arguments related to self-interest can help understand how family ownership dispersion may affect the social conduct of family firms. Indeed, when the shares are concentrated in the hands of a single owner or a small group of owners, there is a strong link, nurtured by family altruism, between the controlling owners' wealth and that of the family (Schulze et al., 2001), since one of their main interests is to maximize both the family's and the firm's welfare. In addition, a relevant share of family wealth is tied to the firm, so it is more likely to invest to generate further wealth (Wiklund, 2006). A family business with ownership highly concentrated among a very few number of family shareholders, in fact, has a long-term perspective because there is usually a greater propensity for the owner(s) to hand the business over to the offspring (Miller and Le Breton-Miller, 2005). Family wealth, career opportunities and corporate reputation are all linked with firm success, so that there might be a greater inclination of family firm owners to care about the long-term interests of all the stakeholders, not only family members. Moreover, it is more likely that family firms invest in building a positive moral capital, in order to prevent both the firm and the family from being acknowledged as irresponsible citizens when risks for their reputation in the community may emerge (Dyer and Whetten, 2006).

As ownership gets dispersed among siblings or cousins, new dynamics emerge and affect the CSR strategies accomplished by family firms. Indeed, new agency issues may hinder the performance of private small- and medium-sized family firms and imply changes to their conduct. Family members who have become new shareholders may claim a legitimate stake in the ownership of the firm, by inheriting it (Stark and Falk, 1998). They may consider CSR as an unnecessary and wasteful activity since it is their dividends that might be kept in the business to invest in CSR. Then, when family ownership gets further dispersed among multiple members of the extended family, these owners usually occupy different roles and thus have diverse incentives and goals (Kotlar and De Massis, 2013). Solving goals misalignment and governing the several roles of family members in the family and the business allows family firms to pursue a common purpose (De Massis, Chirico, Kotlar and Naldi, 2014a), i.e. to enhance firm's reputation by investing in social issues, thus agreeing on unique long-term gains that the business may benefit from. However, usually only a small portion of owners is likely to be directly involved in the company's operations and, on the other hand, each family member is likely to invest only a fractional part of her/his wealth in the family firm (Gersick et al., 1997). In this circumstance, the family firm must respond to the claims of both family owners involved and those not involved in the business, which is likely to be driven by different motivations (Schulze et al., 2003a). It may, therefore, be more difficult to run the business because of possible conflicts that make family issues, politics and agreements, the priority over corporate activities (Pratt and Foreman, 2000). CSR may thus be overshadowed in these cases, despite the importance attached to reputation by the family. In light of the foregoing:

Hypothesis 2

In family firms, intra-family ownership dispersion negatively affects engagement in CSR.

Finally, considering which generation controls the business can be important to predict family firms' engagement in CSR. Generation in control usually implies the increase in the number of family members taking part in the business activities, but more notably it entails the presence of emotional linkages among family members (Le Breton-Miller et al., 2011). This is especially true in first generation family firms, where family members involved in the business aim to building a sustainable business to be passed to their offspring with whom they share everyday life and experience. In this case, reputation is expected to be extremely important, since it allows the family (and the firm) to be labeled as good corporate citizen; the founder is committed to build a solid and profitable business, and thus, personally manage the relationships with the main stakeholders, especially employees, suppliers, and customers. The set of these business relationships are often based on personal bonds, and thus they constitute the social capital that becomes part of the heritage which is handed over to the second generation. Therefore, we expect a high attention paid by the founder to socially responsible practices to build a good reputation for the business and the family and to create and hold good relationships, particularly with proximate stakeholders. The second generation is usually characterized by the presence of siblings who own and manage the family firm. They are grown-up in the family business; they share the same values, principles, and norms of their fathers/mothers, and thus have even more interest in perpetuating what the founder generation started up. There is a strong feeling to carry out what they have inherited: reputation plays in this context a relevant role because second-generation is still committed to raising the image of the family business and nurture stakeholders' relationships in a more strategic way with respect to their predecessors. We expect that building and maintaining the reputation, not only in terms of organizational character but also in terms of symbolic conformity and technical efficacy, becomes a priority for second-generation family firms. Finally, family members in later generations are usually less committed, and thus business interests may displace the family's ones (Le Breton-Miller et al., 2011); moreover, they are usually less talented and entrepreneurial than the former generations (James, 2006), so that it is likely that they rely on more formal and structured ways to manage the external relationships and minimize the efforts towards social activities. In this situation firms may engage less in CSR with respect to prior generation family firms.

Hypothesis 3

In family firms, family generation in control negatively affects engagement in CSR.

To summarize, our hypothesized conceptual model is presented in Figure 16.1, which proposes the relationships between the different dimensions of family involvement in the business and engagement in CSR, as described above.

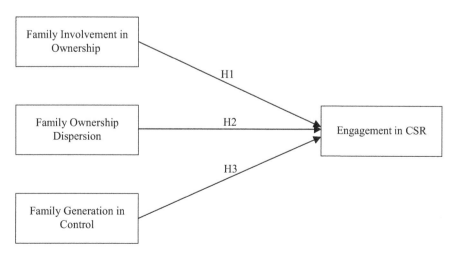

Figure 16.1   Proposed Theoretical Model

Methodology

Sample and Survey Measures

The 136 firms surveyed for this study were drawn from a list of approximately 4000 firms in the Lombardy region, in Northern Italy, selected in order to obtain a homogeneous sample, because previous studies using Italian companies found a significant effect of the geographical location on firm performance (Caselli and Di Giuli, 2010; De Massis et al., 2015). Businesses were selected for inclusion in this list if they have sales between 2 and 50 million Euros and a number of employees in the range between 10 and 250, as suggested by the thresholds set by the European commission.

The survey was conducted as a self-administered questionnaire e-mailed to the contact list. The survey instrument was designed drawing on the contributions provided in past research on family business and corporate social responsibility. It was first tested through a pilot study on a small sample, calculating the Crombach's alpha (α) to measure construct reliability, obtaining values higher than 0.7, that is considered an acceptable value. Therefore, the questions eventually selected for the survey were based on the research team's collective experience working with family businesses as well as the pretest results. Responses were representative of the target population in terms of geography, sales, and industry type, thus, observations were not weighted.

The questionnaire was organized as follows. Section 1 reported questions that sought to obtain general business and demographic information about the firm, which was then triangulated through a research of the firms in the Amadeus database. Section 2 queried respondents on the distinctive characteristics of family-owned firms, including the percentage of business ownership shared by family members, the number of family members employed full time in the business, and family generation involved in the business. Section 3 asked respondents about their reasons for joining the family-owned business, their intentions and their perceptions of trust and pride to work in the family business. Five separate items appeared in this section of the survey with Likert-type scales used to measure the importance level of each item (1 = Extremely Unimportant, 5 = Extremely Important).

Variables

The dependent variable is Engagement in CSR, which we measured by asking the CEO if the firm accomplishes any CSR initiatives according to the CSR definition reported in Italy in the Green Book, a document provided by the European Commission (2011). The following definition: "*A concept whereby companies integrate social and environmental concerns in their business operations and in their interaction with their stakeholders on a voluntary basis*" is conveyed in Italy through its translation into Italian. Each firm's respondent was asked in the survey if any social initiatives are performed so that a dummy variable was computed as a proxy of engagement in CSR within the firm. We also checked that in all the cases the respondent to the survey was involved in the top management of the firm, in order to assert that (s)he was aware of the firm's activities at any level.

The independent variables included family firm measures. Family involvement in ownership is operationalized through the measure of the total percentage of shares owned by the family, namely family ownership concentration. It is a continuous measure of family involvement and to be accountable as a family firm two thresholds have to be overcome: (i) at least one family member serves in the top management team, and (ii) at least 5 percent of the shares are owned by the family. Although different researchers adopt diverse thresholds for the latter, these two criteria are the most used to identify family firms in the field (De Massis et al., 2012). All firms that do not satisfy the ownership and control criteria above mentioned are considered as non-family firms, and are assigned value 0. We adopted dummy variables with different thresholds of family ownership concentration as alternative family firm measures to be used in robustness checks. The second measure is the number of owners belonging to the family, which is used as a proxy of the dispersion of ownership among the members of the family (Bertrand et al., 2008; De Massis et al., 2015).

We considered the number of generations as a variable that encompasses the social and human capital that have been generated and transferred through a number of generational shifts. In particular, we created three dummy variables: the first one takes value 1 when the family firm is in the first generation, controlled by the founder, and 0 otherwise; the second one takes value 1 when there is the second generation who owns the family firm, and 0 otherwise; and finally, the last one takes value 1 when the owning generation is greater or equal than 3, and 0 otherwise (Davis and Harveston, 2001).

We also included a number of control variables. We considered the numbers of years from the incorporation as a measure of the age of the firm. The natural logarithm of firm sales was used to control for firm size; we also collected information on the number of employees and the firm total assets in order to perform sensitivity analyses with alternative measures of firm size. We used the lagged variation of ROE to consider the remuneration of shareholders' equity. We introduced a dummy variable to control for industry, coding the firms in the sample according to their belonging to manufacturing and non-manufacturing industries, used to cluster data. Finally, we included the degree of agreement with family goals, future plans and corporate strategies; and the adoption of beneficial practices for employees, i.e. the possibility to work with flexible hours and the box for ideas, that is an easier and anonymous way to collect new ideas from anyone in the firm, all evaluated as categorical ordered variables measured as Likert scales ranging from 1 to 5. In this way, it was possible to consider also the impact of the social activities actually accomplished by the sampled family firms.

Data Analysis

Descriptive statistics and correlations for the variables used in this study are shown in Table 16.1. Sampled companies had average annual revenues of 15.3 million Euros and were on average 32 years old.

We regressed our data with a hierarchical logit model, controlling for possible correlation heteroskedasticity by using the Huber-White sandwich estimator clustered at industry-level. We performed Pearson goodness-of-fit test to assess whether the model is suitable, and in all the cases we rejected the null hypothesis that the model is not adequate. We also performed a number of sensitivity tests that are in-depth exposed in the Robustness checks section, to assess both robustness of theoretical premises and empirical findings.

Results

Table 16.2 presents the results of the regression analysis using Engagement in CSR as the dependent variable.

Model II significantly supports hypothesis 1, suggesting that family firms with higher family ownership are less likely to engage in CSR (β = -1.24, p < .01). As regards the effect of ownership dispersion among family members on CSR engagement, we find in Model III a significant negative effect (β = -.06, p < .01), thus supporting hypothesis 2. Finally, even

Table 16.1 Means, Standard Deviations, and Correlations

Variable	M	SD	1	2	3	4	5	6	7	8	9	10	11
1. Family Ownership (%)	0.93	0.17											
2. Intra-family Ownership Dispersion	3.32	2.11	.09										
3. First Generation (dummy)	0.26	0.44	-.07	.02									
4. Second Generation (dummy)	0.54	0.50	.14	.03	-.63**								
5. Age (log)	3.34	0.57	-.03	.20*	.08	-.09							
6. Firm Size (log)	9.03	1.10	-.01	.19*	-.04	-.02	.27**						
7. Industry (dummy)	0.71	0.45	-.06	-.01	-.04	.03	-.01	-.05					
8. Performance	-15.16	113.96	.10	.01	-.05	.13	-.07	-.00	.04				
9. Adoption of flexible hours	3.42	1.10	.01	.01	.08	-.23**	.07	.01	-.05	.07			
10. Adoption of box of ideas	3.79	1.06	-.03	-.18*	.06	-.22**	.10	.01	.04	-.01	.08		
11. Agreement with Family Goals	4.10	0.96	-.16	.11	-.02	-.05	.17*	.05	-.07	.02	.02	.02	
12. Engagement in CSR	0.63	0.48	-.10	-.05	.01	.06	.12	-.03	-.06	.09	.07	.12	.06

N = 136 observations

*p < .05; **p < .01

Table 16.2 Hierarchic Logit Regression for CSR Engagement in Family Firms

Variable	Engagement in CSR			
	I	II	III	IV
Age	0.326**	0.324**	0.348**	0.306†
	(0.0592)	(0.0523)	(0.0624)	(0.160)
Firm Size	-0.0420	-0.0463	-0.0348	-0.0802
	(0.133)	(0.145)	(0.149)	(0.173)
Performance	-0.00395*	-0.00398†	-0.00419*	-0.00492*
	(0.00180)	(0.00208)	(0.00213)	(0.00205)
Adoption of flexible hours	0.110*	0.112*	0.120*	0.251**
	(0.0381)	(0.0526)	(0.0610)	(0.0199)
Adoption of box of ideas	0.221†	0.219*	0.200†	0.341**
	(0.117)	(0.106)	(0.119)	(0.0886)
Agreement with Family Goals	0.102**	0.0672**	0.0785**	0.0964*
	(0.00140)	(0.0123)	(0.00824)	(0.0375)
Family Ownership (%)		-1.244**	-1.197**	-1.434**
		(0.0720)	(0.0916)	(0.0432)
Intra-family Ownership Dispersion			-0.0569**	-0.0358*
			(0.0143)	(0.0152)
First Generation (dummy)				0.785**
				(0.167)
Second Generation (dummy)				1.127**
				(0.0583)
Constant	-1.807	-0.451	-0.498	-2.271
	(2.066)	(2.046)	(2.144)	(2.514)
Observations	128	128	128	126
Pseudo R²	0.0234	0.0315	0.0326	0.0529

Robust standard errors in parentheses
** $p < 0.01$, * $p < 0.05$, † $p < 0.1$

the family generation involved in the business emerges as a variable with a significant effect on our analyses. The regression shows that the first generation has a positive and significant effect ($\beta = .78$, $p < .01$) on the dependent variable with respect to the later-generation variable, considered in the analysis as the base case; also the effect of the presence of second generation, with respect to the later-generation variable, on engagement in CSR, is significant and positive ($\beta = 1.13$, $p < .01$), as shown in Model IV. It is notable that the regression coefficient is higher for the second generation stage than for the founder generation stage; we, therefore, performed also the regression using the first-generation dummy variable as the base case, but the regression result is not significant ($\beta = 0.34$, $.10 < p < .15$), thus suggesting that there are no significant differences between first- and second-generation family firms on engagement in CSR. Hypothesis 3 is thus partially supported, since both first-generation and second-generation family firms are more engaged in CSR than later-generation family businesses while it is not possible to infer on the difference between first- and second-generation family firms. Finally, it is worth noting that firms that internally install socially responsible initiatives, such as flexible hours or the box of ideas, consistently declare that they engage in CSR (significant positive results in all models).

Robustness Checks

Overall, our analyses supported all the three hypotheses. Nevertheless, to ensure the robustness of the findings, we conducted additional analyses.

We reran the models to check for the sensitivity of the results to the use of alternative measures for the independent variables. Specifically, family involvement in ownership is alternatively measured by considering dummy variables identified at different thresholds of family ownership concentration. We replicated the analyses by substituting the continuous measure of family involvement in ownership with the dummy variables obtained, respectively, at 30 percent, 50 percent, 70 percent and 90 percent of family ownership concentration. The results confirmed the findings of the main analysis with a negative and significant effect on the dependent variable, with the exception of the case where the threshold is set at 90 percent, which provided no significant effect[1].

In order to check for possible differences between younger and older firms we separated the sample firms in two subsamples based on the median value of age and we replicated the analyses. The signs and significance of the coefficients of all variables relevant to our hypotheses were consistent with the main analysis, providing further support to the hypothesized relationships.

Finally, we checked for the sensitivity of the findings to the use of alternative measures for firm size. We adopt both the logarithmic transformation of firm assets and the number of employees, and our conclusions regarding the hypotheses do not change, since in both the cases the effect of size on the dependent variable is not significant.

Discussion

The analysis presented herein supports the existence of a significant direct relationship between family involvement and engagement in CSR. The findings indicate that the relationship between different dimensions of family involvement in the firm and engagement in corporate social responsibility is not trivial, and family firms differ from their nonfamily counterparts in CSR engagement. Accordingly, the findings of this study contribute to add new insights to previous findings, in the attempt to answer the rising calls for further and detailed research on social issues of family firms (Deniz and Suarez, 2005; Van Gils et al., 2014; Wiklund, 2006), thus contributing to further understanding the social behavior of family firms, as well as shedding new lights on the ongoing debate on the heterogeneity of family firms (Chua et al., 2012; De Massis et al., 2014b). Our findings suggest that the presence of the family in the ownership structure of the firm has an impact on CSR engagement and such impact is multidimensional in scope, as both degree of family ownership and intra-family ownership dispersion, as well as the family generation in control, significantly affect the engagement of the firm in corporate social responsibility. The non-invariant results of this research suggest that it is not possible to just compare family and non-family businesses, entailing the former as a homogeneous sample of firms, which are expected to behave always in the same way. Family business research can benefit from studies in the field of CSR to in-depth analyze the drivers of family firms' behavior, relying also on more specific concepts and theoretical views, like those looking at socioemotional wealth preservation (Chua, Chrisman, and De Massis, 2015; Gómez-Mejía et al., 2007).

Indeed, the findings of this study suggest that a higher degree of family ownership leads to higher importance attached to family issues over business interests, and thus, lower concerns and efforts to build formal relationships with the firm stakeholders, especially those who are distant from the daily activities of the family firm. Our findings thus suggest that self-interest arguments prevail over reputational ones when the degree of family ownership increases, offering new insights to the ongoing debate on the role of reputation as a driver of family firms' behavior (e.g., Deephouse and Jaskiewicz, 2013). Moreover, this finding provides new hints to further discuss previous results showing that family firms invest in socially responsible initiatives in order to protect their socioemotional endowments by enhancing their image and reputation in the community (Berrone et al., 2010); this study shows that reputation is not the only driver to understand family businesses' social investments, but also self-interest can contrast and affect predictions on their behavior, thus contributing to understanding heterogeneity among family firms, who may differently protect their socioemotional wealth.

Moreover, the fact that firms with highly dispersed ownership appear to be less concerned about CSR issues further supports our contention that self-interest and agency issues play a crucial role in explaining the behavior of family firms and their attitude towards CSR. The findings showing a negative relationship between the number of owners of the family business and engagement in CSR imply that, when ownership is concentrated in the hands of few family members, the owners of the family firm invest more on building and maintaining firm reputation through CSR engagement aimed at satisfying long-term interests of all the stakeholders, and not only those of the family, as family wealth, career opportunities, and corporate reputation are all linked to firm success. This is consistent with the idea that family firms are very proactive in the surrounding community with family owners tending to support and subsidize the institutions in the area and committed to the common good (Bird and Wennberg, 2014). Therefore, as few family members are expected to make decisions on how to invest in social initiatives, these efforts may be mainly philanthropic in nature, through donations of money, goods, or services to support a socially beneficial or humanitarian cause (Windsor, 2006). Many family firms, for example, create associations or foundations that are intended for these philanthropic purposes (Gallo, 2004).

Finally, the effect of generational shifts during the family business life cycle is clear-cut and shows that the incoming of a new family generation in control of the business can change engagement in CSR. Indeed, commitment to social issues associated with firm activities decreases across generations, suggesting that later-generation family firms are more concerned about transferring the business to the following generation and less concerned about family reputation. Accordingly, CSR loses its relevance as a strategy to engage in.

Conclusions

This study has shown that family involvement in the business has a direct effect on firm engagement in corporate social responsibility. In particular, our empirical evidence has shown that two different dimensions of family involvement in ownership, namely degree of family ownership and intra-family ownership dispersion, negatively affect CSR engagement. What is more, the generation at the helm of the family business is also important, since later generations engage less in corporate social responsibility. Theoretical arguments related to reputation and self-interest have been used to explain the behavior predicted by the models that we tested through regression analyses.

Academics, practitioners and policy makers may benefit from the results of our study. First, it contributes to the family business literature, since scholars in the field have started only very recently to address the topic of CSR (Van Gils et al., 2014). The results of this study enable us to identify how different dimensions of family involvement affect the social behavior of family firms. The involvement of the family in the organization is a unique trait of family firms (De Massis et al., 2014b), and our study shows that each dimension of family involvement plays a crucial role in explaining engagement in CSR. More specifically, the importance of reputation among their stakeholders and the self-interest that characterizes family firms are two important drivers of CSR engagement. The study findings contribute to the ongoing debate on the heterogeneity of family firms (Chua et al., 2012). Moreover, we also contribute to the emerging stream of research on social issues in small- and medium-sized family firms (e.g., Fitzgerald et al., 2010; Niehm et al., 2008).

Second, this study has implications for managers working in family firms, who are encouraged not to take for granted what corporate social responsibility handbooks propose as universally applicable good practices. They should carefully consider instead how different dimensions of family involvement in their business organization could affect the extent to which they engage in CSR and the effectiveness of these social practices, and how the related activities and norms should be revised to best suit the distinctive characteristics if the family firm.

Finally, this research is expected to suit as a background policy document for policy makers. Corporate social responsibility initiatives are being paid increasing attention to the design of public policies, and particularly family firms, due to their ubiquity (Astrachan and Shanker, 2003; Anderson and Reeb, 2003), are considered critical for the growth of economies around the world (Villalonga and Amit, 2009; La Porta et al., 1999). In this respect, our study's findings are useful since they suggest how to build a system of supporting initiatives for CSR that fits with the idiosyncratic characteristics of family firms. For example, the findings of our study may support policy makers in decisions regarding how to make family firms favor a socially responsible behavior. Nevertheless, we suggest being cautious and considering that these results are valid in a specific regional context, and their generalization cannot be taken for granted.

Our findings are original with regard to previous studies in that they untangle the direct effects of family involvement and also show that family involvement in ownership, intra-family ownership dispersion and family generation in control hinder CSR engagement of small private family firms. Yet, as with all research, our results should be interpreted by acknowledging our study's limitations.

First, the sample used to perform the empirical analyses is modest in size, so it is not straightforward to generalize the findings to all private small- and medium-sized family firms, and there is, therefore, room for additional studies to support our contention. Second, our analysis is cross-sectional, thus, causal relationships can be questionable; therefore, it would be interesting to analyze the relationships under investigation over time in a longitudinal study in order to provide additional insights into the ways in which the evolution in the dimension of family involvement affects private small- and medium-sized family firms' engagement in CSR. Moreover, the dependent variable of our study – namely engagement in CSR – can be measured in a different way, for example adopting a Likert scale to have more nuanced information on family firms' engagement.

In light of the results of our study and the above mentioned limits that are still to be addressed, further investigation of the ways in which family involvement affects private small- and medium-sized family firms' engagement in CSR deserves further attention. First, replicating this study on a sample of both family and non-family firms may enable scholars as well as owners of family firms to gain further insights on the relationship between family involvement and engagement in CSR. Second, what is CSR and how firms behave in a socially responsible manner is strongly dependent on cultural aspects, like values and traditions that differentiate countries (Scholtens and Dam, 2007), religion (Brammer, Williams, and Zinkin, 2007), tradition and legacy in the families (Marques, Presas, and Simon, 2014). Although there are some articles analyzing CSR in studies comparing different contexts, such as the Chinese context as compared to the Western one (Xu and Yang, 2010), studying family business CSR in different cultural contexts, in order to identify whether and to what extent different levels of involvement and diverse conceptions of family are relevant to explain corporate social behaviors, is an area ripe for future research.

In addition, beyond the knowledge and diffusion of CSR within family firms, a related and interesting topic for future investigation relates to social performances. Specifically, it would be interesting to find whether the accomplishment of socially responsible initiatives affects social and economic performances of family firms. We hope that this study will encourage future work contributing to this field at the intersection of CSR and family business.

Note

1 The results of the robustness checks are available upon request from the first author.

References

Adams, J.S., Taschian, A., and Shore, T.H. (1996). Ethics in family and non-family owned firms: An exploratory study. *Family Business Review*, 9(2), 157–170.

Anderson, R.C., and Reeb, D.M. (2003). Founding family ownership and firm performance: Evidence from the S&P 500. *Journal of Finance*, 58(3), 1301–1328.

Astrachan, J.H., and Shanker, M.C. (2003). Family businesses' contribution to the US economy: A closer look. *Family Business Review*, 16(3), 211–219.

Atkinson, L., and Galaskiewicz, J. (1988). Stock ownership and company contributions to charity. *Administrative Science Quarterly*, 33(1), 82–100.

Austin, J., Stevenson, H., and Wei-Skillern, J. (2006). Social and commercial entrepreneurship: same, different, or both?. *Entrepreneurship Theory and Practice*, 30(1), 1–22.

Barney, J. (1991). Firm resources and sustained competitive advantage. *Journal of Management*, 17(1), 99–120.

Beatty, R. P., and Zajac, E. J. (1994). Managerial incentives, monitoring and risk bearing: A study of executive compensation, ownership, and board structure in initial public offerings. *Administrative Science Quarterly*, 39(2), 313–335.

Berrone, P., Cruz, C., Gómez-Mejía, L. R., and Larraza-Kintana, M. (2010). Socioemotional wealth and corporate responses to institutional pressures: Do family-controlled firms pollute less? *Administrative Science Quarterly*, 55(1), 82–113.

Bertrand, M., Johnson, S., Samphantharak, K., and Schoar, A. (2008). Mixing family with business: A study of Thai business groups and the families behind them. *Journal of Financial Economics*, 88(3), 466–498.

Bertrand, M., and Schoar, A. (2006). The role of family in family firms. *Journal of Economic Perspective*, 20(2), 73–96.

Bird, M., and Wennberg, K. (2014). Regional influences on the prevalence of family versus non-family start-ups. *Journal of Business Venturing*, 29(3), 421–436.

Blombäck, A., and Wigren, C. (2009). Challenging the importance of size as determinant for CSR activities. *Management of Environmental Quality: An International Journal*, 20(3), 255–270.

Bloom, N., and Van Reenen, J. (2007). Measuring and explaining management practices across firms and countries. *Quarterly Journal of Economics*, 122(4), 1351–1408.

Brammer, S., Williams, G., and Zinkin, J. (2007). Religion and attitudes to corporate social responsibility in a large cross-country sample. *Journal of Business Ethics*, 71(3), 229–243.

Campopiano, G., and De Massis, A. (2015). Corporate social responsibility reporting: a content analysis in family and non-family firms. *Journal of Business Ethics*, 129(3), 511–534.

Campopiano, G., De Massis, A., and Cassia, L. (2012). The relationship between motivations and actions in corporate social responsibility: An exploratory study. *International Journal of Business and Society*, 13(3), 391–425.

Campopiano, G., De Massis, A., and Chirico, F. (2014). Firm philanthropy in small- and medium-sized family firms: The effects of family involvement in ownership and management. *Family Business Review*, 27(3), 244–258.

Carroll, A. B., and Shabana, K. M. (2010). The business case for corporate social responsibility: A review of concepts, research and practice. *International Journal of Management Reviews*, 12(1), 85–105.

Carter, S. M., and Dukerich, J. M. (1998). Corporate responses to changes in reputation. *Corporate Reputation Review*, 1(3), 250–270.

Caselli, S., and Di Giuli, A. (2010). Does the CFO matter in family firms? Evidence from Italy. *European Journal of Finance*, 16(5), 381–411.

Chen, S., Chen, X., and Cheng, Q. (2008). Do family firms provide more or less voluntary disclosure? *Journal of Accounting Research*, 46(3), 499–536.

Chua, J. H., Chrisman, J. J., De Massis, A. (2015). A closer look at socioemotional wealth: Its flows, stocks, and prospects for moving forward. *Entrepreneurship Theory and Practice*, 39(2), 173–182.

Chua, J. H., Chrisman, J. J., and Sharma, P. (1999). Defining the family business by behavior. *Entrepreneurship Theory and Practice*, 23, 19–40.

Chua, J. H., Chrisman, J. J., Steier, L. P., and Rau, S. B. (2012). Sources of heterogeneity in family firms: An introduction. *Entrepreneurship Theory and Practice*, 36(6), 1103–1113.

Claessens, S., Djankov, S., Fan, J. P. H., and Lang, L. H. P. (2002). Disentangling the incentive and entrenchment effects of large shareholdings. *Journal of Finance*, 57(6), 2741–2771.

Crane, A., and Matten, D. (2007). *Business Ethics: Managing Corporate Citizenship and Sustainability in the Age of Globalization*. New York: Oxford University Press.

Danes, S. M., Loy, T. C. K., and Stafford, K. (2008). Business planning practices of family-owned firms within a quality framework. *Journal of Small Business Management*, 46(3), 395–421.

Davies, G., Chun, R., Da Silva, R. and Roper, S. (2003). *Corporate Reputation and Competitiveness*. London: Routledge.

Davis, P. S., and Harveston, P. D. (2001). The phenomenon of substantive conflict in the family firm: a cross-generational study. *Journal of Small Business Management*, 39(1), 14–30.

De Massis, A., Chirico, F., Kotlar, J., and Naldi, L. (2014a). The temporal evolution of proactiveness in family firms: The horizontal S-curve hypothesis. *Family Business Review*, 27(1), 35–50.

De Massis, A., Kotlar, J., Campopiano, G., and Cassia, L. (2013). Dispersion of family ownership and the performance of small-to-medium size private family firms. *Journal of Family Business Strategy*, 4(3), 166–175.

De Massis, A., Kotlar, J., Campopiano, G., and Cassia, L. (2015). The impact of family involvement on SMEs' performance: Theory and evidence. *Journal of Small Business Management*, 53(4), 924–948.

De Massis, A., Kotlar, J., Chua, J. H., and Chrisman, J. J. (2014b). Ability and willingness as sufficiency conditions for family-oriented particularistic behavior: Implications for theory and empirical studies. *Journal of Small Business Management*, 52(2), 344–364.

De Massis, A., Sharma, P., Chua, J. H., and Chrisman, J. J. (2012). *Family Business Studies: An Annotated Bibliography*. Edward Elgar Publishing.

Deephouse, D. L., and Jaskiewicz, P. (2013). Do family firms have better reputations than non-family firms? An integration of socioemotional wealth and social identity theories. *Journal of Management Studies*, 50(3), 337–360.

Deniz Deniz, M. C., and Suarez, M. K. (2005). Corporate social responsibility and family business in Spain. *Journal of Business Ethics*, 56(1), 27–41.

Dowling, G. R. (1986). Managing your corporate image. *Industrial Marketing Management*, 15(2), 109–115.

Dunn, B. (1996). Family enterprises in the UK: A special sector? *Family Business Review*, 9(2), 139–155.

Dyer, W. G., and Whetten, D. (2006). Family firms and social responsibility: Preliminary evidence from the S&P 500. *Entrepreneurship Theory and Practice*, 30(6), 785–802.

Eddleston, K. A., Kellermanns, F. W., and Sarathy, R. (2008). Resource configuration in family firms: Linking resources, strategic planning and technological opportunities to performance. *Journal of Management Studies*, 45(1), 26–50.

European Commission. (2011). *A Renewed EU Strategy 2011–14 for Corporate Social Responsibility*. Available at http://europa.eu/rapid/press-release_MEMO-11-730_en.htm.

Fitzgerald, M. A., Haynes, G. W., Schrank, H. L., and Danes, S. M. (2010). Socially responsible processes of small family business owners: Exploratory evidence from the national family business survey. *Journal of Small Business Management*, 48(4), 524–551.

Fombrun, C. J. (1996). *Reputation: Realizing Value From the Corporate Image*. Boston: Harvard Business School Press.

Fombrun, C. J., and Van Riel, C. B. M. (2004). *Fame and Fortune: How Successful Companies Build Winning Reputations*. Upper Saddle River, NJ: Pearson Education.

Friedman, M. (1970). The social responsibility of business is to increase its profits. *New York Times Magazine* (13 September), 32–39.

Gallo, M. Á. (2004). The family business and its social responsibilities. *Family Business Review*, 17(2), 135–149.

Gersick, K. E., Davis, J. A., Hampton, M. M., and Lansberg, I. (1997). *Generation to Generation: Life Cycles of the Family Business*. Boston: Harvard Business School Press.

Godfrey, J., Mather, P. R., and Ramsay, A. (2003). Earnings and impression management in financial reports: the case of CEO changes. *Abacus*, 39(1), 95–123.

Godfrey, P. C. (2005). The relationship between corporate philanthropy and shareholder wealth: A risk management perspective. *Academy of Management Review*, 30(4), 777–798.

Granovetter, M. S. (1985). Economic action and social structure: The problem of embeddedness. *American Journal of Sociology*, 91(3), 481–510.

James, H. S. (2006). *Family Capitalism: Wendels, Haniels, Falcks, and the Continental European Model*. Cambridge, MA: Belknap Press of Harvard University Press.

Karra, N., Tracey, P., and Phillips, N. (2006). Altruism and agency in the family firm: Exploring the role of family, kinship, and ethnicity. *Entrepreneurship Theory and Practice*, 30(6), 861–877.

Kotlar, J., and De Massis, A. (2013). Goal setting in family firms: Goal diversity, social interactions, and collective commitment to family-centered goals. *Entrepreneurship Theory and Practice*, 37(6), 1263–1288.

La Porta, R., Lopez-de-Silanes, F., Shleifer, A., and Vishny, R. (1999). Corporate ownership around the world. *Journal of Finance*, 54(2), 471–517.

Le Breton-Miller, I., Miller, D., and Lester, R. H. (2011). Stewardship or agency: A social embeddedness reconciliation of conduct and performance in public family businesses. *Organization Science*, 22(3), 704–721.

Litz, R. A., and Stewart, A.C. (2000). Charity begins at home: Family firms and patterns of community involvement. *Nonprofit and Voluntary Sector Quarterly*, 29(1), 131–148.

Love, E. G., and Kraatz, M. (2009). Character, conformity, or the bottom line? How and why downsizing affected corporate reputation. *Academy of Management Journal*, 52(2), 314–335.

Lundström, A., and Zhou, C. (2014). Rethinking social entrepreneurship and social enterprises: A three-dimensional perspective. In Lundström, A., Zhou, C., von Friedrichs, Y., and Sunin, E. (eds.), *Social Entrepreneurship*. Springer International Publishing, pp. 71–89.

Mair, J., and Marti, I. (2006). Social entrepreneurship research: A source of explanation, prediction, and delight. *Journal of World Business*, 41(1), 36–44.

Marques, P., Presas, P., and Simon, A. (2014). The heterogeneity of family firms in CSR engagement the role of values. *Family Business Review*, 27(3), 206–227.

Matten, D., and Crane, A. (2005). Corporate citizenship: Toward an extended theoretical conceptualization. *Academy of Management Review*, 30(1), 166–179.

McWilliams, A., and Siegel, D. (2001). Corporate social responsibility: A theory of the firm perspective. *Academy of Management Review*, 26(1), 117–127.

Miller, D., and Le Breton-Miller, I. (2005). *Managing for the Long Run: Lessons in Competitive Advantage from Great Family Businesses*. Boston: Harvard Business School Press.

Miller, D., Le Breton-Miller, I., and Lester, R. H. (2013). Family firm governance, strategic conformity, and performance: Institutional vs. strategic perspectives. *Organization Science*, 24(1), 189–209.

Miller, D., Le Breton-Miller, I., and Scholnick, B. (2008). Stewardship vs. stagnation: An empirical comparison of small family and non-family businesses. *Journal of Management Studies*, 45(1), 51–78.

Morck, R., and Yeung, B. (2004). Family control and the rent-seeking society. *Entrepreneurship Theory and Practice*, 28(4), 391–409.

Morck, R. K., Wolfenzon, D., and Yeung, B. (2005). Corporate Governance, Economic Entrenchment, and Growth. *Journal of Economic Literature*, 43(3), 655–720.

Morris, N., Williams, R., Allen, J., and Avilla, R. (1997). Correlates of success in family business. *Journal of Business Venturing*, 12(5), 385–401.

Murillo, D., and Lozano, J. M. (2006). SMEs and CSR: An approach to CSR in their own words. *Journal of Business Ethics*, 67(3), 227–240.

Niehm, L. S., Swinney, J., and Miller, N. J. (2008). Community social responsibility and its consequences for family business performance. *Journal of Small Business Management*, 46(3), 331–350.

Peredo, A. M., and McLean, M. (2006). Social entrepreneurship: A critical review of the concept. *Journal of World Business*, 41(1), 56–65.

Pierre, A., von Friedrichs, Y., and Wincent, J. (2014). A review of social entrepreneurship research. In Lundström, A., Zhou, C., von Friedrichs, Y., and Sunin, E. (eds.), *Social Entrepreneurship*. Springer International Publishing, pp. 43–69.

Pratt, M. G., and Foreman, P. O. (2000). Classifying managerial responses to multiple organizational identities. *Academy of Management Review*, 25(1), 18–42.

Russo, A., and Perrini, F. (2010). Investigating stakeholder theory and social capital: CSR in large firms and SMEs. *Journal of Business Ethics*, 91(2), 207–221.

Scholtens, B., and Dam, L. (2007). Cultural values and international differences in business ethics. *Journal of Business Ethics*, 75(3), 273–284.

Schulze, W. S., Lubatkin, M. H., and Dino, R. N. (2003a). Exploring the agency consequences of ownership dispersion among the directors of private family firms. *Academy of Management Journal*, 46(2), 179–194.

Schulze, W. S., Lubatkin, M. H., and Dino, R. N. (2003b). Toward a theory of agency and altruism in family firms. *Journal of Business Venturing*, 18(4), 473–490.

Schulze, W. S., Lubatkin, M. H., Dino, R. N., and Buchholtz, A. (2001). Agency relationships in family firms: Theory and evidence. *Organization Science*, 12(2), 99–116.

Sciascia, S., and Mazzola, P. (2008). Family involvement in ownership and management: Exploring nonlinear effects on performance. *Family Business Review*, 21(4), 331–345.

Shapiro, C. (1983). Premiums for high quality products as returns to reputations. *Quarterly Journal of Economics*, 98(4), 659–679.

Shleifer, A., and Vishny, R. W. (1986). Large shareholders and corporate control. *Journal of Political Economy*, 94(3), 461–488.

Stark, O., and Falk, I. (1998). Transfers, empathy formation, and reverse transfers. *American Economic Review*, 88(2), 271–276.

Stryker, S. (1987). Identity theory: Developments and extensions. In Yardley, K. and Honess, T. (eds). *Self and Identity: Psychosocial Perspectives*. New York: John Wiley & Sons, pp. 89–103.

Tagiuri, R., and Davis, J. (1996). Bivalent attributes of the family firm. *Family Business Review*, 9(2), 199–208.

Uhlaner, L. M., van Goor-Balk, A., and Masurel, E. (2004). Family business and corporate social responsibility in a sample of Dutch firms. *Journal of Small Business and Enterprise Development*, 11(2), 186–194.

Uzzi, B. (1996). The sources and consequences of embeddedness for the economic performance of organizations: The network effect. *American Sociological Review*, 61(4), 674–698.

Van Gils, A., Dibrell, C., Neubam, D. O., and Craig, J. B. (2014). Social issues in the family enterprise. *Family Business Review*, 27(3), 193–205.

Villalonga, B., and Amit, R. (2006). How do family ownership, control and management affect firm value? *Journal of Financial Economics*, 80(2), 385–417.

Volpin, P. F. (2002). Governance with poor investor protection: Evidence from top executive turnover in Italy. *Journal of Financial Economics*, 64(1), 61–90.

Wasserman, N. (2006). Stewards, agents, and the founder discount. *Academy of Management Journal*, 49(5), 960–976.

Whetten, D. A., and Mackey, A. (2005). *An Identity-congruence Explanation of Why Firms Would Consistently Engage in Corporate Social Performance*. Working Paper, Provo, UT: Brigham Young University.

Wiklund, J. (2006). Commentary: Family firms and social responsibility. Preliminary evidence from the S&P 500. *Entrepreneurship Theory and Practice*, 30(6), 803–808.

Windsor, D. (2006). Corporate social responsibility: Three key approaches. *Journal of Management Studies*, 43(1), 93–114.

Xu, S., and Yang, R. (2010). Indigenous characteristics of Chinese corporate social responsibility conceptual paradigm. *Journal of Business Ethics*, 93(2), 321–333.

17

BAD BLOOD IN THE BOARDROOM

Antecedents and Outcomes of Conflict in Family Firms

Andrew C. Loignon, Franz W. Kellermanns,
Kimberly A. Eddleston, and Roland E. Kidwell

Introduction

Despite the potential benefits afforded to family firms based on close family relationships (Habbershon & Williams, 1999), strife within the dominant coalition of family members can limit the effectiveness of these organizations (Lansberg, 1983). An example of the deleterious effects of conflict within family firms recently unfolded at Market Basket, a chain of U.S.-based grocery stores. A long-simmering power struggle between two family factions erupted when the company's CEO, Arthur T. Demoulas, was forced out by his cousin over making questionable investments and reducing dividends to shareholders (British Broadcasting Corporation, 2014). The conflict eventually spilled out of the boardroom and into the workforce when employees went on strike in support of their ousted boss (Pathe, 2014). Although a settlement was eventually reached (British Broadcasting Corporation, 2014), the strike cost the company more than $10 million each day and jeopardized its standing with its loyal customer base (Pathe, 2014).

Although Market Basket is an extreme example, it highlights how conflict among family members in family firms should not be taken lightly. To address this important topic, this chapter reviews the extant research on conflict in family firms and offers directions for future research on conflict in family businesses. First, we begin by describing how the manifestation of conflict is unique in family firms and presents challenges to these organizations. Next, we discuss the three dominant forms of conflict that have been examined within the family firm literature. Then, we review the main findings from the literature as they pertain to the antecedents, consequences, and moderators of conflict within family firms. We also discuss a type of conflict that is only found in family firms (i.e., the Fredo Effect). Finally, we conclude by providing practical recommendations for addressing conflict within family firms and highlighting some potential avenues for future research.

Conflict in Family Firms

Although conflict is observed across every level of an organization, from entry-level employees to top managers (Amason, 1996; Jehn, 1995), this interpersonal process often unfolds differently in family firms than in other business settings. Most notably, because family members occupy overlapping roles within business and family systems, family members may be more likely to experience conflict (Kellermanns & Eddleston, 2004). That is, in family firms, kinship and business are so entwined that the potential for discord may be greater than in nonfamily firms (Kellermanns & Eddleston, 2004). For example, sibling rivalry, marital strife, identity conflict, and issues of ownership among family members all reflect family-related issues that can contribute to conflict in the family business (Eddleston & Kellermanns, 2007).

In addition to these overlapping systems, the temporal dynamics of family relationships also contribute to unique manifestations of conflict within family firms (Kellermanns & Eddleston, 2004). As each new generation of family members enters the business, existing dynamics in the dominant coalition will likely change. Thus, established relationships, whether pleasant or fraught with conflict, may shift and become even more complex as new generations of family members begin to work in the family firm.

Finally, how members of family firms respond to ongoing conflict may be different than in traditional business settings. Family members are often deeply committed to their family's firm, which increases exit costs (Kellermanns & Eddleston, 2004). Additionally, family members may remain in the family firm despite deep conflicts because they fear that leaving the firm will jeopardize their inheritance or their children's opportunities in the family firm. Equity in the family firm can also induce family members to stay with their family firm despite conflicts. Thus, it may be necessary for family members to reconcile their differences since avoiding or leaving the conflict behind is unlikely.

Forms of Conflict: A Family Firm Application

Although conflict typically holds a negative connotation, researchers have highlighted how this process can yield both positive and negative effects within family firms (Kellermanns & Eddleston, 2004). Thus, even though conflict has the potential to create strife within the dominant coalition, limit cohesion in the family, and therefore reduce the firm's overall effectiveness, there are instances in which disagreements among family members can be beneficial (Kellermanns & Eddleston, 2007). For example, conflict can limit the likelihood that the family firm's dominant coalition reaches consensus prematurely (i.e., groupthink). That is, rather than settling on an initial solution to the challenges facing the organization, conflict may encourage family members to elaborate on their opinions and increase their involvement in organizational decision-making and planning. Likewise, such disagreements and discussions may engender an increased awareness about external information and environmental changes that are confronting the family firm (Kellermanns & Eddleston, 2007). Lastly, conflict can limit the extent to which family firms rely on a single generation to lead the organization (Kellermanns & Eddleston, 2007). Disagreements among family members may provide an opportunity for younger generations to express their opinions and become more involved within the family firm.

One of the primary considerations in determining whether conflict will be beneficial for a family firm is determining the type of conflict being experienced. Researchers have identified three primary forms of conflict: relationship conflict, task conflict and process conflict (de Wit, Greer, & Jehn, 2012; Loughry & Amason, 2014). Relationship conflict refers to perceptions of personal animosities or incompatibilities and includes an emotionally-laden or affective component (e.g., frustration, annoyance, irritation) (Eddleston & Kellermanns, 2007; Jehn & Mannix, 2001). Most research has focused on this form of conflict, which often contributes to negative outcomes within family firms because it redirects family members' attention and efforts away from productive functions and responsibilities (Kellermanns & Eddleston, 2004).

Along with relationship conflict, family members may also experience task conflict, which pertains to disagreements about the tasks or activities that should be completed (Jehn & Mannix, 2001). This form of conflict often revolves around differences of opinion about the appropriate goals or strategies for the family firm (Kellermanns & Eddleston, 2007). Task conflict may benefit family firms by improving the quality of the decision-making process and enhancing the likelihood that the ultimate decision is accepted because family members had the opportunity to express their views (Kellermanns & Eddleston, 2004). Furthermore, task conflict has the potential to help family members develop long-term goals, continuously critique their strategies, better understand the challenges facing the firm, develop new ideas and innovative approaches, enhance creativity, and diminish opportunistic behavior (Kellermanns & Eddleston, 2007). Within a family firm, such benefits may be especially relevant because without effective conflict, family firms can become reliant on subpar traditional strategies and beholden to the outmoded opinions and ideas of the family firm's founders (Eddleston, Kellermanns, Floyd, Crittenden, & Crittenden, 2013).

Finally, family members may also experience process conflict, or disagreements about how work should be accomplished and how family members' skills should be used (Behfar, Mannix, Peterson, & Trochim, 2011; Kellermanns & Eddleston, 2004). For example, family members may disagree about how much responsibility a given person receives within the firm. This form of conflict may be beneficial for family firms because it helps ensure that family members' expertise is being applied appropriately. Rather than hiring or assigning individuals to positions based on seniority or family status, process conflict helps ensure that the most able person is assigned appropriate tasks (Kellermanns & Eddleston, 2004, 2007). Given that family members can feel entitled to specific jobs or occupy high-level positions that exceed their formal credentials, frank and honest discussions about family members' skills and abilities are especially beneficial (Kellermanns & Eddleston, 2004, 2007).

Research Results about Conflict in Family Firms

With task, process and relationship conflict in mind, a body of research examining the antecedents, effects, and moderators of conflict within family firms has begun to emerge. To organize this literature, we have developed a path model that summarizes these relationships (see Figure 17.1). The solid lines in this figure correspond with effects that have been empirically examined while the dashed lines reflect relationships that have been proposed but remain untested. We have also included subscripts that correspond to the specific study that examined a particular effect. In the following paragraphs, we first review antecedents that may limit or exacerbate the level of conflict within family firms. Then, we discuss potential effects of conflict on family firm outcomes (i.e., performance). Finally, we conclude this section by discussing factors that may moderate the effects of conflict within family firms.

Antecedents of Conflict in Family Firms

An initial question when examining conflict within family firms is "What factors contribute to or reduce conflict among family members?." As depicted in Figure 17.1, researchers have examined or proposed three antecedents. First, the degree to which control of the family firm, or power, is concentrated within a single family member may influence how family members experience conflict (Kellermanns & Eddleston, 2004). In family firms in which control is highly concentrated (i.e., sole owners), there is less participative decision making and distinct power differences among family members. Such centralized decision-making diminishes the likelihood that diverse

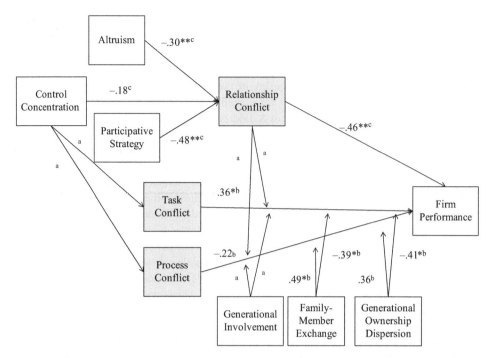

Figure 17.1 Path Model Summarizing Relationships

Note. Solid lines = empirical effects; dashed lines = proposed, but untested effects. Superscripts denote the corresponding study for a particular effect. a Kellermanns & Eddleston (2004); b Kellermanns & Eddleston (2007); c Eddleston & Kellermanns (2007).

perspectives concerning the appropriate tasks and assignments are discussed. Family members may also be less likely to seek the opinions and advice of other members if decision-making is concentrated among a single or handful of individuals. Thus, Kellermanns and Eddleston (2004) proposed that higher levels of control concentration should reduce task and process conflict among family members because there are limited opportunities for such processes to unfold.

Although high levels of control concentration are thought to stifle task and relationship conflict, such an environment may exacerbate the level of relationship conflict within a family firm. That is, this dynamic will likely increase tension and antagonistic behaviors between those who occupy positions of power and those who do not (Kellermanns & Eddleston, 2007). High levels of control concentration, which are emblematic of authoritarian leaders, reflect an environment characterized by minimal trust, which could further increase the likelihood that family members experience relationship conflict (Kellermanns & Eddleston, 2004). Despite the potential for control concentration to increase relationship conflict, Kellermanns and Eddleston (2007) found a non-significant relationship between these two constructs in a sample of 51 family firms. Thus, it remains unclear the extent to which control concentration in family firms influences the level of relationship conflict among family members.

Although high levels of control concentration were found to be unrelated to relationship conflict, an alternative style of decision-making (i.e., participative strategy) was negatively related to this form of conflict among family members. Drawing on stewardship theory, Eddleston and Kellermanns (2007) argued that if more family members are involved in the decision-making process, they are more likely to perceive greater benefits from the business. Furthermore, if family members communicate more in face-to-face settings during strategy processes, there will be less conflict and tension in the dominant coalition because family members have an opportunity to voice their opinions and ideas. Indeed, initial evidence has demonstrated a negative relationship between participative strategy processes and relationship conflict (Eddleston & Kellermanns, 2007).

In addition to control concentration and participative strategy processes, researchers have also proposed that altruism can influence the amount of conflict among family members. More specifically, Kellermanns and Eddleston (2004) proposed that altruism can reduce relationship conflict among family members. Altruism is an individual-level trait that positively links the welfare of an individual to the welfare of others. Thus, the more altruistic family members are, the more likely their primary social functions will be intended to nurture and care for one another and focus on the long-term needs and well-being of other family members (Kellermanns & Eddleston, 2004). Furthermore, higher levels of altruism are associated with a shared or common responsibility to see the firm prosper (Eddleston & Kellermanns, 2007). This collectivist orientation encourages family members to exercise self-restraint and consider the actions of others. Such restraint and empathy should help family members overcome differences and cooperate, which ultimately reduces relationship conflict. Eddleston and Kellermanns (2007) found support for such arguments based on a negative relationship between self-reported levels of altruism and relationship conflict among family members within family firms.

Effects of Conflict within Family Firms

Along with examining the antecedents of conflict among family members, researchers have also explored the extent to which different forms of conflict influence family firm performance (see Figure 17.1). In accordance with earlier propositions, Eddleston and Kellermanns (2007) found a direct, negative effect on relationship conflict and family firm performance. Thus, there is initial evidence suggesting that this particular form of conflict may detract from ongoing business activities by encouraging family members to focus more on reducing threats, attending to internal politics, and building coalitions. Thus, family firms that devote too much attention to addressing relationship conflict may overlook business needs and eventually see their performance suffer (Eddleston & Kellermanns, 2007).

In addition to the deleterious effects of relationship conflict, prior studies have examined the extent to which task and process conflict among family members influence family firm performance. Surprisingly, Kellermanns and Eddleston (2007) observed negative effects for task and process conflict on firm performance; although only the effect of task conflict was statistically significant (see Figure 17.1). Thus, rather than observing a direct benefit for disagreement over tasks and job assignments, as was proposed by Kellermanns and Eddleston (2004), this study found that such conflict may have negative effects on firm performance. Although surprising, these results correspond with recent meta-analyses suggesting that all three forms of conflict are associated with negative performance outcomes (de Wit et al., 2012). Also, it is important to note that these direct effects should be interpreted in the context of moderators. Without the appropriate social environment, disagreements about tasks and processes may be perceived as personal attacks, i.e., relationship conflict, rather than as a constructive dialogue about business needs (Kellermanns & Eddleston, 2007).

Moderators of the Effects of Conflict on Firm Outcomes

To understand when the various forms of conflict may be beneficial or detrimental to family firm performance, researchers have proposed a number of moderators to account for the context in which such disagreements unfold (see Figure 17.1). These moderators reflect both interpersonal relationships among family members, i.e., family-member exchange, and how the family is structured or involved with the firm, i.e., generational ownership dispersion and generational involvement (Eddleston & Kellermanns, 2007; Kellermanns & Eddleston, 2007). Drawing on a complexity model of conflict, researchers have also proposed that the various forms of conflict may interact and exhibit curvilinear effects (Kellermanns & Eddleston, 2004).

Family-Member Exchange

First, researchers have examined the extent to which family-member exchange (FMX) moderates the influence of task and process conflict on family firm performance (Kellermanns & Eddleston, 2007). Similar to team-member exchange (TMX) and leader-member exchange (LMX) (Dulebohn, Bommer, Liden, Brouer, & Ferris, 2012; Seers, 1989), FMX reflects the level of reciprocity among family members and corresponds with the family's willingness to share ideas, feedback, and expectations with one another (Kellermanns & Eddleston, 2007). Thus, with higher levels of FMX, which reflects more open and honest communications among family members, it is more likely that task and process conflict will be perceived as an attempt to improve performance rather than as a personal attack or a political maneuver.

Based on responses from 51 family firms, Kellermanns and Eddleston (2007) found that FMX moderated the direct effects of both task and process conflict on firm performance. In terms of process conflict, the highest performing family firms were those that had high levels of FMX and high levels of process conflict. On the other hand, family firms performed significantly worse when experiencing process conflict in the absence of high levels of FMX. Kellermanns and Eddleston (2007) argued that, based on a stewardship perspective, process conflict can be perceived as a means of assigning individuals to the right tasks, but only if high-quality relationships exist among family members. If there are low levels of FMX, family members may be unable to comfortably critique each other's abilities, and it may be best to limit discussions about roles and position assignments (Kellermanns & Eddleston, 2007).

In terms of task conflict, Kellermanns and Eddleston (2007) found the highest levels of firm performance among family firms with high levels of FMX, but low levels of task conflict. Surprisingly, when family members expressed high levels of task conflict, they performed better if they exhibited low quality exchanges, i.e., low FMX. Kellermanns and Eddleston (2007) concluded that these findings may suggest that more open communication, accompanied by disagreements about specific tasks, may actually limit family members ability to reach consensus. That is, open exchanges centered around task conflict may stymie the decision-making process and ultimately disrupt the family firm's performance.

Generational Ownership Dispersion

Along with the quality of relationships among family members, how the family structures the ownership of the firm may also moderate the effects of conflict on firm performance. Generational ownership dispersion, or the extent to which ownership of the family firm resides within a single generation, influences how conflict is interpreted and influences firm-level outcomes (Kellermanns & Eddleston, 2007). Specifically, higher levels of ownership dispersion (i.e., multiple generations own a firm) increases the likelihood that conflict engenders feuds or coalitions. If ownership is consolidated within a single generation, however, conflict may enhance the quality of the decision-making process by limiting the likelihood that the controlling owners or founders can maintain exclusive control over the strategy of the firm.

The highest levels of performance were, in fact, observed for those with low levels of generational dispersion and high levels of task conflict (Kellermanns & Eddleston, 2007). The lowest levels of performance, on the other hand, were observed among those firms with high levels of generational dispersion and high task conflict. Thus, there is some evidence to suggest that if family firms are controlled by a single generation, task conflict may facilitate higher-quality discussions to establish their strategies and goals (Kellermanns & Eddleston, 2007). However, if the family firm is controlled by a multigenerational coalition, task conflict may be interpreted as one group attempting to jockey for position or to seize control, which may ultimately limit the firm's performance (Kellermanns & Eddleston, 2007).

Generational Involvement

In addition to generational ownership dispersion, researchers have proposed that the extent to which multiple generations are involved within a family firm moderates the effects of task conflict and process conflict on firm performance (Kellermanns & Eddleston, 2004). For multigenerational family firms to succeed, each new generation of family members must acquire the preceding generation's knowledge and expertise, while at the same time providing new insights and diversifying the existing perspectives within the family firm. Task conflict may facilitate this process by deepening debates over what tasks should be completed and the appropriate strategies for the firm (Kellermanns & Eddleston, 2004). Similarly, process conflict may provide a means for older generations to seek out and adopt new strategies from younger generations of family members. As new generations of family members advocate for new approaches for executing the business' strategies, there are bound to be discussions about the roles that each family member will play. Thus, the extent to which particular family members feel entitled to a specific job or role can be clarified and resolved via discussions, which ideally will result in a better fit between work roles and talents (Kellermanns & Eddleston, 2004).

Forms and Levels of Conflict

Finally, as Kellermanns and Eddleston (2004) noted, the different forms of conflict are theorized to coalesce and interact in complex ways. In particular, relationship conflict may moderate the potential beneficial effects of task and process conflict. Given that relationship conflict engenders animosity and frustration among family members, it may limit how well family members incorporate one another's ideas about which tasks to complete or who should be assigned to which activities. More specifically, the emotional distress that arises from relationship conflict among key family members in the firm prevents the integration of ideas. Instead, the firm is more likely to experience inertia in the decision-making process. Thus, despite the potential for task and process conflict to enhance organizational decision-making, when it is accompanied by relationship conflict, the family will likely shift its attention from important, business-related matters to more personal topics, which could ultimately reduce firm performance.

Furthermore, there may be curvilinear effects for each form of conflict (Kellermanns & Eddleston, 2004). That is, despite the potential benefits of task and process conflict, there may be a tipping point at which too much conflict limits the family's ability to reach a decision or come to consensus on assignments or duties. Conversely, too little conflict can cause family members' decision-making to stagnate (De Dreu, 2006; Kellermanns & Eddleston, 2004). Thus, along with the moderating effects of family relationships (i.e., FMX), as well as family governance and generational involvement, the type and level of the three forms of conflict may interact to yield distinct effects for firm level outcomes (Kellermanns & Eddleston, 2004).

Unique Types of Conflict in Family Firms: The Fredo Effect

Along with examining how conflict unfolds within family firms, researchers have proposed elements of conflict that are unique to these types of organizations. In particular, researchers have suggested that family firms may be susceptible to the Fredo Effect (Kidwell, Eddleston, Cater III, & Kellermanns, 2013). This phenomenon refers to a character from Mario Puzo's (1969) novel, *The Godfather*, and subsequent movies, which detail the activities of an infamous crime family. Although the family is successful and overcomes numerous external threats, e.g., rival crime families and law enforcement, it is eventually undone by one of its own members. More specifically, Fredo, the bumbling middle brother, harbors resentment towards his family because he is passed over for a leadership role and only peripherally involved in the family firm. Although his actions in this distal role are troublesome (i.e., he makes questionable business decisions and challenges organizational norms), Fredo's biggest failure is betraying his family, which ultimately leads to his demise (Kidwell et al., 2013).

What is the Fredo Effect?

Drawing on this artistic representation of a phenomenon that is common in family firms, Kidwell et al. (2013) and Kidwell, Kellermanns, and Eddleston (2012) have defined the Fredo Effect as a process by which family leaders' generous actions increase a family member's sense of entitlement, weaken the family member's connection to the firm, and increase the likelihood that this family member will become an impediment to the business. Family members become impediments when they are less capable or competent than other employees and only hold a position within the family firm because of their status within the family (Kidwell et al., 2013). It is important to note that being incompetent does not equate to being unethical (Kidwell et al., 2013). That is, a family member may not commit serious ethical violations, e.g., siphoning resources for their own personal use, but can still cause the firm serious damage simply by being incapable of performing his or her job. Furthermore, the Fredo Effect is distinct from nepotism (Kidwell et al., 2013). Nepotism refers to a bias toward hiring relatives, whereas the Fredo Effect refers to family members that hold family status and can remain in their positions causing long-term damage to the family firm.

How do "Fredos" Affect the Family Firm?

By disrupting the quality of family relationships, contributing to ineffective governance, increasing nepotism, and flaming struggles over family control, the Fredo Effect undermines beneficial resources that are critical for family firms, e.g., entrepreneurial capabilities, implicit knowledge, and social capital (Kidwell et al., 2013). For example, Fredos may be given more leeway than other firm members, which could instill perceptions of injustice or unfair treatment. If non-family employees observe that a Fredo's actions have gone unpunished, then they may withdraw from the firm or engage in similar types of behavior.

The disruptive behavior exhibited by a Fredo may also influence the family firm's leadership. That is, Fredo's parents, or family leaders, may feel guilty and question how their actions contributed to the current situation (Kidwell et al., 2013). To resolve these uncomfortable feelings, the family leader may be tempted to exhibit more altruism towards their relative, e.g., provide additional resources or leeway. Furthermore, family leaders cannot entirely abandon their incompetent family member because of overlapping subsystems. In other words, even if the family leader removes the problematic family member from the business, i.e., fires him or her, they will likely still see each other for family functions such as holiday gatherings (Kidwell et al., 2013). Thus, this family-firm interaction has the potential of forming an escalating cycle of dysfunctional behavior, which could ultimately disrupt the firm's performance as well as the family system (Cooper, Kidwell & Eddleston, 2013).

Fredos are especially problematic if they are directly in line to succeed the current leader of the family firm (Kidwell et al., 2013). If the incompetent family member assumes a leadership position, he or she will likely exhibit poor decision-making and reduce the firm's effectiveness. On the other hand, if this family member is passed over, it could challenge his or her feelings of entitlement, which could lead to more disengagement and an even greater liability.

What Contributes to the Fredo Effect?

As with conflict among family members more generally, the structure of family firms lays the foundation for the Fredo Effect to occur (Kidwell et al., 2013). Because family firms are defined by overlapping family, ownership, and management subsystems (Habbershon, Williams, & Mac-Millian, 2003), it is more likely that family members will be employed, regardless of their skills or level of competence. Thus, the structural characteristics of family firms can directly contribute to the Fredo Effect (Kidwell et al., 2013).

Family leaders may also contribute to the Fredo Effect based on their actions as parents (Kidwell et al., 2013). For example, children whose parents exhibited highly supportive parenting styles, but provided little control are more likely to exhibit delinquent behavior (Eddelston & Kidwell, 2012). Likewise, more hostile behavior towards a child will likely elicit dysfunctional behaviors (Kidwell et al., 2013). As such, children will likely reciprocate the types of behavior they experience from their parents. Thus, the actions of a family leader may set the stage for a future Fredo Effect well before the family member enters the family business (Kidwell et al., 2013).

After the family member enters the firm, the actions of the family leaders are also critical antecedents of the Fredo Effect. For example, family firm leaders who exhibit altruistic behaviors and attempt to preserve a family member's well-being may entice individual family members to adopt the role of Fredo. More specifically, if family leaders reward a family member even when he or she acts incompetently, displays unproductive behaviors, or evades assigned duties, they may be encouraging a sense of entitlement that could eventually become disruptive (Kidwell et al., 2013).

Along with well-intentioned, altruistic behaviors, family leaders who demonstrate clear in-group/out-group preferences may contribute to the Fredo Effect (Kidwell et al., 2013). More specifically, throughout prolonged exchanges over the course of their time together, family leaders form high- and low-quality relationships with their relatives. These preferences may lead family members to compete or challenge one another so as to occupy more favored positions within the family firm. However, if a family member considers himself or herself to be in the out-group (i.e., consistently experiences low-quality exchanges with family leaders), he or she may interpret subsequent interactions through an increasingly negative lens. That is, any acts of altruism from his or her family leader (e.g., forgiving the Fredo's transgressions, offering alternative positions or assignments) may be seen as spiteful or disingenuous. Thus, in-group or out-group preferences may eventually contribute to the Fredo Effect (Eddleston & Kidwell, 2012).

There are also structural characteristics of the family firm that can lead to the Fredo Effect. Most notably, the different norms and logics that underlie decision-making in the family domain compared to those in the business domain may set the stage for Fredos to emerge (Kidwell et al., 2013). In the business domain, positions and jobs are ideally distributed based on one's merit and competence. However, in the family domain, jobs and favors are provided based on a family member's needs. Thus, family leaders and parents may be more inclined to forgive poor performance or incompetence, which could heighten the Fredo Effect.

The Role of Relationship Conflict within the Fredo Effect

Although the actions of a family member and the structure of the family firm may contribute to the Fredo Effect (Kidwell et al., 2013), researchers have found that a key mediating mechanism is the level of relationship conflict within the family firm (Kidwell et al., 2012). Because relationship conflict consists of perceptions of personal animosities and incompatibilities, it also lessens work efforts, reduces cohesion and limits goodwill (Kellermanns & Eddleston, 2004). Thus, the more relationship conflict a family is experiencing, the more likely its members will focus on political issues, like those associated with dealing with a Fredo, instead of on the economic issues facing the family firm.

Support for the mediating role of relationship conflict was demonstrated by Kidwell et al. (2012). This study found that increased harmony, i.e., better quality relationships among family members, higher levels of distributive justice, i.e., increased perceptions of fair reward allocation, and less role ambiguity reduce relationship conflict, which in turn limits the likelihood that there is a family member impeding the firm's performance, i.e., the presence of a Fredo Effect. Furthermore, the authors found empirical evidence to suggest that these characteristics of the family and the firms, i.e., harmony, distributive justice, and relationship conflict, reduced the likelihood of a Fredo Effect by first reducing the level of relationship conflict among family members (Kidwell et al., 2012).

Recommendations for Managing Conflict and Addressing the Fredo Effect in Family Firms

As noted earlier, family firms represent a unique context for addressing issues of conflict. For example, family leaders must manage conflict that can emerge within either the family or business systems limit the extent to which disagreements spill over across these domains (Kellermanns & Eddleston, 2004). Nevertheless, there is a large body of literature within management and organizational behavior that has examined various strategies for managing and reducing conflict within organizational settings (Bergmann & Volkema, 1989; De Dreu & Van Vianen, 2001; Wall & Callister, 1995). In the following section, we draw on these previous findings to offer practical recommendations for family leaders to manage conflict within their organizations and address the Fredo Effect. These recommendations are briefly summarized in Table 17.1.

Managing Conflict in Family Firms

Researchers have proposed five strategies for managing conflict in groups. Each of these strategies is designed to mitigate the potential negative consequences of conflict (Bergmann & Volkema, 1989; De Dreu & Van Vianen, 2001; Wall & Callister, 1995). Below we review each of these strategies and discuss their relevance in a family firm context.

Avoiding

One approach for managing conflict is to simply ignore any disagreements. Thus, avoiding consists of ignoring the source of the conflict. Under some circumstances, avoiding conflict can be beneficial for a group (De Dreu & Van Vianen, 2001; Jehn, 1997). If the conflict can be attributed

Table 17.1 Strategies for Reducing Family Conflict and Limiting the Fredo Effect

Family Conflict		*The Fredo Effect*	
Avoiding	• Ignore minor or inconsequential disagreements between family members • Less effective in family firms because of ongoing relationships inside and outside of work	Set standards for employment	• Vacancy must exist before family employees can be hired • Family members complete the same hiring process as other applicants • Establish clear incentive systems
Contending	• Individual family member forces their ideas or opinions into action while disregarding others' responses • Exacerbates relationship conflict and undermines any potential benefits from task conflict and process conflict	Define clear roles	• Provide job descriptions • Clearly communicate responsibilities and expectations
Compromising	• Identify a solution that partially satisfies all parties • Reduces conflict over the short-term but unlikely to be effective in the long run	Establish family councils	• Provide opportunity for family members to express concerns about family and business systems • Establish code of ethics and transparent termination processes
Collaborating	• Share ideas to identify a mutually agreed upon solution that satisfies all parties • Reduces conflict over the short-term and enhances effectiveness in the long run	Evaluate parent-child relationships	• Assess children's sense of entitlement and ability to contribute to the firm • Monitor quality of relationship between parent and child
Third-Party Intervention	• Invite others outside the family business to mediate or resolve the conflict • Leads to long-term solutions and improves communication among family members		

to petty or frivolous topics, it may be appropriate for group members to simply ignore such disagreements in order to avoid becoming distracted from pressing tasks or deadlines. In fact, some research suggests that avoiding conflict can enhance team members' perceptions of performance (De Dreu & Van Vianen, 2001).

Despite the benefits of avoiding conflict in small groups, this approach may have limited applicability when addressing conflict within a family firm. Because family members will likely remain in the business, work together for the foreseeable future, and interact outside of the workplace, an avoiding strategy may be less feasible (Kellermanns & Eddleston, 2006). That is, by ignoring minor disagreements, family members may be sowing the seeds for greater levels of conflict at a later point in time. In fact, there is some anecdotal evidence to suggest that avoidance tactics in family firms contribute to lower levels of family satisfaction, more sibling rivalry, and less mutual trust (Kaye & McCarthy, 1996). Thus, although avoiding conflict may enhance performance within groups or teams, it may be a limiting approach to conflict management for family businesses.

Contending

Family members may also try a contending, or competing, approach for managing conflict within their firms. This strategy consists of an individual forcing their ideas or opinions into action while disregarding others' thoughts or responses (De Dreu & Van Vianen, 2001). This approach is unlikely to be an effective response to either relationship conflict, task conflict, or process conflict. In response to relationship conflict, this strategy may create greater tension or more negative responses given that it likely benefits a single individual (i.e., the person adopting the contending strategy) (Kellermanns & Eddleston, 2006; Sorenson, 1999). Contending may also undermine any potential benefits of task and process conflict (De Dreu & Van Vianen, 2001). To the extent that a family member uses threats, forces compliance, or promotes his or her personal agenda (Sorenson, 1999), this approach to resolving conflict may stifle decision-making, communication, and strategy formation processes (Kellermanns & Eddleston, 2006). Thus, taken as a whole, contending is unlikely to be an optimal strategy for resolving conflict within family firms.

Compromising

Rather than avoiding or competing over issues, family members may seek to identify a compromise. Compromising consists of identifying solutions to a conflict that partially appease all parties involved. Although a compromise may temporarily resolve conflict, it does not create a long-term solution (Kellermanns & Eddleston, 2006). Some level of negotiation and compromise can initially deescalate existing conflicts and restore lines of communication within a family (Sorenson, 1999). However, compromising can also stifle discussing new ideas and limit the likelihood of finding a more enduring resolution.

Given these considerations, compromising may be a useful way of defusing tension surrounding relationship conflict. By finding a solution that partially satisfies all members, there is an opportunity to reduce tension. However, a compromising approach to managing task and process conflict may actually inhibit the family firm's performance because it undermines the ability of the family members to reach consensus on new ideas (Sorenson, 1999). Thus, compromising should be viewed as an effective strategy for managing conflict over the short-term, but it is ineffective in the long run.

Collaboration

Collaboration consists of family members working together and sharing ideas to develop a solution that mollifies the concerns of all involved parties and is mutually agreed upon (De Dreu & Van Vianen, 2001). By identifying solutions that benefit all parties, collaboration has the greatest potential of identifying actions that can deescalate conflict in the short-term and reduce the reoccurrence of conflict in the future. Because collaboration creates a cooperative environment by considering the interest of all parties, it can help diffuse relationship conflict among family members (Kellermanns & Eddleston, 2006). Furthermore, for task conflict and process conflict, collaboration improves the quality of the decision that is reached by encouraging open communication about the issues at hand (Sorenson, 1999). Given these benefits (De Dreu & Van Vianen, 2001), collaboration has the greatest potential to benefit family firms (Sorenson, 1999).

Third-Party Intervention

The final approach for managing conflict, third-party intervention, consists of inviting others outside the family business to mediate or resolve the conflict (Wall & Callister, 1995). This approach differs from previous strategies in that an external party is included in the conflict management process. Within the context of family firms, third-party interventions may be especially effective because they afford family members the chance to introduce a neutral 'outsider' who provides an unbiased perspective of the conflict (Kaye, 1991). Thus, third-party interventions are beneficial to the extent that the external party can resolve the conflict (either through mediation or arbitration) rather than provide a temporary solution (e.g., compromise). Also, the third-party may provide a fresh perspective and outlet that allows family members to improve their communication and interactions (Kaye, 1991; Kellermanns & Eddleston, 2007). Thus, as a conflict management strategy for family firms, third party interventions may be an appropriate option.

Addressing the Fredo Effect in Family Firms

In addition to managing conflict more generally, it is important for family leaders to be cognizant of the potential for the Fredo Effect to occur (Kidwell et al., 2013). Below we provide recommendations for family leaders that are intended to limit the likelihood that Fredos will emerge. Essentially, each of the prescribed actions contributes to a strong ethical climate. An ethical climate reflects shared or prevailing perceptions among family members and family leaders that typical organizational practices and procedures are ethical (Kidwell et al., 2012). This type of climate limits the likelihood that family members will pursue their own self-interests and focus on their own well-being, which ultimately reduces the likelihood of the Fredo Effect.

Set Standards for Employment

One approach for reducing the Fredo Effect is to minimize the sense of entitlement among family members that are involved with the firm (Kidwell et al., 2013; Kidwell et al., 2012). By setting clear standards for employment within the family firm, family leaders can establish structures that limit the potential for feelings of entitlement. More specifically, these standards could specify a vacancy must exist before a family member can be hired. This practice helps avoid any implicit dependencies between children and the family firm (Kidwell et al., 2013). Family leaders could also require family members to demonstrate they have similar levels of experience, education, and skills as non-family applicants who are vying for the same position. Again, this would ensure that family members are, in fact, qualified for their positions and limit feelings of entitlement. Finally, family leaders could establish a clear incentive system that aligns the behaviors of employees (both family members and non-family workers) with the goals of the organization. This practice demonstrates that all employees, regardless of their family status, must understand that they are rewarded for what they do rather than who they are (Kidwell et al., 2012).

Taken as a whole, these practices help improve perceptions of distributive justice among all members of the family firm. Distributive justice perceptions consist of comparisons between the rewards people receive and what they expect based on principles of reciprocity (Kidwell et al., 2012). To the extent that such expectations are met, and an individual feels their rewards are equitable, they are more likely to feel valued by the firm and express greater commitment. Thus, justice perceptions limit the likelihood of a family member withdrawing from the firm and exhibiting counterproductive or unethical behaviors (e.g., hoarding ideas, providing suboptimal effort).

Define Clear Roles

Along with establishing these standards for employment, it is critical that family leaders establish clear roles for family employees (Sharma & Hoy, 2013). That is, family members should receive clear job descriptions that delineate job expectations and communicate their position's responsibilities (Kidwell et al., 2013). This process may also consist of having an open dialogue about how to limit family and business roles from interfering with one another.

Such actions improve a family member's role clarity (Kidwell et al., 2013). Role clarity ensures that an individual understands what activities are required of their position. If an employee believes that he or she lacks the resources required to perform their assigned duties, then they are likely to experience greater stress, to exhibit diminished job performance, and to engage in unpredictable behavior. For family employees, a lack of role clarity may be especially alarming because it could raise issues around generational succession. If a family employee is not sure how he or she is expected to contribute to the firm, i.e., greater role ambiguity, they will experience stress and could eventually withdraw from the firm (Kidwell et al., 2013). Such disengagement or withdrawal could eventually culminate in the family employee expressing dissent and engaging in unethical behavior.

Establish Family Councils

Family leaders can also establish family councils to limit the occurrence of the Fredo Effect. Family councils reflect formal structures where individuals can share frustrations and concerns about potential conflicts between the family and business systems (Kidwell et al., 2013). Thus, the councils are a formal forum where family employees can voice their grievances. This setting may be especially important if the family firm consists of a single dominant leader or founder, which can stifle open dialogue and increase the likelihood of interpersonal animosity or relationship conflict (Kellermanns & Eddleston, 2004).

Family councils can also create a code of ethics and establish processes for termination (Kidwell et al., 2013). Thus, these structures can clearly communicate the norms and expectations of the firm while also making the consequences for violating these expectations more transparent. Both of these processes have the benefit of increasing perceptions of equity and fairness, which can ultimately reduce the potential for Fredos to emerge.

Evaluate Parent-Child Relationships

Finally, family leaders can limit the likelihood of a Fredo Effect occurring, or at least mitigate the potentially deleterious effects, by evaluating existing parent-child relationships (Kidwell et al., 2013). For example, family leaders could consider which children demonstrate the greatest feelings of entitlement or are ill-suited to work in the family business. These types of reflections provide the family leader with the opportunity to take preventative actions (e.g., re-assigning positions, adjusting policies) (Kidwell et al., 2013). Furthermore, by being cognizant of existing parent-child relationships, the family leader is better able to take action at first sight of any 'Fredo' type of behavior. Although the severity of the family leader's response could vary, e.g., suspension OR firing, they at least have the opportunity to administer some form of punishment and uphold principles of justice and fairness (Kidwell et al., 2013).

Future Research on Conflict in Family Firms

Considering the current state of the literature, it is also important to highlight avenues for future research. By drawing on recent advances in the teams and work groups literature, we identify three areas in which our understanding of conflict within family firms can be extended (i.e., patterns of conflict, conflict asymmetry, and status conflict). Each of these areas is described below.

Patterns of Conflict within Family Firms

As noted earlier, the different forms of conflict within family firms are expected to interact and influence one another (Kellermanns & Eddleston, 2004). However, few studies have considered complex interactions among the different forms of conflict (either two-way or three-way). This oversight may be attributed to the difficulty in recruiting a large enough sample of family firms to ensure there is sufficient power to test such effects (Aguinis & Gottfredson, 2010).

An alternative approach for operationalizing the complexity perspective of conflict consists of classifying teams based on their pattern of conflict (O'Neill, McLarnon, Hoffart, Woodley, & Allen, in press). This team-centric approach assigns groups to categories based on the reported levels of relationship conflict, task conflict, and process conflict. Using this technique, O'Neill et al. (in press) recently found four distinct conflict profiles. The first, labeled as task conflict dominant, consisted of groups that disagreed almost exclusively about the types of tasks that need to be completed (i.e., high task conflict, low relationship conflict, and low process conflict). The second and third profiles, labeled as low-range and mid-range conflict, resembled the initial profile but simply experienced either higher or lower levels of conflict. The final profile, called dysfunctional conflict, consisted of groups that experienced high levels of all three forms of conflict (O'Neill et al., in press). O'Neill et al. (in press) also found that teams classified as "task conflict dominant" were better able to manage their conflict and demonstrated higher levels of performance.

Given these recent findings, a 'family-centric' approach for examining conflict within family firms may be beneficial. This approach may be well-suited for testing existing propositions that suggest the highest degree of family firm performance should occur when families experience moderate levels of task conflict and process conflict and low levels of relationship conflict (Kellermanns & Eddleston, 2004). Thus, rather than considering each form of conflict individually, or examining complex interactions, which require greater statistical power, assigning family firms to categories based on the observed levels of conflict may allow researchers to clarify the complex relationship among these three processes.

Family Conflict Asymmetry

The majority of the research on conflict in family firms assumes that family members perceive conflict similarly (Eddleston & Kellermanns, 2007; Kellermanns & Eddleston, 2007). That is, conflict is assumed to be a homogeneous and shared experience for all members of the dominant family coalition. Although there are certainly instances where family members agree about the level of conflict within the dominant coalition, there may also be times where some family members perceive conflict, while others do not. Drawing on social cognitive theory and social information processing theory (Bandura, 1977; Salancik & Pfeffer, 1978), Jehn, Rispens, and Thatcher (2010) argued that group members are attuned to different stimuli in their teams and thus experience conflict differently. Discrepancies in perceptions of conflict are especially damaging for a group's performance and creativity because they undermine shared understandings of their internal environment and create confusion and inefficiencies (Jehn, Rispens, et al., 2010; Jehn, Rupert, & Nauta, 2006; Jehn, Rupert, Nauta, & van den Bossche, 2010).

Given that conflict asymmetry is due, at least in part, to diversity within a group or team (Jehn, Rispens, et al., 2010), this phenomenon may be likely to occur within the dominant coalition of family firms. Because family members simultaneously occupy distinct roles within the firm (e.g., various positions) and the family hierarchy (e.g., cousins, siblings, children, parents) (Kellermanns & Eddleston, 2004), there is an increased likelihood that they experience their social environment differently. These distinct experiences can then contribute to unique perceptions of the level of conflict that is occurring within the family, which could further limit the firm's performance and ability to respond to its environment.

Conflict asymmetry within family firms may also have implications for the Fredo Effect. Given that Fredos are most disruptive when they become detached from the firm and respond to altruistic behavior cynically (Kidwell et al., 2013; Kidwell et al., 2012), this effect may be exacerbated to the extent that a Fredo perceives more conflict within the family than others. In fact, Jehn, Rispens, et al. (2010) found that team members that experienced more conflict than their teammates perceived lower levels of communication and cooperation within the group, and subsequently withheld their performance. Thus, if Fredos are not in agreement about the level of conflict with their family members, they may be more likely to become detached from the firm and become an even greater impediment.

Status Conflict within Family Firms

Although most research on conflict in family firms has focused on the three dominant forms within the literature (i.e., relationship conflict, task conflict, and process conflict) (Eddleston & Kellermanns, 2007; Kellermanns & Eddleston, 2004, 2007), researchers have recently proposed status conflict as an alternative form of conflict that can occur within groups. Status conflict is defined as disputes over people's relative status position in their group's social hierarchy (Bendersky & Hays, 2012).

This recent form of conflict has three features that make it unique or distinct from the previous types. First, status conflict is more structural. Because this type of conflict focuses on one's position within a group, rather than a specific task or strategy, such disagreements are likely to arise when discussing a number of issues (Bendersky & Hays, 2012). Second, status conflict exhibits more long-term effects. Specifically, because a group's hierarchy is more enduring than a particular issue, disputes over status hierarchies may persist for longer periods of time (Bendersky & Hays, 2012). Finally, Bendersky and Hays (2012) argued that status conflicts may be more disruptive because they undermine the existing structure of the entire group.

Based on evidence from three studies, Bendersky and Hays (2012) found that status conflict was, in fact, empirically distinct from other existing forms of conflict. Furthermore, status conflict exerts unique, negative effects on team performance above and beyond the previous three forms of conflict. Status conflict was especially disruptive for groups because it limits information sharing (Bendersky & Hays, 2012).

Given these findings, future research on conflict in family firms may consider this additional form of conflict. Status conflict may be especially relevant within the context of family firms given the potential for dual, competing status hierarchies, i.e., positions within the family versus the business (Kellermanns & Eddleston, 2004). Furthermore, there is initial evidence to suggest that status conflict could help further elucidate the surprising negative effects of task conflict on family firm performance (Kellermanns & Eddleston, 2007). For instance, teams performed best when high levels of task conflict occurred in the absence of status conflict (Bendersky &

Hays, 2012). Thus, in situations where group members are not competing for high status positions, they are more receptive to one another's ideas about the tasks that need to be completed (Bendersky & Hays, 2012).

Finally, status conflict may be uniquely related to the Fredo Effect. Given that disruptive family members emerge after their sense of entitlement is violated (Kidwell et al., 2012), conflicts over one's relative status (either within the family or the business) may be a bellwether for this effect. In fact, the original Fredo, from *The Godfather*, became especially disruptive after he was passed over for the family leader's position. Thus, conflict over status within family firms may increase the likelihood of the development of a family member impediment.

Conclusion

Although conflict within family firms has only been studied for the past 10 years (Kellermanns & Eddleston, 2004); a sizeable body of research has emerged. Across multiple studies, there is consistent evidence to suggest that conflict can either directly inhibit a family firm's performance (Kellermanns & Eddleston, 2007) or increase the likelihood of a single family member becoming an impediment to the organization (Kidwell et al., 2012). However, it is clear that the effects of conflict depend on structural characteristics of the firm, aspects of internal family dynamics, and the nature of conflict itself (Eddleston & Kellermanns, 2007; Kellermanns & Eddleston, 2004). Despite these robust findings, there are a number of interesting research questions still worth exploring. We hope this chapter provides a useful summary and helps guide subsequent research aimed at expanding our understanding of this important topic.

References

Aguinis, H., & Gottfredson, Ryan K. (2010). Best-practice recommendations for estimating interaction effects using moderated multiple regression. *Journal of Organizational Behavior, 31*, 776–786.

Amason, Allen C. (1996). Distinguishing the effects of functional and dysfunctional conflict on strategic decision making: Resolving a paradox for top management teams. *Academy of Management Journal, 39*(1), 123–148.

Bandura, Albert. (1977). *Social Learning Theory.* Englewood Cliffs, NJ: Prentice-Hall.

Behfar, Kristin J., Mannix, Elizabeth A., Peterson, Randall S., & Trochim, William M. (2011). Conflict in small groups: The meaning and consequences of process conflict. *Small Group Research, 42*(2), 127–176.

Bendersky, Corinne, & Hays, Nicholas. (2012). Status conflict in groups. *Organization Science, 23*(2), 323–340.

Bergmann, T. J., & Volkema, R. J. (1989). Understanding and managing interpersonal conflict at work: Its issues, interactive processes, and consequences. In M. A. Rahim (Ed.), *Managing Conflict: An Interdisciplinary Approach.* (pp. 7–19). New York: Praeger.

British Broadcasting Corporation. (2014). Market Basket dispute sale to former boss ends bitter dispute. Retrieved June 1st, 2015, from http://www.bbc.com/news/business-28972536

De Dreu, Carsten. (2006). When too little or too much hurts: Evidence for a curvlinear relationship between task conflict and innovation in teams. *Journal of Management, 32*, 83–107.

De Dreu, Carsten, & Van Vianen, A. E. M. (2001). Managing relationship conflict and the effectiveness of organizational teams. *Journal of Organizational Behavior, 22*(3), 309–328.

de Wit, Frank R. C., Greer, L. L., & Jehn, K. A. (2012). The paradox of intragroup conflict: A meta-analysis. *Journal of Applied Psychology, 97*(2), 360–390.

Dulebohn, James H., Bommer, William H., Liden, R. C., Brouer, Robyn L., & Ferris, Gerald R. (2012). A meta-analysis of antecedents and consequences of leader-member exchange: Integrating the past with an eye toward the future. *Journal of Management, 38*(6), 1715–1759.

Eddleston, Kimberly A., & Kellermanns, Franz W. (2007). Destructive and productive family relationships: A stewardship theory perspective. *Journal of Business Venturing, 22*, 545–565.

Eddleston, Kimberly A., & Kidwell, Roland E. 2012. Parent-child relationships: Planting the seeds of deviant behavior in the family firm. *Entrepreneurship Theory & Practice, 36*(2): 369–386.

Eddleston, Kimberly A., Kellermanns, Franz W., Floyd, Steven W., Crittenden, Victoria L., & Crittenden, William F. (2013). Planning for growth: Life stage differences in family firms. *Entrepreneurship Theory and Practice, 37*(5), 1177–1202.

Habbershon, Timothy G., & Williams, Mary. (1999). A resource-based framework for assessing the strategic advantages of family firms. *Family Business Review, 12*(1), 1–25.

Habbershon, Timothy G., Williams, Mary, & MacMillian, Ian C. (2003). A unified perspective of family firm performance. *Journal of Business Venturing, 18*, 451–465.

Jehn, K. A. (1995). A multimethod examination of the benefits and detriments of intragroup conflict. *Administrative Science Quarterly, 40*, 265–282.

Jehn, K. A. (1997). A quantitative analysis of conflict types and dimensions in organizational groups. *Administrative Science Quarterly, 42*(3), 530–558.

Jehn, K. A., & Mannix, Elizabeth A. (2001). The dynamic nature of conflict: A longitudinal study of intragroup conflict and group performance. *Academy of Management Journal, 44*(2), 238–251.

Jehn, K. A., Rispens, Sonja, & Thatcher, S. M. B. (2010). The effects of conflict asymmetry on work group and individual outcomes. *Academy of Management Journal, 53*(3), 596–616.

Jehn, K. A., Rupert, Joyce, & Nauta, Aukje. (2006). The effects of conflict asymmetry on mediation outcomes: Satisfaction, work motivation, and absenteeism. *International Journal of Conflict Management, 17*(2), 96–109.

Jehn, K. A., Rupert, Joyce, Nauta, Aukje, & van den Bossche, Seth. (2010). Crooked conflicts: The effects of conflict asymmetry in mediation. *Negotiation and Conflict Management Research, 3*(4), 338–357.

Kaye, K. (1991). Penetrating the cycle of sustained conflict. *Family Business Review, 4*(1), 21–44.

Kaye, K., & McCarthy, C. (1996). Healthy disagreements. *Family Business, Autumn*, 71–72.

Kellermanns, Franz W., & Eddleston, Kimberly A. (2004). Feuding families: When conflict does a family firm good. *Entrepreneurship Theory and Practice, 28*(3), 209–228.

Kellermanns, Franz W., & Eddleston, Kimberly A. (2006). Feuding families: The management of conflict in family firms. In P. Poutziouris, K. Smynrios & B. Klein (Eds.), *Family Business Research Handbook* (pp. 358–368). Northampton, MA: Edward Elgar Publishing.

Kellermanns, Franz W., & Eddleston, Kimberly A. (2007). A family perpsective on when conflict benefits family firm performance. *Journal of Business Research, 60*, 1048–1057.

Kidwell, Roland E., Eddleston, Kimberly A., Cater III, John James, & Kellermanns, Franz W. (2013). How one bad family member can undermine a family firm: Preventing the Fredo effect. *Business Horizons, 56*, 5–12.

Kidwell, Roland E., Kellermanns, Franz W., & Eddleston, Kimberly A. (2012). Harmony, justice, confusion, and conflict in family firms: Implications for ethical climate and the "Fredo Effect." *Journal of Business Ethics, 106*, 503–517.

Lansberg, Ivan S. (1983). Managing human resources in family firms: The problem of institutional overlap. *Organizational Dynamics, 12*(1), 39–46.

Loughry, Misty L., & Amason, Allen C. (2014). Why won't task conflict cooperate? Deciphering stubborn results. *International Journal of Conflict Management, 25*(4), 333–358.

O'Neill, T. A., McLarnon, Matthew J. W., Hoffart, Genevieve, C., Woodley, Hayden J., & Allen, N. J. (in press). The structure and function of team conflict state profiles. *Journal of Management*.

Pathe, Simone. (2014). With jobs on the line, why are Market Basket employees so loyal to Artie T? Retrieved June 1st, 2015, from http://www.pbs.org/newshour/making-sense/with-jobs-on-the-line-why-are-market-basket-employees-so-loyal-to-artie-t/

Puzo, Mario. (1969). *The Godfather*. New York, NY: Penguin.

Salancik, Gerald R., & Pfeffer, Jeffrey. (1978). A social information processing approach to job attitudes and task design. *Administrative Science Quarterly, 23*, 224–253.

Seers, Anson. (1989). Team-member exchange quality: A new construct for role-making research. *Organizational Behavior and Human Decision Processes, 43*, 118–135.

Sharma, Pramodita, & Hoy, Francis. (2013). Family business roles. In R. L. Sorensen, A. Yu, K. H. Brigham & G. T. Lumpkin (Eds.), *The Landscape of Family Business*. (pp. 113–142). Cheltenham, UK: Edward Elgar Publishing Ltd.

Sorenson, R. L. (1999). Conflict management strategies used in successful family businesses. *Family Business Review, 12*(4), 325–339.

Wall, James A., & Callister, Ronda Roberts. (1995). Conflict and its management. *Journal of Management, 21*(3), 515–558.

18

CONFLICT IN FAMILY BUSINESS IN THE LIGHT OF SYSTEMS THEORY

Arist von Schlippe and Hermann Frank

Family Businesses – A "Fertile Environment" for Conflicts

Family businesses are seen as a form of company that, compared to non-family businesses, can enjoy special competitive advantages through the interplay of family and business on the one hand (Hoffmann, Hoelscher, and Sorenson 2006), but on the other hand is characterized by increased complexity (von Schlippe and Frank 2013; Tagiuri and Davis 1996) and a multitude of vulnerabilities. Constant disputes and disagreement about how the family is positioned vis-à-vis the business can be a burden on the firm, make its strategic orientation difficult and might even result in the company's demise as a family business (Grossmann and von Schlippe 2015). According to Hennerkes (2004: 58), disputes are the "greatest destroyers of value" in family businesses.

From the point of view of new systems theory, conflicts are based on communication, in fact, they are communication. Communicated contradictions can lead to internal dynamics taking on a life of their own (Luhmann 1995). How this can develop in family businesses due to their specific characteristics will be discussed in this article. The special connection between family and business entails that family businesses are in a way "a fertile environment for conflict" (Harvey and Evans 1994; von Schlippe 2014). Conflicts, of course, are by no means only negative in nature. "Cognitive conflicts," for instance, involve "tasks" (*what* is there to do?). These, and also "process conflicts" (*how* is it to be done?) can further creativity and innovation, which clearly implies positive effects (McKee et al. 2014). These types are called "functional conflicts" (though whether a conflict is functional or dysfunctional, according to systems theory, depends on the observer's perspective (Lehnert 2006).

Thus conflicts can contribute to a company finding new answers to the challenges of increasing environmental complexity. Therefore, not all types of conflict necessarily have a negative effect on performance (Eddleston, Otondo, and Kellermanns 2008; Frank et al. 2011). When the communicated contradiction is eventually replaced by communicated consensus, the mutual struggle for the best solution can be beneficial not just for the company. In many cases the people involved will also profit. For example, a person can experience growth by dealing with a tricky conflict situation constructively, negotiating compromises and finding solutions nobody had thought of before. And an organization, a family, a group can, in the wake of successfully tackled disagreements about decisions, develop a culture of solving conflicts that enable it to perform extraordinary feats und strengthens cohesion (Kellermanns and von Schlippe 2012; McKee et al. 2014).

Yet in every conflict, and thus also in family businesses, there is also the other option, i.e. the possibility of a dispute about "tasks" and "processes" taking on a life of its own and creating an emotional arena that spins out of control, so that the conflict keeps escalating (Glasl 2008; 2011). Then, relationship conflicts might come up that not only harm performance (e.g. Nosé et al. 2015) but also grow to an extent that they destroy individual relationships, whole groups, and even organizations (see McKee et al. 2014 for a comprehensive and recent overview of works on conflict in family businesses as well as its management and outcomes). Especially in the case of family conflicts, the effects can be dramatic. The map of Europe, for instance, reflects the "solutions" of such conflict situations from past centuries, in fact, the results of more or less successful succession agreements, frequently accompanied by great suffering and a massive death toll. Charlemagne's empire, for instance, fell apart more than 1,000 years ago at the hands of his grandchildren and a series of succession decisions, partly involving wars, resulted in the territory's partition. The borders running through Europe today are solidified testimony of conflicts that can be traced back to that time (Riché 1991: 201).

Conflicts in families, particularly involving inheritance, can have extreme effects. The actors' experiences, the sometimes enormous wealth involved, and the mechanisms of conflict dynamics can turn into an explosive mix. In most cases, the dynamics gain additional momentum as other persons and interests join in, which further increases social complexity and the conflict escalates even more, by for instance interrupting the contact between the parties to the conflict (e.g. through lawyers): one sticks with one's kind and in discussions with such third parties, mostly advisers, self-contained "realities" emerge, mutual interpretation patterns of the other side's activities, the reaction to which then escalates right up to a family war (Gordon and Nicholson 2008; Simon 2012a). Thus, it can be said that, as regards conflicts, family businesses are rarely "middle of the road." Either the parties manage to constructively settle their differences and disagreements or the conflict will be particularly intense and severe. After all, one possibility of conflict resolution, that in most cases, is chosen in other organizations when reaching a dead end, dismissal or resignation, is not equally available in business families: you cannot simply cancel family membership, you cannot simply leave. The working relationship can be dissolved, but shortly thereafter people will meet again at the general meeting and the conflict is perpetuated.

As there are already solid research results on the effects of various types of conflict in family businesses (for an overview see McKee et al. 2014), the following sections will look at the question which conditions there are for family businesses relating to conflict *dynamics* in relationship conflicts from a systems-theoretical perspective. So far, these aspects have not been sufficiently researched in detail. In our opinion, new systems theory (Luhmann 1995; 2000; related to family businesses, von Schlippe and Frank 2013) is particularly suitable to address the complexity of family businesses. The starting point of the analysis is hence a systems-theoretical sketch of the specific complexity of this type of business (Chapter 3), resulting from the interplay of two different systems (family and business). These often operate based on mutually exclusive rules and from these contradictory behavioural expectations paradoxes (Litz 2012) can develop (Chapter 4). Families—and hence also family businesses—are also a field of "disinhibited communication" (Luhmann 1995), which provides a multitude of options for conflicts (Chapter 5). These include e.g. psychological contracts, social comparison processes, and transgenerational stories. In combination with factors that exacerbate conflicts (Chapter 6), conflict dynamics can come into existence that cannot easily be avoided. One systems-theoretical prerequisite is that they are communicated, as not communicated intra-psychic conflict perceptions and emotions will not have any social consequences. The final item will be starting points for interrupting the conflict dynamics, without attributing causes to individual persons or groups (Chapter 7). First, though, systems theory will be presented briefly as a first step (Chapter 2).

The Theory of Social Systems as a Framework for Understanding Family Businesses

Usually, following the theory of open systems, systems are understood in a way that they "consist of individuals" (Pieper and Klein 2007: 302). Luhmann, however, proposes a radical change in defining the elements of systems and suggests rethinking the concept of system. He assumes that "social systems in general and organizations, in particular, do not consist of fixed particles (let alone 'individuals') but of *events* which disappear as they occur" (2000: 152, translated by the authors). He applies the concept of autopoiesis (Maturana and Varela 1980) to social systems. The founders of this originally biological theory had stated that autopoietic ("self-creating") systems are self-organizing, operate autonomously and operationally closed: a cell is a system not due to its parts, or to external structuring influences but only in the way which the network of the parts reproduces itself and thus generates the cell (in contrast to an allopoietic system such as thermostats etc., which cannot exist without external input and governance). By conceptualizing communication as an autopoietic system Luhmann sees the basic elements of social systems as *communicative acts*, which continuously recreate themselves in a self-organizing process (he calls this "temporalization of elements"). Thus, a social system does not consist of human beings but of communications that are related to each other in a meaningful way; the system lies in the rules of the game, not in the pawns.

Communication continuously has to find out about how to connect one communication to the next: families process communication in a totally different way than organizations. Families process mainly "*attachment communication,*" organizations rather "*decision communication*" (von Schlippe and Frank 2013). That means that the expectation of how a communicative act fits the next is totally different in a family and a business. But, in family businesses, the different logics of the systems that are involved are simultaneously present (usually three systems are differentiated: family, business, owners; see more about the "three-circle-model" later in this text). So the expectation of how a communication might be understood can easily be disappointed (e.g., father decides not to take daughter into the company, mother sees this as a sign of disapproval and neglect). Business family members never know exactly in which communication logic they are communicating at a certain point in time, because clear "context-markers" (Bateson 1972: 290) are missing: these markers usually clear up which context a person is in and which logic of communication will be active, e.g., by entering a school a teacher knows which context he/she is in from now on, which "person" he/she "is," which set of expectations has to be met by him/her. When coming home he/she intuitively "becomes another person" as the front door of the home shows clearly; you are no more a teacher but now a father/mother and/or husband/wife. But what if the home does not indicate clearly, which communication logic is active right now? What if even a board meeting doesn't prevent family communication to "break in" (see example below)? In family businesses contexts may be blurred (and so might be the context markers): it might not always be clear in which communication system you act at a particular moment (within seconds it may shift from "By the way, did you check out the options for this opportunity, as we decided yesterday?" to "Clean my glasses, honey!" – so the incident in a board meeting reported by a daughter, successor and CEO of the firm, the two sentences came one directly after another from her father who was head of the board). A communication within the context of "family" might be understood within the context of "business" – and if the persons are not aware of the difference, communicative patterns may arise which can be described as paradox or "skew"; the expectations from the family and the expectations from the business collide and bring about a certain kind of "double-bind" (Litz 2012). Instead of studying roles it may thus be interesting to study the competing system logics that govern the communication and create diffusion.

Dramatic misunderstandings can occur at these points. Since social systems consisting of communications are "invisible" and the context markers often become blurred in family businesses, logical breakdowns may occur in the various communicative connections, depending on which system logic is operating and according to which expectation structures' meaning is generated.

Communicative logics may be "mixed" when one communication is rooted within the expectation structures of the family (attachment-oriented) and the other communication in the expectation structures of the business (decision-oriented; see more details in the following chapters). Many observations of conflict-ridden events in family businesses might be explained by the fact that differing functional logics lead to a kind of "operative displacement" of communicative acts (Fuchs 1993), and then "sloping connections" (von Schlippe 2014) occur: communicative acts connect to each other within different logics, but as the communication is not aware of this "displacement," the attributional processes easily focus on "the other person" who is to be blamed. The problem is that the expectations that are implied within the system logic often create a kind of self-evidence that does not leave any question or even doubt that the communication could connect differently. If the other person behaves in a way that does not fit one's own logic, obviously he or she is "ill, bad, wicked." It is this kind of allegation of motives ("Motivunterstellung") that brings the conflict cycle into motion.

An impressive example: the massive conflict between founder and son became transparent when they found out that the father's offer ("I'd like to hand over our hotel to you, son!") had stood in the context of attachment communication, whereas the answer came in the context of decision communication. The son, then, had come up with a business plan with strategic options etc., while the father had reacted extremely angrily to the "ingratitude" of the son, who felt on his part again massively hurt by the outburst of fury of his father as he was convinced to have done "everything right." In fact, both were "right." The conflict had to do with conflicting logics, not with conflicting persons. But their attributions finally brought out the conflict.

A Special Kind of Complexity

In order to answer the question what makes particularly conflicts in family businesses so special, it is helpful to reconstruct this special type of organizations from a systems-theoretical perspective. When considering the importance of conflicts in family businesses, it is surprising how little we know about the dynamics in detail. Frank et al. (2011) in their literature review point out that we have much too little insight into the intricacies of their development and the progression of these conflicts and underline that it will take a considerable number of qualitative studies to rectify this shortcoming.

Many conflicts in family businesses can be attributed to the actors not being aware of the special complexity of their situation and the internal dynamics of conflicts, and so they simplify and ascribe things to persons in order to explain the situation. Yet the dynamics of social systems cannot be reduced to the properties of psychic and biological systems; a social system is something different than the sum of the experiences and behaviors of its participants. If this complexity now is explained by tying matters to persons, this can lead to dangerous simplifications. Allegations of motives ("You're only doing this because … !") or ascribing the causes of conflicts to individuals ("All your fault!"), though psychologically understandable, still directly propagate the conflict dynamics. They do offer the parties to the conflict a clear and simplified orientation for their actions, but at the same time greatly contribute to escalation (as naturally there is no consensus about who is now finally to blame for the conflict). This is the central proposition of our article: escalating conflicts in family businesses are related to the fact that actors do not sufficiently realize the systemic complexity of the relationships in the system and react to this by simplistically ascribing the causes of a conflict to individuals. This idea is presented in more detail below.

Family businesses have been described as particularly complex systems for a long time. The so-called "three-circle model" states that the actors are overwhelmed by the complexity of the three "circles" of family, business and ownership. Often it is – inaccurately – assumed that these three systems "overlap," that the roles the members play in these systems are blurred, and that there are "overlapping goals," with the result that stakeholder conflicts are more severe (Tagiuri and Davis 1996). But a social system is a third type of entity, detached from experience and perception of the individual persons, and this does not become clear in such "set-theoretical sketches" (Fuchs 1993). What exactly "overlapping" means and how exactly it relates to conflicts is not discussed any further. Von Schlippe und Frank (2013) show that although the three-circle model can be pragmatically suitable to superficially illustrate the complexity of the three systems' connections, the systems theory underlying the model has not been developed properly: What exactly is it that "overlaps," What does it mean to "be" in one of the three circles? Are persons moved about like "pawns"? And how exactly are the "overlaps" related to conflicts? There are doubtless a number of studies describing the particular frequency and intensity of conflicts in business families, typologizing the various forms of conflicts, listing their functions, and analyzing conflict resolution strategies (excellently reviewed in McKee et al. 2014). But the three-circle model does not provide any compelling theory how the specific conflict dynamics in family businesses arise.

In social systems theory, the three "circles" are seen as structurally coupled social systems that each operates on the basis of different logics (von Schlippe and Frank 2013). The resulting complexity can arise, amongst other things, because a multitude of conflicting expectations from the different logics of the respective systems (Lehnert 2006; Luhmann 1995) can be involved in a conflict, as each system implies a bundle of expectations. If in a particular case it is unclear which logic is currently active, it also remains unclear which behaviour expectations are adequate for a particular given situation and there are no orientation markers for communication.

In family businesses, complexity can increase quickly also for another reason. This is due to the strong emotional concern people experience and communicate with the respective topics: it is not just one's professional identity that is at risk, but that of the whole family or branch of the family; not just one person is affected, but always a whole network. It is all about central things in life, one's life's work, experiencing (in-)justice or deeply felt injustice, recognition or non-recognition of loyalty, fulfilled or unfulfilled existential expectations, questions of love and affection, and much more. This collective affectivity results in faster communicative processes with a greater intensity and also in persons that are not directly involved in the conflict quickly being drawn into it. Emotional involvement is at first an "inner-state" of a person, that is, an event that only takes place in the psychic system or the body (e.g. faster breathing). Feelings and emotions cannot be directly observed; they can only be deducted indirectly from behavior. An emotion becomes relevant for a conflict only when it is addressed by the person involved or an observer: only communicating emotions enables their relevance for the system.

It is, as already mentioned, very tempting in confrontational situations to react to complexity by using simple ways of complexity reduction. The greatest danger is to ascribe the causes of the conflict to individual persons: "It's all your fault!"; "If you would only let go, then … !"; "If you turned out to be reliable and competent, then I could … !" Many conflicts arise from such attempts to reduce complexity quickly to simple patterns: "We face a paradox here: each simplification increases complexity […] The simple is not the opposite of the complex, but a moment of coping with complexity that contributes to increased complexity" (Baecker 1999: 28, translation by the authors). To react to complexity with oversimplification is a moment of creating conflict and its chronification. Many problematic decision hubs are, over time, attributed personally: "How can she do that!," "Now he's showing his real face!" The person so addressed, however, is not going to agree with that assessment. He or she is going to react with a counter-simplification ("No, no, on the contrary, it is you!") and so conflict intensity can increase fast following the exchange of communicated contradictions. As early as 1958, Ashby (1991) pointed out that complexity should be countered with complexity ("law of requisite variety") if the aim is to avoid the paradox of increasing complexity by means of too much simplification.

Family Businesses – An "Impossible" Type of Business

Paradox, because in this type of company various social systems couple structurally which as communication systems are based on incompatible communication logics (Simon, Wimmer, and Groth 2005; Simon 2012b), i.e. because the system "family business" is a contradiction in itself. The logics of family, business, and ownership, for instance, are in many ways contradictory: family as a system relying on ties differs completely in its logic from a business, which is orientated towards functions and decisions.

- The function of communication in a family is often redundant and more directed towards a mutual confirmation of relationships.
- The logic of communication in a business is directly or indirectly geared towards decisions (Luhmann 2000).
- The specific communication that establishes the owner's system, is usually governed, formalized, and even ritualized.

So it might be important to differentiate between the functions of communication within the different systems: A kiss or a gesture indicating a family relationship do not add any "new information" to the family system, but serve as a confirmation of the relationship and a signal of belonging. In companies, such forms of shaping relationships are rather inappropriate, as only communication relevant for decision-making is deemed to be organizational communication. Thus, the statement: "I have a headache!," which in the family would prompt a considerate response, would in a company rather lead to the question: "That's a shame. Well, are you able to work or do you have to take the day off sick?" In an ownership assembly, the question again would be different: "Poor guy, but, let's see, if you can't attend the meeting, could you name a representative for you who could speak in your voice when it comes to decisions about the payout of dividends?" The major differences of the logics of these systems are shown in Table 18.1.

Table 18.1 Differences Between the Logics (Translation by Authors)

Type ⇒ Theme ⇓	System "Family"	System "Business"	System "Shareholders"
Membership logic	Closely related persons of all ages	Usually not related persons that fulfil specific qualification demands	In family businesses: relatives (close or distantly related)
Access and exit: How to enter and leave?	Access by birth, marriage, adoption. Exit in principle not possible.	Access by getting the job, entering the company. Exit possible at any time, depending on the contract.	Access by getting/ inheriting property. Exit by sale.
Centre of communication	Confirmation of bonding and attachment (logic of inclusion)	Company decisions (logic of selectivity)	Ownership decisions (logics of law)
Communication paths	Less formal, oral, less hierarchized	Formal, written, hierarchized	Formal, written, protocols
Making decisions	Many chances for negotiation, agreement as goal, seniority or consensus	Little room for negotiation, hierarchical, clarity of decision as goal	Rather hierarchical, majority votes
What/who is important?	The single person (not exchangeable)	Function, competence (person is exchangeable)	Amount of shares, function
"Currency" that is exchanged	Love, attachment, loyalty	Work/effort, career, power	Shares, authority qua competence, seniority etc.
Adequate compensation	Recognition, appreciation, gratitude; long-term (possibly decades)	Salary, short-term (by end of month), appreciation important, but not enforceable	Regular dividend; appreciation value
Logic of justice	Equality: Everybody gets the same (or what he/she needs)	Inequality: Position and salary according to effort, competence	(a) Equal in information (b) Not equal in voice: according to shares

Source: von Schlippe 2014, 32–33

The form of paradox can be illustrated as follows:

- In family businesses, we find system logics and expectation structures that contradict each other.
- The expectation resulting from the bonding logic can be termed: "We are a family!" It follows the logic of inclusion: we are making sure that the ties between the members are maintained and that no one is excluded etc.
- This is in contrast to the expectation from the decision logic: "We are a circle of shareholders, in other words: an organization!" This is implied by the logic of selectivity: we are making sure the company has a competent circle of owners, that always the best person is selected, that decision-making is possible etc.

- At the same time, there is the tertiary rule: "Don't leave the playing field!"
- All this constitutes the formal prerequisites for a paradox double bind (Bateson 1972; Litz 2012).

The logics, which are present simultaneously, are not compatible. As you cannot not act (Watzlawick, Beavin, and Jackson 1969), one communication necessarily follows another. This can lead to communicative situations that can be called paradoxical. A series of such paradox dynamics in family businesses has been described in the literature. These cannot be presented here in detail (see Simon et al. 2005; Wimmer et al. 2005; Brundin and Härtel 2014; Litz 2012; Zellweger 2014). Rather, the discussion will focus on how in family businesses conflict-creating mechanisms build on these paradoxes and how conflicts, once they have emerged, can be communicatively advanced.

Social Systems are "Invisible"

In Chapter 2 we already discussed the basic difference the theory of social systems (also "new systems theory") by Niklas Luhmann (e.g. 1968; 1995; 2000) posits in comparison to other systems theories: Social systems are not designed on the basis of living systems (human beings, individuals), they rather consist of "temporalized elements," i.e. individual communications that all meaningfully connect to each other (Luhmann 1995; 2000). Once a communication comes into existence it is already gone. These are "invisible" meaning systems, which can be defined by how one communication connects to another. Seen like this, a "system" is a series of communications and the way they connect to each other is always determined by a specific logic. This logic provides the framework for how to understand and classify a communication (von Schlippe and Frank 2013): in a university context, for example, things are communicated differently than in a family context or the context of a fleeting interaction system that briefly emerges down the pub of an evening. The same words can assume a different meaning, depending on the context. Normally, "context markers" (see Chapter 2) help to keep the system logics apart. Yet in "poly-contextual inter-system relations" this orientation easily gets lost (Vogd 2013); the actors move in different contexts simultaneously, which cannot always easily be differentiated. So it becomes understandable that it is rather confusing to talk about something "overlapping" or "intersecting" in family businesses. It is the logics that determine the communication systems and in the case of family businesses they happen to be present and active simultaneously. Admittedly, it is theoretically possible to fix the communication context, i.e. to explicitly select "family communication," for instance, but this requires a great deal of awareness reflecting on the differences between social systems. If there are no clear context markers, it is never quite certain which context is activated at any given moment (Jansen, von Schlippe, and Vogd 2015; Vogd 2013); at the breakfast table company communication will suddenly be activated, or family communication can intercede in the company. The people involved often do not realize which of the logics is currently "active" ("Am I talking as a father or a businessman?" – "Am I being addressed as daughter or as successor?"). Thus, they frequently encounter dilemmas they cannot escape from easily or at all. A decision that is correct and appropriate in the context of the company, such as denying a descendant a top-management position, in the context and logic of the family looks like a father's/mothers "betrayal" of a son/daughter, after all, it is the parents' task to provide the best for their children. Yet this is exactly what the logic of the business forbids, as it forces people to act not out of love for their children but according to the logic of the system "business."

Paradoxes and Conflicts

The parallel existence of incompatible behavior expectations is the basis for experiencing para-doxes, or, to be more exact, pragmatic paradoxes[1] (Watzlawick et al. 1969). As the system logics cannot be separated as clearly as in other contexts, in family businesses frequently paradoxical situations arise, where it comes to "skewed connections": one communication is connected in the logic of another system (in a way, the "three-circle model" oscillates constantly and has to be balanced anew in every communication). Conflicts can arise if the people involved are not aware of this complexity. This is because the conflict communication, at the level of psychic systems, is experienced as direct causality; any opponent is "wrong" (or stupid, ill or evil – it is usually one of these three explanations, see von Schlippe 2014). Only from a distance can the paradox be detected, but the more a person is involved in the conflict, the more stressful it is, the less capable he or she is to watch the goings-on from a "higher level." In conflicts, people usually automatically use themselves as a reference point, they feel their own hurt and it is almost "nat-ural" to see the other person as the culprit causing the hurt, who has to be resisted. At this point, mechanisms start to come into play that, if not reflected upon and balanced out, can massively further the escalation of the conflict.

As family businesses are often afraid of conflicts and the related "emotional messiness" (Brundin and Sharma 2012), communication by means of emotions is frequently suppressed. This does not mean, though, that feelings do not enter communication; non-verbal signs are "read," (mis-)interpreted, exchanged with others ("Did you see the face she made?"). At the same time, there can be the expectation in business families that communication should be effected by means of emotions. When the repressed feelings later become active in communi-cation and relevant for the system, rapidly escalating conflicts can be the result that use feelings as the central medium of communication and create specific communication patterns. In this connection, the type of emotion also plays a part.

Family Businesses as "Emotional Arenas"

Family as a Place of "Disinhibited Communication"

Families are seen as "intimate relationship systems" (von Schlippe and Schneewind 2014). Potentially, any and all human topics can be discussed here, at least in principle anything can be addressed. The option available in a company, for instance, to reject an emotionally laden question with a statement like: "Here's not the place for this!," is not available in a family in the "disinhibited communication" framework (Luhmann 1995). In a company, more restric-tive manners determine communicative events. This means that the two systems deal very differently with escalation and the regulation of agitation. While the "disinhibited disputes" in the family can also be controlled spontaneously and intuitively by using appropriate forms of tension control (a tearful embrace following a row, a tentative kiss or a deliberate sulk, angrily keeping one's distance for a lengthy period of time etc.), in organizations these regulations are handled much more formally. Neither is particular physical closeness common to release tensions, nor is keeping your distance possible for long in a work context. In the "paradox space in between" family and business logic, the forms of escalation and tension control of the two systems can now combine in such a way that the people involved get stuck in ongoing tension that is connected with high emotionality (Brundin and Härtel 2014). This increases the probability of a "malign clinch" (Stierlin 2005). From a systems-theoretical point of view, it is once more important for the following sections that it is not states of awareness that are of interest, but communication, when it comes to understanding conflicts; only when a feeling becomes communication does it become relevant in the social system. The feeling of disappointment becomes meaningful only when it becomes part of the communication: "I am disappointed!" The systems-theoretical definition of communication is not based on a transmission model with sender, receiver and information to be transmitted, but on a process of continuous selection of information, utterance and understanding. Communication is a continuing chain of selections; information is selected, a message is opted for (utterance) and from all options the one variant is chosen that is then used for connecting to the communication. "Understanding," by the way, does not mean "understanding correctly"; in the tripartite selection process, also misunderstandings and dissent are included and contribute towards the system's autopoiesis (Luhmann 1995; Lehnert 2006). Written communication as an important type of communication for most social systems, especially organizations, does not require the presence of persons (interactions systems). In the case of written communication the interactional concurrence is dispersed and written communication (e.g. a family constitution) may have a stronger impact on the selection of information than oral communication. Furthermore, implicit knowledge may exert influence on the selection of information, utterance, and understanding. This is valid for all deliberations in the following sections. Even if a person sulks and remains silent, the silence serves as the continuation of the communication as long as it is interpreted as communication (Luhmann and Fuchs 1989), although communication does not necessarily require a reaction.

Psychological Contracts

The concept of "psychological contracts" suggested by Rousseau (Robinson and Rousseau 1994; Rousseau 1989) was taken up in family business research in order to understand the "emotional messiness" and the turbulences frequently arising in business families (Brundin and Härtel 2014; Brundin and Sharma 2012). Psychological contracts describe the self-evident und emotionally highly charged expectations from exchange agreements between two parties that both refer to a kind of promise. This promise is rarely made explicitly, often through verbal insinuation, but often also non-verbally, by means of actions, signals and symbols, and confirmed through long-term, ongoing practice. The promise rests on the expectation that both sides fulfil their part. On the basis of these expectations, a person starts behaving in line with the promise (a child, for instance starts to study business against her vocation because she assumes to get into the company at some point). In many cases the background for such a promise is a deeply felt loyalty, where the assumption is that the other person also feels the same and, predominantly, that one's own commitment is perceived as an expression of this loyalty by the other. However, if a person has entered into a psychological contract in the family's bonding logic ("I am loyal, I will join the company!"), but the other person perceives this following the family's decision logic ("Let's see, whether you're sufficiently qualified. I will make a definite decision later!"), such a contract can be breached at some critical points. In this context, Kaye describes the "successor's trap" the child can fall into; out of natural expectation and because of her own commitment, studies and career planning are oriented towards the family business without explicitly addressing this; alternative offers are rejected, until in middle age, and sometimes only when the last will is revealed, there is the realization that one's own expectations do not match the perceptions of the other party (Kaye 1996).

Social Comparison Processes

The theory of social comparison processes (e.g. Festinger, Torrey, and Willermann 1954) assumes that people assess their self-esteem and the status they believe they have by comparing themselves with personalities they feel close to in respect of aspects they personally deem important. This universal mechanism can convey problematic dynamics in business families, if, for example, a person's position in the family is made dependent on whether she is treated "completely equally" to a sibling. Who has "more," who has "less" – and who therefore receives more or less recognition by the parents, can play a big role in disputes. This may result in difficult situations, if e.g. the business logic calls for a clear difference in how the children are treated, while the family logic demands equality (one of the central paradoxes). In this case, minimal differences can be fought over acrimoniously.

The Logic of Justice and Family-Internal Settlement Systems

Social comparison processes are closely connected with perceptions of justice, a crucial item in business families. A violated sense of justice is generally seen as a conflict driver; a violated normative expectation of how we ourselves or someone else should be treated can result in strong perceptions of indignation (Montada 2003). This indignation can be seen as a "guiding indicator for social conflicts"; ultimately, what underlies every conflict is the feeling that there has been a great injustice that has to be made up for.

In families—and this makes the topic so complicated—there are very individual, different settlement systems that underlie all that what we perceive as "just" or "unjust" (Boszormenyi-Nagy and Spark 1973; Stierlin 2005). In regard to many aspects, members of a social system keep something like a "justice ledger," where the awareness of fairness and appropriateness is "recorded," for instance, regarding our own or others' performance, merits etc. In this "internal account," people assess themselves in comparison to those close to them. As experience has shown, people here normally make the mistake to systematically assess their own performance in too positive a manner (Bruner 1992), and therefore conflicts and feelings of indignation can be expected particularly frequently in families. In business families these processes are even multiplied like through a "magnifying glass," as the question of a family member's "merits" involves not just recognition and appreciation, but also the materialized form of this in the form of an inheritance, a large share of the wealth, or influence in the company. The "great binding effect of such a hoped for or promised inheritance" (Simon 2012b) is in any case directly related to these processes; the feeling to be completely and utterly tied to the family is not exactly a rarity in business families. Solving the conflict by simply withdrawing from close relatives one feels disappointed or betrayed by is not an easily available option.

Us Against Them

A frequently proven socio-psychological mechanism refers to inter-group effects. Within a short time, communication patterns can evolve between groups that facilitate intense conflicts; the respective other side is step-by-step described in more negative terms and at the same time one's own group is idealized. This is particularly true if the two groups are in a competitive relationship. In order to produce these effects, it is sufficient to establish two groups by drawing an arbitrary boundary (for example, in a summer camp for children) and have them compete: this rapidly creates negative stereotypes that might even lead to bitter hostility (Sherif 1966). This phenomenon can become important in business families if the organizational form of "tribal business" has been chosen, if the funder's decision to distribute his inheritance equally between his three or four children but not to split this share any further results in a structure in which the sub-families of the children and grandchildren are tied together as groups. In these cases, dynamics can evolve where the "vertical loyalty" (Stierlin 2005) to the founder slowly fades, which in the first generation after the founder usually is still very strong and so helps to dampen conflicts ("Dad wouldn't have wanted that, let's be friends!"). In later generations, "horizontal loyalty" predominates and one's own sub-group ("us") is sharply set apart from that of the others ("them") and the interests of one's own group are increasingly put before those of the whole. In business families this can often be seen with married couples, whose loyalty to the extended family is naturally less pronounced than that to their own nuclear family. In the latter, sentiment against the larger family and "the others" can then build up ("Why do you put up with that!") that promotes tribal conflicts.

Transgenerational Stories

The communicated sentiments discussed in the previous two sections find their continuation when experiences are passed on to the next generation. Again, this is not specific to business families, but stories can be particularly important for these families as the company remains present in the family as a constant factor through the generations and keeps the families of estranged siblings or cousins together for a very long time, while other families at some point cannot even remember their ever more distant relatives. In business families people constantly encounter each other, in shareholder and board meetings, and old stories about (in)justice, (betrayed) loyalty, wounded honor etc. are passed on or are refreshed. The transgenerational life's work of a family business can be a source of positive stories that convey identity, but equally, it can perpetuate existing conflicts, if in themselves conclusive and consistent, but one-sided, world views are passed on in the extended business family across generations in the form of competing stories (Zwack and von Schlippe 2012).

Conflict Aggravation

The mechanisms described above are typical conditions found at the start of conflicts, they apply universally, but in family businesses they are encouraged by the specific paradox constellation of that type of business. They can also easily escalate into "family wars" (Gordon and Nicholson 2008). To understand these, the interaction of the above-mentioned entry conditions with typical psychological conflict mechanisms has to be taken into account, which apply when a conflict (as the negation of a negation; Simon 2012a) has started. These mechanisms then propel an escalation and chronify the conflict, which quickly turns into an autonomous "system within the system." These mechanisms are described one by one below, although in many cases they obviously occur at the same time and often are interwoven. What has to be kept in mind is that not only paradoxes as features of the system of family business but also persons can shape conflict-related communicative patterns and content, especially if social systems (for want of pronounced structures) enable individual persons to exert a massive influence on the course of conflicts.

The Fundamental Attribution Error

An effect proven in countless psychological studies is the specific tendency to perceive conflict situations in an extremely distorted manner, a phenomenon also known as "correspondence bias" (Gilbert and Malone 1995). One's own position and even one's own aggressive behavior are, quite in contrast to those of the counterparty, seen as honorable, as they are "only" a counter-reaction and a measure of self-defence that has to be taken in order to end the conflict once and for all. Positions and actions of the other party or parties, on the other hand, are seen as an expression of their ill will. Thus, the process of reciprocal escalation is subjectively perceived as one-sided; *they* escalate, *we* only react. As this assumption is made on both sides, this attribution error takes them ever further into the conflict: both sides "defend" themselves against the "evil" opponent and everybody becomes blind to their own part in the conflict dynamics. Both sides do not only feel justified but forced to use ever stronger means to end the conflict.

Hostile Attributional Bias

Closely connected to the perception pattern just mentioned is a second factor, and both together massively intensify the conflict dynamics. This mechanism, called "hostile attributional bias," was originally found in highly aggressive children; these interpret a neutral or even friendly offer to interact as hostile and react accordingly, negatively (Dodge 2006). Apparently a situation of mutual mistrust creates an expectation structure (in a way as a premise for communication), through which this mistrust constantly feeds on itself and so establishes its own, negative conditions for reproductions; if you are convinced the other party wishes you harm, you will consequently show a negative reaction, and the other side might not keep up the originally friendly offer. If this happens, the moments – which occur in every conflict – where one side is more conciliatory and takes careful steps in that direction, are not perceived as such. On the contrary, such offers might even be rejected derisively ("Now they're trying softly-softly; well, not on my watch!"). The other side will then, naturally, feel particularly aggrieved and possibly reacts with further escalation (which then confirms the perception pattern: "I knew it, that was just pretend, now they show their true face!"). It is not easy to detect and see through this mechanism, in order to follow up a rejected offer for de-escalation with another one (which then might circumvent the hostile attribution bias).

The patterns described above strongly further the development of an escalating conflict system; where the fundamental attribution error leads into the conflict, in the next step, the hostile bias makes it impossible to find a way out of escalation once it has been set in motion (Omer, Alon, and von Schlippe 2007).

Losing the Ability to Adopt Perspectives and Demonization

Increasingly, the persons involved thus get tangled up in a vicious circle, in which they change without noticing it. Feelings of wounded honor, a hurt sense of justice, moral indignation, and at the same time helplessness can all result in a specific way of thinking, experiencing and communicating that is characterized by an increasing narrowing of one's field of vision, demonizing descriptions of the other side, and a loss of the ability to adopt different perspectives, of empathy, and of the ability for self-control. Under the tension of a conflict the ability to emphasize with the other person, to see things from his/her perspective, gradually disappears and the structures of thinking begin to match those of feeling (Ciompi 2005;

Simon 2012a). One's own point of reference becomes absolute, the idea that someone else also might feel hurt or treated unjustly gets lost. In communication, people resort to simplified differentiations and all shades and nuances are gone, now it is 'black or white,' 'all or nothing,' 'friend or foe.'

In this change of attention focus, there is also a change in the sense of time (Simon 2012a), it is the present alone that counts. Step by step a "demonized mindset" (Omer et al. 2007) emerges, the other person/side is increasingly described in a totally negative manner. "Demonic narratives" enter the communication, where the other party is depicted as (completely and utterly) evil and thus turns into a "monster" that has to be defeated. Eventually, any means is justified, which at high levels of escalation might even include the (economic or even physical) destruction of the other party. "Demonized zones" (Glasl 2008; 2011) spring into existence, and actions are taken without assuming any responsibility ("Now this is his own bloody fault!"), involving highly destructive processes.

Internal Dynamics of the Conflict: The Conflict as "Parasite"

From a certain point onwards, the internal dynamics of escalating processes increasingly start to elude the actors. In this connection, Luhmann (1995) talks about conflicts as "parasitic social systems." Such a social system intrudes upon an existing communication structure and establishes its own conflict logic. The original communication system is occupied by the conflict and is turned into a new, "highly integrated" communication system with often very predictable expectation structures, where the behavioral options of everybody involved are narrowed down enormously: the statement of one party is immediately followed by a statement from the other, frequently it is already "known" what the other party is going to say. The parties have less and less room for their communicative reactions, the conflict logic can be less and less influenced from outside and forces its own laws onto the parties. At some point it becomes impossible to control the goings-on; "The conflict has got us" (Glasl 2011). Without external support, there is no solution anymore (although conflict counsellors also know how difficult it is to gain access to such highly integrated social systems).

In family businesses this process often takes the form of disputes being avoided for a long time out of the sheer fear of conflicts. Archetypically, the conflict starts with occasional contradictory communication, and over time stable expectation structures focused on dissent develop (by means of the mechanisms described). The content dimension described at the beginning (task or process conflicts) more and more retreats into the background, until finally the focus is exclusively on the social dimension as a pure relationship conflict (Lehnert 2006; Simon 2012a). In the worst case, this process includes the conflicting parties' mutual way into the abyss (Glasl 2008; 2011). This can be the moment where mediation becomes the only option to prevent the destruction of company assets.

Conclusion: Intervention Focus "Consciousness Raising"

All mechanisms described so far are probably phylogenetically predetermined inside us (Riedl 1981). In the course of the conflict they make sure that we mobilize our readiness to fight or flee, and the conflict topics themselves become secondary. In moments of imminent threat from the environments in which these patterns once evolved, this may have been appropriate. In highly complex social situations today, however, they are counter-productive or even dangerous, as they create exceptional situations for the actors that might promote the chronification of conflict systems as soon as these exceptional situations have a communicative effect.

Non-communicated, psychic exceptional situations will not have any social consequences. Even though they are important for the individual they are not in the focus of social systems theory. But once they are communicated, they can still be ignored or they could be answered. While many social systems try to dismiss the communication of conflict-related emotions, especially family businesses or business families are exposed to a greater risk of establishing their own, typical communication patterns as a response to conflict-related, communicated emotions, which rapidly create their own structures with a characteristic development logic and dynamics (Frank et al. 2011). In this connection, also individual persons (for example because of their formal and/or informal power) can gain great influence over these conflict systems. But what basal means of intervention are available to us, apart from well-known conflict management strategies (Eddleston et al. 2008; Kellermanns and von Schlippe 2012; McKee et al. 2014; von Schlippe 2014) and preventive measures such as family governance (Lueger and Frank 2015; Suess 2014) or legal procedures (Fabis 2009; Neuvians 2011)? The major focus from the systems-theoretical perspective assumed here is on avoiding the attribution of reasons for the conflict to individuals, i.e. allegations of motives and person-related attributions (Frank et al. 2011), and on perceiving paradoxes and conflicts as a mutual challenge and task.

At the heart of these efforts to contain already existing conflicts there is "consciousness raising" at the family level and, subsequently, an individual level (Harvey and Evans 1994). The idea is to see through the mechanisms and rules underlying the family system and to understand the dynamics this system is subject to. This includes accepting the different system logics of family, business and ownership, and to balance these in situations when decisions are made. Shared knowledge of these fields of tension can help to keep a certain distance. Depending on the degree of escalation, more or less pronounced external support or even massive intervention will be required. What has proven effective is to properly reflect on the specific initial conditions of family business conflicts and the communication and attribution patterns that have emerged in the course of the conflict. Once the other person is not perceived as an "adversary" anymore, but realization has set in that the real "adversary" is the paradox of the family business, it can become possible to dissolve the highly integrated conflict system carefully. The opponents can realize that they are allies that together might be able to face the challenge posed by this "impossible type of company" that has led them into a debilitating conflict system. It can also be helpful to understand that often in these conflicts the values of all conflict parties are violated, but that these values are rooted in different reference systems and logics. While one party to the conflict is deeply committed to the family in its values, the other party's values might rather be closely connected to the business. If these structures are understood properly, patterns of hostile allegations of motives can be broken and people may be prepared to see the other side's motives as honorable and comprehensible, rather than as malicious. This is an important prerequisite to return to a cooperative state. After all, the essential element that has to be regained is trust—and this means to take the risk to "assume the other party has good intentions" (Luhmann 1968)—and that in a social situation where you can never be absolutely sure what the other one "really" thinks. An intervention focus primarily on changing communication patterns and their underlying rules, that is away from assigning blame to persons or groups, does not only relieve the pressure on the people involved, but also provides a new approach towards understanding one's own family and their position towards the family business. Social systems depend on the structural coupling with psychic systems and people. If the insights generated in the course of reflexion processes accepted as information by a psychic system, i.e. do they become conscious, they can remain there as thoughts or, by means of communication, decisively contribute towards the changes in expectation structures of social (conflict) systems.

Note

1 A "semantic paradox" is a logical contradiction ("The next sentence is wrong!" – "The previous sentence is right!"). These paradoxes are confusing but not relevant for our behavior. Pragmatic paradoxes, on the other hand, emerge when two incompatible behavior expectations are communicated, ("Tell me that you love me! But tell me because you want to, voluntarily, not because I ask you to!"). The parallel existence of two contradictory behavior expectations paralyzes all actions. In family businesses it is possible for the two expectations "family" and "business" to mutually exclude each other.

References

Ashby, W. R. (1991) 'Requisite variety and its implications for the control of complex systems,' in: Klir, G. J. (ed.) *Facets of Systems Science,* New York: Springer Science and Business Media, 405–17.

Baecker, D. (1999) *Organisation als System,* Frankfurt: Suhrkamp.

Bateson, G. (1972) *Steps to an Ecology of Mind,* New York: Ballantine Books.

Boszormenyi-Nagy, I., & Spark, G. (1973). *Invisible loyalties: Reciprocity in intergenerational family therapy.* New York: Harper & Row.

Brundin, E., and C. E. J. Härtel (2014) 'Emotions in family firms,' in: Melin, L., Nordqvist, M., and Sharma, P. (eds.) *The SAGE Handbook of Family Business,* Los Angeles, London: SAGE Publications, 529–48.

Brundin, E., and P. Sharma (2012) 'Love, hate, and desire: The role of emotional messiness in the business family,' in: Carsrud, A. L., and Brännback, M. (eds.) *Understanding Family Business. Undiscovered Approaches, Unique Perspectives, and Neglected Topics,* New York: Springer, 55–71.

Bruner, J. (1992). *Acts of meaning.* Cambridge, Mass.: Harvard University Press.

Ciompi, L. (2005) *Die emotionalen Grundlagen des Denkens,* Göttingen: Vandenhoeck & Ruprecht.

Coyle-Shapiro, J. A.-M., and M.-R. Parzefall (2008) 'Psychological contracts,' in: Cooper, C. L., and Barling, J. (eds.) *The SAGE Handbook of Organizational Behavior,* London: SAGE Publications, 17–34.

Dodge, K. A. (2006) 'Translational science in action: Hostile attributional style and the development of aggressive behavior problems,' *Development and Psychopathology,* 18: 791–814.

Eddleston, K. A., R. F. Otondo, and F. W. Kellermanns (2008) 'Conflict, participative decision-making, and generational ownership dispersion: A Multilevel Analysis,' *Journal of Small Business Management,* 46: 456–84.

Fabis, F. G. (2009) *Gesellschafterkonflikte in Familienunternehmen. Vermeidungs- und Lösungsstrategien auf gesellschaftsvertraglicher und individualvertraglicher Ebene,* Lohmar: Eul.

Festinger, L., J. Torrey, and B. Willermann (1954) 'Self-evaluation as a function of attraction to the group,' *Human Relations,* 7: 161–74.

Frank, H., A. Kessler, L. Nosé, and D. Suchy (2011) 'Conflicts in family firms: State of the art and perspectives for future research,' *Journal of Family Business Management,* 1: 130–53.

Fuchs, P. (1993) *Moderne Kommunikation: zur Theorie des operativen Displacements,* Frankfurt: Suhrkamp.

Gilbert, D. T., and P. S. Malone (1995) 'The Correspondence Biasc, *Psychological Bulletin,'* 117: 21–38.

Gimeno, A., G. Baulenas, and J. Coma-Cros (2010) *Family Business Models: Practical Solutions for the Family Business,* Basingstoke: Palgrave.

Glasl, F. (2008) 'Enriching Conflict Diagnosis and Strategies for Social Change: A Closer Look at Conflict Dynamics. Berghof Handbook Dialogue No. 6,' Berghof center for constructive conflict management. http://www.berghof-handbook.net.

Glasl, F. (2011) *Selbsthilfe in Konflikten.* 6th ed. Stuttgart/Bern: Haupt.

Gordon, G., and N. Nicholson (2008) *Family Wars: Classic Conflicts in Family Business and How to Deal with Them,* London: Kogan.

Grossmann, S., and A. von Schlippe (2015) 'Family Businesses: Fertile Environments for Conflict,' *Journal of Family Business Management,* 5(2): 294–314.

Harvey, M., and R. E. Evans (1994) 'Family business and multiple levels of conflict,' *Family Business Review,* 7: 331–48.

Hennerkes, B.-H. (2004) *Die Familie und ihr Unternehmen. Strategie, Liquidität, Kontrolle,* Frankfurt: Campus.

Hoffmann, J., M. Hoelscher, and R. L. Sorenson (2006) 'Achieving sustained competitive advantage: A family capital theory,' *Family Business Review,* 19: 135–45.

Jansen, T., Schlippe, A.v., Vogd, W. (2015) Contextural Analysis—A Proposal for Reconstructive Social Research in Organisational Contexts. *Forum Qualitative Research* 16(1) (E-Journal) http://nbn-resolving. de/urn:nbn:de:0114-fqs150141.

Kaye, K. (1996) 'When the family business is a sickness,' *Family Business Review*, 9: 347–68.

Kellermanns, F.W., and A. von Schlippe (2012) 'Konflikte in Familie und Unternehmen erkennen, managen und vermeiden,' in: Koeberle-Schmidt, A., Fahrion, H.-J., and Witt, P. (eds.) *Family Business Governance*, Berlin: Erich Schmidt, 429–41.

Lehnert, M. (2006) *Gibt es Konflikte? Eine systemtheoretische Betrachtung*, Heidelberg: Carl Auer Systeme.

Litz, R. A. (2012) 'Double roles, double binds? Double bind theory and family business research,' in: Carsrud, A. L., and Brännback, M. (eds.) *Understanding Family Business: Unique Perspectives, Neglected Topics, and Undiscovered Approaches,* Heidelberg: Springer, 115–32.

Lueger, M., and H. Frank (eds.) (2015) *Zukunftssicherung für Familienunternehmen. Good Practice Fallanalysen zur Family Governance,* Wien: Facultas.

Luhmann, N. (1968) *Vertrauen. Ein Mechanismus der Reduktion sozialer Komplexität*, Stuttgart: Lucius & Lucius.

Luhmann, N. (1995) *Social Systems*, Stanford, CA: Stanford University Press.

Luhmann, N. (2000) *Organisation und Entscheidung*, Wiesbaden: Westdeutscher Verlag.

Luhmann, N., and P. Fuchs (1989) *Reden und Schweigen*, Frankfurt: Suhrkamp.

Maturana, H. R., and F. J. Varela (1980) *Autopoiesis and Cognition*, Boston, MA: Riedel.

McKee, D'L., T. M. Madden, F.W. Kellermanns, and K. A. Eddleston (2014) 'Conflicts in family firms: The good and the bad,' in: Melin, L., Nordqvist, M., and Sharma, P. (eds.) *The SAGE Handbook of Family Business,* Los Angeles, London: SAGE Publications, 514–28.

Montada, L. (2003) 'Justice, equity, and fairness in human relations,' in: Millon, T. J., and Lerner, M. J. (eds.) *Handbook of Psychology.* Vol. 5. Hoboken, NJ: Wiley-Blackwell, 537–68.

Neuvians, N. (2011). *Mediation in Familienunternehmen. Chancen und Grenzen*, Wiesbaden: Gabler.

Nosé, L., C. Korunka, H. Frank, and S. M. Danes (2015) 'Decreasing the effects of relationship conflict on family businesses: The moderating role of family climate,' *Journal of Family Issues.* doi:10.1177/0192513X15573869

Omer, H., N. Alon, and A. von Schlippe (2007) *Feindbilder. Psychologie der Dämonisierung*, Göttingen: Vandenhoeck & Ruprecht.

Pieper, T. M., and S. B. Klein (2007) 'The bulleye: A systems approach to modeling family firms,' *Family Business Review*, XX: 301–19.

Riché, P. (1991) *Die Karolinger. Eine Familie formt Europa*, München: DVA Deutsche Verlagsanstalt.

Riedl, R. (1981) 'Die Folgen des Ursachendenkens,' in: Watzlawick, P. (ed.) *Die erfundene Wirklichkeit*, München: Piper, 67–90.

Robinson, S. L., and D. M. Rousseau (1994) 'Violating the psychological contract: Not the exception but the norm,' *Journal of Organizational Behavior*, 15: 249–59.

Rousseau, D. M. (1989) 'Psychological and implied contracts in organizations,' *Employee Responsibilities and Rights Journal*, 2: 121–39.

von Schlippe, A. (2014) *Das kommt in den besten Familien vor. Systemische Konfliktberatung in Familien und Familienunternehmen*, Stuttgart: Concadora.

von Schlippe, A., and H. Frank (2013) 'The theory of social systems as a framework for understanding family businesses,' *Family Relations,* 62: 384–98.

von Schlippe, A., and K. A. Schneewind (2014) 'Theories from family psychology and family therapy,' in: Melin, L., Nordqvist, M. and Sharma, P. (eds.) *The SAGE Handbook of Family Business Research,* Los Angeles, London: SAGE Publications, 47–65.

Sherif, M. (1966) *In Common Predicament: Social Psychology of Intergroup Conflict and Cooperation*, Boston, MA: Houghton Mifflin.

Simon, F. B. (2012a) *Einführung in die Systemtheorie des Konflikts.* 2nd ed. Heidelberg: Carl Auer Systeme.

Simon, F. B. (2012b) *Einführung in die Theorie des Familienunternehmens*, Heidelberg: Carl Auer Systeme.

Simon, F. B., R. Wimmer, and T. Groth (2005) *Mehr-Generationen-Familienunternehmen*, Heidelberg: Carl Auer Systeme.

Stierlin, H. (2005) *Gerechtigkeit in nahen Beziehungen*, Heidelberg: Carl Auer Systeme.

Suess, J. (2014) 'Family Governance: Literature review and the development of a conceptual model,' *Journal of Family Business Strategy*, 5: 138–55.

Tagiuri, R., and J. A. Davis (1996) 'Bivalent attributes of the family firm,' *Family Business Review,* 9: 199–208.

Vogd, W. (2013) 'Polykontexturalität: Die Erforschung komplexer systemischer Zusammenhänge in Theorie und Praxis,' *Familiendynamik,* 38: 32–41.

Watzlawick, P., J. H. Beavin, and D. D. Jackson (1969) *Menschliche Kommunikation,* Bern: Huber.

Wimmer, R., E. Domayer, M. Oswald, and G. Vater (2005) *Familienunternehmen - Auslaufmodell oder Erfolgstyp?* 2nd ed. Wiesbaden: Gabler.

Zellweger, T. (2014) 'Toward a paradox perspective of family firms: The moderating role of collective mindfulness in controlling families,' in: Melin, L., Nordqvist, M., and Sharma, P. (eds.) *The SAGE Handbook of Family Business,* Los Angeles, London: SAGE Publications, 648–55.

Zwack, M., and A. von Schlippe (2012) 'Eine kurze Geschichte zur Bedeutung von Geschichten in Organisationen,' *Systeme,* 26(1): 23–39.

19

MORE THAN A FEELING

The Promise of Experimental Approaches for Building Affective and Cognitive Microfoundations of Family Firm Behavior

David S. Jiang and Timothy P. Munyon

Introduction

"Do family firms really behave differently from nonfamily firms? If so, how and why are they different?" (Chrisman Chua & Sharma 2005, 567). Family firm scholars have long argued that family involvement and behavior in the firm leads family firms to have unique strategic outcomes relative to their nonfamily counterparts. Overlapping family and firm systems are thought to introduce family members' emotions and goals into management, enabling family firms' unique outcomes (Gómez-Mejía, Cruz, Berrone, & Castro, 2011). Despite intentions to integrate family and firm assumptions, family firm research has traditionally focused on family firms' unique strategic outcomes at the expense of not fully understanding the family members' cognitions, emotions, goals, and behaviors that drive them. Indeed, family firm research often: (1) builds broad assumptions about how structural aspects of the family, such as the number of family members in the firm or the number of generations involved in the firm, will impact strategic and firm-level outcomes and (2) uses distal firm-level proxies to latently measure family behavior (Berrone Cruz & Gómez-Mejía 2012; Morris & Kellermanns 2013). Consequently, the family firm literature's microfoundations, which we characterize as the family firm members' affective, cognitive, and behavioral factors that drive unique family firm outcomes, remain unnaturally constricted and generally untested.

There have been several calls for research to better understand the microfoundations of family firms (Berrone et al. 2012; Morris & Kellermanns, 2013; Pieper, 2010; Sharma, 2004). However, these calls often go unanswered because family firm scholarship lacks appropriate methodological precedent for capturing family emotions, cognitions, goals, and behaviors in family firm environments (Berrone et al. 2012; Kellermanns Dibrell & Cruz 2014; Morris & Kellermanns 2013). Here, recognizing that family firm assumptions are often inherently psychological in nature (Pieper, 2010), we argue that experimental approaches, especially when combined with other methods, can help build and extend research on family firm microfoundations. Psychological scholarship employing experiments finds that different contexts can change the nature and direction of expected relationships (Johns 2006; Taylor & Fiske 1978). With family firm research rarely focusing on how psychological factors and contexts within family firms drive behavior (Pieper 2010), we believe that experimental approaches can, therefore, play a vital role in opening new impactful avenues for family firm scholarship to explore.

Through our efforts, we hope that experimental approaches provide methodological tools that can help move research beyond a dichotomous view of family firms vs. nonfamily firms to an understanding of heterogeneity within and between family firms. However, we recognize that we cannot cover all of the necessary theoretical and methodological ground needed for this venture into the psychological microfoundations of family firm behavior within the page limits of this chapter. Therefore, we have purposefully focused on methodological concerns, recognizing that scholars can use their own theories to specify interesting relationships in experiments that push family firm research forward. In order to motivate our arguments and suggestions, we begin by outlining the shortcomings of correlational approaches and advantages of experimental approaches for the family firm scholarship. Then, we walk through various steps in experimental design processes. Finally, we conclude by discussing future directions and possibilities from which family firm scholars can use experiments to explore family firm microfoundations.

Correlational Approaches to Studying Family Firms

Correlational research approaches, especially archival and survey designs, are sturdy workhorses in family firm scholarship (Berrone et al. 2012). Although these approaches have offered tremendous insights about family firms' unique strategic behaviors and outcomes, they are not particularly suited for examining family firm microfoundations, or the causal effects driving these unique behaviors and outcomes (Kellermanns et al. 2014; Morris & Kellermanns 2013). There are several issues in an extant family firm research that leaves the causal drivers of unique family firm behavior up to question.

A heavy reliance on latent firm-level measures to make dynamic family-related arguments lies at the heart of these issues (Morris & Kellermanns 2013). By its very nature, family firm theorizing inherently involves multiple levels of analysis, spanning from the individual level to the family level and then to the firm level and beyond (Sharma 2004). However, a traditional focus on unique family firm strategic behavior has often led researchers to condense rich theoretical arguments that cross multiple levels into assumptions that are measured latently with only firm level proxies. These approaches not only leave core assumptions untested but can also lead to mixed results when researchers use similar proxies for different theoretical arguments (Boyd Gove & Hitt 2005; Ketchen Boyd & Bergh 2008). Additionally, family firm researchers often draw on atheoretical anecdotes and qualitative research from earlier stages of the field to make broad and general assumptions about how specific generational members in a family firm are expected to behave, using indications that these generations are involved in management or ownership to support their arguments about family firm behavior (Morris & Kellermanns 2013). Such approaches have helped explain unique firm behavior *when* certain family members are involved in the firm. However, these approaches fail to provide sufficient evidence to explain *why* and *how* family members cause unique firm behavior or *what* they do to cause it. Consequently, causal drivers behind unique family firm behaviors generally remain untested.

Why Do Family Firms Experiment? A Brief Overview of Experiments and Their Benefits

It is difficult to infer causality from current approaches to family firm research because family members' behaviors are generally not measured, leaving little room to assess the direction of relationships or account for confounding variables that might instead be driving the results. In order to infer causality, general tenets in philosophy of science argue that a research approach should account for: (1) the cause and effect occurring close in time, (2) the cause occurring before the effect, (3) whether the effect does not occur without the presence of the cause, and (4) how alternative explanations can be ruled out (Hume 1748; Mill 1856). While many of these conditions are often met in family firm studies, few rarely address all four. Experimental designs, in contrast, have long been praised as an ideal gold standard across numerous research domains because they allow researchers enough control over conditions to address all four of the aforementioned principles (Campbell & Stanley 1963). For these reasons, experiments have long been the go-to method for psychologists interested in studying emotions, goal pursuits, and other human behaviors that family firm researchers generally assume but generally do not measure (Harmon-Jones Amodio & Zinner 2007).

Before providing examples of how family firm researchers can use experiments to explore family firm microfoundations, it is important to outline the general tenets and benefits of experiments. Experimental methods have several advantages that allow researchers to make stronger causal inferences than they can with correlational or other methods (Campbell & Stanley 1963). First, psychologists often rely on experiments for studying affective and cognitive phenomena because they allow more control over variables (Wilson Aronson & Carlson 2010). An experiment allows the researcher to isolate and manipulate a theoretically important variable (independent variable) to observe its effect on another important variable (the dependent variable). Random assignment ensures greater control because participants all have an equal chance of being in any group, thus reducing systematic biases and helping control for confounding relationships (Campbell & Stanley, 1963; Wilson et al. 2010). Indeed, random assignment acts as an important equalizer. When there is a large enough sample, random assignment to conditions helps reassure researchers that individual differences among participants are equally distributed across conditions. Any observed differences between conditions in the experiment are then likely due to the manipulation of the independent variable (Campbell & Stanley, 1963; Spencer Zanna & Fong 2005).

A Guide to Designing Experiments That Build and Extend Family Firm Microfoundations

At the core, two key attributes define an experiment: (1) participants are randomly assigned to conditions and (2) researchers manipulate independent variable(s) in conditions while holding other variables constant (Wilson Aronson & Carlsmith 2010). However, when considering how to design and execute an experiment, the process can be broken into five basic steps: 1) setting the stage, 2) constructing the independent variable, 3) measuring the dependent variable, 4) conducting post-experimental procedures, and 5) considering additional steps to extend findings. Capturing these steps and providing recommendations, Table 19.1 summarizes important points that can help family firm scholars design experiments that extend family firm microfoundations. In the following sections, we walk through these steps while considering how different aspects of family firm literature can also be taken into account.

Setting the Stage

Compared to methods that employ archival data or latently measure variables through firm level proxies, experimental efforts to examine the causal root of family firm decision-makers' actions require more invention and direct access to desired family firm populations (cf. Zellweger et al. 2012). When designing a family firm experiment, scholars can manipulate the context within which family firm members make decisions and therefore are afforded opportunities to ascertain the effects of family members' emotions, goals, and other theoretically relevant variables

Table 19.1 Experimental Design Steps and Recommendations

Experimental Design Steps	Recommendations
1. Setting the Stage	– Determine whether experimental (e.g. between subjects or within subjects) design is appropriate
	– Utilize a context that is theoretically relevant and psychologically consistent with the research question
	– Consider using a cover story that maximizes participant attention and minimizes bias
	– Anticipate whether additional methods can be used to offset weaknesses or strengthen findings of the experiment
2. Constructing the Independent Variable	– Assign participants randomly to conditions
	– Keep independent variable free from all other sources of variation
	– Manipulate independent variable seamlessly so participants are unaware
	– Utilize manipulation checks to increase validity and mitigate biases
3. Measuring the Dependent Variable	– If using a cover story, make sure dependent variable fits the story
	– Measure behavior or physiology if possible
	– Disguise self-report dependent variables to reduce bias
4. Conducting Post Experimental Procedures	– Check with participants about research clarity
	– Check for participant bias or suspicions
	– Educate participants about the research
	– Make sure participants leave in a good state of mind
5. Considering Additional Ways to Extend Findings	– If doing programmatic research, consider which methods can offset weaknesses of findings
	– Use different operationalizations of the same variables to increase confidence in findings
	– Replicate and extend findings across studies

on important outcomes. Because researchers have more control in experimental studies than correlational studies, family firm scholars that employ experiments have the ability to examine core but often directly untested assumptions of the family firm literature.

Researchers must, therefore, take great care to set the stage, or context, for family firm experiments so that, theoretically, interesting relationships that extend family firm microfoundations are not confounded but instead shine through. Family firm researchers have several experimental tools at their exposure, such as vignette study and conjoint analysis experimental approaches (e.g. Aguinis & Bradley 2014). However, we believe that traditional social psychological experiment approaches that employ cover stories, or some form of misdirection and/or deception, are especially powerful for research questions intended to extend the affective and cognitive microfoundations of family firm behavior. Indeed, experiment participants are generally intelligent and curious adults that might change responses to conform to social expectations or what they believe the experimenter intends to measure. Cover stories that misdirect participants from the true purpose of the study but still provide a sensible, internally consistent, pretext and rationale for the context enriches both data collection efforts and the chances that participants do not detect the true intent of the study (Wilson Aronson & Carlson 2010).

It is important to note that researchers try to consider fully what is required of the research question, allowing them to frame a cover story that is as theoretically tight and psychologically plausible (Harmon-Jones Amodio & Zinner 2007). Often, less is more with experimental design. If a simple setting or context successfully provides a plausible cover story and captures the attention of participants, then there is little need to expand or embellish a cover story. However, in contrast, for more complex research questions and in-depth micro-oriented theoretical problems, it might be harder to capture the attention of family firm owners than general population managers or employees. In many cases, cover stories that selectively embellish key details can increase the validity of research designs (Harmon-Jones et al. 2007; Wilson et al. 2010).

For example, suppose family firm researchers want to understand how family business members directly respond to the threat of potential family firm failure. Researchers could try addressing this research topic through a vignette experiment asking family business participants what decisions they might pursue or what emotions they might experience if they learned that their business was likely to fail. However, critics argue that a vignette experiment by itself might not necessarily capture how participants react to stimuli in reality (Aguinis & Bradley 2014). Family business experimenters have stronger chances of realistically arousing strong emotions and more realistic decisions when they craft a cover story that is selectively embellished with real contextual features tied to the participant's family business. For instance, experimenters could present family firm decision-makers with a cover story that they are demoing a financial forecasting software program. Using this cover story, participants would enter information about their business in a faux software program with the expectation that they receive realistic feedback about their business' future projections. The plausibility of the cover story can be enhanced by being administered in sales or a professional environment, such as that of a tradeshow. In reality, regardless of what financial and nonfinancial information participants enter into the faux software, they are randomly assigned to a "projected business failure" condition, "projected business survival" condition, or a control condition. One could go further to provide advertisement material for the faux software that also serves as an independent variable manipulation that accompanies the business failure independent variable manipulation. Dependent variables such as family members' emotional reaction to the threat of failure or intended actions to mitigate potential business failure could be captured in a faux customer feedback survey incorporated at the end of this software demo cover story.

The point we are making with the above example is that when conducting a family firm experiment that aims to manipulate and examine aspects of family members' thoughts, feelings, or actions, the reasoning for the cover story should be as airtight as possible. Researchers must carefully set the stage, considering how the context of a cover story addresses the research question of interest while also keeping family business participants unaware of the true intent of the study. There are accumulated benefits that come from carefully designed experiments. Although all variables of interest might not tightly fit into one experiment, as we will elaborate more on later, researchers can combine other similar but slightly differing tightly designed experiments and well-executed research methods with an experiment to make stronger causal inferences for family firm related phenomena (cf. Eid & Diener 2006).

Constructing the Independent Variable

Experiments cannot test their hypotheses unless their independent variables manipulate what they are supposed to manipulate. Consequently, independent variable construction is one of the most important and difficult aspects of experimental design (Wilson et al. 2010). In order to be theoretically rigorous, researchers should design independent variable manipulations that are as free of other sources of variation as possible. Similarly, comparing a manipulation to a control group can be extremely useful. Control groups fundamentally allow researchers to understand how participants not exposed to the stimuli would respond, providing a stronger causal inference than even "high" or "low" levels of a stimulus. In a perfect world, it is useful to randomly assign participants to varying levels of a stimulus or a control. Researchers must also be cautious about priming participants using pre-tests or instructions, as this can introduce a variety of spurious influences into findings via social desirability, self-presentation, and even deviance mechanisms. Pre-recorded instructions are one way of ensuring that participants receive the same information and non-verbal cues concerning an experiment.

When constructing independent variables, researchers begin with conceptual variables, which are the theoretically important variables that the experimenter thinks will have a causal effect on the desired dependent variable (Wilson et al. 2010). Understanding the nature of the conceptual variable, the researcher is tasked with designing a manipulation or procedure in the experiment that captures the nature of the conceptual variable as perfectly as possible without influencing other factors (Harmon-Jones et al. 2007; Wilson et al. 2010). There are several effective vehicles for independent variable manipulation, including audiovisual stimuli (Rottenberg Ray & Gross, 2007), interaction tasks (Roberts Tsai & Coan 2007), mental image or memory recall tasks (e.g. Shteynberg Hirsch Galinsky & Knight 2013), and vignettes (Aguinis & Bradley 2014), that can be used to operationalize a conceptual variable. Recognizing this, below we will discuss how various potential cognitive and affective manipulations can be operationalized in studies intending to extend the microfoundations of family firm behavior.

Cognitive Manipulations

Family firm research has long argued that family firms differ from nonfamily firms because the overlap between family and firm systems leads family members to think differently about their business and pursue different goals than their counterparts in nonfamily firms (Chrisman et al. 2005; Gómez-Mejía et al. 2011). Although latent measures in family firm research often leaves these assumptions untested (Morris & Kellermanns 2013; Kellermanns Dibrell & Cruz 2014), psychological research has long relied on experimental manipulations to activate cognitive constructs and goal-relevant knowledge so that experimenters can examine their effects on behavioral outcomes (Förster Liberman & Friedman 2007; Higgins 1996; Taylor & Fiske 1978). Indeed, working with a limited amount of available attention, the human mental system has a remarkable capacity to both consciously and unconsciously recognize cues that activate goals (Förster et al. 2007). From a cognitive psychological perspective, goals operate as desired end states. Knowledge about specific goals is stored in ways such that certain stimuli can make it accessible and activated in cognition, instigating "top of head phenomena" that guides behavior (Higgins 1996; Taylor & Fiske 1978). Consequently, research finds experimental manipulations can be used to prime goals and cognitive states in ways that mirror real psychological processes (Higgins 1996; Förster et al. 2007). Cognitive priming could especially be useful for manipulating family firm goals such as having better environmental performance (Berrone et al. 2010), ensuring succession (Zellweger et al. 2012), engaging stakeholders (Cennamo Berrone Cruz & Gómez-Mejía 2012), or maintaining a spiritual mission (Kellermanns, 2013), and other goals that are mentioned but often latently measured in the family firm literature.

When manipulating theoretically relevant goals in a family firm experiment, it is important to recognize relevant goal-priming principles (See Förster et al. 2007 for a review) such as *goal shielding*, which occurs when mental representations of competing goals are inhibited by the mere activation of a focal goal (Shah Friedman & Kurglanski 2002). Goal priming principles suggest that successfully manipulated goals will elicit a participant behavioral and/or attitudinal response. Thus, manipulations may be used to prime participants to consider specific family or firm goals during an experiment. For example, maintaining family control has been an important theoretical goal and variable in several family firm studies. If interested in understanding how individual family members actually react to changes in family control, researchers can ask participants in one condition to consider how they would respond if their companies were subjected to an initial public offering (IPO) or hostile takeover that reduces or eliminates family control. The experimenter wouldn't necessarily be interested in their response as much as in eliciting participant cognitions concerning (lost) family control.

Subtle manipulations can also be used to capture the correspondence between goals and participant behaviors. For example, asking participants to show pictures of or discuss loved family members during an interview could be useful for activating goals such as family cohesion, continued family control, or family succession in participants' cognition. On a different note, family firm scholars have used firm level proxies to argue that family firms pay greater attention to environmental performance (Berrone et al. 2010). Yet, research has shown that some companies engage in "greenwashing" to the public when they espouse environmental values only in communications (e.g., Dahl 2010), and it is plausible that the same phenomenon could occur in family firms. To test whether family firm participants actually practice their espoused beliefs concerning environmental practices (cf. Berrone et al. 2010), one could use a subtle manipulation where participants are offered a bottle of water or soda during an interview or task. By continuing the simulation until the bottle was empty, the researchers could see if the participants place the empty bottle in a recycling bin or wastebasket when leaving the interview or task. Placing the wastebasket in the lab and the recycling bin outside would demonstrate additional effort as long as the researchers could demonstrate (perhaps through a pilot) that participants were aware of the recycling bin's presence.

Affect Manipulations

Emotion and affect can be very complex phenomena. There are several differences in emotional states that should be taken into consideration when designing a study. At its core, the choice of emotion, mood, or both must reflect the theoretical questions being asked. It is also critical to measure affective states appropriately since they fluctuate by moment, hour, time of day (e.g., morning, afternoon, evening), day, week, or in general (see Watson & Clark 1997 for related discussion). Affective states are also thought to fluctuate according to set individual rhythms (Frijda 1988). Thus, experiments incorporating affect must first decide which type of affect to use, and then decide at what point in time its measurement is most appropriate. After selecting the appropriate affective state and considering how it will be measured, it is critical to consider how the affective state of the participants will be manipulated (or not altered in the control condition). This is where a cover story can be useful, incorporating details that fit the appropriate affective state researchers are trying to capture while also keeping participants from understanding the true purpose of the experiment itself.

In their research on anxiety and negotiation outcomes, Brooks and Schweitzer (2011) undertook four experiments that manipulated participant anxiety in negotiation tasks. In the first experiment, these researchers exposed participants to several minutes of music from either the movie *Psycho* (anxious condition) or Handel's *Water Music: Air* (neutral condition) while they worked on a negotiations task. In this study, participants were given the cover story that they were needed to evaluate music as part of a separate study unrelated to their negotiations. In the second study, the researchers changed the operationalization of the independent variable so that video clips were used to induce emotions in the negotiation task. Then, Brooks and Schweitzer (2011) used the same video manipulations in study 3 and study 4 but changed the dependent variable to examine different theoretically related outcomes in negotiations. In each of these studies, participants were given a cover story that shrouded the true purpose of the study. However, it is important to note that the cover story did not include a risk of significant harm to participants. The cover stories were also used because of the risk of contamination and bias should participants uncover the true purpose of the study. Of course, this implies that cover stories may be unnecessary in studies where such social desirability or participant awareness concerns are less of a risk.

Cover stories are also less needed when well-validated manipulations are used. For example, Lang, Bradley, and Cuthbert (1999) produced an emotional stimulus measure that exposes participants to a selection of more than 600 pictures that induce discrete emotions. Robinson and Clore (2001) tested this measure to ascertain whether participants would report similar levels of emotion when responding in a concurrent simulation or online context. Their findings suggest that participants in the concurrent simulation experienced more fear, anxiety, and excitement than participants in the online condition when exposed to the commensurate slides. However, it is also notable that participants in both settings had largely convergent estimates, implying that discrete emotions may be consistently manipulated in either setting.

Although such "off the shelf" measures are intuitively attractive, we advocate that researchers consider how the overt manipulation of emotion may inform participants about the underlying purposes of the research, which can result in spurious variance. For example, the Lang et al. (1999) measure has been used to test a variety of physiological responses that accompany emotional activation (reviewed in Robinson & Clore 2001). Such applications are not prone to social desirability or participant awareness concerns in the same manner as social science applications.

Subtle ways of eliciting emotion often rely on the senses or interpersonal interaction (see Harmon-Jones Amodio & Zinner, 2007 and Roberts Tsai & Coan 2007 for reviews). The aforementioned Lang et al. (1999) measure accomplishes this through the visual presentation of pictures. Brooks and Schweitzer (2011) incorporated music (i.e., sound) as their manipulation, and this could easily be modified. For example, unpleasant traffic and construction sounds may be used to elicit negative emotions, while exposure to positive sounds like singing birds may be used to elicit positive emotions or put individuals in positive or negative mood states before completing a family firm related experimental task. Similarly, pleasant or unpleasant odors can activate emotion and modify mood. Certain smells may also elicit memory recall and concomitant emotion in individuals. Even touch may elicit emotions and modify moods based on the participant's comfort and interaction with an environment.

Manipulation Checks

To insure that researchers have indeed manipulated what they intended to manipulate, it is important to incorporate manipulation checks in the experiment. Manipulation checks can be direct or inferential, but are essential to ascertain if and how experiments function. Direct manipulation checks involve interviewing or surveying participants before and after exposure to a given manipulation. Inferential manipulation checks involve observing participants and inferring the presence of manipulated states based on differences in behavior. For example, strong activated emotions, such as anger and surprise, often manifest outward physiological signs in the participant. The advance of inferential manipulation checks is that the researcher reduces the probability of influencing the results through observer- or subject-expectancy effects. However, inferential manipulation checks should only be used when manipulation checks would unduly prime participants or represent an intrusion to the experimental process. Inferential manipulation checks also necessitate coding by outside observers, increasing the research burden.

Conversely, direct manipulation checks often include pre- and post-test surveys or interviews. The former reduces the possibility of observer-expectancy effects; although, subject-expectancy effects are still a possibility. Ideally, manipulation checks are designed in intervals and with a cover story that reduces the prospect of incurring bias. For example, manipulation checks in the software demo example offered earlier could be incorporated in the customer feedback survey part of the cover story under the guise of better understanding how the software affects feelings of prospective customers. In experiments where participant-expectancy effects are not viewed as detrimental, direct manipulation checks may simply involve giving individuals a standard survey to complete while being debriefed. The advantage here is that such scales can easily be interpreted statistically to ascertain if the treatment(s) worked as intended. Such scales can also measure intervening mediator variables thought to underlie affective-cognitive processes.

Measuring the Dependent Variable

As mentioned previously, proper specification of an experiment requires forethought regarding the placement and manipulation of variables. However, there is sometimes a tendency for scholars to focus on manipulations at the expense of the criterion, or dependent, variable. This is certainly a possibility for family firm researchers, so here we will briefly discuss various approaches to collecting dependent variables and then review some of the potential levels of analysis that could be useful for extending family firm microfoundations.

A main dilemma that researchers face in measuring dependent variables in experimental research is whether to use self-report, physiological, or behavioral measures (Harmon-Jones et al. 2007). If researchers are using a cover story, the quality of the cover story and potential tradeoffs between types of measures that can plausibly be incorporated in it should be taken into consideration. Ideally, behavioral and physiological measures are preferred because, if properly disguised in a cover story, they are not as vulnerable to social desirability as self-report measures (Harmon-Jones et al. 2007; Wilson et al. 2010). However, the reality of the context for the cover story helps guide the appropriate use of a dependent variable measure. For example, it would be difficult to plausibly incorporate physiological measures (such as heart rate or hormone levels) in the software demo cover story mentioned earlier but self-reports (e.g. Watson Clark & Tellegen's 1988 PANAS scale) of emotional reactions can more easily be incorporated in the customer feedback survey aspect of the cover story. However, different cover stories that draw on narratives related to participant health and wellness in the workforce might be more suited for using physiological dependent measures.

Additionally, it is important for the dependent variable's level of analysis to fit the context of the research question. Family firm research has a tendency to make arguments about emotion and goal pursuits that are suited to individual and dyadic/family levels of analysis but that are instead measured at the firm level (Morris & Kellermanns, 2013). Research questions and designs aimed at individual and dyadic/family levels, as well as some firm level variables, could therefore be especially fruitful for disentangling theoretical confounds and extending family firm microfoundations. We discuss each of these variables in turn below.

First, there is significant opportunity to craft interesting research questions that measure dependent variables at the individual level of analysis. Researchers also have the widest range of options, such as self-report, behavioral, and physiological approaches, that can be used to measure dependent variables at the individual level. While family firm research often focuses on firm-level variables, individual assumptions about specific generations or family members' emotions, commitments, trust, and actions in the firm often go untested (Gómez-Mejía et al. 2011; Pieper 2010). Additionally, there are opportunities for researchers to capture the subjective well-being or satisfaction that family firm members derive from their position in the firm. Context often drives how people individually respond to a situation (Johns 2006); picking appropriate individual level dependent variables from psychology and organizational behavior research can therefore add much needed depth to the family firm literature.

Second, researchers could develop research questions and designs that examine interpersonal concerns or family member dyads of interest, such as founder and successor or spouse dyads. Testing at the dyadic or family level requires the incorporation of more than one family member either directly within an experiment or indirectly as a part of the experiment. Altruism has long been an important topic in family firm research (Schulze, Lubatkin, Dino, & Buchholtz, 2001). Using multiple family members from a family, economists have used experimental procedures to examine altruism in family contexts (Peters Unur Clark & Schulze 2004). Such approaches could potentially be replicated in family firms or used to show how altruism in family firm contexts might differ. Additionally, researchers could evaluate factors such as shared attention (c.f. Shteynberg, 2015) towards important issues or conflict between family members (c.f. Kellermanns & Eddleston 2004; McKee, Madden, Kellermanns, & Eddleston, 2014) regarding the prioritization of specific goals or potential actions.

Finally, there is the strategic, or firm, unit of analysis. Testing at this level is difficult because the researcher must observe and measure behavior *in situ*, or enable participants to make prospective judgments regarding firm actions under varying conditions. The latter provide less valid results since behavioral intentions, rather than behaviors, are measured. For example, family firm leaders' financial valuations, propensity to sell to non-family members, divestiture or acquisition of units, and expansion goals might provide interesting prescriptions about family decision-makers' financial vs. nonfinancial concerns. When experimenting using firm-level dependent variables in the family firm member population, it is important to consider whether participants are positioned to adequately make the needed inferences. Thus, participant screening can also be a useful tool to ensure that participants are exposed to firm operations in a manner that enables them to adapt firm activities.

Conducting Post-Experimental Procedures

An experiment, especially if it employs a cover story, should not end after the researcher has collected the last dependent variable. When deception is used in an experiment, participants should gently be debriefed about the true purpose of the study as soon as possible after completing it. Debriefing participants has both important ethical implications and research design implications. We will briefly discuss these implications here.

When debriefing participants, researchers have three main goals: (1) to make sure that the participant leaves the experiment in a healthy frame of mind, (2) to explain and make certain that participants understand the importance and purpose of the study's hypotheses, manipulations, and outcomes, and (3) to gain feedback on the effectiveness of the manipulations and procedures so as to discern whether participants were able to identify the true intent of the study (Harmon-Jones et al. 2007; Wilson et al. 2010).

When deception is involved in a research design, depending on the severity, manipulations can pose potential risks such as stress or emotional distress. Therefore, it is important for researchers that use deception to be cognizant of how the study is debriefed.

Consequently, researchers often have to approach debriefing in a thoughtfully deliberate and caring way. A best practice approach to debriefing is to first ask the participants if they have any questions about the experiment. If they do not, then the experimenter should ask the participant to discuss whether they thought the instructions and purpose for the experiment and each part of it was clear. Furthermore, it is good to explain that people react to experimental studies in many ways and ask them how they feel they were affected by the experiment. Following a logical flow like this allows the experimenter to probe for demand bias or participant awareness of the true intent of manipulations while gradually and gently debriefing participants.

Considering Additional Efforts That Can Extend Experimental Findings

We have continually emphasized the importance of using experiments to extend theoretical microfoundations supporting unique family firm behaviors. Indeed, independent variable manipulations allow experimenters to observe how family members actually react to change, helping avoid common pitfalls associated with latent measures in the family firm literature. However, it is important to note that not all variables of interest for a research question can always fit into one study. When researchers want to delve deeper to rule out alternative explanations or explore a family firm phenomenon further, a multimethod approach can be used to triangulate and potentially extend and strengthen the results of an experiment. Indeed, multimethod research programs are a common practice in social psychology and organizational behavior scholarship (Eid & Diener 2006). Scholars in these areas put a great deal of thought into how each study builds on and enhances the previous one. Researchers employ multiple studies to offset weaknesses or alternative explanations for one study with the research design of another study. Such an approach could be extremely useful for scholars who want to extend the microfoundations of family firm behavior. Experiments can be bolstered with several types of research designs, such as additional experiments, experience sampling methods, surveys, qualitative studies, and archival studies. Below we provide some examples of published research and potential methods that can be combined with experiments to create a stronger theoretical impact.

Additional Experiments

It is a common practice in social psychology to offset the weaknesses of one experiment with other experiments. Brooks and Schweitzer's (2011) research on anxiety and negation provides an excellent example of how several experiments can be used to reinforce and enhance research findings. Whether it is with another between-subjects design or a within subjects design, social psychologists often try to replicate but slightly vary the design between experiments. These scholars often use different operationalizations of independent and dependent variables to build additional confidence in the experimental results. This is accomplished by demonstrating what researchers intended to manipulate was indeed manipulated not only once but also across different settings and with different samples.

Surveys

Additionally, an experiment can often be combined with a carefully crafted survey that first helps establish correlational relationships of a phenomenon. After establishing correlational relationships in a survey, an experiment can be used to examine the causal mechanisms underlying the relationships. As an example, Fast and colleagues' (2013) research examined the role of manager self-efficacy in soliciting employee voice. To address this research topic, the researchers first used a field survey to find support that managers who have lower self-efficacy are less likely to solicit employee voice. Then, wanting to establish a stronger causal direction for this relationship, these researchers manipulated low self-efficacy in an experiment to show that it leads to less solicitation of employee input. Considering that there are several psychological relationships in the family firm literature that are implied but not directly tested, similar approaches that first establish a relationship with a survey and then examine the causal roots with an experiment could prove very beneficial for extending family firm microfoundations.

Experience Sampling Methods

Considering that emotions are temporally situated and occur in response to events that change valued goal pursuits, experimental approaches are some of the most appropriate methods for researchers that want to examine different emotional reactions between groups experiencing various levels of a theoretical important variable. However, researchers that want to replicate or extend experimental findings to also account for within person affective or cognitive states over time and in a more ecologically valid setting can pair their experiment's findings with experience sampling methods (Beal & Weiss 2003). Experience sampling methods are useful because they provide a systematic way to collect samples of ongoing affective states, cognitions, and/or behaviors in real time. For example, Seo and Barrett (2007) used experience sampling to examine how emotional and financial concerns interact in decision-making during a stock-investment simulation that went on for 20 consecutive business days, finding interesting results that suggest more intense feelings aided decision-making performance in this financial task. Just as Seo & Barrett (2007) examined emotional and financial tradeoffs, family firm scholars could use experience-sampling methods to test financial and nonfinancial tensions that are often emphasized in several areas of family firm theory. Furthermore, family firm researchers could strategically utilize experience-sampling methods by selecting a specific time where emotions would especially be expected to influence family firm phenomena. For example, Trougakos et al. (2008) conducted an experience sampling study where they were interested in how breaks helped increase positive emotional settings in service related areas of work. Drawing inspiration from this approach, family firm scholars could select specific times that factor into a particular facet of a theory. For family firm scholars that want to examine how specific emotional states change commonly held theoretical relationships, such fine-grained micro-oriented data from experience-sampling approaches could really help increase ecological validity and extend experimental results.

Qualitative Studies

Researchers interested in the processes and the meaning behind family firm decisions might find it worthwhile to explore multimethod investigations that include both experiments and qualitative methods. Indeed, qualitative methods such as ethnographic, case study, grounded theory, content analysis, or discourse analysis, can be used to assess meaning of decisions or the processes that either lead to or follow particular family firm decisions that are examined in an experimental study. For example, consider the approach that Raaijmakers and colleagues (2014) took for understanding tensions in time to compliance decisions under different types of institutional complexity. In this article, the authors were interested in how long it would take decision-makers to comply with a coercive demand. Using a vignette experiment, the experimenters varied institutional pressures from the government to comply with a new law and coworker support of the law. Following the experimental vignette, researchers interviewed participants on the steps and processes they would take to deal with compliance. Using this interview data, they had both information about a experimentally controlled decision and processes that participants would follow to address their decision, allowing them to use grounded theory qualitative methods to come up with a process model for delay in decision compliance. For family business researchers, a similar design approach could be useful for studying family behavior related to succession, reputational concerns, or ties with outside stakeholders to understand the meaning, processes, or sense making behind specific family firm decisions.

Archival Studies

As we mentioned earlier, a large portion of family firm research draws on indirect proxies from archival data. These studies shed light on unique family firm strategic outcomes but are not clear on factors that influence these strategic outcomes. Thus, for researchers interested in delving deeper into causality leading to the unique strategic outcomes examined in these types of studies, it might be fruitful to pair archival data with experiments that mirror conditions believed to precede strategic outcomes of interest. This can help open new possibilities for building research on family member behaviors driving specific strategic outcomes.

Discussion and Future Directions

In this chapter we offered guidelines for designing experiments that can extend family firm scholarship's affective and cognitive microfoundations. Family firm research up to this point has largely used distal firm level proxies across archival and survey studies to infer that emotions, particular goal pursuits, and/or behaviors drive unique family firm decisions. While these methodological approaches have made tremendous strides advancing the family firm literature, they focus on the outcomes and not the causes of unique family firm behavior. Here, we have argued that to better understand causal relationships driving unique behaviors and firm outcomes, researchers cannot only rely on latent measures but must also have enough control over the study to isolate and manipulate variables of interest. Experiments, especially when paired with other studies that complement their strengths and offset their weaknesses, provide researchers with methodological tools that can unpack the family firm literature's microfoundations. The advice that we offer in this chapter is meant to serve as guidelines and is definitively not meant to be exhaustive. Indeed, as we hope we have shown, there are numerous theoretical benefits that experimental design can provide the family firm literature. However, here we would like to discuss what we believe to be three important implications and future research directions.

Motivated to build a body of work that shows how, why, when, and where family firms differ from nonfamily firms, over three decades of family firm scholarship provides evidence that family firms do behave differently than nonfamily firms (Chrisman et al. 2005 Sharma 2004). Focused on differentiating family firms' unique strategic outcomes from nonfamily firms' strategic outcomes, extant family firm scholarship has provided sufficient evidence suggesting that family firms are indeed different. In this way, family firm research has answered its first generation question (Are family firms different from nonfamily firms?) and now faces its second generation questions concerning how, why, and when family firms are not only different from nonfamily firms but also how family firms differ from each other. Experimental methods offer a greater degree of control and precision over variables and study conditions that will allow family firm researchers to get at the heart of the microfoundational relationships supporting unique family firm behaviors.

Applying creative theoretical approaches to the guidelines and suggestions offered in this chapter can help family firm scholars observe family member behavior and processes behind unique family firm outcomes. Manipulating specific emotions and goals in experiments can add depth and a psychological base to the family firm literature in ways that encourage scholars to move beyond structural and dichotomous views of family firm relations. Indeed, family firm research tends to paint broad portraits of how first generation family members might act vs. later generation family members or how family members might react differently to events than nonfamily members. With experiments, first and later generations can be treated as separate samples that receive the same experimental treatment (i.e. replication) and stronger, more nuanced, inferences about each generation's behaviors can therefore be drawn from comparison between samples. The same ideas can be applied to samples of family members vs. nonfamily members to hopefully uncover more nuanced differences and theoretical implications than are currently found in the literature.

Finally, when seeking to extend family firm microfoundations, there is a rich methodological tradition and numerous theoretical models that family firm scholars can exploit in their experiments. Social psychologists and organizational behavior scholars often use experiments to explore research questions tied to emotion and goal theories. By combining family firm scholarship's core assumptions with psychological theories in experiments, family firm scholars have the opportunity not only to extend family firm theory but also to challenge broader management theories. In order to garner interest from other disciplines, family firm experiments can be used to show the limitations or boundaries of commonly held assumptions about emotion and goal pursuits.

In conclusion, there is significant opportunity for both family business and organizational behavior scholars to begin building the microfoundations of family firm behavior. We believe that experiments can play an important role in these efforts. Integrating psychology and family firm theory will surely provide a strong base for interesting research that not only examines family firms' unique strategic outcomes but also the family members' causal roles in shaping those outcomes. As research on family firms continues to grow we hope that researchers will begin exploring these avenues, accounting for unique family behaviors within firm contexts.

References

Aguinis, H. & Bradley, K. (2014) 'Best Practice Recommendations for Designing and Implementing Experimental Vignette Methodology Studies,' *Organizational Research Methods* 17 (4): 351–71.

Beal, D. & Weiss, H. (2003) 'Methods of Ecological Momentary Assessment in Organizational Research,' *Organizational Research Methods* 6 (4): 440–64.

Berrone, P., Cruz, C., & Gómez-Mejía, L. (2012) 'Socioemotional Wealth in Family Firms Theoretical Dimensions, Assessment Approaches, and Agenda for Future Research,' *Family Business Review* 25 (3): 258–79.

Berrone, P., Cruz, C., Gómez-Mejía, L., & Larraza-Kintana, M. (2010) 'Socioemotional Wealth and Corporate Responses to Institutional Pressures: Do Family-Controlled Firms Pollute Less?,' *Administrative Science Quarterly* 55 (1): 82–113.

Boyd, B., Gove, S., & Hitt, M. (2005) 'Construct Measurement in Strategic Management Research: Illusion or Reality?,' *Strategic Management Journal* 26 (3): 239–57.

Brooks, A. & Schweitzer, M. (2011) 'Can Nervous Nelly Negotiate? How Anxiety Causes Negotiators to Make Low First Offers, Exit Early, and Earn Less Profit,' *Organizational Behavior and Human Decision Processes* 115 (1): 43–54.

Campbell, D., Stanley, J., & Gage, N. (1963) *Experimental and Quasi-Experimental Designs for Research*, Boston: Houghton Mifflin.

ınamo, C., Berrone, P., Cruz, C., & Gómez-Mejía, L. (2012) 'Socioemotional Wealth and Proactive Stakeholder Engagement: Why Family-Controlled Firms Care More About Their Stakeholders,' *Entrepreneurship Theory and Practice* 36 (6): 1153–73.

ısman, J., Chua, J., & Sharma, P. (2005) 'Trends and Directions in the Development of a Strategic Management Theory of the Family Firm,' *Entrepreneurship Theory and Practice* 29 (5): 555–76.

ıl, R. (2010) 'Green Washing: Do You Know What You're Buying,' *Environmental Health Perspectives* 118 (6): A246-A52.

, M. & Diener, E. (2006) 'Introduction: The Need for Multimethod Measurement in Psychology,' in: Eid M. & Diener E. (eds.) *Handbook of Multimethod Measurement in Psychology*, Washington DC: American Psychological Association, 3–8.

, N., Burris, E., & Bartel, C. (2014) 'Managing to Stay in the Dark: Managerial Self-Efficacy, Ego Defensiveness, and the Aversion to Employee Voice,' *Academy of Management Journal* 57 (4): 1013–34.

ster, J., Liberman, N., & Friedman, R. (2007) 'Seven Principles of Goal Activation: A Systematic Approach to Distinguishing Goal Priming from Priming of Non-Goal Constructs,' *Personality and Social Psychology Review* 11 (3): 211–33.

da, N. (1988) 'The Laws of Emotion,' *American Psychologist* 43 (5): 349.

nez-Mejía, L., Cruz, C., Berrone, P., & Castro, J. (2011) 'The Bind That Ties: Socioemotional Wealth Preservation in Family Firms,' *The Academy of Management Annals* 5 (1): 653–707.

mon-Jones, E., Amodio, D., & Zinner, L. (2007) 'Social Psychological Methods of Emotion Elicitation,' in: Coan, J. & Allen, J. (eds.) *Handbook of Emotion Elicitation and Assessment*, New York: Oxford University Press 91–105.

gins, E. (1996) 'Knowledge Activation: Accessibility, Applicability, and Salience,' in: Higgins, E. & Kruglanski, A. (eds.) *Social Psychology: Handbook of Basic Principles*, New York: Guilford Press, 133–168.

me, D. (1748) *Philosophical Essays Concerning Human Understanding*, London: A Miller.

ns, G. (2006) 'The Essential Impact of Context on Organizational Behavior,' *Academy of Management Review* 31 (2): 386–408.

lermanns, F. (2013) 'Spirituality and Religion in Family Firms,' *Journal of Management, Spirituality & Religion* 10 (2): 112–15.

lermanns, F. & Eddleston, K. (2004) 'Feuding Families: When Conflict Does a Family Firm Good,' *Entrepreneurship Theory and Practice* 28 (3): 209–28.

lermanns, F., Dibrell, C., & Cruz, C. (2014) 'The Role and Impact of Emotions in Family Business Strategy: New Approaches and Paradigms,' *Journal of Family Business Strategy* 5 (3): 277–79.

chen, D., Boyd, B., & Bergh, D. (2008) 'Research Methodology in Strategic Management: Past Accomplishments and Future Challenges,' *Organizational Research Methods* 11 (4): 643–658.

g, P., Bradley, M., & Cuthbert, B. (1999) 'International Affective Picture System (Iaps): Instruction Manual and Affective Ratings,' *The center for research in psychophysiology, University of Florida.*

Kee, D., Madden, T., Kellermanns, F., & Eddleston, K. (2014) 'Conflicts in family firms: The good and the bad,' in Melin, L., Nordqvist, M., & Sharma, P. (eds.) *SAGE Handbook of Family Business.* London: Sage Publications, 514–528.

l, J. (1856) *A System of Logic, Ratiocinative and Inductive, Being a Connected View of the Principles, and the Methods of Scientific Investigation*, London: JW Parker.

rris, M. & Kellermanns, F. (2013) 'Family Relations and Family Businesses: A Note from the Guest Editors,' *Family Relations* 62 (3): 379–83.

ers, H., Ünür, A., Clark, J., & Schulze, W. (2004) 'Free Riding and the Provision of Public Goods in the Family: A Laboratory Experiment,' *International Economic Review* 45 (1): 283–99.

per, T. (2010) 'Non Solus: Toward a Psychology of Family Business,' *Journal of Family Business Strategy* 1 (1): 26–39.

ıijmakers, A., Vermeulen, P., Meeus, M., & Zietsma, C. (2015) 'I Need Time! Exploring Pathways to Compliance under Institutional Complexity,' *Academy of Management Journal* 58 (1): 85–110.

berts, N., Tsai, J. & Coan, J. (2007) 'Emotion Elicitation Using Dyadic Interaction Tasks,' in: Allen, J. & Coan, J. (eds.) *Handbook of Emotion Elicitation and Assessment*, New York: Oxford University Press, 106–23.

binson, M. & Clore, G. (2001) 'Simulation, Scenarios, and Emotional Appraisal: Testing the Convergence of Real and Imagined Reactions to Emotional Stimuli,' *Personality and Social Psychology Bulletin* 27 (11): 1520–32.

ttenberg, J., Ray, R., & Gross, J. (2007) 'Emotion Elicitation Using Films,' in: Coan, J. & Allen, J. (eds.) *Handbook of Emotion Elicitation and Assessment*, New York: Oxford University Press, 9–28.

Schulze, W., Lubatkin, M., Dino, R., & Buchholtz, A. (2001) 'Agency Relationships in Family Firms: Theory and Evidence,' *Organization Science* 12 (2): 99–116.

Seo, M. & Barrett, L. (2007) 'Being Emotional During Decision Making—Good or Bad? An Empirical Investigation,' *Academy of Management Journal* 50 (4): 923–40.

Shah, J., Friedman, R., & Kruglanski, A. (2002) 'Forgetting All Else: On the Antecedents and Consequences of Goal Shielding,' *Journal of Personality and Social Psychology* 83 (6): 1261.

Sharma, P. (2004) 'An Overview of the Field of Family Business Studies: Current Status and Directions for the Future,' *Family Business Review* 17 (1): 1–36.

Shteynberg, G. (2015) 'Shared Attention,' *Perspectives on Psychological Science* 10 (5): 579–590.

Shteynberg, G., Hirsh, J., Galinsky, A., & Knight, A. (2014) 'Shared Attention Increases Mood Infusion,' *Journal of Experimental Psychology: General* 143 (1): 123.

Spencer, S., Zanna, M., & Fong, G. (2005) 'Establishing a Causal Chain: Why Experiments Are Often More Effective Than Mediational Analyses in Examining Psychological Processes,' *Journal of Personality and Social Psychology* 89 (6): 845.

Taylor, S. & Fiske, S. (1978) 'Salience, Attention, and Attribution: Top of the Head Phenomena,' in: Berkowitz, L. (ed.) *Advances in Experimental Social Psychology*, New York: Academic Press, 249–88.

Trougakos, J., Beal, D., Green, S., & Weiss, H. (2008) 'Making the Break Count: An Episodic Examination of Recovery Activities, Emotional Experiences, and Positive Affective Displays,' *Academy of Management Journal* 51 (1): 131–46.

Watson, D. & Clark, L. (1997) 'Measurement and Mismeasurement of Mood: Recurrent and Emergent Issues,' *Journal of Personality Assessment* 68 (2): 267–96.

Watson, D., Clark, L., & Tellegen, A. (1988) 'Development and Validation of Brief Measures of Positive and Negative Affect: The Panas Scales,' *Journal of Personality and Social Psychology* 54 (6): 1063.

Wilson, T., Aronson, E., & Carlsmith, K. (2010) 'The Art of Laboratory Experimentation,' in: Fiske, S., Gilbert, D., & Lindzey, G. (eds.) *Handbook of Social Psychology*, Hoboken: John Wiley & Sons, 49–79.

Zellweger, T., Kellermanns, F., Chrisman, J., & Chua, J. (2012) 'Family Control and Family Firm Valuation by Family CEOs: The Importance of Intentions for Transgenerational Control,' *Organization Science* 23 (3): 851–68.

20

FINDING BENEVOLENCE IN FAMILY FIRMS
The Case of Stewardship Theory

Matthias Waldkirch and Mattias Nordqvist

Introduction

The view of organizations as "purely rational and calculated systems" (Frost et al. 2006, 843) has a long history, underpinned by a 'model of man' that depicts actors as inherently self-interested, aiming to maximize their economic gain (Donaldson and Davis 1991). Many theories of organizations irrespective of their origin have built upon this simplified view of human action, seeing it as "the pursuit of self-interest by rational, more or less atomized individuals" (Granovetter 1985, 482). As Ghoshal argued, the view of business studies as science has resulted in the "the denial of any moral or ethical considerations in our theories," which in turn has negatively informed management practice (2005, 77). However, there is a recent contra-trend acknowledging the plurality of human behavior and motivation going beyond self-serving behavior. For instance, the rich literature on corporate social responsibility (CSR) has tried to capture and explain responsibility in the context of corporate environments. The concept is thus differentiated from "business fulfillment of core profit-making responsibility and from the social responsibilities of government" (Matten and Moon 2008, 405). Also the growing body of research on social entrepreneurship captures business activity which is not primarily directed towards financial outcomes, but to "pursue opportunities to catalyze social change and address social needs" (Mair and Martí 2006, 37).

A group of firms that is often depicted to represent such non-economically driven behavior is, at least to a certain amount, family firms. The research in the field of family firms paints a comparatively bright picture of such organizations. Miller and Le Breton-Miller (2005) find that family firms are more caring towards their employees, and also Cabrera-Suárez and colleagues argue that the family firm has a strong predisposition to develop "strong ties with nonfamily stakeholders" (2014, 1). Family firms are found to pollute less (Berrone et al. 2010) and are less likely to let their employees go in times of financial crisis (Block 2010; Stavrou, Kassinis, and Filotheou 2007). In general, current research shows that family firms follow non-financial goals (Chrisman et al. 2012; Zellweger et al. 2013) and are not only interested in the pure pursuit of higher profits. In this sense, family firms go beyond what Kochan described as "maximizing shareholder value without regard for the effects of their actions on other stakeholders" (2002, 139).

Such arguments are commonly brought up when comparing family to non-family firms and aiming to describe what is special about family influence. Trying to capture such 'good side' of the family firm has been theoretically complicated, though. A theory that has been increasingly used in the pursuit to capture this benevolent side of family firms has been stewardship theory (Davis, Schoorman, and Donaldson 1997). Oftentimes seen as "reflecting an ongoing sense of obligation or duty to others" (Hernandez 2012, 174), stewardship theory has been applied in the field of family firms, as it is seen to have "a natural application to family businesses" (Blumentritt, Keyt, and Astrachan 2007, 323). Firstly, in our chapter we will introduce different depictions of models of man in organizational theory, using agency and stewardship theory as the point of comparison. Then, we try to show how stewardship theory has been used in family business research, especially in regards to locating the 'good side' of family firms. We highlight how the use of stewardship theory has partially gone beyond its boundaries, and how such use of the theory could potentially turn the idea of stewardship in organizations inside out. We show two issues that hinder basic stewardship theory from locating and grasping the 'good side' of organizations and propose ways to integrate moral behavior into stewardship theory. We believe that such critical discussion about stewardship theory is important since an increasing number of articles make us of it.

The Underlying Models of Man in Organizational Theory

The classic model of man underlying in organizational research is the view of a self-interested and opportunistic actor who will strive for personal economic gain. McGregor (1960) captured the view in his so-called 'Theory X,' according to which management is responsible for organizing the elements of an organization, including people, in order to reach economic ends. The organizational members need to be controlled and directed to fulfill the goals of the company. Without such direction, people would remain "passive—even resistant—to organizational needs" (McGregor 1957, 166). The model of man is depicting human actors as indolent, lacking ambition, gullible and fundamentally self-centered. The view does not at all account for any action going beyond self-serving behavior and draws a sad picture of human actors. The model is close to the *homo oeconomicus* that has dominated economic and organizational research for a long time (Granovetter 1985; Thaler 2000), assuming a purely rational agent.

A theory that has made ample use of such model of man has been agency theory (Jensen and Meckling 1976), which looks at the problem of contracting between a principal and an agent in an organization, arguing that there is a goal conflict between principal and agent (Eisenhardt 1989). Agency Theory builds upon Theory X, depicting principals and agents as "self-interested actor[s] rationally maximizing their own personal economic gain" (Donaldson and Davis 1991, 51). At the heart of agency theory stands the assumption of actors as individual utility maximizers (Jensen and Meckling 1976), which is why actors will choose actions that will heighten their personal utility. The main focus and unit of analysis of agency theory hence is the contract between principal and agent in the company. Owners become principals "when they contract with executives" managing their firm (Davis, Schoorman, and Donaldson 1997, 22). Even though such distinction of principal-owner and agent-manager has become the norm of many theories, it only has been introduced by, amongst others, Berle and Means (1932) who proclaimed the distinction and separation between ownership and management. Before, it was the family businesses that provided the "backbone" (Bird et al. 2002, 337) of economies for hundreds of years. The distinction and reframing of ownership and management were the starting point of agency research since the goals for owners and managers were seen to be diverging, which is why agents would take advantage of their principals to increase their own utility.

Agency theory has been hugely influential in organizational research and was the starting point for much research for instance on top-management teams, remuneration, or governance structures. Researchers using agency theory, unfortunately, adopted its underlying model of man, casting a one-sided picture of interaction in organizations. As Davis and colleagues remark, agency theory and its model of man had become a "self-fulfilling prophecy regarding the nature of relationships" (1997, 32). If we see people as self-serving and inherently self-centered, then we will behave accordingly and design our companies in a way that will encourage such behavior. These structures, however, will not leave much room for benevolence, and most certainly do not account for it.

It was Granovetter in 1985 who saw that such view of human and economic action raised the problem of social embeddedness and the "neglect of social structure" (Granovetter 1985, 506). He argued that by leaving out social factors, we do not see action embedded in social life and hence only contend economic action as 'rational.' Seeing action, however, "closely embedded in networks of interpersonal relations" (1985, 504) opens up the venue for new rationalities. More and more authors argued that there are other models of man that explain behavior and that choosing these for organizational research would "drive [...] the development of management philosophies and management systems" (Davis, Schoorman, and Donaldson 1997, 32). Even though agency theory certainly explains many actions taken by individuals, Davis and Associates correctly argued that its boundaries and limits are "determined by its model of man" of self-serving behavior (1997, 24). Also, Doucouliagos calls for a stronger focus on the relations between the agent's behavior, the institution and the group, claiming that "[i]ndividual, atomistic and self-interested decision making cannot capture the institutional and norm-based nature of the firm" (Doucouliagos 1994, 881).

Another model of man is depicted by McGregor (1960) in his so-called Theory Y. The theory is meant to display the opposite of the self-serving model of man and has laid the foundation of a stronger view on the human side of organizations. People are not seen to be inherently self-serving but only have become so due to their organizational experiences. The motivation for pro-organizational behavior and the readiness to assume responsibility are supposed to be all present in people; it is only up to the management to foster these behavioral patterns. Hence, management needs to arrange organizational conditions in a way so that people can "achieve their own goals best by directing their own efforts toward organizational objectives" (McGregor 1957, 169). The model sees actors as being able to transcend their own self-serving behavior, moving towards self-actualizing and self-fulfillment; in this sense, it is close to Maslow's (1970) famous depiction of the hierarchy of needs and his model of people as self-actualizing.

Stewardship Theory

Maybe the most important organizational theory building on Theory Y is stewardship theory (Davis, Schoorman, and Donaldson 1997; Donaldson and Davis 1991), which in opposite to agency theory presumes that "stewards are motivated to act in the best interest of their principals" (Davis, Schoorman, and Donaldson 1997, 24). Stewardship theory assumes a model whose behavior is ordered in a way "such that pro-organizational, collectivistic behaviors have higher utility than individualistic, self-serving behaviors" (Davis, Schoorman, and Donaldson 1997, 24). The main entrance of Stewardship Theory into the mainstream canon of organizational theory has been the article by Davis, Schoorman and Donaldson (1997) who were able to differentiate stewardship from agency theory (Eisenhardt 1989; Jensen and Meckling 1976) and to elaborate the psychological and situational assumptions and mechanisms inherent in stewardship theory.

It was the paper in 1997 that has proven to start the research stream on stewardship, arguing its implication for the whole of organization research.

Stewardship assumes a convergence in the goals between principal and agent since the collective behavior and orientation of the agent will generally benefit principals such as company owners. The orientation works as well intraorganizationally, where for instance middle managers will profit from the steward-like behavior of their subordinates since they will foster the common goal. The best interest of the group is mostly seen as a "viable, successful enterprise" (Davis, Schoorman, and Donaldson 1997, 25). Since the steward in the organization will work towards organizational ends, the person can and should be trusted and accordingly given more freedom to act pro-organizationally. As such, stewardship theory especially differs from agency theory, which assumes that the agents cannot be trusted and accordingly need to be controlled (Eisenhardt 1989). According to Davis and colleagues (1997), control can even be counterproductive since it may lower the motivation of the steward. Since the principal does not have to control the steward, also the monitoring costs are lowered. Donaldson and Davis (1991) in their study on the positive effect of stewardship in boards and CEOs show that stewardship leads to higher corporate performance. They point out it would ultimately lead to the question why not all companies are structured according to stewardship theory. Davis et al.'s answer seems to be very much grounded in game theory since they argue that if either principal or agent defect from their steward stance, the other party will lose out in the relationship. Especially in case the principal enters the relationship as a steward while the agent acts self-interested, the organizational outcome can be dramatic. From a game theory argument, the principal might, therefore, choose the strategy that would make huge losses unlikely, hence, an agency stance.

Not long ago, one of the authors had a conversation with a fellow researcher about agency and stewardship theory, and the colleague mentioned that he did not 'believe' in stewardship theory, even though he was well aware that agency theory did not cover all aspects of human interaction. Looking at the organizational reality we can see both types of behavior (e.g. Chrisman et al. 2007). Already Donaldson argued, reflecting on the underlying model, that to explain behavior, "some more complex and contingent admixture of the two" approaches would be necessary (1990, 372). In explaining or accounting for benevolent behavior, however, Stewardship theory at first glance seems more prone due to its assumption of the collectivistic orientation of actors.

The Inaugural use of Stewardship Theory

Even before its inaugural article in 1997, stewardship theory had been introduced earlier in the research discussion (Donaldson and Davis 1989; Donaldson 1990), focusing mostly on upper echelons (Donaldson and Davis 1991). By putting the focus on issues in the area of top management, boards, and governance mechanisms, stewardship theory, in the beginning focused on competing with agency theory in its natural setting, questioning the underlying assumptions made by agency theory.

Frankforter, Berman and Jones (2000) for instance investigate the relationship between the adoption of 'shark repellents,' mechanisms that are put in place to fend off hostile takeovers, and several mechanisms that were supposed to align interests between members of the board of directors and the shareholders. These mechanisms were constructed using an agency perspective, but the authors found that only one of the variables they used had an influence on the relationship. Given the "mixed support for an agency theory interpretation of board behavior" (2000, 340), the authors conclude that there had been other factors influencing board decision and hence propose the further use of stewardship theory and agent morality. Much of the stewardship literature furthermore was concerned with differentiating stewardship from agency theory (Hernandez 2012) and seeing which one applies more to organizational studies. Tosi, Brownlee, Silva and Katz (2003) look at the actual decision-making process, using a laboratory experimental setting to see whether the participants make different decisions depending on the control – agency or stewardship – they are under. The authors find that decision-makers under agency control will more likely take profit-maximizing decisions.

Sundaramurthy and Lewis (2003) investigated such tensions between agency and stewardship theory also in regards to corporate governance. However, in opposite to pointing out the opposites of both theories, they try to embrace the paradox by arguing for both the value of agency monitoring as well as stewardship-empowerment. They show reinforcing cycles of collaboration and control, which in themselves are both likely to become pathological and lead to firm failure. The authors promote the need for both control approaches helping to "curb human limitations" as well as collaborative approaches tapping into "individuals' aspirations" (Sundaramurthy and Lewis 2003, 407). Such an integrative framework going beyond "either/or thinking" (Sundaramurthy and Lewis 2003, 411) is very much in line with the stewardship argumentation, arguing that in order to explain behavior we need "some more complex and contingent admixture of the two" approaches (Donaldson 1990, 372).

In these articles, stewardship theory sticks close to its origins, being depicted as basically a collective approach with little regards to what McGregor described as a self-realizing actor. Little is being said about the moral of the actors as being good or responsible as a steward. Even though Frankforter et al. talk about 'morality,' it is only considered as a dilemma of choice in acting in favor of the peers or the decision-maker's actual role. Morality as in "moral standards and norms" (Trinkaus and Giacalone 2005, 238) is not regarded, which Trinkaus and Giacolone criticize especially in the case of Enron.

Stewardship Theory and Family Businesses

Stewardship theory has a short, but impactful history in the field of family business. It is argued to have a "natural application to family businesses" (Blumentritt, Keyt, and Astrachan 2007, 323) and has been widely used and regarded. Taking a look at stewardship in different organizations, Corbetta and Salvato argue that it may "differ between family and non-family firms" (2004, 356), with family businesses rather relying on trust and intra-familial altruism. Family businesses follow family goals, both financial and non-financial in nature (Tagiuri and Davis 1996), an argument that relates back to Granovetter's (1985) point of the rationality of action not being located only in economic reasoning. Hall explains this by arguing that family business is "not irrational but multi-rational" (2002, 43). Also, Corbetta and Salvato (2004) point out that self-actualizing behavior in family firms is not irrational, but that the complex rationality of family firms cannot be captured sufficiently by the self-interested rationality underlying agency theory. Recently, Madison, Holt, Kellermanns and Ranft follow a similar argumentation by combining both agency and stewardship in their review of family business articles, arguing that both theories offer "mutually enabling explanations of the family firm" (2015, 2). Relying on a thorough review of the literature, they show how managers, both family, and non-family, act as stewards as well as agents.

Chrisman, Chua, Kellermanns and Chang (2007) investigate whether family managers in the business behave like agents or stewards. Looking at small family-owned businesses, they find that also family managers are monitored and paid with incentive compensation, and that such agency control results in better performance. Their results are more supportive of the "presence of agency relationships than stewardship relationships" (Chrisman et al. 2007, 1036). Also, Miller and Le Breton-Miller (2006) use stewardship and agency theory in their work on family gover-nance and firm performance as a lens from which to see possible advantages and disadvantages of family businesses on the levels of ownership, family leadership, the involvement of family members and planned/actual participation of future generations. Miller and Le-Breton Miller argue that the assumptions of stewards as being collectively oriented and intrinsically motivated would be "especially prevalent among family businesses" (2006, 74) because of the emotional connection between family and business. Looking through both lenses, the authors draw out several propositions about family business behavior, concluding that family businesses are a heterogeneous group that does best when exploiting "lower agency costs and elicit attitudes of stewardship among leaders and majority owners" "(Miller and Le Breton-Miller 2006, 85). Stewardship is seen as an attitude that is apparent in family businesses and becomes entangled with emotional attachment.

In their paper on the perception of benevolence in the design of agency contracts, Cruz, Gómez-Mejía and Becerra utilize trust literature, thereby positioning themselves in a "middle ground where agency theory and others-oriented theories [such as stewardship] can meet" (2010, 71). They see benevolence as the "extent to which a trustee is believed to want to do good to the trustor" (2010, 70), and utilize it as the opposite of agent opportunism. Yet, through such depiction benevolence stays a one-dimensional construct, especially since it is paired with agency assumptions and its underlying model of man. In another article, Miller, Le Breton-Miller and Scholnick (2008) look at two distinctive perspectives on the nature of family businesses, stewardship and stagnation, developing and comparing them through an empirical study of small businesses, either family- or non-family owned. Looking again at the "significant socio-emotional attachments," the authors argue that family managers might "exhibit especially marked levels of stewardship" (Miller, Le Breton-Miller, and Scholnick 2008, 52) and develop three common forms of stewardship in family-owned businesses. The first is stewardship over the continuity of the business, which can take many different forms such as for instance an increased attention to boosting or keeping a positive reputation of the business (Deephouse and Jaskiewicz 2013) in order to enhance the robustness of the business. This is closely linked to the creation of transgenerational wealth – "a continuous stream of wealth that spans generations" (Habbershon and Pistrui 2002, 223) – in order to keep the family and provide for the next generations. The second form of stewardship is community, i.e. stewardship over employees, that can result for instance in heightened efforts for employee training (Reid and Harris 2002) or the creation of a "flexible, inclusive culture" (Miller, Le Breton-Miller, and Scholnick 2008, 55). The last form of stewardship is connection, i.e. stewardship over customer relationships, which could take place for instance through a more personal contact between the family business and its customers. These three forms of stewardship are accordingly compared to a perspective of stagnation in family businesses, and the authors' initial assumption that stewardship will be more prevailing is confirmed.

The two articles by Miller, Le Breton-Miller and Scholnick (2006; 2008) combine the classic stewardship perspective with a more emotionally-driven family component. The component is apparent in the relationship between the family and the business as well as in the relationship among the family members. Nevertheless, the emotional component seems to not encompass the circle of business. When talking about stewardship with employees, they find an inclusive culture, but their arguments are very much focused on the goals of the business and the family. A stewardship relation hence seems to be only built to "keep the firm healthy and improve pros-pects for its future" (Miller, Le Breton-Miller, and Scholnick 2008, 55). Such view of stewardship stays true to its roots, but interestingly negates the notion of altruism and caring just introduced by taking into consideration family as a variable (Dyer 2003).

Also, Zahra (2003) sees family altruism as a reason why family businesses act as stewards in the international expansion of their businesses. According to the author, this is due to the "desire to build an enduring legacy" for the family's offspring (Zahra 2003, 496). Furthermore, Eddleston and Kellermanns (2007) take a special look at family relationships and conflicts, trying to explain why some family firms are flourishing while other face dire problems. By looking through a lens of stewardship, the authors propose that a participatory strategy process may have a positive influence on a firm's performance and that altruistic family relationships can solve and lower intrafamily conflicts. The authors' stewardship perspective is focused on family members and their stances towards altruism or participative strategy. The integration of altruism into the stewardship perspective is intriguing but needs further clarification. Hernandez in her article on the psychology of stewardship (2012) is correct in pointing out that altruism is theoretically and conceptually different from the stewardship perspective. Stewardship behavior is directed towards the collective well-being, but altruism is directed at increasing the goal of another person "without regard for [one's] own welfare" (Hernandez 2012, 175). Such altruistic behavior, however, is not automatically in line with the collective well-being, and in some cases it can even undermine the collective good (Batson et al. 1995). Hence, altruism is not captured in stewardship behavior itself. But as for instance Corbetta and Salvato (2004) outline, it can be an antecedent for stewardship relationships in the organization.

Already Davis and colleagues argued that the assumption about the model "drives the development of management philosophies and management systems" (1997, 32). For family businesses, Corbetta and Salvato (2004) outline four factors, including altruism among the family members, that would influence the model and accordingly would lead to the prevalence of agency or stewardship relationships in the family firm. The family and their values and behaviors influence the prevalence of stewardship in a business. While the article by Corbetta and Salvato (2004) rather looks at how passive attributes influence possible stewardship behavior, Blumentritt et al. (2007) talk about how family firms can create an environment prone to 'stewardship' relationships, including appropriate governance mechanisms. Family businesses seem to be able to actively shape the conditions for organizational behavior, unwillingly or not. Since stewardship in organizations would only be an outcome of several factors or decisions, it is worth contemplating whether the concept is appropriate in describing family businesses. It also raises the question about the unit of analysis in stewardship theory since its origin in the organization would thus lie in the family itself.

The Problem of Tracing Benevolence in Stewardship Theory

Not surprisingly, stewardship theory has become entangled with emotional constructs and meaning. Since stewardship theory is the most common theory about organizational behavior building upon the self-realizing model, it seems only logical to try to capture 'good' behavior with the theory. The use of stewardship theory in family business research has followed a "call for research that considers the positive aspects and advantages the family can contribute to family firms" (Eddleston and Kellermanns 2007, 549). For instance, emotional attachment and benevolent behavior, which are not accounted for in agency theory and its underlying model of man, can be explained by attributing stewardship to the company or owner family. The problem of accounting for such behavior and action is being solved by including it in an overall frame of 'stewardship,' talking for instance about a "culture of stewardship" (Zahra et al. 2008). Yet, when looking at what is meant by such use of stewardship, it becomes apparent that there are several uses of the concept of stewards that depart from the original idea. We believe that such ambiguity of the concept of stewardship can sometimes lead to misconceptions about the idea behind stewardship theory. First of all, the term 'stewardship' has a strong religious connotation. Referring to the belief that the world has been god's gift, and that we as humans are responsible for taking care of it (see for instance Calvin's writings), stewardship in this sense carries a strong moral component, which is lacking from the theory of stewardship by Davis et al.

In another article, Poza and Messer (2001) for instance use the term 'steward' to talk about the role of the CEO's spouse in family businesses. According to the authors, the spouse's role is that of a "steward of the family legacy, facilitator of communications, and touchstone of emotional intelligence in family relations" (2001, 25). Tilba and McNulty (2013) also talk about stewardship looking at engaged and disengaged ownership in the UK. Their notion of stewardship is however influenced by the UK Stewardship Code (Financial Reporting Council 2012) for institutional investors which for instance talks about the need to strongly monitor the investee companies and engage with them in such matters as strategy or capital structure. Such a use of stewardship is more related to what organizational researchers would see as agency controls (Eisenhardt 1989) and is distinct from the stewardship term coined by Davis and colleagues (1997).

The Missing Ethical Dimension of Stewardship Theory

Yet another idea of stewardship has been introduced by Caldwell, Hayes, Karri and Bernal (2008) who talk about ethical stewards regarding leadership behavior that generates high levels of commitment from followers. The authors thereby define ethical stewardship as the "honoring of duties owed to employees, stakeholders, and society in the pursuit of long-term wealth creation" (2008, 153). This idea of stewardship is linked closely to the concept introduced by Davis and colleagues (1997), yet it adds an ethical dimension that is missing in the original framework. While Davis and associates argued that stewards "work toward organization's goals" (1997, 30), Caldwell and colleagues also include other parties into this framework. In an earlier paper, Caldwell and Karri (2005) compared the assumption of stewardship to agency and stakeholder theory, extending Davis et al.'s perspective of stewardship (1997) with Block's model of stewardship as 'service over self-interest' (Block 1993). Caldwell and Karri add an ethical dimension that takes into consideration the steward's "commitment to society based virtues and rights" (Caldwell and Karri 2005, 254), something that has been absent to stewardship theory before.

Such an absence of a 'moral compass' in the actions and behaviors of the steward is surprising, since already the original stewardship theory is, at first sight, closely related towards ethical behavior due its collective perspective. But as Frankforter and colleagues rightly observed, 'other regarding' is linked to moral obligations and thus inherently different than the goal congruence proposed by Davis et al.'s Stewardship Theory (1997). Continuing such line of thought, what would happen in case organizational goals, values or the general culture are inherently pathologic? Would stewardship behavior then involve the adherence to such pathologic and socially detrimental goals? Should organizational members that behave according to such pathologic norms and values of the organization be called 'stewards'? Since stewards are supposed to help achieve organizational goals, these goals are at the same time the 'roof' for benevolent behavior that has to keep inside the borders of these goals. The conflict was properly outlined by Hernandez (2012) who argued that altruistic behavior and organizational goals do not always go together.

Corbetta and Salvato's (2004) argument that the underlying model of the family ultimately shapes the organizational relationships to either agency- or stewardship-based offers an interesting starting point for situating benevolent behavior. Taking a closer look at the family and its values might yield insights into the benevolent behavior in companies. Since the family values will be present in the organization, benevolent and compassionate values might influence the behavior of organizational actors. Davis and colleagues argue about the "value commitment" (1997, 30) of stewards is closely related to organizational identification. By adopting the benevolent values of the family, the organizational actors will supposedly act according to them. In this case, however, the source of benevolence would lie in the family and be only spread through the adoption of stewardship behavior.

Moreover, in the case of family businesses, the absence of a moral level in the stewardship theory could be mitigated by strong family values. In general, however, Caldwell and colleagues (2008) are right by adding a moral component to the theory of stewardship. Also, Frankforter and associates (2000) explicitly mentioned stewardship and agent morality as two distinct approaches. The "moral commitment" (Hernandez 2012, 173) of the steward is related only to the organization and its goals. In this way, stewardship is more related to a psychological contract (Rousseau 1989) ignoring the all-encompassing moral of behavior and action. Such "lack of meaningful vocal [...] stewardship" resulting from a "temporary lapse in social morality" has been criticized by Trinkaus and Giacalone (2005, 237). Looking at Carroll's (1991) pyramid of corporate social responsibility, the moral of this kind of stewardship would only care about the economic and legal implications. However, without such a 'moral compass' of behavior, benevolence and compassion in organizations are not sufficiently regarded, since such behavior might be accounted for as just unnecessary costs. In order for stewardship theory to include benevolence, it would thus need some kind of extension, enriching it with a 'moral compass' for the stewards.

Capturing Benevolence in the Utility Function

Stewardship theory is inherently a theory based on utility-maximization. In opposite to agency theory, individuals fulfill their personal goals not by defecting behavior and self-interest, but through collective behavior: "utility gained from pro-organizational behavior is higher than the utility that can be gained through individualistic, self-serving behavior" (Davis, Schoorman, and Donaldson 1997, 25). In the classic stewardship sense, individuals will work "toward[s] organizational, collective ends" (Davis, Schoorman, and Donaldson 1997, 25) which mostly are represented through performance and organizational well-being. Looking for benevolence, we have thus to look at the utility function. Personal utility maximization through acting in a collective way would need to encompass a moral 'other-regarding' part (Frankforter, Berman, and Jones 2000). In this regard, the avenue of non-financial goals is interesting as it goes beyond purely economic reasoning. The utility of family firms can be best described through their two-folded goals related to family and business, encompassing both financial and non-financial elements (Hirigoyen and Labaki 2012; Tagiuri and Davis 1996; Chrisman, Memili, and Misra 2014).

Family utility is both directed toward the company and accordingly financial output as well as to the protection of their socioemotional wealth, the "non-financial aspects of the firm that meet the family's affective needs" (Gómez-Mejía et al. 2007, 106). Inherent in this socioemotional wealth perspective is the concern about the family, including intrafamilial altruism as proposed already by other authors (Corbetta and Salvato 2004; Eddleston and Kellermanns 2007), and the wish to preserve this "emotional endowment" (Gómez-Mejía et al. 2011, 654). In an intrafamilial perspective, stewardship might be used to explain and motivate benevolent and altruistic behavior. Paradoxically on an organizational level such intrafamilial benevolence could lead to an agency situation with the owner family trying to work only for their own benefit, putting socioemotional wealth over business goals for instance.

In overall, we are skeptical concerning the use of stewardship in terms of capturing benevolent behavior. Even though its model of man has in a way been 'marketed' as contrary from the rational, self-interested model of man underlying agency theory, its core regarding utility maximization still remains troublesome. Looking for instance at an extreme case of benevolence, the exit of the owner family from a business, DeTienne and Chirico (2013) propose several ways that family businesses exit their business. One of them is explicitly called "stewardship-based exit strategy" which displays the family displaying care for the "firm continuity and care of the firm, the family, and the employees" (DeTienne and Chirico 2013, 4). Looking only at goals and utility-maximization such as stewardship does, such behavior cannot be sufficiently explained. Therefore, in a way stewardship is in danger to become another "self-fulfilling prophecy regarding the nature of relationships" (Davis, Schoorman, and Donaldson 1997, 32), only that this time we believe to have captured all human behavior through the combination of agency and stewardship. Already Chrisman, Chua and Sharma (2005) were critical towards stewardship, arguing that little is known about the basis of stewardship wherefore we "do not really know whether stewardship requires selflessness, self-control, or altruism" (2005, 567).

We believe that too much has been attributed to stewardship theory concerning a positive view on businesses and behavior, which is why we might run into problem using and advocating stewardship as a theory of benevolence and compassion.

Conclusion

Stewardship Theory has rightly earned its merits. However, as we have shown in this chapter, stewardship has its boundaries and is not particularly prone to explain and capture benevolent behavior in organizations due to its utilitarian core and disregard for interpersonal benevolence. More work is needed in situating benevolence both in the goals of the principals as well as in the overall utility function in order to be able to capture benevolence in stewardship theory. Accordingly, stewardship theory in its current state is not well suited to capture moral behavior in organizations, and it certainly cannot explain the benevolent character that is oftentimes attributed to family firms. By relying on stewardship to explain and understand moral behavior, we run into danger to either miss or misinterpret what we are actually looking for. Therefore, we would encourage researchers interested in the 'good' side of firms to dive into theories of psychology and sociology, which are more prone to capture such behavior as they move beyond utility-centred argumentation. Doing so could help expand our understanding of behavior in organizations by moving beyond descriptions of both agency and stewardship theory.

References

Batson, C. Daniel, Tricia R. Klein, Lori Highberger, and Laura L. Shaw. 1995. "Immorality from Empathy-Induced Altruism: When Compassion and Justice Conflict." *Journal of Personality and Social Psychology* 68 (6): 1042–54. doi:http://dx.doi.org.bibl.proxy.hj.se/10.1037/0022-3514.68.6.1042.

Berle, Adolf Augustus, and Gardiner Coit Means. 1932. *The Modern Corporation and Private Property*. New York: McMillan.

Berrone, Pascual, Cristina Cruz, Luis R. Gómez-Mejía, and Martin Larraza-Kintana. 2010. "Socioemotional Wealth and Corporate Responses to Institutional Pressures: Do Family-Controlled Firms Pollute Less?" *Administrative Science Quarterly* 55 (1): 82–113.

Bird, Barbara, Harold Welsch, Joseph H. Astrachan, and David Pistrui. 2002. "Family Business Research: The Evolution of an Academic Field." *Family Business Review* 15 (4): 337–50.

Block, Jörn H. 2010. "Family Management, Family Ownership, and Downsizing: Evidence From S&P 500 Firms." *Family Business Review* 23 (2): 109–30. doi:10.1177/0894486509360520.

Block, Peter. 1993. *Stewardship: Choosing Service Over Self-Interest*. Berrett-Koehler Publishers.

Blumentritt, Timothy P., Andrew D. Keyt, and Joseph H. Astrachan. 2007. "Creating an Environment for Successful Nonfamily CEOs: An Exploratory Study of Good Principals." *Family Business Review* 20 (4): 321–35.

Cabrera-Suárez, M. Katiuska, M. Cruz Déniz-Déniz, and Josefa D. Martín-Santana. 2014. "Family Social Capital, Trust within the TMT, and the Establishment of Corporate Goals Related to Nonfamily Stakeholders." *Family Business Review*, March, 1–19. doi:10.1177/0894486514526754.

Caldwell, Cam, Linda A. Hayes, Patricia Bernal, and Ranjan Karri. 2008. "Ethical Stewardship – Implications for Leadership and Trust." *Journal of Business Ethics* 78 (1–2): 153–64. doi:10.1007/s10551-006-9320-1.

Caldwell, Cam, and Ranjan Karri. 2005. "Organizational Governance and Ethical Systems: A Covenantal Approach to Building Trust." *Journal of Business Ethics* 58 (1–3): 249–59. doi:10.1007/s10551-005-1419-2.

Carroll, A. B. 1991. "The Pyramid of Corporate Social Responsibility: Toward the Moral Management of Organizational Stakeholders." *Business Horizons* 34 (4): 39–48.

Chrisman, James J., Esra Memili, and Kaustav Misra. 2014. "Nonfamily Managers, Family Firms, and the Winner's Curse: The Influence of Noneconomic Goals and Bounded Rationality." *Entrepreneurship Theory and Practice* 38 (5): 1103–27. doi:10.1111/etap.12014.

Chrisman, James J., Jess H. Chua, Allison W. Pearson, and Tim Barnett. 2012. "Family Involvement, Family Influence, and Family-Centered Non-Economic Goals in Small Firms." *Entrepreneurship Theory and Practice* 36 (2): 267–93. doi:10.1111/j.1540-6520.2010.00407.x.

Chrisman, James J., Jess H. Chua, Franz W. Kellermanns, and Erick P.C. Chang. 2007. "Are Family Managers Agents or Stewards? An Exploratory Study in Privately Held Family Firms." *Journal of Business Research* 60 (10): 1030–38. doi:10.1016/j.jbusres.2006.12.011.

Chrisman, James J., Jess H. Chua, and Pramodita Sharma. 2005. "Trends and Directions in the Development of a Strategic Management Theory of the Family Firm." *Entrepreneurship Theory and Practice* 29 (5): 555–76. doi:10.1111/j.1540-6520.2005.00098.x.

Corbetta, Guido, and Carlo Salvato. 2004. "Self-Serving or Self-Actualizing? Models of Man and Agency Costs in Different Types of Family Firms: A Commentary on 'Comparing the Agency Costs of Family and Non-Family Firms: Conceptual Issues and Exploratory Evidence.'" *Entrepreneurship Theory and Practice* 28 (4): 355–62. doi:10.1111/j.1540-6520.2004.00050.x.

Cruz, Cristina, Luis R. Gómez-Mejía, and Manuel Becerra. 2010. "Perceptions of Benevolence and the Design of Agency Contracts: Ceo-Tmt Relationships in Family Firms." *Academy of Management Journal* 53 (1): 69–89.

Davis, James H., F. David Schoorman, and Lex Donaldson. 1997. "Toward a Stewardship Theory of Management." *Academy of Management Review* 22 (1): 20–47.

Deephouse, David L., and Peter Jaskiewicz. 2013. "Do Family Firms Have Better Reputations Than Non-Family Firms? An Integration of Socioemotional Wealth and Social Identity Theories." *Journal of Management Studies* 50 (3): 337–60. doi:10.1111/joms.12015.

DeTienne, Dawn R., and Francesco Chirico. 2013. "Exit Strategies in Family Firms: How Socioemotional Wealth Drives the Threshold of Performance." *Entrepreneurship Theory and Practice* 37 (6): 1297–1318. doi:10.1111/etap.12067.

Donaldson, Lex. 1990. "The Ethereal Hand: Organizational Economics and Management Theory." *Academy of Management Review* 15 (3): 369–81. doi:10.5465/AMR.1990.4308806.

Donaldson, Lex, and James H. Davis. 1991. "Stewardship Theory or Agency Theory: CEO Governance and Shareholder Returns." *Australian Journal of Management* 16 (1): 49–64. doi:10.1177/031289629101600103.

Donaldson, Lex, and John A. Davis. 1989. "CEO Governance and Shareholder Returns: Agency Theory or Stewardship Theory." In. Washington, DC.

Doucouliagos, Chris. 1994. "A Note on the Evolution of Homo Economicus." *Journal of Economic Issues (Association for Evolutionary Economics)* 28 (3): 877–83.

Dyer, W. Gibb Jr. 2003. "The Family: The Missing Variable in Organizational Research." *Entrepreneurship Theory and Practice* 27 (4): 401–16.

Eddleston, Kimberly A., and Franz W. Kellermanns. 2007. "Destructive and Productive Family Relationships: A Stewardship Theory Perspective." *Journal of Business Venturing* 22 (4): 545–65. doi:10.1016/j.jbusvent.2006.06.004.

Eisenhardt, Kathleen M. 1989. "Agency Theory: An Assessment and Review." *The Academy of Management Review* 14 (1): 57–74. doi:http://dx.doi.org/10.2307/258191.

Financial Reporting Council. 2012. "The Stewardship Code 2012, UK." Financial Reporting Council, London.

Frankforter, Steven A., Shawn L. Berman, and Thomas M. Jones. 2000. "Boards of Directors and Shark Repellents:Assessing the Value of an Agency Theory Perspective." *Journal of Management Studies* 37 (3): 321–48. doi:10.1111/1467-6486.00183.

Frost, Peter J., Jane E. Dutton, Sally Maitlis, Jacoba M. Lilius, Jason M. Kanov, and Monica C.Worline. 2006. "Seeing Organizations Differently: Three Lenses on Compassion." In *The SAGE Handbook of Organization Studies*, edited by Stewart R. Clegg, Cynthia Hardy, Thomas B. Lawrence, and Walter R. Nord, 843–66. Thousand Oaks, CA: SAGE Publications Ltd.

Ghoshal, Sumantra. 2005. "Bad Management Theories Are Destroying Good Management Practices." *Academy of Management Learning & Education* 4 (1): 75–91. doi:10.5465/AMLE.2005.16132558.

Gómez-Mejía, Luis R., Cristina Cruz, Pascual Berrone, and Julio De Castro. 2011. "The Bind That Ties: Socioemotional Wealth Preservation in Family Firms." *The Academy of Management Annals* 5 (1): 653–707.

Gómez-Mejía, Luis R., Katalin Takács Haynes, Manuel Núñez-Nickel, Kathyrn JL Jacobson, and José Moyano-Fuentes. 2007. "Socioemotional Wealth and Business Risks in Family-Controlled Firms: Evidence from Spanish Olive Oil Mills." *Administrative Science Quarterly* 52 (1): 106‑37.

Granovetter, Mark. 1985. "Economic Action and Social Structure: The Problem of Embeddedness." *American Journal of Sociology* 91 (3): 481–510.

Habbershon, Timothy G., and Joseph Pistrui. 2002. "Enterprising Families Domain: Family-Influenced Ownership Groups in Pursuit of Transgenerational Wealth." *Family Business Review* 15 (3): 223–37.

Hall, Annika. 2002. "Towards an Understanding of Strategy Processes in Small Family Businesses: A Multi-Rational Perspective." In *Understanding the Small Family Business*, edited by Denise Fletcher, 32–45. London; New York: Routledge.

Hernandez, Morela. 2012. "Toward an Understanding of the Psychology of Stewardship." *Academy of Management Review* 37 (2): 172–93. doi:10.5465/amr.2010.0363.

Hirigoyen, Gérard, and Rania Labaki. 2012. "The Role of Regret in the Owner-Manager Decision-Making in the Family Business: A Conceptual Approach." *Journal of Family Business Strategy* 3 (2): 118–26. doi:10.1016/j.jfbs.2012.03.004.

Jensen, Michael C., and William H. Meckling. 1976. "Theory of the Firm: Managerial Behavior, Agency Costs and Ownership Structure." *Journal of Financial Economics* 3 (4): 305–60. doi:10.1016/0304-405X(76)90026-X.

Kochan, Thomas A. 2002. "Addressing the Crisis in Confidence in Corporations: Root Causes, Victims, and Strategies for Reform." *The Academy of Management Executive (1993–2005)* 16 (3): 139–41.

Madison, Kristen, Daniel T. Holt, Franz W. Kellermanns, and Annette L. Ranft. 2015. "Viewing Family Firm Behavior and Governance through the Lens of Agency and Stewardship Theories." *Family Business Review*, 0894486515594292.

Mair, Johanna, and Ignasi Martí. 2006. "Social Entrepreneurship Research: A Source of Explanation, Prediction, and Delight." *Journal of World Business* 41 (1): 36–44. doi:10.1016/j.jwb.2005.09.002.

Maslow, Abraham H. 1970. *Motivation and Personality*. New York: Harper & Row.

Matten, Dirk, and Jeremy Moon. 2008. "'Implicit' and 'Explicit' CSR: A Conceptual Framework for a Comparative Understanding of Corporate Social Responsibility." *Academy of Management Review* 33 (2): 404–24.

McGregor, Douglas M. 1957. "The Human Side of Enterprise." *Management Review*, November, 41–49.

———. 1960. *The Human Side of Enterprise*. New York: McGraw-Hill.

Miller, Danny, and Isabelle Le Breton-Miller. 2005. "Management Insights from Great and Struggling Family Businesses." *Long Range Planning* 38 (6): 517–30. doi:10.1016/j.lrp.2005.09.001.

———. 2006. "Family Governance and Firm Performance: Agency, Stewardship, and Capabilities." *Family Business Review* 19 (1): 73–87.

Miller, Danny, Isabelle Le Breton-Miller, and Barry Scholnick. 2008. "Stewardship vs. Stagnation: An Empirical Comparison of Small Family and Non-Family Businesses." *Journal of Management Studies* 45 (1): 51–78. doi:10.1111/j.1467-6486.2007.00718.x.

Poza, Ernesto J., and Tracey Messer. 2001. "Spousal Leadership and Continuity in the Family Firm." *Family Business Review* 14 (1): 25–36.

Reid, Renee S., and Richard I. D. Harris. 2002. "The Determinants of Training in SMEs in Northern Ireland." *Education & Training* 44 (8/9): 443–50.

Rousseau, Denise M. 1989. "Psychological and Implied Contracts in Organizations." *Employee Responsibilities and Rights Journal* 2 (2): 121–39. doi:10.1007/BF01384942.

Stavrou, Eleni, George Kassinis, and Alexis Filotheou. 2007. "Downsizing and Stakeholder Orientation Among the Fortune 500: Does Family Ownership Matter?" *Journal of Business Ethics* 72 (2): 149–62. doi:10.1007/s10551-006-9162-x.

Sundaramurthy, Chamu, and Marianne Lewis. 2003. "Control and Collaboration: Paradoxes of Governance." *The Academy of Management Review* 28 (3): 397–415. doi:10.2307/30040729.

Tagiuri, Renato, and John A. Davis. 1996. "Bivalent Attributes of the Family Firm." *Family Business Review* 9 (2): 199–208.

Thaler, Richard H. 2000. "From Homo Economicus to Homo Sapiens." *The Journal of Economic Perspectives* 14 (1): 133–41.

Tilba, Anna, and Terry McNulty. 2013. "Engaged versus Disengaged Ownership: The Case of Pension Funds in the UK." *Corporate Governance: An International Review* 21 (2): 165–82. doi:10.1111/j.1467-8683.2012.00933.x.

Tosi, Henry L., Amy L. Brownlee, Paula Silva, and Jeffrey P. Katz. 2003. "An Empirical Exploration of Decision-Making Under Agency Controls and Stewardship Structure." *Journal of Management Studies* 40 (8): 2053–71. doi:10.1046/j.1467-6486.2003.00411.x.

Trinkaus, John, and Joseph Giacalone. 2005. "The Silence of the Stakeholders: Zero Decibel Level at Enron." *Journal of Business Ethics* 58 (1–3): 237–48. doi:http://dx.doi.org.bibl.proxy.hj.se/10.1007/s10551-005-1418-3.

Zahra, Shaker A. 2003. "International Expansion of U.S. Manufacturing Family Businesses: The Effect of Ownership and Involvement." *Journal of Business Venturing* 18 (4): 495–512. doi:10.1016/S0883-9026(03)00057-0.

Zahra, Shaker A., James C. Hayton, Donald O. Neubaum, Clay Dibrell, and Justin Craig. 2008. "Culture of Family Commitment and Strategic Flexibility: The Moderating Effect of Stewardship." *Entrepreneurship Theory and Practice* 32 (6): 1035–54.

Zellweger, Thomas Markus, Robert S. Nason, Mattias Nordqvist, and Candida G. Brush. 2013. "Why Do Family Firms Strive for Nonfinancial Goals? An Organizational Identity Perspective." *Entrepreneurship Theory and Practice* 37 (2): 229–48. doi:10.1111/j.1540-6520.2011.00466.x.

PART IV

Family Science

21

THE HEART OF THE MATTER

Family Processes Affect Family Businesses

Sharon M. Danes and Kathryn Stafford

In the development of any academic field that is grounded in human behavior such as that of family business, there are three stages of conceptual development (Danes, 2014). The first stage focuses on structure, roles, and rules within the focal group and effects of these structures, roles and rules on the group's outcomes. Within the field of family business, the group being studied could be either the family or the business system. The second stage involves progressing from the investigation of structural concepts to a focus on processes. The third developmental stage is studying those processes over time. This longitudinal lens would bring an understanding of processes not only in times of stability but in times of change. The call then is for the family business field to progress deeper into the second and third stages of its conceptual development in order to refine its behavioral foundations. This chapter's focus is a discussion of conceptual and methodological issues around family processes supported by examples of recently published research by chapter authors that illustrate points being made.

The field of family business is fairly new as academia goes; as a result, it has focused primarily on structural concepts in its research base (Danes, 2014). An example of this initial stage is the use of marital status to explain whether a new business venture succeeds or not. Findings from that research indicate that the family structure of marriage has an impact on new venture viability, a business outcome. However, the inclusion of that concept in an analysis reveals nothing about the processes creating the positive relationship between marital status and new venture viability and limits the applicability of the results. It is the understanding of family processes associated with marriage that expands the applicability of the results and provides a lens into what might be used in education, consulting or training with family firms to guide them in their mission. In other words, research on family processes addresses how to change behavior to obtain better outcomes. Research on processes provides the foundation for results-based education, consulting and owner action.

Dyer and Dyer (2009) state that there is a trend in family firm research to neglect the concept of family and its impact on business success. In doing so, what has been neglected is of vital importance to most family business owners – their family interactions. To move beyond the study of structure, roles, and rules of enterprising families or their businesses, researchers must investigate processes such as interpersonal and resource transactions occurring within families or at the intersection of firm and family (Danes & Brewton, 2012). There are only a few researchers who investigate effects of family processes on firm performance; and their work is often, but not exclusively, published in family science journals, not regularly read by business managers and consultants. Use of Google Scholar (www.scholar.google.com) can readily over-come this historical barrier. A greater obstacle that persists is the difference in concepts and vocabulary between family science and business management and the lack of credibility that accompanies this difference. An iceberg metaphor best epitomizes what results. By primarily measuring structural concepts and neglecting the study of family processes – the fuel of family business management- the current research presents only what is above the water line. The major part of an iceberg is hidden below the water line; if family processes (what is below the water line) are not studied, the major part of the entrepreneurial fuel of family businesses has not been tapped.

With a focus on family processes, defining what we mean by family and processes is important. For the purposes of this chapter, the family consists of two or more people related by blood marriage, adoption or long-term commitment to each other who share resources. This defini-tion of family does not require two or more generations. Neither does it require legal marriage. It does require sharing resources, the financial, physical, human and social capital. In other words, a parent and child who live in separate states and have not spoken to each other for a decade would not qualify as a family by this definition. If there should be a reconciliation, the parent and child would then qualify. The latter part of this family definition is vital because different ethnicities and collectivist cultures define family in varied ways; defining family as those who have a long-term commitment to each other who share resources allows for this ethnic and cultural diversity in definition (Danes, Lee, Stafford & Heck, 2008).

This chapter is about business owning families, not all families. Although defining family is more critical to our chapter discussion, ownership is also important to define. A family is considered to own a business if one or more adults in the family own a portion of a private firm. Although we do not disagree with researchers who include ownership of a publicly traded firm in their definition of an owning family, we exclude them from consideration in our chapter because of their rarity and the lack of data on which to base that discussion. Also, the decisions of those families are circumscribed by a different set of rules from those for private firms.

Family processes are largely unseen patterns created, sustained and modified by the family (Dyer & Dyer, 2009). Processes refer to decision making and acting by family members singly or jointly. Owning family processes transform inputs into family and business system achieve-ment in the short-run and sustainability in the long-term (Danes & Brewton, 2012). With this definition in mind, there are two key points to note when attempting to study underlying family processes.

First, one must identify observable family behaviors that are indicative of underlying family processes of interest. Those might include resource transactions such as utilization or transfor-mation of time, energy, or money. They might also include interpersonal transactions such as communication or relationship interactions such as degree or kind of commitment, support, conflict, or harmony (Danes & Brewton, 2012). An observable behavior for the unobservable family process of trust might be acting on the advice of a spouse.

The second key point in measuring family processes is that once observable behaviors are measured, they must be combined in such a way as to measure the shape or nature and size of the underlying process, the quality, and quantity of the underlying process. There are several typologies commonly used to simplify the description of the "shape" of family processes, ratio-nal versus irrational, interpersonal versus transactional, leisure versus production, for example. Description and analysis of family processes are frequently prescribed by the intended purpose or the goal to be achieved, such as decisions and actions that are taken to acquaint children with the business (Danes et al., 2008).

Tracking family processes can be achieved in a number of ways. Key aspects of tracking family processes are being conceptually precise about the focal type of transaction and its characteristics. For example, having multi-informants about interpersonal interactions is a vital part of creating validity. Processes might be observed qualitatively or quantitatively. Collecting data qualitatively allows for observations of actual interactions containing both verbal and nonverbal cues. It is critical to account for differential, individual interpretations about the group interaction. Another way to track processes is quantitatively through surveys or face-to-face interviews. Measuring the multiple interpretations of a similar interaction is a huge conundrum within surveys about processes because there is expense in time and money to collect data from multi-informants' assessments of interaction patterns. An advantage of face-to-face interviews is an opportunity to probe respondents about their responses to questions and to note some of the nonverbal cues during the interview as they describe family interaction patterns.

Studying family processes within family firms is complex. In this chapter, we will be addressing five points within that complexity. These points include:

(a) informal power of family processes;
(b) value of multiple methods of assessment;
(c) value of data from multiple family members;
(d) direct and indirect indicators of family processes;
(e) long-run and short-run family processes.

For each of these points, there will be a discussion of the issues around the point that will be grounded in a recent study conducted by chapter authors.

Informal Power of Family Processes

Literature on enterprising families has tended to primarily focus solely on the formal power of entrepreneurs when studying their entrepreneurial endeavors. That means that the literature has focused primarily on those family members who work for pay in the business and who have formal titles within the business. In an attempt to draw greater attention to the impact of the informal power generated in entrepreneurial efforts through family processes, Danes and Jang (2013) investigated the development of a copreneurial identity within couples who were starting a new business venture. The identity of the entrepreneurs is clearly established when they begin to operate a business. However, we know little about the couple interactions of the owning couple that contribute or detract from new venture viability. The study was a longitudinal one with multiple informants-the entrepreneur and the entrepreneur's spouse.

Other researchers have recognized the importance of spouses in the entrepreneurial process. Dimov (2007) indicated that although the literature is filled with how entrepreneurs form their identity, we know little about how entrepreneurs and their spouses form a collective, copreneurial identity. Van Auken and Werbel (2006) stated that an entrepreneur's decision to launch a new business venture depends not only on opportunity analyses but also on the degree that an entrepreneur's spouse shares a common vision about firm goals, risks, and rewards. If an entrepreneur's commitment to new venture's goals is shared and verified by the spouse, increased emotional attachment to the new venture develops resulting in increased trust and access to spousal resources (Burke and Stets, 1999; Danes et al., 2009). This study built on the work of Danes et al. (2010) who found that couples with a mutual commitment to new venture goals had a substantial impact on its sustainability over time.

A collective identity such as a copreneurial identity is a dyad-level concept representing shared cognitions that dyad members feel are central, enduring, and distinctive such as goals for the new venture (Pratt and Forman, 2000). This collective identity resides in the couple relationship (Bershcheid, 1994). By its very nature as a social construction between the spouse and entrepreneur, a collective, copreneurial identity involves communicating the sense-making of each member to the other. As couples communicate and clarify their individual social identities in developing shared cognitions for their collective identity related to new business goals, spouses define their meanings through their interactions. The couple's copreneurial identity was not directly assessed in the study but was measured through the interrelationships of the self-report of a spouse's commitment to new venture goals in Time 1 and the assessment of the entrepreneur's evaluation of spousal commitment over time moderated by satisfaction of the entrepreneur with the communication about business issues with the spouse. Conceptual clarity and precision are critical in family process research such as this study.

This study was not about predicting copreneurial identity; it was not about assessing spousal resources that potentially flow from a copreneurial identity, or even to assess whether it existed or not. Rather, this study was about meanings and sense-making that were core to early stages of copreneurial identity formation where identity standards and reflective appraisals of entrepreneurs and spouses are verified. The study's findings reinforced the proposition that the copreneurial identity verification process has two parts. The first part involves the input about the spouse's commitment to new venture goals; the second part has to do with the feedback that the entrepreneur experiences over time-related to that initial spousal commitment. The copreneurial identity has to do not just with the spousal commitment to new venture goals, but it also has to do with the family process interaction of communicating about business issues. Communication is socially constructed and that communication in rooted within the couple relationship. Developing a copreneurial identity is an iterative process between entrepreneurs and their immediate context which includes spousal interaction, a facet of family process.

The message for family firm educators, consultants and to entrepreneurs themselves is that attention needs to be paid not just to business system concerns when starting a new business venture. To increase the probabilities of venture sustainability, attention needs to be given to the creation of a copreneurial identity within owning couples. So not only is available financing and business knowledge and market investigation important when starting a new business venture, but it is important to also assess the strength of the couple relationship of the owning couple. Their mutual commitment cannot develop without satisfying couple communication about new venture goals. It also brings attention to the need to negotiate and reconstruct a different couple relationship that is both personal and professional. It is another example of heeding the power of not only formal power processes but informal power processes within the family system because those processes are a major part of the entrepreneurial fuel that propels the initiation of the venture but also contributes to its sustenance over time.

The Value of Multiple Methods of Assessment

Power is a concept that is of concern within family firms. It is often measured through structure by identifying formal titles that family members hold within the family firm. Power, however, is about the decision-making process, not just who makes the final decision. Assessing power dynamics is more than the formal title or role that a family member holds. The concept of power has both formal and informal dimensions. Within family firms, one is not obtaining the complete picture of power dynamics if assessments approach power in only a structural sense because there is much informal power grounded within the family system that is wielded within family firms. That informal power is expressed across the family, not just within the family members who work for pay within the firm. Family members not having a formal title in the firm can exert informal power in the firm by the nature of their role in the family or the relationship they hold with those working in the firm. An example of such informal power was recognized by Danes in her 2011 editorial in the Entrepreneurship Research Journal when she entitled it "Pillow Talk Leaks: Integrating Couple Interactions into Entrepreneurship Research."

Hedberg and Danes (2012) studied on both formal and informal power by exploring dynamic power processes within family business decision teams as they made a major business change decision. The study was an in-depth investigation of behavioral dynamics of decision-making processes. The focus is important because research indicates that these decision teams are more effective when they exhibit social cohesion (Ensley & Pearson, 2005), when they share leadership (Ensley, Hmieleski & Pearce, 2006; Ensley, Pearson & Pearce, 2003), when they have a unified vision (West 2007), and when they have collective perceptions of how they are working together (Sheperd & Krueger, 2002). However, we know little about what precise conceptual components of individual, dyadic and group dynamics make this happen, especially when family roles overlap with business roles. What we do know about successful communication patterns and productive interactions is that they are based not only in verbal cues but nonverbal cues. Hedberg and Danes' study methodology captured and analyzed both types of cues.

In addressing conceptual complexity and texture of power dynamics, Hedberg and Danes (2012) used four ways to examine power structure and interactions within the family firm decision teams. First, individuals provided written answers to questions about their firm power structure (self-reports). Second, decision teams were interviewed about the process of making a major change within their business. Third, the decision team interview was videotaped and coded for observations of power structures and interactions as well as firm integration. Finally, individual interviews with each spouse were used to contrast with observations from couple interviews to confirm or refute what was said in the team interviews. Through the four analyses, message content could be compared or contrasted with the way messages were conveyed. Likewise, decision team interactions could be examined in comparison to individual perceptions of decision power dynamics. Combined, multiple methods and perspectives allowed for comparisons of message content with nonverbal messages, and dyadic dynamics with individual perceptions.

Induction (Gilgun, 2001) was the analytic procedure used in the study. The procedure requires a theory to guide the analysis; a family theory, Family FIRO theory (Hedberg & Danes, 2012) framed data collection, analysis, organization and presentation of research findings. Power processes were examined from the respondent's perspective with a focus on how people form their own social experiences. To create the power dialogue, interviews were designed around the execution of a planned change. Open-ended questions provided a rich source of information and allowed examination of phenomena using family member words, expressions, and actions resulting in qualitative data rich in content and context without researcher bias from preconceived notions of Family FIRO dimensions. The goal of the analytic induction was to confirm or refute findings from the decision team group interview through an individual member, confidential interviews (Gilgun, 2001). An initial hypothetical conjecture was used to examine cases to determine if the conjecture fit the case observations. The initial conjecture derived from the main Family FIRO tenet was that inclusive power structures lead to more collaborative power interactions resulting in more productive decision teams.

Observational coding from the videos of the decision team interviews was used along with analytic induction to verify decision team power structures and interactions. Group and dyadic interaction scores were coded using Iowa family interaction rating scales (Melby & Conger, 2001). The scales were intended to tap both verbal and nonverbal behaviors and affective and contextual dimensions of interaction. In the observational coding, three coders separately viewed videotaped group interactions. Group consensus among coders determined final scores when differences were detected. Analytical induction analyses were performed by still another coder to prevent introducing bias. To assure consistency in focus, the principle investigator was the one constant in the research project. All these checks and balances created trustworthiness and authenticity. Power structure and interactions were understood through triangulation of multiple perspectives. This form of validation added rigor, breadth, complexity, richness, and depth to any qualitative inquiry (Denzin & Lincoln, 2005).

This study examined power interactions through the use of innovative and diverse methodologies (Helmle et al., 2011). Study findings contributed to understanding how family business decision teams tackle complexities of change and ways in which power processes affect business productivity. Study findings indicated that it was not enough to have an equitable firm power structure; that structure needed to correspond with collaborative power interactions (Edmundson et al., 2003). Family members with business decision teams who listen to each other, who respectfully share ideas and opinions, and who create a positive dynamic do more than communicate well. They provide a platform for constructive discussion of important firm decisions resulting in psychological safety, a situation that mitigates interpersonal risk (Edmondson, 1999). At the very least, repressing a family member's contribution limits resources available to the firm. Creativity in problem solving thrives on the interplay of ideas and insights within an open and respectful team climate where decisions can be discussed without fear of harming interpersonal relationships.

Although the methodologies identified here are time-consuming, they can be quite productive for business decision teams. Videotaping a business decision team while it is making a planned change decision and then analyzing verbal and nonverbal interaction among decision team members can provide some rather insightful observations. The insights might be about its functioning as a group or interactions between dyads within the group. Those insights then might be cross-referenced with the roles and responsibilities of decision group members.

Value of Data from Multiple Family Members

Gudmunson, Danes, Werbel, and Loy (2009) used longitudinal data and structural equation modeling to investigate whether emotional spousal support for business-related concerns was transmitted from spouses to entrepreneurs and whether receipt of this specific type of support would have an impact on business owner's work-family balance. This study demonstrates the use of two family members' views of the same concept by including the spouse's assessment of the emotional support given and the business owner's assessment of the emotional support received. The findings of this study epitomize the benefits of measuring family member interactions at the intersection of family and business systems using information from more than one family member. Within the study's findings, the effects of spousal support were confounded until satisfaction with business communication was introduced. That communication variable was introduced into the model to assess whether spousal support was contributing to the business owner's recognition of its usefulness.

Introducing the family process concept of communication into the model demonstrates some of the subtlety of family processes. The introduction of this firm communication concept revealed competing direct and indirect effects on the firm owner's work/family balance. Owners who sensed that emotional spousal support for firm-related concerns was productive were found to have greater satisfaction with communication about the business and this satisfaction further contributed to his/her sense of work/family balance. On the other hand, once these positive effects of spousal support through satisfying communication were accounted for, we also discovered that the receipt of spousal support could detract from a sense of work/family balance for business owners. Thus, our findings were consistent with Hobfoll's conservation of resources theoretical proposition (2001) that social support is a conditional resource dependent on circumstances.

Resources can be classified as objects, personal characteristics, values, beliefs or energies. There are some family interactions such as the extension of social support that depend on situational needs or that have a time-limited effect (Hobfoll, 1989). In terms of situational context, social support may contribute to resilience when it facilitates the preservation of other resources but it can also have a deleterious effect when it detracts from other personal resources. For example, a spouse might offer support to the entrepreneur by taking sole responsibility for child care during hectic business times and that would create a certain resilience capacity for the entrepreneur. The situation needs at a point in time may dictate the assessment of the giving or receiving of social support as a resource or a constraint. Its positive effect could be time-limited as well. If the full responsibility for child care continues for an extended time period, the spouse's work/family balance could become strained creating a stress contagion effect for the spouse that eventually spills over to the entrepreneurs that gradually leads to a deleterious impact on business performance.

Several lessons may be learned from this example. One of the lessons learned for family business educators, consultants, and business owners alike, is that within family processes there is never just one individual perspective and that perspective might change with time and situational needs. With structure, roles, and rules, generalizations can be made more easily than with family processes. Knowing and understanding context is absolutely critical when assessing family processes and taking account of all players in that social context is part of understanding the context. Another lesson is to think through whether you need input from a family member about her/his processes or input from more than one family member about family processes. Gudmunson et al (2009) obtained results and insights that would not have been possible without responses from more than one family member.

Direct and Indirect Indicators of Family Processes

In their paper on the effects of family capital on family business outcomes, Danes, Stafford, Haynes and Amarapurkar (2009) measured family processes directly and indirectly while controlling for the effects of family and firm structure. They included respondent answers to questions about family processes, the outcomes of family processes and family capital stocks and flows over time. They defined family capital as all resources of owning family members, whether or not employed by the firm. They used data from the first two years in the National Family Business Panel. Respondents were a geographic area probability sample of U.S. business owning families in 1997. Due to the method of sample selection, the results are generalizable to all business owning families in the United States and their businesses. Precisely because the overwhelming majority of family businesses are small and privately owned, so are the businesses in this data. Generalizability to any particular subset of families and businesses is less reliable.

They analyzed effects of three direct measures of family processes during 1997 on both business gross revenue and owner-perceived success in 1997 and later in 2000: family functioning, adjustment strategies and resource family/business intermingling processes. These measures were considered direct because they were based on respondent answers to questions about their processes during telephone interviews. Family functioning type measured how members interacted with each other and their environments during stable periods. Family functioning was classified as either: a) family members negotiate with each other, b) family members act as individuals, and c) the family has ordered decision making. Families with each of these types of functioning in this sample reported fairly consistent interaction patterns; they did not readily switch how they functioned during stable periods. Adjustment strategies indicated how family members changed their routines during "crunch" times, periods of change and pressure on resources. Family members could use all or none of these strategies. In earlier research, five strategies had proved influential on family and business achievements and were included in the analysis. They were: a) use temporary hired help, b) family members volunteer to help, c) business manager takes work home, d) reallocate tasks to other family members and e) reallocate to spend more time with family. For this study, resource intermingling was coded simply as either from the family to the business or vice versa.

After controlling for family and business s structure, direct measures of family processes had statistically significant effects across indicators of success. In both 1997 and 2000, family processes explained less variance in gross revenue than did family and business structure, and in both years, family processes explained more variance in perceived success than did structure. Specifically, adjustment strategies had significant effects on gross revenue and owner's perceived success. Adjustment strategies had similar effects on both gross revenue and perceived success, but resource intermingling did not as indicated by the signs and significance of the coefficients. Differences in the relative size of effects and a qualitative (sign) difference in the effect of a variable have implications for scholars, practitioners and owners alike. Such results mean that it is necessary to identify and keep in mind the desired or important aspect of achievement or sustainability.

Furthermore, effects of direct measures of family processes on both gross revenue and owner's perceived success persisted over time. The relative explanatory power of direct measures of family processes was consistent over time, although it differed between gross revenue and perceived success. Also, the direction of the effects was consistent over time. By 2000, three of the adjustment strategies still had significant effects on business gross revenue and one adjustment strategy still had a significant effect on owner's perceived success. It is worth noting that among the direct measures of family processes those measuring family processes during change had greater effects than processes during stability. After all, families and their businesses are at greatest risk during crunch times or periods of change. Obtaining sound education and advice in preparation for such periods can make or break them.

Danes et al (2009) also analyzed indirect indicators of family processes. They analyzed effects of subjective family outcomes, capital stocks available for use and capital flows. They included two family process outcomes: a) family integrity and b) family/business congruity. Family integrity was measured by the Family APGAR score, a five-item scale assessing respondents' satisfaction with family Adaptation, Partnership, Growth, Affection, and Resolve (Danes & Stafford, 2011). This sample had high family integrity, indicating most were sufficiently strong to be able to withstand the stress of change. Congruity was also high, indicating a high degree of perceived harmony between family and firm systems. Harmony is the absence of conflict.

These family outcomes did not have significant effects on either business gross revenue or owner's perceived success.

Another indirect way to analyze family and firm processes is to track capital stocks available for input and capital flows. Processes require the use of resources; hence, analysis of resource use is one more means by which we may gain information about family business system processes and their effectiveness. Human capital and financial capital explained significant proportions of variance in business gross revenue and owner's perceived success in both 1997, the current year, and three years later in 2000. Social capital in 1997 explained significant proportions of variance in gross revenue and owner's perceived success only in 2000. Capital stocks are resources available for use either before or after a process; whereas, capital flows are changes in capital stocks during a specific time period. This difference in results highlights the importance of distinguishing between stock and flow measures of capital. Sirmon and Hitt (2003), Heck, Danes, Loy and Stafford (2008), and Danes et al. (2009) distinguish between capital stocks and flows and refer to use of capital stock, capital flows) as resource management, a process. Family resource management may be more important to firm achievement in the short run and sustainability in the long run than family capital stock available. The greater effect of the flow measures in the Danes et al. study means that careful attention should be paid to the type of measure used for family capital. One implication is that the assumption that capital available will be used is not safe. Also, nonuse of family capital does not mean that it is not available.

This relatively small body of quantitative research reinforces some of the conclusions drawn from qualitative research on family interpersonal processes earlier in this chapter. Data from multiple perspectives or using multiple dependent variables yields more reliable conclusions. For example, in their analysis of family capital flows over time, Danes, Stafford, Haynes and Amarapurkar (2009) found that family capital accounted for more variance in business gross revenue in the long run, but more variance in owner perceived success in the short run. When comparing contributions of family capital within each time period, in both short and long run, family capital accounted for more variance in gross revenue than in owner perceived success.

The Danes et al. (2009) study findings demonstrated that when business owners assess the short run use of family capital as making a constructive contribution to the business, that dynamic creates a synergistic multiplier effect in management behavior. Management synergy grows out of the psychic energy created from effective contributions of family capital, whether through formal or informal channels and fuels deeper commitment and continuity motivation that is exhibited in measurable outcomes such as gross revenue in the long-term.

For some owners business gross revenue and perceived success move together, while for others they do not. The authors initially believed that business gross revenue was an objective measure of success and owner's perception was a subjective measure of success. However, as the authors collected data from the same owners over time, they found that the two measures did not even reliably move in the same direction. It is possible that just as Hedburg and Danes (2012) found that couples whose power dynamics when together were confirmed through individual and confidential statements and whose power was distributed equitably owned businesses that did better, so we might find that the businesses of owners whose perceptions of success more closely tracked objective measures would do better. More research needs to be done with simultaneous multiple indicators of family processes. More research is also needed that focuses on family business decision team dynamics with individual confirmations or refutations when not within the group setting. Group dynamics and individual members' perceptions about what they actually think occurs can match the group dynamics or be quite different; with the latter, scarce resources tend to be diverted from business goals and vision.

Danes et al. also found that the picture of family business processes is slightly different when based on data from a single period and when based on data from multiple time periods. This phenomenon is well known to economists, but the familiarity of the phenomenon has not meant that we know better how to predict the long run from short run data. That is due to the need for much more research on family processes related to capital flows both within the business and between the business and the family and the recognition of not only formal power of family members working within the business but also the informal power of those members who are committed to the family business but do not have formal business titles.

Referring to the two key points in studying and observing family processes, use of various dimensions of the family capital bundle (human, social, and financial) (Danes et al., 2009) are observable family behaviors. In assessing size and shape of the underlying family processes (fuel for the entrepreneurial engine), one needs to then observe the effects of the use of family capital over time from multiple perspectives (e.g. perceived firm success and gross revenues). True firm success in family businesses is not just a function of financial gains but also of healthy family functioning (Danes et al., 2008; Danes & Brewton, 2012). Strong families beget strong family businesses. Using metaphors, family processes can either be the sturdy foundation for successful family businesses or the quicksand that siphons energies and resources from the core goals of the family business, draining its entrepreneurial fuel.

Long-Run and Short-Run Family Processes

Gudmunson and Danes (2013) analyzed family social capital use processes over time, and their study illustrates the difference between family processes at one point in time and over time. In other words, family processes are not immutable; they are time dependent. They used data collection at three points in time to investigate the direction of effects in associations between family functional strength and business-related tension as related to firm continuation status. Family resilience capacity is embodied in family functional strength and business-related tensions represented business system demands and stresses on family functional strength. The resilience processes of drawing on family functional strength to solve problems around the demands and stresses of business-related tensions occur at the family and business interface. Bubolz (2001) indicates that social capital is a latent resource typically consumed when needed and when it is consumed, it facilitates action and creates value facilitating productivity.

Findings provide an in-depth window into the contribution of family processes to family firm continuity. Only longitudinal data with repeated measures can provide such insight along with following businesses that survive and close over time. Using quantitative structural equation modeling and panel data collected by phone interviews at three points in time, these authors contributed to family process research by: 1) investigating continuity and crossover effects between family functional strength and business-related tensions over time, 2) examining coefficients for multiple group differences, and 3) revealing correlates that retain significance while controlling for past effects of family functioning strength and business-related tension on these same measures. These procedures allowed an investigation of differences in the family functioning strength and business-related tension relationship for family businesses that survived over time and those that did not.

Gudmunson and Danes (2013) assessed the family processes over a three-year period while both groups of family businesses were operating. Continuity status was assessed seven years later.

For the businesses that remained in operation, there was a buffering effect of family functional strength on business-related tensions over time and strong cross-sectional association within each year. For the group of still existing businesses, family processes were part of a pattern of enduring processes that demonstrated the cumulative effect of social capital development over time. For the businesses that were closed seven years later, the relationships between family functional strengths and business-related tensions were the lead-up period to discontinuation of ownership. Family processes for this discontinued group of family businesses indicated that stress evolved when resources were threatened, lost or believed to be unstable or family members could not see a path to fostering or protecting resources through individual or joint efforts (Hobfoll, 2001).

This study's findings tell us that business tensions that do not subside tend to spill over into the family context; they have a stress pile-up effect over time. Ignoring the problem issues does not make them go away. The danger here, however, is that people tend to personalize these issues without delving into or communicating about the root causes of the tension. A neutral third party who understands family process may be needed to negotiate some of the more deep-seeded family concerns, but often a family member who is committed to the business but is not directly impacted by the business issue causing the tension may be able to visualize alternatives. Scenario-building exercises often allow for a more neutral problem-solving atmosphere.

Discussion

At this point, we hope that we have convinced you that family processes are relevant to firm outcomes - firm achievements in the short-term and sustainability in the long-term. We all readily accept the proposition that without processes, we are left with only potential. We less readily accept that processes within the family affect business outcomes. We have endeavored in this chapter to convince you of the latter. In doing so, we have addressed both observable interpersonal and resource transactions and processes that reflect the unseen patterns created, sustained and modified by the owning families. In other words, both the observable behaviors and the unseen family patterns affect family firm outcomes. Evidence for effects of both aspects of family processes is plentiful and growing.

There is evidence that adjustment processes invoked during periods of peak demand in either the family or the firm have greater effects on business outcomes than do routine processes invoked during lulls or relatively stable periods. Having said this, you should not wait until peak demand periods or a crisis to ask about these processes or to give attention to them. Consequently, these family adjustment strategies are a good place to start inquiring about family processes and establishing a desired comfort level. All families have these adjustment processes and our research experience tells us family members can readily tell you about them when asked. Think about and ask yourself or others, "What do you do?"; that approach is much easier than asking about feelings.

For educators, consultants and owners alike, the fact that family processes affect business achievements and sustainability should be viewed as good news because processes are much easier and quicker to change than family structure, roles, and rules. Changing family structure entails such major decisions as marriage and divorce decisions or decisions to have a child. Family structure is also affected by aspects over which we have little or no control such as aging and death. Family roles and rules also can be affected substantially by aspects of life over which we have no control such as ethnicity, gender, age, and birth order. By contrast, members of owning families have much more control over their family processes within the constraints imposed by their resources and environment. In other words, attending to family processes can have a relatively quick beneficial effect on family business achievements and sustainability. Having now convinced you of the benefits of attending to family processes as well as structure, roles and rules, it is imperative that more efforts are spent on collecting data on those processes. Students studying business need to study about family processes as well as business management. Family business consulting teams need to be composed of people who understand family processes and human behavior as well as business management principles.

Useful data on family processes can be obtained via both interview and observation. Both means of obtaining information on family processes have advantages and disadvantages. Interviews, whether oral or written, rely on interviewee honesty and awareness of themselves and others, but can address past and present behavior and future intentions. Observation is more viable with small groups and is limited to the current time period. Unlike interviews, observation does not require subject honesty and self-awareness. Observation does not even require verbal responses. Both data collection methods work very well. The choice of method depends on your purpose, access to the owning family and availability of analytical expertise.

Observation has the advantage of being able to note both verbal and nonverbal responses, and it also enables you to obtain data on interpersonal interactions. However, observation consumes a lot of time and is expensive. Of course, owners also find it difficult to observe themselves. These days, technology has facilitated data collection by observation. Ubiquitous cell phones with cameras have made it easier to record interactions without changing the nature of the interaction itself. They have also made it faster to record a transaction process and then review it. Selfie boom sticks even make it possible to record group interactions with a recorder participant. It is more important than ever before to understand the expertise of business consulting teams because if consultants do not understand more than basic dynamics of human behavior and family processes, they can make disastrous recommendations that could affect not only business success but the healthy functioning of the owning family.

Interview data are more viable when time and expense are issues. These interviews might be for research but they also might be to gather information about owning family members when doing consulting with families. Interviews can be structured and responses precoded. Interviews give you the opportunity to rehearse and pretest questions and their wording. To understand how important this can be, all we have to do is recall a recent news story about an opinion survey in which a question was asked two different ways and the responses changed from the majority in favor to the majority against. The ground-breaking research in heuristics for which a Nobel Prize in Economics was awarded documented the potentially large effects on decisions of small differences in wording. Closer to home, in one of our surveys we asked owners if they had sought help from a list of government agencies. Very few said yes, yet we knew in some cases that they were agency clients. We had made the mistake of using the "H" word (help) instead of a more neutral word such as advice. Interviews allow dress rehearsals and "do overs" that observation does not.

Here is just one example of where information about family processes could be obtained by either observation or interview. An enterprising couple with young children had a growing business; they were expanding the building that housed the business. Before the expansion, the couple had their offices in the same room. During the day, they constantly communicated about business issues and the child care and school decisions simultaneously as the day progressed. A business consultant stated that they needed to totally separate business and family as they grew the firm and recommended having separate offices on opposite ends of the building, which is what they did. However, what eventually happened with this total work/ family separation was a level of couple stress that led to couple tensions that grew to the point of discussion of divorce. It wasn't until they hired a different business consultant that was knowledgeable about family processes that they recognized where they potentially went wrong; they then decided to rearrange the business office space so they could more efficiently organize their family and work responsibilities. By ignoring the measurable couple behavior and the underlying family processes in this example, the first business consultant created a disastrous result. Strong family businesses are based on healthy, strong families. That means paying attention to family processes and business management because of their reciprocal relationship.

Whether you obtain data via observation or interview, we propose you follow a few rules of thumb. Obtain data from more than one source. Talk to more than one family member if possible. Obtain more than one type of data. For example, this might entail obtaining objective *and* subjective measures of achievements, or qualitative *and* quantitative measures of the nature of family conversations. Also, use as many multiple item indicators as possible. For example, we suggest using an indicator such as the Family APGAR to assess family integrity. The assessment is based on responses to five questions, instead of the response to a single question. Direct measures of family processes work better than indirect measures, so if possible, use direct measures. Examples of direct measures would be actions taken and resources used for a particular purpose. An example of an indirect measure would be capital available. Just because capital is available does not mean that it is used. Direct measures assess whether the capital is actually being used in the most efficient and effective manner. More recent processes should be a higher priority when inquiring about family processes. Research results indicate that the further away from the current time period questions refer to, the less reliable the answers unless you provide an event to use as a reference point such as the opening of the first store or the youngest daughter's marriage. Also, the further in the past a process occurred, the smaller the effect is likely to be on current and future achievements and sustainability.

Attending to family processes offers the potential for improving family business achievements and sustainability relatively quickly at relatively little financial cost. Take advantage of the opportunities you have to think about and obtain information about family processes. Start a conversation. Observe and listen. Raise your awareness level. Then you can start to formulate questions. There are good examples of ways to effectively word questions available online, so you do not have to start from scratch. Remember, even poor measures are usually better than none. The emotional cost may be relatively larger than the financial cost. The fundamental justification for incurring this emotional cost is the increase in human and social capital for the family that will pay dividends far into the future.

Attending to family processes offers the potential for improving family business achievements and sustainability relatively quickly at relatively little financial cost. Do not let the perfect be the enemy of the good. In other words, some progress in attending to family processes is better than the current state of ignoring them. In this chapter, we have presented some potential ways that have been used to measure and assess family processes. They may not yet be perfect ways to do so but they are a beginning. More work on family process assessment is needed in the future. But meanwhile, take advantage of the opportunities you have to think about and obtain information about family processes. Start a conversation. Observe and listen. Raise your awareness level. Then you can start to formulate questions. There are good examples of ways to effectively word questions available online, so you do not have to start from scratch. Remember, even poor measures are usually better than none. The emotional cost may be relatively larger than the financial cost. The fundamental justification for incurring this emotional cost is the increase in human and social capital for the family that will pay dividends within the family business far into the future. In other words, family business experts, owning families and their businesses can all benefit from knowing more about family processes and their effects on the family's business.

References

Berscheid, E. (1994). Interpersonal relationships. *Annual Review of Psychology*, Vol. 4, pp. 29–79.

Bubolz, M. (2001). Family as source, user, and builder of social capital. *Journal of Socio-Economics*, *30*, 129–131.

Danes, S.M. (2014). The future of family business research through the family scientist's lens (Chapter 31; pp. 611–619). In *Handbook of Family Business*, Melin, L., Nordqvist, M., & Sharma, P. (Eds.), Sage: NY, NY.

Danes, S.M. & Brewton, K.E. (2012). Follow the Capital: Benefits of Tracking Family Capital across Family and Business Systems (Chapter 14, pp. 227–250). In Alan Carsrud & Malin Brannback (Eds.), *Understanding Family Businesses: Undiscovered Approaches, Unique Perspectives, and Neglected Topics*. Springer.

Danes, S.M., J. Lee, K. Stafford, and R. K. Z. Heck, (2008). The effects of ethnicity, families and culture on entrepreneurial experience: An extension of sustainable family business theory. Invited article for *Journal of Developmental Entrepreneurship, Special Issue* titled Empirical Research on Ethnicity and Entrepreneurship in the U.S., *13*(3), 229–268.

Danes, S.M., Matzek, A. E. and Werbel, J. D. (2010), Spousal context during the venture creation process, in Katz, J. A. and Lumpkin, G. T. (Eds.), *Advances in Entrepreneurship, Firm Emergence and Growth*: Vol. 12, Emerald, New Milford, CT, pp. 113–162.

Danes, S.M. & Stafford, K. (2011). Family social capital as family business resilience capacity. In Richard Sorenson (Ed.), *Family Business and Social Capital* (pp. 79–105, Chapter 7). Edward Elgar: UK.

Danes, S.M., Stafford, K., Haynes, G., & Amarapurkar, S. (2009). Family capital of family firms: Bridging human, Social, and financial capital. *Family Business Review, 22*(3), 199–215.

Denzin, N.K. & Lincoln, Y.S. (2000). *Handbook of Qualitative Research* (2nd Ed.). Thousand Oaks, CA; Sage.

Dimov, D. (2007), 'Beyond the single-person, single-insight attribution in understanding entrepreneurial opportunities,' *Entrepreneurship, Theory, and Practice*, pp. 713–731.

Dyer, W.G. Jr. & Dyer, W.J. (2009). Putting the family into family business research. *Family Business Review*, 22 (1), 216–219.

Edmondson, A. (1999). Psychological safety and learning behavior in work teams. *Administrative Science Quarterly, 44*(4), 350–383.

Edmundson, A., Roberto, A., & Watkins, M. (2003). A dynamic model of top management tam effectiveness: Managing unstructured task streams. *The Leadership Quarterly, 14*, 297–325.

Ensley, M., Hmieleski, K., & Pearce, C. (2006). The importance of vertical and shared leadership within new venture top management teams: Implications for the performance of startups. *The Leadership Quarterly, 17*(3), 217–231.

Ensley, M., & Pearson, A. (2005). An exploratory comparison of the behavioral dynamics of top management teams in family and nonfamily new ventures: Cohesion, conflict, potency, and consensus. *Entrepreneurship Theory and Practice, 29*(3), 267–284.

Gilgun, J. (2001). Grounded theory and other inductive research methods. In Bruce A. Thyer (Ed.), *The Handbook of Social Work Research Methods* (pp. 345–364). Thousand Oaks, CA: Sage.

Gudmunson, C.G. & Danes, S.M. (2013). Family social capital in family businesses; A stocks and flows investigation. *Family Relation, 62*, 399–414. DOI:10.111/fare.12017.

Gudmunson, C.G., Danes, S.M., Loy, J.T., & Werbel, J.D. (2009). Spousal support and work/family balance in launching a family business. *Journal of Family Issues, 30*(8), 1098–1121.

Hedberg, P.R. & Danes, S.M. (2012). Explorations of dynamic power processes within copreneurial couples: *Journal of Family Business Strategy, 3*, 228–238.

Helmle, J., Seibold, D., & Afifi, T. (2011). Work & family in copreneurial family businesses. In C. Salmon (Ed.), *Communication Yearbook 35* (pp. 51–91). New York and London: Routledge.

Hobfoll, S. E. (1989). Conservation of resources: A new attempt at conceptualizing stress. *American Psychologist, 44*, 513–524.

Hobfoll, S. E. (2001). The influence of culture, community, and the nested-self in the stress process: Advancing conservation of resources theory. *Applied Psychology: An International Review, 50*, 337–421.

Melby, J.N. & Conger, R.D. (2001). The Iowa Family Interaction Rating Scales: Instrument summary. In P. Kerig and K. Lindahl (Eds.), *Family Observational Coding Systems: Resources for Systematic Research*, (pp. 33–58). Mahwah, NJ: Erlbaum.

Shepherd, D., & Krueger, N. (2002). An intentions-based model of entrepreneurial teams' social cognition. *Entrepreneurial Theory and Practice, 27*(2), 167–185.

Van Auken, H. and Werbel, J. (2006), Family dynamic and family business financial performance: Spousal commitment, *Family Business Review,* Vol. 19, pp. 49–63.

West, G. (2007). Collective cognition: When entrepreneurial teams, not individuals, make decisions. *Entrepreneurship Theory and Practice, 31*(1), 77–102.

22

UNCOVERING THE 'MISSING VARIABLE'

The Family in Family Business Research

Thomas Rieg and Sabine Rau

Introduction

While the family is undoubtedly the variable that distinguishes family firms from other organizational forms, surprisingly little scholarly attention has been paid to the examination of business-owning families (Dyer 2003). Consequently, scholars have recently called for a greater focus on the family, and accordingly on variables related to the family system, to better understand the behavior and performance of family firms (e.g., Craig and Salvato 2012; Dyer and Dyer 2009; Sharma, Chrisman, and Gersick 2012; Sharma, Melin, and Nordqvist 2014; Yu et al. 2012). To the point is Bertrand and Schoar's (2006; 95) assertion "that much can be learned by taking serious the 'family' part of 'family firms.'" For example, recent studies demonstrate that different family configurations and characteristics are associated with varying levels of entrepreneurial activity in family firms (e.g., Alsos, Carter, and Ljunggren 2014; Jaskiewicz, Combs, and Rau 2015; Michael-Tsabari, Labaki, and Zachary 2014). However, such family related research endeavors require ways to conceptualize and measure the family variable (Dyer and Dyer 2009; Pearson, Holt, and Carr 2014; Sharma, Melin, and Nordqvist 2014). Thus, to pave the way for more family related research in the future, it is essential to synthesize, consolidate, and assess existing knowledge on how to operationalize the family in empirical research and to identify blind spots where new measures need to be developed. Accordingly, the central research question of this paper is: *Which options are available to operationalize 'family' as a variable, and what are avenues for future research?*

To answer this research question, we conduct a structured literature review of articles published in leading outlets for family business research. The remainder of this paper is structured as follows: First, we outline the methodological aspects of the literature selection and analysis. Second, we present an integrative framework to classify different family measures. Third, in the main section of this paper, we analyze the literature and consolidate the findings using the framework. The psychometric quality of the measures employed, a topic of increasing relevance for family business researchers, will also be assessed in this part. The following discussion section will sum up the main findings, discuss research gaps, and provide directions for future research.

This paper offers several contributions: First, we provide family business researchers with an overview and classification of available constructs and measures that can serve as a starting point for studies incorporating the family as a unit of analysis and provide reference points on how to capture the heterogeneity of business-owning families. Second, this paper identifies promising areas for the development of new measures to capture the "striking diversity of family structures, values and interaction patterns" (James, Jennings, and Breitkreuz 2012; 94), as advocated by several leading scholars (e.g., Dyer and Dyer 2009; Sharma, Melin, and Nordqvist 2014; Pearson, Holt, and Carr 2014). Third, by assessing and discussing the psychometric quality of the existing measures, we follow Pearson and Lumpkin's (2011; 288) call to "pay greater attention to measurement issues if the field is to make scientific progress."

Methodology and Literature Selection

This chapter follows the general approach employed by David and Han (2004) for an objective and systematic literature review. A structured literature review employs a transparent and replicable process through which existing knowledge can be identified and evaluated (Mulrow 1994). We focus exclusively on articles published in journals that require a systematic peer review process to ensure a certain quality level and scientific rigor (Light and Pillemer 1984). Although neighboring fields such as psychology and sociology could provide interesting insights on the family variable, we concentrate on articles written in a family business context. We believe that each field merits a separate review regarding how it conceptualizes and operationalizes "family," the results of which could later be used to draw comparisons across fields. The *Academic Journal Quality Guide* (The Association of Business Schools 2010) serves as a baseline to identify relevant journals. Among the different sub-fields of business and management cataloged by the guide, journals listed in *Economics, Entrepreneurship and Small Business Management, Finance, General Management, Organization Studies,* and *Strategic Management* are selected as likely outlets for relevant studies. The Association of Business Schools ranks journal quality using four categories, with grade 1 being the lowest and grade 4 the highest (The Association of Business Schools 2010). Only journals ranked as grade four are included in the list of relevant scientific journals for this review, except for *Entrepreneurship and Small Business Management*, where journals from grades two and three are included to incorporate relevant outlets such as *Family Business Review* or *Journal of Small Business Management*.

In total, this yields 46 journals.[1] We then selected keywords to identify relevant studies. To ensure that no important article is left out, we decided to use initially broad keywords to identify all studies that deal with family firms, and only in subsequent steps to limit the search to articles that focus on the business-owning family. Hence, we used the following keywords to search abstracts, title, and author supplied keywords:

> "family firm" OR "family business" OR "family company" OR "family enterprise" OR "family-controlled" OR "family-managed" OR "family-owned" OR "founding family" OR "privately held firm"

Similar to David and Han (2004), variations of the ending of the words are permitted. Given the abundance of studies focusing on family firms published in *Family Business Review*, all articles published in the relevant timeframe are included in the initial pool of articles. Our review of high-quality peer-reviewed studies is limited to the volumes starting in 1998, thereby connecting to Rothausen's 1999 review on the "family in organizational research." The search was carried out using the bibliographic database Scopus. The articles published in *Family Business Review* plus the articles identified through the keywords yielded an initial sample of 908 articles.

As a third step, we develop criteria for the inclusion or exclusion of specific studies. First, as the goal of this paper is to identify ways to operationalize the business-owning family, we focus on the family sub-system within the family business system (Pieper and Klein 2007). Hence, we exclude studies that concentrate exclusively on the business system, or that assess the family solely based on ownership or involvement in the top management team of the firm (e.g., Anderson and Reeb 2003; Schulze, Lubatkin, and Dino 2003; Villalonga and Amit 2006). Second, due to the fact that a family consists of a "group of people" (Rothausen 1999; 819), we also exclude studies that focus on the characteristics and attitudes of individuals (e.g., Parker and van Praag 2012; Marshall et al. 2006; Zellweger, Sieger, and Halter 2011). Third, we decided to consider conceptual papers only if they go beyond anecdotal evidence and case illustrations (e.g., Abetti and Phan 2004).

Following the process suggested by David and Han (2004), we read the abstracts of the initial 908 articles identified using the keywords to select those that meet the inclusion criteria above. This step drastically reduced the number of articles to a more manageable pool of 135 articles. This is hardly surprising given that the field "is now dominated by topics and theoretical perspectives associated with the business system" (Sharma, Chrisman, and Gersick 2012; 10). The remaining 135 articles were retrieved and read in their entirety. Information including the bibliographic information, the theoretical background, and the independent and dependent variables was extracted from these articles. A closer analysis of the articles revealed that another 67 studies did not meet the inclusion requirements; these were removed from the article pool. The final list consisted of 68 papers in respected journals that focus on or include the business-owning family as a variable. The list of journals, their impact factor, and the number of articles obtained from each journal are summarized in Table 22.1.

Developing a Framework to Categorize Family Measures

An essential aspect in classifying and synthesizing existing research in a systematic manner is a clear conceptual framework. Such a framework allows for the organization and localization of constructs, variables, and findings in a coherent and comprehensive manner. Furthermore, a conceptual framework facilitates the identification of gaps in the literature and accordingly avenues for future research. For this literature review, constructs and measures used for business-owning families were classified in a matrix along two dimensions: a unit of analysis and a type of measure.

Unit of Analysis

On a general level, a family can be defined as a "unit of interacting personalities" (Burgess 1926). As such, it requires several individuals that "cohere in an ongoing structure that are both sustained and altered through interaction" (Handel 1965; 21). However, within each family system, several substructures exist that represent different units of analysis. Common levels of analysis for family assessment are the individual, dyadic, and whole system levels of the family (Jacob and Tennenbaum 1988; Skinner, Steinhauer, and Sitarenios 2000). Given that sociologists treat the dyad as the smallest social group, and given that research related to individual characteristics and their impact on business outcomes represents a different

Table 22.1 Journals and Articles Reviewed for the Literature Review

ABS Journal Categories	Journal	2013 Impact Factor	Number of initial articles through keywords	Number of articles after abstract scan	Number of final articles
Economics	American Economic Review	3.305	2	0	0
	Quarterly Journal of Economics	5.966	2	1	1
	Review of Economics and Statistics	2.718	1	0	0
	Journal of the European Economic Association	3.356	3	0	0
Entrepreneur- ship and Small Business Management	Journal of Business Venturing	3.265	35	5	5
	Entrepreneurship Theory and Practice	2.598	115	32	11
	International Small Business Journal	1.397	20	4	0
	Entrepreneurship and Regional Development	1.000	12	2	1
	Small Business Economics	1.641	46	6	2
	Journal of Small Business Management	1.361	48	8	4
	Strategic Entrepreneurship Journal	1,744	6	0	0
	Journal of Small Business and Enterprise Development	0.289	20	2	1
	International Journal of Entrepreneurial Behavior and Research	0.545	18	1	0
	International Journal of Entrepreneurship and Innovation	0.592	3	0	0
	Family Business Review	4.243	480	61	38
General Management	Academy of Management Review	7.817	2	0	0
	Academy of Management Journal	4.974	3	1	0
	Administrative Science Quarterly	2.394	3	0	0
	Journal of Management	6.862	3	0	0
	Journal of Management Studies	3.277	18	5	2
	Harvard Business Review	1.831	7	0	0
	British Journal of Management	1.909	3	0	0
Organization Studies	Organization Science	3.807	8	2	0
	Organization Studies	2.504	7	1	0
	Leadership Quarterly	2.006	1	1	1
	Human Relations	1.867	1	1	0
Strategic Management	Strategic Management Journal	2.993	10	1	0
Finance	Journal of Finance	6.033	6	0	0
	Review of Financial Studies	3.532	7	0	0
	Journal of Financial and Quantitative Analysis	1.877	3	1	1
	Journal of Financial Economics	3.769	15	1	1
		Ø 3.154	908	135	68

(Note: Journals that produced no results after the keyword search, such as *Econometrica*, are not included in the list above.)
Source: Own

research stream, we exclusively focus on the dyad and the whole family unit of analysis for this review.

In a family firms context, dyads can refer to different combinations of family member pairs, such as siblings, couples, father-daughter pairs, etc., that are shaped by certain characteristics such as trust, marital status, or age relationships. In contrast, the whole family level refers to the family in its entirety. Family business scholars often use expansive definitions of family that goes beyond the nuclear conceptualization prevalent in other social science fields (Anderson, Jack, and Dodd 2005; Distelberg and Blow 2011). Whole families as a group or a network can develop special dynamics, such as cohesion and conflict, that set them apart from other families.

Type of Measure

Measures for family assessment can be separated into two distinct categories: structural-quantitative and psychodynamic measures (Rothausen 1999). Structural measures refer to the biological and legal ties that bind the family together as a social group (Brannon, Wiklund, and Haynie 2013). This approach is closely related to the genograms used in many social science disciplines to describe the family unit in a structured and standardized way. Common variables include the number of children and siblings as well as gender and age spacing that allow the construction of a family tree over multiple generations (Nicholson 2008). Psychodynamic measures, on the other hand, do not refer to the structural dimensions of the family but rather to the internal dynamics and the functioning of the family unit. Over time, family systems develop certain internal cultures and dynamics that are key to understanding why some families function better than others under certain circumstances (Dyer and Dyer 2009). For example, Zahra (2012) finds that the level of family cohesiveness has an influence on organizational learning in family firms while Salvato and Melin (2008) highlight the importance of family cohesion for the development of family social capital.

Figure 22.1 summarizes the two orthogonal dimensions – unit of analysis and type of measure with their binary subcategories – that will be used to classify and consolidate measures to assess the business-owning family.

		TYPE OF MEASURE	
		Assessment of Family Structure	Assessment of Family Dynamics and Functioning
	Dyad	Dyad Structure	Dyad Dynamics and Functioning
UNIT OF ANALYSIS	Whole Family	Whole Family Structure	Whole Family Dynamics and Functioning

Figure 22.1 Analytical Framework for the Literature Review
Source: Own

Literature Analysis and Results

Descriptive Results

Methodologies Applied

The studies identified for this literature review employ a multiplicity of research methodologies. Surprisingly, nearly 31 percent of the studies use a case study approach to collect information on family firms. This is more than twice as many as the average number of papers published using qualitative research methods in the field's major outlet, the *Family Business Review* (Reay 2014). A possible explanation might be that family-related research usually requires a trust-based relationship, which is easier to establish in personal interviews than with mail or online surveys (Eddleston and Kidwell 2012). However, half of the analyzed papers are based on large-scale surveys that were collected via questionnaires or telephone interviews. This mirrors Dawson and Hjorth's (2012) ascertainment that large-scale surveys remain the predominant method of research in the family business field. Furthermore, several studies in the sample are based on the same survey. For example, the papers by Danes and Olson (2003), Danes et al. (2009) and Muske and Fitzgerald (2006) are all based on the National Family Business Survey (NFBS) conducted between 1997 and 2000.

Studies concentrating on conceptual development (10 percent of the studies) or which are based on secondary data (7 percent) are rather scarce. However, several studies have used interesting and noteworthy sources to collect secondary data on the family. For example, Bertrand et al. (2008) as well as Bunkanwanicha, Fan, and Wiwattanakantang (2013) use cremation booklets that detail the deceased's family history to reconstruct the family trees of business-owning families (in Thailand, such books are traditionally distributed as gifts to funeral guests). The distribution of methodologies employed by the studies in this sample is summarized in figure 22.2 below.

Theories Applied

Strong and adequate theoretical foundation is the cornerstone of organizational research and key to understanding the systematic reason for a specific phenomenon (Corley and Gioia 2011; Reay and Whetten 2011; Sutton and Staw 1995). A lack of adequate theory encourages

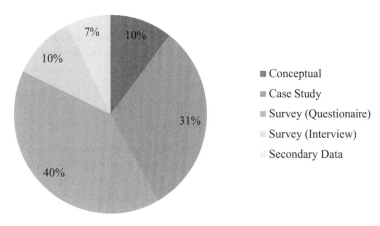

Figure 22.2   Methodologies Employed
Source: Own

the fragmentation of research findings and prohibits the generalization of insights into family business processes and outcomes. This problem is especially apparent for the studies reviewed in this paper – 50 percent of the studies lack an identifiable theoretical foundation. Many studies discuss and list various variables and constructs and connect them based on previous findings documented in the literature, but lack a coherent theory that explains *why* these variables are selected and *how* they influence each other.

Among the studies that have a clear theoretical foundation, nearly half use established family business theories such as agency theory (e.g., Karra, Tracey, and Phillips 2006), social capital theory (e.g., Sorenson et al. 2009), systems theory (e.g., Distelberg and Blow 2011), conflict theory (e.g., Davis and Harveston 2001) or social identity theory (e.g., Brannon, Wiklund, and Haynie 2013). Some papers borrow from related fields. For example, some borrow from psychology: Trevinyo-Rodriguez and Bontis (2010) use Cultural-Historical Activity Theory (Vygotsky 1978). Others borrow from family science: Kwan, Lau, and Au (2012) employ Conservation of Resource Theory (Hobfoll 1989); Haberman and Danes (2007) build upon Fundamental Interpersonal Relations Orientation Theory (Schutz 1958); and Penney and Combs (2013) use the Circumplex Model (Olson, Sprenkle, and Russell 1979). Additionally, several papers use theories that have been developed specifically for family firm research, such as the Sustainable Family Business Theory (e.g., Danes et al. 2009) developed by Stafford et al. (1999). Only a handful studies (e.g., Shepherd 2009) engage in theory building to develop new theoretical foundations for use in family firm research.

Journals

The majority of articles identified for this paper (55 percent) were published in the *Family Business Review*, a premier journal for family firm research. The second major journal for family-related research is *Entrepreneurship Theory and Practice*, with 16 percent, followed by the *Journal of Business Venturing* with 7 percent and *Journal of Small Business Management* with 6 percent of the papers in this sample. Generally, the majority of papers fall into the ABS journal category "Entrepreneurship and Small Business Management," while only a few papers that include the family as a variable were published in journals that belong to fields such as "Economics" (2 percent) or "Finance" (3 percent).

Options for the Assessment of Family Structure

This review of ways to conceptualize and operationalize the business-owning family as a variable will start by classifying and discussing measures that belong to the family structure category in the framework presented in the previous section. As a first step, we examine the structural dimension of the family at the dyad level, followed by the whole family level.

Dyad Structure

Only a very small number of studies have examined the structural dimensions of family dyads in a family firm context. Variables include the *gender* and *age relationship* of dyad members as well as whether they are *romantically linked* or *biologically linked* or *divorced*. For example, Brannon, Wiklund, and Haynie (2013) study dyadic entrepreneurial teams that are either *biologically linked* (e.g., father-son or brother-sister) or *romantically linked* (couples) to examine which is more likely to achieve first sales. By analyzing 295 teams, they find that couples are more successful in terms of first sales than biologically linked entrepreneurial family dyads. The authors also examine the *age relationship* (i.e. age gap) present within the dyads but find no significant effect. While Brannon, Wiklund, and Haynie (2013) do not examine the *gender* of the dyad members, Haberman and Danes (2007), Vera and Dean (2005), and Bunkanwanicha, Fan, and Wiwattanakantang (2013) do. Haberman and Danes (2007) compare two family dyad decision teams in two family firms based on their gender configuration to shed light on the power structures and interactions within the family during succession. Using FIRO theory (Schutz 1958) as a theoretical base, they find that female family members who are not active in the business experience exclusion, high levels of conflict, and low levels of integration in the father-son dyad succession, while such women experience feelings of inclusion and integration from family members in the father-daughter configuration. In a similar study, Vera and Dean (2005) compare ten father-daughter and mother-daughter successions. They find that the mother-daughter dyad is associated with higher levels of conflict compared to the father-daughter dyad. Bunkanwanicha, Fan, and Wiwattanakantang (2013) examine the effect of dyads that are newly formed through marriage on the cumulative abnormal returns of family firms in Thailand. They find that both a son of founder-new spouse and a daughter of founder-new spouse dyads lead to abnormal returns when the new spouse comes from an influential family.

The previous studies examine the case of dyad formation or analyze existing dyads. However, dyads can also disintegrate – mainly through *divorce*. Galbraith (2003) examines the effect of marital dissolution on the short-term financial performance of 52 family firms. He finds that the majority of firms report a decline in revenue and profit in the post-separation year. The author's results also indicate that the financial loss is more severe when the female member of the marriage dyad remains in the business compared to the male member. However, a divorce must not always be associated with a negative impact on the business. For example, Cole and Johnson (2007) examine successful post-divorce "copreneurs," i.e. couples that have joint ownership and responsibility for a business. They find that the breakup of one dyad (i.e. marriage) can potentially lead to the strengthening of another dyad (i.e. successful business team). For instance, they report that divorce enabled the female dyad member to participate more effectively in the business relationship by shifting the balance of power in her favor. While the study of dyad structure and dyad dissolution in family firms is still in its infancy, many interesting research opportunities arise that will be discussed in later parts of this chapter.

Whole Family Structure

Studies on the structural dimension of business-owning families as a whole are quite numerous compared to papers on dyad family structure. Nearly 20 studies in the sample concentrate on aspects related to whole family structure. Major variables include the *family size, birth order, marriage, divorce, death*, and *social status* of the family as a whole.

An essential element of a family's structural configuration is its *size*. For example, Bertrand et al. (2008) find that family size is strongly correlated with the number of family members active in the business. Furthermore, the authors find that business groups run by larger families, especially with many sons, tend to exhibit lower performance. In a similar vein, Bennedsen et al. (2007) use a unique dataset from Denmark to demonstrate that the size of the business-owning family, measured by the number of children and specifically the number of sons, is negatively related to profitability around succession. On the other hand, the authors find that family size has a positive impact on intra-family succession. Wiklund et al. (2013) shed further light on this finding by demonstrating that family size has an impact on the probability of internal succession, but that the children's life stage plays an important role. Wiklund et al. (2013) find that the larger the number of adult heirs, the less likely an internal transition of ownership becomes. On the other hand, a larger number of young children seems to increase the probability of internal ownership transition, indicating that the age levels of family members can have an important influence on family business outcomes. Danes et al. (2009) show that family size is positively related to gross revenue, but do not elaborate on whether or not they control for the age of the firm. Using the same dataset with different dependent variables, Olson et al. (2003) demonstrate that family size can also have a negative impact on the family. They find that family size is strongly negatively correlated with the functional integrity of the business-owning family. Additionally, Michael-Tsabari, Labaki, and Zachary (2014) accentuate the importance of family size by demonstrating in a qualitative setting that the growth of the family in size can trigger entrepreneurial behavior in family firms. On a conceptual level, Arregle et al. (2007) discuss the negative impact that family size can have on the closure and density of the family network and therefore on the level of family social capital (FSC). These results show that family size is an important variable that has the potential to influence family business outcomes in a negative as well as a positive way, depending on the variable of interest.

However, studies have shown that not only the size of the family but also the composition of the family tree, can have a profound influence on family and organizational outcomes. Among the most important variables in this context is the *birth order* of children in the business-owning family. Bennedsen et al. (2007) show that an internal succession is more likely when the first-born child is male. This finding is supported by qualitative case-studies conducted in Brazil by Curimbaba (2002). The author discovers that female members of business-owning families were less likely to be chosen as the successor when older brothers are present. Female family members at the end of the birth order termed 'invisible heiresses,' were not prepared from youth to become professionals in the family business. Firstborn daughters, on the other hand, were accustomed to the family business from a young age (Curimbaba 2002). The results from Vera and Dean (2005) partly support this finding by demonstrating that there is a general preference for the firstborn child as a successor, but that female firstborn children have to work harder to prove themselves. In a different setting, Bunkanwanicha, Fan, and Wiwattanakantang (2013) find that the marriage of sons and daughters of the current CEO to members of well-connected families in Thailand leads to abnormal returns irrespective of birth order.

The above mentioned study by Bunkanwanicha, Fan, and Wiwattanakantang (2013) leads to another important structural variable for business-owning families – *marriage*. Marriage between two individuals is a key structural bond within the family system in most societies. Hence, the marriage of members of business-owning families can have a profound impact on the business as well as the family. On the one hand, individuals who become part of a business-owning family though marriage may bring valuable resources, such as financial assets, family contacts, or managerial knowledge, into the family firm. On the other hand, marriage can disrupt the existing family structure and lead to conflict. In a study of Philippine in-laws, Santiago (2011) found that the inclusion of in-laws is conditional to several factors. For example, the author finds that daughters-in-law were generally more welcome in family firms regardless of their educational level and experience; sons-in-law, in comparison, were only included after they demonstrated their managerial ability. Bunkanwanicha, Fan, and Wiwattanakantang (2013) demonstrate that not only the qualification of an in-law but also the social status and level of influence of the in-law's family can impact the firm. The authors find that a marriage between a member of a business-owning family and a member of another business or political family leads to abnormal stock price increases in the days after the marriage announcement. The marriage status of members of business-owning families not only impacts business outcomes but also impacts family and individual variables. For example, Kwan, Lau, and Au (2012) find that marriage contributes positively to the level of job satisfaction of family business owners. These studies demonstrate that marriage is an important structural variable for business-owning families. Marriage increases the size of the family and provides an opportunity to bind valuable tangible and intangible resources to the family and ultimately the family business. However, the increased complexity of the family system resulting from a marriage can also constitute a challenging change for the family as well as the business system (Stafford et al. 1998; Santiago 2011).

While birth and marriage contribute to the size and resource endowment of the family, *divorce* and *death* curtail the family system. The divorce process within a family usually generates conflict and mistrust, factors that tend to be associated with negative outcomes in family firms. This assumption is supported by an empirical study by Rutherford, Muse, and Oswald (2006) who find that divorce within the business-owning family is associated with lower sales in family firms. In a similar study, Galbraith (2003) examines 52 cases of divorce and its impact on family business performance. He finds that a divorce event in the family system is associated with a decrease in revenue, profitability, and equity. A qualitative study by Santiago (2011) provides a possible explanation for these findings by showing that the termination of a family relationship through a divorce will usually also lead to the cessation of the business relationship regardless of qualification and talent. The resulting conflict and presumably financial settlement can strain the business and result in a dwindling performance. The *death* of a family member is another source of major structural upheaval for the business-owning family (James, Jennings, and Breitkreuz 2012). Michael-Tsabari, Labaki, and Zachary (2014) demonstrate in a qualitative setting that the death of a family member can trigger ownership and management succession in family firms. Bennedsen et al. (2007) use the death of a family CEO as an instrumental variable to determine the effect of intra-family succession on the performance of family firms. Despite the potentially severe impact that the death of a family member can have on the family and the business, no other published studies other than the two above mentioned were identified in the reviewed literature. However, an unpublished paper by Bennedsen, Perez-Gonzalez, and Wolfenzon (2010) using the same dataset from Denmark as Bennedsen et al. (2007) finds that the death of the CEO or another member of the family is strongly related to a decline in firm profitability and sales growth. These findings underscore that disruptions in the family's structure are an important antecedent of family and family business outcomes that merit further research.

Options for the Assessment of Family Dynamics and Functioning

Besides the structural dimension of family assessment detailed in the previous section, business-owning families can also be analyzed by examining the unique dynamics within the family and the functioning of the family unit. Such latent psychodynamic constructs are usually measured using survey-based measures and scales that are designed to capture individuals' perceptions of the family as a group. Alternatively, psychodynamic constructs may be assessed in a qualitative case study approach. Again, the unit of analysis can be divided into dyadic and whole family levels.

Dyad Dynamics and Functioning

Several studies have examined the dynamics and the functioning of dyadic pairs within business-owning families. Variables that have been assessed include the levels of *conflict*, *trust*, *communication* and *emotional connection*. Furthermore, two studies have examined the *overall relationship quality*. Given that family businesses are "fertile fields for conflict" (Harvey and Evans 1994; 331), *conflict* is an important variable on a family level as well as a dyadic level. Aspects such as sibling rivalry or incumbent-successor conflict can have a profound impact on both the family and the business system. In their conceptual paper, De Massis, Chua, and Chrisman (2008) highlight the importance of sibling and parent-child conflict as a major relational factor that prevents succession in family firms. Vera and Dean (2005) observe the role of dyadic conflict in succession. The authors study the succession of 10 female family business owners and find that conflict between the mother and the successor, as well as between the siblings and the successor, can have an impact on the succession process. In one case this culminated in the disbursement of a sibling to keep the business in family hands. The studies identified in the literature all use a conceptual or qualitative approach to study conflict in family business dyads. Hence, no scales or measure could be identified that measure the level of conflict in such dyadic relationships.

While conflict is generally associated with negative outcomes in a succession process, *trust* is antithetic. In a study of 332 South African family firm successions, Venter, Boshoff, and Maas (2005) find that high levels of trust between the owner-manager and the family successor are associated with the successor's increased willingness to take over, ultimately culminating in a successful succession process. This relationship is substantiated by the study of Dawson and Hjorth (2012) who employ narrative analysis to an owner-manager's autobiography to demonstrate that a lack of trust in the incumbent-successor dyad relationship can jeopardize the succession process and lead to its failure. However, trust is critical not only in parent-child dyads but also in couples. Cole and Johnson's (2007) study of successful post-divorce copreneurial couples finds that trust was an important factor that allowed individuals to continue working together effectively even after their marriage disintegrated. The authors also identify another important construct for dyad functioning – *emotional connection*. Economic considerations played only a marginal role in the decision to stay together while the emotional connection was one of the main reasons for continued cooperation post-divorce. Individuals who have shared values and a shared history form a unique emotional tie that allows them to work together effectively even in a difficult environment.

Closely related to the previous constructs is *communication* within the family dyad. Communication is an essential aspect for individuals working together and is especially important when these individuals are in the process of ownership and/or management succession. In their qualitative study, Dawson and Hjorth (2012) clearly identify the role played by a lack of communication in a failed succession process.

The final construct – *overall relationship quality* – is a meta-level construct that combines the constructs previously discussed. Venter, Boshoff, and Maas (2005) measure the relationship quality between the incumbent and the successor based on items from a scale developed by Lansberg and Astrachan (1994). They find that an overall positive relationship quality of the incumbent-successor dyad has significant influence on the satisfaction of the succession process and the profitability of the family business. This finding is underpinned by Cater and Justis' (2009) study on succession in small family firms. Employing a case study approach, they find that a positive parent-child relationship is important for a successful succession and enhances the development of successor leadership.

As the studies discussed above demonstrate family business literature has in recent years introduced and employed several interesting constructs for dyad dynamics and functioning. The nature and quality of dyadic family relationships become especially relevant prior to and during the succession process in family firms, which is highlighted by the large number of studies that focus on succession. Also noteworthy is the fact that the majority of studies that examine business-owning families on the dyadic level employ a case study approach, while only a few collected data using surveys. This results in a particularity small number of scales available for the assessment of dyad dynamics and functioning in a family business context, suggesting a promising avenue for future research.

Whole Family Dynamics and Functioning

Acknowledging that "the family is an organized whole and cannot be understood from the combined characteristics of its members" (Shepard 2009; 84), scholars have investigated the functioning and the dynamics within the business-owning family in its totality. Analogous to the dyadic level, construct measurement can be obtained via self-reported survey procedures, in-depth interviews, content coding of secondary documents, or observed interactions of family members (Jacob and Tennenbaum 1988). Assessed constructs include the level of *conflict, cohesion, communication, trust, altruism, social capital, adaptability,* and *functional integrity present* in the family system.

Among these constructs that reflect the inherent dynamics within the business-owning family, *conflict* stands out as the variable that has received the most scholarly attention to date. This is hardly surprising, given that "family firms are often plagued by substantial conflict" (Kellermanns and Eddleston 2004; 209). Conflict is a prime example of family dysfunction and is traditionally associated with negative outcomes for the family firm (Harvey and Evans 1994; Levinson 1971). However, recent research reveals that different types of conflict – namely task, process, and relationship conflict – exist. While relationship conflict is usually associated with negative outcomes, task, and process conflict can be beneficial up to a certain level (Kellermanns and Eddleston 2004). Eddleston and Kellermanns (2007) survey 60 family firms using an adapted form of the relationship conflict scale developed by Jehn (1997) and Jehn and Mannix (2001) to demonstrate that relationship conflict within the business-owning family does indeed have a negative influence on family firm performance. Using the same scale, Chirico and Salvato (forthcoming) find that relationship conflict in family firms negatively impacts product development by reducing knowledge internalization among family members. The negative influence of relationship conflict on knowledge integration is further studied on a conceptual level in Chirico and Salvato's (2008) paper. The potential negative impact of interpersonal conflict is additionally emphasized by the qualitative studies by Ainsworth and Cox (2003) and Cabrera-Suárez (2005). The authors compare several family firms and find that conflict can prevent intra-family succession, for example by forcing the potential successor out of the firm. Regarding the antecedents of interpersonal conflict, Davis and Harveston (1999) employ a North American sample to find that conflict across generations is influenced by the generation of ownership and the presence of a generational shadow. Eddleston, Otondo, and Kellermanns (2008) study the effect of participative decision-making and generational ownership dispersion on the relationship and cognitive (i.e. task and process conflict) conflict. Using the same scale as Eddleston and Kellermanns (2007) and Chirico and Salvato (forthcoming), they find that participative decision-making is positively related to relationship and cognitive conflict when ownership is dispersed and negatively related when ownership is concentrated.

High levels of conflict in family firms are likely to impact negatively the *functional integrity* of the business-owning family. The integrity of the family as a whole has been examined in serval studies. Using Family APGAR, a scale prominent in the medical field to measure overall family health and functioning by examining an individual's satisfaction with family relationships (Smilkstein 1978), Olson et al. (2003) find that the number of children and level of conflict in the family have a negative impact on its functional integrity, while a negotiating family culture has a positive impact. In a similar study, Danes and Olson (2003) also find that conflict is associated with lower levels of functional integrity. Interestingly, Danes et al. (2009) find no relationship between family integrity measured using the APGAR scale and the perceived success of the family firm, indicating that problematic family dynamics do not necessarily spill over into the business sphere.

The level of *cohesion* within the business-owning family has also been a major variable of interest for family business researchers. Its importance for business-owning families is highlighted by Davis and Herrera (1998; 255), who consider "the cohesiveness of the family shareholder group (…) (as) perhaps the most fundamental measure of its effectiveness." This conclusion receives support from Zahra's (2012) study on the effect of family cohesion on organizational learning. The author finds that cohesion amplifies the positive effect of family ownership on the breadth and speed of organizational learning in family firms. Contrarily, Lee (2006) employs a sample of ethnic Chinese in Singapore and finds no support for the hypothesized relationship between family cohesion and organizational commitment, job satisfaction, or propensity to leave. The two previous authors have adapted different items from the literature to construct scales to measure family cohesion, albeit without going through the psychometric steps for scale development. Björnberg and Nicholson (2007) overcome this problem by developing specific scales for emotional and cognitive cohesion as part of their Family Climate Scales (FCS). Cabrera-Suárez, Déniz-Déniz, and Martín-Santana (2015) employ the cognitive and emotional cohesion items from the FCS to measure the cognitive and structural dimension of family social capital.

While Cabrera-Suárez, Déniz-Déniz, and Martín-Santana (2015) equate social capital and cohesion in their study, Salvato and Melin (2008) find that family cohesion is an important antecedent for the development of family social capital by comparing four family firms in the Italian wine and spirits industry. On a conceptual level, this finding is supported by Arregle et al. (2007), who propose that closure, a construct related to cohesion, strengthens family social capital. However, the importance of family cohesion is recognized not only among family business scholars but also in neighboring fields such as family science. Penney and Combs (2013) use an established theoretical model from family science, the Circumplex Model (Olson, Sprenkle, and Russell 1979), to explain why some families are more innovative than others. They argue that cohesion, one of the two central dimensions of the model, plays a central role in explaining innovation in family firms. A small number of authors, such as Salvato and Melin (2008), have additionally discussed the possibility that an excessive level of cohesion can have a negative influence by exacerbating existing agency problems in family firms.

Cohesion is not the only factor associated with positive outcomes in family firms; aspects such as *harmony*, *trust*, *altruism*, and *reciprocity* are important as well. Using a scale developed by Sharma (1997), Venter, Boshoff, and Maas (2005) we find that more *harmonious* relationships among all members of the family system correspond to a better relationship between the incumbent and the successor. Farrington, Venter, and Boshoff (2012) hypothesize that family harmony is positively related to perceived financial success, but find no statistically significant relationship. However, they find that clear strategic leadership and skill diversity within the family's top management team has a positive impact on the level of family harmony. Closely related to harmony is the level of *trust* present in the business-owning family. A qualitative study by Salvato and Melin (2008) demonstrates that trust is an important antecedent for the development of family cohesion and family social capital. In a similar study, Steier (2001) finds that family trust plays an important role in the governance of family firms. Trust can significantly reduce transaction costs, hence providing an important source of competitive advantage. However, the author also finds that trust slowly erodes as family firms and business-owning families evolve and grow, necessitating an investment into trust-building activities to maintain a healthy level of trust.

Complementary to trust is the concept of *altruism*. Altruism is defined as a trait that links the welfare of an individual to the welfare of others (such as family members) (Kellermanns and Eddleston 2004). Employing a scale developed by Becker and Vance (1993), Eddleston, Kellermans, and Sarathy (2007) find that altruism within the business-owning family is positively associated with family firm performance. Using the same scale, Eddleston and Kellermanns

(2007) offer a more detailed perspective by demonstrating that altruism increases participative strategy processes and decreases relationship conflict, which affects organizational performance accordingly. The negative relationship between altruism and harmful relationship conflict is further discussed on a conceptual level in a paper by Kellermanns and Eddleston (2004). And, in an in-depth case study of a Turkish family firm, Karra, Tracey, and Phillips (2006) find that altruism reduces agency costs and serves as a driver for business growth in the early stages of the firm's development. However, the authors also find that if the welfare of the family is prioritized above the firm's well-being – a case of too much altruism – the firm's development can be hampered. A closely related but distinct concept is family member *reciprocity*. Reciprocity refers to the degree to which family members assist each other and share responsibilities to accomplish organizational tasks. As such, reciprocity facilitates stewardship behavior and serves as a way to channel altruism towards the family firm (Kellermanns et al. 2012). In their empirical study of 70 family firms located in Northeastern USA, Kellermanns et al. (2012) find that reciprocity within the business-owning family has a positive impact on the performance of family firms.

The family-related constructs discussed above all require *communication* and are associated with different levels of *social interaction* within the business-owning family. Björnberg and Nicholson (2007) developed a scale to measure the level of open communication within the business-owning family as part of the FCS. Cabrera-Suárez, Déniz-Déniz, and Martín-Santana (2015) use this scale as a component to develop a family social capital construct and find that this is positively related to the level of trust present in the business-owning family. Distelberg and Blow (2011) use qualitative data and social network analysis to construct communication networks in family firms. They find that too much communication exclusively within the business-owning family can result in the development in further isolated networks, which in turn has the potential to have a negative impact on the family business. *Social interaction* within the family, such as family meetings, facilitates communication between family members active in the business and passive shareholders. Mahto et al. (2010) hypothesize that families that interact a lot with each other will exhibit greater satisfaction with firm performance due to the fact that they are better informed and hence better understand the reasons for a potential deterioration of family firm performance. Their analysis of 2,224 family firms supports this hypothesis, hence emphasizing the importance of communication and social interaction to business-owning families and family firms.

Complex systems such as business-owning families also require a certain level of *adaptability* and *willingness to change* to cope successfully with challenges. Business-owning families that are able and willing to adapt to situational changes are more likely to survive environmental shifts and to pursue beneficial entrepreneurial activities (Kellermanns and Eddleston 2006). Families that lack the capacity to change, however, impair the long-term survival of the family firm. The importance of adaptability to systems has long been recognized by system theorists such as von Bertalanffy (1968), who asserted, "system sickness is system rigidity." Several of the reviewed studies support this assertion. Kellermanns and Eddleston (2006) study 74 family firms and find that families who are more willing to change, have a positive impact on corporate entrepreneurship. Lee (2006) examines 88 family firms in Singapore and finds that family adaptability is positively related to organizational commitment and negatively related to the propensity to leave the family business. The negative impact of low adaptability and an overly strong focus on tradition is underscored by an exploratory inductive study by Miller, Steier, and Le Breton-Miller (2003). The authors find that an excessive attachment to the past has a negative impact on strategy, organization, and governance in family firms and can ultimately culminate in a decline in performance. On a conceptual level, Penney and Combs (2013) and Distelberg and Sorenson (2009) discuss the impact of adaptability. Penney and Combs (2013) employ the Circumplex

Model (Olson, Sprenkle and Russell 1979), an established family science concept, to determine the extent to which the level of adaptability within the family system can impact innovation. The model predicts that balanced levels of adaptability are most beneficial while too much change can be associated with negative outcomes. This accentuates that dynamics within the business-owning family can also be related to family business outcomes in a curvilinear manner.

Among the variables that characterize and differentiate business-owning families, the level of *family social capital* (FSC) plays a special role, given that "the family is a source, builder and user of social capital" (Bubolz 2001; 130). On a conceptual level, Arregle et al. (2007) discuss the importance of FSC to the development of organizational social capital (OSC) and investigate mechanisms that link the spheres of social capital. By adapting a scale by Tsai and Ghoshal (1998), Chirico and Salvato (forthcoming) find that family social capital has a positive impact on the internalization of knowledge among family members, which in turn has a positive impact on the level of product development in family firms. The conceptual relationship between FSC and knowledge integration among family members is examined further in an early paper by Chirico and Salvato (2008). In a recent study, Cabrera-Suárez, Déniz-Déniz, and Martín-Santana (2015) find that family social capital is a determining factor in the establishment of corporate goals related to the interests and needs of key stakeholders. Further insight into how specific components of FSC, namely structural and relational social capital, influence strategic processes and outcomes in family firms is provided by a qualitative study of wine estates by Salvato and Melin (2008). Carr et al. (2011) add a third social capital dimension – cognitive social capital. In the course of their paper, Carr et al. (2011) develop a reliable and valid scale that measures the level of structural, relational, and cognitive social capital present among family members active in the firm, thereby contributing to the current trend towards more accurate construct measurement (Pearson and Lumpkin 2011).

While the constructs discussed above represent the ones that have attracted most attention by family business scholars, several other interesting and relevant family dynamics and functioning variables have been reported and examined in the literature. These include, among others, the level of *intergenerational attention* (e.g., Cabrera-Suárez, Déniz-Déniz, and Martín-Santana 2015; Björnberg and Nicholson 2007), *participative decision making* (e.g., Eddleston et al. 2008), *affective commitment to goals* (e.g., Chirico and Salvato, forthcoming), and *knowledge integration* among family members (e.g., Chirico and Salvato 2008). These are not discussed in further detail in the course of this paper; however, the complete list of options available for the assessment of family functioning and family dynamics can be found at the end of this paper.

Psychometric Quality of Measures

Among the studies that focus on the functioning and dynamics within family dyads and the whole business-owning family, the majority uses scales to measure the construct under examination. The psychometric quality of scales used in family business studies has recently attracted considerable debate among scholars. Pearson and Lumpkin (2011; 287) observe that "valid and reliable measurement is essential to the development of the 'normal science' of family firms" and urge scholars to pay more attention to accurate construct measurement. Scholars should hence only employ scales that demonstrate sufficient validity (Does the scale measure what it pretends to measure?) and reliability (Does the scale measure the construct accurately?). Validity can be assessed *inter alia* by conducting exploratory and confirmatory factor analyses while reliability can be gauged using Cronbach's alpha (Hinkin 1995). Papers that use newly developed scales or adapt existing scales should hence contain, among others, a clear construct definition grounded in theory, item sources/item generation procedure, a construct validity assessment, and a reliability assessment (Pearson and Lumpkin 2011). The scales and measures employed by the articles reviewed for this paper are compared against these criteria to assess their psychometric quality.

While most studies report the scales' reliability, mainly by computing Cronbach's alpha, only a handful of studies assess the scales' validity through exploratory or confirmatory factor analyses. Many studies state that "items were adapted from the literature" or "the construct was measured using the following items," without going into detail where the items come from or what factor structure underlies them. This is especially predominant among studies published in the late-1990's and early to mid-2000's. More than half of the reviewed studies adapt items from existing scales. However, only a few of the adapted measurement instruments meet the criteria laid out by Pearson and Lumpkin (2011). A noteworthy example is the paper by Cabrera-Suárez, Déniz-Déniz, and Martín-Santana (2015), who conduct an exploratory and confirmatory factor analysis to demonstrate the validity of their adapted measures. A small number of authors have engaged in the development of new family related measures. Examples are Björnberg and Nicholson (2007), Carr et al. (2011), Chirico and Salvato (forthcoming) and Zellweger, Nason, and Nordqvist (2012). This mirrors Pearson, Holt, and Carr's (2014; 567) conclusion that "a limited number of measures have been developed for specific use in family firms studies." Although there are some promising developments, the psychometric quality of the scales and measures used in the reviewed studies does not always meet the standards expected in contemporary peer-reviewed research. Scholars should accordingly be careful employing previously used measures before ensuring their validity and reliability.

Discussion

The main purpose of this paper was to synthesize and assess the options available to operationalize the business-owning family in family business research. In the past, scholars have used several interesting constructs and measures to assess the business-owning family's structure as well as its internal dynamics and functioning. These studies provide valuable findings that help scholars to better understand family business outcomes and their antecedents. To a large extent, however, the business-owning family still remains a "missing variable in organizational research" (Dyer 2003), and one that lacks a clear definition and requires further scholarly attention in order for the field to progress (Sharma, Chrisman, and Gersick 2012; Sharma, Melin, and Nordqvist 2014).

This chapter contributes to the literature in several ways. First, we provide a systematic and replicable review that structures and consolidates family measures and constructs in a transparent and logical framework. The paper at hand can consequently serve scholars as a valuable resource to identify a suitable and interesting family construct and measurement tool, hence laying the groundwork for more family-related research. Second, we identify blind spots in the scope of options available to capture family heterogeneity and in this context provide references to avenues for promising future research. Third, the assessment of the psychometric quality of existing measures contributes to the emerging debate on accurate construct measurement in the family business field (e.g., Pearson and Lumpkin 2011; Pearson, Holt, and Carr 2014).

Based on these findings, we highlight starting points for future research and discuss possible options to overcome shortcomings prevalent in the family related constructs and measures currently available. A primary observation in this regard is that the majority of studies are poorly grounded theoretically. As indicated in the previous part, nearly fifty percent of the reviewed studies lack a clear theoretical foundation. This theory deficiency is a possible explanation for the fragmentation and apparent contradictions of research findings. While we would not go as far as Mintzberg (2005; 361) - "no theory, no insight. And if no insight, why do research?" – it is evident that family-related studies in the family business realm require a stronger theoretical base to fully leverage research findings. This conclusion is supported by Dyer and Dyer (2009; 218), who emphasize: "to measure family effectiveness researchers must get at the underlying family processes. This requires the researcher to have a theory of what constitutes effective family functioning." While such theories are not readily available in the management and organization research field, neighboring disciplines such as family science provide rich grazing grounds for theoretical models on family functioning (Dyer & Dyer 2009; James, Jennings, and Breitkreuz 2012; Litz, Pearson, and Litchfield 2012; Sharma, Melin, and Nordqvist 2014). The lack of widespread application of family science theories in family business research is likely attributable to the fact that quite often "substantial theory-building efforts are necessary to bridge the gap between family science and outcomes that interest family business researchers" (Penney and Combs 2013; 1422). In order to enhance the theoretical grounding of family-related studies, future research should accordingly engage in more such theory building and theory transfer to further integrate theoretical models from family science. Penney and Combs (2013) provide an interesting demonstration of such theory transfer by adapting the Circumplex Model (Olson Sprenkle and Russell 1979), a well-established family science model, to discuss how families that differ along the model's two dimensions – cohesion and adaptability – are associated with varying innovation outcomes in family firms. Such studies, well grounded in theory, promise to advance our understanding of business-owning families and their impact on business outcomes. Hence, we urge scholars to devote efforts to embed future family-related studies deeper in theories from organizational and management studies as well as family science.

Furthermore, most studies overlook an important variable – the institutional, cultural, and social contexts (Welter 2011). "Family" can mean something very different depending on the context (Szapocznik and Kurtines 1993). Some family dynamics, such as conflict or low levels of cohesion, might be associated with low family functioning and a negative impact on business outcomes in a certain context, while not posing a problem in another. As such, different findings regarding the role of family cohesion in the studies conducted by Lee (2006) compared to Zahra (2012) and Cabrera-Suárez, Déniz-Déniz, and Martín-Santana (2015) might be attributable to different social and cultural contexts. Lee (2006) examines ethnic Chinese in Singapore while Zahra (2012) uses a North American and Cabrera-Suárez, Déniz-Déniz, and Martín-Santana (2015) a Spanish sample. China has a different attitude towards family and work than Western societies, which could explain the different research findings (Yang et al. 2000). Furthermore, scholars should take into the account whether a nuclear system or an extended, kinship-based family system is the prevalent family institution in a certain context before assessing the business-owning family (Gorall and Olson 1995). Accordingly, we follow Welter's (2011) call that urges scholars to employ a "context lens" when examining family business processes and outcomes.

Another important observation apparent from the reviewed articles is that accurate and reliable construct measurement has not received the level of scholarly attention that it merits. While there are notable exceptions, many scholars adapt existing scales without reporting the information necessary to assess their validity. Even fewer scales were developed specifically to measure family related variables in family business research. This is congruent with Pearson, Holt, and Carr's (2014) assertion that measurement issues are one of the field's greatest challenges. Accordingly, we agree with Sharma, Melin, and Nordqvist (2014; 8) that "great promise lies in devoting efforts to (...) define and develop valid and reliable measures for the family variable." However, the development of valid and reliable scales requires a clear construct definition grounded in theory and a strong theoretical foundation (Hinkin, 1998; Pearson and Lumpkin 2011). Hence, scholars that set out to develop new measurement instruments to assess the functioning and dynamics within business-owning families need to find or develop theories that provide a clear reference point for such scales. As discussed in the previous part, family science offers interesting theoretical concepts that can enrich family business research. While scales exist for most family science theories, they are mostly geared towards the nuclear family and clinical applications and hence not directly applicable to family business research (Björnberg and Nicholson 2007). The development of new scales or adaptation of existing scales according to the psychometric standards laid out by leading scholars (e.g., Hinkin 1995; MacKenzie, Podsakoff, and Podsakoff 2011) to enable the empirical application of family science models in family firm research is hence a promising research endeavor.

While the reviewed studies have predominantly explored the effect of the family structure or family dynamics and functioning on family business outcomes, few have combined the psychodynamic and structural types of measures in one study. Splicing together both approaches is likely to produce valuable insights into family business behavior and outcomes. In their conceptual work on the development of organizational social capital, Arregle et al. (2007; 89) ask the following question: "When the FSC/OSC balance suddenly changes, due to family events (divorce, scandal, etc.) (...) can the OSC be sustained?" Developing this thought further, many research questions remain unexplored that would link alterations in the business-owning family's structure to changes in family dynamics and functioning, which in turn have the potential to impact business outcomes. Studies that examine the effect of profound changes in the family's structure, such as the death of an important family member, are still in their infancy. None of the reviewed studies explore how such a structural upheaval impacts family dynamics like cohesion, conflict, social capital, or trust. Hence, interesting research opportunities arise for studies that examine this interplay between family structure, family dynamics, and functioning, as well as family business variables.

The overwhelming number of studies reviewed for this paper have examined the business-owning family as an independent variable and business outcomes as the dependent variable. However, few studies examine the antecedents of the business-owning family's structure and functioning. For example, how do families maintain adequate levels of cohesion and trust? These family variables have the potential to harm or benefit the family business, but how can the family ensure that they do not reach harmful levels? Take, for instance, the study by Eddleston and Kellermanns (2007) that finds that relationship conflict has a negative impact on family firm performance – what mechanisms can prevent such harmful relationship conflicts? Several scholars have suggested that family governance mechanisms, such as a family constitution or regular family meetings, could have a positive impact on the functioning of business-owning families (e.g., Distelberg and Sorenson 2009). While the impact of family governance mechanisms on business outcomes has been examined by a handful of studies (e.g., Berent-Braun and Uhlaner 2012), research on the impact of such governance mechanisms on the family itself is virtually nonexistent, indicating fertile ground for further research. As also recommended by Dyer and Dyer (2009), future studies should subsequently focus on the business-owning family as a dependent variable and examine the antecedents of important constructs that characterize business-owning families.

This systematic literature review is also associated with some limitations. First, some interesting articles may have been omitted due to the methodology employed. Some articles might examine variables related to the business-owning family without any indication in the articles' abstracts, title, or keywords. We try to mitigate this problem by analyzing the papers cited by the reviewed articles to find papers omitted in the main literature selection process; however, this does not completely assure that all relevant research is captured by this review. Second, by focusing exclusively on studies published in highly ranked journals, we ensure that the studies meet high-quality standards. On the other hand, this might exclude research findings that provide interesting constructs and measures that could be used to assess the business-owning family. Finally, we limited our review to journals that predominantly publish management, organization, strategy, and economics research. As indicated above, promising family related constructs and measures could exist in neighboring fields such as psychology or sociology – these are not captured by the review at hand. Nevertheless, we believe that by following the guidelines for a systematic literature review, we have captured the majority of relevant research for the research question at hand.

Conclusion

In their editorial for the 25th anniversary of the *Family Business Review*, Sharma, Chrisman, and Gersick (2012; 86) argue that it is important to "deepen our knowledge of variables related to the family system so we will better understand why, when, and how its characteristics attributes are likely to influence the behaviors and performance of family firms." Through a systematic and replicable review of constructs and measures to assess the family system, we have laid the groundwork for such family related research to flourish in the future. Our review consolidates and assesses existing constructs and measures and identifies blind spots, which in turn can serve as starting points for prospective research endeavors.

Table 22.2 Classification and Summary of Reviewed Articles

Reviewed Articles on Dyad Structure	† = *empirical* ★★ = *case study/qualitative* ★ = *conceptual*

- **Age Relationship**
Brannon et al. (2013)†

- **Divorce**
Cole & Johnson (2007)★★, Galbraith (2003)†

- **Gender of Dyad Members**
Bunkanwanicha et al. (2013)†, Haberman & Danes (2007)†, Vera & Dean (2005)★★

- **Romantically or Biologically Linked**
Brannon et al. (2013)†

Reviewed Articles on Whole Family Structure	† = *empirical* ★★ = *case study/qualitative* ★ = *conceptual*

- **Adoption**
Bertrand et al. (2008)†

- **Birth Order**
Bennedsen et al. (2007)†, Bertrand et al. (2008)†, Bunkanwanicha et al. (2013)†, Curimbaba (2002)★★, Howorth & Ali (2001)★★, Michael-Tsabari et al. (2014)★★, Stavrou (1999)†, Vera & Dean (2005)★★

- **Death**
Bennedsen et al. (2007)†, Michael-Tsabari et al. (2014)★★

- **Divorce**
Bennedsen et al. (2007)†, Cabrera-Suárez (2005)★★, Galbraith (2003)†, Kwan et al. (2012)★★, Michael-Tsabari et al. (2014)★★, Rutherford et al. (2006)†, Santiago (2011)★★

- **Family Size** (total number, number of spouses, children, siblings, etc.)

Arregle et al. (2007)★, Bennedsen et al. (2007) †, Bertrand et al. (2008)†, Bunkanwanicha et al. (2013) †, Curimbaba (2002)★★, Danes et al. (2009) †, Howorth & Ali (2001)★★, Jaskiewicz et al. (2015)★★, Kwan et al. (2012)★★, Marchisio et al. (2010)★★, Michael-Tsabari et al. (2014)★★, Muske & Fitzgerald (2006) †, Olson et al. (2003) †, Rowe & Hong (2000) †, Thomas (2002) †, Vera & Dean (2005)★★, Wiklund et al. (2013) †

- **Marriage**

Bunkanwanicha et al. (2013) †, Danes et al. (2009) †, Kwan et al. (2012)★★, Michael-Tsabari et al. (2014)★★, Santiago (2011) ★★

- **Social Status of Family**

Bunkanwanicha et al. (2013) †

Reviewed Articles on Dyad Dynamics and Functioning   † = *empirical*
                                                              ★★ = *case study/qualitative*
                                                              ★ = *conceptual*

- **Communication**

Dawson & Hjorth (2012)★★

- **Conflict**

Dawson & Hjorth (2012)★★, De Massis et al. (2008)★, Vera & Dean (2005)★★

- **Emotional Connection**

Cole & Johnson (2007)★★

- **Overall Relationship Quality and Strength**

Eddleston & Kidwell (2012)★, Cater & Justis (2009)★★, Venter et al. (2005) †

- **Trust**

Cole & Johnson (2007)★★, Dawson & Hjorth (2012)★★, Gagné et al. (2011) †, Venter et al. (2005) †

Reviewed Articles on Whole Family Dynamics and Functioning   † = *empirical*
                                                                 ★★ = *case study/qualitative*
                                                                 ★ = *conceptual*

- **Adaptability and Willingness to Change**

Björnberg & Nicholson (2007) †, Distelberg & Sorenson (2009)★, Kellermanns & Eddleston (2006) †, Lee (2006) †, Miller et al. (2003), Penney & Combs (2013)★

- **Affective Commitment to Goals**

Chirico & Salvato (2008)★, Chirico & Salvato (forthcoming) †

- **Altruism**

Eddleston et al. (2007) †, Eddleston et al. (2008) †, Eddleston & Kellermanns (2007) †, Eddleston & Kidwell (2012)★, Karra et al. (2006)★★, Kellermanns & Eddleston (2004)★

- **Cohesion**

Ainsworth & Cox (2003)★★, Arregle et al. (2007)★, Björnberg & Nicholson (2007) †, Cabrera-Suárez et al. (2015) †, Distelberg & Sorenson (2009)★, Jaskiewicz et al. (2015)★★, Lee (2006) †, Marchisio et al. (2010)★★, Penney & Combs (2013)★, Salvato & Melin (2008)★★, Smyrnios et al. (2003) †, Zahra (2012) †

- **Communication**

Björnberg & Nicholson (2007) †, Cabrera-Suárez et al. (2015) †, Distelberg & Blow (2011) ★★

(Continued)

Reviewed Articles on Whole Family Dynamics and Functioning † = *empirical*
★★ = *case study/qualitative*
★ = *conceptual*

- **Conflict and Family Tensions**

Ainsworth & Cox (2003)★★, Cabrera-Suárez (2005)★★, Chirico & Salvato (2008)★, Chirico & Salvato (forthcoming) †, Danes & Olson (2003) †, De Massis et al. (2008)★, Davis & Harveston (1999) †, Davis & Harveston (2001) †, Eddleston & Kellermanns (2007) †, Eddleston et al. (2008) †, Kellermanns & Eddleston (2004)★, Nam & Herbert (1999) †, Olson et al. (2003)★★, Perricone et al. (2001)★★, Santiago (2011) ★★, Trevinyo-Rodriguez & Bontis (2010)★★

- **Emotional Capability**

Shepherd (2009)★

- **Family Entrepreneurial Orientation / Entrepreneurial Legacy**

Jaskiewicz et al. (2015)★★, Zellweger et al. (2012) †

- **Family Functional Integrity**

Danes et al. (2009) †, Danes & Olson (2003) †, Muske & Fitzgerald (2006) †, Olson et al. (2003) †

- **Family Harmony**

Farrington et al. (2012) †, Nam & Herbert (1999) †, Poza et al. (2004) †, Venter et al. (2005) †

- **Family Reciprocity**

Kellermanns et al. (2012) †

- **Family Relationship Style**

Olson et al. (2003) †

- **Family Social Capital**

Arregle et al. (2007)★, Cabrera-Suárez et al. (2015) †, Carr et al. (2011) †, Chirico & Salvato (2008)★, Chirico & Salvato (forthcoming) †, Salvato & Melin (2008)★★, Sorenson et al. (2009)★

- **Family Values**

Koiranen (2002) †, Santiago (2011) ★★

- **Intergenerational Attention**

Björnberg & Nicholson (2007) †, Cabrera-Suárez et al. (2015) †

- **Intergenerational Authority**

Björnberg & Nicholson (2007) †

- **Knowledge Integration among Family Members**

Chirico & Salvato (2008)★

- **Participative Decision Making**

Eddleston et al. (2008) †

- **Strength of Family Ties**

Cabrera-Suárez (2005)★★

- **Social Interaction within the Family**

Davis & Harveston (2001) †, Mahto et al. (2010) †, Nam & Herbert (1999) †, Poza et al. (2004) †, Trevinyo-Rodriguez & Bontis (2010)★★

- **Tolerance of Difference**

Poza et al. (2004) †

- **Trust**

Cabrera-Suárez (2005)★★, Pagliarussi & Rapozo (2011)★★, Salvato & Melin (2008)★★, Steier (2001)★★

Source: Own

Note

Journals include: *Econometrica, Journal of Political Economy, American Economic Review, Quarterly Journal of Economics, Review of Economic Studies, Journal of Economic Literature, Journal Econometrics, Journal of Monetary Economics, Journal of Economic Theory, Review of Economic sand Statistics, International Economic Review, Journal of Economic Perspectives, Economic Journal, Journal of Environmental Economics and Management, Games and Economic Behavior, Journal of Risk and Uncertainty, Journal of the European Economic Association, Journal of Business Venturing, Entrepreneurship Theory and Practice, International Small Business Journal, Entrepreneurship and Regional Development, Small Business Economics, Journal of Small Business Management, Strategic Entrepreneurship Journal, Journal of Small Business and Enterprise Development, International Journal of Entrepreneurial Behavior and Research, Venture Capital: An International Journal of Entrepreneurial Finance, International Journal of Entrepreneurship and Innovation, Family Business Review, Academy of Management Review, Academy of Management Journal, Administrative Science Quarterly, Journal of Management, Journal of Management Studies, Harvard Business Review, British Journal of Management, Organization Science, Organization Studies, Leadership Quarterly, Human Relations, Strategic Management Journal, Journal of Finance, Review of Financial Studies, Journal of Financial and Quantitative Analysis, Journal of Financial Economics, Journal of Money, Credit and Banking.*

References

(Articles denoted ★★★ are part of the reviewed papers.)

Alberti, P. A. & Phan, P. H (2004) 'Zobele chemical industries: The evolution of a family company from flypaper to globalization (1919–2001),' *Journal of Business Venturing*, 19(4): 589–600.

Ainsworth, S., & Cox, J. W. (2003) 'Families divided: culture and control in small family business,' *Organization Studies*, 24(9): 1463–1485. ★★★

Alsos, G. A., Carter, S., & Ljunggren, E. (2014) 'Kinship and business: How entrepreneurial households facilitate business growth,' *Entrepreneurship & Regional Development*, 26(1–2): 97–122.

Anderson, A. R., Jack, S. L., & Dodd, S. D. (2005) 'The role of family members in entrepreneurial networks: Beyond the boundaries of the family firm,' *Family Business Review*, 18(2): 135–154.

Anderson, R. C. & Reeb, D. M. (2003) 'Founding-family ownership and firm performance: Evidence from the S&P 500,' *The Journal of Finance*, 58(3): 1301–1327.

Arregle, J.-L., Hitt, M. A., Sirmon, D. G., & Very, P. (2007) 'The development of organizational social capital: Attributes of family firms,' *Journal of Management Studies*, 44(1): 73–95. ★★★

The Association of Business Schools. (2010) '*The Association of Business Schools Academic Journal Quality Guide*,' Gardners Books.

Becker, T. E. & Vance, R. J. (1993) 'Construct validity of three types of organizational citizenship behavior: An illustration of the direct product model with refinements,' *Journal of Management*, 19: 663–82.

Bennedsen, M., Nielsen, K. M., Perez-Gonzalez, F., & Wolfenzon, D. (2007) 'Inside the family firm: The role of families in succession decisions and performance,' *The Quarterly Journal of Economics*, 122(2): 647–691. ★★★

Bennedsen, M., Perez-Gonzalez, F., & Wolfenzon, D. (2006) 'Do CEOs matter?,' *NYU Working Paper No. FIN-06-032*.

Berent-Braun, M. M. & Uhlaner, L. M. (2012) 'Family governance practices and teambuilding: Paradox of the enterprising family,' *Small Business Economics*, 38(1): 103–119.

Bertrand, M. & Schoar, A. (2006) 'The role of family in family firms,' *Journal of Economic Perspectives*, 20: 73–96.

Bertrand, M., Johnson, S., Samphantharak, K., & Schoar, A. (2008) 'Mixing family with business: A study of Thai business groups and the families behind then,' *Journal of Financial Economics*, 88(3): 466–498. ★★★

Björnberg, Å., & Nicholson, N. (2007) 'The family climate scales—Development of a new measure for use in family business research,' *Family Business Review*, 20(3): 229–246. ★★★

Brannon, D. L., Wiklund, J., & Haynie, J. M. (2013) The varying effects of family relationships in entrepreneurial teams,' *Entrepreneurship Theory and Practice*, 37(1): 107–132. ★★★

Bubolz, M. (2001) 'Family as source, user, and builder of social capital,' *Journal of Socio-Economics*, 30: 129–31.

Bunkanwanicha, P., Fan, J. P. H., & Wiwattanakantang, Y. (2013) 'The value of marriage to family firms,' *Journal of Financial and Quantitative Analysis*, 48(2): 611–636. ★★★

Burgess, E. W. (1926) 'The family as a unit of interacting personalities,' *Family*, 7:3–9.

Cabrera-Suárez, M. K. (2005) 'Leadership transfer and the successor's development in the family firm,' *The Leadership Quarterly*, 16(1): 71–96. ★★★

Cabrera-Suárez, M. K., Déniz-Déniz, M. C., & Martín-Santana, J. D. (2015) 'Family social capital, trust within the TMT, and the establishment of corporate goals related to nonfamily stakeholders,' *Family Business Review*, 28(2): 145–162. ★★★

Carr, J. C., Cole, M. S., Ring, J. K., & Blettner, D. P. (2011) 'A measure of variations in internal social capital among family firms,' *Entrepreneurship Theory and Practice*, 35(6): 1207–1227. ★★★

Cater, J. J. & Justis, R. T. (2009) 'The development of successors from followers to leaders in small family firms: An exploratory study,' *Family Business Review*, 22(2): 109–124. ★★★

Chirico, F. & Salvato, C. (2008) 'Knowledge integration and dynamic organizational adaptation in family firms,' *Family Business Review*, 21(2): 169–181. ★★★

Chirico, F. & Salvato, C. (forthcoming) 'Knowledge integration and product development in family firms: When relational and affective factors matter,' *Entrepreneurship Theory and Practice*, in Press. ★★★

Cole, P. M. & Johnson, K. (2007) 'An exploration of successful copreneurial relationships postdivorce,' *Family Business Review*, 20(3): 185–198. ★★★

Corley, K. G. & Gioia, D. A. (2011) 'Building theory about theory building: What constitutes a theoretical contribution?,' *Academy of Management Review*, 36(1): 12–32.

Craig, J. J. & Salvato, C. (2012) 'The distinctiveness, design, and direction of family business research: Insights from management luminaries,' *Family Business Review*, 25: 109–116.

Curimbaba, F. (2002) 'The dynamics of women's roles as family business managers,' *Family Business Review*, 15(3): 239–252. ★★★

Danes, S. M., & Olson, P. D. (2003) 'Women's role involvement in family businesses, business tensions, and business success,' *Family Business Review*, 16(1): 53–68. ★★★

Danes, S. M., Stafford, K., Haynes, G., & Amarapurkar, S. S. (2009) 'Family capital of family firms: Bridging human, social, and financial capital,' *Family Business Review*, 22(3): 199–215. ★★★

David, R. J. & Han, S.-K. (2004) 'A systematic assessment of the empirical support for transaction cost economics,' *Strategic Management Journal*, 25(1): 39–58.

Davis, J. A. & Herrera, R. M. (1998) 'The social psychology of family shareholder dynamics,' *Family Business Review*, 11(3): 253–260. ★★★

Davis, P. S. & Harveston, P. D. (1999) 'In the founder's shadow: Conflict in the family firm,' *Family Business Review*, 12(4): 311–323. ★★★

Davis, P. S. & Harveston, P. D. (2001) 'The phenomenon of substantive conflict in the family firm: A cross-generational study,' *Journal of Small Business Management*, 39(1): 14–30. ★★★

Dawson, A. & Hjorth, D. (2012) 'Advancing family business research through narrative analysis,' *Family Business Review*, 25(3): 339–355. ★★★

De Massis, A., Chua, J. H., & Chrisman, J. J. (2008) 'Factors preventing intra-family succession,' *Family Business Review*, 21(2): 183–199. ★★★

Distelberg, B. & Sorenson, R. L. (2009) 'Updating systems concepts in family businesses: A focus on values, resource flows, and adaptability,' *Family Business Review*, 22(1): 65–81. ★★★

Distelberg, B. J. & Blow, A. (2011) 'Variations in family system boundaries,' *Family Business Review*, 24(1): 28–46. ★★★

Dyer, W. G. (2003) 'The family: The missing variable in organizational research,' *Entrepreneurship Theory and Practice*, 27(4): 401–416.

Dyer, W. G. & Dyer, W. J. (2009) 'Putting the family into family business research,' *Family Business Review*, 22: 216–219.

Eddleston, K. A. & Kellermanns, F. W. (2007) 'Destructive and productive family relationships: A stewardship theory perspective,' *Journal of Business Venturing*, 22(4): 545–565. ★★★

Eddleston, K. A. & Kidwell, R. E. (2012) 'Parent-child relationships: Planting the seeds of deviant behavior in the family firm,' *Entrepreneurship Theory and Practice*, 36(2): 369–386. ★★★

Eddleston, K. A., Kellermanns, F. W., & Sarathy, R. (2007) 'Resource configuration in family firms: Linking resources, strategic planning and technological opportunities to performance,' *Journal of Management Studies*, 45(1): 26–50. ★★★

Eddleston, K. A., Otondo, R. F., & Kellermanns, F. W. (2008) 'Conflict, participative decision-making, and generational ownership dispersion: A multilevel analysis,' *Journal of Small Business Management*, 46(3): 456–484. ★★★

Farrington, S. M., Venter, E., & Boshoff, C. (2012) 'The role of selected team design elements in successful sibling teams,' *Family Business Review*, 25(2): 191–205. ★★★

Gagné, M., Wrosch, C., & Brun de Pontet, S. (2011) 'Retiring from the family business: The role of goal adjustment capacities,' *Family Business Review*, 24(4): 292–304. ★★★

Galbraith, C. S. (2003) 'Divorce and the financial performance of small family businesses: An exploratory study,' *Journal of Small Business Management*, 41(3): 296–309. ★★★

Gorall, D.M. & Olson, D.H. (1995) 'Circumplex model of family systems: Integrating ethnic diversity and other social systems,' in: Mikesell, R. H., Lusterman, D.-D., & McDaniel, S.H. (eds.), *Integrating Family Therapy: Handbook of Family Psychology and Systems Theory*, Washington, DC: American Psychological Association, 217–233.

Haberman, H. & Danes, S. M. (2007) 'Father-daughter and father-son family business management transfer comparison: Family FIRO model application,' *Family Business Review*, 20(2): 163–184. ★★★

Handel, G. (1965) 'Psychological study of whole families,' *Psychological Bulletin*, 65, 19–41.

Harvey, M. & Evans, R. E. (1994) 'Family business and multiple levels of conflict,' *Family Business Review*, 7(4): 331–348.

Hinkin, T. 1995 'A review of scale development practices in the study of organizations,' *Journal of Management*, 21(5): 967–988.

Hobfoll, S.E. (1989) 'Conservation of resources: A new attempt at conceptualizing stress,' *American Psychologist*, 44(3): 513–524.

Howorth, C. & Ali, Z. A. (2001) 'Family business succession in Portugal: An examination of case studies in the furniture industry,' *Family Business Review*, 14(3): 231–244. ★★★

Jacob, T., & Tennenbaum, D. L. (1988) '*Family Assessment: Rationale, Methods, and Future Directions*,' New York: Plenum Press.

James, A. E., Jennings, J. E., & Breitkreuz, R. S. (2012) 'Worlds apart?: Rebridging the distance between family science and family business research,' *Family Business Review*, 25(1): 87–108.

Jaskiewicz, P., Combs, J., & Rau, S. (2015) 'How an entrepreneurial legacy fosters transgenerational entrepreneurship in multi-generational family firms,' *Journal of Business Venturing*, 30: 29–49. ★★★

Jehn, K.A. (1997) 'A qualitative analysis of conflict types and dimensions in organizational groups,' *Administrative Science Quarterly*, 42(3): 530. 26

Jehn, K. A. & Mannix, E. A. (2001) 'The dynamic nature of conflict: A longitudinal study of intragroup conflict and group performance,' *Academy of Management Journal*, 44(2): 238–251.

Karra, N., Tracey, P., & Phillips, N. (2006) 'Altruism and agency in the family firm: Exploring the role of family, kinship, and ethnicity,' *Entrepreneurship Theory and Practice*, 30(6): 861–877. ★★★

Kellermanns, F. W. & Eddleston, K. A. (2004) 'Feuding families: When conflict does a family firm good,' *Entrepreneurship Theory and Practice*, 28(3): 209–228. ★★★

Kellermanns, F.W. & Eddleston, K.A. (2006) 'Corporate entrepreneurship in family firms: A family perspective,' *Entrepreneurship Theory and Practice*, 30(6): 809–830. ★★★

Kellermanns, F. W., Eddleston, K. A., Sarathy, R., & Murphy, F. (2012) 'Innovativeness in family firms: A family influence perspective,' *Small Business Economics*, 38(1): 85–101. ★★★

Koiranen, M. (2002) 'Over 100 years of age but still entrepreneurially active in business: exploring the values and family characteristics of old Finnish family firms,' *Family Business Review*, 15(3): 175–187. ★★★

Kwan, H. K., Lau, V. P., & Au, K. (2012) 'Effects of family-to-work conflict on business owners: The role of family business,' *Family Business Review*, 25(2): 178–190. ★★★

Lansberg, I. & Astrachan, J.H. (1994) 'Influence of family relationships on succession planning and training: The importance of mediating factors,' *Family Business Review*, 7(1): 39–59.

Lee, J. (2006) 'Impact of family relationships on attitudes of the second generation in family business,' *Family Business Review*, 19(3): 175–191. ★★★

Levinson, H. (1971) 'Conflicts that plague family businesses,' *Harvard Business Review*, 49: 90–98.

Light, R. J., & Pillemer, D. B. (1984) '*Summing Up: The Science of Reviewing Research*,' Cambridge, MA: Harvard University Press.

Litz, R.A., Pearson, A.W., & Litchfield, S. (2012) 'Charting the future of family business research: Perspectives from the field,' *Family Business Review*, 25(1): 16–32.

MacKenzie, S. B., Podsakoff, P. M., & Podsakoff, N. P. (2011) 'Construct measurement and validation procedures in MIS and behavior research: Integrating new and existing techniques,' *MIS Quarterly*, 35: 293–334.

Mahto, R. V., Davis, P. S., Pearce, J. A., & Robinson, R. B. (2010) 'Satisfaction with firm performance in family businesses,' *Entrepreneurship Theory and Practice*, 34(5): 985–1001. ★★★

Marchisio, G., Mazzola, P., Sciascia, S., Miles, M., & Astrachan, J. (2010) 'Corporate venturing in family business: The effects on the family and its members,' *Entrepreneurship & Regional Development*, 22(3–4): 349–377. ★★★

Marshall, J. P., Sorenson, R., Brigham, K., Wieling, E., Reifman, A., & Wampler, R. S. (2006) 'The Paradox for the family firm CEO: Owner age relationship to succession-related processes and plans,' *Journal of Business Venturing*, 21: 348–368.

Michael-Tsabari, N., Labaki, R., & Zachary, R. K. (2014) 'Towards the cluster model: The family firm's entrepreneurial behavior over generations,' *Family Business Review*, 27(2): 161–185. ★★★

Miller, D., Steier, L., & Le Breton-Miller, I. (2003) 'Lost in time: Intergenerational succession, change, and failure in family business,' *Journal of Business Venturing*, 18(4): 513–531. ★★★

Mintzberg, H. (2005) 'Developing theory about the development of theory,' In Smith, K. G. & Hitt, M. A. (eds.), *Great Minds in Management: The Process of Theory Development*, Oxford: Oxford University Press, 355–372.

Mulrow, C. D. (1994) 'Systematic reviews: Rationale for systematic reviews,' *British Medical Journal*, 309 (6954): 597–599.

Muske, G., & Fitzgerald, M. A. (2006) 'A panel study of copreneurs in business: Who enters, continues, and exits?,' *Family Business Review*, 19(3): 193–205. ★★★

Nam, Y.-H. & Herbert, J. I. (1999) 'Characteristics and key success factors in family business: The case of Korean immigrant businesses in metro-Atlanta,' *Family Business Review*, 12(4): 341–352. ★★★

Nicholson, N. (2008) 'Evolutionary psychology and family business: A new synthesis for theory, research, and practice,' *Family Business Review*, 21(1): 103–118.

Olson, D. H., Sprenkle, D. H., & Russell, C. S. (1979) 'Circumplex model of marital and family systems: I. Cohesion and adaptability dimensions, family types, and clinical applications,' *Family Process*, 18(1): 3–28.

Olson, P. D., Zuiker, V. S., Danes, S. M., Stafford, K., Heck, R. K., & Duncan, K. A. (2003) 'The impact of the family and the business on family business sustainability,' *Journal of Business Venturing*, 18(5): 639–666. ★★★

Pagliarussi, M. S. & Rapozo, F. O. (2011) 'Agency relationships in a Brazilian multifamily firm,' *Family Business Review*, 24(2): 170–183. ★★★

Parker, S. C. & van Praag, M. (2012) 'The entrepreneur's mode of entry: Business takeover or new venture start?,' *Journal of Business Venturing*, 27: 31–46.

Pearson, A. W. & Lumpkin, G. T. (2011) 'Measurement in family business research: How do we measure up?,' *Family Business Review*, 24(4): 287–291.

Pearson, A. W., Holt, D. T. & Carr, J. C. (2014) 'Scales in family business studies,' in: Melin, L., Nordqvist, M., & Sharma, P. (eds.), *The Sage Handbook of Family Businesses*, London, England: Sage, 551–572.

Penney, C. R., & Combs, J. G. (2013) 'Insights from family science: The case of innovation,' *Entrepreneurship Theory and Practice*, 37(6): 1421–1427. ★★★

Perricone, P. J., Earle, J. R., & Taplin, I. M. (2001) 'Patterns of succession and continuity in family-owned businesses: Study of an ethnic community,' *Family Business Review*, 14(2): 105–121. ★★★

Pieper, T. M. & Klein, S. B. (2007) 'The bulleye: A systems approach to modeling family firms,' *Family Business Review*, 20(4): 301–319.

Poza, E. J., Hanlon, S., & Kishida, R. (2004) 'Does the family business interaction factor represent a resource or a cost?,' *Family Business Review*, 17(2): 99–118. ★★★

Reay, T. (2014) 'Publishing qualitative research,' *Family Business Review*, 27(2): 95–102.

Reay, T. & Whetten, D. A. (2011) 'What constitutes a theoretical contribution in family business?,' *Family Business Review*, 24(2): 105–110.

Rothausen, T. (1999) '"Family" in organizational research: A review and comparison of definitions and measures,' *Journal of Organizational Behavior*, 20: 817–836.

Rowe, B. R. & Hong, G.-S. (2000) 'The role of wives in family businesses: The paid and unpaid work of women,' *Family Business Review*, 13(1): 1–13. ★★★

Rutherford, M. W., Muse, L. A., & Oswald, S. L. (2006) 'A new perspective on the developmental model for family business,' *Family Business Review*, 19(4): 317–333. ★★★

Salvato, C., & Melin, L. (2008) 'Creating value across generations in family-controlled businesses: The role of family social capital,' *Family Business Review*, 21(3): 259–276. ★★★

Santiago, A. L. (2011) 'The family in family business: Case of the in-laws in Philippine businesses,' *Family Business Review*, 24(4): 343–361. ★★★

lze, W. S., Lubatkin, M. H., & Dino, R. N. (2003) 'Exploring the agency consequences of ownership dispersion among the directors of private family firms,' *The Academy of Management Journal*, 46(2): 179–194.

tz, W.C. (1958) *FIRO: A Three Dimensional Theory of Interpersonal Behavior*, New York: Holt, Rinehart, & Winston.

ma. P. (1997) *'Determinants of the satisfaction of the primary stakeholder with the succession process in family firms,'* unpublished doctoral dissertation. University of Calgary, Canada.

ma, P., Chrisman, J., & Gersick, K. (2012) '25 years of family business review: Reflections on the past and perspectives for the future,' *Family Business Review*, 25(1): 5–15.

ma, P., Melin, L., & Nordqvist, M. (2014) 'Introduction: Scope, evolution and future of family business studies,' in: Melin, L., Nordqvist, M. & Sharma, P. (eds.), *The Sage Handbook of Family Businesses,* London, England: Sage, 1–23.

herd, D. A. (2009) 'Grief recovery from the loss of a family business: A multi- and meso-level theory,' *Journal of Business Venturing*, 24(1): 81–97.★★★

ner, H., Steinhauer, P., & Sitarenios, G. (2000) 'Family assessment measure (FAM) and process model of family functioning,' *Journal of Family Therapy*, 22(2): 190–210.

kstein, G. (1978) 'The Family APGAR: A proposal for a family functioning test and its use by physicians,' *The Journal of Family Practice*, 6(6): 1231–1239.

rnios, K. X., Romano, C. A., Tanewski, G. A., Karofsky, P. I., Millen, R., & Yilmaz, M. R. (2003) 'Work-Family Conflict: A study of American and Australian family businesses,' *Family Business Review*, 16(1): 35–51.

nson, R. L., Goodpaster, K. E., Hedberg, P. R., & Yu, A. (2009) 'The family point of view, family social capital, and firm performance: An exploratory test,' *Family Business Review*, 22(3): 239–253. ★★★

ford, K., Duncan, K. A., Dane, S., & Winter, M. (1999) 'A research model of sustainable family businesses,' *Family Business Review*, 12(3): 197–208.

rou, E. (1999) 'Succession in family businesses: Exploring the effects of demographic factors on offspring intentions to join and take over the business,' *Journal of Small Business Management*, 37(3): 43–61. ★★★

er, L. (2001) 'Family firms, plural forms of governance, and the evolving role of trust,' *Family Business Review*, 14(4): 353–367. ★★★

con, R. I. & Staw, B. M. (1995) 'What theory is not,' *Administrative Science Quarterly*, 40(3): 371–384.

oocznik, J., & Kurtines, W.A. (1993) 'Family psychology and cultural diversity: Opportunities for theory, research, and application,' *American Psychologist*, 48(4): 400–407.

omas, J. (2002) 'Freeing the shackles of family business ownership,' *Family Business Review*, 15(4): 321–336. ★★★

vinyo-Rodríguez, R. N., & Bontis, N. (2010) 'Family ties and emotions: A missing piece in the knowledge transfer puzzle,' *Journal of Small Business and Enterprise Development*, 17(3): 418–436. ★★★

i, W. & Ghosal, S. (1998) 'Social capital and value creation: The role of intrafirm networks,' *Academy of Management Journal*, 41: 464–476.

ter, E., Boshoff, C., & Maas, G. (2005) 'The influence of successor-related factors on the succession process in small and medium-sized family businesses,' *Family Business Review*, 18(4): 283–303. ★★★

a, C. F., & Dean, M. A. (2005) 'An examination of the challenges daughters face in family business succession,' *Family Business Review*, 18(4): 321–345. ★★★

alonga, B. & Amit, R. (2006) 'How do family ownership, control, and management affect firm value?,' *Journal of Financial Economics*, 80(2): 385–417.

. Bertalanffy, K.L. (1968) *'General System Theory: Foundations, Development, Applications,'* New York: George Braziller.

gotsky, L.S. (1978) *'Mind in Society: The Development of Higher Psychological Processes,'* Cambridge, MA: Harvard University Press

lter, F. (2011). Contextualizing entrepreneurship – Conceptual challenges and ways forward, *Entrepreneurship Theory and Practice,* 35(1): 165–184.

klund, J., Nordqvist, M., Hellerstedt, K., & Bird, M. (2013) 'Internal versus external ownership transition in family firms: An embeddedness perspective,' *Entrepreneurship Theory and Practice*, 37(6): 1319–1340. ★★★

ng, N., Chen, C.C., Choi, J., & Zou, Y. (2000) 'Sources of work-family conflict: A Sino-U.S. comparison of the effects of work and family demands,' *Academy of Management Journal*, 43(1): 113–123.

. A., Lumpkin, G. T., Sorenson, R. L., & Brigham, K. H (2012) 'The landscape of family business outcomes: A summary and numerical taxonomy of dependent variables,' *Family Business Review,* 25(1): 33–57.

Zahra, S. A. (2012) 'Organizational learning and entrepreneurship in family firms: Exploring the moderating effect of ownership and cohesion,' *Small Business Economics*, 38(1): 51–65. ★★★

Zellweger, T., Sieger, P., & Halter, F. (2011) 'Should I stay or should I go? Career choice intentions of students with family business background.,' *Journal of Business Venturing*, 26(5): 521–536.

Zellweger, T. M., Nason, R. S., & Nordqvist, M. (2012) 'From longevity of firms to transgenerational entrepreneurship of families: Introducing family entrepreneurial orientation' *Family Business Review*, 25(2): 136–155. ★★★

23

THE JANUS EFFECT

Psychopathy in Family Business

Reginald L. Tucker, Kristen K. Shanine, and James G. Combs

The Janus Effect: The Role of Psychopathy in Family Business

Most firms across the globe are owned and managed by family members, and family firms are critical to most economies (Morck and Yeung 2003; Perman 2006; Sharma, Chrisman, Pablo, & Chua 2001). Accordingly, family business researchers strive to understand factors that contribute to family business success. Studies have uncovered important factors at the environmental- (e.g., culture), firm- (e.g., resource and governance), and individual- (e.g., relational or personal) levels (Filser, Kraus, and Mark 2013; Long and Chrisman 2013; Nordqvist, Wennerg, and Hellerstedt 2013). One particularly fruitful avenue of inquiry involves identifying family leaders' unique psychological traits and the consequences of these traits for key family business outcomes (i.e., Filser et al. 2013; Nordqvist et al. 2013).

One psychological trait that has not received attention, but has the potential to help explain outcomes in some family firms, is psychopathy. Psychopathy is defined as "a lack of concern for both other people and social regulatory mechanisms, impulsivity, and a lack of guilt or remorse when their actions harm others" (O'Boyle, Forsyth, Banks, and McDaniel 2012, 558). Psychopathy concerns an individual's intense focus while disregarding the emotions of others. While psychopathy is a seemingly negative psychological trait, it can have positive effects in the workplace due to the psychopath's charisma, intense focus, and stress tolerance (Babiak and Hare 2006). Similar to the Roman God, Janus, the psychopath has two faces: one that is inherently good and another that is bad. Psychopathy yields dual outcomes.

Understanding the positive side of dark-side traits, such as psychopathy, is a recent area of focus in organizational behavior research (e.g., O'Boyle et al. 2012). The most widely accepted positive side of psychopathy concerns the superficial charm that psychopaths use to influence others and achieve their own desires (Stevens, Deuling, and Armenakis 2012). An individual who exhibits psychopathic tendencies while flourishing in the workplace is termed a "successful psychopath" (Hall and Benning 2006). While much research on successful psychopaths concerns individuals, the positive effects of psychopaths in business can be seen in their ability to instill vision in others, form small productive work teams, and provide strategic thinking across the company (Hall and Benning 2006). In addition, psychopathic leaders are more likely to take bold actions that are beneficial to the business because they are unconcerned with how others view them (Babiak and Hare 2006).

While psychopaths appear to have positive effects in business, their impact on their families is decidedly negative. Children of psychopathic parents are more likely to develop antisocial tendencies, feel neglected and deprived of nurturance, and become depressed, aggressive, and violent towards others (Rockwell 1978). Children of psychopaths are more prone to become psychopaths themselves because they are consistently socialized into psychopathic behaviors and tendencies (Gao, Raine, Chan, Venables, and Mednick 2010). There is also a reciprocal relationship between psychopathy and family outcomes wherein psychopathy influences negative family outcomes and negative family outcomes, in turn, reinforce the psychopathic behavior by the parent(s) and/or child (Tuvblad, Bezdijian, Raine, and Baker 2013). Overall, the negative traits associated with psychopathy provide substantial evidence that psychopaths harm families (Kidwell, Kellermanns, and Eddleston 2012).

Given that psychopaths can have a positive impact in business while their influence on family is universally negative, it seems worthwhile to understand how psychopaths impact family business – where the psychopath's positive impact on business likely collides with their negative impact on family. Psychopathic leaders might develop a superior vision and strategy or take bold actions that benefit the firm, but their callous lack of empathy might also lead to negative emotions and subsequent relationship conflict among family members, undermining the family harmony and effective decision-making (Kellermanns and Eddleston 2004) that is vital to family business success (Filser et al. 2013). Accordingly, we develop a conceptual model that helps explain when a psychopathic family leader can be more versus less beneficial for the family firm. In particular, we draw on Lawler's (2001) affect theory of social exchange to suggest that the presence of family members in family firms interferes with the psychopath's ability to generate positive outcomes for the firm, but that some family characteristics help psychopathic leaders' potentially positive benefits shine through.

Our central contribution is to explain how a potentially important, but previously uninvestigated family business leader psychological trait, – i.e., psychopathy – can interact with family characteristics to influence the success of a family business. In doing so, we also contribute to the limited knowledge of successful psychopathy by explaining how one context – i.e., family business – reshapes their potentially positive impact. This knowledge is important for family business researchers because the same rags-to-riches family background that often produces successful entrepreneurs (Collins and Moore 1964; Kets de Vries 1996; Sarachek 1978; Strenger and Burak, 2005; Wadhwa, Holly, Aggarwal, and Salkever 2009) might also produce psychopathy, which can be harmful when mixed with family. It would be beneficial for family members to recognize psychopathy and learn how the family might structure itself and the business to help the psychopath succeed.

Psychopathy in the Workplace and the Family

To repeat, psychopathy is defined as "a lack of concern for both other people and social regulatory mechanisms, impulsivity, and a lack of guilt or remorse when their actions harm others" (O'Boyle et al., 2012, 558). Psychopathy carries both clinical and subclinical meanings. Clinical psychopathy differs from subclinical psychopathy in terms of degree, magnitude, or frequency of behaviors and cognitions (Gustafson and Ritzer 1995). Clinical psychopathy is an all-encompassing pattern of deviant and dysfunctional behavior, affect, and cognition that affects multiple aspects of an individual's life (e.g., work, family, social) (LeBreton, Binning, and Adorno 2006). They are clinically impaired, chronically dysfunctional employees, spouses, parents, and friends (LeBreton et al. 2006). They are often incapable of living among the general population and commonly end up in criminal or psychiatric institutions (Babiak and Hare

2006). Psychologists estimate that about one percent of the general population meets the clinical criteria for psychopathy (Babiak and Hare 2006). Given the low rate of clinical psychopathy in the general population, most empirical studies are in incarcerated or psychiatric settings (Lebreton et al. 2006). Clinical psychopaths are identified by symptoms such as pathological lying, serial irresponsibility and impulsivity, lack of remorse, failure to accept responsibility for one's actions, superficial charm and charisma, manipulative and self-serving patterns of behavior, and adolescent and adult criminal behavior (Cleckley 1941; Hare 1999).

Subclinical psychopaths differ from clinical psychopaths in that their behaviors are less intense, pervasive, or frequent (Gustafson and Ritzer 1995). For example, where the clinical psychopath might make a career out of violent crime (e.g., armed robbery), the subclinical psychopath is likely to pursue less extreme (and less frequent) forms of antisocial behavior (e.g., inflating expense accounts) (LeBreton et al. 2006). Subclinical psychopaths have less than ideal relationships, but they are capable of maintaining relationships (O'Boyle et al. 2012). While clinical psychopathy occurs in one percent of the population, subclinical psychopathy is more common, with estimates suggesting five to fifteen percent in the general population (Gustafson and Ritzer 1995; Pethman and Erlandsson 2010). Because our theory is about psychopathy in a family business context, our theorizing is constrained to subclinical psychopathy.

Psychopathy in Business

Psychopathic tendencies in organizations can result in several negative outcomes. Employees may perceive psychopaths as overly harsh (e.g., threats of punishment) (Jonason, Li, Webster, and Schmitt 2012), bullies (Boddy 2011), and poor managers (Babiak, Neumann, and Hare 2010). The psychopath is not able to charm all and, as a result, can alienate and sever relationships with employees (Paulhus and Williams, 2002). Also, impulsivity, a characteristic of psychopathy, is associated with workplace deviance, job and work withdrawal, and accidents on the job (Judge and LePine 2007). As psychopaths move into leadership positions, they can have negative effects on other employees who might mimic their socially undesirable or unethical behavior believing that it is necessary for workplace success (i.e., promotion) (Boddy, Ladyshewsky, and Galvin 2010). Additionally, subordinates who suffer abuse from psychopathic leaders might engage in counter-productive work behaviors (e.g., deviance, absenteeism, relationship conflict) in retaliation against the organization (Jones 2009).

Despite evidence that psychopathy sometimes has negative workplace consequences, there is a bright side to psychopathy in organizations. Psychopaths often experience workplace promotion and career mobility due to their careerist orientation (i.e., ability to achieve advancement via non-performance based activities) (Babiak and Hare, 2006; Chiaburu, Muñoz, and Gardner 2013). They can also be perceived as bold, charismatic, and achievement-oriented leaders (Judge and LePine 2007; Lykken 1995; O'Boyle et al. 2012), and while impulsivity can be a negative trait of psychopathy, it can also allow psychopaths to perform better at complex tasks (Anderson, 1994). In concert with the psychopath's charm and cool decisiveness, these factors allow psychopaths to be singled out for rapid promotion (Boddy 2011). In fact, three to four percent of individuals promoted to higher ranks have psychopathic tendencies (Babiak and Hare 2006). (Babiak et al. 2010; Cleckley 1941).

Psychopaths, on average, have disinhibited impulses (O'Boyle et al. 2012), are not prone to get along with others (Stevens et al. 2012), and are often found in authoritative positions (Babiak and Hare 2006). A combination of these factors, along with the psychopath's desire to get ahead (Akhtar et al. 2013), often culminates in a decisive leader – which is particularly important when firms face risk and uncertainty (Miller 2015). Research finds that individuals in psychopath-led firms and teams are less likely to attribute abusive behavior to the psychopathic leader when the firm faces uncertainty, attributing it instead to the environment (Hmieleski and Ensley 2007). Overall, when combined with environmental uncertainty, psychopathic leaders appear able to use their charisma to enhance firm performance (Waldman, Ramírez, House, and Purnam 2001).

Given the positive and negative effects that psychopaths can have on the workplace, perhaps it should not be surprising that a recent meta-analysis covering over 60 years of research found only a very small negative relationship between psychopathy and job performance and a similarly small positive relationship between psychopathy and counterproductive work behaviors (O'Boyle et al. 2012). Importantly, these small harmful effects turn around as psychopaths gain authority (O'Boyle et al. 2012). In other words, psychopaths are more likely to have positive job performance and engage in productive work behaviors as they move up the organization's hierarchy (O'Boyle et al. 2012). One likely reason is that whereas emotional intelligence and team building (i.e., human relation skills) are critical mid-management skills, the ability to discern strategy and offer a clear sense of direction are more important at higher levels (Mumford, Campion, and Morgeson 2007). Thus, while psychopaths clearly have a negative impact in organizations, they can, and more often than not do, have important positive benefits when they move into organizational leadership roles.

Psychopathy in Family

Unlike in the workplace, there is no evidence that psychopathy has positive effects in the family (Farrington 2006). Family is a setting where individuals find warmth, nurture, and perhaps unconditional acceptance (Eagly 1987). Psychopathy, on the other hand, is characterized by a lack of empathy and superficial charm (O'Boyle et al. 2012). Thus, it is intuitive that psychopathy has negative effects on families.

In order to review the psychopathy and family literature, we searched Google Scholar for studies related to psychopathy and family background. Our search returned studies that primarily investigated how family dynamics influenced psychopathic development in adolescents. This was expected because family dynamics are often studied as an antecedent of adolescent psychopathy (Farrington 2006). Regarding research design, we attempted to find studies that tracked psychopathic development and its effects on family members over time; longitudinal studies are considered the best research design when examining the relationship between psychopathy and family dynamics (Farrington 2006). As Lynam (1996, 214) describes, "the most straightforward way to connect a childhood disorder with an adult disorder is through longitudinal research, showing that the children with a given childhood disorder are more likely to become adults with a specific disorder." Accordingly, Table 23.1 summarizes the major longitudinal studies connecting psychopathy with family outcomes.

Consistent themes emerge when examining psychopathy and family. A lack of parent and child interaction, particularly by the mother, and inconsistent parental discipline are fertile grounds for the development of psychopathy in adolescents (Gao et al. 2010). When there is parent and child interaction, the child's warmth, nurture, and acceptance needs are met (Gao et al. 2010). The first five years of a child's life are particularly important regarding the relationship with the mother because an absence of this relationship is more likely to lead to psychopathic tendencies (Gao et al. 2010). A lack of parent and child interaction fosters feelings in children that relationships and social interaction, even with birth parents, is neither important nor something to cherish. This type of parent-child relationship might influence the child to develop an

Table 23.1 Psychopathy and Family Studies

Author/Journal	Year	Title	Method	Sample/Description	Findings
Lykken, *The Antisocial Personalities*	1995	*The Antisocial Personalities*	Book/Review	Book	"The psychopath and the sociopath can be regarded as opposite endpoints on a common dimension with difficult temperament maximized at the psychopathic end and inadequate parenting maximized at the sociopathic end" (p. 7). "Inadequate or incompetent parenting leads to insecure attachment bonding that forecasts 'low levels of empathy, compliance, cooperation, and self control'" (Draper & Belsky, 1990, p. 151) (p. 199).
Lynam, *Psychological Bulletin*	1996	Early identification of chronic offenders: Who is the fledgling psychopath?	Review	Prior studies	The most straightforward way to connect a childhood disorder with an adult disorder is through longitudinal research, showing that the children with a given childhood disorder are more likely to become adults with a specific disorder (p. 214).
Weiler & Widom, *Criminal Behavior and Mental Health*	1996	Psychopathy and violent behavior in abused and neglected young adults	Quantitative	652 abused and neglected individuals/489 control group	The authors found that **childhood victimization** and **psychopathy** were linked. Also, the authors found that **psychopathy** mediated (partial mediation) the relationship between **childhood victimization** and **violent offending**. ★The authors did not identify who the abusers were (e.g., family).
Marshall and Cooke, *Journal of Personality Disorders*	1999	The childhood experiences of psychopaths: A retrospective study of familial and societal factors	Quantitative	105 prisoners; 50 psychopaths/55 non-psychopaths	The authors found that [1] **parental discipline**, [2] **parental indifference/neglect**, [3] **parental supervision**, and [4] **psychological abuse** had high correlations with psychopathy in the criminal psychopath sample.

(Continued)

Author/Journal	Year	Title	Method	Sample/Description	Findings
Farrington, *Behavioral Sciences and the Law*	2000	Psychosocial predictors of adult antisocial personality and adult convictions	Longitudinal (follow up to1977 Cambridge study)	In the first study, psychosocial risk factors measured males from ages 8–10, 411 South London males were followed up since age 8 to see the antisocial personality disorder at ages 18, 32, and their convictions between ages 21–40	The authors found that [1] **large family size**, [2] **poor child rearing**, [3] **poor supervision**, [4] **disrupted family**, and [5] **father uninterested in child** were indicators of antisocial personality disorder at age 18 and at age 32.
Lang, af Klinteberg, and Alm, *Acta Psychiatra Scandinavica*	2002	Adult psychopathy and violent behavior in males with early neglect and abuse	Longitudinal	Swedish males (*N* = 199) recruited from a socially high-risk neighborhood and grouped on an index variable of victimization, yielding high (*N* = 110) and low victimization (*N* = 89) groups. The males examined were from the research program "Follow up of young criminals and controls in Stockholm 1956." The program was initiated by the Swedish government in 1956, and 287 boys aged 11–14 years, from an urban area, were examined in 1959–1963.	*One of the best predictors in the development of psychopathy in young individuals turned out to be a father who is a psychopath, who is an alcoholic, or who shows antisocial behaviors (not a finding, but a statement). *Delayed or inconsistent discipline from the parents is considered to be a cause of confusion about when to resist impulses and temptations, and of a lack of guilt; two qualities common among psychopaths. No significant association between childhood victimization and psychopathy was found. The present results indicated that an association between childhood victimization and adult psychopathy might be mediated by psychosocial components. This suggests that children with psychopathy-related traits and behaviors living in abusive families, with parental impulsivity and impulse control disorders, hyperactivity, alcohol abuse, poor socialization and low tolerance to frustration, are at high risk for eye-witnessing of violence and for developing violent behavior themselves.
Campbell, Porter, and Snow, *Behavioral Sciences and the Law*	2004	Psychopathic traits in adolescent offenders: An evaluation of criminal history, clinical, and psychosocial correlates	Quantitative	226 incarcerated youth (17% female)	The authors found that **history of placement in foster care** had high associations with PCL-YV youth psychopathy while [1] **quality of parental caregiver relationship**, [2] **total number of disruptions in living situation**, [3] **history of sexual abuse**, and [4] **whether offender was raised by a single parent** also had a significant effect on psychopathic tendencies.

Authors, Journal	Year	Title	Method	Participants	Findings
Moffitt, *Psychological Bulletin*	2005	The new look of behavioral genetics in developmental psychopathology: Gene–environment interplay in antisocial behaviors	Review		**Bad parenting** statistically predicts children's aggression.
Lynam, Caspi, Moffitt, Loeber, and Stouthamer-Loeber, *Journal of Abnormal Psychology*	2007	Longitudinal evidence that psychopathy scores in early adolescence predict adult psychopathy	Longitudinal	250 participants (all male) from a Pittsburgh Youth Study. At time 1, participants were 13 years of age, and at time 2, participants were 24 years of age.	The authors found that adolescent boys who were reported by their mothers to have psychopathy at age 13 had psychopathic traits at age 24 as measured by interviews. **Psychopathy can occur in adolescence and continue into adulthood.**
Gao, Raine, Chan, Venables, and Mednick, *Psychological Medicine: A Journal of Research in Psychiatry and the Allied Sciences*	2010	Early maternal and paternal bonding, childhood physical abuse and adult psychopathic personality	Quantitative/ Examined relationship between maternal and paternal bonding, childhood physical abuse and psychopathic personality at 28 years	333 (203 male/ 130 female) from the island of Mauritius	[1] The key finding of this study is that **disrupted parental bonding** is associated with an increased level of adult psychopathic personality. [2] **Low maternal care** was the key aspect of bonding most associated with psychopathy, while **low paternal overprotection** (i.e., increased autonomy and lack of regulatory control) was also important, especially in relation to the emotional detachment factor. [3] **Low maternal care** was the parental variable most strongly associated with both factors of adult psychopathy, reflecting the relatively greater impact of mothers.

(Continued)

Author/Journal	Year	Title	Method	Sample/Description	Findings
McDonald, Dodson, Rosenfield, and Jouriles, *Journal of Abnormal Psychology*	2011	Effects of a parenting intervention on features of psychopathy in children	Longitudinal – Tested at 6 time periods over 20 months	66 families (mother and child) recruited from domestic violence shelters. Each family included at least one child between the ages of 4 and 9 who exhibited clinical levels of conduct problems	The authors found that **parental consistency** (mother) (i.e., "I always follow through on my discipline for my child no matter how long it takes") mediated **child psychopathy** such that child psychopathy was reduced as mothers were more consistent in their parenting.
Fontaine, McCrory, Boivin, Moffitt, and Viding, *Journal of Abnormal Psychology*	2011	Predictors and outcomes of joint trajectories of callous-unemotional traits and conduct problems in childhood	Longitudinal	$N = 9{,}578$/ Twins Early Development Study/ The authors investigated callous-unemotional (CU) and conduct problems (CP). Children were assessed at 4 years of age and again at 12 years of age.	The authors found that **negative parental feelings** had a positive relationship with **chaos in the home** and that negative parental discipline had a positive relationship with chaos in the home.
Tuvblad, Bezdjian, Raine, and Baker, *Journal of Criminal Justice*	2013	Psychopathic personality and negative parent-to-child affect: A longitudinal cross-lag twin study	Longitudinal	1,562 twins. The twins were assessed at ages 9–10, and again at ages 14–15 utilizing both caregiver and youth self-reports.	The authors found that significant parent-driven effects for **negative parent-to-child affect** at ages 9–10 years influenced **psychopathic personality** at ages 14–15 years. Also, **psychopathic personality** at age 9–10 years influenced **negative parent-to-child affect** at age 14–15 years. This study illustrates the bi-directional effects of child psychopathy and negative parenting.

attitude that "others are either for me or against me." This attitude encourages children to learn how to manipulate others and remain emotionally distant.

Inconsistent or delayed discipline from parents will lead to a child's lack of guilt and inability to resist impulses and temptations – two qualities common among psychopaths (Lang, Af Klinteberg, and Alm 2002). An example of inconsistent parenting is when the parent warns the child of consequences for bad behavior but does not follow through (McDonald, Dodson, Rosenfield, and Jouriles 2011). Deciding whether or not to discipline a child, or even delaying discipline, might come across as impulsive to the child. Impulsivity is defined as "the tendency to act with little prior thought, to be prone to sensation and novelty seeking, and to be behaviorally disinhibited" (Judge and LePine, 2007, 338). The inconsistent and impulsive behavior of parents sends mixed signals to children, resulting in children who do not know when and how they will face consequences for their actions. Children who do not experience consequences, or experience consequences that seem unlinked to behavior, are more likely to engage in socially unacceptable behaviors (Lang et al. 2002).

Studies examining the effect of psychopathy on other family members are rare. However, evidence suggests that psychopathy and negative family outcomes have a reciprocal effect (Tuvblad et al. 2013). While psychopathy develops as a result of a negative family environment, psychopathy also perpetuates and reinforces a negative family environment (Tuvblad et al. 2013). Children with psychopathic parents are depressed, aggressive, violent, feel neglected, and develop antisocial tendencies (Rockwell 1978). Research finds that without some measure of intervention, the cycle continues for both child and parent (Lang et al. 2002; McDonald et al. 2011). Overall, the negative traits associated with psychopathy suggest strongly that psychopathy harms families.

Psychopathic Leadership and Family Business Success

While psychopathic leaders clearly can have a negative impact on employees, recent research suggests that, as leaders, their ability to take charge, set direction, and move forward without regard to others' feelings can yield positive benefits for firm performance (O'Boyle et al. 2012). The impact of psychopathy on the family, however, is universally negative, which raises questions about the role of psychopathy in family businesses, which is a context where business and family co-exist.

Psychopathy and Social Exchange in the Family

Social exchange theory (Emerson 1976) explains how exchange processes between individuals influence behavior. An exchange is a joint activity whereby individuals exchange benefits that they cannot achieve alone (Lawler 2001; Thibaut and Kelley 1959). Exchanges are both backward and forward looking in that individuals evaluate the past rewards and costs associated with an ongoing exchange and anticipate potential future rewards and costs (Emerson 1976; Lawler 2001). It is considered a Skinnerian, rational theory of behavior in that it assumes actors are rational. Affect theory of social exchange builds upon the original social exchange theory by adding the insight that successful exchanges produce positive emotions, and ineffective exchanges produce negative emotions (Lawler 2001). It adds a more socialized, non-rational layer to the original exchange theory by incorporating emotions, which are involuntary, internal responses to stimuli (Hochschild 1979; Lawler 2001). Affect theory of social exchange explains that emotions produced by social exchanges can generate stronger or weaker ties to the social unit (e.g., family) (Lawler 2001).

Affect theory of social exchange makes several assumptions and predictions. It assumes that social exchanges produce emotions that are along a positive-negative dimension in that actors either "feel good" or "feel bad" from an exchange; these reactions are considered internal, self-induced rewards or punishments (Lawler 2001). Individuals will then strive to reproduce positive emotions (i.e., rewards) and avoid negative ones (i.e., punishments) that develop from exchanges (Lawler 2001). Additionally, the emotions produced from exchanges will trigger a need to understand the source of the feelings, which results in an attribution process whereby individuals will explain their feelings with reference to social units (Lawler 2001).

Family and business are interdependent in family businesses, and family members form strong, unavoidable emotional bonds with one another and to the business (Daily and Dollinger 1992; Davis 1983; Kellermanns and Eddleston 2004). Additionally, a family business can be considered a "productive" exchange, which is a "single socially produced event or good that occurs only if members perform certain behaviors" (Lawler 2001, 336). A productive exchange occurs whenever "two or more actors bring something specific to a collective endeavor, and the whole of what they produce is greater than the sum of its parts" (Lawler 2001, 336). Productive exchanges entail the highest degree of interdependence compared to other types of exchanges (Lawler 2001). This means that family members involved in family business social exchanges will experience the greatest level of negative emotions when faced with exchange failure, and the greatest level of positive emotions when exchanges go well, compared to the other types of exchanges (Lawler 2001). Thus, family members who are involved in exchanges with a psychopathic leader in a family business will feel strong, negative emotions (e.g., hurt, anger, shame) when the psychopath does not reciprocate appropriately due to his or her inability to socially relate to others (Eddleston and Kidwell 2012). The callousness, lack of empathy, weak social regulatory mechanisms, and impulsivity among psychopaths will likely lead to strong negative emotions among family members, which will then lead to relationship conflict. The negative emotions and conflict that ensue from exchanges between the family members and the psychopath will ultimately, we submit, undermine the psychopath's ability to effectively lead a family business.

Our review of the literature on psychopathy in the workplace suggests that psychopaths can have positive and negative effects in organizations (Boddy et al. 2010; Jones 2009). However, on average, they have an overall positive impact on organizations in that they are rapidly promoted and often are effective leaders at higher levels (Chiaburu et al. 2013; O'Boyle et al. 2012). Their careerist orientation, charismatic leadership, achievement orientation, cool decisiveness, boldness, and impulsivity often result in effective decision-making that increases firm performance. In a family business, however, the callousness and lack of empathy among psychopaths likely lead to heightened perceptions of family discord and, as a result, relationship conflict between the psychopathic family business leader and other family members. Relationship conflict is related to stress (Jehn 1997). Psychopathic leaders create feelings of relationship conflict because their impulsivity results in frequent change and a family culture rife with uncertainty (Harvey and Evans 1994). Kidwell, Kellermanns, and Eddleston (2012) find that perceptions of family harmony are negatively related to relationship conflict, which, in turn, results in lower performance (Kellermanns and Eddleston 2004). When family members get along with one another, they are more productive because they are able to engage in better decision making. When family members do not get along, they focus more on their emotions and not on task performance (Kellermanns and Eddleston 2004). Thus, we predict that family will diminish any positive benefits that psychopathic leadership might otherwise have. Stated formally, we expect that:

Proposition 1

The positive benefits of psychopathic leadership are less when the firm is a family business.

Our central theoretical insight is that because families are harmed by, and likely react negatively to, psychopathic leadership, any benefits of psychopathic leadership that might otherwise be obtained in nonfamily firms becomes elusive in family firms. However, family firms differ dramatically from one another (Filser et al. 2013; Long and Chrisman 2013; Nordqvist et al. 2013). Thus, it seems likely that family characteristics that empower psychopathic family leaders to use their charisma and vision can benefit the firm financially while family characteristics that entangle psychopathic leaders with potentially hostile family members detract from the firm financially.

Based on affect theory of social exchange (Lawler 2001), we propose that family characteristics that increase interaction between the family and the psychopathic family business leader further weaken any positive benefit that psychopathic family business leadership might otherwise have for business success. In essence, the psychopath's callousness and lack of empathy will lead to negative emotions among family members during social exchanges, which create discord that undermines the psychopath's leadership. We build theory around four family characteristics – i.e., cohesiveness, family involvement, ownership dispersion, and generation – that: (1) have been heavily studied in family business research (e.g., Akhtar et al. 2013; Davis 1983; Davis and Harveston 1998; Lansberg and Astrachan 1994; Olson 2000; Schulze, Lubatkin, and Dino 2003, etc.) and (2) are known to be critical factors affecting the extent to which family members and family business leaders interact. Accordingly, they fit with our central insight that the need for family members to interact with psychopathic family business leaders impacts such leaders' overall effectiveness. Figure 23.1 depicts our conceptual model.

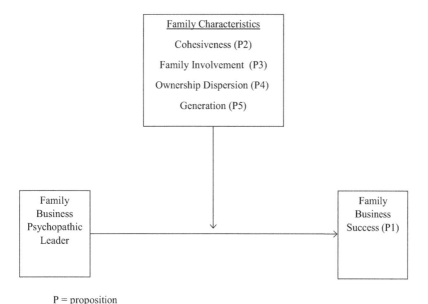

P = proposition

Figure 23.1 Conceptual Model

Family Characteristics that Affect the Quality of Family-member Psychopathic Leadership

We describe four family characteristics that likely shape the potential for positive outcomes from psychopathic leadership in family business. These factors – cohesiveness, family involvement, ownership dispersion, and generation – affect the potential for interference by hostile family members. In essence, it is thought that psychopaths will be successful in business due to their high level of stress tolerance, focused and driven personality, and charisma. However, they will be less successful if success requires interpersonal relations with family members because psychopaths are inherently callous and find interpersonal relationships difficult (O'Boyle et al. 2012). According to affect social exchange theory, such difficult interpersonal exchanges likely result in negative emotions among other family members (Lawler 2001); emotions that likely lead family members to interfere with the psychopathic leader's freedom to act. Thus, we ultimately predict that lower levels of closeness and involvement among family members will, by limiting the influence of conflict-laden family relationships, strengthen the potential for psychopathic family business leadership to benefit the family firm.

Cohesiveness

Cohesiveness is defined as the emotional glue that bonds family members to one another (Olson 2000, 145). According to Olson's (2000) Circumplex Model of Family Functioning, cohesiveness is defined in terms of a continuum. At one extreme, the highest levels of cohesion represent a high degree of enmeshment. Family members are very loyal to one another, dependent upon one another, and there are high levels of emotional connectedness. At the other extreme, the lowest levels of cohesion represent disengagement, and each family member is highly independent. Family members do not feel attached or committed to one another, and there is little emotional connectedness. Family systems with more balanced levels of family cohesiveness are thought to be the most effective in family businesses (Davis 1983; Lansberg and Astrachan 1994). Family cohesiveness impacts succession via the family commitment to the organization (Lansberg and Astrachan 1994).

When family leaders display psychopathic tendencies, we predict that a disengaged family system will work in the psychopath's favor in that it will weaken the negative impact of the family and strengthen the positive impact that psychopathic leadership can have. In terms of the affect theory of social exchange, in a disengaged family system where the family members are not close, actors will engage in fewer exchanges with the psychopathic leader. Thus, they will not respond as negatively to, or care as much about, the psychopathic leader's lack of empathy and callousness. The negative emotions that typically result from exchanges with the psychopathic leader will not lead to as much relationship conflict in a disengaged family system. The opposite is true of enmeshed family systems. Higher levels of cohesiveness in a family unit that contains a psychopathic leader will result in more exchanges that produce negative emotions and relationship conflict that undermines the psychopathic leader's ability to successfully lead the family business. The subsequent relationship conflict would cause family members to become less productive as they focus more on their emotions and not the tasks at hand. Accordingly, we predict that:

Proposition 2

In family businesses with cohesive controlling families, the positive benefits of having a leader with psychopathic tendencies will be less.

Family Involvement

The number of family members involved in the business and the extent of their involvement might also impact the psychopathic leader's ability to influence family business success. In general, the more family members involved and the higher their position in the business hierarchy, the more influence they will exercise (Davis and Harveston 1998).

Although not all family members exercise influence and work closely with the leader in the upper echelons, family involvement still requires the psychopathic family business leader to sustain his or her kinship network. According to affect theory of social exchange, if family members are not involved in the business, they will not be present to engage in exchanges that could produce negative emotions and conflict, which would undermine the psychopath's ability to lead. Thus, the fewer family members actively involved in the business, and the less they are involved in top management decisions, the better it will be for the psychopath's effectiveness. The opposite is also true. The more family members that are involved in the business, especially at higher levels, the more the psychopath will have to engage in interpersonal relationships and social exchanges that lead to negative emotions among his or her family members and greater relationship conflict. Relationship conflict will cause family members to focus more on their emotions than task performance, which would lessen productivity. Such conflict also makes it difficult for the psychopathic family business leader to exercise control and execute decisions that advance the firm financially. Thus, we anticipate that:

Proposition 3

In family businesses with more family involvement, the positive benefits of having a leader with psychopathic tendencies will be less.

Ownership Dispersion

The number of family member owners might also impact the degree to which psychopathic leaders can influence family business success. Concentrated ownership implies a few large owners who will actively engage with and try to influence the psychopathic leader. Fragmented ownership implies a large number of small owners who will be less engaged.

Again, according to the affect theory of social exchange, the more the psychopath engages in interpersonal relations and social exchanges with his or her family, the more such exchanges reduce the psychopathic leader's overall effectiveness. If family members do not exercise influence, they will not generate negative emotions from ongoing social exchanges with the psychopath, which will reduce the overall level of conflict and disharmony in the family. Thus, the more family member owners are fragmented, the better it will be for the psychopath's business success. Therefore:

Proposition 4

In family businesses with concentrated ownership, the positive benefits of having a leader with psychopathic tendencies will be less.

Generation

For two reasons, we predict that psychopathic family business leaders will be more effective, and the negative impact of the family will be less, in first generation family firms. The first reason is that successful psychopathy is more likely to coexist with an entrepreneurial orientation in the first generation. Akhtar et al. (2013) found a relationship between psychopathic tendencies and entrepreneurial abilities (i.e., entrepreneurial awareness, creativity, opportunism, and vision). This finding is in line with the notion that entrepreneurs can be callous, fearless, and persuasive – traits that are needed to explore and exploit opportunities (Akhtar et al. 2013; Kets de Vries 1985). Accordingly, it should not be surprising to find psychopathic tendencies in the founding generation.

Research shows that psychopathic tendencies are also inherited and/or imprinted (Gao et al. 2010; Tuvblad et al. 2013), so it should not be surprising to find second- and later-generation family firms run by psychopathic successors. Orientation toward entrepreneurship, however, is not as easily inherited. Indeed, generation is a key factor that is known to decrease innovation and creativity in family firms; innovation decreases once control is passed from the founder to later generations (Block, Miller, Jaskiewicz, and Spiegel 2013; Jaskiewicz, Combs, and Rau 2015). The founder's entrepreneurial orientation (i.e., preference for autonomy, innovation, risk-taking, proactive behavior, and competition) is what grows the firm (Lumpkin and Dess 1996), and although an entrepreneurial orientation is often passed via imprinting to a second generation, it is rarely as strong as in the first generation (Cruz and Nordqvist 2012). It will certainly disappear by the third generation unless families take active steps to institutionalize and preserve an entrepreneurial mindset (Jaskiewicz et al. 2015). Furthermore, it is not uncommon for exposure to the founding generation's wealth to result in a second- or later-generation "Fredo effect" where "a family member's incompetence, opportunistic behaviors, and/or ethically dubious actions can impede the firm's success" (Kidwell, Kellermanns, and Eddleston 2012, p. 503). Overall, second- and later-generation psychopathic family leaders are less likely to possess the same level of entrepreneurial orientation founding generation.

The second reason why second- and later-generation psychopathic leaders are less likely to be successful is because the relationship among other family members is different. Although family member social exchanges with a psychopath in a first-generation family firm will still lead to negative emotions and conflict, it will be less in the first generation because the family members are willing to overlook their relationship problems due to the firm's growing wealth and the family's increasing dependence on the firm for financial security. Further, because psychopathic founders are legitimately the key players in first-generation family firms, it is easier for them to ignore the input of disgruntled family members. A second- or later-generation psychopath has less legitimacy and, thus, is less likely to get the family to accept their leadership without interference. Stated formally:

Proposition 5

In later generation family firms, the positive benefits of having a leader with psychopathic tendencies will be less.

Discussion

To better understand the psychological factors that contribute to family business success, we examined psychopathy among family business leaders. Like the Roman God, Janus, psychopaths have two faces: one that is inherently good and another that is bad. In essence, psychopathy yields dual outcomes. On one hand, psychopaths can have positive effects in business. For example, they are rapidly promoted (Chiaburu et al. 2013), and many psychopathic traits are also effective leadership traits (i.e., political and organizational savvy, detachment, and capacity to make decisions based on objectivity rather than loyalty, trust, or emotions) (O'Boyle et al. 2012). On the other hand, they have very negative effects on families. For example, children with psychopathic parents are depressed, aggressive, neglected, and antisocial (Rockwell 1978). Given that psychopaths can have a positive impact on business (Babiak and Hare 2006; Chiaburu et al. 2013; Hall and Benning 2006; O'Boyle et al. 2012) while their influence on family is negative (Gao et al. 2010; Rockwell 1978), it seems worthwhile to understand how psychopaths impact family business – which is a context where the psychopath's positive impact on business likely collides with their negative impact on family.

Accordingly, we developed a conceptual model that helps explain when a psychopathic family leader can be more versus less beneficial for the family firm. We used Lawler's (2001) affect theory of social exchange to suggest that the presence of family members in family firms interferes with the psychopath's ability to generate positive outcomes for the firm, but that some family characteristics – i.e., cohesiveness, family involvement, ownership dispersion, and generation – affect the extent to which a psychopathic leader can benefit the firm. In general, these various family and firm factors affect the amount of social interaction, and negative emotions family members experience via social exchanges with the family business psychopathic leader. Psychopathy in the family business is important because the same rags-to-riches family background that often produces successful entrepreneurs (Collins and Moore 1964; Kets de Vries 1996; Sarachek 1978; Strenger and Burak 2005; Wadhwa, Holly, Aggarwal, and Salkever 2009) might also produce psychopathy, which can be harmful when mixed with family. Thus, understanding factors that influence their success as family business leaders are important because it could help family members recognize psychopathy and learn to structure itself and the business to help the psychopath succeed. Our theory also has implications for future family business research and psychopathic leadership.

Implications for Future Family Business Research

While this chapter analyzes one potential dark side psychological trait of family business leaders, future studies might consider other dark side traits. There is an assumption that dark side traits are inherently bad and have no positive outcomes. Other dark side traits that researchers might choose to explore are Machiavellianism and narcissism. Machiavellianism is a personality trait characterized by individuals who manipulate others for personal gain (Jonason et al. 2009). Narcissism is associated with a grandiose view of oneself where individuals take bold actions to receive praise and validation from others (Chatterjee and Hambrick 2007). Along with psychopathy, these two dark side traits comprise what researchers call the dark triad (O'Boyle et al. 2012).

Taking narcissism as an example, Freud insisted that narcissism could be positive and healthy. Researchers have since distinguished between positive "adaptive" narcissism and negative "maladaptive" narcissism based on the dimensions used in the Narcissistic Personality Inventory (NPI; Raskin and Hall 1979). Exploitativeness, Entitlement, and Exhibitionism scales are considered maladaptive narcissism based on their associations with poor social adjustment while Authority and Self-Sufficiency scales are considered adaptive narcissism based on their associations with self-confidence and assertiveness, which have less clear connections to social maladjustment (Barry, Frick, Adler, and Grafeman 2007). In general, narcissism can be healthy in terms of feeling good about oneself, but unhealthy for those who are close to the narcissist (Campbell, Hoffman, Campbell, and Marchisio 2011). In a family business succession, for example, adaptive narcissism (i.e., Authority and Self-Sufficiency) might be particularly beneficial because the successor will feel confident enough to assume a leadership role, and they are less likely to suffer from the negative employee outcomes associated with more maladaptive narcissistic behaviors (i.e., Exploitativeness, Entitlement, and Exhibitionism).

Future research might also consider how firm factors likely influence the degree to which psychopathic leaders are constrained by the family. Factors such as firm size or industry technology are likely to affect the family's ability to interfere with the psychopathic family business leader's positive influence on the family business's success. Small firm size, for example, might work in the psychopath's favor because it means fewer people that the psychopath has to get along with and exchange with while trying to lead the family business. Family firms involved in industries that are risky and uncertain might similarly find psychopathic leadership favorable because psychopaths are less intimidated by uncertainty and thus better equipped to be decisive in high-tech industries (Miller 2015).

Another potential avenue for future research concerns the impact of psychopathic parenting on multiple children. Psychopathic parents are more likely to have children with psychopathic tendencies (Gao et al. 2010; Tuvblad et al. 2013). This raises questions about what happens in family firms when there are multiple psychopathic children who are active in the firm. Our theory is that psychopathic leaders are less successful in family businesses because of the conflict that results from negative emotions that other family members have in their interactions with the psychopathic family leader. If many, or even most, family members are psychopaths, however, it seems less likely that affect social exchange would be the key theoretical mechanism because psychopaths do not care about what other people think and are less likely to respond emotionally to social exchanges (Babiak and Hare 2006; Cleckley 1941). Having multiple family members with blind ambition and an inability to empathize seems like a recipe for a highly politicized environment that will yield negative outcomes for the firm. Accordingly, future inquiry might advance by identifying what theoretical mechanisms drive behavior when multiple psychopaths interact within the same family firm.

Our focus has been on explaining how the interaction between psychopathic leadership and family affects strategic and financial outcomes for the firm. However, family firms are well known to pursue socioemotional wealth goals in addition to financial goals (Gómez-Mejía, Haynes, Núñez-Nickel, Jacobson, and Moyano-Fuentes 2007). Socioemotional wealth goals include, among other things, protecting the family's reputation (Deephouse and Jaskiewicz, 2010), caring for employees (Miller and Miller 2014), investing in local communities (Berrone et al., 2010), and investing in social causes (Cruz, Larraza-Kintana, Garces-Galdeano, and Berrone 2014). Our theory is that factors that buffer the psychopathic leader from the family will allow the leader to be more effective. It seems likely, though, that those same factors will also make it more difficult for the family to achieve socioemotional wealth goals because achieving such goals requires the efforts of multiple engaged family members (Miller and Miller 2014). Thus, it seems likely that psychopathic leadership, at a minimum, would disrupt efforts to achieve socioemotional wealth goals. The investigation of the trade-offs between financial and socioemotional wealth goals in the context of psychopathic leadership might provide a more encompassing theory about the effects of psychopathy in particular, and the dark side traits more generally, in the family business.

Implications for Research on Psychopathic Leadership

Family business is one context in which psychopathic leadership can be positive as well as negative, and it seems likely that there are other important contexts that also moderate the degree to which psychopaths can be beneficial in business. Future research might consider how organizational culture and climate, for example, moderate psychopathic leadership in firms (cf. Schein, 1990). Organizational culture, the underlying atmosphere of the firm, and climate, the daily manifestation of culture (Schein, 1990), are likely to be impacted by psychopathic leadership and also influence the psychopathic leader's effectiveness. For example, where organizational politics are the cultural norm, the ability to exercise political skill leads to individual success (e.g., promotion, pay raise) (Ferris, Treadway, Perrewé, Brouer, Douglas, and Lux 2007). Psychopathic leaders might influence the intensity of organizational politics within the firm through their actions, and they could also be rewarded as a result of their political skill. Additionally, other employees would take notice of the rewards or punishments associated with the psychopathic leader's behavior and attempt to imitate them, resulting in their own individual success or failure.

Leader-member exchange theory might also provide interesting findings regarding psychopathic leadership in firms. Leader-member exchange concerns the process of how leaders form in-groups and out-groups within the firm (Wayne, Shore, and Liden 1997). Leaders delegate responsibilities to members and depending upon the member's success or lack of success with those responsibilities, they are positioned into the in-group or out-group (Wayne et al. 1997). The psychopath's lack of empathy, antisocial tendencies, and demanding standards might heighten the differences between in- and out-group membership and lead toward more deviant behaviors, such as showing up late to work, among out-group members.

Practical Implications

Our theory has implications for family business practitioners. Perceptions of family business leaders are not likely to be associated with the term "psychopath" because of its negative connotations. A family business leader who engages in psychopathic behavior can be positive for the family business because they will be ambitious about achieving financial results and they can furnish a steady direction in an uncertain environment. Our theory, however, is that any positive benefits a psychopathic leader might have in a family firm are diminished by interactions with other family members that create negative emotions and conflict. A logical implication is that when family members see that their leader has psychopathic tendencies, the family will be better off if they can find alternative legitimate ways to monitor and influence the psychopathic leader while minimizing direct interactions that create negative affect. Perhaps this can be achieved by building an advisory board comprising strong external business leaders to act as an intermediary.

Conclusion

Because psychopaths typically harm their families but help business performance, we explore the impact of psychopathic leadership in a family business – a context where the psychopath's positive impact on business likely collides with their negative impact on the family. Based on affect theory of social exchange (Lawler 2001), we proposed that family members' negative emotions regarding the family business psychopathic leader will weaken any positive benefit that s/he might otherwise have for family business success. However, family characteristics such as cohesiveness, family involvement, ownership dispersion, and generation likely moderate the extent to which family members can interfere with the psychopathic leader's ability to shape the firm. We hope that our conceptual model can be the first step toward deeper thinking about psychopathy and other dark traits in family business, and will help family members to recognize psychopathy and find better ways to interact with the psychopath for the benefit of the firm and the family.

References

Akhtar, Reece, Gorkan Ahmetoglu and Tomas Chamorro-Premuzic. (2013) 'Greed is Good? Assessing the Relationship Between Entrepreneurship and Subclinical Psychopathy.' *Personality and Individual Differences* 54(3) : 420–425.

Babiak, Paul. (1995) 'When Psychopaths Go to Work: A Case Study of an Industrial Psychopath.' *Applied Psychology: An International Review* 44(2): 171–188.

Babiak, Paul, and Robert D. Hare. (2006) *Snakes in Suits: When Psychopaths go to Work*, New York: Regan Books.

Babiak, Paul, Craig S. Neumann, and Robert D. Hare. (2010) 'Corporate Psychopathy: Talking the Walk.' *Behavioral Sciences and the Law* 28(2)2010: 174–193.

Bailey, Charles D. (2014) 'Psychopathy, Academic Accountants' Attitudes Towards Unethical Research Practices, and Publication Success.' *The Accounting Review.*

Barry, Christopher, T., Paul J. Frick, Kristy K. Adler, and Sarah J. Grafeman. (2007) 'The Predictive Utility of Narcissism among Children and Adolescents: Evidence for a Distinction Between Adaptive and Maladaptive Narcissism,' *Journal of Child and Family Studies* 16(4): 508–521.

Bass, Bernard M. (1985) *Leadership and Performance Beyond Expectations,* New York: Free Press.

Baumrind, D. (1971) 'Current Patterns of Parental Authority.' *Developmental Psychology* 4(1): 1–103.

Bengston, Vern L., and Robert E.L. Roberts.E.L. (1991) 'Intergenerational Solidarity in Aging Families: An Example of Formal Theory Construction,' *Journal of Marriage and the Family* 53(4): 856–870.

Berrone, Pascalu., Cristina Cruz, C., Luis R. Gómez-Mejía, and Martin Larraza-Kintana. (2010) 'Socioemotional Wealth and Corporate Responses to Institutional Pressures: Do Family-Controlled Firms Pollute Less?' *Administrative Science Quarterly* 55(1): 82–113.

Block, Joern, Danny Miller, Peter Jaskiewicz, and Frank Spiegel. (2013) 'Economic and Technological Importance of Innovations in Large Family and Founder Firms an Analysis of Patent Data.' *Family Business Review* 26(2): 180–199.

Board, Belina Jane, and Katarina Fritzon. (2005) 'Disordered Personalities at Work.' *Psychology, Crime and Law* 11(1): 17–32.

Boddy, Clive R. (2006) 'The Dark Side of Management Decisions: Organisational Psychopaths.' *Management Decision* 44(10): 1461–1475.

Boddy, Clive R. (2011) 'Corporate Psychopaths, Bullying and Unfair Supervision in the Workplace,' *Journal of Business Ethics* 100(3): 367–379.

Boddy, Clive R., Richard K. Ladyshewsky, and Peter Galvin, P. (2010) 'The Influence of Corporate Psychopaths on Corporate Social Responsibility and Organizational Commitment to Employees,' *Journal of Business Ethics* 97(1): 1–19.

Bowlby, John. (1969) *Attachment and Loss: Attachment* (vol. 1), New York: Basic Books.

Campbell, W. Keith, Brian J. Hoffman, Stacey M. Campbell, and Gaia Marchisio. (2011) 'Narcissism in Organizational contexts.' *Human Resource Management Review* 21(4): 268–284.

Caponecchia, Carlo, Andrew Y.Z. Sun, and Anne Wyatt. 2012. "Psychopaths' at Work? Implications of Lay Persons' Use of Labels and Behavioural Criteria for Psychopathy,' *Journal of Business Ethics* 107(4): 399–408.

Chatterjee, Arjit, and Donald C. Hambrick. (2007) 'It's All About Me: Narcissistic Chief Executive Officers and Their Effects on Company Strategy and Performance.' *Administrative Science Quarterly* 52(3): 351–386.

Chiaburu, Dan S., Gonzalo J. Muñoz, and Richard G. Gardner, R. G. (2013) 'How to Spot a Careerist Early on: Psychopathy and Exchange Ideology as Predictors of Careerism,' *Journal of Business Ethics* 118(3): 473–486.

Chrisman, James J., Jess H. Chua, Allison W. Pearson, and Tim Barnett. (2012) 'Family Involvement, Family influence, and Family-centered Non-economic Goals in Small Firms.' *Entrepreneurship Theory and Practice* 36(2): 267–293.

Cleckley, Hervey. (1941) *The Mask of Sanity: An Attempt to Reinterpret the So-Called Psychopathic Personality.* St. Louis: The C.V. Mosby Company.

Collins, Orvis. F., and David G. Moore. (1964) *The Enterprising Man* (Vol. 1), Michigan State University Press.

Cruz, Cristina, and Mattias Nordqvist. (2012) 'Entrepreneurial Orientation in Family Firms: A Generational Perspective.' *Small Business Economics* 38(1): 33–49.

Cruz, Cristina, Martin Larraza-Kintana, Lucía Garcés-Galdeano, and Pascual Berrone. (2014) 'Are Family Firms Really More Socially Responsible?' *Entrepreneurship Theory and Practice* 38(6): 1295–1316.

Daily, Catherine M., and Marc J. Dollinger. (1992) 'An Empirical Examination of Ownership Structure in Family and Professionally Managed Firms.' *Family Business Review* 5(2): 117–136.

Dalal, Reeshad S. (2005) 'A Meta-analysis of the Relationship Between Organizational Citizenship Behavior and Counterproductive Work Behavior,' *Journal of Applied Psychology* 90(6) (2005)1241–1255.

Danco, L.A. (1980) *Inside the Family Business.* Cleveland, OH: The University Press.

Davis, Peter. (1983) 'Realizing the potential of the family business.' *Organizational Dynamics* 12(1): 47–56.

Davis, Peter S., Paula D. Harveston, P. D. (1998) 'The Influence of Family on the Family Business Succession Process: A Multi-generational Perspective.' *Entrepreneurship Theory and Practice* 22(3): 31–54.

De Oliveira-Souza, Ricardo, Jorge Moll, Fátima Azevedo Ignácio, and Robert D. Hare. (2008) 'Psychopathy in a Civil Psychiatric Outpatient Sample.' *Criminal Justice and Behavior* 35(4): 427–437.

Deephouse, David L., and Peter Jaskiewicz. (2013) 'Do Family Firms Have Better Reputations than Non-family firms? An Integration of Socioemotional Wealth and Social Identity Theories,' *Journal of Management Studies* 50(3): 337–360.

Downey, Geraldine, and Scott I. Feldman. (1996) 'Implications of Rejection Sensitivity for Intimate Relationships,' *Journal of Personality and Social Psychology* 70(6): 1327.

Dyer, W. Gibb. (1986) *Cultural Change in Family Firms: Anticipating and Managing Business and Family Transitions,* San Francisco, CA: Jossey-Bass.

Eagly, Alice H. (1987) *Sex Differences in Social Behavior: A Social-Role Interpretation,* London: Lawrence Erlbaum Associates.

Eddleston, Kimberly A., and Roland E. Kidwell. (2012) 'Parent–child Relationships: Planting the Seeds of Deviant Behavior in the Family Firm.' *Entrepreneurship Theory and Practice* 36(2): 369–386.

Feldman, Scott, and Geraldine Downey. (1994) 'Rejection Sensitivity as a Mediator of the Impact of Childhood Exposure to Family Violence on Adult Attachment Behavior.' *Development and Psychopathology* 6(1): 231–247.

Ferris, Gerald R., Darren C. Treadway, Pamela L. Perrewé, Robyn L. Brouer, Ceasar Douglas, and Sean Lux. (2007) 'Political skill in Organizations,' *Journal of Management* 33(3): 290–320.

Filser, Matthias, Sascha Kraus, and Stefan Märk. (2013) 'Psychological Aspects of Succession in Family Business Management.' *Management Research Review* 36(3): 256–277.

Fitzpatrick, Mary Anne, and L. David Ritchie. (1994) 'Communication Schemata Within the Family.' *Human Communication Research* 20(3): 275–301.

Foo, Maw-Der. (2011) 'Emotions and Entrepreneurial Opportunity Evaluation.' *Entrepreneurship Theory and Practice* 35(2): 375–393.

Gómez-Mejía, Luis R., Katalin Takács Haynes, Manuel Núñez-Nickel, Kathryn JL Jacobson, and José Moyano-Fuentes. (2007) 'Socioemotional Wealth and Business Risks in Family-controlled Firms: Evidence from Spanish Olive Oil Mills.' *Administrative Science Quarterly* 52(1): 106–137.

Gustafson, Sigrid B., and Darren R. Ritzer. (1995) 'The Dark side of Normal: A Psychopathy-linked Pattern Called Aberrant Self-promotion,' *European Journal of Personality* 9(3): 147–183.

Hall, J.R., & Benning, S.D. (2006) "The 'Successful' Psychopath: Adaptive and Subclinical Manifestations of Psychopathy in the General Population.' In *Handbook of Psychopathy*, edited by Christopher J. Patrick, 459–478. New York: The Guilford Press.

Hambrick, Donald C., and Phyllis A. Mason. (1984) 'Upper Echelons: The Organization as a Reflection of its Top Managers.' *Academy of Management Review* 9(2): 193–206.

Hare, Robert D. (1996) 'Psychopathy a Clinical Construct Whose Time has Come.' *Criminal Justice and Behavior* 23(1): 25–54.

Hare, Robert D. (1999) *Without Conscience: The Disturbing Word of the Psychopaths Among Us,* New York: Guildford Press.

Harvey, Michael, and Rodney E. Evans. (1994) 'Family Business and Multiple Levels of Conflict.' *Family Business Review* 7(4): 331–348.

Hmieleski, Keith M., and Michael D. Ensley. (2007) 'The Effects of Entrepreneur Abusive Supervision.' *Academy of Management Proceedings* 1–6.

Hochschild, Arlie Russell. (1979) 'Emotion Work, Feeling Rules, and Social Structure,' *American Journal of Sociology* 85(3): 551–575.

Holland, Daniel V., and Dean A. Shepherd. (2013) 'Deciding to Persist: Adversity, Values, and Entrepreneurs' Decision Policies.' *Entrepreneurship Theory and Practice* 37(2): 331–358.

Hopley, Anthony AB, and Caroline Brunelle. (2012) 'Personality Mediators of Psychopathy and Substance Dependence in Male Offenders.' *Addictive Behaviors* 37(8): 947–955.

Howe, Jacqueline, Diana Falkenbach, and Christina Massey. (2014) 'The Relationship Among Psychopathy, Emotional Intelligence, and Professional Success in Finance,' *International Journal of Forensic Mental Health* 13(4): 337–347.

Hutcheson, J.O. (2015, March 11). Addiction and Family Business. Retrieved from http://ffipractitioner. org/2015/03/11/addiction-and-family-business/.

Jaskiewicz, Peter, James G. Combs, and Sabine B. Rau. (2015) 'Entrepreneurial Legacy: Toward a Theory of How some Family Firms Nurture Transgenerational Entrepreneurship,' *Journal of Business Venturing* 30(1): 29–49.

Jehn, Karen A. (1997) 'A Qualitative Analysis of Conflict Types and Dimensions in Organizational Groups.' *Administrative Science Quarterly* 42(3): 530–557.

Jonason, Peter K., Norman P. Li, Gregory D. Webster, and David P. Schmitt. (2009) 'The Dark Triad: Facilitating a Short-term Mating Strategy in Men,' *European Journal of Personality* 23(1): 5–18.

Kellermanns, Franz W., and Kimberly A. Eddleston. (2004) 'Feuding Families: When Conflict Does a Family Firm Good.' *Entrepreneurship Theory and Practice* 28(3): 209–228.

Kellermanns, Franz W., Kimberly A. Eddleston, and Thomas M. Zellweger. (2012) 'Extending the Socioemotional Wealth Perspective: A Look at the Dark Side.' *Entrepreneurship Theory and Practice* 36(6): 1175–1182.

Kets de Vries, M.F.R. (1985) 'The Dark Side of Entrepreneurship.' *Harvard Business Review, 63,* 161–167.

Kets de Vries, M.F.R. (1996) 'The Anatomy of the Entrepreneur: Clinical Observations.' *Human Relations* 49(7): 853–883.

Kidwell, Roland E., Franz W. Kellermanns, and Kimberly A. Eddleston. (2012) 'Harmony, Justice, Confusion, and Conflict in Family Firms: Implications for Ethical Climate and the 'Fredo Effect,'' *Journal of Business Ethics* 106(4): 503–517.

La Porta, Rafael, Florencio Lopez-de-Silanes, and Andrei Shleifer. (1999) 'Corporate Ownership around the World,' *The Journal of Finance* 54(2): 471–517.

Lang, S., B. Af Klinteberg, and P-O. Alm. (2002) 'Adult Psychopathy and Violent Behavior in Males with Early Neglect and Abuse.' *Acta Psychiatrica Scandinavica* 106(s412): 93–100.

Lansberg, Ivan, and Joseph H. Astrachan. (1994) 'Influence of Family Relationships on Succession Planning and Training: The Importance of Mediating Factors.' *Family Business Review* 7(1): 39–59.

Lawler, Edward J. (2001) 'An Affect Theory of Social Exchange,' *American Journal of Sociology* 107(2): 321–352.

LeBreton, J.M., Binning, J.F., & Adorno, A.J. (2006) 'Subclinical Psychopaths.' In: *Comprehensive Handbook of Personality and Psychopathology: Personality and Everyday Functioning*, edited by Jay C. Thomas and Daniel L. Segal, 388–411, Hoboken, NJ: John Wiley.

Long, R. G., & Chrisman, J. J. (2013) "Management Succession in Family Business.' In: L. Melin, M. Nordqvist & P. Sharma (Eds.) *SAGE Handbook of Family Business*, London: Sage.

Lumpkin, G. Tom, and Gregory G. Dess. (1996) 'Clarifying the Entrepreneurial Orientation Construct and Linking it to Performance.' *Academy of Management Review* 21(1): 135–172.

Lykken, David Thoreson. (1995) *The Antisocial Personalities*, Mahwah, NJ: Erlbaum.

McDonald, Renee, Mary Catherine Dodson, David Rosenfield, and Ernest N. Jouriles. (2011) 'Effects of a Parenting Intervention on Features of Psychopathy in Children,' *Journal of Abnormal Child Psychology* 39(7): 1013–1023.

Merari, Ariel, Ilan Diamant, Arie Bibi, Yoav Broshi, and Giora Zakin. (2009) 'Personality Characteristics of 'Self Martyrs'/'Suicide Bombers' and Organizers of Suicide Attacks.' *Terrorism and Political Violence* 22(1): 87–101.

Miller, Danny. (2015) 'A Downside to the Entrepreneurial Personality?' *Entrepreneurship Theory and Practice* 39(1): 1–8.

Miller, Danny, Jangwoo Lee, Sooduck Chang, and Isabelle Le Breton-Miller. (2009) 'Filling the Institutional Void: The Social Behavior and Performance of Family vs Non-family Technology Firms in Emerging Markets.' *Journal of International Business Studies* 40(5): 802–817.

Miller, Danny, and Le Breton-Miller. (2014) 'Deconstructing Socioemotional Wealth.' *Entrepreneurship Theory and Practice* 38(4): 713–720.

Morck, Randall, and Bernard Yeung. (2003) 'Agency Problems in Large Family Business Groups.' *Entrepreneurship Theory and Practice* 27(4): 367–382.

Mumford, Troy V., Michael A. Campion, and Frederick P. Morgeson. (2007) 'The Leadership Skills Strataplex: Leadership Skill Requirements Across Organizational Levels.' *The Leadership Quarterly* 18(2): 154–166.

Nelton, Sharon. (1996) 'Team Playing is on the Rise.' *Nation's Business* 84(6): 53–56.

Nordqvist, Mattias, Karl Wennberg, and Karin Hellerstedt. (2013) 'An Entrepreneurial Process Perspective on Succession in Family Firms.' *Small Business Economics* 40(4): 1087–1122.

O'Boyle Jr, Ernest H., Donelson R. Forsyth, George C. Banks, and Michael A. McDaniel. (2012) 'A Meta-analysis of the Dark Triad and Work Behavior: A Social Exchange Perspective,' *Journal of Applied Psychology* 97(3): 557–579.

Olson, David H. (2000) 'Circumplex Model of Marital and Family Systems,' *Journal of Family Therapy* 22(2) (2000): 144–167.

Perman, S. (2006) 'Taking the Pulse of Family Business.' *Bloomberg Businessweek.* Retrieved from http://www.businessweek.com/ February 13, 2006.

Pethman, Tonya M.I., and Soly I. Erlandsson. (2010) 'Aberrant Self-promotion or Subclinical Psychopathy in a Swedish General Population.' *The Psychological Record* 52(1): 33–50.

Raskin, Robert N., and Calvin S. Hall. (1979) 'A Narcissistic Personality Inventory.' *Psychological Reports* 45(2): 590–590.

Rockwell, D.A. (1978) 'Social and Familial Correlates of Antisocial Disorders.' In *The Psychopath: A Comprehensive Study of Antisocial Disorders and Behaviors*, edited by William H. Reid, 132–145, New York: Brunner-Mazel.

Sanders, Jimy M., and Victor Nee. (1996) 'Immigrant Self-employment: The Family as Social Capital and the Value of Human Capital.' *American Sociological Review* 61(2): 231–249.

Sarachek, Bernard. (1978) 'American Entrepreneurs and the Horatio Alger myth,' *The Journal of Economic History* 38(2): 439–456.

Schein, E.H. (1990) 'Organizational Culture.' *American Psychologist* 45(2): 109–119.

Schulze, William S., Michael H. Lubatkin, and Richard N. Dino. (2003) 'Exploring the Agency Consequences of Ownership Dispersion Among the Directors of Private Family Firms.' *Academy of Management Journal* 46(2): 179–194.

Sharma, Pramodita, James J. Chrisman, Amy L. Pablo, and Jess H. Chua. (2001) 'Determinants of Initial Satisfaction with the Succession Process in Family Firms: A Conceptual Model.' *Entrepreneurship Theory and Practice* 25(3): 17–36.

Smith, Sarah Francis, and Scott O. Lilienfeld. (2013) 'Psychopathy in the Workplace: The Knowns and Unknowns.' *Aggression and Violent Behavior* 18(2): 204–218.

Sorenson, Ritch L. (2000) 'The Contribution of Leadership Style and Practices to Family and Business Success.' *Family Business Review* 13(3): 183–200.

Stevens, Gregory W., Jacqueline K. Deuling, and Achilles A. Armenakis. (2012) 'Successful Psychopaths: Are they Unethical Decision-makers and Why?,' *Journal of Business Ethics* 105(2): 139–149.

Strenger, Carlo, and Jacob Burak. (2005) 'The Leonardo Effect: Why Entrepreneurs Become Their Own Fathers.' *International Journal of Applied Psychoanalytic Studies* 2(2): 103–128.

Thibaut, J.W., & Kelley, H.H. (1959) *The Social Psychology of Groups*, New York: Wiley.

Tuvblad, Catherine, Serena Bezdjian, Adrian Raine, and Laura A. Baker. (2013) 'Psychopathic Personality and Negative Parent-to-child Affect: A Longitudinal Cross-lag Twin Study,' *Journal of Criminal Justice* 41(5): 331–341.

Wadhwa, V., Holly, K., Aggarwal, R., & Salkever, A. (2009) 'Anatomy of an Entrepreneur: Family Background and Motivation.' *Kauffman Foundation Small Research Projects Research.*

Waldman, David A., Gabriel G. Ramirez, Robert J. House, and Phanish Puranam. (2001) 'Does Leadership Matter? CEO Leadership Attributes and Profitability Under Conditions of Perceived Environmental Uncertainty.' *Academy of Management Journal* 44(1): 134–143.

Ward, John L. (1997) 'Growing the Family Business: Special Challenges and Best Practices.' *Family Business Review* 10(4): 323–337.

Wayne, Sandy J., Lynn M. Shore, and Robert C. Liden. (1997) 'Perceived Organizational Support and Leader-member Exchange: A Social Exchange Perspective.' *Academy of Management Journal* 40(1): 82–111.

White, Randall P., and Sandra L. Shullman. (2010) 'Acceptance of Uncertainty as an Indicator of Effective Leadership.' *Consulting Psychology Journal: Practice and Research* 62(2): 94–104.

PART V

Special Topics: Country

24

FAMILY BUSINESS RESEARCH IN CHINA

A Field in the Light of Traditional Culture and Transforming Society*

Jing Xi, Shanshan Zhang, Linlin Jin, and Garrett Holloway

Introduction

Family businesses contribute to a large portion of China's economic development and share in an increasing number of social responsibilities. In general, Chinese family businesses (CFB) face problems similar to those of their counterparts in other parts of the world, including enterprise governance, succession, growth, and management. However, the culture and social situation in which they are embedded are different, which leads to unique phenomena and behavior in Chinese family businesses. Furthermore, due to the short history of most family firms in China, there is little experience for founding families to draw on regarding the preservation of values, culture, heritage, and legacy. Such a reality consequently brings unique opportunities and challenges for researchers interested in Chinese family businesses. Chinese scholars have done a great deal research in the field; however, due to language barriers, the most valuable and interesting Chinese studies cannot be read by researchers in the rest of the world. Therefore, this chapter, by reviewing family business research articles published in Chinese, attempts to outline the research in this field. It also attempts to answer questions such as: who is most active in the family business research field, what insights are available, what topics are the primary focus of Chinese family business research, and what makes this line of research unique.

The following review and analysis are primarily based on open reports (for an introduction to Chinese family business research) and articles collected from the China National Knowledge Infrastructure (CNKI), China's most comprehensive and authoritative academic database (for a review of family business studies).

As for the remainder of the chapter, Section 2 provides a general introduction to the status quo of Chinese family businesses; then bibliometric techniques are used to review the literature in Section 3. In Section 4, we conduct a co-word analysis to identify clusters of research topics, and in Section 5, we illustrate how traditional culture and societal transformation have influenced Chinese family business research. Lastly, we compare family business research published in Chinese with that published in English and offer conclusions.

---

* This research is sponsored by: (1) National Natural Science Foundation of China (71302137); (2) General Fund of the Humanities and Social Science Project of Chinese Ministry of Education (14YJA630018).

Family Businesses in China

Change in Social Status of Chinese Family Businesses

Family businesses have a profound origin in China. Widespread handcraft workshops operated by families supported the economy during China's long feudal history. However, traditional Chinese values ranked businesspeople in the lowest social class, in contrast to government officers, scholars, farmers, and craftsmen, who enjoyed a higher status. As a result, businessmen were looked down upon. After 1949, private enterprise became illegal in China, and entrepreneurs were criticized or even persecuted. Therefore, most family businesses were transformed into state-owned businesses. It was not until 1978—the year China implemented the Reform and Opening-up policy—that private enterprise was once again legalized, enabling the establishment of a growing number of private, family businesses. Meanwhile, some surviving traditional family businesses were returned to their original owners. This is why, nowadays, most family firms in China are first-generation firms with a short history of fewer than 30 years. Although the private economy has prospered during the past 30 years, Chen, one of the most active scholars in Chinese family business research, pointed out that the society is still 'ideologically discriminant' against family businesses. Some have declared that family businesses represent an ineffective business form that lacks prosperity and will eventually be sorted out by modern business mechanisms. Even today, many family business owners deny their identity as family business owners. However, during the past decade, with an effort from scholars and entrepreneurs, family businesses have generally won their social positon. People have realized that privately owned firms play an increasingly important role in national economic activity and that family businesses make up a significant portion of the private economy. A large number of famous family businesses gained recognition, such as Fangtai—a leading brand of kitchen equipment, New Hope—whose founder is among the 100 richest people in China, Biguiyuan—one of the largest real estate corporations, and so forth. Therefore, some sensitive and prospective Chinese scholars recognized the prosperous future of Chinese family businesses and the huge opportunity for relevant research.

Economic Contribution of Chinese Family Businesses

According to data from the State Administration for Industry and Commerce of China and data from the Third National Economic Census[1], there were a total of 18.19 million registered enterprises in China at the end of 2014[2], among which, 15.46 million are domestic private enterprises, with family firms accounting for 80 percent of private sector enterprises and 68 percent of overall enterprises. In terms of tax revenue, family businesses contributed 45 percent of the national amount in 2014, which is more than state-owned and foreign enterprises. Table 24.1 reports the number of different types of enterprises in existence, along with the amount of registered capital and tax contributions from each type during 2013 and 2014.

It can be seen from the data that family businesses make a significant economic contribution to the Chinese economy. Furthermore, family businesses are developing more quickly than non-family businesses. Figures 24.1, 24.2 and 24.3 show the yearly progress of different types of enterprises in terms of total number, the amount of registered capital, and tax contribution, respectively.

Status Quo of Family Businesses in China

In terms of industries, (see Figure 24.2) manufacturing accounts for the largest proportion of Chinese family businesses, with up to 48.59 percent, while education, public management, and

Table 24.1 CFB's Economic Contribution

Types of Enterprise	By December 2014			By December 2013		
	Number (Million)	Registered Capital (Trillion RMB)	Tax Contribution (Billion RMB)	Number (Million)	Registered Capital (Trillion RMB)	Tax Contribution (Billion RMB)
Private entreprise	15.46	59.21	5879.50	12.54	39.32	5349.86
Family business	12.37	47.37	4703.60	4.67	31.45	4279.89
State-owned & foreign enterprise	2.73	64.36	4497.30	2.74	57.56	4187.64
Total	18.19	123.57	10376.80	15.28	96.88	9537.50

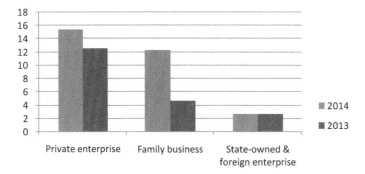

Figure 24.1 Increase in Terms of Enterprise Number During 2013–2014

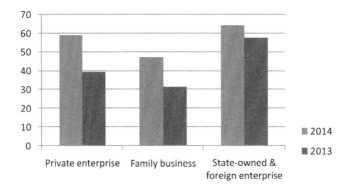

Figure 24.2 Registered Capital of Enterprises During 2013–2014

science and technology industries account for the lowest proportion. Among other industries, both wholesale/retail and construction make up 11.86 percent.

As for time since establishment (see Figure 24.5), about half of Chinese family businesses have existed for 15–36 years, 23.53 percent have existed for 6–10 years, 3.92 percent are 3–5 years old, and another 3.92 percent were established within the past 3 years.

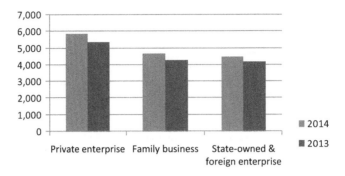

Figure 24.3   Tax Amount of Enterprises During 2013–2014

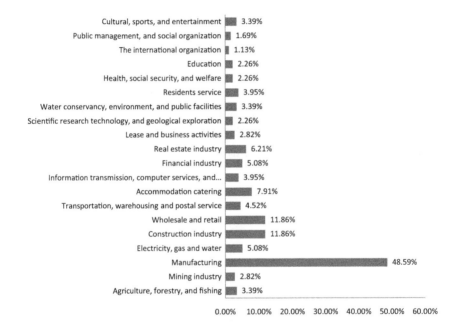

Figure 24.4   Industry Distribution of CFB in 2015

According to their annual revenue, most Chinese family businesses fall into the category of small or medium-sized enterprises, with annual revenues of less than 1.5 billion USD, while 13.19 percent of them are considered large enterprises (see Figure 24.6).

Since most Chinese family businesses were established around 1990 and the first generation of business owners are nearing retirement age, China will see a peak in intergenerational successions within the next 5–10 years. In the 2015 Index for Healthy Chinese Family Business, Ling and colleagues (2015) report that only 3 percent of family businesses had gone through a succession by 2015, 37 percent are in the process of succession while another 60 percent have not yet experienced succession and are still controlled by first generation owners. Figure 24.7 shows the proportion of family businesses in different stages of succession.

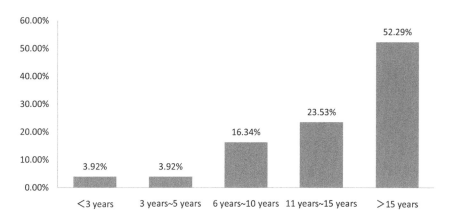

Figure 24.5   Established Time of CFB by 2015

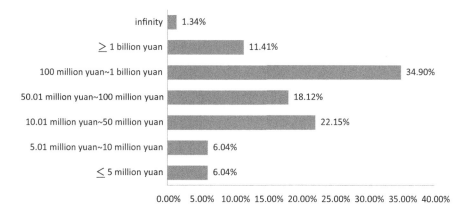

Figure 24.6   Annual Revenue of CFB in 2015

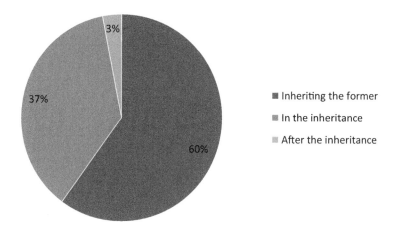

Figure 24.7   Succession Stage of CFB in 2015

According to survey data in the Chinese Family Business Succession Report published in 2015, only 40 percent of second generation members of business-owning families expressed a clear willingness to take over the business, while 15 percent report they are unwilling to take over. The attitudes of the remaining 45 percent are unclear. Such statistics reveal a sobering problem for many family firms—lack of a clear successor.

Scientific Publications on Chinese Family Businesses in Top Ranking Journals: A Bibliometric Approach

Publication Screening Criteria

Although a tremendous amount of family business research has been published in Chinese, much of it has little influence on the global family business research field due to either lack of innovation or limited validity. To provide an in depth and concrete understanding of the interests of Chinese family business researchers, their research methods, and their findings, our study focuses on top journals that have published family business research at any point in the past, including:

1. Top ranking journals approved by the Academic Department of Management of the National Natural Science Foundation of China (NNSFC), of which 24 out of 26 listed journals have published family business research at some point in the past.
2. The top three journals in social science subjects such as social science, psychology, and history: *Chinese Social Science, Social Science Study,* and *Psychology Academy*.
3. A special journal, '*Journal of Sun Yat-sen University (Social Science Edition),*' which was added to our list of journals because it is based at the Management School of Sun Yat-sen University, where half of the most active Chinese family business scholars earned doctorates or serve as professors. Additionally, this journal has published 16 influential family business articles, including a top cited article (cited 138 times).

In total, 28 journals were selected for inclusion in our study.

We searched CNKI for family business articles published in each of the selected journals at any time in history, using the maximum timespan allowed by the search engine. For journals obtained from the list of the Academic Department of Management of NNSFC, the generic term 'family' was entered into the 'title' field of the search engine. For other journals, 'family business,' 'family management,' 'family governance,' 'family owned,' and 'family control' were used. In total, 390 articles were selected for further analysis.

Temporal Distribution Analysis

Compared to publications printed in English, family business research did not appear in Chinese publications until relatively recently. The first notable academic publications regarding family businesses appeared in Chinese journals in 1990. In the following decade, only seven additional articles were published, with an average of 0.7 articles per year. As for authors, with the exception of Professor Ling Chen (published in 1998 in *Economic Study*)—one of the most active family business scholars in China—very few researchers were active in the family business field during this time.

The lack of Chinese family business research continued until 2000. After that year, publications increased dramatically, peaking in 2008 with an average of 25.9 articles annually. Figure 24.8

illustrates the temporal evolution tendency of the research field. Two points should be noted from this evolution. First, the number of publications in 2008 (54) was abnormally high—almost twice as many as in neighboring years. This is because 23 articles appeared in a special issue of *Science Research Management* in 2008. Second, the growth in publications has slowed since 2014. This could be due to changing criteria for academic evaluation in China. That is, universities now seek international top tier publications and are not satisfied with publications in Chinese Journals. As a result, some high-quality studies are now published in English journals, such as Junsheng Dou's 2014 publication in *Family Business Review*.

The year 2000 was a critical point in the evolution of Chinese family business research because a milestone article appeared in *Chinese Social Science* (the top social science journal) that year—'Family Business Research—a Topic with Contemporary Significance.' Its author, Xiaoping Chu, a professor of Sun Yat-sen University, is a pioneer researcher in the field and is still one of the most active family business scholars in China. In this article, Chu analyzed prospective family business research opportunities. He reminded researchers and the public that family businesses are a dominant economic force in China and around the world and that they are an effective mode of organizational operation and management. He argued that extensive and profound Chinese cultural traditions, including family ethics, parental authority, and the pattern of a differentiated order (Chaxu Geju) have differentiated Chinese family businesses from those of western cultures. Chu's statements widely resonated among Chinese academic circles, and many other scholars joined an encouraging wave of family business research. Fan (2002) described family businesses as ' a topic in need of further exploration,' while Zhang, Xu and Zhang (2004) described them as ' a research field worthy of deep exploration,' and Wang and Chen (2006) pointed out that 'family business research is growing.' Thus, in 2000, family business research entered a period of rapid development. Nowadays, family business research is a critically important topic in the management and economics fields[3].

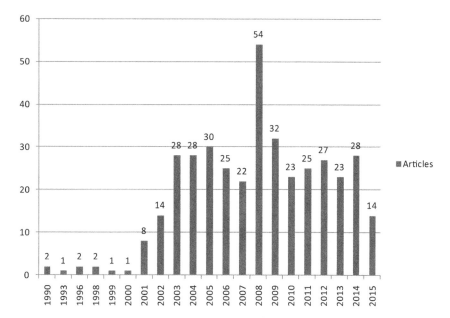

Figure 24.8   Temporal Analysis of Article Publication

Journal Distribution Analysis of Chinese Family Business Articles

The 28 journals we sampled produced 390 family business research articles, averaging 13.92 relevant articles per journal (see Table 24.2).

It can be seen that there is a tremendous variance in productivity between these journals. Thirteen of the journals published more than 10 articles and account for a total of 330 articles, or 84.61 percent of the article pool. Among these 13 journals, *Journal of Sun Yat-sen University* (Social Science Edition) and *Academic Research* are in the social science field, while the rest are in the fields of business and economics. The most productive journal, with a total of 52 publications, is *Management World*, which is considered the best management science journal in China. The fact that *Management World* is the most productive journal indicates that family business research attracts the most outstanding management science scholars whose research earns high praise within the field. *Economic Management Journal* and *Foreign Economics and Management* are next in the rankings based on a number of articles included in the pool.

Table 24.2 Journal Distribution of CFB Articles

Serial	Journal	Articles
1	Management World	52
2	Economic Management Journal	48
3	Foreign Economies And Management	37
4	Science Research Management	37
5	Journal of Business Economics	31
6	Soft Science	21
7	Nankai Business Review	17
8	Journal of Sun Yat-sen University (Social Science Edition)	16
9	Academic Research	16
10	On Economic Problems	15
11	China Industrial Economics	14
12	Chinese Journal of Management	14
13	Management Review	12
14	Economic Research Journal	9
15	Science of Science and Management of S.& T	9
16	China Soft Science	6
17	Forecasting	6
18	Accounting Research	5
19	Journal of Financial Research	5
20	Journal of Industrial Engineering and Engineering Management	4
21	Systems Engineering	3
22	Sociological Studies	3
23	Chinese Rural Econony	2
24	Journal of Management Sciences in China,	2
25	Journal of Management Science	2
26	Studies in Science of Science	2
27	Social Sciences In China	1
28	R&D Management	1
Total		390

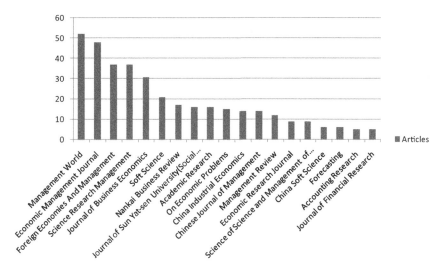

Figure 24.9 Productivity of Journals

Locations and Institutions of Chinese Family Business Research

Early Chinese family business studies were primarily discussions of or introductions to the experiences of family businesses in Hong Kong and Taiwan, rather than empirical research. Later, as family businesses in Mainland China matured, researchers began to conduct empirical studies using domestic samples. Most empirical study samples were from Zhejiang and Guangdong provinces because these two regions are leaders in China's economic development and are the location of over 80 percent of the country's family businesses. In addition to the concentration of family businesses in these regions, key family business researchers are also concentrated in these areas. Take *Management World* as an example, where among the 52 articles, 80 percent of first authors are from Zhejiang and Guangdong.

The three most famous scholars in the field are Professors Xiaoping Chu and Xinchun Li from Sun Yet-sen University and Professor Chen ling from Zhejiang University (determined by our analyses in the following section). On top of that, many Chinese family business researchers are their students.

There are quite a few research and educational institutes that specialize in Chinese family business research. For example, Sun Yet-sen University—the best comprehensive university in Southeast China—hosts the Research Center for Chinese Family Firms (RCF), with Xinchun Li as its current leader. Their research covers various topics, including the nature, characteristics, and forms of family firms, the governance structure of family firms, the leadership and entrepreneurial succession of family firms, comparative systems analysis on family firms, internal governance of family firms, procedures for employing external managers and guarding against risk, financing of family firms, psychological research on family firms, and the managerial culture of family firms and it's reform.

Another even more active family business research center is Zhejiang University's Entrepreneurship and Family Business Research Center (EFBRC). Established in 2004, the EFBRC was China's first family business research center and has successfully hosted an annual international academic conference for the past ten years. Zhejiang also operates Evergreen College for Family Business, a special school for successors of family businesses.

Most Active Researchers in the Chinese Family Business Research Field

There are 20 researchers who have published 5 or more articles in the 28 selected Journals (see Table 24.3). Among them, Xinchun Li is the most published, with a total of 35 publications, while Ling Chen and Lixin Zhou follow him with 23 and 15 publications, respectively. Although Xiaoping Chu ranks fourth based on a number of publications, he has received the largest number of citations, with a total of 2,433 citations and an average of 173.79 citations per article.

Eight of these researchers also publish in English, especially in recent years (see Table 24.4). Many of their articles can be found in *Asia Pacific Journal of Management, Management and Organization Review,* and *Family Business Review.*

Topical Clusters of Chinese Family Business Articles

Xi, Kraus, Filser and Kellermanns (2015) abstracted five topical clusters from virtually all existing family business research published in English; namely, the definition of family business, leadership and management, succession, governance, and competitive advantage. These five topics are also found in Chinese family business research to some degree; however, due to China's specific historical and social context, other topics have aroused Chinese scholars' interests. For instance, Xinchun Li and Xuanyu Wang classified family business research in mainland China into nine topical clusters: family business governance, family control and governance in state-owned versus privately owned enterprises, cultural traditions and family institutional arrangements, introduction and comparisons between Chinese and foreign family businesses,

Table 24.3 Authors with More Than Five Articles

Author	Articles	Cites	Institution
Xinchun Li	35	2080	Sun Yat-sen University
Ling Chen	23	1176	Zhejiang University
Lixin Zhou	15	107	Chongqing Technology and Business University
Xiaoping Chu	14	2433	Sun Yat-sen University
Xiaogang He	13	202	Shanghai University of Finance and Economics
Xuan He	12	149	Guangdong University of Foreign Language and Trade
Qilin Su	11	402	Jinan University
Wenting Chen	10	124	Dongbei University of Finance and Economics
Xiaoming Ou	8	329	South China Agricultural University
Yanling Lian	8	198	Shanghai University of Finance and Economics
Junsheng Dou	8	298	Zhejiang University
Jian'an Zhu	7	41	Zhejiang University
Kang Zhu	7	41	Sun Yat-sen University
Jianlin Chen	7	23	Guangdong University of Finance & Economics,
Minglin Wang	7	268	Hangzhou Normal University
Shenghua Jia	7	231	Zhejiang University
Jing Li	5	57	Shanghai University of Political Science and Law
Xueru Yang	5	73	Sun Yat-sen University
Lin Wang	5	206	Sun Yat-sen University
Shengchun Zhou	15	272	Zhejiang University
Total	212	8710	

Table 24.3 (continued)

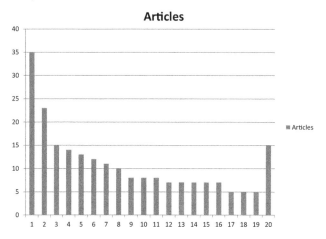

Table 24.4 Researchers and Their Articles in English

Year	Author(s)	Journal	Article
2008	**Shujun Zhang** **Xinchun Li**	Asia Pacific Journal of Management	Managerial Ties, Firm Resources, and Performance
2007	Mike W. Peng **Shujun Zhang** **Xinchun Li**	Management and Organization Review	CEO Duality and Firm Performance during China's Institutional Transitions
2011	**Xuan He**	Frontiers of Business Research in China	Symbiotic Relationship of Modern Contract and Traditional Ethic: Entrepreneur's Zhongyong Rationality and Family Firm Governance Choice
2013	**Junsheng Dou** Shengxiao Li	Asia Pacific Journal of Management	The Succession Process in Chinese Family Firms: A Guanxi Perspective, Asia Pacific Journal of Management
2014	**Junsheng Dou** Zhongyuan Zhang Emma Su	Family Business Review	Does Family Involvement Make Firms Donate More? Empirical Evidence From Chinese Private Firms
2013	Emma Su **Junsheng Dou**	Family Business Review	How Does Knowledge Sharing Among Advisors From Different Disciplines Affect the Quality of the Services Provided to the Family Business Client? An Investigation From the Family Business Advisor's Perspective
2013	**Qiang Liang** **Xinchun Li Xueru** **Yang** Danming Lin Danhui Zheng	Asia Pacific Journal of Management	How Does Family Involvement Affect Innovation in China?
2013	**Hang Zhu** C. Chen Chao **Xinchun Li** Yinhui Zhou	Management and Organization Review	From Personal Relationship to Psychological Ownership: The Importance of Manager-Owner Relationship Closeness in Family Businesses

★Authors in bold words are among the list of most active researchers (see Table 24.3).

trust and professional managers, family business management and operation, succession, literature reviews and introductions to foreign and domestic family business research, and others. The first three clusters relate to the topic of governance and account for more than two-thirds of all Chinese family business literature. Shi and Zhang (2013), in a review of Chinese family business articles published from 1998 to 2012, summarized thirteen topical clusters, including: governance structures and modes, property-ownership-institutional arrangements, succession and continuity, management and motivation, entrepreneurship and growth, family business resources and heterogeneity, internationalization and culture, management modes, investments and financing, trust mechanisms, family business definitions and research methods, altruistic stewardship agency agreement, family business performance and assessment, and stakeholders and social responsibility. These authors present profiles of Chinese family business research; however, their conclusions are based on subjective judgments. To make their conclusions more reliable, we applied a co-word technique to explore the in-depth, logical connections behind the articles so as to build a concrete understanding of the clusters in current Chinese family business research.

For this purpose, we conducted co-words analysis with Bicomb Co-word Analysis Software[4], which is suitable for analyzing Chinese characters and has been deemed reliable by many scholars (Guo & Wan, 2015). First, we downloaded keywords, abstracts, authors, and other general information for each article from CNKI to establish a database. Then, we analyzed the frequency of the keywords. Nine-hundred eight keywords appeared in the database with frequencies ranging from 1–261 and an average of 2.3 different keywords per article, indicating that researchers' interests are widely scattered. Because lower-frequency keywords lack value for identifying research focus, we removed keywords that appeared less than four times to eliminate unnecessary analysis. In the end, 45 keywords were selected for further analysis.

Clustering analysis by Bicomb software produces an eight-cluster structure of Chinese family business research. Table 24.5 shows how the keywords were distributed among these clusters. The following sections discuss the content of each of the eight clusters.

Cluster 1

Familism and Management
As did their English-speaking peers, Chinese family business researchers noticed a unique characteristic of family businesses—familism, and the series of consequences that follow, including lack of trust between family members and non-family members. This lack of trust, in turn, causes high agency costs of authorization and empowerment. Researchers believe that in current Chinese society, the best way for family businesses to optimize governance performance is to establish a modern enterprise system. That is an integration of the traditional family enterprise and the modern enterprise system. This type of system is characterized by a unification of ownership and control, and transparency with regard to positions, stock rights, and financial affairs (Hu, 2007).

Cluster 2

Trust, Social Capital, Agency, and Relational Governance[5]
As mentioned above, as they grow, family businesses encounter challenges with regard to professional management ability. When family businesses try to obtain social capital, especially

Table 24.5 Result of High Frequency Keyword Clustering Analysis

Cluster	Sub-cluster	Key Words
Familinism & Management	1	Family management(15), Family system(7), Family style(5), Enterprise system(6), Professional manager(17)
	2	Agency cost(8), Management model(5)
	3	Familism(5)
Trust & social capital	1	Social capital(7), Trust(4)
Agency	1	Altruism(7), Agency theory(5)
	2	Intergenerational succession(23)
	3	Agency problem(5)
Relational governance	1	Relational governance(5), Power structure(4)
Governance	1	Family authority(6), Family entrepreneur (5)
	2	public company(6), Capital structure(5)
	3	Genetic relationship(5), Governance efficiency(5)
	4	Control power(7), Cash flow right(4)
	5	Governance structure(9)
Entrepreneurship & Growth	1	Sustainable development(6)
	2	Family governance(10), Family entrepreneurship(6), Entrepreneurial orientation(6)
	3	Family involvement(14), Corporate social responsibility(4)
	4	Institutional environment(4)
	5	Enterprise growth(10), Competitive edge(4)
	6	Enterprise performance(11)
Succession	1	Family ownership(4), Succession willingness(4), Social emotional wealth(6)
	2	Successor(5)
Others	1	Social responsibility(4), Pyramid control structure (6)
	2	CEO compensation(4), Enterprise value(5)
	3	Minor enterprises(4)
	4	Finance(4)

from the external labor market, an agency problem arises. To successfully integrate professional managers into family businesses, family businesses must establish trust; but unfortunately, this issue has never been fundamentally solved, which can restrict the performance of professional managers or even remove performance incentives. These studies reflect a series of realistic problems in the development of Chinese family businesses, including the lack of management resources, the introduction of external professional managers, and the traditional governance structure.

Chinese social systems value family ethics and interpersonal relation networks, which causes relational contracts to become the implicit contract form in family businesses. Therefore, relationship governance is a kind of adaptive mechanism for Chinese family businesses. Some scholars try to analyze the family business growth dilemma from this perspective.

In the early stage of relationship governance research, scholars focused on relationships between external agents and family business owners, while in recent years, relationship governance between family members and family business owners—that is, how authority is distributed among family members—has received more attention. Regarding these two types of agents, some researchers point out that strong relationships and strong contract governance should be the optimal mode for reducing agent cost.

Cluster 3

Governance
Generally speaking, studies on governance in Chinese family businesses are mainly based on Tagiuri and Davis's (1982) 'three ring' model of family business governance and Mustakallio's (2002) conclusion that—in addition to the formal contract of the principal-agent relationship—informal relationship governance is also important. Chinese scholars extended these two theories to find the most suitable governance mode for Chinese family businesses. The relationship between governance structure and corporate performance forms the central component of this cluster.

Cluster 4

Family Entrepreneurship and Continuity
In this cluster, Chinese researchers' primary focus is how family businesses seize entrepreneurial opportunities and achieve sustainable growth. Xinchun Li and his students are main researchers in this cluster. Their conclusion is that family involvement, unique family resources, and entrepreneurial orientation have a conjoint influence on family business growth (Li 和 Liu 2008, Yang, Yang 和 Li 2009, Hu 和 Li 2009). Other researchers propose a process-based research paradigm to analyze how family factors affect the recognition of entrepreneurial opportunities and conclude that shifting from an opportunity-orientation to an entrepreneurial orientation strategy is conducive to achieving sustainable growth of Chinese family businesses (Chen, Yang 和 Li 2009)

Cluster 5

Succession
Chinese researchers have conducted a series of succession studies focusing on three main topics: who successors are, what succession means to them, and how the succession process unfolds. Researchers increasingly believe that the traditional 'father-to-son' model of succession is the most suitable and common mode in China. To evaluate whether someone is suitable to become a successor, Yu (2013) established a competency model composed of eight factors: social network, government relations, chance discoveries, risk, resource integration, strategic decision-making, learning innovation, and scientific management. Among these, the first four factors and the last four factors can be attributed to the quality of management and management skill, respectively.

Current research finds that the tacit knowledge, relationship network and entrepreneurial spirit of current family business owners are the three main factors that need to be maintained by successors. Successful inheritance of entrepreneurial spirit influences the sustainable development of enterprises. Research in this field indicates that the relationship between the current owner and the successor—namely, trust and the degree of comfort with concerning power distribution—affects the inheritance of entrepreneurial spirit.

In the process of family business intergenerational succession, developing a succession plan—especially one for cultivating the potential successor's willingness and capability to succeed—is important.

Cluster 6

Others

This cluster covers various research interests such as social responsibility, control structure, CEO compensation, and finance.

Family Business Growth Under Traditional Chinese Culture and Trust Structure

In the broad and profound Chinese traditional culture, family culture and the pattern of a differentiated order (Chaxu Geju) are the two most common perspectives used to understand China's unique interpersonal relationships and social structures, and they have significant effects on family business growth and organizational behavior.

Family Culture in China

The family is one of the most basic parts of human existence. In every country, no matter the culture, there exist families and sets of cultural rules influenced by families. But, only in Chinese history has such an extensive set of ethical norms and social rules developed and extended from 'family culture.' These norms and rules guide the daily routines, social lives, politics, and thought patterns of traditional Chinese people. So, what is Chinese 'family culture,' exactly? Based on numerous explanations, Chu (2003) summarized Chinese 'family culture' as a set of rules and regulations of clans, with clans and families tied together by blood, and with patrilineal authority as a guiding principal. Furthermore, family hierarchy determines the identity and behavioral norms, with ancestor-worship and family proliferation of the utmost importance. These rules and regulations do not just dominate family life—they have been applied to all levels of society, and have therefore become the dominant ideological system of traditional Chinese Society. Hence, 'family culture' is a sort of generalization of internal family identity structure, ethics, morals, and family cognitive and behavioral patterns. These generalizations manifest themselves in many old Chinese sayings, such as 'Monarch and his subjects are as father and sons' and 'One day your teacher, always your father.' In Chinese society, in business or government, if someone has a special relationship with an important person such as a neighbor, schoolmate, or another, he or she will be considered a family member to some degree, and will receive more resources, trust, opportunities, and so on. This is why so many historians, philosophers, and masters of Chinese culture (e.g., Qichao Liang, Xianli Ji, Suming Liang) have held the opinion that family culture and its generalizations form the core of traditional Chinese culture. Yiyuan Li (1998), a famous Taiwanese scholar, stated that "Chinese culture is just 'family culture,'" and as Guoshu Yang (1998) pointed out, the family is not only the key element of Chinese economic, cultural, and social life but also of political life. Dingding Wang (1995) believes that family remains the core concept of Chinese behavioral foundations. Even the great German philosopher Hegel recognized that 'China's invariable constitutional spirit is family spirit' and that 'filial piety is the basis of the Chinese family, and also the basis of the Constitution.' When evaluating the significance of family culture, Chu (2003) argued that, unlike traditional western culture which tends to divide people into different cultural circles, generalization of family concept works as cultural capital by making it easier for Chinese people to break through the barriers between different social strata, so as to enhance their social capital. Therefore, understanding family culture helps us to understand family businesses in China.

The Pattern of a Differentiated Order (Chaxu Geju)

The 'pattern of a differentiated order (*Chaxu Geju*)' was initially proposed by Xiaotong Fei (1939) in his masterpiece *Peasant Life in China: A Field Study of Country Life in the Yangtze Valley*. Fei used the term *Chaxu Geju* ('pattern of a differentiated order') to describe a common Chinese social phenomenon in which people develop different classes of relationships and give differential treatment to the members of the different classes.

By Fei's observation, Chinese people establish social networks primarily based on the intimacy of interpersonal relationships. Each individual is surrounded by a series of concentric circles, at the center of which lies the self. The first, and smallest circle is composed of blood relatives. The next, slightly larger circle is composed of family members who are not blood relatives. Beyond that, an even larger circle is composed of neighbors, classmates, and so forth. Fei used the image of ripples spreading across the water's surface after a rock is dropped into it as a metaphor for this type of relational network.

Fei compared Chaxu Geju to the manner in which western cultures form social relationships and found that, in western societies, each organization has its own boundaries which specify who is part of the organization and who is not, and each individual's relation to the organization is the same. Likewise, all members of an organization are equivalent. Fei calls this the 'organizational mode of association' (Tuanti Geju). In China, by comparison, individuals fall into circles with various distances separating them from the central point of the organization, with distance from the central point determined by one's social influence. Everyone's relational circles are interrelated with those of others, and different circles operate in different times and places. Such differences in social networking lead to two practical consequences. First, in western society, people's rights are determined by laws and regulations; while in China, people seek interests and rights by establishing connections with those in higher positions or with more authority. The second consequence is that, in China, both public officials and private individuals use the same concept of social order to guide their actions, thus mixing private concerns with public issues. In Western society, on the other hand, public and private rights and obligations are divided into distinctly different 'organizations.' In the 'pattern of a differentiated order,' people make personnel decisions according to one another's personal relationships. Individual rights are not considered, and social morality only makes sense regarding personal connections.

Based on such modes of association, corresponding patterns of governance and management developed in Chinese family businesses. The structure of family businesses is a three-level personal relationship network. The owner and owner's family members lie at the center while the next circle includes non-blood relatives and long-time employees, and the outer circle is composed of ordinary employees. With this social structure in mind, it is easier to understand the organizational behavior and decision-making that occurs in Chinese family businesses.

Chinese Traditional Culture, Trust Structure, and Family Business Growth

Chinese family business scholars have noted the differences between the Chinese trust structure and that of western society. Xinchun Li argues that trust should be understood from two perspectives—social and individual. Social trust is founded on law and legal contracts while individual trust is an evolutionary process based on interactions between individuals or organizations. Compared with the developed market economies of the U.S. or Europe, China is characterized by lower levels of social trust, but higher levels of private trust. In other words, in Chinese society, there exists a 'differential order structure' with discrimination occurring against outsiders in favor of insiders. Such a trust structure is defined as a 'trust of association,' and leads to specific problems for Chinese family businesses.

In seeking continuous growth, family businesses inevitably encounter bottlenecks—namely, resource constraints. The reason for this is that, in the early development stage of new ventures, founders can obtain capital, labor, and other resources from within the family relatively easily. However, once firms grow to a certain size, the family's internal resources are no longer sufficient to support firm growth, especially in terms of professional management ability. Therefore, family businesses seek external human resources. In this situation, family culture plays a negative role in the family business' continuous growth in at least two ways. First, because of the existence of 'parental authority' in family culture, decision-making power is controlled by the founder, which prevents mid-level or lower-level managers from gaining experience and practicing their managerial skills. This further contributes to the failure of family businesses to fully utilize internal professional management resources. Second, if family businesses seek external resources, trust becomes an issue. In Chinese society, under family culture, kinship forms the basis for trust, and people tend to place more trust in family members. This makes it difficult for non-family managers to win family members' trust, simply because there is no blood relationship between them. Thus, professional managers' talent is often not utilized effectively. To break the management resources bottleneck and obtain and integrate external resources into family businesses, Chu (2002) proposes that the 'pan-family' concept be adopted. This concept encourages family business owners to expand their concept of family and consider non-family professional managers as family members.

However, because of the immaturity of the Chinese professional-manager market, it is harder to monitor professional managers' agent behavior in China than in the U.S. and Europe. Given this challenge, Chu's (2002) second proposal is to build a social trust mechanism. But, due to the differences in family business owners' family concept and interests and those of professional managers, solutions to issues of trust within family businesses have not been well established.

Other researchers also note the influence of traditional culture on the growth of family businesses. Dai and Li (2012) attempt to apply the logic behind family business growth from the perspective of family systems and business systems using a case study. They believe that the driving force for maintaining family systems is affection while efficiency is the focus of business systems. These two systems both complement and conflict with one another. The growth of family businesses hinges on the balance between family and business logic. The success of the case study organization indicates that family ethics—with filial piety and fraternal duty as its core—affect the family status of entrepreneurs and the social capital within their families, and also influences the culture and social responsibility of family businesses. The authors argue that an ethical culture helps to improve the efficiency of business operations as long as there exists restriction from institutional rationality. Therefore, the basic path for the growth of family businesses lies in the effective balance of family ethics, business ethics, and institutional rationality.

Chinese Traditional Culture and Leadership in Chinese Family Businesses

What is Paternalistic Leadership (PL)?

In Chinese family businesses, Paternalistic Leadership (PL) is a product of family culture and the pattern of a differentiated order. PL, embedded in Chinese culture for thousands of years and distinctly different from Western leadership theories, is a set of leadership philosophies, theories, and methods transferred from traditional Chinese family management to organizational management. It is the basic characteristic of organizations in Chinese culture and is prevalent in various types of Chinese organizations. In 2000, Taiwanese scholars Jingli Fan and Boxun Zheng defined PL as a behavioral leadership style in which the leader shows discipline and authority, as well as kindness and virtue, much like a father. They also put forward the famous three-element PL theory model, in which they state that authoritarianism, benevolence, and moral leadership are basic elements of PL.

1. Authoritarian Leadership

   Family, as a core concept of Chinese culture, also exists in Chinese organizations. Guoshu Yang calls the process whereby Chinese people transfer experiences learned from the family to other organizations 'pan-familism,' meaning that even in non-family organizations, people's psychology and behaviors manifest in much the same way as they do in family settings. Therefore, consistent with the father-son relationship of Chinese families, the leader plays the role of a father, symbolizing authority, while subordinates play the role of sons, who must display loyalty and obedience.

2. Moral Leadership

   As the cornerstone of mainstream Chinese culture, Confucianism emphasizes personal morality, declaring it the most basic requirement of Chinese people. In fact, as China is traditionally a society ruled by man—not by law—the lack of legal constraints raises ordinary people's expectations of public officials' morality. As a result, Chinese society relies on officials' moral self-cultivation to restrain their behavior. In Chinese organizations, the emphasis on morality pressures leaders to maintain fairness and integrity to a certain extent; otherwise, it is hard to earn subordinates' true obedience.

3. Benevolent Leadership

   Chinese social relationships should be understood from a dyadic perspective. That is, Confucius' ideal society is composed of five dyads of interpersonal relationship: gracious monarchs and loyal ministers, friendly older brothers and obedient younger brothers, righteous husbands, and gentle wives, and kind mothers-in-law and filial daughters-in-law. A dyadic culture such as this requires supervisors to be beneficent and subordinates to be obedient and loyal, which forms the root of Benevolent Leadership. Also, in Chinese people's interpersonal communication, 'reward' is a widespread concept with a mutual benefit at its core. So, in Chinese businesses, behaving kindly toward subordinates, caring for them, helping them, preserving their self-esteem, treating them as family members, and similar behaviors are considered an investment in social capital and should lead to positive returns from subordinates—including loyalty, gratitude, and hard work.

Empirical Studies on Paternalistic Leadership

At present, empirical research on PL has two primary focuses. The first seeks evidence that PL exists in various Chinese family and non-family organizations while the other explores the effectiveness of PL.

Most studies agree that in China, PL and the three-element model is widespread, not only in organizations (Zheng & Zhou, 2003), but also in professional sports teams (Tao, 2002), public service organizations (Cai, 2002), science and technology research institutions, and military units (Zhang, 2001). Therefore, PL is one common organizational feature found throughout Chinese culture.

Studies regarding the effectiveness of PL indicate that benevolent leadership and moral leadership have a clear, positive relationship with organization performance, with the latter playing a key role. But, it is hard to draw conclusions about the function of authoritarian leadership. Authoritarian leadership is more likely to be implemented and recognized in: (1) family businesses, (2) organizations without a clear distinction between ownership and management, (3) entrepreneurial organizations, and (4) businesses operating in a simple and stable environment, but leads to resentment and conflict in organizations with standardized management mechanisms and younger and higher-quality employees (Fan, Zheng, 2000).

Researchers are also interested in the interaction among the three elements of PL Theory. Fan and Zheng (2000) believe that the relationship of the three elements can be described as relatively independent and divisible. Benevolence and moral leadership have a clear positive correlation while the relationship between moral leadership and authoritarian leadership is difficult to sort out—it is possible there is no clear correlation. Between authoritarian and benevolent leadership, there may be a negative correlation; but it seems difficult for these two styles to coexist within a single leader. The most typical situation would be that, within a leadership team, different leaders play different roles.

China's Institutional Environment and Its Impact on Family Businesses

Features of China's Institutional Environment

The most interesting feature of China's institutional environment is the current transition period in which the regulatory environment is changing due to government withdrawal and market expansion. However, China's transformation is far from complete. At the core of the economic transformation is the coexistence of two types of regulatory systems: the state-owned socialist command economy on one hand, and the property-based market economy on the other.

Such an environment creates many restrictions for family businesses. First of all, although the laws and rules undergo continuous innovation, China's legislative process tends towards strengthening political control. In China, the degree of protection for private enterprises and private property is significantly weaker than that of public property; but, private enterprises are more willing to take risks to improve performance and shareholder wealth. Secondly, the protection system for property rights is imperfect, leading to a lack of restriction on government violations of private enterprises' property rights. Without a rigid system of property rights and judicial constraints, local governments often create policy burdens and take advantage of private enterprises for political promotion, rent-seeking, and other purposes, which directly damages the interests of private enterprises or creates unfair advantages for state-owned companies.

Also, due to the lack of financial market reform, state-owned banks with monopoly positions show a preference for state-owned enterprises, resulting in institutional constraints for private enterprise financing. Even during the financial crisis, state-owned enterprises could still obtain strong support from state-owned banks, and thus, experienced less decline in capital investment. Simultaneously, private enterprises have had to 'shrink the front.' That is, a large number of small and medium-sized private enterprises were forced to retain profits to implement endogenous financing, thus reducing profit distribution to the household sector.

How China's Institutional Environment Impacts Chinese Family Businesses

Compared to state-owned enterprises, family businesses are at an obvious disadvantage, yet they contribute to a large part of China's economy. These family businesses, in order to adapt to environmental constraints, have established a set of endogenous behaviors and special governance arrangements, including the following.

Political Connections and Social Charity

Political connections and social charity are used by family businesses as a substitute for the property right protection mechanism, and even to gain access to more resources, which is particularly true in regions with poorer property protections, more local government intervention, and lower levels of financial development. Professor Chen's study shows that business owners with political ties receive more bank loans and longer loan terms than those without political ties. Chen and Chen found that family business owners with political connections donate more to charity than those with no political affiliation; and the higher the level of political connection, the larger number of their charitable donations. The reason why family businesses make more charitable donations lies in their ultimate goal; that is, to protect the family reputation and the ensure the family's continuous control over the business.

Family Operation and Management

Chen and Liu's research shows that Chinese family businesses tend to strengthen family involvement and family governance to deal with the problem of internal agency, as well as to allow family members to share corporate earnings. In the current period of economic transformation in which the cost of protecting intellectual property rights and business secrets is rather high, the manager market is far from perfect, there has been a decline of social entrepreneurship and an improved entrepreneurial atmosphere, family businesses would encounter serious competition if their core staff (especially senior managers) turned over and started their own ventures. Therefore, entrepreneurial families apply family governance from the beginning so as to allow more family members to attend to the business.

Family Succession

The perceived hospitability of the institutional environment influences succession decisions. He (2014)'s empirical study indicates that when entrepreneurs perceive the institutional environment to be more hostile, they are less inclined to pass the company to their children. But if entrepreneurs have high political status, the negative effects of institutional environment on internal succession willingness is tempered. For these entrepreneurs, the defects of institutional environmental may not be seen as constraints, but as useful resources. It can be seen that with regard to family businesses' internal authority allocation—no matter if a family business' performance is lower or higher than expected—most family businesses tend to allocate authority to the most capable core family members; but not to distant family members. Only when the institutional environment is quite hostile, do business owners—concerned that involvement in business management will be too taxing for family members to handle on their own—allocate authority to distant relatives instead of core family members. This reflects entrepreneurs' strong benevolent motives towards family members.

Group-Type: Organizational Structure

Once family businesses reach a certain size, they may attempt to build a *group-type organizational structure by which a group of family businesses or a large family business with a close relationship to government forms a large scale family enterprise group so as* to operate in diverse markets. In many emerging markets, including Mainland China, large family enterprise groups are prevalent. The relationship between subsidiary companies in a group is not based on the market, nor on bureaucracies, but on family ties or family-like relationships (e.g., friends, neighbors, partnerships). In the process of market transformation, large networks of family and social ties can provide informal guidelines to strengthen the cooperation between subsidiaries. In particular, such family relations reduce strategic reconstitution and therefore improve governance performance.

Comparisons between Chinese and English Family Business Research

Chinese family business research started almost 20 years later than English family business research. As a result, many Chinese studies are extensions or localizations of English studies of similar topics. However, there exist obvious differences between the two research camps. Comparing the content of the clusters of Chinese family business studies with the studies in English, we found that although both Chinese and English studies are interested in governance, succession, entrepreneurship, strategy, and competition—important in English literature—attract less attention in Chinese family business research. Relevant keywords such as 'strategy decision,' 'strategy entrepreneurship,' 'strategy transforming,' 'competence,' and 'globalization' appear only 15 times in our entire data pool. Table 24.6 shows the respective topics of Chinese and English studies. The reason for these differences needs further analysis.

Conclusion

This chapter aims to create an overall picture of Chinese family business research in order to give readers an idea of what Chinese family businesses are like, how they are studied, who studies them, what topics are discussed, primary conclusions, and how, if at all, is Chinese family business research different from English family business research. Our work, based on data from public reports and a bibliometric analysis of relevant literature, illustrates a temporal distribution of 390 articles published thus far in top-tier Chinese academic journals. It also identifies the most productive journals, authors, and institutions, and also specifies the eight topical clusters of the Chinese family business research field. Furthermore, significant differences between Chinese family business research and that published in English were found. That is, Chinese family business researchers are not as interested as English-speaking researchers in strategy and competence of family businesses.

Table 24.6 Comparison of English and Chinese FB Research

English Literature	Chinese Literature
definition of family business	familinism and management
leadership and management	trust, agency and relational governance
succession	governance
governance	entrepreneurship and growth
competitive advantage	succession
	others

Notes

1 See 'Data Bulletin of the Third National Economic Census,' http://www.stats.gov.cn/tjsj/zxfb/201412/t20141216_653709.html.
2 Chen Yu, The financial management mode of Chinese Family Enterprises [D].Beijing Jiaotong University master degree thesis, 2015.
3 Family business researches were published in top journals in China, 1 in Chinese Social Science, 3 in Economic Study, 56 in Management World.
4 This software was co-developed by Professor Lei Cui of Chinese Medical Sciences University and Hongsheng Computer Technique Co. Ltd, and is available in Cui's blog (http://skydrive.live.com/?cid=3adcb3b569c0a509&id=3ADCB3B569C0A509%211195).
5 Actually, according to the analysis of Bicomb, TRUST, SOCIAL CAPITAL AND RELATION GOVERNANCE are three separate clusters, but by reading relevant articles we find that the core issue they discuss is the same, so we put the three into one cluster.

References

Boxun Zheng, Lifang Zhou, Minping Huang. (2003) 'Three-element pattern of the paternalistic leadership: evidence from Chinese mainland enterprise organizations., 2003' *Local Psychology Research*, no. 20: 209–252.
Chen, Ling. (2003) 'Information Characteristics, Transaction Costs and Family Organization' *Economic Research* (51–60), no. 7.
Chen, Ling, and Lihua Chen. (2014) 'The clan involvement, the socio-emotional wealth and the corporate charitable contributions: A case study based on the survey of the private enterprises all over china' *Management World*, 90–101.188.
Chen, Ling; Ying, Lifen. (2003) 'Hereditary succession: The inheritable management and creation in clannish enterprises' *Management World*, no. 6: 89–97,156.
Chen, Ling; Ying, Lifen. (2014) 'Political connections, institutional environments and charitable contributions by family entrepreneurs' *East China Economic Management* 28, no. 1 : 1–6.
Chen, Wenting, Xueru Yang, and Xinchun Li . (2009) 'A family entreprenuership study on process perspective' *Foreign Economic and Management*, no. 2: 56–64.
Chu, Xiaoping; Li, Huaizu. (2003) 'Trust and chinese family business growth' *Management World*, no. 6: 98–104.
Fei, Xiaotong. (2003) *Peasant Life in China: A Field Study of Country Life in the Yangtze Valley.* New York: Dotton.
He, Xiaogang. (2013 fourth' 4 2013) 'Business expectations and the configuration of authority within the family - a study based on data of Chinese listing Corporation,the Journal of management science.
He, Xuan, Lihong Song, Hang Zhu, and Xinchun Li. (2014) 'Why does the family firm want to let go? The perception of the system environment,the political status, and the succession intention of china's family firms entrepreneurs' *Management World*, 2: 90–110,188.
Hu, Xiaohong, and Xinchun Li. (2014) 'Family business oriented and business growth.' *Academic Research*, no. 4 (2009): 12–21.
Jianan, Zhu; Ling, Chen; Junsheng, Dou; Hao, Wang. (2015) 'The institutional environment, family involvement and enterprise behavior — a review of family business studies from the perspective of economic transformation,2015.2' *Shandong Social Science*,146–152.
Jingli Fan, Lifang Zhou,Boxun Zheng. (2000) 'Paternalistic leadership scale: the construction and measurement of the three element model. Indigenous psychology, 2000,14: 3~64.' *Indigenous Psychology*, no. 3: 53–64.
Li, Xinchun, and Li Liu. (2000) 'Family entrepreneurship research: A new paradigm of theoretical research.' Edited by 23–31. *Journal of Social Sciences of Jilin University*, no. 6.
Li, Xinchun, and Xuanyu Wang. 'Review and prospection of family business research in Mainland China:1988–2007.' *Zhangshan Management Review (Taiwan China)*, 2008: 256–257.
Liu, Chen, and Zhibiao Liu. (2009) 'Separation of core staff in family businesses in the transition period.' *Nankai Business Review* 12, no. 1: 110–117.
Luo, Danglun, and Qingquan Tang. (2009) 'Environment institution and performance of chinese private public entrepreneurs .' *Economic Study*, no. 2: 108–118.

Ancheng. (2009)'Familiness, social-cognitiveness and family entrepreneurship: A case study.' *Nankai Management Review* 14, no. 3 (3 2011): 91–100.

Benren, and Jian Zhang. (2013) 'Family business research review: analysis based on CSSCI literature from 1998–2012.' *Jinan Journal (Philosophy & Social Science Edition)*, 9: 18–29.

g, Hesen. (2012) 'Study on the dual governance of Chinese family enterprise group, the dissertation of Zhejiang University in 2012.'

g, Hesen. (2012) 'Study on the dual governance of Chinese family enterprise groups,' the dissertation of Zhejiang University in 2012.' In *Study on the Dual Governance of Chinese Family Enterprise Groups*. he dissertation of Zhejiang University, 2012.

ing; Wang, Wenfeng. (2007) 'Organizational identification and Chinese family business growth.' *Economy and Managment* 29, no. 23: 59–62.

g, Xueru, Wenting Yang, and Xinchun Li. (2009) 'Yang Xueru, Chen Wenting, Li Xinchun, family orintEntrepreneurial Orientation and Entrepreneurial Performance.' *Economic Management*, no. 3: 85–92.

ng, Xinan; He, Hui; Gu, Feng . (2009) 'The impact of paternalistic leadership on team performance: the mediating role of team conflict management.' *Management World*, no. 3: 122–133.

25

FOUNDERS AND SUCCESSORS IN CHINA'S FAMILY FIRMS

What Should We Expect from the Rising Generation?

Milton Ming Wang and Michael Carney

Beginning in the late 1970s, China's economic reforms created conditions for the emergence of a generation of entrepreneurial, founder-managed family firms. These firms were not universally welcomed by the transitional regime, but they were tolerated, and many went on to play a significant role in China's ascendance as a global economic power. Some four decades later, many of those founder entrepreneurs are considering retirement and planning for the future leadership of the firms they established. China's society and its economy have changed dramatically since the reform period. Socioeconomic changes are reflected in China's rising generation that has little experience of the hardship experienced by the prior generation. The rising generation is much wealthier and better educated than their parents. China confronts continuing economic challenges in migrating from reliance on agriculture and commodity manufacturing towards a higher value-added services and technology centered economy. Fortunately, its rising generation is eager to acquire new skills and is already highly proficient with leading-edge information and communication technologies. Many Chinese family firms (CFFs) have adapted well to the ongoing socioeconomic changes, but many traditional Chinese family values have been retained (Egri & Ralston, 2004; Ralston, Egri, Stewart, Terpstra, & Yu, 1999). In particular, the expectation that a family member should succeed to the leadership of the family firm remains strong.

Given the continuing changes in China's social and economic fabric, what should we expect from the rising generation of family firm leaders? To what extent will successors retain or change the prevailing strategies and management practices of the firms they inherit from founders? How much emphasis will be placed on re-orienting strategies, for example by diversifying the firm's activities? To what extent will successors professionalize management structure and appoint non-family executives to senior positions? Rapid changes in the political and economic environment, especially in the early reform period, required the founding generation to place great emphasis on the management of relationships with governments and business partners, but will the focus on relationships remain so vitally important for the next generation? In this chapter, we consider the question of 'how successors in China's family firms are likely to adopt new management practices and introduce strategic change into the firms they inherit?' We seek to open broader discourse and research interest about how emerging market family firms' strategies and management practices will evolve as the firm ages generationally. Do continuing changes in the structure of Chinese family life herald improvements in or worsening of the quality of management practices?

We are motivated to address these understudied research questions because China, like many emerging markets, presents an interesting challenge to our understanding of family firm succession. Much of the succession literature and received wisdom about the value of family continuity in the family firm and the processes of managing effective succession are largely based on family firms situated in mature and fully developed institutional contexts such as North America and Europe. Under these conditions, it is reasonable to assume that organizational continuity and the intergenerational transfer of accumulated knowledge and skill are important in preserving the competitive advantages of the firm (Cabrera-Suarez, et al. 2001; Steier, 2009). But this assumption may not hold in rapidly changing socioeconomic and institutional environments since strategic continuity, established management practice and accumulated knowledge may be redundant in preparing a family firm to face the challenges of the future. Thus, rather than being a valued asset, the founders' accumulated knowledge and skills may be dysfunctional to the successor and its intergenerational transfer may be 'the teaching of fools' (March 2011).

In this chapter, we approach the question of effective succession as an issue of the generational transfer of human and social capital (Gedajlovic & Carney, 2010). The conventional transfer of formal ownership and control is viewed as the exchange of legal property rights over physical and financial assets, which in most cases is a routine transaction. However, the effective control and use of property rights and financial assets require the exercise of human and social capital, in the form of judgment, business acumen, and skill in trust-building and relationship management. The value and heritability of human and social capital across generations is much more ambiguous. Effective transfer of these intangible assets is a complex process depending upon socialization processes with respect to values and priorities, education and learning, and factors such as career paths and life experience of successors (Dou & Li, 2013). Moreover, we cannot assume that effective transfer is valuable in the context of a changing social and economic environment. If founders are effective in transferring their human social capital to successors, they may lock-in inappropriate and obsolete skills. Indeed, successors may wish to avoid trans-generational learning from founders and focus upon the cultivation of relevant knowledge and contemporary management practices.

Theoretically, we draw upon sociological traditions in family firm research (Martinez & Aldrich, 2013) which view family firms as embedded within a broader sociological context and which must establish legitimacy with the imperatives of the prevailing normative environment. Painting with broad brush strokes, we identify and describe shifting social and economic factors that present today's entrepreneurial family firms with new challenges. Our purpose is to connect the evolving relationships and link them with prevailing academic research findings and popular conceptions of the entrepreneurial family fun.

A Dynamic Economic and Social Context

Out of the chaos the Cultural Revolution and the passing of the Maoist regime, and beginning in 1978, Deng Xiao Ping ushered in a series of experiments in social and economic reform, including the gradual opening of China's economy to trade and investment. What followed was a huge transfer of business and management know-how, first from entrepreneurs from the Chinese diaspora and later by multinational corporations. China's entrepreneurs were quick learners and embraced the opportunities created by reform. Along with public and quasi-public enterprises, China's private family firms contributed to the high levels of economic growth for four decades. Today, mainland China's economy has become the second largest in the world and the industries and cities of its eastern seaboard show high levels of technological and organizational sophistication. Nevertheless, there is continuing room for economic and organizational development.

While the state-owned enterprises (SOEs) continued to control the commanding heights of the economy, the state experimented with a wide range of organizational hybrids (Nee, 1992). However, the Communist Party remained ambiguous about private property and the existence of private entrepreneurship, since public ownership of the means of production continued to be a major plank of socialist ideology. Nevertheless, an entrepreneurial class of domestic founders appeared in a variety of basic industries that proved to be essential to China's economic transformation. The appearance of a new class of private entrepreneurs was accompanied by rapid industrialization, migration, and urbanization as well as substantial improvements in access to education for young people located in the major urban areas. Among those changes were several state sponsored social engineering projects, such as the implementation of a one-child-per-family policy across large sections of the population, which diffused new social norms and produced significant changes in the demographic structure of the contemporary Chinese family (Whyte, 2005). In urban settings, the joint family form has largely been displaced. Instead, families are now overwhelmingly organized as nuclear units in a dominant pattern where males in their mid-to-late twenties marry females in their early to mid-twenties (Whyte, 1996).

Moreover, the single child policy has produced a dearth of male successors, which is a challenge for Chinese family firms who prefer the male family successors (Cao, Cumming, & Wang, 2015). Furthermore, despite the evident trade-off between a number of children and a single child's human capital quality, the one child policy contributed only modestly to improvements in human capital (Rosenzweig & Zhang, 2009). However, in the wake of the single-child policy daughters have more power than ever before to defy disadvantaging gender norms while using equivocal and changing norms to their advantage (Fong, 2002) and many daughters are poised to inherit significant wealth.

Founders Versus Successors: Strategy and Management

Rapid changes in the structure of China's economy and society generated several open questions about the relationship between family and the management of family firms. It remains the norm that a family member, preferably a male son, succeed in managing and controlling family assets. However, the single child policy has created significant human capital constraints on finding suitable successors to perpetuate dynastic management of family firms. Nevertheless, one study found that having only one heir decreases the probability of continuing family management by a relatively minor 3 percent, and reduces the probability of adult children working in the family by 14 percent, (Cao, Cumming, & Wang 2015), suggesting that a significant number of family firms succeed in retaining ownership and management within the family. A study of some 500 publicly listed CFFs established over the last 30 years found that some 120 have completed a succession process of replacing the founder (Zhao, Carney, Zhang, & Zhu, 2015). The vast majority of succession events resulted in a succession to the CEO role by a family member and only six successions involved the introduction of a nonfamily professional manager as a CEO. Thus, given the revolutionary changes in the socioeconomic environment combined with the continued intergenerational involvement of family members, the question about the extent to which CFF founders and their successors maintain or differ in their strategic orientation and management practices needs to be explored and addressed.

To identify potential areas of difference between founders and successors, we dimensionalize six recurring CFF attributes that have attracted theoretical and empirical attention in the academic literature, as illustrated in the hexagram contained in Figure 25.1. We survey this literature and describe the consensus regarding founder attributes and their location along a particular dimension. We then consider factors that are likely to influence successors' likely attributes and the extent to which we should expect to see continuity or change in position on a particular dimension. Going clockwise around the hexagram in Figure 25.1, the dimensions depicted to describe differences in the behavior and preferences of founders and successors are: Strategic focus, firm product market scope and organizational capabilities; Entrepreneurial orientation, conservative, risk-averse or proactive, risk accepting; Governance, the extent to which an entrepreneur adopts a personalized and centralized control structure or a decentralized structure which delegates authority into the hands of a cadre of professional executives; Multiple goals, the extent to which an entrepreneur gives priority to economic or noneconomic goals; Managing network ties, reliance on and reciprocity with family, government and party officials, and business ties; Family ties, the extent to which families retain management and ownership themselves or share with a wider range of nonfamily members. We begin by considering China's founding entrepreneurs' strategic focus and the expected changes likely to be made by the rising generation.

Strategic Focus

At the onset of reform, there were few individuals in China with the capital, know-how, and entrepreneurial insight to establish an internationally competitive firm. The reformist state was largely indifferent, if not openly hostile, towards private enterprises and, to lead the reform process, the state directed available resources toward state-owned and controlled enterprises. Yet the state recognized the importance of foreign investment and entrepreneurial initiative for economic development and provided opportunities for private sector participation in the reform process. In the early stages, these opportunities were seized mostly by entrepreneurs from the Chinese diaspora in Taiwan, Hong Kong and in Southeast Asia, where a class of entrepreneurs had materialized to pioneer the regions' export-oriented industrialization (McVey, 1992). Possessing capital, know-how, and familiarity with foreign markets, these entrepreneurs returned to South China and located their investments in enterprise zones to implement an export-oriented development strategy that had worked so successfully in other parts of East and Southeast Asia. China's returnee entrepreneurs were later joined by Western multinationals that were eager to extend their global supply chains into the region to access the abundant sources of low-cost labor.

The ready availability of foreign export demand, the importation of knowledge, and the utilization of hybrid contracting mechanisms such as original equipment manufacturing, joint ventures, licensing, subcontracting and technology sharing, along with informal means such as overseas training, returnee hiring networks (Hobday, 1995), provided opportunities for nascent entrepreneurs and small family firms. Participation in these markets required domestic firms to develop generic organizational and technical skills directed toward efficient and flexible day-to-day management of operations, the effective use of low-cost labor, and the adoption and application of best practice quality and logistics management. These skills proved to be highly generalizable and could be applied in a variety of sectors, for example, footwear, apparel, commodity manufacturing, and entrepreneurs later expanded into finance-driven sectors such as real estate and property development, forming the basis of diversified family business groups.

As reforms progressed, the state authorized experiments with new hybrid organizational forms in villages and townships up and down China's east coast known as township and village enterprises (TVEs) (Nee, 1992). Some observers consider TVEs to be the primary engine of

China's economic development during the 1980s and 90s (Huang, 2008). Ideologically, TVEs were collective enterprises, owned by the municipalities, workers, and entrepreneurs. But in practice, property rights were ambiguous, and *de facto* control gravitated toward private entrepreneurs and their allies in government. Although research is sparse, it seems probable that the TVE movement generated substantial numbers of family controlled firms who concealed their true identities by appearing to be state authorized organizations. Wearing a 'red hat' is a common term used to describe this common form of organizational ambiguation (Chen, 2007).

Fueling the export-led developments in enterprise zones and TVEs were SOEs in the commanding heights of the economy of banking, telecommunications, airlines, railways, construction and infrastructure, petroleum, steel, and automobile production. However, the interstices of these major industries provided numerous opportunities for perceptive entrepreneurs, in services such as logistics, transportation, retail, and tourism, as well as in the extractive industries and primary manufacturing, and coal mining, minerals, oil exploration and gas production. During the course of reforms, the central state increased its administrative capacity in centralized tax and revenue collection, previously the jurisdiction of provinces, and delegated land reform and land sales to the provinces, which became an important source of revenue for provincial governments. This shift in financing triggered a long-running commercial property and housing construction boom, which is still evident in China's ever-expanding urban agglomerations.

Thus, the export-oriented era of reform produced a generation of entrepreneurial founder managed family firms across a wide range of industries. Research suggests that the salient attributes of this generation consisted of incisive business acumen in perceiving and seizing fleeting opportunities (Tang, 2010), managing relationships with an omnipresent central and local state (Boisot, Child, & Redding, 2011), and the creation of relatively simple, non-bureaucratic, centrally controlled organizational structures (Redding & Witt, 2009). During this era, China's manufacturing and exporting industries moved to the technological frontiers of production and its manufacturing sector became known as 'the workshop of the world' (McNaughton, 1997; Nolan, 2001). However, entrepreneurial family firms, for the most part, did not develop complex and proprietary technological and organizational capabilities and relied heavily on imitation learning of pre-existing know-how. By the beginning of the 21st century, with China being a member of WTO, the economy could be described as "China serves the world." CFFs established factories that served global commodity markets. However, this era has almost reached its apex and will eventually decline with growing urban and infrastructure congestion, the fading advantage of abundant low-cost labor and the accumulating wealth of Chinese people. Hence, there is a growing recognition of a shift toward domestic markets, which we label "China serves China."

With this shift, there is a growing development and integration of nationwide markets and products and services focused on the needs of newly affluent domestic customers, utilizing made-in-China technologies. A generation of highly educated entrepreneurs is now pioneering the new domestic oriented economy in e-commerce platforms, media, software, smartphones, telecoms, online entertainment, and alternative energy. Whereas the state is actively encouraging enterprises to "go out" and become multinational in their scope, contrarily, we expect that internationalization may not be an attractive option for China's second-generation family firms. This is because we believe the primary task for successors of mature founder-led firms will be to reorient and reinvigorate the strategies and capabilities of their firms toward the domestic opportunities emerging in an increasingly integrated domestic market. Seizing emerging domestic opportunities will represent a significant challenge for a generation of firms that are located in maturing industries, and whose management practices are attuned to a socioeconomic era that is now passing. Ironically perhaps, while the founders were oriented to distant export markets in the West, successors are likely to be more preoccupied with local rather than international opportunities. Thus, while much of the western literature is highly attentive to the subject of family-firm internationalization (Singla, Veliyath, & George, 2014; Pukall & Calabrò, 2014), we suspect the strategic focus of second-generation CFFs will contain a decisively domestic agenda. In formal terms.

Proposition 1

Whereas founders focused upon distant export markets, the rising generation is more likely to reorient their firm's strategies and capabilities toward emerging domestic market opportunities.

Entrepreneurial Orientation

In the previous section, we proposed that the strategic focus of the founding generation of CFFs was acutely attuned to fleeting opportunities, accumulating capital, and growing a substantial enterprise. This view accords with the received wisdom that founders typically build the business while second and later generation successors will tend to be risk-averse and more likely to adopt a stewardship orientation, for example, aimed at family wealth preservation rather than further growth (Gersick, 1997). Whether this traditional wisdom applies in CFFs is an open question.

The first generation founders confronted an abundant but restricted range of opportunities. While the state tolerated the existence of entrepreneurial family firms, the legal system afforded ambiguous property rights. As a result, private entrepreneurs tended to focus on short-term opportunities and typically preferred investment in projects that offered rapid payback. These conditions were unfavorable towards long-term exploratory types of opportunity, and family firms ignored creating organizational structures and capabilities associated with such opportunities. The distribution of opportunities favored SOEs, who enjoyed preferential policies regarding market access, monopoly positions in key industries, and soft capital allocation. Even in the late reform era, SOEs retain preferential treatment and do not need to be aggressive in order to retain access to lucrative opportunities. We suspect these SOEs have few incentives to innovate or engage in risky and exploratory projects.

However, in the late reform period, which we have described as "China serves China," we expect that the new generation of private entrepreneurs will adopt more innovative made-in-China business models that rely upon complex organizational capabilities. We suspect that this generation of private entrepreneurs will be formidable competitors and, furthermore, second-generation family firms that choose to remain concentrated in mature industries are likely to sink into irrelevance. Moreover, in the late reform period, the blurred boundaries between state and private sector remain and legal protection with respect to property rights remains ambiguous and contradictory (Peck & Zhang, 2013). Although we see indications that institutional protection for property rights is improving, uncertainty about property ownership is likely to linger. In consequence, compared to SOEs, family firms still have to maintain a posture of alertness toward opportunity. In other words, we expect that the second generation, even with their inherited wealth, faces a strong imperative to remain proactive as entrepreneurs. As Dess, Pinkham and Yang (2011) put it, "unless they are proactive, risk-taking, and innovative, they are likely to be driven out of the market." Accordingly, in Figure 25.1 we show the succeeding generation as facing an imperative to sustain the highly entrepreneurial orientation that characterized their founders; whether they do so will depend on their preferred choices of other dimensions of Figure 25.1. In formal terms.

Proposition 2

Growing market competition will present the rising generation with the imperative to sustain high entrepreneurial orientation.

Governance

There are two distinguishing governance features of CFFs: ownership concentration and the absence of professional executives in senior governance role positions (Zhang & Ma, 2009). Both factors place significant discretion in the hands of the founder entrepreneurs. Ownership concentration is one of the most salient issues of corporate governance in emerging economies. Concentrated ownership is ubiquitous in family firms since families value the freedom and flexibility it provides to owners. Because family firms are not fully accountable to external investors, they can exercise their entrepreneurial acumen and enter into opaque and unwritten agreements with government officials and business partners. However, numerous studies have identified that this upper arrangement is significantly correlated with poor financial performance. Ownership concentration can neutralize the supervisory and advisory capacities of corporate boards, which could serve as a check and balance on ill-considered strategic choices (Hu, Tam & Tan, 2009). Several studies attest to weaknesses in an overly concentrated family and privately owned firms in China (Li, Guo, Yi, & Liu, 2010), finding ownership concentration is negatively related to product innovation. Some scholars find that ownership concentration is associated with an unwillingness to shed underperforming business units and that failure to divest assets aggravates relationships with minority investors (Wu, Xu, & Phan, 2010). Other studies find that ownership concentration was associated with expropriation of minority investors (Luo, Wan, Cai & Liu, 2013). The picture painted by these studies suggests that despite founders' impressive achievements in building firms, deficiencies in corporate governance may leave an accumulating legacy of strategic and investor-relations problems for the next-generation. We suggest that this legacy will reinforce the need for successors to bring about substantial governance reforms and strategic change.

Secondly, founder managed family films have typically been unwilling to appoint professional executives to senior management roles. Scholars have identified numerous impediments to the adoption of professional management in China's reform era (Zhang & Ma, 2009). Perhaps most importantly, founder entrepreneurs severely mistrusted outsiders and feared principal agency risks associated with the appointments of professional managers (Lee, Lim & Lim, 2003). Mistrust of outsiders provided strong incentives for founders to seek successors among more trusted family members. We suggest that the rising generation will be more willing to recruit professional executives into the managerial ranks. Educated in prestigious universities in China and abroad, many of the rising generation have greater experience and understanding of formal business management and its potential contribution. Compared with their parents, the rising generation will have greater familiarity with professional managers, whom they initially encountered as fellow-students at university, and will include them in their personal networks, which is likely to increase the trust between each other. Indeed, it is increasingly common to find private entrepreneurs enrolled in part-time executive MBA programs as a means of increasing their own understanding of professional management.

We expect that the successors will continue to exhibit a strong preference for concentrated ownership, but the greater understanding and familiarity with professional managers will produce beneficial influences on governance choices. Successors are more likely to adopt a less authoritarian management style, preferring to rely on more progressive corporate governance approaches. These approaches may include independent corporate boards, the separation of chairman of the board and CEO roles, or the adoption of top management team performance accountability processes that would constrain their authority over the fund activities. Carney (2013) depicts this approach to corporate governance as "personal rule," a hybrid system which makes greater use of professional management but retains strategic and financial control firmly in the hands of entrepreneurial founders and their successors providing for unchecked personal power discretion or 'rule' over the firm's affairs. Hence, in Figure 25.1, we show founder entrepreneurs to be located at the concentrated ownership/personal management end of the spectrum. We locate successors at the intermediate stage, retaining concentrated ownership and control but with greater reliance on professional management. Nevertheless, successors are unlikely to adopt the North American ideal of separated ownership and control by a professional management team. In formal terms.

Proposition 3

Similar to the founders, the rising generation, will continue to concentrate ownership in the hands of family members, however, they are more likely to incorporate professional management into the senior ranks.

Economic and Noneconomic Goals

A defining feature of family firms around the world is their pursuit of both economic and noneconomic goals (Chrisman, Chua, & Barnett, 2012). The balance in the choice between the two is likely to be determined by several factors, but the received wisdom suggests that noneconomic goals will become more pronounced as the firm ages generationally. There are two leading branches of theory that bear upon the choice of noneconomic goals and family funds. The first is an asymmetric altruism argument, which suggests that founders, motivated by altruism to succeeding generations to seek to provide a lasting legacy for them (Schulze, Lubatkin, Ling, & Dino, 2005). While altruism may not be reciprocated by children, which may be a source of sibling rivalry and conflict, parents are nonetheless highly motivated to provide for their descendants by assuring them of rights in the firm. The second perspective associated with socioemotional wealth theory suggests that families give significant value to their reputation in the community and make significant investments in upholding the family name even though this may entail a loss of economic value (Berrone, Cruz, Gómez-Mejía, & Kintana, 2010). The latter perspective is consistent with theory suggesting that family firms are concerned with the role of corporate social responsibility and a stewardship orientation toward the firm's numerous stakeholders (Le Breton-Miller, Miller, & Lester, 2011) in upholding their reputation.

From the above discussion, it is evident that CFFs have given great emphasis to economic goals in building their businesses by accumulating significant wealth. Moreover, it seems probable that founder entrepreneurs will be concerned with handing down a legacy to family members on noneconomic goals. However, it is far from clear that the founder entrepreneurs have given sufficient attention to reputation-building and strengthening their reputation as good corporate citizens in the wider community. While recent research suggests family firms are paying more attention to issues such as philanthropy and corporate social responsibility (Dou, Zhang, & Su, 2014; Li, Song, Wu, 2014), the interest in CSR comes as a reactive response to a spate of corporate scandals. Increasingly, private firms are becoming associated with poor social responsibility, including a callous disregard for employee safety practices, widespread product adulteration, concealing wealth, and overseas transfer of capital to safe havens. Daily stories of fraud and expropriation of minority investors contribute to these negative perceptions. Moreover, while "guanxi" is often characterized by some researchers as a legitimate "network strategy," private entrepreneurs' fondness for developing political ties is increasingly seen by the general public as illegal influence peddling and corruption. In consequence, there is a growing social resentment of private entrepreneurs' behavior, which is manifested in unhealthy sentiments of 'Chou Fu' (hatred of the rich). Despite their growth in numbers, private sector firms remain low-status organizations (Xu, Lu, & Gu, 2014) and share a collective risk of incurring a legitimacy crisis. We reason that the characteristic founder entrepreneurs' short-term orientation towards wealth accumulation has left a potentially hazardous responsibility deficit that will demand attention from the next generation. Because it is in their interests to project a more socially desirable public image, we suspect the rising generation will pay far more attention to the goal of improving their social, political legitimacy. Accordingly, in Figure 25.1 we show that the rising generation is likely to differ significantly from the previous generation and will invest heavily in building a family firm reputation for corporate social responsibility, even though this may come at a cost to their economic goals. In formal terms.

Proposition 4

Unlike founders who focused exclusively on economic goals, the rising generation will invest more effort in building a family firm reputation and seeking noneconomic goals.

Managing Network Ties

The pervasive influence of the state and party in China's growth and development is uniquely associated with network strategy and the way entrepreneurs manage the relationship with key stakeholders in business and government. In an environment of intense competition, ambiguous protection of individual property rights, and government mediated access to business opportunities and resources, China's founder entrepreneurs devote substantial effort to establishing and maintaining favorable relationships with their business partners and the relevant agencies in government. The experimental, gradual, and opaque approach to economic reform creates much uncertainty for entrepreneurs and relationships with influential individuals, and agencies serve as an important source of information about pending policy changes and emergent opportunities.

Given the ambiguous status of private firms, it is more difficult for private entrepreneurs to connect with the government; because government officials have many suitors they can drive a hard bargain in demanding reciprocity. In contrast, SOEs enjoy a privileged position in establishing and maintaining political ties for two reasons: first, SOEs are charged with multiple social and economic tasks and often seen as a part of government whose executives and managers have a formal position in Chinese political hierarchy (Bai, Lu & Tao, 2006); to appoint and dismiss a manager in the SOE calls for daily operation of the Organization Department of CPC. Secondly, there are substantial legal and administrative constraints that limit entry for private entrepreneurs into major industries including public utilities, telecom, petroleum, etc. (Bai, Li & Wang, 2003). Managers in these industries naturally monopolize the opportunities for building up reciprocity.

Nevertheless, a consensus has formed that the quality of a private firm's relationships has a direct bearing on its competitive and financial performance. In a meta-analysis of 53 studies of network strategy, Luo, Huang, and Wang (2012) found a positive relationship between guanxi-style ties and firm performance. Specifically, business ties (ties with customers, suppliers, competitors) and government ties (ties with the government, industrial bureaus, and other regulatory organizations) were found to boost both economic (financial-based and market-based) and operational (competitive-based and social-based) performance. Also, business ties have a larger impact on operational performance because of their advantage to operational efficiency and effectiveness. At the same time, government ties affect economic performance more since they may help provide extra economic resources and crucial information. Interestingly, some of the most insightful findings of the meta-analysis are: i) that government ties are less important for non-state-owned organizations, and ii) the significance of government ties is declining with the progression of reform and with improvements in the institutional environment progresses. Accordingly, some scholars predict that successors of family firms will continue to cultivate and maintain government ties (Li, Yao, Sue-Chan & Xi, 2011).

However other studies present a more nuanced picture, suggesting that the value of relationships is contextually contingent (Xiao & Tsui, 2007). Guo and Miller (2010) investigated the evolution of guanxi in knowledge-intensive firms longitudinally and found that founders typically rely on a "core circle" of family, kin, and close friends to mobilize start-up financial capital and advice about institutional and legitimacy issues. During the early growth period, they substantially widen their ties to acquire additional resources and information through ties with governmental officials, bankers, and business partners. Guo & Miller (2010) term this widening network as the "intermediary circle." In a later growth period, entrepreneurs further widen the network to include a "periphery circle" through which entrepreneurs can get timely information and potential opportunities. The "periphery circle" consists of a wider mix of individuals with more varied experience and backgrounds. Furthermore, successful entrepreneurs are associated with dyadic reciprocity, a two-way flow of information, that is, the longevity and value of network ties depend on knowledge and information sharing. The implication for successors, who assume leadership at a late-growth or mature stage of firm life cycle, engages more intensively with a "periphery circle" to obtain information and opportunities rather than relying on the core and intermediary circle of family and government.

The suggestion is consistent with social capital imperatives that greater value accrues from bridging forms of social capital that span structural holes providing access to non-redundant information (Adler & Kwon, 2002). Hence, we anticipate, notwithstanding any evolution in the quality of institutions, that the successors continue to cultivate network ties but will do so with a wider and more varied network of individuals and organizations. Moreover, we suspect that while research findings support the positive value of political ties (Luo, Huang, & Wang, 2012), there is a growing unease about the legitimacy of such linkages for private firms (Barkema, Chen, George, Luo, & Tsui, 2015). Given the era of "China serves China" and Chinese industries are becoming increasing knowledge-intensive, the next generation should build more relations with different groups so that they can have access to more diverse information and opportunities. Accordingly, as illustrated in Figure 25.1, successors are more likely to extend their network building strategies to a wider range of business ties, thereby facilitating their strategic redirection and transition to new industries. In formal terms, we propose.

Proposition 5

The rising generation will continue to cultivate ties but will do so with a wider and more varied network of business and government partners.

Family Involvement

Extensive family involvement in ownership and management of the firm by spouses, in-laws, children and the wider family is also viewed as a defining feature of traditional Chinese family firms (Fukuyama, 1997; Redding, 1990). Recent research on the contemporary Chinese family firm suggests family will continue to play an important role and strategic and financial decisions (Liang, Wang, & Cui, 2014). As we had discussed above, family involvement has played an important role in helping entrepreneurs navigate the uncertainties and risks of the reform process. In particular, family ties proved vital in providing financial and human resources to entrepreneurs in the context of institutional voids in capital and labor markets. Moreover, despite changes in social and economic norms and government social engineering projects that have impacted many aspects of the family structure, there remains a deep commitment to family involvement and business matters, which manifests itself most conspicuously in founders' preference for continued family involvement in the firms they founded. We argued that successors are more likely than founders to rely upon professional management and to extend their business networks beyond the family. How then do we expect the family to be involved in the second-generation owner managed firms? We consider four emergent themes that warrant further research: the effects of diluted ownership, the potential for portfolio entrepreneurship, changes in family knowledge sharing behavior, and the role of international networks and escape institutional constraints.

First, we expect the family members to retain share ownership of the founding firm. While we expect founders to prefer to appoint a successor CEO from family, we suspect that founders will continue to divide share ownership among a wider group of family members including spouses, siblings, in-laws, and grandchildren. The effects of continuing divided ownership as the firm ages generationally will be to attenuate family members identification with the firm. Divided ownership is likely to bring about a more instrumental concern about the financial value of their personal stake. These dynamics generate the potential for conflict between central and more distant family members as illustrated by Schulze and his colleagues (2001) in multi-generational U.S. family firms. The solutions to these problems include buying back shares and converting family ownership stakes into financial assets which are managed by trust companies and wealth management firms. The pace at which families can segment firm ownership into active and passive ownership will depend on the extent to which China's financial wealth management sector develops and enables the dilution of family ownership.

Second, founder capital accumulation and successful firms are likely to create free cash flow, cash that cannot be profitably reinvested the founding firm, and which creates the possibility of portfolio entrepreneurship. In the traditional Chinese family firm, scholars such as Wong (1985) and Redding (1990) document the division of a founders' wealth among his or her offspring to allow younger family members to develop their own distinctive and separate lines of business. The tradition continues in the present era in Greater China. Au and his colleagues (2013) document emergent forms of portfolio entrepreneurship in Hong Kong SAR. In this practice family firms serve as incubators for new business ventures, once a new business has demonstrated feasibility could be spun off to form a separate business owned and operated by another a family member, wherein the new entrepreneur may 'borrow' family resources including political and business networks, entrepreneurial knowledge and idiosyncratic competence. Carney (1998) identifies these processes as forming the basis of diversified multigenerational business groups and depending on the availability of human capital may also proliferate among China's second-generation family firms.

Third, we expect successors will adopt a different approach to knowledge sharing within the family firm. Founding generations were frequently dependent upon export markets where there is little requirement for the development of sophisticated marketing and distribution capabilities, little opportunity to develop proprietary organizational capabilities with intense competition and low profitability. In these circumstances, founders sought to protect their sparse competitive capabilities by limiting information and knowledge to trusted family members. On this point, Su and Carney (2012) explored the relationship between social capital, capacity for knowledge transfer, and intellectual capital formation. "Intellectual capital, as the firm's knowledge and knowing capability, can enrich and aggregate the firm's human capital and lead to an advancement of a firm's innovation and strategic differentiation." They propose that in the early stages, China's family firms do not codify knowledge. Instead, knowledge (especially tacit knowledge) sticks to family members or limitedly shared within the scope of family. Meanwhile, potential recipients of knowledge sharing, especially non-family ones, were not well disposed to acquire knowledge. The result was a low knowledge equilibrium with little incentive for the organization to develop intellectual capital that might serve as the basis of competitive advantage. However, in the future family firms will need to give greater attention to strategic differentiation in the development of organizational capabilities. To ensure continued success, family firms are more likely to innovate and seek to upgrade their skills (Yang, Liu, Gao, and Li, 2012). Skill upgrading can be achieved by expanding the radius of trust to a wider range of employees and encourage them to become familiar with the sources of the firm's competitive advantage and seek to apply their talents in the firm more fully.

Finally, contrary to the three adaptive and competitiveness enhancing strategies identified above, an alternative development may arise from the perceived illegitimacy that some family firms have acquired in the eyes of the state and the wider society. To the extent that CFFs are subject to continuing pressure and restrictions from the state, families may choose to close ranks and to maintain a cumulative capital that may seek to reinforce the thick social wall of family ties. In this respect we foresee the possibility that family firms will enact an escape strategy seeking to transfer their capital to safer havens (Yamakawa, Peng, & Deeds, 2008; Boisot & Meyer, 2008; Witt & Lewin, 2007), for example, by investing in overseas networks by means of family controlled foreign ventures. Escape strategies are a response to perceived threats of expropriation

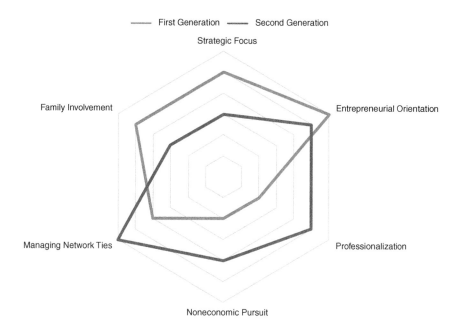

Figure 25.1 Differences Between Founders and Successors

and excessive regulation (Witt & Lewin, 2007) and we expect that family firms may adopt this strategy should such threats materialize. In formal terms.

Proposition 6

The rising generation is likely to reduce family involvement in the management of the firm.

Discussion

Figure 25.1 summarizes our expectations about the strategic and managerial choices that will be adopted by a rising generation of successors to China's founding entrepreneurs. We envisage the co-evolution of CFF's strategic and managerial practices as they age generationally and make adaptive responses to the changing socioeconomic environment. China's ongoing reform process is fraught with uncertainty and contradiction (Peck & Zhang, 2013) and private family firms remain low legitimacy organizations in the Chinese context (Ahlstrom, Bruton, & Yeh, 2008; Xu, Lu, & Gu, 2014) Accordingly, CFFs must navigate an environment containing unforeseen contingencies. However, we have adopted favorable assumptions about the ability of family firms to adapt and thrive in both harsh and munificent conditions. Indeed, the longevity and robustness of family firms to adjust to diverse conditions are suggested by their prevalence around the world.

Overall, we develop several predictions about the expected evolution of the CFF and the logic of its practice. First, unlike founders who focused on distant export markets in the West, we expect that the rising generation may reorient and reinvigorate the strategies and capabilities of firms toward the emerging domestic opportunities. Second, we expect that successors still have the imperative to sustain high entrepreneurial orientation that characterized their founders. Third, in corporate governance, we expect that successors will continue to exhibit a strong preference for concentrated ownership like their fathers but less "person rule" and more professional management. Fourth, the rising generation is likely to notably differ from the previous generation and will invest much in building the family firm reputation and seeking noneconomic goals. Fifth, although the founders depended on network strategy to acquire resource and legitimacy, we expect that the rising generation will continue to cultivate ties with a wider and more varied network of individuals and organizations. Finally, family involvement once was a defining feature of the traditional Chinese family firms. However, we expect that successors are more likely to reduce dependence on family ownership and management. Though, we expect that there is going to be a different generation for Chinese family firms. Successors have their own advantage and way of management.

Currently, it is not hard to find family firm studies with "succession" being one of the keywords. Nevertheless, few studies offered enlightening insights about motives of successors. But motive is not a negligible issue because it is the premise of talking about succession strategy. We also believe there is a necessity to distinguish between economic and noneconomic motives due to their different mechanisms. Scholars, through the lens of institution, explained that family firms can obtain distinctive advantages in emerging markets like China, which implies that even the motive is purely economic, family firms can still have a sustainable legitimacy to maximize profits. As a representative of noneconomic motives, on the other hand, SEW has not drawn enough attention. But similar to developed areas, it is not uncommon to see the refusal of the second generation to inherit.

Here we propose two future directions. First, to further explore what the other possible advantages of family firms are, thus making a contribution to general theories of the family firm.

Especially when successors are going to assume the responsibility of "China serves China," the institutional environments of China cannot be overlooked. In so doing, successors could have a more thorough comprehension of what their firms are good at. Secondly, more importance should be attached to SEW. Family holding and controlling problems in public firms should be the next item on SEW agenda (Berrone, Cruz, & Gómez-Mejía, 2012).

References

Adler, P. S. and Kwon, S. W. (2002) 'Social capital: Prospects for a new concept,' *Academy of Management Review*, 27(1): 17–40.

Ahlstrom, D., Bruton, G. D. and Yeh, K. S. (2008) 'Private firms in China: Building legitimacy in an emerging economy,' *Journal of World Business*, 43(4): 385–399.

Arregle, J. L., Batjargal, B., Hitt, M. A., Webb, J. W., Miller, T. and Tsui, A. S. (2013) 'Family ties in entrepreneurs' social networks and new venture growth,' *Entrepreneurship Theory and Practice*.

Au, K., Chiang, F. F., Birtch, T. A. and Ding, Z. (2013) 'Incubating the next generation to venture: The case of a family business in Hong Kong,' *Asia Pacific Journal of Management*, 30(3): 749–767.

Bai, C. E., Lu, J., & Tao, Z. (2006). 'The multitask theory of state enterprise reform: empirical evidence from China,' *The American Economic Review*, 353–357.

Berrone, P., Cruz, C. and Gómez-Mejía, L. R. (2012) 'Socioemotional wealth in family firms theoretical dimensions, assessment approaches, and agenda for future research,' *Family Business Review*, 25(3): 258–279.

Berrone, P., Cruz, C., Gómez-Mejía, L. R. and Kintana, M. (2010) 'Ownership structure and corporate response to institutional pressures: do family-controlled firms pollute less?,' *Administrative Science Quarterly*, 55(2): 82- 13.

Boisot, M., Child, J. and Redding, G. (2011) 'Working the system: Towards a theory of cultural and institutional competence,' *International Studies in Management and Organization*, 41: 63–96.

Boisot, M. and Meyer, M. W. (2008) 'Which way through the open door? Reflections on the internationalization of Chinese firms,' *Management and Organization Review*, 4(3): 349–365.

Cabrera-Suárez, K., De Saa-Perez, P. and García-Almeida, D. (2001) 'The succession process from a resource- and knowledge-based view of the family firm,' *Family Business Review*, 14(1): 37–46.

Cao, J., Cumming, D. and Wang, X. (2015) 'One-child policy and family firms in China,' *Journal of Corporate Finance*, in press.

Carney, M. (1998). 'A management capacity constraint? Obstacles to the development of the overseas Chinese family business,' *Asia Pacific Journal of Management*, 15(2): 137–162.

Carney, M. (2013) 'Personal rule in Asia' family-controlled Business Groups.' *Global Themes and Local Variations in Organization and Management: Perspectives on Glocalization*, Routledge.

Chen, C. C., Chen, X. P. and Huang, S. (2013) 'Chinese Guanxi: An integrative review and new directions for future research,' *Management and Organization Review*, 9(1), 167–207.

Chen, W. (2007) 'Does the colour of the cat matter? The red hat strategy in China's private enterprises,' *Management and Organization Review*, 3(1): 55–80. the.

Chrisman, J. J., Chua, J. H., Pearson, A. W. and Barnett, T. (2012) 'Family involvement, family influence, and family-centered non-economic goals in small firms,' *Entrepreneurship Theory and Practice*, 36(2): 267–293.

Dess, G. G., Pinkham, B. C. and Yang, H. (2011) 'Entrepreneurial orientation: Assessing the construct's validity and addressing some of its implications for research in the areas of family business and organizational learning,' *Entrepreneurship Theory and Practice*, 35(5): 1077–1090.

Dou, J. and Li, S. (2013), 'The succession process in Chinese family firms: A guanxi perspective,' *Asia Pacific Journal of Management*, 30(3): 893–917.

Dou, J., Zhang, Z. and Su, E. (2014) 'Does family involvement make firms donate more? Empirical evidence from Chinese private firms,' *Family Business Review*, 27(3): 259–274.

Egri, C. P. and Ralston, D. A. (2004) 'Generation cohorts and personal values: A comparison of China and the United States,' *Organization Science*, 15(2): 210–220.

Fong, V. L. (2002). 'China's one-child policy and the empowerment of urban daughters,' *American Anthropologist*, *104*(4): 1098–1109.

Fukuyama, F. (1995) *Trust: The Social Virtues and the Creation of Prosperity*, New York: Free Press.

Gedajlovic, E. and Carney, M. (2010) 'Markets, hierarchies, and families: Toward a transaction cost theory of the family firm,' *Entrepreneurship Theory and Practice*, 34(6): 1145–1172.

Gersick, K. E. (1997) *Generation to generation: Life cycles of the family business*, Harvard Business Press.

Guo, C. and Miller, J. K. (2010) 'Guanxi dynamics and entrepreneurial firm creation and development in China,' *Management and Organization Review*, 6(2): 267–291.

Hobday, M. (1995) 'East Asian latecomer firms: learning the technology of electronics,' *World Development*, 23(7): 1171–1193.

Hu, H.W., Tam, O. K. and Tan, M. G. S. (2010) 'Internal governance mechanisms and firm performance in China,' *Asia Pacific Journal of Management*, 27(4): 727–749.

Huang, Y. (2008) *Capitalism with Chinese Characteristics: Entrepreneurship and the State*, New York: Cambridge University Press.

Le Breton-Miller, I., Miller, D. and Lester, R. H. (2011) 'Stewardship or agency? A social embeddedness reconciliation of conduct and performance in public family businesses,' *Organization Science*, 22(3): 704–721.

Li, S., Song, X. and Wu, H. (2014) 'Political connection, ownership structure, and corporate philanthropy in China: A strategic-political perspective,' *Journal of Business Ethics*, 1–13.

Li, S. X., Yao, X., Sue-Chan, C. and Xi, Y. (2011) 'Where do social ties come from: Institutional framework and governmental tie distribution among Chinese managers,' *Management and Organization Review*, 7(1): 97–124.

Li, Y., Guo, H., Yi, Y. and Liu, Y. (2010) 'Ownership concentration and product innovation in Chinese firms: The mediating role of learning orientation,' *Management and Organization Review*, 6(1): 77–100.

Liang, X., Wang, L. and Cui, Z. (2014) 'Chinese private firms and internationalization effects of family involvement in management and family ownership,' *Family Business Review*, 27(2): 126–141.

Lubatkin, M. H., Schulze, W. S., Ling, Y. and Dino, R. N. (2005) 'The effects of parental altruism on the governance of family-managed firms,' *Journal of Organizational Behavior*, 26(3): 313–330.

Luo, J. H., Wan, D. F., Cai, D. and Liu, H. (2013) 'Multiple large shareholder structure and governance: The role of shareholder numbers, contest for control, and formal institutions in Chinese family firms,' *Management and Organization Review*, 9(2): 265–294.

Luo, Y., Huang, Y. and Wang, S. L. (2012) 'Guanxi and organizational performance: A meta-analysis,' *Management and Organization Review*, 8(1): 139–172.

March, J. G. (2011) *The Ambiguities of Experience*, Cornell University Press.

Martinez, M., & Aldrich, H. (2013) 'Sociological theories applied to family businesses,' in L. Melin, M. Nordqvist & P. Sharma (Eds.), *The SAGE Handbook of Family Business* (pp. 83–99). Thousand Oaks, CA: Sage.

McNaughton, B. (1997) *The China Circle: Economics and Electronics in the PRC, Taiwan, and Hong Kong*, Washington, DC: Brookings Institution.

McVey, R. T. (Ed.). (1992) *Southeast Asian Capitalists (No. 9)*, SEAP Publications.

Nee, V. (1992) 'Organizational Dynamics of Market Transition: Hybrid Forms, Property Rights, and Mixed Economy in China,' *Administrative Science Quarterly*, 37: 1–27.

Nolan, P. (2001) *China and the Global Economy*, Basingstoke: UK Palgrave.

Peck, J. and Zhang, J. (2013) 'A variety of capitalism with Chinese characteristics?,' *Journal of Economic Geography*, 13(3): 357–396.

Pukall, T. J. and Calabrò, A. (2014) 'The internationalization of family firms: A critical review and integrative model,' *Family Business Review*, 27(2): 103–125.

Ralston, D. A., Egri, C. P., Stewart, S., Terpstra, R. H. and Kaicheng, Y. (1999) 'Doing business in the 21st century with the new generation of Chinese managers: A study of generational shifts in work values in China,' *Journal of International Business Studies*, 415–427.

Redding, G. (1990) *The Spirit of Chinese Capitalism*. New York: De Gruyter.

Redding, G. and Witt, M. (2009) 'China's business system in its future trajectory,' *Asia Pacific Journal of Management*, 26(3): 381–399.

Rosenzweig, M. R., & Zhang, J. (2009). 'Do population control policies induce more human capital investment? Twins, birth weight and China's "one-child" policy,' *The Review of Economic Studies*, 76(3): 1149–1174.

Schulze, W., Lubatkin, M. H., Dino, R. N. and Buchholtz, A. K. (2001) 'Agency relationships in family firms,' *Theory and Evidence Organization Science*, 12(2): 99–116.

Singla, C., Veliyath, R. and George, R. (2014) 'Family firms and internationalization-governance relationships: Evidence of secondary agency issues,' *Strategic Management Journal*, 35(4): 606–616.

Steier, L. (2009) 'Where do new firms come from? Households, family capital, ethnicity, and the welfare mix,' *Family Business Review*, 22(3): 273–278.

Su, E. and Carney, M. (2013) 'Can China's family firms create intellectual capital?,' *Asia Pacific Journal of Management*, 30(3): 657–675.

Tang, J. (2010) 'How entrepreneurs discover opportunities in China: An institutional view,' *Asia Pacific Journal of Management*, 27(3): 461–479.

Whyte, M. K. (1996) 'The Chinese family and economic development: obstacle or engine?,' *Economic Development and Cultural Change*, 1–30.

Whyte, M. K. (2005) 'Continuity and change in urban Chinese family life,' *The China Journal*, 9–33.

Witt, M. and Lewin, A. W. (2007) 'Outward foreign direct investment as escape response to home country institutional constraints,' *Journal of International Business Studies*, 38(4): 579–594.

Wong, S.-L. (1985) 'The Chinese family firm: A model,' *British Journal of Sociology*, 36: 58–72.

Wu, J., Xu, D. and Phan, P. H. (2011) 'The effects of ownership concentration and corporate debt on corporate divestitures in Chinese listed firms,' *Asia Pacific Journal of Management*, 28(1): 95–114.

Xiao, Z. and Tsui, A. S. (2007) 'When brokers may not work: The cultural contingency of social capital in Chinese high-tech firms,' *Administrative Science Quarterly*, 52(1): 1–31.

Xu, D., Lu, J. W. and Gu, Q. (2014) 'Organizational forms and multi-population dynamics economic transition in china,' *Administrative Science Quarterly*.

Yamakawa, Y., Peng, M. and Deeds, D. L. (2008) 'What drives new ventures to internationalize from emerging to developed economies?,' *Entrepreneurship: Theory and Practice*, 32(1): 59–82.

Yang, J., Liu, H., Gao, S. and Li, Y. (2012) 'Technological innovation of firms in China: Past, present, and future,' *Asia Pacific Journal of Management*, 29(3): 819–840.

Zhang, J. and Ma, H. (2009) 'Adoption of professional management in Chinese family business: A multilevel analysis of impetuses and impediments,' *Asia Pacific Journal of Management*, 26(1): 119–139.

Zhao, J., Carney, M., Zhang, S. and Zhu, L. (2015) 'Family Firm Succession, Strategic Change, and Performance: Evidence from China's Publicly Listed Family Firms,' *Working Paper*, Beijing: Renmin University.

26

A REVIEW OF THE ACADEMIC LITERATURE ON FAMILY BUSINESS IN SPANISH*

María Concepción López-Fernández, Ana María Serrano-Bedia,
Marta Pérez-Pérez, Remedios Hernández-Linares,
and Manuel Palma-Ruiz

Introduction

The field of family business studies has been of interest to management scholars and writers as a topic of academic inquiry since the 1960s and has been growing over the last decades (Chrisman et al. 2008; Benavides-Velasco, Quintana-García, and Guzmán-Parra 2013). However, the literature on this field is not as extensive as in other management areas (Bird et al. 2002); and it has a clear tendency towards research from Anglo-Saxon countries and the use of the English language as its primary means of publication.

A number of articles have reviewed the literature on family firms of recent decades from both a subjective (e.g. Sharma, Chrisman, and Chua 1996; Sharma, Chrisman, and Chua 1997; Bird et al. 2002; Chrisman, Chua, and Sharma 2003; Sharma 2004; Zahra and Sharma 2004) and objective perspectives (e.g. Casillas and Acedo 2007; Debicki et al. 2009; Yu et al. 2012; Benavides-Velasco, Quintana-García, and Guzmán-Parra 2013); then again, all of these reviews are based on articles in English. Moreover, a research study revealed that 95.06 percent of JCR journals issued in Social Sciences categories were published in English in 2012 (López-Fernández, Serrano-Bedia, and Pérez-Pérez 2016).

Be that as it may, the importance of the Spanish language is undeniable. The United Nations has declared that it is the second most important language in the world, right after Chinese and ahead of English. Spanish is spoken in Spain, Mexico and most countries in Central and South America. In addition, it is the second most spoken language in the USA. Accordingly, it is relevant to acquire an overview of the scientific literature developed in said language. In this line, the objective of this study is to offer a comprehensive view of the family firm literature in Spanish to explore the alternative realities, and geographical and linguistic contexts that have been considered.

To examine the status and trends in the family business literature in Spanish, a comprehensive and systematic review of academic literature was performed by collecting information from different scientific databases (Web of Science, Scopus, and Dialnet). In addition, bibliometric indicators and other methods were applied to obtain a deeper understanding of this literature.

* This work was supported by the Banco Santander Chair of Family Business (University of Cantabria).

This chapter is structured as follows. The next section presents an overview of the literature obtained from the Dialnet database, one of the main bibliographic databases for scientific literature in Spanish. The following section includes a bibliometric analysis of the articles published in journals included in international databases (namely Web of Science and Scopus). Indicators of the publication activity and content analysis of the family business literature in Spanish were incorporated. In this section, a comparison of Spanish and English literature is included. The last section discusses the main results and presents the conclusions.

An Overview of the Scientific Publications on Family Business in Spanish

In this section, the Dialnet database is used for a description of the temporal evolution of the family business literature in Spanish, including existing themes and productivity by countries and journals. Dialnet is one of the largest bibliographic free access online databases, which contains summaries of articles from about 9,000 scientific journals in all subject areas published in Spain and Latin America. To give greater visibility to the Hispanic literature, it is produced cooperatively by university libraries, under the leadership of the Library of the University of La Rioja (Spain). Dialnet allows consultation of summaries and offers a classification of scientific categories and sub-categories.

We accessed Dialnet on April 2015, and searched for journal articles with the Spanish term for "family firm" and published in journals that meet the Latindex[1] quality criteria. With these search criteria, we retrieved an initial sample of 474 documents, with no timespan limit. Later, a filtering process consisting of independent readings of abstracts was carried out, reducing the sample to 210 articles. The main information about the search and filtering process is summarized in Table 26.1.

Finally, we fully reviewed the 210 documents. It is interesting to note that the first article on family business in Spanish was not published until 1982, whereas the first approximation to the field of family business studies can be found about two decades earlier (Trow 1961).

Figure 26.1 shows the total percentages of family business articles retrieved from the Dialnet's categories. It is possible to observe that nearly three-fourths of the published articles are classified within the "Economics and Business" category, whereas the percentage of articles included in any of the other six categories does not exceed 10 percent, even though family business area is considered an interdisciplinary field.

Given the large number of articles included in the "Economics and Business" category (155 from 210), a second classification was carried out to reveal the corresponding sub-categories (see Figure 26.2). More than half of these articles appeared in journals related to the "Business Management," while nearly a third of them belonged to the "Economics and Business" sub-category.

Table 26.1 Search Criteria Used in Dialnet

Search Criteria	Documents Retrieved	Documents Selected
Keyword: "Empresa familiar" *Language:* Spanish *Document type:* Journal article *Journals included in Latindex:* Yes	474	210

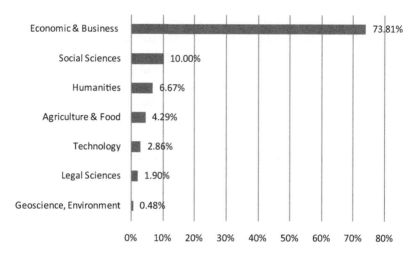

Figure 26.1 Total Percentages of Family Business Articles Retrieved from Dialnet's Categories

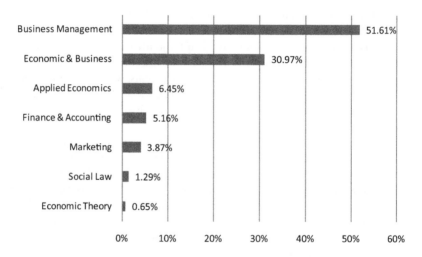

Figure 26.2 Total Percentages of Family Business Articles Retrieved from Dialnet's Sub-Categories

The articles included in this study have been published in journals from eight countries, although only five of these countries exceed one percent of the total production. Figure 26.3 shows the percentage of articles published per country. Figure 26.3 shows that the largest contributor to the family business literature in Spanish is Spain, given that 82.38 percent of the articles were published in journals edited in this country. This fact may be explained by the existence of an important network of Chairs of the family-owned business. This network, possibly the largest in the world in this discipline, is composed of 36 Chairs, where 200 university professors work and train an average of 1,800 students per year (Instituto de la Empresa Familiar, 2015). Also, Spain is the only country in which a specialized journal in Spanish on family business studies has been published, called *Revista de Empresa Familiar*.

Spain is followed far behind by Colombia and Uruguay (4.76 percent of the articles each), and Venezuela and Mexico (2.86 percent of the articles each). The contributions made to the family business field by Argentina and Peru may be considered merely testimonial. Interestingly, we find an

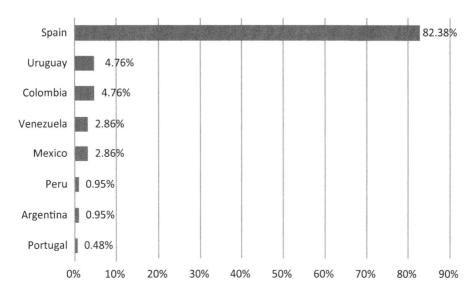

Figure 26.3   Productivity of Family Business Articles per Country

Table 26.2 Number of Articles on Family Business in Spanish per Country

	Argentina	*Colombia*	*Mexico*	*Peru*	*Spain*	*Uruguay*	*Venezuela*
1980–1989	–	–	–	–	2	–	–
1990–1999	–	–	–	–	9	–	–
2000–2009	1	4	2	1	75	4	4
2010–2015	1	6	4	1	87	6	2

Note: Portugal has been excluded from this table considering it is not a Spanish-speaking country.

article published in a Portuguese journal (Bañegil Palacios, Hernández Linares, and Barriuso Iglesias, 2012), which publishes articles in Portuguese, English, and Spanish, thus justifying the presence of Portugal in Figure 26.3. However, the absence of other Latin American countries is noticeable. For example, the lack of Chilean articles in the Dialnet database is particularly striking because there are several papers from this country within the international databases of Web of Science and Scopus.

As shown in Table 26.2, Spain is the country that has contributed the most to family business literature in Spanish, and in which this interest was born earlier. In fact, the first studies on family firms appeared in Spain during the 1980s (Mesanza 1982; Gallo and García-Pont 1989), whereas in Latin America, this interest emerged twenty years later. (Andrade C., 2002; Castillo, 2002; Zouboulakis and Kamarianos, 2002).

Table 26.3 shows the journals that have published at least three articles on family firms. Most of these journals are edited in Spain (specifically 20 of 24 journals included in the table), and the few remaining in Uruguay (2), Colombia (1), and Mexico (1). The journal that has published the most articles is *Revista de Empresa Familiar (REF)*, which (as mentioned before) is the only specialized journal in Spanish. Sponsored by Banco Santander Chair of Family Business at the University of Málaga, this journal started in 2011 with the purpose of becoming a benchmark publication for the family business literature in Spanish. In 2015, this journal changed its editorial policy to English in order to access international indexes (although it still maintains its original title in Spanish). This same decision has been adopted by other journals published initially

Table 26.3 Journals in Dialnet That Have Published at Least Three Articles on Family Business

Journal	Country	Articles
Revista de Empresa Familiar	Spain	28
Pecunia. Revista de la Facultad de Ciencias Económicas y Empresariales	Spain	11
Boletín de Estudios Económicos	Spain	10
Investigaciones Europeas de Dirección y Economía de la Empresa	Spain	10
IEEM. Revista de Negocios	Uruguay	8
Revista Europea de Dirección y Economía de la Empresa	Spain	8
Cuadernos de Economía y Dirección de la Empresa	Spain	5
Economía Industrial	Spain	5
Universia Business Review	Spain	5
3c Empresa. Investigación y Pensamiento Crítico	Spain	4
Ekonomiaz: Revista Vasca de Economía	Spain	4
Entramado	Colombia	4
Revista de Antiguos Alumnos del IEEM	Uruguay	4
Revista de Historia Industrial	Spain	4
ROC Máquina. Piedras Naturales, Maquinaria y Equipos	Spain	4
América Latina en la Historia Económica	Mexico	3
Anuario Jurídico y Económico Escurialense	Spain	3
Cuadernos de Gestión	Spain	3
EsicMarket	Spain	3
Información Comercial Española, ICE: Revista de Economía	Spain	3
Molinería y Panadería: Revista Profesional de Panadería y Pastelería	Spain	3
Papeles de Economía Española	Spain	3
Revista Española de Financiación y Contabilidad	Spain	3
Sociedad y Utopía: Revista de Ciencias Sociales	Spain	3

in Spanish, such as *Cuadernos de Economía y Dirección de la Empresa*, now called *Business Research Quarterly* and *Investigaciones Europeas de Dirección y Economía de la Empresa* now called *European Research on Management and Business Economics*.

Scientific Publications on Family Business Studies in Spanish in Top-Ranking Journals: A Bibliometric Approach

To get a glimpse of the literature on family business studies in Spanish that could be comparable to previous review studies, we performed a bibliometric analysis of this literature in Spanish published in indexed journals included in the Web of Science and Scopus. For this purpose, we carried out a systematic search accessing both databases during the month of March 2015. The selected timespan limit was the maximum allowed in order not to distort the results.

Table 26.4 summarizes the main information about the search and filtering process. To ensure the comprehensive nature of this analysis, two searches were performed. In a first round, the most generic term "famil*" in the business-economics research area was included. In a second round we searched in any possible area employing keywords that are generic to family firm: a) "famil* business*" and "famil* firm*" (Benavides-Velasco, Quintana-García, and Guzmán-Parra 2013) both in Spanish and English, and b) those referring to the family nature of the company ownership or management "famil* own*" and "famil* control*" (Shanker and Astrachan 1996). With regards to the type of document, the decision was made to select the articles and reviews published in journals as the basis for analysis since both are the source of most up-to-date knowledge.

Table 26.4 Search Criteria Used in Web of Science and Scopus Databases

		Search criteria	Documents retrieved	Documents selected
FIRST ROUND	Web of Science	• *Topic*: "Famil★" • *Research area*: Business Economics • *Language*: Spanish • *Document type*: Article or review	641	37
	Scopus	• *Title-abs-key*: "Famil★" • *Sub-area*: "BUSI" OR "ECON" • *Language*: Spanish • *Doctype*: "Ar" OR "re"	261	26
SECOND ROUND	Web of Science	• *Topic*: "famil★ business★" OR "famil★ firm★" OR "famil★ own★" OR "famil★ control★") OR ("empres★" and "famil★") • *Language*: Spanish • *Document type*: Article or review	189	13
	Scopus	• *Title-abs-key*: "famil★ business★" OR "famil★ firm★" OR ("empres★" and "famil★") OR "famil★ own★" OR "famil★ control★") • *Language*: Spanish • *Doctype*: "Ar" OR "re"	129	10
		Total of articles included in the study		86
		Books (at least 5 cites in the 86 articles sample)		5
		Total of documents analyzed		91

FILTERING PROCESS

By following these search criteria, we retrieved a total of 1,220 documents. The filtering process consisted in an independent reading of abstracts to ensure that family business topics were in fact investigated. During this filtering process, different types of errors were also identified (e.g. duplications, classification mismatch, and articles not written in Spanish).

After the filtering process, an initial sample of 86 articles was obtained. Relevant work might have been left out during the first sample, such as books. For this reason, a further analysis of the references cited in these 86 articles was conducted in order to identify relevant books in family business published in Spanish. All references used in each article were recorded in a database. Those books that were cited at least 5 times were identified and added to the sample, resulting in 91 documents.

Regarding the bibliometric analysis, diverse types of indicators were used, which can be classified mainly into two categories:

- *Activity indicators.* Provide data about the volume and impact of research, allowing one to observe the quantitative evolution of the literature. In this particular case, the temporal evolution of the field of study was analyzed, including most productive authors, journals, universities, and countries.
- *Relation indicators.* Particularly, co-words analysis was used. Co-words technique is based on the analysis of the co-occurrences of keywords, which allows the depiction of the state of the art, identifying and classifying clusters or research topics in a strategic matrix associated according to their levels of development. With regard to the tool used for the calculation of these indicators, the free bibliometrics software REDES 2005 was employed.

These indicators have been previously used in other general literature reviews in the field (Benavides-Velasco, Quintana-García, and Guzmán-Parra 2013) allowing a comparison of the results in English and Spanish literature.

Results of the Activity Indicators

Regarding the temporal evolution of the field of study, the analysis shows a relatively recent field. Although the selected timespan limit was the maximum allowed, it was found that the first document is Gallo (1995), one of the five books included in the sample. Gallo can be considered the pioneer of family firm literature in Spanish. He is also the co-author of the first articles published in the journal of *Family Business Review* by a researcher of Spanish language (Gallo and García-Pont 1996; Gallo and Vilaseca 1996).

The temporal evolution confirms the existence of three research cycles (see Figure 26.4). The first period includes studies from 1995 to 2007 with limited scientific production (an average of 1.07 documents annually), and irregular, with several years with no production. It is noteworthy also that all of the books identified and included in the sample are in this first period. The second period is characterized by an increase in research from 2008, the year from which the trend has grown steadily, until 2011 when a maximum of 20 articles is reached. From that moment, a third period is identified, marked with a decline in publications annually, particularly evident in 2014. This may suggest a certain degree of maturity in this field of study. However, data relating to 2014 are to be interpreted with caution, because, as previously stated, these data may still be incomplete.

The nationality of the authors in the sample is summarized in Table 26.5. In this case, the most productive country is Spain with a total of 41 documents, followed by Colombia and Mexico, with a total of 18 and 14 documents respectively, and far away from other Latin American countries. Although researchers affiliated to universities in Spain represent the most productive group, its weight decreases significantly compared to that data obtained from Dialnet. This

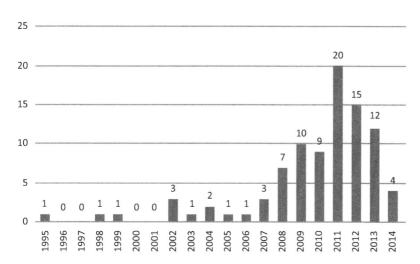

e 26.4   Number of Publications on Family Business per Year
e: Web of Science, Scopus, and Top Books

Table 26.5 Productivity per Country

Country	Authors	Documents	Productivity Average
Spain	94	41	2,29
Colombia	41	18	2,28
Mexico	30	14	2,14
Venezuela	9	6	1,50
Argentina	3	3	1,00
Chile	3	2	1,50
Brazil	2	1	2,00
Greece	2	1	2,00
Canada	1	1	1,00
USA	1	1	1,00
Peru	1	1	1,00
UK	1	1	1,00

Source: Web of Science, Scopus, and Top Books

ance can be attributed to the evaluation system of the scientific activity of university scholars
Spain. The system in place in Spain, established in the early 1990s, demands publications in
journal rankings, prioritizing publications in English for scholars to have a positive evalua-
of their research activities. As a result, the presence of Spaniard authors in leading journals
English has grown significantly since the beginning of this century (Meroño-Cerdán and
to-Sánchez 2015), but at the expense of a minor presence in journals published in Spanish.
vertheless, researchers use journals in Spanish not included in scientific rankings to publish
iminary work or studies focalized on national issues. The evaluation system in effect in Spain
y also explain that the average number of coauthors per work is lower than in Colombia and
xico, as this system penalizes articles signed by more than two authors.
In regards to the productivity of the journals (see Table 26.6), the articles in the sample were
lished in 45 different journals, and only ten of them (22.2 percent) published at least three

articles. These ten journals bring together 49 articles, representing the 57 percent of the articles in our sample. The most productive journal is *Cuadernos de Administración*, with 11 papers (12.8 percent), followed by *Universia Business Review* and *Revista Española de Financiación y Contabilidad*, with 8 and 6 articles respectively (9.3 and 7.0 percent of the sample).

The analysis shows that while these three journals have published articles in the second and third periods of research identified before, their productivity varies in each of them. *Cuadernos de Administración* and *Universia Business Review* are the most productive journals in the period of 2008–2011, meanwhile, the *Spanish Journal of Finance and Accounting* tops the ranking in the period of 2012–2014. In this latter period, other journals appeared, such as *Entramado* or *Estudios Gerenciales* together with *Contaduría y Administración*, which reappears in this period after a first publication in the period of 1995–2007. By contrast, other journals such as *Investigaciones Europeas de Dirección y Economía de la Empresa, Cuadernos de Economía y Dirección de Empresas* o *Revista Venezolana de Gerencia* are not present in the most recent period.

In regards to the research productivity of the authors (see Table 26.7), 192 authors wrote the 91 documents in the sample (2.11 authors per document). Among them, only 22 authors have published more than 1 document in Spanish. This is an indicative of a wide dispersion between the Spanish-speaking scholars interested in the field of Family Business studies, where only five authors seem to have specialized in this field by publishing three or more articles. These results may also indicate that this field of Family Business studies represents a secondary line of research for many of these authors. The most productive scholars in this field are Gómez-Betancourt, Betancourt-Ramírez, López-Vergara, Lozano-Posso, and Cabrera-Suárez. The first three, originally from Colombia, topped the ranking of the most productive and stand out as a well-consolidated research group, signing joint publications during the two main periods of research previously identified (2007–2011 and 2012–2014). By contrast, Lozano-Posso did not continue publishing in the second period of analysis (2012–14). Cabrera-Suárez is the only scholar included in English literature reviews (e.g. Debicki et al., 2009).

The last aspect addressed in this section refers to the analysis of the different academic institutions from which the authors in the sample belong. In this sense, the 192 scholars previously identified come from a total of 66 universities. From the total sample of 91 documents, 37 institutions have at least two authors publishing family business research, which again suggest the wide dispersion that usually exists in this field.

Table 26.6 Most Productive Journals on Family Business Literature in Spanish

Journal	Articles	Country
Cuadernos de Administración	11	Colombia
Universia Business Review	8	Spain
Revista Española de Financiación y Contabilidad – Spanish Journal of Finance and Accounting	6	Spain
Contaduría y Administración	4	Mexico
Entramado	4	Colombia
Revista Europea de Dirección y Economía de la Empresa	4	Spain
Estudios Gerenciales	3	Colombia
Investigaciones Europeas de Dirección y Economía de la Empresa	3	Spain
Revista de Ciencias Sociales	3	Venezuela
Revista Venezolana de Gerencia	3	Venezuela

Note: This table only includes journals with at least three articles published.
Source: Web of Science and Scopus

e 26.7 Most Productive Authors on Family Business Studies in Spanish

ʰor	Documents	Authors	Documents
nez Betancourt, Gonzalo	8	Guzmán Vásquez, Alexander	2
ancourt Ramírez, José Bernardo	7	Hernández Fernández, Lissette	2
ez Vergara, María Piedad	6	Herrera Madueño, Jesús	2
ano Posso, Melquicedec	4	Larrán Jorge, Manuel	2
rera Suárez, María Katiuska	3	Martín Santana, Josefa Delia	2
at, Joan María	2	Moreno Lázaro, Javier	2
tillo, Ramón Amadeo	2	Pombo Vejarano, Carlos	2
ntes Lombardo, Guadalupe	2	Sánchez Gardey, Gonzalo	2
o, Miguel Ángel	2	Trujillo Dávila, María Andrea	2
cía Pérez de Lema, Domingo	2	Vallejo Martos, Manuel Carlos	2
azález Ferrero, Maximiliano	2	Zapata Cuervo, Natalia	2

e: This table only shows authors with at least two articles/books published.

rce: Web of Science, Scopus, and Top Books

e 26.8 Most Productive Institutions on Family Business Studies in Spanish

versity	Documents	University	Documents
iversity of La Sabana, Colombia	17	The National Polytechnic Institute (IPN), Mexico	3
iversity of Las Palmas de Gran Canaria, Spain	10	Pontifical University Javeriana, Colombia	3
iversity of Los Andes, Colombia	9	University of Alicante, Spain	3
iversity of Cádiz, Spain	8	Politechnical University of Cartagena, Spain	3
onomous University of Tamaulipas, México	7	Dr. José María Luis Mora Research Institute, Mexico	2
iversity of Extremadura, Spain	7	Pontifical Catholic University of Chile, Chile	2
iversity of Burgos, Spain	6	University Autonomous of Baja California, U.S.	2
iversity of Jaén, Spain	6	Complutense University of Madrid, Spain	2
iversity of Zulia, Venezuela	6	University of Antioquía, Colombia	2
ular Autonomous University of Puebla, Mexico	5	University of Cantabria, Spain	2
iversity of León, Spain	5	University of Granada, Spain	2
iversity of Valladolid, Spain	5	University of Los Andes, Venezuela	2
iversity of Valle, Colombia	5	University Externado, Colombia	2
iversity of Navarra, Spain	5	Federal University of Sergipe, Brazil	2
iversity of A Coruña, Spain	4	National Autonomous University of Mexico, México	2
iversity of Murcia, Spain	4	University Pompeu Fabra, Spain	2
iversity of Seville, Spain	4	Pontifical University of Salamanca, Spain	2
iversity of Zaragoza, Spain	4	King Juan Carlos University, Spain	2
iversity of Málaga, Spain	3		

te: This table only shows institutions with at least two authors publishing an article or book.

rce: Web of Knowledge, Scopus, and Top Books

Table 26.8 shows the universities with more scholars publishing in family business in Spanish, which are University of La Sabana (Colombia), followed by University of Las Palmas de Gran Canaria (Spain), University of Los Andes (Colombia), and University of Cádiz (Spain). The first two universities match the home universities of the most productive scholars identified in Table 26.7, highlighting the relevance of the research groups at these institutions, one formed by Gómez-Betancourt, Betancourt-Ramírez and López-Vergara, and another by Cabrera-Suárez. In all other cases, it is not possible to identify other consolidated research groups, at least not to this date.

Results of the Relation Indicators

In this case, we propose to use the co-words technique, which identifies cluster or research topics according to their levels of development. The co-words analysis is based on a simple principle: a research specialty can be identified by the particular associations established between its keywords (Callon, Courtial, and Penan 1995). The analysis of citations involves an intrinsic delay, whereas the co-words analysis does not suffer from this limitation; therefore, it does not hamper more recent works. This last analysis requires to manually completing the search results downloaded from Web of Science and Scopus including keywords. In the cases of the articles and books that did not contain keywords, we assigned them based on the titles, abstract, and the full text of the documents.

When adding up all joint appearances and representing their relationships graphically, it is possible to identify various thematic groups or clusters. In these cases, the strength of the union of the words that comprise them is measured by a normalized index, whose value depends on both the appearance of the words individually as well as their joint appearances. This is calculated as:

$$e_{ij} = \frac{c_{ij}^2}{c_i c_j}$$

Where Cij measures the strength of association between two words i and j, and Ci and Cj are the absolute frequency of occurrence of words i and j respectively. The co-words analysis made it possible to obtain two types of results: (1) the definition of the themes present in the field and their classification within the strategic matrix in terms of their different levels of development; and (2) networks of keywords associated with each thematic cluster.

With respect to the first results, the analysis carried out identified a total of six clusters called: Performance, Continuity, Size, Culture, Family Business, and Corporate Governance. We defined the name of the cluster by the central keyword, which is the main node and therefore is better connected with the rest of the cluster's keywords. The results of the strategic matrix (see Figure 26.5) correspond to a field whose structure is mainly distributed around the first bisector (quadrant one – quadrant four), with the only exception of a cluster in quadrant two.

The first quadrant (upper right) defines the widely developed central themes. Within the same, we found the Continuity and Performance clusters. The fourth quadrant (lower left) defines the peripheral and underdeveloped themes, and here we found the Culture, Size, and Corporate Governance clusters. Finally, a Family Business cluster is identified in quadrant two (bottom right), that defines emergent topics that are important for the development of the field. Themes were not identified in quadrant three (upper left corner) that identifies peripheral but well developed themes. In summary, the field is arranged around a core of themes that are well-developed and structured and which are associated with a number of peripheral and underdeveloped themes.

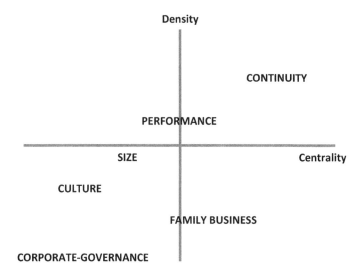

Figure 26.5 Strategic Matrix Results

Table 26.9 Main Groups of Co-words Identified Using Hierarchical Clustering Analysis

Cluster	Co-words
Continuity	Entrepreneurial family; professionalization; family-business relationship; family governance; evolution; succession; conflict
Corporate Governance	Capital structure; firm performance
Culture	Strategic management; family protocol
Family Business	Case study; value; firm; successor; competitive advantage; Spain; cost
Performance	Governance; ownership structure; panel data; ownership; family firm; boards of directors; agency cost
Size	Debt; management

The analysis of co-words has yielded networks of keywords associated with each of the previously identified clusters in the field. These networks of co-words group those keywords that best describe each of the themes present in the field, as we can see in Table 26.9. This information may be of particular interest to help future researchers to define the most important search keywords depending on the specific topic that they seek to address, as they represent the most important words that relate articles to each other and provide more information on the subject. Next, the main lines of research identified in each cluster are described:

Continuity Cluster

This cluster comprises 18 documents (19.8 percent of the total sample) and is one of the largest, a result that complies with the widely developed central themes. Relating to its evolution over time, the subject maintained a constant activity. Also, a high percentage of the documents belonged to the first period of analysis (1995–2007), including all the books present in the sample. It is important to mention that the methodologies used in the empirical studies were exclusively qualitative, and most of them were case studies from a wide geographic variety.

This cluster included five books in the sample since they constituted the precedent on the interest for this subject within Hispanic researchers. These books have served as a base for several universities' programs on family business. The authors of these books are pioneers in this field of study. Gallo and Amat wrote two books each and another book jointly, and Casillas, Díaz, and Vázquez, and Belausteguigoitia wrote the other two. All the writers are Spaniards except for the last one, who is from Mexico. Regarding the content of the books, they analyze the general problems of family businesses, with a special emphasis on the management, dynamic, and continuity of the firms; most of them included case studies. Part of the theoretical articles shared the same proposal: the need of an adequate design of government structures as a key for renovation and continuity of the family business.

The remainder of documents from this cluster was more closely related to succession problems in family businesses. The group included works that were only theoretical on its proposition, defending the need of an adequate succession planning to minimize conflicts. It also contained some empirical observations, exclusively of a qualitative nature. Within these observations, we could identify different case studies that analyzed the succession process from specific points of view like conflict among the founder and the successors, the role of expectations and family relations in the succession process, the perceptions of how a protocol can work as a tool for business continuity, or an analysis of the effect of recruiting an external CEO as a successful factor in the succession stage.

Finally, the other subjects considered within this cluster were the development of concrete activity sectors from a historic point of view, the role of female entrepreneurship and the family structure in the organization of a local productive system.

Corporate Governance Cluster

The cluster comprises six documents (6.6 percent) and, along with the Size cluster, is the shortest in the sample. Located in the fourth quadrant of the matrix, all articles included in this cluster have been published after 2010, and two-thirds of them correspond to the last period of analysis (2012–2014), indicating that the interest of the researchers for the issues included in this cluster is very recent. The documents incorporated in this cluster include literature reviews from a financial perspective (16.6 percent), most of them are quantitative studies (50 percent of the cluster), and the samples are from mixed countries or focalized in geographical areas such as Mexico or Colombia.

With regards to the analyzed subjects, these concentrate on the analysis of government practices and corporate ownership structures. On one hand, the articles examined corporate governance practices and its effects on fraud or performance. The multi-country analysis allowed an exploration of differences in the countries' policies, and it endorsed some suggestions specific for each regulatory and cultural environment. On the other hand, the articles analyzed the relationship between firm ownership structure and economic growth, finding a negative relationship between both variables. On a micro level, the explored subjects included management replacement in relation to property structure and its influence over performance.

Culture Cluster

This cluster comprises seven documents (7.7 percent) and is located in the fourth quadrant of the matrix, reflecting a slow development of the subject and most articles (85.7 percent), have been published during the second period of the analysis (2008–2011). On this cluster, the empirical works prevailed (85.7 percent) and most of them used a qualitative methodology

(66.6 percent), over those of quantitative (16.6 percent) or mixed nature (16.6 percent). The geographical location where the studies took place is varied and included Mexico, Colombia, Spain and some multi-country samples.

The identified subjects included strategic management, culture, and family businesses management. In regards to the first subject, the articles were developed through case studies, and they analyzed strategies conceived by family firms, an endowment for survival and success on the long run. The second group focused on the study of the cultural influence that family businesses have over management, internal communication or strategic direction and their results. Once again, the articles were developed through case studies. The influence of cultural aspects over the management of companies has also been studied from a macro perspective, analyzing through multi-country samples the impact that the different cultural characteristics have over concrete management issues such as remuneration policies. Lastly, the third group included works that studied family protocols as management tools, analyzing the degree of their knowledge and their implementation on family businesses, or pondering from a theoretical view its role on the generational transition in a family firm.

Family Business Cluster

This cluster comprises 33 documents (36.3 percent of the total sample), and it is the largest one; it grouped subjects identified as emergent since it was located at quadrant number two. In reference to its evolution over time, the works were concentrated on the last period; specifically 64 percent of them were published after 2010. Nineteen of the papers in this cluster are qualitative (57.6 percent) with a big variability in the number of cases (from 1 to more than 100). There are also four theoretical papers, as well as one review about knowledge in family firms, and a methodological paper related to the use of the case method in family firm research. Eight of the articles (24.2 percent) are quantitative in nature, and most of them are from Spain, except two that are from Greece and Colombia. The geographical diversity is ample since it included works that analyzed the Greek reality, the Mexican emigration to the USA, and some other cases from Colombia, Spain, Mexico or Venezuela.

In this cluster, we can identify a first subset that groups together seven papers centered in analyzing the history of different family companies, both in America and in Spain, and the way they had faced their development as enterprises in different external and family contexts. All the papers in this subset are qualitative, and most of them studied a singular case.

The second subset is integrated by five papers centered in analyzing the role of next generations, as well as their selection, education, and engagement in their family firms. In this subset, there are three qualitative Colombian papers and two empirical Spanish studies.

A third subset of papers studied the influence of family on the formation of family firm's culture. There are theoretical, qualitative, and quantitative papers, all of them recognizing the importance of values handed down to the business by the founder or/and the family.

There are four pairs of works addressing marginal issues in family firm literature such as the relationship between family and business in ethnic minorities and immigrant context; innovation in family firms; family influence on internationalization and knowledge management in family firms. Only the internationalization works are quantitative in nature while the rest are theoretical and qualitative.

Accordingly, with its emergent nature, the rest of the cluster is integrated by a variety of themes scarcely studied both in the Spanish and in the English literature, such as the paper of women in management positions, emotional intelligence, dynamic capabilities, mechanism for equity succession, and others. Most of the papers are qualitative, and the quantitative papers address the influence of family orientation on management and governance practices, the advantages of a particular corporate system and the collaboration among companies.

Performance Cluster

This cluster comprises 21 documents (23.1 percent of the total sample) and is the second largest. Eleven of the articles in this cluster have been published during the second period (2008–2011). Related to methodologies, the cluster includes a group of four review papers of the research in the field. There are also four qualitative papers, but the majority of the articles (13) employed a quantitative approach. Most studies used large samples and even (22.73 percent) used longitudinal data (all of them written by Spaniard authors, except one from Mexico). The articles in this cluster can be grouped in three main subsets, apart from the reviews previously mentioned.

The bigger subset includes 15 papers that were comparing family and non-family firms and were trying to identify differences in the impact of the familial condition on different aspects. Only two papers exploring managerial practices and employee behavior were qualitative, and in general, papers exploring managerial issues (such as international commerce, intangible resources and leadership styles) tended to employ smaller samples, due to their use of surveys. However, papers researching growth, tax, performance, financial/ownership structure and board/control issues tended to have larger samples, from listed companies and worked with longitudinal data.

The main conclusions from this first subset were that family firms tend to be smaller, to growth slower, to be more effective in the use of resources, to use technologies less intensive in capital, less tax aggressiveness and less prone to accept corporate risk, but they have similar results. In relation to the boards and the control of the managers, they tend to have fewer agency costs and the family control is found to be more effective when there is not a good protection of ownership rights in the markets. These results are in line with those obtained in other geographical context, but it is true that most of the studies use Spanish datasets and differences can arise if Latin American countries were more widely studied.

The second subset included management oriented papers, and the main conclusions were that the influence of family management can lead to different behavior in areas such as internationalization (less aggressive politics and intangible resource endowment as a source of competitive advantage in the development of their international strategies) or human resources (more balanced task/employee organizational focus and higher levels of work engagement, job satisfaction, and lower levels of mobbing).

In addition, we can identify a small third group, which only includes two qualitative papers exploring factors affecting growth in family firms.

Size Cluster

The cluster comprises six documents (6.6 percent), indicating that the aspects investigated in the cluster have been limited. All articles included in this cluster have been published along the two last periods identified and, as for the methodologies used in empirical studies (66.6 percent of the total), all of them are quantitative. All the works studied a variety of Spaniard companies and included regression analysis, path analysis, cluster analysis or analysis of panel data and time series.

One of the main characteristics of the works in this cluster is the sampling of Small and Medium-Sized Enterprises (SMEs) to explore differences in behavior, capital structure or strategic orientation. The analyzed variables included the gender of the manager, the family character of the business, the formality on strategic planning or the age of the director. In other cases, the articles explored the effect that the variable size had over the financial decisions of the family firms, or over the performance of family firms and non-family firms, finding a direct relation between risk and the family businesses managed by its founders.

A Comparison with Family Business Literature in English

The analysis of this section is completed with the comparison between the results obtained in the revision of family businesses articles published in Spanish, and the similar works that have previously done the same but for publications in English. In this case, the work with the most conceptual and methodological similarities is from Benavides-Velasco, Quintana-Garcia, and Guzman-Parra (2013), allowing a comparison between the two works. Concretely, we contrasted the methodology and the topics used in the publications.

Regarding the methodology employed in family business literature, we reviewed the 86 articles in our sample to identify aspects related to data sources, research settings, sample size, etc. Table 26.10 contains information on these methodological parameters as well as the figures obtained by Benavides-Velasco, Quintana-Garcia, and Guzman-Parra in their global review of the family business field. Of the 86 articles, 77.9 percent were categorized as empirical, while the remaining (22.1 percent) were theoretical contributions and review works. The percentage of empirical papers is larger than in Benavides-Velasco, Quintana-Garcia, and Guzman-Parra (2013) work, and the main reason may be that the theoretical roots of the field are developed and published in top academic journals published in English. However, when these main theoretical frames were applied to particular or national cases, it was more likely that the results were published in Spanish.

As for the methods of gathering information, the most common source in our sample were case studies and interviews; both associated to qualitative in nature empirical papers. This percentage was almost four times bigger than the percentage in Benavides-Velasco, Quintana-Garcia, and Guzman-Parra (2013). When the development of the family business research began demanding a broader, more multidisciplinary view with high-quality sources, the percentage of quantitative studies increased in literature in English. However, in our sample, this is not yet a reality.

As for quantitative studies in our sample, both types (survey and database) have the same percentage. This shows a duality between a big amount of qualitative studies and a bigger percentage than in the main field of the use of public information, databases, and other secondary sources, especially in papers written by researchers working at universities located in Spain. The more frequent databases used were SABI[2] and data from listed companies. These databases are of critical importance because they provide systematic and longitudinal data collection.

Related to sample size, Table 26.10 shows that the percentage of small samples is high due to the big number of qualitative studies, which tend to have smaller sample sizes. However, there are not significant differences in the percentage of medium and big samples. The big number of qualitative studies in our sample, cross-sectional in nature, explains the big percentage of this dataset in the papers reviewed.

Table 26.11 compares the results obtained by Benavides-Velasco, Quintana-Garcia, and Guzman-Parra (2013), and those of this work regarding the main topics studied in the family business literature. At first, the table shows that in both reviews the most prevalent research topics were "Succession planning/protocol/continuity," "Strategy/Management" and "Governance/Professionalization"; in all cases, the work of Benavides-Velasco, Quintana-Garcia, and Guzman-Parra (2013) had a higher weight in comparison with the literature in Spanish.

The succession research stream, which is considered one of the biggest challenges for most family firms, included studies on conflict between generations, as well as the influence of different factors, such as CEO characteristics, professionalization, affectionate and normative compromise of the successor, family dynamics, on the favorable outcome of the succession process and the financial performance of family firms. The most significant difference between both samples is the great attention that Hispanic researchers have on protocol as key instrument of generational transition in a family business.

Table 26.10 Comparative Methodological Parameters

		% Articles in Spanish	% Articles in Benavides-Velasco, Quintana-Garcia, and Guzman-Parra 2013
Article Type	Theoretical	22.1	43.7
	Empirical	77.9	56.3
	Total	100	100
Data Source	Case & Interview	40.7	11.4
	Survey	18.6	35.8
	Database	18.6	9.1
	Total	77.9	56.3
Sample Size	< 100	51.2	22.0
	>100/<400	10.4	14.6
	>400	16.3	16.1
	Unknown		3.6
	Total	77.9	56.3
Temporal Dimension	Cross-sectional	26.7	44.9
	Longitudinal	51.2	11.4
	Total	77.9	56.3

Regarding the topic of "Strategy/Management," the studies included the analysis of strategic decisions in subjects such as growth, innovation, internationalization, quality management or human resources management, among others. The descriptive character of the studies in both samples, as well as the small presence of articles with theoretical frameworks, or studying the cultural context and the size of the company as a decision factor in the literature in Spanish, are some of the theoretical and empirical aspects that could be studied in future investigations.

The third research subject shared in both samples is that of "Governance/ Professionalization," and includes aspects related to the composition and size of the board, the selection of external managers, the governance codes or the influence of property structure in aspects such as firm value creation or business performance. Benavides-Velasco, Quintana-Garcia, and Guzman-Parra (2013) argue the need to include bigger samples in the empirical studies, but it is interesting to note that our sample contained several quantitative works that handled large samples and longitudinal data, developed by researchers at universities in Spain.

The main differences between the two samples are centered on the topics "Business History and Culture," which has been showing a greater interest in the literature in Spanish with a largely descriptive treatment, and the topic of "Interpersonal Family Dynamics/Conflict," which has been underdeveloped in our sample. Also notable is the existence of a topic "Review of the Field/Methodology" clearly identified in the literature in Spanish but non-existent in Benavides-Velasco, Quintana-Garcia, and Guzman-Parra (2013) work. The topics "Business Performance and Work," "Gender and Ethnicity," and "Financial management/capital, market/ liquidity, and fiscal issues" are the other thematic areas of interest by scholars in both samples.

Finally, the "Other Subjects" category encompasses a range of issues scarcely addressed by the literature, and therefore could be the subject of further research in the future. In the work of Benavides-Velasco, Quintana-Garcia, and Guzman-Parra (2013) this category is composed of 20.9 percent of the analyzed documents, a higher percentage than those from the Spanish sample (15.1 percent). The topics included in this category were aspects such as entrepreneurship/

Table 26.11 Primary Topics Covered (Benavides-Velasco, Quintana-Garcia, and Guzman-Parra 2013 Versus Web of Science and Scopus)

Topics	Articles in Spanish	% Articles in Spanish	% Articles Benavides-Velasco, Quintana-Garcia, and Guzman-Parra 2013
Succession planning/Protocol/Continuity	11	12.8	17.4
Strategy management/Organizational change/Management	11	12.8	19.3
Business history	9	10.5	2.1
Governance (boards, directors, governance codes)/Professionalization	8	9.3	10.6
Business performance and growth	6	7.0	6.4
Review of the field, methodology	8	9.3	n.a.
Culture	6	7.0	1.3
Interpersonal family dynamics/Conflict	5	5.8	10.3
Gender and ethnicity	5	5.8	3.6
Financial management/Capital market/ Liquidity and fiscal issues	4	4.6	7.2
Other subjects	13	15.1	20.9
Total	**86**	**100**	**100**

innovation, human resource management, internationalization and globalization, family business education and consulting, state and tax planning or distinctiveness and competitive advantage of family firms. Additionally, topics such as corporate social responsibility and ethics marketing, production, and macro systems were found in this section but only addressed on the papers written in English.

Conclusions

This chapter aimed to identify and describe the patterns and trends in the family firm literature published in Spanish, with the purpose of obtaining a general knowledge of the size and characteristics of the research in this language, one of the three most important in the world. Our study identified the countries, individuals, research groups, academic institutions, and journals that have contributed the most to family business research in Spanish, as well as the topics of interest that scholars have investigated.

In doing that, we carried out a general analysis of the papers published in Spanish on scientific journals included in the Dialnet database, as well as a bibliometric analysis of the papers published in Spanish in scientific journals included in the Social Science Citation Index and in Scopus. In an attempt to overcome the limitation of reviewing only journal papers, we included in our bibliometric analysis a number of highly cited books, which are alternative and perhaps equally effective ways to support the development of the field (Sharma et al. 2007; Debicki et al. 2009). Diverse measures and indicators were used to describe the evolution of the production and the structure of the field. A number of conclusions spring from the analysis.

Firstly, there is a time lag between the first scientific family firm papers published in English in the 1960s and the appearance of the first paper in Spanish published in Dialnet (1982) and in Web of Science and Scopus (1999).

Secondly, Spain is the country with more publications in all the analyzed databases, a fact that could be explained by the abundant existence of university Chairs coordinated by the Spaniard

Institute of Family Business (Instituto de la Empresa Familiar). Spain is also the country that has the highest number of productive journals in Dialnet, although its presence is scarce in Web of Science and Scopus. There is also a reduction in the presence of Spaniard researchers publishing in Spanish in Web of Science and Scopus, a fact that could be explained with the bias that the Spaniard university system has on publishing in journals issued in English and with higher rankings. In summary, the researchers are concentrated in four countries, coinciding with the nationality of the journals with the most articles regarding family business within the Hispanic community: Spain, Colombia, Venezuela, and Mexico.

Thirdly, there are two consolidated research groups that systematically publish in Spanish. One is headed by Cabrera-Suarez from the University of Las Palmas in Gran Canaria (Spain), who is also mentioned in the analysis made by Debicki et al. (2009). Gómez-Betancourt, Betancourt-Ramírez and López-Vergara from the University of La Sabana (Colombia) integrate the second group. In both cases, the research on family business constitutes their main line of research. In the case of Spain, the absence of additional specialized groups can be explained by the bias, explained before, towards English publications. It could also be justified with the fact that research on family business is a novel subject, initiated in parallel with the appearance of the university Chairs on the subject and with a coexistence with more traditional lines of research.

Fourthly, in the case of Spain, there are consolidated research groups that publish in English (Meroño-Cerdán and Nieto-Sánchez 2015). The results obtained for the case of Latin American countries indicate a need to promote the subject among the countries where the research activity is null. Our results suggest that family business research centers or Chairs could be a good way to develop this research area. However, it is even more important that universities provide an adequate environment to these centers in terms of funding, along with control and evaluation of the research results and the existence of networks (Debicki et al. 2009).

Regarding support to publish in the Spanish language, this is scattered among different journals, with only one journal specialized in family business. However, it has recently changed its language politics to begin publications in English, facilitating its access to international indexes.

The bibliometric analysis indicates that the field is structured around a core of themes that are well developed and structured (Continuity and Performance clusters), which are associated with a number of peripheral and underdeveloped themes (Culture, Size, and Corporate Governance clusters). Finally, the Family Business cluster group provides an interesting number of emergent topics.

Concerning the content analysis of the study, our review of research areas using the topic classification employed by Benavides-Velasco, Quintana-Garcia, and Guzman-Parra (2013), revealed parallelisms with the main topics and a smaller variety of the secondary topics. This is an indication of the underdevelopment of applied studies to some of the subjects published in English. Regarding methodological issues, we agree with Benavides-Velasco, Quintana-Garcia, and Guzman-Parra (2013) in the need of performing more longitudinal analyses that allow testing the evolution and causality of the variables over time. However, in our case, we also suggest that future research utilize a larger number of quantitative studies and bigger sample sizes for both quantitative and qualitative studies; we further believe that an effort must be made in order to develop theories that had better reflect Latin American reality and particularities.

Lastly, it is noteworthy to mention the difficulty of maintaining literature strongly founded on a theoretical and empirical point of view and written in Spanish. This is true for the journals publishing in Spanish, which have obstacles to enter, maintain, and progress in the international indexes. It is also a reality for the researchers because of the implementation of evaluation systems based on international indicators, increasing the quality of their publications, but decreasing their production in Spanish.

We recognize some limitations of this study. First, the co-word analysis provided a small number of significant clusters taking into account the number of keywords considered. This result could be explained by the high fragmentation of the literature on family business (Casillas and Acedo 2007; Benavides-Velasco, Quintana-García, and Guzmán-Parra 2013). Besides, this study focused on a group of bibliometric indicators and techniques to examine and measure contributions, but other objective indicators, such as the impact of the authors' individual publications and classification methods and schemes, could improve future research.

Articles		Cluster
1	Andrade C., Jesús Alberto. 2002. "Sucesión en la Empresa Familiar: Su Futuro cuando la Muerte se Acerca." *Revista Venezolana de Gerencia* 7 (19):375–389.	Continuity
2	Arenas Cardona, Henry Antonio, and Daniela Rico-Balvín. 2014. "La Empresa Familiar, el Protocolo y la Sucesión Familiar." *Estudios Gerenciales* 30 (132):252–258.	Continuity
3	Bañegil Palacios, Tomás Manuel, Remedios Hernández Linares, and Cristina Barriuso Iglesias. 2012. "El Protocolo Familiar y Sus Instrumentos de Desarrollo en las Empresas Familiares de Extremadura." *Tourism & Management Studies* 8:139–150.	Culture
4	Baracaldo-Lozano, Natalia Andrea. 2013. "Diagnóstico de Gobierno Corporativo como Mecanismo en la Prevención del Fraude en Empresas Familiares (Aplicación de Método de Casos)." *Cuadernos de Contabilidad* 14 (35):581–615.	Corporate Governance
5	Barbeito Roibal, Susana, Eduardo Guillén Solórzano, Manuel Martínez Carballo, and Gerardo Domínguez Feijoó. 2006. "El Criterio de Elección del Sucesor en las Empresas Familiares Gallegas." *Revista Galega de Economía* 15 (2):81–96.	Family Business
6	Barros-Contreras, Ismael, Juan Hernangómez-Barahona, and Natalia Martín-Cruz. 2014. "La Familiaridad Dinámica de las Empresas Familiares. El Caso del Grupo Yllera." *Universia Business Review* 42:88–109.	Family Business
7	Barros Nock, Magdalena. 2007. "El Matrimonio y las Pequeñas Empresas Comerciales: El Caso de los Salvadoreños y Mexicanos en Los Ángeles." *Revista Mexicana de Sociología* 69 (1):109–138.	Family Business
8	Basco, Rodrigo. 2010. "Tipo de Orientación Familiar y Prácticas de Dirección de Gobierno: Un Estudio Aplicado a las Empresas Familiares Españolas." *Revista Europea de Dirección y Economía de la Empresa* 19 (2):129–144.	Family Business
9	Benavides Velasco, Carlos A., Vanesa F. Guzmán Parra, and Cristina Quintana García. 2011. "Evolución de la Literatura sobre Empresa Familiar como Disciplina Científica." *Cuadernos de Economía y Dirección de la Empresa* 14 (2):78–90.	Performance
10	Betancourt Ramírez, José Bernardo, Gonzalo Gómez Betancourt, María Piedad López Vergara, Francisco Pamplona Beltrán, and Claudia Beltrán Ruget. 2013. "Ventajas y Desventajas de la Sociedad por Acciones Simplificada para la Empresa Familiar en Colombia. Estudio Exploratorio." *Estudios Gerenciales* 29 (127):213–221.	Family Business
11	Blanco Mazagatos, Virginia, Esther de Quevedo Puente, and Juan Bautista Delgado García. 2009. "La Estructura Financiera de la Empresa Familiar: El Cambio Generacional." *Revista Española de Financiación y Contabilidad-Spanish Journal of Finance and Accounting* 38 (141):57–73.	Performance

(Continued)

Articles	Cluster
12 Bona Sánchez, Carolina, Jerónimo Pérez Alemán, and Domingo Javier Santana Martín. 2009. "Capacidad Informativa de los Resultados Contables en la Empresa Familiar." *Cuadernos de Gestión* 9 (2):17–30.	Performance
13 Cabrera Suárez, María Katiuska, and Arístides Olivares Mesa. 2012. "La Influencia de los Recursos de Capital Humano, Social y Financiero sobre la Velocidad del Proceso Exportador de las Empresas Familiares." *Revista Europea de Dirección y Economía de la Empresa* 21 (4):306–315.	Family Business
14 Cabrera Suárez, María Katiuska, and Josefa Delia Martín Santana. 2010. "La Influencia de las Relaciones Intergeneracionales en la Formación y el Compromiso del Sucesor: Efectos sobre el Proceso de Sucesión en la Empresa Familiar." *Revista Europea de Dirección y Economía de la Empresa* 19 (2):111–128.	Family Business
15 Cabrera Suárez, María Katiuska, María de la Cruz Déniz Déniz, and Josefa Delia Martín Santana. 2011. "Consejos de Administración y Potencial para la Responsabilidad Social de las Empresas Familiares No Cotizadas Españolas." *Investigaciones Europeas de Dirección y Economía de la Empresa* 17 (3):47–67.	Performance
16 Castillo, Ramón A. 2002. "Protección de los Derechos de Propiedad y Selección de la Estructura de Propiedad Corporativa." *Trimestre Económico* 69 (273):37–63.	Performance
17 Castrillo Lara, Luis Ángel, and Juan Manuel San Martín Reyna. 2007. "La Propiedad Familiar como Mecanismo de Gobierno Disciplinador de la Dirección en las Empresas Mexicanas: Una Evidencia Empírica." *Contaduría y Administración* 222:59–82.	Performance
18 Caula, Elsa. 2013. "Sociabilidades Mercantiles y Prácticas Comerciales de los Mercaderes Vascos en el Buenos Aires Virreinal." *Caravelle. Cahiers du Monde Hispanique et Luso-Brésilien* 101:193–216.	Continuity
19 Ceja, Lucía, Jordi Escartín, and Álvaro Rodríguez-Carballeira. 2012. "Contextos Organizativos que Fomentan el Comportamiento Positivo y el Bienestar de los Trabajadores: Una Comparación entre Empresas Familiares y No Familiares." *Revista de Psicología Social* 27 (1):69–84.	Performance
20 Cercós, Mabel. 2013. "Castro Hermanos. El Éxito de una Empresa Familiar Vitivinícola de San Juan Durante el Primer Peronismo." *Revista de Historia Americana y Argentina* 48 (1):135–157.	Family Business
21 Chiner, Alfonso. 2011. "La Necesidad de un Buen Gobierno de la Familia en las Empresas Familiares." *Universia Business Review* 32:102–110.	Continuity
22 Claver Cortés, Enrique, Laura Rienda García, and Diego Quer Ramón. 2008. "Factores Familiares y Compromiso Internacional: Evidencia Empírica en Empresas Españolas." *Cuadernos de Economía y Dirección de la Empresa* 35 (2): 7–25.	Family Business
23 Del Pozo, José. 2004. "Los Empresarios del Vino en Chile y su Aporte a la Transformación de la Agricultura, de 1870 a 1930." *Universum (Talca)* 19 (2):12–27.	Family Business
24 Díez Esteban, José María, Conrado Diego García Gómez, and Félix J. López-Iturriaga. 2013. "Evidencia Internacional sobre la Influencia de los Grandes Accionistas en el Riesgo Corporativo." *Revista Española de Financiación y Contabilidad-Spanish Journal of Finance and Accounting* 42 (160):487–511.	Performance
25 Echaiz Moreno, Daniel. 2010. "El Protocolo Familiar. La Contractualización en las Familias Empresarias para la Gestión de las Empresas Familiares." *Boletín Mexicano de Derecho Comparado* 127:101–130.	Culture

Articles		Cluster
26	Esparza Aguilar, José Luis, and Domingo García Pérez de Lema. 2011. "La Cultura de las Empresas Familiares Turísticas Mexicanas y su Influencia en la Gestión Estratégica." *Cuadernos de Administración* 24 (42):295–313.	Culture
27	Espinoza Aguiló, Tomás Ignacio, and Nicolás Felipe Espinoza Aguiló. 2012. "El Desempeño de las Empresas Familiares: Evidencias del Caso Mexicano." *Cuadernos de Administración* 25 (44):39–61.	Corporate Governance
28	Fuentes Lombardo, Guadalupe, María Jesús Hernández Ortiz, and Manuel Carlos Vallejo Martos. 2008. "Razones para Crecer en la Empresa Familiar: Un Análisis Comparativo." *Investigaciones Europeas de Dirección y Economía de la Empresa* 14 (3):15–34.	Performance
29	Fuentes-Lombardo, Guadalupe, Rubén Fernández-Ortiz, and Miriam Cano-Rubio. 2011. "Intangibles en la Internacionalización de las Bodegas Españolas: Percepción Directiva y Comparada entre Empresas Familiares y No Familiares." *Intangible Capital* 7 (2):428–473.	Performance
30	Galve-Górriz, Carmen, and Vicente Salas-Fumás. 2011. "Determina la propiedad familiar diferencias en las relaciones entre preferencias, comportamiento y resultados en las empresas españolas cotizadas?." *Revista de Economia Aplicada* 19 (57): 5–34.	Performance
31	García Berumen González, José, Pablo García Soto, and Rogerio Domenge Muñoz. 2012. "Determinantes de la Estructura de Capital en la Pequeña y Mediana Empresa Familiar en México." *Contaduría y Administración* 57 (3):67–96.	Size
32	García-Borbolla Fernández, Amalia, Jesús Herrera Madueño, Manuel Larrán Jorge, Gonzalo Sánchez Gardey, and Alfonso Suárez Llorens. 2009. "Análisis Empírico de la Influencia de la Propiedad Familiar sobre la Orientación Estratégica de las Pequeñas y Medianas Empresas." *Investigaciones Europeas de Dirección y Economía de la Empresa* 15 (1):45–59.	Size
33	García-Meneses, Erika, María de Lourdes Rodríguez-Espinosa, and Ramón A. Castillo-Ponce. 2012. "Estructura de Propiedad Corporativa y Crecimiento Económico." *Innovar* 23(49):31–39.	Corporate Governance
34	García-Ramos, Rebeca, and Myriam García Olalla. 2011. "La Estructura de la Junta Directiva de las Empresas Familiares Frente a las No Familiares: La Evidencia Empírica en España." *Revista Española de Financiación y Contabilidad-Spanish Journal of Finance and Accounting* 40 (149):35–64.	Performance
35	García Solarte, Mónica, Domingo García Pérez de Lema, and Antonia Madrid Guijarro. 2012. "Caracterización del Comportamiento de las Pymes según el Género del Gerente: Un Estudio Empírico." *Cuadernos de Administración* 28 (47):37–52.	Size
36	Garza Ramos, María Isabel, José Melchor Medina Quintero, Nazlhe Faride Cheín Schekaibán, Karla Paola Jiménez Almaguer, Jannett Ayup González, and José Guillermo Díaz Figueroa. 2011. "Los Valores Familiares y la Empresa Familiar en el Nordeste de México." *Cuadernos de Administración* 24 (42):315–333.	Family Business
37	Gómez, Diana Marcela, and Kewy Sarsosa Prowesk. 2011. "Características de la Cultura Organizacional y Comunicación Interna en una Comercializadora de Lácteos de Cali." *Pensamiento Psicológico* 9 (17):57–68.	Culture

(Continued)

Articles	Cluster
38 Gómez-Betancourt, Gonzalo, and Natalia Zapata-Cuervo. 2013. "Gobierno Corporativo: Una Comparación de Códigos de Gobierno en el Mundo, un Modelo para Empresas Latinoaméricanas Familiares y No Familiares." *Entramado* 9 (2):98–117.	Corporate Governance
39 Gómez-Betancourt, Gonzalo, José Bernardo Betancourt Ramírez, and Natalia Zapata Cuervo. 2012. "Empresas Familiares Multigeneracionales." *Entramado* 8 (2):38–49.	Family Business
40 Gómez-Betancourt, Gonzalo, José Bernardo Betancourt Ramírez, and María Piedad López Vergara. 2013. "Factores que Influyen en la Inteligencia Emocional de los Miembros de una Empresa Familiar." *Entramado* 9 (1):12–25.	Family Business
41 Gómez-Betancourt, Gonzalo, María Piedad López Vergara, and José Bernardo Betancourt Ramírez. 2008. "Estudio Exploratorio de los Factores que Influyen en la Selección de un Mecanismo de Sucesión Patrimonial en las Empresas Familiares Colombianas." *Cuadernos de Administración* 21 (37):269–292.	Family Business
42 Gómez-Betancourt, Gonzalo, María Piedad López Vergara, and José Bernardo Betancourt Ramírez. 2009. "Estudio Exploratorio sobre la Influencia de la Visión Familiar y la Visión Patrimonial en el Crecimiento en Ventas de la Empresa Familiar Colombiana." *Cuadernos de Administración* 22 (39):163–190.	Performance
43 Gómez-Betancourt, Gonzalo, María Pilar López Vergara, José Bernardo Betancourt Ramírez, and Javier Olmedo Millán Payán. 2012. "Estudio sobre el Desempeño de las Empresas Familiares Colombianas que Cotizan en la Bolsa de Valores, Frente a las Empresas No Familiares." *Entramado* 8 (1):28–42.	Performance
44 González Ferrero, Maximiliano, Alexander Guzmán Vásquez, Carlos Pombo Bejarano, and María Andrea Trujillo Dávila. 2010. "Empresas Familiares: Revisión de la Literatura desde una Perspectiva de Agencia." *Cuadernos de Administración* 23 (40):11–33.	Performance
45 González Ferrero, Maximiliano, Alexander Guzmán Vásquez, Carlos Pombo Vejarano, and María Andrea Trujillo Dávila. 2011. "Revisión de la literatura de empresas familiares: una perspectiva financiera." *Academia. Revista Latinoamericana de Administración* 47 :18–42	Corporate Governance
46 Hernández Fernández, Lissette. 2007. "Competencias Esenciales para las Pequeñas y Medianas Empresas Familiares: Un Modelo para el Éxito Empresarial." *Revista de Ciencias Sociales* 13 (2):249–263.	Family Business
47 Herrera Madueño, Jesús, Manuel Larrán Jorge, and Gonzalo Sánchez Gardey. 2012. "Una Propuesta Metodológica para el Análisis de la Eficiencia en la PYME." *Revista Española de Financiación y Contabilidad-Spanish Journal of Finance and Accounting* 41 (154):291–307.	Size
48 Jiménez, Magda, and Henri Piña Zambrano. 2011. "Capital Social en Empresas Familiares." *Revista Venezolana de Gerencia* 16 (54):255–273.	Family Business
49 López Castro, Natalia. 2009. "Cuando la Persistencia es una Cuestión de Familia: Relaciones Familiares, Traspaso y Género en Explotaciones Agropecuarias del Sudoeste Bonaerense (198 7–2007)." *Mundo Agrario* 10 (19).	Continuity
50 López Vergara, María Piedad, Gonzalo Gómez-Betancourt, and José Bernardo Betancourt Ramírez. 2011. "Factores que Influyen en la Participación de las Mujeres en Puestos de Dirección y Órganos de Gobierno de las Empresas Familiares Colombianas." *Cuadernos de Administración* 24 (42):231–252.	Family Business

Articles	Cluster
51	Lozano Posso, Melquicedec. 2011. "El Modelo IEI, un Nuevo Concepto en la Vinculación de Potenciales Sucesores a la Empresa Familiar." *Cuadernos de Administración* 24 (42):275–293.	Family Business
52	Lozano Posso, Melquicedec. 2008. "Elementos del Proceso de Formación de Descendientes Antes de su Vinculación a la Empresa Familiar: Un Estudio de Casos Colombianos." *Cuadernos de Administración* 21 (37):243–268.	Family Business
53	Lozano Posso, Melquicedec. 2009. "Elementos para la Consultoría en Empresas Familiares." *Pensamiento & Gestión* 26:214–237.	Family Business
54	Lozano Posso, Melquicedec, and David Urbano. 2010. "Primer Empleo a Jornada Completa de Descendientes de la Empresa Familiar. Un Estudio Cualitativo en Colombia." *Revista Venezolana de Gerencia* 15 (50):183–206.	Family Business
55	Macho Morales, Elisa Antonia, and Rocío Rosales Ortega. 2011. "Empresarialidad Femenina y Redes Sociales en San Pedro Tultepec de Quiroga, estado de México." *Cuadernos de Geografía: Revista Colombiana de Geografía* 20 (1):85–101.	Continuity
56	Marcelino Aranda, Mariana, Francisco Alfredo Baldazo Molotla, and Oscar Valdés Nieto. 2012. "El Método del Estudio de Caso para Estudiar las Empresas Familiares," *Pensamiento & Gestión* 33:125–139.	Family Business
57	Meira Teixeira, Rivanda, and Felipe Carvalhal. 2013. "Sucesión y Conflictos en Empresas Familiares: Estudio de Casos Múltiples en Pequeñas Empresas Hoteleras." *Estudios y Perspectivas en Turismo* 22 (5):854–874.	Continuity
58	Miralles Marcelo, José Luis, María del Mar Miralles Quirós, and Inés Lisboa. 2012. "Empresa Familiar y Bolsa: Análisis de Rentabilidad y Estrategias de Inversión." *Revista Española de Financiación y Contabilidad-Spanish Journal of Finance and Accounting* 41 (155):393–416.	Size
59	Molins, Casimiro. 2011. "Cementos Molins: Una Empresa Familiar y Casi Centenaria." *Universia Business Review* 32:132–138.	Family Busines
60	Monterrey Mayoral, Juan, and Amparo Sánchez Segura. 2010. "Diferencias en Agresividad Fiscal entre Empresas Familiares y No Familiares." *Revista Española de Financiación y Contabilidad-Spanish Journal of Finance And Accounting* 39 (145):65–97.	Performance
61	Moreno Lázaro, Javier. 2009. "La Formación de la Gran Empresa Galletera Mexicana, 1907–2007." *Historia Mexicana* 58 (3):1045–1092.	Continuity
62	Moreno-Lázaro, Javier. 2009. "Las Estrategias de Expansión de una Empresa Familiar Catalana: Agrolimen, 1937–2007." *Revista de Historia Industrial* 41:49–89.	Family Business
63	Navarro de Granadillo, Ketty. 2008. "Estado Actual de la Investigación sobre la Gestión del Conocimiento en la Empresa Familiar." *Revista de Ciencias Sociales* 14 (1):30–45.	Family Business
64	Nueno, Pedro. 2011. "Iniciativa Emprendedora y Empresa Familiar: Emprendiendo a través de Generaciones." *Universia Business Review* 32:96–101.	Continuity
65	Omaña Guerrero, Lenix Margarita, and María Auxiliadora Briceño Barrios. 2013. "Gerencia de las Empresas Familiares y No Familiares: Análisis Comparativo." *Estudios Gerenciales* 29 (128):293–302.	Performance
66	Ortiz García, Pilar, and Ángel José Olaz Capitán. 2015. "La Mujer en la Empresa Familiar Española desde la Perspectiva del Familiness." *Política y Sociedad* 51 (2):481–506.	Family Business

(Continued)

Articles	Cluster
67	Pablo Cereceda, Felipe de. 1999. "La Empresa Gráfica Familiar: Cómo Hacer el Relevo Generacional." *Gráficas: Revista Técnica de las Artes del Libro* 663:494–499.	Continuity
68	Pedraja Iglesias, Marta, and Mercedes Marzo Navarro. 2014. "Desarrollo del Enoturismo desde la Perspectiva de las Bodegas Familiares." *Cuadernos de Turismo* 34:415.	Family Business
69	Pureco Ornelas, Alfredo. 2010. "Prácticas y Estrategias Empresariales en el Sector Arrocero. Los Cusi en Michoacán (México), 1884–1915." *América Latina en la Historia Económica* 34:67–92.	Culture
70	Raventós, María del Mar. 2011. "Codorníu, la Historia de una Familia que Elabora Vinos desde Hace Quinientos Años." *Universia Business Review* 32:126–131.	Family Business
71	Rodríguez Díaz, M. del Rosario. 2008. "Negocios de Familia: Valores Específicos de su Esencia." *International Journal of Interdisciplinary Social Sciences* 3 (1):275–284.	Continuity
72	Rodríguez Romero, Carlos Alberto, and Edison Jair Duque Oliva. 2008. "El Grupo Santodomingo: El Pez Chico se Come al Grande de Generación en Generación." *Innovar* 18 (32):127–152.	Culture
73	Rodríguez-Suárez, Pedro Manuel, Beatriz Pico-González, and Francisco Javier Méndez-Ramírez. 2013. "Capacidad Innovadora en la Empresa Familiar como Área de Oportunidad hacia el Desarrollo de México." *Economía, Sociedad y Territorio* 13 (43):779–794.	Family Business
74	Romero B., Jenny, Lissette Hernández, and Neida Bracho. 2012. "Comparación de la Actividad Exportadora Entre Empresas Familiares y No Familiares de la Región Zuliana en Venezuela." *Revista de Ciencias Sociales* 18 (3):553–565.	Performance
75	Saiz Álvarez, José Manuel, and Beatriz Olalla Caballero. 2010. "Gestión del Conocimiento y Sistemas de Calidad en los Clusters de Empresas Familiares." *Revista Escuela de Administración de Negocios* 68:70–85.	Size
76	San Román, Elena. 2009. "Un Zaibatsu Fuera de Lugar: Los Orígenes del Grupo Fierro (1870–1939)." *Revista de Historia Económica* 27 (3):499–532.	Family Business
77	Sánchez Marín, Gregorio, Antonio José Carrasco Hernández, and Sergio Manuel Madero Gómez. 2011. "Retribución de los Empleados en la Empresa Familiar: Un Análisis Comparativo Regional España-México." *Cuadernos de Administración* 23 (41):37–59.	Culture
78	Serna, María Guadalupe. 2012. "Empresas Familiares Frente a las Crisis." *Economía, Sociedad y Territorio* 12 (38):43–80.	Continuity
79	Serra, José María. 2011. "Grupo Catalana Occidente: Una Empresa Familiar entre los Mayores Grupos Aseguradores Españoles." *Universia Business Review* 32:120–125.	Family Business
80	Soto Maciel, Argentina. 2013. "La Empresa Familiar en México. Situación Actual de la Investigación." *Contaduría y Administración* 58 (2):135–171.	Performance
81	Tàpies, Josep. 2011. "Empresa Familiar: Un Enfoque Interdisciplinario." *Universia Business Review* 32:12–25.	Performance
82	Vallejo Martos, Manuel Carlos. 2009. "Liderazgo Transformacional y Sus Efectos en Las Empresas Familiares: Un Análisis Diferencial y Evolutivo." *Revista Europea de Dirección y Economía de la Empresa* 18 (1):105–122.	Performance
83	Villares Varela, María. 2012. "¿Gracias al Negocio o a Pesar del Negocio? La Intersección entre Familia y Empresa para los Emprendedores Inmigrantes en Galicia." *Papers: Revista de Sociología*, 97:641–660.	Family Business

Articles	Cluster
84	Watkins Fassler, Karen, and Martín Dávila Delgado. 2012. "Reemplazos de Directivos en México: de la Teoría a la Práctica." *Contaduría y Administración* 57 (1):13–28.	Corporate Governance
85	Zouboulakis, Michel S., and John Kamarianos. 2002. "Racionalidad y Cooperación entre Firmas. Examen del Comportamiento Habitual de las Industrias Griegas." *Revista de Economía Institucional* 4 (7):98–113.	Family Business
86	Zuñiga-Vicente, José Ángel, and María Sacristán-Navarro. 2009. "Los directivos externos y la sucesión en la empresa familiar: un caso de estudio." *Universia Business Review* 22:74–87.	Continuity

Books	Cluster
87	Amat, Joan María. 1998. *La Continuidad de la Empresa Familiar.* Barcelona: Gestión 2000.	Continuity
88	Belausteguigoita, Imanol. 2006. *Empresas Familiares. Su Dinámica, Equilibrio y Consolidación.* México: McGraw-Hill.	Continuity
89	Casillas, José Carlos, Carmen Díaz, and Adolfo Vázquez. 2005. *La Gestión de la Empresa Familiar. Conceptos, Casos y Soluciones.* Madrid: Thomson Editores.	Continuity
90	Gallo, Miguel Ángel. 1995. *Empresa Familiar. Texto y Casos.* Barcelona: Editorial Praxis.	Continuity
91	Gallo, Miguel Ángel, and Joan María Amat. 2003. *Los Secretos de las Empresas Familiares Centenarias: Claves del Éxito de las Empresas Familiares Multigeneracionales.* Barcelona: Ediciones Deusto.	Continuity

Note: This table literally collects the data contained in published articles. There are three cases in which, even though the names of the authors are slightly different, they correspond to the same person: Carlos Pombo Bejarano (44) and Carlos Pombo Vejarano (45); Lissette Hernández Fernández (46) and Lissette Hernández (74); Ramón A. Castillo (16) and Ramón A. Castillo-Ponce (33).

Notes

1 Latindex is a regional cooperative online information system for scholarly journals from Latin America, the Caribbean, Spain, and Portugal. Latindex is composed of three main features: Directory, Catalogue, and Index. Journals must fulfill certain criteria to be included in this catalogue. More information at: http://digital.csic.es/handle/10261/20851.
2 SABI (Sistema de Análisis de Balances Ibéricos, Analysis System of Spanish Balance Sheets) database is an enhanced version of Amadeus for Spain and Portugal provided by Bureau Van Dijk.

References

Andrade C., Jesus Alberto. 2002. "Sucesion en la Empresa Familiar: Su Futuro cuando la Muerte se Acerca." *Revista Venezolana de Gerencia* 7(19):375–389.

Banegil Palacios, Tomas Manuel, Remedios Hernández-Linares, and Cristina Barriuso Iglesias. 2012. "El Protocolo Familiar y Sus Instrumentos de Desarrollo en las Empresas Familiares de Extremadura." *Tourism & Management Studies* 8:139–150.

Benavides-Velasco, Carlos A., Cristina Quintana-García, and Vanesa F. Guzmán-Parra. 2013. "Trends in Family Business Research." *Small Business Economics* 40 (1) (August): 41–57. doi:10.1007/s11187-011-9362-3. http://link.springer.com/10.1007/s11187-011-9362-3.

Bird, Barbara, Harold Welsch, Joseph H. Astrachan, and David Pistrui. 2002. "Family Business Research: The Evolution of an Academic Field." *Family Business Review* 15 (4) (December): 337–350. doi:10.1111/j.1741-6248.2002.00337.x. http://fbr.sagepub.com/cgi/ doi/10.1111/j.1741-6248.2002.00337.x.

Callon, Michel, Jean Pierre Courtial, and Hervé Penan. 1995. *Cienciometría. La Medición de La Actividad Científica: De la Bibliometría a la Vigilancia Tecnológica.* Gijón: Ediciones Trea.

Casillas, José C., and Francisco Acedo. 2007. "Evolution of the Intellectual Structure of Family Business Literature: A Bibliometric Study of FBR." *Family Business Review* 20 (2) (June): 141–162. doi:10.1111/j.1741-6248.2007.00092.x. http://onlinelibrary.wiley.com/doi/ 10.1111/j.1741-6248.2007.00092.x/full.

Castillo, Ramon A. 2002. "Proteccion de los Derechos de Propiedad y Seleccion de la Estructura de Propiedad Corporativa." *Trimestre Económico* 69 (273):37–63.

Chrisman, James J., Jess H. Chua, Franz W. Kellermanns, Curtis F. Matherne III, and Bart J. Debicki. 2008. "Management Journals as Venues for Publication of Family Business Research." *Entrepreneurship Theory and Practice* 32 (5) (September): 927–934. doi:10.1111/j.1540-6520.2008.00263.x. http://doi.wiley.com/10.1111/j.1540-6520.2008. 00263.x.

Chrisman, James J., Jess H. Chua, and Pramodita Sharma. 2003. "Current Trends and Future Directions in Family Business Management Studies: Toward a Theory of the Family Firm." *Coleman White Paper Series.*

Debicki, Bart J., Curtis F. Matherne, Franz W. Kellermanns, and James J. Chrisman. 2009. "Family Business Research in the New Millennium: An Overview of the Who, the Where, the What, and the Why." *Family Business Review* 22 (2) (April): 151–166. doi:10.1177/0894486509333598. http://fbr.sagepub.com/content/22/2/151.short.

Gallo, Miguel Ángel. 1995. *Empresa Familiar. Texto y Casos.* Barcelona: Editorial Praxis.

Gallo, Miguel Angel, and Alvaro Vilaseca. 1996. "Finance in Family Business." *Family Business Review* 9 (4) (December): 387–401. doi:10.1111/j.1741-6248.1996.00387.x. http://fbr.sagepub.com/cgi/doi/10.1111/j.1741-6248.1996.00387.x.

Gallo, Miguel Ángel, and Carlos García-Pont. 1989. "La Empresa Familiar en la Economía Española." *Papeles de Economía Española* 39: 67–85.

———. 1996. "Important Factors in Family Business Internationalization." *Family Business Review* 9 (1) (March): 45–59. doi:10.1111/j.1741-6248.1996.00045.x. http://fbr.sagepub.com/cgi/doi/10.1111/j.1741-6248.1996.00045.x.

López-Fernández, Mª. Concepción, Ana Mª. Serrano-Bedia, and Marta Pérez-Pérez. 2016. "Entrepreneurship and Family Firm Research: A Bibliometric Analysis of an Emerging Field." *Journal of Small Business Management* 54(2) (April): 622–639. doi:10.1111/jsbm.12161. http://doi.wiley.com/10.1111/jsbm.12161.

Meroño-Cerdán, Ángel L., and M. Jesús Nieto-Sánchez. 2015. *25 Años de Historia. Evolución de la Investigación en Economía Y Dirección de la Empresa en España.* Alcalá de Henares: Asociación Científica de Economía y Dirección de la Empresa (ACEDE).

Mesanza, Bernardo de. 1982. "La Empresa Familiar." *Agricultura: Revista Agropecuaria* (596): 219–220.

Shanker, Melissa C., and Joseph H. Astrachan. 1996. "Myths and Realities: Family Businesses' Contribution to the US Economy-A Framework for Assessing Family Business Statistics." *Family Business Review* 9 (2) (June): 107–123. doi:10.1111/j.1741-6248.1996.00107.x. http://fbr.sagepub.com/cgi/doi/10.1111/j.1741-6248.1996.00107.x.

Sharma, Pramodita. 2004. "An Overview of the Field of Family Business Studies: Current Status and Directions for the Future." *Family Business Review* 17 (1) (March): 1–36. http://dx.doi.org/10.1111/j.1741-6248.2004.00001.x.

Sharma, Pramodita, Frank Hoy, Joseph H. Astrachan, and Matti Koiranen. 2007. "The Practice-Driven Evolution of Family Business Education." *Journal of Business Research* 60 (10) (October): 1012–1021. doi:10.1016/j.jbusres.2006.12.010. http://linkinghub.elsevier.com/ retrieve/pii/S0148296307000732.

Sharma, Pramodita, James J. Chrisman, and Jess H. Chua. 1996. *A Review and Annotated Bibliography of Family Business Studies.* Boston, MA: Kluwer Academic Publishers.

Sharma, Pramodita, James J. Chrisman, and Jess H. Chua. 1997. "Strategic Management of the Family Business: Past Research and Future Challenges." *Family Business Review* 10 (1) (March): 1–35. doi:10.1111/j.1741-6248.1997.00001.x. http://fbr.sagepub.com/cgi/doi/ 10.1111/j.1741-6248.1997.00001.x.

Trow, Donald B. 1961. "Executive Succession in Small Companies." *Administrative Science Quarterly* 6 (2): 228–239.

Yu, Andy, G. Thomas Lumpkin, Ritch L. Sorenson, and Keith. H. Brigham. 2012. "The Landscape of Family Business Outcomes: A Summary and Numerical Taxonomy of Dependent Variables." *Family Business Review* 25 (1) (March): 33–57. doi:10.1177/0894486511430329. http://fbr.sagepub.com/cgi/doi/10.1177/ 0894486511430329.

Zahra, Shaker A., and Pramodita Sharma. 2004. "Family Business Research: A Strategic Reflection." *Family Business Review* 17 (4) (December): 331–346. doi:10.1111/j.1741-6248.2004.00022.x. http://dx.doi.org/10.1111/j.1741-6248.2004.00022.x.

Zouboulakis, Michel S., and John Kamarianos. 2002. "Racionalidad y Cooperacion entre Firmas. Examen del Comportamiento Habitual de las Industrias Griegas." *Revista de Economía Institucional* 4 (7):98–113.

27

CONTEXTUAL FACTORS THAT AFFECT SELECTION AND USE OF GOVERNANCE STRUCTURES IN LATIN AMERICAN FAMILY ENTERPRISES

Isabel C. Botero and Gonzalo Gómez Betancourt

Introduction

In its most general form, corporate governance describes "the study of power and influence over decision making within a corporation" (Aguilera and Jackson 2010: 487). For family enterprises[1], the study of corporate governance encompasses the exploration of the different systems and structures that are put in place to help the family business and the business family make decisions regarding the direction of the business and to assure accountability and control in the relationships of the business, family and ownership of the firm (Gallo and Kenyon-Rouvinez 2006). Thus, decisions about governance are important because the success in this context is closely tied to the structures and processes that are in place to help the family and the business adapt to the environment and disruptions that occur (Miller and Le Breton-Miller 2006, Suess 2014).

Although corporate governance is the area of family business research that has received the most attention in the last two decades (De Massis et al. 2012; Debicki et al. 2009), we know very little about the role that cultural contexts[2] have in the practice of governance in family enterprises. This is very interesting given the growth in the study international corporate governance and findings that suggest that national culture influences the policies that governments have regarding in the use of governance structures (Aguilar and Jackson 2010). Similarly, family business researchers indicate that we need to pay closer attention to the cultural context because it can affect our understanding of the relationship between variables (Sharma and Chua 2013), the way that family business is defined (Astrachan, Klein and Smyrnios 2002), and different considerations that are important in corporate governance decisions (Monteferrante and Piñango 2011). With this in mind, this chapter focuses on the Latin American[3] context to explore how characteristics of Latin American families, family enterprises, and cultural context affect corporate governance choices that family enterprises make.

Latin America countries have many differences between them, yet they share common characteristics that come from similar cultural, political, economic, and historical similarities (Hoy and

Mendoza-Abarca 2014). Historically, archeologists can place the first settlers in Latin America approximately 10,000 years ago (Britannica.com). Starting in the 16th century, Europeans (primarily Spanish and Portuguese) and African immigrants started coming to this part of the world and mixing with the indigenous population to create a new type of society (Nicholson 2011). The combination of these diverse backgrounds resulted in a new culture that shared religious beliefs (i.e., Catholicism as the most influential religion), class structure, and authority dynamics that influenced how society and families work. As a result, they share great similarities in how they think about family, business, and relationships.

Research in corporate governance in the context of family firms suggests that the way individuals think about business and relationships can play an important role in how they select and use corporate governance systems (Steier 2001, Steier et al. 2015). Building on this knowledge, this chapter identifies the unique characteristics of families, family enterprises, and economic, socio-cultural, political, and legal systems, and explains how these factors influence the selection and use of governance structures in family enterprises. This work contributes to our understanding of family enterprises in at least two ways. First, we explicitly highlight factors that can play a role in choices about governance. In this area, we build on the work of Steier (2001), Astrachan and colleagues (2002), Miller and Le-Breton-Miller (2006), Aguilar and Jackson (2010), and Steier and colleagues (2015) to identify how family, family business, and cultural contextual factors that can affect decision about which corporate governance structures and procedures to use and why they affect decision making about this issue. And, second, we contribute to a growing body of literature that explores the characteristics of family businesses in emerging economies such as Latin America. Particularly, we highlight the characteristics of the Latin American culture that create family enterprises that are unique and different from other family businesses around the world.

To achieve our goal the following sections summarize the literature on corporate governance in family firms and the different factors that can affect the choices about how to govern a firm. Following this, the Latin American context is described. This section focuses on the unique characteristics of the cultural context, the family, and the family business. Using this description, we explain how and why these unique factors need to be considered to understand how family businesses practice governance in this part of the world. We then use the Colombian context as an example of how characteristics of the cultural context, the family, and the family business affect decisions about corporate governance in family firms. We conclude by highlighting unique considerations for studying and practicing corporate governance in the family business context of Latin America.

Understanding Corporate Governance in Family Enterprises

Corporate governance describes the systems (i.e., structures, processes, and policies) by which corporations are managed/directed and controlled (Aguilera and Jackson 2010). The purpose of having these structures, processes, and policies is to diminish the problems that can arise from a conflict of interest between different stakeholders of the firm (Cadbury 1999, Suáre and Santana-Martin 2004). Governance systems are important because they help the firm direct their efforts to achieve prosperity and long-term value, have a clear structure for accountability of actions and guide internal stakeholders to help achieve organizational goals (Gersick and Feliu 2014, Suess 2014). These actions, in turn, can help with the success of the firm (Steier et al. 2015).

Mainstream understanding of corporate governance is based on the separation between ownership and control/management within an organization (Pieper 2003). However, in family enterprises, this clear separation is not always possible. Researchers acknowledge that family involvement in the firm introduces unique considerations in corporate governance (Chua et al. 1999, Gómez-Mejía et al. 2011, Sirmon and Hitt 2003). For example, the introduction of the family into the business can affect the type of goals that become prevalent for the business, the short- or long-term focus of the firm, the relationships between owners of the firm, and the importance that is given to family members within the business system (Gómez-Mejía et al. 2011). Given this, family businesses require governance systems that facilitate the development of structures that will help the family, ownership (i.e., stockholders) and the business (i.e., control/management of the business) in their planning, decision making, and problem solving (Carlock and Ward 2003).

On the *business* side, the function of governance systems is to help outline the practices that managers need to engage in to help the organization achieve its goals (Gersick and Feliu 2014). This is done through the board of directors and the executive leadership of the firm (i.e., CEO and Management). In the *ownership* system, the function of the governance is to serve the equity of the owners. This is done by establishing and monitoring structures and procedures that will help owners comply with the legal and accounting requirements, setting risk and return parameters, and tracking all data on performance to ensure that owners maintain their equity in the firm (Gersick and Feliu 2014). The governance practices include shareholder's meetings, shareholder council/assembly, shareholder agreements, family offices, and family foundations (Gersick and Feliu 2014, Suess 2014). It is important to note that, in family firms, the ownership system can overlap greatly with the family system and the business system, which makes it difficult if the goal is to clearly separate each area of governance. Finally, within the *family system*, governance structures help the family by organizing and managing the relationships between the family and the business (Berent-Braun and Uhlaner 2012), the family and ownership (Montemerlo and Ward 2011), and the family and management (Mustakallio et al. 2002). Researchers suggest that the governance of the family system is one of the critical components of the family enterprise (Suess 2014). The purpose of the family governance structures is to make explicit and clear the rewards and demands of being part of the family enterprise, to clearly identify the opportunities for family members to be involved in the business, and to ease the flow of information that is trustworthy among family members (Gersick and Feliu 2014). Examples of the governance practices in this area include: family meetings[4], family council[5], family committees, and family constitution/protocol[6] (Suess 2014).

The study of governance in family businesses in the last 25 years has evolved greatly. Early on, work in this area was scattered and focused on individual governance bodies and structures, with emphasis on the role of the board of directors in the family firm (Pieper 2003). Later the focused shifted to understanding the link between governance and family firm performance (Pieper 2003). More recently, the focus of governance research has been to understand the different factors that may play a role in choices about governance systems, and the governance challenges that family business and business families face (Steier et al. 2015). This chapter focuses on the factors that influence decisions about which corporate governance systems to use.

Factors that Influence Corporate Governance Choices

Research suggests that family business characteristics, and broader contextual factors both play a role in determining how a family decides to govern their business. At the family business level, Miller and Le Breton-Miller (2006) suggest that concentration of ownership/control, family management, the involvement of multiple family owners and /or managers in the business, and the involvement of multiple generations in the firm can all impact the governance choices that a family business makes. They argue that these four factors will affect governance choices that can enhance the presence of agency problems or stewardship behaviors on behalf of the business, which can result in benefits and/or challenges for the firm. Steier (2001) complements this by highlighting that organizational size and the level of development of the family firm influence the governance choices that family businesses decide to exercise. He argues that smaller firms that are early in their developmental stage rely on trust as a mechanism to govern the firm. In these circumstances there is a very close relationship between members and there is no need for explicit structures that help make decisions, which reduces transactions costs and provides a strategic advantage to the family firm. However, as families and businesses grow and evolve, there are forces that will diminish the trust between family members, managers, and owners, which will require the investment in activities to enhance their trust or the implementation of governance structures that can help build accountability and trust between stakeholders in the firm.

Context matters greatly when trying to understand family businesses (Sharma and Chua, 2012, Steier et al. 2015). Thus, although not directly studied in the family business area, there is a growing body of literature that explores the role that cultural context can play in how corporate governance is practiced in different countries. In their review of international corporate governance, Aguilera and Jackson (2010) indicate that there are four contextual environments that need to be considered to understand the use of corporate governance structures and policies across cultural contexts. The *economic environment* describes external factors in a business market and broader economy that influences the functioning of the business. At a macro level, this includes interest rates, taxation system, and inflation just to mention a few. At a micro level, it includes characteristics such as market size, supply, demand and the distribution chain. Economic environments are likely to affect how the business needs to be structured to respond to the environment. Thus, affecting how a business needs to be governed. Table 27.1 provides examples of the factors from the cultural context that influence corporate governance and the type of governance decisions and practices that it can affect.

The *social environment* has characteristics (i.e., beliefs, customs, practices, and behaviors) of the immediate social setting in which the organization exists. Projects that explore the influence of culture on corporate governance taking the *socio-cultural approach* focus on two issues. First, they explore how individual cultural orientation (i.e., perceptions of power distance, individualism, uncertainty avoidance, masculinity, and long-term orientation) affects managerial decision making in a firm (Hofstede 2001, House et al. 2001). Second, it explores how national culture can affect societal norms that play a role in the management of a firm (Aguilera and Jackson 2010). These researchers argue that a national culture may support certain kinds of behaviors that are seen as acceptable. Thus, organizations will be more likely to include them as part of their governance considerations to be able to survive.

The *legal environment* is the third component of the cultural context and describes the rules and regulations that define the boundaries of the business activity in a country. This approach centers on the boundaries of property rights within each national culture and the regulations that affect how organizations are governed. Research that studies corporate governance in this area explores the extent to which the corporate legal system of a nation protects minority shareholders, which can influence the governance structure that a business will use. Researchers argue that the level of protection given to minority shareholders affects the ownership structure and, in turn, all structures that deal with decision-making within the firm (La Porta et al. 1999).

Finally, the *political environment* describes the actions taken by a government that can affect the daily business activities of a company. Research from this approach examines how the

Table 27.1 Effects of Culture on Corporate Governance Based on Each Environment

Environment	Factors the Environment Influences	Examples of Governance Issues
Economic	Structure of the firm	• Financial systems used and financial choices available based on these systems. • Accounting practices that are prevalent • Board of Directors (e.g., size, type of board, power of board) • Hierarchy and power distribution within the organization • Executive compensation • Which stakeholders have a voice and how they participate in decision making?
Socio-cultural	Manager Behaviors	• Importance given to different governance practices • Priority given to different managerial activities. • How decisions about the organization are made.
	Societal Norms	• What are the accounting norms used by a company? • What are the different factors that a company needs to disclose?
Legal	Structure of Legal System	• Who has rights over a property? • Who has voice in the decision making about the firm?
Political	Political factors that are salient in society	• Degree and form of competition available in an industry. • Different political interest and how they affect a company behavior. • The degree of loyalty that managers have towards different stakeholders.
	Power and level of activity of political institutions	• The role that political institutions have in the state. • How prevalent is political activity in society.

introduction of particular laws in a country can change how organizations are governed. From this view, political actions within a country require organizations to adapt their structure to avoid having problems that can negatively reflect on the corporation. Thus, politics are likely to influence the governance structure of a company.

Aguilera and Jackson (2010) suggest that to fully understand the role that culture play in corporate governance choices, it is necessary to integrate ideas from these four environments. Each environment offers a unique lens through which governance systems and practices can be explained. They argue that corporate governance decisions are influenced by multiple interrelated factors that need to be considered in conjunction because they affect individual and group normative expectations. Building on this idea, we argue that the four environments contexts provide a general picture of a region's culture. In particular, these characteristics describe the economic, social, legal and political systems that compose a cultural context, and determine the norm and expectations that individuals within a cultural context have about behavior. Using the theory of reasoned action, researchers argue that societal values and norms play an important role in the choices and behaviors that individuals decide to enact (Park and Smith 2007). Building on this approach, we believe that the effects that culture has on the selection and use of corporate governance systems can be explained by the influence that these societal characteristics have on individual and organizational normative behaviors and expectations. These, in turn, play a role the selection and use of corporate governance structures and policies within a firm (See Figure 27.1). Applying this idea to the family business area, we believe that societal factors also play a role in the selection and use of corporate governance practices.

This chapter focuses on the Latin American context and how characteristics of this context influence decisions about corporate governance in family enterprises. Emerging economies in developing regions such as Latin America play an important role in the economy of the world. However, there is very little research conducted and published on how family businesses in these contexts survive, stay competitive, and grow (Astrachan, 2010). Building on our discussion above regarding the factors that play a role in the selection and use of corporate governance systems and policies, the following section describes the Latin American context. We focus on characteristics of the cultural context and the family firm that have been linked to the selection and use of corporate governance structures and policies. We also discuss the view of family in this region of the world and explain how it can also influence decisions about governance.

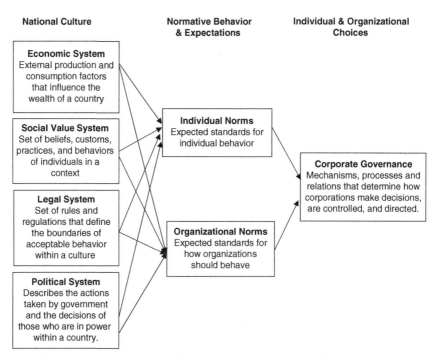

Figure 27.1   Influence of Societal Culture on Selection and Use of Corporate Governance Structures and Policies

The Latin American Context

Latin America constitutes a rapidly growing and influential economic region with a population of more than 600 million people[7]. It extends from Mexico to Tierra del Fuego in Chile and includes many of the Caribbean Islands. Latin American countries are major providers of strategic commodities (i.e., iron, copper, zinc), they represent an important market for manufacturers, and have unique natural resources that make this region a significant partner to major players around the world (i.e., Asia, Europe and North America; Nicholson 2011). Throughout its history, the Latin American region has experienced times of economic hardships and political instability that have affected the structure, governance and development of their businesses. Because of these challenges, family controlled enterprises have always been the driver of growth for the region (Nicholson 2011).

Although there are many differences between Latin American countries, their shared history has influenced their perceptions that individuals in this part of the world hold. We begin describing the cultural context (i.e., economic, socio-cultural, legal and political systems) and explaining how these characteristics affect our understanding of family enterprises and their behavior.

The Latin American Cultural Context

The economic, social, political, and legal environment in Latin American countries has been influenced by the multiple changes that have occurred in this region since the 1960s. Back then the economic environment was characterized by regional protectionism, which promoted the development of small national markets (Lansberg and Perrow 1991). However, between 1970 and 2000 there was a big shift towards international trade and open markets that created higher instability, and market changes (Britanica.com). The push towards internationalization also promoted the shift in many countries from state-owned enterprises to privatization (Hoy and Mendoza-Abarca 2014). Countries like Mexico, Colombia, and Chile have seen major changes in their business structures (Britanica.com). At the same time, other countries in the region have changed from private to state ownership (Lansberg and Perrow 1991). Two examples of this are Venezuela and Ecuador, who have moved towards a more socialist government since 2000. The combination of these factors has created an economic environment characterized as fragile, volatile, and in constant flux. Because of this, it is common for corporations have difficult times accessing funding due to constant currency devaluation concerns, and structural changes in the market (Lansberg and Perrow 1991, Nicholson 2011).

At a social level, the constant change of economic conditions has created an environment of social unrest where social conflict has been normal in these countries. These conflicts have led to civil wars that have mobilized most of the population into urban settings were 79 percent of the population now resides (UNEP, 2010). This shift in the locations of the population has resulted in high levels of unemployment, underdeveloped infrastructures, and poor education systems that make the acquisition of skilled workers a difficult task (Poza 1991, Nordqvist et al. 2011). These social issues are also manifested in political and legal environments that are constant flux and require organizations to adapt to the changing regulations and policies that are initiated by the government (Lansberg & Perrow, 1991).

In the legal environment, it is important to know that Latin American countries are governed by the civil law system. Countries governed by civil law have an explicit set of rules that provide a normative approach to how corporations should work and the responsibilities of those who are in charge of the firm. This is different from common law, which is the legal system prevalent in North America[8]. Common law is based on precedence and does not have a codified system. When applied to corporate governance, having a legal system based on civil law requires that organizations follow specific codes and rules that will determine the different governance structures and procedures that organizations need to implement. Thus, Latin American countries have prescribed characteristics that require specific governance structures that need to be used for an organization to be considered legal. This results in rigid regulations for the local companies.

When taken together, all of these issues have created climates of uncertainty, and the need for adaptive structures in the business environment. For family enterprises, this uncertainty means that they require governance structures that differ from other regions of the world (Monteferrante and Piñango 2011). For example, the presence of political corruption requires family enterprises to have structures that enable them to have people with good negotiation skills and with power within the company to negotiate with officials at various levels within the public bureaucracy to facilitate the practice of their business within their industry and country (Lansberg and Perrow, 1991). At the family and ownership levels, these characteristics require that governance choices can protect the family and its property. Thus, as highlighted by previous researchers, cultural contexts need to be considered to better understand and help Latin American family businesses. In the next section, we talk about the unique characteristics of family enterprises in Latin America and how these factors also influence choices about governance systems.

The Family Business in Latin America

Throughout its history, the Latin American region has experienced times of economic hardships and political instability that have created an environment for the development of family businesses with unique characteristics (Hoy and Mendoza-Abarca 2014; Lansberg and Perrow 1991; Nordqvist et al. 2011; Poza, 1995). Historically, family businesses in Latin America are very young (i.e., most likely to be in their first or second generation), have a high concentration of ownership in the family (Poza 1995), and are born from the entrepreneur's need to support themselves or their families (Nordqvist et al 2011). Family enterprises in this region are likely to be organized based on a multi-business portfolio structure often labeled "grupo" (Brenes et al 2006, Lansberg and Perrow 1991, Nicholson, 2011).

"Grupos" are large holding companies that include a group of businesses that are owned by a family or group of families. This form of organizing offers several benefits to the entrepreneurial family. First, it allows for the participation and involvement of more family members. "Grupos" tend to grow through diversification. Thus, by having more companies, there are more ways to involve family members into the business. Second, having multiple companies also allows multiple generations of the family to work in the business at the same time and have power and autonomy over their decisions. A multi-business structure does not require younger generations to wait until older generations leave the organization to have a position of authority and to be independent. Given that, younger generations are given the opportunity to create spinoffs that are related to the family enterprise (Lansberg and Perrow, 1991). This enables new generations to enter the business and have their independent firm but still get the benefits of the family enterprise. Third, this multi-business structure can prevent stock values from being diluted when new members of the family become owners in the family enterprise. As explained above, a family member can own their business and still be under the umbrella of the family enterprise. Thus, having multiple members of the family enter the business is not always harmful to the value of the stocks. And, fourth, the group structure can also make financing new family ventures much easier (Lansberg and Perrow, 1991). By having multiple organizations, the family enterprise can have access to more family capital and use this capital to fund the new ventures. However, this business structure creates interesting challenges to the way family enterprises are governed. The majority of the governance models discussed by family business scholars assume a single-family and single-business structure and do not provide clear explanations of how different structures (i.e., the "grupo") could align their governance systems with their goals (Steier et al. 2015). Thus, we need new approaches to governance to be able to deal with these challenges.

Understanding the Latin American Family

A third aspect that we believe influences the selection and use of corporate governance structures and policies is how a culture defines who is included in the family. The definition of family is important because it can change the number of family members that are involved in the business, which is an important consideration when selecting which governance structures to use (Miller and Le Breton-Miller 2006). While some regions around the world define the term family as equivalent to nuclear family (i.e., father, mother, and children), in Latin America the understanding of family is broader. In this part of the world, the idea of "family" includes the nuclear family, the extended family (i.e., grandparents, aunts, uncles, cousins; in-laws), and others related by friendship (e.g., best friends of parents that grew in the parents family) (Georgas 2003). In the context of family enterprises, this broader definition has several implications. First, it affects who is considered a "family member" when determining the involvement of family in the family business. In this case, while other cultures may only include a single individual in the dominant coalition, Latin American family businesses can have multiple individuals of the family with decision-making power in the organization (Lansberg and Perrow, 1991). Having more people with decision-making power will influence what structures and policies need to be in place to manage the family enterprise. Second, this broader definition also affects the number of family members that are involved and may depend on the family business, indirectly affecting the degree of involvement of the family in the business. And, third, this broader definition can also play a role in determining the number of generations that are involved in the business at the same type.

The dominant role that the Roman Catholic religion has historically played in Latin American society has influenced a family-centered culture. Latin American families place greater importance on family relationships, family harmony, family unity, and family cohesion instead of profit maximization (Hoy and Mendoza-Abarca 2014, Poza 1995). This concern for maintaining relationships has important implications for family businesses. First, it affects the influence level of nepotism that is present in the business. Given that family is more important than the business, family membership trumps ability when hiring people for important managerial positions inside the business (Poza 1995). Additional, family rules are more prominent than business rules, which can affect the decision-making dynamics in the business. Second, a greater concern for maintaining harmony in the family prevents enforcing the accountability in the performance of family members (Poza 1995). Because of this, governance structures need to be adapted to allow for different decision-making mechanisms. And, third, the concern for relationships leads to a culture that avoids conflict and is less accepting of constructive criticisms (Hoy and Mendoza-Abarca 2014, Poza 1995). Thus, governance structures are less likely to rely on direct accountability of family members.

The influence of the Roman Catholic religion is also evident in the traditional view of the family structure (i.e., a man and a woman getting married to have children). Latin American cultures are patriarchal in nature[9] (Lansberg and Perrow 1991). This characteristic promotes traditional gender roles in which women act as the glue that keeps the family together while men are expected to take roles that involve greater authority and decision making. For family businesses, this traditional structure can be problematic when families have businesses in male dominated industries and have junior generations in which women are prevalent. This traditional view is also problematic when younger generations of females want to enter the business and either their fathers or their mothers, expect them to engage in behaviors that are consistent with their gender. This traditional view can also have implications for who can participate in the governance of the firm.

A final characteristic that is important to highlight about Latin American families is the sense of obligation that they feel towards family members. Given the belief that family always comes first, family members feel a collective obligation for all other members of their group. For example, if there is a family member that is going through a rough time, it is common that other family members will help them any way that they can. This can take the form of either moral or financial support. Because of this, family businesses tend to engage in cross-shareholder arrangements (i.e., when a family member lends their money to the business in a time of need). These types of arrangements can affect the degree to which family believes that they have a say in the business or the level of intrusion that family members will have over business affairs. And, both of these factors also play an important role.

Figure two combines the characteristics that the Latin American context has that we believe affect the use and selection of corporate governance systems. We complement the work of Steier (2001), Miller and Le Breton-Miller (2006), and Aguilera and Jackson (2010), by including family factors as important predictors of corporate governance choices in family enterprises. As Mustakallio and colleagues (2002), Pieper (2003), Berent-Braun and Uhlaner (2012), and Suess (2014) argue, the understanding of governance in family enterprises requires consideration of both the family and the business. And, given that all families have unique factors that affect the way the operate (Pieper), we believe that choices about governing the family enterprise also require considerations about the characteristics of the family.

The Colombian Context as an Example

Colombia is located on the northern tip of South America. It is the third largest country in Latin America with a population surpassing 48 million people. Seventy percent of this population lives in urban areas[10]. There are close to 1 million companies in the country (30 percent are formal organizations listed within chambers of commerce, and 70 percent are informal in nature). Broadly speaking, the *legal system* of Colombia is based on the French Civil Law system. This means that there are legal codes that determine what constitutes the different types of corporations and what type of governance structures these entities should have to be considered formal businesses. The *societal value system* is greatly influenced by Roman Catholic religion. Church has historically been very influential in personal and family lives of Colombians. There is a strong hierarchical structure and social stratification that affects who individuals interact with and the types of roles they expect to do when they join a business. Additionally, the family system is central in Colombian social structure and has a patrilineal structure. Finally, the *political system* is characterized by a two party system (i.e., conservatives and liberals) and a three-branch structure for the government (i.e., executive, legislative and judicial). There are a lot of connections between the personal/social network and the political system. Guerrillas have become an important component of the political system in Colombia. It is estimated that there have been more than three thousand kidnappings per year since the late 1970's. This has created a tense political environment because many of those that are targeted by the guerrilla are politicians or business owners.

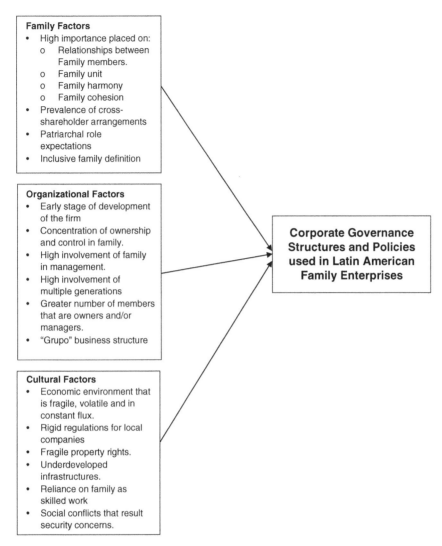

Family Factors
- High importance placed on:
  - o   Relationships between Family members.
  - o   Family unit
  - o   Family harmony
  - o   Family cohesion
- Prevalence of cross-shareholder arrangements
- Patriarchal role expectations
- Inclusive family definition

Organizational Factors
- Early stage of development of the firm
- Concentration of ownership and control in family.
- High involvement of family in management.
- High involvement of multiple generations
- Greater number of members that are owners and/or managers.
- "Grupo" business structure

Cultural Factors
- Economic environment that is fragile, volatile and in constant flux.
- Rigid regulations for local companies
- Fragile property rights.
- Underdeveloped infrastructures.
- Reliance on family as skilled work
- Social conflicts that result security concerns.

Corporate Governance Structures and Policies used in Latin American Family Enterprises

Figure 27.2   Characteristics of Latin American Enterprises That Affect the Selection and Use of Governance Structures

The cultural issues mentioned above affect the norms and behaviors that individuals and organizations follow. At the *individual level*, laws, individual values and political connections affect manager expectations and behaviors. For example, depending on the type of business that a manager works for, they are expected to create specific reports for the organization or pay attention to specific aspects of the firm for which they are held liable. Similarly, due to social class and hierarchical stratification, those in higher roles are expected to make decisions. The respect of an individual is based on their age, title, and social class. Thus, managers are expected to be older, have a higher level of education, and belong to a higher social class. These three characteristics give managers the responsibility of making decisions on behalf of the organization. Although "machismo" [11] can be present in the working environment it is not the norm, especially in urban centers of the country. Regarding gender roles, men are more likely to occupy dominant positions, and women are not considered fit for jobs that are seen as very masculine. Finally, at the individual level, the connections that a person has with those in political roles or those in a higher class are likely to determine the types of actions that are seen as required for a role. For example, in cases where there are political favors that are owed, rules can be flexible to make sure that the favor is returned.

Cultural characteristics also play a role in the expectations of what organizations are required to do. As mentioned earlier, the legal system in Colombia clearly identifies the laws that organizations need to obey by to remain a legal entity. Societal values suggest that respect for hierarchy is very important. In this sense, respect and power are given to those higher up in the organization, while lower level employees are seen as followers. Because of this, titles within an organization are seen as important. Finally, political conditions in Colombia have created informal norms for organizations to show less profit to avoid being targeted by guerrilla and avoid paying full tax to the government who will use this capital inefficiently.

When taken together, the cultural characteristics do have an influence in the selection and use of corporate governance structures and strategies through the effects they have on the norms that organizations need to follow and the individual behaviors of managers. In the case of family enterprises, the influence is augmented by the inclusion of family in the business and the strong role that family plays in society. In Colombia, 90 percent of all formal organizations are family owned or operated, and out of all these firms it is estimated that 70 percent are in the first generation, 25 percent are in the second generation, and 5 percent are in the third or greater generation (Gómez Betancourt et al. 2012). There are several cultural characteristics that need to be highlighted when focusing on family enterprises. First, it is important to note that there are no specific laws that pertain exclusively to family enterprises. Similar to other countries, Colombia relied on information from chambers of commerce, government control agencies, business associations, and universities to develop voluntary governance codes for close and open companies (Gómez Betancourt and Zapata Cuervo 2013). These codes are greatly influenced by developed countries that tend to have larger corporations and rely on trust and delegation of responsibilities to different components of the governance structure. However, characteristics of businesses in Colombia do not have similar conditions. For example, the most common form of formal organization in Colombia is the "Sociedad Anonima" (i.e., S.A., "Anonymous Company; equivalent to a public limited company in the USA). These organizations are required to have at least five partners, and need to have three mandated governance structures: shareholder's meeting (this convene at least once a year and elects the board of directors and the auditor); a board of directors with at least three principles and three replacements; and an auditor. On top of this, the partners who own the company are also required to create regulations of how they will manage their relations. When family firms are incorporated as an anonymous company, they need to create their legal document of how they will manage their relationships. Because family enterprise owners have a familial relationship, the regulations they require can be seen as similar to a family protocol. Thus, in Colombia, the use of family protocol as part of family governance of the firm is perceived as common and important.

The board of directors is another area that presents interesting differences for the context in Colombia. Internationally, researchers indicate that board of directors in family firms should have a good percentage of external members that can provide an outside perspective to the business (Bammens et al. 2008, Bettinelli 2011, Corbetta & Salvato, 2004). Our research has found that boards of directors in family enterprises in Colombia have between 20 percent and 25 percent of independent members of the board. There are at least two reasons for this. First, families have great loyalty to family members. Thus, family enterprises are more likely to include members that are considered part of the family. By doing this, they are ensuring that there are people who will protect the interest of the family when making decisions about the firm. In this case, outsiders are not seen as having the best interest of the family in mind, thus, they are not seen as viable candidates for the board. Second, as we mentioned earlier, in Colombia families are defined as including nuclear, extended, and strong friendship ties. Thus, it is much more difficult to claim full independence from the family when being part of the board. From our observations, those who get trusted with the responsibilities of a board member tend to have some form of long-term relationship with the family or the business, which makes them part of the family.

Another important aspect when thinking about decision-making as a part of corporate governance of a family enterprise is the hierarchical nature of Colombian families and societies. There are two issues that are important in this hierarchy: (1) who should make the decision? and (2) Who has greater influence in the decision? In Colombian families, senior/older members have the responsibility to make the decision, and those younger are expected to respect their decisions. Thus, senior family members are the ones that are more likely to participate and make decisions about the family firm. Their decisions and opinions are also seen as important and representative. Therefore, younger generations are less likely to have voice and influence during the decision-making process. Implied in this notion is the idea that older family members will play a central role in the governance of family enterprises. This could be done through formalized participation or informal interactions. Similarly, younger generations are expected to defer to the decisions of older family members.

Although these are just a small sample of the different ways that the Colombian cultural orientation can affect the selection and use of corporate governance structures and policies, it shows that some cultures may emphasize different structures and aspect of governance. In this sense, our knowledge about corporate governance in family enterprises may not apply to all cultures.

Conclusion

The purpose of this chapter was two-fold. First, we wanted to identify characteristics of families, family enterprises, and cultural context that play a role in the selection and use of governance systems and policies in family enterprises. Second, we wanted to explain how and why these factors played a role in decisions about governance. We build on previous work from Steier (2001), Astrachan and colleagues (2002), Miller and Le-Breton-Miller (2006), Aguilar and Jackson (2010), and Steier and colleagues (2015) to identify the three sets of factors presented in Figure 27.2 that play a role in how Latin American families make decisions about governing their enterprises. We argued that cultural, family business, and family characteristics affect the way individuals and organizations are expected to act, which, in turn, will affect the corporate governance choices. We suggest that countries in Latin America share similarities in their history that affect their beliefs about what constitutes a family and the role that families play in their lives, which influences the way that they think about the family enterprise, who gets to be part of it, and who gets to make and respect the decisions of the family enterprise. We also describe similarities in the cultural context and family business characteristics that can affect the normative expectations individuals and organizations have when determining how to govern an organization (see Figure 27.2). Finally, we illustrate how some of these ideas work using the Colombian context to illustrate our ideas.

Based on our observations, there are several implications for research and practice of corporate governance in family enterprises. First, we believe that the way that family is conceptualized influences who can be part of the family enterprise and in what type of interactions they can have with the business. For example, a broader definition would imply that there are more members that can participate and play a role in the business. This creates a greater overlap between family and business systems, which can blur the distinction between family and business governance structure. A smaller separation between family and business is likely to result in complex choices regarding the governance of the business and the family. This blurring of lines can also occur between the ownership and the family system, which can have similar implications when making decisions about the family enterprise. Some of these ideas have been indirectly explored in the work of Poza (1995) and Lansberg and Perrow (1991). These authors argue that the Latin American context is unique because of the family culture that exists in this environment and how it affects the behaviors of family businesses. Thus, we complement these ideas by explaining how these unique views about families could affect selection and use of family and business governances systems. Second, we also argue that the central role that family has in the social structure can also affect corporate governance, especially in decision-making situations. For example, in a context like Colombia older family members have greater influence over decision even if they are not active members of the family enterprise. Because Colombian people have such respect for older members of their families, they are less likely to contradict or not follow opinions and suggestions from older family members. This contradicts how we currently conceptualize governance and who influences the governance of the firm. This complements the work of Steier (2001) who suggests that in some family firms trust can work as a governance mechanism that can help in making decisions about the firm. In particular, we argue that the family culture in Latin America works by trusting family members who will often participate or be part of the governance of the firm, even when they are not active owners or members of the firm.

Third, legal systems also affect the different governance structures that family enterprises use. For example, although there are no specific policies about what family enterprises need to do in Colombia, they are bounded by the legal requirements of the type of Legal Corporation they represent. Different codes of commerce may require for organizations to have specific governance structures or procedures. Thus, affecting the legal requirements of a country can affect which governance structures are used and how they are used. This complements the work of Gómez Betancourt and Zapata Cuervo (2013) who analyze the different business codes around the world to present governance structures that can be useful for Latin American family enterprises. A fourth aspect that is noteworthy is the effect that political systems and contexts have to the way family enterprises are controlled and make decisions. Political contexts like Colombia, where there is turmoil can influence how the governance is structured and how closely policies are followed. For example, having social conflicts can lead to concerns about the personal of family members, how legal information is presented to outside stakeholders, and how financial information is reported. We believe that these considerations have important implications for the transparency of governance structures and decisions.

Up to date, there is not much research that explores how characteristics of the cultural context affect the selection and use of governance structures in Latin American family firms. The two studies that we found (Monteferrante and Piñago 2011; Ross Schneider, 2008) do suggest that Latin American family business groups behave differently than those in other parts of the world. In particular, Ross Schneider (2008) suggests that family business groups in this part of the world are more resilient and can adapt to changes in the environment that are brought by globalization. These characteristics challenge the traditional theorizing about corporate governance. Thus, there needs to be further understanding of all the factors that can play a role in decisions about governance, and how these decisions are made. The work of Monteferrante and Piñago (2011) sheds some light on this idea. They argue that family firms that are in their early stages of development rely less on formal structures of governance because they have fewer family members involved in the firm. This enables businesses to be more adaptable early on and rely on trust as an aid to governance. However, as businesses grow and more family members become involved in the business, there will be a need for formal structures that can provide transparency and accountability during decision making.

Based on these observations we believe that there is a great opportunity for future research that can help us better understand decisions and use of corporate governance structures in Latin American family enterprises. Initially, we believe that research could provide descriptive information about the governance practices that are used in the family, the business, and ownership components of the family enterprise. This can give us important background necessary to explore other issues. For example, once we know what are the practices used in Latin America we could compare with other regions in the globe to understand the similarities and differences that are present in the governance of family enterprises. These initial findings can shed light into which corporate governance choices are affected by the culture context in which the family enterprise exists? Understanding this can open different lines of research to understand the unique effects of culture on governance.

Another area that could be developed in future research are the similarities and differences between governance structures between family enterprises in Latin American countries. Although this chapter argues for the prevalence of similarities in decisions regarding choice and use of corporate governance systems, it would be interesting to explore whether this assumption is correct, and cultural characteristics could affect who influences the decision making of a family enterprise. This within culture exploration would be very interesting for practitioners and consultants throughout Latin America.

Finally, it would also be useful to explore the predictors and effects of governance choices in Latin American family enterprises. In this chapter, we present a set of factors that we believe influence the decisions that family enterprises make about governance. However, our ideas are conceptual in nature. Thus, it would be really interesting to explore whether the factors we highlight do influence these choices. At the same time, it would be really interesting to explore the consequences of the use of different governance structures in Latin American family firms. There is some research that suggests that governance structures can affect the profitability of the family enterprise (Steier et al. 2015), thus it would be interesting to understand effect that using different structures has on the performance of a firm.

Latin American family enterprises have unique characteristics and are the drivers of the economy in this part of the world. Unfortunately, there is not much published about them in academic and practice-oriented journals. Given this, we would like to conclude our chapter encouraging researchers and practitioners to explore the uniqueness and contribution of family enterprises in this part of the world and to share this knowledge through the publication of their work.

Notes

1 In this paper we view family firms/family businesses as a single organization that "is governed and/or managed with the intention to shape and pursue the vision of the business held by a dominant coalition controlled by members of the same family or a small number of families in a manner that is potentially sustainable across generations of the family or families" (p.24, Chua et al., 1999). On the other hand we view family enterprises as a group of organizations that are "governed and/or managed with the intention to shape and pursue the vision of the business held by a dominant coalition controlled by members of the same family or a small number of families in a manner that is potentially sustainable across generations of the family or families" (p.24, Chua et al., 1999).
2 In this paper we use the term cultural context to describe the economic, social, political and legal environments of a region.

3 We define Latin America to include the countries from the Americas where Romance languages (Spanish & Portuguese) are predominant.

4 Family meetings are "a recurring assembly of family members to discuss business and /or family issues" (p. 140; Suess, 2014). It constitutes the simplest form of family governance.

5 Family Council represents a group of family members that is selected to represent multiple generations and branches of the family. They meet regularly to discuss matters that involve the family's involvement in the business (Suess, 2014).

6 Family constitution or protocol represents a normative agreement that results from a process that establishes fundamental principles and guidelines to organize the family's relation with the business (Berent-Braun & Uhlaner, 2012). It addresses fundamental questions about the governance of the family in relation to the business (Suess, 2014).

7 Population based on estimates from the different countries. Accessed from: https://en.wikipedia.org/wiki/List_of_Latin_American_countries_by_population.

8 An exception is Louisiana, which is governed by civil law.

9 Although society is changing and more accepting of the role of women in corporations today, Latin America is still considered a patriarchal culture.

10 The information for this section was complied from the CIA Fact Book.

11 Machismo describes the attitudes and beliefs that agree with traditional ideas about gender roles and men being strong and aggressive.

References

Aguilera, R.V., and Jackson, G. (2010) 'Comparative and international corporate governance,' *The Academy of Management Annals* 4(1): 485–556.

Astrachan, J. S. (2010) 'Strategy in family business: toward a multidimensional research agenda,' *Journal of Family Business Strategy* 1(1): 6–14.

Astrachan, J. S., Klein, S. B., and Smyrnios, K. X. (2002) 'The F-PEC Scale of family influence: A proposal for solving the family business definition problem,' *Family Business Review* 15(1): 45–58.

Bammens, Y., Voordeckers, W., and Van Gils, A. (2008) 'Boards of directors in family firms: A generational perspective,' *Small Business Economics* 21(2): 163–180.

Berent-Braun, M. M., and Uhlaner, L. M. (2012) 'Family governance practices and team building: Paradox of the enterprising family,' *Small Business Economics* 38(1): 103–119.

Bettinelli, C. (2011) 'Boards of Directors in Family Firms: An exploratory study of structure and group processes,' *Family Business Review* 24(2): 151–169.

Brenes, E.R. Madrigal, K. and Molina-Navarro, G. E. (2006) 'Family business structure and succession: Critical topics in Latin American experience,' *Journal of Business Research* 59(3): 372–374.

Britannica.com Retrieved on October 30, 2015 from: http://www.britannica.com/place/Latin-America.

Cadbury, Sir A. (1999) 'What are the trends in corporate governance? How will they impact your company?' *Long Range Planning* 32(1): 12–19.

Carlock, R.S. and Ward, J. L. (2003) *Strategic planning for the family businesses – Parallel planning to unify the family business*, New York, Palgrave.

Chua, J. H., Chrisman, J. J., and Sharma, P. (1999) 'Defining the family business by behavior,' *Entrepreneurship Theory and Practice* 23(4): 19–39.

CIA World Fact Book, accessed on October 20th on https://www.cia.gov/library/publications/the-world-factbook/geos/co.html.

Corbetta, G., and Salvato, C. A. (2004) 'The board of directors in family firms: One size fits all?,' *Family Business Review* 17(2): 119–134.

Davis, G.F. (2005). New directions in corporate governance. *Annual Review of Sociology* 31: 143–162.

De Massis, A., Sharma, P., Chua, J., and Chrisman, J. (2012) '*Family Business Studies an Annotated Bibliography*' Northhampton, UK: Edward Elgar Publishing Inc.

Debicki, B. J., Matherne, C. F., Kellermanns, F. W., and Chrisman, J. J. (2009) 'Family business research in the new millenium: An overview of the who, the where, the what, and the why' *Family Business Review* 22(2): 151–166.

Gallo, M. A., and Kenyon-Rouvinez, D. (2006) 'The importance of family and business governance,' in: D. Kenyon-Rouvinez and J. L. Ward (Eds.) *Family Business: Key Issues*, New York: Palgrave –MacMillan, 45–57.

Georgas, J. (2003) 'Family: Variations and changes across cultures,' in W. J. Lonner, D. L. Dinnel, S. A. Hayes, & D. N. Sattler (Eds.) *Online Readings in Psychology and Culture* (Unit 13, Chapter 3) Washington, Center for Cross-Cultural Research, Western Washington University, Bellingham.

Gersick, K. E., and Feliu, N. (2014) 'Governing the family enterprise: Practices, performance, and research,' in: L. Melin, M. Nordqvist, & P. Sharma (Eds.) *The Sage Handbook of Family Business*, London, UK: Sage Publications: 196–225.

Gómez Betancourt, G., Lopez Vergara, M.P., Betancourt Ramirez, J. B., and Millan Payan, J. O. (2012) 'Estudio sobre el desempeño de las empresas familiars colombianas que cotizan en la bolsa de valores, frente a las no familiares,' *Entramado* 8(1): 28–42.

Gómez Betancourt, G. and Zapata Cuervo, N. (2013) 'Gobierno corporativo: Una comparacion de codigos de gobierno en el mundo, un modelo para empresas Latinoamericanas familiars y no familiars,' *Entramado* 9(2): 98–117.

Gómez-Mejía, L. R., Cruz, C., Berrone, P., and De Castro, J. (2011) 'The bind that ties: Socioemotional wealth preservation in family,' *The Academy of Management Annals* 5(1): 653–707.

Hofstede, G.H. (2001) *Culture's Consequences: Comparing Values, Behaviors, Institutions, and Organizations Across Nations* (2nd ed.), Thousand Oaks, CA: Sage.

House, R., Javidan, M., and Dorfman, P. (2001) Project GLOBE: An introduction. *Applied Psychology—An International Review* 50(4): 489–505.

Hoy, F. and Mendoza-Abarca K. (2014) 'Latin America,' in S.M. Carraher and D.H.B. Welsh (Eds) *Global Entrepreneurship* (2nd Edition), Iowa, Kendall Hunt Publishing: 293–312.

La Porta, R., Lopez-de-Silanes, F., and Shleifer, A. (1999) 'Corporate ownership around the world,' *Journal of Finance* 54(2): 471–517.

Lansberg, I., and Perrow, E. (1991) 'Understanding and working with leading family businesses in Latin America,' *Family Business Review* 4(2): 127–147.

Miller, D., and Le Breton-Miller, I. (2006) 'Family governance and firm performance: Agency, stewardship, and capabilities,' *Family Business Review* 19(1): 73–87.

Monteferrante, P., and Piñango, R. (2011) 'Governance structures and entrepreneurial performance in family firms: An exploratory study of Latin American family firms,' in: M. Nordqvist, G. Marzano, E. R. Brenes, G. Jimenez, and M. Fonseca-Paredes (Eds.) *Understanding Entrepreneurial Family Businesses in Uncertain Environments: Opportunities and Research in Latin America*, Cheltenham, UK: Edward Elgar Publishing: 91–124.

Montemerlo, D., and Ward, J. L. (2011) *The Family Constitution – Agreements to Secure and Perpetuate Your Family and Your Business*, New York: Palgrave Macmillan.

Mustakallio, M., Autio, E., and Zahra, S. A. (2002) 'Relational and contractual governance in family firms: Effects on strategic decision making,' *Family Business Review* 15(3): 205–222.

Nicholson, E. (2011) 'Discovering Latin America and its family businesses' Tharawat Magazine. Accessed at: http://www.tharawat-magazine.com/en/family-business-articles/1888-discovering-latin-america-and-its-family-businesses-3.html.

Nordqvist, M., Marzano, G., Brenes E. R., Jimenez, G., and Fonseca-Paredes, M. (2011) 'Understanding entrepreneurial family businesses in uncertain environments: The case of Latin America,' in: M. Nordqvist, G. Marzano, E. R. Brenes, G. Jimenez, and M. Fonseca-Paredes (Eds.) *Understanding Entrepreneurial Family Businesses in Uncertain Environments: Opportunities and Research in Latin America*, Cheltenham, UK: Edward Elgar Publishing: 1–28.

Park, H. S., and Smith, S. W. (2007) 'Distinctiveness and influence of subjective norms, personal descriptive and injunctive norms, and societal descriptive and injunctive norms on behavioral intent: A case of two behaviors critical to organ donation,' *Human Communication Research* 33(2): 194–218.

Pieper, T. (2003) 'Corporate governance in family firms: A literature review,' Working paper series, INSEAD 2003/97/IIFE.

Poza, E.J. (1995) 'Global competition and the family owned business in Latin America,' *Family Business Review* 8(4): 301–311.

Sharma, P., and Chua, J. H. (2013) 'Asian family enterprises and family business research,' *Asian Pacific Journal of Management* 30(3): 641–656.

Sirmon, D.G. & Hitt, M.A. (2003) 'Managing resources: Linking unique resources, management and wealth creation in family firms' *Entrepreneurship Theory and Practice* 27(4): 339–358.

Steier, L. P. (2001) 'Family firms, plural forms of governance, and the evolving role of trust,' *Family Business Review* 14(4): 353–368.

Steier, L. P., Chrisman, J. J., and Chua, J. H. (2015) 'Governance challenges in family businesses and business families,' *Entrepreneurship Theory and Practice'* Published on-line first.

Suáre, K. C., and Santana-Martín, D. J. (2004) 'Governance in Spanish Family Business,' *International Journal of Entrepreneurial Behavior and Research* 10(1/2): 141–163.

Suess, J. (2014) 'Family governance–Literature review and the development of a conceptual model,' *Journal of Family Business Strategy* 5(2): 138–155.

UNEP (2010) 'Latin America and the Caribbean Environment Outlook,' UNEP, Panama, GEO LAC 3.

28

FAMILY BUSINESS IN LATIN AMERICA

The Case of Mexico

*Edgar Rogelio Ramírez Solís, Verónica Ilián Baños Monroy,
and Lucía Alejandra Rodríguez Acevez*

Introduction

The study of family businesses in Latin America has attracted the attention of researchers only recently (Soto 2013), despite the economic importance of these kinds of firms. The aim of this chapter is to present the current state of research on family businesses in Latin America and particularly in Mexico.

There are two characteristics that define family businesses in Latin America: the first is that firms typically consist of multi-business portfolios with investments in several activities, often with no synergies between them. The second is that historically the strategy adopted by many families consciously includes the introduction of external capital to accelerate growth because debt markets are underdeveloped, and interest rates can be prohibitively high. The risk of loss of control is less than in many other countries because different classes of shares can be used, making it possible to retain control with a shareholding as low as 17 percent. In a region where debt markets are limited, the ability to raise additional equity to dilute below the normal 50 percent level without losing control, provides added flexibility to business owners to maintain their competitive position in a rapidly growing market. Lack of capital can be a constraint for those companies deciding to remain fully private.

The introduction of external capital to Latin American family businesses has greatly improved "governance and transparency" with benefits for family and shareholders. Only 15 years ago, it was unusual for a Latin American family company to have an international presence. Since then, a number of regional champions have internationalized their businesses in a series of well-planned opportunistic moves, and this is the case in the following Mexican firms: Bimbo, América Movil, Cemex, and Televisa.

Understanding the region is important, but understanding the specifics of each country is critical because the key factors influencing decisions may be very individual and imply a different risk for family firms. Foreign investment has primarily focused their interest on Brazil, Mexico, and Chile although Peru has also received considerable investment in mining. For the new entrant to the region, Brazil, Chile, and Mexico have usually been the first markets with which people are likely to be acquainted.

Family-controlled businesses have been the driver of growth and employment in Latin America. With the exception of a handful of state-controlled champions such as CODELCO in Chile, Petrobras in Brazil, PDVSA in Venezuela, as well as PEMEX in Mexico, the majority of economic activity is seeded and controlled by private family-owned companies or foreign multinationals, often in partnership with local family firms. There are, however, few businesses which can trace their family ownership back more than three generations, with the majority of businesses still in the founding or second generation. Diniz, De Moraes, De Andrade Faria and Marinho in Brazil; Matte and Said in Chile; Garza Lagüera, Zambrano, Azcárraga, Romo Garza, Saba, Arango, Peralta, and Salinas-Pliego in Mexico, and Perez-Companc and Rocca in Argentina are all family names readily identifiable with prominent businesses in their home countries (Kirkman 1999).

An example of a successful regional entrepreneur is Carlos Slim Helú, considered the world's richest man, and who controls Conglomerate Grupo Carso, Grupo Financiero Inbursa and Carso Global Telecom. In Brazil, the Egydio de Souza Aranha and Moreira Salles families have a controlling position in Itau Unibanco—the region's most successful bank—and the Emirio de Moraes family controls the Votorantim Group with interests including basic materials, mining, pulp, and paper. In Chile, the Luksic family has extensive interests including mining, banking, and shipping. In Peru, the Romero family controls Banco de Credito, the country's major bank (América Economía 2015).

This chapter is organized as follows: we will start with an economic overview of Latin America as a region, then we will present the current status of research on family businesses in the region and subsequently focus on research carried out using Mexican companies as the subject, as the country offers unique characteristics within the Latin American context. We conclude with some challenges that family companies in Latin America face.

Latin America's Economic Outlook

The growing interest in Latin American economic and social history began in the 1960's and led to the publication of many sectorial studies that became standard reference works. The study of family firms in the same region can be traced to the 1970's. In the decades of the 80's and 90's the economic sectors in which family businesses operated became relevant, because the number of companies starting operations was different in the sector of interest in each country. For example, in Brazil, family firms were involved in coffee, sugar and some specific manufacturing branches predominantly located in Sao Paulo and Rio de Janeiro. In Colombia, the companies are still working in sectors related to coffee, tobacco and banana production, particularly in the Antioquia region (Barbero 2008).

Family businesses generate 60 percent of Latin America's GDP and employ 70 percent of the workforce in the region. Regarding the generations leading those companies we can say that 47 percent of them are managed by the first generation, 29 percent of the companies are managed by the second generation, 14 percent are managed jointly by the first and second generations at the same time and only 10 percent are led by the third or fourth generations (Ernst and Young 2014).

Potential growth in Latin America has been estimated at between 3 percent and 4 percent per annum over the past ten years, which is slightly below the growth recorded during the most recent period of expansion, from 2004 to 2008. However, the slowdown has continued since 2010 as the international situation, which undoubtedly boosted economic activity in the past, has worsened, so the "new normal" for the region may well be lower than previously expected. Latin America's productivity in recent years has been disappointing compared with that of both OECD countries and emerging economies.

Moderate poverty fell from more than 40 percent in 2000 to less than 30 percent in 2010. This decline in poverty implies that 50 million Latin Americans saw improved living conditions in the first decade of the 21st century. The Latin American middle class grew very substantially: from 100 million people in 2000, to around 150 million in 2012. The emerging middle class differs, of course, from country to country, but there are a number of common threads. Middle-class entrants are more educated than those they have left behind. They are also more likely to live in urban areas and to work in formal sector jobs. Middle-class women are more likely to have fewer children and to participate in the labor force than women in the poor or vulnerable groups (Ferreira et al. 2013).

Stronger productivity would lead to more growth and would reduce the significant rates of inequality and poverty found in the region. Education and innovation reforms must ensure equal opportunities for access to a complete, high-quality cycle of education and a workforce with better skills: this can be achieved with better matches to the labor market. There must also be measures to promote formal employment. In Latin America and the Caribbean, 36 percent of companies operating in the formal economy struggle to find a properly trained workforce, compared to a global average of 21 percent per country and an OECD average of 15 percent. Latin American firms are 3 times more likely than South Asian firms, and 13 times more likely than Pacific-Asian firms to face serious operational problems due to a shortage of human capital (OECD 2014).

Furthermore, Latin America is a major manufacturing hub with growing importance in retail and is increasingly a supplier of services. Ford, Toyota, VW, General Motors, and Renault amongst others manufacture cars in the region while Rio de Janeiro is the support center for offshore oil exploration. The size and growth potential of the regional market has encouraged global brands such as Nestle, Unilever, and Kraft to develop significant local production facilities encouraged by low labor costs. Embraer, a manufacturer of short/medium-haul aircraft, while not privately controlled, also has a presence in the region. It sells its aircraft worldwide and enjoys an excellent reputation for quality. Latin America is also a leader in financial services, suffering no significant impact from the credit crunch of 2008. Banks like Itau Unibanco and BTG Pactual, both privately controlled, have built strong franchises in retail/commercial and investment banking respectively. The top 10 family businesses generated approximately US$290 billion out of Latin America's US$5.3 trillion GDP in 2012 and employ almost one million people (Ernst and Young 2014).

On the other hand, the main risks to Latin America's economy lie in structural weaknesses. Most countries need to upgrade their infrastructure and logistics to boost competitiveness across more international markets and global value chains. As shown in the Latin American Economic Outlook 2013, logistics costs in the regions are almost nine times larger than tariffs, and far greater than in the OECD area. One way of reducing costs might be increased competition, which might also serve to discourage and monopolistic practices (Daude 2013).

Despite these structural weaknesses, some firms have been able to perform successfully. Of these, family businesses often show leadership and pave the way for other companies in Latin America, hence the growing enthusiasm for research into this topic. In the next section, we will focus briefly on research into family businesses.

Research on Family Firms in Latin America

Family business research has been approached from different perspectives (e.g. management, economics) and substantially enriched during the last twenty years. Today, one of the most relevant findings is that the distinctiveness and heterogeneous features of family business depend on four key factors: family business definition, geographic location, industry affiliation, and inter-temporal variation in economic conditions (Amit and Villalonga 2014). In this section, we attempt to identify major themes in extant research about particular aspects of family firms in Latin America. We approached three topics that we found the research has in common. First, ownership, control and management structure that significantly differs from other geographical locations. Then, features of Latin American businesses related to the structure, size and preferences of the business, as well as power and political process and size. Finally, entrepreneurial family businesses as a response to the adverse context in emerging economies.

Control and Management Structure

Research into ownership, control, and management structure in family firms has various lines of inquiry. For example, features related to the level of ownership concentration, corporate governance and the impact of the internationalization processes. In this regard, family-owned or controlled companies are the leading form of business organization in Latin American countries, and this has been true for some time, even among large listed companies. Some of the oldest family businesses in Latin America are located in Mexico and Brazil. For example, we have the Ypióca Group founded in 1846 which is involved in the beverage industry and belongs to the Telles family. Also from Brazil we have two more examples: Rotermund S.A. Indústria E Comércio founded in 1877 and which delivers specialized design services and Klabin which was founded in 1890 by the Klabin family and which produces paper products. In Mexico, the oldest family business is Tardan Hermanos Sucesores S.A., which belongs to the Tardan family and which produces and sells hats and caps (Ernst and Young 2014).

In the Latin American context, the ownership structure of listed firms is characterized by high levels of concentrated possession where many firms are directly controlled by one of the industrial or financial conglomerates that operate in the region (López and Saona 2005; Céspedes et al. 2010). Such control is exerted through the use of pyramidal structures that enable controlling shareholders to separate their voting and cash flow rights (Mendes and Mazzer, 2005) and by the notable presence of family groups among such owners (La Porta et al. 1999; Castañeda 2000; Santiago et al. 2009). Moreover, the control exerted by these family owners is not usually limited solely to their participation in the firm's ownership since they usually play an active role in management (La Porta et al. 1999). In the early 2000s over 90 per cent of 33 of the largest businesses in Latin America were family-owned and managed (La Porta et al. 1999). In addition, family ownership in Latin America typically involves multiple generations of managers and superimposes generational hierarchy on managerial relationships. Brenes, Madrigal and Molina-Navarro (2006) analyzed three cases of family businesses in Latin America and found that for family members, succession and control are sensitive topics which need to be resolved to avoid family conflict and business disruption. Formal family tiers act as corner stones in the company structure and reliance on external members was found to be a central issue when seeking a balance between business and family.

Boards of Directors in Latin American firms are not as independent as those in developed countries, making them less effective in monitoring the decisions made by managers (Santiago and Baek 2003; Lefort 2005). Sáenz and García-Meca (2014) examined the relationship between the internal mechanisms of Corporate Governance and Earnings Management as measured by discretionary accrual in a sample of 435 listed Latin American non-financial companies from the period 2006–2009. Their results showed that in the region the role of external directors is limited, and in addition ownership concentration might be a manipulative practice/constrictor mechanism when the ownership of the main shareholders is moderate.

Shen and Pereira (2013) extended the agency literature on ownership structure by investigating the effects of the degree of internationalization and main entry modes on ownership structure using a sample of listed companies from Argentina, Brazil, and Chile.

In total, they studied 425 Latin American firms between 2007 and 2011. Their results supported the negative relationship predicted by principal-agent theory (Bhaumik et al. 2010; Oesterle. 2013).

Features of Latin American Businesses

In Latin America the structure of business, the preferences of business, and the power in the political process differ from those in other regions and are likely to be quite stable (Schneider and Karcher 2012). The structure is characterized by a larger share of small and informal firms, the dominant role of multinational corporations (MNCs) and economic groups, and comparatively large firms which are smaller than in other regions. MNCs, which are key elements in the business structure, have different preferences depending on their strategic orientation and whether they invest in Latin America to gain access to resources, to new markets, or to enhance their global productivity.

Regarding large domestic groups, four main features can be identified (Schneider 2009). Firstly, they are widely diversified into subsidiaries that have little or no market or technological relation to one another. Secondly, each large group maintains direct hierarchical control over dozens of separate firms. Thirdly, small numbers of huge groups account for a large proportion of economic activity, sometimes estimated as high as a fifth or more of GDP. Fourthly, groups are mostly owned and managed by families, and often have been for several generations (Khanna and Yafeh 2005). In addition, business groups are often particularly strong in non-competitive industries such as the supply of resources and small firms have little political influence due to their informal nature. In the same vein, large firms have various ways of influencing the political processes in Latin America. Business leaders are well represented in governments and are often included in advisory councils which can play crucial roles in affecting policy.

An inductive survey of corporate governance and the organization of production in the larger countries of Latin America over the past half-century revealed four enduring features: diversified business groups, MNCs, atomistic labor and employee relations, and low-skilled labor (Schneider 2009). There are major variations within Latin America, especially in terms of country size, commodity rents and the degree of integration with the US economy. What is remarkable is that despite these variations, the similarities on the four core features remain significant. The huge size of most groups, both in terms of overall proportion of GDP and market dominance in certain sectors, means that relations with competitors, suppliers and clients are often unequal and imbued with a hint of coercive hierarchy (Schneider 2009).

Entrepreneurial Family Businesses

Many government leaders see entrepreneurial development as a gateway to economic development (Habbershon, et al. 2010; Nordqvist and Melin 2010). Recently, authors have begun to offer useful conceptual frameworks and some empirical evidence regarding the peculiarities of entrepreneurial family businesses. One conclusion of such previous studies is that the heterogeneity of family business matters when studying entrepreneurship because one family is similar to another. Therefore, internal and external contexts are essential in order to understand the phenomenon. As an example of an internal context, Dyer highlighted "strong organizational cultures" as a general characteristic of family business (1986). As an external context, Gupta and Levenburg studied the impact of the industry environment and national culture on an organization's entrepreneurial capabilities (2010).

Regarding entrepreneurial family businesses, while a paternalistic organizational culture may be associated with business activities in Latin America, studies reveal that these patterns are often challenged (Lenartowicz and Johnson 2003). In such a region, family business cultures have to adapt rapidly to uncertainty and change with a high degree of flexibility and often have to consider initiating new business ventures (Hall, Melin and Nordqvist 2001). In the same vein, most entrepreneurial ventures receive support from family members both financially and physically (Astrachan, Zahra, and Sharma 2003) as well as access to economic, market and social networks (Pistrui, Welsch, and Roberts 1997). This is especially true in developing economies that cannot rely on sophisticated regulatory systems or systems that provide financial support and venture capital, which is the case in Latin America. Family businesses are often a substitute for a lack of regulation by financial markets in developing economies and are found to offer effective protection to minority shareholders (Bertrand and Schoar 2006; Khanna and Palepu 2000; Khanna and Rivkin 2006).

As previously seen, the Latin American context has a variety of features that in some cases present similarities across countries. Nevertheless, each country has interesting peculiarities depending on its history and identity, current political system, geographical location and trade agreements among many other factors. In the next section, we will focus on an economy that has many of the characteristics of other countries in Latin America, but that also has special features: the case of Mexico.

Family Firms in Mexico

Why Mexico?

Mexico is maybe the most representative country in Latin America given its historic and economic characteristics. Mexico was the first Spanish colony to break away from Spain and help to pave the way for other wars of independence in Latin America. Nowadays, Mexico is the 14th largest economy in the world (CIA 2015); three of the Top Ten Latin American family businesses are Mexican firms: América Movil, which belongs to the Slim family (No. 1 of the top 10), Cemex, owned by the Zambrano family (No.8 of the top 10) and Grupo Bimbo, owned by the Servitje family (No. 10 of the top 10) (Ernst and Young 2014).

As in most developing countries, the majority of Mexican firms are family businesses. Regardless of size, the most dominant ones are owned and managed by one or more families or descendants of the founding family. Five of the top ten biggest companies in Mexico are family businesses (Expansion 2008). These companies are América Movil, Cemex, Femsa, Telmex, and Telcel. The other five companies in the top ten are Pemex and CFE (government companies) and Walmart, GM and BBVA-Bancomer (Global Companies) (Avendaño, Kelly, Treviño and Madero 2009). More than 90 percent of the firms listed on the Mexican stock exchange (BMV) have a clear family representation in both capital and control (KPMG 2013).

In Mexico, micro and small and medium-sized (SMEs) enterprises represent 99.8 percent of the total businesses, contribute 52 percent of the GDP and generate more than 71.9 percent of the jobs (INEGI 2010). According to the SME Observatory (Observatorio Pyme), 65 percent of these companies are family businesses (CIPI 2003). Therefore, family businesses represent the largest number of enterprises that currently exist in Mexico. Additionally, 60 percent of jobs are generated by FB, and they contribute half of the gross domestic product (GDP); around 90 percent of the more than three million businesses are managed by a family. According to the National Institute of Statistics, Geography and Informatics (INEGI), 57 percent of the companies have been in existence for less than five years, and these small, more recently founded companies are made up of one family and several non-related workers. They also experience family conflicts in the course of their day-to-day operations and the new generations faced more challenges than the founders did (García Fuentes 2015).

La Porta, López-de Silanes, and Shleifer (1999) stated that families control nearly 100 percent of Mexico's largest firms, and this number has remained largely stable in the 2000´s since the aforementioned companies are still under the control of the founding families. Unlike large businesses, there is not enough statistical information on medium and small family firms; there is no census to define the type of businesses (family and non-family) in Mexico, and no official agency has registered firms in this sector to date (Avendaño, Kelly, Treviño and Madero 2009).

The lack of accurate statistical information about family businesses in Mexico leaves us with many unanswered questions. This is because in Mexico there is no legal entity called "family business" which could be classified as an official entity like small or medium enterprises with rights and obligations. That is one of the reasons why many contemporary family businesses are operating outside the legal and regulatory framework, therefore there is no information about how many of them exists nowadays.

Research on Culture in Mexican Family Firms

Despite the lack of statistical information, there are some studies about family businesses that indicate that entrepreneurial behavior is related to the culture of the business, as this is where members of the family have a strong influence (Adler and Pérez 1993; Athanassiou et al. 2002; Belausteguigoitia 2006; Astrachan 1988). For example, 76 percent of Mexican family firms lack policies regarding succession and in 78 percent of these kinds of companies, family members do not compete with other candidates for a position in the company (Durán and San Martín 2013).

Hoshino's work (2005) and De Clercq and Belausteguigoitia (2007) focused on non-family employees. Hoshino (2005) begins by establishing that in large family businesses there is a negative tendency of family members to participate which leads to his interest in identifying the development of managerial profiles. The results of De Clercq et al. (2007) validate the positive and important relationship of employee commitment to factors such as employment status, the perception of organizational climate, and the administrative orientation of the company.

Athanassiou et al. (2002) found that consistency in the perception of the Mexican management team on issues such as corporate culture, strategic vision, and organizational goals appeared linked to a high level of goal achievement in those areas associated with finance, society, and family.

Belausteguigoitia et al. (2007) were interested in determining whether the variable of Psychological Climate is associated with organizational commitment, entrepreneurial orientation, and employee effort. The sample took into account both family and non-family companies. Overall, the results showed some similarity in both types of companies and demonstrate a relationship between organizational climate and entrepreneurial orientation.

Ayup et al. (2008) focused on the recognition of the relationship between brand image, organizational culture and organizational continuity of family firms in Mexico. The results showed that organizational culture determines the permanence and positioning of the family business, and as a result, the company relies on the brand image generated and promoted within a strong organizational culture.

Maubert (2008) shows us a series of data which postulate the weight that values, ethics, and management have within the FB in Mexico. The data highlights that where 75 percent of the companies are managed by their founder, 58 percent have a business plan and in 27 percent the succession plan is known by family members; 31 percent of homeowners have a will; 43 percent of the businesses have a Board of Directors, 21 percent of this percentage includes external advisors; 26 percent have a Family Constitution; 39 percent give access to key positions only to relatives, and; 27 percent have rules guiding the work of family members within the company.

Research on Succession in Mexican Family Firms

Other authors also focus on the succession problem. For example, the relationship between the impact of human resources development and succession in Mexican family businesses represents for Hoshino (2004) the main topic of his research. The author recognizes two patterns: the first concerns those cases where a woman is the natural descendant of the company and, in general, it is not a participant in the succession; the second relates to the lack of anticipation of the succession and the sudden loss of a family member, which ordinarily involves the deterioration in performance of the firm. On his side, Navarrete (2008) analyzes the factors of family business and property that help explain the continuity of Mexican family businesses. The author includes the influence in the succession process of certain characteristics of the family as the strength of the relationship in terms of interdependence, cohesion, and adaptability.

The work of Flores et al. (2008; 2010) is also focused on succession and shows significant common features with the work of Hoshino; for example, in the first study, the authors mention that more than half of the children questioned hope to replace their parents at retirement; in the second case, 70 percent of owners expect to be succeeded by the children. However, the owners do not have a family succession plan despite recognizing that this situation has the potential to cause serious problems for the company such as stagnation or even bankruptcy.

The study of Ramírez and Fonseca (2010) shows that social capital in the Mexican family business is the result of the intersection of the relationships between the owning family, family interaction and the participation of other members in the business. That intersection influences the willingness and commitment of the members of the network, notably when new projects are proposed. The authors, therefore, maintain that in the company family members belonging to previous generations facilitate influence and access to existing relationships, in addition to building new relationships with new generations and improving the capabilities of the network.

Often, knowledge is the source of the development of competitive advantages, therefore understanding the way in which it is integrated and shared within the family business can significantly contribute to the continuity of the company. In this perspective, Sandoval et al. (2010) are interested in understanding how knowledge is revealed in different models of family businesses.

Corporate Governance in Mexico

As we mentioned previously for Latin America, in Mexico families also play an essential role defining corporate governance practices. For example, the purpose of most board members in Mexican companies is to control shareholders through family ties, friendship, business relationships and labor contracts (Espinoza and Espinoza, 2012). Babatz (1997) and Husted and Serrano (2002) show that 53 percent of a company's managers or senior executives are also managers of other companies of the same group, or are relatives of the executives of the company.

According to Castañeda (2000), in most Mexican firms the president of the board is the main stockholder and the general manager. They, therefore, experience little in the way of opposition from independent board members. This author shows that, on average, only 20 percent of firms allow a majority of external members on the board, and this fact does not necessarily mean independence since those external members can also be involved with another company within the same business group. In addition, an average of 35.2 percent of board members belong to the president's family while 38.7 percent are executive managers and around 57 percent are employees or relatives of the CEO.

Castrillo (2007) highlights the relationship between the mechanisms of corporate governance and managerial discretion using a sample of companies listed on the Mexican Stock Exchange. The author wondered whether these mechanisms were conditioned by the ownership structure of the company; the results suggest less managerial discretion in family firms than in non-family firms.

It is worth mentioning that the Mexican corporate system has more in common with the European or Latin-American corporate governance models than with the Anglo-Saxon ones (San Martin-Reyna and Duran-Encalada 2012). In Mexican companies, as in other European or Latin American enterprises, ownership is relatively more concentrated (La Porta et al. 1999).

Esparza et al. (2010) analyzed the main differences between the financial management of micro, small and medium-sized Mexican tourism firms (family and non-family), considering variables such as financing, profitability, growth and the use of accounting and financial information. Through the results of their study, they recognize that family businesses get higher returns and accounting and financial information to a lesser extent than non-family firms. In addition, they corroborated that family businesses are older than non-family enterprises.

Treviño and Bontis (2007) through the analysis of several cases of mergers and acquisitions in family businesses, propose to introduce the concepts of human capital, structural capital and relational capital as an important part of the qualitative factors for assessing family businesses in these strategic processes.

Conclusions

Family business ownership could be an opportunity or a threat, depending on a variety of factors. Family business ownership and commitment may be understood as adding value if the company and the controlling family can respond to the concerns of the investor's community. On the other hand, in Latin America, as elsewhere, family fights have destroyed companies to the detriment of all stakeholders.

Main Challenges

In Latin America, especially in Mexico, family firms are smaller and younger than their counterparts in the rest of the world; almost half of them are in fact first-generation. Research shows that there is a lack of strategic planning and had centralized decision making (Burgoa et al. 2013; Durán and San Martín 2013); this situation implies a major problem for Latin American entrepreneurs because they need faster and more modern organizational systems to compete globally.

The challenges that family business owners face in Latin American countries are influenced by the countries in which they operate but common to all are the following:

- How to sustain growth to remain competitive in a rapidly changing environment and balance this with the financial needs of the family shareholders. The issues here being the retention of control, the debate over re-investment versus higher dividends, and the level of additional risk to be assumed.
- How to obtain external capital in a turbulent economic environment.
- The role the family should have in the business whereby the main challenge is to recognize the need to professionalize management.
- How to attract and retain the best talent in a competitive labor market.

For a small minority, how to mitigate the impact of political risk can also be of major concern. This may range from excessively onerous taxes or constraints on the export of capital to the other extreme of expropriation. Fortunately, the latter is rare in Latin America but it does demonstrate the need for geographic diversification to lower risk. Interestingly, families impacted by political risk often tend to believe that things will improve with time – a state of denial likely to end up in destroying significant value.

Within the "family" dimension, family governance is a constant topic of discussion and this includes pressure to diversify portfolio risk and increase dividend levels. Another widely debated subject concerns the treatment of share ownership in case of generational change or marriage. Families develop their own policies for this depending on the specific circumstances but there have been a few well-publicized cases where rifts and conflicts have been exposed. This usually originates in the failure to define the ground rules at an earlier time, when this would have been less controversial, or reliance on goodwill in the family, which may be absent in the subsequent generation. Fortunately, advance planning and harmony are the norm. Moreover, the predominance of family companies shapes both, opportunities and particular corporate governance challenges that not always are considered in markets where ownership is dispersed and management is mainly composed of hired external specialists.

Suggestions for Future Research

The success of many economies in Latin America like in Mexico, Brazil and Chile is such that they are rapidly becoming major economic forces in the world. Family firms play a key role in this economic development. To date, little is known about family business in emerging economies.

Our review of the literature suggests there is a gap in relation to the impact of country culture or contextual factors and its consequences for family-firm outcomes. Very few studies investigate the specific characteristics of this type of company in each country and make a comparison between them. This suggests important questions, for example: what are the contextual characteristics that promote variation across countries in Latin America? And how do contextual characteristics or specific industries affect outcomes for family firms?

It would also be interesting to know how specific processes like succession may vary in each country; what specific skills, resources and relations make family successors more or less able than their counterparts in developed regions?

Recently research has focused on entrepreneurial family firms because of the economic impact that they may generate. Therefore, we need more studies on the related factors that encourage professionalism in this kind of entrepreneurship for example spin-offs.

We also found some gaps in methodological aspects. The literature on family firms in Latin America shows that the methods and research designs are fragmented; there is a lack of longitudinal studies and some of the works are theoretical and have never been empirically tested. Some others are case studies and we need more quantitative analysis; typically research has relied on convenient samples, and there is, therefore, a need for more sophisticated approaches to explain the uniqueness (or not) of family firms in the region.

We believe that local or regional context should be incorporated within the study of family business; Latin America deserves more research attention, and we are sure that a greater quantity of high-quality research on this topic will generate insights for literature, practice, and public policy.

References

Adler, L. and Pérez, M. (1993). *Una familia de la élite mexicana*, México: Alianza Editorial.
Amit, R., and Villalonga, B. (2014). Financial performance of FBs. *Sage Handbook of Family Business*. Thousand Oaks, CA: Sage.

Astrachan, J.H. (1988). 'Family firm and community culture.' *Family Business Review*, 1: 165–189.

Astrachan, J.H., Zahra, S. A., and Sharma, P. (2003). *Family-sponsored Ventures*. Kansas, MO: Kauffman Foundation.

Athanassiou, N, Crittenden, W.F., Kelly, L., and Marquez, P. (2002) 'Founder centrality effects on the Mexican Family Firm's top management group: firm, culture, strategic vision and goals and firm performance.' *Journal of World Business*, (37): 139–150.

Avendaño, J., Kelly, L., Treviño, R.N., and Madero, S. (2009) 'A Family Based Competitive Advantage: Handling key success family factors in Mexican family firms.' *Cuad. Adm. Bogotá, Colombia*, 22(39): 191–212.

Ayup, J., De la Garza, M., and Cheín, N. (2008). 'La imagen de marca: un reflejo de la cultura organizacional de la empresa familiar.' X Asamblea General de la ALAFEC, No. 22, República Dominicana.

Babatz, G. (1997). 'Agency problems, ownership structure, and voting structure under lax corporate governance rules: The case of Mexico.' Ph.D. thesis, Harvard University.

Barbero, M.I. (2008) 'Business History in Latin America: A Historiographical Perspective.' *Business History Review*, 82(3): 555–575.

Belausteguigoitia, I. (2006). *Empresas familiares, su dinámica, equilibrio y consolidación*, 2ª. ed. México: McGraw-Hill.

Belausteguigoitia, I., Patlán, J., and Navarrete, M. (2007). 'Organizational climate as antecedent of commitment, effort and entrepreneurial orientation in Mexican family and non family firms.' *Revista del Centro de Investigación*, 7(27): 5–25.

Bertrand, M., and Schoar, A. (2006). 'The role of family in family firms.' *The Journal of Economic Perspectives*, 73–96.

Bhaumik, S.K., Driffield, N., and Pal, S. (2010). 'Does ownership structure of emerging-market firms affect their outward FDI and quest; the case of the Indian automotive and pharmaceutical sectors.' *Journal of International Business Studies*, 41(3): 437–450.

Brenes, E.R., Madrigal, K., and Molina-Navarro, G. E. (2006). 'Family business structure and succession: Critical topics in Latin American experience.' *Journal of Business Research*, 59(3): 372–374.

Burgoa, T., Herrera, E., and Treviño, J. (2013) 'Study on Family Business Administration in Mexico: Main Problems and Challenges Confronted.' *International Journal of Good Conscience*, 8(2): 01–22.

Castañeda, G. (2000). 'Governance of large corporations in Mexico and productivity implications.' *Avante, Studies in Business Management*, 3(1): 57–89.

Castrillo, L. and J. San Martín. (2007). 'La propiedad familiar como mecanismo de gobierno disciplinador de la dirección en las empresas mexicanas, una evidencia empírica.' *Contaduría y Administración*, mayo-agosto (222): 59–82.

Céspedes, J., González, M., and Molina, C.A. (2010). Ownership and capital structure in Latin America. *Journal of Business Research*, 63(3): 248–254.

CIA. (2015). 'The World Factbook. Mexico' Retrieved on August 19th from: https://www.cia.gov/library/publications/the-world-factbook/geos/mx.html.

Daude C. (2013). Latin America's challenge. Organisation for Economic Cooperation and Development. *The OECD Observer 2013*, 4(297): 38–39.

De Clercq, D. and Belausteguigoitia, I. (2007). 'Organizational commitment in mexican small and medium-sized firms: the role of work status, organizational climate, and entrepreneurial orientation.' *Journal of Small Business Management*, 45(4): 467–490.

Durán, J.A and San Martín, J.M. (2013). 'Estudio comparativo de la empresa familiar mexicana en el contexto mundial.' *Revista de Contaduría, Administración e Informática*. Año 2, No. 5 (septiembre-diciembre): 21–54.

Durand, F. (1996). *Incertidumbre y soledad: reflexiones sobre los grandes empresarios de América Latina*. Friedrich Ebert.

Dyer, W.G. (1986). *Cultural change in family firms*. Jossey-Bass.

Economía, A. (2015). 'Las 500 mayores empresas de América Latina,' retrieved on August 19th from: http://rankings.americaeconomia.com/las-500-mayores-empresas-de-latinoamerica-2014/.

Ernst and Young (2014). *Family Business Yearbook*. retrieved on July 13th, 2015 from: https://familybusiness.ey-vx.com/insights/family-business-yearbook-2014.aspx.

Esparza, J.D., García, D., and Duréndez, A. (2010). 'Diferencias de gestión financiera entre empresas familiares y no familiares del sector turístico mexicano.' *Actualidad Contable*, 13(20): 29–48.

Espinoza, T.I. and Espinoza, N.C. (2012) 'Family business performance: Evidence from Mexico.' *Cuaderno de Administración de Servicios Organizacionales* Vol 25, No. 44: 39–61.

Fernández, P. (2001). *El rostro familiar de los nuevos global players: la gran empresa familiar en México, Brasil y China en el siglo XXI.* (U. d. Barcelona, Ed.) Centro de Investigación de la Universidad del Pacífico, XXXVIII(68): 267–277.

Ferreira, F.H., Messina, J., Rigolini, J., López Calva, L.F., Lugo, M.A., and Vakis R. (2013). '*Economic Mobility and the Rise of the Latin American Middle Class.*' Washington, DC: The World Bank.

Flores, M., and Vega, A. (2010). 'La sucesión en las empresas familiares del sector textil en Tijuana, B.C., México,' Global Conference on Business and Finance, No. 10, México.

Flores, M., Vega A., and Ahumada, E. (2008). 'La sucesión en la pequeña empresa familiar de prendas de vestir en Tijuana: capital humano y desarrollo.' X Asamblea General de la ALAFEC, No. 15, República Dominicana.

García Fuentes, M. (2015). 'Negocios en familia. Herencia multiplicada.' *Entrepreneur, Emprende, Crece y Triunfa.* Septiembre. Digital edition available at: https://mx.zinio.com/www/browse/product.jsp?rf=sch&productId=500662334#/.

González, J.S. and García-Meca, E. (2014). 'Does corporate governance influence earnings management in Latin American markets?' *Journal of Business Ethics*, 121(3): 419–440.

Gupta, V., and Levenburg, N. (2010). 'A thematic analysis of cultural variations in family businesses: The CASE project.' *Family Business Review*, 23(2): 155–169.

Hall, A., Melin, L., and Nordqvist, M. (2001). 'Entrepreneurship as radical change in the family business: Exploring the role of cultural patterns.' *Family Business Review*, 14(3): 193–208.

Hoshino, T. (2004). '*Family business in Mexico: Response to Human Resource Limitations and Management Succession.*' Discussion paper No 12, Chiba: Institute of Developing Economies.

Hoshino, T. (2005). 'La estructura propietaria y el mecanismo de control de las grandes empresas familiares en México.' In M.A. Pozas ed. *Estructura y dinámica de la Gran Empresa en México: Cinco estudios sobre su realidad reciente*, México. El Colegio de México.

Husted, B. and Serrano, C. (2002). 'Corporate governance in México.' *Journal of Business Ethics.* Vol. 37, Issue 3: 337–348.

Khanna, T. and Palepu, K. (2000). 'Is group affiliation profitable in emerging markets? An analysis of diversified Indian business groups.' *Journal of Finance*, 867–891.

Khanna, T. and Rivkin, J.W. (2006). 'Interorganizational ties and business group boundaries: Evidence from an emerging economy.' *Organization Science*, 17(3), 333–352.

Khanna, T., and Yafeh, Y. (2005). 'Business groups in emerging markets: Paragons or parasites?.' ECGI-Finance Working Paper, (92).

Kirkman, A. (1999) 'The Americas.' Forbes Magazine retrieved on May 13th, 2015 from: http://www.forbes.com/global/1999/0705/0213097a.html.

KPMG (2013) 'Empresas familiares en México: El desafío de crecer, madurar y permanecer.' KPMG de México.

La Porta, R., Lopez-de-Silanes, F., and Shleifer, A. (1999). 'Corporate ownership around the world.' *The Journal of Finance*, 54(2): 471–517.

Lefort, F. (2005). 'Ownership structure and corporate governance in Latin America.' *Revista Abante*, 8, 55–84.

Lenartowicz, T., and Johnson, J.P. (2003). 'A cross-national assessment of the values of Latin America managers: Contrasting hues or shades of gray?' *Journal of International Business Studies*, 34(3): 266–281.

López, F.J. and Saona, P. (2005). 'Earnings Management and Internal Mechanism of Corporate Governance: Empirical Evidence from Chilean Firms.' *Corporate Ownership and Control*, 3: 17–29.

Maubert, I. (2008) 'Empresa y Familia ¿Amigos o Enemigos?' Retrieved on June 16th 2015 from http://www.soyentrepreneur.com/empresa-y-familia-amigos-o-enemigos.html.

Mendes, D. and Mazzer, R. (2005). 'Estrutura de propriedade e de controle das empresas de capital aberto no Brasil.' *Revista de Economia Política*, 25(2): 115–137.

Navarrete, M. (2008). 'Transición generacional en las empresas familiares mexicanas fabricantes de pinturas y tintas.' Premio UDEM-Adalberto Viesca Sada, No. 16, Centro de Empresas Familiares de la Universidad de Monterrey, México.

Nordqvist, M., and Melin, L. (2010). 'Entrepreneurial families and family firms.' *Entrepreneurship and Regional Development*, 22(3–4): 211–239.

OECD (2014). 'Latin American Economic Outlook 2015.' OECD iLibrary available at: http://www.oecd-ilibrary.org/development/latin-american-economic-outlook-2015_leo-2015-en.

Oesterle, M.J., Richta, H.N., and Fisch, J.H. (2013). 'The influence of ownership structure on internationalization.' *International Business Review*, 22: 187–201.

Pistrui, D., Welsch, H.P., and Roberts, J.S. (1997). 'The re-emergence of family businesses in the transform-ing soviet bloc: Family contributions to entrepreneurship development in Romania.' *Family Business Review*, *10*(3), 221–238.

Ramírez, M. and Fonseca, M. (2010). 'Building social capital across generations,' Family Enterprise Research Conference, México.

San Martin-Reyna, J. and Duran-Encalada, J.A. (2012). 'The relationship among family business, corporate governance and firm performance: Evidence from the Mexican stock exchange.' *Journal of Family Business Strategy*, 3 (Family Businesses from a World Perspective - Strategic, Ownership, Governance, and Socio-Psychological Heterogeneity), 106–117. doi:10.1016/j.jfbs.2012.03.001.

Sandoval, F., Gimeno, A., and Fonseca, M. (2010). 'Knowledge within family business models: Mexican family firm case studies.' Family Enterprise Research Conference, México.

Santiago, M., and Brown, C. (2009). 'An empirical analysis of Latin American board of directors and minority shareholders' rights.' *Forum Empresarial*, 14(2): 1–18.

Santiago-Castro, M., and Baek, H.Y. (2004). 'Board composition and firm performance of large Latin American firms: An exploratory view.' *Latin American Business Review*, 4(2): 1–19.

Sheng, H.H., and Pereira, V.S. (2014). 'Effects of internationalization on ownership structure: Evidence from latin american firms.' *BAR-Brazilian Administration Review*, 11(3): 323–339.

Schneider, B.R. (2009). 'A comparative political economy of diversified business groups, or how states organize big business.' *Review of International Political Economy*, 16(2): 178–201.

Schneider, B.R. and Karcher, S. (2012). 'La política de las empresas en Latinoamérica: investigando sus estructuras, preferencias e influencia.' *Apuntes: Revista de Ciencias Sociales*, 39(70): 7–28.

Soto Maciel, A. (2013). 'La empresa familiar en México Situación actual de la investigación.' *Contaduría y Administración*, 58135–171. doi:10.1016/S0186-1042(13)71213-0.

Trevinyo, R. and Bontis, N. (2007). 'The role of intellectual capital in mexican family-based business: understanding their soul, brain and heart.' *Journal of Information & Knowledge Management*, 6(3): 189–200.

29

FAMILY BUSINESS CENTERS

Donna Boone Parsons and Cindy Clarke

Introduction

Local family business centers (FBCs) serve to bring together a community of stakeholders interested in the ongoing success of family businesses. To varying degrees, FBCs bring together family business members, consulting and advising practitioners who work with family businesses, undergraduate and graduate students and family business scholars. Whether they focus on teaching, professional development, research or networking, local family business centers exist to strengthen and perpetuate the family-owned businesses in their areas.

Leon and Katie Danco created the first family business center in 1962 in Cleveland, Ohio. The Dancos' Center for Family Business was independent of any supporting organization (Sharma, Hoy, Astrachan, and Koiranen 2007). At present, only a few centers, like The Legacy Center in Knoxville, Tennessee operate as independent entities. The vast majority of family business centers are affiliated in some way with a college or university, although the nature of that affiliation and the location of the FBC within the university vary greatly. Most university-affiliated FBCs are housed in the school or college of business. Additionally, most of these university programs are professional development or executive education organizations specifically designed for members who identify themselves as participants in a family-owned business. However, more organizations that serve family business owners in the private sector, such as law practices, accounting firms, and investment advisors, are offering similar programming. This expansion in the private sector has led to an increase in the expectations of FBC participants for program quality and usefulness. (Sharma et al. 2007).

Following the Dancos, The Wharton School at the University of Pennsylvania started a university-based Family Business Center in 1979. For the next 20 years, the number of FBCs grew quickly from about 20 centers in 1988 (Sharma et al. 2007) to approximately 90 in 1995 (Carlock 1995). Sharma et al. (2007) reported 110 on the Family Firm Institute's (FFI) list of "Centers and Related Organizations" at the time of their review article. A current count of FFI's list of Education Centers reveals 139 centers worldwide. Of those, over ninety percent are affiliated with a college or university. This growth in the numbers of FBCs appears to be occurring outside of the United States and Canada. A panel presentation about Family Business Centers at the 2012 FFI Global Conference pointed to a vast reduction in the number of Centers based on declining membership of only 40 centers in the Family Business Alliance, an association of directors of university-affiliated family business centers in the United States and Canada (Clark, Feth, Houden, and van der Vliet 2012).

In general, university centers or institutes tend to be founded on the specific research interests of one or a small group of faculty members. Centers are created as a way to attract private and government funding and as a way for universities to interact with industry for research around specific topics or outcomes. Examples of university research centers exist across disciplines, although they tend to be clustered in the sciences and medicine (Bozeman and Boardman 2003; Stahler and Teish 1994). The creation of FBCs follows the patterns of other university centers in many ways. FBCs have often been created to increase university outreach and as a way to attract additional university funding. Additionally, the early formation of FBCs demonstrates university and industry collaboration. As an example, Mass Mutual Life Insurance initiated a family business survey to privately held companies which appears to be one of the cornerstones of family business centers. Mr. Richard Narva helped found the Northeastern University family business program in 1991 in partnership with Northeastern's Director of Executive Education. The initial funding was from Mass Mutual Life Insurance that subsequently went on to fund many university programs, as well as the inaugural 1992 conference of the Family Firm Institute. In other ways, however, the creation of FBCs tends to be unique. Early FBCs were, with a few exceptions, not organized around a research function. The early FBCs were created as entrepreneurial ventures based on the efforts of a champion for the idea. In several examples, this champion was someone serving in an advisory or support role outside of the research or teaching functions of the university. For example, Ken Austin, a successful alumnus, was the driving force in the creation of the Austin Family Business Program at Oregon State. At UNC Asheville, George Groome, the Chair of the Board of Trustees, championed the formation of the Family Business Forum. The focus on research has been a more recent phenomenon for FBCs as newer programs have become concerned with academics and practitioners have begun to be concerned with sharing insights about successful family enterprises (Bird, Welsch, Astrachan, and Pistrui 2002).

This chapter will investigate past and current issues facing family business centers. First, we will explore the types of family business centers and discuss the comparative strengths and weaknesses of each type. Next, the chapter will discuss challenges that family business centers face in integrating the work of the family business center with the mission and strategic direction of the supporting university or organization. The next section of this chapter will examine the issue of how the function of family business centers should be assessed. Finally, we will propose some future directions for local FBCs and research on FBCs.

About Family Business Centers

Sharma et al. (2007) suggested that all centers focus, to varying degrees of research, outreach and curriculum development. Birdthistle and Fleming (2003) identified two distinct operational models under which FBCs operate. The Forum Model or the Kennesaw Model, named after a pioneering program at Kennesaw State University, has many variations, but all centers operating under this model focus heavily on providing family business education as an outreach to the community. The vast majority of these programs are university-affiliated, but a few are associated with a local chamber of commerce. Programs operating in the Kennesaw Model offer executive education and programs for members who pay a yearly membership fee. Sponsors – typically professional service providers – contribute financial and other resources to the university, but are often forbidden from directly soliciting members. Kennesaw Model centers are member-based organizations that provide resources and programming to help businesses with issues specific to family businesses such as transition planning for leadership succession, and also assist members in maximizing the overall well-being of their company in traditional terms of finance and management. Under this model, the director is often *not* a faculty member. Thus involvement in curriculum and research is not inherently part of this model (McCann 2003). The Forum Model creates a tie between the university and local businesses. The thinking is that, because most donors to universities are family businesses, a natural reciprocity exists. The family business center helps sustain local family businesses and, in return, they help sustain the university.

The advantages of the Forum Model are many and are the foundation for the proliferation of this model. Anecdotal evidence suggests that the majority of family business centers continue to operate in this way. University advancement and development offices are charged with finding links between the university and the community because they know that donors with a connection are more likely to give. Because a large percentage of donors to most colleges and universities are business owners, family business centers present the opportunity to engage that group of stakeholders in a meaningful way. Secondly, the Forum Model includes the financial support of sponsors who allow programs to run with minimal cost burden to the university. Sponsors usually represent industries that benefit from the success of family businesses. Sponsor annual dues range from $2,500 to $10,000 (USD). Finally, many university-based centers operate outside of academic affairs with a staff director (McCann 2003). This structure allows Forum Model centers to operate with fewer constraints and less accountability. This means that center directors may make more timely decisions and, in many cases, operate autonomously.

There are also potential disadvantages to the Forum Model. One is the probable lack of a champion for the center other than the director. If there is no integration with the other parts of the university, specifically in academic affairs, the return on investment to the university may be seen as limited to donations received rather than viewed as a significant facet of the university's community involvement. If the director is not a faculty member, there may be restricted access to university resources (e.g., faculty, students, funding) and limited research. Few connections to the core of a university's mission can result in less or no perceived ownership by administrators, putting the center at risk in terms of longevity (McCann 2003).

The Holistic Model was proposed by McCann and Upton (2000) from Stetson University. The Holistic Model is a strategic approach to integrating the FBC with the affiliated university. In theory, programs operating under the Holistic Model focus on the three basic elements of the academy – teaching, research, and outreach. The FBC is aligned with the academic side of the university, not merely an external extension of it. In practice, these FBCs, such as the one at Stetson, are geared toward students in degree programs and are focused on curriculum. At Stetson, the world's first family business major and minor degrees were developed as part of their business curriculum (McCann 2000). Since Stetson graduated its first majors in 2006, a few other universities have developed majors or minors in family business, and many other universities have begun offering undergraduate family business courses (Marklein 2013). A few others offer graduate-level family business courses.

The Holistic Model analyzes the impact that students might have on their family and business systems. During the start-up phase of their own family business center, a Stetson University survey of students found that 42 percent of business majors self-identified as coming from families that own businesses (DeMoss 1999). Similarly, the course in the MBA curriculum at the Kenan-Flagler School of Business at the University of North Carolina–Chapel Hill includes a family enterprise course that requires students to interview their own families about their businesses and business strategies. Another example of this academic programming specifically for family business members is the EMBA for Families in Business program at Kennesaw State University. This objective learning opportunity can have a profound effect on family businesses, bringing faculty, students, and business families together in mutually beneficial and meaningful ways (McCann 2003).

Potential challenges for centers based on the Holistic Model are largely based on internal competition from other academic programs for financial support or other resources. Another challenge is that, often, the center is very dependent on the passion and energy of the director. That leaves centers vulnerable to the possibility that a center director is recruited to another university or leaves under other circumstances (McCann 2003). This is a risk especially for those centers that focus primarily on research. Because the field of family business research is so small and individual research interests are narrow, the departure of a family business researcher can potentially be difficult to overcome. Lastly, for centers to focus on curriculum, they must be associated with a university that has significant student interest and needs in this area. Public universities or smaller, private universities with higher percentages of first-generation college students might have much lesser demand for family business curriculum than the large number of students with family business backgrounds supporting the curricular programs at Stetson, for example.

Executive directors, hired by sponsors or the affiliated organization are responsible for maintaining direction, program planning, recruiting and maintaining members, membership services and the overall direction and focus of the center. Directors are housed in many different locations within supporting universities or organizations. In the cases of the UNC Asheville Family Business Forum and the Elizabethtown College High Center for Family Business, the director is housed within the Advancement Division of the University. In many university settings (e.g., Northeastern University, California State University Fullerton), the director is housed as part of the school of business. The Family Business Center at Wake Forest University is part of the Career Center. Two FBCs, the Institute for Family Business in Fresno, California, and the Family Business Alliance in Grand Valley, Michigan, are housed in local universities but are supported entirely by local chambers of commerce and sponsors.

Integration

Regardless of the form, an FBC takes, the best way to protect and to increase perceived significance of family business centers is through balancing sustained cooperation among the stakeholders in research, teaching and outreach. The outcome of cooperation develops credibility and mutually perceived value for each area. The Holistic Model of FBC operation is based on a program that integrates focus and activities in all three areas. Much of the literature warns of the risks of focusing on one area to the exclusion of others. This is particularly true if the primary focus is on outreach for the reasons outlined above.

McCann (2003) suggested that an FBC must be built on an "academic base of either teaching or research" (p. 125) whichever is more consistent with the mission and strategic focus of the university. At Stetson University, the Family Business Center was structured around teaching and curriculum because of the University's stated focus on the "primacy of teaching" (McCann p. 129). However, the Family Business Center balanced that focus by organizing research conferences and by becoming a founding member of the STEP project, a global collaboration in applied family business research (Sharma et al. 2007; Babson).

Exemplar programs at the University of Alberta have balanced the FBC functions by creating two centers that work together. The University of Alberta's Center for Entrepreneurship and Family Enterprise focuses on teaching and research and the Alberta Business Family Institute provides the outreach component. The two programs share an academic director and work together to provide value to the stakeholders. Although Kennesaw State was the foundation for the Forum Model of FBC operation and its original focus was on outreach, it has strived for integration by providing, at one time, an academic home for the *Family Business Review*, coordination of large research studies on family business and classroom materials for family business courses (Sharma et al. 2007). While the argument is strong for the integration of FBCs with their academic homes, it is this integration that makes the assessment of FBCs particularly difficult.

Assessment of Family Business Centers

Several searches on the topic of *family business centers* produced only one article in the academic literature about assessment of family business centers. Kaplan, George, and Rimler (2000) studied member perceptions and satisfaction in twenty-one university-based family business centers. The study surveyed 333 family business member firms and twenty-one directors. Their instrument was aimed at Forum Model programs. This survey measured center members' perception of the usefulness of center programming in terms of how much value the center programs provided for educating family members and for aiding in family business decision making around major business issues and succession. The survey also examined program performance, operationalized as program quality, program satisfaction, and service quality. Most FBCs utilize some form of assessment of program quality for individual programs. Often, they include questions about the usefulness of speaker content. It stands to reason that because FBCs often operate as a university outreach function, that community perceptions of that outreach would be assessed as measures of program success. McCann et al. (2004) suggest that any assessment of FBCs must include perceptions of all key stakeholders.

The lack of existing literature on FBC assessment is, perhaps, an indication of the lack of integration of FBCs into their affiliated universities. Much of the direction of assessment of the academic endeavors of teaching and research are driven by university accrediting bodies who are urging colleges and universities to create a "real culture of assessment" where every curricular and co-curricular program is assessed to ensure outcomes and to build continuous improvement (Wehlburg 2014). This culture of assessment is also driven by organizations such as AACSB International, an external accrediting agency for schools of business. Since 2003, AACSB standards have "placed emphasis on direct measures of student learning" (Wehlburg) to assess progress on achieving Student Learning Outcome goals.

AACSB has also completed an exploratory study to investigate how AACSB-accredited schools of business assess the impact of research. This study was driven by recognition of the increasing demands for universities to measure return on research investment. University stakeholders, particularly donors, granting foundations and governments are asking for universities to measure the outcomes of research because of the large investment in it (AACSB 2012). In practice, large research-based institutions have always measured the impact of faculty research in some way. With the new AACSB standards, it is likely that all colleges and universities will have increasing pressure to measure research impact.

What this increasing culture of assessment means for FBCs is that centers will likely be asked to assess their ability to reach desired outcomes. As discussed above, it is likely that the teaching and research components of FBCs are already being evaluated, but likely as part of an evaluation of degree programs, departments or colleges in which these functions reside. It is also likely that the outreach function of FBCs is evaluated as part of the evaluation of university outreach or development. As FBCs move toward integration of these three areas, the challenge will be to create assessment programs that measure the synergy and integration of these areas and measure specific outcomes related to the FBC. As any assessment should be based on program goals, FBCs could begin by developing program goals that go beyond outreach and include goals for integration. For example, goals could include simple target numbers for FBC staff member involvement in classroom activities or research or student participation in FBC programming. Additionally, these goals could involve quantity and impact of action research done in conjunction with the FBC or its members. Once goals for integration are developed, assessment is a matter of measuring progress toward the goal.

Future Direction of Family Business Centers

In 1998, Frishkoff outlined the key questions facing FBCs at the time. She suggested that the core question was, "Why should this college or university have a family business program"? Other key questions that should be addressed, according to Frishkoff were:

- Where is the program located within the University?
- Who are the clients?
- Who heads the program?
- What services are provided?
- How is the program funded?

DeMoss (2002) argued that the key question no longer remains unanswered. She suggested that it is clear that, for many colleges and universities, family business programming is an important element of university outreach. We agree that the core question and many of the other questions Frishkoff posed about FBCs have been answered. The question of long-term funding remains, as it likely always will. Additionally, the questions facing FBCs in the future are those about alignment, integration, and assessment.

Alignment

While the literature presents the models of FBCs as existing neatly in one of two categories, in reality, family business centers seem to operate on a continuum from pure Forum Model to entirely Holistic. Based on our interaction with most of the university-based centers in North America, we suggest that even centers that tend more toward the Holistic end of the continuum do not fully integrate the functions of teaching, research, and outreach. Centers tend to focus heavily on one area. A majority of centers operate closer to the Forum Model end of the spectrum, and many do not focus on activities not directly related to outreach. Therefore, a future direction for FBCs is to consider is increasing integration across the three functions.

The literature clearly suggests that to survive, the mission of a Family Business Center needs to be closely aligned with the mission or core activities (DeMoss 2002) of the university with which it is affiliated (Sharma et. al, 2007). This means that mission and goals of the FBC must be aligned with those of the university. Although we are not aware of any examples of this practice, the FBC should be a stakeholder in strategic planning for the academic area in which it resides and for the university.

Integration

Centers should position themselves as legitimate participants in academic activities (McCann 2000). FBCs that operate purely as outreach functions of the affiliated university risk being evaluated only in terms of money raised and are likely to be undervalued by the university (McCann et al. 2004). Any center affiliated with a college or university cannot base long-term survival on an outreach-only model. Because institutions of higher learning exist to teach and conduct research (to varying degrees), affiliated centers must be built, at least in part on this academic base (McCann 2003). McCann's plea that each FBC needs a champion still resounds. To fully integrate with the academic side of a university, that champion likely needs to come from faculty or academic affairs administration.

To do this, FBCs, particularly those with a primary outreach mission, should explore integration with the academic side of the university with which they are affiliated. For example, the Family Business Forum at the University of North Carolina Asheville recognizes that, at a teaching institution, activities should be more aligned with the curriculum. The Family Business Forum gave financial support for faculty development for the creation of a family business course. Another example is at Cornell where FBC members regularly volunteer to participate in curricular activities as guest speakers, panelists or reviewers in classrooms. FBCs at teaching-centered universities also involve students with the programming of the FBC. Many FBCs offer students of the affiliated university (and often their parents) the opportunity to attend center programs without charge. For example, Tulane Family Business Center at the Levy-Rosenblum Institute offers free memberships to family businesses who have offspring attending Tulane University. As another case in point, at Wilkes University, the Family Business Alliance launched a program that offers tuition discounts to members and sponsors, their employees, spouses, domestic partners and dependent children as a way to support the University's goal of enrollment growth.

According to McCann's (2003) argument, FBCs at research-centered institutions should integrate with and support the research activities of the university's family business scholars. Research originating in universities with strong family business research faculty (e.g., Mississippi State University, the Brigham Young University Marriott School of Business, Belk College of Business at UNC Charlotte, University of Vermont) is at the core of developing the body of knowledge about family business. FBCs in these research institutions could further support these efforts in several ways. Because family businesses tend to closely hold information about the family and the business, the FBC could facilitate researcher access to members for research studies. Also, the FBC could be involved in developing and providing funding for faculty members doing research in family business.

Another example of integration is from the University of Toledo. Filbeck (1999) described a program of faculty internships at the university. This program places faculty members in on-site internships with local family businesses for a minimum of 160 hours. This allows faculty members to experience the issues in family businesses and to incorporate that into their teaching. This idea might be especially valuable now in the family business field that is calling for increased interdisciplinarity to give experience to those faculty members with little or no business experience. It is also valuable for increasing the scope of business school curricula which is often based on large, corporate examples and cases.

For most FBCs, integration likely means increased focus on teaching and research. However, fully integrated programs cannot ignore the outreach or service function. The work of the FBC must apply to the practice of family business to serve the family business stakeholders. From a systems perspective, a fully integrated program values the input of the parts (teaching, research, outreach) to the whole and the value of the whole to the parts. To do this, FBCs must bring students, scholars, and business-owning families together in meaningful ways (McCann 2003).

Assessment

Jaffe suggested that to provide sustained benefits to members, FBCs must offer programming that creates opportunities for deep learning. According to Jaffe, deep learning or what he calls double-loop learning happens when FBC programming goes beyond providing content through lectures to create a shift in how people see things (Jaffe 1998). Likewise, Kaplan et al. (2000) found that members had a higher perception of program usefulness in a learning workshop environment rather than a lecture format. This is consistent with work about learning in college which suggests that deep learning occurs when assumptions are challenged and when learners are asked to synthesize information to solve problems (Bain 2012). McCann (2003) proposed that one of the pressing questions is how to measure or assess this deep, value-providing learning in center members/participants. He suggests that assessment should measure financial sustainability as well.

FBCs that are successful in the future will not only move toward the Holistic end of the spectrum but will see their mission as being a long-term one. McCann et al. (2004) use the analogy of health care to describe an ideal perspective for FBCs. Using this analogy, long-term FBCs are those that are concerned with preventive medicine and wellness rather than critical or acute care. In other words, centers should focus on preparing family businesses to deal with difficult issues before they occur rather than on crisis intervention (McCann et al. 2004). In order to do this, FBCs need to build ongoing and lasting relationships with family business members. Many FBCs have long-tenured members, and this should be another key measure of FBC performance. This long-term perspective will also aid FBCs in integrating research and teaching and in bridging the gap between family businesses and academia. Academic timelines tend to be longer than those in the business world for several reasons. Research by its nature requires a long-term perspective and requires time to complete a full cycle. Likewise, student learning occurs over a period of years and in a sequence of courses.

Funding

Long-term funding for FBCs remains as central an issue as it was in 1998 (Frishkoff). Clark, Feth, Houden, and van der Vliet (2012) reported that 30 percent of FBCs in the Family Business Alliance are experiencing financial difficulty while another 11 percent report breaking even consistently. It seems evident that FBCs must look beyond annual recurring income from member dues and sponsorships (Sharma et al. 2007). Long-term sustainability will depend on funding from research grants, sponsored research and endowments. The Family Business Alliance reports only 10 percent of FBC funding comes from endowments. As FBCs move toward greater alignment with university missions and increased integration with academic functions, it should increase the centers' ability to attract research funding.

Collaborative research efforts, like the STEP project, focus the research of many different centers. STEP (Successful Transgenerational Entrepreneurship Practices) was founded in 2005 by six university partners as a way to produce research collaboration on family business research. The STEP project now has over 40 affiliate universities who are involved in this global research project. The STEP project has produced case studies and, in 2015, released the STEP Survey, a quantitative comparison of family businesses across the six continents represented by STEP (Babson). The large scale and visibility of projects such as STEP will likely attract larger, more consistent financing for research.

Future Research

Future research in the area of family business centers should focus on three areas. First, qualitative case studies could examine the issue of integration. Such studies could examine the degree to which centers are integrating teaching, research and outreach. Additionally, case studies could highlight best practices of and outcomes from integration. Finally, case studies would be useful in determining what organizational, and structural factors might contribute to success in integrating.

Another area of future research should focus on assessment of FBCs. This work could examine how FBCs are currently assessing their outcomes. Also, existing research on how different kinds of university centers and institutes (e.g., university medical research centers, technology transfer centers) are assessed could be reviewed. Ultimately, models for assessing synergy and outcomes of fully integrated programs should be proposed.

Lastly, research could examine the level of applicability of research produced by FBCs. If family business research is to be valued for its usefulness in practice, it must be measured by metrics other than (or in addition to) standard metrics for academic research such as impact or citation usage. Researchers could suggest instruments for evaluating the level of dissemination of research findings and the application of those findings by family business practitioners.

Conclusion

The future of family business centers is promising. The family business community is a very supportive and collaborative one. Family business centers work together through their directors and the Family Business Alliance to share best practices. The small, but growing group of family business researchers collaborates at conferences like FERC (Family Enterprise Research Conference). This culture of collaboration allows new ideas to grow quickly as successes, and new knowledge is shared easily.

Outreach, education, and research all contribute to a continuous cycle of improvement and sustenance for family-owned businesses. (Sharma et al. 2007). It is likely that new funding resources for family business research will dictate research that is practical and applicable. The ideal future is that research will be providing practical answers that, in turn, will have a greater impact on students, feeding the cycle of family business education, and stimulating a change in mindset about family businesses from a public perspective and for family businesses themselves. As more and more understand that the legacy of family businesses is worth protecting, the importance of family business centers will become increasingly apparent, and the success of the family business center will become self-perpetuating.

References

'AACSB assurance of learning standards: An interpretation, [White Paper]' *AACSB.edu*, 2003, http://www.aacsb.edu/~/media/AACSB/Publications/white-papers/wp-assurance-of-learning-standards.ashx.

'Successful transgenerational entrepreneurship practices (STEP),' *Babson.edu*, accessed October 1, 2015, http://www.babson.edu/Academics/centers/blank-center/global-research/step/Pages /home.aspx.

Bain, K. (2012) *What the Best College Students Do*, Cambridge, MA: Harvard University Press.

Bird, B., Welsch, H., Astrachan, J.H., Pistrui, D. (2002) 'Family business research: The evolution of an academic field,' *Family Business Review* 15(4): 337–350.

Bozeman, B. and Boardman, C. (2003) *Managing the New Multipurpose, Multidiscipline University Research Center: Institutional Innovation in the Academic Community*, Washington, DC: IBM Endowment for the Business of Government.

Clark, T., Feth, S., Houden, D., and van der Vliet, D. 'Lessons learned from the frontlines: Navigating the challenging waters where academia meets business.' Presentation at the Family Firm Institute Global Conference, Brussels, October, 2012.

DeMoss, M. (2002) 'Developing consumer-driven services in university-based family business programs,' *Family Business Review* 15(2): 119–129.

Filbeck, G., Skutch, D., & Dwyer, D. (1999) 'Faculty internships in family business,' *American Journal of Business* 14(12): 47–56.

Frishkoff, P.A. (1998) 'Strategic questions for university-based family business programs,' *Family Business Review* 11(4): 355–362.

Jaffe, D.T. (1998) 'Building communities of learning in family business programs,' *Family Business Review* 11(4): 363.

Kaplan, T. E., George, G., and Rimler, G.W. (2000) 'University-sponsored family business programs: Program characteristics, perceived quality and member satisfaction,' *Entrepreneurship Theory and Practice* 24(3): 65–75.

Marklein, M.B. 'College courses enlighten family businesses.' *USA Today,* Feb. 25, 2013.

McCann, G. (2003) 'Where do we go from here? Strategic answers for university-based family business programs,' *Family Business Review* 16(2): 125–144.

McCann, G., DeMoss, M., Dascher, P., and Barnett, S. (2003) 'Educational needs of family businesses: Perceptions of university directors,' *Family Business Review* 16(4): 283–291.

McCann, G., Hammond, C., Keyt, A., Schrank, H., and Fujiuchi, K. (2004) 'A view from afar: Rethinking the director's role in university-based family business programs,' *Family Business Review* 17(3): 203–219.

McCann, G., Upton, N. (2000) *Rethinking the Role of the University-Based Family Business Center,* DeLand, FL: Stetson University.

Sharma, P., Hoy, F., Astrachan, J.H., and Koiranen, M. (2007), 'The practice-driven evolution of family business education,' *Journal of Business Research* 60: 1012–1021.

Stahler, G.J. and Tash, W.R. (1994) 'Centers and institutes in the research university: Issues, problems and prospects,' *Journal of Higher Education* 65(5): 540–554.

Wehlburg, C. 'Transformative assessment and student learning.' Presentation at the SACSCOC Summer Institute, New Orleans, LA, July, 2014.

INDEX

AACSB International 584
Abdellatif, M. 127
ability to innovate 232–3, 258
ability-willingness perspective to innovation 4, 232–5, 258
absorptive capacity 230, 245, 246, 247, 248, 250, 251, 252, 253
Academic Research 490
Academy of Management Journal 211
accountant, use of 169
accounting 3; choices 107–9; controls and long-term orientation (LTO) 73–74
activity content 196, 198
activity governance 197, 198
activity structure 196, 198
activity systems 196–8; heterogeneous 201–2
Adams, Janet S. 270, 321
adaptability 221, 445, 448, 451
adaptive narcissism 473–4
adjustment strategies 424, 427
adolescents and psychopathy 467
adopting perspectives, losing ability to 379–80
adoption and whole family structure 450
adverse selection problem 46, 48, 177
advisors facilitating leadership transfer 27
advisor/successor relationship 169
affective behavior 385–98
affective commitment to goals 446
affective state and manipulations in experiments 391–2
affect theory of social exchange 467–8, 469, 473
affluent families: business models of multi-family offices 196–9; internationalization of 195, 203–4
af Klinteberg, B. 464
agency 46–60; in Chinese family businesses (CFB) 494–5; costs 49–60; governance 60–61; and supply of bank debt 178–9

agency theory 2, 45–65, 77, 81, 168, 183, 215, 217, 220, 225, 226, 228, 247, 249, 402–5, 438; causality 63; and family firm literature review 2, 47–59; future research opportunities 63–64; and innovation 212–13; overview 45–47; research methodology 61–63
agent-manager 402, 404
agent morality 409
age of firm and corporate social responsibility (CSR) 339
age relationship and dyad family structure 439, 450
aggregation bias problem 180
Aguilera, R. V. 550, 552, 553, 558, 561
Aguinis, Herman 271
Ainsworth, S. 443
Akhtar, Reece 472
Alberta Business Family Institute 583
Ali, A. 49
Allison, T. H. 217, 230, 233
Alm, P-O. 464
Alsos, Gry Agnete 313, 314, 315, 317, 320
alternative explanations elimination 62
altruism 48, 58, 148, 405, 409, 444–5; *see also* family altruism; asymmetric 48, 60, 63, 513; and whole family dynamics 451
Amarapurkar, S. 423, 425
América Movil 572
Amit, R. 59, 144, 145, 149, 202
Amman, B. 127
Amore, M. D. 34, 102
Andersén, J. 230, 233
Anderson, R. C. 49, 60, 102, 148, 150
André, P. 50
Andres, C. 49, 102
Anokhin, Sergey 253
Antcliff, V. 299
anxiety with ownership transfer 25
APGAR scale 443

apprenticeship 149
Aquino, K. 58
archival studies 397
Argentina 524
Arosa, B. 55
Arregle, J.-L. 123, 440, 444, 449
Asaba, S. 50
Ashby, W. R. 372
Asia: internationalization of affluent families 195; and multi-family offices 201; percentage of family firms 119; and succession planning 23
asset substitution 177
Astrachan, J. H. 58, 120, 133, 295, 442, 550, 561
asymmetric altruism 48, 60, 63, 513
asymmetric information 213
Athanassiou, N. 573
attachment communication 369
attention-based view 221
Au, K. 299, 438, 440, 516
Austin, Ken 581
Austin Family Business Program 581
Australia and export orientation 126
authoritarian leadership 500
Autio, E. 56
autopoiesis 369
Ayup, J. 573

Babatz, G. 574
BaFin 200
Baker, Laura A. 466
balance method of leadership transfer 27
Bammens, Yannick 246
Banco de Credito 568
bank debt: and agency problems 178–9; control considerations and demand for 178
bank-optimal interest rate 176, 180
bankruptcy 52
Barbera, F. 169
Barbero, J. L. 103
Barclay, M. J. 177
Barge-Gil, Andrés 245, 256
Barnett, T. 105, 170, 294
Barrett, L. 396
Barrick, M. R. 99
Barth, E. 50
Bartholomeusz, S. 50
Basel I Capital Accord 189
Bau, M. 51
Bauman, Zygmunt 72
B dimension 124, 133
Becerra, M. 52, 406
Beck, L. 217, 232
Becker, T. E. 444
behavioral agency model 122, 144, 165, 218, 220, 222, 226, 227; and innovation 214, 215, 218
behavioral measures in experiments 393

behavioral theory 220, 223, 246, 247, 248
Belausteguigoitia, I. 573
Belgium: case study in credit rationing 175, 179–91; and open innovation 257
Ben-Amar, W. 50
Benavides-Velasco, Carlos A. 537, 538, 540
Bendersky, Corinne 364
benevolence 401–10; during leadership transfer 27; in stewardship theory 407–10; in the utility function 409–10
benevolent leadership 500, 501
Bennedsen, M. 25, 33, 439, 440, 441
Berent-Braun, M. M. 558
Berger, Allen N. 177
Bergfeld, M.-M. H. 99
Berman, Shawn L. 404
Bernal, Patricia 408
Berrone, P. 94, 122, 168, 236, 271, 297
Bertrand, M. 432, 439
Bessemer Trust 197
Betancourt-Ramírez, José Bernardo 530, 540
Bettinelli, Cristina 267
Bezdijan, Serena 466
Bhaumik, S. 127
Biais, Bruno 183
Bianchi, Mattia 245, 248, 254
bias in conflict 379
Bicomb Co-word Analysis Software 494
Biguiyuan 484
binding social ties 124, 133
Bingham, J. B. 168
biologically linked dyad structures 438, 450
Bird, B. 120
Bird, Miriam 26
Birtch, T. A. 299
birth order of children: and family structure 440; and succession 22; and whole family structure 450
Björnberg, Å. 444, 445, 447
Block, J. H. 50, 94, 102, 147, 213, 217, 218, 231, 233, 298, 408
blockholders 151–2
Bloom, N. 102
Bloomberg Top 50 ranking 200, 204
Blow, A. 445
Bluedorn, Allen C. 74
Blumentritt, Tim 31, 34, 407
board of directors 60–61, 570; in Colombia 560–1; composition of 54; family involvement 53, 57
Boivin, M. 466
Bontis, N. 438, 575
Boroditsky, Lera 72
borrower-lender agency costs 128
Boshoff, C. 442, 444
Boter, Håkan 253
Bradley, B. H. 99
Bradley, M. 392

Brandon, G. L. 100, 101
Brannon, D. L. 438, 439
Braun, M. 51
Brazil 568, 570; gender and likelihood of
    succession 440
Brenes, E. R. 570
Brigham, K. H. 75, 80, 295
Brooks, A. 391, 392, 395
Brown, Bonnie M. 23
Brownlee, Amy L. 405
Brunswicker, Sabine 245
Buchholtz, A. K. 58
Bunkanwanicha, P. 439, 440
Burcharth, Ana Luiza Araújo 246
Business Developmental Dimension (BDD) 287–8,
    290–1, 294–301
business models: global standardization of 199–200,
    203–4; heterogeneity of 201–4; homogeneity
    of 202–3; local adaptation of 200–1;
    of multi-family offices 196–9
buyer-seller relationship and long-term orientation
    (LTO) 73

Cabela Family Foundation 168
Cabrera-Suárez, M. K. 28, 401, 443, 444, 445, 446,
    447, 448, 530, 540
Cai, D. 51
Calabrò, A. 122, 123, 126, 130
Caldwell, Cam 408, 409
Callimaci, A. 105
Campbell, M. A. 464
Campodall'Orto, Sergio 245
Campopiano, G. 53, 169
Canada and succession 22
Canadian Association of Family
    Enterprises 166
Cannella, Albert A. 277
capital flows 425
capital stocks 425
capital structure 108–9, 176
Carney, M. 513, 516, 517
Carpenter, Robert E. 188
Carr, J. C. 446, 447, 448
Carree, Martin 246
Carroll, A. B. 409
Carso Global Telecom 568
Carter, Sara 313, 314, 316, 318, 319, 320, 322
Casasanto, Daniel 72
Caselli, S. 93, 103
case study approach to family as a variable 437
Casillas, J. C. 93, 94, 102, 103, 249
Caspi, A. 465
Cassia, L. 53, 80, 247, 298
Castañeda, G. 574
Castrillo, L. 575
Cater, J. J. 442
causality 61, 63, 386–7

cause: and effect variables covariation 61; precedes
    the effect 61–62
Cemex 572
CEOs 96–97, 221–2; death of 441; duality 60–61;
    family 167; and family-TMT-involvement
    93; and firm performance 30, 144, 148; and
    innovation output 231; and noneconomic goals
    234; non-family 96–97, 144; pay structure 55;
    risk taking propensity 215, 224, 232; succession
    and post-succession performance 33; tenure of
    148; as visionary 169
CEO-TMT interface 98–99
Chang, C.-Y. 51
Chang, E. P. 52, 405
Chang, S.-C. 297
Chang, Y. C. 127
Chao, C. Chen 493
charitable organizations 168
Charlemagne 368
Chaxu Geju 497, 498
Chen, E. T. 51
Chen, H.-L. 51
Chen, L.-Y. 297
Chen, Lihua 502
Chen, Ling 484, 486, 488, 492, 502
Chen, S. 51
Chen, T.-Y. 49
Chen, X. 51
Cheng, Q. 51
Chesbrough, Henry W. 242, 243
Chiang, F. F. 299
Chile 568
China 8, 9, 448; emerging domestic markets
    510–11; entrepreneurship in 507–8; export-
    oriented era of reform 509–10; family culture
    497; and family ownership 290; and foreign
    direct investment 127; and generational stages of
    the firm 167; and illegal entrepreneurship 321;
    and institutional efficiency 149; institutional
    environment and Chinese family businesses
    (CFB) 501–3; and internationalization 137; and
    leadership transfer 27; pattern of a differentiated
    order 497, 498; property ownership 511;
    single child policy 508; traditional culture and
    Chinese family businesses (CFB) 498–500; trust
    structure in 498–9
China National Knowledge Infrastructure
    (CNKI) 483
"China serves China" era 510, 511
Chinese family businesses (CFB) 483–504; change
    in social status 484; changing strategic focus to
    domestic opportunities 510–11; and China's
    institutional environment 501–3; continuity in
    496; economic and noneconomic goals 513–14;
    economic contribution of 484–7; enterprise
    system 494; entrepreneurial orientation 511–12;
    entrepreneurship 496; familism 494; family

involvement 515–18; family operation and management 502; founders and successors in 506–19; governance 496, 512–13; group-type organizational structure 503; growth of 497–501; knowledge sharing 516–17; lack of research on 488–9; literature review of 488–97; locations and institutions of 491; managing network ties 514–15; paternalistic leadership 499–501; political connections 502; relationship governance 494–6; researchers in 492; social charity 502; status quo of 484–8; succession in 496, 502; topical clusters of articles on 492–7; trust 494–5

Chirico, F. 51, 107, 169, 295, 296, 300, 315, 316, 318, 323, 410, 443, 446, 447

Chittenden, Francis 177

Chittoor, Raveendra 30, 33

Chiu, C. 127

Choi, S. B. 51

Chou Fu 514

Chrisman, J. J. 24, 52, 60, 91, 103, 108, 125, 129, 134, 152, 165, 214, 218, 226, 234, 281, 283, 284, 405, 410, 442, 450

Chu, Xiaoping 489, 491, 497, 499

Chua, J. H. 24, 52, 91, 108, 125, 129, 134, 144, 284, 405, 410, 442

Chung, Chi-Nien 31, 34, 55

Circumplex Model 438, 444, 445–6, 448, 470

civil law system 555–6

Clark, T. 587

Clarkson, M. E. 161

Classen, N. 218, 219, 229, 233, 246, 257

Claver, E. 103, 134, 135, 136

clinical psychopathy 460–1

clock-time 72

Clore, G. 392

club deals 203

co-CEO 99; and family involvement 96–97

CODELCO 568

cognitive behavior 385–98

cognitive conflicts 367

cognitive manipulations in experiments 390–1

cognitive priming 390

cognitive social capital 446

cohesion within the family 444, 448; impacting psychopathic leadership 469, 470; and whole family dynamics 451

Colbert, A. E. 99

Cole, P. M. 439, 442

collaboration: and conflict in family firms 359, 360; technological 247, 249, 253–5

collateral requirements for bank debt 189

collective identity 420

collectivism 100–1

Colombia 9, 524, 528; corporate governance of family business in 558–61

Combs, J. G. 438, 444, 445, 448

commitment to goals and whole family dynamics 451

common law 555–6

communication 5; among family members 445; attachment 369; and conflicts 367; in the copreneurial identity 420; decision 369; differing contexts of 369–70; disinhibited 368, 375–6; on dyad dynamics 451; within family dyad 442; and spousal support 422–3; and whole family dynamics 451

communicative logics 369–70, 372–4

community and stewardship 406

Community Innovation Survey 244

community service 149

competitor orientation 268

complementarities 197, 198, 202–3

compromising and conflict in family firms 359, 360

conceptual variable in experiments 390

configuration theory 250

conflict 6, 11, 349–65; aggravation of 378–80; antecedents of 351–3; avoiding 358–60; collaboration 359, 360; compromising 359, 360; contending 359, 360; and defining clear roles 362; differing perceptions of 363–4; on dyadic level 441–2, 451; effects of 353–5; and establishing family councils 362; between family members and non-family members 146; and family-TMT-involvement 96; forms of 350–1, 355; Fredo Effect 6, 349, 356–8, 361, 364, 365; future research 363–5; managing 6, 8–62; as a parasite 380; and parent-child relationships 362; patterns of 363; research results of 351–6; and setting employment standards 361–2; status conflict 364–5; and systems theory 367–82; theory 438; third-party intervention to handle 359, 361; and whole family dynamics 443, 452

Confucian dynamism 71

Confucianism 27, 500

Conglomerate Grupo Carso 568

connection and stewardship 406

conscious raising 7, 380–1

Conservation of Resource Theory 438

conservatism 269

conservative succession 35

consumption and long-term orientation (LTO) 73

context: blurring of markers 369, 374; and corporate governance 552–4

continuity of the business 151, 406; in Chinese family businesses (CFB) 496; in Spanish literature on family business 532–4

contracts, use of 57

control concentration: and conflict in family firms 351–2

control group in experiments 390

controlling owner stage of ownership 166–7, 286, 289–90

control orientation of family 95
Cooke, D. J. 463
Cooper, D. 98
copreneurial identity 419–20
copreneurs 439
Corbett, A. C. 297
Corbetta, G. 56, 102, 169, 405, 407, 408
core circle of network ties 515
Cornell University 586
corporate entrepreneurship 281–305; *see also* entrepreneurship; definition 283; and developmental dimensions of family firm 284–305; literature review 292–301
corporate governance 291; in Colombia 558–61; definition 550; factors influencing 551–4; in Latin American family enterprises 549–64; in Mexican family firms 574–5; in Spanish literature on family business 534, 538
corporate myopia 73
corporate social performance 167–8
corporate social responsibility (CSR) 6, 149, 268, 270–1, 276, 331–45, 401; by Chinese family businesses (CFB) 513–14; hypotheses 335–8; survey 338–43; theoretical background 333–5
corporate venturing 283, 293–300
correspondence bias 379
couple relationship and firm performance 419–20
cousin consortium stage of ownership 166–7, 287, 290, 301
cover story 391–3; in experimental design 388–9
Covin, Jeffrey G. 81
co-words analysis 532–3
Cox, J. W. 443
Craig, J. B. 219, 230, 233, 272
credit demand factors 176
creditors 152
credit rationing 4, 175–91; background 176–7; for long-term *vs.* short-term bank debt 177–91
Crespi, Rafel 180
Cronbach's alpha 446–7
cross-cultural differences with predecessor's withdrawal 29
Cruz, Allan 313, 315, 316
Cruz, C. 236, 297, 298, 301, 406
Cruz, C. C. 52, 61, 94, 122, 148
Cucculelli, M. 33, 52, 103, 148
Cui, Z. 126, 131
Cultural-Historical Activity Theory 438
culture: in Colombia impacting corporate governance 558–61; and controlling owner stage of ownership 290; and corporate governance in Latin American family enterprises 549–64; differing treatment of time 71–72; family in China 497; impacting Chinese family businesses (CFB) 483, 498–500; impacting leadership transfer 27; impacting market orientation 268–71, 276; impacting

multi-family offices 201; in Latin America 555–6; in Mexican family firms 573; in Spanish literature on family business 534–5
Curimbaba, F. 440
customer: involvement in innovation 254; orientation 268
Cuthbert, B. 392

Dahlander, Linus 244
Daily, C. M. 135
Daly, Kerry 72
Danco, Katie 580
Danco, Leon 580
Dancos' Center for Family Business 580
Danes, S. M. 419, 421, 422, 423, 424, 425, 426, 437, 438, 439, 440, 443
Das, Ranjan 30, 33
daughters-in-law 440
daughters joining family business 17, 22, 440
David, R. J. 433, 434
Davis, J. 284
Davis, J. A. 135, 444
Davis, James H. 403, 404, 407, 409
Davis, P. S. 272, 443
Dawson, A. 52, 437, 442
Dean, M. A. 439, 440, 442
death impacting family structure 441, 450
Debicki, Bart J. 540
debriefing experimental participants 394–5
debt: long-term *vs.* short-term 177–91; maturity 189; maturity and firm size 177; ratios of family firms 175; and succession 31, 34
De Castro, J. 297
decision making 144, 145, 146, 150–2; casuality of 387; in Colombia 561; communication 369; and conflict 443; and long-term orientation (LTO) 74; participative 446; and power 420–2; and stakeholder relationships 159–71; and temporal orientation 72–73; of top management team (TMT) 97–98
decision to join family business 18, 22
Decker, C. 200
De Clerq, D. 573
declining stage 300
De Jong, Jeroen P. J. 252
Dekker, J. 93, 103
Del Aguila-Obra, Ana R. 250
Delmas, Magali A. 271
de Luque, S. 169
De Maere, J. 52
demand and supply market for bank debt 176–8
demand equation in demand-supply disequilibrium model 5, 182–3
demand-supply disequilibrium model 180–90; estimation of 183–4
De Massis, A. 35, 53, 80, 91, 103, 211, 216, 220, 222, 229, 235, 247, 248, 298, 442

Demil, Benoît 248
demonization 379–80
demonized zones 380
DeMoss, M. 585
Demoulas, Arthur T. 349
Deng Xiao Ping 506
Déniz-Déniz, M. C. 334, 444, 445, 446, 447, 448
Depaire, B. 93, 103
dependent variable 393–4, 449
Deprez-Sims, A.-S. 296
De Rochemont, Maurice 252
Dess, G. G. 511
DeTienne, D. R. 315, 316, 318, 323, 410
developmental dimensions of family firm and
    entrepreneurship 284–305
De Zutter, Stijn 253
Dibrell, C. 219, 230, 233, 272
differentiated order in China 497, 498
Di Giuli, A. 93, 103
diluted ownership of Chinese family businesses
    (CFB) 516
DiMaggio, P. J. 200, 202
Dimov, D. 419
Ding, Z. 299
Dino, R. N. 57, 58
direct manipulation checks 392–3
discontinuous technology change 231
disinhibited communication 368, 375–6
Distelberg, B. J. 445
distributive justice perceptions 361
diversification, corporate, lack of 146, 147, 152
diversity: as disparity 97–98; as separation 97–98; in
    top management team 97–98; as variety 97–98
dividend payments 57
divorce: on dyadic level 450; impacting family
    structure 441, 450; impacting on family
    business 439
Diwisch, Denise S. 31, 33
Djoundourian, Salpie 32
Dodson, M. C. 466
Dollinger, M. J. 135
domain redefinition 283
Donaldson, Lex 403, 404
Dou, Junsheng 78, 489, 493
Doucouliagos, Chris 403
downsizing 50
Drechsler, Wenzel 247
Driffield, N. 127
duality of family members' role 146
Duran, P. 123, 216, 235, 241, 259
Duru, A. 49
Dutch and open innovation 257
duty impacting top management team (TMT) 101
dyad dynamics 441–2, 451
dyads 8
dyad structure of the family 8, 434, 436, 438–9
Dyer, W. G. 270, 448, 449, 571

Dyer, W. G. Jr. 417
Dyer, W. J. 417, 448, 449
dynamic capabilities 251
dynastic succession 150–1
dysfunctional conflict 363

early exit of shareholders 25
Economic Management Journal 490
economics: of business and succession planning
    23; context and post-succession performance
    31, 34; and corporate governance 552; and
    ownership transfer 26
economic values 169
Eddleston, K. A. 34, 79, 105, 121, 294, 352, 354,
    355, 356, 407, 443, 444, 445, 449, 468
E dimension of FIBER model 124, 134
efficiency 197, 198, 203
Egydio de Souza Aranha family 568
Emirio de Moraes family 568
emotional aspects of ownership transfer 25–26
emotional attachment to venture 419–20
emotional capability and whole family
    dynamics 452
emotional connection on dyadic level
    442, 451
emotional detachment of family members
    124, 134
emotional endowment 409
emotional support 422
emotions: affecting behavior 7; and
    communication 371–2; eliciting in experiments
    391–2; and experience sampling methods 396;
    in family business 375–8; and social exchange
    467–8; and stewardship 406
employment: opportunities of family members
    165; setting standards for 361–2
Ensley, M. D. 93, 98, 104
entering the business stage 288, 291–2
enterprise governance 9
enterprise system in Chinese family businesses
    (CFB) 494
entitlement, minimizing among family
    members 361–2
entrenched family ownership 60
entrepreneurial legacy 452
entrepreneurial orientation (EO) 81, 99, 103–12,
    212, 283–4, 294–9, 301, 452; in Chinese
    family businesses (CFB) 496, 502, 511–12;
    and family-TMT-involvement 96; and
    psychopathic leaders 472
entrepreneurship 4–6, 11, 59; *see also* corporate
    entrepreneurship; portfolio entrepreneurship; in
    China 509; in Chinese family businesses (CFB)
    496, 502; decrease of 146; entrepreneur and
    entrepreneur's spouse 419; illegal 321; informal
    321; in Latin American firms 571–2; and
    long-term orientation (LTO) 79; and market

orientation 267–78; portfolio 311–24; social 331; transgenerational 322
Entrepreneurship and Family Business Research Center (EFBRC) 491
environmental friendly practices 168, 230
equity-based modes of internationalization 124, 127–38
Esparza, J. D. 575
Essen, Marc 78
estate tax rates and ownership transfer 26
ethical behaviors 270
ethical stewardship 408–9
ethnicity and succession planning 23
Europe 9; and gender in succession 17, 22; internationalization of affluent families 195; and portfolio entrepreneurship 321
Evans, Rodney E. 23
Evergreen College for Family Business 491
exclusiveness of financial products 197–9
executive entrenchment 53
exit strategy 410
expansion and crisis periods 175, 180
expansion/formalization business stage 287, 291
experience sampling methods 396
experiments 386–98; additional to extend findings 395; conducting post experimental procedures 394–5; constructing the independent variable 389–93; extending experimental findings 395–7; future directions 397–8; measuring the dependent variable 393–4, 449; setting the stage 387–9; vignette 389
exploitation activities as innovation 230
exploration: and implementation stage of succession 25–29; as innovation 230
export behavior 123–4
export orientation 125–7, 129–35
extended family 557
external environment and entrepreneurship 267–78
external market opportunities 254
external successors 25
external technology acquisition 222, 257–8

Faccio, M. 148
Fahed-Sreih, Josiane 32
failed succession 21
familiness 78, 121–2, 137, 214, 230, 269
familism 38; in Chinese family businesses (CFB) 494
family: adaptability 23, 231; cohesion 23, 44; and corporate social responsibility (CSR) 336–7, 339, 341, 343; culture in China 497; definition 7, 8, 418; dynamics and functioning 441–6; entry into the business 23; flourishing 36–37; influencing innovation 211–38, 256–8; integrity 424; and internationalization 126; involvement in top management team (TMT)

90–112; literature review 433–5; measuring family variable 436; member ratio in the top management team 98; members becoming impediments 356; and nonfamily members relationship 63–65; perceptions influenced by factors 8; preserving influence on business 36; psychopathy in 462, 467; role in succession 37–38; as supra-TMT, 95–96, 99–100; as a system 373; tensions 452; ties 452; as unit of analysis 434, 436; as a variable 432–53
family altruism 334–5, 357, 394, 407; *see also* altruism; and conflict in family firms 353
Family APGAR 424, 429, 443
family business: in China 483–521; in Latin America 556–7, 567–76; local and regional context 8–10; next generation joining 17, 22; organizational behavior 329–413; review of Spanish literature 522–47; strategic management 13–207; and tacit knowledge transfer 28
Family Business Alliance 580–1, 586, 587
family business associations 165–6
family business centers 10, 580–8; assessment of 584–7; funding 587; future direction of 585; future research 587–8; integration 583–6
Family Business Consulting Group 166
Family Business Forum 581
family business forums 165
Family Business Review 169
Family Business System Model 282
family capital 423
family centered culture 557
family-centric behavior 146
Family Climate Scales (FCS) 444, 445
family conflict asymmetry 363–4
family control 55, 124; in internationalization 126, 128, 129–32
family councils 53; to avoid conflict in family firms 362
Family Developmental Dimension (FDD) 288, 291–2, 294–301
Family Firm Institute (FFI) 580
family firms: correlational research approaches 386; definition 119, 160, 281; as a differentiated organizational form 120–3; as a dominant organizational form 119–20; as emotional arenas 375–8; experiments on 386–98; as nested stakeholder relationships 163
Family FIRO theory 421–2
family foundation 168
family funds in Chinese family businesses (CFB) 513
family-internal settlement systems 377
family involvement 6, 121; on the board 53, 55; in business impacting psychopathic leadership 469, 471; in Chinese family businesses (CFB) 502, 515–18; and corporate social responsibility 332–45; on performance 3

family management: and ability to innovate 232; and firm performance 148–9; and internationalization 126, 128

family managers: as agents or stewards 94; managerial skills 93–94

family member exchange (FMX) and conflict in family firms 354

family offices 4

family ownership 3, 6; and corporate entrepreneurship 285–90; entrenched 60; influencing firm performance 143–8; and innovation 232, 235, 236, 246; proportion of 57

family processes 8, 417–30; direct and indirect indicators of 423–6; informal power of 419–20; long-run and short-run 426–7; value of data from multiple family members 422–3; value of multiple methods of assessment 420–2

family protocol as part of corporate governance 560

family resource management 425

family science 1, 7–8, 11, 448, 449

family shareholders conflicting with non-family shareholders 143

family size impacting family structure 439–40, 451

family social capital (FSC) 446

family stakeholder group 164–7

family structure 438–41; and ownership transfer 26; as a whole 439–41

family-TMT-involvement: forms of 93; influencing organizational outcomes 93–97; literature review 91–92; strategic preferences 94, 102

family-TMT-ratio 95

family utility 409–10

family wars 378

Fan, J. P. H. 439, 440

Fan, Jingli 500

Fang, H. 223, 248

Fangtai 484

Far East and gender in succession 17, 22

Farrington, D. P. 464

Farrington, S. M. 444

Fast, N. 395

father–daughter dyad 439

fathers/mothers resigning from family business 17

father–son dyad 439

father-to-son model of succession 496

Fayolle, Alain 267

FBCs. *see* family business centers

F dimension in FIBER model 124, 128, 129–32

Fei, Xiaotong 498

Feldman, E. R. 147

Feliu, Neus 64

female: as heirs 17, 22; lack of heirs 36–37; leaders and succession planning 23; likelihood of succession of 440; oldest children not as successor 25

Femsa 572

FERC (Family Enterprise Research Conference) 588

Fernández, Z. 125, 130, 225, 230, 233, 249, 257

Feth, S. 587

Fialko, A. S. 55

FIBER model 122, 123, 236

FIDC 200

Fiegener, Mark K. 23

Fiet, James O. 79

Filbeck, G. 93, 104, 586

File, Karen M. 23

finance 3–4

financial capital 425

financial performance 59, 103–12

financial products, exclusiveness of 197–9

financial services industry and multi-family offices 195

firm: growth and bank debt 183, 188; identity 121; innovativeness 272

firm performance: below aspiration levels 234; and conflict in family firms 353–5; and impact of family 417–30; multidimensional perspective 145, 146; negatively impacted by family management 148–9; and portfolio entrepreneurship 313; post-succession 30–34; and ratio of family members in the top management team 98; in Spanish literature on family business 536; and stakeholder relationships 159–60

FIRO theory 439

firstborn daughters as heirs 440

Fisscher, Olaf A. M. 250

Fitzgerald, M. A. 437

Fleming family 197

Fleming Family & Partners 197

Flores, M. 574

Focam 197, 199

Fonseca, M. 574

Fontaine, N. M. 466

foreign direct investment (FDI) 124, 127–8, 137

Foreign Economics and Management 490

Fortin, A. 105

Forum Model 581–2, 584, 585

Fosfuri, Andrea 246

founder-achiever 24

founder and controlling owner stage of ownership 286, 289–90

founder-inventor 24

founder involvement 150

founder of family tradition 24

founders of Chinese family businesses (CFB) 506–19

founder-strategist 24

founding family name and innovation 231, 234

Frank, H. 370, 371

Frankforter, Steven A. 404, 408, 409

Frattini, F. 211, 216, 235, 245, 247, 248

Fredo Effect 6, 349, 356–8, 361, 364, 365, 472
free cash flow 54
Freeman, R. E. 159, 160, 161
Freud, Sigmund 473
Friedman, Milton 73
Frishammar, Johan 250
Frishkoff, P. A. 585
Fu, Xiaolan 247
full information maximum likelihood model (FIML) 184
functional conflicts 367
functional integrity of family 452; and conflict 443
fundamental attribution error 379
Fundamental Interpersonal Relations Orientation 438
futurity 151

Galbraith, C. S. 439, 441
Gallo, M. A. 126, 129, 130, 134, 270, 528
Ganesan, Shankar 73
Gann, David M. 244
Ganter, M. 221, 231, 234
Gao, F. Y. 105
García-Álvarez, Ercilia 24, 80
García-Vazquez, J. M. 128
Garrett, R. 219, 230, 233
Gatti, S. 93, 103
gender: and dyad family structure 439; of dyad members 450; and female heirs 36–37; and likelihood of succession 440; and potential family heirs 17, 22, 38; roles in businesses in Latin America 557–60
generation: diversity in top management team (TMT) 95, 96; first to second generation transfer of firm 31, 33; impacting psychopathic leader 469, 471–2; involvement and conflict in family firms 355; multiple and family-TMT-involvement 96; number of and corporate social responsibility (CSR) 336–7, 339, 341, 343; transfer and innovativeness 271
generational stage of firm 166–7; and innovation 232, 260
geographic dispersion of affluent families 195
George, G. 53, 584
Gergaud, Olivier 271
Gersick, K. E. 64, 135, 271, 284, 285, 286, 290, 450
Ghobadian, A. 299
Ghoshal, Sumantra 401, 446
Giacalone, Joseph 405, 409
Ginsberg, A. 283
Glavas, Ante 271
global standardization *versus* local adaptation 196, 200–1, 203–4
Gnan, L. 53, 58
goal-priming 390–1

goals 214; affecting behavior 7; affective commitment to 446; conflict between principal and agent 402, 404; family 143–4; family mixed with business goals 121–3; and innovation 260; shielding 390–1
Godfather, The (Puzo) 356
Goel, S. 57, 319
Gollier, Christian 183
Gómez Betancourt, Gonzalo 462, 530, 540
Gómez-Mejía, L. R. 52, 53, 77, 94, 122, 134, 144, 147, 148, 152, 214, 220, 236, 297, 406
Gonzâlez, M. 53
Gonzalvo, Pilar Saldaña 24, 80
governance 2, 9, 50, 56, 59–61, 197, 198, 291, 449; in Chinese family businesses (CFB) 494–6, 512–13; corporate 534, 538, 549–64, 574–5; relational 494–6
government ties by Chinese family businesses (CFB) 514–15
Granovetter, Mark 403, 405
Graves, C. 54, 126, 132, 134
Gray, S. 51
Green, Leonard 73
"greenwashing," 391
Groen, Aard J. 250
Groome, George 581
gross revenue 424
grounded theory 80
group-type organizational structure in Chinese family businesses (CFB) 503
Grundström, C. 220, 231
Grupo Bimbo 572
Grupo Financiero Inbursa 568
grupos 556
Guangdong province 491
guanxi 514–15
Gudmunson, C. G. 422, 423, 426
Guiso, Luigi 177
Gulbrandsen, T. 50, 95, 104
Gummesson, Evert 73
Guo, C. 515
Gupta, V. 571
Guth, W. D. 283
Gutierrez, I. 53
Guzmán, A. 53

Habbershon, Timothy G. 322
Haberman, H. 438, 439
Hack, A. 215, 224, 231, 232, 235, 236
Hall, Annika 405
Hall, Graham C. 177
Hambrick, D. C. 90, 97, 100, 101
Hamilton, Eleanor 315, 316
Hampton, M. M. 135
Han, S.-K. 433, 434
Handler, W. C. 15

harmony: among family members 444, 468;
    and whole family dynamics 452
Harris, D. 135
Harrison, D. A. 97
Harrison, J. S. 152
Hart, T. A. 295
Harveston, P. D. 23, 443
Harvey, Michael 23
Harzing, Anne-Will 243
Hasso, T. 169
Hauck, J. 221, 231
Hauser, B. R. 203
Hayes, Linda A. 408
Haynes, G. 423, 425
Haynie, J. M. 438, 439
Hays, Nicholas 364
He, Xuan 493, 502
Hedberg, P. R. 421, 425
Hegel, Georg 497
heir: female 17, 22; lack of 36–37; male *versus*
    female 440; potential 17, 22, 38; preparation
    and post-succession performance 32;
    qualifications of 36
Hellerstedt, Karin 26
Hennerkes, B.-H. 367
Hernandez, Morela 407, 408
Herreo, I. 104
Herrera, R. M. 444
Herrero, I. 54
heterogeneity of firm 63–64; and
    innovativeness 277
heterogeneous activity systems 201–2
Hewitt-Dundas, Nola 251
"Hidden Champions," 211
hierarchy of needs 403
higher owner age impacting succession
    planning 22
high risk/high return paradigm 146
Hitt, M. A. 123, 150, 151, 214, 257, 259
Hjorth, D. 437, 442
Hobfoll's conservation of resources theoretical
    proposition 423
Hofstede, Geert 71
Holistic Model 582–3, 585
Holliday, Ruth 319
Holt, D. T. 405, 447, 448
homo oeconomicus 402
Hong, P. 51
Hoopes, David G. 75
horizontal loyalty 378
Hoshino, T. 573, 574
hostile attributional bias 379
Houden, D. 587
House, R. J. 169
Howorth, C. 59
Hoy, Frank 259, 284, 294
Hsu, H.-T. 51

Hu, S.-y. 94, 105
Huang, Fang 247
Huang, Y. 514
human capital 214, 425
Hung, J.-H. 54, 59
Huovinen, Jari 314
Huse, M. 53

Iacobucci, Donato 313, 314, 315, 316
identification of family members with the firm
    124, 132
I dimension in FIBER model 124, 132
illegal entrepreneurship 321
imbalance and disintegration method of leadership
    transfer 27
impulsivity 467
inbound innovation 259
inbound open innovation 242
incentive compensation 60
incumbent: characteristics impacting succession
    planning 22; withdrawal 20, 29
independent variable construction 389–93
Index for Healthy Chinese Family Business
    (2015) 486
individual trust 498–9
inferential manipulation checks 392–3
informal entrepreneurship 321
informal power 421–2
informational opacity 177
information asymmetry 31, 50, 54; and credit
    rationing 176–8
information load increase 200
in-group/out-group preferences 357
in-laws impacting family structure 440–1
innovation 4, 5, 51, 211–38, 283, 448; ability-
    willingness perspective 232–5, 258; activities
    216, 229, 230–1, 236; and conflict 444;
    efficiency 259; lack of 147; open 241–61;
    research review 216–35; theoretical perspectives
    212–15; types of studies 212–13
innovation inputs 216, 229, 230, 235
innovation outputs 216, 229–30, 231–2, 236, 241
innovativeness and market orientation 267–78
input-mediation-output (IMO) for innovation
    4, 211
institutional context 448
institutional environment in China 501–3
institutionalism 199–200
institutionalizing succession processes 37
instrumental approach to stakeholders 161,
    163, 164
intangible assets 128
intellectual capital 517
interest rate, increasing 176–7
interfunctional coordination 268–9
intergenerational attention 446; and whole family
    dynamics 452

intergenerational authority and whole family
    dynamics 452
intermediary circle of network ties 515
internal cash flow 188
internationalization 3, 53, 58, 111, 118–38, 216,
    570; of affluent families 195, 203–4; equity-
    based modes of 124, 127–38; future research
    137; motivations and capabilities for 123–37;
    non-equity based modes of 124, 125–7, 129–38
interviews as data collection method 428
intrafamilial altruism 409
intra-family ownership dispersion and corporate
    social responsibility (CSR) 336, 343
intra-family succession 24, 26, 30, 36; and death
    of family CEO, 441; failed 35; and family size
    439–40
investment costs 50
invisible heiresses 440
Ireland, R. D. 295
Italy and illegal entrepreneurship 321
Itau Unibanco 568
Iturralde, X. 55

Jackson, G. 550, 552, 553, 558, 561
Jacobs, Andreas 197, 199
Jaffe, D. T. 314, 316, 586
Jaffee, Dwight M. 176
James, Albert E. 37
James, Harvey S. 77
Janus 459, 472
Janus effect 459–76
Japan: and family ownership 290; and joint
    ventures 127; keeping business in the family 38
Jaskiewicz, P. 28, 54, 57
Jaussaud, J. 127
Jehn, K. A. 363, 364, 443
Johnson, K. 439, 442
joint ventures 127, 128
Jones, O. 299
Jones, Thomas M. 404
Jorissen, A. 52
Jouriles, E. N. 466
Journal of Product Innovation Management 211
Journal of Sun Yat-sen University 488, 490
justice, logic of 377
Justis, R. T. 442

Kammerlander, N. 221, 231, 234
Kansas Family Business Forum 165
Kao, M. S. 127
Kaplan, T. E. 584, 586
Kappes, I. 54
Karra, N. 445
Karri, Ranjan 408
Kashmiri, S. 221, 231, 234
Katz, Jeffrey P. 405
Kaye, K. 376

Keating, Norah C. 24
Kellermanns, F. W. 52, 105, 121, 125, 129, 134, 146,
    169, 171, 215, 224, 231, 232, 235, 236, 260, 294,
    352, 353, 354, 355, 356, 405, 407, 443, 444, 445,
    449, 468
Kennesaw Model 581–2
Kennesaw State 583
Ketchen, D. J. 295
Kidwell, Roland E. 356, 358, 468
Kierkegaard, Søren 83
Kim, Y. 105
King, Sandra 32
Klabin 570
Klein, K. J. 97
Klein, P. 54
Klein, S. 54
Klein, S. B. 57
knowledge: integration among family members
    446, 452; sharing in Chinese family businesses
    (CFB) 516–17
Knudsen, Mette Praest 246
Kochan, Thomas A. 401
Kodithuwakku, S. S. 294, 300
Kolvereid, Lars 317
Kontinen, T. 123
Kotlar, J. 53, 222, 223, 248, 257
Kowalewski, O. 105
Kraiczy, N. D. 96, 105, 215, 224, 231, 232, 235, 236
Kristof-Brown, A. L. 99
Kuo, A. 127
Kuo, L. 59
Kuo, Y.-C. 59
Kuo, Y.-P. 54
Kwan, H. K. 438, 440

Labaki, R. 440, 441
Laforet, Sylvie 79
Lambrecht, Johan 24, 27
Landry, S. 105
Lane, Sam H. 314, 316
Lang, P. 392
Lang, S. 464
Lange, K. S. G. 200
language influencing concept of time 72
Lansberg, I. 442, 562
Lansberg, I. S. 135
La Porta, R. 573
Larraza-Kintana, M. 53
Lasagni, Andea 248
later-generation psychopathic leaders 472
later stage generational control 6
Latin America 8, 9; contextual factors influencing
    corporate governance 549–64; control and
    management structure of firms 570–1; cultural
    context 555–6; economic outlook 568–9;
    entrepreneurship 571–2; family business in
    556–7, 567–76; family structure in 557–8;

features of businesses 571; role of Roman Catholic religion 557–8

Lau, V. P. 438, 440

Laursen, Keld 248

Lawler, Edward J. 460, 473

leader–member exchange theory 475

leader personality and post-succession performance 32

leadership: authoritarian 500, 501; benevolent 500, 501; in Chinese family businesses (CFB) 499–501; dyadic perspective to 500; moral 500, 501; paternalistic 499–501; psychopathic 461–2, 467–76; transfer of 26–28

Le Breton-Miller, I. 15, 35, 36, 56, 75, 83, 93, 105, 106, 277, 401, 405–6, 445, 550, 551, 558, 561

Lecocq, Xavier 248

Lee, J. 444, 445, 448

Lee, Khai S. 24

Lee, S. 93, 104

Lee, Sungjoo 249

Legacy Center, The 580

legal environment and corporate governance 552

legal issues impacting ownership transfer 26

legitimacy of stakeholders 161

Lester, R. H. 93, 277

Levenburg, N. 571

Lewis, Marianne 405

Li, X. 55

Li, Xinchun 491, 492, 493, 496, 498

Li, Yiyuan 497

Liang, Qiang 55, 493

Liang, X. 126, 127, 131

Lichtenthaler, U. 211, 216, 235

life cycles of firm and entrepreneurship 5, 282, 284–5, 304

Lim, Guan H. 24

Lim, Wei S. 24

Lin, D. 55, 493

Lin, S.-h. 94, 105

Ling, Chen 491

Little, Heather M. 24

Litz, R. A. 52, 321

Liu, Chen 502

Llach, J. 224, 229

local adaptation *versus* global standardization 196, 200–1, 203–4

Lockett, Nigel 250

lock-in 197, 198, 202

Loeber, R. 465

Loedstar 166

logic of justice 377

lone founder firms and innovativeness 277

longevity goals and family-TMT-involvement 97

longitudinal research 5

long-term bank debt rationing 176, 177–91

long-term credit rationed firms: and non credit rationed firms 187–8

long-term debt 4

long-termism 71

long-term orientation (LTO) 2, 57, 70–83, 150, 151, 154, 168, 169, 234; antecedents 77–78, 82; and bank debt 179; in the business and economics literature 72–74; consequences 78–79; definitions 75–77; development of construct 71; differences within family businesses 82; and entrepreneurship 79; in family business literature 74–75; from financial investment perspective 75; future research 80–83; and internationalization 125, 128; measures of 79–80; and performance 78; from planning perspective 75; and resilience 78; and risk-taking 78; and sustainability efforts 78

López-deSilanes, F. 572

López-Sintas, Jordi 24

López-Vergara, María Piedad 530

loss aversion 3, 144–9, 214; framework 218; and value creation 149–53; and value destruction 146–9, 153–5

Love, James H. 252, 255

low-range conflict 363

Loy, J. T. 422

Lozano-Posso, Melquicedec 530

Lubtakin, M. H. 57, 58

Luhmann, N. 368, 374, 380

Luksic family 568

Lumpkin, G. T. 75, 79, 81, 295, 297, 433, 446, 447

Luo, J. 51

Luo, X. R. 31, 34, 55

Luo, Y. 514

Lybaert, N. 56, 93, 103

Lykken, David Thoreson 463

Lynam, D. R. 462, 463, 465

Maas, G. 442, 444

Machiavellianism 473

machismo 559

Maddala, G. S. 180

Madison, Kristen 405

Madrigal, K. 570

Mahajan, V. 221, 231, 234

Mahto, R. V. 445

Maignan, Isabelle 270

Makri, M. 53

maladaptive narcissism 473–4

male heirs 17, 22, 508; eldest children as successor 25; and likelihood of succession 440

male leaders and succession planning 23

malign clinch 375

man, self-serving model of 402–3

management: family managers *versus* non-family managers 93–94; of Latin American family enterprises 570–1; professionalization of

and succession 30, 33; and separation from ownership 48, 60
management buy-in (MBI) 31, 35
management buyout (MBO) 31, 35
Management World 490
managerial entrenchment 148
Manikutty, S. 322
manipulation checks in experiments 392–3
Mannarino, L. 52
Mannix, E. A. 443
Mansi, S. A. 49
Marchisio, G. 31, 293, 295
Margolis, J. D. 168
marital status on business success 417
Markarian, G. 57
Market Basket 349
market orientation 5, 267–78; hypotheses 269–71; and innovativeness 267–78; literature review 268–9; research methodology 271–2
marriage enterprise 288
marriage impacting family structure 440–1, 451
Marshall, L. A. 463
Martinez, J. I. 135
Martin-Oliver, Alfredo 180
Martín-Santana, J. D. 444, 445, 446, 447, 448
Maseda, A. 55
Maslow, Abraham H. 403
Mason, P. A. 90, 100
Mass Mutual Life Insurance 581
materialism impacting top management team (TMT) 101
Mathews, Timothy 31
Matthews, C. H. 55
mature business stage 287–8, 291
Matzler, K. 214, 225, 229
Maubert, I. 573
Mauer, David C. 177
Maury, B. 55
Mazzi, Chiara 31
Mazzola, P. 58, 107, 133, 295
McCann, G. 582, 583, 584, 586, 587
McConaughy, D. L. 55, 148
McCrory, E. J. 466
McDonald, R. 466
McGaughey, Sara L. 314
McGregor, Douglas M. 402, 403, 405
McKenny, A. F. 145, 217, 230, 233
McKenny, Aaron 267
McNulty, Terry 408
McVey, Henry 78
measurement issues 446, 448
Mehrotra, Vikas 38
Melin, L. 436, 444, 446, 448
Memili, E. 299
Merino, F. 127, 133
Messer, Tracey 408

Mexico 10, 528; culture and family firms 573; family business in 567–76; and illegal entrepreneurship 321; succession in family firms 574
Michael-Tsabari, N. 315, 440, 441
Michiels, A. 56
microfoundations of family firms 385–98
Micucci, G. 33, 148
mid-range conflict 363
Miles, M. 295
Miller, D. 56, 93, 96, 99, 105, 106, 144, 283, 401, 445, 550, 551, 558, 561
Miller, Danny 35, 75, 83, 277, 405–6
Miller, J. K. 515
Minichilli, A. 56, 95, 98, 102, 106
minority shareholders 49, 50, 51, 55, 60; legal protection of 26
Mintzberg, H. 447
Mirabella, D. 297
Mitchell, J. 33
Mitchell, J. R. 295
Mitchell, R. K. 161
models of man in organizational theory 402–3
Moffitt, M. 466
Moffitt, T. E. 465, 466
Molina-Navarro, G. E. 570
Molly, Vincent 33
monitoring 57, 60–61
Monreal-Pérez, J. 127, 133
Monteferrante, P. 562
Montemerlo, D. 53
Moog, P. 297
moral compass 408, 409
moral hazard agency problem 46, 48, 50, 60, 177, 188, 213
morality 405
moral leadership 500, 501
Morck, R. 38, 168, 260
Moreira Salles family 568
Moreno, A. M. 93, 94, 102, 103
Moreno-Menéndez, Ana M. 249
Morris, Michael H. 32
Moss, T. W. 295
mother-daughter dyad 439
mother influencing family succession 23
motivation for internationalization 123–37
Motwani, Jaideep 23
multi-family offices 195–205; business models of 196–9; heterogeneous activity systems 201–2; information load increase 200; institutional perspectives on 199–201; interaction among 200; interorganizational patterns of coalition among 200; mutual awareness among 200; national contexts of 196
multigenerational involvement and entrepreneurship 294, 299, 300
multiple-constituency theory 159

Múñez-Nickel, M. 53
Muñoz-Bullón, F. 132, 225, 233, 234
Murphy, P. J. 296
Muse, L. A. 441
Muske, G. 437
Mussolino, D. 126, 130
Mustakallio, M. 56, 496, 558
Myers, Steward C. 188
Myerson, Joel 73

Naldi, L. 57, 107, 144, 169
narcissism 473–4
Narcissistic Personality Inventory (NPI) 473
Narva, Richard 581
Narver, John C. 268, 270, 272
Nason, R. S. 447
national and cultural differences 8
national contexts of multi-family offices 196, 200–1
national culture and corporate governance 552
National Family Business Panel 423
National Family Business Survey (NFBS) 437
Natter, Martin 247
Navarrete, M. 574
nepotism 356, 557
networking 249, 250, 253, 254; in Chinese family businesses (CFB) 514–15
New Hope 484
new product portfolio 224; performance 231
new systems theory 374
next generation joining family business 17, 22
Nicholson, N. 444, 445, 447
Nielsen, Kasper M. 25
Nielsen, S. 98
Nieto, M. J. 125, 130, 225, 230, 233
Nieto, María 249, 257
non credit rational firms compared to long-term credit rationed firms 187–8
noneconomic goals 169, 221, 231; of Chinese family businesses (CFB) 513–14; and innovation 234
noneconomic outcomes 165
non-equity based modes of internationalization 124, 125–7, 129–38
non-family business and tacit knowledge transfer 28
non-family managers 51, 166–7; and firm performance 30, 31; managerial skills 93–94
non-family shareholders conflicting with family shareholders 143
non-financial goals 401, 409
non-financial wealth 121
Nordqvist, M. 26, 57, 296, 298, 301, 322, 447, 448
normative approach to stakeholders 161, 163, 164
North America 8, 9, 10
not-invented-here (NIH) syndrome 246, 255
not-shared-here (NSH) syndrome 246, 255

novelty 197, 198, 202; impacting top management team (TMT) 101
Nowland, J. 51
Nowotny, Helga 72
nuclear family 557

Oakey, Raymond P. 250
Öberg, C. 220, 231
observation as data collection method 428
Ojala, A. 123
Okoroafo, S. 125, 130
Olson, David H. 470
Olson, P. D. 437, 440, 443
O'Neill, T. A. 363
open innovation 5, 241–61; challenges 255–6; literature overview 245–53; opportunities and challenges 243–4, 254
opportunism 49, 63
O'Regan, N. 299
organizational ambidexterity 217, 230
organizational behavior 6–7, 11
organizational characteristics and needs impacting choice of successor 24–25
organizational mode of associations 498
organizational rejuvenation 283
organizational social capital (OSC) 446, 449
organizational social consciousness 272–3; and market orientation 267–78
organizational socialization 246
organizational theory and role of man 402–3
Ortiz-Molina, Hernan 177
Oswald, S. L. 441
Otondo, R. F. 443
outbound innovation 259
outbound open innovation 242
out-group/in-group preferences 357
out-licensing proprietary technology 254
outsiders. *see* non-family managers
outward foreign direct investment 124
owner and controlling owner stage 286, 289–90
owner-manager: conflict 48, 60; and family successor 442
owner-perceived success 424
ownership: concentration in Chinese family businesses (CFB) 512–13; controlled by predecessor 29; definition 418; diluted in Chinese family businesses (CFB) 516; and separation from management 48, 60; transfer of 25–26
Ownership Developmental Dimension (ODD) 285–90, 294–301
ownership dispersion 9, 100, 166–7; and conflict in family firms 354–5, 443; and corporate social responsibility (CSR) 336, 339–40, 343; impacting psychopathic leadership 469, 471; and intra-family ownership transfer 6, 26, 35
ownership group in a family firm 163

Padilla-Meléndez, Antonio 250
Pal, S. 127
pan-familism 500; in China 499
parent-child relationship: and conflict in family firms 362; conflict on dyadic level 442; and psychopathy 462, 467
parenting: inconsistent 467; psychopathic 474
Parida, Vinit 250
Park, B. I. 51
Park, Gwangman 249
Parker, S. C. 298, 300, 315
participative decision making 446, 452
participative strategy 407
particularism 121
passing the baton stage 289, 292
past experiences and portfolio entrepreneurship 317
Patel, P. C. 79, 98, 152, 214, 218, 226, 234
paternalism in Latin American firms 571
paternalistic leadership (PL) 499–501; model 500; studies on 500–1
patient capital 150, 151, 154, 214
Payne, G. Tyge 267
pay structures 53; of CEOs 55
Pazzaglia, F. 107
PDVSA, 568
Peake, W. O. 57
Pearson, A. 78
Pearson, A. W. 93, 98, 104, 105, 433, 446, 447, 448
pecking order theory 182–3
PEMEX, 568
Penas, Maria 177
Peng, Mike W. 493
Penney, C. R. 438, 444, 445, 448
Pérez, P. F. 128
Perez-Gonzalez, F. 25, 33
periphery circle of network ties 515
permanent income hypothesis 73
Perrow, E. 562
Perryy, M. 125, 130
perservance 151
personality characteristics 8
personal rule in Chinese family businesses (CFB) 513
Person-Organization (PO) Fit 82
Peru 524, 568
Petersen, Bruce C. 188
Petrobras 568
Phillips, N. 445
Phipps family 197
physiological measures in experiments 393
Pictet & Cie 199
Pieper, T. 558
Pieper, T. M. 57, 58, 133
Piñango, R. 562
Pindado, J. 57

Pinkkam, B. C. 511
Pistrui, D. 120, 296
Pittino, D. 56
Pizzurno, E. 80, 247, 298
planning and post-succession performance 32
political connections and Chinese family businesses (CFB) 502
political environment and corporate governance 552–3
Pombo, C. 53
Pont, C. 126
Pont, C. G. 130, 134
Porter, S. 464
portfolio entrepreneurship 5–6, 311–24; *see also* entrepreneurship; performance and outcome 322–4; prior research 316–18; research methodology 216, 312–13; studies on 314–15; triggers for 313, 319–20
Portugal 525; and leadership transfer 27
post-succession stage of succession 21, 30–35
Poutziouris, P. 296
Powell, W. W. 200, 202
power: dynamics and decision making process 420–2; informal 421–2; of stakeholders 161
Poza, E. J. 167, 408, 562
Pozza, L. 57
predecessor 23; conflicts with successor 29; goal adjustment capacities 22; new role in the business 29
Prencipe, A. 57
Priem, R. L. 170
primogeniture 22, 24, 37
Prince, Russ A. 23
principal-manager agency 49, 51, 54
principal-owner 402, 404
principal-principal agency problems 49, 50, 51
private enterprises in China 483–504
problem framing 214
process conflict 351, 353–6, 367, 443
productivity, decreased 50
professional-manager in Chinese family businesses (CFB) 499, 512–13
profitability and succession 30
profit margins 54
profit maximization 165
property ownership in China 501, 511
Prügl, R. 221, 231
psychodynamic measures of the family 436
psychological contracts 376
psychological ownership 58
psychological predispositions 7
psychopathic leaders constrained by family members 474
psychopathic leadership: family characteristics impacting 470–73
psychopathic parenting 474

psychopathy: clinical 460–1; definition 459, 460; in family 462, 467; in the family business 459–76; and family business success 467–76; literature review 463–6; positive and negative impacts 460; and positive impacts of 8, 11; and social exchange in the family 467–9; subclinical 460, 461
publicly funded research 251
Puig, N. 128
Pukall, T. J. 122, 123
Pullen, Annemien 250
Pupo, V. 52
Puzo, Mario 356

Quer, D. 103, 134, 136
Quirke, L. 201

Raaijmakers, A. 396
Radhakrishnan, S. 49
Raine, Adrian 466
Ram, Monder 313, 314, 316, 318, 319, 322
Ramírez, M. 574
Randerson, Kathleen 267
Randøy, T. 57
Ranft, Annette L. 405
Rao, A. Srinivas 24
rationality impacting top management team (TMT) 101
Rau, S. B. 137
R&D expenditures as measure of long-term orientation (LTO) 79
R dimension of FIBER model 124, 134
R&D intensity 216, 217, 225, 226, 227, 229, 235
R&D investment 55, 147, 150, 152, 213, 214, 216, 218, 220, 222, 223, 226, 227, 230, 234, 235
rebellious succession 35
reciprocal escalation 379
reciprocity: within the family 445; and whole family dynamics 452
Reeb, D. M. 49, 60, 102, 148, 150
Reform and Opening-up policy 484
relational governance in Chinese family businesses (CFB) 494–6
relationship conflict 350–6, 368, 443, 449, 468; within the Fredo Effect 358
relationship conflict scale 443
relationship quality on dyad dynamics 442, 451
relationship style and whole family dynamics 452
renewal of family bonds 124, 134
reputation and corporate social responsibility (CSR) 333–4, 342–3
Requejo, I. 57
Rerup, Claus 314
research methodologies 9
resource-based view of innovation 213–14, 219, 220, 225, 227, 228, 247, 249, 251
resource dependency theory 223

resource family/business intermingling processes 424
retirement age/date impacting succession planning 22
Revista de Empresa Familiar 524, 525
reward delay and value 73
Rice, John 247
Ricotta, F. 52
Rienda, L. 103, 134, 136
Rimler, G. W. 584
risk 122–3; abatement 226; aversion 225, 233, 235; in internationalization 128; preferences 144
risk-taking behavior 57, 214, 215, 224, 232; and long-term orientation (LTO) 78
Rispens, Sonja 363, 364
Robinson, M. 392
Robson, Paul J. A. 315
Roijakkers, Nadine 251, 254
role clarity among family members 362
Roman Catholic religion in Latin America 557–8
romantically linked dyad structure 438, 450
Romero family 568
Rönnbäck, A. Ö. 220, 231
Roper, Stephen 251, 252, 255
Rosa, P. 294, 300, 313, 314, 315, 316
Rosell-Martinez, J. 128
Rosenfield, D. 466
Rosplock, K. 203, 299
Rotermund S.A. Indústria E Comércio 570
Rothausen, T. 433
Roure, J. 299
Rousseau, Jean Jacques 376
Russell, Thomas 176
Rutherford, M. W. 441

sales, international 135
saliency theory of stakeholders 161–3
Salter, Ammon 248
Salvato, C. 169, 295, 300, 303, 405, 407, 408, 436, 443, 444, 446, 447
Sanchez-Bueno, M. J. 132, 225, 233, 234
Sánchez-Marìn, G. 127, 133
Sánchez-Sellero, P. 128
Sandoval, F. 574
Santamaria, L. 225, 230, 233, 249, 257
Santiago, A. L. 440, 441
Santor, D. 464
Sarathy, R. 444
Sardeshmukh, S. R. 297
scales 446, 448
Schlepphorst, S. 297
Schmid, T. 54, 234
Schneider, Ross 562
Schoar, A. 432, 439
Scholnick, Barry 406
Schonea, P. 50
Schoorman, F. David 403

Schulze, W. 516
Schulze, W. S. 48, 57, 58, 146, 148
Schumpeter, Joseph A. 242
Schumpeter Mark II view of innovation 241–2
Schweitzer, M. 391, 392, 395
Sciascia, S. 58, 96, 107, 133, 227, 234, 295
search breadth 229
SEC 200
second-generation psychopathic leaders 472
Segaro, E. 137
Segurado, J. L. 299
self-categorization process and leadership transfer 27
self-interest and corporate social responsibility (CSR) 334–5, 342–3
self-report in experiments 393
self-serving model of man 402–3
semantic paradox 382
sense-making theory 221
Seo, M. 396
separation of ownership and management 48, 60
settings for portfolio entrepreneurship 313, 320–2
settlement systems in families 377
Shan, Y. G. 54
Shapiro, D. 54
shareholders: conflict between majority and minority 60; legal protection of 26; as a system 373
shark repellents 404
Sharma, A. 51
Sharma, P. 24, 52, 91, 168, 281, 283, 284, 295, 300, 322, 410, 444, 448, 450, 580, 581
Sharma, S. 168, 270
Shepherd, Dean A. 314
Shevlin, T. 51
Shi, Benren 494
Shim, Jungwook 38
Shleifer, A. 572
shocks impacting leadership transfer 28–29
Shore, Ted H. 270, 321
Short, J. C. 217, 230, 233, 267
short-term bank debt rationing 176, 177–91
short-term orientation 73
sibling conflict on dyadic level 442
sibling partnership stage of ownership 166–7, 286, 290, 300
Sieger, P. 58, 299, 301, 315, 316
Silva, Paula 405
Singapore 445
single child policy in China 508
single-family offices 195
Sirmon, D. G. 107, 150, 151, 214, 216, 227, 234, 257, 259
Sirmon, H. 232
size of firm: and corporate social responsibility 332, 339; and debt maturity 177; in Spanish

literature on family business 536–7; and succession planning 23; and successor selection 25
Sjöberg, K. 57
Slater, Stanley F. 268, 270, 272
Slim, Carlos Helú 568
small- and medium-sized enterprises (SMEs) 227, 572; and corporate social responsibility 332; and innovation 241–61
smallness liability 243, 244, 250, 254
small-sized enterprises 536
smells to elicit emotions 392
Smith, C. 177
social capital 56, 214, 250, 425, 444, 446, 574; in Chinese family businesses (CFB) 494–5; and innovation 258–9; theory 78, 438; transfer 28; and whole family dynamics 452
social charity and Chinese family businesses (CFB) 502
social consciousness 5; and market orientation 267–78
social context 448
social embeddedness 403
social entrepreneurship 331, 401
social environment and corporate governance 552
social exchange: in the family and psychopathy 467–9; theory 460, 467
social identity theory 221, 246, 438
social insurance 334
social interaction among family members 445, 452
socialization of the next generation 24
social status of family on whole family structure 451
social support 422–3
social systems: theory and conflict 367–82; theory of 369–70
social transformation 9
social trust 498–9
Sociedad Anonima 560
society impacting Chinese family businesses (CFB) 483
socio-cultural approach to corporate governance 552
socio-emotional wealth (SEW) 3, 11, 37, 56, 77, 121–5, 165–6, 214, 218, 221, 224, 227; and benevolence 409; and demand for bank debt 178; and equity modes of internationalization 127; and family CEOs 97, 99; and family-TMT-involvement 95, 97; goals 474; and innovation 214–15, 236, 246, 276–7; and internationalization 137; and lack of willingness to innovate 233, 258; and portfolio entrepreneurship 320; theory 144–5; value creation of 149–53; value destruction of 146–9, 153

sole owners and conflict in family firms 351–2
Søndergaard, Helle Alsted 246
Songini, L. 58
sons-in-law 440
Sorenson, R. L. 445
sounds to elicit emotions 392
South America 64
South Asia and leadership transfer 27
Spain 9, 448; and export orientation 127; and foreign direct investment 128; and internationalization 125, 126; literature on family business 524–5, 528–9, 539; and open innovation 257
Spanish literature on family business 522–47; activity indicators 528–32; authors on 530–1; bibliometric analysis of 526–39; compared to English literature 537–9; corporate governance 534, 538; culture cluster 534–5; family business cluster 535–6; institutions on 530–2; overview 523–6; performance cluster 536; relation indicators 532–7; size cluster 536–7
Spiegel, F. 217, 231
spiral theory 83
Spithoven, André 251, 254
spousal support for business concerns 420, 422–3
spouses: of CEO, role of 408; in the entrepreneurial process 419–20
Spriggs, M. 228, 233
Sraer, D. 108
Stafford, K. 423, 425, 438
stakeholders 3, 151–2; and corporate social responsibility (CSR) 335–6; creating value for 196–7; definition 160–3; descriptive approach to 161, 163, 164; external 167–8; family group as 164–7; internal 167; as nested relationships 163; relationships with family film 159–71; synergy 170–1
stakeholder theory 159–63
Standifer, Rhetta L. 74
Stanhope family 197
start-up business stage 287, 290–1
state-owned enterprises (SOEs) 508, 510, 511, 514; in China 501
status conflict in family firms 364–5
Stavrou, E. T. 17, 32
Steier, L. 297, 444, 445
Steier, L. P. 28, 35, 550, 552, 558, 561, 562
Steijvers, T. 56, 93, 103, 189
STEP project 587
Stetson University 582, 583
Stetsyuk, I. 105
stewardship-based exit strategy 410
stewardship theory 7, 53, 77, 79, 81, 219, 220, 247, 334–5, 401–10; and benevolence 407–10; by Chinese family businesses (CFB) 513–14;

inaugural use of 404–5; missing ethical dimension 408–9
Stiglitz, Joseph 176–7, 180
Stockmans, A. 108
Stohs, Mark Hoven 177
Stouthamer-Loeber, M. 465
strategic alliances 134
strategic focus of Chinese family businesses (CFB) 509–11
strategic reference point theory 222
strategic renewal 283, 295–9
structural-quantitative measures of the family 436
Su, E. 493, 517
Suarez, M. K. 334
subclinical psychopathy 460, 461
successful psychopath 459
succession 2, 9, 166–7, 169; affecting firm performance 30–34; assessment of studies on 16–21; in Chinese family businesses (CFB) 486, 487–8, 496, 502; choosing a successor 24–25; competing for 37; and conflict impeding 442; conservative 35; definition 15; exploration and implementation stage 25–29; failed family 35; five stages of 15–16; holistic framework for studying 36–37; incumbent's withdrawal stage 29; and innovation 231, 260–1; intra-family 24, 35–36, 439–40; and maintaining stakeholder relationships 171; male *versus* female heir 440; in Mexican family firms 574; and owner-manager trust relationship 442; planning stage 17–24; and portfolio entrepreneurship 318, 319–20; post-succession stage 30–35; predictors of an effective succession 30; preparation 17–22; rebellious 35; satisfaction from 31, 35; and socialization of the next generation 24; in Spanish literature on family business 534, 537–8; time and firm performance 30; wavering 35
successor: attributes of 24; availability of 23; capability and post-succession performance 32; of Chinese family businesses (CFB) 506–19; choosing 19, 24–25; development system 23; discretion 31, 33; external 25
successor's trap 376
Suess, J. 558
Sundarmurthy, Chamu 405
Sun Yet-sen University 491
superficial charm 459
supply equation in demand-supply disequilibrum model 183, 185
supra-TMT, 3, 92, 95–96, 97; family as 99–100
surveys 395–6
survivability capital 150, 214
Sustainable Family Business Theory 438

sustained regeneration 283
Sveen, J. 129
Sweden: family advisors 169; and ownership transfer 26
Swinth, R. L. 128
systems theory 438; and conflict in family firms 367–82

tacit knowledge: and succession planning 23; transfer 28
Tagiuri, R. 135, 284, 496
Taiwan 31; and internationalization 137
Talavera, O. 105
Tanewski, G. A. 50
Tantalo, C. 170
Tardan family 570
Tardan Hermanos Sucesores S.A. 570
Taschian, Armen 270, 321
task conflict 351, 353–6, 363, 443
task conflict dominant 363
tax aggressiveness 51
technological collaboration 230
technology acquisition 244, 246, 248, 254
technology sourcing 243
Teece, David 242
Telcel 572
Telles family 570
Telmex 572
temporal dimension to corporate entrepreneurship 282–305
temporal discounting 73
temporal factors 70
temporal orientation 71, 151–2; and decision making 72–73
tensions in business 427
tenure 148; of CEO, 96–97
Thailand's marriages impacting family structure 440
Thatcher, S. M. B. 363, 364
theory deficiency 447
Theory X 402
Theory Y 403
Thesmar, D. 108
Theyel, Nelli 251
third generation and firm performance 31
third-party intervention for handling conflict in family firms 359, 361
Thomas, J. 126, 134
Thorgren, Sara 315, 317
threats and opportunities for the business after leadership transfer 29
threats of imitation 216
three-circle model of family firms 284–5, 371, 496
Three-Dimensional Developmental Model 285, 287–8, 290–1, 294–301
Thurik, Roy 177

Tihula, Sanna 314
Tilba, Anna 408
time: concept of 71–72; influencing family business 70; temporal and family firms 284–5
time horizons 54
TMT. *see* top management team (TMT)
tolerance of difference 452
Tomlinson, Philip R. 251
top management team (TMT) 3, 51, 61, 224; CEO-TMT interface 98–99; composition of 94–95; decision making process 97–98; family involvement in 90–112; impact of values 100–1; and innovation 215; and innovation output 231–2
"top of head phenomena," 390
Torre, C 57
Tosi, Henry L. 405
Townsend, D. M. 295
township and village enterprises (TVEs) 509–10
Tracey, P. 445
trade credit 183, 188
traditional culture 9
Tranfield, David 16, 35
transfer of knowledge and social capital 19
transfer of leadership 19, 26–28
transfer of ownership 20, 25–26; *see also* ownership dispersion
transformational leadership 99
transgenerational entrepreneurship 281–2, 322
transgenerational stories 378
transgenerational succession and export orientation 125, 128
transgenerational wealth 406
Treviñyo, R. 575
Trevinyo-Rodrízquez, R. N. 438
tribal business 378
triggers for portfolio entrepreneurship 313, 319–20
Trinkaus, John 405, 409
Trougakos, J. 396
Trujillo, M.-A. 53
trust: among family members 444; of association 499; in Chinese family businesses (CFB) 494–5; and corporate governance 562–3; on dyad dynamics 451, 452; structure in China 498–9; and whole family dynamics 452
trustworthiness 259
Tsai, W. 446
Tsai, W.-H. 59
Tsang, E. W. K. 137
Tuanti Geju 498
Tulane Family Business Center 586
Tulane University 586
Turner, Nick 321
Tuvblad, Catherine 466
Type I agency problem 48, 60
Type II agency problem 60

Ucbasaran, Deniz 314, 315
Uhlaner, L. M. 52, 558
UK Stewardship Code 408
United States 10; and illegal entrepreneurship 321;
    percentage of family firms 119
university affiliated family business
    centers 580–1
University of Alberta 583
University of Cádiz 532
University of La Sabana 532
University of Las Palmas de Gran
    Canaria 532
University of Los Andes 532
University of North Carolina 582, 585
University of Toledo 586
university outreach programs for family
    businesses 165
upper echelons research 90–112; literature
    review 91–92
upper echelon theory (UET) 215, 219, 224
Upton, N. 582
Uruguay 524
U.S. and internationalization 125, 126
"us against them" mechanism 377–8
utility-maximization 7, 409–10

Vahter, Pritt 252, 255
Valcea, S. 295
value 148; commitment 409; creation 196–7, 205;
    creation due to socio-emotional wealth (SEW)
    149–53; destruction and loss aversion 146–9;
    loss due to socio-emotional wealth (SEW)
    146–9, 153
value chain perspective 251
values: and benevolence 409; impacting top
    management team (TMT) 100–1; and
    innovation 276–7; and whole family
    dynamics 452
Van Auken, H. 419
Vancauteren, M. 97, 108
Vance, R. J. 444
Vandemaele, S. 97, 108
Van der Meer, Han 252
Van der Stede, Wim A. 74
van der Vliet, D. 587
Van der Wijst, Nico 177
Van de Vrande, V. 243, 252, 255
van Essen, M. 123
Van Gils, A. 182, 246
Vanhaverbeke, Wim 245, 251, 252, 253, 254
Van Praag, C. M. 298, 300
van Reenen, J. 102
variable: conceptual 390; dependent 393–4, 449;
    independent in experimental design 389–93
Venezuela 568
Venter, E. 30, 32, 442, 444
venturing. *see* corporate venturing

Vera, C. F. 439, 440, 442
Vercesi, Paolo 245
Vermeersch, Ine 253
vertical loyalty 378
Viding, E. 466
vignette experiment 389
Villalonga, B. 59, 144, 145
Vinton, K. L. 128
von Bertalanffy, K. L. 445
Von Schlippe, A. 371
Voordeckers, W. 56, 182, 189
Votorantim Group 568
Vredenburg, Harrie 270

Wagner, M. 228, 233
Waldman, D. A. 169
Walrasian market clearing level 176, 180
Walsh, J. P. 168
Wan, D. 51, 497
Wang, Hesen 489
Wang, L. 126, 131
Wang, S. L. 514
Wang, Xuanyu 492
Wang, Y. 296
Ward, J. L. 135
Washburn, M. F. 169
Watson, W. 57
wavering succession 35
wealth: conserving and growing 4; financial and
    non-financial 121; management centralization
    197; preservation 269
Webb, J. W. 293, 295, 321
Weber, F.-M. 99
Weerd-Nederhof, Petra C. 250
Weiler, B. L. 463
Weiss, Andrew 176–7, 180
Welsch, H. 120
Welsh, D. H. 300
Welsh, D. H. B. 299
Welter, F. 448
Werbel, J. 419
Werbel, J. D. 422
Westerberg, Mats 250
Western Europe, percentage of family firms 119
Westhead, P. 59, 314
Wharton School at the University of
    Pennsylvania 580
Whetten, David A. 270
whole family 8; dynamics 443–6, 451–2;
    psychometric quality of measures 446–7
whole family structure 439–41; variables 450–1
whole family unit of analysis 434, 436
Wichita State University 165
Widom, C. S. 463
Wiklund, J. 26, 53, 57, 314, 438, 439
Wilkes University 586
willingness to change 445

willingness to innovate 233–5, 258
willingness to take over and post-succession
    performance 32
Wincent, Joakim 253, 315, 317
Witten Institute for Family Business 166
Wiwattanakantang, Y. 38, 439, 440
Wolfenzon, D. 25, 441
Wong, S.-L. 516
Wong, Y.-J. 297
work/family balance 423
working together stage 289
Wright, M. 297, 314
Wu, Z. 108, 125, 129, 134
Wynarczyk, Pooran 253

Xi, Jing 492

Yacob, S. 297, 301, 303
Yang, Guoshu 497, 500
Yang, H. 511
Yang, M. L. 108
Yang, X. 55
Yang, Xueru 493
Yeung, B. 168, 260

Yoon, Byungun 249
Young, J. 54
young business family stage 288, 291
Ypióca Group 570

Zachary, Miles A. 267
Zachary, R. K. 440, 441
Zahra, S. A. 53, 56, 59, 96, 108, 126, 133,
    135, 150, 283, 294, 296, 407, 436, 444, 448
Zapata Cuervo, N. 562
Zellweger, T. 58, 80, 121, 299, 301, 313, 315,
    316, 320, 322, 447
Zhang, Jian 494
Zhang, Shujun 493
Zhang, Xinan 489
Zhang, Zhongyuan 493
Zhejiang province 491
Zhejiang University 491
Zheng, Boxun 500
Zheng, D. 55, 493
Zhou, Lixin 492
Zhou, Yinhui 493
Zhu, Hang 493
Zott, C. 202

For Product Safety Concerns and Information please contact our EU
representative GPSR@taylorandfrancis.com Taylor & Francis Verlag GmbH,
Kaufingerstraße 24, 80331 München, Germany

Printed and bound by CPI Group (UK) Ltd, Croydon, CR0 4YY
01/05/2025
01858412-0003